PETER CLARK
1959

4.5

The People Shall Judge

The People Shall Judge

Readings in the Formation of American Policy

VOLUME I

Selected and Edited by

THE STAFF, SOCIAL SCIENCES 1

The College of the University of Chicago

"Who shall be judge whether the prince or legislative act contrary to their trust? . . . The people shall be judge; for who shall be judge whether the trustee or deputy acts well and according to the trust reposed in him, but he who deputes him. . . ."—LOCKE, *Second Treatise of Civil Government*, chap. XIX.

THE UNIVERSITY OF CHICAGO PRESS
CHICAGO · ILLINOIS

THE UNIVERSITY OF CHICAGO PRESS, CHICAGO 37
Cambridge University Press, London, N.W. 1, England
The University of Toronto Press, Toronto 5, Canada

PREFACE

THIS book expresses the faith of one American college in the usefulness of liberal education to American democracy. If the United States is to be a democracy, its citizens must be free. If citizens are to be free, they must be their own judges. If they are to judge well, they must be wise. Citizens may be born free; they are not born wise. Therefore, the business of liberal education in a democracy is to make free men wise. Democracy declares that "the people shall judge." Liberal education must help the people to judge well.

The teachers who have prepared this volume have been practicing the creed which is merely preached above. Insistently, they have asked themselves, "How can we help Americans to study their own past in such a way that they will grow in practical wisdom?" Their attempt to answer this question has determined both the content and the method of the course for which these teachers are responsible.

Since the wise citizen is more than the informed citizen, he needs to learn more than a summary of the facts of American history. Accordingly, these teachers have placed at the center of their course, not textbooks, but the primary materials which appear in this volume. Instead of the usual later summaries of events and controversies, the firsthand reports and original

arguments of those who took part in them have been selected.

But original documents, no less than secondhand materials, might be so presented as to add to the student's information without improving his judgment. Aware of this danger, these teachers have arranged their materials problematically. They have invited the student to see how human judgments such as those he will himself have to make as citizen have been real causes in his country's history. The materials are grouped around a series of moments of decision in the American past, and they have been so selected as to present the diverse arguments and interests, the hopes and fears, the gains, losses, and compromises, of those who actively affected the character and outcome of those moments.

Yet even this open and problematic arrangement of materials could not, by itself, insure the development of practical wisdom in the citizen. Practical wisdom is an active virtue, to be acquired and perfected through exercise. It is not enough to show students how the judgments of their forefathers helped to make their nation's history. The students must themselves practice judgment. This is why the course is conducted by means of discussion classes in which the readings this volume contains and the historical decisions they illumine are subjected to critical examination. In these discussions "learning" and "thinking" advance together in so close an alliance that, in the end, what the student "knows" is not what he has been told to learn but what his own active analysis of the problems of the course has led him to believe or to doubt. He and his fellow-students have been engaged not only in claiming a heritage of wisdom and achievement in the American past but in forming habits of open discussion and independent judgment which will lead to wise decisions and new achievements in the American future. Surely, a democracy should invite its citizens to learn and to think in this inquiring way. Surely, a democracy whose citizens do so learn and think will be well and freely served.

Is national improvement the final good to be expected from this undertaking? Indifferent to political frontiers, liberal education seeks a universal good; and free men, when they have also become wise, discover a concern for freedom everywhere. The college teachers who prepared this book can fairly claim that even those most general ends of education and politics are served by the kind of study of American history in which they and their students are engaged. They need only to pursue a major American issue to its roots in order to discover that, for all its local idiom and occasion, it was and is a universal human issue, too. The protagonists in the American controversies over federation and slavery and revolution were joining Locke and Pericles, Rousseau and Ghandi, in that "great conversation" about Man and among all men which Chancellor Hutchins has recently proposed as the touchstone of civilization. This "civilization of the dialogue" may someday culminate in an hour when the great conversation will be carried on by men without a country speaking Esperanto without an accent. Pending that hour, it may well be that the most authentic citizens of the world will not be rootless cosmopolites but active citizens of those nations which have sought to liberate their people not from but through a knowledge of their own history. He who would move the world must first be given a place to stand.

F. CHAMPION WARD
Dean of the College

UNIVERSITY OF CHICAGO
November 1, 1948

INTRODUCTION

THE purpose underlying these two volumes is the promotion of intelligent citizenship. They were prepared by a teaching staff who hoped to accomplish certain definite ends by introducing their students to the political experience of the American people. This staff has three chief aims. The first is to enable the student to acquire some basic historical knowledge about American ideas and institutions. The second is to develop competence in the analysis of social issues by giving special prominence to the process of deliberation and decision through which policy is formulated. The third is to encourage the student to acquire a sense of responsibility about public issues and to examine his own standards in an atmosphere of free inquiry and discussion.

To understand the past is to know how we have come to be what we are. We learn to see ourselves as the heirs of a particular tradition, thinking, feeling, and acting along lines suggested by our previous national experience. We find that much of our political thought has revolved around an eighteenth-century creed of natural rights; that our Constitution bears the ineffaceable marks of the initial struggle with English despotism and American radicalism; that our attitude to the institution of private property is strongly affected by an experience in which the rights of property have been

widely shared; that our national character reflects the exhilarations and excesses of the frontier long after the last acre of free land has disappeared. We understand why our foreign policy has often seemed to be directed from the graves of Washington and Monroe and why the names of Jefferson and Lincoln are used by party politicians to exorcise the demons in our midst. We uncover the roots of some of our problems in the Civil War; of others in the industrialism which swept away the fabric of rural society without being able to obliterate its ideals. In short, we acquire the kind of national self-knowledge—about our emotional constitution, our mental furnishings, our institutions, our established policies—which only a study of the past can give.

The first object of the editors was to find some satisfactory means of putting this general knowledge within the students' reach. This might have been done in any one of several ways. Here we have presented the historical record in a particular way because we also wanted to develop a certain kind of competence. As a citizen the student will be confronted with issues of public policy. He will join an endless debate in which these issues are perpetually arising, provoking argument, and forcing decisions on individuals, organized groups, and agencies of government. This process of deliberation and decision is the same activity in which our predecessors were involved as they faced their problems. In many cases the basic questions are the same. What is the end of man? What are the ends of government? What compromise should be sought between freedom and authority? What position should government occupy in relation to the economic system? On what principles should one nation conduct its relations with others? In all cases, however much conditions may alter, there is a certain constancy about the pattern of controversy. Interests clash; values are affirmed; argument proliferates; personality asserts itself. And all calculations have to reckon with the unknown or the unknowable. The function of intelligence in this conflict of opinion is to analyze and to clarify. If we want to develop competence in current controversies, one obvious method is to practice the same kind of talent on past controversies. And this discipline has the added advantage that, where the past is concerned, events have already passed some sort of judgment on the plans of the policy-makers.

Skill in analysis can be made to serve any scheme of values. Are the editors of these volumes, as a teaching staff, trying to promote any particular scheme? They are innocent, they hope, of any desire to indoctrinate their students with their own nostrums, but they are acting within some assumptions which ought to be made explicit. They think that their students ought to have convictions. They want them to feel responsible for the decisions which a self-governing society makes. And they believe that the beginning of wisdom is a willingness to submit all opinions to the test of free and rigorous inquiry. These considerations have led them to organize a course of study which will enable their students to feel the force of the convictions that have molded American values, to examine their own beliefs in the light of this wider world of human experience, and to accept the challenge of criticism and discussion.

Both these volumes consist of readings which might be briefly described as ideas about public policy. They have been drawn from systematic philosophies; from opinions crystallized in law and judicial decision; from speeches or pamphlets struck off in the heat of controversy; from political and diplomatic correspondence; from sermons, lectures, and newspapers. They range from the speculative to the practical, from the nature of man and society to specific issues of political, economic, and social policy in domestic and foreign affairs. These opinions have been organized in a series of units, each corresponding with a historical situation in which the American people were encountering critical problems of government. The first unit deals with the problem of freedom and authority in the seventeenth century; the second, with the American Revolution; the third, with the organization of a federal constitution; etc. No material has been used in any of these units in which the actors or observers in the actual situation are not speaking for themselves. Their language throughout has been modernized in spelling, in capitalization, and in punctuation; but no other labor-saving device has been inserted between the reader and the original ideas. Wherever feasible, an attempt has been made to reproduce the atmosphere of a debate rather than a monologue. Locke's views have been set side by side with those of Hobbes; Boucher's with Paine's; Jefferson's with Hamilton's; William Graham Sumner's with those of Henry Demarest Lloyd. Each unit is preceded by a brief introduction indicating the scope of the material and suggesting its significance, without prejudging the issues involved.

These readings are not intended to supplement lectures or textbooks. They are the basic material to which lectures and textbooks are subsidiary. In any given year a selection from these readings is assigned for study, and the student is asked to prepare himself for classroom discussion by careful reading and critical analysis of the documents. This effort of his requires an exertion of historical imagination, an exercise of clear thinking, and a continuous interest in the light which past experience can shed on present problems. He begins with an argument in a particular historical setting. To understand it at all, he has to make the effort to see the problems of that age as they were seen then and to resist any superficial insinuation of his own standards. He identifies the problem which the author is facing and sees how the author defines his position; what his asumptions are, whether ex-

plicit or hidden; what alternatives he formulates; how he estimates the consequences of different courses of action. The student compares other approaches to the problem and asks himself what his own opinion would have been in the same situation. He tries to assess the historical significance of the debate and its sequel. He then examines the arguments in their wider bearing on our own times. What has Locke's liberalism to contribute to an industrial democracy? How relevant is Adam Smith's inquiry into the wealth of nations to present-day America? What conduct would Jefferson have stigmatized as disloyal to American ideals? What can be learned by our present international society from a study of American experience under the Articles of Confederation? These are a few of the questions which might be usefully raised in the subsequent discussions.

The materials in these volumes have survived the test of considerable teaching experience. Many other readings have been tried and eliminated when they seemed unprofitable. The responsibility for this selection rests with the past and present staff of "Social Sciences 1," the first in a three-year sequence of general social science courses in the College of the University of Chicago. The basic principles of this course were first explicitly formulated and applied in 1944 by Bernard Drell, Robert E. Keohane (then chairman of the course), George Probst, Malcolm P. Sharp, Milton B. Singer, and O. Meredith Wilson. To Clarence H. Faust, Dean of the College at the time, should go the credit for convincing the staff of the possibility and desirability of this approach and for the encouragement he gave to the first efforts. Others who have contributed to the development and teaching of the course since 1945 have included Edward Bastian, Richard Birnberg, Earl Edgar, Millard Hansen, Ira Kipnis, Laurence Leamer, William Ludlow, D. Eldridge McBride, Edmund S. Morgan, Harvey Perloff, Kramer Rohfleisch, Lester Seligman, Alan Simpson, Ben Stephansky, Rexford Tugwell, and Jay C. Williams, Jr. Valuable advice has at various times been given by Maure E. Goldschmidt, Reuben Frodin, Maynard C. Krueger, and Gerhard E. O. Meyer.

The first printed edition of these materials has been, like the previous mimeographed and planographed editions, a co-operative staff undertaking. To Robert E. Keohane and Bernard Drell should go special mention for the time and energy they have given during the last four years to finding and modernizing texts, preparing footnotes, and otherwise making materials suitable for classroom use. They, together with Millard Hansen, George Probst, and Alan Simpson, have been responsible for the editorial direction of this edition. Mr. Simpson has prepared the final drafts of the unit introductions. The staff is indebted to Miss Margaret Maddox for editorial assistance and to Miss Margaret Perry for securing permissions. It also wishes to express its thanks to Morton Grodzins (chairman of "Social Sciences 2"), Donald Meiklejohn (chairman of "Social Sciences 3"), and Milton Singer (chairman of the social sciences in the College) for a critical reading of the introductions and footnotes and to F. Champion Ward, Dean of the College, for guidance and encouragement. Publication of Volume I of this work has been aided by a grant from the Charles R. Walgreen Foundation for the Study of American Institutions of the University of Chicago.

THE STAFF, SOCIAL SCIENCE 1

UNIVERSITY OF CHICAGO
October 29, 1948

TABLE OF CONTENTS

UNIT I. AUTHORITY AND LIBERTY IN THE SEVENTEENTH CENTURY

SECTION A. AUTHORITY AND LIBERTY IN COLONIAL AMERICA

SECTION B. AUTHORITY AND LIBERTY IN ENGLAND

UNIT II. THE AMERICAN REVOLUTION

SECTION A. THE REVOLUTIONARY DEBATE

SECTION B. DEMOCRACY AND ARISTOCRACY IN THE NEW REPUBLIC

CONTENTS

UNIT III. CONFEDERATION AND CONSTITUTION

UNIT IV. ECONOMIC PROBLEMS OF THE NEW REPUBLIC

SECTION A. PROBLEMS OF ECONOMIC LIBERALISM

SECTION B. THE HAMILTONIAN AND JEFFERSONIAN SYSTEMS

UNIT V. CONSTITUTIONAL PROBLEMS
OF THE NEW REPUBLIC

UNIT VI. THE BEGINNINGS OF AMERICAN
FOREIGN POLICY

CONTENTS

CONTENTS

SECTION D. THE CIVIL WAR AND RECONSTRUCTION

UNIT 1

AUTHORITY AND LIBERTY IN THE
SEVENTEENTH CENTURY

MOST Americans think of themselves as citizens of a free country. If a modern American could step back into early seventeenth-century England—about the time when the first colonies in America were being founded—how "free" would life there seem to him? If he were a businessman, he would notice that there were laws fixing prices and wages, that labor had none of its modern freedom to move around in search of a job, and that many businessmen were doing business under some kind of official monopoly. If he were a churchgoer, he would discover that there was only one official religion, the rest being banned by law. If he listened to sermons, he might get the impression that the clergy were part of an official conspiracy to prevent a man from making money by denouncing all sorts of modern practices as immoral. If he had "a mind of his own," he would find it unhealthy to give it too much exercise in matters of religion, politics, or morals. If he wanted to publish his opinions, he would need official permission. If he wanted to treat all the English people he met—lords, gentry, merchants, yeomen, craftsmen, laborers—as social equals, he would be viewed with wonder and embarrassment. If he asked whether Englishmen could change their nationality, he would learn that they were born subjects of the king and that once a subject they were always a subject, no matter where they went. If he visited the House of Commons, he would hear a great deal of talk about "rights" and "liberties"—much of it earnest and angry—but he would also hear King James I telling his Commons that they were not to meddle with the high secrets of government but to leave such matters to the fatherly care of God's lieutenant on earth. If he looked into the careers of recent statesmen, he would find that the penalty of political failure sometimes included death as well as dismissal.

In short, he would soon convince himself that there was no freedom of enterprise, no freedom of worship, no liberty of opinion, no freedom of the press, no self-government, and not the remotest suspicion in anyone's mind that one man was "equal" to another. Of course, if he were wise, he would examine these first impressions a little more carefully after a longer visit; but he would still be much impressed with the difference between "liberty" then and now.

If the same American could repeat

this experiment a century later—in the reign of James I's great-granddaughter, Queen Anne—he would find the experience much less bewildering. For one thing, he would learn that there had been two revolutions since his last visit, and this would not surprise him at all. For another, he would find not only that Britain was more to his liking but that there was also an America—twelve flourishing colonies strung along the seaboard from South Carolina to Maine.

In Britain he would see that social inequality was still a religion in spite of some idle phrases among the philosophers and more opportunities than there used to be for converting wealth into nobility. But the British people would strike him as far more business-like. He would notice that a lot of the old restrictions on business freedom were not being enforced: in the old days the king had councils which were constantly meddling, but these were gone. If he listened to the morality which the churches were preaching, he would hear a different note—a suggestion, perhaps, that someday business might be business and not clergymen's business. If he wanted to worship outside the established church, he could do so—under all sorts of illogical conditions, but still it was possible. If he wanted to read a logical defense of toleration, which summarized one aspect of the revolution in men's minds, he could find it in Locke. Wherever he looked he would see that religion was falling into its modern place—one claim over the human spirit among many rather than the one which strove

to unify all effort in a single purpose. The national states of Europe, whose religious character had now been stabilized, were disentangling religion from their national policies and freeing themselves for purely secular struggles. Branches of knowledge, like physics, politics, economics, which in the old days had been branches of theology, were largely secularized. Scientists were showing that physical phenomena were subject to law and so were undermining the faith which had seen the hand of God or the devil in the behavior of nature. They were also raising hopes in the power of reason to subdue the natural world to man's convenience. Of course, there was a wide gulf between the educated and the uneducated classes, but our visitor would certainly feel that the former were much more interested in what he would call "progress and happiness" than they had been before.

Lastly, he would see the difference in government. There was still a king, a House of Lords, and a House of Commons; but, where before there had been an absolute monarchy, there was now a limited monarchy. It had always been an Englishman's boast that he was ruled by law; but he now knew that the law was one which Parliament made and which independent judges enforced. To achieve this result, one king had been executed and another expelled. These revolutions had not made the king a cipher; he was his own prime minister. But he ruled by a parliamentary, not a divine, title, and he could not get along without Parliament. Of course, this Parliament was a highly aristocratic body—a gentle-men's club. But, once it had been settled that government depended upon consent, then the field was free for argument about whose consent.

So much for Britain. But what of America—where this particular argument was to be so vigorously developed? He would find it in many ways a provincial reproduction of Britain: there was a ruling class in every colony, just as there was a ruling class in Britain; there was a governor and two houses in the typical colony, just as there was a king and two houses in Britain. The chief executive was not elected, any more than the chief executive in Britain, but, like the latter, he was constantly reminded of the rights and powers of representative assemblies. In social morality generally, there was an obvious family resemblance between the colonies and the mother-country.

But there were differences. Some were implicit in the colonial status: the fact that the colonies, though far freer to manage their own affairs than any other colonies in the world, were still subordinate to British authority. Others were implicit in frontier conditions which were bound to modify European customs. If colonial society seemed aristocratic, it was less so than British. If property was usually the basis of social prestige and political privilege, access to property was very much easier. Though princely estates were common enough, many fewer colonists than Englishmen were in the position of living their lives under the shadow of the squirearchy. In situa-

tions where British standards had given no guidance, the colonists had learned to rely on themselves, and the habit of self-reliance had bred independence.

Anyone who compares the outlook of Englishmen in 1600 with their outlook a century later will be struck by the growth of those ideas which we call "liberal." It is the first phase in the development of that tradition which was to dominate both England and America in the eighteenth and nineteenth centuries. Some characteristics of the values which are loosely suggested by this label have already been suggested—in particular, the growing faith in individualism with all its implications for business, worship, opinion, government, and the search for happiness—and others will be discovered in the documents which follow.

The writings in this unit are divided into two sections. The first (A) represents the views of certain Englishmen in America; the second (B), the views of Englishmen in England. The first begins with the Mayflower Compact—an example of how a group of common people solved the problem of government when they found themselves on the frontier. This is followed by four documents from the early history of Massachusetts. One is an explanation and defense of Puritan institutions in the colony for the information of certain nobles in England who were interested in emigrating. Two are from the pen of John Winthrop, the first governor: one providing a revealing glimpse into the commercial ethics of a Puritan commonwealth; the other, a famous statement of Winthrop's own views about liberty. The last is a series of extracts from the Massachusetts Body of Liberties (1641). Roger Williams, whose views on liberty in church and state may be contrasted with those of the magistrates and elders in Massachusetts, is represented by *The Bloody Tenent of Persecution*. The final documents are taken from a later period. William Penn, proprietor of Pennsylvania, prepared a "Frame of Government" for his colony in 1682, a portion of which is here reprinted. John Wise, who embodies the spirit of homespun democracy which had rooted itself in the life of New England villages, is represented by a defense of the congregational principle in church government, which was published in 1772.

The second section begins with a selection from a debate held in 1647 among members of the Army Council in England. This includes the views of the Levellers, a group of radicals who appeared during the turmoil of the English Rebellion and whose opinions are a startling anticipation of some of the ideas which we associate with modern democracy. Then follow extracts from the writings of the two political thinkers who made the most famous contributions to the theory of government in this century—Thomas Hobbes and John Locke. Hobbes wrote *The Leviathan* in the middle of the civil wars when the central problem in English political life was to find some escape from anarchy. His solution was a sovereign invested with irresistible and arbitrary power. Locke wrote his treatises on civil government to justify the Revolution of 1688. Explicitly, his defense of limited government was directed against Sir Robert Filmer, an apologist for the "divine right of kings" and the subject's duty of passive obedience. Implicitly, Locke's arguments may be considered an answer to Hobbes, a far more acute and powerful antagonist. Extracts from the Bill of Rights, the statute which embodied the results of the Revolution of 1688, accompany the reading from the *Second Treatise . . . of Civil Government*. The other reading from Locke is taken from the *Letter on Toleration*.

SECTION A. AUTHORITY AND LIBERTY IN COLONIAL AMERICA

1. THE MAYFLOWER COMPACT[1]

EDITORS' NOTE.—This famous social contract is the first agreement for a self-governing community in America created by the people of the community to which the contract was to apply. The Separatists, or "Pilgrims," had accepted voluntary exile in the Netherlands from their homes in Nottinghamshire, England. After an exile of more than a decade they applied to the Virginia Company for a patent for a private plantation. From Leiden, Holland, they sailed to Plymouth, where seventy recruits from London were added to their group. Their landfall was off Cape Cod, some two hundred miles north of the limit of their patent. This compact was drawn up just before they left the ship which had brought them across the Atlantic. William Bradford says that the agreement was occasioned partly by the fact that some of the "strangers" argued that none had power to command them, for the patent they had was for Virginia and not for New England, and New England belonged to another company with which the Virginia Company had nothing to do. The forty-one signers included all the male adults in the colonizing group except eight servants and a dying Pilgrim. The compact is a plantation covenant, providing for local government, and can be regarded as an unauthorized extension of the customary church covenant to civil life; the Pilgrims were never able to obtain a charter of their own from the crown. In 1691 the Plymouth colony was annexed by Massachusetts Bay. For further discussion see C. M. Andrews, *The Fathers of New England* (New Haven, 1921); *The Colonial Period of American History* (New Haven, 1934), Vol. I; or H. L. Osgood, *American Colonies in the Seventeenth Century* (New York, 1904), Vol. I.

In the name of God, Amen. We, whose names are underwritten, the loyal subject of our dread sovereign Lord, King James, by the grace of God, of Great Britain, France, and Ireland, King, Defender of the Faith, etc., having undertaken, for the glory of God, and advancement of the Christian faith, and honor of our king and country, a voyage to plant the first colony in the northern parts of Virginia, do by these presents solemnly and mutually in the presence of God, and of one another, covenant and combine ourselves together into a civil body politic, for our better ordering and preservation and furtherance of the ends aforesaid; and by virtue hereof to enact, constitute, and frame such just and equal

1. The text is adapted from William Bradford, *History of Plymouth Plantation* ("Massachusetts Historical Collections," Fourth Series), III, 89–90.

laws, ordinances, acts, constitutions, and offices, from time to time, as shall be thought most meet and convenient for the general good of the colony, unto which we promise all due submission and obedience. In witness whereof we have

hereunder subscribed our names at Cape Cod the eleventh of November, in the year of the reign of our sovereign Lord, King James, of England, France, and Ireland the eighteenth, and of Scotland the fifty-fourth. *Anno Domini*, 1620.

2. EQUALITY AND INEQUALITY IN PURITAN MASSACHUSETTS[1]

By John Cotton

EDITORS' NOTE.—The political and religious situation of Puritans in England was so bad at this time that several Puritan peers, including Lord Brook and Lord Say and Sele, considered emigrating to Massachusetts Bay in the middle 1630's. When their demands were not granted, the "noble lords" turned their attention to Providence Island in the Caribbean, a venture which proved unsuccessful, but which led to a later controversy between Winthrop and Lord Say and Sele.

A. CERTAIN PROPOSALS MADE BY LORD SAY, LORD BROOKE, AND OTHER PERSONS OF QUALITY, AS CONDITIONS OF THEIR REMOVING TO NEW ENGLAND, WITH THE ANSWERS THERETO

DEMAND 1. That the commonwealth should consist of two distinct ranks of men, whereof the one should be for them and their heirs, gentlemen of the country, the other for them and their heirs, freeholders.

ANSWER. Two distinct ranks we willingly acknowledge, from the light of nature and Scripture; the one of them called princes, or nobles, or elders (among whom gentlemen have their place), the other the people. Hereditary dignity or honors we willingly allow to the former, unless, by the scandalous and base conversation of any of them, they become degenerate. Hereditary liberty, or estate of freemen, we willingly allow to the other, unless they also, by some unworthy and slavish carriage, do disfranchise themselves.

1. Thomas Hutchinson, *History of the Colony and Province of Massachusetts Bay*, ed. L. S. Mayo (3 vols.; Cambridge, Mass., 1936), I, 410–13, 414–17.

DEM. 2. That in these gentlemen and freeholders, assembled together, the chief power of the commonwealth shall be placed, both for making and repealing laws.

ANS. So it is with us.

DEM. 3. That each of these two ranks should, in all public assemblies, have a negative voice, so as without a mutual consent nothing should be established.

ANS. So it is agreed among us.

DEM. 4. That the first rank, consisting of gentlemen, should have power, for them and their heirs, to come to the parliaments or public assemblies and there to give their free votes personally; the second rank of freeholders should have the same power for them and their heirs of meeting and voting, but by their deputies.

ANS. Thus far this demand is practiced among us. The freemen meet and vote by their deputies; the other rank give their votes personally, only with this difference: there be no more of the gentlemen that give their votes personally, but such as are chosen to places of office, either governors, deputy governors, counselors, or assistants. All gentlemen in England have not that honor to meet and vote personally in Parliament, much less all their heirs. But of this more fully, in an answer to the ninth and tenth demand[s].

DEM. 5. That for facilitating and dispatch of business, and other reasons, the gentlemen and freeholders should sit and hold their meetings in two distinct houses.

ANS. We willingly approve the motion, only as yet it is not so practiced among us, but in time, the variety and discrepancy of sundry occurrences will put them upon a necessity of sitting apart.

DEM. 6. That there shall be set times for these meetings, annually or half-yearly, or as shall be thought fit by common consent, which meetings should have a set time for their continuance, but should be adjourned or broken off at the discretion of both houses.

ANS. Public meetings, in general courts, are by charter appointed to be quarterly, which, in this infancy of the colony, wherein many things frequently occur which need settling, have been of good use, but when things are more fully settled in due order, it is likely that yearly or half-yearly meetings will be sufficient. For the continuance or breaking-up of these courts, nothing is done but with the joint consent of both branches.

DEM. 7. That it shall be in the power of this parliament, thus constituted and assembled, to call the governor and all public officers to account, to create new officers, and to determine them already set up; and, the better to stop the way to insolence and ambition, it may be ordered that all offices and fees of office shall, every parliament, determine, unless they be new confirmed the last day of every session.

ANS. This power to call governors and all officers to account, and to create new and determine the old, is settled already in the general court or parliament, only it is not put forth but once in the year, viz., at the great and general court in May, when the governor is chosen.

DEM. 8. That the governor shall ever be chosen out of the rank of gentlemen.

ANS. We never practice otherwise, choosing the governor either out of the assistants, which is our ordinary course, or out of approved known gentlemen, as this year [1636] Mr. Vane.[2]

DEM. 9. That, for the present, the Right Honorable the Lord Viscount Say and Seale, the Lord Brooke, who have already been at great disbursements for the public works in New England, and such other gentlemen of approved sincerity and worth, as they, before their personal remove, shall take into their number, should be admitted for them and their heirs, gentlemen of the country. But, for the future, none shall be admitted into this rank but by the consent of both houses.

ANS. The great disbursements of these noble personages and worthy gentlemen we thankfully acknowledge, because the safety and presence of our brethren at Connecticut is no small blessing and comfort to us. But, though that charge had never been disbursed, the worth of the honorable persons named is so well known to all, and our need of such supports and guides is so sensible to ourselves, that we do not doubt the country would thankfully accept it, as a singular favor from God and from them, if he should bow their hearts to come into this wilderness and help us. As for accepting them and their heirs into the number of gentlemen of the country, the custom of this country is, and readily would be, to receive and acknowledge, not only all

2. Sir Henry Vane, the Younger (1613–62), prominent in the English Civil War, friend of Cromwell (for a time), executed after the Restoration.

such eminent persons as themselves and the gentlemen they speak of, but others of meaner estate, so be it is of some eminency, to be for them and their heirs, gentlemen of the country. Only, thus standeth our case. Though we receive them with honor and allow them pre-eminence and accommodations according to their condition, yet we do not, ordinarily, call them forth to the power of election or administration of magistracy until they be received as members into some of our churches, a privilege, which we doubt not religious gentlemen will willingly desire (as David did in Psal. xxvii. 4) and Christian churches will as readily impart to such desirable persons. Hereditary honors both nature and Scripture does acknowledge (Eccles. xix. 17), but hereditary authority and power stands only by the civil laws of some commonwealths, and yet, even among them, the authority and power of the father is nowhere communicated, together with his honors, unto all his posterity. Where God blesses any branch of any noble or generous family with a spirit and gifts fit for government, it would be a taking of God's name in vain to put such a talent under a bushel, and a sin against the honor of magistracy to neglect such in our public election. But if God should not delight to furnish some of their posterity with gifts fit for magistracy, we should expose them rather to reproach and prejudice, and the commonwealth with them, than exalt them to honor, if we should call them forth, when God does not, to public authority.

DEM. 10. That the rank of freeholders shall be made up of such, as shall have so much personal estate there, as shall be thought fit for men of that condition, and have contributed, some fit proportion, to the public charge of the country, either by their disbursements or labors.

ANS. We must confess our ordinary practice to be otherwise. For, excepting the old planters, i.e., Mr. Humphry,[3] who himself was admitted an assistant at London, and all of them freemen, before the churches here were established, none are admitted freemen of this commonwealth but such as are first admitted members of some church or other in this country, and, of such, none are excluded from the liberty of freemen. And out of such only, I mean the more eminent sort of such, it is that our magistrates are chosen. Both which points we should willingly persuade our people to change, if we could make it appear to them, that such a change might be made according to God; for, to give you a true account of the grounds of our proceedings herein, it seems to them, and also to us, to be a divine ordinance (and moral) that none should be appointed and chosen by the people of God, magistrates over them, but men fearing God (Ex. xviii. 21) chosen out of their brethren (Deut. xvii. 15) saints (1 Cor. vi. 1). Yes, the apostle makes it a shame to the church, if it be not able to afford wise men from out of themselves, which shall be able to judge all civil matters between their brethren (ver. 5). And Solomon makes it the joy of a commonwealth, when the righteous are in authority, and the calamity thereof, when the wicked bear rule (Prov. xxix. 2).

OBJ. If it be said, there may be many carnal men whom God has invested with sundry eminent gifts of wisdom, courage, justice, fit for government.

ANS. Such may be fit to be consulted with and employed by governors, according to the quality and use of their gifts and parts, but yet are men not fit to be trusted with place of standing power or settled authority. Ahitophel's wisdom

3. John Humfry had been interested in New England settlement and active in colonizing groups in the region from 1623. As one of the leaders in the formation of the Massachusetts Bay Company he could not be disregarded in a new colony whose relative independence of English control had a very precarious legal basis. There probably were a few church members who were not admitted as freemen (Andrews, *op. cit.*, p. 437).

may be fit to be heard (as an oracle of God) but not fit to be trusted with power of settled magistracy, lest he at last call for 12,000 men to lead them forth against David (2 Sam. xvii. 1, 2, 3). The best gifts and parts, under a covenant of works (under which all carnal men and hypocrites be), will at length turn aside by crooked ways, to depart from God, and, finally, to fight against God, and are therefore, herein, opposed to good men and upright in heart (Psal. cxxv. 4, 5).

OBJ. If it be said again, that then the church estate could not be compatible with any commonwealth under heaven.

ANS. It is one thing for the church or members of the church loyally to submit unto any form of government, when it is above their calling to reform it, another thing to choose a form of government and governors discrepant from the rule. Now, if it be a divine truth that none are to be trusted with public permanent authority but godly men, who are fit materials for church fellowship, then from the same grounds it will appear that none are so fit to be trusted with the liberties of the commonwealth as church members. For the liberties of the freemen of this commonwealth are such as require men of faithful integrity to God and the state to preserve the same. Their liberties, among others are chiefly these: 1. To choose all magistrates, and to call them to account at their general courts. 2. To choose such burgesses, every general court, as with the magistrates shall make or repeal all laws. Now both these liberties are such, as carry along much power with them, either to establish or subvert the commonwealth, and therewith the church, which power, if it be committed to men not according to their godliness, which makes them fit for church fellowship, but according to their wealth, which, as such, makes them no better than worldly men, then, in case worldly men shrould prove the major part, as soon they might do, they would as readily set over us magistrates like themselves, such as might hate us according to the curse (Levit. xxvi. 17) and turn the edge of all authority and laws against the church and the members thereof, the maintenance of whose peace is the chief end which God aimed at in the institution of magistracy (1. Tim. ii. 1. 2).

B. COPY OF A LETTER FROM MR. COTTON TO LORD SAY AND SELE IN THE YEAR 1636

RIGHT HONORABLE,

... I know no man under heaven (I speak in God's fear without flattery) whose counsel I should rather depend upon, for the wise administration of a civil state according to God, than upon your Lordship, and such confidence have I (not in you) but in the Lord's presence in Christ with you that I should never fear to betrust a greater commonwealth than this (as much as in us lieth) under such a *perpetuâ dictaturâ* as your Lordship should prescribe. For I nothing doubt, but that either your Lordship would prescribe all things according to the rule, or be willing to examine again, and again, all things according to it. ...
It is very suitable to God's all-sufficient wisdom, and to the fulness and perfection of Holy Scriptures, not only to prescribe perfect rules for the right ordering of a private man's soul to everlasting blessedness with himself, but also for the right ordering of a man's family, yea, of the commonwealth too, so far as both of them are subordinate to spiritual ends. ... God's institutions (such as the government of church and of commonwealth be) may be close and compact, and co-ordinate one to another, and yet not confounded. God hath so framed the state of church government and ordinances that they may be compatible to any commonwealth, though never so much disordered in his frame. But yet when a commonwealth hath liberty to

mold his own frame. . . . I conceive the Scripture hath given full direction for the right ordering of the same, and that, in such sort as may best maintain the *euexia*[4] of the church. Mr. Hooker[5] doth often quote a saying out of Mr. Cartwright[6] (though I have not read it in him) that no man fashioneth his house to his hangings, but his hangings to his house. It is better that the commonwealth be fashioned to the setting-forth of God's house, which is his church, than to accommodate the church frame to the civil state. Democracy, I do not conceive that ever God did ordain as a fit government either for church or commonwealth. If the people be governors, who shall be governed? As for monarchy, and aristocracy, they are both of them clearly approved, and directed in Scripture, yet so as referreth the sovereignty to himself, and setteth up theocracy in both, as the best form of government in the commonwealth, as well as in the church.

The law which your Lordship instanceth in (that none shall be chosen to magistracy among us but a church member) was made and enacted before I came into the country; but I have hitherto wanted sufficient light to plead against it. 1st. The rule that directeth the choice of supreme governors is of like equity and weight in all magistrates, that one of their brethren (not a stranger) should be set over them . . . nonmembership may be a just cause of nonadmission to the place of magistracy, but yet, ejection out of his membership will not be a just cause of ejecting him out of his magistracy. A godly woman, being to make choice of an husband, may justly refuse a man that is either cast out of church fellowship or is not yet received into it, but yet, when she is once given to him, she may not reject him then for such defect. Mr. Humfrey was chosen for an assistant (as I hear) before the colony came over hither; and, though he be not as yet joined into church fellowship (by reason of the unsettledness of the congregation where he liveth), yet the commonwealth do still continue his magistracy to him, as knowing he waiteth for opportunity of enjoying church fellowship shortly.

When your Lordship doubteth that this course will draw all things under the determination of the church . . . (seeing the church is to determine who shall be members, and none but a member may have to do in the government of a commonwealth) be pleased (I pray you) to conceive that magistrates are neither chosen to office in the church nor do govern by directions from the church, but by civil laws, and those enacted in general courts, and executed in courts of justice, by the governors and assistants. In all which the church (as the church) hath nothing to do: only, it prepareth fit instruments both to rule, and to choose rulers, which is no ambition in the church, nor dishonor to the commonwealth, the apostle, on the contrary, thought it a great dishonor and reproach to the church of Christ, if it were not able to yield able judges to hear and determine all causes amongst their brethren . . . it will be no arrogance nor folly in church members, nor prejudice to the commonwealth, if voluntarily they never choose any civil judges, but from amongst the saints, such as church members are called to be. . . . If this therefore be (as your Lordship rightly conceiveth one of the main objections if not the only one) which hindereth this commonwealth from the entertainment of the propositions of those worthy gentlemen, we entreat them, in the name of the Lord Jesus, to consider, in meekness of wisdom, it is not any conceit or will of

4. Health or well-being.
5. Richard Hooker (1554?–1600), Anglican clergyman, upholder of the Elizabethan religious settlement, author of the *Laws of Ecclesiastical Polity*.
6. Thomas Cartwright (1535–1603), leading Puritan clergyman who is credited with writing an important criticism of Hooker's work.

ours, but the holy counsel and will of the Lord Jesus (whom they seek to serve as well as we) that overruleth us in this case: and we trust will overrule them also, that the Lord only may be exalted amongst all his servants. What pity and grief were it that the observance of the will of Christ should hinder good things from us!

But your Lordship doubteth that if such a rule were necessary, then the church estate and the best-ordered commonwealth in the world were not compatible. But let not our Lordship so conceive. For the church submitteth itself to all the laws and ordinances of men, in what commonwealth soever they come to dwell. But it is one thing to submit unto what they have no calling to reform; another thing voluntarily to ordain a form of government which to the best discerning of many of us (for I speak not of myself) is expressly contrary to rule. Nor need your Lordship fear (which yet I speak with submission to your Lordship's better judgment) that this course will lay such a foundation, as nothing but a mere democracy can be built upon it. Bodin[7] confesseth that though it be *status popularis*,[8] where a people choose their own governors, yet the government is not a democracy if it be administered, not by the people, but by the governors, whether one (for then it is a monarchy, though elective) or by many, for then (as you know) it is aristocracy. In which respect it is that church government is justly denied (even by Mr. Robinson)[9] to be democratical, though the people choose their own officers and rulers.

Nor need we fear that this course will, in time, cast the commonwealth into distractions and popular confusions. For (under correction) these three things do not undermine, but do mutually and strongly maintain one another (even those three which we principally aim at): authority in magistrates, liberty in people, purity in the church. Purity, preserved in the church, will preserve well-ordered liberty in the people, and both of them establish well-balanced authority in the magistrates. God is the author of all these three, and neither is himself the God of confusion, nor are his ways the ways of confusion but of peace.

3. ON EARLY NEW ENGLAND ECONOMY, 1633[1]

By JOHN WINTHROP

EDITORS' NOTE.—John Winthrop (1587/88–1649), Puritan lawyer and country gentleman in England, was the first governor of the colony of Massachusetts Bay. For the main parts of his life, see the *Dictionary of American Biography* (20 vols. and index; New York, 1928–37), XX, 408–11.

These extracts from Winthrop's *Journal* reveal the gap between an inherited economic theory and actual practice. They also suggest that strict governmental regulation of economic enterprise is an old element in the American tradition.

7. Jean Bodin (1530–96), French political theorist.
8. "Popular state."
9. Probably a reference to the John Robinson (1576?–1625), who was pastor of the church of the Pilgrims at Leiden before their emigration to Plymouth from the Netherlands and England.
1. John Winthrop, *Winthrop's Journal: History of New England* ("Original Narratives of Early American History," ed. J. K. Hosmer [New York, 1908]), I, 112, 152, 315–18; II, 228.

The scarcity of workmen had caused them to raise their wages to an excessive rate, so as a carpenter would have three shillings the day, a laborer two shillings and six pence, etc.; and accordingly those who had commodities to sell advanced their prices sometime double to that they cost in England, so as it grew to a general complaint, which the court, taking knowledge of, as also of some further evils, which were springing out of the excessive rates of wages, they made an order that carpenters, masons, etc., should take but two shillings the day, and laborers but eighteen pence, and that no commodity should be sold at above four pence in the shilling more than it cost for ready money in England; oil, wine, etc., and cheese, in regard of the hazard of bringing, etc. (excepted). The evils which were springing, etc., were: 1. Many spent much time idly, etc., because they could get as much in four days as would keep them a week. 2. They spent much in tobacco and strong waters, etc., which was a great waste to the commonwealth, which, by reason of so many foreign commodities expended, could not have subsisted to this time, but that it was supplied by the cattle and corn, which were sold to newcomers at very dear rates, viz., corn at six shillings the bushel, a cow at £20—yea, some at £24, some £26—a mare at £35, an ewe goat at 3 or £4; and yet many cattle were every year brought out of England, and some from Virginia. Soon after order was taken for prices of commodities, viz., not to exceed the rate of four pence in the shilling above the price in England, except cheese and liquors, etc....

[JUNE 1635]

For preventing the loss of time, and drunkenness, which sometimes happened, by people's running to the ships, and the excessive prices of commodities, it was ordered that one in each town should buy for all, etc., and should retail the same within twenty days at five per hundred, if any came to buy in that time. But this took no good effect, for most of the people would not buy, except they might buy for themselves; and the merchants appointed could not disburse so much money, etc.; and the seamen were much discontented, yet some of them brought their goods on shore and sold them there....

[NOVEMBER 1639]

At a general court holden at Boston, great complaint was made of the oppression used in the country in sale of foreign commodities; and Mr. Robert Keaine, who kept a shop in Boston, was notoriously above others observed and complained of; and, being convented, he was charged with many particulars; in some, for taking above six pence in the shilling profit; in some above eight pence; and, in some small things, above two for one; and being hereof convict (as appears by the records), he was fined £200, which came thus to pass: The deputies considered, apart, of his fine, and set it at £200; the magistrates agreed but to £100. So, the court being divided, at length it was agreed that his fine should be £200, but he should pay but £100, and the other should be respited to the further consideration of the next general court. By this means the magistrates and deputies were brought to an accord, which otherwise had not been likely, and so much trouble might have grown, and the offender escaped censure. For the cry of the country was so great against oppression, and some of the elders and magistrates had declared such detestation of the corrupt practice of this man (which was the more observable, because he was wealthy and sold dearer than most other tradesmen, and for that he was of ill report for the like covetous practice in England, that incensed the deputies very much against him). And sure the course was very evil, especial circumstances considered: 1. He being an ancient professor of the gospel; 2. A man of eminent parts; 3. Wealthy, and having but one child; 4. Having come over for conscience' sake, and for the advancement of the gospel here; 5. Having been formerly dealt with and admonished, both by private friends and also by some of the magistrates and elders, and having promised reformation; being a member of a church and commonwealth now in their infancy, and under the curious observation of all churches and civil states in the world. These added much aggravation to his sin in the judgment of all men of understanding. Yet most of the magistrates (though they discerned of the offense clothed with all these circumstances) would have been more moderate in their censure: 1. Because there was no law in force to limit or direct men in point of profit in their trade. 2. Because it is the common practice, in all countries, for men to make use of advantages for raising the prices of their commodities. 3. Because (though he were chiefly aimed at, yet) he was not alone in this fault. 4. Because all men through the country, in sale of cattle, corn, labor, etc., were guilty of the like excess in prices. 5. Because a certain rule could not be found out for an equal rate between buyer and seller, though much labor had been bestowed in it, and divers laws had been made, which, upon experience, were repealed, as being neither safe nor equal. Lastly, and especially, because the law of God appoints no other punishment but double restitution; and, in some cases, where the offender freely confesseth, and brings his offering, only half added to the principal. After the court had censured him, the church of Boston called him also in question, where (as before he had done in the court) he did, with tears, acknowledge and bewail his covetous and corrupt heart, yet making some excuse for many of the particulars, which were charged upon him, as partly by pretense of ignorance of the true price

of some wares, and chiefly by being misled by some false principles, as 1. That, if a man lost in one commodity, he might help himself in the price of another. 2. That if, through want of skill or other occasion, his commodity cost him more than the price of the market in England, he might then sell it for more than the price of the market in New England, etc. These things gave occasion to Mr. Cotton, in his public exercise the next lecture day, to lay open the error of such false principles, and to give some rules of direction in the case.

Some false principles were these:

1. That a man might sell as dear as he can and buy as cheap as he can.

2. If a man lose by casualty of sea, etc., in some of his commodities, he may raise the price of the rest.

3. That he may sell as he bought, though he paid too dear, etc., and though the commodity be fallen, etc.

4. That, as a man may take the advantage of his own skill or ability, so he may of another's ignorance or necessity.

5. Where one gives time for payment, he is to take like recompense of one as of another.

The rules for trading were these:

1. A man may not sell above the current price, i.e., such a price as is usual in the time and place, and as another (who knows the worth of the commodity) would give for it, if he had occasion to use it; as that is called current money, which every man will take, etc.

2. When a man loseth in his commodity for want of skill, etc., he must look at it as his own fault or cross, and therefore must not lay it upon another.

3. Where a man loseth by casualty of sea, or, etc., it is a loss cast upon himself by Providence, and he may not ease himself of it by casting it upon another; for so a man should seem to provide against all providences, etc., that he should never lose; but where there is a scarcity of the commodity, there men may raise their

price; for now it is a hand of God upon the commodity, and not the person.

4. A man may not ask any more for his commodity than his selling price, as Ephron to Abraham, the land is worth thus much.

The cause being debated by the church, some were earnest to have him excommunicated; but the most thought an admonition would be sufficient. Mr. Cotton opened the causes, which required excommunication, out of that in 1 Cor. 5. 11. The point now in question was whether these actions did declare him to be such a covetous person, etc. Upon which he showed that it is neither the habit of covetousness (which is in every man in some degree) nor simply the act that declares a man to be such, but when it appears that a man sins against his conscience, or the very light of nature, and when it appears in a man's whole conversation. But Mr. Keaine did not appear to be such, but rather upon an error in his judgment, being led by false

principles; and, beside, he is otherwise liberal, as in his hospitality, and in church communion, etc. So, in the end, the church consented to an admonition....

[APRIL 1645]

The wars in England kept servants from coming to us, so as those we had could not be hired, when their times were out, but upon unreasonable terms, and we found it very difficult to pay their wages to their content (for money was very scarce). I may upon this occasion report a passage between one of Rowley and his servant. The master, being forced to sell a pair of his oxen to pay his servant his wages, told his servant he could keep him no longer, not knowing how to pay him the next year. The servant answered, he would serve him for more of his cattle. But how shall I do (saith the master) when all my cattle are gone? The servant replied, you shall then serve me, and so you may have your cattle again.[2]

4. ON LIBERTY[1]

By John Winthrop

EDITORS' NOTE.—In 1645, while he was deputy-governor, Winthrop and his fellow-magistrates had interfered in a local election of a militia officer. When the dispute flared into a war of words, the magistrates bound over some of the dissidents to the next court and summoned others to appear. In this controversy the magistrates were ac-

cused of having exceeded their powers, and Winthrop was impeached. After a controversy of almost three months Winthrop was fully acquitted and some of his opponents fined. It was after this test and vindication that Winthrop made his famous "little speech" here quoted.

I suppose something may be expected from me, upon this charge that is befallen me, which moves me to speak now

to you; yet I intend not to intermeddle in the proceedings of the court or with any of the persons concerned therein. Only I bless God that I see an issue of this troublesome business. I also acknowl-

2. The editor of Winthrop's *Journal* comments that this passage is the most nearly humorous item in the work. Opposite this passage in the manuscript Winthrop wrote "insolent."

1. John Winthrop, *History of New England, 1630–1649*, ed. James Savage (Boston, 1853), II, 279–82.

edge the justice of the court, and, for mine own part, I am well satisfied, I was publicly charged, and I am publicly and legally acquitted, which is all I did expect or desire. And though this be sufficient for my justification before men, yet not so before the God, who hath seen so much amiss in my dispensations (and even in this affair) as calls me to be humble. For to be publicly and criminally charged in this court is matter of humiliation (and I desire to make a right use of it), notwithstanding I be thus acquitted. If her father had spit in her face (saith the Lord concerning Miriam), should she not have been ashamed seven days? Shame had lien upon her, whatever the occasion had been. I am unwilling to stay you from your urgent affairs, yet give me leave (upon this special occasion) to speak a little more to this assembly. It may be of some good use, to inform and rectify the judgments of some of the people, and may prevent such distempers as have arisen amongst us. The great questions that have troubled the country are about the authority of the magistrates and the liberty of the people. It is yourselves who have called us to this office, and, being called by you, we have our authority from God, in way of an ordinance, such as hath the image of God eminently stamped upon it, the contempt and violation whereof hath been vindicated with examples of divine vengeance. I entreat you to consider that, when you choose magistrates, you take them from among yourselves, men subject to like passions as you are. Therefore, when you see infirmities in us, you should reflect upon your own, and that would make you bear the more with us, and not be severe censurers of the failings of your magistrates, when you have continual experience of the like infirmities in yourselves and others. We account him a good servant who breaks not his covenant. The covenant between you and us is the oath you have taken of us, which is to this purpose: that we shall govern you and judge your causes by the rules of God's laws and our own, according to our best skill. When you agree with a workman to build you a ship or house, etc., he undertakes as well for his skill as for his faithfulness, for it is his profession, and you pay him for both. But when you call one to be a magistrate, he doth not profess nor undertake to have sufficient skill for that office, nor can you furnish him with gifts, etc., therefore you must run the hazard of his skill and ability. But if he fail in faithfulness, which by his oath he is bound unto, that he must answer for. If it fall out that the case be clear to common apprehension, and the rule clear also, if he transgress here, the error is not in the skill, but in the evil of the will: it must be required of him. But if the case be doubtful, or the rule doubtful, to men of such understanding and parts as your magistrates are, if your magistrates should err here, yourselves must bear it.

For the other point concerning liberty, I observe a great mistake in the country about that. There is a twofold liberty, natural (I mean as our nature is now corrupt) and civil or federal. The first is common to man with beasts and other creatures. By this, man, as he stands in relation to man simply, hath liberty to do what he lists; it is a liberty to evil as well as to good. This liberty is incompatible and inconsistent with authority and cannot endure the least restraint of the most just authority. The exercise and maintaining of this liberty makes men grow more evil and in time to be worse than brute beasts: *omnes sumus licentia deteriores*. This is that great enemy of truth and peace, that wild beast, which all of the ordinances of God are bent against, to restrain and subdue it. The other kind of liberty I call civil or federal; it may also be termed moral, in reference to the covenant between God and man, in the moral law, and the politic covenants and constitutions amongst men themselves. This liberty is the proper end and object of authority and cannot subsist without it; and it is a liberty to that only which is good, just, and honest. This liberty you are to stand for, with the hazard (not only of your goods, but) of your lives, if need be. Whatsoever crosseth this is not authority but a distemper thereof. This liberty is maintained and exercised in a way of subjection to authority; it is of the same kind of liberty wherewith Christ hath made us free. The women's own choice makes such a man her husband; yet, being so chosen, he is her lord, and she is to be subject to him, yet in a way of liberty, not of bondage; and a true wife accounts her subjection her honor and freedom and would not think her condition safe and free but in her subjection to her husband's authority. Such is the liberty of the church under the authority of Christ, her king and husband; his yoke is so easy and sweet to her as a bride's ornaments; and if through forwardness or wantonness, etc., she shake it off, at any time, she is at no rest in her spirit, until she take it up again; and whether her lord smiles upon her and embraceth her in his arms, or whether he frowns, or rebukes, or smites her, she apprehends the sweetness of his love in all, and is refreshed, supported, and instructed by every such dispensation of his authority over her. On the other side, ye know who they are that complain of this yoke and say, Let us break their bands, etc.; we will not have this man to rule over us. Even so, brethren, it will be between you and your magistrates. If you want to stand for your natural corrupt liberties, and will do what is good in your own eyes, you will not endure the least weight of authority, but will murmur, and oppose, and be always striving to shake off that yoke; but if you will be satisfied to enjoy such civil and lawful liberties, such as Christ allows you, then will you quietly and cheerfully submit unto that authority which is set over you, in all the administrations of it, for your good. Wherein, if we fail at any time, we hope we shall be willing (by God's assistance) to hearken to good advice from any of you, or in any other way of God; so shall your liberties be preserved in upholding the honor and power of authority amongst you.

5. MASSACHUSETTS BODY OF LIBERTIES, 1641[1]

The free fruition of such liberties, immunities, and privileges as humanity, civility, and Christianity call for as due to every man in his place and proportion without impeachment and infringement hath ever been and ever will be the tranquillity and stability of churches and commonwealths. And the denial or deprival thereof, the disturbance if not the ruin of both.

We hold it, therefore, our duty and safety whilst we are about the further establishing of this government to collect and express all such freedoms as for present we foresee may concern us, and our posterity after us, and to ratify them with our solemn consent.

We do, therefore, this day religiously and unanimously decree and confirm these following rights, liberties, and privileges concerning our churches and civil state to be respectively, impartially, and inviolably enjoyed and observed throughout our jurisdiction forever.

1. No man's life shall be taken away, no man's honor or good name shall be stained, no man's person shall be arrested, restrained, banished, dismembered, nor

1. "Massachusetts Body of Liberties," *The Colonial Laws of Massachusetts* ..., ed. W. H. Whitmore (Boston, 1890), pp. 33, 35, 37, 43, 47, 49, 51, 53, 55, 57, 61.

any ways punished, no man shall be deprived of his wife or children, no man's goods or estate shall be taken away from him, nor any way indamaged under color of law or countenance of authority, unless it be by virtue or equity of some express law of the country warranting the same, established by a general court and sufficiently published, or in case of the defect of a law in any particular case by the word of God. And in capital cases, or in cases concerning dismembring or banishment, according to that word to be judged by the General Court.

2. Every person within this jurisdiction, whether inhabitant or foreigner, shall enjoy the same justice and law that is general for the plantation, which we constitute and execute one toward another without partiality or delay. . . .

7. No man shall be compelled to go out of the limits of this plantation upon any offensive wars which this Commonwealth or any of our friends or confederates shall voluntarily undertake. But only upon such vindictive and defensive wars in our own behalf or the behalf of our friends and confederates as shall be enterprised by the counsel and consent of a court general, or by authority derived from the same.

No man's cattle or goods of what kind soever shall be pressed or taken for any public use or service, unless it be by warrant grounded upon some act of the General Court, nor without such reasonable prices and hire as the ordinary rates of the country do afford. And if his cattle or goods shall perish or suffer damage in such service, the owner shall be sufficiently recompensed.

9. No monopolies shall be granted or allowed amongst us, but of such new inventions that are profitable to the country, and that for a short time. . . .

17. Every man of, or within, this jurisdiction shall have free liberty, notwithstanding any civil power to remove both himself and his family at their pleasure out of the same, provided there be no legal impediment to the contrary.

RITES, RULES, AND LIBERTIES CONCERNING JUDICIAL PROCEEDINGS

18. No man's person shall be restrained or imprisoned by any authority whatsoever, before the law hath sentenced him thereto, if he can put in sufficient security, bail, or mainprise, for his appearance, and good behavior in the meantime, unless it be in crimes capital, and contempts in open court, and in such cases where some express act of court doth allow it. . . .

41. Every man that is to answer for any criminal cause, whether he be in prison or under bail, his cause shall be heard and determined at the next court that hath proper cognizance thereof, and may be done without prejudice of justice.

42. No man shall be twice sentenced by civil justice for one and the same crime, offense, or trespass.

43. No man shall be beaten with above forty stripes, nor shall any true gentleman, nor any man equal to a gentleman be punished with whipping, unless his crime be very shameful, and his course of life vicious and profligate.

44. No man condemned to die shall be put to death within four days next after his condemnation, unless the court see special cause to the contrary, or in case of martial law, nor shall the body of any man so put to death be unburied twelve hours, unless it be in case of anatomy.

45. No man shall be forced by torture to confess any crime against himself nor any other, unless it be in some capital case where he is first fully convicted by clear and sufficient evidence to be guilty, after which if the cause be of that nature, that it is very apparent there be other conspirators, or confederates with him, then he may be tortured, yet not with such tortures as be barbarous and inhumane.

46. For bodily punishments we allow

amongst us none that are inhumane, barbarous, or cruel. . . .

58. Civil authority hath power and liberty to see the peace, ordinances, and rules of Christ observed in every church according to his Word. So it be done in a civil and not in an ecclesiastical way.

59. Civil authority hath power and liberty to deal with any church member in a way of civil justice, notwithstanding any church relation, office, or interest.

60. No church censure shall degrade or depose any man from any civil dignity, office, or authority he shall have in the Commonwealth. . . .

62. Any shire or town shall have liberty to choose their deputies whom and where they please for the General Court. So be it they be freemen, and have taken their oath of fealty, and inhabiting in this jurisdiction. . . .

66. The freemen of every township shall have power to make such by-laws and constitutions as may concern the welfare of their town, provided they be not of a criminal, but only of a prudential nature, and that their penalties exceed not 20 shillings for one offense, and that they be not repugnant to the public laws and orders of the country. And if any inhabitant shall neglect or refuse to observe them, they shall have power to levy the appointed penalties by distress.

67. It is the constant liberty of the freemen of this plantation to choose yearly at the Court of Election out of the freemen all the general officers of this jurisdiction. If they please to discharge them at the day of election by way of vote, they may do it without showing cause. But if at any other general court, we hold it due justice that the reasons thereof be alleged and proved. By general officers we mean our governor, deputy governor, assistants, treasurer, general of our wars. And our

admiral at sea, and such as are, or hereafter may be, of the like general nature.

68. It is the liberty of the freemen to choose such deputies for the General Court out of themselves, either in their own towns or elsewhere as they judge fittest. And because we cannot foresee what variety and weight of occasions may fall into future consideration and what counsels we may stand in need of, we decree, that the deputies (to attend the General Court in the behalf of the country) shall not any time be stated or inacted, but from court to court, or at the most but for one year, that the country may have an annual liberty to do in that case what is most behooveful for the best welfare thereof.

69. No General Court shall be dissolved or adjourned without the consent of the major party thereof.

70. All freemen called to give any advice, vote, verdict, or sentence in any court, counsel, or civil assembly shall have full freedom to do it according to their true judgments and consciences, so it be done orderly and inoffensively for the manner. . . .

79. If any man at his death shall not leave his wife a competent portion of his estate, upon just complaint made to the General Court she shall be relieved.

80. Every married woman shall be free from bodily correction or stripes by her husband, unless it be in his own defense upon her assault. If there be any just cause of correction, complaint shall be made to authority assembled in some court, from which only she shall receive it.

81. When parents die intestate, the elder son shall have a double portion of his whole estate real and personal, unless the General Court upon just cause alleged shall judge otherwise.

82. When parents die intestate having

no heirs males of their bodies, their daughters shall inherit as copartners, unless the General Court upon just reason shall judge otherwise.

83. If any parents shall wilfully and unreasonably deny any child timely or convenient marriage, or shall exercise any unnatural severity toward them, such children shall have free liberty to complain to authority for redress.

84. No orphan during their minority which was not committed to tuition or service by the parents in their lifetime shall afterward be absolutely disposed of by any kindred, friend, executor, township, or church, nor by themselves without the consent of some court, wherein two assistants at least shall be present.

LIBERTIES OF SERVANTS

85. If any servants shall flee from the tyranny and cruelty of their masters to the house of any freeman of the same town, they shall be there protected and sustained till due order be taken for their relief. Provided due notice thereof be speedily given to their masters from whom they fled. And the next assistant or constable where the party flying is harbored.

86. No servant shall be put off for above a year to any other neither in the lifetime of their master nor after their death by their executors or administrators unless it be by consent of authority assembled in some court or two assistants.

87. If any man smite out the eye or tooth of his manservant, or maidservant, or otherwise maim or much disfigure him, unless it be by mere casualty, he shall let them go free from his service, and shall have such further recompense as the court shall allow him.

88. Servants that have served diligently and faithfully to the benefit of their masters seven years shall not be sent away empty. And if any have been unfaithful, negligent, or unprofitable in their service, notwithstanding the good usage of their masters, they shall not be dismissed till they have made satisfaction according to the judgment of authority.

LIBERTIES OF FOREIGNERS AND STRANGERS

89. If any people of other nations professing the true Christian religion shall flee to us from the tyranny or oppression of their persecutors, or from famine, wars, or the like necessary and compulsory cause, they shall be entertained and succored amongst us, according to that power and prudence God shall give us.

90. If any ships or other vessels, be it friend or enemy, shall suffer shipwreck upon our coast, there shall be no violence or wrong offered to their persons or goods. But their persons shall be harbored, and relieved, and their goods preserved in safety till authority may be certified thereof, and shall take further order therein.

91. There shall never be any bond slavery, villeinage, or captivity amongst us unless it be lawful captives taken in just wars, and such strangers as willingly sell themselves or are sold to us. And these shall have all the liberties and Christian usages which the law of God established in Israel concerning such persons doth morally require. This exempts none from servitude who shall be judged thereto by authority.

OF THE BRUTE CREATURE

92. No man shall exercise any tyranny or cruelty toward any brute creature which are usually kept for man's use. . . .

94. CAPITAL LAWS

1

If any man after legal conviction shall have or worship any other god, but the Lord God, he shall be put to death.

2

If any man or woman be a witch (that

is, hath or consulteth with a familiar spirit), they shall be put to death.

3

If any man shall blaspheme the name of God, the Father, Son, or Holy Ghost, with direct, express, presumptuous, or high-handed blasphemy, or shall curse God in the like manner, he shall be put to death. . . .

95. A DECLARATION OF THE LIBERTIES THE LORD JESUS HATH GIVEN TO THE CHURCHES

1

All the people of God within this jurisdiction who are not in a church way, and be orthodox in judgment, and not scandalous in life, shall have full liberty to gather themselves into a church estate. Provided they do it in a Christian way, with due observation of the rules of Christ revealed in his Word.

2

Every church hath full liberty to exercise all the ordinances of God, according to the rules of Scripture.

3

Every church hath free liberty of election and ordination of all their officers from time to time, provided they be able, pious, and orthodox.

4

Every church hath free liberty of admission, recommendation, dismission, and expulsion, or deposal of their officers and members, upon due cause, with free exercise of the discipline and censures of Christ according to the rules of his Word.

5

No injunctions are to be put upon any church, church officers, or member in point of doctrine, worship, or discipline, whether for substance or circumstance besides the institutions of the Lord. . . .

98. Lastly, because our duty and desire is to do nothing suddenly which fundamentally concern us, we decree that these rights and liberties shall be audibly read and deliberately weighed at every General Court that shall be held, within three years next ensuing, and such of them as shall not be altered or repealed they shall stand so ratified, that no man shall infringe them without due punishment. . . .

6. A PLEA FOR RELIGIOUS LIBERTY[1]

By ROGER WILLIAMS

EDITORS' NOTE.—Roger Williams (*ca.* 1603–83), religious leader and one of the founders of Rhode Island, was the son of a well-to-do London businessman. Educated at Cambridge (A.B., 1627) he became a clergyman and in 1630 sailed for Massachusetts. He refused a call to the church of Boston because it had not formally broken with the Church of England, but after two invitations he became the assistant pastor, later pastor, of the church at Salem. He questioned the right of the colonists to take the Indians' land from them merely on the legal basis of the royal charter and in other ways ran afoul of the oligarchy then ruling Massachusetts. In 1635 he was found guilty of spreading "new and dangerous opinions against the

1. Roger Williams, *The Bloudy Tenent of Persecution* . . . ("Publications of the Narragansett Club" [Providence, R.I.], Vol. III [1867]), pp. 3–4, 63, 58–59, 138–39, 148, 170–71, 201, 247–50, 372–73, 424–25.

authority of magistrates" and was ordered to be banished from the colony. He lived briefly with friendly Indians and then, in 1636, founded Providence in what was to be the colony of Rhode Island and Providence Plantations. His religious views led him to become briefly a Baptist, later a Seeker. In 1644, while he was in England getting a charter for his colony from Parliament, he wrote the work from which this dialogue is taken. During much of his later life he was engaged in polemics on political and religious questions. He was an important figure in the intellectual life of his time, though the direct influence of his writings is considered by Professor Brockunier to have been slight: "Earliest of the fathers of American democracy, he owes his enduring fame to his humanity and breadth of view, his untiring devotion to the cause of democracy and free opportunity, and his long record of opposition to the privileged and self-seeking" (*DAB*, XX, 289).

First, that the blood of so many hundred thousand souls of Protestants and Papists, spilt in the wars of present and former ages, for their respective consciences, is not required nor accepted by Jesus Christ the Prince of Peace.

Secondly, pregnant scriptures and arguments are throughout the work proposed against the doctrine of persecution for cause of conscience.

Thirdly, satisfactory answers are given to scriptures, and objections produced by Mr. Calvin, Beza, Mr. Cotton, and the ministers of the New English churches and others former and later, tending to prove the doctrine of persecution for cause of conscience.

Fourthly, the doctrine of persecution for cause of conscience is proved guilty of all the blood of the souls crying for vengeance under the altar.

Fifthly, all civil states with their officers of justice in their respective constitutions and administrations are proved essentially civil, and therefore not judges, governors, or defenders of the spiritual or Christian state and worship.

Sixthly, it is the will and command of God that (since the coming of his Son the Lord Jesus) a permission of the most paganish, Jewish, Turkish, or antichristian consciences and worships, be granted to all men in all nations and countries; and they are only to be fought against with that sword which is only (in soul matters) able to conquer, to wit, the sword of God's Spirit, the Word of God.

Seventhly, the state of the Land of Israel, the kings and people thereof in peace and war, is proved figurative and ceremonial, and no pattern nor president for any kingdom or civil state in the world to follow.

Eighthly, God requireth not a uniformity of religion to be enacted and enforced in any civil state; which enforced uniformity (sooner or later) is the greatest occasion of civil war, ravishing of conscience, persecution of Christ Jesus in his servants, and of the hypocrisy and destruction of millions of souls.

Ninthly, in holding an enforced uniformity of religion in a civil state, we must necessarily disclaim our desires and hopes of the Jew's conversion to Christ.

Tenthly, an enforced uniformity of religion throughout a nation or civil state, confounds the civil and religious, denies the principles of Christianity and civility, and that Jesus Christ is come in the flesh.

Eleventhly, the permission of other consciences and worships than a state professeth only can (according to God) procure a firm and lasting peace (good assurance being taken according to the wisdom of the civil state for uniformity of civil obedience from all forts).

Twelfthly, lastly, true civility and Christianity may both flourish in a state or kingdom, notwithstanding the permission of divers and contrary consciences, either of Jew or Gentile....

TRUTH. I acknowledge that to molest any person, Jew or Gentile, for either professing doctrine, or practicing worship merely religious or spiritual, it is to persecute him, and such a person (whatever his doctrine or practice be, true or false) suffereth persecution for conscience.

But withal I desire it may be well observed that this distinction is not full and complete: for beside this that a man may be persecuted because he holds or practices what he believes in conscience to be a truth (as Daniel did, for which he was cast into the lions' den, Dan. 6), and many thousands of Christians, because they durst not cease to preach and practice what they believed was by God commanded, as the Apostles answered (Acts 4 & 5), I say besides this a man may also be persecuted, because he dares not be constrained to yield obedience to such doctrines and worships as are by men invented and appointed....

Dear TRUTH, I have two sad complaints:

First, the most sober of the witnesses, that dare to plead thy cause, how are they charged to be mine enemies, contentious, turbulent, seditious?

Secondly, thine enemies, though they speak and rail against thee, though they outrageously pursue, imprison, banish, kill thy faithful witnesses, yet how is all vermilion'd o'er for justice against the heretics? Yea, if they kindle coals, and blow the flames of devouring wars, that leave neither spiritual nor civil state, but burn up branch and root, yet how do all pretend an holy war? He that kills, and

he that's killed, they both cry out: "It is for God, and for their conscience."

'Tis true, nor one nor other seldom dare to plead the mighty Prince Christ Jesus for their author, yet (both Protestant and Papist) pretend they have spoke with Moses and the Prophets, who all, say they (before Christ came), allowed such holy persecutions, holy wars against the enemies of holy church.

TRUTH. Dear PEACE (to ease thy first complaint), 'tis true, thy dearest sons, most like their mother, peacekeeping, peacemaking sons of God, have borne and still must bear the blurs of troublers of Israel, and turners of the world upside down. And 'tis true again, what Solomon once spake: "The beginning of strife is as when one letteth out water, therefore (saith he) leave off contention before it be meddled with. This caveat should keep the banks and sluices firm and strong, that strife, like a breach of waters, break not in upon the sons of men."

Yet strife must be distinguished: It is necessary or unnecessary, godly or ungodly, Christian or unchristian, etc.

It is unnecessary, unlawful, dishonorable, ungodly, unchristian, in most cases in the world, for there is a possibility of keeping sweet peace in most cases, and, if it be possible, it is the express command of God that peace be kept (Rom. 13).

Again, it is necessary, honorable, godly, etc., with civil and earthly weapons to defend the innocent and to rescue the oppressed from the violent paws and jaws of oppressing persecuting Nimrods[2] (Psal. 73; Job 29).

It is as necessary, yea more honorable, godly, and Christian, to fight the fight of faith, with religious and spiritual artillery, and to contend earnestly for the faith of Jesus, once delivered to the saints against all opposers, and the gates of earth and hell, men or devils, yea against Paul himself, or an angel from

2. See Gen. 10:8–9.

heaven, if he bring any other faith or doctrine. . . .

PEACE. I add that a civil sword (as woeful experience in all ages has proved) is so far from bringing or helping forward an opposite in religion to repentance that magistrates sin grievously against the work of God and blood of souls by such proceedings. Because as (commonly) the sufferings of false and antichristian teachers harden their followers, who being blind, by this means are occasioned to tumble into the ditch of hell after their blind leaders, with more inflamed zeal of lying confidence. So, secondly, violence and a sword of steel begets such an impression in the sufferers that certainly they conclude (as indeed that religion cannot be true which needs such instruments of violence to uphold it so) that persecutors are far from soft and gentle commiseration of the blindness of others. . . .

For (to keep to the similitude which the Spirit useth, for instance) to batter down a stronghold, high wall, fort, tower, or castle, men bring not a first and second admonition, and after obstinacy, excommunication, which are spiritual weapons concerning them that be in the church: nor exhortation to repent and be baptized, to believe in the Lord Jesus, etc., which are proper weapons to them that be without, etc. But to take a stronghold, men bring cannons, culverins, saker, bullets, powder, muskets, swords, pikes, etc., and these to this end are weapons effectual and proportionable.

On the other side, to batter down idolatry, false worship, heresy, schism, blindness, hardness, out of the soul and spirit, it is vain, improper, and unsuitable to bring those weapons which are used by persecutors, stocks, whips, prisons, swords, gibbets, stakes, etc. (where these seem to prevail with some cities or kingdoms, a stronger force sets up again, what a weaker pull'd down), but against these spiritual strongholds in the souls of men, spiritual artillery and weapons are proper, which are mighty through God to subdue and bring under the very thought to obedience, or else to bind fast the soul with chains of darkness, and lock it up in the prison of unbelief and hardness to eternity. . . .

PEACE. I pray descend now to the second evil which you observe in the answerer's position, viz., that it would be evil to tolerate notorious evildoers, seducing teachers, etc.

TRUTH. I say the evil is that he most improperly and confusedly joins and couples seducing teachers with scandalous livers.

PEACE. But is it not true that the world is full of seducing teachers, and is it not true that seducing teachers are notorious evildoers?

TRUTH. I answer, far be it from me to deny either, and yet in two things I shall discover the great evil of this joining and coupling seducing teachers, and scandalous livers as one adequate or proper object of the magistrate's care and work to suppress and punish.

First, it is not an homogeneal (as we speak) but an hetergeneal[3] commixture or joining together of things most different in kinds and natures, as if they were both of one consideration. . . .

TRUTH. I answer, in granting with Brentius[4] that man hath not power to make laws to bind conscience, he overthrows such his tenent and practice as restrain men from their worship, according to their conscience and belief, and constrain them to such worships (though it be out of a pretense that they are convinced) which their own souls tell them they have no satisfaction nor faith in.

Secondly, whereas he affirms that men may make laws to see the laws of God observed.

3. Old forms for "homogeneous" and "heterogeneous."
4. Johann Brenz (1499–1570), German Lutheran theologian.

I answer, as God needeth not the help of a material sword of steel to assist the sword of the Spirit in the affairs of conscience, to those men, those magistrates, yea that commonwealth which makes such magistrates, must needs have power and authority from Christ Jesus to fit judge and to determine in all the great controversies concerning doctrine, discipline, government, etc.

And then I ask whether upon this ground it must not evidently follow that:

Either there is no lawful commonwealth nor civil state of men in the world, which is not qualified with this spiritual discerning (and then also that the very commonweal hath more light concerning the church of Christ than the church itself).

Or, that the commonweal and magistrates thereof must judge and punish as they are persuaded in their own belief and conscience (be their conscience paganish, Turkish, or antichristian) what is this but to confound heaven and earth together, and not only to take away the being of Christianity out of the world, but to take away all civility, and the world out of the world, and to lay all upon heaps of confusion? . . .

PEACE. The fourth head is the proper means of both these powers to attain their ends.

First, the proper means whereby the civil power may and should attain its end are only political, and principally these five.

First, the erecting and establishing what form of civil government may seem in wisdom most meet, according to general rules of the world, and state of the people.

Secondly, the making, publishing, and establishing of wholesome civil laws, not only such as concern civil justice, but also the free passage of true religion; for outward civil peace ariseth and is maintained from them both, from the latter as well as from the former.

Civil peace cannot stand entire, where religion is corrupted (2 Chron. 15. 3. 5. 6; and Judges 8). And yet such laws, though conversant about religion, may still be counted civil laws, as, on the contrary, an oath doth still remain religious though conversant about civil matters.

Thirdly, election and appointment of civil officers to see execution to those laws.

Fourthly, civil punishments and rewards of transgressors and observers of these laws.

Fifthly, taking up arms against the enemies of civil peace.

Secondly, the means whereby the church may and should attain her ends are only ecclesiastical, which are chiefly five.

First, setting up that form of church government only of which Christ hath given them a pattern in his Word.

Secondly, acknowledging and admitting of no lawgiver in the church but Christ and the publishing of His laws.

Thirdly, electing and ordaining of such officers only, as Christ hath appointed in his Word.

Fourthly, to receive into their fellowship them that are approved and inflicting spiritual censures against them that offend.

Fifthly, prayer and patience in suffering any evil from them that be without, who disturb their peace.

So that magistrates, as magistrates, have no power of setting up the form of church government, electing church officers, punishing with church censures, but to see that the church does her duty herein. And on the other side, the churches as churches, have no power (though as members of the commonweal they may have power) of erecting or altering forms of civil government, electing of civil officers, inflicting civil punishments (no not on persons excommunicate) as by deposing magistrates from their civil authority, or withdrawing the hearts of the people against them, to their laws, no more than to discharge wives, or children, or servants, from due obedience to their husbands, parents, or masters; or by taking up arms against their magistrates, though he persecute them for conscience: for though members of churches who are public officers also of the civil state may suppress by force the violence of usurpers, as Iehoiada did Athaliah, yet this they do not as members of the church but as officers of the civil state.

TRUTH. Here are divers considerable passages which I shall briefly examine, so far as concerns our controversy.

First, whereas they say that the civil power may erect and establish what form of civil government may seem in wisdom most meet, I acknowledge the proposition to be most true, both in itself and also considered with the end of it, that a civil government is an ordinance of God, to conserve the civil peace of people, so far as concerns their bodies and goods, as formerly hath been said.

But from this grant I infer (as before hath been touched) that the sovereign, original, and foundation of civil power lies in the people (whom they must needs mean by the civil power distinct from the government set up). And, if so, that a people may erect and establish what form of government seems to them most meet for their civil condition; it is evident that such governments as are by them erected and established have no more power, nor for no longer time, than the civil power or people consenting and agreeing shall betrust them with. This is clear not only in reason but in the experience of all commonweals, where the people are not deprived of their natural freedom by the power of tyrants.

And, if so, that the magistrates receive their power of governing the church from the people, undeniably it follows that a people, as a people, naturally considered (of what nature or nation soever in Europe, Asia, Africa, or America), have fundamentally and originally, as

men, a power to govern the church, to see her do her duty, to correct her, to redress, reform, establish, etc. And if this be not to pull God and Christ and Spirit out of heaven, and subject them unto natural, sinful, inconstant men, and so consequently to Satan himself, by whom all peoples naturally are guided, let heaven and earth judge. . . .

PEACE. Some will here ask: What may the magistrate then lawfully do with his civil horn or power in matters of religion?

TRUTH. His horn not being the horn of that unicorn or rhinoceros, the power of the Lord Jesus in spiritual cases, his sword not the two-edged sword of the spirit, the word of God (hanging not about the loins or side, but at the lips, and proceeding out of the mouth of his ministers) but of an humane and civil nature and constitution, it must consequently be of a humane and civil operation, for who knows not that operation follows constitution? And therefore I shall end this passage with this consideration:

The civil magistrate either respecteth that religion and worship which his conscience is persuaded is true, and upon which he ventures his soul; or else that and those which he is persuaded are false.

Concerning the first, if that which the magistrate believeth to be true, be true, I say he owes a threefold duty unto it:

First, approbation and countenance, a reverent esteem and honorable testimony, according to Isa. 49, and Revel. 21, with a tender respect of truth, and the professors of it.

Secondly, personal submission of his own soul to the power of the Lord Jesus in that spiritual government and kingdom, according to Matt. 18 and 1 Cor. 5.

Thirdly, protection of such true professors of Christ, whether apart, or met together, as also of their estates from violence and injury, according to Rom. 13.

Now, secondly, if it be a false religion

(unto which the civil magistrate dare not adjoin, yet) he owes:

First, permission (for approbation he owes not what is evil) and this according to Matthew 13. 30 for public peace and quiet's sake.

Secondly, he owes protection to the persons of his subjects (though of a false worship), that no injury be offered either to the persons or goods of any....

...The God of Peace, the God of Truth will shortly seal this truth, and confirm this witness, and make it evident to the whole world, that the doctrine of persecution for cause of conscience, is most evidently and lamentably contrary to the doctrine of Christ Jesus the Prince of Peace. Amen.

7. FRAME OF GOVERNMENT OF PENNSYLVANIA, 1682[1]

By WILLIAM PENN

EDITORS' NOTE.—William Penn (1644–1718), founder of Pennsylvania, as a young man joined the persecuted sect of Friends, or Quakers, despite the opposition of his father. As a leader of this group he became interested in the management of the Jerseys, then largely under Quaker control and, in the later days of Charles II, secured the grant of Pennsylvania, including three counties now in Delaware. Penn then set about attracting settlers for the new colony and later, after consultation with Algernon Sidney and other friends, drew up the "Frame of Government" and a penal code far in advance of his time. Actually the governmental structure here provided for proved unworkable and, within a year, was supplanted. Only in 1701, with Penn's "Charter of Privileges," was the proprietary government established upon the formal basis on which it continued to 1776.

For a full picture of the constitutional structure of colonial Pennsylvania more than the "Frame" is needed; the latter must be read in light of the royal charter. The charter grants to Penn and his heirs the usual proprietary rights over taxation (which required the assent of the freemen), the appointment of officers, the administration of justice, the incorporation of towns, and the sale and disposal of land. This grant is subject, of course, to the usual proviso that the provincial laws be in harmony with those of England, a point for the royal courts ultimately to decide.

THE PREFACE

When the great and wise *God* had made the world, of all his creatures it pleased him to choose man his deputy to rule it; and to fit him for so great a charge and trust, he did not only qualify him with skill and power but with integrity to use them justly. This native goodness was equally his honor and his happiness; and whilst he stood here, all went well; there was no need of coercive or compulsive means; the precept of divine love and truth, in his bosom, was

1. *The Federal and State Constitutions, Colonial Charters, and Other Organic Laws of the States, Territories, and Colonies, Now or Heretofore Forming the United States of America,* ed. F. N. Thorpe (7 vols.; Washington, 1909), V, 3052–55, 3056, 3057, 3058–59.

the guide and keeper of his innocency. But lust prevailing against duty made a lamentable breach upon it; and the law, that before had no power over him, took place upon him, and his disobedient posterity, that such as would not live comformable to the holy law within should fall under the reproof and correction of the just law without in a judicial administration.

This the Apostle teaches in divers of his epistles: "The law," says he, "was added because of transgressions." In another place, "Knowing that the law was not made for the righteous man; but for the disobedient and ungodly, for sinners, for unholy and profane, for murderers, for whoremongers, for them that defile themselves with mankind, and for mansteelers, for liars, for perjured persons," etc.; but this is not all, he opens and carries the matter of government a little further: "Let every soul be subject to the higher powers; for there is no power but of *God*. The powers that be are ordained of *God:* whosoever therefore resisteth the power, resisteth the ordinance of *God*. For rulers are not a terror to good works, but to evil: wilt thou then not be afraid of the power? Do that which is good, and thou shalt have praise of the same." "He is the minister of God to thee for good." "Wherefore ye must needs be subject, not only for wrath, but for conscience' sake."

This settles the divine right of government beyond exception, and that for two ends: first, to terrify evildoers; secondly, to cherish those that do well; which gives government a life beyond corruption and makes it as durable in the world, as good men shall be. So that government seems to me a part of religion itself, a thing sacred in its institution and end. For, if it does not directly remove the cause, it crushes the effects of evil and is, as such (though a lower, yet), an emanation of the same Divine Power that is both author and object of pure religion; the difference lying here, that the

one is more free and mental, the other more corporal and compulsive in its operations; but that is only to evildoers; government itself being otherwise as capable of kindness, goodness, and charity, as a more private society. They weakly err that think there is no other use of government than correction, which is the coarsest part of it: daily experience tells us that the care and regulation of many other affairs, more soft, and daily necessary, make up much of the greatest part of government; and which must have followed the peopling of the world, had Adam never fell, and will continue among men, on earth, under the highest attainments they may arrive at, by the coming of the blessed *Second Adam*, the *Lord* from heaven. Thus much of government in general, as to its rise and end.

For particular *frames* and *models*, it will become me to say little; and comparatively I will say nothing. My reasons are:

First. That the age is too nice and difficult for it; there being nothing the wits of men are more busy and divided upon. It is true, they seem to agree to the end, to wit, happiness; but, in the means, they differ, as to divine, so to this human felicity; and the cause is much the same, not always want of light and knowledge, but want of using them rightly. Men side with their passions against their reason, and their sinister interests have so strong a bias upon their minds that they lean to them against the good of the things they know.

Secondly. I do not find a model in the world, that time, place, and some singular emergencies have not necessarily altered; nor it is easy to frame a civil government that shall serve all places alike.

Thirdly. I know what is said by the several admirers of *monarchy, aristocracy,* and *democracy,* which are the rule of one, a few, and many, and are the three common ideas of government, when men discourse on the subject. But

I choose to solve the controversy with this small distinction, and it belongs to all three: *Any government is free to the people under it* (whatever be the frame) *where the laws rule, and the people are a party to those laws,* and more than this is tyranny, oligarchy, or confusion.

But, lastly, when all is said, there is hardly one frame of government in the world so ill designed by its first founders that, in good hands, would not do well enough; and story tells us, the best, in ill ones, can do nothing that is great or good; witness the *Jewish* and *Roman states*. Governments, like clocks, go from the motion men give them, and as governments are made and moved by men, so by them they are ruined too. Wherefore governments rather depend upon men than men upon governments. Let men be good, and the government cannot be bad; if it be ill, they will cure it. But, if men be bad, let the government be ever so good, they will endeavor to warp and spoil it to their turn.

I know some say, "Let us have good laws, and no matter for the men that execute them"; but let them consider that, though good laws do well, good men do better, for good laws may want good men and be abolished or evaded [*invaded* in Franklin's print] by ill men; but good men will never want good laws nor suffer ill ones. It is true, good laws have some awe upon ill ministers, but that is where they have not power to escape or abolish them, and the people are generally wise and good, but a loose and depraved people (which is the question) love laws and an administration like themselves. That, therefore, which makes a good constitution, must keep it, *viz.*: men of wisdom and virtue, quali-

ties that, because they descend not with wordly inheritances, must be carefully propagated by a virtuous education of youth; for which after ages will owe more to the care and prudence of founders, and the successive magistracy, than to their parents, for their private patrimonies.

These considerations of the weight of government, and the nice and various opinions about it, made it uneasy to me to think of publishing the ensuing frame and conditional laws, forseeing both the censures they will meet with from men of differing humors and engagements and the occasion they may give of discourse beyond my design.

But, next to the power of necessity (which is a solicitor that will take no denial), this induced me to a compliance: that we have (with reverence to God, and good conscience to men), to the best of our skill, contrived and composed the *frame* and *laws* of this government, to the great end of all government, *viz.*: *To support power in reverence with the people, and to secure the people from the abuse of power;* that they may be free by their just obedience, and the magistrates honorable, for their just administration; for liberty without obedience is confusion, and obedience without liberty is slavery. To carry this evenness is partly owing to the constitution and partly to the magistracy; where either of these fail, government will be subject to convulsions; but, where both are wanting, it must be totally subverted; then where both meet, the government is like to endure. Which I humbly pray and hope *God* will please to make the lot of this of *Pennsylvania.* Amen.

THE FRAME, &C.—APRIL 25, 1682

To all persons to whom these presents may come. Whereas, King Charles the Second ... hath been graciously pleased to give and grant unto me, *William Penn,* ... all that tract of land, or province, called *Pennsylvania,* in *America* ... I, the said *William Penn,* have declared, granted, and conformed ... these liberties, franchises, and properties, to be held, enjoyed, and kept by the freemen, planters, and inhabitants of the said province of *Pennsylvania* for ever.

Imprimis. That the government of this province shall, according to the powers of the patent, consist of the governor and freemen of the said province, in form of a provincial Council and General Assembly, by whom all laws shall be made, officers chosen, and public affairs transacted, as is hereafter respectively declared. . . .

II. That the freemen of the said province shall . . . choose out of themselves *seventy-two* persons of most note for their wisdom, virtue, and ability, who shall meet . . . and act as, the provincial Council. . . .

IV. That, after the first seven years, every one of the said third parts, that goeth yearly off, shall be uncapable of being chosen again for one whole year following; that so all may be fitted for government and have experience of the care and burden of it. . . .

VI. That, in this provincial Council, the governor or his deputy shall, or may, always preside and have a treble voice. . . .

VII. That the governor and provincial Council shall prepare and propose to the General Assembly, hereafter mentioned, all bills which they shall, at any time, think fit to be passed into laws. . . .

VIII. That the governor and provincial Council shall take care that all laws, statutes, and ordinances which shall at any time be made within the said province be duly and diligently executed. . . .

XII. That the governor and the provincial Council shall erect and order all public schools and encourage and reward the authors of useful sciences and laudable inventions in the said province. . . .

XIV. And, to the end that all laws prepared by the governor and provincial Council aforesaid may yet have the more full concurrence of the freemen of the province . . . the said freeman shall yearly choose members to serve in a General Assembly, as their representatives, not exceeding two hundred persons, who shall yearly meet . . . in the capital town, or city, of the said province, where, during eight days, the several members may freely confer with one another . . . and, on the ninth day from their so meeting, the said General Assembly, after reading over the proposed bills by the clerk of the provincial Council, and the occasions and motives for them being opened by the governor or his deputy, shall give their affirmative or negative. . . .

XVI. That, for the establishment of the government and laws of this province, and to the end there may be an universal satisfaction in the laying of the fundamentals thereof: The General Assembly shall, or may, for the first year, consist of all the freemen of and in the said province; and ever after it shall be yearly chosen, as aforesaid; which number of two hundred shall be enlarged as the country shall increase in people, so as it do not exceed five hundred, at any time; the appointment and proportioning of which, as also the laying and methodizing of the choice of the provincial Council and General Assembly, in future times, most equally to the divisions of the hundreds and counties, which the country shall hereafter be divided into, shall be in the power of the provincial Council to propose, and the General Assembly to resolve.

XVII. That the governor and the proprovincial Council shall erect, from time to time, standing courts of justice in such places and number as they shall judge convenient for the good government of the said province. . . .

XVIII. But forasmuch as the present condition of the province requires some immediate settlement, and admits not of so quick a revolution of officers; and to the end the said Province may, with all convenient speed, be well ordered and settled, I, *William Penn*, do therefore think fit to nominate and appoint such persons for judges, treasurers, masters of the rolls, sheriffs, justices of the peace, and coroners, as are most fitly qualified for those employments; to whom I shall make and grant commissions for the said offices, respectively, to hold to them, to whom the same shall be granted, for so long time as every such person shall well behave himself in the office, or place, to him respectively granted, and no longer. And upon the decease or displacing of any of the said officers, the succeeding officer, or officers, shall be chosen, as aforesaid. . . .

XXIII. That no act, law, or ordinance whatsoever shall at any time hereafter be made or done by the governor of this province, his heirs or assigns, or by the freemen in the provincial Council, or the General Assembly, to alter, change, or diminish the form, or affect, of this charter, or any part, or clause thereof, without the consent of the governor, his heirs, or assigns, and six parts of seven of the said freemen in provincial Council and General Assembly.

XXIV. And, lastly, that I, the said *William Penn*, for myself, my heirs, and assigns, have solemnly declared, granted, and confirmed, and do hereby solemnly declare, grant, and confirm, that neither I, my heirs, nor assigns, shall procure or do anything or things, whereby the liberties in this charter contained and expressed shall be infringed or broken; and if anything be procured by any person or persons contrary to these premises, it shall be held of no force or effect. In witness whereof, I, the said *William Penn*, have unto this present character [*sic*] of liberties set my hand and broad seal, this five and twentieth day of the second month, vulgarly called April,[2] in the year of our *Lord* one thousand six hundred and eighty-two.

8. DEMOCRACY IN CHURCH AND STATE[1]

By JOHN WISE

EDITORS' NOTE.—John Wise (1652–1725), Congregational pastor of Chebacco Parish, Ipswich, Massachusetts, from 1680 to 1725, was perhaps the "first colonial to justify village democracy by an appeal to political philosophy" (V. L. Parrington, *The Colonial Mind* [1927], p. 124). His defense of democracy in church government was occasioned by proposals which, had they been carried into effect, would have greatly reduced the influence of the laity and diminished the independence of the individual congregation in the Massachusetts churches. Opposing this scheme, Wise upheld the congregational principle, defining a church as "a society of Christians, meeting together in one place, under their proper pastors, for the performance of religious worship, and the exercising of Christian discipline," which has "complete power, when rightly constituted, to exercise all the ordinances of God."

CHAPTER II

I. I shall disclose several principles of natural knowledge, plainly discovering the law of nature or the true sentiments of natural reason, with respect to man's being and government. And in this essay

2. The reference to April as the "second month" is based on the custom then extant in England of beginning the legal new year on March 25.

1. John Wise, *A Vindication of the Government of New England Churches* (Boston, 1772), pp. 22–30, 31–33, 34, 35, 37, 39–41, 62.

I shall peculiarly confine the discourse to two heads:

Of the natural (in distinction to the civil).

Of the civil being of man. I shall principally take Baron Puffendorff for my chief guide and spokesman.

First

I shall consider man in a state of natural being, as a free-born subject under the crown of heaven, and owing homage to none but God himself. It is certain civil government in general is a very admirable result of Providence and an incomparable benefit to mankind, yet must needs be acknowledged to be the effect of human free compacts and not of divine institution. It is the produce of man's reason, of human and rational combinations, and not from any direct orders of infinite wisdom, in any positive law wherein is drawn up this or that scheme of civil government. Government . . . is necessary—in that no society of men can subsist without it. That particular form of government is necessary which best suits the temper and inclination of a people. Nothing can be God's ordinance but what he has particularly declared to be such. There is no particular form of civil government described in God's word; neither does nature prompt it. The government of the Jews was changed five times. Government is not formed by nature, as other births or productions. If it were, it would be the same in all countries because nature keeps the same method, in the same thing, in all climates. If a commonwealth be changed into a monarchy, is it nature that forms and brings forth the monarch? Or if a royal family be wholly extinct (as in Noah's case, being not heir apparent from descent from Adam), is it nature that must go to work (with the king bees, who themselves alone preserve the royal race in that empire) to breed a monarch before the people can have a king or a government set over them?

And thus we must leave kings to resolve which is their best title to their crowns, whether natural right, or the constitution of government settled by human compacts, under the direction and conduct of reason. But to proceed under the head of a state of natural being. . . .

1. The prime immunity in man's state is that he is most properly the subject of the law of nature. He is the favorite animal on earth; in that this part of God's image, namely, reason, is congenate with his nature, wherein by a law immutable, stamped upon his frame, God has provided a rule for men in all their actions, obliging each one to the performance of that which is right, not only as to justice, but likewise as to all other moral virtues, which is nothing but the dictate of right reason founded in the soul of man. That which is to be drawn from man's reason, flowing from the true current of that faculty, when unperverted, may be said to be the law of nature, on which account the Holy Scriptures declare it written on men's hearts. For being endowed with a soul, you may know from yourself how and what you ought to act (Romans 2:14). *These having not a law, are a law to themselves.* So that the meaning is: when we acknowledge the law of nature to be the dictate of right reason, we must mean that the understanding of man is endowed with such a power as to be able, from the contemplation of human conditions, to discover a necessity of living agreeably with this law. And likewise to find out some principle by which the precepts of it may be clearly and solidly demonstrated. The way to discover the law of nature in our own state is by a narrow watch and accurate contemplation of our natural condition and propensities. Others say this is the way to find out the law of nature. To wit, if a man doubts whether what he is going to do to another man be agreeable to the law of nature, then let him suppose himself to be in that other man's room and by this rule effectually exe-

cuted. A man must be a very dull scholar of nature not to make proficiency in the knowledge of her laws. But more particularly in pursuing our conditions for the discovery of the law of nature, this is very obvious to view, namely:

(1) A principle of self-love and self-preservation is very predominant in every man's being.

(2) A sociable disposition.

(3) An affection or love to mankind in general. And to give such sentiments the force of a law, we must suppose a God who takes care of all mankind and has thus obliged each one, as a subject of higher principles of being, than mere instincts. . . . All law, properly considered, supposes a capable subject and a superior power; and the law of God, which is binding, is published by the dictates of right reason as other ways: Therefore, says Plutarch, "to follow God and obey reason is the same thing." But, moreover, that God has established the law of nature as the general rule of government is further illustrable from the many sanctions in Providence, and from the peace and guilt of conscience in them that either obey or violate the law of nature. But, moreover, the foundation of the law of nature with relation to government may be thus discovered. To wit, man is a creature extremely desirous of his own preservation. Of himself he is plainly exposed to many wants, unable to secure his own safety and maintenance without the assistance of his fellows; and he is also able of returning kindness by the furtherance of mutual good; but yet man is often found to be malicious, insolent, and easily provoked, and as powerful in effecting mischief as he is ready in designing it. Now that such a creature may be preserved, it is necessary that he be sociable; that is, that he be capable and disposed to unite himself to those of his own species and to regulate himself toward them, that they may have no fair reason to do him harm but rather incline to promote his

interests and secure his rights and concerns. This then is a fundamental law of nature, that every man, as far as in him lies, do maintain a sociableness with others, agreeable with the main end and disposition of human nature in general. For this is very apparent, that reason and society render man the most potent of all creatures. And, finally, from the principles of sociableness it follows as a fundamental law of nature that man is not so wedded to his own interest but that he can make the common good the mark of his aim. Hence he becomes capacitated to enter into a civil state by the law of nature; for without this property in nature, namely, sociableness, which is for cementing of parts, every government would soon molder and dissolve.

2. The second great immunity of man is an original liberty stamped upon his rational nature. He that intrudes upon this liberty violates the law of nature. In this discourse I shall waive the consideration of man's moral turpitude, but shall view him physically as a creature which God has made and furnished essentially with many enobling immunities, which render him the most august animal in the world, and still, whatever has happened since his creation, he remains at the upper end of nature, and as such is a creature of a very noble character. . . . The whole frame of the lower part of the universe is devoted to his use and at his command, and his liberty under the conduct of right reason is equal with his trust, which liberty may be briefly considered, internally as to his mind and externally as to his person.

(1) The internal, native liberty of man's nature in general implies a faculty of doing or omitting things according to the direction of his judgment. But in a more special meaning this liberty does not consist in a loose and ungovernable freedom or in an unbounded license of acting. Such license is disagreeing with the condition and dignity of man and would make man of a lower and meaner

constitution than brute creatures, who in all their liberties are kept under a better and more rational government by their instincts. Therefore, as Plutarch says, those persons only who live in obedience to reason are worthy to be accounted free; they alone live as they will who have learned what they ought to will. So that the true natural liberty of man, such as really and truly agrees with him, must be understood, as he is guided and restrained by the ties of reason and laws of nature; all the rest is brutal, if not worse.

(2) Man's external, personal, natural liberty, antecedent to all human parts or alliances, must also be considered. And so every man must be conceived to be perfectly in his own power and disposal and not to be controlled by the authority of any other. And thus every man must be acknowledged equal to every man, since all subjection and all command are equally banished on both sides. And considering all men thus at liberty, every man has a prerogative to judge for himself, viz., what shall be most for his behoof, happiness, and well-being.

3. The third capital immunity belonging to man's nature is an equality amongst men, which is not to be denied by the law of nature till man has resigned himself with all his rights for the sake of a civil state; and then his personal liberty and equality is to be cherished and preserved to the highest degree as will consist with all just distinctions amongst men of honor, and shall be agreeable with the public good. For man has a high valuation of himself, and the passion seems to lay its first foundation (not in pride, but) really in the high and admirable frame and constitution of human nature. The word "man," says my author, is thought to carry somewhat of dignity in its sound; and we commonly make use of this as the most proper and prevailing argument against a rude insulter, viz., I am not a beast or a dog, but am a man as well as yourself. Since then

human nature agrees equally with all persons, and since no one can live a sociable life with another that does not own or respect him as a man, it follows as a command of the law of nature that every man esteem and treat another as one who is naturally his equal or who is a man as well as he. There be many popular or plausible reasons that greatly illustrate this equality, viz., that we all derive our being from one stock, the same common father of the human race. On this consideration Boethius[2] checks the pride of the insulting nobility. . . .

> Fondly our first descent we boast,
> If whence at first our breath we drew
> The common springs of life we view,
> The airy notion soon is lost.
> The Almighty made us equal all;
> But he that slavishly complies
> To do the Drudgery of Vice,
> Denies his high original.

And also that our bodies are composed of matter, frail, brittle, and liable to be destroyed by a thousand accidents; we all owe our existence to the same method of propagation. The noblest mortal in his entrance on the stage of life is not distinguished by any pomp or of passage from the lowest of mankind; and our life hastens to the same general mark; death observes no ceremony but knocks as loud at the barriers of the court as at the door of the cottage. This equality, being admitted, bears a very great force in maintaining peace and friendship amongst men. For that he who would use the assistance of others in promoting his own advantage ought as freely to be at their service when they want his help on the like occasions. One good turn requires another is the common proverb; for otherwise he must need esteem others unequal to himself, who constantly demands their aid and as constantly denies his own. And whoever is of this insolent

2. Boethius (480–524), Roman philosopher and statesman, author of the *De consolatione philosophiae* ("Of the Consolation of Philosophy").

temper cannot but highly displease those about him and soon give occasion of the breach of the common peace. It was a manly reproof which Charactacus[3] gave the Romans.... What! Because you desire to be masters of all men, does it follow therefore that all men should desire to be your slaves, for that it is a command of nature's law that no man that has not obtained a particular and special right shall arrogate to himself a larger share than his fellows, but shall admit others to equal privileges with himself. So that the principle of equality in a natural state is peculiarly transgressed by pride, which is when a man without sufficient reason prefers himself to others.... As Hensius[4] paraphrases upon Aristotle's *Politics* to this purpose: ... Nothing is more suitable to nature than that those who excel in understanding and prudence should rule and control those who are less happy in those advantages.... Yet we must note ... that there is room for an answer. That it would be the greatest absurdity to believe that nature actually invests the wise with a sovereignty over the weak or with a right of forcing them against their wills, for that no sovereignty can be established unless some human deed or covenant precede. Nor does natural fitness for government make a man presently governor over another, for ... as Ulpian says, by a natural right all men are born free; and nature having set all men upon a level and made them equals, no servitude or subjection can be conceived without inequality; and this cannot be made without usurpation or force in others or voluntary compliance in those who resign their freedom and give away their degree of natural being. And thus we come,

3. Charactacus, or Caractacus, leader of British resistance to the Roman invasions of A.D. 48–51.

4. Hensius, properly Heinsius, Daniel (1580–1655), one of the greatest scholars of the Dutch Renaissance, professor at Leiden.

Second

To consider man in a civil state of being, wherein we shall observe the great difference between a natural and political state, for in the latter state many great disproportions appear, or at least many obvious distinctions are soon made amongst men, which doctrine is to be laid upon under a few heads.

1. Every man considered in a natural state must be allowed to be free and at his own disposal; yet to suit man's inclinations to society, and in a peculiar manner to gratify the necessity he is in of public rule and order, he is impelled to enter into a civil community and divests himself of his natural freedom and puts himself under government, which amongst other things comprehends the power of life and death over him, together with authority to enjoin him some things to which he has an utter aversion and to prohibit him other things for which he may have as strong an inclination, so that he may be often under this authority obliged to sacrifice his private for the public good.... Though man is inclined to society, yet he is driven to a combination by great necessity.... The true and leading cause of forming governments and yielding up natural liberty and throwing man's equality into a common pile to be new cast by the rules of fellowship was really and truly to guard themselves against the injuries man were liable to interchangeably; for none so good to man as man and yet none a greater enemy....

2. The first human subject and origin of civil power is the people. For as they have a power every man over himself in a natural state, so upon a combination they can and do bequeath this power unto others and settle it according as their united discretion shall determine. For that this is very plain, that when the subject of sovereign power is quite extinct, that power returns to the people again. And when they are free, they may set up what species of government they

please; or if they rather incline to it, they may subside into a state of natural being, if it be plainly for the best. In the eastern country of the Mogul[5] we have some resemblance of the case, for, upon the death of an absolute monarch, they live so many days without a civil head; but, in that interregnum, those who survive the vacancy are glad to get into a civil state again, and usually they are in a very bloody condition when they return under the cover of a new monarch: This project is to endear the people to a tyranny from the experience they have so lately had of an anarchy.

3. The formal reason of government is the will of a community, yielded up and surrendered to some other subject, either of one particular person, or more, conveyed in the following manner:

Let us conceive in our mind a multitude of men, all naturally free and equal, going about voluntarily to erect themselves into a new commonwealth. Now their condition being such, to bring themselves into a political body, they must needs enter into diverse covenants.

(1) They must interchangeably each man covenant to join in one lasting society, that they may be capable to concert the measures of their safety, by a public vote.

(2) A vote or decree must then nextly pass to set up some particular species of government over them. And if they are joined in their first compact upon absolute terms to stand to the decision of the first vote concerning the species of government, then all are bound by the majority to acquiesce in that particular form thereby settled, though their own private opinion incline them to some other model.

(3) After a decree has specified the particular form of government, then there will be need of a new covenant,

5. Mogul, form of Mongul, or Mongol, usually applied to the Mohammedan empire of India; here refers to the Mongols proper in eastern Asia whose custom was to elect a successor after the death of the khan or ruler.

whereby those on whom sovereignty is conferred engage to take care of the common peace and welfare. And the subjects, on the other hand, to yield them faithful obedience. In which covenant is included that submission and union of wills by which a state may be conceived to be but one person. So that the most proper definition of a civil state is this, namely, a civil state is a compound moral person whose will (united by those covenants before passed) is the will of all; to the end it may use and apply the strength and riches of private persons toward maintaining the common peace, security, and well-being of all. That may be conceived as though the whole state was now become but one man, in which the aforesaid covenants may be supposed, under God's Providence, to be the divine fiat, pronounced by God: Let us make man. And by way of resemblance the aforesaid being may be thus anatomized.

i. The sovereign power is the soul infused, giving life and motion to the whole body.

ii. Subordinate officers are the joints by which the body moves.

iii. Wealth and riches are the strength.

iv. Equity and laws are the reason.

v. Counselors the memory.

vi. *Salus populi*, or the happiness of the people, is the end of its being or main business to be attended and done.

vii. Concord amongst the members, and all estates, is the health.

viii. Sedition is sickness, and civil war death.

(4) The parts of sovereignty may be considered: so,

   i. As it prescribes the rule of action, it is rightly termed legislative power.

   ii. As it determines the controversies of subjects by the standard of those rules, so is it justly termed judiciary power.

   iii. As it arms the subjects against foreigners or forbids hostility, so it is called the power of peace and war.

iv. As it takes in ministers for the discharge of business, so it is called the right of appointing magistrates. So that all great officers and public servants must needs owe their original to the creating power of sovereignty. So that those whose right it is to create may dissolve the being of those who are created, unless they cast them into an immortal frame, and yet must needs be dissoluble if they justly forfeit their being to their creators.

v. The chief end of civil communities is that men thus conjoined may be secured against the injuries they are liable to from their own kind. For if every man could secure himself singly, it would be great folly for him to renounce his natural liberty, in which every man is his own king and protector....

II. The forms of a regular state are three only, which forms arise from the proper and particular subject in which the supreme power resides. As,

1. A democracy, which is when the sovereign power is lodged in a council consisting of all the members and where every member has the privilege of a vote. This form of government appears in the greatest part of the world to have been the most ancient.... That reason seems to show it to be most probable, that when men (being originally in a condition of natural freedom and equality) had thoughts of joining in a civil body, [they] would without question be inclined to administer their common affairs by their common judgments and so must necessarily to gratify that inclination to establish a democracy. Neither can it be rationally imagined that fathers of families being yet free and independent should in a moment or little time take off their own delight in governing their own affairs and devolve all upon some single sovereign commander.... It seems to have been thought more equitable that what belonged to all should be managed

by all, when all had entered by compact into one community. The original of our government, says Plato (speaking of the Athenian commonwealth), was taken from the equality of our race. Other states there are composed of different blood and of unequal lines, the consequence of which are disproportionable sovereignty, tyrannical or oligarchical sway, under which men live in such a manner as to esteem themselves partly lords and partly slaves to each other. But we and our countrymen, being all born brethren of the same mother, do not look upon ourselves to stand under so hard a relation as that of lords and slaves, but the parity of our descent inclines us to keep up the like parity by our laws and to yield the precedency to nothing but to superior virtue and wisdom. And, moreover, it seems very manifest that most civil communities arose at first from the union of families that were nearly allied in race and blood. And though ancient story makes frequent mention of kings, yet it appears that most of them were such that had an influence rather in persuading than in any power of commanding....

A democracy is then erected when a number of free persons do assemble together in order to enter into a covenant for uniting themselves in a body, and such a preparative assembly hath some appearance already of a democracy. It is a democracy in embryo properly in this respect, that every man hath the privilege freely to deliver his opinion concerning the common affairs. Yet he who dissents from the vote of the majority is not in the least obliged by what they determine, till by a second covenant a popular form be actually established, for not before then can we call it a democratic government, namely, till the right of determining all matters relating to the public safety is actually placed in a general assembly of the whole people, or by their own compact and mutual agreement [they] determine themselves the proper subject for the exercise of sovereign power. And to complete this state and render it capable to exert its power to answer the end of a civil state, these conditions are necessary:

(1) That a certain time and place be assigned for assembling.

(2) That when the assembly be orderly met, as to time and place, that then the vote of the majority must pass for the vote of the whole body.

(3) That magistrates be appointed to exercise the authority of the whole for the better dispatch of business, of every day's occurrence, who also may, with more mature diligence, search into more important affairs. . . . If in case anything happens of greater consequence, [they] may report it to the assembly and be peculiarly serviceable in putting all public decrees into execution, because a large body of people is almost useless in respect of the last service, and of many others, as to the more particular application and exercise of power. Therefore, it is most agreeable with the law of nature that they institute their officers to act in their name and stead.

2. The second species of regular government is an aristocracy. . . . This is said then to be constituted when the people or assembly, united by a first covenant and having thereby cast themselves into the first rudiments of a state, do then by common decree devolve the sovereign power on a council consisting of some select members. . . . These having accepted of the designation are then properly invested with sovereign command, and then an aristocracy is formed.

3. The third species of a regular government is a monarchy, which is settled when the sovereign power is conferred on some one worthy person. It differs from the former, because a monarch . . . is but one person in natural, as well as in moral, account, and so is furnished with an immediate power of exercising sovereign command in all instances of government, but the forenamed must needs have particular time and place assigned; but the power and authority is equal in each.

III. Mixed governments . . . are various and of diverse kinds. . . . Yet possibly the fairest in the world is that which has a regular monarchy settled upon a noble democracy as its basis. And each part of the government is so adjusted by pacts and laws that render the whole constitution an Elysium. It is said of the British Empire that it is such a monarchy, as that by the necessary subordinate concurrence of the Lords and Commons in the making and repealing all statutes or acts of Parliament it hath the main advantages of an aristocracy and of a democracy and yet free from the disadvantages and evils of either. It is such a monarchy as by most admirable temperament affords very much to the industry, liberty, and happiness of the subject and reserves enough for the majesty and prerogative of any king, who will own his people as subjects, not as slaves. It is a kingdom that, of all the kingdoms of the world, is most like to the kingdom of Jesus Christ, whose yoke is easy and burden light. . . .

In general, concerning rebellion against government, for particular subjects to break in upon regular communities duly established is from the premises to violate the law of nature and is a high usurpation upon the first grand immunities of mankind. Such rebels in states and usurpers in churches affront the world with a presumption that the best of the brotherhood are a company of fools and that themselves have fairly monopolized all the reason of human nature. . . . They take upon them the boldness to assure a prerogative of trampling underfoot the natural original equality and liberty of their fellows. For to push the proprietors of settlements out of possession of their old, and impose new, schemes upon them is virtually to declare them in a state of vassalage or that they were born so, and therefore will the usurper be so gracious as to insure them they shall not be sold at the next market. . . .

Says my author, where the constitution of a nation is such that the laws of the land are the measures both of the sovereign's commands and the obedience of the subjects, whereby it is provided that as the one are not to invade what by concessions and stipulations is granted to the ruler, so the other is not to deprive them of their lawful and determined rights and liberties. Then the prince who strives to subvert the fundamental laws of the society is the traitor and the rebel and not the people, who endeavor to preserve and defend their own. It is very applicable to particular men in their rebellions or usurpations in church or state. . . .

An aristocracy . . . places the supreme power in a select company of choice persons. . . . This government might do to support the church in its most valuable rights . . . if we could be assured they would make the Scripture, and not their private will, the rule of their personal and ministerial actions. And indeed upon these terms any species of government might serve the great design of redemption; but considering how great an interest is embarked and how frail a bottom we trust, though we should rely upon the best of men, especially if we remember what is in the hearts of good men (namely, much ignorance, abundance of small ends, many times cloaked with a high pretense in religion, pride skulking and often breeding revenge upon a small affront and blown up by a pretended zeal, yet really and truly by nothing more divine than interest or ill nature) and also considering how very uncertain we are of the real goodness of those we esteem good men and also how

impossible it is to secure the entail of it to successors. . . .

In a word, an aristocracy is a dangerous constitution in the church of Christ, as it possesses the presbytery of all church power: what has been observed sufficiently evinces it . . . from the nature of the constitution, for it has no more barrier to it against the ambition, insults, and arbitrary measures of men than an absolute monarchy. But, to abbreviate, it seems most agreeable with the light of nature that, if there be any of the regular government settled in the church of God, it must needs be:

A democracy. This is a form of government which the light of nature does highly value and often directs to as most agreeable to the just and natural prerogatives of human beings. This was of great account in the early times of the world. And not only so, but, upon the experience of several thousand years after the world had been tumbled and tossed from one species of government to another at a great expense of blood and treasure, many of the wise nations of the world have sheltered themselves under it again. . . .

It is certainly a great truth that man's original liberty, after it is resigned (under due restrictions), ought to be cherished in all wise governments. . . . Otherwise a man in making himself a subject . . . alters himself from a freeman into a slave, which to do is repugnant to the law of nature. Also the natural equality of men amongst men must be duly favored in that government was never established by God or nature to give one man a prerogative to insult over another. Therefore, in a civil as well as in a natural state of being, a just equality is to be indulged so far as that every man is bound to honor every man, which is agreeable both with nature and religion (1 Peter 2:17). *Honor all men.* The end of all good government is to cultivate humanity and promote the happiness of all and the good of every man in all his rights, his life, liberty, estate, honor, etc., without injury or abuse done to any. Then certainly it cannot easily be thought that a company of men that shall enter into a voluntary compact to hold all power in their own hands, thereby to use and improve their united force, wisdom, riches, and strength for the common and particular good of every member, as is the nature of a democracy; I say it cannot be that this sort of constitution will so readily furnish those in government with an appetite or disposition to prey upon each other or embezzle the common stock, as some particular persons may be apt to do when set off and intrusted with the same power. And, moreover, this appears very natural that when the aforesaid government or power settled in all, when they have elected certain capable persons to minister in their affairs, and the said ministers remain accountable to the assembly, these officers must needs be under the influence of many wise cautions from their own thoughts (as well as under confinement by their commission) in their whole administration: And from thence it must needs follow that they will be more apt and inclined to steer right for the main point, viz., the peculiar good and benefit of the whole and every particular member fairly and sincerely. And why may not these stand for very rational pleas in church order?

For certainly if Christ has settled any form of power in his church, he has done it for his church's safety and for the benefit of every member: Then he must needs be presumed to have made choice of that government as should least expose his people to hazard, either from the fraud or arbitrary measures of particular men. And it is as plain as daylight, there is no species of government like a democracy to attain this end. There are but about two steps from an aristocracy to a monarchy and from thence but one to a tyranny. An able standing force and an ill nature, *ipso facto*, turns an absolute monarch into a tyrant. This is obvious among the Roman Caesars and through the world. And all these direful transmutations are easier in church affairs (from the different qualities of things) than in civil states. For what is it that cunning and learned men cannot make the world swallow as an article of their creed, if they are once invested with an uncontrollable power and are to be the standing orators to mankind in matters of faith and obedience? ...

But at present I shall leave it to other men to run the parallel between our constitution and the several governments I have mentioned, and infer what more they shall think proper, only leaving to myself the liberty to conclude that the several examples of civil states which I have named do serve abundantly to justify the noble nature of our constitution in church order, for that the several famous and august nations which I have mentioned, in all their glory at home and success in arms and trade abroad; their several governments, which have brought them to all this, are either a perfect democracy or very much mixed and blended with it.

Then why should we in New England be any more ashamed or less careful of our church government, which keeps us from tyranny and slavery in the concerns of our consciences, than those nations are of their civil government, whereby they are preserved from the like damnable circumstances in the concerns of their outward life and natural rights and fortunes?

SECTION B. AUTHORITY AND LIBERTY IN ENGLAND

1. PROPERTY AND SUFFRAGE[1]

EDITORS' NOTE.—At the time this debate was held (October, 1647), the English people had recently emerged from the First Civil War (1642–46) and were shortly to be involved in the Second (May–August, 1648). The defeat of the Royalists, by the New Model Army, had been followed by a triangular struggle for power between the army, the Parliament, and the captured king, in which each was striving for a settlement on its own terms. No settlement, in fact, was possible, and the upshot was a war between the army on the one side and a combination of Royalists and Presbyterians on the other, which ended in Cromwell's victory and the king's execution (1649).

These debates show that opinion within the army itself was sharply divided. They were held within the General Council of the army, a body which at this time included elected representatives (two officers and two "agitators") of each regiment as well as the high command. Levelling sentiment had spread through many of the regiments, particularly among the rank and file, and the speeches here printed turned on a proposal for manhood suffrage which had been put forward by the Levellers as part of a draft constitution (called "An Agreement of the People"). The Rainborough brothers, Petty, and Wildman, supported the proposal. Cromwell, and his son-in-law Ireton, the real masters of the situation, reflected the opposition of the propertied classes.

The Levellers had their brief hour of importance during this period of turmoil, but, when their dissatisfaction led to a mutiny in 1649, they were quickly suppressed. They are interesting to us as the earliest exponents in English history of modern democratic principles.

MAJOR [WILLIAM] RAINBOROUGH:[2] I desire we may come to that end we all strive after. I humbly desire you will fall upon that which is the engagement of all, which is the rights and freedoms of the people, and let us see how far we have made sure to them a right and freedom, and if anything be tendered as to that [in this paper]. And when that engagement is gone through, then, let us consider of those [things only] that are of greater weight.

(The paper called the Agreement[3] read. Afterward the first article read by itself.)

1. *Puritanism and Liberty*, ed. A. S. P. Woodhouse (London, 1938), pp. 52–59, 61–67, 71–73.

2. Major William Rainborough (also spelled Rainsborough, Rainborow, or Rainborowe), was a brother of Colonel Thomas Rainborough (d. 1648), who was a leader of the Leveller group in the army and who takes a leading part in this debate.

3. One of several statements so designated. The "Agreement" of October–November, 1647, represented the Levellers' program as of that date. The part of it relevant to this

IRETON:[4] The exception that lies in it is this. It said, they are to be distributed according to the number of the inhabitants, "The people of England," &c. And this doth make me think that the meaning is that every man that is an inhabitant is to be equally considered and to have an equal voice in the election of those representers, the persons that are for the general representative; and, if that be the meaning, then I have something to say against it. But if it be only that those people that by the civil constitution of this kingdom, which is original and fundamental, and beyond which I am sure no memory of record does go . . . should

debate is here quoted:

"AN AGREEMENT OF THE PEOPLE—NOV. 3, 1647

"I. That the people of England, being at this day very unequally distributed by counties, cities, and boroughs, for the election of their deputies in Parliament, ought to be more indifferently proportioned, according to the number of the inhabitants; the circumstances whereof, for number, place, and manner, are to be set down before the end of this present Parliament.

"II. That to prevent the many inconveniences apparently arising from the long continuance of the same persons in authority, this present Parliament be dissolved upon the last day of September, which shall be in the year of our Lord 1648. . . .

"These things we declare to be our native rights, and therefore are agreed and resolved to maintain them with our utmost possibilities against all opposition whatsoever, being compelled thereunto not only by the examples of our ancestors, whose blood was often spent in vain for the recovery of their freedoms, suffering themselves, through fraudulent accommodations, to be still deluded of the fruit of their victories, but also by our own woeful experience, who, having long expected, and dearly earned, the establishment of these certain rules of government, are yet made to depend for the settlement of our peace and freedom upon him that intended our bondage and brought a cruel war upon us" (*Puritanism and Liberty*, ed. Woodhouse, pp. 444–45).

4. Henry Ireton (1611–51), cavalry leader on the parliamentary side; son-in-law of Oliver Cromwell; led Independents in debates against the Levellers in 1647–49; leader in the reconquest of Ireland (1649–51).

be [still] the electors, I have no more to say against it. . . .

RAINBOROUGH: For really I think that the poorest he that is in England hath a life to live, as the greatest he; and therefore truly, sir, I think it is clear that every man that is to live under a government ought first by his own consent to put himself under that government; and I do think that the poorest man in England is not at all bound in a strict sense to that government that he hath not had a voice to put himself under; and I am confident that, when I have heard the reasons against it, something will be said to answer those reasons, insomuch that I should doubt whether he was an Englishman or no that should doubt of these things. . . .

IRETON: Give me leave to tell you that, if you make this the rule, I think you must fly for refuge to an absolute natural right, and you must deny all civil right; and I am sure it will come to that in the consequence. This, I perceive, is pressed as that which is so essential and due: the right of the people of this kingdom, and as they are the people of this kingdom, distinct and divided from other people, and that we must for this right lay aside all other considerations; this is so just, this is so due, this is so right to them. . . . For my part, I think it is no right at all. I think that no person hath a right to an interest or share in the disposing of the affairs of the kingdom, and in determining or choosing those that shall determine what laws we shall be ruled by here—no person hath a right to this that hath not a permanent fixed interest in this kingdom, and those persons together are properly the represented of this kingdom, and consequently are [also] to make up the representers of this kingdom, who taken together do comprehend whatsoever is of real or permanent interest in the kingdom. And I am sure otherwise I cannot tell what any man can say why a foreigner coming in amongst us—or as many as will come in amongst us, or by force or other-wise settling themselves here, or at least by our permission having a being here—why they should not as well lay claim to it as any other. We talk of birthright. Truly [by] birthright there is thus much claim. Men may justly have by birth-right, by their very being born in England, that we should not seclude them out of England, that we should not re-fuse to give them air and place and ground, and the freedom of the high-ways and other things, to live amongst us—not any man that is born here, though by his birth there come nothing at all (that is part of the permanent interest of this kingdom) to him. That, I think, is due to a man by birth. But that by a man's being born here he shall have a share in that power that shall dispose of the lands here, and of all things here, I do not think it a sufficient ground. I am sure if we look upon that which is the utmost (within [any] man's view) of what was originally the constitution of this kingdom, upon that which is most radical and fundamental, and which if you take away, there is no man hath any land, any goods, [or] any civil interest, that is this: that those that choose the representers for the making of laws by which this state and kingdom are to be governed are the persons who, taken to-gether, do comprehend the local interest of this kingdom; that is, the persons in whom all land lies, and those in corpora-tions in whom all trading lies. This is the most fundamental constitution of this kingdom and [that] which, if you do not allow, you allow none at all. This consti-tution hath limited and determined it that only those shall have voices in elec-tions. It is true, as was said by a gentle-man near me, the meanest man in Eng-land ought to have [a voice in the elec-tion of the government he lives under—but only if he has some local interest]. I say this: that those that have the meanest local interest—that man that hath but forty shillings a year, he hath as

great voice in the election of a knight for the shire as he that hath ten thousand a year, or more if he had never so much; and therefore there is that regard had to it. But this [local interest], still the con-stitution of this government hath had an eye to (and what other government hath not an eye to this?). It doth not re-late to the interest of the kingdom if it do not lay the foundation of the power that is given to the representers, in those who have a permanent and a local inter-est in the kingdom, and who taken all together do comprehend the whole [in-terest of the kingdom]. There is all the reason and justice that can be [in this]: if I will come to live in a kingdom, being a foreigner to it, or live in a kingdom, having no permanent interest in it, [and] if I will desire as a stranger, or claim as one freeborn here, the air, the free pas-sage of highways, the protection of laws, and all such things—if I will either desire them or claim them, [then] I (if I have no permanent interest in that kingdom) must submit to those laws and those rules [which they shall choose], who, taken together, do comprehend the whole in-terest of the kingdom. And if we shall go to take away this, we shall plainly go to take away all property and interest that any man hath either in land by in-heritance, or in estate by possession, or anything else—[I say], if you take away this fundamental part of the civil con-stitution.

RAINBOROUGH: Truly, sir, I am of the same opinion I was and am resolved to keep it till I know reason why I should not. . . . I do hear nothing at all that can convince me why any man that is born in England ought not to have his voice in election of burgesses. It is said that if a man have not a permanent interest, he can have no claim; and [that] we must be no freer than the laws will let us be, and that there is no [law in any] chron-icle will let us be freer than that we [now] enjoy. Something was said to this yesterday. I do not think that the main cause why Almighty God gave men reason, it was that they should make use of that reason, and that they should improve it for that end and purpose that God gave it them. And truly, I think that half a loaf is better than none if a man be hungry: [this gift of reason without other property may seem a small thing], yet I think there is nothing that God hath given a man that any[one] else can take from him. And therefore I say that either it must be the Law of God or the law of man that must prohibit the meanest man in the kingdom to have this benefit as well as the greatest. I do not find anything in the Law of God that a lord shall choose twenty burgesses, and a gentleman but two, or a poor man shall choose none; I find no such thing in the Law of Nature, nor in the Law of Nations. But I do find that all Englishmen must be subject to English laws, and I do verily believe that there is no man but will say that the foundation of all law lies in the people, and if [it lie] in the people, I am to seek for this exemption.

And truly I have thought something [else]: in what a miserable distressed condition would many a man that hath fought for the Parliament in this quarrel be! I will be bound to say that many a man whose zeal and affection to God and this kingdom hath carried him forth in this cause hath so spent his estate that, in the way the state [and] the army are going, he shall not hold up his head, if when his estate is lost, and not worth forty shillings a year, a man shall not have any interest. And there are many other ways by which [the] estates men have (if that be the rule which God in his providence does use) do fall to decay. A man, when he hath an estate, hath an interest in making laws, [but] when he hath none, he hath no power in it; so that a man cannot lose that which he hath for the maintenance of his family but he must [also] lose that which God and nature hath given him! And there-

fore I do [think], and am still of the same opinion, that every man born in England cannot, ought not, neither by the Law of God nor the Law of Nature, to be exempted from the choice of those who are to make laws for him to live under and for him, for aught I know, to lose his life under. And therefore I think there can be no great stick in this.

Truly I think that there is not this day reigning in England a greater fruit or effect of tyranny than this very thing would produce. Truly I know nothing free but only the knight of the shire, nor do I know anything in a parliamentary way that is clear from the height and fulness of tyranny, but only [that]. As for this of corporations [which you also mentioned], it is as contrary to freedom as may be. For, sir, what is it? The king he grants a patent under the broad seal of England to such a corporation to send burgesses, he grants to [such] a city to send burgesses. When a poor base corporation from the king['s grant] shall send two burgesses, when five hundred men of estate shall not send one, when those that are to make their laws are called by the king, or cannot act [but] by such a call, truly I think that the people of England have little freedom.

IRETON: I think there was nothing that I said to give you occasion to think that I did contend for this, that such a corporation [as that] should have the electing of a man to the Parliament. I think I agreed to this matter that all should be equally distributed. But the question is whether it should be distributed to all persons, or whether the same persons that are the electors [now] should be the electors still, and it [be] equally distributed amongst them. . . .

All the main thing that I speak for is because I would have an eye to property. I hope we do not come to contend for victory—but let every man consider with himself that he do not go that way to take away all property. For here is the case of the most fundamental part of the constitution of the kingdom, which, if you take away, you take away all by that. Here men of this and this quality are determined to be the electors of men to the Parliament, and they are all those who have any permanent interest in the kingdom, and who, taken together, do comprehend the whole [permanent, local] interest of the kingdom. I mean by permanent [and] local, that [it] is not [able to be removed] anywhere else. As, for instance, he that hath a freehold, and that freehold cannot be removed out of the kingdom; and so there is a [freeman of a] corporation, a place which hath the privilege of a market and trading, which, if you should allow to all places equally, I do not see how you could preserve any peace in the kingdom, and that is the reason why in the constitution we have but some few market towns. Now those people [that have freeholds] and those [that] are the freemen of corporations were looked upon by the former constitution to comprehend the permanent interest of the kingdom. For, [first], he that hath his livelihood by his trade, and by his freedom of trading in such a corporation, which he cannot exercise in another, he is tied to that place, [for] his livelihood depends upon it. And, secondly, that man hath an interest, hath a permanent interest there, upon which he may live, and live a freeman without dependence. These [things the] constitution [of] this kingdom hath looked at. Now I wish we may all consider of what right you will challenge that all the people should have right to elections. Is it by the right of nature? If you will hold forth that as your ground, then I think you must deny all property too, and this is my reason. For thus: by that same right of nature (whatever it be) that you pretend, by which you can say one man hath an equal right with another to the choosing of him that shall govern him—by the same right of nature, he hath the same [equal] right in any goods he sees—

meat, drink, clothes—to take and use them for his sustenance. He hath a freedom to the land, [to take] the ground, to exercise it, till it; he hath the [same] freedom to anything that anyone doth account himself to have any propriety in. Why now I say then, if you, against the most fundamental part of [the] civil constitution (which I have now declared), will plead the Law of Nature, that a man should (paramount [to] this, and contrary to this) have a power of choosing those men that shall determine what shall be law in this state, though he himself have no permanent interest in the state, [but] whatever interest he hath he may carry about with him—if this be allowed, [because by the right of nature] we are free, we are equal, one man must have as much voice as another, then show me what step or difference [there is] why [I may not] by the same right [take your property, though not] of necessity to sustain nature. It is for my better being, and [the better settlement of the kingdom]. Possibly not for it, neither: possibly I may not have so real a regard to the peace of the kingdom as that man who hath a permanent interest in it. He that is here today, and gone tomorrow, I do not see that he hath such a permanent interest. Since you cannot plead to it by anything but the Law of Nature, [or for anything] but for the end of better being, and [since] that better being is not certain, and [what is] more, destructive to another; upon these grounds, if you do, paramount [to] all constitutions, hold up this Law of Nature, I would fain have any man show me their bounds, where you will end, and [why you should not] take away all property.

RAINBOROUGH: . . . Sir, to say because a man pleads that every man hath a voice [by right of nature] that therefore it destroys [by] the same [argument all property—this is to forget the Law of God]. That there is a property, the Law of God says it; else why [hath] God made that law, Thou shalt not steal? I am a poor man; therefore, I must be [op]pressed: if I have no interest in the kingdom, I must suffer by all their laws be they right or wrong. Nay thus: a gentleman lives in a country and hath three or four lordships, as some men have (God knows how they got them); and when a Parliament is called, he must be a Parliament-man; and it may be he sees some poor men, they live near this man, he can crush them—I have known an invasion to make sure he hath turned the poor men out of doors; and I would fain know whether the potency of [rich] men do not this and so keep them under the greatest tyranny that was [ever] thought of in the world. And therefore I think that to that it is fully answered: God hath set down that thing as to propriety with this law of his, Thou shalt not steal. And for my part I am against any such thought, and, as for yourselves, I wish you would not make the world believe that we are for anarchy.

CROMWELL: . . . But really, sir, this is not right as it should be. No man says that you have a mind to anarchy, but [that] the consequence of this rule tends to anarchy, must end in anarchy; for where is there any bound or limit set if you take away this [limit], that men that have no interest but the interest of breathing [shall have no voice in elections]? Therefore I am confident on't, we should not be so hot one with another. . . .

PETTY:[5] I desire to add one word concerning the word *property*. It is for something that anarchy is so much talked of. For my own part I cannot believe in the least that it can be clearly derived from that paper. 'Tis true that somewhat may be derived in the paper against the king, the power of the king, and somewhat against the power of the Lords; . . . for this of changing the representative of the nation, of changing

those that choose the representative, making of them more full, taking more into the number than formerly, I had verily thought we had all agreed in it that more should have chosen—all that had desired a more equal representation than we now have. For now those only choose who have forty shillings freehold.[6] A man may have a lease for one hundred pounds a year, a man may have a lease for three lives, [but he has no voice]. But [as] for this [argument], that it destroys all right [to property] that every Englishman that is an inhabitant of England should choose and have a voice in the representatives, I suppose it is, [on the contrary], the only means to preserve all property. For I judge every man is naturally free; and I judge the reason why men [chose representatives] when they were in so great numbers that every man could not give his voice [directly] was that they who were chosen might preserve property [for all]; and therefore men agreed to come into some form of government that they might preserve property, and I would fain know, if we were to begin a government, [whether you would say], "You have not forty shillings a year, therefore you shall not have a voice." Whereas before there was a government every man had such a voice, and afterward, and for this very cause, they did choose representatives, and put themselves into forms of government that they may preserve property, and therefore it is not to destroy it, [to give every man a voice].

IRETON: I think we shall not be so apt to come to a right understanding in this business if one man, and another man, and another man do speak their several thoughts and conceptions to the same purpose, as if we do consider where

6. A statute of 1430, which remained in force until 1832, had restricted the franchise in English counties to the "forty-shilling freeholders," i.e., to holders of free land (as distinct from leaseholders or those who held under other forms of tenure), the annual value of which was forty shillings.

5. Maximilian Petty, or Pettus, one of the agents of the Levellers.

the objection lies, and what the answer is which is made to it; and therefore I desire we may do so. To that which this gentleman spake last. The main thing that he seemed to answer was this: that he would make it appear that the going about to establish this government, [or] such a government, is not a destruction of property, nor does not tend to the destruction of property, because the people's falling into a government is for the preservation of property. What weight there [is in it] lies in this: since there is a falling into a government, and government is to preserve property, therefore this cannot be against property. The objection does not lie in that, the making of the representation more equal, but [in] the introducing of men into an equality of interest in this government, who have no property in this kingdom, or who have no local permanent interest in it. For if I had said that I would not wish at all that we should have any enlargement of the bounds of those that are to be the electors, then you might have excepted against it. But [what I said was] that I would not go to enlarge it beyond all bounds, so that upon the same ground you may admit of so many men from foreign states as would outvote you. The objection lies still in this. I do not mean that I would have it restrained to that proportion [that now obtains], but to restrain it still to men who have a local, a permanent interest in the kingdom, who have such an interest that they may live upon it as freemen, and who have such an interest as is fixed upon a place, and is not the same equally everywhere. . . . But if you go beyond this law, if you admit any man that hath a breath and being, I did show you how this will destroy property. It may come to destroy property thus. You may have such men chosen, or at least the major part of them, [as have no local and permanent interest]. Why may not those men vote against all property? [Again] you may admit strangers by this rule, if you admit

them once to inhabit, and those that have interest in the land may be voted out of their land. It may destroy property that way. But here is the rule that you go by. You infer this to be the right of the people, of every inhabitant, because man hath such a right in nature, though it be not of necessity for the preserving of his being; [and] therefore you are to overthrow the most fundamental constitution for this. By the same rule, show me why you will not, by the same right of nature, make use of anything that any man hath, [though it be not] for the necessary sustenance of men. Show me what you will stop at; wherein you will fence any man in a property by this rule.

RAINBOROUGH: I desire to know how this comes to be a property in some men and not in others.

COLONEL [NATHANIEL] RICH:[7] I confess [there is weight in] that objection that the Commissary-General last insisted upon; for you have five to one in this kingdom that have no permanent interest. Some men [have] ten, some twenty servants, some more, some less. If the master and servant shall be equal electors, then clearly those that have no interest in the kingdom will make it their interest to choose those that have no interest. It may happen that the majority may by law, not in a confusion, destroy property; there may be a law enacted that there shall be an equality of goods and estate. I think that either of the extremes may be urged to inconveniency; that is, [that] men that have no interest as to estate should have no interest as to election [and that they should have an equal interest]. But there may be a more equitable division and distribution than that he that hath nothing should have an equal voice; and certainly there may be some other way thought of that there may be a representative of the poor as

7. Colonel Nathaniel Rich (d. 1701), lawyer; cavalry captain on parliamentary side (1643), colonel in New Model Army (1645); in debates of 1647–48 Rich favored wide toleration but feared "extreme democracy."

well as the rich and not to exclude all. I remember there were many workings and revolutions, as we have heard, in the Roman Senate; and there was never a confusion that did appear (and that indeed was come to) till the state came to know this kind of distribution of election. That is how the people's voices were bought and sold, and that by the poor; and thence it came that he that was the richest man, and [a man] of some considerable power among the soldiers, and one they resolved on, made himself a perpetual dictator. And if we strain too far to avoid monarchy in kings [let us take heed] that we do not call for emperors to deliver us from more than one tyrant....

WILDMAN:[8] ... Our case is to be considered thus, that we have been under slavery. That is acknowledged by all. Our very laws were made by our conquerors; and whereas it is spoken much of chronicles, I conceive there is no credit to be given to any of them; and the reason is because those that were our lords, and made us their vassals, would suffer nothing else to be chronicled. We are now engaged for our freedom. That is the end of parliaments: not to constitute what is already [established, but to act] according to the just rules of government. Every person in England hath as clear a right to elect his representative as the greatest person in England. I conceive that is the undeniable maxim of government: that all government is in the free consent of the people. If [so], then upon that account there is no person that is under a just government, or hath justly his own, unless he by his own free consent be put under that government. This he cannot be unless he be consenting to it, and therefore, according to this maxim, there is never a person in Eng-

land [but ought to have a voice in elections]. If [this], as that gentleman says, be true, there are no laws that in this strictness and rigor of justice [any man is bound to], that are not made by those who[m] he doth consent to. And therefore I should humbly move, that if the question be stated—which would soonest bring things to an issue—it might rather be thus: Whether any person can justly be bound by law, who doth not give his consent that such persons shall make laws for him?

IRETON: ... I do acknowledge that which you take to be so general a maxim, that in every kingdom, within every land, the original of power of making laws, of determining what shall be law in the land, does lie in the people—[but by the people is meant those] that are possessed of the permanent interest in the land....

RAINBOROUGH: Sir, I see that it is impossible to have liberty but all property must be taken away. If it be laid down for a rule, and if you will say it, it must be so. But I would fain know what the soldier hath fought for all this while. He hath fought to enslave himself, to give power to men of riches, men of estates, to make him a perpetual slave. We do find in all presses that go forth none must be pressed that are freehold men. When these gentlemen fall out among themselves, they shall press the poor scrubs to come and kill [one another for] them.

IRETON: ... Give me leave [to say] but this one word. I [will] tell you what the soldier of the kingdom hath fought for. First, the danger that we stood in was that one man's will must be a law. The people of the kingdom must have this right at least, that they should not be concluded [but] by the representative of those that had the interest of the kingdom. So[m]e men fought in this, because they were immediately concerned and engaged in it. Other men who had no other interest in the kingdom but this, that they should have the benefit of those laws made by the representative,

8. Sir John Wildman (1621?–93), served briefly on parliamentary side in the First Civil War; was one of the chief spokesmen of the Levellers (1647–49); in prison under Cromwell and later in exile; returned to England with William of Orange; made alderman of London and knighted (1692).

yet [fought] that they should have the benefit of this representative. They thought it was better to be concluded by the common consent of those that were fixed men, and settled men, that had the interest of this kingdom [in them]. "And from that way," [said they], "I shall know a law and have a certainty." Every man that was born [in the country, that] is a denizen in it, that hath a freedom, he was capable of trading to get money, to get estates by; and therefore this man, I think, had a great deal of reason to build up such a foundation of interest to himself: that is, that the will of one man should not be a law, but that the law of this kingdom should be by a choice of persons to represent, and that choice to be made by, the generality of the kingdom. Here was a right that induced men to fight, and those men that had this interest, though this be not the utmost interest that other men have, yet they had *some* interest. Now [tell me] why we should go to plead whatsoever we can challenge by the right of nature against whatsoever any man can challenge by constitution. I do not see where that man will stop, as to point of property, [so] that he shall not use [against other property] that right he hath [claimed] by the Law of Nature against that constitution. I desire any man to show me where there is a difference. I have been answered, "Now we see liberty cannot stand without [destroying] property." Liberty may be had and property not be destroyed. First, the liberty of all those that have the permanent interest in the kingdom, *that* is provided for [by the constitution]. And, [secondly, by an appeal to the Law of Nature], liberty cannot be provided for in a general sense if property be preserved.

2. LEVIATHAN[1]

By THOMAS HOBBES

EDITORS' NOTE.—Thomas Hobbes (1588–1679), the English philosopher, son of a clergyman, early became dissatisfied with the scholastic teaching to which he had been subjected at Oxford in one of its darker periods. His first work was a translation of Thucydides' *History*. While tutor and companion to the Earl of Cavendish, Hobbes as a young man traveled abroad, becoming familiar with the skeptical ideas of Montaigne and of Galileo and Kepler, the astronomers. Hobbes also grew fond of Euclid's geometrical method of reasoning. He set himself the task of explaining natural bodies, man's nature, and the state in terms of elementary propositions deriving from "motion." Of this great project, *De corpore* ("On Body") and *De cive* ("On the State") were later published, the parts on man eventuating only in a theory of vision and two small early works on *Human Nature* and *De corpore politico* ("On the Body Politic"). His political classic, *The Leviathan*, was completed at Paris, whence Hobbes had fled from England at the outbreak of the Civil War and where he acted as tutor to the Prince of Wales. He thought the book, published after the king had been executed in England, favorable to the royal cause. But the work alienated him from the royal circle of exiles, pos-

1. Thomas Hobbes, *Leviathan* (London, 1914), pp. 63–69, 87–97, 110, 114–16, 170–73, 176–78. Reprinted from *The Leviathan*, by Thomas Hobbes, published by E. P. Dutton & Co., Inc., New York.

sibly because of its light treatment of divine right and church authority; and he returned in some panic to Cromwell's England, after sending in his submission to the Council of State. Young King Charles befriended Hobbes again after the Restoration. But Hobbes had become the type figure of "atheism" and could not get the censor's permission to publish further works on human nature. The superstitious believed "Hobbesism"

responsible for the London plague and fire. He was, in any case, more and more interested in mathematical controversy. Just before he died, the censor permitted *Behemoth*, a history of the Civil War and a study of the state in disorder, to see the light. Hobbes was the first to attempt to apply "mechanical philosophy" as understood in the seventeenth century to man and the state.

Nature has made men so equal in the faculties of body and mind as that, though there be found one man sometimes manifestly stronger in body, or of quicker mind than another, yet, when all is reckoned together, the difference between man and man is not so considerable as that one man can thereupon claim to himself any benefit to which another may not pretend as well as he. For as to the strength of body, the weakest has strength enough to kill the strongest either by secret machination or by confederacy with others that are in the same danger with himself.

And as to the faculties of the mind (setting aside the arts grounded upon words, and especially that skill of proceeding upon general and infallible rules called science, which very few have, and but in few things, as being not a native faculty born with us nor attained—as prudence—while we look after somewhat else), I find yet a greater equality amongst men than that of strength. For prudence is but experience which equal time equally bestows on all men in those things they equally apply themselves unto. That which may perhaps make such equality incredible is but a vain concept of one's own wisdom which almost all men think they have in a greater degree than the vulgar, that is, than all men but themselves, and a few others, who by fame, or for concurring with

themselves, they approve. For such is the nature of men that howsoever they may acknowledge many others to be more witty or more eloquent or more learned, yet they will hardly believe there be many so wise as themselves, for they see their own wit at hand, and other men's at a distance. But this proves rather that men are in that point equal, than unequal, for there is not ordinarily a greater sign of the equal distribution of anything than that every man is contented with his share.

From this equality of ability arises equality of hope in the attaining of our ends. And, therefore, if any two men desire the same thing, which nevertheless they cannot both enjoy, they become enemies, and in the way to their end (which is principally their own conservation and sometimes their delectation only) endeavor to destroy, or subdue one another. And from hence it comes to pass that where an invader has no more to fear than another man's single power, if one plant, sow, build, or possess a convenient seat, others may probably be expected to come prepared with forces united, to dispossess and deprive him, not only of the fruit of his labor, but also of his life, or liberty. And the invader again is in the like danger of another.

And from this diffidence of one another there is no way for any man to secure himself so reasonable as anticipation, that is, by force, or wiles, to master the persons of all men he can, so long, till he see no other power great enough to endanger him. And this is no more than his own conservation requires and is generally allowed. Also, because there be some, that taking pleasure in contemplating their own power in the acts of conquest which they pursue farther than their security requires; if others, that otherwise would be glad to be at ease within modest bounds, should not by invasion increase their power, they would not be able, long time, by standing only on their defense, to subsist. And by consequence, such augmentation of dominion over men, being necessary to a man's conservation, it ought to be allowed him.

Again, men have no pleasure (but on the contrary, a great deal of grief) in keeping company where there is no power able to overawe them all. For every man looks that his companion should value him, at the same rate he sets upon himself, and upon all signs of contempt, or undervaluing, naturally endeavors, as far as he dares (which amongst them that have no common power to keep them in quiet is far enough to make them destroy each other), to extort a greater value from his contemners, by damage, and from others, by the example.

So that in the nature of man we find three principal causes of quarrel: first, competition; secondly, diffidence; thirdly, glory.

The first makes men invade for gain; the second, for safety; and the third, for reputation. The first use violence to make themselves masters of other men's persons, wives, children, and chattels; the second, to defend them; the third, for trifles, as a word, a smile, a different opinion, and any other sign of undervalue, either direct to their persons or by reflection on their kindred, their friends, their nation, their profession, or their name.

Hereby it is manifest that, during the time men live without a common power to keep them all in awe, they are in that condition which is called war, and such a war, as is of every man, against every man. . . .

In such condition there is no place for industry, because the fruit thereof is uncertain, and consequently no culture of the earth, no navigation, nor use of the commodities that may be imported by sea, no commodious building, no instruments of moving and removing such things as require much force, no knowledge of the face of the earth, no account of time, no arts, no letters, no society, and, which is worst of all, continual fear, and danger of violent death, and the life of man, solitary, poor, nasty, brutish, and short.

It may seem strange to some man that has not well weighed these things that nature should thus dissociate and render men apt to invade and destroy one another, and he may therefore, not trusting to this inference made from the passions, desire perhaps to have the same confirmed by experience. Let him therefore consider with himself when taking a journey; he arms himself and seeks to go well accompanied; when going to sleep, he locks his doors; when even in his house he locks his chests, and this when he knows there be laws, and public officers armed to revenge all injuries shall be done him; what opinion he has of his fellow-subjects when he rides armed; of his fellow-citizens when he locks his doors; of his children and servants when he locks his chests. Does he not there as much accuse mankind by his actions as I do by my words? But neither of us accuse man's nature in it. The desires, and other passions of man, are in themselves no sin. No more are the actions that proceed from those passions till they know a law that forbids them; which, till laws be made, they cannot know, nor can any law be made till they have agreed upon the person that shall make it.

It may peradventure be thought there was never such a time nor condition of war as this, and I believe it was never generally so, over all the world, but there are many places where they live so now. For the savage people in many places of America, except the government of small families, the concord whereof depends on natural lust, have no government at all and live at this day in that brutish manner, as I said before. Howsoever, it may be perceived what manner of life there would be where there were no common power to fear, by the manner of life which men that have formerly lived under a peaceful government use to degenerate into in a civil war. . . .

To this war of every man against every man, this also is consequent, that nothing can be unjust. The notions of right and wrong, justice and injustice, have there no place. Where there is no common power, there is no law: where no law, no injustice. Force and fraud are in war the two cardinal virtues. Justice and injustice are none of the faculties either of the body or mind. If they were, they might be in a man that were alone in the world, as well as his senses and passions. They are qualities that relate to men in society, not in solitude. It is consequent also to the same condition that there be no propriety, no dominion, no mine and thine distinct, but only that to be every man's, that he can get, and for so long as he can keep it. And thus much for the ill condition which man by mere nature is actually placed in, though with a possibility to come out of it, consisting partly in the passions, partly in his reason.

The passions that incline men to peace are fear of death, desire of such things as are necessary to commodious living, and a hope by their industry to obtain them. And reason suggests convenient articles of peace, upon which men may be drawn to agreement. These articles are they which otherwise are called the laws of nature, whereof I shall speak more particularly in the two following chapters.

OF THE FIRST AND SECOND NATURAL LAWS AND OF CONTRACTS

THE RIGHT OF NATURE which writers commonly call *jus naturale* is the liberty each man has to use his own power as he will himself for the preservation of his own nature, that is to say, of his own life; and, consequently, of doing anything, which in his own judgment, and reason, he shall conceive to be the aptest means thereunto.

By LIBERTY is understood, according to the proper signification of the word, the absence of external impediments, which impediments may often take away part of a man's power to do what he would, but cannot hinder him from using the power left him, according as his judgment, and reason shall dictate to him.

A LAW OF NATURE (*lex naturalis*) is a precept, or general rule, found out by reason, by which a man is forbidden to do that which is destructive of his life, or takes away the means of preserving the same, and to omit that by which he thinks it may be best preserved. For though they that speak of this subject use to confound *jus* and *lex*, *right* and *law*, yet they ought to be distinguished, because *right* consists in liberty to do or to forbear, whereas *law* determines and binds to one of them, so that *law* and *right* differ as much as *obligation* and *liberty*, which in one and the same matter are inconsistent.

And because the condition of man (as has been declared in the preceding chapter) is a condition of war of everyone against everyone, in which case everyone is governed by his own reason, and there is nothing he can make use of that may not be a help unto him in preserving his life against his enemies; it follows that in such a condition every man has a right to everything, even to one another's body. And therefore, as long as this natural right of every man to everything endures, there can be no security to any man (how strong or wise soever he be) of living out the time which nature ordinarily allows men to live. And consequently it is a precept or general rule of reason that every man ought to endeavor peace, as far as he has hope of obtaining it, and, when he cannot obtain it, that he may seek, and use, all helps and advantages of war. The first branch of which rule contains the first, and fundamental law of nature, which is to seek peace and follow it. The second, the sum of the right of nature, which is, by all means we can, to defend ourselves.

From this fundamental law of nature by which men are commanded to endeavor peace is derived this second law; that a man be willing, when others are so too, as far-forth, as for peace and defense of himself, he shall think it necessary to lay down this right to all things and be contented with so much liberty against other men as he would allow other men against himself. For as long as every man holds this right of doing anything he likes, so long are all men in the condition of war. But if other men will not lay down their right, as well as he, then there is no reason for anyone to divest himself of his, for that were to expose himself to prey (which no man is bound to) rather than to dispose himself to peace. This is that law of the gospel: Whatsoever you require that others should do to you, that do ye to them. And that law of all men, *Quod tibi fieri non vis, alteri ne feceris.*

To lay down a man's right to anything is to divest himself of the liberty of hindering another of the benefit of his own right to the same. For he that renounces, or passes away his right, gives not to any other man a right which he had not before, because there is nothing to which every man had not right by nature, but only stands out of his way, that he may enjoy his own original right without hin-

drance from him, not without hindrance from another. So that the effect which redounds to one man by another man's defect of right is but so much diminution of impediments to the use of his own right original.

Right is laid aside either by simply renouncing it or by transferring it to another. By simply renouncing, when he cares not to whom the benefit thereof redounds. By transferring, when he intends the benefit thereof to some certain person, or persons. And when a man has in either manner abandoned or granted away his right, then is he said to be obliged or bound not to hinder those to whom such right is granted or abandoned, from the benefit of it, and that he ought, and it is his duty, not to make void that voluntary act of his own, and that such hindrance is injustice, and injury, as being *sine jure*, the right being before renounced or transferred. So that injury or injustice, in the controversies of the world, is somewhat like to that which in the disputations of scholars is called absurdity. For as it is there called an absurdity to contradict what one maintained in the beginning, so in the world it is called injustice and injury voluntarily to undo that which from the beginning he had voluntarily done. The way by which a man either simply renounces or transfers his right is a declaration or signification by some voluntary and sufficient sign, or signs, that he does so renounce, or transfer, or has so renounced, or transferred, the same, to him that accepts it. And these signs are either words only, or actions only, or (as it happens most often) both words and actions. And the same are the bonds by which men are bound and obliged: Bonds that have their strength, not from their own nature (for nothing is more easily broken than a man's word), but from fear of some evil consequence upon the rupture.

Whenever a man transfers his right, or renounces it, it is either in consideration of some right reciprocally transferred to himself or for some other good he hopes for thereby. For it is a voluntary act, and of the voluntary acts of every man the object is some good to himself. And, therefore, there be some rights which no man can be understood by any words, or other signs, to have abandoned or transferred. As first a man cannot lay down the right of resisting them that assault him by force to take away his life, because he cannot be understood to aim thereby at any good to himself, the same may be said of wounds, and chains, and imprisonment, both because there is no benefit consequent to such patience, as there is to the patience of suffering another to be wounded or imprisoned, as also because a man cannot tell, when he sees men proceed against him by violence, whether they intend his death or not. And, lastly, the motive and end for which this renouncing and transferring of right is introduced is nothing else but the security of a man's person, in his life, and in the means of so preserving life, as not to be weary of it. And, therefore, if a man by words, or other signs, seem to despoil himself of the end for which those signs were intended, he is not to be understood as if he meant it, or that it was his will, but that he was ignorant of how such words and actions were to be interpreted.

The mutual transferring of right is that which men call CONTRACT.

There is difference between transferring of right to the thing, and transferring, or tradition; that is, delivery of the thing itself. For the thing may be delivered together with the translation of the right, as in buying and selling with ready money, or exchange of goods, or lands, and it may be delivered some time after.

Again, one of the contractors may deliver the thing contracted for on his part, and leave the other to perform his part at some determinate time after, and in the meantime be trusted; and then the contract on his part is called PACT, or COVENANT....

OF THE CAUSES, GENERATION, AND DEFINITION OF A COMMONWEALTH

The final cause, end, or design of men (who naturally love liberty and dominion over others), in the introduction of that restraint upon themselves (in which we see them live in commonwealths), is the foresight of their own preservation, and of a more contented life thereby; that is to say, of getting themselves out from that miserable condition of war, which is necessarily consequent (as has been shown) to the natural passions of men, when there is no visible power to keep them in awe and tie them by fear of punishment to the performance of their covenants, and observation of those laws of nature set down in the fourteenth and fifteenth chapters....

The only way to erect such a common power as may be able to defend them from the invasion of foreigners, and the injuries of one another, and thereby to secure them in such sort, as that by their own industry, and by the fruits of the earth, they may nourish themselves and live contentedly is to confer all their power and strength upon one man, or upon one assembly of men, that may reduce all their wills, by plurality of voices, unto one will, which is as much as to say to appoint one man, or assembly of men, to bear their person, and everyone to own and acknowledge himself to be author of whatsoever he that so bears their person shall act, or cause to be acted, in those things which concern the common peace and safety, and therein to submit their wills, everyone to his will, and their judgments, to his judgment. This is more than consent, or concord; it is a real unity of them all, in one and the same person, made by covenant of every man with every man, in such manner, as if every man should say to every man, I authorize and give up my right of governing myself to this man, or to this assembly of men, on this condition, that thou give up thy right to him, and authorize all his actions in like manner. This done, the multitude so united in one person is called a COMMONWEALTH, Latin *Civitas*. This is the generation of that great LEVIATHAN, or rather (to speak more reverently) of that mortal God, to which we owe, under the immortal God, our peace and defense. For by this authority, given him by every particular man in the commonwealth, he has the use of so much power and strength conferred on him that, by terror thereof, he is enabled to form the wills of them all to peace at home and mutual aid against their enemies abroad. And in him consists the essence of the commonwealth, which (to define it) is one person, of whose acts a great multitude, by mutual covenants one with another, have made themselves everyone the author, to the end he may use the strength and means of them all as he shall think expedient for their peace and common defense.

And he that carries this person is called sovereign and said to have sovereign power, and everyone besides, his SUBJECT.

<h3>OF THE RIGHTS OF SOVEREIGNS BY INSTITUTION</h3>

A commonwealth is said to be instituted when a multitude of men do agree, and covenant, everyone with everyone, that to whatsoever man, or assembly of men, shall be given by the major part the right to present the person of them all (that is to say, to be their representative), everyone, as well he that voted for it as he that voted against it, shall authorize all the actions and judgments of that man, or assembly of men, in the same manner as if they were his own, to the end, to live peaceably amongst themselves and be protected against other men.

From this institution of a commonwealth are derived all the rights and faculties of him, or them, on whom the sovereign power is conferred by the consent of the people assembled.

First, because they covenant, it is to be understood, they are not obliged by former covenant to anything repugnant hereunto. And, consequently, they that have already instituted a commonwealth, being thereby bound by covenant to own the actions and judgments of one, cannot lawfully make a new covenant amongst themselves to be obedient to any other, in anything whatsoever, without his permission. And, therefore, they that are subjects to a monarch cannot without his leave cast off monarchy and return to the confusion of a disunited multitude, nor transfer their person from him that bears it to another man or other assembly of men, for they are bound, every man to every man, to own and be reputed author of all that he that already is their sovereign shall do and judge fit to be done, so that any one man, dissenting all the rest, should break their covenant made to that man, which is injustice, and they have also every man given the sovereignty to him that bears their person; and therefore if they depose him, they take from him that which is his own, and so again it is injustice. Besides, if he that attempts to depose his sovereign be killed or punished by him for such attempt, he is author of his own punishment, as being by the institution author of all his sovereign shall do; and, because it is injustice for a man to do anything for which he may be punished by his own authority, he is also upon that title, unjust. And whereas some men have pretended for their disobedience to their sovereign, a new covenant, made, not with men, but with God; this also is unjust, for there is no covenant with God, but by mediation of somebody that represents God's person, which none do but God's lieutenant, who has the sovereignty under God. But this pretense of covenant with God is so evident a lie, even in the pretenders' own consciences, that it is not only an act of an unjust but also of a vile and unmanly disposition.

Secondly, because the right of bearing the person of them all is given to him they make sovereign, by covenant only of one to another, and not of him to any of them, there can happen no breach of covenant on the part of the sovereign, and consequently none of his subjects, by any pretense of forfeiture, can be freed from his subjection. That he which is made sovereign makes no covenant with his subjects beforehand is manifest, because either he must make it with the whole multitude, as one party to the covenant, or he must make a several covenant with every man. With the whole as one party, it is impossible, because as yet they are not one person, and if he make so many several covenants as there be men, those covenants after he has the sovereignty are void, because what act soever can be pretended by any one of them for breach thereof is the act both of himself and of all the rest, because done in the person, and by the right of everyone of them in particular. Besides, if any one or more of them pretend a breach of the covenant made by the sovereign at his institution, and others, or one other of his subjects, or himself alone, pretend there was no such breach, there is in this case no judge to decide the controversy, it returns therefore to the sword again, and every man recovers the right of protecting himself by his own strength, contrary to the design they had in the institution. It is therefore in vain to grant sovereignty by way of precedent covenant. The opinion that any monarch receives his power by covenant, that is to say, on condition, proceeds from want of understanding this easy truth, that covenants, being but words and breath, have no force to oblige, contain, constrain, or protect any man, but what it has from the public sword; that is, from the untied hands of that man, or assembly of men, that

has the sovereignty, and whose actions are avouched by them all, and performed by the strength of them all, in him united. But, when an assembly of men is made sovereign, then no man imagines any such covenant to have past in the institution, for no man is so dull as to say, for example, the people of Rome made a covenant with the Romans to hold the sovereignty on such or such conditions which, not performed, the Romans might lawfully depose the Roman people. That men see not the reason to be alike in a monarchy, and in a popular government, proceeds from the ambition of some, that are kinder to the government of an assembly, whereof they may hope to participate, than of monarchy, which they despair to enjoy.

Thirdly, because the major part has by consenting voices declared a sovereign, he that dissented must now consent with the rest, that is, be contented to avow all the actions he shall do, or else, justly be destroyed by the rest. For if he voluntarily entered into the congregation of them that were assembled, he sufficiently declared thereby his will (and therefore tacitly covenanted), to stand to what the major part should ordain, and therefore, if he refuse to stand thereto, or make protestation against any of their decrees, he does contrary to his covenant, and therefore unjustly. And whether he be of the congregation or not, and whether his consent be asked or not, he must either submit to their decrees or be left in the condition of war he was in before, wherein he might without injustice be destroyed by any man whatsoever.

Fourthly, because every subject is by this institution author of all the actions and judgments of the sovereign instituted, it follows that whatsoever he does it can be no injury to any of his subjects, nor ought he to be by any of them accused of injustice. For he that does anything by authority from another does therein no injury to him by whose authority he acts; but by this institution of a commonwealth, every particular man is author of all the sovereign does, and consequently he that complains of injury from his sovereign complains of that whereof he himself is author, and therefore ought not to accuse any man but himself; no nor himself of injury; because to do injury to one's self is impossible. It is true that they that have sovereign power may commit iniquity, but not injustice, or injury in the proper signification.

Fifthly, and consequently to that which was said last, no man that has sovereign power can justly be put to death or otherwise in any manner by his subjects punished. For, seeing every subject is author of the actions of his sovereign, he punishes another for the actions committed by himself.

And because the end of this institution is the peace and defense of them all, and whosoever has right to the end has right to the means; it belongs of right, to whatsoever man, or assembly that has the sovereignty, to be judge both of the means of peace and defense and also of the hindrances and disturbances of the same, and to do whatsoever he shall think necessary to be done, both beforehand, for the preserving of peace and security by prevention of discord at home and hostility from abroad; and, when peace and security are lost, for the recovery of the same. And, therefore,

Sixthly, it is annexed to the sovereignty to be judge of what opinions and doctrines are averse and what conducing to peace; and, consequently, on what occasions, how far, and what, men are to be trusted withal, in speaking to multitudes of people; and who shall examine the doctrines of all books before they be published. For the actions of men proceed from their opinions, and in the well governing of opinions consists the well governing of men's actions, in order to their peace, and concord. And though in matter of doctrine, nothing ought to be regarded but the truth; yet this is not repugnant to regulating of the same by peace. For doctrine repugnant to peace can no more be true than peace and concord can be against the law of nature. It is true that in a commonwealth, where by the negligence, or unskilfulness of governors, and teachers, false doctrines are by time generally received, the contrary truths may be generally offensive: Yet the most sudden and rough busting in of a new truth that can be does never break the peace but only sometimes awake the war. For those men that are so remissly governed that they dare take up arms to defend, or introduce, an opinion are still in war, and their condition not peace but only a cessation of arms for fear of one another; and they live, as it were, in the precincts of battle continually. It belongs therefore to him that has the sovereign power to be judge, or constitute all judges of opinions and doctrines, as a thing necessary to peace, thereby to prevent discord and civil war.

Seventhly, is annexed to the sovereignty the whole power of prescribing the rules whereby every man may know what goods he may enjoy, and what actions he may do, without being molested by any of his fellow-subjects; and this is it men call propriety. For before constitution of sovereign power (as has already been shown), all men had right to all things, which necessarily causes war; and therefore this propriety, being necessary to peace, and depending on sovereign power, is the act of that power, in order to the public peace. These rules of propriety (or *Meum* and *Tuum*) and of good, evil, lawful, and unlawful in the actions of subjects, are the civil laws; that is to say, the laws of each commonwealth in particular, though the name of civil law be now restrained to the ancient civil laws of the city of Rome, which, being the head of a great part of the world, her laws at that time were in these parts the civil law.

Eighthly, is annexed to the sovereignty

the right of judicature; that is to say, of hearing and deciding all controversies which may arise concerning law, either civil or natural, or concerning fact. For without the decision of controversies, there is no protection of one subject against the injuries of another; the laws concerning *Meum* and *Tuum* are in vain; and to every man remains, from the natural and necessary appetite of his own conservation, the right of protecting himself by his private strength, which is the condition of war and contrary to the end for which every commonwealth is instituted.

Ninthly, is annexed to the sovereignty the right of making war and peace with other nations and commonwealths, that is to say, of judging when it is for the public good, and how great forces are to be assembled, armed, and paid for that end; and to levy money upon the subjects to defray the expenses thereof. For the power by which the people are to be defended consists in their armies, and the strength of an army, in the union of their strength under one command, which command the sovereign instituted, therefore has, because the command of the militia, without other institution, makes him that has it sovereign. And, therefore, whosoever is made general of an army, he that has the sovereign power is always generalissimo.

Tenthly, is annexed to the sovereignty the choosing of all counselors, ministers, magistrates, and officers, both in peace and war. For seeing the sovereign is charged with the end, which is the common peace and defense, he is understood to have power to use such means as he shall think most fit for his discharge.

Eleventhly, to the sovereign is committed the power of rewarding with riches or honor, and of punishing with corporal or pecuniary punishment, or with ignominy, every subject according to the law he has formerly made; or if there be no law made, according as he shall judge most to conduce to the en-

couraging of men to serve the commonwealth, or deterring of them from doing disservice to the same.

Lastly, considering what values men are naturally apt to set upon themselves, what respect they look for from others, and how little they value other men, from whence continually arise amongst them emulation, quarrels, factions, and at last war, to the destroying of one another, and diminution of their strength against a common enemy: It is necessary that there be laws of honor, and a public rate of the worth of such men as have deserved, or are able to deserve well of the commonwealth; and that there be force in the hands of some or others to put those laws in execution. But it has already been shown that not only the whole militia or forces of the commonwealth but also the judicature of all controversies is annexed to the sovereignty. To the sovereign therefore it belongs also to give titles of honor and to appoint what order of place and dignity each man shall hold and what signs of respect, in public or private meetings, they shall give to one another.

These are the rights which make the essence of sovereignty and which are the marks whereby a man may discern in what man, or assembly of men, the sovereign power is placed and resides. For these are incommunicable and inseparable. The power to coin money, to dispose of the estate and persons of infant heirs, to have pre-emption in markets, and all other statute prerogatives may be transferred by the sovereign, and yet the power to protect his subjects be retained. But if he transfer the militia, he retains the judicature in vain, for want of execution of the laws; or, if he grant away the power of raising money, the militia is in vain, or if he give away the government of doctrines, men will be frightened into rebellion with the fear of spirits. And so if we consider any one of the said rights, we shall presently see that the holding of all the rest will pro-

57

duce no effect in the conservation of peace and justice, the end for which all commonwealths are instituted. And this division is it, whereof it is said, a kingdom divided in itself cannot stand; for, unless this division precede, division into opposite armies can never happen. If there had not first been an opinion received of the greatest part of England that these powers were divided between the king and the Lords, and the House of Commons, the people had never been divided and fallen into this Civil War, first, between those that disagreed in politics and, after, between the dissenters about the liberty of religion, which have so instructed men in this point of sovereign right that there be few now (in England) that do not see that these rights are inseparable and will be so generally acknowledged at the next return of peace and so continue till their miseries are forgotten, and no longer, except the vulgar be better taught than they have hitherto been.

And because they are essential and inseparable rights, it follows necessarily that in whatsoever words any of them seem to be granted away, yet if the sovereign power itself be not in direct terms renounced, and the name of sovereign no more given by the grantees to him that grants them, the grant is void; for when he has granted all he can, if we grant back the sovereignty, all is restored, as inseparably annexed thereunto.

This great authority being indivisible, and inseparably annexed to the sovereignty, there is little ground for the opinion of them that say of sovereign kings, though they be *singulis majores*, of greater power than every one of their subjects, yet they be *universis minores*, of less power than them all together. For if by all together, they mean not the collective body as one person, then all together, and every one, signify the same; and the speech is absurd. But if by all together, they understand them as one person (which person the sover-

eign bears), then the power of all together is the same with the sovereign's power, and so again the speech is absurd; which absurdity they see well enough when the sovereignty is in an assembly of the people; but in a monarch they see it not; and yet the power of sovereignty is the same in whomsoever it be placed.

And as the power, so also the honor of the sovereign, ought to be greater than that of any, or all, the subjects. For in the sovereignty is the fountain of honor. The dignities of lord, earl, duke, and prince are his creatures. As in the presence of the masters, the servants are equal and without any honor at all, so are the subjects in the presence of the sovereign. And though they shine, some more, some less, when they are out of his sight, yet in his presence they shine no more than the stars in presence of the sun.

But a man may here object that the condition of subjects is very miserable, as being obnoxious to the lusts and other irregular passions of him, or them that have so unlimited a power in their hands. And commonly they that live under a monarch think it the fault of monarchy, and they that live under the government of democracy or other sovereign assembly attribute all the inconvenience to that form of commonwealth; whereas the power in all forms, if they be perfect enough to protect them, is the same; not considering that the estate of man can never be without some incommodity or other; and that the greatest, that in any form of government can possibly happen to the people in general, is scarce sensible, in respect of the miseries and horrible calamities, that accompany a civil war; or that dissolute condition of masterless men, without subjection to laws, and a coercive power to tie their hands from rapine and revenge: nor considering that the greatest pressure of sovereign governors proceeds not from any delight or profit they can expect in the damage or weakening of their subjects, in whose vigor consists their own strength and glory; but in the restiveness of themselves, that unwillingly contributing to their own defense, make it necessary for their governors to draw from them what they can in time of peace, that they may have means on any emergent occasion, or sudden need, to resist or take advantage of their enemies. For all men are by nature provided of notable multiplying glasses (that is their passions and self-love), through which every little payment appears a great grievance; but are destitute of those prospective glasses (namely, moral and civil science) to see afar off the miseries that hang over them and cannot without such payments be avoided.

OF THE SEVERAL KINDS OF COMMON-WEALTH BY INSTITUTION

The difference of commonwealths consists in the difference of the sovereign, or the person representative of all and every one of the multitude. And because the sovereignty is either in one man or in an assembly of more than one, and into that assembly either every man has right to enter, or not everyone but certain men distinguished from the rest, it is manifest there can be but three kinds of commonwealth. For the representative must needs be one man, or more; and, if more, then it is the assembly of all, or but of a part. When the representative is one man, then is the commonwealth a MONARCHY; when an assembly of all that will come together, then it is a DEMOCRACY, or popular commonwealth; when an assembly of a part only, then it is called an ARISTOCRACY. Other kind of commonwealth there can be none; for either one, or more, or all, must have the sovereign power (which I have shown to be indivisible) entire.

There be other names of government in the histories and books of policy, as tyranny and oligarchy; but they are not the names of other forms of government but of the same forms misliked. For they that are discontented under monarchy call it tyranny; and they that are displeased with aristocracy call it oligarchy. So also, they which find themselves grieved under a democracy call it anarchy (which signifies want of government); and yet I think no man believes that want of government is any new kind of government; nor by the same reason ought they to believe that the government is of one kind when they like it and another when they mislike it or are oppressed by the governors. . . .

OF THE LIBERTY OF SUBJECTS

. . . To come now to the particulars of the true liberty of a subject; that is to say, what are the things which, though commanded by the sovereign, he may, nevertheless, without injustice refuse to do; we are to consider what rights we pass away when we make a commonwealth, or (which is all one) what liberty we deny ourselves by owning all the actions (without exception) of the man or assembly we make our sovereign. For in the act of our submission consists both our obligation and our liberty, which must therefore be inferred by arguments taken from thence; there being no obligation on any man which arises not from some act of his own; for all men equally are by nature free. And because such arguments must either be drawn from the express words, "I authorize all his actions," or from the intention of him that submits himself to his power (which intention is to be understood by the end for which he so submits); the obligation, and liberty of the subject, is to be derived, either from those words (or others equivalent) or else from the end of the institution of sovereignty; namely, the peace of the subjects within themselves, and their defense against a common enemy.

First, therefore, seeing sovereignty by institution, is by covenant of every one to every one; and sovereignty by acquisition, by covenants of the vanquished to the victor, or child to the parent. It is manifest that every subject has liberty in all those things, the right whereof cannot by covenant be transferred. I have shown before in the 14th chapter that covenants not to defend a man's own body are void. Therefore,

If the sovereign command a man (though justly condemned) to kill, wound, or maim himself; or not to resist those that assault him; or to abstain from the use of food, air, medicine, or any other thing, without which he cannot live; yet has that man the liberty to disobey.

If a man be interrogated by the sovereign, or his authority, concerning a crime done by himself, he is not bound (without assurance of pardon) to confess it, because no man (as I have shown in the same chapter) can be obliged by covenant to accuse himself.

Again, the consent of a subject to sovereign power is contained in these words, "I authorize, or take upon me, all his actions"; in which there is no restriction at all, of his own former natural liberty. For, by allowing him to kill me, I am not bound to kill myself when he commands me. 'Tis one thing to say, "Kill me, or my fellow, if you please"; another thing to say, "I will kill myself, or my fellow." It follows therefore, that

No man is bound by the words themselves, either to kill himself, or any other man; and, consequently, that the obligation a man may sometimes have upon the command of the sovereign to execute any dangerous or dishonorable office depends not on the words of our submission but on the intention, which is to be understood by the end thereof. When therefore our refusal to obey frustrates the end for which the sovereignty was ordained, then there is no liberty to refuse; otherwise there is.

Upon this ground a man that is commanded as a soldier to fight against the enemy, though his sovereign have right enough to punish his refusal with death, may nevertheless in many cases refuse, without injustice; as when he substitutes a sufficient soldier in his place; for in this case he deserts not the service of the commonwealth. And there is allowance to be made for natural timorousness, not only to women (of whom no such dangerous duty is expected), but also to men of feminine courage. When armies fight, there is on one side, or both, a running-away; yet, when they do it not out of treachery but fear, they are not esteemed to do it unjustly but dishonorably. For the same reason, to avoid battle is not injustice but cowardice. But he that enrols himself a soldier, or takes impressed money, takes away the excuse of a timorous nature and is obliged, not only to go to the battle, but also not to run from it, without his captain's leave. And when the defense of the commonwealth requires at once the help of all that are able to bear arms, everyone is obliged; because otherwise the institution of the commonwealth, which they have not the purpose or courage to preserve, was in vain.

To resist the sword of the commonwealth, in defense of another man, guilty or innocent, no man has liberty, because such liberty takes away from the sovereign the means of protecting us and is therefore destructive of the very essence of government. But in case a great many men together have already resisted the sovereign power unjustly, or committed some capital crime, for which every one of them expects death, whether have they not the liberty then to join together, and assist, and defend one another? Certainly they have. For they but defend their lives, which the guilty man may as well do as the innocent. There was indeed injustice in the first breach of their duty; their bearing of arms subsequent to it, though it be to maintain what they have done, is no new unjust act. And if it be only to defend their persons, it is not unjust at all. But the offer of pardon takes from them, to whom it is offered, the plea of self-defense and makes their perseverance in assisting or defending the rest unlawful.

As for other liberties, they depend on the silence of the law. In cases where the sovereign has prescribed no rule, there the subject has the liberty to do or forbear, according to his own discretion. And therefore such liberty is in some places more, and in some less, and in some times more, in other times less, according as they that have the sovereignty shall think most convenient. As, for example, there was a time when in England a man might enter into his own land (and dispossess such as wrongfully possessed it) by force. But in aftertimes that liberty of forcible entry was taken away by a statute made (by the king) in Parliament. And in some places of the world men have the liberty of many wives; in other places, such liberty is not allowed.

If a subject have a controversy with his sovereign, of debt, or of right of possession of lands or goods, or concerning any service required at his hands, or concerning any penalty, corporal or pecuniary, grounded on a precedent law, he has the same liberty to sue for his right as if it were against a subject, and before such judges as are appointed by the sovereign. For seeing the sovereign demands by force of a former law, and not by virtue of his power, he declares thereby that he requires no more than shall appear to be due by that law. The suit therefore is not contrary to the will of the sovereign, and consequently the subject has the liberty to demand the hearing of his cause and sentence according to that law. But if he demand or take anything by pretense of his power, there lies in that case no action of law; for all that is done by him in Virtue of his power is done by the authority of every subject, and, consequently, he that brings an action against the sovereign brings it against himself. . . .

The obligation of subjects to the sovereign is understood to last as long, and no longer, than the power lasts by which he is able to protect them. For the right men have by nature to protect themselves, when none else can protect them, can by no covenant be relinquished. The sovereignty is the soul of the commonwealth, which, once departed from the body, the members do no more receive their motion from it. The end of obedience is protection, which, wheresoever a man sees it, either in his own or in another's sword, nature applies his obedience to it, and his endeavor to maintain it. And though sovereignty, in the intention of them that make it, be immortal, yet is it in its own nature not only subject to violent death, by foreign war, but also, through the ignorance and passions of men, it has in it, from the very institution, many seeds of a natural mortality by intestine discord. . . .

OF THOSE THINGS THAT WEAKEN OR TEND TO THE DISSOLUTION OF A COMMONWEALTH

. . . Amongst the infirmities therefore of a commonwealth I will reckon in the first place those that arise from an imperfect institution and resemble the diseases of a natural body which proceed from a defective procreation.

Of which this is one: that a man to obtain a kingdom is sometimes content with less power than to the peace and defense of the commonwealth is necessarily required. From whence it comes to pass that, when the exercise of the power laid by is for the public safety to be resumed, it has the resemblance of an unjust act, which disposes great numbers of men (when occasion is presented) to rebel. In the same manner as the bodies of children, gotten by diseased parents, are subject either to untimely death or to purge the ill quality derived from their vicious conception by breaking out into boils and scabs. And when kings deny themselves some such necessary power, it is not always (though sometimes) out of ignorance of what is necessary to the office they undertake but many times out of a hope to recover the same again at their pleasure, wherein they reason not well, because such as will hold them to their promises shall be maintained against them by foreign commonwealths. . . .

In the second place I observe the diseases of a commonwealth that proceed from the poison of seditious doctrines, whereof one is that every private man is judge of good and evil actions. This is true in the condition of meet nature, where there are no civil laws, and also under civil government in such cases as are not determined by the law. But otherwise it is manifest that the measure of good and evil actions is the civil law; and the judge the legislator, who is always representative of the commonwealth. From this false doctrine men are disposed to debate with themselves and dispute the commands of the commonwealth and afterwards to obey, or disobey them, as in their private judgments they shall think fit. Whereby the commonwealth is distracted and weakened.

Another doctrine repugnant to civil society is that whatsoever a man does against his conscience is sin, and it depends on the presumption of making himself judge of good and evil. For a man's conscience and his judgment is the same thing, and as the judgment, so also the conscience may be erroneous. Therefore, though he that is subject to no civil law sins in all he does against his conscience, because he has no other rule to follow but his own reason; yet it is not so with him that lives in a commonwealth, because the law is the public conscience, by which he has already undertaken to be guided. Otherwise in such diversity as there is of private consciences, which are but private opinions, the commonwealth must needs be distracted, and no man dare to obey the

sovereign power farther than it shall seem good in his own eyes.

It has been also commonly taught that faith and sanctity are not to be attained by study and reason but by supernatural inspiration or infusion, which granted, I see not why any man should render a reason of this faith, or why every Christian should not be also a prophet, or why any man should take the law of his country rather than his own inspiration for the rule of his action. And thus we fall again into the fault of taking upon us to judge of good and evil. . . .

A fourth opinion, repugnant to the nature of a commonwealth, is this: that he that has the sovereign power is subject to the civil laws. It is true that sovereigns are all subject to the laws of nature, because such laws be divine and cannot, by any man or commonwealth, be abrogated. But to those laws which the sovereign himself, that is, which the commonwealth makes, he is not subject. For to be subject to laws is to be subject to the commonwealth, that is, to the sovereign representative, that is, to himself, which is not subjection but freedom from the laws. Which error, because it sets the laws above the sovereign, sets also a judge above him, and a power to punish him; which is to make a new sovereign, and again for the same reason a third, to punish the second, and so continually without end, to the confusion and dissolution of the commonwealth.

A fifth doctrine that tends to the dissolution of a commonwealth is that every private man has an absolute propriety in his goods, such as excludes the right of every other subject; and he has it only from the sovereign power, without the protection whereof, every other man should have equal right to the same. But if the right of the sovereign also be excluded, he cannot perform the office they have put him into, which is to defend them both from foreign enemies and from the injuries of one another, and consequently there is no longer a commonwealth.

And if the propriety of subjects exclude not the right of the sovereign representative to their goods, much less to their offices of judicature, or execution, in which they represent the sovereign himself.

There is a sixth doctrine, plainly and directly against the essence of a commonwealth, and 'tis this: that the sovereign power may be divided. For what is it to divide the power of a commonwealth but to dissolve it, for powers divided mutually destroy each other. . . .

As when the power of levying money (which is the nutritive faculty) has depended on a general assembly, the power of conduct and command (which is the motive faculty on one man, and the power of making laws (which is the rational faculty) on the accidental consent, not only of those two, but also of a third. This endangers the commonwealth, sometimes for want of consent to good laws, but most often for want of such nourishment as is necessary to life and motion. For although few perceive that such government is not government, but division of the commonwealth into three factions, and call it mixed monarchy, yet the truth is that it is not one independent commonwealth but three independent factions, nor one representative person, but three. In the Kingdom of God there may be three persons independent, without breach of unity in God that reigns, but where men reign, that be subject to diversity of opinions, it cannot be so. And therefore if the king bear the person of the people, and the general assembly bear also the person of the people, and another assembly bear the person of a part of the people, they are not one person, nor one sovereign, but three persons, and three sovereigns.

To what disease in the natural body of man I may exactly compare this irregurality of a commonwealth, I know not.

But I have seen a man that had another man growing out of his side, with a head, arms, breast, and stomach of his own. If he had another man growing out of his other side, the comparison might then have been exact.

Hitherto I have named such diseases of a commonwealth as are of the greatest and most present danger. There be other, not so great, which nevertheless are not unfit to be observed. At first, the difficulty of raising money for the necessary uses of the commonwealth, especially in the approach of war. This difficulty arises from the opinion that every subject has of a propriety in his lands and goods, exclusive of the sovereign's right to the use of the same. From whence it comes to pass that the sovereign power, which foresees the necessities and dangers of the commonwealth (finding the passage of money to the public treasure obstructed by the tenacity of the people), whereas it ought to extend itself to encounter and prevent such dangers in their beginnings, contracts itself as long as it can, and, when it cannot longer, struggles with the people by stratagems of law to obtain little sums, which, not sufficing, he is fain at last violently to open the way for present supply or perish; and being put often to these extremities, at last reduces the people to their due temper; or else the commonwealth must perish. Insomuch as we may compare this distemper very aptly to an ague, wherein the fleshly parts being congealed, or by venomous matter obstructed; the veins which by their natural course empty themselves into the heart are not (as they ought to be) supplied from the arteries, whereby there succeeds at first a cold contraction and trembling of the limbs; and afterward a hot and strong endeavor of the heart to force a passage for the blood; and, before it can do that, contents itself with the small refreshments of such things as cool for a time, till (if nature be strong enough) it break at last the contumacy of the parts obstructed and dissipates the venom into sweat; or (if nature be too weak) the patient dies.

Again, there is sometimes in a commonwealth a disease which resembles the pleurisy; and that is when the treasure of the commonwealth, flowing out of its due course, is gathered together in too much abundance in one or a few private men, by monopolies or by farms of the public revenues; in the same manner as the blood in a pleurisy, getting into the membrane of the breast, breeds there an inflammation, accompanied with a fever and painful stitches.

Also, the popularity of a potent subject (unless the commonwealth have very good caution of his fidelity) is a dangerous disease, because the people (which should receive their motion from the authority of the sovereign), by the flattery and by the reputation of an ambitious man, are drawn away from their obedience to the laws to follow a man of whose virtues and designs they have no knowledge. And this is commonly of more danger in a popular government than in a monarchy, because an army is of so great force and multitude as it may easily be made believe they are the people. By this means it was that Julius Caesar, who was set up by the people against the Senate, having won to himself the affections of his army, made himself master, both of Senate and people. And this proceeding of popular and ambitious men is plain rebellion and may be resembled to the effects of witchcraft.

Lastly, when in a war (foreign or intestine) the enemies get a final victory, so as (the forces of the commonwealth keeping the field no longer) there is no further protection of subjects in their loyalty, then is the commonwealth DISSOLVED, and every man at liberty to protect himself by such courses as his own discretion shall suggest unto him. For the sovereign is the public soul, giving life and motion to the commonwealth, which, expiring, the members are governed by it no more than the carcass of a man by his departed (though immortal) soul. For though the right of a sovereign monarch cannot be extinguished by the act of another, yet the obligation of the members may. For he that wants protection may seek it anywhere; and, when he has it, is obliged (without fraudulent pretense of having submitted himself out of fear) to protect his protection as long as he is able. But when the power of an assembly is once suppressed, the right of the same perishes utterly, because the assembly itself is extinct, and, consequently, there is no possibility for the sovereignty to re-enter. . . .

3. ENGLISH BILL OF RIGHTS OF 1688–89[1]

AN ACT FOR DECLARING THE RIGHTS AND LIBERTIES OF THE SUBJECT AND SETTLING THE SUCCESSION OF THE CROWN

Whereas the Lords Spiritual and Temporal, and Commons, assembled at Westminster, lawfully, fully, and freely representing all the estates of the people of this realm, did, upon the thirteenth day of February, in the year of our Lord 1688, present unto their majesties, then called and known by the names and style of William and Mary, Prince and Princess of Orange, being present in their proper persons, a certain declaration in writing, made by the said Lords and Commons, in the words following, viz.:

Whereas the late King James II, by the assistance of divers evil counselors, judges, and ministers employed by him, did endeavor to subvert and extirpate the Protestant religion and the laws and liberties of this kingdom:

1. William and Mary to 8 William III, c. 36, *The Statutes at Large*, ed. Danby Pickering (London, 1764), IX, 67–72. By our present calendar, 1689; at this time the new year legally began in England on March 25.

1. By assuming and exercising a power of dispensing with, and suspending of, laws, and the execution of laws, without consent of Parliament.

2. By committing and prosecuting divers worthy prelates, for humbly petitioning to be excused from concurring to the said assumed power.

3. By issuing and causing to be executed a commission under the great seal for erecting a court called the Court of Commissioners for Ecclesiastical Causes.

4. By levying money for and to the use of the crown, by pretense of prerogative, for other time, and in other manner, than the same was granted by Parliament.

5. By raising and keeping a standing army within this kingdom in time of peace, without consent of Parliament, and quartering soldiers, contrary to law.

6. By causing several good subjects, being Protestants, to be disarmed, at the same time when Papists were both armed and employed, contrary to law.

7. By violating the freedom of election of members to serve in Parliament.

8. By prosecutions in the Court of King's Bench for matters and causes cognizable only in Parliament; and by divers other arbitrary and illegal courses.

9. And whereas of late years partial, corrupt, and unqualified persons have been returned and served on juries in trials, and particularly divers jurors in trials for high treason, which were not freeholders.

10. And excessive bail hath been required of persons committed in criminal cases, to elude the benefits of the laws made for the liberty of the subjects.

11. And excessive fines have been imposed, and illegal and cruel punishments inflicted.

12. And several grants and promises made of fines and forfeitures, before any conviction or judgment against the persons upon whom the same were to be levied.

All which are utterly and directly contrary to the known laws and statutes and freedom of this realm.

And whereas the said late King James II, having abdicated the government, and the throne being thereby vacant, His Highness the Prince of Orange (whom it hath pleased Almighty God to make the glorious instrument of delivering this kingdom from popery and arbitrary power) did (by the advice of the Lords Spiritual and Temporal, and diverse principal persons of the Commons) cause letters to be written to the Lords Spiritual and Temporal, being Protestants, and other letters to the several counties, cities, universities, boroughs, and cinque ports, for the choosing of such persons to represent them, as were of right to be sent to Parliament, to meet and sit at Westminster upon the two-and-twentieth day of January, in this year one thousand six hundred eighty and eight, in order to such an establishment, as that their religion, laws, and liberties might not again be in danger of being subverted; upon which letters, elections have been accordingly made.

And thereupon the said Lords Spiritual and Temporal, and Commons, pursuant to their respective letters and elections, being now assembled in a full and free representation of this nation, taking into their most serious consideration the best means for attaining the ends aforesaid, do in the first place (as their ancestors in like case have usually done), for the vindicating and asserting their ancient rights and liberties, declare:

1. That the pretended power of suspending of laws, or the execution of laws, by regal authority, without consent of Parliament, is illegal.

2. That the pretended power of dispensing with laws, or the execution of laws, by regal authority, as it hath been assumed and exercised of late, is illegal.

3. That the commission for erecting the late Court of Commissioners for Ecclesiastical Causes, and all other commissions and courts of like nature, are illegal and pernicious.

4. That levying money for or to the

use of the crown, by pretense of prerogative, without grant of Parliament, for longer time or in other manner than the same is or shall be granted, is illegal.

5. That it is the right of the subjects to petition the king, and all commitments and prosecutions for such petitioning are illegal.

6. That the raising or keeping of a standing army within the kingdom in time of peace, unless it be with consent of Parliament, is against law.

7. That the subjects which are Protestants may have arms for their defense suitable to their conditions and as allowed by law.

8. That election of members of Parliament ought to be free.

9. That the freedom of speech, and debates or proceedings in Parliament, ought not to be impeached or questioned in any court or place out of Parliament.

10. That excessive bail ought not to be required, nor excessive fines imposed; nor cruel and unusual punishments inflicted.

11. That jurors ought to be duly impaneled and returned, and jurors which pass upon men in trials for high treason ought to be freeholders.

12. That all grants and promises of fines and forfeitures of particular persons before conviction are illegal and void.

13. And that for redress of all grievances, and for the amending, strengthening, and preserving of the laws, Parliament ought to be held frequently.

And they do claim, demand, and insist upon all and singular the premises as their undoubted rights and liberties; and that no declarations, judgments, doings, or proceedings, to the prejudice of the people in any of the said premises, ought in any wise to be drawn hereafter into consequence or example.

To which demand of their rights they are particularly encouraged by the declaration of His Highness the Prince of Orange, as being the only means for obtaining a full redress and remedy therein:

Having therefore an entire confidence that his said Highness the Prince of Orange will perfect the deliverance so far advanced by him, and will still preserve them from the violation of their rights, which they have here asserted and from all other attempts upon their religion, rights, and liberties:

II. The said Lords Spiritual and Temporal, and Commons, assembled at Westminster, do resolve that William and Mary, Prince and Princess of Orange, be, and be declared, king and queen of England, France, and Ireland, and the dominions thereunto belonging, to hold the crown and royal dignity of the said kingdoms and dominions to them the said prince and princess during their lives, and the life of the survivor of them; and that the sole and full exercise of the regal power be only in and executed by the said Prince of Orange, in the names of the said prince and princess, during their joint lives; and after their deceases, the said crown and royal dignity of the said kingdoms and dominions to be to the heirs of the body of the said princess; and, for default of such issue, to the Princess Anne of Denmark and the heirs of her body; and, for default of such issue, to the heirs of the body of the said Prince of Orange. And the Lords Spiritual and Temporal, and Commons, do pray the said prince and princess to accept the same accordingly.

III. And that the oaths hereafter mentioned be taken by all persons of whom the oaths of allegiance and supremacy might be required by law, instead of them; and that the said oaths of allegiance and supremacy be abrogated.

I, A.B., do sincerely promise and swear that I will be faithful and bear true allegiance to their majesties King William and Queen Mary; so help me God.

I, A.B., do swear that I do from my heart abhor, detest, and adjure as impious and heretical that damnable doctrine and position that princes excommunicated or deprived by the pope, or any authority of the see of Rome, may be deposed or murdered by their subjects, or any other whatsoever. And I do declare that no foreign prince, person, prelate, state, or potentate hath, or ought to have any jurisdiction, power, superiority, preeminence, or authority, ecclesiastical or spiritual, within this realm; so help me God.

IV. Upon which their said majesties did accept the crown and royal dignity of the kingdoms of England, France, and Ireland, and the dominions thereunto belonging, according to the resolution and desire of the said Lords and Commons contained in the said declaration.

V. And thereupon their majesties were pleased that the said Lords Spiritual and Temporal, and Commons, being the two houses of Parliament, should continue to sit and with their majesties' royal concurrence make effectual provision for the settlement of the religion, laws, and liberties of this kingdom, so that the same for the future might not be in danger again of being subverted; to which the said Lords Spiritual and Temporal, and Commons, did agree and proceed to act accordingly.

VI. Now, in pursuance of the premises, the said Lords Spiritual and Temporal, and Commons, in Parliament assembled, for the ratifying, declaration, and the articles, clauses, matters, and things therein contained, by the force of a law made in due form by authority of Parliament, do pray that it may be declared and enacted that all and singular the rights and liberties asserted and claimed in the said declaration are the true, ancient, and indubitable rights and liberties of the people of this kingdom, and so shall be esteemed, allowed, adjudged, deemed, and taken to be, and that all and every the particulars aforesaid shall be firmly and strictly holden and observed, as they are expressed in the said declaration; and all officers and ministers whatsoever shall serve their

majesties and their successor according to the same in all times to come.

VII. And the said Lords Spiritual and Temporal, and Commons, seriously considering how it hath pleased Almighty God, in his marvelous providence and merciful goodness to this nation, to provide and preserve their said majesties' royal persons most happily to reign over us upon the throne of their ancestors, for which they render unto Him from the bottom of their hearts their humblest thanks and praises, do truly, firmly, assuredly, and in the sincerity of their hearts, think, and do hereby recognize, acknowledge, and declare that King James II, having abdicated the government, and their majesties having accepted the crown and royal dignity as aforesaid, their said majesties did become, were, are, and of right ought to be, by the laws of this realm, our sovereign liege lord and lady, king and queen of England, France, and Ireland, and the dominions thereunto belonging, in and to whose princely persons the royal state, crown, and dignity of the said realms, with all honors, styles, titles, regalities, prerogatives, powers, jurisdictions, and authorities to the same belonging and appertaining, are most fully, rightfully, and entirely invested and incorporated, united and annexed.

VIII. And for preventing all questions and divisions in this realm, by reason of any pretended titles to the crown, and for preserving a certainty in the succession thereof, in and upon which the unity, peace, tranquillity, and safety of this nation doth, under God, wholly consist and depend, the said Lords Spiritual and Temporal, and Commons, do beseech their majesties that it may be enacted, established, and declared that the crown and regal government of the said kingdoms and dominions, with all and singular the premises thereunto belonging and appertaining, shall be and continue to their said majesties and the survivor of them, during their lives, and the life of the survivor of them. And that the entire, perfect, and full exercise of the regal power and government be only in and executed by His Majesty, in the names of both their majesties during their joint lives; and after their deceases the said crown and premises shall be and remain to the heirs of the body of Her Majesty; and, for default of such issue, to Her Royal Highness the Princess Anne of Denmark and the heirs of her body; and, for default of such issue, to the heirs of the body of his said majesty. And thereunto the said Lords Spiritual and Temporal, and Commons, do, in the name of all the people aforesaid, most humbly and faithfully submit themselves, their heirs and posterities forever; and do faithfully promise that they will stand to, maintain, and defend their said majesties, and also the limitation and succession of the crown herein specified and contained, to the utmost of their powers, with their lives and estates, against all persons whatsoever that shall attempt anything to the contrary.

IX. And whereas it hath been found by experience that it is inconsistent with the safety and welfare of this Protestant kingdom to be governed by a popish prince, or by any king or queen marrying a Papist, the said Lords Spiritual and Temporal, and Commons, do further pray that it may be enacted that all and every person and persons that is, are, or shall be reconciled to, or shall hold communion with, the see or church of Rome, or shall profess the popish religion, or shall marry a Papist, shall be excluded, and be forever incapable to inherit, possess, or enjoy the crown and government of this realm and Ireland, and the dominions thereunto belonging, or any part of the same, or to have, use, or exercise any regal power, authority, or jurisdiction within the same; and in all and every such case or cases the people of these realms shall be and are hereby absolved of their allegiance; and the said crown and government shall from time to time descend to, and be enjoyed by such person or persons, being Protestants, as should have inherited and enjoyed the same in case the said person or persons so reconciled, holding communion, or profession, or marrying as aforesaid, were naturally dead. . . .

4. SECOND TREATISE . . . ON CIVIL GOVERNMENT[1]

By John Locke

EDITORS' NOTE.—John Locke (1632–1704), English philosopher, wrote three works which have become foundation stones of the modern liberal tradition. The *Essay concerning the Human Understanding* (begun in 1671 but not published until 1690) presented his theory of the origins and validity of knowledge. It puts forward Locke's famous proposition that the mind is at birth a *tabula rasa* ("white sheet") upon which "the experience of the senses and reflection" inscribes knowledge. *A Letter concerning Toleration* (1689) is what its name indicates: an argument for the toleration by the state of all theistic sects except those holding allegiance to an outside temporal power. The third work comprises *Two Treatises of Government*. The first of these two treatises is routine polemics against Sir Robert Filmer's *Patriarcha*, a defense of the ab-

1. John Locke, *Second Treatise . . . of Civil Government*, in *English Philosophers from Bacon to Mill*, ed. E. A. Burtt (New York, 1939), 403–23, 437–43, 449–69, 484–503. Reprinted by permission of the Modern Library, New York.

solute dominion of kings in terms of Adam's god-given rule over his children. The second treatise, from which the excerpts below are taken, is a classic defense of private property and free government as they came to be understood in England and especially, one hundred years later, in the American colonies.

Educated at Oxford, Locke later studied medicine but abandoned it to become secretary to Anthony Ashley Cooper (later Earl of Shaftesbury). As Ashley's helper, Locke had a major part in drafting the "Fundamental Constitution for the Government of Carolina." The downfall of the Whigs in the early 1680's led Locke to follow his patron into exile in the Netherlands, whence Locke returned in 1689 during the "Glorious Revolution." After 1689 Locke carried on some minor official duties and wrote essays on religious, fiscal, educational, and other social problems. Throughout his lifetime John Locke was interested in the growing natural sciences. He was a member of the Royal Society and friend and admirer of natural scientists, among them, Sir Isaac Newton and Robert Boyle, whose *History of the Air* he edited.

Locke's first treatise was probably written between the publication of the first edition of *Patriarcha* and the appearance of the second. The essay was probably "substantially completed" during the last year or two of Locke's stay in Holland; but it was polished up and published in the first year of his return. In his prefatory note Locke remarks that a middle portion, longer than the two published essays, had been lost. In this Preface Locke also remarked that he hoped that "these papers would be sufficient to establish the throne of our great restorer, our present King William, to make good his title in the consent of the people, which, being the only one of all lawful governments, he has more fully and clearly than any prince in Christendom, and to justify to the world the people of England, whose love of their natural rights, with their resolution to preserve them, saved the nation when it was on the very brink of slavery and ruin."

The best biography of Locke is the two-volume work by H. R. Fox Bourne (New York, 1876). See, for further references, articles in the *Encyclopaedia of the Social Sciences* on "Locke" and "Property."

CHAPTER I

THE INTRODUCTION

1. It having been shown in the foregoing discourse:[2]

(i) That Adam had not, either by natural right of fatherhood or by positive donation from God, any such authority over his children, nor dominion over the world, as is pretended.[3]

(ii) That if he had, his heirs yet had no right to it.

(iii) That if his heirs had, there being no law of nature nor positive law of God that determines which is the right heir in all cases that may arise, the right of succession, and consequently of bearing

2. "In the foregoing discourse," i.e., in the first of the *Two Treatises of Government*, which was entitled "An Essay concerning Certain False Principles."

3. "As is pretended," i.e., by Sir Robert Filmer.

rule, could not have been certainly determined.

(iv) That if even that had been determined, yet the knowledge of which is the eldest line of Adam's posterity, being so long since utterly lost, that in the races of mankind and families of the world there remains not to one above another the least pretense to be the eldest house, and to have the right of inheritance.

All these premises having, as I think, been clearly made out, it is imposible that the rulers now on earth should make any benefit, or derive any the least shadow of authority from that which is held to be the foundation of all power, Adam's private dominion and paternal jurisdiction; so that he that will not give just occasion to think that all government in the world is the product only of force and violence, and that men live together by no other rules but that of beasts, where the strongest carries it, and so lay a foundation for perpetual disorder and mischief, tumult, sedition, and rebellion (things that the followers of that hypothesis so loudly cry out against), must of necessity find out another rise of government, another original of political power, and another way of designing and knowing the persons that have it, than what Sir Robert Filmer hath taught us.[4]

2. To this purpose, I think it may not be amiss to set down what I take to be political power; that the power of a magistrate over a subject may be distinguished from that of a father over his children, a master over his servant, a husband over his wife, and a lord over his slave. All which distinct powers happening sometime together in the same man, if he be considered under these different

relations, it may help us to distinguish these powers one from another, and show the difference betwixt a ruler of a commonwealth, a father of a family, and a captain of a galley.

3. Political power, then, I take to be a right of making laws with penalties of death, and consequently all less penalties, for the regulating and preserving of property, and of employing the force of the community in the execution of such laws, and in the defense of the commonwealth from foreign injury, and all this only for the public good.

CHAPTER II
OF THE STATE OF NATURE

4. To understand political power aright, and derive it from its original, we must consider what state all men are naturally in, and that is a state of perfect freedom to order their actions and dispose of their possessions and persons as they think fit, within the bounds of the law of nature, without asking leave, or depending upon the will of any other man.

A state also of equality, wherein all the power and jurisdiction is reciprocal, no one having more than another; there being nothing more evident than that creatures of the same species and rank, promiscuously born to all the same advantages of nature, and the use of the same faculties, should also be equal one amongst another without subordination or subjection, unless the Lord and Master of them all should by any manifest declaration of His will set one above another, and confer on him by an evident and clear appointment an undoubted right to dominion and sovereignty.

5. This equality of men by nature the judicious Hooker[5] looks upon as so evident in itself and beyond all question, that he makes it the foundation of that

4. Sir Robert Filmer published numerous works on the authority of kings, among them *The Anarchy of a Limited and Mixed Monarchy* in 1646 and *The Power of Kings* in 1648. His *Patriarcha*, to which Locke's *Treatises* were an answer, was written about 1642 but not published until 1680, by Filmer's son. A second edition of *Patriarcha* appeared in 1685.

5. Richard Hooker (1554?–1600), English divine and author of *The Laws of Ecclesiastical Polity*, an early classic of English prose and political thought.

obligation to mutual love amongst men on which he builds the duties they owe one another, and from whence he derives the great maxims of justice and charity. His words are:

"The like natural inducement hath brought men to know that it is no less their duty to love others than themselves; for seeing those things which are equal must needs all have one measure, if I cannot but wish to receive good, even as much at every man's hands as any man can wish unto his own soul, how should I look to have any part of my desire herein satisfied, unless myself be careful to satisfy the like desire, which is undoubtedly in other men weak, being of one and the same nature. To have anything offered them repugnant to this desire, must needs in all respects grieve them as much as me, so that, if I do harm, I must look to suffer, there being no reason that others should show greater measures of love to me than they have by me showed unto them. My desire, therefore, to be loved of my equals in nature as much as possible may be, imposeth upon me a natural duty of bearing to them-ward fully the like affection; from which relation of equality between ourselves and them that are as ourselves, what several rules and canons natural reason hath drawn for direction of life no man is ignorant" (*Eccl. Pol.*, lib. i).

6. But though this be a state of liberty, yet it is not a state of license; though man in that state have an uncontrollable liberty to dispose of his person or possessions, yet he has not liberty to destroy himself, or so much as any creature in his possession, but where some nobler use than its bare preservation calls for it. The state of nature has a law of nature to govern it, which obliges everyone; and reason, which is that law, teaches all mankind who will but consult it, that, being all equal and independent, no one ought to harm another in his life, health, liberty, or possessions. For men being all the workmanship of one omnipotent and infinitely wise Maker—all the servants of one sovereign Master, sent into the world by His order, and about His business— they are His property, whose workmanship they are, made to last during His, not one another's pleasure; and being furnished with like faculties, sharing all in one community of nature, there cannot be supposed any such subordination among us, that may authorize us to destroy one another, as if we were made for one another's uses, as the inferior ranks of creatures are for ours. Everyone, as he is bound to preserve himself, and not to quit his station wilfully, so, by the like reason, when his own preservation comes not in competition, ought he, as much as he can, to preserve the rest of mankind, and not, unless it be to do justice on an offender, take away or impair the life, or what tends to the preservation of the life, the liberty, health, limb, or goods of another.

7. And that all men may be restrained from invading others' rights, and from doing hurt to one another, and the law of nature be observed, which willeth the peace and preservation of all mankind, the execution of the law of nature is in that state put into every man's hand, whereby everyone has a right to punish the transgressors of that law to such a degree as may hinder its violation. For the law of nature would, as all other laws that concern men in this world, be in vain if there were nobody that, in the state of nature, had a power to execute that law, and thereby preserve the innocent and restrain offenders. And if anyone in the state of nature may punish another for any evil he has done, everyone may do so. For in that state of perfect equality, where naturally there is no superiority or jurisdiction of one over another, what any may do in prosecution of that law, everyone must needs have a right to do.

8. And thus in the state of nature one man comes by a power over another; but yet no absolute or arbitrary power, to use a criminal, when he has got him

in his hands, according to the passionate heats or boundless extravagance of his own will; but only to retribute to him so far as calm reason and conscience dictate what is proportionate to his transgression, which is so much as may serve for reparation and restraint. For these two are the only reasons why one man may lawfully do harm to another, which is that we call punishment. In transgressing the law of nature, the offender declares himself to live by another rule than that of common reason and equity, which is that measure God has set to the actions of men, for their mutual security; and so he becomes dangerous to mankind, the tie which is to secure them from injury and violence being slighted and broken by him. Which, being a trespass against the whole species, and the peace and safety of it, provided for by the law of nature, every man upon this score, by the right he hath to preserve mankind in general, may restrain, or, where it is necessary, destroy things noxious to them, and so may bring such evil on anyone who hath transgressed that law, as may make him repent the doing of it, and thereby deter him, and by his example others, from doing the like mischief. And in this case, and upon this ground, every man hath a right to punish the offender, and be executioner of the law of nature.

9. I doubt not but this will seem a very strange doctrine to some men: but before they condemn it, I desire them to resolve me by what right any prince or state can put to death or punish an alien, for any crime he commits in their country. 'Tis certain their laws, by virtue of any sanction they receive from the promulgated will of the legislative, reach not a stranger: they speak not to him, nor, if they did, is he bound to hearken to them. The legislative authority, by which they are in force over the subjects of that commonwealth, hath no power over him. Those who have the supreme power of making laws in England, France, or Holland, are to an Indian but like the rest of the world—men without authority. And, therefore, if by the law of nature every man hath not a power to punish offenses against it, as he soberly judges the case to require, I see not how the magistrates of any community can punish an alien of another country; since in reference to him they can have no more power than what every man naturally may have over another.

10. Besides the crime which consists in violating the law, and varying from the right rule of reason, whereby a man so far becomes degenerate, and declares himself to quit the principles of human nature, and to be a noxious creature, there is commonly injury done, and some person or other, some other man receives damage by his transgression, in which case he who hath received any damage, has, besides the right of punishment common to him with other men, a particular right to seek reparation from him that has done it. And any other person who finds it just, may also join with him that is injured, and assist him in recovering from the offender so much as may make satisfaction for the harm he has suffered.

11. From these two distinct rights—the one of punishing the crime, for restraint and preventing the like offense, which right of punishing is in everybody; the other of taking reparation, which belongs only to the injured party—comes it to pass that the magistrate, who by being magistrate hath the common right of punishing put into his hands, can often, where the public good demands not the execution of the law, remit the punishment of criminal offenses by his own authority, but yet cannot remit the satisfaction due to any private man for the damage he has received. That he who has suffered the damage has a right to demand in his own name, and he alone can remit. The damnified person has this power of appropriating to himself the goods or service of the of-

fender, by right of self-preservation, as every man has a power to punish the crime, to prevent its being committed again, by the right he has of preserving all mankind, and doing all reasonable things he can in order to that end. And thus it is that every man in the state of nature has a power to kill a murderer, both to deter others from doing the like injury, which no reparation can compensate, by the example of the punishment that attends it from everybody, and also to secure men from the attempts of a criminal who having renounced reason, the common rule and measure God hath given to mankind, hath by the unjust violence and slaughter he hath committed upon one, declared war against all mankind, and therefore may be destroyed as a lion or a tiger, one of those wild savage beasts with whom men can have no society nor security. And upon this is grounded that great law of nature. "Whoso sheddeth man's blood, by man shall his blood be shed." And Cain was so fully convinced that everyone had a right to destroy such a criminal, that after the murder of his brother he cries out, "Every one that findeth me shall slay me"; so plain was it writ in the hearts of mankind.

12. By the same reason may a man in the state of nature punish the lesser breaches of that law. It will perhaps be demanded, With death? I answer, each transgression may be punished to that degree, and with so much severity, as will suffice to make it an ill bargain to the offender, give him cause to repent, and terrify others from doing the like. Every offense that can be committed in the state of nature, may in the state of nature be also punished equally, and as far forth as it may, in a commonwealth. For though it would be beside my present purpose to enter here into the particulars of the law of nature, or its measures of punishment, yet it is certain there is such a law, and that, too, as intelligible and plain to a rational creature and a studier of that law as the positive laws of commonwealths; nay, possibly plainer, as much as reason is easier to be understood than the fancies and intricate contrivances of men, following contrary and hidden interests put into words; for truly so are a great part of the municipal laws of countries, which are only so far right as they are founded on the law of nature, by which they are to be regulated and interpreted.

13. To this strange doctrine—viz., that in the state of nature everyone has the executive power of the law of nature—I doubt not but it will be objected that it is unreasonable for men to be judges in their own cases, that self-love will make men partial to themselves and their friends. And on the other side, that ill-nature, passion, and revenge will carry them too far in punishing others; and hence nothing but confusion and disorder will follow; and that therefore God hath certainly appointed government to restrain the partiality and violence of men. I easily grant that civil government is the proper remedy for the inconveniences of the state of nature, which must certainly be great where men may be judges in their own case, since 'tis easy to be imagined that he who was so unjust as to do his brother an injury, will scarce be so just as to condemn himself for it. But I shall desire those who make this objection, to remember that absolute monarchs are but men, and if government is to be the remedy of those evils which necessarily follow from men's being judges in their own cases, and the state of nature is therefore not to be endured, I desire to know what kind of government that is, and how much better it is than the state of nature, where one man commanding a multitude, has the liberty to be judge in his own case, and may do to all his subjects whatever he pleases, without the least question or control of those who execute his pleasure; and in whatsoever he doth, whether led by reason, mistake, or pas-

sion, must be submitted to, which men in the state of nature are not bound to do one to another? And if he that judges, judges amiss in his own or any other case, he is answerable for it to the rest of mankind.

14. 'Tis often asked as a mighty objection, Where are, or ever were there, any men in such a state of nature? To which it may suffice as an answer at present: That since all princes and rulers of independent governments all through the world are in a state of nature, 'tis plain the world never was, nor ever will be, without numbers of men in that state. I have named all governors of independent communities, whether they are or are not in league with others. For 'tis not every compact that puts an end to the state of nature between men, but only this one of agreeing together mutually to enter into one community, and make one body politic; other promises and compacts men may make one with another, and yet still be in the state of nature. The promises and bargains for truck, etc., between the two men in Soldania,[6] in or between a Swiss and an Indian, in the woods of America, are binding to them, though they are perfectly in a state of nature in reference to one another. For truth and keeping of faith belong to men as men, and not as members of society.

15. To those that say there were never any men in the state of nature, I will not only oppose the authority of the judicious Hooker (*Eccl. Pol.*, lib. i., sec. 10), where he says, "The laws which have been hitherto mentioned," i.e., the laws of nature, "do bind men absolutely, even as they are men, although they have never any settled fellowship, and never any solemn agreement amongst themselves what to do or not to do; but forasmuch as we are not by ourselves sufficient to furnish ourselves with competent store of things needful for such a

6. In the realms of the Sultans, probably those of North Africa.

life as our nature doth desire—a life fit for the dignity of man—therefore to supply those defects and imperfections which are in us, as living single and solely by ourselves, we are naturally induced to seek communion and fellowship with others; this was the cause of men's uniting themselves at first in politic societies"—but I moreover affirm that all men are naturally in that state, and remain so, till by their own consents they make themselves members of some politic society; and I doubt not, in the sequel of this discourse, to make it very clear.

CHAPTER III
OF THE STATE OF WAR

16. The state of war is a state of enmity and destruction; and therefore declaring by word or action, not a passionate and hasty, but a sedate, settled design upon another man's life, puts him in a state of war with him against whom he has declared such an intention, and so has exposed his life to the other's power to be taken away by him, or anyone that joins with him in his defense and espouses his quarrel; it being reasonable and just I should have a right to destroy that which threatens me with destruction. For by the fundamental law of nature, man being to be preserved as much as possible, when all cannot be preserved, the safety of the innocent is to be preferred; and one may destroy a man who makes war upon him, or has discovered an enmity to his being, for the same reason that he may kill a wolf or a lion; because they are not under the ties of the common law of reason, have no other rule but that of force and violence, and so may be treated as a beast of prey, those dangerous and noxious creatures that will be sure to destroy him whenever he falls into their power.

17. And hence it is that he who attempts to get another man into his absolute power does thereby put himself into a state of war with him; it being to be understood as a declaration of a

design upon his life. For I have reason to conclude that he who would get me into his power without my consent, would use me as he pleased when he had got me there, and destroy me too, when he had a fancy to it; for nobody can desire to have me in his absolute power, unless it be to compel me by force to that which is against the right of my freedom, i.e., make me a slave. To be free from such force is the only security of my preservation; and reason bids me look on him as an enemy to my preservation who would take away that freedom which is the fence to it; so that he who makes an attempt to enslave me, thereby puts himself into a state of war with me. He that in the state of nature would take away the freedom that belongs to any one in that state, must necessarily be supposed to have a design to take away everything else, that freedom being the foundation of all the rest; as he that in the state of society would take away the freedom belonging to those of that society or commonwealth, must be supposed to design to take away from them everything else, and so be looked on as in a state of war.

18. This makes it lawful for a man to kill a thief who has not in the least hurt him, nor declared any design upon his life, any farther than by the use of force, so to get him in his power as to take away his money, or what he pleases, from him; because using force, where he has no right to get me into his power, let his pretense be what it will, I have no reason to suppose that he who would take away my liberty would not, when he had me in his power, take away everything else. And, therefore, it is lawful for me to treat him as one who has put himself into a state of war with me—i.e., kill him if I can; for to that hazard does he justly expose himself whoever introduces a state of war, and is aggressor in it.

19. And here we have the plain difference between the state of nature and the state of war, which however some men have confounded, are as far distant as a state of peace, good will, mutual assistance and preservation, and a state of enmity, malice, violence and mutual destruction, are one from another. Men living together according to reason, without a common superior on earth with authority to judge between them, is properly the state of nature. But force, or a declared design of force, upon the person of another, where there is no common superior on earth to appeal to for relief, is the state of war; and 'tis the want of such an appeal gives a man the right of war even against an aggressor, though he be in society and a fellow-subject. Thus a thief, whom I cannot harm, but by appeal to the law, for having stolen all that I am worth, I may kill, when he sets on to rob me but of my horse or coat; because the law, which was made for my preservation where it cannot interpose to secure my life from present force, which if lost is capable of no reparation, permits me my own defense, and the right of war, a liberty to kill the aggressor, because the aggressor allows not time to appeal to our common judge, nor the decision of the law, for remedy in a case where the mischief may be irreparable. Want of a common judge with authority puts all men in a state of nature; force without right, upon a man's person, makes a state of war, both where is, and is not, a common judge.

20. But when the actual force is over, the state of war ceases between those that are in society, and are equally on both sides subject to the judge.

21. And, therefore, in such controversies, where the question is put, Who shall be judge? it cannot be meant, Who shall decide the controversy? Everyone knows what Jephtha here tells us, that the "Lord the Judge"[7] shall judge. Where there is no judge on earth, the appeal lies to God in Heaven. That question, then, cannot mean, Who shall judge

7. One of the early Hebrew judges. The reference is to Judg. 11:27.

Whether another hath put himself in a state of war with me, and whether I may, as Jephtha did, appeal to Heaven in it? Of that I myself can only be judge in my own conscience, as I will answer it at the great day, to the supreme Judge of all men.

CHAPTER IV

OF SLAVERY

22. The natural liberty of men is to be free from any superior power on earth, and not to be under the will or legislative authority of man, but to have only the law of nature for his rule. The liberty of man in society is to be under no other legislative power but that established by consent in the commonwealth; nor under the dominion of any will or restraint of any law, but what that legislative shall enact according to the trust put in it. Freedom then is not what Sir Robert Filmer tells us (O. A. 55),[8] "a liberty for everyone to do what he lists, to live as he pleases, and not to be tied by any laws." But freedom of men under government is to have a standing rule to live by, common to everyone of that society, and made by the legislative power erected in it; a liberty to follow my own will in all things, where that rule prescribes not; and not to be subject to the inconstant, uncertain, unknown, arbitrary will of another man: as freedom of nature is to be under no other restraint but the law of nature.

23. This freedom from absolute arbitrary power is so necessary to, and closely joined with, a man's preservation, that he cannot part with it but by what forfeits his preservation and life together. For a man not having the power of his own life cannot by compact, or his own consent, enslave himself to anyone, nor put himself under the absolute arbitrary power of another to take away his life when he pleases. Nobody can give more power than he has himself; and he that

8. A reference to Filmer's *Observations upon Aristotle's Politiques* (1679).

cannot take away his own life, cannot give another power over it. Indeed, having by his fault forfeited his own life by some act that deserves death, he to whom he has forfeited it may (when he has him in his power) delay to take it, and make use of him to his own service; and he does him no injury by it. For whenever he finds the hardship of his slavery outweigh the value of his life, 'tis in his power by resisting the will of his master to draw on himself the death he desires.

24. This is the perfect condition of slavery, which is nothing else but the state of war continued between a lawful conqueror and a captive, for if once compact enter between them, and make an agreement for a limited power on the one side, and obedience on the other, the state of war and slavery ceases as long as the compact endures; for, as has been said, no man can by agreement pass over to another that which he hath not in himself—a power over his own life.

I confess, we find among the Jews, as well as other nations, that men did sell themselves; but it is plain this was only to drudgery, not to slavery; for it is evident the person sold was not under an absolute, arbitrary, despotical power, for the master could not have power to kill him at any time, whom at a certain time he was obliged to let go free out of his service; and the master of such a servant was so far from having an arbitrary power over his life that he could not at pleasure so much as maim him, but the loss of an eye or tooth set him free (Exod. xxi).

CHAPTER V

OF PROPERTY

25. Whether we consider natural reason, which tells us that men being once born have a right to their preservation, and consequently to meat and drink and such other things as nature affords for their subsistence; or revelation, which gives us an account of those grants God made of the world to Adam, and to

Noah and his sons, 'tis very clear that God, as King David says, Psalm cxv. 16, "has given the earth to the children of men," given it to mankind in common. But this being supposed, it seems to some a very great difficulty how anyone should ever come to have a property in anything. I will not content myself to answer that if it be difficult to make out property upon a supposition that God gave the world to Adam and his posterity in common, it is impossible that any man but one universal monarch should have any property upon a supposition that God gave the world to Adam and his heirs in succession, exclusive of all the rest of his posterity. But I shall endeavor to show how men might come to have a property in several parts of that which God gave to mankind in common, and that without any express compact of all the commoners.[9]

26. God, who hath given the world to men in common, hath also given them reason to make use of it to the best advantage of life and convenience. The earth and all that is therein is given to men for the support and comfort of their being. And though all the fruits it naturally produces, and beasts it feeds, belong to mankind in common, as they are produced by the spontaneous hand of nature; and nobody has originally a private dominion exclusive of the rest of mankind in any of them as they are thus in their natural state; yet being given for the use of men, there must of necessity be a means to appropriate them some way or other before they can be of any use or at all beneficial to any particular man. The fruit or venison which nourishes the wild Indian, who knows no enclosure, and is still a tenant in common, must be his, and so his, i.e., a part of him, that another can no longer have any right to it, before it can do any good for the support of his life.

27. Though the earth and all inferior

creatures be common to all men, yet every man has a property in his own person; this nobody has any right to but himself. The labor of his body and the work of his hands we may say are properly his. Whatsoever, then, he removes out of the state that nature hath provided and left it in, he hath mixed his labor with, and joined to it something that is his own, and thereby makes it his property. It being by him removed from the common state nature placed it in, it hath by this labor something annexed to it that excludes the common right of other men. For this labor being the unquestionable property of the laborer, no man but he can have a right to what that is once joined to, at least where there is enough, and as good left in common for others.

28. He that is nourished by the acorns he picked up under an oak, or the apples he gathered from the trees in the wood, has certainly appropriated them to himself. Nobody can deny but the nourishment is his. I ask, then, When did they begin to be his—when he digested, or when he ate, or when he boiled, or when he brought them home, or when he picked them up? And 'tis plain if the first gathering made them not his, nothing else could. That labor put a distinction between them and common; that added something to them more than nature, the common mother of all, had done, and so they became his private right. And will anyone say he had no right to those acorns or apples he thus appropriated, because he had not the consent of all mankind to make them his? Was it a robbery thus to assume to himself what belonged to all in common? If such a consent as that was necessary, man had starved, notwithstanding the plenty God had given him. We see in commons which remain so by compact that 'tis the taking any part of what is common and removing it out of the state nature leaves it in, which begins the property; without which the common is of no use. And

9. Here, one of those having the right of use in common.

the taking of this or that part does not depend on the express consent of all the commoners. Thus the grass my horse has bit, the turfs my servant has cut, and the ore I have dug in any place where I have a right to them in common with others, become my property without the assignation or consent of anybody. The labor that was mine removing them out of that common state they were in, hath fixed my property in them.

29. By making an explicit consent of every commoner necessary to anyone's appropriating to himself any part of what is given in common.[10] Children or servants could not cut the meat which their father or master had provided for them in common without assigning to everyone his peculiar part. Though the water running in the fountain be everyone's, yet who can doubt but that in the pitcher is his only who drew it out? His labor hath taken it out of the hands of Nature where it was common, and belonged equally to all her children, and hath thereby appropriated it to himself.

30. Thus this law of reason makes the deer that Indian's who hath killed it; it is allowed to be his goods who hath bestowed his labor upon it, though, before, it was the common right of everyone. And amongst those who are counted the civilized part of mankind, who have made and multiplied positive laws to determine property, this original law of nature for the beginning of property, in what was before common, still takes place, and by virtue thereof, what fish anyone catches in the ocean, that great and still remaining common of mankind; or what ambergris anyone takes up here is by the labor that removes it out of that common state nature left it in, made his property who takes that pains about it. And even amongst us, the hare that anyone is hunting is thought his who pursues her during the chase. For being a beast that is still looked upon as com-

10. This sentence and the preceding should be read as one.

mon, and no man's private possesion, whoever has employed so much labor about any of that kind as to find and pursue her has thereby removed her from the state of nature wherein she was common, and hath began a property.

31. It will perhaps be objected to this, that if gathering the acorns, or other fruits of the earth, etc., makes a right to them, then anyone may engross as much as he will. To which I answer, Not so. The same law of nature that does by this means give us property, does also bound that property too. "God has given us all things richly" (1 Tim. vi. 17), is the voice of reason confirmed by inspiration. But how far has He given it us? To enjoy. As much as anyone can make use of to any advantage of life before it spoils, so much he may by his labor fix a property in; whatever is beyond this, is more than his share, and belongs to others. Nothing was made by God for man to spoil or destroy. And thus considering the plenty of natural provisions there was a long time in the world, and the few spenders, and to how small a part of that provision the industry of one man could extend itself, and engross it to the prejudice of others—especially keeping within the bounds, set by reason, of what might serve for his use—there could be then little room for quarrels or contentions about property so established.

32. But the chief matter of property being now not the fruits of the earth, and the beasts that subsist on it, but the earth itself, as that which takes in and carries with it all the rest, I think it is plain that property in that, too, is acquired as the former. As much land as a man tills, plants, improves, cultivates, and can use the product of, so much is his property. He by his labor does as it were enclose it from the common. Nor will it invalidate his right to say, everybody else has an equal title to it; and therefore he cannot appropriate, he cannot enclose, without the consent of all his fellow-com-

moners, all mankind. God, when He gave the world in common to all mankind, commanded man also to labor, and the penury of his condition required it of him. God and his reason commanded him to subdue the earth, i.e., improve it for the benefit of life, and therein lay out something upon it that was his own, his labor. He that, in obedience to this command of God, subdued, tilled, and sowed any part of it, thereby annexed to it something that was his property, which another had no title to, nor could without injury take from him.

33. Nor was this appropriation of any parcel of land, by improving it, any prejudice to any other man, since there was still enough and as good left; and more than the yet unprovided could use. So that in effect there was never the less left for others because of his enclosure for himself. For he that leaves as much as another can make use of, does as good as take nothing at all. Nobody could think himself injured by the drinking of another man, though he took a good draught, who had a whole river of the same water left him to quench his thirst; and the case of land and water, where there is enough of both, is perfectly the same.

34. God gave the world to men in common; but since He gave it them for their benefit, and the greatest conveniences of life they were capable to draw from it, it cannot be supposed He meant it should always remain common and uncultivated. He gave it to the use of the industrious and rational (and labor was to be his title to it), not to the fancy or covetousness of the quarrelsome and contentious. He that had as good left for his improvement as was already taken up, needed not complain, ought not to meddle with what was already improved by another's labor; if he did, it is plain he desired the benefit of another's pains, which he had no right to, and not the ground which God had given him in common with others to labor on, and

whereof there was as good left as that already possessed, and more than he knew what to do with, or his industry could reach to.

35. It is true, in land that is common in England, or any other country where there is plenty of people under government, who have money and commerce, no one can enclose or appropriate any part without the consent of all his fellow-commoners:[11] because this is left common by compact, i.e., by the law of the land, which is not to be violated. And though it be common in respect of some men, it is not so to all mankind; but is the joint property of this country, or this parish. Besides, the remainder, after such enclosure, would not be as good to the rest of the commoners as the whole was, when they could all make use of the whole; whereas in the beginning and first peopling of the great common of the world it was quite otherwise. The law man was under was rather for appropriating. God commanded, and his wants forced him, to labor. That was his property, which could not be taken from him wherever he had fixed it. And hence subduing or cultivating the earth, and having dominion, we see are joined together. The one gave title to the other. So that God, by commanding to subdue, gave authority so far to appropriate. And the condition of human life, which requires labor and materials to work on, necessarily introduces private possessions.

36. The measure of property nature has well set by the extent of men's labor and the conveniency of life. No man's labor could subdue or appropriate all, nor could his enjoyment consume more than a small part; so that it was impossible for any man, this way, to entrench upon the right of another or acquire to himself a property to the prejudice of his neighbor, who would still have room for as good and as large a possession

11. In English communities certain parts of the land were used in common by all the villagers, as grazing land, peat bogs, and woods.

(after the other had taken out his) as before it was appropriated. Which measure did confine every man's possession to a very moderate proportion, and such as he might appropriate to himself without injury to anybody in the first ages of the world, when men were more in danger to be lost, by wandering from their company, in the then vast wilderness of the earth than to be straitened for want of room to plant in.

The same measure may be allowed still, without prejudice to anybody, full as the world seems. For, supposing a man or family, in the state they were at first, peopling of the world by the children of Adam or Noah, let him plant in some inland vacant places of America. We shall find that the possessions he could make himself, upon the measures we have given, would not be very large, nor, even to this day, prejudice the rest of mankind or give them reason to complain or think themselves injured by this man's encroachment, though the race of men have now spread themselves to all the corners of the world, and do infinitely exceed the small number was at the beginning. Nay, the extent of ground is of so little value without labor that I have heard it affirmed that in Spain itself a man may be permitted to plough, sow, and reap, without being disturbed, upon land he has no other title to, but only his making use of it. But, on the contrary, the inhabitants think themselves beholden to him who, by his industry on neglected, and consequently waste land, has increased the stock of corn, which they wanted. But be this as it will, which I lay no stress on, this I dare boldly affirm, that the same rule of propriety—viz., that every man should have as much as he could make use of, would hold still in the world, without straitening anybody, since there is land enough in the world to suffice double the inhabitants, had not the invention of money, and the tacit agreement of men to put a value on it, introduced (by consent) larger possessions and a right to them; which, how it has done, I shall by and by show more at large.

37. This is certain, that in the beginning, before the desire of having more than man needed had altered the intrinsic value of things, which depends only on their usefulness to the life of man; or had agreed that a little piece of yellow metal which would keep without wasting or decay should be worth a great piece of flesh or a whole heap of corn, though men had a right to appropriate by their labor, each one to himself, as much of the things of nature as he could use, yet this could not be much, nor to the prejudice of others, where the same plenty was still left to those who would use the same industry.

Before the appropriation of land, he who gathered as much of the wild fruit, killed, caught, or tamed as many of the beasts as he could; he that so employed his pains about any of the spontaneous product of nature as any way to alter them from the state which nature put them in, by placing any of his labor on them, did thereby acquire a propriety in them. But if they perished in his possession without their due use; if the fruits rotted, or the venison putrefied before he could spend it, he offended against the common law of nature, and was liable to be punished; he invaded his neighbor's share, for he had no right further than his use called for any of them and they might serve to afford him conveniences of life.

38. The same measures governed the possessions of land, too. Whatsoever he tilled and reaped, laid up, and made use of before it spoiled, that was his peculiar right; whatsoever he enclosed and could feed and make use of, the cattle and product was also his. But if either the grass of his enclosure rotted on the ground, or the fruit of his planting perished without gathering and laying up, this part of the earth, notwithstanding his enclosure, was still to be looked on as

waste, and might be the possession of any other. Thus, at the beginning, Cain might take as much ground as he could till and make it his own land, and yet leave enough for Abel's sheep to feed on; a few acres would serve for both their possessions. But as families increased, and industry enlarged their stocks, their possessions enlarged with the need of them; but yet it was commonly without any fixed property in the ground they made use of, till they incorporated, settled themselves together, and built cities; and then, by consent, they came in time to set out the bounds of their distinct territories, and agree on limits between them and their neighbors, and, by laws within themselves, settled the properties of those of the same society. For we see that in that part of the world which was first inhabited, and therefore like to be best peopled, even as low down as Abraham's time, they wandered with their flocks and their herds, which was their substance, freely up and down—and this Abraham did in a country where he was a stranger; whence it is plain that, at least, a great part of the land lay in common, that the inhabitants valued it not, nor claimed property in any more than they made use of; but when there was not room enough in the same place for their herds to feed together, they, by consent, as Abraham and Lot did (Gen. xiii. 5), separated and enlarged their pasture where it best liked them. And for the same reason, Esau went from his father and his brother, and planted in Mount Seir (Gen. xxxvi. 6).

39. And thus, without supposing any private dominion and property in Adam over all the world, exclusive of all other men, which can no way be proved, nor any one's property be made out from it, but supposing the world, given as it was to the children of men in common, we see how labor could make men distinct titles to several parcels of it for their private uses, wherein there could be no doubt of right, no room for quarrel.

40. Nor is it so strange, as perhaps before consideration it may appear, that the property of labor should be able to overbalance the community of land. For it is labor indeed that puts the difference of value on everything; and let anyone consider what the difference is between an acre of land planted with tobacco or sugar, sown with wheat or barley, and an acre of the same land lying in common without any husbandry upon it, and he will find that the improvement of labor makes the far greater part of the value. I think it will be but a very modest computation to say that of the products of the earth useful to the life of man nine-tenths are the effects of labor; nay, if we will rightly estimate things as they come to our use, and cast up the several expenses about them—what in them is purely owing to nature, and what to labor—we shall find that in most of them ninety-nine hundredths are wholly to be put on the account of labor.

41. There cannot be a clearer demonstration of anything than several nations of the Americans are of this, who are rich in land and poor in all the comforts of life; whom nature, having furnished as liberally as any other people with the materials of plenty—i.e., a fruitful soil, apt to produce in abundance what might serve for food, raiment, and delight; yet, for want of improving it by labor, have not one hundredth part of the conveniences we enjoy, and a king of a large and fruitful territory there feeds, lodges, and is clad worse than a day laborer in England.[12]

42. To make this a little clearer, let us but trace some of the ordinary provisions of life, through their several progresses, before they come to our use, and see how much they receive of their value from human industry. Bread, wine, and cloth are things of daily use and

12. Contrary to the knowledge of Locke's time, there was much farming among the American Indians, although they used the hoe rather than the plow.

great plenty; yet, notwithstanding, acorns, water, and leaves or skins, must be our bread, drink, and clothing, did not labor furnish us with these more useful commodities. For whatever bread is more worth than acorns, wine than water, and cloth or silk than leaves, skins, or moss, that is wholly to labor and industry: the one of these being the food and raiment which unassisted nature furnishes us with; the other, provisions which our industry and pains prepare for us; which how much they exceed the other in value when anyone hath computed, he will then see how much labor makes the far greatest part of the value of things we enjoy in this world. And the ground which produces the materials is scarce to be reckoned in as any, or at most but a very small, part of it; so little that even amongst us land that is left wholly to nature, that hath no improvement of pasturage, tillage, or planting, is called, as indeed it is, "waste," and we shall find the benefit of it amount to little more than nothing.

43. An acre of land that bears here twenty bushels of wheat, and another in America which, with the same husbandry, would do the like, are without doubt of the same natural intrinsic value; but yet the benefit mankind receives from the one in a year is worth £5, and from the other possibly not worth a penny, if all the profit an Indian received from it were to be valued and sold here; at least, I may truly say, not one-thousandth. 'Tis labor, then, which puts the greatest part of value upon land, without which it would scarcely be worth anything; 'tis to that we owe the greatest part of all its useful products, for all that the straw, bran, bread, of that acre of wheat is more worth than the product of an acre of as good land which lies waste, is all the effect of labor. For 'tis not barely the ploughman's pains, the reaper's and thresher's toil, and the baker's sweat, is to be counted into the bread we eat; the labor of those who broke the oxen, who dug and wrought the iron and stones, who felled and framed the timber employed about the plough, mill, oven, or any other utensils, which are a vast number, requisite to this corn, from its sowing, to its being made bread, must all be charged on the account of labor, and received as an effect of that. Nature and the earth furnished only the almost worthless materials as in themselves. 'Twould be a strange catalogue of things that industry provided, and made use of, about every loaf of bread before it came to our use, if we could trace them—iron, wood, leather, bark, timber, stone, bricks, coals, lime, cloth, dyeing drugs, pitch, tar, masts, ropes, and all the materials made use of in the ship that brought any of the commodities made use of by any of the workmen to any part of the work all which it would be almost impossible—at least, too long—to reckon up.

44. From all which it is evident that, though the things of nature are given in common, yet man, by being master of himself and proprietor of his own person and the actions or labor of it, had still in himself the great foundation of property; and that which made up the great part of what he applied to the support or comfort of his being, when invention and arts had improved the conveniences of life, was perfectly his own, and did not belong in common to others.

45. Thus labor, in the beginning, gave a right of property, wherever anyone was pleased to employ it upon what was common, which remained a long while the far greater part, and is yet more than mankind makes use of. Men at first, for the most part, contented themselves with what unassisted nature offered to their necessities; and though afterward in some parts of the world (where the increase of people and stock,[13] with the use of money, had made land scarce, and so of some value), the several communi-

13. Here, capital and capital goods, accumulated raw materials, equipment, buildings, and other forms of wealth.

ties settled the bounds of their distinct territories, and, by laws within themselves, regulated the properties of the private men of their society, and so, by compact and agreement, settled the property which labor and industry began—and the leagues that have been made between several states and kingdoms, either expressly or tacitly disowning all claim and right to the land in the other's possession, have, by common consent, given up their pretenses to their natural common right, which originally they had to those countries; and so have, by positive agreement, settled a property amongst themselves in distinct parts of the world—yet there are still great tracts of ground to be found which, the inhabitants thereof not having joined with the rest of mankind in the consent of the use of their common money, lie waste, and are more than the people who dwell on it do or can make use of, and so still lie in common; though this can scarce happen amongst that part of mankind that have consented to the use of money.

46. The greatest part of things really useful to the life of man, and such as the necessity of subsisting made the first commoners of the world look after, as it doth the Americans now, are generally things of short duration, such as, if they are not consumed by use, will decay and perish of themselves: gold, silver, and diamonds are things that fancy or agreement have put the value on more than real use and the necessary support of life. Now, of those good things which nature hath provided in common, everyone hath a right, as hath been said, to as much as he could use, and had a property in all he could effect with his labor—all that his industry could extend to, to alter from the state nature had put it in, was his. He that gathered a hundred bushels of acorns or apples had thereby a property in them; they were his goods as soon as gathered. He was only to look that he used them before they spoiled, else he took more than his share, and robbed others; and, indeed, it was a foolish thing, as well as dishonest, to hoard up more than he could make use of. If he gave away a part to anybody else, so that it perished not uselessly in his possession, these he also made use of; and if he also bartered away plums that would have rotted in a week, for nuts that would last good for his eating a whole year, he did no injury; he wasted not the common stock, destroyed no part of the portion of goods that belonged to others, so long as nothing perished uselessly in his hands. Again, if he would give his nuts for a piece of metal, pleased with its color, or exchange his sheep for shells, or wool for a sparkling pebble or a diamond, and keep those by him all his life, he invaded not the right of others; he might heap up as much of these durable things as he pleased, the exceeding of the bounds of his just property not lying in the largeness of his possessions, but the perishing of anything uselessly in it.

47. And thus came in the use of money —some lasting thing that men might keep without spoiling, and that, by mutual consent, men would take in exchange for the truly useful but perishable supports of life.

48. And as different degrees of industry were apt to give men possesions in different proportions, so this invention of money gave them the opportunity to continue and enlarge them; for supposing an island, separate from all possible commerce with the rest of the world, wherein there were but a hundred families—but there were sheep, horses, and cows, with other useful animals, wholesome fruits, and land enough for corn for a hundred thousand times as many, but nothing in the island, either because of its commonness or perishableness, fit to supply the place of money—what reason could anyone have there to enlarge his possessions beyond the use of his family and a plentiful supply to its

consumption, either in what their own industry produced, or they could barter for like perishable useful commodities with others? Where there is not something both lasting and scarce, and so valuable to be hoarded up, there men will not be apt to enlarge their possessions of land, were it never so rich, never so free for them to take; for I ask, what would a man value ten thousand or a hundred thousand acres of excellent land, ready cultivated, and well stocked too with cattle, in the middle of the inland parts of America, where he had no hopes of commerce with other parts of the world, to draw money to him by the sale of the product? It would not be worth the enclosing, and we should see him give up again to the wild common of nature whatever was more than would supply the conveniences of life to be had there for him and his family.

49. Thus in the beginning all the world was America, and more so than that is now, for no such thing as money was anywhere known. Find out something that hath the use and value of money amongst his neighbors, you shall see the same man will begin presently to enlarge his possessions.

50. But since gold and silver, being little useful to the life of man in proportion to food, raiment, and carriage, has its value only from the consent of men, whereof labor yet makes, in great part, the measure, it is plain that the consent of men have agreed to a disproportionate and unequal possession of the earth—I mean out of the bounds of society and compact; for in governments the laws regulate it; they having, by consent, found out and agreed in a way how a man may rightfully and without injury possess more than he himself can make use of by receiving gold and silver, which may continue long in a man's possession, without decaying for the overplus, and agreeing those metals should have a value.

51. And thus, I think, it is very easy to conceive without any difficulty how labor could at first begin a title of property in the common things of nature, and how the spending it upon our uses bounded it; so that there could then be no reason of quarreling about title, nor any doubt about the largeness of possession it gave. Right and conveniency went together; for as a man had a right to all he could employ his labor upon, so he had no temptation to labor for more than he could make use of. This left no room for controversy about the title, nor for encroachment on the right of others; what portion a man carved to himself was easily seen, and it was useless, as well as dishonest, to carve himself too much, or take more than he needed.

CHAPTER VII
OF POLITICAL OR CIVIL SOCIETY

87. Man being born, as has been proved, with a title to perfect freedom, and an uncontrolled enjoyment of all the rights and privileges of the law of nature equally with any other man or number of men in the world, hath by nature a power not only to preserve his property—that is, his life, liberty, and estate—against the injuries and attempts of other men, but to judge of and punish the breaches of that law in others as he is persuaded the offense deserves, even with death itself, in crimes where the heinousness of the fact in his opinion requires it. But because no political society can be nor subsist without having in itself the power to preserve the property, and, in order thereunto, punish the offenses of all those of that society, there, and there only, is political society, where every one of the members hath quitted this natural power, resigned it up into the hands of the community in all cases that exclude him not from appealing for protection to the law established by it; and thus all private judgment of every particular member being excluded, the community comes to be umpire; and by understanding indifferent rules and men

authorized by the community for their execution, decides all the differences that may happen between any members of that society concerning any matter of right, and punishes those offenses which any member hath committed against the society with such penalties as the law has established; whereby it is easy to discern who are and who are not in political society together. Those who are united into one body, and have a common established law and judicature to appeal to, with authority to decide controversies between them and punish offenders, are in civil society one with another; but those who have no such common appeal—I mean on earth—are still in the state of nature, each being, where there is no other, judge for himself and executioner, which is, as I have before shown it, the perfect state of nature.

88. And thus the commonwealth comes by a power to set down what punishment shall belong to the several transgressions which they think worthy of it committed amongst the members of that society, which is the power of making laws, as well as it has the power to punish any injury done unto any of its members by anyone that is not of it, which is the power of war and peace; and all this for the preservation of the property of all the members of that society as far as is possible. But though every man entered into civil society, has quitted his power to punish offenses against the law of nature in prosecution of his own private judgment, yet with the judgment of offenses, which he has given up to the legislative in all cases where he can appeal to the magistrate, he has given a right to the commonwealth to employ his force for the execution of the judgments of the commonwealth whenever he shall be called to it; which, indeed, are his own judgments, they being made by himself or his representative. And herein we have the original of the legislative and executive power of civil society, which is to judge by standing laws how far offenses are to be punished when committed within the commonwealth, and also by occasional judgments founded on the present circumstances of the fact, how far injuries from without are to be vindicated; and in both these to employ all the force of all the members when there shall be need.

89. Wherever, therefore, any number of men so unite into one society, as to quit everyone his executive power of the law of nature, and to resign it to the public, there, and there only, is a political, or civil society. And this is done wherever any number of men, in the state of nature, enter into society to make one people, one body politic, under one supreme government, or else when anyone joins himself to, and incorporates with, any government already made. For hereby he authorizes the society, or, which is all one, the legislative thereof, to make laws for him, as the public good of the society shall require, to the execution whereof his own assistance (as to his own decrees) is due. And this puts men out of a state of nature into that of a commonwealth, by setting up a judge on earth with authority to determine all the controversies and redress the injuries that may happen to any member of the commonwealth; which judge is the legislative, or magistrates appointed by it. And wherever there are any number of men, however associated, that have no such decisive power to appeal to, there they are still in the state of nature.

90. Hence it is evident that absolute monarchy, which by some men is counted the only government in the world, is indeed inconsistent with civil society, and so can be no form of civil government at all. For the end of civil society being to avoid and remedy those inconveniences of the state of nature which necessarily follow from every man's being judge in his own case, by setting up a known authority to which

everyone of that society may appeal upon any injury received or controversy that may arise, and which every one of the society ought to obey; wherever any persons are who have not such an authority to appeal to and decide any difference between them there, those persons are still in the state of nature. And so is every absolute prince, in respect of those who are under his dominion.

91. For he being supposed to have all, both legislative and executive power in himself alone, there is no judge to be found; no appeal lies open to anyone who may fairly and indifferently and with authority decide, and from whence relief and address may be expected of any injury or inconvenience that may be suffered from or by his order; so that such a man, however entitled—Czar, or Grand Seignior,[14] or how you please—is as much in the state of nature, with all under his dominion, as he is with the rest of mankind. For wherever any two men are, who have no standing rule and common judge to appeal to on earth for the determination of controversies of right betwixt them, there they are still in the state of nature, and under all the inconveniences of it, with only this woeful difference to the subject, or rather slave, of an absolute prince: that, whereas in the ordinary state of nature he has a liberty to judge of his right, and according to the best of his power to maintain it, now, whenever his property is invaded by the will and order of his monarch, he has not only no appeal, as those in the society ought to have, but, as if he were degraded from the common state of rational creatures, is denied a liberty to judge of or to defend his right; and so is exposed to all the misery and inconveniences that a man can fear from one who, being in the unrestrained state of nature, is yet corrupted with flattery, and armed with power.

92. For he that thinks absolute power

14. Name of the sultan of Turkey, so called by Western nations in Locke's time.

purifies men's blood, and corrects the baseness of human nature, need read but the history of this or any other age, to be convinced of the contrary. He that would have been insolent and injurious in the woods of America, would not probably be much better in a throne; where, perhaps, learning and religion shall be found out to justify all that he shall do to his subjects, and the sword presently silence all those that dare question it. For what the protection of absolute monarchy is, what kind of fathers of their countries it makes princes to be, and to what a degree of happiness and security it carries civil society, where this sort of government is grown to perfection, he that will look into the late relation of Ceylon may easily see.

93. In absolute monarchies, indeed, as well as other governments of the world, the subjects have an appeal to the law, and judges to decide any controversies and restrain any violence that may happen betwixt the subjects themselves, one amongst another. This everyone thinks necessary, and believes he deserves to be thought a declared enemy to society and mankind who should go about to take it away. But whether this be from a true love of mankind and society, and such a charity as we owe all one to another, there is reason to doubt. For this is no more than that every man who loves his own power, profit, or greatness may, and naturally must do, keep those animals from hurting or destroying one another who labor and drudge only for his pleasure and advantage; and so are taken care of, not out of any love the master has for them, but love of himself, and the profit they bring him. For if it be asked, what security, what fence is there, in such a state, against the violence and oppression of this absolute ruler, the very question can scarce be borne. They are ready to tell you that it deserves death only to ask after safety. Betwixt subject and subject they will grant there must be measures, laws and judges, for

their mutual peace and security; but as for the ruler, he ought to be absolute, and is above all such circumstances; because he has power to do more hurt and wrong, 'tis right when he does it. To ask how you may be guarded from harm or injury on that side where the strongest hand is to do it, is presently the voice of faction and rebellion. As if when men quitting the state of nature entered into society, they agreed that all of them but one should be under the restraint of laws, but that he should still retain all the liberty of the state of nature, increased with power, and made licentious by immunity. This is to think that men are so foolish that they take care to avoid what mischiefs may be done them by polecats or foxes, but are content, nay, think it safety, to be devoured by lions.

94. But, whatever flatterers may talk to amuse people's understandings, it never hinders men from feeling; and when they perceive that any man, in what station soever, is out of the bounds of the civil society they are of, and that they have no appeal on earth against any harm they may receive from him, they are apt to think themselves in the state of nature in respect of him whom they find to be so; and to take care, as soon as they can, to have that safety and security in civil society for which it was first instituted, and for which only they entered into it. And, therefore, though perhaps at first (as shall be shown more at large hereafter in the following part of this discourse), some one good and excellent man, having got a pre-eminence amongst the rest, had this deference paid to his goodness and virtue, as to a kind of natural authority, that the chief rule, with arbitration of their differences, by a tacit consent devolved into his hands, without any other caution but the assurance they had of his uprightness and wisdom; yet when time, giving authority and (as some men would persuade us) sacredness to customs which the negligent and unforeseeing inno-

cence of the first ages began, had brought in successors of another stamp, the people finding their properties not secure under the government, as then it was (whereas government has no other end but the preservation of property), could never be safe nor at rest, nor think themselves in civil society, till the legislative was placed in collective bodies of men, call them Senate, Parliament, or what you please. By which means every single person became subject, equally with other the meanest men, to those laws, which he himself, as part of the legislative, had established; nor could anyone by his own authority avoid the force of the law when once made, nor by any pretense of superiority plead exemption, thereby to license his own, or the miscarriages of any of his dependents. No man in civil society can be exempted from the laws of it. For if any man may do what he thinks fit, and there be no appeal on earth for redress or security against any harm he shall do, I ask whether he be not perfectly still in the state of nature, and so can be no part or member of that civil society; unless anyone will say the state of nature and civil society are one and the same thing, which I have never yet found anyone so great a patron of anarchy as to affirm.

CHAPTER VIII

OF THE BEGINNING OF POLITICAL SOCIETIES

95. Men being, as has been said, by nature all free, equal, and independent, no one can be put out of this estate, and subjected to the political power of another, without his own consent, which is done by agreeing with other men to join and unite into a community for their comfortable, safe, and peaceable living one amongst another, in a secure enjoyment of their properties, and a greater security against any that are not of it. This any number of men may do, because it injures not the freedom of the rest; they are left as they were in the

liberty of the state of nature. When any number of men have so consented to make one community or government, they are thereby presently incorporated, and make one body politic, wherein the majority have a right to act and conclude the rest.

96. For when any number of men have, by the consent of every individual, made a community, they have thereby made that community one body, with a power to act as one body, which is only by the will and determination of the majority. For that which acts any community being only the consent of the individuals of it, and it being one body must move one way, it is necessary the body should move that way whither the greater force carries it, which is the consent of the majority; or else it is impossible it should act or continue one body, one community, which the consent of every individual that united into it agreed that it should; and so everyone is bound by that consent to be concluded by the majority.[15] And therefore we see that in assemblies empowered to act by positive laws, where no number is set by that positive law which empowers them, the act of the majority passes for the act of the whole, and of course determines, as having by the law of nature and reason the power of the whole.

97. And thus every man, by consenting with others to make one body politic under one government, puts himself under an obligation to every one of that society, to submit to the determination of the majority, and to be concluded by it; or else this original compact, whereby he with others incorporates into one society, would signify nothing, and be no compact, if he be left free and under no other ties than he was in before in the state of nature. For what appearance would there be of any compact? What new engagement if he were no farther

tied by any decrees of the society, than he himself thought fit, and did actually consent to? This would be still as great a liberty as he himself had before his compact, or anyone else in the state of nature hath, who may submit himself and consent to any acts of it if he thinks fit.

98. For if the consent of the majority shall not in reason be received as the act of the whole and conclude every individual, nothing but the consent of every individual can make anything to be the act of the whole, which considering the infirmities of health and avocations of business, which in a number, though much less than that of a commonwealth, will necessarily keep many away from the public assembly, and the variety of opinions, and contrariety of interest, which unavoidably happen in all collections of men, 'tis next to impossible ever to be had. And therefore if the coming into society be upon such terms it will be only like Cato's coming into the theater, *tantum ut exiret*.[16] Such a constitution as this would make the mighty leviathan of a shorter duration than the feeblest creatures, and not let it outlast the day it was born in; which cannot be supposed till we can think that rational creatures should desire and constitute societies only to be dissolved. For where the majority cannot conclude the rest, there they cannot act as one body, and consequently will be immediately dissolved again.

99. Whosoever therefore out of a state of nature unite into a community must be understood to give up all the power necessary to the ends for which they unite into society, to the majority of the community, unless they expressly agreed in any number greater than the majority. And this is done by barely agreeing to unite into one political society, which is all the compact that is, or needs be, between the individuals that enter into or make up a commonwealth. And thus that which begins and actually constitutes

15. Accept the decision as binding upon them, as the entire nation concludes a treaty through the signers thereof.

16. "That he may be as promptly expelled."

any political society is nothing but the consent of any number of freemen capable of a majority to unite and incorporate into such a society. And this is that, and that only, which did or could give beginning to any lawful government in the world.

100. To this I find two objections made.

First, that there are no instances to be found in story of a company of men independent, and equal one amongst another, that met together and in this way began and set up a government.

Secondly, 'tis impossible of right that men should do so, because all men being born under government, they are to submit to that, and are not at liberty to begin a new one. . . .

The other objection I find urged against the beginning of polities in the way I have mentioned is this, viz.:

113. That all men being born under government, some or other, it is impossible any of them should ever be free and at liberty to unite together and begin a new one, or ever be able to erect a lawful government.

If this argument be good, I ask, how came so many lawful monarchies into the world? For if anybody, upon this supposition, can show me any one man, in any age of the world, free to begin a lawful monarchy, I will be bound to show him ten other free men at liberty at the same time to unite and begin a new government under a regal, or any other form, it being demonstration that if anyone, born under the dominion of another, may be so free as to have a right to command others in a new and distinct empire, everyone that is born under the dominion of another may be so free too, and may become a ruler or subject of a distinct separate government. And so by this their own principle either all men, however born, are free, or else there is but one lawful prince, one lawful government in the world. And then they

have nothing to do but barely to show us which that is; which, when they have done, I doubt not but all mankind will easily agree to pay obedience to him.

114. Though it be a sufficient answer to their objection to show that it involves them in the same difficulties that it doth those they use it against, yet I shall endeavor to discover the weakness of this argument a little farther.

"All men," say they, "are born under government, and therefore they cannot be at liberty to begin a new one. Everyone is born a subject to his father, or his prince, and is therefore under the perpetual tie of subjection and allegiance." It is plain mankind never owned nor considered any such natural subjection that they were born in, to one or to the other that tied them without their own consents, to a subjection to them and their heirs.

115. For there are no examples so frequent in history, both sacred and profane, as those of men withdrawing themselves and their obedience from the jurisdiction they were born under, and the family or community they were bred up in, and setting up new governments in other places; from whence sprang all that number of petty commonwealths in the beginning of ages, and which always multiplied, as long as there was room enough, till the stronger or more fortunate swallowed the weaker; and those great ones again breaking to pieces, dissolved into lesser dominions, all which are so many testimonies against paternal sovereignty, and plainly prove that it was not the natural right of the father descending to his heirs that made government in the beginning, since it was impossible upon that ground there should have been so many little kingdoms, but only one universal monarchy if men had not been at liberty to separate themselves from their families and their government, be it what it will, that was set up in it, and go and make distinct

commonwealths and other governments as they thought fit.

116. This has been the practice of the world from its first beginning to this day; nor is it now any more hindrance to the freedom of mankind that they are born under constituted and ancient polities that have established laws and set forms of government, than if they were born in the woods amongst the unconfined inhabitants that run loose in them. For those who would persuade us that by being born under any government we are naturally subjects to it, and have no more any title or pretense to the freedom of the state of nature, have no other reason (bating that of paternal power, which we have already answered) to produce for it, but only because our fathers or progenitors passed away their natural liberty, and thereby bound up themselves and their posterity to a perpetual subjection to the government which they themselves submitted to. It is true that whatever engagements or promises anyone made for himself, he is under the obligation of them, but cannot by any compact whatsoever bind his children or posterity. For his son when a man being altogether as free as his father, any act of the father can no more give away the liberty of the son than it can of anybody else. He may indeed annex such conditions to the land he enjoyed as a subject of any commonwealth as may oblige his son to be of that community, if he will enjoy those possessions which were his father's, because that estate being his father's property he may dispose or settle it as he pleases.

117. And this has generally given the occasion to the mistake in this matter, because commonwealths not permitting any part of their dominions to be dismembered, nor to be enjoyed by any but those of their community, the son cannot ordinarily enjoy the possessions of his father but under the same terms his father did: by becoming a member of the society; whereby he puts himself presently under the government he finds there established as much as any other subject of that commonwealth. And thus the consent of freemen, born under government, which only makes them members of it, being given separately in their turns, as each comes to be of age, and not in a multitude together. People take no notice of it, and thinking it not done at all, or not necessary, conclude they are naturally subjects as they are men.

118. But it is plain governments themselves understand it otherwise; they claim no power over the son, because of that they had over the father; nor look on children as being their subjects by their father's being so. If a subject of England have a child by an English woman in France, whose subject is he? Not the king of England's, for he must have leave to be admitted to the privileges of it; nor the king of France's, for how then has his father a liberty to bring him away and breed him as he pleases? And whoever was judged as a traitor or deserter, if he left or warred against a country, for being barely born in it of parents that were aliens there? It is plain then by the practice of governments themselves, as well as by the law of right reason, that a child is born a subject of no country or government. He is under his father's tuition and authority till he comes to age of discretion, and then he is a freeman, at liberty what government he will put himself under, what body politic he will unite himself to. For if an Englishman's son, born in France, be at liberty, and may do so, it is evident there is no tie upon him by his father's being a subject of that kingdom; nor is he bound up by any compact of his ancestors. And why then hath not his son by the same reason, the same liberty, though he be born anywhere else? Since the power that a father hath naturally over his children is the same wherever they be born, and the ties of natural ob-

ligations are not bounded by the positive limits of kingdoms and commonwealths.

119. Every man being, as has been shown, naturally free, and nothing being able to put him into subjection to any earthly power but only his own consent, it is to be considered what shall be understood to be sufficient declaration of a man's consent to make him subject to the laws of any government. There is a common distinction of an express and a tacit consent, which will concern our present case. Nobody doubts but an express consent of any man entering into any society makes him a perfect member of that society, a subject of that government. The difficulty is, what ought to be looked upon as a tacit consent, and how far it binds, i.e., how far anyone shall be looked on to have consented, and thereby submitted to any government, where he has made no expressions of it at all. And to this I say that every man that hath any possession or enjoyment of any part of the dominions of any government doth thereby give his tacit consent, and is as far forth obliged to obedience to the laws of that government during such enjoyment as anyone under it; whether this his possession be of land to him and his heirs for ever, or a lodging only for a week; or whether it be barely traveling freely on the highway; and in effect it reaches as far as the very being of anyone within the territories of that government.

120. To understand this the better, it is fit to consider that every man when he at first incorporates himself into any commonwealth, he, by his uniting himself thereunto, annexed also, and submits to the community those possessions which he has or shall acquire that do not already belong to any other government; for it would be a direct contradiction for anyone to enter into society with others for the securing and regulating of property, and yet to suppose his land, whose property is to be regulated by the laws of the society, should be exempt from the jurisdiction of that government to which he himself, and the property of the land, is a subject. By the same act, therefore, whereby anyone unites his person, which was before free, to any commonwealth, by the same he unites his possessions, which was before free, to it also; and they become, both of them, person and possession, subject to the government and dominion of that commonwealth as long as it hath a being. Whoever therefore from thenceforth by inheritance, purchases, permission, or otherwise, enjoys any part of the land so annexed to, and under the government of that commonwealth, must take it with the condition it is under, that is, of submitting to the government of the commonwealth under whose jurisdiction it is as far forth as any subject of it.

121. But since the government has a direct jurisdiction only over the land, and reaches the possessor of it (before he has actually incorporated himself in the society), only as he dwells upon, and enjoys that: the obligation anyone is under, by virtue of such enjoyment, to submit to the government, begins and ends with the enjoyment; so that whenever the owner, who has given nothing but such a tacit consent to the government, will by donation, sale, or otherwise, quit the said possession, he is at liberty to go and incorporate himself into any other commonwealth, or to agree with others to begin a new one (*in vacuis locis*)[17] in any part of the world they can find free and unpossessed. Whereas he that has once by actual agreement and any express declaration given his consent to be of any commonweal is perpetually and indispensably obliged to be and remain unalterably a subject to it, and can never be again in the liberty of the state of nature; unless, by any calamity, the government he was under comes to be dissolved, or else by some public acts cuts him off from being any longer a member of it.

17. "In unappropriated places."

122. But submitting to the laws of any country, living quietly and enjoying privileges and protection under them makes not a man a member of that society. This is only a local protection and homage due to and from all those who, not being in the state of war, come within the territories belonging to any government to all parts whereof the force of its law extends. But this no more makes a man a member of that society a perpetual subject of that commonwealth, than it would make a man a subject to another in whose family he found it convenient to abide for some time; though whilst he continued in it he were obliged to comply with the laws, and submit to the government he found there. And thus we see, that foreigners by living all their lives under another government, and enjoying the privileges and protection of it, though they are bound even in conscience to submit to its administration as far forth as any denizen, yet do not thereby come to be subjects or members of that commonwealth. Nothing can make any man so, but his actually entering into it by positive engagement, and express promise and compact. This is that, which I think, concerning the beginning of political societies, and that consent which makes anyone a member of any commonwealth.

CHAPTER IX
OF THE ENDS OF POLITICAL SOCIETY AND GOVERNMENT

123. If man in the state of nature be so free, as has been said, if he be absolute lord of his own person and possessions, equal to the greatest, and subject to nobody, why will he part with his freedom, this empire, and subject himself to the dominion and control of any other power? To which, it is obvious to answer, that though in the state of nature he hath such a right, yet the enjoyment of it is very uncertain, and constantly exposed to the invasions of others. For all being kings as much as he, every man

his equal, and the greater part no strict observers of equity and justice, the enjoyment of the property he has in this state is very unsafe, very unsecure. This makes him willing to quit this condition, which, however free, is full of fears and continual dangers; and it is not without reason that he seeks out and is willing to join in society with others, who are already united, or have a mind to unite, for the mutual preservation of their lives, liberties, and estates, which I call by the general name, property.

124. The great and chief end, therefore, of men's uniting into commonwealths, and putting themselves under government, is the preservation of their property; to which in the state of nature there are many things wanting.

First, there wants an established, settled, known law, received and allowed by common consent to be the standard of right and wrong, and the common measure to decide all controversies between them. For though the law of nature be plain and intelligible to all rational creatures; yet men, being biased by their interest, as well as ignorant for want of study of it, are not apt to allow of it as a law binding to them in the application of it to their particular cases.

125. Secondly, in the state of nature there wants a known and indifferent judge, with authority to determine all differences according to the established law. For everyone in that state, being both judge and executioner of the law of nature, men being partial to themselves, passion and revenge is very apt to carry them too far, and with too much heat in their own cases, as well as negligence and unconcernedness, to make them too remiss in other men's.

126. Thirdly, in the state of nature there often wants power to back and support the sentence when right, and to give it due execution. They who by any injustice offend, will seldom fail, where they are able by force to make good their injustice; such resistance many times

makes the punishment dangerous, and frequently destructive to those who attempt it.

127. Thus mankind, notwithstanding all the privileges of the state of nature, being but in an ill condition, while they remain in it, are quickly driven into society. Hence it comes to pass that we seldom find any number of men live any time together in this state. The inconveniences that they are therein exposed to by the irregular and uncertain exercise of the power every man has of punishing the transgressions of others, make them take sanctuary under the established laws of government, and therein seek the preservation of their property. It is this makes them so willingly give up everyone his single power of punishing, to be exercised by such alone, as shall be appointed to it amongst them; and by such rules as the community, or those authorized by them to that purpose, shall agree on. And in this we have the original right and rise of both the legislative and executive power, as well as of the governments and societies themselves.

128. For in the state of nature, to omit the liberty he has of innocent delights, a man has two powers.

The first is to do whatsoever he thinks fit for the preservation of himself, and others within the permission of the law of nature, by which law, common to them all, he and all the rest of mankind are of one community, make up one society, distinct from all other creatures. And were it not for the corruption and viciousness of degenerate men there would be no need of any other, no necessity that men should separate from this great and natural community, and associate into lesser combinations.

The other power a man has in the state of nature is the power to punish the crimes committed against that law. Both these he gives up when he joins in a private, if I may so call it, or particular political society, and incorporates into any commonwealth separate from the rest of mankind.

129. The first power, viz., of doing whatsoever he thought fit for the preservation of himself and the rest of mankind, he gives up to be regulated by laws made by the society, so far forth as the preservation of himself and the rest of that society shall require; which laws of the society in many things confine the liberty he had by the law of nature.

130. Secondly, the power of punishing he wholly gives up, and engages his natural force (which he might before employ in the execution of the law of nature, by his own single authority as he thought fit), to assist the executive power of the society, as the law thereof shall require. For being now in a new state, wherein he is to enjoy many conveniences, from the labor, assistance, and society of others in the same community, as well as protection from its whole strength; he has to part also with as much of his natural liberty, in providing for himself, as the good, prosperity and safety of the society shall require; which is not only necessary but just, since the other members of the society do the like.

131. But though men when they enter into society give up the equality, liberty and executive power they had in the state of nature into the hands of the society, to be so far disposed of by the legislative as the good of the society shall require; yet it being only with an intention in everyone the better to preserve himself, his liberty and property (for no rational creature can be supposed to change his condition with an intention to be worse), the power of the society, or legislative constituted by them, can never be supposed to extend farther than the common good, but is obliged to secure everyone's property by providing against those three defects above-mentioned that made the state of nature so unsafe and uneasy. And so whoever has the legislative or supreme power of any commonwealth is bound to govern by

established standing laws, promulgated and known to the people, and not by extemporary decrees; by indifferent and upright judges, who are to decide controversies by those laws; and to employ the force of the community at home only in the execution of such laws, or abroad, to prevent or redress foreign injuries, and secure the community from inroads and invasion. And all this to be directed to no other end but the peace, safety, and public good of the people.

CHAPTER X

OF THE FORMS OF A COMMONWEALTH

132. The majority having, as has been shown, upon men's first uniting into society, the whole power of the community, naturally in them, may employ all that power in making laws for the community from time to time, and executing those laws by officers of their own appointing: and then the form of the government is a perfect democracy; or else may put the power of making laws into the hands of a few select men, and their heirs or successors, and then it is an oligarchy; or else into the hands of one man and then it is a monarchy; if to him and his heirs, it is an hereditary monarchy; if to him only for life, but upon his death the power only of nominating a successor to return to them, an elective monarchy. And so accordingly of these, the community may make compounded and mixed forms of government, as they think good. And if the legislative power be at first given by the majority to one or more persons only for their lives, or any limited time, and then the supreme power to revert to them again; when it is so reverted, the community may dispose of it again anew into what hands they please, and so constitute a new form of government. For the form of government depending upon the placing of the supreme power, which is the legislative, is being impossible to conceive that an inferior power should prescribe to a superior, or any but the

supreme make laws, according as the power of making laws is placed, such is the form of the commonwealth.

133. By commonwealth, I must be understood all along to mean, not a democracy, or any form of government, but any independent community which the Latins signified by the word *civitas*, to which the word which best answers in our language is commonwealth, and most properly expresses such a society of men, which community does not, for there may be subordinate communities in a government; and city much less. And therefore to avoid ambiguity I crave leave to use the word commonwealth in that sense, in which I find it used by King James himself, which I think to be its genuine signification; which if anybody dislike, I consent with him to change it for a better.[18]

CHAPTER XI

OF THE EXTENT OF THE
LEGISLATIVE POWER

134. The great end of men's entering into society being the enjoyment of their properties in peace and safety, and the great instrument and means of that being the laws established in that society: the first and fundamental positive law of all commonwealths, is the establishing of the legislative power; as the first and fundamental natural law, which is to govern even the legislative itself, is the preservation of the society, and (as far as will consist with the public good) of every person in it. This legislative is not only the supreme power of the commonwealth, but sacred and unalterable in the hands where the community have once placed it; nor can any edict of anybody else, in what form soever conceived, or by what power soever backed, have the force and obligation of a law, which has not its sanction from that legislative which the public has chosen and

18. See below, in chap. xviii of the *Second Treatise*, for the quotation from King James I's speech using this term.

appointed. For without this the law could not have that, which is absolutely necessary to its being a law, the consent of the society over whom nobody can have a power to make laws; but by their own consent, and by authority received from them; and therefore all the obedience, which by the most solemn ties anyone can be obliged to pay, ultimately terminates in this supreme power, and is directed by those laws which it enacts; nor can any oaths to any foreign power whatsoever, or any domestic subordinate power discharge any member of the society from his obedience to the legislative, acting pursuant to their trust; nor oblige him to any obedience contrary to the laws so enacted, or farther than they do allow; it being ridiculous to imagine one can be tied ultimately to obey any power in the society which is not the supreme.

135. Though the legislative, whether placed in one or more, whether it be always in being, or only by intervals, though it be the supreme power in every commonwealth, yet,

First, it is not nor can possibly be absolutely arbitrary over the lives and fortunes of the people. For it being but the joint power of every member of the society given up to that person, or assembly, which is legislator; it can be no more than those persons had in a state of nature before they entered into society, and gave it up to the community. For nobody can transfer to another more power than he has in himself; and nobody has an absolute arbitrary power over himself, or over any other to destroy his own life, or take away the life or property of another. A man as has been proved cannot subject himself to the arbitrary power of another; and having in the state of nature no arbitrary power over the life, liberty, or possession of another, but only so much as the law of nature gave him for the preservation of himself, and the rest of mankind; this is all he doth, or can give up to the commonwealth, and by it to the legislative power, so that the legislative can have no more than this. Their power in the utmost bounds of it, is limited to the public good of the society. It is a power that hath no other end but preservation, and therefore can never have a right to destroy, enslave, or designedly to impoverish the subjects. The obligations of the law of nature cease not in society, but only in many cases are drawn closer, and have by human laws known penalties annexed to them to enforce their observation. Thus the law of nature stands as an eternal rule of all men, legislators as well as others. The rules that they make for other men's actions must, as well as their own, and other men's actions be comformable to the law of nature, i.e., to the will of God, of which that is a declaration, and the fundamental law of nature being the preservation of mankind, no human sanction can be good or valid against it.

136. Secondly, the legislative, or supreme authority, cannot assume to itself a power to rule by extemporary arbitrary decrees, but is bound to dispense justice, and decide the rights of the subject by promulgated standing laws, and known authorized judges. For the law of nature being unwritten, and so nowhere to be found but in the minds of men, they who through passion or interest shall miscite or misapply it, cannot so easily be convinced of their mistake where there is no established judge. And so it serves not, as it ought, to determine the rights, and fence the properties of those that live under it, especially where everyone is judge, interpreter, and executioner of it too, and that in his own case; and he that has right on his side, having ordinarily but his own single strength hath not force enough to defend himself from injuries, or punish delinquents. To avoid these inconveniences, which disorder men's properties in the state of nature, men unite into societies that they may have the united strength

of the whole society to secure and defend their properties, and may have standing rules to bound it, by which everyone may know what is his. To this end it is that men give up all their natural power to the society which they enter into, and the community put the legislative power into such hands as they think fit, with this trust, that they shall be governed by declared laws, or else their peace, quiet, and property, will still be at the same uncertainty as it was in the state of nature.

137. Absolute arbitrary power, or governing without settled standing laws, can neither of them consist with the ends of society and government, which men would not quit the freedom of the state of nature for, and tie themselves up under, were it not to preserve their lives, liberties, and fortunes; and by stated rules of right and property to secure their peace and quiet. It cannot be supposed that they should intend, had they a power so to do, to give to anyone, or more, an absolute arbitrary power over their persons and estates, and put a force into the magistrate's hand to execute his unlimited will arbitrarily upon them. This were to put themselves into a worse condition than the state of nature, wherein they had a liberty to defend their right against the injuries of others, and were upon equal terms of force to maintain it, whether invaded by a single man or many in combination. Whereas, by supposing they have given up themselves to the absolute arbitrary power and will of a legislator, they have disarmed themselves, and armed him, to make prey of them when he pleases. He being in a much worse condition that is exposed to the arbitrary power of one man who has the command of 100,000, than he that is exposed to the arbitrary power of 100,-000 single men; nobody being secure that his will, who hath such a command, is better than that of other men, though his force be 100,000 times stronger. And, therefore, whatever form the common-wealth is under, the ruling power ought to govern by declared and received laws, and not by extemporary dictates and undetermined resolutions. For then mankind will be in a far worse condition than in the state of nature, if they shall have armed one, or a few men, with the joint power of a multitude to force them to obey at pleasure the exorbitant and unlimited decrees of their sudden thoughts, or unrestrained, and, till that moment, unknown wills, without having any measures set down which may guide and justify their actions. For all the power the government has, being only for the good of the society, as it ought not to be arbitrary and at pleasure, so it ought to be exercised by established and promulgated laws; that both the people may know their duty and be safe and secure within the limits of the law; and the rulers too kept within their due bounds, and not be tempted by the power they have in their hands to employ it to such purposes, and by such measures, as they would not have known, and own not willingly.

138. Thirdly, the supreme power cannot take from any man any part of his property without his own consent. For the preservation of property being the end of government, and that for which men enter into society, it necessarily supposes and requires that the people should have property, without which they must be supposed to lose that by entering into society, which was the end for which they entered into it, too gross an absurdity for any man to own. Men, therefore, in society having property, they have such a right to the goods which by the law of the community are theirs, that nobody hath a right to take them or any part of them from them, without their own consent; without this they have no property at all. For I have truly no property in that which another can by right take from me when he pleases, against my consent. Hence it is a mistake to think that the supreme or legislative

power of any commonwealth can do what it will, and dispose of the estates of the subjects arbitrarily, or take any part of them at pleasure. This is not much to be feared in governments where the legislative consists wholly, or in part, in assemblies which are variable, whose members, upon the dissolution of the assembly, are subjects under the common laws of their country, equally with the rest. But in governments where the legislative is in one lasting assembly, always in being, or in one man, as in absolute monarchies, there is danger still, that they will think themselves to have a distinct interest from the rest of the community, and so will be apt to increase their own riches and power by taking what they think fit from the people. For a man's property is not at all secure, though there be good and equitable laws to set the bounds of it between him and his fellow subjects, if he who commands those subjects have power to take from any private man what part he pleases of his property, and use and dispose of it as he thinks good.

139. But government, into whosesoever hands it is put, being, as I have before shown, entrusted with this condition, and for this end, that men might have and secure their properties, the prince, or senate, however it may have power to make laws for the regulating of property between the subjects one amongst another, yet can never have a power to take to themselves the whole or any part of the subject's property without their own consent. For this would be in effect to leave them no property at all. And to let us see that even absolute power, where it is necessary, is not arbitrary by being absolute, but is still limited by that reason, and confined to those ends which required it in some cases to be absolute, we need look no farther than the common practice of martial discipline. For the preservation of the army, and in it the whole commonwealth, requires an absolute obedience to the command of every superior officer, and it is justly death to disobey or dispute the most dangerous or unreasonable of them; but yet we see that neither the sergeant, that could command a soldier to march up to the mouth of a cannon, or stand in a breach, where he is almost sure to perish, can command that soldier to give him one penny of his money; nor the general, that can condemn him to death for deserting his post, or not obeying the most desperate orders, cannot yet, with all his absolute power of life and death, dispose of one farthing of that soldier's estate, or seize one jot of his goods, whom yet he can command anything, and hang for the least disobedience. Because such a blind obedience is necessary to that end for which the commander has his power, viz., the preservation of the rest; but the disposing of his goods has nothing to do with it.

140. 'Tis true governments cannot be supported without great charge, and it is fit everyone who enjoys a share of the protection should pay out of his estate his proportion for the maintenance of it. But still it must be with his own consent, i.e., the consent of the majority giving it either by themselves or their representatives chosen by them. For if anyone shall claim a power to lay and levy taxes on the people, by his own authority, and without such consent of the people, he thereby invades the fundamental law of property, and subverts the end of government. For what property have I in that which another may by right take when he pleases to himself?

141. Fourthly, the legislative cannot transfer the power of making laws to any other hands; for it being but a delegated power from the people, they who have it cannot pass it over to others. The people alone can appoint the form of the commonwealth, which is by constituting the legislative, and appointing in whose hands that shall be. And when the people have said we will submit to rules, and be governed by laws made by such men,

and in such forms, nobody else can say other men shall make laws for them; nor can the people be bound by any laws but such as are enacted by those whom they have chosen and authorized to make laws for them.

142. These are the bounds which the trust that is put in them by the society, and the law of God and Nature, have set to the legislative power of every commonwealth, in all forms of government.

First, they are to govern by promulgated established laws, not to be varied in particular cases, but to have one rule for rich and poor, for the favorite at court and the countryman at plough.

Secondly, these laws also ought to be designed for no other end ultimately but the good of the people.

Thirdly, they must not raise taxes on the property of the people without the consent of the people, given by themselves or their deputies. And this properly concerns only such governments where the legislative is always in being, or at least where the people have not reserved any part of the legislative to deputies, to be from time to time chosen by themselves.

Fourthly, the legislative neither must nor can transfer the power of making laws to anybody else, or place it anywhere but where the people have.

CHAPTER XII

OF THE LEGISLATIVE, EXECUTIVE, AND FEDERATIVE POWER OF THE COMMONWEALTH

143. The legislative power is that which has a right to direct how the force of the commonwealth shall be employed for preserving the community and the members of it. Because those laws which are constantly to be executed, and whose force is always to continue, may be made in a little time, therefore there is no need that the legislative should be always in being, not having always business to do; and because it may be too great a temptation to human frailty, apt to grasp at power for the same persons, who have the power of making laws, to have also in their hands the power to execute them, whereby they exempt themselves from obedience to the laws they make, and suit the law, both in its making and execution to their own private advantage, and thereby come to have a distinct interest from the rest of the community, contrary to the end of society and government. Therefore, in well-ordered commonwealths, where the good of the whole is so considered as it ought, the legislative power is put into the hands of divers persons who duly assembled, have by themselves or jointly with others a power to make laws, which when they have done, being separated again, they are themselves subject to the laws they have made; which is a new and near tie upon them, to take care that they make them for the public good.

144. But because the laws that are at once and in a short time made, have a constant and lasting force and need a perpetual execution or an attendance thereunto; therefore, it is necessary there should be a power always in being, which should see to the execution of the laws that are made and remain in force; and thus the legislative and executive power come often to be separated.

145. There is another power in every commonwealth, which one may call natural, because it is that which answers to the power every man naturally had before he entered into society; for though in a commonwealth the members of it are distinct persons still in reference to one another, and as such are governed by the laws of the society, yet in reference to the rest of mankind they make one body, which is, as every member of it before was still in the state of nature with the rest of mankind. So that the controversies that happen between any man of the society with those that are out of it are managed by the public, and an injury done to a member of their body engages the whole in the reparation of it. So that

under this consideration the whole community is one body in the state of nature in respect of all other states or persons out of its community.

146. This therefore contains the power of war and peace, leagues and alliances, and all the transactions with all persons and communities without the commonwealth, and may be called federative if anyone pleases. So the thing be understood, I am indifferent as to the name.

147. These two powers, executive and federative, though they be really distinct in themselves, yet one comprehending the execution of the municipal laws of the society within itself upon all that are parts of it; the other the management of the security and interest of the public without, with all those that it may receive benefit or damage from, yet they are always almost united. And though this federative power in the well or ill management of it be of great moment to the commonwealth, yet it is much less capable to be directed by antecedent, standing, positive laws than the executive; and so must necessarily be left to the prudence and wisdom of those whose hands it is in to be managed for the public good. For the laws that concern subjects one amongst another, being to direct their actions, may well enough precede them. But what is to be done in reference to foreigners, depending much upon their actions and the variation of designs and interests, must be left in great part to the prudence of those who have this power committed to them, to be managed by the best of their skill for the advantage of the commonwealth.

148. Though, as I said, the executive and federative power of every community be really distinct in themselves, yet they are hardly to be separated and placed at the same time in the hands of distinct persons; for both of them requiring the force of the society for their exercise, it is almost impracticable to place the force of the commonwealth in distinct and not subordinate hands; or

that the executive and federative power should be placed in persons that might act separately, whereby the force of the public would be under different commands, which would be apt some time or other to cause disorder and ruin.

CHAPTER XIII

OF THE SUBORDINATION OF THE POWERS OF THE COMMONWEALTH

149. Though in a constituted commonwealth, standing upon its own basis, and acting according to its own nature, that is, acting for the preservation of the community, there can be but one supreme power, which is the legislative, to which all the rest are and must be subordinate, yet the legislative being only of fiduciary power to act for certain ends, there remains still in the people a supreme power to remove or alter the legislative when they find the legislative act contrary to the trust reposed in them; for all power given with trust for the attaining an end, being limited by that end, whenever that end is manifestly neglected or opposed, the trust must necessarily be forfeited, and the power devolve into the hands of those that gave it who may place it anew where they shall think best for their safety and security. And thus the community perpetually retains a supreme power of saving themselves from the attempts and designs of anybody, even of their legislators whenever they shall be so foolish or so wicked as to lay and carry on designs against the liberties and properties of the subject; for no man or society of men, having a power to deliver up their preservation, or consequently the means of it to the absolute will and arbitrary dominion of another, whenever anyone shall go about to bring them into such a slavish condition they will always have a right to preserve what they have not a power to part with; and to rid themselves of those who invade this fundamental, sacred and unalterable law of self-preser-

vation for which they entered into society; and thus the community may be said in this respect to be always the supreme power, but not as considered under any form of government, because this power of the people can never take place till the government be dissolved.

150. In all cases whilst the government subsists, the legislative is the supreme power; for what can give laws to another must needs be superior to him, and since the legislative is no otherwise legislative of the society but by the right it has to make laws for all the parts and for every member of the society, prescribing rules to their actions, and giving power of execution where they are transgressed, the legislative must needs be the supreme, and all other powers in many members or parts of the society derived from and subordinate to it.

151. In some commonwealths where the legislative is not always in being, and the executive is vested in a single person who has also a share in the legislative, there that single person, in a very tolerable sense, may also be called supreme; not that he has in himself all the supreme power, which is that of lawmaking, but because he has in him the supreme execution from whom all inferior magistrates derive all their several subordinate powers, or, at least, the greatest part of them; having also no legislative superior to him, there being no law to be made without his consent, which cannot be expected should ever subject him to the other part of the legislative, he is properly enough in this sense supreme. But yet it is to be observed that though oaths of allegiance and fealty are taken to him, it is not to him as supreme legislator, but as supreme executor of the law made by a joint power of him with others, allegiance being nothing but an obedience according to law, which, when he violates, he has no right to obedience, nor can claim it otherwise than as the public person vested with the power of the law, and so is to be considered as the image, phantom,

or representative of the commonwealth, acted by the will of the society declared in its laws, and thus he has no will, no power, but that of the law. But when he quits this representation, this public will, and acts by his own private will, he degrades himself, and is but a single private person without power and without will; the members owing no obedience but to the public will of the society.

152. The executive power placed anywhere but in a person that has also a share in the legislative is visibly subordinate and accountable to it, and may be at pleasure changed and displaced; so that it is not the supreme executive power that is exempt from subordination, but the supreme executive power vested in one, who having a share in the legislative, has no distinct superior legislative to be subordinate and accountable to, farther than he himself shall join and consent, so that he is no more subordinate than he himself shall think fit, which one may certainly conclude will be but very little. Of other ministerial and subordinate powers in a commonwealth we need not speak, they being so multiplied with infinite variety in the different customs and constitutions of distinct commonwealths, that it is impossible to give a particular account of them all. Only thus much which is necessary to our present purpose we may take notice of concerning them, that they have no manner of authority, any of them, beyond what is by positive grant and commission delegated to them, and are all of them accountable to some other power in the commonwealth.

153. It is not necessary—no, nor so much as convenient—that the legislative should be always in being; but absolutely necessary that the executive power should, because there is not always need of new laws to be made, but always need of execution of the laws that are made. When the legislative hath put the execution of the laws they make into other hands, they have a power still to resume

it out of those hands when they find cause, and to punish for any maladministration against the laws. The same holds also in regard of the federative power, that and the executive being both ministerial and subordinate to the legislative, which, as has been shown, in a constituted commonwealth is the supreme, the legislative also in this case being supposed to consist of several persons; for if it be a single person it cannot but be always in being, and so will, as supreme, naturally have the supreme executive power, together with the legislative, may assemble and exercise their legislative at the times that either their original constitution or their own adjournment appoints, or when they please, if neither of these hath appointed any time, or there be no other way prescribed to convoke them. For the supreme power being placed in them by the people, it is always in them, and they may exercise it when they please, unless by their original constitution they are limited to certain seasons, or by an act of their supreme power they have adjourned to a certain time, and when that time comes they have a right to assemble and act again.

154. If the legislative, or any part of it, be of representatives, chosen for that time by the people, which afterward return into the ordinary state of subjects, and have no share in the legislature but upon a new choice, this power of choosing must also be exercised by the people, either at certain appointed seasons, or else when they are summoned to it; and, in this latter case, the power of convoking the legislative is ordinarily placed in the executive, and has one of these two limitations in respect of time:—that either the original constitution requires their assembling and acting at certain intervals; and then the executive power does nothing but ministerially issue directions for their electing and assembling according to due forms; or else it is left to his prudence to call them by new elections when the occasions or exigencies

of the public require the amendment of old or making of new laws, or the redress or prevention of any inconveniencies that lie on or threaten the people.

155. It may be demanded here, what if the executive power, being possessed of the force of the commonwealth, shall make use of that force to hinder the meeting and acting of the legislative, when the original constitution or the public exigencies require it? I say, using force upon the people, without authority, and contrary to the trust put in him that does so, is a state of war with the people, who have a right to reinstate their legislative in the exercise of their power. For having erected a legislative with an intent they should exercise the power of making laws, either at certain set times, or when there is need of it, when they are hindered by any force from what is so necessary to the society, and wherein the safety and preservation of the people consists, the people have a right to remove it by force. In all states and conditions the true remedy of force without authority is to oppose force to it. The use of force without authority always puts him that uses it into a state of war as the aggressor, and renders him liable to be treated accordingly.

156. The power of assembling and dismissing the legislative, placed in the executive, gives not the executive a superiority over it, but is a fiduciary trust placed in him for the safety of the people in a case where the uncertainty and variableness of human affairs could not bear a steady fixed rule. For it not being possible that the first framers of the government should by any foresight be so much masters of future events as to be able to prefix so just periods of return and duration to the assemblies of the legislative, in all times to come, that might exactly answer all the exigencies of the commonwealth, the best remedy that could be found for this defect was to trust this to the prudence of one who was always to be present, and whose

business it was to watch over the public good. Constant, frequent meetings of the legislative, and long continuations of their assemblies, without necessary occasion, could not but be burdensome to the people, and must necessarily in time produce more dangerous inconveniencies, and yet the quick turn of affairs might be sometimes such as to need their present help; any delay of their convening might endanger the public; and sometimes, too, their business might be so great that the limited time of their sitting might be too short for their work, and rob the public of that benefit which could be had only from their mature deliberation. What, then, could be done in this case to prevent the community from being exposed some time or other to imminent hazard on one side or the other, by fixed intervals and periods set to the meeting and acting of the legislative, but to intrust it to the prudence of some who, being present and acquainted with the state of public affairs, might make use of this prerogative for the public good? And where else could this be so well placed as in his hands who was intrusted with the execution of the laws for the same end? Thus, supposing the regulation of times for the assembling and sitting of the legislative not settled by the original constitution, it naturally fell into the hands of the executive; not as an arbitrary power depending on his good pleasure, but with this trust always to have it exercised only for the public weal, as the occurrences of times and change of affairs might require. Whether settled periods of their convening, or a liberty left to the prince for convoking the legislative, or perhaps a mixture of both, hath the least inconvenience attending it, it is not my business here to inquire, but only to show that, though the executive power may have the prerogative of convoking and dissolving such conventions of the legislative, yet it is not thereby superior to it.

157. Things of this world are in so

constant a flux that nothing remains long in the same state. Thus people, riches, trade, power, change their stations; flourishing mighty cities come to ruin, and prove in time neglected desolate corners, whilst other unfrequented places grow into populous countries filled with wealth and inhabitants. But things not always changing equally, and private interest often keeping up customs and privileges when the reasons of them are ceased, it often comes to pass that in governments where part of the legislative consists of representatives chosen by the people, that in tract of time this representation becomes very unequal and disproportionate to the reasons it was at first established upon. To what gross absurdities the following of custom when reason has left it may lead, we may be satisfied when we see the bare name of a town, of which there remains not so much as the ruins, where scarce so much housing as a sheepcote, or more inhabitants than a shepherd is to be found, send as many representatives to the grand assembly of lawmakers as a whole county numerous in people and powerful in riches. This strangers stand amazed at, and everyone must confess needs a remedy; though most think it hard to find one, because the constitution of the legislative being the original and supreme act of the society, antecedent to all positive laws in it, and depending wholly on the people, no inferior power can alter it. And, therefore, the people when the legislative is once constituted, having in such a government as we have been speaking of no power to act as long as the government stands, this inconvenience is thought incapable of a remedy.

158. *Salus populi suprema lex*[19] is certainly so just and fundamental a rule that he who sincerely follows it cannot dangerously err. If therefore the executive, who has the power of convoking

19. "The welfare of the people is the highest law."

the legislative, observing rather the true proportion than fashion of representation, regulates, not by old custom, but true reason, the number of members in all places that have a right to be distinctly represented, which no part of the people however incorporated can pretend to, but in proportion to the assistance which it affords to the public, it cannot be judged to have set up a new legislative, but to have restored the old and true one, and to have rectified the disorders which succession of time had insensibly as well as inevitably introduced. For it being the interest, as well as intention of the people, to have a fair and equal representative, whoever brings it nearest to that is an undoubted friend to and establisher of the government, and cannot miss the consent and approbation of the community. Prerogative being nothing but a power in the hands of the prince to provide for the public good in such cases which, depending upon unforseen and uncertain occurrences, certain and unalterable laws could not safely direct. Whatsoever shall be done manifestly for the good of the people, and the establishing the government upon its true foundations is, and always will be, just prerogative. The power of erecting new corporations,[20] and therewith new representatives, carries with it a supposition that in time the measures of representation might vary, and those have a just right to be represented which before had none; and by the same reason those cease to have a right, and be too inconsiderable for such a privilege which before had it. It is not a change from the present state, which perhaps corruption or decay has introduced, that makes an inroad upon the government, but the tendency of it to injure or oppress the people, and to set up one part or party with a distinction from, and an unequal subjection of the rest. Whatsoever cannot but be acknowledged to be of ad-

20. Incorporated municipalities, as borough, town, or city.

vantage to the society and people in general upon just and lasting measures, will always, when done, justify itself; and whenever the people shall choose their representatives upon just and undeniably equal measures, suitable to the original frame of the government, it cannot be doubted to be the will and act of the society who ever permitted or proposed to them so to do.

CHAPTER XVII

OF USURPATION

197. As conquest may be called a foreign usurpation, so usurpation is a kind of domestic conquest, with this difference—that an usurper can never have right on his side, it being no usurpation but where one is got into the possession of what another has right to. This, so far as it is usurpation, is a change only of persons, but not of the forms and rules of the government; for if the usurper extend his power beyond what, of right, belonged to the lawful princes or governors of the commonwealth, it is tyranny added to usurpation.

198. In all lawful governments the designation of the persons who are to bear rule being as natural and necessary a part as the form of the government itself, and that which had its establishment originally from the people—the anarchy being much alike, to have no form of government at all, or to agree that it shall be monarchical, yet appoint no way to design the person that shall have the power and be the monarch—all commonwealths, therefore, with the form of government established, have rules also of appointing and conveying the right to those who are to have any share in the public authority; and whoever gets into the exercise of any part of the power by other ways than what the laws of the community have prescribed hath no right to be obeyed, though the form of the commonwealth be still preserved, since he is not the person the laws have appointed, and, consequently, not the

person the people have consented to. Nor can such an usurper, or any deriving from him, ever have a title till the people are both at liberty to consent, and have actually consented, to allow and confirm in him the power he hath till then usurped.

CHAPTER XVIII

OF TYRANNY

199. As usurpation is the exercise of power which another hath a right to, so tyranny is the exercise of power beyond right, which nobody can have a right to; and this is making use of the power any-one has in his hands, not for the good of those who are under it, but for his own private, separate advantage. When the governor, however entitled, makes not the law, but his will, the rule, and his commands and actions are not directed to the preservation of the properties of his people, but the satisfaction of his own ambition, revenge, covetousness, or any other irregular passion.

200. If one can doubt this to be truth or reason because it comes from the obscure hand of a subject, I hope the authority of a king will make it pass with him. King James, in his speech to the Parliament, 1603, tells them thus: "I will ever prefer the weal of the public and of the whole commonwealth, in making of good laws and constitutions, to any particular and private ends of mine, thinking ever the wealth and weal of the commonwealth to be my greatest weal and wordly felicity—a point wherein a lawful king doth directly differ from a tyrant; for I do acknowledge that the special and greatest point of difference that is between a rightful king and an usurping tyrant is this—that whereas the proud and ambitious tyrant doth think his kingdom and people are only or-dained for satisfaction of his desires and unreasonable appetites, the righteous and just king doth, by the contrary, acknowl-edge himself to be ordained for the pro-curing of the wealth and property of his people." And again, in his speech to the Parliament, 1609, he hath these words: "The king binds himself, by a double oath, to the observation of the funda-mental laws of his kingdom—tacitly, as by being a king, and so bound to protect, as well the people as the laws of his king-dom; and expressly by his oath at his coronation; so as every just king, in a settled kingdom, is bound to observe that paction made to his people, by his laws, in framing his government agreeable thereunto, according to that paction which God made with Noah after the deluge: 'Hereafter, seed-time, and har-vest, and cold, and heat, and summer, and winter, and day, and night, shall not cease while the earth remaineth.' And therefore a king, governing in a settled kingdom, leaves to be a king, and degen-erates into a tyrant, as soon as he leaves off to rule according to his laws." And a little after: "Therefore, all kings that are not tyrants, or perjured, will be glad to bound themselves within the limits of their laws, and they that persuade them the contrary are vipers, pests, both against them and the commonwealth." Thus, that learned king, who well under-stood the notions of things, makes the difference betwixt a king and a tyrant to consist only in this: that one makes the laws the bounds of his power and the good of the public the end of his govern-ment; the other makes all give way to his own will and appetite.

201. It is a mistake to think this fault is proper only to monarchies. Other forms of government are liable to it as well as that; for wherever the power that is put in any hands for the govern-ment of the people and the preservation of their properties is applied to other ends, and made use of to impoverish, harass, or subdue them to the arbitrary and irregular commands of those that have it, there it presently becomes tyr-anny, whether those that thus use it are one or many. Thus we read of the thirty

tyrants at Athens,[21] as well as one at Syracuse;[22] and the intolerable dominion of the Decemviri[23] at Rome was nothing better.

202. Wherever law ends, tyranny begins, if the law be transgressed to another's harm; and whosoever in authority exceeds the power given him by the law, and makes use of the force he has under his command to compass that upon the subject which the law allows not, ceases in that to be a magistrate, and acting without authority may be opposed, as any other man who by force invades the right of another. This is acknowledged in subordinate magistrates. He that hath authority to seize my person in the street may be opposed as a thief and a robber if he endeavors to break into my house to execute a writ, notwithstanding that I know he has such a warrant and such a legal authority as will empower him to arrest me abroad. And why this should not hold in the highest, as well as in the most inferior magistrate, I would gladly be informed. Is it reasonable that the eldest brother, because he has the greatest part of his father's estate, should thereby have a right to take away any of his younger brothers' portions? Or, that a rich man, who possessed a whole country, should from thence have a right to seize, when he pleased, the cottage and garden of his poor neighbor? The being rightfully possessed of great power and riches, exceedingly beyond the greatest part of the sons of Adam, is so far from

21. After the Peloponnesian Wars, Athens was briefly ruled by thirty oligarchs, who abused their power and were removed by the people.

22. Dion of Syracuse had liberal theories about government until he supplanted the tyrant Dionysius the Younger, whose adviser he had been. He then became a military despot and had to be removed.

23. Literally, "ten men," a temporary commission which succeeded all other Roman magistrates from 451 to 449 B.C., mainly for the purpose of drawing up a code of laws. Their rule became violent and tyrannical, and they were forced to abdicate in 449 B.C.

being an excuse, much less a reason for rapine and oppression, which the endamaging another without authority is, that it is a great aggravation of it. For the exceeding the bounds of authority is no more a right in a great than a petty officer, no more justifiable in a king than a constable. But so much the worse in him as that he has more trust put in him, is supposed, from the advantage of education and counselors to have better knowledge and less reason to do it, having already a greater share than the rest of his brethren.

203. May the commands, then, of a prince be opposed? May he be resisted, as often as anyone shall find himself aggrieved, and but imagine he has not right done him? This will unhinge and overturn all polities, and instead of government and order, leave nothing but anarchy and confusion.

204. To this I answer: That force is to be opposed to nothing but to unjust and unlawful force. Whoever makes any opposition in any other case draws on himself a just condemnation, both from God and man; and so no such danger or confusion will follow, as is often suggested. For—

205. First, as in some countries the person of the prince by the law is sacred, and so whatever he commands or does, his person is still free from all question or violence, not liable to force, or any judicial censure or condemnation. But yet opposition may be made to the illegal acts of any inferior officer or other commissioned by him, unless he will, by actually putting himself into a state of war with his people, dissolve the government, and leave them to that defense, which belongs to everyone in the state of nature. For of such things, who can tell what the end will be? And a neighbor kingdom has showed the world an odd example. In all other cases the sacredness of the person exempts him from all inconveniencies, whereby he is secure, whilst the government stands, from all

violence and harm whatsoever, than which there cannot be a wiser constitution. For the harm he can do in his own person not being likely to happen often, nor to extend itself far, nor being able by his single strength to subvert the laws nor oppress the body of the people, should any prince have so much weakness and ill nature as to be willing to do it. The inconveniency of some particular mischiefs that may happen sometimes when a heady prince comes to the throne are well recompensed by the peace of the public and security of the government in the person of the chief magistrate, thus set out of the reach of danger; it being safer for the body that some few private men should be sometimes in danger to suffer than that the head of the republic should be easily and upon slight occasions exposed.

206. Secondly, but this privilege, belonging only to the king's person, hinders not but they may be questioned, opposed, and resisted, who use unjust force, though they pretend a commission from him which the law authorizes not; as is plain in the case of him that has the king's writ to arrest a man which is a full commission from the king, and yet he that has it cannot break open a man's house to do it, nor execute this command of the king upon certain days nor in certain places, though this commission have no such exception in it; but they are the limitations of the law, which, if anyone transgress, the king's commission excuses him not. For the king's authority being given him only by the law, he cannot empower anyone to act against the law, or justify him by his commission in so doing. The commission or command of any magistrate where he has no authority, being as void and insignificant as that of any private man, the difference between the one and the other being that the magistrate has some authority so far and to such ends, and the private man has none at all; for it is not the commission but the authority that gives the right

of acting, and against the laws there can be no authority. But notwithstanding such resistance, the king's person and authority are still both secured, and so no danger to governor or government.

207. Thirdly, supposing a government wherein the person of the chief magistrate is not thus sacred, yet this doctrine of the lawfulness of resisting all unlawful exercises of his power will not, upon every slight occasion, endanger him or embroil the government; for where the injured party may be relieved and his damages repaired by appeal to the law, there can be no pretense for force, which is only to be used where a man is intercepted from appealing to the law. For nothing is to be accounted hostile force but where it leaves not the remedy of such an appeal, and it is such force alone that puts him that uses it into a state of war, and makes it lawful to resist him. A man with a sword in his hand demands my purse in the highway, when perhaps I have not 12d. in my pocket. This man I may lawfully kill. To another I deliver £100 to hold only whilst I alight, which he refuses to restore me when I am got up again, but draws his sword to defend the possession of it by force. I endeavor to retake it. The mischief this man does me is a hundred, or possibly a thousand times more than the other perhaps intended me (whom I killed before he really did me any); and yet I might lawfully kill the one and cannot so much as hurt the other lawfully. The reason whereof is plain; because the one using force which threatened my life, I could not have time to appeal to the law to secure it, and when it was gone it was too late to appeal. The law could not restore life to my dead carcass. The loss was irreparable; which to prevent the law of nature gave me a right to destroy him who had put himself into a state of war with me and threatened my destruction. But in the other case, my life not being in danger, I might have the benefit of appealing to

the law, and have reparation for my £100 that way.

208. Fourthly, but if the unlawful acts done by the magistrate be maintained (by the power he has got), and the remedy, which is due by law, be by the same power obstructed, yet the right of resisting, even in such manifest acts of tyranny, will not suddenly, or on slight occasions, disturb the government. For if it reach no farther than some private men's cases, though they have a right to defend themselves, and to recover by force what by unlawful force is taken from them, yet the right to do so will not easily engage them in a contest wherein they are sure to perish; it being as impossible for one or a few oppressed men to disturb the government where the body of the people do not think themselves concerned in it, as for a raving madman or heavy malcontent to overturn a well-settled state, the people being as little apt to follow the one as the other.

209. But if either these illegal acts have extended to the majority of the people, or if the mischief and oppression has light only on some few, but in such cases as the precedent and consequences seem to threaten all, and they are persuaded in their consciences that their laws, and with them, their estates, liberties, and lives are in danger, and perhaps their religion too, how they will be hindered from resisting illegal force used against them I cannot tell. This is an inconvenience, I confess, that attends all governments whatsoever, when the governors have brought it to this pass, to be generally suspected of their people, the most dangerous state they can possibly put themselves in; wherein they are the less to be pitied, because it is so easy to be avoided. It being as impossible for a governor, if he really means the good of his people, and the preservation of them and their laws together, not to make them see and feel it, as it is for the father of a family not to let his children see he loves and takes care of them.

210. But if all the world shall observe pretenses of one kind, and actions of another, arts used to elude the law, and the trust of prerogative (which is an arbitrary power in some things left in the prince's hand to do good, not harm, to the people) employed contrary to the end for which it was given; if the people shall find the ministers and subordinate magistrates chosen, suitable to such ends, and favored or laid by proportionably as they promote or oppose them; if they see several experiments made of arbitrary power, and that religion underhand favored, though publicly proclaimed against, which is readiest to introduce it, and the operators in it supported as much as may be; and when that cannot be done, yet approved still, and liked the better, and a long train of acting show the counsels all tending that way, how can a man any more hinder himself from being persuaded in his own mind which way things are going; or, from casting about how to save himself, than he could from believing the captain of a ship he was in was carrying him and the rest of the company to Algiers, when he found him always steering that course, though cross-winds, leaks in his ship, and want of men and provisions did often force him to turn his course another way for some time, which he steadily returned to again as soon as the wind, weather, and other circumstances would let him?

CHAPTER XIX

OF THE DISSOLUTION OF GOVERNMENT

211. He that will with any clearness speak of the dissolution of government ought, in the first place, to distinguish between the dissolution of the society and the dissolution of the government. That which makes the community, and brings men out of the loose state of nature into one politic society, is the agreement which everyone has with the rest to incorporate and act as one body, and so be one distinct commonwealth. The

usual and almost only way whereby this union is dissolved, is the inroad of foreign force making a conquest upon them. For in that case (not being able to maintain and support themselves as one entire and independent body) the union belonging to that body which consisted therein must necessarily cease, and so everyone return to the state he was in before, with a liberty to shift for himself and provide for his own safety as he thinks fit in some other society. Whenever the society is dissolved, it is certain the government of that society cannot remain. Thus conquerors' swords often cut up governments by the roots, and mangle societies to pieces, separating the subdued or scattered multitude from the protection of and dependence on that society which ought to have preserved them from violence. The world is too well instructed in, and too forward to allow of this way of dissolving of, governments to need any more to be said of it; and there wants not much argument to prove that where the society is dissolved, the government cannot remain—that being as impossible as for the frame of a house to subsist when the materials of it are scattered and displaced by a whirlwind, or jumbled into a confused heap by an earthquake.

212. Besides this overturning from without, governments are dissolved from within.

First, when the legislative is altered. Civil society being a state of peace amongst those who are of it, from whom the state of war is excluded by the umpirage which they have provided in their legislative for the ending all differences that may arise amongst any of them, it is in their legislative that the members of a commonwealth are united and combined together in one coherent living body. This is the soul that gives form, life, and unity to the commonwealth. From hence the several members have their mutual influence, sympathy, and connection. And, therefore, when the legislative is broken or dissolved, dissolution and death follow. For the essence and union of the society consisting in having one will, the legislative, when once established by the majority, has the declaring and, as it were, keeping of, that will. The constitution of the legislative is the first and fundamental act of the society, whereby provision is made for the continuation of their union, under the direction of persons and bonds of laws made by persons authorized thereunto by the consent and appointment of the people, without which no one man or number of men amongst them can have authority of making laws that shall be binding to the rest. When any one or more shall take upon them to make laws, whom the people have not appointed so to do, they make laws without authority, which the people are not therefore bound to obey; by which means they come again to be out of subjection, and may constitute to themselves a new legislative, as they think best, being in full liberty to resist the force of those who without authority would impose anything upon them. Everyone is at the disposure of his own will when those who had by the delegation of the society the declaring of the public will, are excluded from it, and others usurp the place who have no such authority or delegation.

213. This being usually brought about by such in the commonwealth who misuse the power they have, it is hard to consider it aright, and know at whose door to lay it, without knowing the form of government in which it happens. Let us suppose, then, the legislative placed in the concurrence of three distinct persons.

(1) A single hereditary person having the constant supreme executive power, and with it the power of convoking and dissolving the other two within certain periods of time.

(2) An assembly of hereditary nobility.

(3) An assembly of representatives chosen *pro tempore* by the people. Such

a form of government supposed, it is evident,

214. First, that when such a single person or prince sets up his own arbitrary will in place of the laws which are the will of the society, declared by the legislative, then the legislative is changed. For that being in effect the legislative whose rules and laws are put in execution and required to be obeyed when other laws are set up, and other rules pretended and enforced, than what the legislative constituted by the society have enacted, it is plain that the legislative is changed. Whoever introduces new laws, not being thereunto authorized by the fundamental appointment of the society, or subverts the old, disowns and overturns the power by which they were made, and so sets up a new legislative.

215. Secondly, when the prince hinders the legislative from assembling in its due time, or from acting freely, pursuant to those ends for which it was constituted, the legislative is altered. For it is not a certain number of men, no, nor their meeting, unless they have also freedom of debating and leisure of perfecting what is for the good of the society, wherein the legislative consists. When these are taken away or altered so as to deprive the society of the due exercise of their power, the legislative is truly altered. For it is not names that constitute governments, but the use and exercise of those powers that were intended to accompany them; so that he who takes away the freedom, or hinders the acting of the legislative in its due seasons, in effect takes away the legislative, and puts an end to the government.

216. Thirdly, when, by the arbitrary power of the prince, the electors or ways of elections are altered, without the consent and contrary to the common interest of the people, there also the legislative is altered. For if others than those whom the society hath authorized thereunto, do choose, or in another way than what the society hath prescribed, those chosen are not the legislative appointed by the people.

217. Fourthly, the delivery also of the people into the subjection of foreign power, either by the prince, or by the legislative, is certainly a change of the legislative, and so a dissolution of the government. For the end why people entered into society being to be preserved one entire, free, independent society, to be governed by its own laws, this is lost whenever they are given up into the power of another.

218. Why, in such a constitution as this, the dissolution of the government in these cases is to be imputed to the prince is evident, because he, having the force, treasure, and offices of the state to employ, and often persuading himself or being flattered by others, that, as supreme magistrate, he is incapable of control; he alone is in a condition to make great advances toward such changes under pretense of lawful authority, and has it in his hands to terrify or suppress opposers as factious, seditious, and enemies to the government; whereas no other part of the legislative, or people, is capable by themselves to attempt any alteration of the legislative without open and visible rebellion, apt enough to be taken notice of, which, when it prevails, produces effects very little different from foreign conquest. Besides, the prince, in such a form of government, having the power of dissolving the other parts of the legislative, and thereby rendering them private persons, they can never, in opposition to him, or without his concurrence, alter the legislative by a law, his consent being necessary to give any of their decrees that sanction. But yet so far as the other parts of the legislative any way contribute to any attempt upon the government, and do either promote, or not, what lies in them, hinder such designs, they are guilty, and partake in this, which is certainly the greatest crime men can be guilty of one toward another.

219. There is one way more whereby such a government may be dissolved, and that is, when he who has the supreme executive power neglects and abandons that charge, so that the laws already made can no longer be put in execution. This is demonstratively to reduce all to anarchy, and so effectually to dissolve the government. For laws not being made for themselves, but to be by their execution the bonds of the society, to keep every part of the body politic, in its due place and function, when that totally ceases, the government visibly ceases, and the people become a confused multitude without order or connection. Where there is no longer the administration of justice, for the securing of men's rights, nor any remaining power within the community to direct the force, or provide for the necessities of the public, there certainly is no government left. Where the laws cannot be executed, it is all one as if there were no laws; and a government without laws is, I suppose, a mystery in politics, inconceivable to human capacity, and inconsistent with human society.

220. In these and the like cases, when the government is dissolved, the people are at liberty to provide for themselves by erecting a new legislative, differing from the other, by the change of persons, or form, or both, as they shall find it most for their safety and good. For the society can never, by the fault of another, lose the native and original right it has to preserve itself, which can only be done by a settled legislative, and a fair and impartial execution of the laws made by it. But the state of mankind is not so miserable that they are not capable of using this remedy, till it be too late to look for any. To tell people they may provide for themselves by erecting a new legislative, when by oppression, artifice, or being delivered over to a foreign power, their old one is gone, is only to tell them they may expect relief when it is too late, and the evil is past cure. This is in effect no more than to bid them first be slaves, and then to take care of their liberty; and when their chains are on tell them they may act like free men. This, if barely so, is rather mockery than relief; and men can never be secure from tyranny if there be no means to escape it till they are perfectly under it. And therefore it is that they have not only a right to get out of it, but to prevent it.

221. There is therefore secondly another way whereby governments are dissolved, and that is when the legislative or the prince, either of them, act contrary to their trust.

First, the legislative acts against the trust reposed in them when they endeavor to invade the property of the subject, and to make themselves or any part of the community masters or arbitrary disposers of the lives, liberties, or fortunes of the people.

222. The reason why men enter into society is the preservation of their property; and the end why they choose and authorize a legislative is that there may be laws made, and rules set, as guards and fences to the properties of all the members of the society to limit the power and moderate the dominion of every part and member of the society. For since it can never be supposed to be the will of the society that the legislative should have a power to destroy that which everyone designs secure by entering into society, and for which the people submitted themselves to legislators of their own making, whenever the legislators endeavor to take away and destroy the property of the people, or to reduce them to slavery under arbitrary power, they put themselves into a state of war with the people, who are thereupon absolved from any further obedience, and are left to the common refuge which God hath provided for all men against force and violence. Whensoever, therefore, the legislative shall transgress this fundamental rule of society, and either by ambition, fear, folly, or corruption, en-

deavor to grasp themselves or put into the hands of any other an absolute power over the lives, liberties, and estates of the people, by this breach of trust they forfeit the power the people had put into their hands, for quite contrary ends, and it devolves to the people, who have a right to resume their original liberty, and by the establishment of the new legislative (such as they shall think fit) provide for their own safety and security, which is the end for which they are in society.

What I have said here concerning the legislative in general, holds true also concerning the supreme executor, who having a double trust put in him, both to have a part in the legislative and the supreme execution of the law, acts against both when he goes about to set up his own arbitrary will as the law of the society. He acts also contrary to his trust when he either employs the force, treasure, and offices of the society, to corrupt the representatives, and gain them to his purposes; or openly pre-engages the electors, and prescribes to their choice such whom he has by solicitations, threats, promises, or otherwise won to his designs, and employs them to bring in such, who have promised beforehand what to vote and what to enact. Thus to regulate candidates and electors, and new-model the ways of election, what is it but to cut up the government by the roots, and poison the very fountain of public security? For the people having reserved to themselves the choice of their representatives as the fence to their properties, could do it for no other end but that they might always be freely chosen, and, so chosen, freely act and advise as the necessity of the commonwealth and the public good should upon examination and mature debate be judged to require. This those who give their votes before they hear the debate, and have weighed the reason on all sides, are not capable of doing. To prepare such an assembly as this, and endeavor to set up the declared abet-

tors of his own will for the true representatives of the people and the lawmakers of the society, is certainly as great a breach of trust and as perfect a declaration of a design to subvert the government as is possible to be met with. To which if one shall add rewards and punishments visibly employed to the same end and all the arts of perverted law made use of to take off and destroy all that stand in the way of such a design, and will not comply and consent to betray the liberties of their country, it will be past doubt what is doing. What power they ought to have in the society who thus employ it contrary to the trust that went along with it in its first institution is easy to determine; and one cannot but see that he who has once attempted any such thing as this cannot any longer be trusted.

223. To this perhaps it will be said that, the people being ignorant and always discontented, to lay the foundation of government in the unsteady opinion and uncertain humor of the people is to expose it to certain ruin; and no government will be able long to subsist if the people may set up a new legislative whenever they take offense at the old one. To this I answer: Quite the contrary. People are not so easily got out of their old forms as some are apt to suggest. They are hardly to be prevailed with to amend the acknowledged faults in the frame they have been accustomed to. And if there be any original defects, or adventitious ones introduced by time or corruption, it is not an easy thing to get them changed, even when all the world sees there is an opportunity for it. This slowness and aversion in the people to quit their old constitutions has, in the many revolutions which have been seen in this kingdom, in this and former ages still kept us to, or after some interval of fruitless attempts still brought us back again to, our old legislative of kings, Lords, and Commons. And whatever provocations have made the crown be taken from some of

our princes' heads, they never carried the people so far as to place it in another line.

224. But it will be said, this hypothesis lays a ferment for frequent rebellion. To which I answer:

First, no more than any other hypothesis. For when the people are made miserable, and find themselves exposed to the ill-usage of arbitrary power, cry up their governors as much as you will for sons of Jupiter, let them be sacred and divine, descended, or authorized from heaven, give them out for whom or what you please, the same will happen. The people generally ill-treated, and contrary to right, will be ready upon any occasion to ease themselves of a burden that sits heavy upon them. They will wish and seek for the opportunity, which in the change, weakness, and accidents of human affairs seldom delays long to offer itself. He must have lived but a little while in the world who has not seen examples of this in his time, and he must have read very little who cannot produce examples of it in all sorts of governments in the world.

225. Secondly, I answer, such revolutions happen not upon every little mismanagement in public affairs. Great mistakes in the ruling part, many wrong and inconvenient laws, and all the slips of human frailty will be borne by the people without mutiny or murmur. But if a long train of abuses, prevarications and artifices, all tending the same way, make the design visible to the people—and they cannot but feel what they lie under, and see whither they are going—it is not to be wondered that they should then rouse themselves and endeavor to put the rule into such hands which may secure to them the ends for which government was at first erected, and without which ancient names and specious forms are so far from being better that they are much worse than the state of nature or pure anarchy; the inconveniences being all as great and as near, but the remedy farther

off and more difficult.

226. Thirdly, I answer that this power in the people of providing for their safety anew by a new legislative when their legislators have acted contrary to their trust by invading their property, is the best fence against rebellion, and the probablest means to hinder it. For rebellion being an opposition, not to persons, but authority, which is founded only in the constitutions and laws of the government, those whoever they be who by force break through, and by force justify their violation of them, are truly and properly rebels. For when men by entering into society and civil government have excluded force, and introduced laws for the preservation of property, peace, and unity amongst themselves, those who set up force again in opposition to the laws do *rebellare*[24]—that is, bring back again the state of war—and are properly rebels; which they who are in power (by the pretense they have to authority, the temptation of force they have in their hands, and the flattery of those about them) being likeliest to do, the properest way to prevent the evil is to show them the danger and injustice of it who are under the greatest temptation to run into it.

227. In both the forementioned cases, when either the legislative is changed or the legislators act contrary to the end for which they were constituted, those who are guilty are guilty of rebellion. For if anyone by force takes away the established legislative of any society, and the laws by them made pursuant to their trust, he thereby takes away the umpirage which everyone had consented to for a peaceable decision of all their controversies, and a bar to the state of war amongst them. They who remove or change the legislative, take away this decisive power, which nobody can have but by the appointment and consent of

24. There is a play here upon the literal meaning of *rebello*—"to wage war again," as well as "to rebel."

the people, and so destroying the authority which the people did, and nobody else can, set up; and introducing a power which the people hath not authorized, actually introduce a state of war which is that of force without authority. And thus by removing the legislative established by the society (in whose decisions the people acquiesced and united as to that of their own will), they untie the knot and expose the people anew to the state of war. And if those who by force take away the legislative are rebels, the legislators themselves, as has been shown, can be no less esteemed so, when they who were set up for the protection and preservation of the people, their liberties and properties, shall by force invade and endeavor to take them away; and so they, putting themselves into a state of war with those who made them the protectors and guardians of their peace, are properly and with the greatest aggravation *rebellantes* (rebels).

228. But if they who say it lays a foundation for rebellion mean that it may occasion civil wars or intestine broils, to tell the people they are absolved from obedience when illegal attempts are made upon their liberties or properties, and may oppose the unlawful violence of those who were their magistrates when they invade their properties contrary to the trust put in them and that therefore this doctrine is not to be allowed, being so destructive to the peace of the world: they may as well say upon the same ground that honest men may not oppose robbers or pirates because this may occasion disorder or bloodshed. If any mischief come in such cases, it is not to be charged upon him who defends his own right, but on him that invades his neighbor's. If the innocent honest man must quietly quit all he has for peace's sake to him who will lay violent hands upon it, I desire it may be considered what a kind of peace there will be in the world which consists only in violence and rapine, and which is to be maintained only for the benefit of robbers and oppressors. Who would not think it an admirable peace betwixt the mighty and the mean when the lamb without resistance yielded his throat to be torn by the imperious wolf? Polyphemus's den[25] gives us a perfect pattern of such a peace and such a government, wherein Ulysses and his companions had nothing to do but quietly to suffer themselves to be devoured. And no doubt Ulysses, who was a prudent man, preached up passive obedience, and exhorted them to a quiet submission by representing to them of what concernment peace was to mankind, and by showing the inconveniences which might happen if they should offer to resist Polyphemus, who had now the power over them.

229. The end of government is the good of mankind, and which is best for mankind, that the people should be always exposed to the boundless will of tyranny, or that the rulers should be sometimes liable to be opposed when they grow exorbitant in the use of their power, and employ it for the destruction and not the preservation of the properties of their people?

230. Nor let anyone say that mischief can arise from hence as often as it shall please a busy head or turbulent spirit to desire the alteration of the government. It is true such men may stir whenever they please, but it will be only to their own just ruin and perdition. For till the mischief be grown general, and the ill designs of the rulers become visible, or their attempts sensible to the greater part, the people, who are more disposed to suffer than right themselves by resistance, are not apt to stir. The examples of particular injustice or oppression of here and there an unfortunate man moves them not. But if they universally have a

25. Polyphemus was the Cyclops who shut up Ulysses with twelve comrades in his cave. Ulysses (Gk., Odysseus) was the king of Ithaca whose voyages constitute the theme of the *Odyssey*.

persuasion grounded upon manifest evidence that designs are carrying on against their liberties, and the general course and tendency of things cannot but give them strong suspicions of the evil intention of their governors, who is to be blamed for it? Who can help it, if they, who might avoid it, bring themselves into this suspicion? Are the people to be blamed if they have the sense of rational creatures, and can think of things no otherwise than as they find and feel them? And is it not rather their fault who put things in such a posture that they would not have them thought as they are? I grant that the pride, ambition, and turbulency of private men have sometimes caused great disorders in commonwealths, and factions have been fatal to states and kingdoms. But whether the mischief hath oftener begun in the people's wantonness, and a desire to cast off the lawful authority of their rulers, or in the rulers' insolence and endeavors to get and exercise an arbitrary power over their people, whether oppression or disobedience gave the first rise to the disorder, I leave it to impartial history to determine. This I am sure, whoever, either ruler or subject, by force goes about to invade the rights of either prince or people, and lays the foundation for overturning the constitution and frame of any just government, he is guilty of the greatest crime I think a man is capable of, being to answer for all those mischiefs of blood, rapine, and desolation, which the breaking to pieces of governments bring on a country; and he who does it is justly to be esteemed the common enemy and pest of mankind, and is to be treated accordingly.

231. That subjects or foreigners attempting by force on the properties of any people may be resisted with force is agreed on all hands; but that magistrates doing the same thing may be resisted, hath of late been denied; as if those who had the greatest privileges and advantages by the law had thereby a power to break those laws by which alone they were set in a better place than their brethren; whereas their offense is thereby the greater, both as being ungrateful for the greater share they have by the law, and breaking also that trust which is put into their hands by their brethren.

232. Whosoever uses force without right—as everyone does in society who does it without law—puts himself into a state of war with those against whom he so uses it, and in that state all former ties are canceled, all other rights cease, and everyone has a right to defend himself, and to resist the aggressor. This is so evident that Barclay himself[26]—that great asserter of the power and sacredness of kings—is forced to confess that it is lawful for the people, in some cases, to resist their king, and that, too, in a chapter wherein he pretends to show that the Divine law shuts up the people from all manner of rebellion. Whereby it is evident, even by his own doctrine, that since they may, in some cases, resist, all resisting of princes is not rebellion. His words are these:[27]

233. "But if anyone should ask: Must the people, then, always lay themselves open to the cruelty and rage of tyranny—must they see their cities pillaged and laid in ashes, their wives and children exposed to the tyrant's lust and fury, and themselves and families reduced by their king to ruin and all the miseries of want and oppression, and yet sit still—must men alone be debarred the common privilege of opposing force with force, which nature allows so freely to all other creatures for their preservation from injury? I answer: Self-defense is a part of the law of nature; nor can it be denied the community, even against the king himself; but to revenge themselves upon him must, by no means, be allowed them,

26. William Barclay (1546–1608), Scottish jurist who defended the rights of kings against the temporal powers of the popes.
27. Here and later in this chapter the original Latin text given by Locke is omitted.

it being not agreeable to that law. Wherefore, if the king shall show a hatred, not only to some particular persons, but sets himself against the body of the commonwealth, whereof he is the head, and shall, with intolerable ill usage, cruelly tyrannize over the whole, or a considerable part of the people; in this case the people have a right to resist and defend themselves from injury; but it must be with this caution, that they only defend themselves, but do not attack their prince. They may repair the damages received, but must not, for any provocation, exceed the bounds of due reverence and respect. They may repulse the present attempt, but must not revenge past violences. For it is natural for us to defend life and limb, but that an inferior should punish a superior is against nature. The mischief which is designed them the people may prevent before it be done, but, when it is done, they must not revenge it on the king, though author of the villainy. This, therefore, is the privilege of the people in general above what any private person hath: That particular men are allowed, by our adversaries themselves (Buchanan only excepted), to have no other remedy but patience; but the body of the people may, with respect, resist intolerable tyranny, for when it is but moderate they ought to endure it."

234. Thus far that great advocate of monarchical power allows of resistance.

235. It is true, he has annexed two limitations to it, to no purpose:

First, he says it must be with reverence.

Secondly, it must be without retribution or punishment; and the reason he gives is, "because an inferior cannot punish a superior."

236. First, how to resist force without striking again, or how to strike with reverence, will need some skill to make intelligible. He that shall oppose an assault only with a shield to receive the blows, or in any more respectful posture, without a sword in his hand to abate the confidence and force of the assailant, will quickly be at an end of his resistance, and will find such a defense serve only to draw on himself the worse usage. This is as ridiculous a way of resisting as Juvenal thought it of fighting: *Ubi tu pulsas, ego vapulo tantum.*[28] And the success of the combat will be unavoidably the same he there describes it:

Libertas pauperis haec est:
Pulsatus, rogat, et pugnis concisus, adorat,
Ut liceat paucis cum dentibus inde reverti.[29]

This will always be the event of such an imaginary resistance, where men may not strike again. He, therefore, who may resist must be allowed to strike. And then let our author, or anybody else, join a knock on the head or a cut on the face with as much reverence and respect as he thinks fit. He that can reconcile blows and reverence may, for aught I know, deserve for his pains a civil, respectful cudgeling wherever he can meet with it.

Secondly, as to this second—"An inferior cannot punish a superior"—that is true, generally speaking, whilst he is his superior. But to resist force with force, being the state of war that levels the parties, cancels all former relation of reverence, respect, and superiority; and then the odds that remains is—that he who opposes the unjust aggressor has this superiority over him, that he has a right, when he prevails, to punish the offender, both for the breach of the peace and all the evils that followed upon it. Barclay, therefore, in another place, more coherently to himself, denies it to be lawful to resist a king in any case. But he there assigns two cases whereby a king may unking himself. His words are:

28. "He does all the beating, and I am only beaten" (Evans translation).

29. "This is a poor man's liberty! When thrashed he humbly begs, and pummelled with fistycuffs, supplicates to be allowed to quit the spot with a few teeth left in his head" (Evans translation).

237. "What, then, can there no case happen wherein the people may of right, and by their own authority, help themselves, take arms, and set upon their king, imperiously domineering over them? None at all whilst he remains a king. 'Honor the king,' and 'he that resists the power, resists the ordinance of God,' are divine oracles that will never permit it. The people, therefore, can never come by a power over him unless he does something that makes him cease to be a king; for then he divests himself of his crown and dignity, and returns to the state of a private man, and the people become free and superior; the power which they had in the interregnum, before they crowned him king, devolving to them again. But there are but few miscarriages which bring the matter to this state. After considering it well on all sides, I can find but two. Two cases there are, I say, whereby a king, *ipso facto*, becomes no king, and loses all power and regal authority over his people, which are also taken notice of by Winzerus.[30] The first is, if he endeavor to overturn the government—that is, if he have a purpose and design to ruin the kingdom and commonwealth, as it is recorded of Nero that he resolved to cut off the senate and people of Rome, lay the city waste with fire and sword, and then remove to some other place; and of Caligula, that he openly declared that he would be no longer a head to the people or senate, and that he had it in his thoughts to cut off the worthiest men of both ranks, and then retire to Alexandria; and he wished that the people had but one neck that he might dispatch them all at a blow. Such designs as these, when any king harbors in his thoughts, and seriously promotes, he immediately gives up all care and thought of the commonwealth,

30. Probably Ninian Winzet (1518–92), a Scottish priest who wrote a number of tracts including *The Buke of Four Scoir Thre Questions* (1563), which treated of church doctrine, sacraments, obedience to rulers, and other matters.

and, consequently, forfeits the power of governing his subjects, as a master does the dominion over his slaves whom he hath abandoned.

238. "The other case is, when a king makes himself the dependent of another, and subjects his kingdom, which his ancestors left him, and the people put free into his hands, to the dominion of another. For however, perhaps, it may not be his intention to prejudice the people, yet because he has hereby lost the principal part of regal dignity—viz., to be next and immediately under God, supreme in his kingdom; and also because he betrayed or forced his people, whose liberty he ought to have carefully preserved, into the power and dominion of a foreign nation. By this, as it were, alienation of his kingdom, he himself loses the power he had in it before, without transferring any the least right to those on whom he would have bestowed it; and so by this act sets the people free, and leaves them at their own disposal. One example of this is to be found in the Scotch annals."

239. In these cases Barclay, the great champion of absolute monarchy, is forced to allow that a king may be resisted, and ceases to be a king. That is, in short, not to multiply cases! In whatsoever he has no authority, there he is no king, and may be resisted: for wheresoever the authority ceases, the king ceases too, and becomes like other men who have no authority. And these two cases that he instances differ little from those above mentioned, to be destructive to governments, only that he has omitted the principle from which his doctrine flows, and that is the breach of trust in not preserving the form of government agreed on, and in not intending the end of government itself, which is the public good and preservation of property. When a king has dethroned himself, and put himself in a state of war with his people, what shall hinder them from prosecuting him who is no king, as they

would any other man, who has put himself into a state of war with them, Barclay, and those of his opinion, would do well to tell us. Bilson,[31] a bishop of our church, and a great stickler for the power and prerogative of princes, does, if I mistake not, in his treatise of "Christian Subjection," acknowledge that princes may forfeit their power and their title to the obedience of their subjects; and if there needed authority in a case where reason is so plain, I could send my reader to Bracton,[32] Fortescue,[33] and the author of the "Mirror,"[34] and others, writers that cannot be suspected to be ignorant of our government, or enemies to it. But I thought Hooker alone might be enough to satisfy those men who, relying on him for their ecclesiastical polity, are by a strange fate carried to deny those principles upon which he builds it. Whether they are herein made the tools of cunninger workmen, to pull down their own fabric, they were best look. This I am sure, their civil policy is so new, so dangerous, and so destructive to both rulers and people, that as former ages never could bear the broaching of it, so it may be hoped those to come, redeemed from the impositions of these Egyptian under-taskmasters, will abhor the memory of such servile flatterers,

31. Thomas Bilson (1546/1547–1616), bishop of Winchester; author of the *True Difference between Christian Subjection and Unchristian Rebellion* (Oxford, 1585). This argument in defense of the Church of England against the Catholics allowed liberty for the subjects to cast off their obedience. Although it was written to uphold the authority of the Tudor Elizabeth, it was later used against the Stuart kings.
32. Henry de Bracton (d. 1268), author of the leading medieval treatise on the laws of England, *De legibus et consuetudinibus Angliae*.
33. Probably Sir John Fortescue (1394?–1476?), English jurist and political theorist who wrote on the laws and government of England.
34. Probably the *Mirror of Justices*, a treatise on the English law, written anonymously but attributed to Andrew Horne, who died in 1328. It has been reissued under the editorship of Sir Henry Maitland.

who, whilst it seemed to serve their turn, resolved all government into absolute tyranny, and would have all men born to what their mean souls fitted them—slavery.

240. Here, it is likely, the common question will be made: Who shall be judge whether the prince or legislative act contrary to their trust? This, perhaps, ill-affected and factious men may spread amongst the people when the prince only makes use of his due prerogative. To this I reply: The people shall be judge; for who shall be judge whether the trustee or deputy acts well and according to the trust reposed in him, but he who deputes him, and must, by having deputed him, have still the power to discard him when he fails in his trust? If this be reasonable in particular cases of private men, why should it be otherwise in that of the greatest moment, where the welfare of millions is concerned, and also where the evil, if not prevented, is greater, and the redress very difficult, dear, and dangerous?

241. But farther, this question, who shall be judge, cannot mean that there is no judge at all; for where there is no judicature on earth to decide controversies amongst men, God in heaven is Judge. He alone, it is true, is Judge of the right; but every man is judge for himself, as in all other cases, so in this, whether another hath put himself into a state of war with him, and whether he should appeal to the Supreme Judge as Jephtha did.

242. If a controversy arise betwixt a prince and some of the people in a matter where the law is silent or doubtful, and the thing be of great consequence, I should think the proper umpire in such a case should be the body of the people; for in cases where the prince hath a trust reposed in him, and is dispensed from the common ordinary rules of the law; there, if any men find themselves aggrieved, and think the prince acts contrary to or beyond that trust, who so proper to

judge as the body of the people (who at first lodged that trust in him) how far they meant it should extend? But if the prince or whoever they be in the administration decline that way of determination, the appeal then lies nowhere but to heaven; force between either persons who have no known superior on earth, or which permits no appeal to a judge on earth, being properly a state of war, wherein the appeal lies only to heaven, and in that state the injured party must judge for himself when he will think fit to make use of that appeal and put himself upon it.

243. To conclude: The power that every individual gave the society when he entered into it, can never revert to the individuals again as long as the society lasts, but will always remain in the community, because without this there can be no community, no commonwealth, which is contrary to the original agreement; so also when the society hath placed the legislative in any assembly of men to continue in them and their successors, with direction and authority for providing such successors, the legislative can never revert to the people whilst that government lasts, because having provided a legislative with power to continue forever, they have given up their political power to the legislative and cannot resume it. But if they have set limits to the duration of their legislative, and made this supreme power in any person or assembly only temporary; or else when by the miscarriages of those in authority it is forfeited; upon the forfeiture, or at the determination of the time set, it reverts to the society, and the people have a right to act as supreme, and continue the legislative in themselves; or place it in a new form, or new hands as they think good.

5. ON TOLERATION[1]

By JOHN LOCKE

EDITORS' NOTE.—As early as 1666 Locke wrote in his commonplace book an "Essay on Toleration." He wrote and extended this work in a letter of 1685 which was published, first in Latin and later in English, in 1689. He wrote two other letters on the same subject in 1690 and 1692 and was writing a fourth when he died. The parts of his work printed here are from the first letter and contain his most important arguments for toleration.

The toleration of those that differ from others in matters of religion is so agreeable to the Gospel of Jesus Christ, and to the genuine reason of mankind, that it seems monstrous for men to be so blind as not to perceive the necessity and advantage of it in so clear a light. I will not here tax the pride and ambition of some, the passion and uncharitable zeal of others. These are faults from which

1. John Locke, *Treatise of Civil Government and a Letter concerning Toleration*, ed. Charles L. Sherman (New York, 1937), pp. 171–76, 179–81, 186, 192–93, 197–98, 204–6, 210–13, 220–21.

human affairs can perhaps scarce ever be perfectly freed; but yet such as nobody will bear the plain imputation of, without covering them with some specious color; and so pretend to commendation, whilst they are carried away by their own irregular passions. But, however, that some may not color their spirit of persecution and unchristian cruelty with a pretense of care of the public weal and observation of the laws; and that others, under pretense of religion, may not seek impunity for their libertinism and licentiousness; in a word, that none may impose either upon himself or others, by the pretenses of loyalty and obedience to the prince, or of tenderness and sincerity in the worship of God; I esteem it above all things necessary to distinguish exactly the business of civil government from that of religion, and to settle the just bounds that lie between the one and the other. If this be not done, there can be no end put to the controversies that will be always arising between those that have, or at least pretend to have, on the one side, a concernment for the interests of men's souls, and, on the other side, a care of the commonwealth.

The commonwealth seems to me to be a society of men constituted only for the procuring, preserving, and advancing their own civil interests.

Civil interests I call life, liberty, health, and indolency of body; and the possession of outward things, such as money, lands, houses, furniture, and the like. . . .

Now that the whole jurisdiction of the magistrate reaches only to these civil concernments, and that all civil power, right and dominion, is bounded and confined to the only care of promoting these things; and that it neither can nor ought in any manner to be extended to the salvation of souls, these following considerations seem unto me abundantly to demonstrate.

First, because the care of souls is not committed to the civil magistrate, any more than to other men. It is not committed unto him, I say, by God; because it appears not that God has ever given any such authority to one man over another, as to compel anyone to his religion. Nor can any such power be vested in the magistrate by the consent of the people, because no man can so far abandon the care of his own salvation as blindly to leave to the choice of any other, whether prince or subject, to prescribe to him what faith or worship he shall embrace. For no man can, if he would, conform his faith to the dictates of another. All the

life and power of true religion consist in the inward and full persuasion of the mind; and faith is not faith without believing. Whatever profession we make, to whatever outward worship we conform, if we are not fully satisfied in our own mind that the one is true, and the other well pleasing unto God, such profession and such practice, far from being any furtherance, are indeed great obstacles to our salvation. For in this manner, instead of expiating other sins by the exercise of religion, I say, in offering thus unto God Almighty such a worship as we esteem to be displeasing unto Him, we add unto the number of our other sins those also of hypocrisy, and contempt of His Divine Majesty.

In the second place, the care of souls cannot belong to the civil magistrate, because his power consists only in outward force; but true and saving religion consists in the inward persuasion of the mind, without which nothing can be acceptable to God. And such is the nature of the understanding that it cannot be compelled to the belief of anything by outward force. Confiscation of estate, imprisonment, torments, nothing of that nature can have any such efficacy as to make men change the inward judgment that they have framed of things. . . .

In the third place, the care of the salvation of men's souls cannot belong to the magistrate, because, though the rigor of laws and the force of penalties were capable to convince and change men's minds, yet would not that help at all to the salvation of their souls. For there being but one truth, one way to heaven, what hope is there that more men would be led into it if they had no rule but the religion of the court, and were put under the necessity to quit the light of their own reason, and oppose the dictates of their own consciences, and blindly to resign themselves up to the will of their governors, and to the religion which either ignorance, ambition, or superstition had chanced to establish in the countries where they were born? In the variety and contradiction of opinions in religion, wherein the princes of the world are as much divided as in their secular interests, the narrow way would be much straitened; one country alone would be in the right, and all the rest of the world put under an obligation of following their princes in the ways that lead to destruction; and that which heightens the absurdity, and very ill suits the notion of a Deity, men would owe their eternal happiness or misery to the places of their nativity....

Let us now consider what a church is. A church, then, I take to be a voluntary society of men, joining themselves together of their own accord in order to the public worshiping of God in such manner as they judge acceptable to Him, and effectual to the salvation of their souls.

I say it is a free and voluntary society. Nobody is born a member of any church; otherwise the religion of parents would descend unto children by the same right of inheritance as their temporal estates, and everyone would hold his faith by the same tenure he does his lands, than which nothing can be imagined more absurd. Thus, therefore, that matter stands. No man by nature is bound unto any particular church or sect, but everyone joins himself voluntarily to that society in which he believes he has found that profession and worship which is truly acceptable to God. The hope of salvation, as it was the only cause of his entrance into that communion, so it can be the only reason of his stay there. For if afterward he discover anything either erroneous in the doctrine or incongruous in the worship of that society to which he has joined himself, why should it not be as free for him to go out as it was to enter? No member of a religious society can be tied with any other bonds but what proceed from the certain expectation of eternal life. A church,

then, is a society of members voluntarily uniting to that end....

These things being thus determined, let us inquire, in the next place: How far the duty of toleration extends, and what is required from everyone by it?

And, first, I hold that no church is bound, by the duty of toleration, to retain any such person in her bosom as, after admonition, continues obstinately to offend against the laws of the society. For these being the condition of communion and the bond of the society, if the breach of them were permitted without any animadversion, the society would immediately be thereby dissolved. But, nevertheless, in all such cases care is to be taken that the sentence of excommunication, and the execution thereof, carry with it no rough usage of word or action whereby the ejected person may any wise be damnified in body or estate. For all force (as has often been said) belongs only to the magistrate, nor ought any private persons at any time to use force, unless it be in self-defense against unjust violence. Excommunication neither does, nor can, deprive the excommunicated person of any of those civil goods that he formerly possessed. All those things belong to the civil government, and are under the magistrate's protection. The whole force of excommunication consists only in this: that the resolution of the society in that respect being declared, the union that was between the body and some member comes thereby to be dissolved; and that relation ceasing, the participation of some certain things which the society communicated to its members, and unto which no man has any civil right, comes also to cease. For there is no civil injury done unto the excommunicated person by the church minister's refusing him that bread and wine, in the celebration of the Lord's Supper, which was not bought with his but other men's money.

Secondly, no private person has any right in any manner to prejudice another person in his civil enjoyments because he is of another church or religion. All the rights and franchises that belong to him as a man, or as a denizen, are inviolably to be preserved to him. These are not the business of religion. No violence nor injury is to be offered him, whether he be Christian or pagan. . . .

What I say concerning the mutual toleration of private persons differing from one another in religion, I understand also of particular churches which stand, as it were, in the same relation to each other as private persons among themselves: nor has any one of them any manner of jurisdiction over any other; no, not even when the civil magistrate (as it sometimes happens) comes to be of this or the other communion. For the civil government can give no new right to the church, nor the church to the civil government. So that whether the magistrate join himself to any church, or separate from it, the church remains always as it was before—a free and voluntary society. It neither requires the power of the sword by the magistrate's coming to it, nor does it lose the right of instruction and excommunication by his going from it. This is the fundamental and immutable right of a spontaneous society—that it has power to remove any of its members who transgress the rules of its institution; but it cannot, by the accession of any new members, acquire any right of jurisdiction over those that are not joined with it. And therefore peace, equity, and friendship are always mutually to be observed by particular churches, in the same manner as by private persons, without any pretense of superiority or jurisdiction over one another. . . .

In the last place, let us now consider what is the magistrate's duty in the business of toleration, which certainly is very considerable. . . .

. . . Although the magistrate's opinion in religion be sound, and the way that he appoints be truly evangelical, yet, if I be not thoroughly persuaded thereof

in my own mind, there will be no safety for me in following it. No way whatsoever that I shall walk in against the dictates of my conscience will ever bring me to the mansions of the blessed. I may grow rich by an art that I take not delight in, I may be cured of some disease by remedies that I have not faith in; but I cannot be saved by a religion that I distrust, and by a worship that I abhor. It is in vain for an unbeliever to take up the outward show of another man's profession. Faith only and inward sincerity are the things that procure acceptance with God. The most likely and most approved remedy can have no effect upon the patient if his stomach reject it as soon as taken; and you will in vain cram a medicine down a sick man's throat which his particular constitution will be sure to turn into poison. In a word, whatsoever may be doubtful in religion, yet this at least is certain, that no religion which I believe not to be true can be either true or profitable unto me. In vain, therefore, do princes compel their subjects to come into their church communion, under pretense of saving their souls. If they believe, they will come of their own accord; if they believe not, their coming will nothing avail them. How great soever, in fine, may be the pretense of good will and charity, and concern for the salvation of men's souls, men cannot be forced to be saved whether they will or no. And therefore, when all is done, they must be left to their own consciences.

Having thus at length freed men from all dominion over one another in matters of religion, let us now consider what they are to do. All men know and acknowledge that God ought to be publicly worshiped; why otherwise do they compel one another unto the public assemblies? Men, therefore, constituted in this liberty are to enter into some religious society, that they meet together, not only for mutual edification, but to own to the world that they worship God, and offer unto His Divine Majesty such service as they themselves are not ashamed of, and such as they think not unworthy of Him, nor unacceptable to Him; and finally, that by the purity of doctrine, holiness of life, and decent form of worship, they may draw others unto the love of the true religion, and perform such other things in religion as cannot be done by each private man apart.

These religious societies I call churches; and these, I say, the magistrate ought to tolerate, for the business of these assemblies of the people is nothing but what is lawful for every man in particular to take care of—I mean the salvation of their souls; nor in this case is there any difference between the national church and other separated congregations.

But as in every church there are two things especially to be considered—the outward form and rites of worship, and the doctrines and articles of faith—these things must be handled each distinctly, that so the whole matter of toleration may the more clearly be understood.

Concerning outward worship, I say, in the first place, that the magistrate has no power to enforce by law, either in his own church, or much less in another, the use of any rites or ceremonies whatsoever in the worship of God. And this, not only because these churches are free societies, but because whatsoever is practiced in the worship of God is only so far justifiable as it is believed by those that practice it to be acceptable unto Him. . . .

In the next place: As the magistrate has no power to impose by his laws the use of any rites and ceremonies in any church, so neither has he any power to forbid the use of such rites and ceremonies as are already received, approved, and practiced by any church; because, if he did so, he would destroy the church itself, the end of whose institution is only

to worship God with freedom after its own manner. . . .

Thus far concerning outward worship. Let us now consider articles of faith.

The articles of religion are some of them practical and some speculative. Now, though both sorts consist in the knowledge of truth, yet these terminate simply in the understanding, those influence the will and manners. Speculative opinions, therefore, and articles of faith (as they are called) which are required only to be believed, cannot be imposed on any church by the law of the land. For it is absurd that things should be enjoined by laws which are not in men's power to perform. . . .

Further, the magistrate ought not to forbid the preaching or professing of any speculative opinions in any church, because they have no manner of relation to the civil rights of the subjects. If a Roman Catholic believe that to be really the body of Christ which another man calls bread, he does no injury thereby to his neighbor. If a Jew do not believe the New Testament to be the Word of God, he does not thereby alter anything in men's civil rights. . . .

. . . Thus much for speculative opinions. Let us now proceed to practical ones.

A good life, in which consists not the least part of religion and true piety, concerns also the civil government; and in it lies the safety both of men's souls and of the commonwealth. Moral actions belong therefore to the jurisdiction both of the outward and inward court; both of the civil and domestic governor; I mean both of the magistrate and conscience. Here, therefore, is great danger, lest one of these jurisdictions intrench upon the other, and discord arise between the keeper of the public peace and the overseers of souls. But if what has been already said concerning the limits of both these governments be rightly considered, it will easily remove all difficulty in this matter. . . .

. . . To come to particulars. I say, first, no opinions contrary to human society, or to those moral rules which are necessary to the preservation of civil society, are to be tolerated by the magistrate. But of these, indeed, examples in any church are rare. For no sect can easily arrive to such a degree of madness as that it should think fit to teach, for doctrines of religion, such things as manifestly undermine the foundations of society, and are, therefore, condemned by the judgment of all mankind; because their own interest, peace, reputation, everything would be thereby endangered.

Another more secret evil, but more dangerous to the commonwealth, is when men arrogate to themselves, and to those of their own sect, some peculiar prerogative covered over with a specious show of deceitful words, but in effect opposite to the civil right of the community. For example, we cannot find any sect that teaches, expressly and openly, that men are not obliged to keep their promise; that princes may be dethroned by those that differ from them in religion; or that the dominion of all things belongs only to themselves. . . . But, nevertheless, we find those that say the same things in other words. What else do they mean, who teach that faith is not to be kept with heretics? Their meaning, forsooth, is that the privilege of breaking faith belongs unto themselves; for they declare all that are not of their communion to be heretics, or at least may declare them so whensoever they think fit. What can be the meaning of their asserting that kings excommunicated forfeit their crowns and kingdoms? It is evident that they thereby arrogate unto themselves the power of deposing kings, because they challenge the power of excommunication, as the peculiar right of their hierarchy. That dominion is founded in grace is also an assertion by which those that maintain it do plainly

lay claim to the possession of all things. For they are not so wanting to themselves as not to believe, or at least as not to profess themselves to be the truly pious and faithful. These therefore, and the like, who attribute unto the faithful, religious, and orthodox, that is, in plain terms, unto themselves, any peculiar privilege or power above other mortals, in civil concernments; or who upon pretense of religion do challenge any manner of authority over such as are not associated with them in their ecclesiastical communion, I say these have no right to be tolerated by the magistrate; as neither those that will not own and teach the duty of tolerating all men in matters of mere religion. For what do all these and the like doctrines signify but that they may, and are ready upon any occasion to seize the government, and possess themselves of the estates and fortunes of their fellow-subjects; and that they only ask leave to be tolerated by the magistrate so long until they find themselves strong enough to effect it?

Again, that church can have no right to be tolerated by the magistrate which is constituted upon such a bottom that all those who enter into it do thereby *ipso facto* deliver themselves up to the protection and service of another prince. For by this means the magistrate would give way to the settling of a foreign jurisdiction in his own country, and suffer his own people to be listed, as it were, for soldiers against his own government. . . .

Lastly, those are not at all to be tolerated who deny the being of a God. Promises, covenants, and oaths, which are the bonds of human society, can have no hold upon an atheist. The taking-away of God, though but even in thought, dissolves all; besides also, those that by their atheism undermine and destroy all religion, can have no pretense of religion whereupon to challenge the privilege of a toleration. As for other practical opinions, though not absolutely free from all error, if they do not tend to establish domination over others, or civil impunity to the Church in which they are taught, there can be no reason why they should not be tolerated.

It remains that I say something concerning those assemblies which being vulgarly called, and perhaps having sometimes been conventicles and nurseries of factions and seditions, are thought to afford the strongest matter of objection against this doctrine of toleration. But this has not happened by anything peculiar unto the genius of such assemblies, but by the unhappy circumstances of an oppressed or ill-settled liberty. These accusations would soon cease if the law of toleration were once so settled that all churches were obliged to lay down toleration as the foundation of their own liberty, and teach that liberty of conscience is every man's natural right, equally belonging to dissenters as to themselves; and that nobody ought to be compelled in matters of religion either by law or force. The establishment of this one thing would take away

all ground of complaints and tumults upon account of conscience; and these causes of discontents and animosities being once removed, there would remain nothing in these assemblies that were not more peaceable and less apt to produce disturbance of state than in any other meetings whatsoever. . . .

God Almighty grant, I beseech Him, that the gospel of peace may at length be preached, and that civil magistrates, growing more careful to conform their own consciences to the law of God and less solicitous about the binding of other men's consciences by human laws, may, like fathers of their country, direct all their counsels and endeavors to promote universally the civil welfare of all their children, except only of such as are arrogant, ungovernable, and injurious to their brethren; and that all ecclesiastical men, who boast themselves to be the successors of the Apostles, walking peaceably and modestly in the Apostles' steps, without intermeddling with state affairs, may apply themselves wholly to promote the salvation of souls.

UNIT II

THE AMERICAN REVOLUTION

WHEN Britain decided, in the aftermath of the Seven Years' War to make the colonies contribute to the cost of imperial defense, it embarked upon a course of action which eventually led Americans to raise all the fundamental questions of government. The agitation began with such specific questions as the right of the mother-country to tax a colony, but it developed into an unrestricted inquiry into the nature of political authority and the rights of those who lived under it. It is important to realize that such a debate involved more than an argument between the colonies and Britain about the constitution of the empire. It also involved a conflict within the colonies, foreshadowed by many earlier struggles between different groups and regions, over the distribution of power and privilege. For this reason "The American Revolution" must be considered in a dual character, as embracing both a struggle for independence and a contest for more democratic institutions.

In the first part of this unit, attention is concentrated on the development of the conflict with Britain, which culminated in the Declaration of Independence. As an illustration of the struggles for local democracy, which became entangled in the imperial quarrel, we have included a petition by the Regulators of North Carolina. These back-country settlers protested in 1769 against the mistreatment which they suffered at the hands of their own ruling class. Their grievances included the familiar ones of overtaxation and underrepresentation. In this particular instance the dissatisfaction led to a revolt, which was suppressed by force, and many of the Regulators subsequently fought on the Loyalist side. Elsewhere, however, the democratic discontent, of which this movement was one symptom, became a powerful element in the agitation against British rule.

The Declaration of Independence meant that British authority, at both the general and the state level, would have to be replaced by American institutions. In the next unit we shall be considering the Articles of Confederation and the Constitution of the United States as attempts to solve the "federal" problem. The second section of this unit deals with some of the problems involved in the organization of state constitutions. Certain basic questions about the nature of republican institutions were common to both areas of government. It will be obvious from the title of this second section—"Democracy and Aristocracy in the New Republics"—that the issues which are discussed here in connection with state constitutions will appear again at the federal level.

THE REVOLUTIONARY DEBATE

The extent to which the British system of commercial regulation was a contributory factor to the American Revolution has been the subject of much controversy among historians. Adam Smith, author of the *Wealth of Nations*, included in that work an analysis of the effect of the system on the liberty and prosperity of the colonies. An extract is given here as a basis for discussing the mercantilist background of the Revolution.

Smith's opinions are followed by three letters written by Benjamin Franklin to Governor Shirley of Massachusetts in 1754. These refer to an abortive plan for a new imperial constitution, which was rejected at that time by both the British and the colonial governments. Franklin discusses the related problems of commercial regulation, taxation, and representation. These were issues which had to be faced again in the aftermath of the Seven Years' War by a mother-country saddled with debts and commitments and by colonists from whom the chief foreign danger had been removed.

Britain first requested the colonies, and then required them, to bear a larger share of the costs of empire. The tax imposed by the Stamp Act fell on the most articulate groups— merchants, lawyers, newspapermen, tavern-keepers, clergymen—and opinion was skilfully organized against it. The Stamp Act Congress of 1765, the first intercolonial meeting of its kind

summoned solely on colonial initiative, drew up a Declaration of Rights in which the leaders affirmed their loyalty but petitioned for the repeal of the Stamp Act on the ground that Englishmen could not be taxed without their own consent. The act was repealed, under pressure from British merchants whose American sales had fallen, but Parliament simultaneously adopted the Declaratory Act to prevent the principle of parliamentary sovereignty from being compromised by the concession. This brief but emphatic statute asserted the authority of the British Parliament to legislate for the colonies "in all cases whatsoever."

In 1767 a new British ministry revived the attempt to tax the colonies, confining themselves on this occasion to external taxation. The Townshend duties, and the enforcement measures which accompanied them, were followed by further acts of colonial resistance, in the course of which the so-called "Boston Massacre" occurred. But the agitation was less extensive than that which followed the Stamp Act, and it subsided in 1770 when the North Ministry repealed all the Townshend duties except that on tea.

The next three years were an interlude of prosperity and peace, with discontent confined to a few radicals. But when Parliament authorized the East India Company to sell its tea directly through its agents—thus setting up the eighteenth-century equivalent to the "chain store"—the radicals were joined by indignant colonial merchants in the use of intimidation and force. The Boston Tea Party led to retaliatory acts of Parliament, which in turn increased colonial opposition. Virginia legislators initiated the organization of the First Continental Congress, which met at Philadelphia in September, 1774. At first it seemed as though the conservative members might carry a plan of union within the empire similar to that proposed by Franklin twenty years earlier. Their failure enabled the radicals to organize the Declaration of Colonial Rights and an economic boycott of British goods.

It was the discussion of this declaration in London which prompted Dr. Johnson to write his pamphlet *Taxation No Tyranny*, extracts from which are inserted here as a sample of Tory opinion in Britain. Another British view of the same imperial dilemma is presented in a second selection from the *Wealth of Nations*.

For more than a year after Lexington (April 19, 1775), the American revolutionists fought for their rights, as they saw them, within the British Empire. The Declaration on Taking Up Arms, passed by the second Continental Congress in July, 1775, disclaimed any desire for independence. Many Americans were neutral. Others, especially among the privileged, preferred the distant rule of Britain to any radical change which threatened their authority on this side of the Atlantic. Jonathan Boucher represents at once this opposition to rebellion and the tradition which John Winthrop and John Cotton had expressed in an earlier period. On the other hand, *Common Sense* was published in January, 1776. Written by a recent immigrant, Thomas Paine, it acted as a powerful tonic on the minds of reluctant rebels and made more converts for independence than any other argument before the appearance of the Declaration of Independence itself.

The ideas of natural law and natural rights, half-remembered phrases of Locke, some of the ideas of the Virginia Declaration of Rights—all these and more were fused by Thomas Jefferson and his colleagues of the Second Continental Congress into that superb "expression of the American mind" which we know as the Declaration of Independence. Here the American Revolution was rationalized in universal terms. The appeal to charter rights and the rights of Englishmen was abandoned in favor of the "inalienable rights" of mankind.

DEMOCRACY AND ARISTOCRACY IN THE NEW REPUBLICS

Independence meant that each state had to adopt its own form of government and to decide how much it should differ from its government of the colonial period. To us it may seem natural that the first state constitutions took the form that they did; but to the world of that day, with its monarchical and aristocratic traditions, and its reliance on custom as a basis for authority, it was a very novel experience to embark on republican experiments.

Some decisions were made relatively simple by the general acceptance of the natural rights philosophy. Each state embodied its own "social compact" in a written constitution. Many drew up bills of rights or arranged for such guaranties by other means. Several of these features are illustrated by extracts from the Virginia Declaration of Rights of 1776. But other decisions were reached only after conflicts of opinion involving deep-seated questions of principle. Who was to have the vote? How was the electoral power to be distributed between coastal and back-country regions? Would the legislative body consist of one or two houses, and, if so, on what basis would it be elected? How would the different branches of government be organized so as to eliminate any risk of tyranny? Two of these questions are discussed by Franklin in connection with a proposed amendment of the Pennsylvania constitution. All of them are raised by Thomas Jefferson in the extracts from his famous *Notes on the State of Virginia*. These writings also include his educational plans for a self-governing society and his eloquent defense of religious liberty as a fundamental right of citizenship.

John Adams was more skeptical than Thomas Jefferson. In his *Defense of the Constitutions of Government of the United States* he disassociated himself from any uncritical worship

of democracy and substituted his own cautious creed for the glowing hopes of some of his contemporaries. This work was published in 1787. Many years later, after he and Jefferson had resumed a friendship which political life had interrupted, they entered into a correspondence which does much to clarify the meaning of the Declaration of Independence by exploring the problem of equality. The selections are focused on the discussion which developed about the differences in the abilities of human beings and the distinctions which might be drawn between natural and artificial aristocracy. Adams disliked hereditary distinctions as much as Jefferson and had no illusions about the conduct of aristocratic regimes; at the same time he had none of Jefferson's faith in the goodness and judgment of the people, and he refused to believe that differences of birth and wealth could ever be eliminated. Where Jefferson trusted the people, rightly educated, to govern themselves through a "natural aristocracy" of virtue and talent, Adams pinned his faith on safeguards which would curb both the pretensions of aristocracy and the violence of popular majorities.

SECTION A. THE REVOLUTIONARY DEBATE

1. COLONIAL POLICY AND MERCANTILISM[1]

By ADAM SMITH

EDITORS' NOTE.—Adam Smith was one of Britain's best-informed scholars on colonial policy. For details on Smith see page 348.

CHAPTER VII

OF COLONIES

PART SECOND

Causes of the Prosperity of New Colonies

The colony of a civilized nation which takes possession either of a waste country, or of one so thinly inhabited, that the natives easily give place to the new settlers advances more rapidly to wealth and greatness than any other human society.

The colonists carry out with them a knowledge of agriculture and of other useful arts, superior to what can grow up of its own accord in the course of many centuries among savage and barbarous nations. They carry out with them too the habit of subordination, some notion of the regular government which takes place in their own country, of the system of laws which supports it, and of a regular administration of justice; and they naturally establish something of the same kind in the new settlement. But among savage and barbarous nations, the natural progress of law and government is still slower than the natural progress of arts, after law and government have been so far established, as is necessary for their protection. Every colonist gets more land than he can possibly cultivate. He has no rent and scarce any

taxes to pay. No landlord shares with him in its produce, and the share of the sovereign is commonly but a trifle. He has every motive to render as great as possible a produce, which is thus to be almost entirely his own. But his land is commonly so extensive that with all his own industry, and with all the industry of other people whom he can get to employ, he can seldom make it produce the tenth part of what it is capable of producing. He is eager, therefore, to collect laborers from all quarters and to reward them with the most liberal wages. But those liberal wages, joined to the plenty and cheapness of land, soon make those laborers leave him, in order to become landlords themselves, and to reward, with equal liberality, other laborers, who soon leave them for the same reason that they left their first master. The liberal reward of labor encourages marriage. The children, during the tender years of infancy, are well fed and properly taken care of, and, when they are grown up, the value of their labor greatly overpays their maintenance. When arrived at maturity, the high price of labor and the low price of land enable them to establish themselves in the same manner as their fathers did before them.

In other countries rent and profit eat up wages, and the two superior orders of people oppress the inferior one. But in new colonies the interest of the two superior orders obliges them to treat the

1. Adam Smith, *An Enquiry into the Nature and Causes of the Wealth of Nations* (New York, 1937), pp. 531-33, 538-52, and 579-91. First published in 1776. Reprinted by permission of the Modern Library, New York.

inferior one with more generosity and humanity; at least, where that inferior one is not in a state of slavery. Waste lands of the greatest natural fertility are to be had for a trifle. The increase of revenue which the proprietor, who is always the undertaker, expects from their improvement constitutes his profit; which in these circumstances is commonly very great. But this great profit cannot be made without employing the labor of other people in clearing and cultivating the land; and the disproportion between the great extent of the land and the small number of the people, which commonly takes place in new colonies, makes it difficult for him to get this labor. He does not, therefore, dispute about wages but is willing to employ labor at any price. The high wages of labor encourage population. The cheapness and plenty of good land encourage improvement and enable the proprietor to pay those high wages. In those wages consists almost the whole price of the land; and though they are high, considered as the wages of labor, they are low, considered as the price of what is so very valuable. What encourages the progress of population and improvement encourages that of real wealth and greatness. . . .

But there are no colonies of which the progress has been more rapid than that of the English in North America.

Plenty of good land and liberty to manage their own affairs their own way seem to be the two great causes of the prosperity of all new colonies.

In the plenty of good land the English colonies of North America, though, no doubt, very abundantly provided, are, however, inferior to those of the Spaniards and Portuguese and not superior to some of those possessed by the French before the late war. But the political institutions of the English colonies have been more favorable to the improvement and cultivation of this land than those of any of the other three nations.

First, the engrossing of uncultivated land, though it has by no means been prevented altogether, has been more restrained in the English colonies than in any other. The colony law which imposes upon every proprietor the obligation of improving and cultivating, within a limited time, a certain proportion of his lands, and which, in case of failure, declares those neglected lands grantable to any other person; though it has not, perhaps, been very strictly executed, has, however, had some effect.

Secondly, in Pennsylvania there is no right of primogeniture, and lands, like movables, are divided equally among all the children of the family. In three of the provinces of New England the oldest has only a double share, as in the Mosaical law. Though in those provinces, therefore, too great a quantity of land should sometimes be engrossed by a particular individual, it is likely, in the course of a generation or two, to be sufficiently divided again. In the other English colonies, indeed, the right of primogeniture takes place, as in the law of England. But in all the English colonies the tenure of the lands, which are all held by free socage, facilitates alienation, and the grantee of any extensive tract of land generally finds it for his interest to alienate, as fast as he can, the greater part of it, reserving only a small quit-rent. . . . The plenty and cheapness of good land, it has already been observed, are the principal causes of the rapid prosperity of new colonies. The engrossing of land, in effect, destroys this plenty and cheapness. The engrossing of uncultivated land, besides, is the greatest obstruction to its improvement. But the labor that is employed in the improvement and cultivation of land affords the greatest and most valuable produce to the society. The produce of labor, in this case, pays not only its own wages, and the profit of the stock which employs it, but the rent of the land too upon which it is employed. The labor of the English colonists, therefore, being more employed in the improvement and cultivation of land, is likely to afford a greater and more valuable produce than that of any of the other three nations, which, by the engrossing of land, is more or less diverted toward other employments.

Thirdly, the labor of the English colonists is not only likely to afford a greater and more valuable produce, but, in consequence of the moderation of their taxes, a greater proportion of this produce belongs to themselves, which they may store up and employ in putting into motion a still greater quantity of labor. The English colonists have never yet contributed anything toward the defense of the mother-country or toward the support of its civil government. They themselves, on the contrary, have hitherto been defended almost entirely at the expense of the mother-country. But the expense of fleets and armies is out of all proportion greater than the necessary expense of civil government. The expense of their own civil government has always been very moderate. It has generally been confined to what was necessary for paying competent salaries to the governor, to the judges, and to some other offices of police, and for maintaining a few of the most useful public works. The expense of the civil establishment of Massachusetts Bay, before the commencement of the present disturbances, used to be but about 18,000*l.* a year. That of New Hampshire and Rhode Island 3,500*l.* each. That of Connecticut 4,000*l.* That of New York and Pennsylvania 4,500*l.* each. That of New Jersey, 1,200*l.* That of Virginia and South Carolina 8,000*l.* each. The civil establishments of Nova Scotia and Georgia are partly supported by an annual grant of Parliament. But Nova Scotia pays, besides, about 7,000*l.* a year toward the public expense of the colony; and Georgia about 2,500*l.* a year. All the different civil establishments in North America, in short, exclusive of those of Maryland and North Carolina, of which no exact account has been got, did not,

before the commencement of the present disturbances, cost the inhabitants above 64,700*l.* a year; an ever memorable example at how small an expense three millions of people may not only be governed but well governed. The most important part of the expense of government, indeed, that of defense and protection, has constantly fallen upon the mother-country. The ceremonial too of the civil government in the colonies, upon the reception of a new governor, upon the opening of a new assembly, etc., though sufficiently decent, is not accompanied with any expensive pomp or parade. Their ecclesiastical government is conducted upon a plan equally frugal. Tithes are unknown among them; and their clergy, who are far from being numerous, are maintained either by moderate stipends or by the voluntary contributions of the people. . . .

Fourthly, in the disposal of their surplus produce, or of what is over and above their own consumption, the English colonies have been more favored, and have been allowed a more extensive market, than those of any other European nation. Every European nation has endeavored more or less to monopolize to itself the commerce of its colonies and, upon that account, has prohibited the ships of foreign nations from trading to them and has prohibited them from importing European goods from any foreign nation. But the manner in which this monopoly has been exercised in different nations has been very different.

Some nations have given up the whole commerce of their colonies to an exclusive company, of whom the colonies were obliged to buy all such European goods as they wanted, and to whom they were obliged to sell the whole of their own surplus produce. It was the interest of the company, therefore, not only to sell the former as dear and to buy the latter as cheap as possible, but to buy no more of the latter, even at this low price, than what they could dispose of for a very high price in Europe. It was their interest, not only to degrade in all cases the value of the surplus produce of the colony, but in many cases to discourage and keep down the natural increase of its quantity. Of all the expedients that can well be contrived to stunt the natural growth of a new colony, that of an exclusive company is undoubtedly the most effectual. . . .

. . . Other nations, without establishing an exclusive company, have confined the whole commerce of their colonies to a particular port of the mother-country, from whence no ship was allowed to sail, but either in a fleet and at a particular season, or, if single, in consequence of a particular license, which in most cases was very well paid for. This policy opened, indeed, the trade of the colonies to all the natives of the mother-country, provided they traded from the proper port, at the proper season, and in the proper vessels. But as all the different merchants, who joined their stocks in order to fit out those licensed vessels, would find it for their interest to act in concert, the trade which was carried on in this manner would necessarily be conducted very nearly upon the same principles as that of an exclusive company. The profit of those merchants would be almost equally exorbitant and oppressive. The colonies would be ill supplied and would be obliged both to buy very dear and to sell very cheap. This, however, till within these few years, had always been the policy of Spain, and the price of all European goods, accordingly, is said to have been enormous in the Spanish West Indies. At Quito, we are told by Ulloa, a pound of iron sold for about four and six-pence, and a pound of steel for about six and nine-pence sterling. But it is chiefly in order to purchase European goods that the colonies part with their own produce. The more, therefore, they pay for the one, the less they really get for the other, and the dearness of the one is the same thing

with the cheapness of the other. . . .

Other nations leave the trade of their colonies free to all their subjects, who may carry it on from all the different ports of the mother-country, and who have occasion for no other license than the common dispatches of the custom-house. In this case the number and dispersed situation of the different traders renders it impossible for them to enter into any general combination, and their competition is sufficient to hinder them from making very exorbitant profits. Under so liberal a policy the colonies are enabled both to sell their own produce and to buy the goods of Europe at a reasonable price. But since the dissolution of the Plymouth company, when our colonies were but in their infancy, this has always been the policy of England. It has generally too been that of France and has been uniformly so since the dissolution of what, in England, is commonly called their Mississippi company. The profits of the trade, therefore, which France and England carry on with their colonies, though no doubt somewhat higher than if the competition was free to all other nations, are, however, by no means exorbitant; and the price of European goods accordingly is not extravagantly high in the greater part of the colonies of either of those nations.

In the exportation of their own surplus produce, too, it is only with regard to certain commodities that the colonies of Great Britain are confined to the market of the mother-country. These commodities, having been enumerated in the act of navigation and in some other subsequent acts, have upon that account been called *numerated commodities*. The rest are called *nonenumerated;* and may be exported directly to other countries, provided it is in British or Plantation ships, of which the owners and three-fourths of the mariners are British subjects.

Among the nonenumerated commodities are some of the most important productions of America and the West Indies: grain of all sorts, lumber, salt provisions, fish, sugar, and rum.

Grain is naturally the first and principal object of the culture of all new colonies. By allowing them a very extensive market for it, the law encourages them to extend this culture much beyond the consumption of a thinly inhabited country, and thus to provide beforehand an ample subsistence for a continually increasing population.

In a country quite covered with wood, where timber consequently is of little or no value, the expense of clearing the ground is the principal obstacle to improvement. By allowing the colonies a very extensive market for their lumber, the law endeavors to facilitate improvement by raising the price of a commodity which would otherwise be of little value, and thereby enabling them to make some profit of what would otherwise be mere expense.

In a country neither half-peopled nor half-cultivated, cattle naturally multiply beyond the consumption of the inhabitants and are often upon that account of little or no value. But it is necessary, it has already been shown, that the price of cattle should bear a certain proportion to that of corn before the greater part of the lands of any country can be improved. By allowing to American cattle, in all shapes, dead and alive, a very extensive market, the law endeavors to raise the value of a commodity of which the high price is so very essential to improvement. The good effects of this liberty, however, must be somewhat diminished by the 4th of George III, c. 15, which puts hides and skins among the enumerated commodities and thereby tends to reduce the value of American cattle.

To increase the shipping and naval power of Great Britain, by the extension of the fisheries of our colonies, is an object which the legislature seems to have had almost constantly in view. Those fisheries, upon this account, have had all the encouragement which freedom can give them, and they have flourished accordingly. The New England fishery in particular was, before the late disturbances, one of the most important, perhaps, in the world. The whale fishery which, notwithstanding an extravagant bounty, is in Great Britain carried on to so little purpose that in the opinion of many people (which I do not, however, pretend to warrant) the whole produce does not much exceed the value of the bounties which are annually paid for it, is in New England carried on without any bounty to a very great extent. Fish is one of the principal articles with which the North Americans trade to Spain, Portugal, and the Mediterranean.

Sugar was originally an enumerated commodity which could be exported only to Great Britain. But in 1731, upon a representation of the sugar planters, its exportation was permitted to all parts of the world. The restrictions, however, with which this liberty was granted, joined to the high price of sugar in Great Britain, have rendered it, in a great measure, ineffectual. Great Britain and her colonies still continue to be almost the sole market for all the sugar produced in the British plantations. Their consumption increases so fast that, though in consequence of the increasing improvement of Jamaica, as well as of the Ceded Islands, the importation of sugar has increased very greatly within these twenty years, the exportation to foreign countries is said to be not much greater than before.

Rum is a very important article in the trade which the Americans carry on to the coast of Africa, from which they bring back Negro slaves in return.

If the whole surplus produce of America in grain of all sorts, in salt provisions, and in fish had been put into the enumeration, and thereby forced into the market of Great Britain, it would have interfered too much with the produce of the industry of our own people. It was probably not so much from any regard to the interest of America, as from a jealousy of this interference, that those important commodities have not only been kept out of the enumeration, but that the importation into Great Britain of all grain, except rice, and of salt provisions, has, in the ordinary state of the law, been prohibited.

The nonenumerated commodities could originally be exported to all parts of the world. Lumber and rice, having been once put into the enumeration, when they were afterward taken out of it, were confined, as to the European market, to the countries that lie south of Cape Finisterre.[2] By the 6th of George III, c. 52, all nonenumerated commodities were subjected to the like restriction. The parts of Europe which lie south of Cape Finisterre are not manufacturing countries, and we were less jealous of the colony ships carrying home from them any manufactures which could interfere with our own.

The enumerated commodities are of two sorts: first, such as are either the peculiar produce of America, or as cannot be produced, or at least are not produced, in the mother-country. Of this kind are molasses, coffee, cacao nuts, tobacco, pimento, ginger, whale fins, raw silk, cotton wool, beaver, and other peltry of America, indigo, fustic, and other dying woods; secondly, such as are not the peculiar produce of America, but which are and may be produced in the mother-country, though not in such quantities as to supply the greater part of her demand, which is principally supplied from foreign countries. Of this kind are all naval stores, masts, yards, and bowsprits, tar, pitch, and turpentine, pig and bar iron, copper ore, hides and skins, pot and pearl ashes. The largest importation of commodities of the first kind could not discourage the growth or

2. Cape Finisterre is located on the northwest corner of the Iberian (Spanish) Peninsula.

interfere with the sale of any part of the produce of the mother-country. By confining them to the home market, our merchants, it was expected, would not only be enabled to buy them cheaper in the Plantations, and consequently to sell them with a better profit at home, but to establish between the Plantations and foreign countries an advantageous carrying trade, of which Great Britain was necessarily to be the center or emporium, as the European country into which those commodities were first to be imported. The importation of commodities of the second kind might be so managed too, it was supposed, as to interfere, not with the sale of those of the same kind which were produced at home, but with that of those which were imported from foreign countries; because, by means of proper duties, they might be rendered always somewhat dearer than the former and yet a good deal cheaper than the latter. By confining such commodities to the home market, therefore, it was proposed to discourage the produce, not of Great Britain, but of some foreign countries with which the balance of trade was believed to be unfavorable to Great Britain.

The prohibition of exporting from the colonies, to any other country but Great Britain, masts, yards, and bowsprits, tar, pitch, and turpentine, naturally tended to lower the price of timber in the colonies and consequently to increase the expense of clearing their lands, the principal obstacle to their improvement. But about the beginning of the present century, in 1703, the pitch and tar company of Sweden endeavored to raise the price of their commodities to Great Britain by prohibiting their exportation, except in their own ships, at their own price, and in such quantities as they thought proper. In order to counteract this notable piece of mercantile policy, and to render herself as much as possible independent, not only of Sweden, but of all the other northern powers, Great Britain gave a bounty upon the importation of naval stores from America, and the effect of this bounty was to raise the price of timber in America much more than the confinement to the home market could lower it; and, as both regulations were enacted at the same time, their joint effect was rather to encourage than to discourage the clearing of land in America.

Though pig and bar iron too have been put among the enumerated commodities, yet as, when imported from America, they are exempted from considerable duties to which they are subject when imported from any other country, the one part of the regulation contributes more to encourage the erection of furnaces in America than the other to discourage it. There is no manufacture which occasions so great a consumption of wood as a furnace, or which can contribute so much to the clearing of a country overgrown with it.

The tendency of some of these regulations to raise the value of timber in America, and thereby to facilitate the clearing of the land, was neither, perhaps, intended nor understood by the legislature. Though their beneficial effects, however, have been in this respect accidental, they have not upon that account been less real.

The most perfect freedom of trade is permitted between the British colonies of America and the West Indies, both in the enumerated and in the nonenumerated commodities. Those colonies are now become so populous and thriving that each of them finds in some of the others a great and extensive market for every part of its produce. All of them taken together, they make a great internal market for the produce of one another.

The liberality of England, however, toward the trade of her colonies has been confined chiefly to what concerns the market for their produce, either in its rude state, or in what may be called the very first stage of manufacture. The more advanced or more refined manufactures even of the colony produce, the merchants and manufactures of Great Britain choose to reserve to themselves and have prevailed upon the legislature to prevent their establishment in the colonies, sometimes by high duties, and sometimes by absolute prohibitions. . . .

While Great Britain encourages in America the manufactures of pig and bar iron, by exempting them from duties to which the like commodities are subject when imported from any other country, she imposes an absolute prohibition upon the erection of steel furnaces and slit-mills in any of her American plantations. She will not suffer her colonists to work in those more refined manufactures even for their own consumption but insists upon their purchasing of her merchants and manufacturers all goods of this kind which they have occasion for.

She prohibits the exportation from one province to another by water, and even the carriage by land upon horseback or in a cart, of hats, of wools and woolen goods, of the produce of America; a regulation which effectually prevents the establishment of any manufacture of such commodities for distant sale, and confines the industry of her colonists in this way to such coarse and household manufactures, as a private family commonly makes for its own use, or for that of some of its neighbors in the same province.

To prohibit a great people, however, from making all that they can of every part of their own produce, or from employing their stock and industry in the way that they judge most advantageous to themselves, is a manifest violation of the most sacred rights of mankind. Unjust, however, as such prohibitions may be, they have not hitherto been very hurtful to the colonies. Land is still so cheap and, consequently, labor so dear among them that they can import from the mother-country almost all the more refined or more advanced manufactures cheaper than they could make them for themselves. Though they had not, therefore, been prohibited from establishing such manufactures, yet in their present state of improvement, a regard to their own interest would probably have prevented them from doing so. In their present state of improvement, those prohibitions, perhaps, without cramping their industry, or restraining it from any employment to which it would have gone of its own accord, are only impertinent badges of slavery imposed upon them, without any sufficient reason, by the groundless jealousy of the merchants and manufacturers of the mother-country. In a more advanced state they might be really oppressive and insupportable.

Great Britain, too, as she confines to her own market some of the most important productions of the colonies, so in compensation she gives to some of them an advantage in that market; sometimes by imposing higher duties upon the like productions when imported from other countries and sometimes by giving bounties upon their importation from the colonies. In the first way she gives an advantage in the home market to the sugar, tobacco, and iron of her own colonies, and in the second to their raw silk, to their hemp and flax, to their indigo, to their naval stores, and to their building timber. This second way of encouraging the colony produce by bounties upon importation is, so far as I have been able to learn, peculiar to Great Britain. The first is not. Portugal does not content herself with imposing higher duties upon the importation of tobacco from any other country but prohibits it under the severest penalties.

With regard to the importation of goods from Europe, England has likewise dealt more liberally with her colonies than any other nation.

Great Britain allows a part, almost always the half, generally a larger portion, and sometimes the whole, of the duty which is paid upon the importation of foreign goods to be drawn back upon their exportation to any foreign country. No independent foreign country, it was easy to foresee, would receive them if they came to it loaded with the heavy duties to which almost all foreign goods are subjected on their importation into Great Britain. Unless, therefore, some part of those duties was drawn back upon exportation, there was an end of the carrying trade; a trade so much favored by the mercantile system.

Our colonies, however, are by no means independent foreign countries; and Great Britain, having assumed to herself the exclusive right of supplying them with all goods from Europe, might have forced them (in the same manner as other countries have done their colonies) to receive such goods, loaded with all the same duties which they paid in the mother-country. But, on the contrary, till 1763, the same drawbacks were paid upon the exportation of the greater part of foreign goods to our colonies as to any independent foreign country. In 1763, indeed, by the 4th of Geo. III, c. 15, this indulgence was a good deal abated, and it was enacted, "That no part of the duty called the old subsidy should be drawn back for any goods of the growth, production, or manufacture of Europe or the East Indies, which should be exported from this kingdom to any British colony or plantation in America; wines, white callicoes and muslins excepted." Before this law, many different sorts of foreign goods might have been bought cheaper in the plantations than in the mother-country; and some may still.

Of the greater part of the regulations concerning the colony trade, the merchants who carry it on, it must be observed, have been the principal advisers. We must not wonder, therefore, if, in the greater part of them, their interest has been more considered than either that of the colonies or that of the mother-country. In their exclusive privilege of supplying the colonies with all the goods which they wanted from Europe, and of purchasing all such parts of their surplus produce as could not interfere with any of the trades which they themselves carried on at home, the interest of the colonies was sacrificed to the interest of those merchants. In allowing the same drawbacks upon the re-exportation of the greater part of European and East India goods to the colonies, as upon their re-exportation to any independent country, the interest of the mother-country was sacrified to it, even according to the mercantile ideas of that interest. It was for the interest of the merchants to pay as little as possible for the foreign goods which they sent to the colonies and, consequently, to get back as much as possible of the duties which they advanced upon their importation into Great Britain. They might thereby be enabled to sell in the colonies, either the same quantity of goods with a greater profit, or a greater quantity with the same profit, and, consequently, to gain something either in the one way or the other. It was, likewise, for the interest of the colonies to get all such goods as cheap and in as great abundance as possible. But this might not always be for the interest of the mother-country. She might frequently suffer both in her revenue, by giving back a great part of the duties which had been paid upon the importation of such goods; and in her manufactures, by being undersold in the colony market, in consequence of the easy terms upon which foreign manufactures could be carried thither by means of those drawbacks. The progress of the linen manufacture of Great Britain, it is commonly said, has been a good deal retarded by the drawbacks upon the re-exportation of German linen to the American colonies.

But though the policy of Great Britain with regard to the trade of her colonies has been dictated by the same mercantile spirit as that of other nations, it has, however, upon the whole, been less illiberal and oppressive than that of any of them.

In everything except their foreign trade the liberty of the English colonists to manage their own affairs their own way is complete. It is in every respect equal to that of their fellow-citizens at home and is secured in the same manner by an assembly of the representatives of the people, who claim the sole right of imposing taxes for the support of the colony government. The authority of this assembly overawes the executive power, and neither the meanest nor the most obnoxious colonist, as long as he obeys the law, has anything to fear from the resentment either of the governor or any other civil or military officer in the province. The colony assemblies, though, like the House of Commons in England, they are not always a very equal representation of the people, yet they approach more nearly to that character; and as the executive power either has not the means to corrupt them, or, on account of the support which it receives from the mother-country, is not under the necessity of doing so, they are perhaps in general more influenced by the inclinations of their constituents. The councils, which, in the colony legislatures, correspond to the House of Lords in Great Britain, are not composed of a hereditary nobility. In some of the colonies, as in three of the governments of New England, those councils are not appointed by the king but chosen by the representatives of the people. In none of the English colonies is there any hereditary nobility. In all of them, indeed, as in all other free countries, the descendant of an old colony family is more respected than an upstart of equal merit and fortune; but he is only more respected, and he has no privileges by which he can be troublesome to his neighbors. Before the commencement of the present disturbances, the colony assemblies had not only the legislative but a part of the executive power. In Connecticut and Rhode Island they elected the governor. In the other colonies they appointed the revenue officers who collected the taxes imposed by those respective assemblies, to whom those officers were immediately responsible. There is more equality, therefore, among the English colonists than among the inhabitants of the mother-country. Their manners are more republican, and their governments, those of three of the provinces of New England in particular, have hitherto been more republican too. . . .

PART THIRD

Of the Advantages Which Europe Has Derived from the Discovery of America, and from That of Passage to the East Indies by the Cape of Good Hope

. . . To found a great empire for the sole purpose of raising up a people of customers may at first sight appear a project fit only for a nation of shopkeepers. It is, however, a project altogether unfit for a nation of shopkeepers but extremely fit for a nation whose government is influenced by shopkeepers. Such statesmen, and such statesmen only, are capable of fancying that they will find some advantage in employing the blood and treasure of their fellow-citizens to found and maintain such an empire. Say to a shopkeeper, "Buy me a good estate, and I shall always buy my clothes at your shop, even though I should pay somewhat dearer than what I can have them for at other shops," and you will not find him very forward to embrace your proposal. But should any other person buy you such an estate, the shopkeeper would be much obliged to your benefactor if he would enjoin you to buy all your clothes at his shop. England purchased for some of her subjects, who found themselves uneasy at home, a great estate in a distant country. The price, indeed, was very small, and instead of thirty years' purchase, the ordinary price

of land in the present times, it amounted to little more than the expense of the different equipments which made the first discovery, reconnoitered the coast, and took a fictitious possession of the country. The land was good and of great extent, and the cultivators having plenty of good ground to work upon, and being for some time at liberty to sell their produce where they pleased, became in the course of little more than thirty or forty years (between 1620 and 1660) so numerous and thriving a people that the shopkeepers and other traders of England wished to secure to themselves the monopoly of their custom. Without pretending, therefore, that they had paid any part, either of the original purchase money or of the subsequent expense of improvement, they petitioned the Parliament that the cultivators of America might for the future be confined to their shop; first, for buying all the goods which they wanted from Europe; and, secondly, for selling all such parts of their own produce as those traders might find it convenient to buy. For they did not find it convenient to buy every part of it. Some parts of it imported into England might have interfered with some of the trades which they themselves carried on at home. Those particular parts of it, therefore, they were willing that the colonists should sell where they could; the farther off the better; and upon that account proposed that their market should be confined to the countries south of Cape Finisterre. A clause in the famous act of navigation established this truly shopkeeper proposal into a law.

The maintenance of this monopoly has hitherto been the principal, or more properly perhaps the sole, end and purpose of the dominion which Great Britain assumes over her colonies. In the exclusive trade, it is supposed, consists the great advantage of provinces, which have never yet afforded either revenue or military force for the support of the civil government or the defense of the mother-country. The monopoly is the principal badge of their dependency, and it is the sole fruit which has hitherto been gathered from that dependency. Whatever expense Great Britain has hitherto laid out in maintaining this dependency has really been laid out in order to support this monopoly. The expense of the ordinary peace establishment of the colonies amounted, before the commencement of the present disturbances, to the pay of twenty regiments of foot; to the expense of the artillery, stores, and extraordinary provisions with which it was necessary to supply them; and to the expense of a very considerable naval force which was constantly kept up, in order to guard, from the smuggling vessels of other nations, the immense coast of North America and that of our West Indian islands. The whole expense of this peace establishment was a charge upon the revenue of Great Britain and was, at the same time, the smallest part of what the dominion of the colonies has cost the mother-country. If we would know the amount of the whole, we must add to the annual expense of this peace establishment the interest of the sums which, in consequence of her considering her colonies as provinces subject to her dominion, Great Britain has upon different occasions laid out upon their defense. We must add to it, in particular, the whole expense of the late war, and a great part of that of the war which preceded it. The late war was altogether a colony quarrel, and the whole expense of it, in whatever part of the world it may have been laid out, whether in Germany or the East Indies, ought justly to be stated to the account of the colonies. It amounted to more than ninety millions sterling, including not only the new debt which was contracted, but the two shillings in the pound additional land tax, and the sums which were every year borrowed from the sinking fund. The

Spanish war, which began in 1739, was principally a colony quarrel. Its principal object was to prevent the search of the colony ships which carried on a contraband trade with the Spanish main. This whole expense is, in reality, a bounty which has been given in order to support a monopoly. The pretended purpose of it was to encourage the manufactures and to increase the commerce of Great Britain. But its real effect has been to raise the rate of mercantile profit and to enable our merchants to turn into a branch of trade, of which the returns are more slow and distant than those of the greater part of other trades, a greater proportion of their capital than they otherwise would have done; two events which, if a bounty could have prevented, it might perhaps have been very well worth while to give such a bounty.

Under the present system of management, therefore, Great Britain derives nothing but loss from the dominion which she assumes over her colonies.

To propose that Great Britain should voluntarily give up all authority over her colonies, and leave them to elect their own magistrates, to enact their own laws, and to make peace and war as they might think proper would be to propose such a measure as never was, and never will be, adopted by any nation in the world. No nation ever voluntarily gave up the dominion of any province, how troublesome soever it might be to govern it, and how small soever the revenue which it afforded might be in proportion to the expense which it occasioned. Such sacrifices, though they might frequently be agreeable to the interest, are always mortifying to the pride of every nation, and, what is perhaps of still greater consequence, they are always contrary to the private interest of the governing part of it, who would thereby be deprived of the disposal of many places of trust and profit, of many opportunities of acquiring wealth and distinction, which the possession of the most turbulent and, to the great body of the people, the most unprofitable province seldom fails to afford. The most visionary enthusiast would scarce be capable of proposing such a measure, with any serious hopes at least of its ever being adopted. If it was adopted, however, Great Britain would not only be immediately freed from the whole annual expense of the peace establishment of the colonies but might settle with them such a treaty of commerce as would effectually secure to her a free trade, more advantageous to the great body of the people, though less so to the merchants, than the monopoly which she at present enjoys. By thus parting good friends, the natural affection of the colonies to the mother-country, which, perhaps, our late dissensions have well-nigh extinguished, would quickly revive. It might dispose them not only to respect, for whole centuries together, that treaty of commerce which they had concluded with us at parting, but to favor us in war as well as in trade, and, instead of turbulent and factious subjects, to become our most faithful, affectionate, and generous allies; and the same sort of parental affection on the one side, and filial respect on the other, might revive between Great Britain and her colonies which used to subsist between those of ancient Greece and the mother-city from which they descended.

In order to render any province advantageous to the empire to which it belongs, it ought to afford, in time of peace, a revenue to the public sufficient not only for defraying the whole expense of its own peace establishment but for contributing its proportion to the support of the general government of the empire. Every province necessarily contributes, more or less, to increase the expense of that general government. If any particular province, therefore, does not contribute its share toward defraying this expense, an unequal burden must be thrown upon some other part of the empire. The extraordinary revenue too which every province affords to the public in time of war ought, from parity of reason, to bear the same proportion to the extraordinary revenue of the whole empire which its ordinary revenue does in time of peace. That neither the ordinary nor extraordinary revenue which Great Britain derives from her colonies bears this proportion to the whole revenue of the British Empire will readily be allowed. The monopoly, it has been supposed, indeed, by increasing the private revenue of the people of Great Britain, and thereby enabling them to pay greater taxes, compensates the deficiency of the public revenue of the colonies. But this monopoly, I have endeavored to show, though a very grievous tax upon the colonies, and though it may increase the revenue of a particular order of men in Great Britain, diminishes instead of increasing that of the great body of the people and consequently diminishes instead of increasing the ability of the great body of the people to pay taxes. The men too whose revenue the monopoly increases constitute a particular order, which it is both absolutely impossible to tax beyond the proportion of other orders and extremely impolitic even to attempt to tax beyond that proportion, as I shall endeavor to show in the following book. No particular resource, therefore, can be drawn from this particular order.

The colonies may be taxed either by their own assemblies or by the Parliament of Great Britain.

That the colony assemblies can ever be so managed as to levy upon their constituents a public revenue sufficient, not only to maintain at all times their own civil and military establishment, but to pay their proper proportion of the expense of the general government of the British empire seems not very probable. It was a long time before even the Parliament of England, though placed immediately under the eye of the sovereign, could be brought under such a system of management or could be rendered sufficiently liberal in their grants for supporting the civil and military establishments even of their own country. It was only by distributing among the particular members of Parliament a great part either of the offices or of the disposal of the offices arising from this civil and military establishment that such a system of management could be established even with regard to the Parliament of England. But the distance of the colony assemblies from the eye of the sovereign, their number, their dispersed situation, and their various constitutions would render it very difficult to manage them in the same manner, even though the sovereign had the same means of doing it; and those means are wanting. It would be absolutely impossible to distribute among all the leading members of all the colony assemblies such a share, either of the offices or of the disposal of the offices arising from the general government of the British Empire, as to dispose them to give up their popularity at home and to tax their constituents for the support of that general government of which almost the whole emoluments were to be divided among people who were strangers to them. The unavoidable ignorance of administration, besides, concerning the relative importance of the different members of those different assemblies, the offenses which must frequently be given, the blunders which must constantly be committed in attempting to manage them in this manner, seems to render such a system of management altogether impracticable with regard to them.

The colony assemblies, besides, cannot be supposed the proper judges of what is necessary for the defense and support of the whole empire. The care of that defense and support is not intrusted to them. It is not their business, and they have no regular means of information concerning it. The assembly of a province, like the vestry of a parish, may judge very properly concerning the affairs of its own particular district but can have no proper means of judging concerning those of the whole empire. It cannot even judge properly concerning the proportion which its own province bears to the whole empire or concerning the relative degree of its wealth and importance, compared with the other provinces, because those other provinces are not under the inspection and superintendency of the assembly of a particular province. What is necessary for the defense and support of the whole empire, and in what proportion each part ought to contribute, can be judged of only by that assembly which inspects and superintends the affairs of the whole empire.

It has been proposed, accordingly, that the colonies should be taxed by requisition, the Parliament of Great Britain determining the sum which each colony ought to pay, and the provincial assembly assessing and levying it in the way that suited best the circumstances of the province. What concerned the whole empire would in this way be determined by the assembly which inspects and superintends the affairs of the whole empire, and the provincial affairs of each colony might still be regulated by its own assembly. Though the colonies should in this case have no representatives in the British Parliament, yet, if we may judge by experience, there is no probability that the parliamentary requisition would be unreasonable. The Parliament of England has not upon any occasion shown the smallest disposition to overburden those parts of the empire which are not represented in Parliament. The islands of Guernsey and Jersey, without any means of resisting the authority of Parliament, are more lightly taxed than any part of Great Britain. Parliament, in attempting to exercise its supposed right, whether well or ill grounded, of taxing the colonies, has never hitherto demanded of them anything which even approached to a just proportion to what was paid by their fellow-subjects at home. If the contribution of the colonies, besides, was to rise or fall in proportion to the rise or fall of the land tax, Parliament could not tax them without taxing at the same time its own constituents, and the colonies might in this case be considered as virtually represented in Parliament.

Examples are not wanting of empires in which all the different provinces are not taxed, if I may be allowed the expression, in one mass but in which the sovereign regulates the sum which each province ought to pay and in some provinces assesses and levies it as he thinks proper, while in others he leaves it to be assessed and levied as the respective states of each province shall determine. In some provinces of France the king not only imposes what taxes he thinks proper but assesses and levies them in the way he thinks proper. From others he demands a certain sum but leaves it to the states of each province to assess and levy that sum as they think proper. According to the scheme of taxing by requisition, the Parliament of Great Britain would stand nearly in the same situation toward the colony assemblies as the king of France does toward the states of those provinces which still enjoy the privilege of having states of their own, the provinces of France which are supposed to be the best governed.

But though, according to this scheme, the colonies could have no just reason to fear that their share of the public burdens should ever exceed the proper proportion to that of their fellow-citizens at home, Great Britain might have just reason to fear that it never would amount to that proper proportion. The Parliament of Great Britain has not for some time past had the same established authority in the colonies which the French king has in those provinces of France which still enjoy the privilege of having states of their own. The colony assem-

blies, if they were not very favorably disposed (and unless more skilfully managed than they ever have been hitherto, they are not very likely to be so), might still find many pretenses for evading or rejecting the most reasonable requisitions of Parliament. A French war breaks out, we shall suppose; ten millions must immediately be raised in order to defend the seat of the empire. This sum must be borrowed upon the credit of some parliamentary fund mortgaged for paying the interest. Part of this fund Parliament proposes to raise by a tax to be levied in Great Britain, and part of it by a requisition to all the different colony assemblies of America and the West Indies. Would people readily advance their money upon the credit of a fund, which partly depended upon the good humor of all those assemblies, far distant from the seat of the war, and sometimes, perhaps, thinking themselves not much concerned in the event of it? Upon such a fund no more money would probably be advanced than what the tax to be levied in Great Britain might be supposed to answer for. The whole burden of the debt contracted on account of the war would in this manner fall, as it always has done hitherto, upon Great Britain, upon a part of the empire and not upon the whole empire. Great Britain is, perhaps, since the world began, the only state which, as it has extended its empire, has only increased its expense without once augmenting its resources. Other states have generally disburdened themselves upon their subject and subordinate provinces of the most considerable part of the expense of defending the empire. Great Britain has hitherto suffered her subject and subordinate provinces to disburden themselves upon her of almost this whole expense. In order to put Great Britain upon a footing of equality with her own colonies, which the law has hitherto supposed to be subject and subordinate, it seems necessary, upon the scheme of taxing them by parliamentary requisition, that Parliament should have some means of rendering its requisitions immediately effectual, in case the colony assemblies should attempt to evade or reject them; and what those means are, it is not very easy to conceive, and it has not yet been explained.

Should the Parliament of Great Britain, at the same time, be ever fully established in the right of taxing the colonies, even independent of the consent of their own assemblies, the importance of those assemblies would from that moment be at an end and, with it, that of all the leading men of British America. Men desire to have some share in the management of public affairs chiefly on account of the importance which it gives them. Upon the power which the greater part of the leading men, the natural aristocracy of every country, have of preserving or defending their respective importance depends the stability and duration of every system of free government. In the attacks which those leading men are continually making upon the importance of one another, and in the defense of their own, consists the whole play of domestic faction and ambition. The leading men of America, like those of all other countries, desire to preserve their own importance. They feel, or imagine, that if their assemblies, which they are fond of calling parliaments, and of considering as equal in authority to the Parliament of Great Britain, should be so far degraded as to become the humble ministers and executive officers of that Parliament, the greater part of their own importance would be at an end. They have rejected, therefore, the proposal of being taxed by parliamentary requisition and, like other ambitious and high-spirited men, have rather chosen to draw the sword in defense of their own importance.

Toward the declension of the Roman republic, the allies of Rome, who had borne the principal burden of defending the state and extending the empire, demanded to be admitted to all the privileges of Roman citizens. Upon being refused, the social war broke out. During the course of that war Rome granted those privileges to the greater part of them, one by one, and in proportion as they detached themselves from the general confederacy. The Parliament of Great Britain insists upon taxing the colonies, and they refuse to be taxed by a Parliament in which they are not represented. If to each colony which should detach itself from the general confederacy Great Britain should allow such a number of representatives as suited the proportion of what it contributed to the public revenue of the empire, in consequence of its being subjected to the same taxes, and in compensation admitted to the same freedom of trade with its fellow-subjects at home, the number of its representatives to be augmented as the proportion of its contribution might afterward augment, a new method of acquiring importance, a new and more dazzling object of ambition, would be presented to the leading men of each colony. Instead of piddling for the little prizes which are to be found in what may be called the paltry raffle of colony faction, they might then hope, from the presumption which men naturally have in their own ability and good fortune, to draw some of the great prizes which sometimes come from the wheel of the great state lottery of British politics. Unless this or some other method is fallen upon, and there seems to be none more obvious than this, of preserving the importance and of gratifying the ambition of the leading men of America, it is not very probable that they will ever voluntarily submit to us; and we ought to consider that the blood which must be shed in forcing them to do so is, every drop of it, the blood either of those who are or of those whom we wish to have for our fellow-citizens. They are very weak who flatter themselves that, in the state to which things have come, our colonies will be easily conquered by force alone. The persons who now govern the resolutions of what they call their continental congress feel in themselves at this moment a degree of importance which perhaps the greatest subjects in Europe scarce feel. From shopkeepers, tradesmen, and attorneys they are become statesmen and legislators and are employed in contriving a new form of government for an extensive empire which, they flatter themselves, will become, and which, indeed, seems very likely to become, one of the greatest and most formidable that ever was in the world. Five hundred different people, perhaps, who in different ways act immediately under the continental congress; and five hundred thousand, perhaps, who act under those five hundred, all feel in the same manner a porportionable rise in their own importance. Almost every individual of the governing party in America fills, at present in his own fancy, a station superior, not only to what he had ever filled before, but to what he had ever expected to fill; and unless some new object of ambition is presented either to him or to his leaders, if he has the ordinary spirit of a man, he will die in defense of that station. . . .

. . . Our colonies, unless they can be induced to consent to a union, are very likely to defend themselves against the best of all mother-countries as obstinately as the city of Paris did against one of the best of kings.

The idea of representation was unknown in ancient times. When the people of one state were admitted to the right of citizenship in another, they had no other means of exercising that right but by coming in a body to vote and deliberate with the people of that other state. The admission of the greater part of the inhabitants of Italy to the privileges of Roman citizens completely ruined the Roman republic. It was no longer possible to distinguish between who was and who was not a Roman citizen. No tribe could know its own members. A rabble of any kind could be introduced into the assemblies of the people, could drive out the real citizens, and decide upon the affairs of the republic as if they themselves had been such. But though America were to send fifty new representatives to Parliament, the doorkeeper of the House of Commons could not find any great difficulty in distinguishing between who was and who was not a member. Though the Roman constitution, therefore, was necessarily ruined by the union of Rome with the allied states of Italy, there is not the least probability that the British constitution would be hurt by the union of Great Britain with her colonies. That constitution, on the contrary, would be completed by it and seems to be imperfect without it. The assembly which deliberates and decides concerning the affairs of every part of the empire, in order to be properly informed, ought certainly to have representatives from every part of it. That this union, however, could be easily effectuated, or that difficulties and great difficulties might not occur in the execution, I do not pretend. I have yet heard of none, however, which appear insurmountable. The principal perhaps arise, not from the nature of things, but from the prejudices and opinions of the people both on this and on the other side of the Atlantic.

We, on this side of the water, are afraid lest the multitude of American representatives should overturn the balance of the constitution and increase too much either the influence of the crown, on the one hand, or the force of the democracy, on the other. But if the number of American representatives were to be in proportion to the produce of American taxation, the number of people to be managed would increase exactly in proportion to the means of managing them; and the means of managing, to the number of people to be managed. The monarchical and democratical parts of the constitution would, after the union, stand exactly in the same degree of relative force with regard to one another as they had done before.

The people on the other side of the water are afraid lest their distance from the seat of government might expose them to many oppressions. But their representatives in Parliament, of which the number ought from the first to be considerable, would easily be able to protect them from all oppression. The distance could not much weaken the dependency of the representatives upon the constituent, and the former would still feel that he owed his seat in Parliament, and all the consequence which he derived from it, to the good will of the latter. It would be the interest of the former, therefore, to cultivate that good will by complaining, with all the authority of a member of the legislature, of every outrage which any civil or military officer might be guilty of in those remote parts of the empire. The distance of America from the seat of government, besides, the natives of that country might flatter themselves, with some appearance of reason too, would not be of very long continuance. Such has hitherto been the rapid progress of that country in wealth, population, and improvement that in the course of little more than a century, perhaps, the produce of American might exceed that of British taxation. The seat of the empire would then naturally remove itself to that part of the empire which contributed most to the general defense and support of the whole.

The discovery of America and that of a passage to the East Indies by the Cape of Good Hope are the two greatest and most important events recorded in the history of mankind. Their consequences have already been very great; but, in the short period of between two and three centuries which has elapsed since these discoveries were made, it is impossible that the whole extent of their consequences can have been seen. What benefits or what misfortunes to mankind may hereafter result from those great events no human wisdom can foresee. By uniting, in some measure, the most distant parts of the world, by enabling them to relieve one another's wants, to increase one another's enjoyments, and to encourage one another's industry, their general tendency would seem to be beneficial. To the natives, however, both of the East and West Indies, all the commercial benefits which can have resulted from those events have been sunk and lost in the dreadful misfortunes which they have occasioned. These misfortunes, however, seem to have arisen rather from accident than from anything in the nature of those events themselves. At the particular time when these discoveries were made, the superiority of force happened to be so great on the side of the Europeans that they were enabled to commit with impunity every sort of injustice in those remote countries. Hereafter, perhaps, the natives of those countries may grow stronger, or those of Europe may grow weaker, and the inhabitants of all the different quarters of the world may arrive at that equality of courage and force which, by inspiring mutual fear, can alone overawe the injustice of independent nations into some sort of respect for the rights of one another. But nothing seems more likely to establish this equality of force than that mutual communication of knowledge and of all sorts of improvements which an extensive commerce from all countries to all countries naturally, or rather necessarily, carries along with it. . . .

2. A PLAN FOR COLONIAL UNION[1]

By BENJAMIN FRANKLIN

EDITORS' NOTE.—Benjamin Franklin (1706–90), philosopher and statesman, was one of America's most versatile leaders. His services in the Second Continental Congress, as agent and minister to France during the Revolutionary War, and his work in the Federal Convention of 1787 are only a few of his outstanding civic accomplishments. For an excellent biography see Carl Van Doren, *Benjamin Franklin* (New York, 1938); for a very good selection from his writings see *Benjamin Franklin: Representative Selections . . .*, ed. F. L. Mott and C. E. Jorgenson (New York, 1936).

The following letters, though first published in 1766, were dated late in 1754, the year that the actual fighting of the French and Indian War began in the Ohio Valley. They were addressed to William Shirley (1694–1771), governor of Massachusetts. In June and July of 1754 Franklin had attended the Albany Conference, where negotiations with the Indian allies of the colonies and discussion of plans for

colonial union had been carried on simultaneously. At that time his famous "Albany Plan," somewhat modified from his original proposals, was unanimously accepted and recommended to the British and colonial governments (*Complete Works . . .*, II, 343–75). In his *Autobiography* Franklin briefly summarizes his plan and sets forth the circumstances in which his letters to Shirley were written:

By this plan the general government was to be administered by a President-General appointed and supported by the Crown, and a Grand Council was to be chosen by the representatives of the people of the several colonies, met in their respective assemblies. . . . Its fate was singular: the assemblies did not adopt it, as they all thought there was too much *prerogative* in it, and in England it was judged to have too much of the *democratic*. . . .

Another scheme was formed . . . whereby the governors of the provinces, with some members of their respective councils, were to meet and order the raising of troops, building of forts, etc., and to draw on the treasury of Great Britain for the expense, which afterward to be refunded by an act of Parliament laying a tax on America . . . [*ibid.*, I, 243–44].

LETTER I

CONCERNING THE VOICE OF THE PEOPLE IN CHOOSING THE RULERS BY WHOM TAXES ARE IMPOSED

TUESDAY MORNING
[December 17, 1754]

SIR:

I return you the loose sheets of the plan, with thanks to your Excellency for communicating them.

I apprehend that excluding the *people* of the colonies from all share in the choice of the grand council will give extreme dissatisfaction, as well as the taxing them by act of Parliament, where they have no representative. It is very possible that this general government might be as well and faithfully administered without the people as with them; but where heavy burthens have been laid on them, it has been found useful to make it as much as possible their own act; for they bear better, when they have,

1. Benjamin Franklin, *Complete Works . . .*, ed. John Bigelow (New York, 1887), II, 376–87.

or think they have, some share in the direction; and when any public measures are generally grievous, or even distasteful, to the people, the wheels of government move more heavily.

LETTER II

ON THE IMPOSITION OF DIRECT TAXES UPON THE COLONIES WITHOUT THEIR CONSENT

WEDNESDAY MORNING
[December 18, 1754]

SIR:

I mentioned it yesterday to your Excellency as my opinion that excluding the *people* of the colonies from all share in the choice of the grand council would probably give extreme dissatisfaction, as well as the taxing them by act of Parliament, where they have no representative. In matters of general concern to the people, and especially where burthens are to be laid upon them, it is of use to consider, as well what they will be apt to think and say, as what they ought to think. I shall therefore, as your Excellency requires it of me, briefly mention what of either kind occurs to me on this occasion.

First, they will say, and perhaps with justice, that the body of the people in the colonies are as loyal and as firmly attached to the present constitution and reigning family as any subjects in the king's dominions.

That there is no reason to doubt the readiness and willingness of the representatives they may choose to grant from time to time such supplies for the defense of the country as shall be judged necessary, so far as their abilities will allow.

That the people in the colonies who are to feel the immediate mischiefs of invasion and conquest by an enemy, in the loss of their estates, lives, and liberties, are likely to be better judges of the quantity of forces necessary to be raised and maintained, forts to be built and supported, and of their own abilities to bear the expense than the Parliament of England at so great a distance.

That governors often come to the colonies merely to make fortunes, with which they intend to return to Britain; are not always men of the best abilities and integrity; have many of them no estates here, nor any natural connections with us that should make them heartily concerned for our welfare; and might possibly be fond of raising and keeping up more forces than necessary, from the profits accruing to themselves, and to make provision for their friends and dependents.

That the conselors in most of the colonies being appointed by the crown, on the recommendation of governors, are often persons of small estates, frequently dependent on the governors for offices, and therefore too much under influence.[2]

That there is therefore great reason to be jealous of a power in such governors and councils to raise such sums as they shall judge necessary, by draft on the Lords of the Treasury, to be afterward laid on the colonies by act of Parliament, and paid by the people here; since they might abuse it by projecting useless expeditions, harassing the people, and taking them from their labor to execute such projects, merely to create offices and employments, and gratify their dependents, and divide profits.

That the Parliament of England is at a great distance, subject to the misinformed and misled by such governors and councils, whose united interests might probably secure them against the effect of any complaint from hence.

That it is supposed an undoubted right

2. Here Franklin refers to the members of the governor's councils which in most of the colonies served as one house of the colonial legislature. They were usually appointed by the crown on the recommendations of the British Board of Trade. In proprietary colonies they were appointed by the proprietor(s), and in Massachusetts, Rhode Island, and Connecticut they were elected. The councils also served as judicial and executive bodies.

of Englishmen not to be taxed but by their own consent, given through their representatives.

That the colonies have no representatives in Parliament.

That to propose taxing them by Parliament, and refuse them the liberty of choosing a representative council to meet in the colonies, and consider and judge of the necessity of any general tax and the quantum, shows a suspicion of their loyalty to the crown, or of their regard for their country, or of their common sense and understanding, which they have not deserved.

That compelling the colonies to pay money without their consent would be rather like raising contributions in an enemy's country than taxing of Englishmen for their own public benefit.

That it would be treating them as a conquered people and not as true British subjects.

That a tax laid by the representatives of the colonies might easily be lessened as the occasions should lessen; but being once laid by Parliament, under the influence of the representations made by governors, would probably be kept up and continued for the benefit of governors, to the grievous burthen and discouragement of the colonies, and prevention of their growth and increase.

That a power in governors to march the inhabitants from one end of the British and French colonies to the other, being a country of at least 1,500 square miles, without the approbation or the consent of their representatives first obtained to such expeditions, might be grievous and ruinous to the people, and would put them on a footing with the subjects of France in Canada, that now groan under such oppression from their governor, who for two years past has harassed them with long and destructive marches to Ohio.

That if the colonies in a body may be well governed by governors and councils appointed by the crown, without representatives, particular colonies may as well or better be so governed; a tax may be laid upon them all by act of Parliament for support of government, and their assemblies may be dismissed as a useless part of the constitution.

That the powers, proposed by the Albany Plan of Union to be vested in a grand council representative of the people, even with regard to military matters, are not so great as those the colonies of Rhode Island and Connecticut are intrusted with by their charters and have never abused; for, by this plan, the president-general is appointed by the crown and controls all by his negative; but in those governments the people choose the governor and yet allow him no negative.

That the British colonies bordering on the French are properly frontiers of the British Empire; and the frontiers of an empire are properly defended at the joint expense of the body of the people in such empire. It would now be thought hard by act of Parliament to oblige the Cinque Ports or seacoasts of Britain to maintain the whole navy, because they are more immediately defended by it, not allowing them at the same time a vote in choosing members of the Parliament;[3] and if the frontiers of America bear the expense of their own defense, it seems hard to allow them no share in voting the money, judging of the necessity and sum, or advising the measures.

That, besides the taxes necessary for the defense of the frontiers, the colonies pay yearly great sums to the mother-country unnoticed: for

1. Taxes paid in Britain by the land-holder or artificer must enter into and increase the price of the produce of land and of manufactures made of it; and a

3. In the Middle Ages the Cinque Ports (originally Dover, Sandwich, Hastings, Hythe, and Romney—other towns added later) fulfilled their feudal obligations to the king of England by furnishing him with the ships and sailors for his expeditionary forces to the Continent or to Ireland. In return these towns received important privileges.

great part of this is paid by consumers in the colonies, who thereby pay a considerable part of the British taxes.

2. We are restrained in our trade with foreign nations; and where we could be supplied with any manufacture cheaper from them, but must buy the same dearer from Britain, the difference of price is a clear tax to Britain.

3. We are obliged to carry a great part of our produce directly to Britain; and where the duties laid upon it lessen its price to the planter, or it sells for less than it would in foreign markets, the difference is a tax paid to Britain.

4. Some manufactures we could make, but are forbidden, and must take them of British merchants; the whole price is a tax paid to Britain.

5. By our greatly increasing the demand and consumption of British manufactures, their price is considerably raised of late years; the advantage is clear profit to Britain and enables its people better to pay great taxes; and much of it, being paid by us, is clear tax to Britain.

6. In short, as we are not suffered to regulate our trade and restrain the importation and consumption of British superfluities, as Britain can the consumption of foreign superfluities, our whole wealth centers finally amongst the merchants and inhabitants of Britain; and if we make them richer, and enable them better to pay their taxes, it is nearly the same as being taxed ourselves and equally beneficial to the crown.

These kinds of secondary taxes, however, we do not complain of, though we have no share in the laying or disposing of them; but to pay immediate heavy taxes, in the laying, appropriation, and disposition of which we have no part, and which perhaps we may know to be as unnecessary as grievous, must seem hard measure to Englishmen, who cannot conceive that by hazarding their lives and fortunes in subduing and settling new countries, extending the dominion and increasing the commerce of the mother-nation, they have forfeited the native rights of Britons, which they think ought rather to be given to them, as due to such merit, if they had been before in a state of slavery.

These, and such kind of things as these, I apprehend will be thought and said by the people, if the proposed alteration of the Albany plan should take place. Then the administration of the board of governors and council so appointed, not having any representative body of the people to approve and unite in its measures, and conciliate the minds of the people to them, will probably become suspected and odious, dangerous animosities and feuds will arise between the governors and governed, and every thing go into confusion.

Perhaps I am too apprehensive in this matter; but, having freely given my opinion and reasons, your Excellency can judge better than I whether there be any weight in them; and the shortness of the time allowed me will, I hope, in some degree excuse the imperfections of this scrawl.

With the greatest respect and fidelity, I have the honor to be

Your Excellency's most obedient and most humble servant,

B. FRANKLIN

LETTER III

ON THE SUBJECT OF UNITING THE COLONIES MORE INTIMATELY WITH GREAT BRITAIN BY ALLOWING THEM REPRESENTATIVES IN PARLIAMENT

BOSTON, December 22, 1754

SIR:

Since the conversation your Excellency was pleased to honor me with, on the subject of *uniting the colonies* more intimately with Great Britain, by allowing them *representatives in Parliament*, I have something further considered that matter and am of opinion that such a union would be very acceptable to the colonies, provided they had a reasonable number of representatives allowed them; and that all the old acts of Parliament restraining the trade or cramping the manufactures of the colonies be at the same time repealed, and the British subjects *on this side the water* put, in those respects, on the same footing with those in Great Britain, till the new Parliament, representing the whole, shall think it for the interest of the whole to re-enact some or all of them. It is not that I imagine so many representatives will be allowed the colonies as to have any great weight by their numbers, but I think there might be sufficient to occasion those laws to be better and more impartially considered, and perhaps to overcome the interest of a petty corporation, or of any particular set of artificers or traders in England, who heretofore seem, in some instances, to have been more regarded than all the colonies or than was consistent with the general interest or best national good. I think, too, that the government of the colonies by a Parliament in which they are fairly represented would be vastly more agreeable to the people than the method lately attempted to be introduced by royal instructions, as well as more agreeable to the nature of an English constitution and to English liberty;[4] and that such laws as now seem to bear hard on the colonies would (when judged by such a Parliament for the best interest of the whole) be more cheerfully submitted to and more easily executed.

I should hope, too, that by such a union the people of Great Britain and the people of the colonies would learn to consider themselves as not belonging to a different community with different interests but to one community with one interest, which I imagine would con-tribute to strengthen the whole and greatly lessen the danger of future separations.

It is, I suppose, agreed to be the general interest of any state that its people be numerous and rich; men enough to fight in its defense and enough to pay sufficient taxes to defray the charge; for these circumstances tend to the security of the state and its protection from foreign power. But it seems not of so much importance whether the fighting be done by John or Thomas, or the tax paid by William or Charles. The iron manufacture employs and enriches British subjects, but is it of any importance to the state whether the manufacturers live at Birmingham, or Sheffield, or both, since they are still within its bounds, and their wealth and persons still at its command? Could the Goodwin Sands be laid dry by banks,[5] and land equal to a large country thereby gained to England, and presently filled with English inhabitants, would it be right to deprive such inhabitants of the common privileges enjoyed by other Englishmen—the right of vending their produce in the same ports, or of making their own shoes, because a merchant or a shoemaker living on the old land might fancy it more for his advantage to trade or make shoes for them? Would this be right even if the land were gained at the expense of the state? And would it not seem less right if the charge and labor of gaining the additional territory to Britain had been borne by the settlers themselves? And would not the hardship appear yet greater if the people of the new country should be allowed no representatives in the Parliament enacting such impositions?

Now, I look on the colonies as so many countries gained to Great Britain, and more advantageous to it than if they had been gained out of the seas around its coasts and joined to its land; for, being

4. When a royal governor was appointed, the British Privy Council gave him a set of instructions to indicate his powers and to serve as a guide to important problems of colonial administration.

5. The Goodwin Sands are a range of shoals at the entrance to the North Sea from the Straits of Dover.

in different climates, they afford greater variety of produce, and being separated by the ocean, they increase much more its shipping and seamen; and since they are all included in the British Empire, which has only extended itself by their means, and the strength and wealth of the parts are the strength and wealth of the whole, what imports it to the general state whether a merchant, a smith, or a hatter grow rich in Old or New England? And if, through increase of people, two smiths are wanted for one employed before, why may not the *new* smith be allowed to live and thrive in the *new* country, as well as the *old* in the *old?* In fine, why should the coun-tenance of a state be *partially* afforded to its people, unless it be most in favor of those who have most merit? And if there be any difference, those who have most contributed to enlarge Britain's empire and commerce, increase her strength, her wealth, and the numbers of her people, at the risk of their own lives and private fortunes in new and strange countries, methinks ought rather to expect some preference. With the greatest respect and esteem, I have the honor to be

Your Excellency's most obedient
and most humble servant,

B. FRANKLIN

3. THE DECLARATION OF RIGHTS OF THE STAMP ACT CONGRESS, OCTOBER 19, 1765[1]

EDITORS' NOTE.—On the motion of James Otis, on June 8, the Massachusetts legislature sent a circular inviting all the colonies to send delegates to a congress at New York in October, 1765. Representatives from only nine colonies appeared. Virginia, New Hampshire, North Carolina, and Georgia were not represented. The Congress agreed upon the Declaration of Rights reproduced here and, further, petitioned the king and Parliament. Because the credentials of certain delegates authorized them merely to consult and not to take action, the petition was signed by the members of only six colonies.

Saturday, Oct. 19th, 1765, A.M.—The congress met according to adjournment, and resumed, etc., as yesterday; and upon mature deliberation, agreed to the following declaration of the rights and grievances of the colonists in America, which were ordered to be inserted.

DECLARATION OF RIGHTS

The members of this congress, sincerely devoted, with the warmest sen-timents of affection and duty to His Majesty's person and government, inviolably attached to the present happy establishment of the Protestant succession, and with minds deeply impressed by a sense of the present and impending misfortunes of the British colonies on this continent; having considered as maturely as time would permit, the circumstances of said colonies, esteem it our indispensable duty to make the following declarations, of our humble opinions, respecting the most essential rights and liberties of the colonists, and of the grievances under which they labor, by reason of several late acts of Parliament.

1. *Journal of the First Congress of the American Colonies, in Opposition to the Tyrannical Acts of the British Parliament. Held at New York, October 7, 1765* (New York, 1845), pp. 27–29.

1st. That His Majesty's subjects in these colonies owe the same allegiance to the crown of Great Britain that is owing from his subjects born within the realm, and all due subordination to that august body, the Parliament of Great Britain.

2d. That His Majesty's liege subjects in these colonies are entitled to all the inherent rights and privileges of his natural born subjects within the kingdom of Great Britain.

3d. That it is inseparably essential to the freedom of a people, and the undoubted rights of Englishmen, that no taxes should be imposed on them, but with their own consent, given personally, or by their representatives.

4th. That the people of these colonies are not, and from their local circumstances cannot be, represented in the House of Commons in Great Britain.

5th. That the only representatives of the people of these colonies are persons chosen therein, by themselves; and that no taxes ever have been or can be constitutionally imposed on them but by their respective legislatures.

6th. That all supplies to the crown, being free gifts of the people, it is unreasonable and inconsistent with the principles and spirit of the British constitution for the people of Great Britain to grant to His Majesty the property of the colonists.

7th. That trial by jury is the inherent and invaluable right of every British subject in these colonies.

8th. That the late act of Parliament entitled, "An act for granting and applying certain stamp duties, and other duties in the British colonies and plantations in America, etc.," by imposing taxes on the inhabitants of these colonies, and the said act, and several other acts, by extending the jurisdiction of the courts of admiralty beyond its ancient limits, have a manifest tendency to subvert the rights and liberties of the colonists.

9th. That the duties imposed by several late acts of Parliament, from the peculiar circumstances of these colonies, will be extremely burthensome and grievous, and, from the scarcity of specie, the payment of them absolutely impracticable.

10th. That as the profits of the trade of these colonies ultimately center in Great Britain, to pay for the manufactures which they are obliged to take from thence, they eventually contribute very largely to all supplies granted there to the crown.

11th. That the restrictions imposed by several late acts of Parliament on the trade of these colonies will render them unable to purchase the manufactures of Great Britain.

12th. That the increase, prosperity, and happiness of these colonies depend on the full and free enjoyment of their rights and liberties, and an intercourse, with Great Britain, mutually affectionate and advantageous.

13th. That it is the right of the British subjects in these colonies to petition the king or either house of Parliament.

Lastly, That it is the indispensable duty of these colonies to the best of sovereigns, to the mother-country, and to themselves, to endeavor, by a loyal and dutiful address to His Majesty, and humble application to both houses of Parliament, to procure the repeal of the act for granting and applying certain stamp duties, of all clauses of any other acts of Parliament whereby the jurisdiction of the admiralty is extended as aforesaid, and of the other late acts for the restriction of the American commerce.

4. THE DECLARATORY ACT, MARCH 18, 1766[1]

EDITORS' NOTE.—To the Rockingham ministry it became apparent that to attempt to enforce the Stamp Act would be politically dangerous, both in Britain and in the colonies. The nature of the situation may be understood in part from the motion to repeal the law, which stated that "the continuance of the said act would be attended with many inconveniencies, and may be productive of consequences greatly detrimental to the commercial interests of these kingdoms." The debate in Parliament proved to be bitter and was climaxed by the cogent testimony of Benjamin Franklin on behalf of the colonists.

On the same day that the House of Commons repealed the stamp duties it adopted the Declaratory Act, without a division—i.e., without a recorded vote. However, in the Lords, Pitt's friends attacked the measure strongly because it did not exclude internal taxation of the colonists from the scope of parliamentary supremacy. For the text of the law repealing the Stamp Act see 6 George III, c. 11, *The Statutes at Large*, p. 19.

AN ACT FOR THE BETTER SECURING THE DEPENDENCY OF HIS MAJESTY'S DOMINIONS IN AMERICA UPON THE CROWN AND PARLIAMENT OF GREAT BRITAIN

Whereas several of the houses of representatives in His Majesty's colonies and plantations in America have of late, against law, claimed to themselves, or to the general assemblies of the same, the sole and exclusive right of imposing duties and taxes upon His Majesty's subjects in the said colonies and plantations; and have, in pursuance of such claim, passed certain votes, resolutions, and orders derogatory to the legislative authority of Parliament, and inconsistent with the dependency of the said colonies and plantations upon the crown of Great Britain: may it therefore please Your Most Excellent Majesty that it may be declared, and be it declared by the king's Most Excellent Majesty, by and with the advice and consent of the Lords Spiritual and Temporal, and Commons, in this present Parliament assembled, and by the authority of the same, That the said colonies and plantations in *America* have been, are, and of right ought to be, subordinate unto, and dependent upon the imperial crown and Parliament of *Great Britain;* and that the king's Majesty, by and with the advice and consent of the Lords Spiritual and Temporal, and Commons, of *Great Britain*, in Parliament assembled, had, hath, and of right ought to have, full power and authority to make laws and statutes of sufficient force and validity to bind the colonies and people of *America*, subjects of the crown of *Great Britain*, in all cases whatsoever.

II. And be it further declared and enacted by the authority aforesaid, That all resolutions, votes, orders, and proceedings, in any of the said colonies or plantations, whereby the power and authority of the Parliament of *Great Britain* to make laws and statutes as aforesaid is denied, or drawn into question, are, and are hereby declared to be, utterly null and void to all intents and purposes whatsoever.

1. 6 George III, c. 12, *The Statutes at Large*, ed. Danby Pickering (London, 1767), XXVII, 19–20.

5. FRONTIER GRIEVANCES[1]

EDITORS' NOTE.—The importance of the difficulties between Britain and the American colonies should not be allowed to obscure the fact that a similar problem had already arisen in the New World where the settlers of the back country felt oppressed by those who lived in the older communities along the seacoast. Provoked by long-standing disregard of their complaints, many residents of Orange, Anson, and other western counties of North Carolina banded together in 1768 and resolved to pay no more taxes until their grievances were adjusted. This led to sporadic instances of violence by the Regulators, as the aroused settlers were known, against the unpopular colonial officers. In 1769 the Regulators elected a number of delegates to the colonial assembly. It was to this session of the legislature that the Regulators of Anson County directed the petition which is reprinted here.

Impatient with legislative delay, another band of Regulators assembled at Hillsboro, in September, 1770, to demand that the judges of the superior court redress such of the grievances

MR. SPEAKER AND GENT OF THE
    ASSEMBLY

The Petition of the Inhabitants of Anson County, being part of the Remonstrance of the Province of North Carolina,

HUMBLY SHEWETH

That the Province in general labor

as were local in nature. Violence again flared up. The house and barns of one of the justices were ransacked and burned. Governor Tryon then called out the militia and with a force of about a thousand men confronted about twice as many Regulators on the banks of the Alamance, in the western country, on May 16, 1770. After a two-hour battle and many casualties, the poorly organized insurgents were driven from the field. Several of their leaders were executed for treason; numbers of the rank and file fled the colony; and the movement was thus effectively crushed. During the Revolution, therefore, hatred of the ruling class led many former Regulators, unlike back-country people in most of the other colonies, to support the British cause. Nevertheless, it was not until the conflict with Britain led to independence that a deep-seated reform of internal conditions within the colonies became possible. James S. Bassett, "The Regulators of North Carolina," *American Historical Association Report* (1894), pp. 141–212, gives the standard account of the movement.

under general grievances, and the western part thereof under particular ones; which we not only see, but very sensibly feel, being crouch'd beneath our sufferings: and notwithstanding our sacred privileges, have too long yielded ourselves slaves to remorseless oppression.— Permit us to conceive it to be our inviolable right to make known our grievances, and to petition for redress; as appears in the Bill of Rights pass'd in the

1. *The Colonial Records of North Carolina* ..., ed. William L. Saunders (Raleigh, N.C., 1890), VIII, 75–78.

reign of King Charles the First,[2] as well as the act of settlement of the Crown of the Revolution. We therefore beg leave to lay before you a specimen thereof that your compassionate endeavors may tend to the relief of your injured constituents, whose distressed condition calls aloud for aid. The alarming cries of the oppressed possibly may reach your ears; but without your zeal how shall they ascend the throne—how relentless is the breast without sympathy, the heart that cannot bleed on a view of our calamity; to see tenderness removed, cruelty stepping in; and all our liberties and privileges invaded and abridg'd (by as it were) domestics: who are conscious of their guilt and void of remorse.—O how daring! how relentless! whilst impending judgments loudly threaten and gaze upon them, with every emblem of merited destruction.

A few of the many grievances are as follows (viz.):

1. That the poor inhabitants in general are much oppress'd by reason of disproportionate taxes, and those of the western counties in particular; as they are generally in mean circumstances.

2. That no method is prescribed by law for the payment of the taxes of the western counties in produce (in lieu of a currency) as is in other counties within this Province; to the people's great oppression.

3. That lawyers, clerks, and other pentioners; in place of being obsequious servants for the country's use, are become a nuisance, as the business of the people is often transacted without the least degree of fairness, the intention of the law evaded, exorbitant fees extorted, and the sufferers left to mourn under their oppressions.

4. That an attorney should have it in his power, either for the sake of ease or interest, or to gratify their malevolence and spite, to commence suits to what courts he pleases, however inconvenient it may be to the defendant: is a very great oppression.

5. That all unlawful fees taken on indictment, where the defendant is acquitted by his country (however customary it may be), is an oppression.

6. That lawyers, clerks, and others, extorting more fees than is intended by law, is also an oppression.

7. That the violation of the king's instructions to his delegates, their artfulness in concealing the same from him; and the great injury the people thereby sustains: is a manifest oppression.

And for remedy whereof, we take the freedom to recommend the following mode of redress, not doubting audience and acceptance; which will not only tend to our relief, but command prayers as a duty from your humble petitioners.

1. That at all elections each suffrage be given by ticket and ballot.

2. That the mode of taxation be altered, and each person to pay in proportion to the profits arising from his estate.[3]

3. That no future tax be laid in money, until a currency is made.

4. That there may be established a western as well as a northern and southern district, and a treasurer for the same.[4]

5. That when a currency is made it may be let out by a loan office (on land security) and not to be call'd in by a tax.[5]

---

3. Under existing law a poll tax was laid on all adult white males and on all adult Negroes, male and female. It was often charged, therefore, that this required that rich and poor pay the same tax. This was not quite accurate, since the wealthy also had to pay the head tax upon their slaves.

4. The purpose of this measure was to make it unnecessary to travel long distances in order to transact business with the government.

5. This reflects a demand for a more permanent issue of paper money. Paper currency issued during the last French and Indian War was to be retired in part each year, based on the revenue from an annual levy of 3s. per person.

2. I.e., the Petition of Right (1628). The Bill of Rights was not passed until 1689, in the reign of William and Mary.

6. That all debts above 40s. and under £10 be tried and determined without lawyers, by a jury of six freeholders, impaneled by a Justice, and that their verdict be enter'd by the said Justice, and be a final judgment.

7. That the chief justice have no perquisites, but a salary only.

8. That clerks be restricted in respect to fees, costs, and other things within the course of their office.

9. That lawyers be effectually barr'd from exacting and extorting fees.

10. That all doubts may be removed in respect to the payment of fees and costs on indictments where the defendant is not found guilty by the jury, and therefore acquitted.

11. That the Assembly make known by remonstrance to the king, the conduct of the cruel and oppressive receiver of the quit rents, for omitting the customary easy and effectual method of collecting by distress, and pursuing the expensive mode of commencing suits in the most distant courts.

12. That the Assembly in like manner make known that the governor and Council do frequently grant lands to as many as they think proper without regard to head rights, notwithstanding the contrariety of His Majesty's instructions; by which means immense sums have been collected, and numerous patents granted, for much of the most fertile lands in this province, that is yet uninhabited and uncultivated, environed by great numbers of poor people who are necessitated to toil in the cultivation of bad lands whereon they hardly can subsist, who are thereby deprived of His Majesty's liberality and bounty: nor is there the least regard paid to the cultivation clause in said patent mentioned, as many of the said Council as well as their friends and favorites enjoy large quantities of lands under the above-mentioned circumstances.

13. That the Assembly communicates in like manner the violation of His Majesty's instructions respecting the land office by the governor and Council, and of their own rules, customs and orders, if it be sufficiently proved, that after they had granted warrants for many tracts of land, and that the same was in due time survey'd and return'd, and the patent fees timely paid into the said office; and that if a private Council was called on purpose to avoid spectators, and peremptory orders made that patents should not be granted; and warrants by their orders arbitrarily to have issued in the names of other persons for the same lands, and if when intreated by a solicitor they refus'd to render so much as a reason for their so doing, or to refund any part of the money by them extorted.

14. That some method may be pointed out that every improvement on lands in any of the proprietors part be proved when begun, by whom, and every sale made, that the eldest may have the preference of at least 300 acres.

15. That all taxes in the following counties be paid as in other counties in the Province (i.e.) in the produce of the country and that warehouses be erected. . . .

16. That every denomination of people may marry according to their respective mode ceremony and custom after due publication or license.—

17. That Doctor Benjamin Franklin or some other known patriot be appointed agent, to represent the unhappy state of this Province to His Majesty, and to solicit the several boards in England:— [260 signatures follow.]

6. DECLARATION OF COLONIAL RIGHTS: RESOLUTIONS OF THE FIRST CONTINENTAL CONGRESS, OCTOBER 14, 1774[1]

EDITORS' NOTE.—Following the Boston Tea Party and the adoption of the Intolerable Acts, delegates gathered on September 5, 1774, at Philadelphia, in what was to become the First Continental Congress. Every colony but Georgia was represented. They voted on September 6 to appoint a committee "to state the rights of the Colonies in general, the several instances in which these rights are violated or infringed, and the means most proper to be pursued for obtaining a restoration of them" (*Journals of the Continental Congress, 1774-1789* [Washington, 1904], I, 26).

Joseph Galloway (1731–1803), a Philadelphia merchant and lawyer, led a conservative attempt to unite the colonies within the Empire. He had served as speaker of the Pennsylvania Assembly from 1766 to 1774. In the war Galloway supported the British cause and after 1778 became spokesman for the Loyalists in England. In the First Continental Congress the more radical delegates thrust aside Galloway's proposal and on October 14 adopted instead, by unanimous action, the Declaration of Colonial Rights reproduced here. The first draft of these resolutions was written by Major John Sullivan (1740–95), delegate from New Hampshire, lawyer, major of the New Hampshire militia, major general in the Continental Army, judge, and eventually governor of his state.

Before they dissolved, on October 26, the members voted to meet again in the same city on May 10, 1775, "unless the redress of grievances . . . be obtained before that time" (*ibid.*, p. 102).

The Congress met according to adjournment, and resuming the consideration of the subject under debate—came into the following resolutions:

SULLIVAN'S DRAUGHT

. . . Whereas, since the close of the last war, the British Parliament, claiming a power of right to bind the people of America, by statute in all cases whatsoever, hath in some acts expressly imposed taxes on them, and in others, under various pretenses, but in fact for the purpose of raising a revenue, hath imposed rates and duties payable in these colonies, established a board of commissioners, with unconstitutional powers, and extended the jurisdiction of courts of ad-

miralty, not only for collecting the said duties, but for the trial of causes merely arising within the body of a county.

And whereas, in consequence of other statutes, judges, who before held only estates at will in their offices, have been made dependent upon the crown alone for their salaries, and standing armies kept in times of peace:

And it has lately been resolved in Parliament, that by force of a statute, made in the thirty-fifth year of the reign of King Henry the Eighth, colonists may be transported to England, and tried there upon accusations for treasons, and misprisions, or concealments of treasons committed in the colonies; and by a late statute, such trials have been directed in cases therein mentioned.

1. *Journals of the Continental Congress, 1774-1789* (Washington, 1904), I, 63–73.

And whereas, in the last session of Parliament, three statutes were made; one, entitled "An act to discontinue, in such manner and for such time as are therein mentioned, the landing and discharging, lading, or shipping of goods, wares and merchandise, at the town, and within the harbor of Boston, in the province of Massachusetts Bay, in North America"; another, entitled "An act for the better regulating the government of the province of the Massachusetts Bay in New England"; and another, entitled "An act for the impartial administration of justice, in the cases of persons questioned for any act done by them in the execution of the law, or for the suppression of riots and tumults, in the province of the Massachusetts Bay, in New England." And another statute was then made, "for making more effectual provision for the government of the province of Quebec, etc." All which statutes are impolitic, unjust, and cruel, as well as unconstitutional, and most dangerous and destructive of American rights.

And whereas, assemblies have been frequently dissolved, contrary to the rights of the people, when they attempted to deliberate on grievances; and their dutiful, humble, loyal, and reasonable petitions to the crown for redress have been repeatedly treated with contempt by His Majesty's ministers of state:

The good people of the several colonies of New Hampshire, Massachusetts Bay, Rhode Island and Providence Plantations, Connecticut, New York, New Jersey, Pennsylvania, Newcastle, Kent and Sussex on Delaware, Maryland, Virginia, North Carolina, and South Carolina, justly alarmed at these arbitrary proceedings of Parliament and administration, have severally elected, constituted, and appointed deputies to meet and sit in General Congress, in the city of Philadelphia, in order to obtain such establishment, as that their religion, laws, and liberties may not be subverted:

Whereupon the deputies so appointed being now assembled, in a full and free representation of these colonies, taking into their most serious consideration, the best means of attaining the ends aforesaid, do, in the first place, as Englishmen, their ancestors in like cases have usually done, for asserting and vindicating their rights and liberties, declare,

That the inhabitants of the English Colonies in North America, by the immutable laws of nature, the principles of the English constitution, and the several charters or compacts, have the following rights:

Resolved, N.C.D.[2] 1. That they are entitled to life, liberty, and property, and they have never ceded to any sovereign power whatever, a right to dispose of either without their consent.

Resolved, N.C.D. 2. That our ancestors, who first settled these colonies, were, at the time of their emigration from the mother-country, entitled to all the rights, liberties, and immunities of free and natural-born subjects, within the realm of England.

Resolved, N.C.D. 3. That by such emigration they by no means forfeited, surrendered, or lost any of those rights, but that they were, and their descendants now are, entitled to the exercise and enjoyment of all such of them, as their local and other circumstances enable them to exercise and enjoy.

Resolved, 4. That the foundation of English liberty, and of all free government, is a right in the people to participate in their legislative council: and as the English colonists are not represented,

2. I.e., *nemine contradicente*, meaning without a dissenting vote or unanimously. Commenting on these proceedings before a committee of the British House of Commons, in June, 1779, Galloway stated that, although the resolutions were recorded as having been passed unanimously, this meant not that they were approved by every member present but by a majority of each delegation (*The Examination of Joseph Galloway . . . before the House of Commons . . .* [2d ed.; London, 1780], p. 61).

and from their local and other circumstances, cannot properly be represented in the British Parliament, they are entitled to a free and exclusive power of legislation in their several provincial legislatures, where their right of representation can alone be preserved, in all cases of taxation and internal polity, subject only to the negative of their sovereign, in such manner as has been heretofore used and accustomed. But, from the necessity of the case, and a regard to the mutual interest of both countries, we cheerfully consent to the operation of such acts of the British Parliament, as are bona fide, restrained to the regulation of our external commerce, for the purpose of securing the commercial advantages of the whole empire to the mother-country, and the commercial benefits of its respective members; excluding every idea of taxation, internal or external, for raising a revenue on the subjects in America, without their consent.

Resolved, N.C.D. 5. That the respective colonies are entitled to the common law of England, and more especially to the great and inestimable privilege of being tried by their peers of the vicinage, according to the course of that law.

Resolved, 6. That they are entitled to the benefit of such of the English statutes as existed at the time of their colonization; and which they have, by experience, respectively found to be applicable to their several local and other circumstances.

Resolved, N.C.D. 7. That these His Majesty's colonies, are likewise entitled to all the immunities and privileges granted and confirmed to them by royal charters, or secured by their several codes of provincial laws.

Resolved, N.C.D. 8. That they have a right peaceably to assemble, consider of their grievances, and petition the king; and that all prosecutions, prohibitory proclamations, and commitments for the same are illegal.

Resolved, N.C.D. 9. That the keeping a standing army in these colonies, in times of peace, without the consent of the legislature of that colony, in which such army is kept, is against law.

Resolved, N.C.D. 10. It is indispensably necessary to good government, and rendered essential by the English constitution, that the constituent branches of the legislature be independent of each other; that, therefore, the exercise of the legislative power in several colonies, by a council appointed, during pleasure, by the crown, is unconstitutional, dangerous, and destructive to the freedom of American legislation.

All and each of which the aforesaid deputies, in behalf of themselves and their constituents, do claim, demand, and insist on, as their indubitable rights and liberties; which cannot be legally taken from them, altered or abridged by any power whatever, without their own consent, by their representatives in their several provincial legislatures.

In the course of our inquiry, we find many infringements and violations of the foregoing rights, which, from an ardent desire, that harmony and mutual intercourse of affection and interest may be restored, we pass over for the present, and proceed to state such acts and measures as have been adopted since the last war, which demonstrate a system formed to enslave America.

Resolved, N.C.D. That the following acts of Parliament are infringements and violations of the rights of the colonists; and that the repeal of them is essentially necessary in order to restore harmony between Great Britain and the American colonies, viz.:

The several acts of 4 Geo. 3, ch. 15, and ch. 34.—5 Geo. 3, ch. 25.—6 Geo. 3, ch. 52.—7 Geo. 3, ch. 41, and ch. 46.—8 Geo. 3, ch. 22, which impose duties for the purpose of raising a revenue in America, extend the powers of the admiralty courts beyond their ancient limits, deprive the American subject of trial by jury, authorize the judges' certificate to indemnify the prosecutor from damages, that he might otherwise be liable to, requiring oppressive security from a claimant of ships and goods seized, before he shall be allowed to defend his property, and are subversive of American rights.

Also the 12 Geo. 3, ch. 24, entitled "An act for the better securing His Majesty's dockyards, magazines, ships, ammunition, and stores," which declares a new offense in America, and deprives the American subject of a constitutional trial by a jury of the vicinage, by authorizing the trial of any person, charged with the committing any offense described in the said act, out of the realm, to be indicted and tried for the same in any shire or county within the realm.

Also the three acts passed in the last session of Parliament, for stopping the port and blocking up the harbor of Boston, for altering the charter and government of the Massachusetts Bay, and that which is entitled "An act for the better administration of justice," etc.

Also the act passed in the same session for establishing the Roman Catholic religion in the Province of Quebec, abolishing the equitable system of English laws, and erecting a tyranny there, to the great danger, from so total a dissimilarity of religion, law, and government of the neighboring British colonies, by the assistance of whose blood and treasure

the said country was conquered from France.

Also the act passed in the same session for the better providing suitable quarters for officers and soldiers in His Majesty's service in North America.

Also, that the keeping a standing army in several of these colonies, in time of peace, without the consent of the legislature of that colony in which such army is kept, is against law.

To these grievous acts and measures, Americans cannot submit, but in hopes that their fellow-subjects in Great Britain will, on a revision of them, restore us to that state in which both countries found happiness and prosperity, we have for the present only resolved to pursue the following peaceable measures:

Resolved, unanimously, That from and after the first day of December next, there be no importation into British America, from Great Britain or Ireland of any goods, wares or merchandise whatsoever, or from any other place of any such goods, wares or merchandise.[3]

1st. To enter into a nonimportation, nonconsumption, and nonexportation agreement or association.

2. To prepare an address to the people of Great Britain, and a memorial to the inhabitants of British America, and

3. To prepare a loyal address to His Majesty; agreeable to resolutions already entered into.

7. DECLARATION OF TAKING UP ARMS: RESOLUTIONS OF THE SECOND CONTINENTAL CONGRESS, JULY 6, 1775[1]

EDITORS' NOTE.—Since the colonial governors had taken steps to prevent the assemblies from naming delegates to the Second Continental Congress, the representatives to that body were

3. This paragraph was struck out.
1. *Journals of the Continental Congress, 1774-1789*, II, 140–57.

chosen by irregular conventions. For this reason the Second Continental Congress was, from the beginning, an extra-legal, if not a revolutionary, assembly rather than a constitutionally authorized gathering. While it took steps to defend the colonies, it did not gather in a mood to declare immediate independence. To clarify its position, Congress adopted the Declaration reproduced below. The first draft is said to have been written by John Rutledge, but no copy of it has been found (for a brief sketch of the life of Rutledge see p. 258). An early draft of this document, written by Jefferson,

proved too strong for the committee (*Journals of the Continental Congress, 1774–1789*, II, 128 n.). It was redrafted and toned down by John Dickinson (cf. p. 261) and adopted after debate, on July 6, in order that Washington might publish it on his arrival at the camp before Boston.

A declaration by the representatives of the United Colonies of North America, now met in general Congress at Philadelphia, setting forth the causes and necessity of their taking up arms.

If it was possible for men, who exercise their reason, to believe, that the Divine Author of our existence intended a part of the human race to hold an absolute property in, and an unbounded power over others, marked out by his infinite goodness and wisdom, as the objects of a legal domination never rightfully resistible, however severe and oppressive, the inhabitants of these colonies might at least require from the Parliament of Great Britain some evidence that this dreadful authority over them has been granted to that body. But a reverence for our great Creator, principles of humanity, and the dictates of common sense must convince all those who reflect upon the subject that government was instituted to promote the welfare of mankind and ought to be administered for the attainment of that end. The legislature of Great Britain, however, stimulated by an inordinate passion for a power, not only unjustifiable, but which they know to be peculiarly reprobated by the very constitution of that kingdom, and desperate of success in any mode of contest, where regard should be had to truth, law, or right, have at length, deserting those, attempted to effect their cruel and impolitic purpose of enslaving these colonies by violence, and have thereby rendered it necessary for

us to close with their last appeal from reason to arms.

Yet, however blinded that assembly may be, by their intemperate rage for unlimited domination, so to slight justice and the opinion of mankind, we esteem ourselves bound, by obligations of respect to the rest of the world, to make known the justice of our cause.

Our forefathers, inhabitants of the island of Great Britain, left their native land to seek on these shores a residence for civil and religious freedom. At the expense of their blood, at the hazard of their fortunes, without the least charge to the country from which they removed, by unceasing labor, and an unconquerable spirit, they effected settlements in the distant and inhospitable wilds of America, then filled with numerous and warlike nations of barbarians. Societies or governments, vested with perfect legislatures, were formed under charters from the crown, and a harmonious intercourse was established between the colonies and the kingdom from which they derived their origin. The mutual benefits of this union became in a short time so extraordinary as to excite astonishment. It is universally confessed that the amazing increase of the wealth, strength, and navigation of the realm arose from this source; and the minister, who so wisely and successfully directed the measures of Great Britain in the late war, publicly declared that these colonies enabled her to triumph over her enemies.

Toward the conclusion of that war, it pleased our sovereign to make a change in his counsels. From that fatal moment, the affairs of the British Empire began to fall into confusion, and gradually sliding from the summit of glorious prosperity, to which they had been advanced by the virtues and abilities of one man, are at length distracted by the convulsions that now shake it to its deepest foundations. The new ministry finding the brave foes of Britain, though frequently defeated, yet still contending, took up the unfortunate idea of granting them a hasty peace and of then subduing her faithful friends.

These devoted colonies were judged to be in such a state, as to present victories without bloodshed, and all the easy emoluments of statutable plunder. The uninterrupted tenor of their peaceable and respectful behavior from the beginning of colonization, their dutiful, zealous, and useful services during the war, though so recently and amply acknowledged in the most honorable manner by His Majesty, by the late king, and by Parliament, could not save them from the meditated innovations.

Parliament was influenced to adopt the pernicious project, and assuming a new power over them, have, in the course of eleven years, given such decisive specimens of the spirit and consequences attending this power, as to leave no doubt concerning the effects of acquiescence under it. They have undertaken to give and grant our money without our consent, though we have ever exercised an exclusive right to dispose of our own property; statutes have been passed for extending the jurisdiction of courts of admiralty and vice-admiralty beyond their ancient limits; for depriving us of the accustomed and inestimable privilege of trial by jury, in cases affecting both life and property; for suspending the legislature of one of the colonies; for interdicting all commerce to the capital of another; and for altering fundamentally the form of government established by charter and secured by acts of its own legislature solemnly confirmed by the crown; for exempting the "murderers" of colonists from legal trial and, in effect, from punishment; for erecting in a neighboring province, acquired by the joint arms of Great Britain and America, a despotism dangerous to our very existence; and for quartering soldiers upon the colonists in time of profound peace. It has also been resolved in Parliament that colonists charged with committing certain offenses shall be transported to England to be tried.

But why should we enumerate our injuries in detail? By one statute it is declared, that Parliament can "of right make laws to bind us IN ALL CASES WHATSOEVER." What is to defend us against so enormous, so unlimited a power? Not a single man of those who assume it is chosen by us or is subject to our control or influence; but, on the contrary, they are all of them exempt from the operation of such laws, and an American revenue, if not diverted from the ostensible purposes for which it is raised, would actually lighten their own burdens in proportion as they increase ours. We saw the misery to which such despotism would reduce us. We for ten years incessantly and ineffectually besieged the throne as suppliants; we reasoned, we remonstrated with Parliament, in the most mild and decent language. But administration, sensible that we should regard these oppressive measures as freemen ought to do, sent over fleets and armies to enforce them. The indignation of the Americans was roused, it is true; but it was the indignation of a virtuous, loyal, and affectionate people. A Congress of Delegates from the United Colonies was assembled at Philadelphia, on the fifth day of last September. We resolved again to offer a humble and dutiful petition to the king, and also addressed our fellow-subjects of Great Britain. We have pursued every temperate, every respectful, measure: we have even proceeded to break off our commercial intercourse with our fellow-subjects, as the last peaceable admonition, that our attachment to no nation upon earth should supplant our attachment to liberty. This, we flattered ourselves, was the ultimate step of the controversy. But subsequent events have shown how vain was this hope of finding moderation in our enemies.

Several threatening expressions against the colonies were inserted in His Majesty's speech; our petition, though we were told it was a decent one, and that His Majesty had been pleased to receive it graciously, and to promise laying it before his Parliament, was huddled into both houses amongst a bundle of American papers, and there neglected. The Lords and Commons in their address, in the month of February, said, that "a rebellion at that time actually existed within the province of Massachusetts Bay; and that those concerned in it, had been countenanced and encouraged by unlawful combinations and engagements, entered into by His Majesty's subjects in several of the other colonies; and therefore they besought His Majesty, that he would take the most effectual measures to enforce due obedience to the laws and authority of the supreme legislature." Soon after, the commercial intercourse of whole colonies, with foreign countries, and with each other, was cut off by an act of Parliament; by another, several of them were entirely prohibited from the fisheries in the seas near their coasts, on which they always depended for their sustenance; and large reinforcements of ships and troops were immediately sent over to General Gage.

Fruitless were all the entreaties, arguments, and eloquence of an illustrious band of the most distinguished Peers, and Commoners, who nobly and strenuously asserted the justice of our cause, to stay, or even to mitigate the heedless fury with which these accumulated and unexampled outrages were hurried on. Equally fruitless was the interference of the city of London, of Bristol, and many other respectable towns in our favor. Parliament adopted an insidious maneuver calculated to divide us, to establish a perpetual auction of taxations where colony should bid against colony, all of them uninformed what ransom would redeem their lives; and thus to extort from us, at the point of the bayonet, the unknown sums that should be sufficient to gratify, if possible to gratify, ministerial rapacity, with the miserable indulgence left to us of raising, in our own mode, the prescribed tribute. What terms more rigid and humiliating could have been dictated by remorseless victors to conquered enemies? In our circumstances to accept them would be to deserve them.

Soon after the intelligence of these proceedings arrived on this continent, General Gage, who in the course of the last year had taken possession of the town of Boston, in the province of Massachusetts Bay, and still occupied it as a garrison, on the 19th day of April, sent out from that place a large detachment of his army, who made an unprovoked assault on the inhabitants of the said province, at the town of Lexington, as appears by the affidavits of a great number of persons, some of whom were officers and soldiers of that detachment, murdered eight of the inhabitants, and wounded many others. From thence the troops proceeded in warlike array to the town of Concord, where they set upon another party of the inhabitants of the same province, killing several and wounding more, until compelled to retreat by the country people suddenly assembled to repel this cruel aggression. Hostilities, thus commenced by the British troops, have been since prosecuted by them without regard to faith or reputation. The inhabitants of Boston being confined within that town by the General, their Governor, and having, in order to procure their dismission, entered into a treaty with him, it was stipulated that the said inhabitants, having deposited their arms with their own magistrates, should have liberty to depart, taking with them their other effects. They accordingly delivered up their arms, but in open violation of honor, in defiance of the obligation of treaties, which even savage nations esteemed sacred, the Governor ordered the arms deposited as aforesaid, that they might be preserved for their owners, to be seized by a body of soldiers; detained the greatest part of the inhabitants in the town, and compelled the few who were permitted to retire to leave their most valuable effects behind.

By this perfidy wives are separated from their husbands, children from their parents, the aged and the sick from their relations and friends, who wish to attend and comfort them; and those who have been used to live in plenty and even elegance are reduced to deplorable distress.

The General, further emulating his ministerial masters, by a proclamation bearing date on the 12th day of June, after venting the grossest falsehoods and calumnies against the good people of these colonies, proceeds to "declare them all, either by name or description, to be rebels and traitors, to supersede the course of the common law, and instead thereof to publish and order the use and exercise of the law martial." His troops have butchered our countrymen, have wantonly burned Charles-Town, besides a considerable number of houses in other places; our ships and vessels are seized; the necessary supplies of provisions are intercepted, and he is exerting his utmost power to spread destruction and devastation around him.

We have received certain intelligence that General Carleton, the Governor of Canada, is instigating the people of that province and the Indians to fall upon us; and we have but too much reason to apprehend that schemes have been formed to excite domestic enemies against us. In brief, a part of these colonies now feels, and all of them are sure of feeling, as far as the vengeance of administration can inflict them, the complicated calamities of fire, sword, and famine. We are reduced to the alternative of choosing an unconditional submission to the tyranny of irritated ministers, or resistance by force. The latter is our choice. We have counted the cost of this contest and find nothing so dreadful as voluntary slavery. Honor, justice, and humanity forbid us tamely to surrender that freedom which we received from our gallant ancestors, and which our innocent posterity have a right to receive from us. We cannot endure the infamy and guilt of resigning succeeding generations to that wretchedness which inevitably awaits them, if we basely entail hereditary bondage upon them.

Our cause is just. Our union is perfect. Our internal resources are great, and, if necessary, foreign assistance is undoubtedly attainable. We gratefully acknowledge, as signal instances of the Divine favor toward us, that his Providence would not permit us to be called into this severe controversy, until we were grown up to our present strength, had been previously exercised in warlike operation, and possessed of the means of defending ourselves. With hearts fortified with these animating reflections, we most solemnly, before God and the world, declare that, exerting the utmost energy of those powers which our beneficent Creator hath graciously bestowed upon us, the arms we have been compelled by our enemies to assume we will, in defiance of every hazard, with unabating firmness and perseverance, employ for the preservation of our liberties; being with our [one] mind resolved to die free men rather than live slaves.

Lest this declaration should disquiet the minds of our friends and fellow-subjects in any part of the Empire, we assure them that we mean not to dissolve that union which has so long and so happily subsisted between us, and which we sincerely wish to see restored. Necessity has not yet driven us into that desperate measure, or induced us to excite any other nation to war against them. We have not raised armies with ambitious designs of separating from Great Britain and establishing independent states. We fight not for glory or for conquest. We exhibit to mankind the remarkable spectacle of a people attacked by unprovoked enemies, without any imputation or even suspicion of offense. They boast of their privileges and civilization and yet proffer no milder conditions than servitude or death.

In our own native land, in defense of the freedom that is our birthright, and which we ever enjoyed till the late violation of it—for the protection of our property, acquired solely by the honest industry of our forefathers and ourselves, against violence actually offered, we have taken up arms. We shall lay them down when hostilities shall cease on the part of the aggressors, and all danger of their being renewed shall be removed, and not before.

With a humble confidence in the mercies of the supreme and impartial Judge and Ruler of the universe, we most devoutly implore his divine goodness to protect us happily through this great conflict, to dispose our adversaries to reconciliation on reasonable terms, and thereby to relieve the Empire from the calamities of civil war.

By order of Congress,

JOHN HANCOCK,
President

Attested,

CHARLES THOMSON,
Secretary

PHILADELPHIA, July 6th, 1775

8. TAXATION NO TYRANNY[1]

By SAMUEL JOHNSON

EDITORS' NOTE.—Samuel Johnson (1709–84), the lexicographer, conversationalist, and critic. Shortly after the accession of George III, Johnson was granted a pension by the government. Boswell states: "That this pamphlet was written at the desire of those who were then in power, I have no doubt; and, indeed, he owned to me, that it had been revised and curtailed by some of them" (... *Life of Johnson*, ed. C. B. Tinker [New York, 1933], I, 560).

In all the parts of human knowledge, whether terminating in science merely speculative or operating upon life private or civil, are admitted some fundamental principles or common axioms, which being generally received are little doubted, and being little doubted have been rarely proved....

Of this kind is the position that *the supreme power of every community has the right of requiring from all its subjects such contributions as are necessary to the public safety or public prosperity,* which was considered by all mankind as comprising the primary and essential condition of all political society till it became disputed by those zealots of anarchy who have denied to the Parliament of Britain the right of taxing the American colonies. ...

We are told how their industry is obstructed by unnatural restraints and their trade confined by rigorous prohibitions; how they are forbidden to enjoy the products of their own soil, to manufacture the materials which nature spreads

1. By Samuel Johnson, *Works* ... (London, 1796), VIII, 155–59, 162–64, 168–76, 178–81, 183–85, 187–93.

before them, or to carry their own goods to the nearest market; and surely the generosity of English virtue will never heap new weight upon those that are already overladen; will never delight in that dominion which cannot be exercised but by cruelty and outrage.

But while we are melting in silent sorrow and in the transports of delirious pity dropping both the sword and balance from our hands, another friend of the Americans thinks it better to awaken another passion and tries to alarm our interest, or excite our veneration, by accounts of their greatness and their opulence, of the fertility of their land, and the splendor of their towns. We then begin to consider the question with more evenness of mind, are ready to conclude that those restrictions are not very oppressive which have been found consistent with this speedy growth of prosperity, and begin to think it reasonable that they, who thus flourish under the protection of our government, should contribute something toward its expense.

But we are soon told that the Americans, however wealthy, cannot be taxed; that they are the descendants of men who left all for liberty and that they have constantly preserved the principles and stubbornness of their progenitors; that they are too obstinate for persuasion and too powerful for constraint; that they will laugh at argument and defeat violence; that the continent of North America contains three millions, not of men merely, but of Whigs, of Whigs fierce for liberty, and disdainful of dominion; that they multiply with the fecundity of their own rattlesnakes, so that every quarter of a century doubles their numbers. Men accustomed to think themselves masters do not love to be threatened. This talk is, I hope, commonly thrown away or raises passions different from those which it was intended to excite. Instead of terrifying the English hearer to tame acquiescence, it disposes him to hasten the experiment

of bending obstinacy before it is become yet more obdurate and convinces him that it is necessary to attack a nation thus prolific while we may yet hope to prevail. When he is told through what extent of territory we must travel to subdue them, he recollects how far, a few years ago, we traveled in their defense. . . .

But terrors and pity are not the only means by which the taxation of the Americans is opposed. There are those who profess to use them only as auxiliaries to reason and justice, who tell us that to tax the colonies is usurpation and oppression, an invasion of natural and legal rights, and a violation of those principles which support the constitution of English government.

This question is of great importance. That the Americans are able to bear taxation is indubitable; that their refusal may be overruled is highly probable; but power is no sufficient evidence of truth. Let us examine our own claim and the objections of the recusants with caution proportioned to the event of the decision, which must convict one part of robbery or the other of rebellion.

A tax is a payment exacted by authority from part of the community for the benefit of the whole. From whom, and in what proportion such payment shall be required, and to what uses it shall be applied, those only are to judge to whom government is intrusted. In the British dominion taxes are apportioned, levied, and appropriated by the states assembled in Parliament.

Of every empire all the subordinate communities are liable to taxation, because they all share the benefits of government and therefore ought all to furnish their proportion of the expense.

This the Americans have never openly denied. That it is their duty to pay the costs of their own safety they seem to admit; nor do they refuse their contribution to the exigencies, whatever they may be, of the British Empire; but they make this participation of the public burden a duty of very uncertain extent and imperfect obligation, a duty temporary, occasional, and elective, of which they reserve to themselves the right of settling the degree, the time, and the duration, of judging when it may be required and when it has been performed.

They allow to the supreme power nothing more than the liberty of notifying to them its demands or its necessities. Of this notification they profess to think for themselves, how far it shall influence their counsels, and, of the necessities alleged, how far they shall endeavor to relieve them. They assume the exclusive power of settling not only the mode but the quantity of this payment. They are ready to co-operate with all the other dominions of the king, but they will co-operate by no means which they do not like and at no greater charge than they are willing to bear. . . .

For the satisfaction of this inquiry, it is necessary to consider how a colony is constituted, what are the terms of migration as dictated by nature, or settled by compact, and what social or political rights the man loses, or acquires, that leaves his country to establish himself in a distant plantation. . . .

The colonies of England differ no otherwise from those of other nations than as the English constitution differs from theirs. All government is ultimately and essentially absolute, but subordinate societies may have more immunities, or individuals greater liberty, as the operations of government are differently conducted. An Englishman in the common course of life and action feels no restraint. An English colony has very liberal powers of regulating its own manners and adjusting its own affairs. But an English individual may by the supreme authority be deprived of liberty, and a colony divested of its powers, for reasons of which that authority is the only judge.

In sovereignty there are no gradations.

There may be limited royalty, there may be limited consulship; but there can be no limited government. There must in every society be some power or other from which there is no appeal, which admits no restrictions, which pervades the whole mass of the community, regulates and adjusts all subordination, enacts laws or repeals them, erects or annuls judicatures, extends or contracts privileges, exempts itself from question or control, and [is] bounded only by physical necessity. . . .

An English colony is a number of persons to whom the king grants a charter permitting them to settle in some distant country, and enabling them to constitute a corporation, enjoying such powers as the charter grants, to be administered in such forms as the charter prescribes. As a corporation they make laws for themselves, but as a corporation subsisting by a grant from higher authority, to the control of that authority they continue subject.

As men are placed at a greater distance from the supreme council of the kingdom, they must be intrusted with ampler liberty of regulating their conduct by their own wisdom. As they are more secluded from easy recourse to national judicature, they must be more extensively commissioned to pass judgment on each other.

For this reason our more important and opulent colonies see the appearance and feel the effect of a regular legislature, which in some places has acted so long with unquestioned authority that it has forgotten whence that authority was originally derived.

To their charters the colonies owe, like other corporations, their political existence. The solemnities of legislation, the administration of justice, the security of property, are all bestowed upon them by the royal grant. Without their charter there would be no power among them, by which any law could be made, or duties enjoined, any debt recovered, or criminal punished.

A charter is a grant of certain powers or privileges given to a part of the community for the advantage of the whole and is therefore liable by its nature to change or to revocation. Every act of government aims at public good. A charter which experience has shown to be detrimental to the nation is to be repealed, because general prosperity must always be preferred to particular interest. If a charter be used to evil purposes, it is forfeited, as the weapon is taken away which is injuriously employed. . . .

A colony is to the mother-country as a member to the body, deriving its action and its strength from the general principle of vitality; receiving from the body, and communicating to it, all the benefits and evils of health and disease; liable in dangerous maladies to sharp applications, of which the body however must partake the pain; and exposed, if incurably tainted, to amputation, by which the body likewise will be mutilated.

The mother-country always considers the colonies thus connected, as parts of itself; the prosperity or unhappiness of either is the prosperity or unhappiness of both; not perhaps of both in the same degree, for the body may subsist, though less commodiously, without a limb, but the limb must perish if it be parted from the body.

Our colonies therefore, however distant, have been hitherto treated as constituent parts of the British Empire. The inhabitants incorporated by English charters are entitled to all the rights of Englishmen. They are governed by English laws, entitled to English dignities, regulated by English counsels, and protected by English arms; and it seems to follow by consequence not easily avoided that they are subject to English government and chargeable by English taxation.

To him that considers the nature, the original, the progress, and the constitution of the colonies, who remembers that the first discoveries had commissions from the crown, that the first settlers owe to a charter their civil forms and regular magistracy, and that all personal immunities and legal securities, by which the condition of the subject has been from time to time improved, have been extended to the colonists, it will not be doubted but the Parliament of England has a right to bind them by statutes, and *to bind them in all cases whatsoever*, and has therefore a natural and constitutional power of laying upon them any tax or impost, whether external or internal, upon the product of land, or the manufactures of industry, in the exigencies of war, or in the time of profound peace, for the defense of America, *for the purpose of raising a revenue*, or for any other end beneficial to the empire.

There are some, and those not inconsiderable for number, nor contemptible for knowledge, who except the power of taxation from the general dominion of Parliament, and hold that, whatever degrees of obedience may be exacted, or whatever authority may be exercised in other acts of government, there is still reverence to be paid to money and that legislation passes its limits when it violates the purse.

Of this exception, which by a head not fully impregnated with politics is not easily comprehended, it is alleged as an unanswerable reason that the colonies send no representatives to the House of Commons.

It is, say the American advocates, the natural distinction of a freeman, and the legal privilege of an Englishman, that he is able to call his possessions his own, that he can sit secure in the enjoyment of inheritance or acquisition, that his house is fortified by the law, and that nothing can be taken from him but by his own consent. This consent is given for every man by his representative in Parliament. The Americans unrepresented cannot consent to English taxations as a corporation, and they will not consent as individuals.

Of this argument, it has been observed by more than one that its force extends equally to all other laws, for a freeman is not to be exposed to punishment or be called to any onerous service but by his own consent. The Congress has extracted a position from the fanciful Montesquieu[2] that *in a free state every man being a free agent ought to be concerned in his own government.* Whatever is true of taxation is true of every other law, that he who is bound by it, without his consent, is not free, for he is not concerned in his own government.

He that denies the English Parliament the right of taxation denies it likewise the right of making any other laws civil or criminal, yet this power over the colonies was never yet disputed by themselves. They have always admitted statutes for the punishment of offenses and for the redress or prevention of inconveniencies, and the reception of any law draws after it, by a chain which cannot be broken, the unwelcome necessity of submitting to taxation.

That a free man is governed by himself, or by laws to which he has consented, is a position of mighty sound; but every man that utters it, with whatever confidence, and every man that hears it, with whatever acquiescence, if consent be supposed to imply the power of refusal, feels it to be false. We virtually and implicitly allow the institutions of any government of which we enjoy the benefit and solicit the protection. In wide-extended dominions, though power has been diffused with the most even hand, yet a very small part of the people are either primarily or secondarily consulted in legislation. The business of the public must be done by delegation. The

choice of delegates is made by a select number, and those who are not electors stand idle and helpless spectators of the commonweal, *wholly unconcerned in the government of themselves.*

Of electors the hap is but little better. They are often far from unanimity in their choice, and where the numbers approach to equality, almost half must be governed not only without, but against, their choice.

How any man can have consented to institutions established in distant ages, it will be difficult to explain. In the most favorite residence of liberty, the consent of individuals is merely passive, a tacit admission in every community of the terms which that community grants and requires. As all are born the subjects of some state or other, we may be said to have been all born consenting to some system of government. Other consent than this, the condition of civil life does not allow. It is the unmeaning clamour of the pedants of policy, the delirious dream of republican fanaticism. . . .

They say that by such emigration they by no means forfeited, surrendered, or lost any of those rights; but that *they were, and their descendants now are, entitled to the exercise and enjoyment of all such of them as their local and other circumstances enable them to exercise and enjoy.*

That they who form a settlement by a lawful charter, having committed no crime, forfeit no privileges, will be readily confessed, but what they do not forfeit by any judicial sentence, they may lose by natural effects. As man can be but in one place at once, he cannot have the advantages of multiplied residence. He that will enjoy the brightness of sunshine must quit the coolness of the shade. He who goes voluntarily to America cannot complain of losing what he leaves in Europe. He perhaps had a right to vote for a knight or burgess; by crossing the Atlantic he has not nullified his right, but he has made its exertion no

2. Charles Louis de Secondat, Baron de la Brède et de Montesquieu (1689–1755), political philosopher, author of *The Spirit of the Laws* (Geneva, 1748).

longer possible.[3] By his own choice he has left a country where he had a vote and little property, for another where he has great property but no vote. But as this preference was deliberate and unconstrained, he is still concerned in the government of himself; he has reduced himself from a voter to one of the innumerable multitude that have no vote. He has truly ceded his right, but he still is governed by his own consent; because he has consented to throw his atom of interest into the general mass of the community. Of the consequences of his own act he has no cause to complain; he has chosen, or intended to choose, the greater good; he is represented, as himself desired, in the general representation. . . .

The colonists are the descendants of men who either had no vote in elections, or who voluntarily resigned them for something, in their opinion, of more estimation; they have therefore exactly what their ancestors left them, not a vote in making laws, or in constituting legislators, but the happiness of being protected by law and the duty of obeying it.

What their ancestors did not carry with them, neither they nor their descendants have since acquired. They have not, by abandoning their part in one legislature, obtained the power of constituting another, exclusive and independent, any more than the multitudes, who are now debarred from voting, have a right to erect a separate Parliament for themselves. . . .

The necessary connection of representatives with taxes seems to have sunk deep into many of those minds that admit sounds without their meaning.

Our nation is represented in Parliament by an assembly as numerous as can well consist with order and dispatch, chosen by persons so differently qualified in different places that the mode of choice seems to be, for the most part, formed by chance and settled by custom. Of individuals far the greater part have no vote, and of the voters few have any personal knowledge of him to whom they intrust their liberty and fortune.

Yet this representation has the whole effect expected or desired; that of spreading so wide the care of general interest, and the participation of public counsels, that the advantage or corruption of particular men can seldom operate with much injury to the public.

For this reason many populous and opulent towns neither enjoy nor desire particular representatives; they are included in the general scheme of public administration and cannot suffer but with the rest of the empire.

It is urged that the Americans have not the same security, and that a British legislator may wanton with their property; yet if it be true that their wealth is our wealth, and that their ruin will be our ruin, the Parliament has the same interest in attending to them as to any other part of the nation. The reason why we place any confidence in our representatives is that they must share in the good or evil which their counsels shall produce. Their share is indeed commonly consequential and remote; but it is not often possible that any immediate advantage can be extended to such numbers as may prevail against it. We are therefore as secure against intentional depravations of government as human wisdom can make us, and upon this security the Americans may venture to repose. . . .

It must always be remembered that they are represented by the same virtual representation as the greater part of Englishmen; and that if by change of place they have less share in the legislature than is proportionate to their opulence, they by their removal gained that opulence and had originally and

3. Of this reasoning, I owe part to a conversation with Sir John Hawkins.—AUTHOR'S NOTE. Sir John Hawkins (1719–89) essayist; author of a *History of Music;* boon companion of Johnson; later a rival to Boswell in publication of Johnson's life and letters.

have now their choice of a vote at home or riches at a distance. . . .

The friends of the Americans are of different opinions. Some think that, being unrepresented they ought to tax themselves, and others that they ought to have representatives in the British Parliament.

If they are to tax themselves, what power is to remain in the supreme legislature? That they must settle their own mode of levying their money is supposed. May the British Parliament tell them how much they shall contribute? If the sum may be prescribed, they will return few thanks for the power of raising it; if they are at liberty to grant or to deny, they are no longer subjects.

If they are to be represented, what number of these western orators are to be admitted? This I suppose the Parliament must settle; yet if men have a natural and unalienable right to be represented, who shall determine the number of their delegates? Let us however suppose them to send twenty-three, half as many as the kingdom of Scotland, what will this representation avail them? To pay taxes will be still a grievance. The love of money will not be lessened, nor the power of getting it increased.

Whither will this necessity of representation drive us? Is every petty settlement to be out of the reach of government, till it has sent a senator to Parliament; or may two of them or a greater number be forced to unite in a single deputation? What at last is the difference between him that is taxed by compulsion without representation and him that is represented by compulsion in order to be taxed? . . .

The friends of the Americans indeed ask for them what they do not ask for themselves. This inestimable right of representation they have never solicited. They mean not to exchange solid money for such airy honor. They say, and say willingly, that they cannot conveniently be represented; because their inference is that they cannot be taxed. They are too remote to share the general government and therefore claim the privilege of governing themselves. . . .

When they apply to our compassion by telling us that they are to be carried from their own country to be tried for certain offenses, we are not so ready to pity them as to advise them not to offend. While they are innocent, they are safe.

When they tell of laws made expressly for their punishment, we answer that tumults and sedition were always punishable and that the new law prescribes only the mode of execution.

When it is said that the whole town of Boston is distressed for a misdemeanor of a few, we wonder at their shamefulness; for we know that the town of Boston, and all the associated provinces, are now in rebellion to defend or justify the criminals.

If frauds in the imposts of Boston are tried by commission without a jury, they are tried here in the same mode; and why should the Bostonians expect from us more tenderness for them than for ourselves?

If they are condemned unheard, it is because there is no need of a trial. The crime is manifest and notorious. All trial is the investigation of something doubtful. An Italian philosopher observes that no man desires to hear what he has already seen.

If their assemblies have been suddenly dissolved, what was the reason? Their deliberations were indecent, and their intentions seditious. The power of dissolution is granted and reserved for such times of turbulence. Their best friends have been lately soliciting the king to dissolve his Parliament, to do what they so loudly complain of suffering.

That the same vengeance involves the innocent and guilty is an evil to be lamented, but human caution cannot prevent it, nor human power always redress it. To bring misery on those who have not deserved it is part of the aggregated guilt of rebellion.

That governors have been sometimes given them only that a great man might get ease from importunity, and that they have had judges not always of the deepest learning, or the purest integrity, we have no great reason to doubt, because such misfortunes happen to ourselves. Whoever is governed will sometimes be governed ill, even when he is most *concerned in his own government*.

That improper officers or magistrates are sent is the crime or folly of those that sent them. When incapacity is discovered, it ought to be removed; if corruption is detected, it ought to be punished. No government could subsist for a day if single errors could justify defection.

One of their complaints is not such as can claim much commiseration from the softest bosom. They tell us that we have changed our conduct and that a tax is now laid by Parliament on those who were never taxed by Parliament before. To this we think it may be easily answered that the longer they have been spared, the better they can pay.

It is certainly not much their interest to represent innovation as criminal or invidious, for they have introduced into the history of mankind a new mode of disaffection and have given, I believe, the first example of a proscription published by a colony against the mother-country.

To what is urged of new powers granted to the courts of admiralty, or the extension of authority conferred on the judges, it may be answered in a few words that they have themselves made such regulations necessary; that they are established for the prevention of greater evils; at the same time, it must be observed that these powers have not been extended since the rebellion in America.

One mode of persuasion their ingenuity has suggested. which it may perhaps be less easy to resist. That we may not look with indifference on the American contest, or imagine that the struggle is for a claim, which, however, decided, is of small importance and remote consequence, the Philadelphian Congress has taken care to inform us, that they are resisting the demands of Parliament, as well for our sakes as their own. . . .

We are told by these croakers of calamity, not only that our present ministers design to enslave us, but that the same malignity of purpose is to descend through all their successors and that the wealth to be poured into England by the Pactolus[4] of America will, whenever it comes, be employed to purchase the remains of liberty.

Of those who now conduct the national affairs we may, without much arrogance, presume to know more than themselves, and of those who shall succeed them, whether minister or king, not to know less.

The other position is that the crown, if this laudable opposition should not be successful, *will have the power of taxing* America *at pleasure*. Surely they think rather too meanly of our apprehensions, when they suppose us not to know what they well know themselves, that they are taxed, like all other British subjects, by Parliament; and that the crown has not by the new imposts, whether right or wrong, obtained any additional power over their possessions.

4. Pactolus, a river in Lydia celebrated for its gold-bearing sands.

9. ON CIVIL LIBERTY, PASSIVE OBEDIENCE, AND NONRESISTANCE[1]

By JONATHAN BOUCHER

EDITORS' NOTE.—Jonathan Boucher (1738–1804) was born in Cumberland, England. At the age of twenty-one he went to Port Royal, Virginia, as tutor to a gentleman's sons. He later took orders in the Episcopal ministry and, in addition, conducted a school of thirty boys. Among his pupils was John Parke Custis, George Washington's stepson. This connection with George Washington was important to Boucher's material success in the colonies.

Always a firm supporter of established authority, Boucher used his pulpit to combat the forces of revolution that began to sweep the country after 1764. His opposition to popular discontent led to threats on his life, and

his last sermons in America were preached while loaded pistols lay on the pulpit. Finally, in fear of his life, he left for England in September, 1775. In 1797 he published thirteen of the discourses he had preached in America under the title, *A View of the Causes and Consequences of the American Revolution*. The following extract includes the bulk of the twelfth discourse, which was preached in answer to a sermon on the same text and subjects delivered by the Reverend Mr. Duché in Philadelphia in 1775. Boucher's remarks may be considered as fairly representative of the conservative Loyalist position toward revolution and authority in the America of 1775.

Stand fast, therefore, in the liberty wherewith Christ hath made us free (Galatians 5:1).

... I entreat your indulgence, whilst, without too nicely scrutinizing the propriety of deducing from a text a doctrine which it clearly does not suggest, I once more adopt a plan already chalked out for me, and deliver to you what occurs to me as proper for a Christian audience to attend to on the subject of Liberty....

Obedience to government is every man's duty, because it is every man's interest; but it is particularly incumbent on Christians, because (in addition to its moral fitness) it is enjoined by the positive commands of God; and, therefore, when Christians are disobedient to

human ordinances, they are also disobedient to God. If the form of government under which the good providence of God has been pleased to place us be mild and free, it is our duty to enjoy it with gratitude and with thankfulness and, in particular, to be careful not to abuse it by licentiousness. If it be less indulgent and less liberal than in reason it ought to be, still it is our duty not to disturb and destroy the peace of the community by becoming refractory and rebellious subjects and *resisting the ordinances of God*. However humiliating such acquiescence may seem to men of warm and eager minds, the wisdom of God in having made it our duty is manifest. For, as it is the natural temper and bias of the human mind to be impatient under restraint, it was wise and merciful in the blessed Author of our religion not to add any new impulse to the natural

1. Jonathan Boucher, *A View of the Causes and Consequences of the American Revolution, with an Historical Preface* (London, 1797), pp. 495, 505–6, 507–21, 534, 543–44, 545–46, 549–50, 552, 553–58, 558–60.

force of this prevailing propensity but, with the whole weight of his authority, altogether to discountenance every tendency to disobedience.

If it were necessary to vindicate the Scriptures for this their total unconcern about a principle which so many other writings seem to regard as the first of all human considerations, it might be observed that, avoiding the vague and declamatory manner of such writings, and avoiding also the useless and impracticable subtleties of metaphysical definitions, these Scriptures have better consulted the great general interests of mankind, by summarily recommending and enjoining a conscientious reverence for law whether human or divine. To respect the laws is to respect liberty in the only rational sense in which the term can be used, for liberty consists in a subserviency to law. "Where there is no law," says Mr. Locke, "there is no freedom." The mere man of nature (if such an one there ever was) has no freedom: *all his lifetime he is subject to bondage*. It is by being included within the pale of civil polity and government that he takes his rank in society as a free man.

Hence it follows that we are free, or otherwise, as we are governed by law, or by the mere arbitrary will, or wills, of any individual, or any number of individuals. And liberty is not the setting at nought and despising established laws—much less the making our own wills the rule of our own actions, or the actions of others—and not bearing (whilst yet we dictate to others) the being dictated to, even by the laws of the land; but it is the being governed by law and by law only. The Greeks described Eleutheria, or Liberty, as the daughter of Jupiter, the supreme fountain of power and law. And the Romans, in like manner, always drew her with the pretor's wand (the emblem of legal power and authority), as well as with the cap. Their idea, no doubt, was that liberty was the fair fruit of just authority and that it consisted in

men's being subjected to law. The more carefully well-devised restraints of law are enacted, and the more rigorously they are executed in any country, the greater degree of civil liberty does that country enjoy. To pursue liberty, then, in a manner not warranted by law, whatever the pretense may be, is clearly to be hostile to liberty; and those persons who thus *promise you liberty* are themselves *the servants of corruption*.

"Civil liberty (says an excellent writer) is a severe and a restrained thing; implies, in the notion of it, authority, settled subordinations, subjection, and obedience; and is altogether as much hurt by too little of this kind, as by too much of it. And the love of liberty, when it is indeed the love of liberty, which carries us to withstand tyranny, will as much carry us to reverence authority, and to support it; for this most obvious reason, that one is as necessary to the being of liberty, as the other is destructive of it. And, therefore, the love of liberty which does not produce this effect, the love of liberty which is not a real principle of dutiful behavior toward authority, is as hypocritical as the religion which is not productive of a good life. Licentiousness is, in truth, such an excess of liberty as is of the same nature with tyranny. For, what is the difference betwixt them, but that one is lawless power exercised under pretense of authority, or by persons vested with it; the other, lawless power exercised under pretense of liberty, or without any pretense at all? A people, then, must always be less free in proportion as they are more licentious, licentiousness being not only different from liberty but directly contrary to it—a direct breach upon it."

True liberty, then, is a liberty to do everything that is right, and the being restrained from doing anything that is wrong. So far from our having a right to do everything that we please, under a notion of liberty, liberty itself is limited and confined—but limited and confined only by laws which are at the same time both its foundation and its support. It can, however, hardly be necessary to inform you that ideas and notions respecting liberty, very different from these, are daily suggested in the speeches and the writings of the times; and also that some opinions on the subject of government at large, which appear to me to be particularly loose and dangerous, are advanced in the sermon now under consideration; and that, therefore, you will acknowledge the propriety of my bestowing some farther notice on them both.

It is laid down in this sermon, as a settled maxim, that the end of government is "the common good of mankind." I am not sure that the position itself is indisputable; but, if it were, it would by no means follow that "this common good being matter of common feeling, government must therefore have been instituted by common consent." There is an appearance of logical accuracy and precision in this statement; but it is only an appearance. The position is vague and loose; and the assertion is made without an attempt to prove it. If by men's "common feelings" we are to understand that principle in the human mind called common sense, the assertion is either unmeaning and insignificant, or it is false. In no instance have mankind ever yet agreed as to what is, or is not, "the common good." A form or mode of government cannot be named, which these "common feelings" and "common consent," the sole arbiters, as it seems, of "common good," have not, at one time or another, set up and established, and again pulled down and reprobated. What one people in one age have concurred in establishing as the "common good," another in another age have voted to be mischievous and big with ruin. The premises, therefore, that "the common good is matter of common feeling," being false, the consequence drawn from it, viz., that government was instituted by "common consent," is of course equally false.

This popular notion, that government was originally formed by the consent or by a compact of the people, rests on, and is supported by, another similar notion, not less popular, nor better founded. This other notion is that the whole human race is born equal; and that no man is naturally inferior, or, in any respect, subjected to another; and that he can be made subject to another only by his own consent. The position is equally ill-founded and false both in its premises and conclusions. In hardly any sense that can be imagined is the position strictly true; but, as applied to the case under consideration, it is demonstrably not true. Man differs from man in everything that can be supposed to lead to supremacy and subjection, *as one star differs from another star in glory*. It was the purpose of the Creator that man should be social; but, without government, there can be no society; nor, without some relative inferiority and superiority, can there be any government. A musical instrument composed of chords, keys, or pipes, all perfectly equal in size and power, might as well be expected to produce harmony, as a society composed of members all perfectly equal to be productive of order and peace. If (according to the idea of the advocates of this chimerical scheme of equality) no man could rightfully *be compelled to come in* and be a member even of a government to be formed by a regular compact, but by his own individual consent, it clearly follows, from the same principles, that neither could he rightfully be made or compelled to submit to the ordinances of any government already formed, to which he has not individually or actually consented. On the principle of equality, neither his parents, nor even the vote of a majority of the society (however virtuously and honorably that vote might be obtained), can have any such authority over any man. Neither can it be maintained that acquiescence implies consent; because acquiescence may have been extorted from impotence or incapacity. Even an explicit consent can bind a man no longer than he chooses to be bound. The same principle of equality that exempts him from being governed without his own consent clearly entitles him to recall and resume that consent whenever he sees fit; and he alone has a right to judge when and for what reasons it may be resumed.

Any attempt, therefore, to introduce this fantastic system into practice would reduce the whole business of social life to the wearisome, confused, and useless task of mankind's first expressing, and then withdrawing, their consent to an endless succession of schemes of government. Governments, though always forming, would never be completely formed; for the majority today might be the minority tomorrow, and, of course, that which is now fixed might and would be soon unfixed. Mr. Locke indeed says that, "by consenting with others to make one body-politic under government, a man puts himself under an obligation to every one of that society to submit to the determination of the majority, and to be concluded by it." For the sake of the peace of society, it is undoubtedly reasonable and necessary that this should be the case; but, on the principles of the system now under consideration, before Mr. Locke or any of his followers can have authority to say that it actually is the case, it must be stated and proved that every individual man, on entering into the social compact, did first consent, and declare his consent, to be concluded and bound in all cases by the vote of the majority. In making such a declaration, he would certainly consult both his interest and his duty; but at the same time he would also completely relinquish the principle of equality, and eventually subject himself to the possibility of being governed by ignorant and corrupt tyrants. Mr. Locke

himself afterward disproves his own position respecting this supposed obligation to submit to the "determination of the majority," when he argues that a right of resistance still exists in the governed; for, what is resistance but a recalling and resuming the consent heretofore supposed to have been given, and in fact refusing to submit to the "determination of the majority"? It does not clearly appear what Mr. Locke exactly meant by what he calls "the determination of the majority"; but the only rational and practical public manner of declaring "the determination of the majority" is by law: the laws, therefore, in all countries, even in those that are despotically governed, are to be regarded as the declared "determination of a majority" of the members of that community; because, in such cases, even acquiescence only must be looked upon as equivalent to a declaration. A right of resistance, therefore, for which Mr. Locke contends, is incompatible with the duty of submitting to the determination of "the majority," for which he also contends.

It is indeed impossible to carry into effect any government which, even by compact, might be framed with this reserved right of resistance. Accordingly there is no record that any such government ever was so formed. If there had, it must have carried the seeds of its decay in its very constitution. For, as those men who make a government (certain that they have the power) can have no hesitation to vote that they also have the right to unmake it, and as the people, in all circumstances, but more especially when trained to make and unmake governments, are at least as well disposed to do the latter as the former, it is morally impossible that there should be anything like permanency or stability in a government so formed. Such a system, therefore, can produce only perpetual dissensions and contests and bring back mankind to a supposed state of nature, arming every man's hand, like Ishmael's, against every man, and rendering the world an *aceldama*, or field of blood.

Such theories of government seem to give something like plausibility to the notions of those other modern theorists who regard all governments as invasions of the natural rights of men, usurpations, and tyranny. On this principle it would follow, and could not be denied, that government was indeed fundamentally, as our people are sedulously taught it still is, an evil. Yet it is to government that mankind owe their having, after their fall and corruption, been again reclaimed, from a state of barbarity and war, to the conveniency and the safety of the social state; and it is by means of government that society is still preserved, the weak protected from the strong, and the artless and innocent from the wrongs of proud oppressors. It was not without reason, then, that Mr. Locke asserted that a greater wrong cannot be done to prince and people than is done by "propagating wrong notions concerning government."

Ashamed of this shallow device, that government originated in superior strength and violence, another party, hardly less numerous, and certainly not less confident than the former, fondly deduce it from some imaginary compact. They suppose that, in the decline perhaps of some fabulous age of old, a multitude of human beings, who, like their brother-beasts, had hitherto ranged the forests, *without guide, overseer, or ruler*—at length convinced, by experience, of the impossibility of living either alone with any degree of comfort or security, or together in society, with peace, without government, had (in some lucid interval of reason and reflection) met together in a spacious plain for the express purpose of framing a government. Their first step must have been the transferring to some individual, or individuals, some of those rights which are supposed to have been in-herent in each of them: of these it is essential to government that they should be divested; yet can they not, rightfully, be deprived of them, otherwise than by their own consent. Now, admitting this whole supposed assembly to be perfectly equal as to rights, yet all agreed as to the propriety of ceding some of them, on what principles of equality is it possible to determine, either who shall relinquish such a portion of his rights, or who shall be invested with such new accessory rights? By asking another to exercise jurisdiction over me, I clearly confess that I do not think myself his equal; and by his consenting to exercise such authority, he also virtually declares that he thinks himself superior. And, to establish this hypothesis of a compact, it is farther necessary that the whole assembly should concur in this opinion—a concurrence so extremely improbable that it seems to be barely possible. The supposition that a large concourse of people, in a rude and imperfect state of society, or even a majority of them, should thus rationally and unanimously concur to subject themselves to various restrictions, many of them irksome and unpleasant, and all of them contrary to all their former habits, is to suppose them possessed of more wisdom and virtue than multitudes in any instance in real life have ever shown. Another difficulty respecting this notion may yet be mentioned. Without a power of life and death, it will, I presume, be readily admitted that there could be no government. Now, admitting it to be possible that men, from motives of public and private utility, may be induced to submit to many heavy penalties, and even to corporal punishment, inflicted by the sentence of the law, there is an insuperable objection to any man's giving to another a power over his life: this objection is that no man has such a power over his own life and cannot therefore transfer to another, or to others, be they few or many, on any conditions, a right which he does not himself possess. He only who gave life can give the authority to take it way; and as such authority is essential to government, this argument seems very decidedly to prove, not only that government did not originate in any compact, but also that it was originally from God. . . .

. . . The glory of God is much concerned that there should be good government in the world; it is, therefore, the uniform doctrine of the Scriptures that it is under the deputation and authority of God alone that *kings reign and princes decree justice*. Kings and and princes (which are only other words for supreme magistrates) were doubtless created and appointed, not so much for their own sakes, as for the sake of the people committed to their charge; yet are they not, therefore, the creatures of the people. So far from deriving their authority from any supposed consent or suffrage of men, they receive their commission from Heaven; they receive it from God, the source and original of all power. However obsolete, therefore, either the sentiment or the language may now be deemed, it is with the most perfect propriety that the supreme magistrate, whether consisting of one or of many, and whether denominated an emperor, a king, an archon, a dictator, a consul, or a senate, is to be regarded and venerated as the vicegerent of God. . . .

Nor let this be deemed a degrading and servile principle: it is the very reverse; and it is this its superior dignity which proves its celestial origin. For, whilst other doctrines and other systems distract the world with disputes and debates which admit of no decision, and of *wars and fightings* which are almost as endless as they are useless, it is the glory of Christianity to teach her votaries patiently to bear imperfections, inconveniences, and evils in government, as in everything else that is human. This patient acquiescence under some remediless evils is not more our duty than it is our interest: for, the only very intolerable grievance in government is when men allow themselves to disturb and destroy the peace of the world by vain attempts to render that perfect which the laws of our nature have ordained to be imperfect. And there is more magnanimity, as well as more wisdom, in enduring some present and certain evils than can be manifested by any projects of redress that are uncertain; but which, if they fail, may bring down irretrievable ruin on thousands of others, as well as on ourselves, since to suffer nobly indicates more greatness of mind than can be shown even by acting valiantly. Wise men, therefore, in the words of a noted philosopher, will "rather choose to brook with patience some inconveniences under government" (because human affairs cannot possibly be without some) than self-opinionatedly disturb the quiet of the public. And, weighing the justice of those things you are about, not by the persuasion and advice of private men, but by the laws of the realm, you will no longer suffer ambitious men, through the streams of your blood, to wade to their own power but esteem it better to enjoy ourselves in the present state, though perhaps not the best, than, by waging war, endeavor to procure a reformation. . . .

All government, whether lodged in one or in many, is, in its nature, absolute and irresistible. It is not within the competency even of the supreme power to limit itself, because such limitation can emanate only from a superior. For any government to make itself irresistible, and to cease to be absolute, it must cease to be supreme, which is but saying, in other words, that it must dissolve itself or be destroyed. If, then, to resist government be to destroy it, every man who is a subject must necessarily owe to the government under which he lives an obedience either active or passive: active, where the duty enjoined may be performed without offending God; and passive (that is to say, patiently to submit to the penalties annexed to disobedience), where that which is commanded by man is forbidden by God. No government upon earth can rightfully compel any one of its subjects to an active compliance with anything that is, or that appears to his conscience to be, inconsistent with, or contradictory to, the known laws of God, because every man is under a prior and superior obligation to *obey God in all things*. When such cases of incompatible demands of duty occur, every well-informed person knows what he is to do; and every well-principled person will do what he ought, viz., he will submit to the ordinances of God rather than comply with the commandments of men. In thus acting, he cannot err, and this alone is "passive obedience," which I entreat you to observe is so far from being "unlimited obedience" (as its enemies wilfully persist to miscall it) that it is the direct contrary. Resolute not to disobey God, a man of good principles determines, in case of competition, as the lesser evil, to disobey man; but he knows that he should also disobey God, were he not, at the same time, patiently to submit to any penalties incurred by his disobedience to man. . . .

A nonresisting spirit never yet made any man a bad subject. And if men of such mild and yielding tempers have shown less ardor than many others do, in the pursuit of that liberty which makes so conspicuous a figure in the effusions of orators and poets, it can be only for this reason: that they think it is precisely that kind of liberty which has so often set the world in an uproar, and that therefore it would be better for the world if it were never more heard of. If they are mistaken, their mistakes are at least harmless; and there is much justice, as well as great good sense, in Bishop Hall's remark that "some quiet errors are better than some unruly truths." . . .

Mr. Locke, like many inferior writers, when defending resistance, falls into inconsistencies and is at variance with himself. "Rebellion being," as he says, "an opposition not to persons, but to authority, which is founded only in the constitution and laws of the government, those, whoever they be, who by force break through, and by force justify their violation of them, are truly and properly rebels." To this argument no one can object; but it should be attended to that, in political consideration, it is hardly possible to dissociate the ideas of authority in the abstract from persons vested with authority. To resist a person legally vested with authority is, I conceive, to all intents and purposes, the same thing as to resist authority. Nothing but its success could have rescued the revolution from this foul imputation, had it not been for the abdication. Accordingly this great event has always hung like a millstone on the necks of those who must protest against rebellions; whilst yet their system of politics requires that they should approve of resistance, and the revolution. . . .

. . . "The Divine Author of our existence" has beyond all question given to "one part of the human race" to hold over another. Without some paramount and irresistible power, there can be no government. In our constitution this supremacy is vested in the king and the Parliament; and, subordinate to them, in our provincial legislatures. If you were now released from this constitutional power, you must differ from all others "of the human race" if you did not soon find yourselves under a necessity of submitting to a power no less absolute, though vested in other persons, and a government differently constituted. And much does it import you to consider whether those who are now so ready to promise to make *the grievous yoke of your fathers lighter* may not themselves verify Rehoboam's assertion and make you feel that *their little fingers are thicker than your father's loins.*

Be it (for the sake of argument) admitted that the government under which till now you have lived happily is, most unaccountably, all at once become *oppressive and severe;* did you, of yourselves, make the discovery? No. I affirm, without any apprehension of being contradicted, that you are acquainted with these oppressions only from the report of others. For what, then (admitting you have a right to resist in any case), are you now urged to resist and rise against those whom you have hitherto always regarded (and certainly not without reason) as your *nursing fathers and nursing mothers?* Often as you have already heard it repeated without expressing any disapprobation, I assure myself it will afford you no pleasure to be reminded that it is on account of an insignificant duty on tea, imposed by the British Parliament, and which, for aught we know, may or may not be constitutionally imposed, but which, we well know, two-thirds of the people of America can never be called on to pay. Is it the part of an *understanding people*, of loyal subjects, or of good Christians, instantly to resist and rebel for a cause so trivial? O my brethren, consult your own hearts and follow your own judgments! and learn not your "measures of obedience" from men who weakly or wickedly imagine there can be liberty unconnected with law—and whose aim it is to drive you on, step by step, to a resistance which will terminate, if it does not begin, in rebellion! On all such trying occasions, learn the line of conduct which it is your duty and interest to observe, from our constitution itself, which, in this particular, is a fair transcript or exemplification of the ordinance of God. Both the one and the other warn you against resistance; but you are not forbidden either to remonstrate or to petition. And can it be humiliating to any man, or any number of men, to ask when we have but to *ask and it shall be given?* Is prayer an abject duty, or do men ever

appear either so great, or so amiable, as when they are modest and humble? However meanly this privilege of petitioning may be regarded by those who claim everything as a right, they are challenged to show an instance in which it has failed when it ought to have succeeded. If, however, our grievances, in any point of view, be of such moment as that other means of obtaining redress should be judged expedient, happily we enjoy those means. In a certain sense, some considerable portion of legislation is still in our own hands. We are supposed to have chosen "fit and able" persons to represent us in the great council of our country; and they only can constitutionally interfere either to obtain the enacting of what is right or the repeal of what is wrong. If we, and our fellow-subjects, have been conscientiously faithful in the discharge of our duty, we can have no reason to doubt that our delegates will be equally faithful in the discharge of theirs. Our provincial assemblies, it is true, are but one part of our colonial legislature; they form, however, that part which is the most efficient. If the present general topic of complaint be, in their estimation, well founded, and a real and great grievance, what reason have you to imagine that all the assemblies on the continent will not concur and be unanimous in so representing it? And if they should all concur so to represent it, it is hardly within the reach of supposition that all due attention will not be paid to their united remonstrances. So many and such large concessions have often been made, at the instance only of individual assemblies, that we are warranted in relying that nothing which is reasonable and proper will ever be withheld from us, provided only it be asked for with decency, and that we do not previously forfeit our title to attention by becoming refractory and rebellious.

Let it be supposed, however, that even the worst may happen, which can happen: that our remonstrances are disregarded, our petitions rejected, and our grievances unredressed: what, you will naturally ask—what, in such a case, would I advise you to do? . . . To your question, therefore, I hesitate not to answer that I wish and advise you to act the part of reasonable men and of Christians. You will be pleased to observe, however, that I am far from thinking that your virtue will ever be brought to so severe a test and trial. The question, I am aware, was an ensnaring one, suggested to you by those who are as little solicitous about your peace as they are for my safety; the answer which, in condescension to your wishes, I have given to it is direct and plain and not more applicable to you than it is to all the people of America. If you think the duty of three pence a pound upon tea laid on by the British Parliament a grievance, it is your duty to instruct your members to take all the constitutional means in their power to obtain redress; if those means fail of success, you cannot but be sorry and grieved, but you will better bear your disappointment by being able to reflect that it was not owing to any

misconduct of your own. And, what is the whole history of human life, public or private, but a series of disappointments? It might be hoped that Christians would not think it grievous to be doomed to submit to disappointments and calamities, as their Master submitted, even if they were as innocent. His disciples and first followers shrunk from no trials nor dangers. Treading in the steps of him who, *when he was reviled, blessed, and when he was persecuted, suffered it*, they willingly laid down their lives rather than resist some of the worst tyrants that ever disgraced the annals of history. Those persons are as little acquainted with general history, as they are with the particular doctrines of Christianity, who represent such submission as abject and servile. I affirm, with great authority, that "there can be no better way of asserting the people's lawful rights, than the disowning unlawful commands, by thus patiently suffering." When this doctrine was more generally embraced, our holy religion gained as much by submission as it is now in a fair way of losing for want of it. . . .

10. COMMON SENSE[1]

By THOMAS PAINE

EDITORS' NOTE.—Thomas Paine (1737–1809), a self-taught Anglo-American writer, was the author of *Common Sense* (1776); the *American Crisis* papers ("these are the times that try men's souls" was the opening phrase of the first *Crisis*, read to the soldiers in camp by Washington's order) (1776–83); *The Rights of Man*, defending the French Revolu-

tion (1791–92); and *The Age of Reason* (1802), a deistic tract on religion. Paine, a former small tradesman and government employee, came to America in 1774. He enlisted in the army and undertook special tasks of Congress and the Pennsylvania Assembly. In the last-mentioned post he was instrumental in securing the prohibition of slavery in Pennsylvania. Returning to Europe in 1787, Paine was obliged successively to flee from England, as a result of the publication of

1. Thomas Paine, *Selections from the Works of* . . . , ed. A. W. Peach (New York, 1928), pp. 4–32. Reprinted by permission of Harcourt, Brace and Company, Boston.

The Rights of Man, and then France, where, although a member of the National Convention, he was imprisoned ten months under the Terror. He returned and died in New York State in 1809, but burial in any cemetery was denied him because of his "atheism." A favorite saying of Paine's was a paraphrase of Franklin: "Where liberty is *not,* there is my country."

Common Sense was published anonymously at two shillings in Philadelphia. In all, 500,000 copies were sold. Paine's forthrightness worked, in Washington's words, "a powerful change" in a large section of American public opinion.

ON THE ORIGIN AND DESIGN OF GOVERNMENT IN GENERAL, WITH CONCISE REMARKS ON THE ENGLISH CONSTITUTION

Some writers have so confounded society with government as to leave little or no distinction between them, whereas they are not only different but have different origins. Society is produced by our wants and government by our wickedness; the former promotes our happiness *positively* by uniting our affections, the latter *negatively* by restraining our vices. The one encourages intercourse, the other creates distinctions. The first is a patron, the last a punisher.

Society in every state is a blessing, but government, even in its best state, is but a necessary evil; in its worst state an intolerable one: for when we suffer, or are exposed to the same miseries *by a government,* which we might expect in a country *without government,* our calamity is heightened by reflecting that we furnish the means by which we suffer. Government, like dress, is the badge of lost innocence; the palaces of kings are built upon the ruins of the bowers of paradise. For were the impulses of conscience clear, uniform, and irresistibly obeyed, man would need no other lawgiver; but that not being the case, he finds it necessary to surrender up a part of his property to furnish means for the protection of the rest; and this he is induced to do by the same prudence which in every other case advises him, out of two evils, to choose the least. *Wherefore,* security being the true design and end of government, it unanswerably follows that whatever *form* thereof appears most likely to insure it to us, with the least expense and greatest benefit, is preferable to all others.

In order to gain a clear and just idea of the design and end of government, let us suppose a small number of persons settled in some sequestered part of the earth, unconnected with the rest; they will then represent the first peopling of any country or of the world. In this state of natural liberty, society will be their first thought. A thousand motives will excite them thereto; the strength of one man is so unequal to his wants, and his mind so unfitted for perpetual solitude, that he is soon obliged to seek assistance and relief of another, who in his turn requires the same. Four or five united would be able to raise a tolerable dwelling in the midst of a wilderness, but *one* man might labor out the common period of life without accomplishing anything; when he had felled his timber, he could not remove it nor erect it after it was removed; hunger in the meantime would urge him to quit his work, and every different want would call him a different way. Disease, nay even misfortune, would be death; for though neither might be mortal, yet either would disable him from living and reduce him to a state in which he might rather be said to perish than to die.

Thus necessity, like a gravitating power, would soon form our newly arrived emigrants into society, the reciprocal blessings of which would supersede and render the obligations of law and government unnecessary while they remained perfectly just to each other; but, as nothing but Heaven is impregnable to vice, it will unavoidably happen that in proportion as they surmount the first difficulties of emigration, which bound them together in a common cause, they will begin to relax in their duty and attachment to each other; and this remissness will point out the necessity of establishing some form of government to supply the defect of moral virtue.

Some convenient tree will afford them a state-house, under the branches of which the whole colony may assemble to deliberate on public matters. It is more than probable that their first laws will have the title only of REGULATIONS and be enforced by no other penalty than public disesteem. In this first parliament every man by natural right will have a seat.

But as the colony increases, the public concerns will increase likewise, and the distance at which the members may be separated will render it too inconvenient for all of them to meet on every occasion as at first, when their number was small, their habitations near, and the public concerns few and trifling. This will point out the convenience of their consenting to leave the legislative part to be managed by a select number chosen from the whole body, who are supposed to have the same concerns at stake which those have who appointed them and who will act in the same manner as the whole body would act were they present. If the colony continue increasing, it will become necessary to augment the number of representatives; and, that the interest of every part of the colony may be attended to, it will be found best to divide the whole into convenient parts, each part sending its proper number; and, that the *elected* might never form to

themselves an interest separate from the *electors*, prudence will point out the propriety of having elections often, because as the *elected* might by that means return and mix again with the general body of the *electors* in a few months, their fidelity to the public will be secured by the prudent reflection of not making a rod for themselves. And as this frequent interchange will establish a common interest with every part of the community, they will mutually and naturally support each other, and on this (not on the unmeaning name of king) depends the *strength of government and the happiness of the governed*.

Here, then, is the origin and rise of government; namely, a mode rendered necessary by the inability of moral virtue to govern the world; here, too, is the design and end of government, viz., freedom and security. And however our eyes may be dazzled with show, or our ears deceived by sound, however prejudice may warp our wills, or interest darken our understanding, the simple voice of nature and reason will say, 'Tis right.

I draw my idea of the form of government from a principle in nature which no art can overturn, viz., that the more simple anything is, the less liable it is to be disordered and the easier repaired when disordered; and with this maxim in view I offer a few remarks on the so much boasted constitution of England. That it was noble for the dark and slavish times in which it was erected is granted. When the world was overrun with tyranny, the least remove therefrom was a glorious rescue. But that it is imperfect, subject to convulsions, and incapable of producing what it seems to promise is easily demonstrated.

Absolute governments (though the disgrace of human nature) have this advantage with them: they are simple. If the people suffer, they know the head from which their suffering springs; know likewise the remedy and are not bewildered by a variety of causes and cures. But the constitution of England is so exceedingly complex that the nation may suffer for years together without being able to discover in which part the fault lies; some will say in one and some in another, and every political physician will advise a different medicine.

I know it is difficult to get over local or long-standing prejudices, yet if we will suffer ourselves to examine the component parts of the English constitution, we shall find them to be the base remains of two ancient tyrannies, compounded with some new republican materials.

First, the remains of monarchical tyranny in the person of the king.

Secondly, the remains of aristocratical tyranny in the persons of the peers.

Thirdly, the new republican materials, in the persons of the Commons, on whose virtue depends the freedom of England.

The two first, by being hereditary, are independent of the people; wherefore in a *constitutional sense* they contribute nothing toward the freedom of the state.

To say that the constitution of England is a *union* of three powers, reciprocally *checking* each other, is farcical; either the words have no meaning or they are flat contradictions.

To say that the Commons is a check upon the king, presupposes two things.

First, that the king is not to be trusted without being looked after; or, in other words, that a thirst for absolute power is the natural disease of monarchy.

Secondly, that the Commons, by being appointed for that purpose, are either wiser or more worthy of confidence than the crown.

But as the same constitution which gives the Commons a power to check the king by withholding the supplies gives afterward the king a power to check the Commons by empowering him to reject their other bills, it again supposes that the king is wiser than those whom it has already supposed to be wiser than him. A mere absurdity!

There is something exceedingly ridiculous in the composition of monarchy; it first excludes a man from the means of information, yet empowers him to act in cases where the highest judgment is required. The state of a king shuts him from the world, yet the business of a king requires him to know it thoroughly; wherefore the different parts, by unnaturally opposing and destroying each other, prove the whole character to be absurd and useless.

Some writers have explained the English constitution thus: the king, say they, is one, the people another; the Peers are a house in behalf of the king, the Commons in behalf of the people. But this hath all the distinctions of a house divided against itself, and though the expressions be pleasantly arranged, yet when examined, they appear idle and ambiguous; and it will always happen that the nicest construction that words are capable of, when applied to the description of something which either cannot exist, or is too incomprehensible to be within the compass of description, will be words of sound only, and, though they may amuse the ear, they cannot inform the mind: for this explanation includes a previous question, viz., *how came the king by power which the people are afraid to trust and always obliged to check?* Such a power could not be the gift of a wise people, neither can any power, *which needs checking*, be from God; yet the provision which the constitution makes supposes such a power to exist.

But the provision is unequal to the task; the means either cannot or will not accomplish the end, and the whole affair is a *Felo de se:* for as the greater weight will always carry up the less, and as all the wheels of a machine are put in motion by one, it only remains to know which power in the constitution has the most weight, for that will govern: and though the others, or a part of them, may clog, or check the rapidity of its motion, yet so long as they cannot stop it, their endeavors will be ineffectual. The first moving power will at last have its way, and what it wants in speed is supplied by time.

That the crown is this overbearing part in the English constitution needs not be mentioned, and that it derives its whole consequence merely from being the giver of places and pensions is self-evident; wherefore, though we have been wise enough to shut and lock a door against absolute monarchy, we at the same time have been foolish enough to put the crown in possession of the key.

The prejudice of Englishmen in favor of their own government, by king, Lords, and Commons, arises as much or more from national pride than reason. Individuals are undoubtedly safer in England than in some other countries; but the will of the king is as much the law of the land in Britain as in France, with this difference: that, instead of proceeding directly from his mouth, it is handed to the people under the formidable shape of an act of Parliament. For the fate of Charles the First hath only made kings more subtle—not more just.

Wherefore, laying aside all national pride and prejudice in favor of modes and forms, the plain truth is that *it is wholly to the constitution of the people and not to the constitution of the government* that the crown is not as oppressive in England as in Turkey.

An inquiry into the *constitutional errors* in the English form of government is at this time highly necessary, for as we are never in a proper condition of doing justice to others, while we continue under the influence of some leading partiality, so neither are we capable of doing it to ourselves while we remain fettered by any obstinate prejudice. And as a man who is attached to a prosti-tute is unfitted to choose or judge of a wife, so any prepossession in favor of a rotten constitution of government will disable us from discerning a good one.

OF MONARCHY AND HEREDITARY SUCCESSION

Mankind being originally equals in the order of creation, the equality could only be destroyed by some subsequent circumstance; the distinctions of rich and poor may in a great measure be accounted for, and that without having recourse to the harsh ill-sounding names of oppression and avarice. Oppression is often the *consequence* but seldom or never the *means* of riches; and though avarice will preserve a man from being necessitously poor, it generally makes him too timorous to be wealthy.

But there is another and greater distinction for which no truly natural or religious reason can be assigned, and that is the distinction of men into KINGS and SUBJECTS. Male and female are the distinctions of nature, good and bad the distinctions of Heaven; but how a race of men came into the world so exalted above the rest, and distinguished like some new species, is worth inquiring into, and whether they are the means of happiness or of misery to mankind.

In the early ages of the world, according to the Scripture chronology, there were no kings; the consequence of which was there were no wars; it is the pride of kings which throws mankind into confusion. Holland without a king hath enjoyed more peace for this last century than any of the monarchical governments in Europe.[2] Antiquity favors the same remark, for the quiet and rural lives of the first Patriarchs have a happy something in them which vanishes when we come to the history of Jewish royalty.

Government by kings was first intro-

2. The Dutch Republic lasted from the seventeenth century to the first decade of the nineteenth century.

duced into the world by the heathens, from whom the children of Israel copied the custom. It was the most prosperous invention the devil ever set on foot for the promotion of idolatry. The heathens paid divine honors to their deceased kings, and the Christian world has improved on the plan by doing the same to their living ones. How impious is the title of sacred majesty applied to a worm, who in the midst of his splendor is crumbling into dust!

As the exalting one man so greatly above the rest cannot be justified on the equal rights of nature, so neither can it be defended on the authority of Scripture, for the will of the Almighty as declared by Gideon, and the prophet Samuel, expressly disapproves of government by kings. All anti-monarchical parts of Scripture have been very smoothly glossed over in monarchical governments, but they undoubtedly merit the attention of countries which have their governments yet to form. "Render unto Caesar the things which are Caesar's" is the Scripture doctrine of courts, yet it is no support of monarchical government, for the Jews at that time were without a king and in a state of vassalage to the Romans.

Near three thousand years passed away, from the Mosaic account of the creation, till the Jews under a national delusion requested a king. Till then, their form of government (except in extraordinary cases where the Almighty interposed) was a kind of republic, administered by a judge and the elders of the tribes. Kings they had none, and it was held sinful to acknowledge any Being under that title but the Lord of Hosts. And when a man seriously reflects on the idolatrous homage which is paid to the persons of kings, he need not wonder that the Almighty, ever jealous of his honor, should disapprove a form of government which so impiously invades the prerogative of Heaven.

Monarchy is ranked in Scripture as one of the sins of the Jews, for which a course in reserve is denounced against them. The history of that transaction is worth attending to.

The children of Israel, being oppressed by the Midianites, Gideon marched against them with a small army, and victory through the Divine interposition decided in his favor. The Jews elate with success, and attributing it to the generalship of Gideon, proposed making him a king, saying, "Rule thou over us, thou and thy son, and thy son's son." Here was temptation in its fullest extent, not a kingdom only but a hereditary one. But Gideon in the piety of his soul replied, "I will not rule over you, neither shall my son rule over you." THE LORD SHALL RULE OVER YOU. Words need not be more explicit; Gideon doth not *decline* the honor but denieth their right to give it; neither doth he compliment them with invented declarations of his thanks, but in the positive style of a prophet charges them with disaffection to their proper Sovereign, the King of Heaven.[3]

About one hundred and thirty years after this, they fell again into the same error. The hankering which the Jews had for the idolatrous customs of the heathens is something exceedingly unaccountable; but so it was that, laying hold of the misconduct of Samuel's two sons,[4] who were intrusted with some secular concerns, they came in an abrupt and clamorous manner to Samuel, saying, "Behold thou art old, and thy sons walk not in thy ways, now make us a king to judge us like all the other nations."[5] And here we cannot but observe that their motives were bad, viz., that they might be *like* unto other nations, i.e., the heathens, whereas their true glory lay in being as much *unlike* them

3. See Judg. 8:22, 23, for Gideon's refusal to govern.
4. Samuel's sons, Joel and Abiah, corrupted judges (I Sam. 8:2, 3).
5. I Sam. 8:4-22.

as possible. "But the thing displeased Samuel when they said, Give us a king to judge us; and Samuel prayed unto the Lord, and the Lord said unto Samuel, Hearken unto the voice of the people in all that they say unto thee, for they have not rejected thee, but they have rejected me, THAT I SHOULD NOT REIGN OVER THEM. According to all the works which they have done since the day that I brought them up out of Egypt even unto this day, wherewith they have forsaken me, and served other gods: so do they also unto thee. Now therefore hearken unto their voice, howbeit, protest solemnly unto them and show them the manner of the king that shall reign over them," i.e., not of any particular king but the general manner of the kings of the earth whom Israel was so eagerly copying after. And notwithstanding the great distance of time and difference of manners, the character is still in fashion. "And Samuel told all the words of the Lord unto the people, that asked of him a king. And he said, This shall be the manner of the king that shall reign over you. He will take your sons and appoint them for himself for his chariots and to be his horsemen, and some shall run before his chariots" (this description agrees with the present mode of impressing men) "and he will appoint him captains over thousands and captains over fifties, will set them to ear his ground and to reap his harvest, and to make his instruments of war, and instruments of his chariots. And he will take your daughters to be confectionaries, and to be cooks, and to be bakers" (this describes the expense and luxury as well as the oppression of kings) "and he will take your fields and your vineyards, and your olive yards, even the best of them, and give them to his servants. And he will take the tenth of your seed, and of your vineyards, and give them to his officers and to his servants" (by which we see that bribery, corruption, and favoritism are the standing vices of kings) "and he will take the tenth of

your menservants, and your maidservants, and your goodliest young men, and your asses, and put them to his work: and he will take the tenth of your sheep, and ye shall be his servants, and ye shall cry out in that day because of your king which ye shall have chosen, AND THE LORD WILL NOT HEAR YOU IN THAT DAY." This accounts for the continuation of monarchy; neither do the characters of the few good kings which have lived since either sanctify the title or blot out the sinfulness of the origin; the high encomium given of David takes no notice of him *officially as a king*, but only as a *man* after God's own heart. "Nevertheless the people refused to obey the voice of Samuel, and they said, Nay but we will have a king over us, that we may be like all the nations, and that our king may judge us, and go out before us and fight our battles." Samuel continued to reason with them but to no purpose; he set before them their ingratitude, but all would not avail; and seeing them fully bent on their folly, he cried out, "I will call unto the Lord, and he shall send thunder and rain" (which was then a punishment, being in the time of wheat harvest) "that ye may perceive and see that your wickedness is great which ye have done in the sight of the Lord, IN ASKING YOU A KING. So Samuel called unto the Lord, and the Lord sent thunder and rain that day, and all the people greatly feared the Lord and Samuel. And all the people said unto Samuel, Pray for thy servants unto the Lord, thy God that we die not, for WE HAVE ADDED UNTO OUR SINS THIS EVIL, TO ASK A KING." These portions of Scripture are direct and positive. They admit of no equivocal construction. That the Almighty hath here entered his protest against monarchical government is true, or the Scripture is false. And a man hath good reason to believe that there is as much of kingcraft as priestcraft in withholding the Scripture from the public in popish countries.

For monarchy in every instance is the property of government.

To the evil of monarchy we have added that of hereditary succession; and as the first is a degradation and lessening of ourselves, so the second, claimed as a matter of right, is an insult and imposition on posterity. For all men being originally equals, no *one* by *birth* could have a right to set up his own family in perpetual preference to all others for ever, and though himself might deserve *some* decent degree of honors of his contemporaries, yet his descendants might be far too unworthy to inherit them. One of the strongest *natural* proofs of the folly of hereditary right in kings is that nature disapproves it, otherwise she would not so frequently turn it into ridicule by giving mankind an *ass for a lion.*

Secondly, as no man at first could possess any other public honors than were bestowed upon him, so the givers of those honors could have no power to give away the right of posterity, and though they might say, "We choose you for our head," they could not without manifest injustice to their children say "that your children and your children's children shall reign over ours forever." Because such an unwise, unjust, unnatural compact might (perhaps) in the next succession put them under the government of a rogue or a fool. Most wise men in their private sentiments have ever treated hereditary right with contempt; yet it is one of those evils which when once established is not easily removed; many submit from fear, others from superstition, and the more powerful part shares with the king the plunder of the rest.

This is supposing the present race of kings in the world to have had an honorable origin. Whereas it is more than probable that, could we take off the dark covering of antiquity and trace them to their first rise, we should find the first of them nothing better than the principal ruffian of some restless gang, whose savage manners or pre-eminence in subtility obtained him the title of chief among plunderers, and who, by increasing in power and extending his depredations, overawed the quiet and defenseless to purchase their safety by frequent contributions. Yet his electors could have no idea of giving hereditary right to his descendants, because such a perpetual exclusion of themselves was incompatible with the free and unrestrained principles they profess to live by. Wherefore, hereditary succession in the early ages of monarchy could not take place as a matter of claim, but as something casual or complemental; but as few or no records were extant in those days, and traditionary history stuffed with fables, it was very easy, after the lapse of a few generations, to trump up some superstitious tale conveniently timed, Mahomet-like, to cram hereditary right down the throats of the vulgar. Perhaps the disorders which threatened, or seemed to threaten, on the decease of a leader and the choice of a new one (for elections among ruffians could not be very orderly) induced many at first to favor hereditary pretensions; by which means it happened, as it hath happened since, that what at first was submitted to as a convenience was afterward claimed as a right.

England since the conquest hath known some few good monarchs but groaned beneath a much larger number of bad ones; yet no man in his senses can say that their claim under William the Conqueror is a very honorable one. A French bastard landing with an armed banditti and establishing himself king of England against the consent of the natives is in plain terms a very paltry rascally original. It certainly hath no divinity in it. However, it is needless to spend much time in exposing the folly of hereditary right; if there are any so weak as to believe it, let them promiscuously worship the ass and the lion, and welcome. I shall neither copy their humility nor disturb their devotion.

Yet I should be glad to ask how they suppose kings came at first? The question admits but of three answers, viz., either by lot, by election, or by usurpation. If the first king was taken by lot, it establishes a precedent for the next, which excludes hereditary succession. Saul was by lot,[6] yet the succession was not hereditary, neither does it appear from that transaction that there was any intention it ever should. If the first king of any country was by election, that likewise establishes a precedent for the next; for to say that the right of all future generations is taken away by the act of the first electors in their choice not only of a king but of a family of kings forever hath no parallel in or out of Scripture but the doctrine of original sin, which supposes the free will of all men lost in Adam; and from such comparison, and it will admit of no other, hereditary succession can derive no glory. For as in Adam all sinned, and as in the first electors all men obeyed; as in the one all mankind were subjected to Satan, and in the other to sovereignty; as our innocence was lost in the first, and our authority in the last; and as both disable us from reassuming some former state and privilege, it unanswerably follows that original sin and hereditary succession are parallels. Dishonorable rank! inglorious connection! yet the most subtle sophist cannot produce a juster simile.

As to usurpation, no man will be so hardy as to defend it; and that William the Conqueror was an usurper is a fact not to be contradicted. The plain truth is that the antiquity of English monarchy will not bear looking into.

But it is not so much the absurdity as the evil of hereditary succession which concerns mankind. Did it insure a race of good and wise men, it would have the seal of divine authority, but, as it

opens a door to the *foolish*, the *wicked*, and the *improper*, it hath in it the nature of oppression. Men who look upon themselves born to reign, and others to obey, soon grow insolent. Selected from the rest of mankind, their minds are early poisoned by importance; and the world they act in differs so materially from the world at large that they have but little opportunity of knowing its true interest and, when they succeed to the government, are frequently the most ignorant and unfit of any throughout the dominions.

Another evil which attends hereditary succession is that the throne is subject to be possessed by a minor at any age; all which time the regency acting under the cover of a king have every opportunity and inducement to betray their trust. The same national misfortune happens when a king worn out with age and infirmity enters the last stage of human weakness. In both these cases the public becomes a prey to every miscreant who can temper successfully with the follies either of age or infancy.

The most plausible plea which hath ever been offered in favor of hereditary succession is that it preserves a nation from civil wars, and, were this true, it would be weighty; whereas it is the most barefaced falsity ever imposed upon mankind. The whole history of England disowns the fact. Thirty kings and two minors have reigned in that distracted kingdom since the conquest, in which time there has been (including the Revolution) no less than eight civil wars and nineteen rebellions. Wherefore instead of making for peace, it makes against it and destroys the very foundation it seems to stand upon.

The contest for monarchy and succession between the houses of York and Lancaster laid England in a scene of blood for many years. Twelve pitched battles besides skirmishes and sieges were fought between Henry and Edward. Twice was Henry prisoner to Edward,

6. Saul, first king of Israel, was selected by lot (I Sam. 10:9–23 and Esther 3:7).

who in his turn was prisoner to Henry. And so uncertain is the fate of war and the temper of a nation, when nothing but personal matters are the ground of a quarrel, that Henry was taken in triumph from a prison to a palace, and Edward obliged to fly from a palace to a foreign land; yet, as sudden transitions of temper are seldom lasting, Henry in his turn was driven from the throne, and Edward recalled to succeed him, the Parliament always following the strongest side.

This contest began in the reign of Henry the Sixth and was not entirely extinguished until Henry the Seventh, in whom the families were united. Including a period of sixty-seven years, viz., from 1422 to 1489.

In short, monarchy and succession have laid (not this or that kingdom only) but the world in blood and ashes. 'Tis a form of government which the word of God bears testimony against, and blood will attend it.

If we inquire into the business of a king, we shall find that in some countries they may have none; and after sauntering away their lives without pleasure to themselves or advantages to the nation, withdraw from the scene, and leave their successors to tread the same idle round. In absolute monarchies the whole weight of business civil and military lies on the king; the children of Israel in their request for a king urged this plea, "that he may judge us, and go out before us and fight our battles." But in countries where he is neither a judge nor a general, as in England, a man would be puzzled to know what *is* his business.

The nearer any government approaches to a republic, the less business there is for a king. It is somewhat difficult to find a proper name for the government of England. Sir William Meredith[7] calls it a republic; but in its present state it is unworthy of the name, because

7. Sir William Meredith (d. 1790), member of Parliament and Whig politician.

the corrupt influence of the crown, by having all the places in its disposal, hath so effectually swallowed up the power and eaten out the virtue of the House of Commons (the republican part in the constitution) that the government of England is nearly as monarchical as that of France or Spain. Men fall out with names without understanding them. For 'tis the republican and not the monarchical part of the constitution of England which Englishmen glory in, viz., the liberty of choosing a House of Commons from out of their own body—and it is easy to see that, when republican virtues fail, slavery ensues. Why is the constitution of England sickly? but because monarchy hath poisoned the republic; the crown has engrossed the Commons.

In England a king hath little more to do than to make war and give away places, which in plain terms is to impoverish the nation and set it together by the ears. A pretty business indeed for a man to be allowed eight hundred thousand sterling a year for and worshiped into the bargain! Of more worth is one honest man to society, and in the sight of God, than all the crowned ruffians that ever lived.

THOUGHTS ON THE PRESENT STATE
OF AMERICAN AFFAIRS

In the following pages I offer nothing more than simple facts, plain arguments, and common sense: and have no other preliminaries to settle with the reader than that he will divest himself of prejudice and prepossession and suffer his reason and his feelings to determine for themselves; that he will put on, or rather that he will not put off, the true character of a man and generously enlarge his views beyond the present day.

Volumes have been written on the subject of the struggle between England and America. Men of all ranks have embarked in the controversy, from different motives, and with various designs;

but all have been ineffectual, and the period of debate is closed. Arms as the last resource decide the contest; the appeal was the choice of the king, and the continent has accepted the challenge.

It hath been reported of the late Mr. Pelham (who though an able minister was not without his faults) that on his being attacked in the House of Commons on the score that his measures were only of a temporary kind, replied, "they will last my time."[8] Should a thought so fatal and unmanly possess the colonies in the present contest, the name of ancestors will be remembered by future generations with detestation.

The sun never shined on a cause of greater worth. 'Tis not the affair of a city, a county, a province, or a kingdom but of a continent—of at least one-eighth part of the habitable globe. 'Tis not the concern of a day, a year, or an age; posterity are virtually involved in the contest and will be more or less affected even to the end of time by the proceedings now. Now is the seedtime of continental union, faith, and honor. The least fracture now will be like a name engraved with the point of a pin on the tender rind of a young oak; the wound would enlarge with the tree, and posterity read it in full-grown characters.

By referring the matter from argument to arms, a new era for politics is struck—a new method of thinkings has arisen. All plans, proposals, etc., prior to the nineteenth of April, i.e., to the commencement of hostilities, are like the almanacs of the last year, which, though proper then, are superseded and useless now. Whatever was advanced by the advocates on either side of the question then, terminated in one and the same point, viz., a union with Great Britain; the only difference between the parties was the method of effecting it; the one

proposing force, the other friendship; but it has so far happened that the first has failed, and the second has withdrawn her influence.

As much has been said of the advantages of reconciliation, which, like an agreeable dream, has passed away and left us as we were, it is but right that we should examine the contrary side of the argument and inquire into some of the many material injuries which these colonies sustain, and always will sustain, by being connected with and dependent on Great Britain. To examine that connection and dependence, on the principles of nature and common sense, to see what we have to trust to, if separated, and what we are to expect, if dependent.

I have heard it asserted by some that, as America has flourished under her former connection with Great Britain, the same connection is necessary toward her future happiness and will always have the same effect. Nothing can be more fallacious than this kind of argument. We may as well assert that, because a child has thrived upon milk, that it is never to have meat, or that the first twenty years of our lives is to become a precedent for the next twenty. But even this is admitting more than is true; for I answer roundly that America would have flourished as much, and probably much more, had no European power taken any notice of her. The commerce by which she hath enriched herself are the necessaries of life and will always have a market while eating is the custom of Europe.

But she has protected us, say some. That she hath engrossed us is true, and defended the continent at our expense as well as her own, is admitted; and she would have defended Turkey from the same motive, viz., for the sake of trade and dominion.

Alas! we have been long led away by ancient prejudices and made large sacrifices to superstition. We have boasted the protection of Great Britain without

8. Henry Pelham was prime minister of England from 1743 to 1746 and from 1746 to 1754, when he was succeeded by his brother, Thomas Pelham, Duke of Newcastle.

considering that her motive was *interest* not *attachment* and that she did not protect us from *our enemies* on *our account* but from her enemies on her own account, from those who had no quarrel with us on any *other account*, and who will always be our enemies on the *same account*. Let Britain waive her pretensions to the continent, or the continent throw off the dependence, and we should be at peace with France and Spain were they at war with Britain. The miseries of Hanover's last war ought to warn us against connections.[9]

It hath lately been asserted in Parliament that the colonies have no relation to each other but through the parent-country, i.e., that Pennsylvania and the Jerseys, and so on for the rest, are sister-colonies by the way of England; this is certainly a very roundabout way of proving relationship, but it is the nearest and only true way of proving enmity (or enemyship, if I may so call it). France and Spain never were, nor perhaps ever will be, our enemies as *Americans* but as our being the *subjects of Great Britain*.

But Britain is the parent-country, say some. Then the more shame upon her conduct. Even brutes do not devour their young, nor savages make war upon their families; wherefore, the assertion, if true, turns to her reproach; but it happens not to be true, or only partly so, and the phrase *parent-* or *mother-country* hath been jesuitically adopted by the king and his parasites, with a low papistical design of gaining an unfair bias on the credulous weakness of our minds. Europe, and not England, is the parent-country of America. This New World hath been the asylum for the persecuted lovers of civil and religious liberty from *every part* of Europe. Hither have they fled, not from the tender embraces of the mother, but from the cruelty of the monster; and it is so far true of England that the same tyranny which drove the

9. The French and Indian War, concluded in 1763.

first emigrants from home pursues their descendants still.

In this extensive quarter of the globe, we forget the narrow limits of three hundred and sixty miles (the extent of England) and carry our friendship on a larger scale; we claim brotherhood with every European Christian, and triumph in the generosity of the sentiment.

It is pleasant to observe by what regular gradations we surmount the force of local prejudices as we enlarge our acquaintance with the world. A man born in any town in England divided into parishes will naturally associate most with his fellow-parishioners (because their interests in many cases will be common) and distinguish him by the name of *neighbor;* if he meet him but a few miles from home, he drops the narrow idea of a street and salutes him by the name of *townsman;* if he travel out of the country and meet him in any other, he forgets the minor divisions of street and town, and calls him *country-man*, i.e., *countyman;* but if in their foreign excursions they should associate in France, or any other part of *Europe*, their local remembrance would be enlarged into that of *Englishman*. And by a just parity of reasoning, all Europeans meeting in America, or any other quarter of all the globe, are *countrymen;* for England, Holland, Germany, or Sweden, when compared with the whole, stand in the same places on the larger scale, which the divisions of street, town, and county do on the smaller ones; distinctions too limited for Continental minds. Not one-third of the inhabitants, even of this province, are of English descent. Wherefore, I reprobate the phrase of parent- or mother-country applied to England only, as being false, selfish, narrow, and ungenerous.

But, admitting that we were all of English descent, what does it amount to? Nothing. Britain, being now an open enemy, extinguishes every other name and title: and to say that reconciliation is our duty is truly farcical. The first king of England, of the present line (William the Conqueror) was a Frenchman, and half the peers of England are descendants from the same country; wherefore, by the same method of reasoning, England ought to be governed by France.

Much hath been said of the united strength of Britain and the colonies, that in conjunction they might bid defiance to the world. But this is mere presumption, the fate of war is uncertain, neither do the expressions mean anything, for this continent would never suffer itself to be drained of inhabitants, to support the British arms in either Asia, Africa, or Europe.

Besides, what have we to do with setting the world at defiance? Our plan is commerce, and that, well attended to, will secure us the peace and friendship of all Europe, because it is the interest of all Europe to have America a *free port*. Her trade will always be a protection, and her barrenness of gold and silver secure her from invaders.

I challenge the warmest advocate for reconciliation to show a single advantage that this continent can reap by being connected with Great Britain. I repeat the challenge, not a single advantage is derived. Our corn will fetch its price in any market in Europe, and our imported goods must be paid for, buy them where we will.

But the injuries and disadvantages which we sustain by that connection, are without number; and our duty to mankind at large, as well as to ourselves, instructs us to renounce the alliance. Because, any submission to, or dependence on, Great Britain, tends directly to involve this continent in European wars and quarrels and set us at variance with nations who would otherwise seek our friendship and against whom we have neither anger nor complaint. As Europe is our market for trade, we ought to form no partial connection with any part of it. 'Tis the true interest of America to steer clear of European contentions, which she never can do, while by her dependence on Britain, she is made the makeweight in the scale of British politics.

Europe is too thickly planted with kingdoms to be long at peace, and whenever a war breaks out between England and any foreign power, the trade of America goes to ruin *because of her connection with Britain*. The next war may not turn out like the last, and, should it not, the advocates for reconciliation now will be wishing for separation then, because neutrality in that case would be a safer convoy than a man-of-war. Everything that is right or reasonable pleads for separation. The blood of the slain, the weeping voice of nature cries, 'TIS TIME TO PART. Even the distance at which the Almighty hath placed England and America is a strong and natural proof that the authority of the one over the other was never the design of heaven. The time likewise at which the continent was discovered adds weight to the argument, and the manner in which it was peopled increases the force of it. The Reformation was preceded by the discovery of America. As if the Almighty graciously meant to open a sanctuary to the persecuted in future years, when home should afford neither friendship nor safety.

The authority of Great Britain over this continent is a form of government which sooner or later must have an end. And a serious mind can draw no true pleasure by looking forward, under the painful and positive conviction that what he calls "the present constitution" is merely temporary. As parents, we can have no joy, knowing that *this government* is not sufficiently lasting to insure anything which we may bequeath to posterity. And by a plain method of argument, as we are running the next generation into debt, we ought to do the work of it, otherwise we use them meanly and pitifully. In order to discover the line of our duty rightly, we should take our children in our hand and fix our station a few years farther into life; that eminence will present a prospect which a few present fears and prejudices conceal from our sight.

Though I would carefully avoid giving unnecessary offense, yet I am inclined to believe that all those who espouse the doctrine of reconciliation may be included within the following descriptions.

Interested men, who are not to be trusted, weak men who *cannot* see, prejudiced men who *will not* see, and a certain set of moderate men who think better of the European world than it deserves; and this last class, by an ill-judged deliberation, will be the cause of more calamities to this continent than all the other three.

It is the good fortune of many to live distant from the scene of present sorrow; the evil is not sufficiently brought to *their* doors to make *them* feel the precariousness with which all American property is possessed. But let our imaginations transport us a few moments to Boston; that seat of wretchedness will teach us wisdom and instruct us forever to renounce a power in whom we can have no trust.[10] The inhabitants of that unfortunate city, who but a few months ago were in ease and affluence, have now no other alternative than to stay and starve or turn out to beg. Endangered by the fire of their friends if they continue within the city, and plundered by the soldiery if they leave it, in their present situation they are prisoners without the hope of redemption, and in a general attack for their relief they would be exposed to the fury of both armies.

Men of passive tempers look somewhat lightly over the offenses of Great Britain, and, still hoping for the best, are apt to call out, "Come, come, we shall be friends again for all this." But examine the passions and feelings of mankind. Bring the doctrine of reconciliation to the touchstone of nature, and then tell me whether you can hereafter love, honor, and faithfully serve the power that hath carried fire and sword into your land? If you cannot do all these, then are you only deceiving yourselves, and by your delay bringing ruin upon posterity. Your future connection with Britain, whom you can neither love nor honor, will be forced and unnatural, and being formed only on the plan of present convenience, will in a little time fall into a relapse more wretched than the first. But if you say, you can still pass the violations over, then I ask, Hath your house been burned? Hath your property been destroyed before your face? Are your wife and children destitute of a bed to lie on, or bread to live on? Have you lost a parent or child by their hands, and yourself the ruined and wretched survivor? If you have not, then are you not a judge of those who have. But if you have, and can still shake hands with the murderers, then are you unworthy the name of husband, father, friend, or lover, and whatever may be your rank or title in life, you have the heart of a coward, and the spirit of a sycophant.

This is not inflaming or exaggerating matters, but trying them by those feelings and affection which nature justifies, and without which we should be incapable of discharging the social duties of life or enjoying the felicities of it. I mean not to exhibit horror for the purpose of provoking revenge, but to awaken us from fatal and unmanly slumbers, that we may pursue determinately some fixed object. 'Tis not in the power of Britain or of Europe to conquer America, if she doth not conquer herself by *delay* and *timidity*. The present winter is worth an age if rightly

10. Boston, still held precariously by the British, was under siege by Washington at the time of Paine's writing. In the spring of 1776 the British left by sea for Halifax.

employed, but if lost or neglected the whole continent will partake of the misfortune; and there is no punishment which that man doth not deserve, be he who, or what, or where he will, that may be the means of sacrificing a season so precious and useful.

'Tis repugnant to reason, to the universal order of things, to all examples from former ages, to suppose that this continent can long remain subject to any external power. The most sanguine in Britain doth not think so. The utmost stretch of human wisdom cannot, at this time, compass a plan, short of separation, which can promise the continent even a year's security. Reconciliation is *now* a fallacious dream. Nature has deserted the connection, and art cannot supply her place. For, as Milton wisely expresses, "never can true reconcilement grow where wounds of deadly hate have pierced so deep."

Every quiet method for peace hath been ineffectual. Our prayers have been rejected with disdain and hath tended to convince us that nothing flatters vanity or confirms obstinacy in kings more than repeated petitioning—and nothing hath contributed more than that very measure to make the kings of Europe absolute. Witness Denmark and Sweden.[11] Wherefore, since nothing but blows will do, for God's sake let us come to a final separation and not leave the next generation to be cutting throats under the violated unmeaning names of parent and child.

To say they will never attempt it again is idle and visionary; we thought so at the repeal of the Stamp Act, yet a year or two undeceived us; as well may we suppose that nations which have been once defeated will never renew the quarrel.

As to government matters, 'tis not in the power of Britain to do this continent justice: the business of it will soon be too weighty and intricate to be managed with any tolerable degree of convenience, by a power so distant from us, and so very ignorant of us; for if they cannot conquer us, they cannot govern us. To be always running three or four thousand miles with a tale or a petition, waiting four or five months for an answer, which, when obtained, requires five or six more to explain it in, will in a few years be looked upon as folly and childishness. There was a time when it was proper, and there is a proper time for it to cease.

Small islands not capable of protecting themselves are the proper objects for government to take under their care; but there is something absurd in supposing a continent to be perpetually governed by an island. In no instance hath nature made the satellite larger than its primary planet; and as England and America, with respect to each other, reverse the common order of nature, it is evident that they belong to different systems. England to Europe; America to itself.

I am not induced by motives of pride, party, or resentment to espouse the doctrine of separation and independence; I am clearly, positively, and conscientiously persuaded that 'tis the true interest of this continent to be so; that everything short of *that* is mere patchwork, that it can afford no lasting felicity—that it is leaving the sword to our children and shrinking back at a time when a little more, a little further, would have rendered this continent the glory of the earth.

As Britain hath not manifested the least inclination toward a compromise, we may be assured that no terms can be obtained worthy the acceptance of the continent, or any ways equal to the expense of blood and treasure we have been already put to.

The object contended for ought always to bear some just proportion to the

11. Denmark and Sweden were among the absolute monarchies of Paine's time. They have since become constitutional monarchies.

expense. The removal of North,[12] or the whole detestable junto, is a matter unworthy the millions we have expended. A temporary stoppage of trade was an inconvenience, which would have sufficiently balanced the repeal of all the acts complained of, had such repeals been obtained; but if the whole continent must take up arms, if every man must be a soldier, 'tis scarcely worth our while to fight against a contemptible ministry only. Dearly, dearly do we pay for the repeal of the acts, if that is all we fight for; for, in a just estimation 'tis as great a folly to pay a bunker-hill price for law as for land.[13] As I have always considered the independency of this continent as an event which sooner or later must arrive, so from the late rapid progress of the continent to maturity, the event cannot be far off. Wherefore, on the breaking-out of the hostilities, it was not worth the while to have disputed a matter which time would have finally redressed, unless we meant to be in earnest; otherwise it is like wasting an estate on a suit at law, to regulate the trespasses of a tenant whose lease is just expiring. No man was a warmer wisher for a reconciliation than myself, before the fatal nineteenth of April, 1775, but the moment the event of that day was made known, I rejected the hardened, sullen-tempered Pharaoh of England forever; and disdain the wretch that, with the pretended title of FATHER OF HIS PEOPLE, can unfeelingly hear of their slaughter and composedly sleep with their blood upon his soul.

But admitting that matters were now made up, what would be the event? I answer: the ruin of the continent. And that for several reasons.

First, the powers of governing still remaining in the hands of the king, he will have a negative over the whole legislation of this continent. And as he hath shown himself such an inveterate enemy to liberty, and discovered such a thirst for arbitrary power, is he, or is he not, a proper person to say to these colonies, "You shall make no laws but what I please?" And is there any inhabitant of America so ignorant as not to know that, according to what is called the *present constitution*, this continent can make no laws but what the king gives leave to; and is there any man so unwise as not to see that (considering what has happened) he will suffer no law to be made here but such as suits his purpose? We may be as effectually enslaved by the want of laws in America as by submitting to laws made for us in England. After matters are made up (as it is called), can there be any doubt but the whole power of the crown will be exerted to keep this continent as low and humble as possible? Instead of going forward we shall go backward, or be perpetually quarrelling, or ridiculously petitioning. We are already greater than the king wishes us to be, and will he not hereafter endeavor to make us less? To bring the matter to one point: Is the power who is jealous of our prosperity a proper power to govern us? Whoever says "No" to this question is an Independent, for independency means no more than this, whether we shall make our own laws or whether the king, the greatest enemy this continent hath, or can have, shall tell us, "there shall be no laws but such as I like."

But the king, you'll say, has a negative in England; the people there can make no laws without his consent. In point of right and good order, it is something very ridiculous that a youth of twenty-one (which hath often happened) shall

12. Frederick North (1732–92), who became the second Earl of Guilford, was prime minister of England from 1770 to 1782. He was a "pliant instrument" of George III and retained the tea duty and introduced the Boston Port Bill to Parliament in 1774. After Cornwallis' defeat North resigned, but he returned briefly to the premiership with Fox in 1790.

13. Paine here refers to the famous Battle of Bunker Hill, which resulted in such heavy losses to the "Redcoats" that the Americans considered it a victory for them.

say to several millions of people older and wiser than himself, "I forbid this or that act of yours to be law." But in this place I decline this sort of reply, though I will never cease to expose the absurdity of it, and only answer that England, being the king's residence, and America not so, makes quite another case. The king's negative here is ten times more dangerous and fatal than it can be in England; for *there* he will scarcely refuse his consent to a bill for putting England into as strong a state of defense as possible, and in America he would never suffer such a bill to be passed.

America is only a secondary object in the system of British politics; England consults the good of *this* country no further than it answers her *own* purpose. Wherefore, her own interest leads her to suppress the growth of *ours* in every case which doth not promote *her* advantage, or in the least interfere with it. A pretty state we should soon be in under such a secondhand government, considering what has happened! Men do not change from enemies to friends by the alteration of a name. And in order to show that reconciliation *now* is a dangerous doctrine, I affirm, *that it would be policy in the king at this time to repeal the acts, for the sake of reinstating himself in the government of the provinces;* In order that HE MAY ACCOMPLISH BY CRAFT AND SUBTLETY, IN THE LONG RUN, WHAT HE CANNOT DO BY FORCE AND VIOLENCE IN THE SHORT ONE. Reconciliation and ruin are nearly related.

Secondly, that as even the best terms which we can expect to obtain can amount to no more than a temporary expedient, or a kind of government by guardianship, which can last no longer than till the colonies come of age, so the general face and state of things in the interim will be unsettled and unpromising. Emigrants of property will not choose to come to a country whose form of government hangs but by a thread, and who is every day tottering on the brink of commotion and disturbance. And numbers of the present inhabitants would lay hold of the interval to dispose of their effects and quit the continent.

But the most powerful of all arguments is that nothing but independence, i.e., a continental form of government, can keep the peace of the continent and preserve it inviolate from civil wars. I dread the event of a reconciliation with Britain *now*, as it is more than probable that it will be followed by a revolt somewhere or other, the consequences of which may be far more fatal than all malice of Britain.

Thousands are already ruined by British barbarity (thousands more will probably suffer the same fate). Those men have other feelings than us who have nothing suffered. All they *now* possess is liberty; what they before enjoyed is sacrificed to its service, and, having nothing more to lose, they disdain submission. Besides, the general temper of the colonies toward a British government will be like that of a youth who is nearly out of his time;[14] they will care very little about her. And a government which cannot preserve the peace is no government at all, and in that case we pay our money for nothing; and pray what is it that Britain can do, whose power will be wholly on paper, should a civil tumult break out the very day after reconciliation? I have heard some men say, many of whom I believe spoke without thinking, that they dreaded an independence, fearing that it would produce civil wars. It is but seldom that our first thoughts are truly correct, and that is the case here; for there is ten times more to dread from a patched-up connection than from independence. I make the sufferer's case my own, and I protest that, were I driven from house and home, my property destroyed, and my circumstances ruined, that as a man, sensible of injuries, I could

14. A youth about to finish his apprenticeship.

never relish the doctrine of reconciliation or consider myself bound thereby.

The colonies have manifested such a spirit of good order and obedience to continental government as is sufficient to make every reasonable person easy and happy on that head. No man can assign the least pretense for his fears on any other ground than such as are truly childish and ridiculous, viz., the one colony will be striving for superiority over another.

Where there are no distinctions there can be no superiority; perfect equality affords no temptation. The republics of Europe are all (and we may say always) in peace. Holland and Switzerland are without wars, foreign or domestic. Monarchical governments, it is true, are never long at rest; the crown itself is a temptation to enterprising ruffians at *home;* and that degree of pride and insolence, ever attendant on regal authority, swells into a rupture with foreign powers in instances where a republican government, by being formed on more natural principles, would negociate the mistake.

If there is any true cause of fear respecting independence, it is because no plan is yet laid down. Men do not see their way out. Wherefore, as an opening into that business I offer the following hints, at the same time modestly affirming that I have no other opinion of them myself than that they may be the means of giving rise to something better. Could the straggling thoughts of individuals be collected, they would frequently form materials for wise and able men to improve into useful matter.

Let the assemblies be annual, with a president only. The representation more equal, their business wholly domestic, and subject to the authority of a Continental Congress.

Let each colony be divided into six, eight, or ten convenient districts, each district to send a proper number of delegates to Congress, so that each colony send at least thirty. The whole number in Congress will be at least 390. Each Congress to sit and to choose a president by the following method. When the delegates are met, let a colony be taken from the whole thirteen colonies by lot, after which let the Congress choose (by ballot) a president from out of the delegates of that province. In the next Congress, let a colony be taken by lot from twelve only, omitting that colony from which the president was taken in the former Congress, and so proceeding on till the whole thirteen shall have had their proper rotation. And in order that nothing may pass into a law but what is satisfactorily just, not less than three-fifths of the Congress to be called a majority. He that will promote discord, under a government so equally formed as this would have joined Lucifer in his revolt.

But as there is a peculiar delicacy from whom, or in what manner, this business must first arise, and as it seems most agreeable and consistent that it should come from some intermediate body between the governed and the governors, that is, between the Congress and the people, let a CONTINENTAL CONFERENCE be held in the following manner, and for the following purpose,

A committee of twenty-six members of Congress, viz., two for each colony. Two members from each house of assembly, or provincial convention; and five representatives of the people at large, to be chosen in the capital city or town of each province, for, and in behalf of the whole province, by as many qualified voters as shall think proper to attend from all parts of the province for that purpose; or, if more convenient, the representatives may be chosen in two or three of the most populous parts thereof. In this CONFERENCE, thus assembled, will be united the two grand principles of business, *knowledge* and *power.* The members of Congress, assemblies, or conventions, by having had experience in national concerns, will be able and useful counselors, and the whole, being empowered by the people, will have a truly legal authority.

The conferring members being met, let their business be to frame a CONTINENTAL CHARTER, or Charter of the United Colonies (answering to what is called the Magna Charta of England), fixing the number and manner of choosing members of Congress, members of Assembly, with their date of sitting; and drawing the line of business and jurisdiction between them. Always remembering, that our strength is continental, not provincial. Securing freedom and property to all men, and, above all things, the free exercise of religion, according to the dictates of conscience; with such other matter as it is necessary for a charter to contain. Immediately after which, the said conference to dissolve, and the bodies which shall be chosen conformable to the said charter, to be the legislators and governors of this continent for the time being, whose peace and happiness, may God preserve. AMEN.

Should any body of men be hereafter delegated for this or some similar purpose, I offer them the following extracts from that wise observer on governments, DRAGONETTI.[15] "The science," says he, "of the politician consists in fixing the true point of happiness and freedom. Those men would deserve the gratitude of ages who should discover a mode of government that contained the greatest sum of individual happiness with the least national expense."

But where, say some, is the king of America? I'll tell you, Friend, he reigns above, and doth not make havoc of mankind like the Royal Brute of Great Britain. Yet that we may not appear to be defective even in earthly honors, let a day be solemnly set apart for proclaiming the charter; let it be brought forth

placed on the divine law, the Word of God; let a crown be placed thereon, by which the world may know that, so far as we approve of monarchy, that in America THE LAW IS KING. For as in absolute governments the king is law, so in free countries the law *ought* to BE king, and there ought to be no other. But lest any ill use should afterward arise, let the crown at the conclusion of the ceremony be demolished, and scattered among the people whose right it is.

A government of our own is our natural right, and when a man seriously reflects on the precariousness of human affairs, he will become convinced that it is infinitely wiser and safer to form a constitution of our own in a cool deliberate manner, while we have it in our power, than to trust such an interesting event to time and chance. If we omit it now, some Massanello[16] may hereafter arise, who, laying hold of popular disquietudes, may collect together the desperate and the discontented and, by assuming to themselves the powers of government, finally sweep away the liberties of the continent like a deluge. Should the government of America return again into the hands of Britain, the tottering situation of things will be a temptation for some desperate adventurer to try his fortune; and in such a case, what relief can Britain give? Ere she could hear the news, the fatal business might be done; and ourselves suffering like the wretched Britons under the oppression of the conqueror. Ye that oppose independence now, ye know not what ye do; ye are opening a door to eternal tyranny by keeping vacant the seat of government. There are thousands and tens of thousands who would think it glorious to expel from the continent

16. Thomas Anello, otherwise Massanello, a fisherman of Naples, who, after spiriting up his countrymen in the public market place against the oppression of the Spaniards, to whom the place was then subject, prompted them to revolts and in the space of a day became king. Paine's note to a later edition.

15. Dragonetti, an Italian jurist (1738–1818). Paine's note reads: "Dragonetti on 'Virtues and Rewards.'"

that barbarous and hellish power, which hath stirred up the Indians and the Negroes to destroy us; the cruelty hath a double guilt, it is dealing brutally by us, and treacherously by them.

To talk of friendship with those in whom our reason forbids us to have faith, and our affections wounded through a thousand pores instruct us to detest, is madness and folly. Every day wears out the little remains of kindred between us and them; and can there be any reason to hope that, as the relationship expires, the affection will increase or that we shall agree better when we have ten times more and greater concerns to quarrel over than ever?

Ye that tell us of harmony and reconciliation, can ye restore to us the time that is past? Can ye give to prostitution its former innocence? Neither can ye reconcile Britain and America. The last cord now is broken; the people of England are presenting addresses against us. There are injuries which nature cannot forgive; she would cease to be nature if she did. As well can the lover forgive the ravisher of his mistress as the continent forgive the murders of Britain. The Almighty hath implanted in us these inextinguishable feelings for good and wise purposes. They are the guardians of his image in our hearts. They distinguish us from the herd of common animals. The social compact would dissolve, and justice be extirpated from the earth, or have only a casual existence, were we callous to the touches of affection. The robber and the murderer would often escape unpunished did not the injuries which our tempers sustain provoke us into justice.

O! ye that love mankind! Ye that dare oppose not only the tyranny but the tyrant, stand forth! Every spot of the Old World is overrun with oppression. Freedom hath been hunted round the globe. Asia and Africa have long expelled her. Europe regards her like a stranger, and England hath given her warning to depart. O receive the fugitive and prepare in time an asylum for mankind. . . .

11. THE DECLARATION OF INDEPENDENCE, JULY 4, 1776[1]

EDITORS' NOTE.—Many revolutionary leaders still hoped for reconciliation with England even after hostilities had broken out on April 19, 1775. The Second Continental Congress on July 6, 1775, disclaimed the intention of rebelling in a resolution that set forth their grievances and expressed a hope for reconciliation (p. 160). On the day that this petition was to be presented, the king proclaimed a state of rebellion in America. Gradually the demand grew for independence. On June 7, 1776, Richard Henry Lee, following the instructions of the Virginia Convention, submitted to the Second Continental Congress three resolutions.

Resolved, That these United Colonies are, and of right ought to be, free and independent states, that they are absolved from all allegiance to the British Crown, and that all political connection between them and the State of Great Britain is, and ought to be, totally dissolved.

That it is expedient forthwith to take the most effectual measures for forming foreign Alliances.

That a plan of confederation be prepared and transmitted to the respective Colonies for their consideration and approbation.

During the debate on the motion it was strongly urged that a French alliance was more probable if independence was declared. A few days later

1. *Documents Illustrative of the Formation of the Union* . . ., ed. C. C. Tansill (Washington, 1927), pp. 22–25.

Congress appointed a committee consisting of Thomas Jefferson, John Adams, Benjamin Franklin, Roger Sherman, and Robert R. Livingston to prepare a declaration of independence. On June 28 the committee reported the draft of a declaration written almost entirely by Jefferson, who had incorporated changes and additions suggested by Adams and Franklin. Congress adopted Lee's first resolution on July 2. This is sometimes called the "real" declaration of independence. On the following two days Congress debated, in committee of the whole, the final form in which the declaration was to be given to the world. After a few changes the Declaration of Independence was adopted on July 4, 1776.

John Adams commented in 1822 in regard to Jefferson's authorship of the Declaration of Independence that "there is not an idea in it, but what had been hackneyed in Congress for two years before." Jefferson replied to this charge that it might well be true. "Of that I am not to be the judge. Richard H. Lee charged it as copied from Locke's treatise on Government. . . . I know only that I turned to neither book nor pamphlet while writing it. I did not consider it as any part of my charge to invent new ideas altogether and to offer no sentiment which had ever been expressed before." In writing to Lee, in 1825, Jefferson said that the essential thing was "to place before mankind the common sense of the subject, in terms so plain and firm as to command their assent. . . . Neither aiming at originality of principles or sentiments, nor yet copied from any particular and previous writing, it was intended to be an expression of the American mind. . . . All its authority rests then on the harmonizing sentiments of the day, whether expressed in conversation, in letters, printed essays, or the elementary books of public right, as Aristotle, Cicero, Locke, Sidney, etc." See Carl Becker, *The Declaration of Independence* (New York, 1922), or J. H. Hazelton, *The Declaration of Independence* (New York, 1906).

IN CONGRESS, JULY 4, 1776

THE UNANIMOUS DECLARATION OF THE THIRTEEN
UNITED STATES OF AMERICA

When, in the course of human events, it becomes necessary[*] for one people to dissolve the political bands which have connected them with another, and to assume, among the powers of the earth, the separate and equal station to which the laws of nature and of nature's God entitle them, a decent respect to the opinions of mankind requires that they should declare the causes which impel them to the separation.

We hold these truths to be self-evident: that all men are created equal; that they are endowed by their Creator with certain unalienable rights; that among these are life, liberty, and the pursuit of happiness.[2] That, to secure these rights,

2. In Jefferson's first drafting of this paragraph, this statement was phrased as follows: "We hold these truths to be sacred and undeniable; that all men are created equal and independent; that from that equal creation they derive in rights inherent and inalienable, among which are the preservation of life, and liberty, and the pursuit of happiness. . . ."

governments are instituted among men, deriving their just powers from the consent of the governed. That, whenever any form of government becomes destructive of these ends, it is the right of the people to alter or to abolish it and to institute new government, laying its foundation on such principles and organizing its powers in such form as to them shall seem most likely to effect their safety and happiness. Prudence, indeed, will dictate that governments long established should not be changed for light and transient causes; and accordingly all experience hath shown that mankind are more disposed to suffer, while evils are sufferable, than to right themselves by abolishing the forms to which they are accustomed. But when a long train of abuses and usurpations, pursuing invariably the same object, evinces a design to reduce them under absolute despotism, it is their right, it is their duty, to throw off such government, and to provide new guards for their future security. Such has been the patient sufferance of these colonies; and such is now the necessity which constrains them to alter their former systems of government. The history of the present king of Great Britain is a history of repeated injuries and usurpations, all having in direct object the establishment of an absolute tyranny over these states. To prove this, let facts be submitted to a candid world.

He has refused his assent to laws, the most wholesome and necessary for the public good.

He has forbidden his governors to pass laws of immediate and pressing importance, unless suspended in their operation till his assent should be obtained; and, when so suspended, he has utterly neglected to attend to them.

He has refused to pass other laws for the accommodation of large districts of people, unless those people would relinquish the right of representation in the legislature, a right inestimable to

them and formidable to tyrants only.

He has called together legislative bodies at places unusual, uncomfortable, and distant from the depository of their public records, for the sole purpose of fatiguing them into compliance with his measures.

He has dissolved representative houses repeatedly, for opposing with manly firmness his invasions on the rights of the people.

He has refused for a long time, after such dissolutions, to cause others to be elected; whereby the legislative powers, incapable of annihilation, have returned to the people at large for their exercise; the state remaining in the meantime exposed to all the dangers of invasion from without, and convulsions within.

He has endeavored to prevent the population of these states; for that purpose obstructing the laws for naturalization of foreigners, refusing to pass others to encourage their migration hither, and raising the conditions of new appropriations of lands.

He has obstructed the administration of justice by refusing his assent to laws for establishing judiciary powers.

He has made judges dependent on his will alone, for the tenure of their offices, and the amount and payment of their salaries.

He has erected a multitude of new offices, and sent hither swarms of officers to harass our people, and eat out their substance.

He has kept among us, in times of peace, standing armies, without the consent of our legislatures.

He has affected to render the military independent of, and superior to, the civil power.

He has combined with others to subject us to a jurisdiction foreign to our constitution and unacknowledged by our laws, giving his assent to their acts of pretended legislation:

For quartering large bodies of armed troops among us;

For protecting them, by a mock trial, from punishment for any murders which they should commit on the inhabitants of these states;

For cutting off our trade with all parts of the world;

For imposing taxes on us without our consent;

For depriving us, in many cases, of the benefits of trial by jury;

For transporting us beyond seas to be tried for pretended offenses;

For abolishing the free system of English laws in a neighboring province, establishing therein an arbitrary government, and enlarging its boundaries so as to render it at once an example and fit instrument for introducing the same absolute rule into these colonies;

For taking away our charters, abolishing our most valuable laws, and altering fundamentally the forms of our governments;

For suspending our own legislatures, and declaring themselves invested with power to legislate for us in all cases whatsoever.

He has abdicated government here, by declaring us out of his protection and waging war against us.

He has plundered our seas, ravaged our coasts, burned our towns, and destroyed the lives of our people.

He is at this time transporting large armies of foreign mercenaries to complete the works of death, desolation, and tyranny, already begun with circumstances of cruelty and perfidy scarcely paralleled in the most barbarous ages, and totally unworthy the head of a civilized nation.

He has constrained our fellow-citizens taken captive on the high seas to bear arms against their country, to become the executioners of their friends and brethren, or to fall themselves by their hands.

He has excited domestic insurrections amongst us, and has endeavored to bring on the inhabitants of our frontiers, the merciless Indian savages, whose known rule of warfare is an undistinguished destruction of all ages, sexes, and conditions.[3]

In every stage of these oppressions we have petitioned for redress in the most humble terms: Our repeated petitions have been answered only by repeated injury. A prince, whose character is thus marked by every act which may define a tyrant is unfit to be the ruler of a free people.

Nor have we been wanting in attentions to our British brethren. We have warned them from time to time of attempts by their legislature to extend an unwarrantable jurisdiction over us. We have reminded them of the circumstances of our emigration and settlement here. We have appealed to their native justice and magnanimity, and we have conjured them by the ties of our common kindred to disavow these usurpations which would inevitably interrupt our connections and correspondence. They too have been deaf to the voice of justice and of consanguinity. We must, therefore, acquiesce in the necessity, which denounces our separation, and hold them, as we hold the rest of mankind, enemies in war, in peace friends.

We, therefore, the Representatives of the United States of America, in General Congress assembled, appealing to the Supreme Judge of the world for the rectitude of our intentions, do, in the name, and by authority of the good

3. A paragraph condemning the king for having promoted the slave trade appeared at this point in the original draft but was deleted by Congress. Of this action Jefferson wrote: "The clause too, reprobating the enslaving the inhabitants of Africa, was struck out in complaisance to South Carolina and Georgia, who had never attempted to restrain the importation of slaves, and who on the contrary still wished to continue it. Our Northern brethren also I believe felt a little tender under those censures; for though their people have very few slaves themselves, yet they had been pretty considerable carriers of them to others."

people of these colonies, solemnly publish and declare, That these United Colonies are, and of right ought to be, free and independent states; that they are absolved from all allegiance to the British crown, and that all political connection between them and the state of Great Britain, is and ought to be, totally dissolved; and that, as free and independent states, they have full power to levy war, conclude peace, contract alliances, establish commerce, and to do all other acts and things which independent states may of right do. And for the support of this declaration, with a firm reliance on the protection of Divine Providence, we mutually pledge to each other our lives, our fortunes, and our sacred honor.

SECTION B. DEMOCRACY AND ARISTOCRACY IN THE NEW REPUBLIC

1. THE VIRGINIA DECLARATION OF RIGHTS[1]

EDITORS' NOTE.—On May 15, 1776, the Virginia Convention "resolved unanimously that the delegates appointed to represent this colony in General Congress be instructed to propose to that respectable body to declare the United Colonies free and independent states . . . [and] that a committee be appointed to prepare a DECLARATION OF RIGHTS and . . . plan of government." R. H. Lee's resolution of June 7, 1776, implemented the first of these resolutions and precipitated the appointment of the committee to draw up the Declaration of Independence; the second proposal was carried out by the framing of Virginia's first state constitution, of which this declaration was an integral part.

As passed, the Virginia Declaration was largely the work of George Mason; the committee and the Convention made some verbal changes and added Sections 10 and 14. This declaration served as a model for bills of rights in several other state constitutions and was a source of the French Declaration of the Rights of Man and of the Citizen, though its degree of influence upon the latter document is a highly controversial question. The reference to "property" in Section 1 may be compared with the use of the word by John Locke (p. 84), its omission by Thomas Jefferson (p. 201) from the second paragraph of the Declaration of Independence, and its use in the Constitution, Amendments V and XIV (pp. 282 and 284).

George Mason (1725–92), one of Virginia's wealthiest planters, a neighbor and friend of Washington, is best remembered for his part in drafting the Virginia constitution of 1776. In 1787 he was a leader in the Federal Convention (p. 257). Refusing to sign the completed document, Mason, along with Patrick Henry and others, opposed its ratification in the Virginia Convention of 1788.

A declaration of rights made by the representatives of the good people of Virginia, assembled in full and free convention; which rights do pertain to them and their posterity, as the basis and foundation of government.

SECTION 1. That all men are by nature equally free and independent and have certain inherent rights, of which, when they enter into a state of society, they cannot, by any compact, deprive or divest their posterity; namely, the enjoyment of life and liberty, with the means of acquiring and possessing property, and pursuing and obtaining happiness and safety.

SEC. 2. That all power is vested in, and consequently derived from, the people; that magistrates are their trustees

1. *The Federal and State Constitutions, Colonial Charters . . .*, ed. F. N. Thorpe (Washington, 1909), VII, 3812–14.

and servants and at all times amenable to them.

SEC. 3. That government is, or ought to be, instituted for the common benefit, protection, and security of the people, nation, or community; of all the various modes and forms of government, that is best which is capable of producing the greatest degree of happiness and safety and is most effectually secured against the danger of maladministration; and that, when any government shall be found inadequate or contrary to these purposes, a majority of the community hath an indubitable, inalienable, and indefeasible right to reform, alter, or abolish it, in such manner as shall be judged most conducive to the public weal.

SEC. 4. That no man, or set of men, are entitled to exclusive or separate emoluments or privileges from the community, but in consideration of public services; which, not being descendible, neither ought the offices of magistrate, legislator, or judge to be hereditary.

SEC. 5. That the legislative and executive powers of the state should be separate and distinct from the judiciary; and that the members of the two first may be restrained from oppression, by feeling and participating the burdens of the people, they should, at fixed periods, be reduced to a private station, return into that body from which they were originally taken, and the vacancies be supplied by frequent, certain, and regular elections, in which all, or any part, of the former members, to be again eligible, or ineligible, as the laws shall direct.

SEC. 6. That elections of members to serve as representatives of the people, in assembly, ought to be free; and that all men, having sufficient evidence of permanent common interest with, and attachment to, the community, have the right of suffrage and cannot be taxed or deprived of their property for public uses without their own consent, or that of their representatives so elected, nor bound by any law to which they have not, in like manner, assented for the public good.

SEC. 7. That all power of suspending laws, or the execution of laws, by any authority, without consent of the representatives of the people, is injurious to their rights and ought not to be exercised.

SEC. 8. That in all capital or criminal prosecutions a man hath a right to demand the cause and nature of his accusation, to be confronted with the accusers and witnesses, to call for evidence in his favor, and to a speedy trial by an impartial jury of twelve men of his vicinage, without whose unanimous consent he cannot be found guilty; nor can he be compelled to give evidence against himself; that no man be deprived of his liberty, except by the law of the land or the judgment of his peers.

SEC. 9. That excessive bail ought not to be required, nor excessive fines imposed, nor cruel and unusual punishments inflicted.

SEC. 10. That general warrants, whereby an officer or messenger may be commanded to search suspected places without evidence of a fact committed, or to seize any person or persons not named, or whose offense is not particularly described and supported by evidence, are grievous and oppressive and ought not to be granted.

SEC. 11. That in controversies respecting property, and in suits between man and man, the ancient trial by jury is preferable to any other and ought to be held sacred.

SEC. 12. That the freedom of the press is one of the great bulwarks of liberty and can never be restrained but by despotic governments.

SEC. 13. That a well-regulated militia, composed of the body of the people, trained to arms, is the proper, natural, and safe defense of a free state; that standing armies, in time of peace, should be avoided as dangerous to liberty; and that in all cases the military should be under strict subordination to, and governed by, the civil power.

SEC. 14. That the people have a right to uniform government; and, therefore, that no government separate from or independent of the government of Virginia ought to be erected or established within the limits thereof.

SEC. 15. That no free government, or the blessings of liberty, can be preserved to any people, but by a firm adherence to justice, moderation, temperance, frugality, and virtue, and by frequent recurrence to fundamental principles.

SEC. 16. That religion, or the duty which we owe to our Creator, and the manner of discharging it, can be directed only by reason and conviction, not by force or violence; and therefore all men are equally entitled to the free exercise of religion, according to the dictates of conscience; and that it is the mutual duty of all to practice Christian forbearance, love, and charity toward each other.

2. ON GOVERNMENT

By JOHN ADAMS

EDITORS' NOTE.—John Adams (1735–1826) was the first distinguished member of a family prominent in American life for more than four generations. As a lawyer, before the Revolution, Adams was among the leaders of the opposition to British policies; but he criticized the violence of a Stamp Act riot, and in the face of popular hostility he defended British soldiers who participated in the "Boston Massacre." He served in Congress and was a leader in organizing the Revolution. From 1778 to 1788 he spent most of his time representing the United States abroad. As President he deliberately sacrificed his political position by ending the undeclared war with France. For a very readable biography see Gilbert Chinard, *Honest John Adams* (Boston, 1933).

The first selection is from a letter written to George Wythe, the Virginia lawyer and political leader, in January, 1776, and published as an anonymous pamphlet later in the same year. The other selections, arranged by topic, are from *A Defense of the Constitutions of Government of the United States of America.* Adams wrote the book while he was minister to England. The first volume was published in 1787 and reached this country in time for the Constitutional Convention, according to Adam's intention for the work. The second and third volumes appeared in the following year.

A. LETTER TO GEORGE WYTHE, JANUARY, 1776[1]

...I think a people cannot be long free, nor ever happy, whose government is in one assembly. My reasons for this opinion are as follows:

1. A single assembly is liable to all the vices, follies, and frailties of an indi-

1. John Adams, *Works*..., ed. Charles Francis Adams (Boston, 1851), IV, 195–96.

vidual; subject to fits of humor, starts of passion, flights of enthusiasm, partialities, or prejudice, and consequently productive of hasty results and absurd judgments. And all these errors ought to be corrected and defects supplied by some controlling power.

2. A single assembly is apt to be avari-

cious and in time will not scruple to exempt itself from burdens, which it will lay, without compunction, on its constituents.

3. A single assembly is apt to grow ambitious and after a time will not hesitate to vote itself perpetual. This was one fault of the Long Parliament; but more remarkably of Holland, whose assembly first voted themselves from annual to septennial, then for life, and after a course of years, that all vacancies happening by death or otherwise should be filled by themselves, without any application to constituents at all.

4. A representative assembly, although extremely well qualified, and absolutely necessary, as a branch of the legislative, is unfit to exercise the executive power, for want of two essential properties, secrecy and dispatch.

5. A representative assembly is still less qualified for the judicial power, because it is too numerous, too slow, and too little skilled in the laws.

6. Because a single assembly, possessed of all the powers of government, would make arbitrary laws for their own interest, execute all laws arbitrarily for their own interest, and adjudge all controversies in their own favor.

But shall the whole power of legislation rest in one assembly? Most of the foregoing reasons apply equally to prove that the legislative power ought to be more complex; to which we may add, that if the legislative power is wholly in one assembly, and the executive in another, or in a single person, these two powers will oppose and encroach upon each other, until the contest shall end in war, and the whole power, legislative and executive, be usurped by the strongest.

The judicial power, in such case, could not mediate, or hold the balance between the two contending powers, because the legislative would undermine it. And this shows the necessity, too, of giving the executive power a negative upon the legislative, otherwise this will be continually encroaching upon that.

To avoid these dangers, let a distinct assembly be constituted as a mediator between the two extreme branches of the legislature, that which represents the people, and that which is vested with the executive power. . . .

B. FROM THE *DEFENSE OF THE CONSTITUTIONS OF GOVERNMENT OF THE UNITED STATES AGAINST THE ATTACK OF M. TURGOT* (1787–88)[2]

I shall cheerfully agree with M. Turgot that it is very possible that laws, and even equal laws, made by common consent may deprive the minority of the citizens of their rights.[3] A society, by a majority, may govern itself, even by equal laws, that is, by laws to which all, majority and minority, are *equally* subject, so as to oppress the minority. It may establish a uniformity in religion; it may restrain trade; it may confine the personal liberty of all equally and against the judgment of many, even of the best and wisest, without reasonable motives, use, or benefit. We may go farther and say that a nation may be unanimous in consenting to a law restraining its natural liberty, property, and commerce, and its moral and religious liberties too, to a degree that may be prejudicial to the nation and to every individual in it. A nation of Catholics might unanimously

2. *Ibid.*, IV, 402; VI, 145, 118; IV, 405; VI, 114–15; IV, 406–7; VI, 7–9, 10, 57–58; IV, 583–84.
3. Anne Robert Jacques Turgot, Baron de Laune (1727–81), French economist, administrator, and, in 1774–76, a minister of Louis XVI, whose support he lost by the vigor with which he pushed a program of moderate reform. In a letter to Dr. Price in 1778 he criticized the constitutions of the American states for violating orderly French ideas of sovereignty and government by employing the principles of a separation of powers. Turgot thought the principle unnecessary in a democracy. This letter was the occasion of Adams' *Defense*.

consent to prohibit labor upon one-half the days in the year, as feast days. The whole American nation might unanimously consent to a Sunday law and a warden act, which should deprive them of the use of their limbs one day in seven. A nation may unanimously agree to a navigation act, which should shackle the commerce of all. Yet Dr. Price's definition of civil liberty is as liable to this objection as any other.[4] These would all be *equal laws* made with *common consent;* these would all be acts of legitimate government. To take in M. Turgot's idea, then, we must add to Dr. Price's ideas of *equal laws* by *common consent* this other—for the *general interest* or the *public good.* But it is generally supposed that nations understand their own interest better than another [*sic*], and, therefore, they may be trusted to judge of the public good; and in all the cases above supposed, they will be as free as they desire to be; and, therefore, they may with great propriety be called free nations, and their constitutions free republics. There can be no way of compelling nations to be more free than they choose to be....

The majesty of the people is a very venerable, sublime, and affecting idea; but, in human theory, every government, despotism, monarchy, aristocracy, and every mixture is created by the people, continued by their sovereign will, and represents their majesty, their august body....

The people are the fountain and original of the power of kings and lords, governors and senates, as well as the house of commons, or assembly of representatives. And if the people are sufficiently enlightened to see all the dangers that surround them, they will always be represented by a distinct personage to manage the whole executive power; a distinct senate, to be guardians of property against levelers for the purposes of plunder, to be a repository of the national tradition of public maxims, customs, and manners, and to be controllers, in turn, both of kings and their ministers on one side, and the representatives of the people on the other, when either discover a disposition to do wrong; and a distinct house of representatives, to be the guardians of the public purse, and to protect the people, in their turn, against both kings and nobles....

In a monarchy the laws, being made according to the interest of one man, or a few men, must needs be more private and partial than suits with the nature of justice; but in a commonwealth the laws, being made by the whole people, must come up to the public interest, which is common right and justice; and if a man know not what is his own interest, who should know it? And that which is the interest of the most or greatest number of particular men, being summed up in the common vote, is the public interest....

If Socrates and Plato, Cicero and Seneca, Hutcheson[5] and Butler,[6] are to be credited, reason is rightfully supreme in man, and, therefore, it would be most suitable to the reason of mankind to have no civil or political government at all. The moral government of God, and his vicegerent, Conscience, ought to be sufficient to restrain men to obedience, to justice, and benevolence, at all times and in all places; we must therefore descend from the dignity of our nature when we think of civil government at all. But the nature of mankind is one

4. Richard Price (1723–91), English liberal minister, philosopher, economist, and political writer; a defender of the American and French revolutions. He attributed moral judgments to intuitive reason.

5. Evidently Francis Hutcheson (1694–1746), English Presbyterian minister and philosopher, who attributed moral judgments to a moral sense, benevolent as well as egoistic; one of the forerunners of Bentham.

6. Bishop Joseph Butler (1692–1752), English churchman and philosopher. Like Dr. Price, he emphasized the part played by reason in practical decisions.

thing, and the reason of mankind another; and the first has the same relation to the last as the whole to a part. The passions and appetites are parts of human nature, as well as reason and the moral sense. In the institution of government, it must be remembered that, although reason ought always to govern individuals, it certainly never did since the Fall, and never will, till the Millennium; and human nature must be taken as it is, as it has been, and will be.

. . . The first inquiry should be, What kind of beings men are. You and I admire the fable of Tristram Shandy[7] more than the fable of the bees,[8] and agree with Butler rather than Hobbes. It is weakness rather than wickedness which renders men unfit to be trusted with unlimited power. The passions are all unlimited; nature has left them so; if they could be bounded, they would be extinct; and there is no doubt they are of indispensable importance in the present system. They certainly increase too, by exercise, like the body. The love of gold grows faster than the heap of acquisition; the love of praise increases by every gratification till it stings like an adder and bites like a serpent; till the man is miserable every moment when he does not snuff the incense. Ambition strengthens at every advance and at last takes possession of the whole soul so absolutely that a man sees nothing in the world of importance to others or himself but in his object. The subtlety of these three passions, which have been selected from all the others because they are aristocratical passions, in subduing all others, and even the understanding itself, if not the conscience too, until they become absolute and imperious masters of the whole mind, is a curious subject of speculation. The cunning with which

7. *Tristram Shandy* (1758–67), a novel by Laurence Sterne (1713–68).

8. *The Fable of the Bees* (1705), a book by Bernard Mandeville (1670?–1733), maintaining that selfish desires, though vicious, promote spending and prosperity.

they hide themselves from others and from a man himself too; the patience with which they wait for opportunities; the torments they voluntarily suffer for a time to secure a full enjoyment at length; the inventions, the discoveries, the contrivances they suggest to the understanding, sometimes in the dullest dunces in the world, if they could be described in writing, would pass for great genius. . . .

Men should endeavor at a *balance* of affections and appetites, under the monarchy of reason and conscience, within, as well as at a balance of power without. . . . They were intended by nature to live together in society and in this way to restrain one another, and in general they are a very good kind of creatures; but they know each other's imbecility so well that they ought never to lead one another into temptation. [Here there is a note, found in the margin of John Adams' copy: "The majority are wicked."] . . . But who would trust his life, liberty, and property to a madman or an assembly of them? It would be safer to confide in knaves. Five hundred or five thousand together, in an assembly, are not less liable to this extravagance than one. The nation that commits its affairs to a single assembly will assuredly find that its passions and desires augment as fast as those of a king. And, therefore, a constitution with a single assembly must be essentially defective. . . .

An excellent writer has said, somewhat incautiously, that "a people will never oppress themselves or invade their own rights." This compliment, if applied to human nature, or to mankind, or to any nation or people in being or in memory, is more than has been merited. . . .

"The people never think of usurping over other men's rights."

What can this mean? Does it mean that the people never *unanimously* think of usurping over other men's rights? This would be trifling, for there would, by the supposition, be no other men's rights to usurp. But if the people never, jointly nor severally, think of usurping the rights of others, what occasion can there be for any government at all? Are there no robberies, burglaries, murders, adulteries, thefts, nor cheats? Is not every crime a usurpation over other men's rights? Is not a great part, I will not say the greatest part, of men detected every day in some disposition or other, stronger or weaker, more or less, to usurp over other men's rights? . . . If we should extend our candor so far as to own that the majority of men are generally under the dominion of benevolence and good intentions, yet, it must be confessed that a vast majority frequently transgresses; and, what is more directly to the point, not only a majority, but almost all, confine their benevolence to their families, relations, personal friends, parish, village, city, county, province, and that very few, indeed, extend it impartially to the whole community. Now, grant but this truth, and the question is decided. If a majority are capable of preferring their own private interest, or that of their families, counties, and party, to that of the nation collectively, some provision must be made in the constitution, in favor of justice, to compel all to respect the common right, the public good, the universal law, in preference to all private and partial considerations.

The proposition of our author, then, should be reversed, and it should have been said that they mind so much their own that they never think enough of others. Suppose a nation, rich and poor, high and low, ten millions in number, all assembled together; not more than one or two millions will have lands, houses, or any personal property; if we take into the account the women and children, or even if we leave them out of the question, a great majority of every nation is wholly destitute of property, except a small quantity of clothes, and a few trifles of other movables. Would Mr. Nedham[9] be responsible that, if all were to be decided by a vote of the majority, the eight or nine millions who have no property would not think of usurping over the rights of the one or two millions who have? Property is surely a right of mankind as really as liberty. Perhaps, at first, prejudice, habit, shame or fear, principle or religion, would restrain the poor from attacking the rich, and the idle from usurping on the industrious; but the time would not be long before courage and enterprise would come, and pretexts be invented by degrees, to countenance the majority in dividing all the property among them, or, at least, in sharing it equally with its present possessors. Debts would be abolished first; taxes laid heavy on the rich, and not at all on the others; and at last a downright equal division of everything be demanded, and voted. What would be the consequence of this? The idle, the vicious, the intemperate, would rush into the utmost extravagance of debauchery, sell and spend all their share, and then demand a new division of those who purchased from them. The moment the idea is admitted into society that property is not as sacred as the laws of God, and that there is not a force of law and public justice to protect it, anarchy and tyranny commence. If "Thou shalt not covet," and "Thou shalt not steal," were not commandments of heaven, they must be made inviolable precepts in every society before it can be civilized or made free.

If the first part of the proposition, namely, that "the people never think of usurping over other men's rights," cannot be admitted, is the second, namely, "they mind which way to preserve their own," better founded?

There is in every nation and people

9. Marchamont Nedham (1620–78), outspoken and volatile English journalist, successively attacked Charles I and supported Charles I, the Commonwealth, and Charles II. During the Commonwealth his paper was under the supervision of Milton.

under heaven a large proportion of persons who take no rational and prudent precautions to preserve what they have, much less to acquire more. Indolence is the natural character of man to such a degree that nothing but the necessities of hunger, thirst, and other wants equally pressing, can stimulate him to action, until education is introduced in civilized societies, and the strongest motives of ambition to excel in arts, trades, and professions are established in the minds of all men. Until this emulation is introduced, the lazy savage holds property in too little estimation to give himself trouble for the preservation or acquisition of it. . . .

It is very easy to flatter the democratical portion of society, by making such distinctions between them and the monarchical and aristocratical; but flattery is as base an artifice, and as pernicious a vice, when offered to the people, as when given to the others. There is no reason to believe the one much honester or wiser than the other; they are all of the same clay; their minds and bodies are alike. The two latter have more knowledge and sagacity, derived from education, and more advantages for acquiring wisdom and virtue. As to usurping others' rights, they are all three equally guilty when unlimited in power. No wise man will trust either with an opportunity; and every judicious legislator will set all three to watch and control each other. . . .

Though we allow benevolence and generous affections to exist in the human breast, yet every moral theorist will admit the selfish passions in the generality of men to be the strongest. There are few who love the public better than themselves, though all may have some affection for the public. We are not, indeed, commanded to love our neighbor better than ourselves. Self-interest, private avidity, ambition, and avarice will exist in every state of society and under every form of government. A succession of powers and persons, by frequent elections, will not lessen these passions in any case, in a governor, senator, or representative; nor will the apprehension of an approaching election restrain them from indulgence if they have the power. The only remedy is to take away the power, by controlling the selfish avidity of the governor, by the senate and house; of the senate, by the governor and house; and of the house, by the governor and senate. Of all possible forms of government, a sovereignty in one assembly, successively chosen by the people, is perhaps the best calculated to facilitate the gratification of self-love, and the pursuit of the private interest of a few individuals; a few eminent conspicuous characters will be continued in their seats in the sovereign assembly, from one election to another, whatever changes are made in the seats around them; by superior art, address, and opulence, by more splendid birth, reputations, and connections, they will be able to intrigue with the people and their leaders, out of doors, until they worm out most of their opposers and introduce their friends; to this end, they will bestow all offices, contracts, privileges in commerce, and other emoluments on the latter and their connections and throw every vexation and disappointment in the way of the former, until they establish such a system of hopes and fears throughout the state as shall enable them to carry a majority in every fresh election of the house. The judges will be appointed by them and their party and, of consequence, will be obsequious enough to their inclinations. The whole judicial authority, as well as the executive, will be employed, perverted, and prostituted to the purposes of electioneering. No justice will be attainable, nor will innocence or virtue be safe, in the judicial courts but for the friends of the prevailing leaders; legal prosecutions will be instituted and carried on against opposers, to their vexation and ruin; and as they have the public purse at command, as well as the executive and judicial power, the public money will be expended in the same way. . . .

The next inquiry is concerning the administration of justice. Shall every criminal be brought before this assembly and tried; shall he be there accused before five hundred men; witnesses introduced, counsel heard? This again would take up more than the whole year; and no man, after all, would consider his life, liberty, or property safe in such a tribunal. These all depend upon the disquisitions of the counsel, the knowledge of the law in the judges, the confrontation of parties and witnesses, the forms of proceedings, by which the facts and the law are fairly stated before the jury for their decision, the rules of evidence, by which the attention of the jury is confined to proper points, and the artifices of parties and counsel avoided. An assembly of five hundred men are totally incapable of this order, as well as knowledge. . . .

Will it be said that the assembly shall appoint committees to try causes? But who are to make these appointments? Will not a few haughty palatines in the assembly have influence enough to determine the election in favor of their friends, and will not this make the judges the tools of a party? If the leaders are divided into parties, will not one prevail at one year, and another the next, and will not this introduce the most wretched of servitudes, an uncertain jurisprudence?

3. GOVERNMENT AND LIBERTY[1]

By THOMAS JEFFERSON

EDITORS' NOTE.—From his numerous accomplishments, Thomas Jefferson (1743–1826) selected for his epitaph the following words ("and not a word more"): "Here was buried Thomas Jefferson, Author of the Declaration of American Independence, of the Statute of Virginia for religious freedom and Father of the University of Virginia." He explained his choice thus: "Because by these, as testimonials that I have lived, I wish most to be remembered."

The Notes on the State of Virginia were written hastily in 1781–82 to answer questions about Virginia which the Marquis de Barbé-Marbois, secretary of the French legation in Philadelphia, had propounded. In addition to the subjects discussed in these extracts, Jefferson described the physical features and natural resources of the state, its climate, population, and armed forces, the Indians, manufacturers, commerce, money, and public finance. Fuller selections are accessible in The Complete Jefferson, ed. Saul K. Padover (New York, 1943), pp. 567–697, or, in the Modern Library edition, The Life and Selected Writings of Thomas Jefferson, ed. Adrienne Koch and William Peden (New York, 1944), pp. 187–288.

1. Notes on the State of Virginia (London, 1787), pp. 190–201, 202–13, 243–49, 261–63, 265–70.

QUERY XIII

THE CONSTITUTION OF THE STATE AND ITS SEVERAL CHARTERS

... No alternative was presented but resistance, or unconditional submission. Between these could be no hesitation. They closed in the appeal to arms. They declared themselves independent states. They confederated together into one great republic, thus securing to every state the benefit of an union of their whole force. In each state separately a new form of government was established. Of ours particularly the following are the outlines. The executive powers are lodged in the hands of a governor, chosen annually, and incapable of acting more than three years in seven. He is assisted by a council of eight members. The judiciary powers are divided among several courts, as will be hereafter explained. Legislation is exercised by two houses of assembly, the one called the House of Delegates, composed of two members from each county, chosen annually by the citizens possessing an estate for life in 100 acres of uninhabited land, or 25 acres with a house on it, or in a house or lot in some town; the other called the Senate, consisting of twenty-four members, chosen quadrenially by the same electors, who for this purpose are distributed into twenty-four districts. The concurrence of both houses is necessary to the passage of a law. They have the appointment of the governor and council, the judges of the superior courts, auditors, attorney-general, treasurer, register of the land office, and delegates to Congress. As the dismemberment of the state had never had its con-

firmation but, on the contrary, had always been the subject of protestation and complaint, that it might never be in our own power to raise scruples on that subject, or to disturb the harmony of our new confederacy, the grants to Maryland, Pennsylvania, and the two Carolinas, were ratified.

This constitution was formed when we were new and unexperienced in the science of government. It was the first, too, which was formed in the whole United States. No wonder then that time and trial have discovered very capital defects in it.

1. The majority of the men in the state, who pay and fight for its support, are unrepresented in the legislature, the roll of freeholders entitled to vote not including generally the half of those on the roll of the militia, or of the taxgatherers.

2. Among those who share the representation, the shares are very unequal. Thus the county of Warwick, with only one hundred fighting men, has an equal representation with the county of Loudon, which has 1,746. So that every man in Warwick has as much influence in the government as seventeen men in Loudon. But lest it should be thought that an equal interspersion of small among large counties, through the whole state, may prevent any danger of injury to particular parts of it, we will divide it into districts, and show the proportions of land, of fighting men, and of representation in each.

	Square Miles	Fighting Men	Delegates	Senators
Between the seacoast and falls of the rivers.....	11,205	19,012	71	12
Between the falls of the rivers and the Blue Ridge Mountains	18,759	18,828	46	8
Between the Blue Ridge and the Alleghany......	11,911	7,673	16	2
Between the Alleghany and Ohio..............	79,650	4,458	16	2
Total	121,525	49,971	149	24

An inspection of [the accompanying] table will supply the place of commentaries on it. It will appear at once that 19,000 men, living below the falls of the rivers, possess half the Senate, and want four members only of possessing a majority of the House of Delegates; a want more than supplied by the vicinity of their situation to the seat of government, and of course the greater degree of convenience and punctuality with which their members may and will attend in the legislature. These 19,000 therefore, living in one part of the country, give law to upward of 30,000 living in another, and appoint all their chief officers, executive and judiciary. From the difference of their situation and circumstances, their interests will often be very different.

3. The Senate is, by its constitution, too homogenous with the House of Delegates. Being chosen by the same electors, at the same time, and out of the same subjects, the choice falls, of course, on men of the same description. The purpose of establishing different houses of legislation is to introduce the influence of different interests or different principles. Thus in Great Britain it is said their constitution relies on the House of Commons for honesty, and the Lords for wisdom; which would be a rational reliance if honesty were to be bought with money, and if wisdom were hereditary. In some of the American states the delegates and senators are so chosen, as that the first represent the persons, and the second the property, of the state. But, with us, wealth and wisdom have equal chance for admission into both houses. We do not therefore derive from the separation of our legislature into two houses those benefits which a proper complication of principles is capable of producing, and those which alone can compensate the evils which may be produced by their dissensions.

4. All the powers of government, legislative, executive, and judiciary, result to the legislative body. The concentrating these in the same hands is precisely the definition of despotic government. It will be no alleviation that these powers will be exercised by plurality of hands, and not by a single one. One hundred and seventy-three despots would surely be as oppressive as one. Let those who doubt it turn their eyes on the republic of Venice. As little will it avail us that they are chosen by ourselves. An *elective despotism* was not the government we fought for; but one which should not only be founded on free principles, but in which the powers of government should be so divided and balanced among several bodies of magistracy, as that no one could transcend their legal limits, without being effectually checked and restrained by the others. For this reason that convention, which passed the ordinance of government, laid its foundation on this basis, that the legislative, executive, and judiciary departments should be separate and distinct, so that no person should exercise the powers of more than one of them at the same time. But no barrier was provided between these several powers. The judiciary and executive members were left dependent on the legislative for their subsistence in office, and some of them for their continuance in it. If therefore the legislature assumes executive and judiciary powers, no opposition is likely to be made; nor, if made, can it be effectual; because in that case they may put their proceedings into the form of an act of assembly, which will render them obligatory on the other branches. They have accordingly, in many instances, decided rights which should have been left to judiciary controversy; and the direction of the executive, during the whole time of their session, is becoming habitual and familiar. And this is done with no ill intention. The views of the present members are perfectly upright. When they are led out of their regular province, it is by art in others, and inad-

vertence in themselves. And this will probably be the case for some time to come. But it will not be a very long time. Mankind soon learn to make interested uses of every right and power which they possess or may assume. The public money and public liberty, intended to have been deposited with three branches of magistracy, but found inadvertently to be in the hands of one only, will soon be discovered to be sources of wealth and dominion to those who hold them; distinguished, too, by this tempting circumstance, that they are the instrument as well as the object of acquisition. With money we will get men, said Caesar, and with men we will get money. Nor should our assembly be deluded by the integrity of their own purposes, and conclude that these unlimited powers will never be abused, because themselves are not disposed to abuse them. They should look forward to a time, and that not a distant one, when corruption in this, as in the country from which we derive our origin, will have seized the heads of government, and be spread by them through the body of the people; when they will purchase the voices of the people and make them pay the price. Human nature is the same on every side of the Atlantic and will be alike influenced by the same causes. The time to guard against corruption and tyranny is before they shall have gotten hold on us. It is better to keep the wolf out of the fold than to trust to drawing his teeth and talons after he shall have entered. To render these considerations the more cogent, we must observe in addition:

5. That the ordinary legislature may alter the constitution itself. On the discontinuance of assemblies, it became necessary to substitute in their place some other body, competent to the ordinary business of government, and to the calling forth the powers of the state for the maintenance of our opposition to Great Britain. Conventions were therefore introduced, consisting of two delegates from each county, meeting together and forming one house, on the plan of the former House of Burgesses, to whose places they succeeded. These were at first chosen anew for every particular session. But in March, 1775, they recommended to the people to choose a convention, which should continue in office a year. This was done accordingly in April, 1775, and in the July following that convention passed an ordinance for the election of delegates in the month of April annually. It is well known that in July, 1775, a separation from Great Britain and establishment of republican government had never yet entered into any person's mind. A convention, therefore, chosen under that ordinance cannot be said to have been chosen for purposes which certainly did not exist in the minds of those who passed it. Under this ordinance, at the annual election in April, 1776, a convention for the year was chosen. Independence and the establishment of a new form of government were not even yet the objects of the people at large. One extract from the pamphlet called *Common Sense* had appeared in the Virginia papers in February, and copies of the pamphlet itself had got into a few hands. But the idea had not been opened to the mass of the people in April, much less can it be said that they had made up their minds in its favor. So that the electors of April, 1776, no more than the legislators of July, 1775, not thinking of independence and a permanent republic, could not mean to vest in these delegates powers of establishing them, or any authorities other than those of the ordinary legislature. So far as a temporary organization of government was necessary to render our opposition energetic, so far their organization was valid. But they received in their creation no powers but what were given to every legislature before and since. They could not therefore pass an act transcendent to the powers of other legislatures. If the present assembly pass any act, and

declare it shall be irrevocable by subsequent assemblies, the declaration is merely void, and the act repealable, as other acts are. So far, and no farther authorized, they organized the government by the ordinance entitled a constitution or form of government. It pretends to no higher authority than the other ordinances of the same session; it does not say that it shall be perpetual; that it shall be unalterable by other legislatures; that it shall be transcendent above the powers of those who they knew would have equal power with themselves. Not only the silence of the instrument is a proof they thought it would be alterable, but their own practice also; for this very convention, meeting as a House of Delegates in general assembly with the Senate in the autumn of that year, passed acts of assembly in contradiction to their ordinance of government; and every assembly from that time to this has done the same.

I am safe therefore in the position that the constitution itself is alterable by the ordinary legislature. Though this opinion seems founded on the first elements of common sense, yet is the contrary maintained by some persons. 1. Because, say they, the conventions were vested with every power necessary to make effectual opposition to Great Britain. But, to complete this argument, they must go on and say further that effectual opposition could not be made to Great Britain without establishing a form of government perpetual and unalterable by the legislature, which is not true. An opposition which at some time or other was to come to an end could not need a perpetual institution to carry it on; and a government, amendable as its defects should be discovered, was as likely to make effectual resistance, as one which should be unalterably wrong. Besides, the assemblies were as much vested with all powers requisite for resistance as the conventions were. If therefore these powers included that of modeling the

form of government in the one case, they did so in the other. The assemblies then as well as the conventions may model the government; that is, they may alter the ordinance of government. 2. They urge that if the convention had meant that this instrument should be alterable, as their other ordinances were, they would have called it an ordinance; but they have called it a constitution, which *ex-vi termini*[2] means "an act above the power of the ordinary legislature." I answer that *constitutio, constitutum, statutum, lex*, are convertible terms. . . .

To get rid of the magic supposed to be in the word *constitution*, let us translate it into its definition as given by those who think it above the power of the law; and let us suppose the convention, instead of saying, "We, the ordinary legislature, establish a *constitution*," had said, "We, the ordinary legislature, establish an act *above the power of the ordinary legislature*." Does not this expose the absurdity of the attempt? 3. But, say they, the people have acquiesced, and this has given it an authority superior to the laws. It is true that the people did not rebel against it; and was that a time for the people to rise in rebellion? Should a prudent acquiescence, at a critical time, be construed into a confirmation of every illegal thing done during that period? Besides, why should they rebel? At an annual election they had chosen delegates for the year, to exercise the ordinary powers of legislation, and to manage the great contest in which they were engaged. These delegates thought the contest would be best managed by an organized government. They therefore, among others, passed an ordinance of government. They did not presume to call it perpetual and unalterable. They well knew they had no power to make it so; that our choice of them had been for no such purpose, and at a time when we could have no such purpose in contemplation. Had an unalterable form of

2. By force of the term.

government been meditated, perhaps we should have chosen a different set of people. There was no cause then for the people to rise in rebellion. But to what dangerous lengths will this argument lead? Did the acquiescence of the colonies under the various acts of power exercised by Great Britain in our infant state confirm these acts, and so far invest them with the authority of the people as to render them unalterable, and our present resistance wrong? On every unauthoritative exercise of power by the legislature must the people rise in rebellion, or their silence be construed into a surrender of that power to them? If so, how many rebellions should we have had already? One, certainly, for every session of assembly. The other states in the Union have been of opinion that, to render a form of government unalterable by ordinary acts of assembly, the people must delegate persons with special powers. They have accordingly chosen special conventions to form and fix their governments. The individuals then who maintained the contrary opinion in this country should have the modesty to suppose it possible that they may be wrong and the rest of America right. But if there be only a possibility of their being wrong, if only a plausible doubt remains of the validity of the ordinance of government, is it not better to remove that doubt by placing it on a bottom which none will dispute? If they be right, we shall only have the unnecessary trouble of meeting once in convention. If they be wrong, they expose us to the hazard of having no fundamental rights at all. True it is, this is no time for deliberating on forms of government. While an enemy is within our bowels, the first object is to expel him. But when this shall be done, when peace shall be established, and leisure given us for intrenching within good forms the rights for which we have bled, let no man be found indolent enough to decline a little more trouble for placing them beyond the reach of

question. If anything more be requisite to produce a conviction of the expediency of calling a convention, at a proper season, to fix our form of government, let it be the reflection:

6. That the assembly exercises a power of determining the quorum of their own body which may legislate for us. . . . When, therefore, it is considered that there is no legal obstacle to the assumption by the assembly of all the powers, legislative, executive, and judiciary, and that these may come to the hands of the smallest rag of delegation, surely the people will say, and their representatives, while yet they have honest representatives, will advise them to say that they will not acknowledge as laws any acts not considered and assented to by the major part of their delegates.

In enumerating the defects of the constitution, it would be wrong to count among them what is only the error of particular persons. In December, 1776, our circumstances being much distressed, it was proposed in the House of Delegates to create a *dictator*, invested with every power legislative, executive, and judiciary, civil and military, of life and of death, over our persons and over our properties: and in June, 1781, again under calamity, the same proposition was repeated and wanted a few votes only of being passed. One who entered into this contest from a pure love of liberty, and a sense of injured rights, who determined to make every sacrifice, and to meet every danger, for the re-establishment of those rights on a firm basis, who did not mean to expend his blood and substance for the wretched purpose of changing this master for that, but to place the powers of governing him in a plurality of hands of his own choice, so that the corrupt will of no one man might in future oppress him, must stand confounded and dismayed when he is told that a considerable portion of that plurality had mediated the surrender of them into a single hand, and, in lieu of a limited monarch, to delivery him over to a despotic one! How must we find his efforts and sacrifices abused and baffled, if he may still by a single vote be laid prostrate at the feet of one man! In God's name from whence have they derived this power? . . . Is it from any principle in our new constitution, expressed or implied? Every lineament of that, expressed or implied, is in full opposition to it. Its fundamental principle is that the state shall be governed as a commonwealth. It provides a republican organization, proscribes under the name of *prerogative* the exercise of all powers undefined by the laws; places on this basis the whole system of our laws; and, by consolidating them together, chooses that they shall be left to stand or fall together, never providing for any circumstances, nor admitting that such could arise, wherein either should be suspended, no, not for a moment. Our ancient laws expressly declare that those who are but delegates themselves shall not delegate to others powers which require judgment and integrity in their exercise. Or was this proposition moved on a supposed right in the movers of abandoning their posts in a moment of distress? The same laws forbid the abandonment of that post, even on ordinary occasions; and much more a transfer of their powers into other hands and other forms, without consulting the people. They never admit the idea that these, like sheep or cattle, may be given from hand to hand without an appeal to their own will. Was it from the necessity of the case? Necessities which dissolve a government do not convey its authority to an oligarchy or a monarchy. They throw back, into the hands of the people, the powers they had delegated, and leave them as individuals to shift for themselves. A leader may offer, but not impose himself, nor be imposed on them. Much less can their necks be submitted to his sword, their breath to be held at his will or caprice. The necessity which

should operate these tremendous effects should at least be palpable and irresistible. Yet in both instances, where it was feared, or pretended with us, it was belied by the event. It was belied, too, by the preceding experience of our sister-states, several of whom had grappled through greater difficulties without abandoning their forms of government. When the proposition was first made, Massachusetts had found even the government of committees sufficient to carry them through an invasion. But we at the time of that proposition were under no invasion. When the second was made, there had been added to this example those of Rhode Island, New York, New Jersey, and Pennsylvania, in all of which the republican form had been found equal to the task of carrying them through the severest trials. In this state alone did there exist so little virtue that fear was to be fixed in the hearts of the people, and to become the motive of their exertions and principle of their government? The very thought alone was treason against the people; was treason against mankind in general, as riveting forever the chains which bow down their necks, by giving to their oppressors a proof, which they would have trumpeted through the universe, of the imbecility of republican government, in times of pressing danger, to shield them from harm. Those who assume the right of giving away the reins of government, in any case, must be sure that the herd, whom they hand on to the rods and hatchet of the dictator,[3] will lay their necks on the block when he shall nod to them. But if our assemblies supposed such a resignation in the people, I hope they mistook their character. I am of opinion that the government, instead of being braced and invigorated for greater

3. Refers to the ancient Roman emblem, the *fasces*, a bundle of rods, tied together by a red strap, and inclosing an ax with its head outside. Revived in modern times as the emblem of the Fascist party in Italy; displayed on the United States dime.

exertions under their difficulties, would have been thrown back upon the bungling machinery of county committees for administration, till a convention could have been called, and its wheels again set into regular motion. What a cruel moment was this for creating such an embarrassment, for putting to the proof the attachment of our countrymen to republican government! Those who meant well, of the advocates for this measure (and most of them meant well, for I know them personally, had been their fellow-laborer in the common cause, and had often proved the purity of their principles), had been seduced in their judgment by the example of an ancient republic, whose constitution and circumstances were fundamentally different. They had sought this precedent in the history of Rome, where alone it was to be found, and where at length, too, it had proved fatal. They had taken it from a republic rent by the most bitter factions and tumults, where the government was of a heavy-handed unfeeling aristocracy, over a people ferocious, and rendered desperate by poverty and wretchedness; tumults which could not be allayed under the most trying circumstances, but by the omnipotent hand of a single despot. Their constitution therefore allowed a temporary tyrant to be erected, under the name of a dictator; and that temporary tyrant, after a few examples, became perpetual. They misapplied this precedent to a people, mild in their dispositions, patient under their trial, united for the public liberty, and affectionate to their leaders. But if from the constitution of the Roman government there resulted to their Senate a power of submitting all their rights to the will of one man, does it follow that the assembly of Virginia have the same authority? What clause in our constitution has substituted that of Rome, by way of residuary provision, for all cases not otherwise provided for? Or if they may step *ad libitum*[4] into any other form of government for precedents to rule us by, for what oppression may not a precedent be found in this world of the *bellum omnium in omnia?*[5] Searching for the foundations of this proposition, I can find none which may pretend a color of right or season, but the defect before developed, that there being no barrier between the legislative, executive, and judiciary departments, the legislature may seize the whole; that having seized it, and possessing a right to fix their own quorum, they may reduce that quorum to one, whom they may call a chairman, speaker, dictator, or by any other name they please. Our situation is indeed perilous, and I hope my countrymen will be sensible of it and will apply, at a proper season, the proper remedy; which is a convention to fix the constitution, to amend its defects, to bind up the several branches of government by certain laws, which when they transgress their acts shall become nullities; to render unnecessary an appeal to the people, or in other words a rebellion, on every infraction of their rights, on the peril that their acquiescence shall be construed into an intention to surrender those rights.

QUERY XIV

THE ADMINISTRATION OF JUSTICE AND THE
DESCRIPTION OF THE LAWS

... Another object of the revisal is to diffuse knowledge more generally through the mass of the people. This bill proposes to lay off every county into small districts of five or six miles square, called hundreds, and in each of them to establish a school for teaching reading,

4. Freely.

5. "War of all against all."

writing, and arithmetic. The tutor to be supported by the hundred, and every person in it entitled to send their children three years gratis, and as much longer as they please, paying for it. These schools to be under a visitor, who is annually to choose the boy of best genius in the school, of those whose parents are too poor to give them further education, and to send him forward to one of the grammar schools, of which twenty are proposed to be erected in different parts of the country for teaching Greek, Latin, geography, and the higher branches of numerical arithmetic. Of the boys thus sent in any one year, trial is to be made at the grammar schools one or two years, and the best genius of the whole selected, and continued six years, and the residue dismissed. By this means twenty of the best geniuses will be raked from the rubbish annually, and be instructed, at the public expense, so far as the grammar schools go. At the end of six years' instruction, one half are to be discontinued (from among whom the grammar schools will probably be supplied with future masters); and the other half, who are to be chosen for the superiority of their parts and disposition, are to be sent and continued three years in the study of such sciences as they shall choose, at William and Mary College, the plan of which is proposed to be enlarged, as will be hereafter explained, and extended to all the useful sciences. The ultimate result of the whole scheme of education would be the teaching all the children of the state reading, writing, and common arithmetic; turning out ten annually, of superior genius, well taught in Greek, Latin, geography, and the higher branches of arithmetic; turning out ten others annually, of still superior parts, who to those branches of learning shall have added such of the sciences as their genius shall have led them to; the furnishing to the wealthier part of the people convenient schools at which their children may be educated at their own expense.

The general objects of this law are to provide an education adapted to the years, to the capacity, and the condition of every one, and directed to their freedom and happiness. Specific details were not proper for the law. These must be the business of the visitors intrusted with its execution. The first stage of this education being the schools of the hundreds wherein the great mass of the people will receive their instruction, the principal foundations of future order will be laid here. Instead, therefore, of putting the Bible and Testament into the hands of the children at an age when their judgments are not sufficiently matured for religious inquiries, their memories may here be stored with the most useful facts from Grecian, Roman, European, and American history. The first elements of morality, too, may be instilled into their minds; such as, when further developed as their judgments advance in strength, may teach them how to work out their own greatest happiness, by showing them that it does not depend on the condition of life in which chance has placed them but is always the result of a good conscience, good health, occupation and freedom in all just pursuits.

Those whom either the wealth of their parents or the adoption of the state shall destine to higher degrees of learning will go on to the grammar schools, which constitute the next stage, there to be instructed in the languages. The learning of Greek and Latin, I am told, is going into disuse in Europe. I know not what their manners and occupations may call for; but it would be very ill judged in us to follow their example in this instance. There is a certain period of life, say, from eight to fifteen or sixteen years of age, when the mind, like the body, is not yet firm enough for laborious and close operations. If applied to such, it falls an early victim to premature exertion, exhibiting, indeed at first, in these young and tender subjects the flattering appearance of their being men while they are yet children, but ending in reducing them to be children when they should be men. The memory is then most susceptible and tenacious of impressions; and the learning of languages being chiefly a work of memory, it seems precisely fitted to the powers of this period, which is long enough too for acquiring the most useful languages, ancient and modern. I do not pretend that language is science. It is only an instrument for the attainment of science. But that time is not lost which is employed in providing tools for future operation; more especially as in this case the books put into the hands of the youth for this purpose may be such as will at the same time impress their minds with useful facts and good principles. If this period be suffered to pass in idleness, the mind becomes lethargic and impotent, as would the body it inhabits if unexercised during the same time. The sympathy between body and mind during their rise, progress, and decline is too strict and obvious to endanger our being misled while we reason from the one to the other. As soon as they are of sufficient age, it is supposed they will be sent on from the grammar schools to the university, which constitutes our third and last stage, there to study those sciences which may be adapted to their views. By that part of our plan which prescribes the selection of the youths of genius from among the classes of the poor, we hope to avail the state of those talents which nature has sown as liberally among the poor as the rich but which perish without use if not sought for and cultivated.

But of all the views of this law none is more important, none more legitimate, than that of rendering the people the safe, as they are the ultimate, guardians of their own liberty. For this purpose the reading in the first stage, where they will receive their whole education, is proposed, as has been said, to be chiefly historical. History, by apprizing them of the past, will enable them to judge of the future; it will avail them of the experience of other times and other nations; it will qualify them as judges of the actions and designs of men; it will enable them to know ambition under every disguise it may assume and, knowing it, to defeat its views. In every government on earth is some trace of human weakness, some germ of corruption and degeneracy, which cunning will discover and wickedness insensibly open, cultivate, and improve. Every government degenerates when trusted to the rulers of the people alone. The people themselves, therefore, are its only safe depositories; and, to render even them safe, their minds must be improved to a certain degree. This indeed is not all that is necessary, though it be essentially necessary. An amendment of our constitution must here come in aid of the public education. The influence over government must be shared among all the people. If every individual which composes their mass participates of the ultimate authority, the government will be safe, because the corrupting the whole mass will exceed any private resources of wealth, and public ones cannot be provided but by levies on the people. In this case every man would have to pay his own price. The government of Great Britain has been corrupted, because but one man in ten has a right to vote for members of Parliament. The sellers of the government therefore get nine-tenths of their price clear. It has been thought that corruption is restrained by confining the right of suffrage to a few of the wealthier of the people; but it would be more effectually restrained by an extension of that right to such numbers as would bid defiance to the means of corruption.

Lastly, it is proposed by a bill in this revisal, to begin a public library and gallery by laying out a certain sum annually in books, paintings, and statues. . . .

QUERY XVII

THE DIFFERENT RELIGIONS RECEIVED INTO THAT STATE

The first settlers in this country were emigrants from England, of the English church, just at a point of time when it was flushed with complete victory over the religious of all other persuasions. Possessed, as they became, of the powers of making, administering, and executing the laws, they showed equal intolerance in this country with their Presbyterian brethren, who had emigrated to the northern government. The poor Quakers were flying from persecution in England. They cast their eyes on these new countries as asylums of civil and religious freedom; but they found them free only for the reigning sect. Several acts of the Virginia assembly of 1659, 1662, and 1693 had made it penal in parents to refuse to have their children baptized; had prohibited the unlawful assembling of Quakers; had made it penal for any master of a vessel to bring a Quaker into the state; had ordered those already here, and such as should come thereafter, to be imprisoned till they should abjure the country; provided a milder punishment for their first and second return but death for their third; had inhibited all persons from suffering their meetings in or near their houses, entertaining them individually, or disposing of books which supported their tenets. If no capital execution took place here, as did in New England, it was not owing to the moderation of the church, or spirit of the legislature, as may be inferred from the law itself, but to historical circumstances which have not been handed down to us. The Anglicans retained full possession of the country about a century. Other opinions began then to creep in, and the great care of the government to support their own church, having begotten an equal degree of indolence in its clergy, two-thirds of the people had become dissenters at the commencement of the present revolution. The laws indeed were still oppres-

sive on them, but the spirit of the one party had subsided into moderation, and of the other had risen to a degree of determination which commanded respect.

The present state of our laws on the subject of religion is this. The convention of May, 1776, in their declaration of rights, declared it to be a truth, and a natural right, that the exercise of religion should be free; but when they proceeded to form on that declaration the ordinance of government, instead of taking up every principle declared in the Bill of Rights, and guarding it by legislative sanction, they passed over that which asserted our religious rights, leaving them as they found them.[6] The same convention, however, when they met as a member of the general assembly in October, 1776, repealed all *acts of Parliament* which had rendered criminal the maintaining any opinions in matters of religion, the forbearing to repair to church, and the exercising any mode of worship; and suspended the laws giving salaries to the clergy, which suspension was made perpetual in October, 1779. Statutory oppressions in religion being thus wiped away, we remain at present under those only imposed by the common law or by our own acts of assembly. . . .

Our rulers can have authority over such natural rights only as we have submitted to them. The rights of conscience we never submitted, we could not submit. We are answerable for them to our God. The legitimate powers of government extend to such acts only as are injurious to others. But it does me no injury for my neighbor to say there are twenty gods or no god. It neither picks my pocket nor breaks my leg. If it be said, his testimony in a court of justice can-

6. Cf. the Virginia Declaration of Rights, pp. 205-7.

not be relied on, reject it then, and be the stigma on him. Constraint may make him worse by making him a hypocrite, but it will never make him a truer man. It may fix him obstinately in his errors but will not cure them. Reason and free inquiry are the only effectual agents against error. Give a loose to them, they will support the true religion, by bringing every false one to their tribunal, to the test of their investigation. They are the natural enemies of error and of error only. Had not the Roman government permitted free inquiry, Christianity could never have been introduced. Had not free inquiry been indulged, at the era of the Reformation, the corruptions of Christianity could not have been purged away. If it be restrained now, the present corruptions will be protected, and new ones encouraged. Was the government to prescribe to us our medicine and diet, our bodies would be in such keeping as our souls are now. Thus in France the emetic was once forbidden as a medicine, and the potato as an article of food. Government is just as infallible, too, when it fixes systems in physics. Galileo was sent to the Inquisition for affirming that the earth was a sphere; the government had declared it to be as flat as a trencher, and Galileo was obliged to abjure his error. This error however at length prevailed, the earth became a globe, and Descartes declared it was whirled round its axis by a vortex. The government in which he lived was wise enough to see that this was no question of civil jurisdiction, or we should all have been involved by authority in vortices. In fact, the vortices have been exploded, and the Newtonian principle of gravitation is now more firmly established, on the basis of reason, than it would be were the government to step in and to make it an article of necessary faith. Reason and experiment have been indulged, and error has fled before them. It is error alone which needs the support of government. Truth can stand by itself.

Subject opinion to coercion; whom will you make your inquisitors? Fallible men: men governed by bad passions, by private as well as public reasons. And why subject it to coercion? To produce uniformity. But is uniformity of opinion desirable? No more than of face and stature. Introduce the bed of Procrustes then, and, as there is danger that the large men may beat the small, make us all of a size, by lopping the former and stretching the latter. Difference of opinion is advantageous in religion. The several sects perform the office of a *Censor morum*[7] over each other. Is uniformity attainable? Millions of innocent men, women, and children, since the introduction of Christianity, have been burned, tortured, fined, imprisoned; yet we have not advanced one inch toward uniformity. What has been the effect of coercion? To make one half the world fools, and the other half hypocrites. To support roguery and error all over the earth. Let us reflect that it is inhabited by a thousand millions of people. That these profess probably a thousand different systems of religion. That ours is but one of that thousand. That if there be but one right, and ours that one, we should wish to see the 999 wandering sects gathered into the fold of truth. But against such a majority we cannot effect this by force. Reason and persuasion are the only practicable instruments. To make way for these, free inquiry must be indulged; and how can we wish others to indulge it while we refuse it ourselves. But every state, says an inquisitor, has established some religion. No two, say I, have established the same. Is this a proof of the infallibility of establishments? Our sister-states of Pennsylvania and New York,

7. Censor or guardian of morals; Roman officers whose duty originally was to take the census. Their powers were later extended to include the right to degrade individuals for offenses for which there was no legal punishment; thus the censors came to have a general supervision over conduct.

however, have long subsisted without any establishment at all. The experiment was new and doubtful when they made it. It has answered beyond conception. They flourish infinitely. Religion is well supported; of various kinds, indeed, but all good enough; all sufficient to preserve peace and order; or if a sect arises whose tenets would subvert morals, good sense has fair play and reasons and laughs it out of doors without suffering the state to be troubled with it. They do not hang more malefactors than we do. They are not more disturbed with religious dissensions. On the contrary, their harmony is unparalleled and can be ascribed to nothing but their unbounded tolerance, because there is no other circumstance in which they differ from every nation on earth. They have made the happy discovery that the way to silence religious disputes is to take no notice of them. Let us too give this experiment fair play and get rid, while we may, of those tyrannical laws. It is true, we are as yet secured against them by the spirit of the times. I doubt whether the people of this country would suffer an execution for heresy or a three years'

imprisonment for not comprehending the mysteries of the Trinity. But is the spirit of the people an infallible, a permanent reliance? Is it government? Is this the kind of protection we receive in return for the rights we give up? Besides, the spirit of the times may alter, will alter. Our rulers will become corrupt, our people careless. A single zealot may commence persecutor, and better men be his victims. It can never be too often repeated that the time for fixing every essential right on a legal basis is while our rulers are honest and ourselves united. From the conclusion of this war we shall be going downhill. It will not then be necessary to resort every moment to the people for support. They will be forgotten, therefore, and their rights disregarded. They will forget themselves, but in the sole faculty of making money, and will never think of uniting to effect a due respect for their rights. The shackles, therefore, which shall not be knocked off at the conclusion of this war will remain on us long, will be made heavier and heavier, till our rights shall revive or expire in a convulsion.

4. REPRESENTATION AND SUFFRAGE[1]

By Benjamin Franklin

EDITORS' NOTE.—Franklin wrote this paper in reply to an item, entitled "Hints for the Members of Convention," which had appeared in the *Federal Gazette,* November 3, 1789. The first and third paragraphs of the text are quoted from this article; the second and fourth, which are Franklin's comments on it, constitute an interesting evaluation of democracy.

ON THE LEGISLATIVE BRANCH

A plural legislature is as necessary to good government as a single executive. It is not enough that your legislature should be numerous; it should also be divided. Numbers alone are not a sufficient barrier against the impulses of passion, the combination of

interest, the intrigues of faction, the haste of folly, or the spirit of encroachment. One division should watch over and control the other, supply its wants, correct its blunders and cross its designs, should they be criminal or erroneous. Wisdom is the specific quality of the legislature, grows out of the number of the body, and is made up of the portions of sense and knowledge which each member brings to it.

1. Benjamin Franklin, *The Complete Works* ..., ed. John Bigelow (New York, 1888), X, 184–91.

On this it may be asked: May not the wisdom brought to the legislature by each member be as effectual a barrier against the impulses of passion, etc., when the members are united in one body as when they are divided? If one part of the legislature may control the operations of the other, may not the impulses of passion, the combinations of interest, the intrigues of faction, the haste of folly, or the spirit of encroachment in one of those bodies obstruct the good proposed by the other and frustrate its advantages to the public? Have we not experienced in this state, when a province under the government of the proprietors, the mischiefs of a second branch existing in the proprietary family, countenanced and aided by an aristocratic council? How many delays and what great expenses were occasioned in carrying on the public business; and what a train of mischiefs, even to the preventing of the defense of the province during several years, when distressed by an Indian war, by the iniquitous demand that the proprietary property should be exempt from taxation? The wisdom of a few members in one single legislative body, may it not frequently stifle bad motions in their infancy and so prevent their being adopted? whereas, if those wise men, in case of a double legislature, should happen to be in that branch wherein the motion did not arise, may it not, after being adopted by the other, occasion long disputes and contentions between the two bodies, expensive to the public, obstructing the public business, and promoting factions among the people, many tempers naturally adhering obstinately to measures they have once publicly adopted? Have we not seen, in one of our neighboring states, a bad measure, adopted by one branch of the legislature, for want of the assistance of some more intelligent members who had been packed into the other, occasion many debates, conducted with much asperity, which could not be settled but by an expensive general appeal to the public?

And have we not seen, in another neighboring state, a similar difference between the two branches, occasioning long debates and contentions, whereby the state was prevented for many months enjoying the advantage of having senators in the Congress of the United States? And has our present legislature in one Assembly committed any errors of importance which they have not remedied or may not easily remedy, more easily, probably, than if divided into branches? And if the wisdom brought by the members to the Assembly is divided into two branches, may it not be too weak in each to support a good measure or obstruct a bad one? The division of the legislature into two or three branches in England, was it the product of wisdom, or the effect of necessity, arising from the pre-existing prevalence of an odious feudal system? which government, notwithstanding this division, is now become, in fact, an absolute monarchy, since . . . by bribing the representative with the people's money, carries, by his ministers, all the measures that please him; which is equivalent to governing without a parliament, and renders the machine of government much more complex and expensive, and, from its being more complex, more easily put out of order. Has not the famous political fable of the snake, with two heads and one body, some useful instruction contained in it? She was going to a brook to drink, and on her way was to pass through a hedge, a twig of which opposed her direct course; one head chose to go on the right side of the twig, the other on the left; so that time was spent in the contest, and, before the decision was completed, the poor snake died with thirst.

Hence it is that the two branches should be elected by persons differently qualified; and in short, that, as far as possible, they should be made to represent different interests. Under this reason I would establish a legislature of two houses. The upper should represent the property; the lower, the population of the state. The upper should be chosen by freemen possessing in land and houses one thousand pounds; the lower, by all such as had resided four years in the country and paid taxes. The first should be chosen for four, the last for two years. They should be in authority co-equal.

Several questions may arise upon this proposition. 1st. What is the proportion of freemen possessing lands and houses of one thousand pounds' value compared to that of freemen whose possessions are inferior? Are they as one to ten? Are they even as one to twenty? I should doubt whether they are as one to fifty. If this minority is to choose a body expressly to control that which is to be chosen by the great majority of the freemen, what have this great majority done to forfeit so great a portion of their right in elections? Why is this power of control, contrary to the spirit of all democracies, to be vested in a minority, instead of a majority? Then, is it intended, or is it not, that the rich should have a vote in the choice of members for the lower house, while those of inferior property are deprived of the right of voting for members of the upper house? And why should the upper house, chosen by a minority, have equal power with the lower chosen by a majority? Is it supposed that wisdom is the necessary concomitant of riches and that one man worth a thousand pounds must have as much wisdom as twenty who have each only nine hundred and ninety-nine; and why is property to be represented at all? Suppose one of our Indian nations should now agree to form a civil society; each individual would bring into the stock of the society little more property than his gun and his blanket, for at present he has no other. We know that, when one of them has attempted to keep a few swine, he has not been able to maintain a property in them, his neighbors thinking they have a right to kill and eat them whenever they want provision, it being one of their maxims that hunting is free to all;

the accumulation therefore of property in such a society, and its security to individuals in every society, must be an effect of the protection afforded to it by the joint strength of the society in the execution of its laws. Private property therefore is a creature of society and is subject to the calls of that society whenever its necessities shall require it, even to its last farthing; its contributions to the public exigencies are not to be considered as conferring a benefit on the public, entitling the contributors to the distinctions of honor and power, but as the return of an obligation previously rceived, or the payment of a just debt. The combinations of civil society are not like those of a set of merchants, who club their property in different proportions for building and freighting a ship, and may therefore have some right to vote in the disposition of the voyage in a greater or less degree according to their respective contributions; but the important ends of civil society, and the personal securities of life and liberty there, remain the same in every member of the society; and the poorest continues to have an equal claim to them with the most opulent, whatever difference time, chance, or industry may occasion in their circumstances. On these considerations I am sorry to see the signs this paper I have been considering affords, of a disposition among some of our people to commence an aristrocracy, by giving the rich a predominancy in government, a choice peculiar to themselves in one-half the legislature to be proudly called the Upper House, and the other branch, chosen by the majority of the people, degraded by the denomination of the Lower; and giving to this Upper House a permanency of four years, and but two to the Lower. I hope, therefore, that our representatives in the convention will not hastily go into these innovations but take the advice of the Prophet: "Stand in the old ways, view the ancient paths, consider them well, and be not among those that are given to change."

5. ON ARISTOCRACY[1]

By JOHN ADAMS and THOMAS JEFFERSON

EDITORS' NOTE.—For more than a half-century John Adams and Thomas Jefferson maintained, with some interruptions occasioned by political differences, one of the most interesting friendships in our history. Members of both Continental Congresses, they cooperated in writing the Declaration of Independence and in promoting its adoption. Both contributed much to the organization of government in their respective native states of Massachusetts and Virginia. During the mid-1780's Adams represented the United States at London and Jefferson at Paris. Party controversies in the 1790's ranged them on opposite sides, but, after both had retired from active political life, they renewed their friendship and began the correspondence from which the following "debate" is taken. For a selection from these letters, with editorial comments, see *Correspondence of John Adams and Thomas Jefferson, 1812–1826*, ed. Paul Wilstach (Indianapolis, 1925). By a remarkable coincidence, both died on the same day, July 4, 1826, exactly fifty years after the passage of the Declaration of Independence.

ADAMS TO JEFFERSON

July 9, 1813

... I recollect, near thirty years ago, to have said carelessly to you that I wished I could find time and means to write something upon aristocracy. You seized upon the idea and encouraged me to do it with all that friendly warmth that is natural and habitual to you. I soon began and have been writing upon that subject ever since. I have been so unfortunate as never to be able to make myself understood. Your "*aristoi*" are the most difficult animals to manage of anything in the whole theory and practice of government.[2] They will not suffer themselves to be governed. They not only exert all their subtilty, industry, and courage, but they employ the commonalty to knock to pieces every plan and model that the most honest architects in legislation can invent to keep them within bounds. Both patricians and plebeians are as furious as the workmen in England to demolish labor-saving machinery.

But who are these "*aristoi*"? Who shall judge? Who shall select these choice spirits from the rest of the congregation? Themselves? We must first find out and determine who themselves are.....

"Nobility in men is worth as much as it is in horses, asses, or rams; but the meanest-blooded puppy in the world, if he gets a little money, is as good a man as the best of them." Yet birth and wealth together have prevailed over virtue and talents in all ages. The many will acknowledge no other "*aristoi*." Your experience of this truth will not much differ from that of your old friend....

ADAMS TO JEFFERSON

August, 1813

... Has science, or morals, or philosophy, or criticism, or Christianity, advanced, or improved, or enlightened mankind upon this subject and shown them that the idea of the "well-born" is

1. Microfilm reproduction, Reels 77–78, of the *Papers of Thomas Jefferson*, Library of Congress, Vol. 198, fols. 35312–13; Vol. 199, fols. 35381–82, 35425–26, 35488–91; Vol. 200, fols. 35526–27, 35378–79, 35638–40.
2. Greek word meaning, literally, "best"; here use as equivalent to "aristocrats."

a prejudice, a phantom, a point-no-point, a Cape Fly-away, a dream?

I say it is the ordinance of God Almighty in the constitution of human nature and wrought into the fabric of the universe. Philosophers and politicians may nibble and quibble, but they never will get rid of it. Their only resource is to control it. Wealth is another monster to be subdued. Hercules could not subdue both or either. To subdue them by regular approaches, by a regular siege and strong fortifications, was my object in writing on aristocracy, as I proposed to you in Grosvenor Square.[3]

If you deny any one of these positions, I will prove them to demonstration by examples drawn from your own Virginia, and from every other state in the Union, and from the history of every nation, civilized and savage, from all we know of the time of the creation of the world. . . .

We may call this sentiment a prejudice, because we can give what names we please to such things as we please; but in my opinion it is a part of the natural history of man, and politicians and philosophers may as well project to make the animal live without bones or blood as society can pretend to establish a free government without attention to it. . . .

ADAMS TO JEFFERSON

September 2, 1813

. . . Now, my friend, who are the *"aristoi"*? Philosophers may answer, "The wise and good." But the world, mankind, have, by their practice, always answered, "The rich, the beautiful, and well-born." And philosophers themselves, in marrying their children, prefer the rich, the handsome, and the well-descended to the wise and good.

What chance have talents and virtues,

3. During most of his three years as minister to Great Britain (1785–88), John Adams and his family lived in a large house in Grosvenor Square near Hyde Park in the West End of London.

in competition with wealth and birth? and beauty? . . .

One truth is clear, by all the world confessed,
Slow rises worth, by poverty oppressed.

The five pillars of aristocracy are beauty, wealth, birth, genius, and virtue. Any one of the three first can, at any time, overbear any one or both of the two last.

Let me ask again, what a wave of public opinion, in favor of birth, has been spread over the globe by Abraham, by Hercules, by Mahomet, by Guelphs, Ghibellines, Bourbons, and a miserable Scottish chief Stuart? By Zingis [Genghis Khan], by, by, by a million others. And what a wave will be spread by Napoleon and by Washington? Their remotest cousins will be sought and will be proud and will avail themselves of their descent. Call this principle prejudice, folly, ignorance, baseness, slavery, stupidity, adulation, superstition, or what you will, I will not contradict you. But the fact in natural, moral, political, and domestic history I cannot deny, or dispute, or question.

And is this great fact in the natural history of man, this unalterable principle of morals, philosophy, policy, domestic felicity, and daily experience from the Creation, to be overlooked, forgotten, neglected, or hypocritically waved out of sight by a legislator? By a professed writer upon civil government and upon constitution of civil government? . . .

JEFFERSON TO ADAMS

October 28, 1813

. . . I agree with you that there is a natural aristocracy among men. The grounds of this are virtue and talents. Formerly, bodily powers gave place among the *aristoi*. But since the invention of gunpowder has armed the weak as well as the strong with missile death, bodily strength, like beauty, good humor, politeness, and other accomplishments, has become but an auxiliary ground of distinction.

There is also an artificial aristocracy, founded on wealth and birth, without either virtue or talents; for with these it would belong to the first class. The natural aristocracy I consider as the most precious gift of nature, for the instruction, the trusts, and government of society. And, indeed, it would have been inconsistent in Creation to have formed man for the social state and not to have provided virtue and wisdom enough to manage the concerns of the society. May we not even say that that form of government is the best which provides the most effectually for a pure selection of these natural *aristoi* into the offices of government? The artificial aristocracy is a mischievous ingredient in government, and provision should be made to prevent its ascendancy. On the question, What is the best provision? you and I differ; but we differ as rational friends, using the free exercise of our own reason and mutually indulging its errors. *You* think it best to put the *pseudo-aristoi* into a separate chamber of legislation, where they may be hindered from doing mischief by their co-ordinate branches, and where also they may be a protection to wealth against the agrarian and plundering enterprises of the majority of the people.[4] I think that to give them power in order to prevent them from doing mischief is arming them for it and increasing instead of remedying the evil. For if the co-ordinate branches can arrest their action, so may they that of the co-ordinates. Mischief may be done negatively as well as positively. Of this, a cabal in the Senate of the United States has furnished many proofs. Nor do I believe them necessary to protect the

wealthy; because enough of these will find their way into every branch of the legislation to protect themselves. From fifteen to twenty legislatures of our own, in action for thirty years past, have proved that no fears of an equalization of property are to be apprehended from them. *I* think the best remedy is exactly that provided by all our constitutions: to leave to the citizens the free election and separation of the *aristoi* from the *pseudo-aristoi*, of the wheat from the chaff. In general they will elect the real good and wise. In some instances, wealth may corrupt and birth blind them, but not in sufficient degree to endanger society.

It is probable that our difference of opinion may, in some measure, be produced by a difference of character in those among whom we live. From what I have seen of Massachusetts and Connecticut myself, and still more from what I have heard, and the character given of the former by yourself, who know them so much better, there seems to be in those two states a traditionary reverence for certain families which has rendered the offices of the government nearly hereditary in those families. I presume that, from an early period of your history, members of those families happening to possess virtue and talents have honestly exercised them for the good of the people and by their services have endeared their names to them. In coupling Connecticut with you, I mean it politically only, not morally. For having made the Bible the common law of their land, they seemed to have modeled their morality on the story of Jacob and Laban.[5] But although this hereditary succession to office with you may, in some degree, be founded in real family merit, yet in a much higher degree it has proceeded from your strict alliance of church and state. These families are canonized in the eyes of the people on

4. "Agrarian" here refers to movements for uniform division or more equalizing redistribution of landed property. Conflicts of this character were familiar to students of Roman history.

5. Cf. Genesis, chaps. 29-31.

the common principle. "You tickle me, and I will tickle you." In Virginia we have nothing of this. Our clergy, before the Revolution, having been secured against rivalship by fixed salaries, did not give themselves the trouble of acquiring influence over the people. Of wealth, there were great accumulations in particular families, handed down from generation to generation, under the English law of entails. But the only object of ambition for the wealthy was a seat in the king's Council. All their court then was paid to the crown on its creatures; and they Philipized in all collisions between the king and the people.[6] Hence they were unpopular; and that unpopularity continues attached to their names. A Randolph, a Carter, or a Burwell must have great personal superiority over a common competitor to be elected by the people even at this day.[7] At the first session of our legislature after the Declaration of Independence, we passed a law abolishing entails. And this was followed by one abolishing the privilege of primogeniture and dividing the lands of intestates equally among all their children or other representatives. These laws, drawn by myself, laid the ax to the foot of pseudo-aristocracy. And had another which I prepared been adopted by the legislature, our work would have been complete. It was a bill for the more general diffusion of learning. This proposed to divide every country into wards of five or six miles square, like your townships; to establish in each ward a free school for reading, writing, and common arithmetic; to provide for the annual selection of the best subjects from

these schools, who might receive, at the public expense, a higher degree of education at a district school; and from these district schools to select a certain number of the most promising subjects, to be completed at an university, where all the useful sciences should be taught. Worth and genius would thus have been sought out from every condition of life and completely prepared by education for defeating the competition of wealth and birth for public trusts. My proposition had, for a further object, to impart to these wards those portions of self-government for which they are best qualified, by confiding to them the care of their poor, their roads, police, elections, the nomination of jurors, administration of justice in small cases, elementary exercises of militia; in short, to have made them little republics, with a warden at the head of each, for all those concerns which, being under their eye, they would better manage than the larger republics of the county or state. A general call of ward meetings by their wardens on the same day through the state would at any time produce the genuine sense of the people on any required point and would enable the state to act in mass, as your people have so often done, and with so much effect by their town meetings. The law for religious freedom, which made a part of this system, having put down the aristocracy of the clergy, and restored to the citizen the freedom of the mind, and those of entails and descents nurturing an equality of condition among them, this on education would have raised the mass of the people to the high ground of moral respectability necessary to their own safety and to orderly government and would have completed the great object of qualifying them to select the veritable *aristoi*, for the trusts of government, to the exclusion of the pseudalists;[8] and the same Theognis who has furnished

6. "To speak or write as one corruptly inspired or influenced," as did pre-Macedonian leaders in the Greek city-states of the fourth century B.C. The modern phrases for such persons, which are roughly equivalent, are "quisling" and "fifth columnist."

7. Here Jefferson names three of the most prominent and influential families of Virginia before the Revolution.

8. False or spurious.

the epigraphs of your two letters assures us that "good men never destroyed any state."[9] Although this law has not yet been acted on but in a small and inefficient degree, it is still considered as before the legislature, with other bills of the revised code, not yet taken up, and I have great hope that some patriotic spirit will, at a favorable moment, call it up and make it the keystone of the arch of our government.

With respect to aristocracy, we should further consider that, before the establishment of the American states, nothing was known to history but the man of the Old World, crowded within limits either small or overcharged and steeped in the vices which that situation generates. A government adapted to such men would be one thing; but a very different one, that for the man of these states. Here every one may have land to labor for himself, if he chooses; or, preferring the exercise of any other industry, may exact for it such compensation as not only to afford a comfortable subsistence but wherewith to provide for a cessation from labor in old age. Every one, by his property, or by his satisfactory situation, is interested in the support of law and order. And such men may safely and advantageously reserve to themselves a wholesome control over their public affairs, and a degree of freedom which, in the hands of the *canaille* of the cities of Europe, would be instantly perverted to the demolition and destruction of everything public and private. The history of the last twenty-five years of France, and of the last forty years in America, nay, of its last two hundred years, proves the truth of both parts of this observation.

But even in Europe a change has sensibly taken place in the mind of man. Science had liberated the ideas of those who read and reflect, and the American example had kindled feelings of right in the people. An insurrection has consequently begun, of science, talents, and courage, against rank and birth, which have fallen into contempt. It has failed in its first effort, because the mobs of the cities, the instrument used for its accomplishment, debased by ignorance, poverty, and vice, could not be restrained to rational action. But the world will recover from the panic of this first catastrophe. Science is progressive, and talents and enterprise on the alert. Resort may be had to the people of the country, a more governable power from their principles and subordination; and rank, and birth, and tinsel-aristocracy will finally shrink into insignificance even there. This, however, we have no right to meddle with. It suffices for us if the moral and physical condition of our own citizens qualifies them to select the able and good for the direction of their government with a recurrence of elections at such short periods as will enable them to displace an unfaithful servant before the mischief he meditates may be irremediable.

I have thus stated my opinion on a point on which we differ, not with a view to controversy, for we are both too old to change opinions which are the result of a long life of inquiry and reflection, but on the suggestions of a former letter of yours, that we ought not to die before we have explained ourselves to each other. We acted in perfect harmony, through a long and perilous contest for our liberty and independence. A constitution has been acquired, which, though neither of us thinks perfect, yet both consider as competent to render our fellow-citizens the happiest and the securest on whom the sun has ever shone. If we do not think exactly alike as to imperfections, it matters little to our country which, after devoting to it long lives of disinterested labor, we have delivered over to our successors in

9. Theognis of Megara (sixth century B.C.), a Greek poet and moralist to whom most of the elegies before the Alexandrian period have been attributed.

life, who will be able to take care of it and of themselves. . . .

ADAMS TO JEFFERSON
November 15, 1813

. . . We are now explicitly agreed on one important point, viz., that "there is a natural aristocracy among men, the grounds of which are virtue and talents." You very justly indulge a little merriment upon this solemn subject of aristocracy. I often laugh at it too, for there is nothing in this laughable world more ridiculous than the management of it by almost all the nations of the earth; but while we smile, mankind have reason to say to us, as the frogs said to the boys, what is sport to you are wounds and death to us. When I consider the weakness, the folly, the pride, the vanity, the selfishness, the artifice, the low craft and mean cunning, the want of principle, the avarice, the unbounded ambition, the unfeeling cruelty of a majority of those (in all nations) who are allowed an aristocratical influence, and, on the other hand, the stupidity with which the more numerous multitude not only become their dupes, but even love to be taken in by their tricks, I feel a stronger disposition to weep at their destiny than to laugh at their folly.

But though we have agreed in one point, in words, it is not yet certain that we are perfectly agreed in sense. Fashion has introduced an indeterminate use of the word "talents." Education, wealth, strength, beauty, stature, birth, marriage, graceful attitudes and motions, gait, air, complexion, physiognomy, are talents, as well as genius, science, and learning. Any one of these talents that in fact commands or influences two votes in society gives to the man who possesses it the character of an aristocrat, in my sense of the word. Pick up the first hundred men you meet and make a republic. Every man will have an equal vote; but when deliberations and discussions are opened, it will be found that twenty-five, by their talents, virtues being equal, will be able to carry fifty votes. Every one of these twenty-five is an aristocrat in my sense of the word; whether he obtains his one vote in addition to his own, by his birth, fortune, figure, eloquence, science, learning, craft, cunning, or even his character for good fellowship, and a *bon vivant*.

What gave Sir William Wallace his amazing aristocratical superiority?[10] His strength. What gave Mrs. Clark her aristocratical influence—to create generals, admirals, and bishops?[11] Her beauty. What gave Pompadour and Du Barry the power of making cardinals and popes? And I have lived for years in the Hotel de Valentinois, with Franklin, who had as many virtues as any of them. In the investigation of the meaning of the word "talents," I could write 630 pages as pertinent as John Taylor's, of Hazelwood,[12] but I will select a single example; for female aristocrats are nearly as formidable in society as male. A daughter of a greengrocer walks the streets in London daily, with a basket of cabbage, sprouts, dandelions, and spinach on her head. She is observed by the painters to have a beautiful face, an elegant figure, a graceful step, and a *débonnaire*. They hire her to sit. She complies and is painted by forty artists in a circle around her. The scientific Sir William Hamilton outbids the painters, sends her to school for a genteel education, and marries her. This

10. Scottish popular hero (*ca.* 1270–1305) who led the resistance to Edward I, king of England.
11. Mary Anne Clarke (*ca.* 1776–1852), mistress of Frederick, Duke of York, second son of George III.
12. John Taylor of Caroline (1753?–1824), Virginia planter and United States senator; interested in the improvement of agriculture and the maintenance of republican government; a founder of the state-rights school of strict interpretation of the Constitution. The work referred to by Adams was Taylor's longest and most systematic book, *An Inquiry into the Principles and Policy of the Government of the United States of America.*

lady not only causes the triumphs of the Nile, Copenhagen, and Trafalgar but separates Naples from France and finally banishes the king and queen from Sicily.[13] Such is the aristocracy of this natural talent of beauty. . . .

Your distinction between natural and artificial aristocracy does not appear to me founded. Birth and wealth are conferred on some men as imperiously by nature as genius, strength, or beauty. The heir to honors and riches and power has often no more merit in procuring these advantages than he has in obtaining a handsome face or an elegant figure. When aristocracies are established by human laws, and honor, wealth, and power are made hereditary by municipal laws and political institutions, then I acknowledge artificial aristocracy to commence; but this never commences till corruption in elections becomes dominant and uncontrollable. But this artificial aristocracy can never last. The everlasting envies, jealousies, rivalries, and quarrels among them; their cruel rapacities upon the poor ignorant people, their followers, compel these to set up Caesar, a demagogue, to be a monarch and master; *pour mettre chacun à sa place*.[14] Here you have the origin of all artificial aristocracy, which is the origin of all monarchy. And both artificial aristocracy and monarchy, and civil, military, political, and hierarchical despotism, have all grown out of the natural aristocracy of "virtues and talents." . . .

Your distinction between the *aristoi* and *pseudo-aristoi* will not help the matter. I would trust one as soon as the other with unlimited power. . . .

You suppose a difference of opinion between you and me on the subject of aristocracy. I can find none. I dislike and detest hereditary honors, offices, emol-

uments established by law. So do you. I am for excluding legal hereditary distinctions from the United States as long as possible. So are you. I only say that mankind have not yet discovered any remedy against irresistible corruption in elections to offices of great power and profit, but making them hereditary. But will you say our elections are pure? Be it so, upon the whole. But do you recollect in history a more corrupt election than that of Aaron Burr to be President,[15] or that of De Witt Clinton last year.[16] By corruption here I mean a sacrifice of every national interest and honor to private and party objects. . . .

Where tends the mania of banks? At my table in Philadelphia, I once proposed to you to unite in endeavors to obtain an amendment of the Constitution, prohibiting to the separate states the power of creating banks; but giving Congress authority to establish one bank, with a branch in each state, the whole limited to ten millions of dollars. . . . But you spurned the proposition from you with disdain. This system of banks, begotten, brooded, and hatched by Duer,[17] Robert and Gouverneur Morris, Hamilton, and Washington, I have always considered as a system of national injustice, a sacrifice of public and private interest to a few

13. Sir William Hamilton (1730–1803), British archeologist and diplomat whose wife, the famous Lady Emma Hamilton, was the mistress of Lord Nelson.
14. "To put everyone in his place."
15. In 1801, when Jefferson was finally chosen by the House.
16. De Witt Clinton (1769–1828), New York lawyer and politician, mayor of New York City for ten years, governor of New York State (1817–23), largely responsible for the construction of the Erie Canal. The election here referred to was the unsuccessful attempt, in 1812, of New York Republicans and the Federalists to elect Clinton to the presidency. The electoral vote was as follows: Madison, 128; Clinton, 89.
17. William Duer (1747–99), merchant and financier; born in Devonshire, England; educated at Eton; ensign in the British army; became permanent resident of New York from 1773; patriot leader, signer of the Articles of Confederation; helped to draft first constitution of New York State; failure of his speculations precipitated a financial panic in New York City (1792).

aristocratical friends and favorites. My scheme could have had no such effect. Verres[18] plundered temples and robbed a few rich men; but he never made such ravages among private property in general nor swindled so much out of the pockets of the poor and the middle class of people as these banks have done! . . . What inequalities of talent have been introduced into this country by these aristocratical banks! Our Winthrops, Winslows, Bradfords, Saltonstalls, Quinceys, Chandlers, Leonards, Hutchinsons, Olivers, Sewalls, etc., are precisely in the situation of your Randolphs, Carters, and Burwells and Harrisons. Some of them unpopular for the part they took in the late Revolution, but all respected for their names and connections; and whenever they fall in with the popular sentiments, are preferred, *cateris paribus*,[19] to all others. . . .

ADAMS TO JEFFERSON
December 19, 1813

[After a long dissertation on the aristocratic standing of the Bowdoin and other families in Massachusetts, Adams goes

18. Gaius Verres (*ca.* 120–43 B.C.), Roman magistrate, successfully prosecuted by Cicero for his misgovernment of Sicily.
19. More usually, *ceteris paribus*, "other things being equal."

on:] . . . Aristocracy, like waterfowl, dives for ages and then rises with brighter plumage. It is a subtle venom that diffuses itself unseen over oceans and continents and triumphs over time. If I could prevent its deleterious influence, I would put it all into "the Hole" of Calcutta. But as this is impossible as it is a phoenix that rises again out of its own ashes, I know no better way than to chain it in a "hole by itself" and place a watchful sentinel on each side of it.

A hundred other foreign aristocracies have sown and are sowing their seeds in this country; and we have an abundance of them springing up in this country, not from virtues and talents, but from banks and land-jobbing. . . .

JEFFERSON TO ADAMS
January 24, 1814

. . . You surprise me with the account you give of the strength of family distinction still existing in your state. With us it is so totally extinguished that not a spark of it is to be found but lurking in the hearts of some of our old Tories. But all bigotries hang to one another; and this, in the eastern states, hangs, as I suspect, to that of the priesthood. Here youth, beauty, mind, and manners are more valued than a pedigree. . . .

UNIT III

CONFEDERATION AND CONSTITUTION

IN THE twelve years which preceded the Declaration of Independence leaders in Britain and in British America had failed to solve the imperial problem—that of reconciling the freedom of each colony, as its members understood it, with the degree of central control which the rulers of the British Empire thought desirable. At the same time, sharp differences of opinion existed within each colony about the proper structure and purpose of government. Together these are the two central problems of the American Revolution. The elimination of British authority did not solve them. It simply transferred to Americans the sole responsibility for finding a solution. The Articles of Confederation represents the first attempt to create a constitution which would preserve the advantages of a common association among the colonies while at the same time safeguarding the other interests involved. It was replaced by the Constitution of the United States. In this process the old problem of reconciling colonial (or state) self-government with imperial (or national) unity was faced and, for seven decades, solved. So also was the problem of defining the purposes of government, so far as this fell within the scope of the federal Constitution.

"That a plan of confederation be prepared and transmitted to the respective Colonies for their consideration and approbation" was the third and last of Richard Henry Lee's resolutions of June 7, 1776. After a year and a half the Continental Congress framed the "Articles of Confederation and Perpetual Union" and transmitted them to the states for ratification. Ten states ratified within the first year; the last, Maryland, accepted the Articles early in 1781. A first reading of the Articles against the Constitution will show how much the latter is indebted to the former; a closer reading will reveal serious defects in the Articles. But, when one recalls the issues of the conflict with Britain, it is not difficult to understand why Congress lacked the power to tax and to regulate commerce, why there was no strong and independent executive, why practically all the general government's activities required state action or acquiescence instead of operating upon individual citizens. Articles II and XIII left no doubt that ultimate authority remained with the several states.

How did this government work? Incredibly badly, said its critics then and since. Congress brought on the worst monetary inflation in our history (excepting that of the southern Confederacy near its end) and could

236

do nothing effective about the deflation which followed. Congress once had to leave Philadelphia hastily to escape an outbreak of dissatisfied soldiers. "Are you one nation or thirteen?" was a legitimate question of foreign statesmen as they saw the states ignoring the requisitions of Congress and apparently violating solemn treaty obligations. America was in no position to protect her vital interests in foreign affairs. States engaged in trade and tax "wars"; sectional jealousies threatened the disruption of the Confederation.

But there was another side. The Confederation did formalize and, for a brief but critical period, did maintain the union of the states and people. Under that union gains in freedom from foreign control and in the greater democratization of our political and social institutions were made. And the Congress of the Confederation initiated the land policy of the general government and provided for the establishment of a generous policy of increasing self-government and ultimate statehood for the West, as outlined in the Ordinance of 1787.

Between 1781 and 1786 there were several unsuccessful attempts to increase the power of Congress by amending the Articles. In the latter year a commercial convention meeting at Annapolis suggested a convention to revise the Articles. Congress accepted the suggestion, and all the states except Rhode Island eventually elected delegates. In this action many were undoubtedly influenced by their fears for the security of property

rights which Shays's Rebellion in 1786, together with other incidents and conditions, had thoroughly aroused. The records of the debates at Philadelphia and the character of the subsequent constitution attest the rallying of conservative interests to the defense of private rights.

Naturally enough, the delegates to the Federal Convention were drawn largely from the upper groups of society, in terms of property, education, and political experience. A few distinguished leaders of the Revolutionary period were unwilling or unable to serve. Patrick Henry, who suspected an attempt to curtail popular liberties, refused to be elected; Thomas Jefferson and John Adams were absent overseas. But Washington and the aging Franklin lent their prestige; James Madison, James Wilson, George Mason, Oliver Ellsworth, Gouverneur Morris, and the two Pinckneys were most active in the debates. Some of the problems which they faced in those debates, and some of the sectional and ideological differences there expressed, may be found in the selections from their several draft plans and from the notes taken by Madison and others. Their solutions are embodied in the text of the Constitution.

The Federal Convention proposed; it was for the states, through specially elected conventions, to ratify or not. The issue was decided between December, 1787, and the end of June, 1788, when ten of the thirteen states had ratified. In more than one important state the margin was very narrow—so much so that some historians have suggested that the Constitution would have been defeated if a popular referendum had been held. Its success seems to have been due to the masterly tactics adopted by its supporters and to the inferior organization of their opponents. The *Federalist Papers*, published to promote ratification, served an essential purpose in the politics of persuasion, though the extent of its direct influence may not have been so great. Hastily written as it was, this work remains one of the profoundest commentaries on the theme of government ever written by Americans.

These divisions among the leaders and the people reflected important differences in interests and ideologies—differences which are suggested in Jefferson's correspondence and in the *Letters of a Federal Farmer*. Most ironically, the author of the tenth number of the *Federalist*, Madison, later helped Jefferson to unite the democratic forces into a great political party against the Hamiltonian program.

In this era "a more perfect union" was obtained to protect the independence of the new nation from the foreign perils which were soon apparent. The real freedom of the states was made possible within the limits of a federal system which, with all its imperfections and ambiguities, reconciled a high degree of "states' rights" with some general supervision of those matters which concerned all. Bills of rights and other provisions in the new constitutions, state and federal, afforded protection to the personal and property rights of individuals. The breakup of the Union was postponed to a time when the forces of unity would be strong enough to prevail. Even though it be granted that most of the elements which coalesced in the Constitution of 1787 were present in the British and colonial heritage and in subsequent American experience, their combination was a great achievement in the field of political invention.

1. THE ARTICLES OF CONFEDERATION[1]

EDITORS' NOTE.—It has been traditional to interpret the Articles as the "product of ignorance and inexperience and the parent of chaos"; the period during which they were in force was called by John Fiske the "Critical Period" of American history. Whatever the causes of the difficulties of the country after 1781, there can be no doubt that later propagandists blamed the government of the Articles for much that was the product of other causes.

For good statements of the orthodox interpretation see A. C. McLaughlin, *A Constitutional History of the United States* (New York, 1935), chapter 12; for a "revisionist" view see Merrill Jensen, *The Articles of Confederation . . . 1774–1781* (Madison, 1940).

. . . Articles of Confederation and Perpetual Union between the states of New Hampshire, Massachusetts Bay, Rhode Island and Providence Plantations, Connecticut, New York, New Jersey, Pennsylvania, Delaware, Maryland, Virginia, North Carolina, South Carolina, and Georgia.

ARTICLE I. The style of this confederacy shall be "The United States of America."

ART. II. Each state retains its sovereignty, freedom, and independence, and every power, jurisdiction, and right which is not by this confederation expressly delegated to the United States in Congress assembled.[2]

ART. III. The said states hereby severally enter into a firm league of friendship with each other, for their common defense, the security of their liberties, and their mutual and general welfare, binding themselves to assist each other against all force offered to, or attacks made upon them, or any of them, on account of religion, sovereignty, trade, or any other pretense whatever.

ART. IV. The better to secure and perpetuate mutual friendship and intercourse among the people of the different states in this union, the free inhabitants of each of these states, paupers, vagabonds, and fugitives from justice excepted, shall be entitled to all privileges and immunities of free citizens in the several states; and the people of each state shall have free ingress and regress to and from any other state and shall enjoy therein all the privileges of trade and commerce, subject to the same duties, impositions, and restrictions as the inhabitants thereof respectively, provided that such restrictions shall not extend so far as to prevent the removal of property imported into any state, to any other state, of which the owner is an inhabitant; provided also that no imposition, duties, or restriction shall be laid by any state on the property of the United States, or either of them.

If any person guilty of or charged with treason, felony, or other high misdemeanor in any state shall flee from justice, and be found in any of the United

---

1. *Journals of the Continental Congress, 1774–1789,* XIX (1912), 214–22.

2. This guaranty of state supremacy in the confederation was originally proposed as an amendment to Dickinson's draft by Dr. Thomas Burke of North Carolina. Its effect was to limit Congress strictly to the powers expressly delegated to it (see the Constitution, Art. I, Sec. 8, Par. 18, and Amendment X).

States, he shall, upon demand of the governor or executive power of the state from which he fled, be delivered up and removed to the state having jurisdiction of his offense.

Full faith and credit shall be given in each of these states to the records, acts, and judicial proceedings of the courts and magistrates of every other state.

ART. V. For the more convenient management of the general interests of the United States, delegates shall be annually appointed in such manner as the legislature of each state shall direct, to meet in Congress on the first Monday in November, in every year, with a power reserved to each state to recall its delegates, or any of them, at any time within the year and to send others in their stead for the remainder of the year.

No state shall be represented in Congress by less than two nor by more than seven members; and no person shall be capable of being a delegate for more than three years in any term of six years; nor shall any person, being a delegate, be capable of holding any office under the United States for which he, or another for his benefit, receives any salary, fees, or emolument of any kind.

Each state shall maintain its own delegates in a meeting of the states and while they act as members of the Committee of the States.

In determining questions in the United States in Congress assembled, each state shall have one vote.[3]

Freedom of speech and debate in Congress shall not be impeached or questioned in any court, or place out of Congress, and the members of Congress shall be protected in their persons from arrests and imprisonments during the time of their going to and from, and attendance

3. Adopted over the opposition of delegates from the large states, which at that time were (in this order) Virginia, Massachusetts, and Pennsylvania. For the same issue in the Federal Convention of 1787 see pp. 258–62.

on, Congress, except for treason, felony, or breach of the peace.

ART. VI. No state, without the consent of the United States in Congress assembled, shall send any embassy to, or receive any embassy from, or enter into any conference, agreement, alliance, or treaty with any king, prince, or state; nor shall any person holding any office of profit or trust under the United States, or any of them, accept of any present, emolument, office, or title of any kind whatever from any king, prince, or foreign state; nor shall the United States in Congress assembled, or any of them, grant any title of nobility.

No two or more states shall enter into any treaty, confederation, or alliance whatever between them without the consent of the United States in Congress assembled, specifying accurately the purposes for which the same is to be entered into and how long it shall continue.

No state shall lay any imposts or duties which may interfere with any stipulations in treaties entered into by the United States in Congress assembled with any king, prince, or state, in pursuance of any treaties already proposed by Congress, to the courts of France and Spain.

No vessels of war shall be kept up in time of peace by any state except such number only as shall be deemed necessary by the United States in Congress assembled for the defense of such state or its trade; nor shall any body of forces be kept up by any state in time of peace except such number only as in the judgment of the United States in Congress assembled shall be deemed requisite to garrison the forts necessary for the defense of such state; but every state shall always keep up a well-regulated and disciplined militia, sufficiently armed and accoutered, and shall provide and constantly have ready for use, in public stores, a due number of field pieces and tents and a proper quantity of arms, ammunition, and camp equipage.

No state shall engage in any war without the consent of the United States in Congress assembled unless such state be actually invaded by enemies, or shall have received certain advice of a resolution being formed by some nation of Indians to invade such state, and the danger is so imminent as not to admit of a delay till the United States in Congress assembled can be consulted; nor shall any state grant commissions to any ships or vessels of war, nor letters of marque or reprisal,[4] except it be after a declaration of war by the United States in Congress assembled, and then only against the kingdom or state and the subjects thereof against which war has been so declared and under such regulations as shall be established by the United States in Congress assembled, unless such state be infested by pirates, in which case vessels of war may be fitted out for that occasion and kept so long as the danger shall continue or until the United States in Congress assembled shall determine otherwise.

Art. VII. When land forces are raised by any state for the common defense, all officers of or under the rank of colonel shall be appointed by the legislature of each state respectively, by whom such forces shall be raised, or in such manner as such state shall direct, and all vacancies shall be filled up by the state which first made the appointment.

Art. VIII. All charges of war and all other expenses that shall be incurred for the common defense or general welfare, and allowed by the United States in Congress assembled, shall be defrayed out of a common treasury, which shall be supplied by the several states in proportion to the value of all land within each state, granted to or surveyed for any person, as such land the buildings and improvements thereon shall be estimated according to such mode as the United States in Congress assembled shall from time to time direct and appoint.[5] The taxes for paying that proportion shall be laid and levied by the authority and direction of the legislatures of the several states within the time agreed upon by the United States in Congress assembled.

Art. IX. The United States in Congress assembled shall have the sole and exclusive right and power of determining on peace and war, except in the cases mentioned in the sixth article—of sending and receiving ambassadors—entering into treaties and alliances, provided that no treaty of commerce shall be made whereby the legislative power of the respective states shall be restrained from imposing such imposts and duties on foreigners as their own people are subjected to or from prohibiting the exportation or importation of any species of goods or commodities whatsoever—of establishing rules for deciding in all cases what captures on land or water shall be legal, and in what manner prizes taken by land or naval forces in the service of the UNITED STATES shall be divided or appropriated—of granting letters of marque and reprisal in times of peace—appointing courts for the trial of piracies and felonies committed on the high seas and establishing courts for receiving and determining finally appeals in all cases of captures, provided that no member of Congress shall be appointed a judge of any of the said courts.

4. Before the Declaration of Paris (1856) it was common and lawful for the government of a country at war to authorize privately owned vessels to seize the ships and goods of an enemy by issuing letters of marque and reprisal. The vessels which were so authorized were known as privateers.

5. The original (Dickinson) draft had apportioned payments according to population, excluding Indians not taxed. This proposal naturally met with strong opposition from the states with a large Negro population, and the southern states favored basing contributions upon the value of lands already granted and surveyed. A proposal that payments be based on white population alone was voted down by the New England and the Middle States except Delaware. The clause finally voted was carried against the solid opposition of New England.

The United States in Congress assembled shall also be the last resort on appeal in all disputes and difference now subsisting or that hereafter may arise between two or more states concerning boundary, jurisdiction, or any other cause whatever, which authority shall always be exercised in the manner following: Whenever the legislative or executive authority or lawful agent of any state in controversy with another shall present a petition to Congress stating the matter in question and praying for a hearing, notice thereof shall be given by order of Congress to the legislative or executive authority of the other state in controversy, and a day assigned for the appearance of the parties by their lawful agents, who shall then be directed to appoint, by joint consent, commissioners or judges to constitute a court for hearing and determining the matter in question; but if they cannot agree, Congress shall name three persons out of each of the United States, and from the list of such persons each party shall alternately strike out one, the petitioners beginning, until the number shall be reduced to thirteen; and from that number not less than seven nor more than nine names, as Congress shall direct, shall in the presence of Congress be drawn out by lot, and the persons whose names shall be so drawn, or any five of them, shall be commissioners or judges to hear and finally determine the controversy, so always as a major part of the judges who shall hear the cause shall agree in the determination; and if either party shall neglect to attend at the day appointed, without showing reasons, which Congress shall judge sufficient, or being present shall refuse to strike, the Congress shall proceed to nominate three persons out of each state, and the secretary of Congress shall strike in behalf of such party absent or refusing; and the judgment and sentence of the court to be appointed, in the manner before prescribed, shall be final and conclusive;

and if any of the parties shall refuse to submit to the authority of such court, or to appear or defend their claim or clause, the court shall nevertheless proceed to pronounce sentence, or judgment, which shall in like manner be final and decisive, the judgment or sentence and other proceedings being in either case transmitted to Congress and lodged among the acts of Congress for the security of the parties concerned: provided that every commissioner, before he sits in judgment, shall take an oath to be administered by one of the judges of the supreme or superior court of the state where the cause shall be tried, "well and truly to hear and determine the matter in question, according to the best of his judgment, without favor, affection, or hope of reward": provided, also, that no state shall be deprived of territory for the benefit of the United States.[6]

All controversies concerning the private right of soil claimed under different grants of two or more states, whose jurisdictions as they may respect such lands, and the states which passed such grants are adjusted, the said grants or either of them being at the same time claimed to have originated antecedent to such settlement of jurisdiction shall, on the petition of either party to the Congress of the United States, be finally determined as near as may be in the same manner as is before prescribed for deciding disputes respecting territorial jurisdiction between different states.

The United States in Congress assembled shall also have the sole and exclusive right and power of regulating the alloy and value of coin struck by their own authority or by that of the respective states—fixing the standard of weights and measures throughout the United States—regulating the trade and managing all affairs with the Indians not

6. A clause inserted on the motion of R. H. Lee to protect the states with claims based on colonial charters to land west of the Appalachians.

members of any of the states, provided that the legislative right of any state within its own limits be not infringed or violated—establishing or regulating post offices from one state to another, throughout all the United States, and exacting such postage on the papers passing through the same as may be requisite to defray the expenses of the said office—appointing all officers of the land forces, in the service of the United States, excepting regimental officers—appointing all the officers of the naval forces, and commissioning all officers whatever in the service of the United States—making rules for the government and regulation of the said land and naval forces, and directing their operations.

The United States in Congress assembled shall have authority to appoint a committee, to sit in the recess of Congress, to be denominated "A Committee of the States," and to consist of one delegate from each state; and to appoint such other committees and civil officers as may be necessary for managing the general affairs of the United States under their direction—to appoint one of their number to preside, provided that no person be allowed to serve in the office of President more than one year in any term of three years; to ascertain the necessary sums of money to be raised for the service of the United States, and to appropriate and apply the same for defraying the public expenses—to borrow money or emit bills on the credit of the United States, transmitting every half-year to the respective states an account of the sums of money so borrowed or emitted—to build and equip a navy—to agree upon the number of land forces, and to make requisitions from each state for its quota, in proportion to the number of white inhabitants in such state, which requisition shall be binding; and thereupon the legislature of each state shall appoint the regimental officers, raise the men and cloth, arm, and equip them in a soldier-like manner, at the expense of the United States; and the officers and men so clothed, armed, and equipped shall march to the place appointed and within the time agreed on by the United States in Congress assembled. But if the United States in Congress assembled shall, on consideration of circumstances, judge proper that any state should not raise men or should raise a smaller number than its quota and that any other state should raise a greater number of men than the quota thereof, such extra number shall be raised, officered, clothed, armed, and equipped in the same manner as the quota of such state, unless the legislature of such state shall judge that such extra number cannot be safely spared out of the same, in which case they shall raise officer, cloth, arm, and equip as many of such extra number as they judge can be safely spared. And the officers and men so clothed, armed, and equipped shall march to the place appointed and within the time agreed on by the United States in Congress assembled.

The United States in Congress assembled shall never engage in a war, nor grant letters of marque and reprisal in time of peace, nor enter into any treaties or alliances, nor coin money, nor regulate the value thereof, nor ascertain the sums and expenses necessary for the defense and welfare of the United States, or any of them, nor emit bills, nor borrow money on the credit of the United States, nor appropriate money, nor agree upon the number of vessels of war to be built or purchased or the number of land or sea forces to be raised, nor appoint a commander-in-chief of the army or navy, unless nine states assent to the same;[7] nor shall a question on any other point, except for adjourning from day to day, be determined unless by the votes

7. Often criticized as making it difficult for Congress to function effectively; actually arrived at as a compromise on representation by which it was made impossible for the six largest states to be outvoted by the seven smallest ones on any important issue (Jensen, *op. cit.*, p. 144).

of a majority of the United States in Congress assembled.

The Congress of the United States shall have power to adjourn to any time within the year, and to any place within the United States, so that no period of adjournment be for a longer duration than the space of six months, and shall publish the Journal of their proceedings monthly, except such parts thereof relating to treaties, alliances, or military operations, as in their judgment require secrecy; and the yeas and nays of the delegates of each state on any question shall be entered on the Journal when it is desired by any delegate; and the delegates of a state, or any of them, at his or their request, shall be furnished with a transcript of the said Journal, except such parts as are above excepted, to lay before the legislatures of the several states.

ART. X. The Committee of the States, or any nine of them, shall be authorized to execute, in the recess of Congress, such of the powers of Congress as the United States in Congress assembled, by the consent of nine states, shall from time to time think expedient to vest them with; provided that no power be delegated to the said Committee, for the exercise of which, by the Articles of Confederation, the voice of nine states in the Congress of the United States assembled is requisite.

ART. XI. Canada acceding to this Confederation, and joining in the measures of the United States, shall be admitted into and entitled to all the advantages of this union; but no other colony shall be admitted into the same unless such admission be agreed to by nine states.

ART. XII. All bills of credit emitted, moneys borrowed, and debts contracted by or under the authority of Congress, before the assembling of the United States, in pursuance of the present Confederation, shall be deemed and considered as a charge against the United States,

for payment and satisfaction whereof the said United States and the public faith are hereby solemnly pledged.

ART. XIII. Every state shall abide by the determinations of the United States in Congress assembled on all questions which by this Confederation are submitted to them. And the Articles of this Confederation shall be inviolably observed by every state, and the union shall be perpetual; nor shall any alteration at any time hereafter be made in any of them; unless such alteration be agreed to in a Congress of the United States and be afterward confirmed by the legislatures of every state.[8]

And whereas it hath pleased the Great Governor of the World to incline the hearts of the legislatures we respectively represent in Congress to approve of, and to authorize us to ratify the said Articles of Confederation and Perpetual Union. Know ye that we the undersigned delegates, by virtue of the power and authority to us given for that purpose, do by these presents, in the name and in behalf of our respective constituents, fully and entirely ratify and confirm each and every of the said Articles of Confederation and Perpetual Union and all and singular the matters and things therein contained. And we do further solemnly plight and engage the faith of our respective constituents that they shall abide by the determinations of the United States in Congress assembled on all questions which by the said Confederation are submitted to them. And that the articles thereof shall be inviolably observed by the states we respectively represent and that the union shall be perpetual. In witness whereof we have hereunto set our hands in Congress. . . .

8. Note the difficulty of amending the Articles; cf. the Constitution, Art. VII, to see how the method by which the Articles were later superseded violated the express provisions of the older document.

2. ON DISBANDING THE ARMY[1]

By George Washington

EDITORS' NOTE. — Those students who wish to read a recent full-length biography should consult the two-volume life of Washington by N. W. Stephenson and W. H. Dunn (New York, 1940). *The Writings . . .* , ed. John C. Fitzpatrick, is the most recent and most nearly complete edition of his writings. For his daily life at Mount Vernon and elsewhere see *The Diaries of George Washington*, ed. John C. Fitzpatrick (4 vols.; Boston, 1925).

When Washington wrote this address, the general government was more than usually in need of money to pay something on its debts, especially the back pay due to the soldiers. In the April preceding the Congress had appealed to the states to give it a limited taxing power and to raise additional revenue themselves for the general government. Although neither the congressional address written by James Madison nor this letter of Washington's had more than a transitory influence, both are able statements of the problems facing the Confederation.

CIRCULAR LETTER ADDRESSED TO THE GOVERNORS OF ALL THE STATES ON DISBANDING THE ARMY (JUNE 8, 1783)

There are four things which, I humbly conceive, are essential to the well-being, I may even venture to say, to the existence of the United States as an independent power:

1st. An indissoluble union of the states under one federal head.

2dly. A sacred regard to public justice.

3dly. The adoption of a proper peace establishment, and

4thly. The prevalence of that pacific and friendly disposition, among the people of the United States, which will induce them to forget their local prejudices and policies, to make those mutual concessions which are requisite to the general prosperity, and, in some instances, to sacrifice their individual advantages to the interest of the community.

These are the pillars on which the glorious fabric of our independency and national character must be supported; liberty is the basis, and whoever would dare to sap the foundation, or overturn the structure, under whatever specious pretexts he may attempt it, will merit the bitterest execration and the severest punishment which can be inflicted by his injured country.

On the three first articles I will make a few observations, leaving the last to the good sense and serious consideration of those immediately concerned.

Under the first head, although it may not be necessary or proper for me in this place to enter into a particular disquisition of the principles of the Union, and to take up the great question which has been frequently agitated, whether it be expedient and requisite for the states to delegate a larger proportion of power to Congress, or not, yet it will be a part of my duty, and that of every true patriot, to assert without reserve, and to insist upon the following positions: That, unless the states will suffer Congress to exercise those prerogatives they are undoubtedly invested with by the Consti-

1. *The Writings of George Washington, from the Original Manuscript Sources, 1745–1799. . . , Prepared under the Direction of the U.S. George Washington Bicentennial Commission. . .* , ed. John C. Fitzpatrick (39 vols.; Washington, 1933–44), XXVI, 487–95.

tution, everything must very rapidly tend to anarchy and confusion. That it is indispensable to the happiness of the individual states that there should be lodged somewhere a supreme power to regulate and govern the general concerns of the Confederated Republic, without which the Union cannot be of long duration. That there must be a faithful and pointed compliance on the part of every state with the late proposals and demands of Congress, or the most fatal consequences will ensue. That whatever measures have a tendency to dissolve the Union, or contribute to violate or lessen the sovereign authority, ought to be considered as hostile to the liberty and independency of America, and the authors of them treated accordingly, and, lastly, that unless we can be enabled by the concurrence of the states to participate of the fruits of the Revolution, and enjoy the essential benefits of civil society, under a form of government so free and uncorrupted, so happily guarded against the danger of oppression, as has been devised and adopted by the Articles of Confederation, it will be a subject of regret that so much blood and treasure have been lavished for no purpose, that so many sufferings have been encountered without a compensation, and that so many sacrifices have been made in vain. Many other considerations might here be adduced to prove that, without an entire conformity to the spirit of the Union, we cannot exist as an independent power; it will be sufficient for my purpose to mention but one or two which seem to me of the greatest importance. It is only in our united character as an empire that our independence is acknowledged, that our power can be regarded, or our credit supported among foreign nations. The treaties of the European powers with the United States of America will have no validity on a dissolution of the Union. We shall be left nearly in a state of nature, or we may find, by our own unhappy experience, that there is a natural and necessary progression, from the extreme of anarchy to the extreme of tyranny; and that arbitrary power is most easily established on the ruins of liberty abused to licentiousness.

As to the second article, which respects the performance of public justice, Congress have, in their late Address to the United States, almost exhausted the subject; they have explained their ideas so fully, and have enforced the obligations the states are under to render complete justice to all the public creditors, with so much dignity and energy, that, in my opinion, no real friend to the honor and independency of America can hesitate a single moment respecting the propriety of complying with the just and honorable measures proposed; if their arguments do not produce conviction, I know of nothing that will have greater influence, especially when we recollect that the system referred to, being the result of the collected wisdom of the continent, must be esteemed, if not perfect, certainly the least objectionable of any that could be devised; and that if it shall not be carried into immediate execution, a national bankruptcy, with all its deplorable consequences, will take place, before any different plan can possibly be proposed and adopted; so pressing are the present circumstances! and such is the alternative now offered to the states!

The ability of the country to discharge the debts which have been incurred in its defense is not to be doubted; an inclination, I flatter myself, will not be wanting, the path of our duty is plain before us, honesty will be found on every experiment to be the best and only true policy, let us then as a nation be just, let us fulfil the public contracts, which Congress had undoubtedly a right to make for the purpose of carrying on the war, with the same good faith we suppose ourselves bound to perform our private engagements; in the meantime, let an attention to the cheerful performance of their proper business, as individuals, and as members of society, be earnestly inculcated on the citizens of America, that will they strengthen the hands of government, and be happy under its protection: everyone will reap the fruit of his labors, everyone will enjoy his own acquisitions without molestation and without danger.

In this state of absolute freedom and perfect security, who will grudge to yield a very little of his property to support the common interest of society and insure the protection of government? Who does not remember the frequent declarations, at the commencement of the war, that we should be completely satisfied, if, at the expense of one-half, we could defend the remainder of our possessions? Where is the man to be found who wishes to remain indebted, for the defense of his own person and property, to the exertions, the bravery, and the blood of others, without making one generous effort to repay the debt of honor and of gratitude? In what part of the continent shall we find any man, or body of men, who would not blush to stand up and propose measures, purposely calculated to rob the soldier of his stipend, and the public creditor of his due? And were it possible that such a flagrant instance of injustice could ever happen, would it not excite the general indignation and tend to bring down upon the authors of such measures the aggravated vengeance of heaven? If, after all, a spirit of disunion or a temper of obstinacy and perverseness should manifest itself in any of the states, if such an ungracious disposition should attempt to frustrate all the happy effects that might be expected to flow from the Union, if there should be a refusal to comply with the requisitions for funds to discharge the annual interest of the public debts, and if that refusal should revive again all those jealousies and produce all those evils, which are now happily removed, Congress, who have in all their transac-

tion shown a great degree of magnanimity and justice, will stand justified in the sight of God and man, and the state alone which puts itself in opposition to the aggregate wisdom of the continent, and follows such mistaken and pernicious councils, will be responsible for all the consequences.

For my own part, conscious of having acted while a servant of the public, in the manner I conceived best suited to promote the real interests of my country; having, in consequence of my fixed belief in some measure, pledged myself to the Army that their country would finally do them complete and ample justice; and not wishing to conceal any instance of my official conduct from the eyes of the world, I have thought proper to transmit to your Excellency the inclosed collection of papers, relative to the half-pay and commutation granted by Congress to the officers of the Army. From these communications, my decided sentiment will be clearly comprehended, together with the conclusive reasons which induced me, at an early period, to recommend the adoption of the measure in the most earnest and serious manner. As the proceedings of Congress, the Army, and myself are open to all, and contain, in my opinion, sufficient information to remove the prejudices and errors which may have been entertained by any, I think it unnecessary to say anything more than just to observe that the resolutions of Congress, now alluded to, are undoubtedly as absolutely binding upon the United States as the most solemn acts of confederation or legislation. As to the idea, which I am informed has in some instances prevailed, that the half-pay and commutation are to be regarded merely in the odious light of a pension, it ought to be exploded forever; that provision should be viewed as it really was, a reasonable compensation offered by Congress, at a time when they had nothing else to give, to the officers of the Army, for services then to be performed. It was the only means to prevent a total dereliction of the service; it was a part of their hire; I may be allowed to say, it was the price of their blood and of your independency; it is therefore more than a common debt; it is a debt of honor; it can never be considered as a pension or gratuity, nor be canceled until it is fairly discharged.

With regard to a distinction between officers and soldiers, it is sufficient that the uniform experience of every nation of the world, combined with our own, proves the utility and propriety of the discrimination. Rewards in proportion to the aids the public derives from them are unquestionably due to all its servants. In some lines, the soldiers have perhaps generally had as ample a compensation for their services by the large bounties which have been paid to them, as their officers will receive in the proposed commutation; in others, if besides the donation of lands, the payment of arrearages of clothing and wages (in which articles all the component parts of the Army must be put upon the same footing), we take into the estimate the bounties many of the soldiers have received and the gratuity of one year's full pay, which is promised to all, possibly their situation (every circumstance being duly considered) will not be deemed less eligible than that of the officers. Should a farther reward, however, be judged equitable, I will venture to assert, no one will enjoy greater satisfaction than myself on seeing an exemption from taxes for a limited time (which has been petitioned for in some instances), or any other adequate immunity or compensation, granted to the brave defenders of their country's cause; but neither the adoption or rejection of this proposition will in any manner affect, much less militate against, the act of Congress, by which they have offered five years' full pay, in lieu of the half-pay for life, which had been before promised to the officers of the Army.

Before I conclude the subject of public justice, I cannot omit to mention the obligations this country is under to that meritorious class of veteran noncommissioned officers and privates who have been discharged for inability, in consequence of the Resolution of Congress of the 23d of April, 1782, on an annual pension for life, their peculiar sufferings, their singular merits and claims to that provision need only be known to interest all the feelings of humanity in their behalf: nothing but a punctual payment of their annual allowance can rescue them from the most complicated misery, and nothing could be a more melancholy and distressing sight than to behold those who have shed their blood or lost their limbs in the service of their country without a shelter, without a friend, and without the means of obtaining any of the necessaries or comforts of life, compelled to beg their daily bread from door to door! Suffer me to recommend those of this description, belonging to your state, to the warmest patronage of your Excellency and your legislature.

It is necessary to say but a few words on the third topic which was proposed and which regards particularly the defense of the Republic. As there can be little doubt but Congress will recommend a proper peace establishment for the United States, in which a due attention will be paid to the importance of placing the militia of the Union upon a regular and respectable footing; if this should be the case, I would beg leave to urge the great advantage of it in the strongest terms. The militia of this country must be considered as the palladium of our security and the first effectual resort in case of hostility; it is essential, therefore, that the same system should pervade the whole; that the formation and discipline of the militia of the continent should be absolutely uniform and that the same species of arms, accouterments, and military apparatus should be introduced in every part of the United States. No one who has not learned it from experience can conceive the difficulty, expense, and confusion which result from a contrary system or the vague arrangements which have hitherto prevailed.

If in treating of political points, a greater latitude than usual has been taken in the course of this address, the importance of the crisis, and the magnitude of the objects in discussion, must be my apology. It is, however, neither my wish or expectation that the preceding observations should claim any regard, except so far as they shall appear to be dictated by a good intention, consonant to the immutable rules of justice; calculated to produce a liberal system of policy and founded on whatever experience may have been acquired by a long and close attention to public business. Here I might speak with the more confidence from my actual observations and, if it would not swell this letter (already too prolix) beyond the bounds I had prescribed myself, I could demonstrate to every mind open to conviction, that in less time and with much less expense than has been incurred, the war might have been brought to the same happy conclusion if the resources of the continent could have been properly drawn forth; that the distresses and disappointments which have very often occurred have, in too many instances, resulted more from a want of

energy in the continental government than a deficiency of means in the particular states. That the inefficiency of measures, arising from the want of an adequate authority in the supreme power, from a partial compliance with the requisitions of Congress in some of the states, and from a failure of punctuality in others, while it tended to damp the zeal of those which were more willing to exert themselves, served also to accumulate the expenses of the war and to frustrate the best concerted plans; and that the discouragement occasioned by the complicated difficulties and embarrassments, in which our affairs were by this means involved, would have long ago produced the dissolution of any Army, less patient, less virtuous, and less persevering than that which I have had the honor to command. But while I mention these things, which are notorious facts, as the defects of our Federal Constitution, particularly in the prosecution of a war, I beg it may be understood that, as I have ever taken a pleasure in gratefully acknowledging the assistance and support I have derived from every class of citizens, so shall I always be happy to do justice to the unparalleled exertion of the individual states, on many interesting occasions.

3. THE NORTHWEST ORDINANCE OF 1787[1]

EDITORS' NOTE.—The Northwest Ordinance of July 13, 1787, was the culmination of almost a decade of intermittent debate in Congress on the problem of providing for the region beyond the Appalachians. The cessions by Virginia and other states having claims to land north and west of the Ohio River made such congressional action possible; Jefferson's *Report of Government for Western Lands* (1784) and the Land Ordinance

of 1785 were important stages in its development. The complaints of the western settlers and the plan of Revolutionary veterans for exchanging congressional promises to pay into titles to western land were important factors in bringing about the passage of this ordinance in the summer of 1787. In these acts of the Congress of the Confederation are formulated a distinctive American solution for the problems of western government.

1. *Documents Illustrative of the Formation of the Union of the American States* (69th Cong.; 1st Sess., House Doc. No. 238 [Washington, 1927]), pp. 47–54.

SECTION 1. *Be it ordained by the United States in Congress assembled,* That the said Territory, for the purpose of temporary government, be one district, subject, however, to be divided into two districts, as future circumstances may, in the opinion of Congress, make it expedient.

SEC. 2. *Be it ordained by the authority aforesaid,* That the estates both of resident and nonresident proprietors in the said territory, dying intestate, shall descend to, and be distributed among, their children and the descendants of a deceased child in equal parts, the descendants of a deceased child or grandchild to take the share of their deceased parent in equal parts among them; and where there shall be no children or descendants, then in equal parts to the next of kin, in equal degree; and among collaterals, the children of a deceased brother or sister of the intestate shall have, in equal parts among them, their deceased parent's share; and there shall, in no case, be a distinction between kindred of the whole and half blood; saving in all cases to the widow of the intestate, her third part of the real estate for life, and one-third part of the personal estate; and this law relative to descents and dower shall remain in full force until altered by the legislature of the district. And until the governor and judges shall adopt laws as hereinafter mentioned, estates in the said territory may be devised or bequeathed by wills in writing, signed and sealed by him or her in whom the estate may be (being of full age), and attested by three witnesses; and real estates may be conveyed by lease and release, or bargain and sale, signed, sealed, and delivered by the person, being of full age, in whom the estate may be, and attested by two witnesses, provided such wills be duly proved, and such conveyances be acknowledged, or the execution thereof duly proved, and be recorded within one year after proper magistrates, courts, and registers shall be appointed for that pur-

pose; and personal property may be transferred by delivery, saving, however, to the French and Canadian inhabitants, and other settlers of the Kaskaskies, Saint Vincents, and the neighboring villages, who have heretofore professed themselves citizens of Virginia, their laws and customs now in force among them, relative to the descent and conveyance of property.

SEC. 3. *Be it ordained by the authority aforesaid,* That there shall be appointed, from time to time, by Congress, a governor, whose commission shall continue in force for the term of three years, unless sooner revoked by Congress; he shall reside in the district, and have a freehold estate therein, in one thousand acres of land, while in the exercise of his office.

SEC. 4. There shall be appointed from time to time, by Congress, a secretary, whose commission shall continue in force for four years, unless sooner revoked; he shall reside in the districts, and have a freehold estate therein, in five hundred acres of land, while in the exercise of his office. It shall be his duty to keep and preserve the acts and laws passed by the legislature, and the public records of the district, and the proceedings of the governor in his executive department, and transmit authentic copies of such acts and proceedings every six months to the Secretary of Congress. There shall also be appointed a court, to consist of three judges, any two of whom to form a court, who shall have a common-law jurisdiction and reside in the district, and have each therein a freehold estate, in five hundred acres of land, while in the exercise of their offices; and their commissions shall continue in force during good behavior.

SEC. 5. The governor and judges, or a majority of them, shall adopt and publish in the district such laws of the original states, criminal and civil, as may be necessary, and best suited to the circumstances of the district, and report them to Congress from time to time, which laws shall be in force in the district until the organization of the general assembly therein, unless disapproved of by Congress; but afterward the legislature shall have authority to alter them as they shall think fit.

SEC. 6. The governor, for the time being, shall be commander-in-chief of the militia, appoint and commission all officers in the same below the rank of general officers; all general officers shall be appointed and commissioned by Congress.

SEC. 7. Previous to the organization of the general assembly the governor shall appoint such magistrates, and other civil officers, in each county or township, as he shall find necessary for the preservation of the peace and good order in the same. After the general assembly shall be organized, the powers and duties of magistrates and other civil officers shall be regulated and defined by the said assembly; but all magistrates and other civil officers, not herein otherwise directed, shall, during the continuance of this temporary government, be appointed by the governor.

SEC. 8. For the prevention of crimes, and injuries, the laws to be adopted or made shall have force in all parts of the district, and for the execution of process, criminal and civil, the governor shall make proper divisions thereof; and he shall proceed, from time to time, as circumstances may require, to lay out the parts of the district in which the Indian titles shall have been extinguished, into counties and townships, subject, however, to such alterations as may thereafter be made by the legislature.

SEC. 9. So soon as there shall be five thousand free male inhabitants, of full age, in the district, upon giving proof thereof to the governor, they shall receive authority, with time and place, to elect representatives from their counties or townships, to represent them in the general assembly: *Provided*, That for every five hundred free male inhabitants there shall be one representative, and so on, progressively, with the number of free male inhabitants, shall the right of representation increase, until the number of representatives shall amount to twenty-five; after which the number and proportion of representatives shall be regulated by the legislature: *Provided*, That no person be eligible or qualified to act as a representative unless he shall have been a citizen of one of the United States three years, and be a resident in the district, or unless he shall have resided in the district three years; and, in either case, shall likewise hold in his own right, in fee-simple, two hundred acres of land within the same: *Provided also*, That a freehold in fifty acres of land in the district, having been a citizen of one of the states, and being resident in the district, or the like freehold and two years' residence in the district, shall be necessary to qualify a man as an elector of a representative.

SEC. 10. The representatives thus elected shall serve for the term of two years; and in case of the death of a representative, or removal from office, the governor shall issue a writ to the county or township, for which he was a member, to elect another in his stead, to serve for the residue of the term.

SEC. 11. The general assembly, or legislature, shall consist of the governor, legislative council, and a house of representatives. The legislative council shall consist of five members, to continue in office five years, unless sooner removed by Congress; any three of them to be a quorum; and the members of the council shall be nominated and appointed in the following manner, to wit: As soon as representatives shall be elected the governor shall appoint a time and place for them to meet together, and when met they shall nominate ten persons, resident in the district, and each possessed of a freehold in five hundred acres of land, and return their names to Congress, five of whom Congress shall appoint and commission to serve as aforesaid; and whenever a vacancy shall happen in the Council, by death or removal from office, the house of representatives shall nominate two persons, qualified as aforesaid, for each vacancy, and return their names to Congress, one of whom Congress shall appoint and commission for the residue of the term; and every five years, four months at least before the expiration of the time of service of the members of the council, the said house shall nominate ten persons, qualified as aforesaid, and return their names to Congress, five of whom Congress shall appoint and commission to serve as members of the council five years, unless sooner removed. And the governor, legislative council, and house of representatives shall have authority to make laws in all cases for the good government of the district, not repugnant to the principles and articles in this ordinance established and declared. And all bills, having passed by a majority in the house, and by a majority in the council, shall be referred to the governor for his assent; but no bill, or legislative act whatever, shall be of any force without his assent. The governor shall have power to convene, prorogue, and dissolve the general assembly when, in his opinion, it shall be expedient.

Sec. 12. The governor, judges, legislative council, secretary, and such other officers as Congress shall appoint in the district shall take an oath or affirmation of fidelity, and of office; the governor before the president of Congress, and all other officers before the governor. As soon as a legislature shall be formed in the district, the council and house assembled, in one room, shall have authority, by joint ballot, to elect a delegate to Congress, who shall have a seat in Congress, with a right of debating, but not of voting, during this temporary government.

Sec. 13. And for extending the fundamental principles of civil and religious liberty, which form the basis whereon these republics, their laws, and constitutions are erected; to fix and establish those principles as the basis of all laws, constitutions, and governments, which forever hereafter shall be formed in the said territory; to provide, also, for the establishment of states, and permanent government therein, and for their admission to a share in the Federal councils on an equal footing with the original states, at as early periods as may be consistent with the general interest:

Sec. 14. It is hereby ordained and declared, by the authority aforesaid, that the following articles shall be considered as articles of compact between the original states and the people and states in the said territory, and forever remain unalterable, unless by common consent, to wit:

ARTICLE I

No person, demeaning himself in a peaceable and orderly manner, shall ever be molested on account of his mode of worship, or religious sentiments, in the said territory.

ARTICLE II

The inhabitants of the said territory shall always be entitled to the benefits of the writs of habeas corpus and of the trial by jury, of a proportionate representation of the people in the legislature, and of judicial proceedings according to the course of the common law. All persons shall be bailable, unless for capital offenses, where the proof shall be evident, or the presumption great. All fines shall be moderate; and no cruel or unusual punishment shall be inflicted. No man shall be deprived of his liberty or property, but by the judgment of his peers, or the law of the land, and, should the public exigencies make it necessary, for the common preservation, to take any person's property, or to demand his particular services, full compensation shall be made for the same. And, in the just preservation of rights and property, it is understood and declared that no law ought ever to be made or have force in the said territory that shall, in any manner whatever, interfere with or affect private contracts, or engagements, bona fide, and without fraud previously formed.

ARTICLE III

Religion, morality, and knowledge being necessary to good government and the happiness of mankind, schools and the means of education shall forever be encouraged. The utmost good faith shall always be observed toward the Indians; their lands and property shall never be taken from them without their consent; and in their property, rights, and liberty they never shall be invaded or disturbed unless in just and lawful wars authorized by Congress; but laws founded in justice and humanity shall, from time to time, be made, for preventing wrongs being done to them and for preserving peace and friendship with them.

ARTICLE IV

The said territory, and the states which may be formed therein, shall forever remain a part of this confederacy of the United States of America, subject to the Articles of Confederation, and to such alterations therein as shall be constitutionally made; and to all the acts and ordinances of the United States in Congress assembled, conformable thereto. The inhabitants and settlers in the said territory shall be subject to pay a part of the federal debts contracted, or to be contracted, and a proportional part of the expenses of government to be apportioned on them by Congress, according to the same common rule and measure by which apportionments thereof shall be made on the other states; and the taxes for paying their proportion shall be laid and levied by the authority and direction of the legislatures of the district, or districts, or new states, as in the original states, within the time agreed upon by the United States in Congress assembled. The legislatures of those districts, or new states, shall never interfere with the primary disposal of the soil by the United States in Congress assembled, nor with any regulations Congress may find necessary for securing the title in such soil to the bona fide purchasers. No tax shall be imposed on lands the property of the United States; and in no case shall nonresident proprietors be taxed higher than residents. The navigable waters leading into the Mississippi and Saint Lawrence, and the carrying places between the same, shall be common highways, and forever free, as well to the inhabitants of the said territory as to the citizens of the United States, and those of any other states that may be admitted into the confederacy, without any tax, impost, or duty therefor.

ARTICLE V

There shall be formed in the said territory not less than three nor more than five states; and the boundaries of the states, as soon as Virginia shall alter her act of cession and consent to the same, shall become fixed and established as follows, to wit: The western state, in the said territory, shall be bounded by the Mississippi, the Ohio, and the Wabash rivers; a direct line drawn from the Wabash and Post Vincents, due north, to the territorial line between the United States and Canada; and by the said territorial line to the Lake of the Woods and Mississippi. The middle state shall be bounded by the said direct line, the Wabash from Post Vincents to the Ohio, by the Ohio, by a direct line drawn due north from the mouth of the Great Miami to the said territorial line, and by the said territorial line. The eastern state shall be bounded by the last-mentioned direct line, the Ohio, Pennsylvania, and the said territorial line: *Provided, however,* and it is further understood and declared, that the boundaries of these three states shall be subject so far to be altered, that, if Congress shall hereafter find it expedient, they shall have authority to form one or two states in that part of the said territory which lies north of an east and west line drawn through the southerly bend or extreme of Lake Michigan. And when-t.er any of the said states shall have sixty thousand free inhabitants therein, such state shall be admitted by its delegates into the Congress of the United States, on an equal footing with the original states, in all respects whatever; and shall be at liberty to form a permanent constitution and state government: *Provided,* The constitution and government, so to be formed, shall be republican, and in conformity to the principles contained in these articles, and, so far as it can be consistent with the general interest of the confederacy, such admission shall be allowed at an earlier period, and when there may be a less number of free inhabitants in the state than sixty thousand.

ARTICLE VI

There shall be neither slavery nor involuntary servitude in the said territory, otherwise than in the punishment of crimes, whereof the party shall have been duly convicted: *Provided always,* That any person escaping into the same, from whom labor or service is lawfully claimed in any one of the original states, such fugitive may be lawfully reclaimed, and conveyed to the person claiming his or her labor or service as aforesaid.

Be it ordained by the authority aforesaid, That the resolutions of the 23d of April, 1784, relative to the subject of this ordinance, be, and the same are hereby, repealed, and declared null and void.[2]

Done by the United States, in Congress assembled, the 13th day of July, in the year of our Lord 1787, and of their sovereignty and independence the twelfth.

4. DEBATES IN THE FEDERAL CONVENTION OF 1787[1]

EDITORS' NOTE. — The selections which follow were chosen to illuminate some of the more pressing problems which faced the Convention. The Virginia plan, largely Madison's work, though presented to the Convention by Governor Randolph, served as the basis of discussion for the opening weeks; the New Jersey plan represented an alternative which, if adopted, would have made a much less drastic change from the Articles of Confederation. The debates of May 31, June 6, and August 7 indicate the several views of the part which the mass of the people should have in the new government. It is interesting to compare Madison's text of his speech of June 6 with Hamilton's notes of the same speech, and both with Number 10 of *The Federalist.* The debates of June 16, 18, and 19 (including the summary of Hamilton's speech) underline the problem of representing sovereign or near-sovereign political entities of greatly varying sizes. The debate of July 13 suggests that sectional divisions underlay much of the argument about the rights of the small states and the extent to which population should be the basis for representation in Congress. Madison's account

1. *Documents Illustrative of the Formation of the Union of the American States* (Washington, 1927), pp. 953–56, 124–27, 130–31, 159–67, 916–17, 967–70, 208–10, 211, 213, 214, 215–18, 219, 220, 221, 222, 233, 237, 238, 239, 487, 488–90, 491, 738–45.

2. I.e., Jefferson's plan, which had never actually gone into effect but which had been formally passed by the Confederation Congress.

of the last session is given, practically in full.

Those who wish to read more extensively on the Convention will find useful the writings of Max Farrand, Charles Warren, and A. C. McLaughlin. For a study of the economic interests of the delegates see Charles A. Beard, *An Economic Interpretation of the Constitution* (New York, 1913). A recent work is Carl Van Doren's *The Great Rehearsal: The Story of the Making and Ratifying of the Constitution of the United States* (New York, 1948).

A. THE VIRGINIA (RANDOLPH) PLAN

1. *Resolved,* That the Articles of Confederation ought to be so corrected and enlarged as to accomplish the objects proposed by their institution, namely "common defense, security of liberty, and general welfare."

2. *Resolved,* therefore, That the rights of suffrage in the National Legislature ought to be proportioned to the quotas of contribution or to the number of free inhabitants, as the one or the other rule may seem best in different cases.

3. *Resolved,* That the National Legislature ought to consist of two branches.

4. *Resolved,* That the members of the first branch of the National Legislature ought to be elected by the people of the several states every ————[2] for the term of ————, to be of the age of ———— years at least; to receive liberal stipends by which they may be compensated for the devotion of their time to public service; to be ineligible to any office established by a particular state, or under the authority of the United States, except those peculiarly belonging to the functions of the first branch, during the term of service and for the space of ———— after its expiration; to be incapable of re-election for the space of ———— after the expiration of their term of service; and to be subject to recall.

5. *Resolved,* That the members of the second branch of the National Legislature ought to be elected by those of the first, out of a proper number of persons nominated by the individual legisla-

tures,[3] to be of the age of ———— years at least; to hold their offices for a term sufficient to insure their independency; to receive liberal stipends, by which they may be compensated for the devotion of their time to public service; and to be ineligible to any office established by a particular state, or under the authority of the United States, except those peculiarly belonging to the functions of the second branch, during the term of service and for the space of ———— after the expiration thereof.

6. *Resolved,* That each branch ought to possess the right of originating acts; that the National Legislature ought to be empowered to enjoy the legislative rights vested in Congress by the Confederation and moreover to legislate in all cases to which the separate states are incompetent, or in which the harmony of the United States may be interrupted by the exercise of individual legislation; to negative all laws passed by the several states, contravening in the opinion of the National Legislature, the Articles of Union, and to call forth the force of the Union against any member of the Union failing to fulfil its duty under the Articles thereof.[4]

7. *Resolved,* That a National Executive be instituted; to be chosen by the National Legislature for the term of ———— years, to receive punctually at stated times a fixed compensation for the services rendered, in which no increase

2. Left blank deliberately, here and later, to be filled in after discussion in the Convention.

3. I.e., the *state* legislatures.

4. Cf. Madison's speech on this clause at the end of the debate of May 31.

or diminution shall be made so as to affect the magistracy existing at the time of increase or diminution, and to be ineligible a second time; and that, besides a general authority to execute the national laws, it ought to enjoy the Executive rights vested in Congress by the Confederation.

8. *Resolved,* That the Executive and a convenient number of the National Judiciary ought to compose a Council of revision with authority to examine every act of the National Legislature before it shall operate, and every act of a particular legislature before a negative thereon shall be final; and that the dissent of the said Council shall amount to a rejection, unless the Act of the National Legislature be again passed or that of a particular legislature be again negatived by ——— of the members of each branch.

9. *Resolved,* That a National Judiciary be established to consist of one or more supreme tribunals, and of inferior tribunals to be chosen by the National Legislature, to hold their offices during good behavior; and to receive punctually at stated times fixed compensation for their services, in which no increase or diminution shall be made so as to affect the persons actually in office at the time of such increase or diminution. That the jurisdiction of the inferior tribunals shall be to hear and determine in the first instance, and of the supreme tribunal to hear and determine in the dernier resort, all piracies and felonies on the high seas, captures from an enemy; cases in which foreigners or citizens of other states applying to such jurisdictions may be interested, or which respect the collection of the national revenue; impeachments of any national officers, and questions which may involve the national peace and harmony.

10. *Resolved,* That provision ought to be made for the admission of states lawfully arising within the limits of the United States, whether from a voluntary junction of government and territory or otherwise, with the consent of a number of voices in the National Legislature less than the whole.

11. *Resolved,* That a republican government and the territory of each state, except in the instance of a voluntary junction of government and territory, ought to be guaranteed by the United States to each state.

12. *Resolved,* That provision ought to be made for the continuance of Congress and their authorities and privileges, until a given day after the reform of the Articles of Union shall be adopted, and for the completion of all their engagements.

13. *Resolved,* That provision ought to be made for the amendment of the Articles of Union whensoever it shall seem necessary and that the assent of the National Legislature ought not to be required thereto.

14. *Resolved,* That the legislative, executive, and judiciary powers within the several states ought to be bound by oath to support the Articles of Union.

15. *Resolved,* That the amendments which shall be offered to the Confederation by the Convention ought at a proper time, or times, after the approbation of Congress to be submitted to an assembly or assemblies of representatives, recommended by the several legislatures to be expressly chosen by the people, to consider and decide thereon.

B. DEBATE OF MAY 31

The third resolution "that the National Legislature ought to consist of two branches" was agreed to without debate or dissent, except that of Pennsylvania. . . .

Resolution 4, first clause, "that the members of the first branch of the National Legislature ought to be elected by the people of the several states," being taken up,

MR. SHERMAN[5] opposed the election by the people, insisting that it ought to be by the state legislatures. The people, he said, immediately should have as little to do as may be about the government. They want information and are constantly liable to be misled.

MR. GERRY.[6] The evils we experience flow from the excess of democracy. The people do not want virtue but are the dupes of pretended patriots. . . . He had, he said, been too republican heretofore; he was still, however, republican, but had been taught by experience the danger of the leveling spirit.

MR. MASON[7] argued strongly for an election of the larger branch by the people. It was to be the grand depository of the democratic principle of the government. . . . It ought to know and sympathize with every part of the community; and ought therefore to be taken not only from different parts of the whole republic but also from different districts of the larger members of it, which had . . . different interests and views arising from difference of produce, of habits, etc. He admitted that we had been too democratic but was afraid we should run in-

cautiously into the opposite extreme. We ought to attend to the rights of every class of the people. He had often wondered at the indifference of the superior classes of society to this dictate of humanity and policy, considering that . . . the course of a few years . . . certainly would distribute their posterity throughout the lowest classes of society. . . .

MR. WILSON[8] contended strenuously for drawing the most numerous branch of the Legislature immediately from the people. He was for raising the Federal pyramid to a considerable altitude and for that reason wished to give it as broad a basis as possible. No government could long subsist without the confidence of the people. . . . He also thought it wrong to increase the weight of the state legislatures by making them electors of the National Legislature. . . .

MR. MADISON[9] considered the popular election of one branch of the National Legislature as essential to every plan of free government. . . . He was an advocate for the policy of refining the popular appointments by successive filtrations but thought it might be pushed too far. He wished the expedient to be resorted to only in the appointment of the second branch of the Legislature and in the executive and judiciary branches. . . .

MR. GERRY did not like the election by the people. . . . He had no objection, however, to an election by the people if it were so qualified that men of honor and character might not be unwilling to be joined in the appointments. He seemed to think the people might nom-

5. Roger Sherman (1721–93), Connecticut; surveyor, merchant, shoemaker, lawyer, judge; signer of all three documents—the Declaration, the Articles, and the Constitution; later member of the House of Representatives and of the Senate. In this, and succeeding biographical notes to the Convention debates, "later" means "after 1787."

6. Elbridge Gerry (1744–1814), Massachusetts; educated at Harvard; merchant; Massachusetts legislature, Continental and Confederation congresses; and later in the House of Representatives; special envoy to France (with C. C. Pinckney and John Marshall); governor of Massachusetts; Vice-President of the United States (1813–14); gave his name to "gerrymander."

7. George Mason (1725–92), Virginia; planter; neighbor and friend of Washington; leader in drafting the Virginia Declaration of Rights of 1776 and in determining Virginia's western land policy; though a leader in the Convention, Mason refused to sign the completed Constitution and opposed its ratification in the Virginia Convention of 1788.

8. James Wilson (1742–98), Pennsylvania; educated at Glasgow and Edinburgh; lawyer, businessman, and judge; signer of the Declaration; one of the ablest thinkers in the Convention; later a member of the United States Supreme Court.

9. James Madison (1750–1836), Virginia; Princeton; lawyer and planter; Virginia legislature and Confederation Congress; "father of the Constitution"; later Jefferson's lieutenant in the Republican party; secretary of state; President (1809–17); author of the most complete notes on the Federal Convention.

inate a certain number out of which the state legislatures should be bound to choose.

Mr. Butler[10] thought an election by the people an impracticable mode. . . . [Popular election was voted, 6 for, 2 against, 2 divided. The remaining clauses of the fourth resolution were then postponed. Debate on the fifth resolution followed, and the resolution was voted down, 3 for, 7 against. The first two clauses of Resolution 6 were then adopted.]

The other clauses giving powers necessary to preserve harmony among the states to negative all state laws contravening in the opinion of the National Legislature the Articles of Union, down to the last clause (the words "or any treaties subsisting under the authority of the Union" being added after the words "contravening, etc., the Articles of the Union," on motion of Dr. Franklin),

were agreed to without debate or dissent.

The last clause of Resolution 6 authorizing an exertion of the force of the whole against a delinquent state came next into consideration.

Mr. Madison observed that the more he reflected on the use of force, the more he doubted the practicability, the justice, and the efficacy of it when applied to people collectively and not individually. A union of the states containing such an ingredient seemed to provide for its own destruction. The use of force against a state would look more like a declaration of war than an infliction of punishment and would probably be considered by the party attacked as a dissolution of all previous compacts by which it might be bound. He hoped that such a system would be framed as might render this recourse unnecessary and moved that the clause be postponed. This motion was agreed to *nem. con.*[11]

C. DEBATE OF JUNE 6 (MADISON)

Mr. Pinckney,[12] according to previous notice and rule obtained, moved that "the first branch of the national Legislature be elected by the state legislatures, and not by the people," contending that the people were less fit judges in such a case, and that the legislatures would be less likely to promote the adop-

tion of the new government if they were to be excluded from all share in it.

Mr. Rutledge[13] seconded the motion.

Mr. Gerry. Much depends on the mode of election. In England the people will probably lose their liberty from the smallness of the proportion having a right of suffrage. Our danger arises from the opposite extreme; hence in Massachusetts the worst men get into the legislature. Several members of that body had lately been convicted of infamous crimes. Men of indigence, ignorance, and baseness spare no pains, however dirty, to carry their point against men who are superior to the artifices practiced. He was not disposed to run into extremes. He was as much principled as ever against aristocracy and monarchy. It

10. Pierce Butler (1744–1822), South Carolina; former officer of the British army; adjutant-general of South Carolina; later a member of the United States Senate (1789–96, 1802–6).

11. "No one contradicting" (unanimously).

12. In Madison's notes "General Pinkney" (as Madison wrote it) refers to Charles Cotesworth Pinckney (1746–1825), South Carolina; Oxford, law study in Middle Temple at London, Military Academy at Caen; lawyer; American officer in the Revolution; later minister and special envoy to France; Federalist candidate for Vice-President (1800), and for President (1804, 1808). His younger cousin (referred to as "Mr. Pinkney"), Charles Pinckney (1757–1824), South Carolina; planter and lawyer; American officer in the Revolution; state legislature and Confederation Congress; later governor of South Carolina; member of both houses of Congress; minister to Spain.

13. John Rutledge (1739–1800), South Carolina; law study in Middle Temple; lawyer, attorney-general, and president of South Carolina; member of Continental and Confederation congresses; later appointed second chief justice of the United States Supreme Court but did not serve.

was necessary, on the one hand, that people should appoint one branch of the government in order to inspire them with the necessary confidence. But he wished the election, on the other, to be so modified as to secure more effectually a just preference of merit. His idea was that people should nominate certain persons in certain districts, out of whom the state legislatures should make the appointment.

MR. WILSON. He wished for vigor in the government, but he wished that vigorous authority to flow immediately from the legitimate source of all authority. The government ought to possess not only, first, the *force* but, secondly, the *mind or sense* of the people at large. The legislature ought to be the most exact transcript of the whole society. Representation is made necessary only because it is impossible for the people to act collectively. The opposition was to be expected, he said, from the *governments*, not from the citizens of the states. The latter had parted as was observed (by MR. KING)[14] with all the necessary powers; and it was immaterial to them, by whom they were exercised, if well exercised. The state officers were to be the losers of power. The people, he supposed, would be rather more attached to the national government than to the state governments as being more important in itself and more flattering to their pride. There is no danger of improper elections if made by *large* districts. Bad elections proceed from the smallness of the districts which give an opportunity to bad men to intrigue themselves into office.

MR. SHERMAN. If it were in view to abolish the state governments, the elections ought to be by the people. If the state governments are to be continued, it is necessary, in order to preserve harmony between the national and state governments, that the elections to the former should be made by the latter. The right of participating in the national government would be sufficiently secured to the people by their election of the state legislatures. The objects of the Union, he thought were few: (1) defense against foreign danger; (2) against internal disputes and a resort to force; (3) treaties with foreign nations; (4) regulating foreign commerce and drawing revenue from it. These, and perhaps a few lesser objects, alone rendered a confederation of the states necessary. All other matters, civil and criminal, would be much better in the hands of the states. The people are more happy in small than large states. States may indeed be too small, as Rhode Island, and thereby be too subject to faction. Some others were perhaps too large, the powers of government not being able to pervade them. He was for giving the general government power to legislate and execute within a defined province.

COL. MASON. Under the existing Confederacy, Congress represents the *states*, not the *people* of the states; their acts operate on the *states*, not on the individuals. The case will be changed in the new plan of government. The people will be represented; they ought therefore to choose the representatives. The requisites in actual representation are that the representatives should sympathize with their constituents, should think as they think and feel as they feel, and that, for these purposes, should even be residents among them. Much, he said, had been alleged against democratic elections. He admitted that much might be said; but it was to be considered that no government was free from imperfections and evils and that improper elections, in many instances, were inseparable from republican governments. But compare these with the advantage of this form in

14. Rufus King (1755–1827), Massachusetts; Harvard; businessman and lawyer; soldier of Revolution; Massachusetts legislature and Confederation Congress; later minister to Great Britain; Federalist candidate for Vice-President (1804, 1808) and for President (1816); served in the United States Senate.

favor of the rights of the people, in favor of human nature. He was persuaded there was a better chance for proper elections by the people, if divided into large districts, than by the state legislatures. Paper money had been issued by the latter when the former were against it. Was it to be supposed that the state legislatures then would not send to the National Legislature patrons of such projects if the choice depended on them?

MR. MADISON considered an election of one branch at least of the legislature by the people immediately as a clear principle of free government and that this, made under proper regulations, had the additional advantage of securing better representatives as well as of avoiding too great an agency of the state governments in the general one. He differed from the member from Connecticut (MR. SHERMAN) in thinking the objects mentioned to be all the principal ones that required a National Government. Those were certainly important and necessary objects; but he combined with them the necessity of providing more effectually for the security of private rights and the steady dispensation of justice. Interferences with these were evils which had more, perhaps, than anything else produced this convention. Was it to be supposed that republican liberty could long exist under the abuses of it practiced in some of the states? The gentleman (MR. SHERMAN) had admitted that, in a very small state, faction and oppression would prevail. It was to be inferred then that, wherever these prevailed, the state was too small. Had they not prevailed in the largest as well as the smallest though less than in the smallest; and were we not thence admonished to enlarge the sphere as far as the nature of the government would admit? This was the only defense against the inconveniencies of democracy consistent with the democratic form of government. All civilized societies would be divided into different sects, factions, and interests, as they happened to consist of rich and poor, debtors and creditors, the landed, the manufacturing, the commercial interests, the inhabitants of this district or that district, the followers of this political leader or that political leader, the disciples of this religious sect or that religious sect. In all cases where a majority are united by a common interest of passion, the rights of the minority are in danger. What motives are to restrain them? A prudent regard to the maxim that honesty is the best policy is found by experience to be as little regarded by bodies of men as by individuals. Respect for character is always diminished in proportion to the number among whom the blame or praise is to be divided. Conscience, the only remaining tie, is known to be inadequate in individuals; in large numbers, little is to be expected from it. Besides, religion itself may become a motive to persecution and oppression. These observations are verified by the histories of every country, ancient and modern. In Greece and Rome the rich and poor, the creditors and debtors, as well as the patricians and plebians, alternately oppressed each other with equal unmercifulness. What a source of oppression was the relation between the parent-cities of Rome, Athens, and Carthage and their respective provinces; the former possessing the power, and the latter being sufficiently distinguished to be separate objects of it? Why was America so justly apprehensive of parliamentary injustice? Because Great Britain had a separate interest, real or supposed, and, if her authority had been admitted, could have pursued that interest at our expense. We have seen the mere distinction of color made in the most enlightened period of time, a ground of the most oppressive dominion ever exercised by man over man. What has been the source of those unjust laws complained of among ourselves? Has it not been the real or supposed interest of the major number? Debtors have defrauded their creditors. The landed interest has borne hard on the mercantile interest. The holders of one species of property have thrown a disproportion of taxes on the holders of another species. The lesson we are to draw from the whole is that where a majority are united by a common sentiment, and have an opportunity, the rights of the minor party become insecure. In a republican government the majority, if united, have always an opportunity. The only remedy is to enlarge the sphere and thereby divide the community into so great a number of interests and parties that, in the first place, a majority will not be likely at the same moment to have a common interest separate from that of the whole or of the minority; and, in the second place, that, in case they should have such an interest, they may not be apt to unite in the pursuit of it. It was incumbent on us then to try this remedy, and with that view to frame a republican system on such a scale and in such a form as will control all the evils which have been experienced.

MR. DICKINSON[15] considered it as essential that one branch of the legislature should be drawn immediately from the people and as expedient that the other should be chosen by the legislatures of the states. This combination of the state governments with the National Government was as politic as it was unavoidable. In the formation of the Senate we ought to carry it through such a refining process as will assimilate it as near as may be to the House of Lords in England. He repeated his warm eulogiums on the British constitution. He was for a strong National Government but for leaving the states a considerable agency in the system. The objection against making the former dependent on the latter might

be obviated by giving to the Senate an authority permanent and irrevocable for three, five, or seven years. Being thus independent, they would speak and decide with becoming freedom.

MR. READ.[16] Too much attachment is betrayed to the state governments. We must look beyond their continuance. A National Government must soon of necessity swallow all of them up. They will soon be reduced to the mere office of electing the National Senate. He was against patching up the old federal system; he hoped the idea would be dismissed. It would be like putting new cloth on an old garment. The Confederation was founded on temporary principles. It cannot last; it cannot be amended. If we do not establish a good government on new principles, we must either go to ruin or have the work to do over again. The people at large are wrongly suspected of being averse to a General Government. The aversion lies among interested men who possess their confidence.

MR. PIERCE[17] was for an election by the people as to the first branch and by the states as to the second branch, by which means the citizens of the states would be represented both *individually* and *collectively*.

GENERAL PINCKNEY wished to have a good National Government and at the same time to leave a considerable share of power in the states. An election of either branch by the people scattered as they are in many states, particularly in South Carolina, was totally impracticable. He differed from gentlemen who thought that a choice by the people

15. John Dickinson (1732–1808), Delaware; law in Middle Temple; lawyer; Delaware and Pennsylvania assemblies, Stamp Act Congress, both Continental congresses; signer of the Articles of Confederation; Annapolis Convention.

16. George Read (1733–98); Delaware; lawyer and judge; Delaware legislature, both Continental congresses, signer of the Declaration; Annapolis Convention; later served in the United States Senate.

17. William Leigh Pierce (1740–89), Georgia, businessman; American officer in the Revolution; Confederation Congress; remembered for character sketches of delegates to the Federal Convention.

would be a better guard against bad measures than by the legislatures. A majority of the people in South Carolina were notoriously for paper money as a legal tender; the legislature had refused to make it a legal tender. The reason was that the latter had some sense of character and were restrained by that consideration. The state legislatures also, he said, would be more jealous, and more ready to thwart the National Government, if excluded from a participation in it. The idea of abolishing these legislatures would never go down.

Mr. WILSON would not have spoken again but for what had fallen from Mr. Read; namely, that the idea of preserving the state governments ought to be abandoned. He saw no incompatibility between the National and state governments, provided the latter were restrained to certain local purposes; nor any probability of their being devoured by the former. In all confederated systems, ancient and modern, the reverse had happened; the generality being destroyed gradually by the usurpations of the parts composing it.

On the question for electing the first branch by the state legislatures as moved by Mr. PINCKNEY: it was negatived: [3 for, 8 against].

Mr. WILSON moved to reconsider the vote excluding the judiciary from a share in the revision of the laws and to add after "National Executive" the words "with a convenient number of the national Judiciary"; remarking the expediency of reinforcing the Executive with the influence of that Department.

Mr. MADISON seconded the motion. He observed that the great difficulty in rendering the Executive competent to its own defense arose from the nature of republican government, which would not give to an individual citizen that settled pre-eminence in the eyes of the rest, that weight of property, that personal interest against betraying the na-

tional interest, which appertain to an hereditary magistrate. In a republic personal merit alone could be the ground of political exaltation, but it would rarely happen that this merit would be so pre-eminent as to produce universal acquiescence. The Executive Magistrate would be envied and assailed by disappointed competitors; his firmness therefore would need support. He would not possess those great emoluments from his station, nor that permanent stake in the public interest which would place him out of the reach of foreign corruption. He would stand in need, therefore, of being controlled as well as supported. An association of the judges in his revisionary function would both double the advantage and diminish the danger. It would also enable the Judiciary Department the better to defend itself against Legislative encroachments. Two objections had been made: first, that the judges ought not to be subject to the bias which a participation in the making of laws might give in the exposition of them; secondly, that the Judiciary Department ought to be separate and distinct from the other great departments. The first objection had some weight; but it was much diminished by reflecting that a small proportion of the laws coming in question before a judge would be such wherein he had been consulted; that a small part of this proportion would be so ambiguous as to leave room for his prepossessions; and that but a few cases would probably arise in the life of a judge under such ambiguous passages. How much good, on the other hand, would proceed from the perspicuity, the conciseness, and the systematic character which the code of laws would receive from the Judiciary talents. As to the second objection, it either had no weight, or it applied with equal weight to the Executive and to the Judiciary revision of the laws. The maxim on which the objection was founded required a separation of the Executive as well as of the Judiciary from the Legislature and from each other. There would in truth, however, be no improper mixture of these distinct powers in the present case. In England, whence the maxim itself had been drawn, the Executive had an absolute negative on the laws; and the supreme tribunal of Justice (the House of Lords) formed one of the other branches of the legislature. In short, whether the object of the revisionary power was to restrain the legislature from encroaching on the other co-ordinate departments, or on the rights of the people at large, or from passing laws unwise in their principle, or incorrect in their form, the utility of annexing the wisdom and weight of the Judiciary to the Executive seemed incontestable.

Mr. Gerry thought the Executive, whilst standing alone, would be more impartial than when they could be covered by the sanction and seduced by the sophistry of the judges.

Mr. King. If the unity of the executive was preferred for the sake of responsibility, the policy of it is as applicable to the revisionary as to the Executive power.

Mr. Pinckney had been at first in favor of joining the heads of the principal departments, the Secretary of War, of foreign affairs, [etc.], in the Council of Revision. He had, however, relinquished the idea from a consideration that these could be called in by the Executive Magistrate whenever he pleased to consult them. He was opposed to an introduction of the judges into the business.

Col. Mason was for giving all possible weight to the revisionary institution. The Executive power ought to be well secured against Legislative usurpations on it. The purse and the sword ought never to get into the same hands, whether Legislative or Executive.

Mr. Dickinson. Secrecy, vigor, and dispatch are not the principal properties required in the Executive. Important as these are, that of responsibility is more so, which can only be preserved by leaving it singly to discharge its functions. He thought, too, a junction of the judiciary to it involved an improper mixture of powers.

Mr. Wilson remarked that the responsibility required belonged to his Executive duties. The revisionary duty was an extraneous one, calculated for collateral purposes. . . .

D. DEBATE OF JUNE 6 (HAMILTON)

I—Human mind fond of compromise— Madison's theory—

I. That they have such extent as to render combinations on the ground of interest difficult—

II. By a process of election calculated to refine the representation of the people—

Answer—There is truth in both these principles but they do not conclude so strongly as he supposes—

—The Assembly when chosen will meet in one room if they are drawn from half the globe—and will be liable to all the passions of popular assemblies.

If more *minute links* are wanting, others will supply them—Distinction of eastern, middle, and southern states will come into view; between commercial and noncommercial states—imaginary lines will influence, etc. Human mind prone to limit its view by near and local objects—

Paper money is capable of giving a general impulse—It is easy to conceive a popular sentiment pervading the eastern states—

Observation: large districts less liable to be influenced by factious demagogues than small—

Note—This is in some degree true but not so generally as may be supposed—Frequently small portions of the large districts carry elections—An influential demogogue will give an impulse to the whole—Demagogues are not always *inconsiderable* persons—Patricians were frequently demagogues—Characters are less known and a less active interest taken in them—

E. THE NEW JERSEY (PATERSON) PLAN[18]

1. *Resolved*, That the Articles of Confederation ought to be so revised, corrected, and enlarged as to render the federal Constitution adequate to the exigencies of government and the preservation of the Union.

2. *Resolved*, That in addition to the powers vested in the United States in Congress, by the present existing Articles of Confederation, they be authorized to pass acts for raising a revenue, by levying a duty or duties on all goods or merchandises of foreign growth or manufacture, imported into any part of the United States, by stamps on paper, vellum or parchment, and by a postage on all letters or packages passing through the general post office, to be applied to such federal purposes as they shall deem proper and expedient; to make rules and regulations for the collection thereof; and the same from time to time, to alter and amend in such manner as they shall think proper; to pass acts for the regulation of trade and commerce as well with foreign nations as with each other; provided that all punishments, fines, forfeitures, and penalties to be incurred for contravening such Acts, rules, and regulation shall be adjudged by the common-law judiciaries of the state in which any offense contrary to the true intent and meaning of such acts, rules, and regulations shall have been committed or perpetrated, with liberty of commencing in the first instance all suits and prosecutions for that purpose in the superior common-law judiciary in such state, subject nevertheless, for the correction of all errors, both in law and fact, in

rendering judgment, to an appeal to the Judiciary of the United States.

3. *Resolved*, That whenever requisitions shall be necessary, instead of the rule for making requisitions mentioned in the Articles of Confederation, the United States in Congress be authorized to make such requisitions in proportion to the whole number of white and other free citizens and inhabitants of every age, sex, and condition including those bound to servitude for a term of years and three-fifths of all other persons not comprehended in the foregoing description, except Indians not paying taxes; that if such requisitions be not complied with, in the time specified therein, to direct the collection thereof in the non-complying states and for that purpose to devise and pass acts directing and authorizing the same; provided that none of the powers hereby vested in the United States in Congress shall be exercised without the consent of at least ____ states, and in that proportion if the number of confederated states should hereafter be increased or diminished.

4. *Resolved*, That the United States in Congress be authorized to elect a federal Executive to consist of ____ persons, to continue in office for the term of ____ years, to receive punctually at stated times a fixed compensation for their services, in which no increase or diminution shall be made so as to affect the persons composing the Executive at the time of such increase or diminution, to be paid out of the federal treasury; to be incapable of holding any other office or appointment during their time of service and for ____ years thereafter; to be ineligible a second time, and removable by Congress on application by

18. Presented by William Paterson of New Jersey on June 15. Probably Paterson, Roger Sherman, and Luther Martin were the chief authors.

a majority of the executives of the several states; that the executives, besides their general authority to execute the federal acts, ought to appoint all federal officers not otherwise provided for and to direct all military operations, provided that none of the persons composing the federal Executive shall on any occasion take command of any troops so as personally to conduct any enterprise as general or in other capacity.

5. *Resolved*, That a federal Judiciary be established to consist of a supreme tribunal the judges of which to be appointed by the Executive and to hold their offices during good behavior, to receive punctually at stated times a fixed compensation for their services in which no increase or diminution shall be made so as to affect the persons actually in office at the time of such increase or diminution; that the Judiciary so established shall have authority to hear and determine in the first instance on all impeachments of federal officers, and by way of appeal in the dernier resort in all cases touching the rights of ambassadors, in all cases of captures from an enemy, in all cases of piracies and felonies on the high seas, in all cases in which foreigners may be interested, in the construction of any treaty or treaties, or which may arise on any of the Acts for regulation of trade, or the collection of the federal revenue; that none of the Judiciary shall during the time they remain in office be capable of receiving or holding any other office or appointment

during their time of service or for thereafter.

6. *Resolved*, That all acts of the United States in Congress made by virtue and in pursuance of the powers hereby and by the Articles of Confederation vested in them, and all treaties made and ratified under the authority of the United States, shall be the supreme law of the respective states so far forth as those acts or treaties shall relate to the said states or their citizens, and that the judiciary of the several states shall be bound thereby in their decisions, anything in the respective laws of the individual states to the contrary notwithstanding; and that if any state, or any body of men in any state, shall oppose or prevent the carrying into execution such acts or treaties, the federal Executive shall be authorized to call forth the power of the confederated states, or so much thereof as may be necessary to enforce and compel an obedience to such acts or an observance of such treaties.

7. *Resolved*, That provision be made for the admission of new states into the Union.

8. *Resolved*, That the rule for naturalization ought to be the same in every state.

9. *Resolved*, That a citizen of one state committing an offense in another state of the Union shall be deemed guilty of the same offense as if it had been committed by a citizen of the state in which the offense was committed.

F. DEBATES ON THE VIRGINIA AND NEW JERSEY PLANS; HAMILTON'S PLAN: JUNE 16, 18, 19

June 16. MR. PATERSON[19] [commenting on his small states plan] ... preferred it because it accorded (1) with the powers of the Convention, (2) with the sen-

19. William Patterson (1745–1806), New Jersey; Princeton; lawyer; New Jersey Convention; attorney-general of New Jersey; Continental Congress; later governor of New Jersey; associate justice of the United States Supreme Court (1793–1806).

timents of the people. If the confederacy was radically wrong, let us return to our states and obtain larger powers, not assume them of ourselves. ... If the sovereignty of the states is to be maintained, the representatives must be drawn immediately from the states, not from the people; and we have no power to vary the idea of equal sovereignty.

The only expedient that will cure the difficulty is that of throwing the states into hotchpot. . . . It will be objected that coercion will be impracticable. But will it be more so in one plan than the other? Its efficacy will depend on the quantum of power collected, not on its being drawn from the states or from the individuals; and according to his plan it may be exerted on individuals as well as according [to] that of Mr. Randolph. . . . The plan of Mr. Randolph will also be enormously expensive. . . . You have 270 members coming once at least a year from the most distant . . . parts of the Republic. In the present deranged state of our finances can so expensive a system be seriously thought of? By enlarging the powers of Congress the greatest part of this expense will be saved, and all purposes will be answered. At least a trial ought to be made.

Mr. Wilson . . . could not persuade himself that the state government and sovereignties were so much the idols of the people, nor a National Government so obnoxious to them, as some supposed. Why should a National Government be unpopular? Has it less dignity? Will each citizen enjoy under it less liberty or protection? Will a citizen of *Delaware* be degraded by becoming a citizen of the *United States?* . . .

Mr. Randolph[20] was not scrupulous on the point of power. When the salvation of the Republic was at stake, it would be treason to our trust not to propose what we found necessary. . . . The true question is whether we shall adhere to the federal plan or introduce the national plan. The insufficiency of the former has been fully displayed by the trial already made. There are but two modes, by which the end of a general government can be attained: the 1st is by coercion as proposed by Mr. Pater-

son's plan; [the] 2[d] by real legislation as proposed by the other plan. Coercion he pronounced to be *impracticable, expensive, cruel to individuals.* . . . We must resort therefore to a national *legislation over individuals.* . . .

June 18. Mr. Hamilton . . . was particularly opposed to that [plan] from New Jersey, being fully convinced that no amendment of the Confederation, leaving the states in possession of their sovereignty, could possibly answer the purpose. . . . The great and essential principles necessary for the support of government are (1) an active and constant interest in supporting it. . . . (2) the love of power. Men love power. . . . (3) a habitual attachment of the people. . . . (4) *Force* . . . of *laws* or . . . of *arms.* . . . (5) *influence.* . . . All the passions then we see . . . which govern most individual and all public bodies, fall into the current of the states and do not flow in the stream of the General Government . . . and render any confederacy in its very nature precarious. . . . How are all these evils to be avoided? Only by such a complete sovereignty in the General Government as will turn all the strong principles and passions above mentioned on its side. . . . The general power . . . must swallow up the state powers. Otherwise it will be swallowed up by them. . . . Two sovereignties cannot coexist within the same limits. . . . In his private opinion he had no scruple in declaring, supported as he was by the opinions of so many of the wise and good, that the British government was the best in the world and that he doubted much whether anything short of it would do in America. . . . It was once thought that the power of Congress was amply sufficient to secure the end of their institution. The error was now seen by everyone. . . . In every community where industry is encouraged, there will be a division of it into the few and the many. . . . Give all power to the many; they will oppress the few. Give all power to the few; they will oppress the many. Both therefore ought to

20. Edmund Randoph (1753–1813), Virginia; William and Mary; lawyer; attorney-general and governor of Virginia; Continental Congress and Annapolis Convention; later a member of Washington's cabinet.

have power that each may defend itself against the other. . . . We ought to go as far in order to obtain stability and permanency as republican principles will admit. Let one branch of the legislature hold their places for life or at least during good behavior. Let the Executive also be for life. . . .

June 19. MR. MADISON. . . . The great difficulty lies in the affair of representation; and if this could be adjusted, all others would be surmountable. It was admitted by both the gentlemen from New Jersey . . . that it would not be *just to allow Virginia,* which was sixteen times as large as Delaware, an equal vote only. Their language was that it would not be *safe for Delaware* to allow Virginia sixteen times as many votes. . . .

MR. WILSON observed that by a National Government he did not mean one that would swallow up the state governments as seemed to be wished by some gentlemen. He was tenacious of the idea of preserving the latter. He thought, contrary to the opinion of the former speaker (COL. HAMILTON), that they might not only subsist but subsist on friendly terms with the former. They were absolutely necessary for certain purposes which the former could not reach.

COL. HAMILTON. . . . He had not been understood yesterday. By abolition of the states, he meant that no boundary could be drawn between the national and state legislatures; that the former must therefore have indefinite authority. . . . As *states,* he thought they ought to be abolished. But he admitted the necessity of leaving in them subordinate jurisdictions.

MR. KING wished, as everything depended on this proposition, that no objection might be improperly indulged against the phraseology of it. . . . The states were not "sovereigns" in the sense contended for by some. They did not possess the peculiar features of sovereignty; they could not make war, nor peace, nor alliances, nor treaties. Considering them as political beings, they were dumb, for they could not speak to any foreign sovereign whatever. They were deaf, for they could not hear any propositions from such sovereign. They had not even the organs or faculties of defense or offense, for they could not of themselves raise troops, or equip vessels, for war. On the other side . . . Congress can act alone without the states —they can act, and their acts will be binding against the instructions of the states. If they declare war, war is *de jure* declared, captures made in pursuance of it are lawful. . . . If the states therefore retained some portion of their sovereignty, they had certainly divested themselves of essential portions of it. If they formed a confederacy in some respects —they formed a nation in others. . . . He doubted much the practicability of annihilating the states but thought that much of their power ought to be taken from them.

MR. MARTIN[21] said he considered that the separation from Great Britain placed the thirteen states in a state of nature toward each other; that they would have remained in that state till this time but for the Confederation; that they entered into the Confederation on the footing of equality; that they met now to amend it on the same footing; and that he could never accede to a plan that would introduce an inequality and lay ten states at the mercy of Virginia, Massachusetts, and Pennsylvania.

MR. WILSON could not admit the doctrine that, when the Colonies became independent of Great Britain, they became independent also of each other. He read the Declaration of Independence, observing thereon that the *United Colonies* were declared to be free and independent states and inferring that they were independent, not *individually* but *unitedly,* and that they were confederated, as they were independent, states. . . .

21. Luther Martin (1748–1826), Maryland; Princeton; lawyer; attorney-general of Maryland; one of the lawyers in the trial of Aaron Burr and in the case of *McCulloch* v. *Maryland.*

G. PROPERTY, SECTIONALISM, AND SUFFRAGE

On the motion of Mr. Randolph, the vote of Saturday[22] last authorizing the legislature to adjust from time to time the representation upon the principles of wealth and numbers of inhabitants, was reconsidered by common consent in order to strike out "wealth" and adjust the resolution to that requiring periodical revisions, according to the number of whites and three-fifths of the blacks. The motion was in the words following—"But as the present situation of the states may probably alter in the number of their inhabitants, that the legislature of the U.S. be authorized from time to time to apportion the number of representatives; and in case any of the states shall hereafter be divided, or any two or more states united, or new states created within the limits of the U.S., the legislature of U.S. shall possess authority to regulate the number of representatives in any of the foregoing cases upon the principle of their number of inhabitants, according to the provisions hereafter mentioned."

Mr. Gouverneur Morris opposed the alteration as leaving still an incoherence. If Negroes were to be viewed as inhabitants and the revision was to proceed on the principle of numbers of inhabitants, they ought to be added in their entire number and not in the proportion of three-fifths. If as property, the word "wealth" was right, and striking it out would produce the very inconsistency which it was meant to get rid of.—The train of business and the late turn which it had taken had led him, he said, into deep meditation on it, and he would candidly state the result. A distinction had been set up and urged between the northern and southern states. He had hitherto considered this doctrine as heretical. He still thought the distinction groundless. He sees, however, that it is persisted in, and that southern gentlemen will not be satisfied unless they see the way open to their gaining a majority in the public councils. The consequence of such a transfer of power from the maritime to the interior and landed interest will, he foresees, be such an oppression of commerce that he shall be obliged to vote for the vicious principle of equality in the second branch in order to provide some defense for the northern states against it. But to come more to the point; either this distinction is fictitious or real; if fictitious, let it be dismissed and let us proceed with due confidence. If it be real, instead of attempting to blend incompatible things, let us at once take a friendly leave of each other. There can be no end of demands for security if every particular interest is to be entitled to it. The eastern states may claim it for their fishery, and for other objects, as the southern states claim it for their peculiar objects. In this struggle between the two ends of the Union, what part ought the middle states in point of policy to take: to join their eastern brethren according to his ideas. If the southern states get the power into their hands, and be joined as they will be with the interior country, they will inevitably bring on a war with Spain for the Mississippi. This language is already held. The interior country, having no property nor interest exposed on the sea, will be little affected by such a war. He wished to know what security the northern and middle states will have against this danger. It has been said that N.C., S.C., and Georgia only will in a little time have a majority of the people of America. They must in that case include the great interior country, and everything was to be apprehended from their getting the power into their hands.

Mr. Butler. The security the south-

22. On the night before this debate the weather turned cool, after more than a week's "heat wave." Apparently temper followed the weather, for, three days later, the "Great Compromise" of the Convention was adopted.

ern states want is that their Negroes may not be taken from them, which some gentlemen within or without doors have a very good mind to do. It was not supposed that N.C., S.C., and Georgia would have more people than all the other states, but many more relatively to the other states than they now have. The people and strength of America are evidently bearing southwardly and southwestwardly.

Mr. Wilson. If a general declaration would satisfy any gentleman, he had no indisposition to declare his sentiments. Conceiving that all men wherever placed have equal rights and are equally entitled to confidence, he viewed without apprehension the period when a few states should contain the superior number of people. The majority of people wherever found ought in all questions to govern the minority. If the interior country should acquire this majority, it will not only have the right but will avail themselves of it whether we will or no. This jealousy misled the policy of Great Britain with regard to America. The fatal maxims espoused by her were that the colonies were growing too fast, and their growth must be stinted in time. What were the consequences? First. Enmity on our part, then actual separation. Like consequences will result on the part of the interior settlements if like jealousy and policy be pursued on ours. Further, if numbers be not a proper rule, why is not some better rule pointed out? No one has yet ventured to attempt it. Congresses have never been able to discover a better. No state, as far as he had heard, has suggested any other. In 1783, after elaborate discussion of a measure of wealth, all were satisfied then as they are now that the rule of numbers does not differ much from the combined rule of numbers and wealth. Again he could not agree that property was the sole or the primary object of government and society. The cultivation and improvement of the human mind was the most noble object. With respect to this object, as well as to other personal rights, numbers were surely the natural and precise measure of representation. And with respect to property, they could not vary much from the precise measure. In no point of view, however, could the establishment of numbers as the rule of representation in the first branch vary his opinion as to the impropriety of letting a vicious principle into the second branch.—On the question to strike out wealth, and to make the change as moved by Mr. Randolph, it passed in the affirmative—[10 for, 0 against, 1 divided].

H. DEBATE OF AUGUST 7[23]

Mr. Wilson ... did not think it [the Report] could be changed for the better....

Mr. Ellsworth[24] thought ... the states are the best judges of the circumstances and temper of their own people....

Mr. Dickinson ... considered them [freeholders] as the best guardians of liberty; and the restriction of the right to them as a necessary defense against the dangerous influence of those multitudes without property and without principle with which our country, like all others, will in time abound. ... The great mass of our citizens is composed at this time of freeholders and will be pleased with it. ...

23. By this date, August 7, the provision had been made that members of the House of Representatives should be elected by the people who met the requirements set by each state for the election of its lower house. Gouverneur Morris moved to strike out the latter part of the clause to allow an amendment to restrict suffrage to freeholders, i.e., to landowners.

24. Oliver Ellsworth (1745–1807), Connecticut; Yale and Princeton; lawyer, judge; Continental and Confederation congresses; United States Senate; chief author of Judiciary Act of 1789; third chief justice of the United States Supreme Court; special commissioner to France.

MR. GOUVERNEUR MORRIS.[25] He had long learned not to be the dupe of words. The sound of aristocracy, therefore, had no effect on him. It was the thing, not the name, to which he was opposed, and one of his principal objections to the Constitution, as it is now before us, is that it threatens this country with an aristocracy. The aristocracy will grow out of the House of Representatives. Give the votes to people who have no property, and they will sell them to the rich who will be able to buy them. . . . The time is not distant when this country will abound with mechanics and manufacturers who will receive their bread from their employers. Will such men be the secure and faithful guardians of liberty? . . . The man who does not give his vote freely is not represented. It is the man who dictates the vote. . . . Nine-tenths of the people are at present freeholders. . . . As to merchants, etc., if they have wealth and value the right, they can acquire it. If not, they don't deserve it.

COL. MASON. We all feel too strongly the remains of ancient prejudices. . . . The true idea, in his opinion, was that every man having evidence of attachment to and permanent common interest with the society ought to share in all its rights and privileges. . . . Does no other kind of property but land evidence a common interest in the proprietor? Does nothing besides property mark a permanent attachment?

MR. MADISON. The right of suffrage is certainly one of the fundamental articles of republican government and ought not to be regulated by the legislature. . . . Viewing the subject on its merits alone, the freeholders of the country would be the safest depositories of republican liberty. In future times a great majority of the people will not only be without landed, but any other sort of, property. These will either combine under the influence of their common situation; in which case, the rights of property and the public liberty, will not be secure in their hands; or which is more probable, they will become the tools of opulence and ambition, in which case there will be equal danger on another side. . . . [After a few more remarks Morris' motion was beaten, 7 noes, 1 aye, 1 divided, 1 not present.]

I. THE CLOSING DAY, SEPTEMBER 17

DR. FRANKLIN rose with a speech in his hand, which he had reduced to writing for his own convenience, and which MR. WILSON read in the words following:

Mr. President, I confess that there are several parts of this Constitution which I do not at present approve, but I am not sure I shall never approve them. For having lived long, I have experienced many instances of being obliged by better information, or fuller consideration, to change opinions even on important

25. Gouverneur Morris (1752–1816), Pennsylvania; Columbia; lawyer, merchant, financier; New York Convention, Continental Congress; signer of the Articles of Confederation; either alone, or with James Wilson, the author of the final draft of the Constitution; later minister to France; United States Senate.

subjects, which I once thought right but found to be otherwise. It is therefore that, the older I grow, the more apt I am to doubt my own judgment and to pay more respect to the judgment of others. Most men indeed, as well as most sects in religion, think themselves in possession of all truth, and that wherever others differ from them it is so far error. Steele, a Protestant, in a dedication tells the Pope that the only difference between our churches in their opinions of the certainty of their doctrines is [that] the Church of Rome is infallible and the Church of England is never in the wrong. But though many private persons think almost as highly of their own infallibility as that of their sect, few express it so naturally as a certain French lady who, in a dispute with her sister, said, "I don't know how it happens, Sister, but I meet with nobody but myself that's always in the right—*Il n'y a que moi qui a toujours raison*."

In these sentiments, Sir, I agree to this Constitution with all its faults, if they are such; because I think a general government necessary for us, and there is no form of government but what may be a blessing to the people if well administered, and believe farther that this is likely to be well administered for a course of years, and can only end in despotism, as other forms have done before it, when the people shall become so corrupted as to need despotic government, being incapable of any other. I doubt, too, whether any other Convention we can obtain may be able to make a better Constitution. For when you assemble a number of men to have the advantage of their joint wisdom, you inevitably assemble with those men all their prejudices, their passions, their errors of opinion, their local interests, and their selfish views. From such an assembly can a perfect production be expected? It, therefore, astonishes me, Sir, to find this system approaching so near to perfection as it does; and I think it will astonish our enemies, who are waiting with confidence to hear that our councils are confounded like those of the builders of Babel; and that our states are on the point of separation, only to meet hereafter for the purpose of cutting one another's throats. Thus I consent, Sir, to this Constitution because I expect no better, and because I am not sure that it is not the best. The opinions I have had of its errors, I sacrifice to the public good. I have never whispered a syllable of them abroad. Within these walls they were born, and here they shall die. If every one of us in returning to our constituents were to report the objections he has had to it, and endeavor to gain partisans in support of them, we might prevent its being generally received and thereby lose all the salutary effects and great advantages resulting naturally in our favor among foreign nations as well as among ourselves, from our real or apparent unanimity. Much of the strength and efficiency of any government in procuring and securing happiness to the people depends on opinion, on the general opinion of the goodness of the government, as well as of the wisdom and integrity of its governors. I hope, therefore, that for our own sakes as a part of the people, and for the sake of posterity, we shall act heartily and unanimously in recommending this Constitution (if approved by Congress and confirmed by the Conventions) wherever our influence may extend, and turn our future thoughts and endeavors to the means of having it well administered.

On the whole, Sir, I cannot help expressing a wish that every member of the Convention who may still have objections to it would, with me, on this occasion doubt a little of his own infallibility and, to make manifest our unanimity, put his name to this instrument.

He then moved that the Constitution be signed by the members and offered the following as a convenient form, viz., "Done in Convention by unanimous consent of *the States* present the 17th of September, etc.—In Witness whereof we have hereunto subscribed our names."

This ambiguous form had been drawn up by MR. G. M.[26] in order to gain the dissenting members and put into the hands of DOCTOR FRANKLIN that it might have the better chance of success.

MR. GORHAM[27] said if it was not too late he could wish, for the purpose of lessening objection to the Constitution, that the clause declaring "the number of

26. Gouverneur Morris.
27. Nathaniel Gorham (1738–96), Massachusetts; merchant; Massachusetts legislature and Constitutional Convention; Confederation Congress.

representatives shall not exceed one for every forty thousand," which had produced so much discussion, might be yet reconsidered in order to strike out "forty thousand" and insert "thirty thousand." This would not, he remarked, establish that as an absolute rule but only give Congress a greater latitude which could not be thought unreasonable.

Mr. KING and Mr. CARROLL[28] seconded and supported the idea of Mr. GORHAM.

When the PRESIDENT[29] rose, for the purpose of putting the question, he said that, although his situation had hitherto restrained him from offering his sentiments on questions depending in the House, and it might be thought, ought now to impose silence on him, yet he could not forbear expressing his wish that the alteration proposed might take place. It was much to be desired that the objections to the plan recommended might be made as few as possible. The smallness of the proportion of representatives had been considered by many members of the Convention an insufficient security for the rights and interests of the people. He acknowledged that it had always appeared to himself among the exceptionable parts of the plan, and, late as the present moment was for admitting amendments, he thought this of so much consequence that it would give much satisfaction to see it adopted.

No opposition was made to the proposition of Mr. GORHAM, and it was agreed to unanimously.

On the question to agree to the Constitution enrolled in order to be signed. It was agreed to all the states answering Aye.

Mr. RANDOLPH then rose and with an allusion to the observations of DOCTOR FRANKLIN apologized for his refusing to sign the Constitution notwithstanding the vast majority and venerable names that would give sanction to its wisdom and its worth. He said, however, that he did not mean by this refusal to decide that he should oppose the Constitution without doors. He meant only to keep himself free to be governed by his duty as it should be prescribed by his future judgment. He refused to sign, because he thought the object of the Convention would be frustrated by the alternative which it presented to the people. Nine states will fail to ratify the plan and confusion must ensue. With such a view of the subject he ought not, he could not, by pledging himself to support the plan, restrain himself from taking such steps as might appear to him most consistent with the public good.

Mr. GOUVERNEUR MORRIS said that he too had objections, but, considering the present plan as the best that was to be attained, he should take it with all its faults. The majority had determined in its favor, and by that determination he should abide. The moment this plan goes forth all other considerations will be laid aside, and the great question will be: Shall there be a national government or not? And this must take place or a general anarchy will be the alternative. He remarked that the signing in the form proposed related only to the fact that the *States* present were unanimous.

Mr. WILLIAMSON[30] suggested that the signing should be confined to the letter accompanying the Constitution to Congress, which might perhaps do nearly as well, and would, he found, be satisfactory to some members who disliked the Constitution. For himself he did not think a better plan was to be expected

28. Daniel Carroll (1730–96), Maryland; planter (brother of John Carroll, first Roman Catholic bishop in the United States); Continental Congress; signer of the Articles of Confederation; later commissioner of the District of Columbia.

29. General George Washington.

30. Hugh Williamson (1735–1819), North Carolina; studied at universities of Pennsylvania, Edinburgh, and Utrecht; physician, merchant, and scientist; North Carolina legislature; Confederation Congress; later House of Representatives.

and had no scruples against putting his name to it.

Mr. Hamilton expressed his anxiety that every member should sign. A few characters of consequence, by opposing or even refusing to sign the Constitution, might do infinite mischief by kindling the latent sparks which lurk under an enthusiasm in favor of the Convention which may soon subside. No man's ideas were more remote from the plan than his were known to be; but is it possible to deliberate between anarchy and convulsion, on one side, and the chance of good to be expected from the plan, on the other?

Mr. Blount[31] said he had declared that he would not sign, so as to pledge himself in support of the plan, but he was relieved by the form proposed and would without committing himself attest the fact that the plan was the unanimous act of the states in Convention.

Dr. Franklin expressed his fears from what Mr. Randolph had said that he thought himself alluded to in the remarks offered this morning to the House. He declared that when drawing up that paper he did not know that any particular member would refuse to sign his name to the instrument and hoped to be so understood. He professed a high sense of obligation to Mr. Randolph for having brought forward the plan in the first instance, and for the assistance he had given in its progress, and hoped that he would yet lay aside his objections and, by concurring with his brethren, prevent the great mischief which the refusal of his name might produce.

Mr. Randolph could not but regard the signing in the proposed form as the same with signing the Constitution. The change of form therefore could make no difference with him. He repeated that,

31. William Blount (1749–1800), North Carolina, politician and landowner; North Carolina legislature and Confederation Congress; later territorial governor of Tennessee, expelled from the United States Senate (1798); Tennessee legislature.

in refusing to sign the Constitution, he took a step which might be the most awful of his life, but it was dictated by his conscience, and it was not possible for him to hesitate, much less, to change. He repeated also his persuasion, that the holding out this plan with a final alternative to the people, of accepting or rejecting it *in toto*, would really produce the anarchy and civil convulsions which were apprehended from the refusal of individuals to sign it.

Mr. Gerry described the painful feelings of his situation, and the embarrassment under which he rose to offer any further observations on the subject which had been finally decided. Whilst the plan was depending, he had treated it with all the freedom he thought it deserved. He now felt himself bound as he was disposed to treat it with the respect due to the Act of the Convention. He hoped he should not violate that respect in declaring on this occasion his fears that a civil war may result from the present crisis of the United States. In Massachusetts, particularly, he saw the danger of this calamitous event. In that state there are two parties, one devoted to democracy, the worst, he thought, of all political evils; the other as violent in the opposite extreme. From the collision of these in opposing and resisting the Constitution, confusion was greatly to be feared. He had thought it necessary, for this and other reasons, that the plan should have been proposed in a more mediating shape in order to abate the heat and opposition of parties. As it has been passed by the Convention, he was persuaded it would have a contrary effect. He could not, therefore, by signing the Constitution pledge himself to abide by it at all events. The proposed form made no difference with him. But if it were not otherwise apparent, the refusals to sign should never be known from him. Alluding to the remarks of Doctor Franklin, he could not, he said, but view them as leveled at himself and

273

the other gentlemen who meant not to sign.

GENERAL PINCKNEY. We are not likely to gain many converts by the ambiguity of the proposed form of signing. He thought it best to be candid and let the form speak the substance. If the meaning of the signers be left in doubt, his purpose would not be answered. He should sign the Constitution with a view to support it with all his influence and wished to pledge himself accordingly.

DOCTOR FRANKLIN. It is too soon to pledge ourselves before Congress and our constituents shall have approved the plan.

MR. INGERSOLL[32] did not consider the signing, either as a mere attestation of the fact, or as pledging the signers to support the Constitution at all events, but as a recommendation of what, all things considered, was the most eligible.

On the motion of DOCTOR FRANKLIN. ... [10, yes; 1 divided; 0, no.]

MR. KING suggested that the Journals of the Convention should be either destroyed or deposited in the custody of the President. He thought, if suffered to be made public, a bad use would be made of them by those who would wish to prevent the adoption of the Constitution.

MR. WILSON preferred the second expedient; he had at one time liked the first best; but, as false suggestions may be

32. Jared Ingersoll (1749–1822), Pennsylvania; Yale; lawyer and judge; Continental Congress; later attorney-general of Pennsylvania.

propagated, it should not be made impossible to contradict them.

A question was then put on depositing the Journals and other papers of the Convention in the hands of the President, on which. ... [10, yes; 1, no.]

The President having asked what the Convention meant should be done with the Journals, etc., whether copies were to be allowed to the members if applied for. It was resolved, nem. con., "that he retain the Journal and other papers, subject to the order of the Congress, if ever formed under the Constitution."

The members then proceeded to sign the instrument.

Whilst the last members were signing it, DOCTOR FRANKLIN, looking toward the president's chair, at the back of which a rising sun happened to be painted, observed to a few members near him that painters had found it difficult to distinguish in their art a rising from a setting sun. "I have," said he, "often and often in the course of the session, and the vicissitudes of my hopes and fears as to its issue, looked at that behind the president without being able to tell whether it was rising or setting. But now at length I have the happiness to know that it is a rising and not a setting sun."

The Constitution being signed by all members except Mr. Randolph, Mr. Mason, and Mr. Gerry, who declined giving it the sanction of their names, the Convention dissolved itself by an adjournment sine die. ...

5. THE CONSTITUTION OF THE UNITED STATES[1]

We, the people of the United States, in order to form a more perfect union, establish justice, insure domestic tranquility, provide for the common defense, promote the general welfare, and secure the blessings of liberty to ourselves and our posterity, do ordain and establish this Constitution for the United States of America.

ARTICLE I

SECTION 1. All legislative powers herein granted shall be vested in a Congress of the United States, which shall consist

1. Documents Illustrative of the Formation of the Union ... , pp. 989–1001, 1066–72. Cf. The Federalist ... (New York, 1937), pp. 603–4. Reprinted by permission of the Modern Library, New York.

of a Senate and House of Representatives.

SEC. 2. The House of Representatives shall be composed of members chosen every second year by the people of the several states, and the electors in each state shall have the qualifications requisite for electors of the most numerous branch of the state legislature.

No person shall be a Representative who shall not have attained to the age of twenty-five years, and been seven years a citizen of the United States, and who shall not, when elected, be an inhabitant of that state in which he shall be chosen.

Representatives and direct taxes shall be apportioned among the several states which may be included within this Union, according to their respective numbers, which shall be determined by adding to the whole number of free persons, including those bound to service for a term of years, and excluding Indians not taxed, three-fifths of all other persons. The actual enumeration shall be made within three years after the first meeting of the Congress of the United States, and within every subsequent term of ten years, in such manner as they shall by law direct. The number of Representatives shall not exceed one for every thirty thousand, but each state shall have at least one Representative; and until such enumeration shall be made, the state of New Hampshire shall be entitled to choose three, Massachusetts eight, Rhode Island and Providence Plantations one, Connecticut five, New York six, New Jersey four, Pennsylvania eight, Delaware one, Maryland six, Virginia ten, North Carolina five, South Carolina five, and Georgia three.

When vacancies happen in the representation from any state, the executive authority thereof shall issue writs of election to fill such vacancies.

The House of Representatives shall choose their speaker and other officers; and shall have the sole power of impeachment.

SEC. 3. The Senate of the United States shall be composed of two Senators from each state, chosen by the legislature thereof, for six years; and each Senator shall have one vote.[2]

Immediately after they shall be assembled in consequence of the first election, they shall be divided as equally as may be into three classes. The seats of the Senators of the first class shall be vacated at the expiration of the second year, of the second class at the expiration of the fourth year, and of the third class at the expiration of the sixth year, so that one-third may be chosen every second year; and if vacancies happen by resignation, or otherwise, during the recess of the legislature of any state, the executive thereof may make temporary appointments until the next meeting of the legislature, which shall then fill such vacancies.[3]

No person shall be a Senator who shall not have attained to the age of thirty years, and been nine years a citizen of the United States, and who shall not, when elected, be an inhabitant of that state for which he shall be chosen.

The Vice-President of the United States shall be president of the Senate, but shall have no vote, unless they be equally divided.

The Senate shall choose their other officers, and also a president pro tempore, in the absence of the Vice-President, or when he shall exercise the office of President of the United States.

The Senate shall have the sole power to try all impeachments. When sitting for that purpose, they shall be on oath or affirmation. When the President of the United States is tried, the Chief Justice shall preside. And no person shall be convicted without the concurrence of two-thirds of the members present.

2. See Amendment XVII.
3. For the current method of filling vacancies see Amendment XVII, sec. 2.

Judgment in cases of impeachment shall not extend further than to removal from office, and disqualification to hold and enjoy any office of honor, trust, or profit under the United States; but the party convicted shall nevertheless be liable and subject to indictment, trial, judgment, and punishment, according to law.

SEC. 4. The times, places, and manner of holding elections for Senators and Representatives shall be prescribed in each state by the legislature thereof; but the Congress may at any time by law make or alter such regulations, except as to the places of choosing Senators.

The Congress shall assemble at least once in every year, and such meeting shall be on the first Monday in December, unless they shall by law appoint a different day.[4]

SEC. 5. Each house shall be the judge of the elections, returns, and qualifications of its own members, and a majority of each shall constitute a quorum to do business; but a smaller number may adjourn from day to day, and may be authorized to compel the attendance of absent members, in such manner, and under such penalties as each house may provide.

Each house may determine the rules of its proceedings, punish its members for disorderly behavior, and, with the concurrence of two-thirds, expel a member.

Each house shall keep a journal of its proceedings, and from time to time publish the same, excepting such parts as may in their judgment require secrecy; and the yeas and nays of the members of either house on any question shall, at the desire of one-fifth of those present, be entered on the journal.

Neither house, during the session of Congress, shall, without the consent of the other, adjourn for more than three days, nor to any other place than that in which the two houses shall be sitting.

4. See Amendment XX.

SEC. 6. The Senators and Representatives shall receive a compensation for their services, to be ascertained by law, and paid out of the treasury of the United States. They shall in all cases, except treason, felony, and breach of the peace, be privileged from arrest during their attendance at the session of their respective houses, and in going to and returning from the same; and for any speech or debate in either house, they shall not be questioned in any other place.

No Senator or Representative shall, during the time for which he was elected, be appointed to any civil office under the authority of the United States, which shall have been created, or the emoluments whereof shall have been increased during such time; and no person holding any office under the United States shall be a member of either house during his continuance in office.

SEC. 7. All bills for raising revenue shall originate in the House of Representatives; but the Senate may propose or concur with amendments as on other bills.

Every bill which shall have passed the House of Representatives and the Senate shall, before it become a law, be presented to the President of the United States. If he approve, he shall sign it, but, if not, he shall return it, with his objections to that house in which it shall have originated, who shall enter the objections at large on their journal, and proceed to reconsider it. If after such reconsideration two-thirds of that house shall agree to pass the bill, it shall be sent, together with the objections, to the other house, by which it shall likewise be reconsidered, and if approved by two-thirds of that house, it shall become a law. But in all such cases the votes of both houses shall be determined by yeas and nays, and the names of the persons voting for and against the bill shall be entered on the journal of each house respectively. If any bill shall not be returned by the President within ten days (Sundays excepted) after it shall have been presented to him, the same shall be a law, in like manner as if he had signed it, unless the Congress by their adjournment prevent its return, in which case it shall not be a law.

Every order, resolution, or vote to which the concurrence of the Senate and House of Representatives may be necessary (except on a question of adjournment) shall be presented to the President of the United States and, before the same shall take effect, shall be approved by him, or, being disapproved by him, shall be repassed by two-thirds of the Senate and House of Representatives, according to the rules and limitations prescribed in the case of a bill.

SEC. 8. The Congress shall have power To lay and collect taxes, duties, imposts and excises, to pay the debts and provide for the common defense and general welfare of the United States; but all duties, imposts, and excises shall be uniform throughout the United States;

To borrow money on the credit of the United States;

To regulate commerce with foreign nations, and among the several states, and with the Indian tribes;

To establish a uniform rule of naturalization, and uniform laws on the subject of bankruptcies throughout the United States;

To coin money, regulate the value thereof, and of foreign coin, and fix the standard of weights and measures;

To provide for the punishment of counterfeiting the securities and current coin of the United States;

To establish post offices and post roads;

To promote the progress of science and useful arts, by securing for limited times to authors and inventors the exclusive right to their respective writings and discoveries;

To constitute tribunals inferior to the Supreme Court;

To define and punish piracies and felonies committed on the high seas, and offenses against the law of nations;

To declare war, grant letters of marque and reprisal,[5] and make rules concerning captures on land and water;

To raise and support armies, but no appropriation of money to that use shall be for a longer term than two years;

To provide and maintain a navy;

To make rules for the government and regulation of the land and naval forces;

To provide for calling forth the militia to execute the laws of the Union, suppress insurrections and repel invasions;

To provide for organizing, arming, and disciplining the militia, and for governing such part of them as may be employed in the service of the United States, reserving to the states, respectively, the appointment of the officers, and the authority of training the militia according to the discipline prescribed by Congress;

To exercise exclusive legislation in all cases whatsoever, over such district (not exceeding ten miles square) as may, by cession of particular states, and the acceptance of Congress, become the seat of the government of the United States, and to exercise like authority over all places purchased by the consent of the legislature of the state in which the same shall be, for the erection of forts, magazines, arsenals, dockyards, and other needful buildings; and

To make all laws which shall be necessary and proper for carrying into execution the foregoing powers, and all other powers vested by this Constitution in the government of the United States, or in any department or officer thereof.[6]

SEC. 9. The migration or importation of such persons as any of the states now existing shall think proper to admit shall not be prohibited by the Congress prior to the year one thousand eight hundred

5. See n. 4, p. 241.
6. This is the famous "elastic" clause. For two quite different interpretations of it by Jefferson and by Hamilton see Unit IV.

and eight, but a tax or duty may be imposed on such importation, not exceeding ten dollars for each person.[7]

The privilege of the writ of habeas corpus shall not be suspended, unless when in cases of rebellion or invasion the public safety may require it.

No bill of attainder or ex post facto law shall be passed.[8]

No capitation,[9] or other direct, tax shall be laid, unless in proportion to the census or enumeration herein before directed to be taken.

No tax or duty shall be laid on articles exported from any state.

No preference shall be given by any regulation of commerce or revenue to the ports of one state over those of another; nor shall vessels bound to, or from, one state, be obliged to enter, clear, or pay duties in another.

No money shall be drawn from the treasury, but in consequence of appropriations made by law; and a regular statement and account of the receipts and expenditures of all public money shall be published from time to time.

No title of nobility shall be granted by the United States. And no person holding any office of profit or trust under them, shall, without the consent of the Congress, accept of any present, emolument, office, or title, of any kind whatever, from any king, prince, or foreign state.

SEC. 10. No state shall enter into any treaty, alliance, or confederation; grant letters of marque and reprisal; coin money; emit bills of credit; make any-

thing but gold and silver coin a tender in payment of debts; pass any bill of attainder, ex post facto law, or law impairing the obligation of contracts, or grant any title of nobility.

No state shall, without the consent of the Congress, lay any imposts or duties on imports or exports, except what may be absolutely necessary for executing its inspection laws: and the net produce of all duties and imposts, laid by any state on imports or exports shall be for the use of the treasury of the United States; and all such laws shall be subject to the revision and control of the Congress.

No state shall, without the consent of Congress, lay any duty of tonnage,[10] keep troops, or ships of war in time of peace, enter into any agreement or compact with another state, or with a foreign power, or engage in war, unless actually invaded, or in such imminent danger as will not admit of delay.

ARTICLE II

SECTION 1. The executive power shall be vested in a President of the United States of America. He shall hold his office during the term of four years, and, together with the Vice-President, chosen for the same term, be elected as follows:

Each state shall appoint, in such manner as the legislature thereof may direct, a number of electors,[11] equal to the whole number of Senators and Representatives to which the state may be entitled in the Congress; but no Senator or Representative, or person holding an office of trust or profit under the United States, shall be appointed an elector.

The electors shall meet in their respective states, and vote by ballot for two persons, of whom one at least shall not be an inhabitant of the same state with

7. This clause empowered Congress to end the *foreign* slave trade after South Carolina and Georgia had had twenty years in which to increase their supply of slave labor. It embodied one of the agreements which settled a controversy in the Federal Convention.

8. By a bill of attainder a *legislature* formerly had inflicted punishments on persons without trial. This clause also prohibits a law to punish a person for actions which were legal at the time they were done.

9. I.e., head or poll tax.

10. I.e., a tax on ships proportioned to their tonnage.

11. These electors are members of the Electoral College and are to be distinguished from electors (voters) in the sense used in Article I, sec. 2, clause 1.

themselves. And they shall make a list of all the persons voted for, and of the number of votes for each; which list they shall sign and certify, and transmit sealed to the seat of the government of the United States, directed to the president of the Senate. The president of the Senate shall, in the presence of the Senate and House of Representatives, open all the certificates, and the votes shall then be counted.

The person having the greatest number of votes shall be the President, if such number be a majority of the whole number of electors appointed; and if there be more than one who have such majority, and have an equal number of votes, then the House of Representatives shall immediately choose by ballot one of them for President; and if no person have a majority, then from the five highest on the list the said house shall in like manner choose the President. But in choosing the President, the votes shall be taken by states, the representation from each state having one vote; a quorum for this purpose shall consist of a member or members from two-thirds of the states, and a majority of all the states shall be necessary to a choice. In every case, after the choice of the President, the person having the greatest number of votes of the electors shall be the Vice-President. But if there should remain two or more who have equal votes, the Senate shall choose from them by ballot the Vice-President.[12]

The Congress may determine the time of choosing the electors, and the day on which they shall give their votes; which day shall be the same throughout the United States.

No person except a natural-born citizen, or a citizen of the United States, at

the time of the adoption of this Constitution, shall be eligible to the office of President; neither shall any person be eligible to that office who shall not have attained to the age of thirty-five years, and been fourteen years a resident within the United States.

In case of the removal of the President from office, or of his death, resignation, or inability to discharge the powers and duties of the said office, the same shall devolve on the Vice-President, and the Congress may by law provide for the case of removal, death, resignation, or inability, both of the President and Vice-President, declaring what officer shall then act as President, and such officer shall act accordingly, until the disability be removed, or a President shall be elected.[13]

The President shall, at stated times, receive for his services, a compensation, which shall neither be increased nor diminished during the period for which he shall have been elected, and he shall not receive within that period any other emolument from the United States, or any of them.

Before he enter on the execution of his office, he shall take the following oath or affirmation: "I do solemnly swear (or affirm) that I will faithfully execute the office of President of the United States, and will to the best of my ability, preserve, protect, and defend the Constitution of the United States."

Sec. 2. The President shall be commander-in-chief of the army and navy of the United States, and of the militia of the several states, when called into the actual service of the United States; he may require the opinion, in writing, of

12. To understand the election of Jefferson and Burr in 1801, it is necessary to understand the electoral system here set forth. Amendment XII was adopted during Jefferson's first administration to avoid a recurrence of the embarrassing tie of 1801; in 1933 Amendment XX provided for other changes.

13. By a law of 1947, if neither the President nor the Vice-President is able to carry out the duties of the President, the speaker of the House of Representatives gives up that office and acts as President until a President or Vice-President qualifies. If the speaker cannot serve, the president *pro tempore* of the Senate fills the vacancy. From him the succession passes to members of the President's cabinet.

the principal officer in each of the executive departments, upon any subject relating to the duties of their respective offices, and he shall have power to grant reprieves and pardons for offenses against the United States, except in cases of impeachment.

He shall have power, by and with the advice and consent of the Senate, to make treaties, provided two-thirds of the Senators present concur; and he shall nominate, and by and with the advice and consent of the Senate, shall appoint ambassadors, other public ministers and consuls, judges of the Supreme Court, and all other officers of the United States, whose appointments are not herein otherwise provided for, and which shall be established by law; but the Congress may by law vest the appointment of such inferior officers, as they think proper, in the President alone, in the courts of law, or in the heads of departments.

The President shall have power to fill up all vacancies that may happen during the recess of the Senate, by granting commissions which shall expire at the end of their next session.

Sec. 3. He shall from time to time give to the Congress information of the state of the Union, and recommend to their consideration such measures as he shall judge necessary and expedient; he may, on extraordinary occasions, convene both houses, or either of them, and in case of disagreement between them, with respect to the time of adjournment, he may adjourn them to such time as he shall think proper; he shall receive ambassadors and other public ministers; he shall take care that the laws be faithfully executed, and shall commission all the officers of the United States.

Sec. 4. The President, Vice-President, and all civil officers of the United States shall be removed from office on impeachment for, and conviction of, treason, bribery, or other high crimes and misdemeanors.

ARTICLE III

Section 1. The judicial power of the United States shall be vested in one Supreme Court, and in such inferior courts as the Congress may from time to time ordain and establish. The judges, both of the Supreme and inferior courts, shall hold their offices during good behavior, and shall, at stated times, receive for their services, a compensation, which shall not be diminished during their continuance in office.

Sec. 2. The judicial power shall extend to all cases, in law and equity, arising under this Constitution, the laws of the United States, and treaties made, or which shall be made, under their authority—to all cases affecting ambassadors, other public ministers and consuls—to all cases of admiralty and maritime jurisdiction—to controversies to which the United States shall be a party—to controversies between two or more states, between a state and citizens of another state—between citizens of different states—between citizens of the same state claiming lands under grants of different states, and between a state, or the citizens thereof, and foreign states, citizens, or subjects.

In all cases affecting ambassadors, other public ministers and consuls, and those in which a state shall be party, the Supreme Court shall have original jurisdiction.[14] In all the other cases before mentioned, the Supreme Court shall have appellate jurisdiction, both as to law and fact, with such exceptions, and under such regulations as the Congress shall make.

The trial of all crimes, except in cases of impeachment, shall be by jury; and such trial shall be held in the state where the said crimes shall have been committed; but when not committed within

14. By "original jurisdiction" is meant the legal power to hear a case in the first instance. For example, a case between two states would not be heard by a federal court lower than the Supreme Court.

any state, the trial shall be at such place or places as the Congress may by law have directed.

SEC. 3. Treason against the United States shall consist only in levying war against them, or in adhering to their enemies, giving them aid and comfort. No person shall be convicted of treason unless on the testimony of two witnesses to the same overt act, or on confession in open court.

The Congress shall have power to declare the punishment of treason, but no attainder of treason shall work corruption of blood, or forfeiture except during the life of the person attainted.

ARTICLE IV

SECTION 1. Full faith and credit shall be given in each state to the public acts, records, and judicial proceedings of every other state. And the Congress may by general laws prescribe the manner in which such acts, records, and proceedings shall be proved, and the effect thereof.

SEC. 2. The citizens of each state shall be entitled to all privileges and immunities of citizens in the several states.

A person charged in any state with treason, felony, or other crime, who shall flee from justice, and be found in another state, shall, on demand of the executive authority of the state from which he fled, be delivered up, to be removed to the state having jurisdiction of the crime.[15]

No person held to service or labor in one state, under the laws thereof, escaping into another, shall, in consequence of any law or regulation therein, be discharged from such service or labor, but shall be delivered up on claim of the party to whom such service or labor may be due.

SEC. 3. New states may be admitted by the Congress into this Union; but no new state shall be formed or erected within the jurisdiction of any other state; nor any state be formed by the junction of two or more states, or parts of states, without the consent of the legislatures of the states concerned as well as of the Congress.

The Congress shall have power to dispose of and make all needful rules and regulations respecting the territory or other property belonging to the United States; and nothing in this Constitution shall be so construed as to prejudice any claims of the United States, or of any particular state.

SEC. 4. The United States shall guarantee to every state in this Union a republican form of government, and shall protect each of them against invasion; and on application of the legislature, or of the executive (when the legislature cannot be convened), against domestic violence.

ARTICLE V

The Congress, whenever two-thirds of both houses shall deem it necessary, shall propose amendments to this Constitution, or, on the application of the legislatures of two-thirds of the several states, shall call a convention for proposing amendments, which, in either case, shall be valid to all intents and purposes, as part of this Constitution, when ratified by the legislatures of three-fourths of the several states, or by conventions in three-fourths thereof, as the one or the other mode of ratification may be proposed by the Congress; provided that no amendment which may be made prior to the year one thousand eight hundred and eight shall in any manner affect the first and fourth clauses in the ninth section of the First Article; and that no state, without its consent, shall be deprived of its equal suffrage in the Senate.

ARTICLE VI

All debts contracted and engagements entered into, before the adoption of this Constitution, shall be as valid against the

15. In spite of the strong language of the Constitution, governors sometimes refuse to extradite persons accused of crime in other states.

United States under this Constitution, as under the Confederation.

This Constitution, and the laws of the United States which shall be made in pursuance thereof, and all treaties made, or which shall be made, under the authority of the United States, shall be the supreme law of the land; and the judges in every state shall be bound thereby, anything in the Constitution or laws of any state to the contrary notwithstanding.[16]

The Senators and Representatives before mentioned, and the members of the several state legislatures, and all executive judicial officers, both of the United States and of the several states, shall be bound, by oath or affirmation, to support this Constitution; but no religious test shall ever be required as a qualification to any office or public trust under the United States.

ARTICLE VII

The ratification of the conventions of nine states shall be sufficient for the establishment of this Constitution between the states so ratifying the same.

. . . Done in convention by the unanimous consent of the states present, the seventeenth day of September, in the year of our Lord one thousand seven hundred and eighty-seven and of the Independence of the United States of America the twelfth. . . . In witness whereof we have hereunto subscribed our names.

GEORGE WASHINGTON, *President and Deputy from Virginia. . . .*

CONSTITUTIONAL AMENDMENTS[17]
ARTICLE I

Congress shall make no law respecting an establishment of religion, or prohibiting the free exercise thereof; or abridging the freedom of speech, or of the press; or the right of the people peaceably to assemble, and to petition the government for a redress of grievances.

ARTICLE II

A well-regulated militia being necessary to the security of a free state, the right of the people to keep and bear arms shall not be infringed.

ARTICLE III

No soldier shall, in time of peace, be quartered in any house, without the consent of the owner, nor in time of war, but in a manner to be prescribed by law.

ARTICLE IV

The right of the people to be secure in their persons, houses, papers, and effects against unreasonable searches and seizures shall not be violated, and no warrants shall issue, but upon probable cause, supported by oath or affirmation, and particularly describing the place to be searched, and the persons or things to be seized.

ARTICLE V

No person shall be held to answer for a capital or otherwise infamous crime, unless on a presentment or indictment of a grand jury, except in cases arising in the land or naval forces, or in the militia, when in actual service in time of war or public danger; nor shall any person be subject for the same offense to be twice put in jeopardy of life or limb; nor shall be compelled in any criminal case to be a witness against himself, nor be deprived of life, liberty, or property, without due process of law; nor shall private property be taken for public use, without just compensation.

16. This paragraph is often called the "keystone clause" of the Constitution because of its significance in establishing the supremacy of the Constitution as national *law.*

17. The first ten amendments resulted from an understanding arrived at during the controversy over the ratification of the Constitution. The advocates of immediate ratification won over some of those who originally preferred a second convention to revise the original draft before ratification. Twelve amendments were proposed by Congress in 1789; of the twelve, ten were ratified by the necessary number of states by the end of 1791.

ARTICLE VI

In all criminal prosecutions, the accused shall enjoy the right to a speedy and public trial, by an impartial jury of the state and district wherein the crime shall have been committed, which district shall have been previously ascertained by law, and to be informed of the nature and cause of the accusation; to be confronted with the witnesses against him; to have compulsory process for obtaining witnesses in his favor, and to have the assistance of counsel for his defense.

ARTICLE VII

In suits at common law, where the value in controversy shall exceed twenty dollars, the right of trial by jury shall be preserved, and no fact tried by a jury, shall be otherwise re-examined in any court of the United States, than according to the rules of the common law.

ARTICLE VIII

Excessive bail shall not be required, nor excessive fines imposed, nor cruel and unusual punishments inflicted.

ARTICLE IX

The enumeration in the Constitution, a certain rights, shall not be construed to deny or disparage others retained by the people.

ARTICLE X

The powers not delegated to the United States by the Constitution, nor prohibited by it to the states, are reserved to the states respectively, or to the people.

ARTICLE XI[18]

The judicial power of the United States shall not be construed to extend to any suit in law or equity, commenced or prosecuted against one of the United States by citizens of another state, or by citizens or subjects of any foreign state.

18. Proposed in 1794 and ratified early in 1798.

ARTICLE XII[19]

The electors shall meet in their respective states, and vote by ballot for President and Vice-President, one of whom, at least, shall not be an inhabitant of the same state with themselves; they shall name in their ballots the person voted for as President, and in distinct ballots the person voted for as Vice-President, and they shall make distinct lists of all persons voted for as President, and of all persons voted for as Vice-President, and of the number of votes for each, which lists they shall sign and certify, and transmit sealed to the seat of the government of the United States, directed to the president of the Senate;—The president of the Senate shall, in the presence of the Senate and House of Representatives, open all the certificates and the votes shall then be counted;—The person having the greatest number of votes for President, shall be the President, if such number be a majority of the whole number of electors appointed; and if no person have such majority, then from the persons having the highest numbers not exceeding three on the list of those voted for as President, the House of Representatives shall choose immediately, by ballot, the President. But in choosing the President, the votes shall be taken by states, the representation from each state having one vote; a quorum for this purpose shall consist of a member or members from two-thirds of the states, and a majority of all the states shall be necessary to a choice. And if the House of Representatives shall not choose a President whenever the right of choice shall devolve upon them, before the fourth day of March next following, then the Vice-President shall act as President, as in the case of the death or other constitutional disability of the President. The person having the greatest number of votes as Vice-President shall be the Vice-Pres-

19. Proposed in December, 1803, and ratified within ten months.

ident, if such number be a majority of the whole number of electors appointed, and if no person have a majority, then from the two highest numbers on the list, the Senate shall choose the Vice-President; a quorum for the purpose shall consist of two-thirds of the whole number of Senators, and a majority of the whole number shall be necessary to a choice. But no person constitutionally ineligible to the office of President shall be eligible to that of Vice-President of the United States.

ARTICLE XIII[20]

SECTION 1. Neither slavery nor involuntary servitude, except as a punishment for crime whereof the party shall have been duly convicted, shall exist within the United States, or any place subject to their jurisdiction.

SEC. 2. Congress shall have power to enforce this article by appropriate legislation.

ARTICLE XIV[21]

SECTION 1. All persons born or naturalized in the United States, and subject to the jurisdiction thereof, are citizens of the United States and of the state wherein they reside. No state shall make or enforce any law which shall abridge the privileges or immunities of citizens of the United States; nor shall any state deprive any person of life, liberty, or property, without due process of law; nor deny to any person within its jurisdiction the equal protection of the laws.

SEC. 2. Representatives shall be apportioned among the several states according to their respective numbers, counting the whole number of persons in each state, excluding Indians not taxed. But

20. The earliest of the three "Civil War amendments"; proposed in February and ratified by December, 1865.

21. From the standpoint of later interpretation the first section of this amendment is probably the most important historically of all the amendments. Proposed in 1866 and ratified by July, 1868.

when the right to vote at any election for the choice of electors for President and Vice-President of the United States, Representatives in Congress, the executive and judicial officers of a state, or the members of the legislature thereof, is denied to any of the male inhabitants of such state, being twenty-one years of age, and citizens of the United States, or in any way abridged, except for participation in rebellion, or other crime, the basis of representation therein shall be reduced in the proportion which the number of such male citizens shall bear to the whole number of male citizens twenty-one years of age in such state.

SEC. 3. No person shall be a Senator or Representative in Congress, or elector of President and Vice-President, or hold any office, civil or military, under the United States, or under any state, who, having previously taken an oath, as a member of Congress, or as an officer of the United States, or as a member of any state legislature, or as an executive or judicial officer of any state, to support the Constitution of the United States, shall have engaged in insurrection or rebellion against the same, or given aid or comfort to the enemies thereof. But Congress may, by a vote of two-thirds of each House, remove such disability.

SEC. 4. The validity of the public debt of the United States, authorized by law, including debts incurred for payment of pensions and bounties for services in suppressing insurrection or rebellion, shall not be questioned. But neither the United States nor any state shall assume or pay any debt or obligation incurred in aid of insurrection or rebellion against the United States, or any claim for the loss or emancipation of any slave; but all such debts, obligations, and claims shall be held illegal and void.

SEC. 5. The Congress shall have power to enforce, by appropriate legislation, the provisions of this article.

ARTICLE XV[22]

SECTION 1. The right of citizens of the United States to vote shall not be denied or abridged by the United States or by any state on account of race, color, or previous condition of servitude.

SEC. 2. The Congress shall have power to enforce this article by appropriate legislation.

ARTICLE XVI[23]

The Congress shall have power to lay and collect taxes on incomes, from whatever source derived, without apportionment among the several states, and without regard to any census or enumeration.

ARTICLE XVII[24]

SECTION 1. The Senate of the United States shall be composed of two Senators from each state, elected by the people thereof, for six years; and each Senator shall have one vote. The electors in each state shall have the qualifications requisite for electors of the most numerous branch of the state legislatures.

SEC. 2. When vacancies happen in the representation of any state in the Senate, the executive authority of such state shall issue writs of election to fill such vacancies: *Provided,* That the legislature of any state may empower the executive thereof to make temporary appointments until the people fill the vacancies by election as the legislature may direct.

SEC. 3. This amendment shall not be so construed as to affect the election or term of any Senator chosen before it becomes valid as part of the Constitution.

ARTICLE XVIII[25]

SECTION 1. After one year from the ratification of this article the manufacture, sale, or transportation of intoxicating liquors within, the importation thereof into, or the exportation thereof from the United States and all territory subject to the jurisdiction thereof for beverage purposes is hereby prohibited.

SEC. 2. The Congress and the several states shall have concurrent power to enforce this article by appropriate legislation.

SEC. 3. This article shall be inoperative unless it shall have been ratified as an amendment to the Constitution by the legislatures of the several states, as provided in the Constitution, within seven years from the date of the submission hereof to the states by the Congress.[26]

ARTICLE XIX[27]

SECTION 1. The right of citizens of the United States to vote shall not be denied or abridged by the United States or by any state on account of sex.

SEC. 2. Congress shall have power to enforce this article by appropriate legislation.

ARTICLE XX[28]

SECTION 1. The terms of the President and Vice-President shall end at noon on the twentieth day of January, and the terms of Senators and Representatives at noon on the third day of January, of the years in which such terms would

---

22. Note the negative form of statement in this amendment. It was proposed in 1869 and ratified by early 1870.

23. This amendment was made necessary, if the national government was to levy a graduated income tax, by the five-to-four decision in *Pollock* v. *Farmers Loan and Trust Co.* in 1895. Proposed in 1909 and ratified by February, 1913.

24. A result of the demand of the Progressives for a more direct participation of the electorate in government. Proposed in 1912 and ratified within thirteen months.

25. Proposed in 1917; ratified by 1919; effective in 1920; repealed in 1933.

26. A clause to prevent a proposed amendment from pending for an indefinite period.

27. Proposed in 1919 and ratified within fifteen months.

28. The so-called "lame-duck" amendment, sponsored by the late Senator George W. Norris. Proposed in 1932; ratified by January, 1933. It shortened President F. D. Roosevelt's first term by about six weeks.

have ended if this article had not been ratified; and the terms of their successors shall then begin.

SEC. 2. The Congress shall assemble at least once in every year, and such meeting shall begin at noon on the third day of January, unless they shall by law appoint a different day.

SEC. 3. If, at the time fixed for the beginning of the term of the President, the President-elect shall have died, the Vice-President-elect shall become President. If a President shall not have been chosen before the time fixed for the beginning of his term, or if the President-elect shall have failed to qualify, then the Vice-President-elect shall act as President until a President shall have been qualified; and the Congress may by law provide for the case wherein neither a President-elect nor a Vice-President-elect shall have qualified, declaring who shall then act as President, or the manner in which one who is to act shall be selected, and such person shall act accordingly until a President or Vice-President shall have qualified.

SEC. 4. The Congress may by law provide for the case of the death of any of the persons from whom the House of Representatives may choose a President whenever the right of choice shall have developed upon them, and for the case of the death of any of the persons from whom the Senate may choose a Vice-President whenever the right of choice shall have devolved upon them.

SEC. 5. Sections 1 and 2 shall take effect on the fifteenth day of October following the ratification of this article.

SEC. 6. This article shall be inoperative unless it shall have been ratified as an amendment to the Constitution by the legislatures of three-fourths of the several states within seven years from the date of its submission.

ARTICLE XXI[29]

SECTION 1. The eighteenth article of amendment to the Constitution of the United States is hereby repealed.

SEC. 2. The transportation or importation into any state, territory, or possession of the United States for delivery or use therein of intoxicating liquors, in violation of the laws thereof, is hereby prohibited.

SEC. 3. This article shall be inoperative unless it shall have been ratified as an amendment to the Constitution by conventions in the several states, as provided in the Constitution, within seven years from the date of the submission hereof to the states by the Congress.

29. Proposed and ratified in 1933.

6. THE FEDERALIST[1]

By ALEXANDER HAMILTON, JAMES MADISON, *and* JOHN JAY

EDITORS' NOTE.—By far the ablest exposition of the new Constitution during the fight over ratification was a series of essays published in several New York newspapers between October, 1787, and April, 1788. Under the pseudonym of "Publius," Alexander Hamilton, James Madison, and John Jay sought to persuade their readers of the necessity for, and the relative excellence of, the proposed government. Convenient editions of the complete text may be found in the "Everyman" and the "Modern Library" series.

1. *The Federalist* (New York, 1937), pp. 3–7, 53–62, 79–82, 86–95, 95–101, 242–49, 312–16, 327–31, 335–41, 502–11. Reprinted by permission of the Modern Library, New York.

A. THE FEDERALIST NO. 1 (HAMILTON)

To the People of the State of New York:

After an unequivocal experience of the inefficacy of the subsisting federal government, you are called upon to deliberate on a new Constitution for the United States of America. The subject speaks its own importance; comprehending in its consequences nothing less than the existence of the UNION, the safety and welfare of the parts of which it is composed, the fate of an empire in many respects the most interesting in the world. It has been frequently remarked that it seems to have been reserved to the people of this country, by their conduct and example, to decide the important question whether societies of men are really capable or not of establishing good government from reflection and choice, or whether they are forever destined to depend for their political constitutions on accident and force. If there be any truth in the remark, the crisis at which we are arrived may with propriety be regarded as the era in which that decision is to be made; and a wrong election of the part we shall act may, in this view, deserve to be considered as the general misfortune of mankind.

This idea will add the inducements of philanthropy to those of patriotism, to heighten the solicitude which all considerate and good men must feel for the event. Happy will it be if our choice should be directed by a judicious estimate of our true interests, unperplexed and unbiased by considerations not connected with the public good. But this is a thing more ardently to be wished than seriously to be expected. The plan offered to our deliberations affects too many particular interests, innovates upon too many local institutions, not to involve in its discussion a variety of objects foreign to its merits, and of views, passions, and prejudices little favorable to the discovery of truth.

Among the most formidable of the obstacles which the new Constitution will have to encounter may readily be distinguished the obvious interest of a certain class of men in every state to resist all changes which may hazard a diminution of the power, emolument, and consequence of the offices they hold under the state establishments; and the perverted ambition of another class of men who will either hope to aggrandize themselves by the confusions of their country or will flatter themselves with fairer prospects of elevation from the subdivision of the empire into several partial confederacies than from its union under one government.

It is not, however, my design to dwell upon observations of this nature. I am well aware that it would be disingenuous to resolve indiscriminately the opposition of any set of men (merely because their situations might subject them to suspicion) into interested or ambitious views. Candor will oblige us to admit that even such men may be actuated by upright intentions; and it cannot be doubted that much of the opposition which has made its appearance, or may hereafter make its appearance, will spring from sources, blameless at least, if not respectable—the honest errors of minds led astray by preconceived jealousies and fears. So numerous, indeed, and so powerful are the causes which serve to give a false bias to the judgment that we, upon many occasions, see wise and good men on the wrong as well as on the right side of questions of the first magnitude to society. This circumstance, if duly attended to, would furnish a lesson of moderation to those who are ever so much persuaded of their being in the right in any controversy. And a further reason for caution, in this respect, might be drawn from the reflection that we are not always sure that those who advocate the truth are influenced by purer principles than their antagonists.

Ambition, avarice, personal animosity, party opposition, and many other motives not more laudable than these, are apt to operate as well upon those who support as those who oppose the right side of a question. Were there not even these inducements to moderation, nothing could be more ill judged than that intolerant spirit which has, at all times, characterized political parties. For in politics, as in religion, it is equally absurd to aim at making proselytes by fire and sword. Heresies in either can rarely be cured by persecution.

And yet, however just these sentiments will be allowed to be, we have already sufficient indications that it will happen in this as in all former cases of great national discussion. A torrent of angry and malignant passions will be let loose. To judge from the conduct of the opposite parties, we shall be led to conclude that they will mutually hope to evince the justness of their opinions, and to increase the number of their converts by the loudness of their declamations and the bitterness of their invectives. An enlightened zeal for the energy and efficiency of government will be stigmatized as the offspring of a temper fond of despotic power and hostile to the principles of liberty. An overscrupulous jealousy of danger to the rights of the people, which is more commonly the fault of the head than of the heart, will be represented as mere pretense and artifice, the stale bait for popularity at the expense of public good. It will be forgotten, on the one hand, that jealousy is the usual concomitant of violent love, and that the noble enthusiasm of liberty is too apt to be infected with a spirit of narrow and illiberal distrust. On the other hand, it will be equally forgotten that the vigor of government is essential to the security of liberty; that, in the contemplation of a sound and well-informed judgment, their interest can never be separated; and that a dangerous ambition more often lurks behind the specious mask of zeal for the rights of the people than under the forbidding appearance of zeal for the firmness and efficiency of government. History will teach us that the former has been found a much more certain road to the introduction of despotism than the latter, and that of those men who have overturned the liberties of republics, the greatest number have begun their career by paying an obsequious court to the people, commencing demagogues and ending tyrants.

In the course of the preceding observations, I have had an eye, my fellow-citizens, to putting you upon your guard against all attempts, from whatever quarter, to influence your decision in a matter of the utmost moment to your welfare, by any impressions other than those which may result from the evidence of truth. You will, no doubt, at the same time, have collected from the general scope of them that they proceed from a source not unfriendly to the new Constitution. Yes, my countrymen, I own to you that, after having given it an attentive consideration, I am clearly of opinion it is your interest to adopt it. I am convinced that this is the safest course for your liberty, your dignity, and your happiness. I affect not reserves which I do not feel. I will not amuse you with an appearance of deliberation when I have decided. I frankly acknowledge to you my convictions, and I will freely lay before you the reasons on which they are founded. The consciousness of good intentions disdains ambiguity. I shall not, however, multiply professions on this head. My motives must remain in the depository of my own breast. My arguments will be open to all, and may be judged of by all. They shall at least be offered in a spirit which will not disgrace the cause of truth.

I propose, in a series of papers, to discuss the following interesting particulars: *The utility of the* UNION *to your political prosperity—The insufficiency of the present Confederation to preserve that Union—The necessity of a government at least equally energetic with the one proposed, to the attainment of this object—The conformity of the proposed Constitution to the true principles of republican government—Its analogy to your own state constitution—and, lastly, The additional security which its adoption will afford to the preservation of that species of government, to liberty, and to property.*

In the progress of this discussion I shall endeavor to give a satisfactory answer to all the objections which shall have made their appearance that may seem to have any claim to your attention.

It may perhaps be thought superfluous to offer arguments to prove the utility of the UNION, a point, no doubt, deeply engraved on the hearts of the great body of the people in every state, and one which, it may be imagined, has no ad-versaries. But the fact is that we already hear it whispered in the private circles of those who oppose the new Constitution that the thirteen states are of too great extent for any general system, and that we must of necessity resort to separate confederacies of distinct portions of the whole. This doctrine will, in all probability, be gradually propagated, till it has votaries enough to countenance an open avowal of it. For nothing can be more evident, to those who are able to take an enlarged view of the subject, than the alternative of an adoption of the new Constitution or a dismemberment of the Union. It will therefore be of use to begin by examining the advantages of that Union, the certain evils, and the probable dangers, to which every state will be exposed from its dissolution. This shall accordingly constitute the subject of my next address.

PUBLIUS

B. THE FEDERALIST NO. 10 (MADISON)

To the People of the State of New York:

Among the numerous advantages promised by a well-constructed Union, none deserves to be more accurately developed than its tendency to break and control the violence of faction. The friend of popular governments never finds himself so much alarmed for their character and fate as when he contemplates their propensity to this dangerous vice. He will not fail, therefore, to set a due value on any plan which, without violating the principles to which he is attached, provides a proper cure for it. The instability, injustice, and confusion introduced into the public councils have, in truth, been the mortal diseases under which popular governments have everywhere perished; as they continue to be the favorite and fruitful topics from which the adversaries to liberty derive their most specious declamations. The valuable improvements made by the American constitutions on the popular models, both ancient and modern, can-not certainly be too much admired; but it would be an unwarrantable partiality to contend that they have as effectually obviated the danger on this side, as was wished and expected. Complaints are everywhere heard from our most considerate and virtuous citizens, equally the friends of public and private faith, and of public and personal liberty, that our governments are too unstable, that the public good is disregarded in the conflicts of rival parties, and that measures are too often decided, not according to the rules of justice and the rights of the minor party, but by the superior force of an interested and overbearing majority. However anxiously we may wish that these complaints had no foundation, the evidence of known facts will not permit us to deny that they are in some degree true. It will be found, indeed, on a candid review of our situation, that some of the distresses under which we labor have been erroneously charged on the operation of our governments;

but it will be found, at the same time, that other causes will not alone account for many of our heaviest misfortunes; and, particularly, for that prevailing and increasing distrust of public engagements, and alarm for private rights, which are echoed from one end of the continent to the other. These must be chiefly, if not wholly, effects of the unsteadiness and injustice with which a factious spirit has tainted our public administrations.

By a faction, I understand a number of citizens, whether amounting to a majority or minority of the whole, who are united and actuated by some common impulse of passion, or of interest, adverse to the rights of other citizens, or to the permanent and aggregate interests of the community.

There are two methods of curing the mischiefs of faction: the one, by removing its causes; the other, by controlling its effects.

There are again two methods of removing the causes of faction: the one, by destroying the liberty which is essential to its existence; the other, by giving to every citizen the same opinions, the same passions, and the same interests.

It could never be more truly said than of the first remedy that it was worse than the disease. Liberty is to faction what air is to fire, an aliment without which it instantly expires. But it could not be less folly to abolish liberty, which is essential to political life, because it nourishes faction, than it would be to wish the annihilation of air, which is essential to animal life, because it imparts to fire its destructive agency.

The second expedient is as impracticable as the first would be unwise. As long as the reason of man continues fallible, and he is at liberty to exercise it, different opinions will be formed. As long as the connection subsists between his reason and his self-love, his opinions and his passions will have a reciprocal influence on each other; and the former

will be objects to which the latter will attach themselves. The diversity in the faculties of men, from which the rights of property originate, is not less an insuperable obstacle to a uniformity of interests. The protection of these faculties is the first object of government. From the protection of different and unequal faculties of acquiring property, the possession of different degrees and kinds of property immediately results; and from the influence of these on the sentiments and views of the respective proprietors ensues a division of the society into different interests and parties.

The latent causes of faction are thus sown in the nature of man; and we see them everywhere brought into different degrees of activity, according to the different circumstances of civil society. A zeal for different opinions concerning religion, concerning government, and many other points, as well of speculation as of practice; an attachment to different leaders ambitiously contending for pre-eminence and power; or to persons of other descriptions whose fortunes have been interesting to the human passions, have, in turn, divided mankind into parties, inflamed them with mutual animosity, and rendered them much more disposed to vex and oppress each other than to co-operate for their common good. So strong is this propensity of mankind to fall into mutual animosities that, where no substantial occasion presents itself, the most frivolous and fanciful distinctions have been sufficient to kindle their unfriendly passions and excite their most violent conflicts. But the most common and durable source of factions has been the various and unequal distribution of property. Those who hold and those who are without property have ever formed distinct interests in society. Those who are creditors and those who are debtors fall under a like discrimination. A landed interest, a manufacturing interest, a mercantile interest, a moneyed interest, with many lesser interests, grow up of necessity in civilized nations and divide them into different classes, actuated by different sentiments and views. The regulation of these various and interfering interests forms the principal task of modern legislation and involves the spirit of party and faction in the necessary and ordinary operations of the government.

No man is allowed to be a judge in his own cause, because his interest would certainly bias his judgment and, not improbably, corrupt his integrity. With equal, nay with greater, reason, a body of men are unfit to be both judges and parties at the same time; yet what are many of the most important acts of legislation but so many judicial determinations, not indeed concerning the rights of single persons, but concerning the rights of large bodies of citizens? And what are the different classes of legislators but advocates and parties to the causes which they determine? Is a law proposed concerning private debts? It is a question to which the creditors are parties on one side and the debtors on the other. Justice ought to hold the balance between them. Yet the parties are, and must be, themselves the judges; and the most numerous party or, in other words, the most powerful faction must be expected to prevail. Shall domestic manufacturers be encouraged, and in what degree, by restrictions on foreign manufacturers? are questions which would be differently decided by the landed and the manufacturing classes, and probably by neither with a sole regard to justice and the public good. The apportionment of taxes on the various descriptions of property is an act which seems to require the most exact impartiality; yet there is, perhaps, no legislative act in which greater opportunity and temptation are given to a predominant party to trample on the rules of justice. Every shilling with which they overburden the inferior number is a shilling saved to their own pockets.

It is in vain to say that enlightened statesmen will be able to adjust these clashing interests and render them all subservient to the public good. Enlightened statesmen will not always be at the helm. Nor, in many cases, can such an adjustment be made at all without taking into view indirect and remote considerations, which will rarely prevail over the immediate interest which one party may find in disregarding the rights of another or the good of the whole.

The inference to which we are brought is that the *causes* of faction cannot be removed and that relief is only to be sought in the means of controlling its *effects*.

If a faction consists of less than a majority, relief is supplied by the republican principle, which enables the majority to defeat its sinister views by regular vote. It may clog the administration, it may convulse the society; but it will be unable to execute and mask its violence under the forms of the Constitution. When a majority is included in a faction, the form of popular government, on the other hand, enables it to sacrifice to its ruling passion or interest both the public good and the rights of other citizens. To secure the public good and private rights against the danger of such a faction, and at the same time to preserve the spirit and the form of popular government, is then the great object to which our inquiries are directed. Let me add that it is the great desideratum by which this form of government can be rescued from the opprobrium under which it has so long labored and be recommended to the esteem and adoption of mankind.

By what means is this object attainable? Evidently by one of two only. Either the existence of the same passion or interest in a majority at the same time must be prevented, or the majority, having such coexistent passion or interest, must be rendered, by their number and local situation, unable to concert and carry into effect schemes of oppression. If the impulse and the opportunity be suffered to coincide, we well know that neither moral nor religious motives can be relied on as an adequate control. They are not found to be such on the injustice and violence of individuals and lose their efficacy in proportion to the number combined together, that is, in proportion as their efficacy becomes needful.

From this view of the subject it may be concluded that a pure democracy, by which I mean a society consisting of a small number of citizens who assemble and administer the government in person, can admit of no cure for the mischiefs of faction. A common passion or interest will, in almost every case, be felt by a majority of the whole; a communication and concert result from the form of government itself; and there is nothing to check the inducements to sacrifice the weaker party or an obnoxious individual. Hence it is that such democracies have ever been spectacles of turbulence and contention; have ever been found incompatible with personal security or the rights of property; and have in general been as short in their lives as they have been violent in their deaths. Theoretic politicians, who have patronized this species of government, have erroneously supposed that, by reducing mankind to a perfect equality in their political rights, they would, at the same time, be perfectly equalized and assimilated in their possessions, their opinions, and their passions.

A republic, by which I mean a government in which the scheme of representation takes place, opens a different prospect and promises the cure for which we are seeking. Let us examine the points in which it varies from pure democracy, and we shall comprehend both the nature of the cure and the efficacy which it must derive from the Union.

The two great points of difference between a democracy and a republic are: first, the delegation of the government, in the latter, to a small number of citizens elected by the rest; secondly, the greater number of citizens, and greater sphere of country, over which the latter may be extended.

The effect of the first difference is, on the one hand, to refine and enlarge the public views, by passing them through the medium of a chosen body of citizens, whose wisdom may best discern the true interest of their country, and whose patriotism and love of justice will be least likely to sacrifice it to temporary or partial considerations. Under such a regulation, it may well happen that the public voice, pronounced by the representatives of the people, will be more consonant to the public good than if pronounced by the people themselves, convened for the purpose. On the other hand, the effect may be inverted. Men of factious tempers, of local prejudices, or of sinister designs may, by intrigue, by corruption, or by other means, first obtain the suffrages, and then betray the interests, of the people. The question resulting is, whether small or extensive republics are more favorable to the election of proper guardians of the public weal; and it is clearly decided in favor of the latter by two obvious considerations:

In the first place, it is to be remarked that, however small the republic may be, the representatives must be raised to a certain number, in order to guard against the cabals of a few; and that, however large it may be, they must be limited to a certain number, in order to guard against the confusion of a multitude. Hence, the number of representatives in the two cases not being in proportion to that of the two constituents, and being proportionally greater in the small republic, it follows that, if the proportion of fit characters be not less in the large than in the small republic, the former will present a greater option, and consequently a greater probability of a fit choice.

In the next place, as each representative will be chosen by a greater number of citizens in the large than in the small republic, it will be more difficult for unworthy candidates to practice with success the vicious arts by which elections are too often carried and, the suffrages of the people being more free, will be more likely to center in men who possess the most attractive merit and the most diffusive and established characters.

It must be confessed that in this, as in most other cases, there is a mean, on both sides of which inconveniences will be found to lie. By enlarging too much the number of electors, you render the representative too little acquainted with all their local circumstances and lesser interests; as by reducing it too much, you render him unduly attached to these and too little fit to comprehend and pursue great and national objects. The federal Constitution forms a happy combination in this respect; the great and aggregate interests being referred to the national, the local, and particular to the state legislatures.

The other point of difference is the greater number of citizens and extent of territory which may be brought within the compass of republican than of democratic government; and it is this circumstance principally which renders factious combinations less to be dreaded in the former than in the latter. The smaller the society, the fewer probably will be the distinct parties and interests composing it; the fewer the distinct parties and interests, the more frequently will a majority be found of the same party; and the smaller the number of individuals composing a majority, and the smaller the compass within which they are placed, the more easily will they concert and execute their plans of oppression. Extend the sphere and you take in a greater variety of parties and interests; you make it less probable that a majority of the whole will have a common motive to invade the rights of other citizens; or

if such a common motive exists, it will be more difficult for all who feel it to discover their own strength and to act in unison with each other. Besides other impediments, it may be remarked that, where there is a consciousness of unjust or dishonorable purposes, communication is always checked by distrust in proportion to the number whose concurrence is necessary.

Hence, it clearly appears that the same advantage which a republic has over a democracy, in controlling the effects of factions, is enjoyed by a large over a small republic—is enjoyed by the Union over the states composing it. Does the advantage consist in the substitution of representatives whose enlightened views and virtuous sentiments render them superior to local prejudices and to schemes of injustice? It will not be denied that the representation of the Union will be most likely to possess these requisite endowments. Does it consist in the greater security afforded by a greater variety of parties, against the event of any one party being able to outnumber and oppress the rest? In an equal degree does the increased variety of parties comprised within the Union, increase this security. Does it, in fine, consist in the greater obstacles opposed to the concert and accomplishment of the secret wishes of an unjust and interested majority? Here, again, the extent of the Union gives it the most palpable advantage.

The influence of factious leaders may kindle a flame within their particular states but will be unable to spread a general conflagration through the other states. A religious sect may degenerate into a political faction in a part of the Confederacy; but the variety of sects dispersed over the entire face of it must secure the national councils against any danger from that source. A rage for paper money, for an abolition of debts, for an equal division of property, or for any other improper or wicked project will be less apt to pervade the whole body of the Union than a particular member of it; in the same proportion as such a malady is more likely to taint a particular county or district than an entire state.

In the extent and proper structure of the Union, therefore, we behold a re-

publican remedy for the diseases most incident to republican government. And according to the degree of pleasure and pride we feel in being republicans, ought to be our zeal in cherishing the spirit and supporting the character of Federalists.

PUBLIUS

C. THE FEDERALIST NO. 14 (MADISON)

To the People of the State of New York:

We have seen the necessity of the Union, as our bulwark against foreign danger, as the conservator of peace among ourselves, as the guardian of our commerce and other common interests, as the only substitute for those military establishments which have subverted the liberties of the Old World, and as the proper antidote for the diseases of faction, which have proved fatal to other popular governments, and of which alarming symptoms have been betrayed by our own. All that remains, within this branch of our inquiries, is to take notice of an objection that may be drawn from the great extent of country which the Union embraces. A few observations on this subject will be the more proper, as it is perceived that the adversaries of the new Constitution are availing themselves of a prevailing prejudice with regard to the practicable sphere of republican administration, in order to supply, by imaginary difficulties, the want of those solid objections which they endeavor in vain to find.

The error which limits republican government to a narrow district has been unfolded and refuted in preceding papers. I remark here only that it seems to owe its rise and prevalence chiefly to the confounding of a republic with a democracy and applying to the former reasonings drawn from the nature of the latter. The true distinction between these forms was also adverted to on a former occasion. It is that, in a democracy, the people meet and exercise the government in person; in a republic, they assemble and administer it by their

representatives and agents. A democracy, consequently, will be confined to a small spot. A republic may be extended over a large region.

To this accidental source of the error may be added the artifice of some celebrated authors, whose writings have had a great share in forming the modern standard of political opinions. Being subjects either of an absolute or limited monarchy, they have endeavored to heighten the advantages, or palliate the evils, of those forms, by placing in comparison the vices and defects of the republican, and by citing as specimens of the latter the turbulent democracies of ancient Greece and modern Italy. Under the confusion of names, it has been an easy task to transfer to a republic observations applicable to a democracy only; and, among others, the observation that it can never be established but among a small number of people, living within a small compass of territory.

Such a fallacy may have been the less perceived, as most of the popular governments of antiquity were of the democratic species; and even in modern Europe, to which we owe the great principle of representation, no example is seen of a government wholly popular, and founded, at the same time, wholly on that principle. If Europe has the merit of discovering this great mechanical power in government, by the simple agency of which the will of the largest political body may be concentrated, and its force directed to any object which the public good requires, America can claim the merit of making the discovery the basis of unmixed and extensive republics. It is only to be lamented that any of her citizens should wish to deprive her of the additional merit of displaying its full efficacy in the establishment of the comprehensive system now under her consideration.

As the natural limit of a democracy is that distance from the central point which will just permit the most remote citizens to assemble as often as their public functions demand, and will include no greater number than can join in those functions; so the natural limit of a republic is that distance from the center which will barely allow the representatives of the people to meet as often as may be necessary for the administration of public affairs. Can it be said that the limits of the United States exceed this distance? It will not be said by those who recollect that the Atlantic coast is the longest side of the Union, that during the term of thirteen years the representatives of the states have been almost continually assembled, and that the members from the most distant states are not chargeable with greater intermissions of attendance than those from the states in the neighborhood of Congress.

That we may form a juster estimate with regard to this interesting subject, let us resort to the actual dimensions of the Union. The limits, as fixed by the treaty of peace, are: on the east the Atlantic, on the south the latitude of thirty-one degrees, on the west the Mississippi, and on the north an irregular line running in some instances beyond the forty-fifth degree, in others falling as low as the forty-second. The southern shore of Lake Erie lies below that latitude. Computing the distance between the thirty-first and forty-fifth degrees, it amounts to nine hundred and seventy-three common miles; computing it from thirty-one to forty-two degrees, to seven hundred and sixty-four miles and a half. Taking the mean for the distance, the amount will be eight hundred and sixty-eight miles and three-fourths. The mean distance from the Atlantic to the Mississippi does not probably exceed seven hundred and fifty miles. On a comparison of this extent with that of several countries in Europe, the practicability of rendering our system commensurate to it appears to be demonstrable. It is not a great deal larger than Germany, where a diet representing the whole empire is continually assembled; or than Poland before the late dismemberment, where another national diet was the depositary of the supreme power. Passing by France and Spain, we find that in Great Britain, inferior as it may be in size, the representatives of the northern extremity of the island have as far to travel to the national council as will be required of those of the most remote parts of the Union. . . .

D. THE FEDERALIST NO. 15 (HAMILTON)

To the People of the State of New York:

In the course of the preceding papers, I have endeavored, my fellow-citizens, to place before you, in a clear and convincing light, the importance of Union to your political safety and happiness. I have unfolded to you a complication of dangers to which you would be exposed, should you permit that sacred knot which binds the people of America together to be severed or dissolved by ambition or by avarice, by jealousy or by misrepresentation. In the sequel of the inquiry through which I propose to accompany you, the truths intended to be inculcated will receive further confirmation from facts and arguments hitherto unnoticed. If the road over which you will still have to pass should in some places appear to you tedious or irksome, you will recollect that you are in quest of information on a subject the most momentous which can engage the attention of a free people, that the field through which you have to travel is in itself spacious, and that the difficulties of the journey have been unnecessarily increased by the mazes with which sophistry has beset the way. It will be my aim to remove the obstacles to your progress in as compendious a manner as it can be done, without sacrificing utility to dispatch.

In pursuance of the plan which I have laid down for the discussion of the subject, the point next in order to be examined is the "insufficiency of the present Confederation to the preservation of the Union." It may perhaps be asked what need there is of reasoning or proof to illustrate a position which is not either controverted or doubted, to which the understandings and feelings of all classes of men assent, and which in substance is admitted by the opponents as well as by the friends of the new Constitution? It must in truth be acknowledged that, however these may differ in other respects, they in general appear to harmonize in this sentiment, at least, that there are material imperfections in our national system and that something is necessary to be done to rescue us from impending anarchy. The facts that support this opinion are no longer objects of speculation. They have forced themselves upon the sensibility of the people at large and have at length extorted from those, whose mistaken policy has had the principal share in precipitating the extremity at which we are arrived, a reluctant confession of the reality of those defects in the scheme of our federal government, which have been long pointed out and regretted by the intelligent friends of the Union.

We may indeed with propriety be said to have reached almost the last stage of national humiliation. There is scarcely anything that can wound the pride or degrade the character of an independent nation which we do not experience. Are there engagements to the performance of which we are held by every tie respectable among men? These are the subjects of constant and unblushing viola-

tion. Do we owe debts to foreigners and to our own citizens contracted in a time of imminent peril for the preservation of our political existence? These remain without any proper or satisfactory provision for their discharge. Have we valuable territories and important posts in the possession of a foreign power which, by express stipulations, ought long since to have been surrendered? These are still retained, to the prejudice of our interests not less than of our rights. Are we in a condition to resent or to repel the aggression? We have neither troops, nor treasury, nor government.[2] Are we even in a condition to remonstrate with dignity? The just imputations on our own faith, in respect to the same treaty, ought first to be removed. Are we entitled by nature and compact to a free participation in the navigation of the Mississippi? Spain excludes us from it. Is public credit an indispensable resource in time of public danger? We seem to have abandoned its cause as desperate and irretrievable. Is commerce of importance to national wealth? Ours is at the lowest point of declension. Is respectability in the eyes of foreign powers a safeguard against foreign encroachments? The imbecility of our government even forbids them to treat with us. Our ambassadors abroad are the mere pageants of mimic sovereignty. Is a violent and unnatural decrease in the value of land a symptom of national distress? The price of improved land in most parts of the country is much lower than can be accounted for by the quantity of waste land at market, and can only be fully explained by that want of private and public confidence, which are so alarmingly prevalent among all ranks, and which have a direct tendency to depreciate property of every kind. Is private credit the friend and patron of industry? That most useful kind which relates to borrowing and lending is re-

2. "I mean for the Union."—*Publius.* AUTHOR'S NOTES.

duced within the narrowest limits, and this still more from an opinion of insecurity than from the scarcity of money. To shorten an enumeration of particulars which can afford neither pleasure nor instruction, it may in general be demanded, what indication is there of national disorder, poverty, and insignificance that could befall a community so peculiarly blessed with natural advantages as we are, which does not form a part of the dark catalogue of our public misfortunes?

This is the melancholy situation to which we have been brought by those very maxims and councils which would now deter us from adopting the proposed Constitution; and which, not content with having conducted us to the brink of a precipice, seem resolved to plunge us into the abyss that awaits us below. Here, my countrymen, impelled by every motive that ought to influence an enlightened people, let us make a firm stand for our safety, our tranquility, our dignity, our reputation. Let us at last break the fatal charm which has too long seduced us from the paths of felicity and prosperity.

It is true, as has been before observed, that facts, too stubborn to be resisted, have produced a species of general assent to the abstract proposition that there exist material defects in our national system; but the usefulness of the concession, on the part of the old adversaries of federal measures, is destroyed by a strenuous opposition to a remedy, upon the only principles that can give it a chance of success. While they admit that the government of the United States is destitute of energy, they contend against conferring upon it those powers which are requisite to supply that energy. They seem still to aim at things repugnant and irreconcilable; at an augmentation of federal authority, without diminution of state authority; at sovereignty in the Union, and complete independence in the members. They still, in fine, seem to cherish with blind devotion the political monster of an *imperium in imperio*. This renders a full display of the principal defects of the Confederation necessary, in order to show that the evils we experience do not proceed from minute or partial imperfections but from fundamental errors in the structure of the building which cannot be amended otherwise than by an alteration in the first principles and main pillars of the fabric.

The great and radical vice in the construction of the existing Confederation is in the principle of LEGISLATION for STATES or GOVERNMENTS, in their CORPORATE or COLLECTIVE CAPACITIES, and as contradistinguished from the INDIVIDUALS of which they consist. Though this principle does not run through all the powers delegated to the Union, yet it pervades and governs those on which the efficacy of the rest depends. Except as to the rule of apportionment, the United States has an indefinite discretion to make requisitions for men and money; but they have no authority to raise either, by regulations extending to the individual citizens of America. The consequence of this is that, though in theory their resolutions concerning those objects are laws, constitutionally binding on the members of the Union, yet in practice they are mere recommendations which the states observe or disregard at their option.

It is a singular instance of the capriciousness of the human mind that, after all the admonitions we have had from experience on this head, there should still be found men who object to the new Constitution, for deviating from a principle which has been found the bane of the old, and which is in itself evidently incompatible with the idea of GOVERNMENT; a principle, in short, which, if it is to be executed at all, must substitute the violent and sanguinary agency of the sword to the mild influence of the magistracy.

There is nothing absurd or impracticable in the idea of a league or alliance between independent nations for certain defined purposes precisely stated in a treaty regulating all the details of time, place, circumstance, and quantity; leaving nothing to future discretion; and depending for its execution on the good faith of the parties. Compacts of this kind exist among all civilized nations, subject to the usual vicissitudes of peace and war, of observance and nonobservance, as the interests or passions of the contrasting powers dictate. In the early part of the present century there was an epidemical rage in Europe for this species of compacts, from which the politicians of the times fondly hoped for benefits which were never realized. With a view to establishing the equilibrium of power and the peace of that part of the world, all the resources of negotiations were exhausted, and triple and quadruple alliances were formed; but they were scarcely formed before they were broken, giving an instructive but afflicting lesson to mankind, how little dependence is to be placed on treaties which have no other sanction than the obligations of good faith, and which oppose general considerations of peace and justice to the impulse of any immediate interest or passion.

If the particular states in this country are disposed to stand in a similar relation to each other, and to drop the project of a general DISCRETIONARY SUPERINTENDENCE, the scheme would indeed be pernicious, and would entail upon us all the mischiefs which have been enumerated under the first head; but it would have the merit of being, at least, consistent and practicable. Abandoning all views toward a confederate government, this would bring us to a simple alliance offensive and defensive and would place us in a situation to be alternately friends and enemies of each other, as our mutual jealousies and rivalships, nourished by the intrigues of foreign nations, should prescribe to us.

But if we are unwilling to be placed in this perilous situation, if we still will adhere to the design of a national government, or, which is the same thing, of a superintending power, under the direction of a common council, we must resolve to incorporate into our plan those ingredients which may be considered as forming the characteristic difference between a league and a government; we must extend the authority of the Union to the persons of the citizens—the only proper objects of government.

Government implies the power of making laws. It is essential to the idea of a law that it be attended with a sanction, or, in other words, a penalty or punishment for disobedience. If there be no penalty annexed to disobedience, the resolutions or commands which pretend to be laws will, in fact, amount to nothing more than advice or recommendation. This penalty, whatever it may be, can only be inflicted in two ways: by the agency of the courts and ministers of justice, or by military force; by the COERCION of the magistracy, or by the COERCION of arms. The first kind can evidently apply only to men, the last kind must, of necessity, be employed against bodies politic, or communities, or states. It is evident that there is no process of a court by which the observance of the laws can, in the last resort, be enforced. Sentences may be denounced against them for violations of their duty, but these sentences can only be carried into execution by the sword. In an association where the general authority is confined to the collective bodies of the communities that compose it, every breach of the laws must involve a state of war, and military execution must become the only instrument of civil obedience. Such a state of things can certainly not deserve the name of government, nor would any prudent man choose to commit his happiness to it.

There was a time when we were told that breaches, by the states, of the regulations of the federal authority were not to be expected; that a sense of common interest would preside over the conduct of the respective members and would beget a full compliance with all the constitutional requisitions of the Union. This language, at the present day, would appear as wild as a great part of what we now hear from the same quarter will be thought, when we shall have received further lessons from that best oracle of wisdom, experience. It at all times betrayed an ignorance of the true springs by which human conduct is actuated, and belied the original inducements to the establishment of civil power. Why has government been instituted at all? Because the passions of men will not conform to the dictates of reason and justice without constraint. Has it been found that bodies of men act with more rectitude or greater disinterestedness than individuals? The contrary of this has been inferred by all accurate observers of the conduct of mankind; and the inference is founded upon obvious reasons. Regard to reputation has a less active influence, when the infamy of a bad action is to be divided among a number, than when it is to fall singly upon one. A spirit of faction, which is apt to mingle its poison in the deliberations of all bodies of men, will often hurry the persons of whom they are composed into improprieties and excesses, for which they would blush in a private capacity.

In addition to all this, there is, in the nature of sovereign power, an impatience of control that disposes those who are invested with the exercise of it to look with an evil eye upon all external attempts to restrain or direct its operations. From this spirit it happens that, in every political association which is formed upon the principle of uniting in a common interest a number of lesser sovereignties, there will be found a kind of eccentric tendency in the subordinate or inferior orbs, by the operation of which there will be a perpetual effort in each to fly off from the common center. This tendency is not difficult to be accounted for. It has its origin in the love of power. Power controlled or abridged is almost always the rival and enemy of that power by which it is controlled or abridged. This simple proposition will teach us how little reason there is to expect that the persons intrusted with the administration of the affairs of the particular members of a confederacy will at all times be ready, with perfect good humor, and an unbiased regard to the public weal, to execute the resolutions or decrees of the general authority. The reverse of this results from the constitution of human nature.

If, therefore, the measures of the Confederacy cannot be executed without the intervention of the particular administrations, there will be little prospect of their being executed at all. The rulers of the respective members, whether they have a constitutional right to do it or not, will undertake to judge of the propriety of the measures themselves. They will consider the conformity of the thing proposed or required to their immediate interests or aims; the momentary conveniences or inconveniences that would attend its adoption. All this will be done; and in a spirit of interested and suspicious scrutiny, without that knowledge of national circumstances and reasons of state which is essential to a right judgment, and with that strong predilection in favor of local objects which can hardly fail to mislead the decision. The same process must be repeated in every member of which the body is constituted; and the execution of the plans, framed by the councils of the whole, will always fluctuate on the discretion of the ill-informed and prejudiced opinion of every part. Those who have been conversant in the proceedings of popular assemblies; who have seen how difficult it often is, where there is no exterior pressure of circumstances, to bring them to harmonious resolutions on important points, will readily conceive how impossible it must be to induce a number of such assemblies, deliberating at a distance from each other, at different times, and under different impressions, long to co-operate in the same views and pursuits.

In our case, the concurrence of thirteen distinct sovereign wills is requisite, under the Confederation, to the complete execution of every important measure that proceeds from the Union. It has happened as was to have been foreseen. The measures of the Union have not been executed; the delinquencies of the states have, step by step, matured themselves to an extreme which has, at length, arrested all the wheels of the national government and brought them to an awful stand. Congress at this time scarcely possess the means of keeping up the forms of administration, till the states can have time to agree upon a more substantial substitute for the present shadow of a federal government. Things did not come to this desperate extremity at once. The causes which have been specified produced at first only unequal and disproportionate degrees of compliance with the requisitions of the Union. The greater deficiencies of some states furnished the pretext of example and the temptation of interest to the complying, or to the least delinquent states. Why should we do more in proportion than those who are embarked with us in the same political voyage? Why should we consent to bear more than our proper share of the common burden? These were suggestions which human selfishness could not withstand, and which even speculative men, who looked forward to remote consequences, could not, without hesitation, combat. Each state, yielding to the persuasive voice of immediate interest or convenience, has successively withdrawn its support, till the frail and tottering edifice seems ready to fall upon our heads and to crush us beneath its ruins.

PUBLIUS

E. THE FEDERALIST NO. 16 (HAMILTON)

To the People of the State of New York:

The tendency of the principle of legislation for states, or communities, in their political capacities, as it has been exemplified by the experiment we have made of it, is equally attested by the events which have befallen all other governments of the confederate kind, of which we have any account, in exact proportion to its prevalence in those systems. The confirmations of this fact will be worthy of a distinct and particular examination. I shall content myself with barely observing here, that, of all the confederacies of antiquity which history has handed down to us, the Lycian and Achaean leagues, as far as there remain vestiges of them, appear to have been most free from the fetters of that mistaken principle, and were accordingly those which have best deserved, and have most liberally received, the applauding suffrages of political writers.[3]

This exceptionable principle may, as truly as emphatically, be styled the parent of anarchy: It has been seen that delinquencies in the members of the Union are its natural and necessary offspring and that, whenever they happen, the only constitutional remedy is force, and the immediate effect of the use of it, civil war.

It remains to inquire how far so odious an engine of government, in its application to us, would even be capable of answering its end. If there should not be a large army constantly at the disposal of the national government, it would

3. Two leagues of ancient Greece; for Madison's notes on confederacies, ancient and modern, see his *Writings*, ed. Gaillard Hunt (9 vols.; New York, 1900–1910), II, 369–90.

either not be able to employ force at all, or, when this could be done, it would amount to a war between parts of the Confederacy concerning the infractions of a league, in which the strongest combination would be most likely to prevail, whether it consisted of those who supported or of those who resisted the general authority. It would rarely happen that the delinquency to be redressed would be confined to a single member, and if there were more than one who had neglected their duty, similarity of situation would induce them to unite for common defense. Independent of this motive of sympathy, if a large and influential state should happen to be the aggressing member, it would commonly have weight enough with its neighbors to win over some of them as associates to its cause. Specious arguments of danger to the common liberty could easily be contrived; plausible excuses for the deficiencies of the party could, without difficulty, be invented to alarm the apprehensions, inflame the passions, and conciliate the good will even of those states which were not chargeable with any violation or omission of duty. This would be the more likely to take place, as the delinquencies of the larger members might be expected sometimes to proceed from an ambitious premeditation in their rulers, with a view to getting rid of all external control upon their designs of personal aggrandizement; the better to effect which it is presumable they would tamper beforehand with leading individuals in the adjacent states. If associates could not be found at home, recourse would be had to the aid of foreign powers, who would seldom be disinclined to encouraging the dissensions of a Confederacy, from the firm union of which they had so much to fear. When the sword is once drawn, the passions of men observe no bounds of moderation. The suggestions of wounded pride, the instigations of irritated resentment, would be apt to carry the states against which the arms of the Union were exerted to any extremes necessary to avenge the affront or to avoid the disgrace of submission. The first war of this kind would probably terminate in a dissolution of the Union.

This may be considered as the violent death of the Confederacy. Its more natural death is what we now seem to be on the point of experiencing, if the federal system be not speedily renovated in a more substantial form. It is not probable, considering the genius of this country, that the complying states would often be inclined to support the authority of the Union by engaging in a war against the noncomplying states. They would always be more ready to pursue the milder course of putting themselves upon an equal footing with the delinquent members by an imitation of their example. And the guilt of all would thus become the security of all. Our past experience has exhibited the operation of this spirit in its full light. There would, in fact, be an insuperable difficulty in ascertaining when force could with propriety be employed. In the article of pecuniary contribution, which would be the most usual source of delinquency, it would often be impossible to decide whether it had proceeded from disinclination or inability. The pretense of the latter would always be at hand. And the case must be very flagrant in which its fallacy could be detected with sufficient certainty to justify the harsh expedient of compulsion. It is easy to see that this problem alone, as often as it should occur, would open a wide field for the exercise of factious views, of partiality, and of oppression, in the majority that happened to prevail in the national council.

It seems to require no pains to prove that the states ought not to prefer a national Constitution which could only be kept in motion by the instrumentality of a large army continually on foot to execute the ordinary requisitions or decrees of the government. And yet this is the plain alternative involved by those who wish to deny it the power of extending its operations to individuals. Such a scheme, if practicable at all, would instantly degenerate into a military despotism; but it will be found in every light impracticable. The resources of the Union would not be equal to the maintenance of an army considerable enough to confine the larger states within the limits of their duty; nor would the means ever be furnished of forming such an army in the first instance. Whoever considers the populousness and strength of several of these states singly at the present juncture, and looks forward to what they will become, even at the distance of half a century, will at once dismiss as idle and visionary any scheme which aims at regulating their movements by laws to operate upon them in their collective capacities and to be executed by a coercion applicable to them in the same capacities. A project of this kind is little less romantic than the monster-taming spirit which is attributed to the fabulous heroes and demigods of antiquity.

Even in those confederacies which have been composed of members smaller than many of our counties, the principle of legislation for sovereign states, supported by military coercion, has never been found effectual. It has rarely been attempted to be employed but against the weaker members; and in most instances attempts to coerce the refractory and disobedient have been the signals of bloody wars, in which one half of the confederacy has displayed its banners against the other half.

The result of these observations to an intelligent mind must be clearly this, that if it be possible at any rate to construct a federal government capable of regulating the common concerns, and preserving the general tranquillity, it must be founded, as to the objects committed to its care, upon the reverse of the principle contended for by the opponents of the proposed Constitution. It must carry its agency to the persons of the citizens. It must stand in need of no intermediate legislations but must itself be empowered to employ the arm of the ordinary magistrate to execute its own resolutions. The majesty of the national authority must be manifested through the medium of the courts of justice. The government of the Union, like that of each state, must be able to address itself immediately to the hopes and fears of individuals; and to attract to its support those passions which have the strongest influence upon the human heart. It must, in short, possess all the means, and have a right to resort to all the methods, of executing the powers with which it is intrusted, that are possessed and exercised by the governments of the particular states.

To this reasoning it may perhaps be objected, that if any state should be disaffected to the authority of the Union, it could at any time obstruct the execution of its laws and bring the matter to the same issue of force, with the necessity of which the opposite scheme is reproached.

The plausibility of this objection will vanish the moment we advert to the essential difference between a mere NON-COMPLIANCE and a DIRECT and ACTIVE RESISTANCE. If the interposition of the state legislatures be necessary to give effect to a measure of the Union, they have only NOT TO ACT, or TO ACT EVASIVELY, and the measure is defeated. This neglect of duty may be disguised under affected but unsubstantial provisions, so as not to appear, and of course not to excite any alarm in the people for the safety of the Constitution. The state leaders may even make a merit of their surreptitious invasions of it on the ground of some temporary convenience, exemption, or advantage.

But if the execution of the laws of the national government should not require the intervention of the state legislatures, if they were to pass into immediate operation upon the citizens themselves, the particular governments could not interrupt their progress without an open and violent exertion of an unconstitutional power. No omissions nor evasions would answer the end. They would be obliged to act, and in such a manner as would leave no doubt that they had encroached on the national rights. An experiment of this nature would always be hazardous in the face of a constitution in any degree competent to its own defense, and of a people enlightened enough to distinguish between a legal exercise and an illegal usurpation of auauthority. The success of it would require not merely a factious majority in the legislature, but the concurrence of the courts of justice and of the body of the people. If the judges were not embarked in a conspiracy with the legislature, they would pronounce the resolutions of such a majority to be contrary to the supreme law of the land, unconstitutional and void. If the people were not tainted with the spirit of their state representatives, they, as the natural guardians of the Constitution, would throw their weight into the national scale and give it a decided preponderancy in the contest. Attempts of this kind would not often be made with levity or rashness because they could seldom be made without danger to the authors, unless in cases of a tyrannical exercise of the federal authority.

If opposition to the national government should arise from the disorderly conduct of refractory or seditious individuals, it could be overcome by the same means which are daily employed against the same evil under the state governments. The magistracy, being equally the ministers of the law of the land, from whatever source it might emanate, would doubtless be as ready to guard the national as the local regulations from the inroads of private licentiousness. As to those partial commotions and insurrections, which sometimes disquiet society, from the intrigues of an inconsiderable faction, or from sudden or occasional ill humors that do not infect the great body of the community, the general government could command more extensive resources for the suppression of disturbances of that kind than would be in the power of any single member. And as to those mortal feuds which, in certain conjunctures, spread a conflagration through a whole nation, or through a very large proportion of it, proceeding either from weighty causes of discontent given by the government or from the contagion of some violent popular paroxysm, they do not fall within any ordinary rules of calculation. When they happen, they commonly amount to revolutions and dismemberments of empire. No form of government can always either avoid or control them. It is in vain to hope to guard against events too mighty for human foresight or precaution, and it would be idle to object to a government because it could not perform impossibilities.

PUBLIUS

F. THE FEDERALIST NO. 39 (MADISON)

To the People of the State of New York:

The last paper having concluded the observations which were meant to introduce a candid survey of the plan of government reported by the convention, we now proceed to the execution of that part of our undertaking.

The first question that offers itself is whether the general form and aspect of the government be strictly republican. It is evident that no other form would be reconcilable with the genius of the people of America; with the fundamental principles of the Revolution; or with that honorable determination which animates every votary of freedom, to rest all our political experiments on the capacity of mankind for self-government.

If the plan of the convention, therefore, be found to depart from the republican character, its advocates must abandon it as no longer defensible.

What, then, are the distinctive characters of the republican form? Were an answer to this question to be sought, not by recurring to principles, but in the application of the term by political writers, to the constitutions of different states, no satisfactory one would ever be found. Holland, in which no particle of the supreme authority is derived from the people, has passed almost universally under the denomination of a republic. The same title has been bestowed on Venice, where absolute power over the great body of the people is exercised, in the most absolute manner, by a small body of hereditary nobles. Poland, which is a mixture of aristocracy and of monarchy in their worst forms, has been dignified with the same appellation. The government of England, which has one republican branch only, combined with an hereditary aristocracy and monarchy, has, with equal impropriety, been frequently placed on the list of republics. These examples, which are nearly as dissimilar to each other as to a genuine republic, show the extreme inaccuracy with which the term has been used in political disquisitions.

If we resort for a criterion to the different principles on which different forms of government are established, we may define a republic to be, or at least may bestow that name on, a government which derives all its powers directly or indirectly from the great body of the people, and is administered by persons holding their offices during pleasure, for a limited period, or during good behavior. It is essential to such a government that it be derived from the great body of the society, not from an inconsiderable proportion, or a favored class of it; otherwise a handful of tyrannical nobles, exercising their oppressions by a delegation of their powers, might aspire to the rank of republicans, and claim for their government the honorable title of republic. It is sufficient for such a government that the persons administering it be appointed, either directly or indirectly, by the people; and that they hold their appointments by either of the tenures just specified; otherwise every government in the United States, as well as every other popular government that has been or can be well organized or well executed, would be degraded from the republican character. According to the constitution of every state in the Union, some or other of the officers of government are appointed indirectly only by the people. According to most of them, the chief magistrate himself is so appointed. And according to one, this mode of appointment is extended to one of the co-ordinate branches of the legislature. According to all the constitutions, also, the tenure of the highest offices is extended to a definite period, and in many instances, both within the legislative and executive departments, to a period of years. According to the provisions of most of the constitutions, again, as well as according to the most respectable and received opinions on the subject, the members of the judiciary department are to retain their offices by the firm tenure of good behavior.

On comparing the Constitution planned by the convention with the standard here fixed, we perceive at once that it is, in the most rigid sense, conformable to it. The House of Representatives, like that of one branch at least of all the state legislatures, is elected immediately by the great body of the people. The Senate, like the present Congress, and the senate of Maryland, derives its appointment indirectly from the people. The President is indirectly derived from the choice of the people, according to the example in most of the states. Even the judges, with all other officers of the Union, will, as in the several states, be the choice, though a remote choice, of the people themselves. The duration of the appointments is equally conformable to the republican standard and to the model of state constitutions. The House of Representatives is elective, for the period of six years; and for the period of two years as in the state of South Carolina. The Senate is elective, for the period of six years; which is but one year more than the period of the senate of Maryland, and but two more than that of the senates of New York and Virginia. The President is to continue in office for the period of four years; as in New York and Delaware the chief magistrate is elected for three years, and in South Carolina for two years. In the other states the election is annual. In several of the states, however, no constitutional provision is made for the impeachment of the chief magistrate. And in Delaware and Virginia he is not impeachable till out of office. The President of the United States is impeachable at any time during his continuance in office. The tenure by which the judges are to hold their places is, as it unquestionably ought to be, that of good behavior. The tenure of the ministerial offices generally will be a subject of legal regulation, conformably to the reason of the case and the example of the state constitutions.

Could any further proof be required of the republican complexion of this system, the most decisive one might be found in its absolute prohibition of titles of nobility, both under the federal and the state governments; and in its express guaranty of the republican form to each of the latter.

"But it was not sufficient," say the adversaries of the proposed Constitution, "for the convention to adhere to the republican form. They ought, with equal care, to have preserved the federal form, which regards the Union as a Confederacy of sovereign states; instead of which, they have framed a national government, which regards the Union as a consolida-

tion of the states." And it is asked by what authority this bold and radical innovation was undertaken? The handle which has been made of this objection requires that it should be examined with some precision.

Without inquiring into the accuracy of the distinction on which the objection is founded, it will be necessary to a just estimate of its force, first, to ascertain the real character of the government in question; secondly, to inquire how far the convention were authorized to propose such a government; and, thirdly, how far the duty they owed to their country could supply any defect of regular authority.

First. In order to ascertain the real character of the government, it may be considered in relation to the foundation on which it is to be established; to the sources from which its ordinary powers are to be drawn; to the operation of those powers; to the extent of them; and to the authority by which future changes in the government are to be introduced.

On examining the first relation, it appears, on one hand, that the Constitution is to be founded on the assent and ratification of the people of America, given by deputies elected for the special purpose; but, on the other, that this assent and ratification is to be given by the people, not as individuals composing one entire nation, but as composing the distinct and independent states to which they respectively belong. It is to be the assent and ratification of the several states, derived from the supreme authority in each state—the authority of the people themselves. The act, therefore, establishing the Constitution will not be a national but a federal act.

That it will be a federal and not a national act, as these terms are understood by the objectors; the act of the people, as forming so many independent states, not as forming one aggregate nation, is obvious from this single consideration, that it is to result neither from the decision of a majority of the people of the Union nor from that of a majority of the states. It must result from the unanimous assent of the several states that are parties to it, differing no otherwise from their ordinary assent than in its being expressed, not by the legislative authority, but by that of the people themselves. Were the people regarded in this transaction as forming one nation, the will of the majority of the whole people of the United States would bind the minority, in the same manner as the majority in each state must bind the minority; and the will of the majority must be determined either by a comparison of the individual votes, or by considering the will of the majority of the states as evidence of the will of a majority of the people of the United states. Neither of these rules has been adopted. Each state, in ratifying the Constitution, is considered as a sovereign body, independent of all others, and only to be bound by its own voluntary act. In this relation, then, the new Constitution will, if established, be a federal, and not a national constitution.

The next relation is to the sources from which the ordinary powers of government are to be derived. The House of Representatives will derive its powers from the people of America; and the people will be represented in the same proportion, and on the same principle, as they are in the legislature of a particular state. So far the government is national, not federal. The Senate, on the other hand, will derive its powers from the states, as political and coequal societies; and these will be represented on the principle of equality in the Senate, as they now are in the existing Congress. So far the government is federal, not national. The executive power will be derived from a very compound source. The immediate election of the President is to be made by the states in their political characters. The votes allotted to them are in a compound ratio, which

considers them partly as distinct and coequal societies, partly as unequal members of the same society. The eventual election, again, is to be made by that branch of the legislature which consists of the national representatives; but in this particular act they are to be thrown into the form of individual delegations, from so many distinct and coequal bodies politic. From this aspect of the government, it appears to be of a mixed character, presenting at least as many federal as national features.

The difference between a federal and national government, as it relates to the operation of the government, is supposed to consist in this, that in the former the powers operate on the political bodies composing the Confederacy, in their political capacities; in the latter, on the individual citizens composing the nation, in their individual capacities. On trying the Constitution by this criterion, it falls under the national, not the federal, characters; though perhaps not so completely as has been understood. In several cases, and particularly in the trial of controversies to which states may be parties, they must be viewed and proceeded against in their collective and political capacities only. So far the national countenance of the government on this side seems to be disfigured by a few federal features. But this blemish is perhaps unavoidable in any plan; and the operation of the government on the people, in their individual capacities, in its ordinary and most essential proceedings, may, on the whole, designate it, in this relation, a national government.

But if the government be national with regard to the operation of its powers, it changes its aspect again when we contemplate it in relation to the extent of its powers. The idea of a national government involves in it, not only an authority over the individual citizens, but an indefinite supremacy over all persons and things, so far as they are objects of lawful government. Among a people consolidated into one nation, this supremacy is completely vested in the national legislature. Among communities united for particular purposes, it is vested partly in the general and partly in the municipal legislatures. In the former case, all local authorities are subordinate to the supreme; and may be controlled, directed, or abolished by it at pleasure. In the latter, the local or municipal authorities form distinct and independent portions of the supremacy, no more subject, within their respective spheres, to the general authority, than the general authority is subject to them, within its own sphere. In this relation, then, the proposed government cannot be deemed a national one; since its jurisdiction extends to certain enumerated objects only, and leaves to the several states a residuary and inviolable sovereignty over all other objects. It is true that in controversies relating to the boundary between the two jurisdictions, the tribunal which is ultimately to decide is to be established under the general government. But this does not change the principle of the case. The decision is to be impartially made, according to the rules of the Constitution; and all the usual and most effectual precautions are taken to secure this impartiality. Some such tribunal is clearly essential to prevent an appeal to the sword and a dissolution of the compact; and that it ought to be established under the general rather than under the local governments, or, to speak more properly, that it could be safely established under the first alone, is a position not likely to be combated.

If we try the Constitution by its last relation to the authority by which amendments are to be made, we find it neither wholly national nor wholly federal. Were it wholly national, the supreme and ultimate authority would reside in the majority of the people of the Union; and this authority would be competent at all times, like that of a majority of every national society, to alter or abolish its established government. Were it wholly federal, on the other hand, the concurrence of each state in the Union would be essential to every alteration that would be binding on all. The mode provided by the plan of the convention is not founded on either of these principles. In requiring more than a majority, and particularly in computing the proportion by states, not by citizens, it departs from the national and advances toward the federal character; in rendering the concurrence of less than the whole number of states sufficient, it loses again the federal and partakes of the national character.

The proposed Constitution, therefore, is, in strictness, neither a national nor a federal Constitution, but a composition of both. In its foundation it is federal, not national; in the sources from which the ordinary powers of the government are drawn, it is partly federal and partly national; in the operation of these powers, it is national, not federal; in the extent of them, again, it is federal, not national; and, finally, in the authoritative mode of introducing amendments, it is neither wholly federal nor wholly national.

PUBLIUS

G. THE FEDERALIST NO. 47 (MADISON)

To the People of the State of New York:

Having reviewed the general form of the proposed government and the general mass of power allotted to it, I proceed to examine the particular structure of this government, and the distribution of this mass of power among its constituent parts.

One of the principal objections inculcated by the more respectable adversaries to the Constitution is its supposed violation of the political maxim that the legislative, executive, and judiciary departments ought to be separate and distinct. In the structure of the federal government, no regard, it is said, seems to have been paid to this essential precaution in favor of liberty. The several departments of power are distributed and blended in such a manner as at once to destroy all symmetry and beauty of form, and to expose some of the essential parts of the edifice to the danger of being crushed by the disproportionate weight of other parts.

No political truth is certainly of greater intrinsic value, or is stamped with the authority of more enlightened patrons of liberty, than that on which the objection is founded. The accumulation of all powers, legislative, executive, and judiciary, in the same hands, whether of one, a few, or many, and whether hereditary, self-appointed, or elective, may justly be pronounced the very definition of tyranny. Were the federal Constitution, therefore, really chargeable with the accumulation of power, or with a mixture of powers, having a dangerous tendency to such an accumulation, no further arguments would be necessary to inspire a universal reprobation of the system. I persuade myself, however, that it will be made apparent to everyone that the charge cannot be supported, and that the maxim on which it relies has been totally misconceived and misapplied. In order to form correct ideas on this important subject, it will be proper to investigate the sense in which the preservation of liberty requires that the three great departments of power should be separate and distinct.

The oracle who is always consulted and cited on this subject is the celebrated Montesquieu. If he be not the author of this invaluable precept in the science of politics, he has the merit at least of displaying and recommending it most effectually to the attention of mankind. Let us endeavor, in the first place, to ascertain his meaning on this point.

The British constitution was to Montesquieu what Homer has been to the didactic writers on epic poetry. As the latter have considered the work of the immortal bard as the perfect model from which the principles and rules of the epic art were to be drawn, and by which all similar works were to be judged, so this great political critic appears to have viewed the constitution of England as the standard, or, to use his own expression, as the mirror of political liberty; and to have delivered, in the form of elementary truths, the several characteristic principles of that particular system. That we may be sure, then, not to mistake his meaning in this case, let us recur to the source from which the maxim was drawn.

On the slightest view of the British constitution, we must perceive that the legislative, executive, and judiciary departments are by no means totally separate and distinct from each other. The executive magistrate forms an integral part of the legislative authority. He alone has the prerogative of making treaties with foreign sovereigns, which, when made, have, under certain limitations, the force of legislative acts. All the members of the judiciary department are appointed by him, can be removed by him on the address of the two houses of Parliament, and form, when he pleases to consult them, one of his constitutional councils. One branch of the legislative department forms also a great constitutional council to the executive chief, as, on another hand, it is the sole depositary of judicial power in cases of impeachment, and is invested with the supreme appellate jurisdiction in all other cases. The judges, again, are so far connected with the legislative department as often to attend and participate in its deliberations, though not admitted to a legislative vote.

From these facts, by which Montesquieu was guided, it may clearly be inferred that in saying "there can be no liberty where the legislative and executive powers are united in the same person or body of magistrates," or, "if the power of judging be not separated from the legislative and executive powers," he did not mean that these departments ought to have no *partial agency*, in, or no *control* over, the acts of each other. His meaning, as his own words import, and still more conclusively as illustrated by the example in his eye, can amount to no more than this: that where the *whole* power of one department is exercised by the same hands which possess the *whole* power of another department, the fundamental principles of a free constitution are subverted. This would have been the case in the constitution examined by him, if the king, who is the sole executive magistrate, had possessed also the complete legislative power, or the supreme administration of justice; or if the entire legislative body had possessed the supreme judiciary, or the supreme executive authority. This, however, is not among the vices of that constitution. The magistrate in whom the whole executive power resides cannot of himself make a law, though he can put a negative on every law; nor administer justice in person, though he has the appointment of those who do administer it. The judges can exercise no executive prerogative, though they are shoots from the executive stock; nor any legislative function, though they may be advised with by the legislative councils. The entire legislature can perform no judiciary act, though by the joint act of two of its branches, the judges may be removed from their offices, and though one of its branches is possessed of the judicial power in the last resort. The entire legislature, again, can exercise no executive prerogative, though one of its branches constitutes the supreme executive magistracy, and another, on the impeachment of a third, can try and condemn all the subordinate officers in the executive department.

The reasons on which Montesquieu grounds his maxim are a further demonstration of his meaning. "When the legislative and executive powers are united in the same person or body," says he, "there can be no liberty, because apprehensions may arise lest *the same* monarch or senate should *enact* tyrannical laws to *execute* them in a tyrannical manner." Again: "Were the power of judging joined with the legislative, the life and liberty of the subject would be exposed to arbitrary control, for *the judge* would then be *the legislator*. Were it joined to the executive power, *the judge* might behave with all the violence of *an oppressor*." Some of these reasons are more fully explained in other passages; but, briefly stated as they are here, they sufficiently establish the meaning which we have put on this celebrated maxim of this celebrated author.

If we look into the constitutions of the several states, we find that, not withstanding the emphatical and, in some instances, the unqualified terms in which this axiom has been laid down, there is not a single instance in which the several departments of power have been kept absolutely separate and distinct. New Hampshire, whose constitution was the last formed, seems to have been fully aware of the impossibility and inexpediency of avoiding any mixture whatever of these departments, and has qualified the doctrine by declaring "that the legislative, executive, and judiciary powers ought to be kept as separate from, and independent of, each other *as the nature of a free government will admit; or as is consistent with that chain of connection that binds the whole fabric of the constitution in one indissoluble bond of unity and amity*." Her constitution accordingly mixes these departments in several respects. The senate, which is a branch of the legislative department, is also a judicial tribunal for the trial of impeachments. The president, who is the head of the executive department, is the presiding member also of the senate; and, besides an equal vote in all cases, has a casting vote in case of a tie. The executive head is himself eventually elective every year by the legislative department, and his council is every year chosen by and from the members of the same department. Several of the officers of state are also appointed by the legislature. And the members of the judiciary department are appointed by the executive department....

H. THE FEDERALIST NO. 49 (HAMILTON *or* MADISON)

To the People of the State of New York:

The author of the *Notes on the State of Virginia,* quoted in the last paper, has subjoined to that valuable work the draught of a constitution, which had been prepared in order to be laid before a convention expected to be called in 1783, by the legislature, for the establishment of a constitution for that commonwealth.[4] The plan, like everything from the same pen, marks a turn of thinking, original, comprehensive, and accurate; and is the more worthy of attention as it equally displays a fervent attachment to republican government and an enlightened view of the dangerous propensities against which it ought to be guarded. One of the precautions which he proposes, and on which he appears ultimately to rely as a palladium to the weaker departments of power against the invasions of the stronger, is perhaps altogether his own and, as it immediately relates to the subject of our present inquiry, ought not to be overlooked.

His proposition is: "that whenever any two of the three branches of government shall concur in opinion, each by the voices of two-thirds of their whole number, that a convention is necessary for altering the constitution, or *correcting breaches of it,* a convention shall be called for the purpose."

As the people are the only legitimate fountain of power, and it is from them that the constitutional charter, under which the several branches of government hold their power, is derived, it seems strictly consonant to the republican theory to recur to the same original authority, not only whenever it may be necessary to enlarge, diminish, or new-model the powers of the government, but also whenever any one of the departments may commit encroachments on the chartered authorities of the others. The several departments being perfectly co-ordinate by the terms of their common commission, neither of them, it is evident, can pretend to an exclusive or superior right of settling the boundaries between their respective powers; and how are the encroachments of the stronger to be prevented, or the wrongs of the weaker to be redressed, without an appeal to the people themselves, who, as the grantors of the commission, can alone declare its true meaning, and enforce its observance?

There is certainly great force in this reasoning, and it must be allowed to prove that a constitutional road to the decision of the people ought to be marked out and kept open, for certain great and extraordinary occasions. But there appear to be insuperable objections against the proposed recurrence to the people, as a provision in all cases for keeping the several departments of power within their constitutional limits.

In the first place, the provision does not reach the case of a combination of two of the departments against the third. If the legislative authority, which possesses so many means of operating on the motives of the other departments, should be able to gain to its interest either of the others, or even one-third of its members, the remaining department could derive no advantage from its remedial provision. I do not dwell, however, on this objection, because it may be thought to lie rather against the modification of the principle than against the principle itself.

In the next place, it may be considered

4. See Jefferson's "Government and Liberty" (p. 215).

as an objection inherent in the principle that, as every appeal to the people would carry an implication of some defect in the government, frequent appeals would, in a great measure, deprive the government of that veneration which time bestows on everything, and without which perhaps the wisest and freest governments would not possess the requisite stability. If it be true that all governments rest on opinion, it is no less true that the strength of opinion in each individual, and its practical influence on his conduct, depend much on the number which he supposes to have entertained the same opinion. The reason of man, like man himself, is timid and cautious when left alone, and acquires firmness and confidence in proportion to the number with which it is associated. When the examples which fortify opinion are *ancient* as well as *numerous*, they are known to have a double effect. In a nation of philosophers, this consideration ought to be disregarded. A reverence for the laws would be sufficiently inculcated by the voice of an enlightened reason. But a nation of philosophers is as little to be expected as the philosophical race of kings wished for by Plato. And in every other nation, the most rational government will not find it a superfluous advantage to have the prejudices of the community on its side.

The danger of disturbing the public tranquility by interesting too strongly the public passions is a still more serious objection against a frequent reference of constitutional questions to the decision of the whole society. Notwithstanding the success which has attended the revisions of our established forms of government, and which does so much honor to the virtue and intelligence of the people of America, it must be confessed that the experiments are of too ticklish a nature to be unnecessarily multiplied. We are to recollect that all the existing constitutions were formed in the midst of a danger which repressed the passions most unfriendly to order and concord; of an enthusiastic confidence of the people in their patriotic leaders, which stifled the ordinary diversity of opinions on great national questions; of a universal ardor for new and opposite forms, produced by a universal resentment and indignation against the ancient government; and whilst no spirit of party connected with the changes to be made, or the abuses to be reformed, could mingle its leaven in the operation. The future situations in which we must expect to be usually placed do not present any equivalent security against the danger which is apprehended.

But the greatest objection of all is that the decisions which would probably result from such appeals would not answer the purpose of maintaining the constitutional equilibrium of the government. We have seen that the tendency of republican governments is to an aggrandizement of the legislative at the expense of the other departments. The appeals to the people, therefore, would usually be made by the executive and judiciary departments. But whether made by one side or the other, would each side enjoy equal advantages on the trial? Let us view their different situations. The members of the executive and judiciary departments are few in number and can be personally known to a small part only of the people. The latter, by the mode of their appointment, as well as by the nature and permanency of it, are too far removed from the people to share much in their prepossessions. The former are generally the objects of jealousy, and their administration is always liable to be discolored and rendered unpopular. The members of the legislative department, on the other hand, are numerous. They are distributed and dwell among the people at large. Their connections of blood, of friendship, and of acquaintance embrace a great proportion of the most influential part of the society. The nature of their public trust implies a personal influence among the people, and that they are more immediately the confidential guardians of the rights and liberties of the people. With these advantages, it can hardly be supposed that the adverse party would have an equal chance for a favorable issue.

But the legislative party would not only be able to plead their cause most successfully with the people. They would probably be constituted themselves the judges. The same influence which had gained them an election into the legislature would gain them a seat in the convention. If this should not be the case with all, it would probably be the case with many, and pretty certainly with those leading characters, on whom everything depends in such bodies. The convention, in short, would be composed chiefly of men who had been, who actually were, or who expected to be, members of the department whose conduct was arraigned. They would consequently be parties to the very question to be decided by them.

It might, however, sometimes happen that appeals would be made under circumstances less adverse to the executive and judiciary departments. The usurpations of the legislature might be so flagrant and so sudden as to admit of no specious coloring. A strong party among themselves might take side with the other branches. The executive power might be in the hands of a peculiar favorite of the people. In such a posture of things, the public decision might be less swayed by prepossessions in favor of the legislative party. But still it could never be expected to turn on the true merits of the question. It would inevitably be connected with the spirit of pre-existing parties, or of parties springing out of the question itself. It would be connected with persons of distinguished character and extensive influence in the community. It would be pronounced by the very men who had been agents in, or opponents of, the measures to which the decision would relate. The *passions*, therefore, not the *reason*, of the public would sit in judgment. But it is the reason of the public, alone, that ought to control and regulate the government. The passions ought to be controlled and regulated by the government. . . .

I. THE FEDERALIST NO. 51 (HAMILTON *or* MADISON)

To the People of the State of New York:

To what expedient, then, shall we finally resort for maintaining in practice the necessary partition of power among the several departments, as laid down in the Constitution? The only answer that can be given is that, as all these exterior provisions are found to be inadequate, the defect must be supplied, by so contriving the interior structure of the government as that its several constituent parts may, by their mutual relations, be the means of keeping each other in their proper places. Without presuming to undertake a full development of this important idea, I will hazard a few general observations, which may perhaps place it in a clearer light, and enable us to form a more correct judgment of the principles and structure of the government planned by the convention.

In order to lay a due foundation for that separate and distinct exercise of the different powers of government, which to a certain extent is admitted on all hands to be essential to the preservation of liberty, it is evident that each department should have a will of its own; and consequently should be so constituted that the members of each should have as little agency as possible in the appointment of the members of the others. Were this principle rigorously adhered to, it would require that all the appointments for the supreme executive, legislative, and judiciary magistracies should be drawn from the same fountain of authority, the people, through channels having no communication whatever with one another. Perhaps such a plan of constructing the several departments would be less difficult in practice than it may in contemplation appear. Some difficulties, however, and some additional expense would attend the execution of it. Some deviations, therefore, from the principle must be admitted. In the constitution of the judiciary department in particular, it might be inexpedient to insist rigorously on the principle: first, because peculiar qualifications being essential in the members, the primary consideration ought to be to select that mode of choice which best secures these qualifications; secondly, because the permanent tenure by which the appointments are held in that department must soon destroy all sense of dependence on the authority conferring them.

It is equally evident that the members of each department should be as little dependent as possible on those of the others, for the emoluments annexed to their offices. Were the executive, magistrate, or the judges not independent of the legislature in this particular, their independence in every other would be merely nominal.

But the great security against a gradual concentration of the several powers in the same department consists in giving to those who administer each department the necessary constitutional means and personal motives to resist encroachments of the others. The provision for defense must in this, as in all other cases, be made commensurate to the danger of attack. Ambition must be made to counteract ambition. The interest of the man must be connected with the constitutional rights of the place. It may be a reflection on human nature that such devices should be necessary to control the abuses of government. But what is government itself but the greatest of all reflections on human nature? If men were angels, no government would be necessary. If angels were to govern men, neither ex-

ternal nor internal controls on government would be necessary. In framing a government which is to be administered by men over men, the great difficulty lies in this: you must first enable the government to control the governed; and in the next place oblige it to control itself. A dependence on the people is, no doubt, the primary control on the government; but experience has taught mankind the necessity of auxiliary precautions.

This policy of supplying, by opposite and rival interests, the defect of better motives might be traced through the whole system of human affairs, private as well as public. We see it particularly displayed in all the subordinate distributions of power, where the constant aim is to divide and arrange the several offices in such a manner as that each may be a check on the other—that the private interest of every individual may be a sentinel over the public rights. These inventions of prudence cannot be less requisite in the distribution of the supreme powers of the state.

But it is not possible to give to each department an equal power of self-defense. In republican government, the legislative authority necessarily predominates. The remedy for this inconveniency is to divide the legislature into different branches; and to render them, by different modes of election and different principles of action, as little connected with each other as the nature of their common functions and their common dependence on the society will admit. It may even be necessary to guard against dangerous encroachments by still further precautions. As the weight of the legislative authority requires that it should be thus divided, the weakness of the executive may require, on the other hand, that it should be fortified. An absolute negative on the legislature appears, at first view, to be the natural defense with which the executive magistrate should be armed. But perhaps it would be neither altogether safe nor alone sufficient. On ordinary occasions it might not be exerted with the requisite firmness, and on extraordinary occasions it might be perfidiously abused. May not this defect of an absolute negative be supplied by some qualified connection between this weaker department and the weaker branch of the stronger department, by which the latter may be led to support the constitutional rights of the former, without being too much detached from the rights of its own department?

If the principles on which these observations are founded be just, as I persuade myself they are, and they be applied as a criterion to the several state constitutions, and to the federal constitution, it will be found that if the latter does not perfectly correspond with them, the former are infinitely less able to bear such a test.

There are, moreover, two considerations particularly applicable to the federal system of America which place that system in a very interesting point of view.

First. In a single republic, all the power surrendered by the people is submitted to the administration of a single government; and the usurpations are guarded against by a division of the government into distinct and separate departments. In the compound republic of America, the power surrendered by the people is first divided between two distinct governments, and then the portion allotted to each subdivided among distinct and separate departments. Hence a double security arises to the rights of the people. The different governments will control each other at the same time that each will be controlled by itself.

Second. It is of great importance in a republic not only to guard the society against the oppression of its rulers, but to guard one part of the society against the injustice of the other part. Different interests necessarily exist in different classes of citizens. If a majority be united by a common interest, the rights of the minority will be insecure. There are but two methods of providing against this evil: the one by creating a will in the community independent of the majority —that is, of the society itself; the other, by comprehending in the society so many separate descriptions of citizens as will render an unjust combination of a majority of the whole very improbable, if not impracticable. The first method prevails in all governments possessing a hereditary or self-appointed authority. This, at best, is but a precarious security; because a power independent of the society may as well espouse the unjust views of the major, as the rightful interests of the minor party, and may possibly be turned against both parties. The second method will be exemplified in the federal republic of the United States. Whilst all authority in it will be derived from and dependent on the society, the society itself will be broken into so many parts, interests, and classes of citizens that the rights of individuals, or of the minority, will be in little danger from interested combinations of the majority. In a free government the security for civil rights must be the same as that for religious rights. It consists in the one case in the multiplicity of interests, and in the other in the multiplicity of sects. The degree of security in both cases will depend on the number of interests and sects; and this may be presumed to depend on the extent of country and number of people comprehended under the same government. This view of the subject must particularly recommend a proper federal system to all the sincere and considerate friends of republican government, since it shows that in exact proportion as the territory of the Union may be formed into more circumscribed confederacies, or states, oppressive combinations of a majority will be facilitated, the best security under the republican forms for the rights of every class of citizens will be diminished; and consequently the stability and independence of some member of the government, the only other security, must be proportionally increased. Justice is the end of government. It is the end of civil society. It ever has been and ever will be pursued until it be obtained, or until liberty be lost in the pursuit. In a society under the forms of which the stronger faction can readily unite and oppress the weaker, anarchy may as truly be said to reign as in a state of nature, where the weaker individual is not secured against the violence of the stronger; and as, in the latter state, even the stronger individuals are prompted, by the uncertainty of their condition, to submit to a government which may protect the weak as well as themselves; so, in the former state, will the more powerful factions or parties be gradually induced, by a like motive, to wish for a government which will protect all parties, the weaker as well as the more powerful. It can be little doubted that if the state of Rhode Island was separated from the Confederacy and left to itself, the insecurity of rights under the popular form of government within such narrow limits would be displayed by such reiterated oppressions of factious majorities that some power altogether independent of the people would soon be called for by the voice of the very factions whose misrule had proved the necessity of it. In the extended republic of the United States, and among the great variety of interests, parties, and sects which it embraces, a coalition of a majority of the whole society could seldom take place on any other principles than those of justice and the general good; whilst there being thus less danger to a minor from the will of a major party, there must be less pretext, also, to provide for the security of the former, by introducing into the government a will not dependent on the latter, or, in other words, a will independent of the society itself. It is no less certain than it is important, notwithstanding the contrary opinions which have been entertained, that the larger the society, provided it lie within a practical sphere, the more duly capable it will be of self-government. And happily for the *republican cause,* the practicable sphere may be carried, to a very great extent, by a judicious modification and mixture of the *federal principle.*

PUBLIUS

J. THE FEDERALIST NO. 78 (HAMILTON)

To the People of the State of New York:

We proceed now to an examination of the judiciary department of the proposed government.

In unfolding the defects of the existing Confederation, the utility and necessity of a federal judicature have been clearly pointed out. It is the less necessary to recapitulate the considerations there urged, as the propriety of the institution in the abstract is not disputed; the only questions which have been raised being relative to the manner of constituting it, and to its extent. To these points, therefore, our observations shall be confined.

The manner of constituting it seems to embrace these several objects: 1st, the mode of appointing the judges. 2d, The tenure by which they are to hold their places. 3d, The partition of the judiciary authority between different courts, and their relations to each other.

First. As to the mode of appointing the judges: this is the same with that of appointing the officers of the Union in general, and has been so fully discussed in the last two numbers that nothing can be said here which would not be useless repetition.

Second. As to the tenure by which the judges are to hold their places: this chiefly concerns their duration in office; the provisions for their support; the precautions for their responsibility.

According to the plan of the Convention, all judges who may be appointed by the United States are to hold their offices *during good behavior;* which is conformable to the most approved of the state constitutions, and among the rest, to that of this state. Its propriety, having been drawn into question by the adversaries of that plan, is no light symptom of the rage for objection which disorders their imaginations and judgments. The standard of good behavior for the continuance in office of the judicial magistracy is certainly one of the most valuable of the modern improvements in the practice of government. In a monarchy it is an excellent barrier to the despotism of the prince; in a republic it is a no less excellent barrier to the encroachments and oppressions of the representative body. And it is the best expedient which can be devised in any government to secure a steady, upright, and impartial administration of the laws.

Whoever attentively considers the different departments of power must perceive that, in a government in which they are separated from each other, the judiciary, from the nature of its functions, will always be the least dangerous to the political rights of the Constitution, because it will be least in a capacity to annoy or injure them. The executive not only dispenses the honors but holds the sword of the community. The legislature not only commands the purse but prescribes the rules by which the duties and rights of every citizen are to be regulated. The judiciary, on the contrary, has no influence over either the sword or the purse; no direction either of the strength or of the wealth of the society; and can take no active resolution whatever. It may be truly said to have neither FORCE nor WILL, but merely judgment; and must ultimately depend upon the aid of the executive arm even for the efficacy of its judgments.

This simple view of the matter suggests several important consequences. It proves incontestably that the judiciary is beyond comparison the weakest of the three departments of power;[5] that it can never attack with success either of the other two; and that all possible care is requisite to enable it to defend itself against their attacks. It equally proves that, though individual oppression may now and then proceed from the courts of justice, the general liberty of the people can never be endangered from that quarter; I mean so long as the judiciary remains truly distinct from both the legislature and the executive. For I agree, that "there is no liberty, if the power of judging be not separated from the legislative and executive powers."[6] And it proves, in the last place, that as liberty can have nothing to fear from the judiciary alone, but would have everything to fear from its union with either of the other departments; that as all the effects of such a union must ensue from a dependence of the former on the latter, notwithstanding a nominal and apparent separation; that as, from the natural feebleness of the judiciary, it is in continual jeopardy of being overpowered, awed, or influenced by its co-ordinate branches; and that as nothing can contribute so much to its firmness and independence as permanency in office, this quality may therefore be justly regarded as an indispensable ingredient in its constitution; and, in a great measure, as the citadel of the public justice and the public security.

The complete independence of the courts of justice is peculiarly essential in a limited constitution. By a limited constitution, I understand one which contains certain specified exceptions to the legislative authority; such, for instance, as that it shall pass no bills of attainder, no ex post facto laws, and the like. Limi-

5. The celebrated Montesquieu, speaking of them, says: "Of the three powers above mentioned, the judiciary is next to nothing" (*Spirit of Laws*, I, 186).—*Publius.* AUTHOR'S NOTE.

6. *Ibid.,* p. 181.—*Publius.* AUTHOR'S NOTE.

tations of this kind can be preserved in practice no other way than through the medium of courts of justice, whose duty it must be to declare all acts contrary to the manifest tenor of the constitution void. Without this, all the reservations of particular rights or privileges would amount to nothing.

Some perplexity respecting the rights of the courts to pronounce legislative acts void, because contrary to the constitution, has arisen from an imagination that the doctrine would imply a superiority of the judiciary to the legislative power. It is urged that the authority which can declare the acts of another void must necessarily be superior to the one whose acts may be declared void. As this doctrine is of great importance in all the American constitutions, a brief discussion of the ground on which it rests cannot be unacceptable.

There is no position which depends on clearer principles than that every act of a delegated authority, contrary to the tenor of the commission under which it is exercised, is void. No legislative act, therefore, contrary to the Constitution, can be valid. To deny this would be to affirm that the deputy is greater than his principal; that the servant is above his master; that the representatives of the people are superior to the people themselves; that men acting by virtue of powers may do not only what their powers do not authorize but what they forbid.

If it be said that the legislative body are themselves the constitutional judges of their own powers, and that the construction they put upon them is conclusive upon the other departments, it may be answered that this cannot be the natural presumption, where it is not to be collected from any particular provisions in the Constitution. It is not otherwise to be supposed that the Constitution could intend to enable the representatives of the people to substitute their *will*

to that of their constituents. It is far more rational to suppose that the courts were designed to be an intermediate body between the people and the legislature, in order, among other things, to keep the latter within the limits assigned to their authority. The interpretation of the laws is the proper and peculiar province of the courts. A constitution is in fact, and must be regarded by the judges as, a fundamental law. It therefore belongs to them to ascertain its meaning, as well as the meaning of any particular act proceeding from the legislative body. If there should happen to be an irreconcilable variance between the two, that which has the superior obligation and validity ought, of course, to be preferred; or, in other words, the Constitution ought to be preferred to the statute; the intention of the people to the intention of their agents.

Nor does this conclusion by any means suppose a superiority of the judicial to the legislative power. It only supposes that the power of the people is superior to both; and that where the will of the legislature, declared in its statutes, stands in opposition to that of the people, declared in the Constitution, the judges ought to be governed by the latter rather than the former. They ought to regulate their decisions by the fundamental laws, rather than by those which are not fundamental.

This exercise of judicial discretion, in determining between two contradictory laws, is exemplified in a familiar instance. It not uncommonly happens that there are two statutes existing at one time, clashing in whole or in part with each other, and neither of them containing any repealing clause or expression. In such a case, it is the province of the courts to liquidate and fix their meaning and operation. So far as they can, by any fair construction, be reconciled to each other, reason and law conspire to dictate that this should be done; where this is impracticable, it becomes a matter of necessity to give effect to one, in exclusion of the other. The rule which has obtained in the courts for determining their relative validity is that the last in order of time shall be preferred to the first. But this is a mere rule of construction, not derived from any positive law, but from the nature and reason of the thing. It is a rule not enjoined upon the courts by legislative provision but adopted by themselves, as consonant to truth and propriety, for the direction of their conduct as interpreters of the law. They thought it reasonable that, between the interfering acts of an *equal* authority, that which was the last indication of its will should have the preference.

But in regard to the interfering acts of a superior and subordinate authority, of an original and derivative power, the nature and reason of the thing indicate the converse of that rule as proper to be followed. They teach us that the prior act of a superior ought to be preferred to the subsequent act of an inferior and subordinate authority; and that accordingly, whenever a particular statute contravenes the Constitution, it will be the duty of the judicial tribunals to adhere to the latter and disregard the former.

It can be of no weight to say that the courts, on the pretense of a repugnancy, may substitute their own pleasure to the constitutional intentions of the legislature. This might as well happen in the case of two contradictory statutes; or it might as well happen in every adjudication upon any single statute. The courts must declare the sense of the law; and if they should be disposed to exercise WILL instead of JUDGMENT, the consequence would equally be the substitution of their pleasure to that of the legislative body. The observation, if it proved anything, would prove that there ought to be no judges distinct from that body.

If, then, the courts of justice are to be considered as the bulwarks of a limited constitution against legislative encroachments, this consideration will afford a strong argument for the permanent tenure of judicial offices, since nothing will contribute so much as this to that independent spirit in the judges which must be essential to the faithful performance of so arduous a duty.

This independence of the judges is equally requisite to guard the Constitution and the rights of individuals from the effects of those ill humors which the arts of designing men, or the influence of particular conjunctures, sometimes disseminate among the people themselves, and which, though they speedily give place to better information, and more deliberate reflection, have a tendency, in the meantime, to occasion dangerous innovations in the government, and serious oppressions of the inner party in the community. Though I trust the friends of the proposed Constitution will never concur with its enemies, in questioning that fundamental principle of republican government, which admits the right of the people to alter or abolish the established Constitution, whenever they find it inconsistent with their happiness, yet it is not to be inferred from this principle that the representatives of the people, whenever a momentary inclination happens to lay hold of the majority of their constituents, incompatible with the provisions in the existing Constitution, would, on that account, be justifiable in a violation of those provisions; or that the courts would be under a greater obligation to connive at infractions in this shape, than when they had proceeded wholly from the cabals of the representative body. Until the people have, by some solemn and authoritative act, annulled or changed the established form, it is binding upon themselves collectively, as well as individually; and no presumption, or even knowledge, of their sentiments can warrant their representatives in a departure from it, prior to such an act. But it is easy to see that it would require an uncommon portion of fortitude in the judges to do their duty as faithful guardians of the Constitution, where the legislative invasions of it had been instigated by the major voice of the community.

But it is not with a view to infractions of the Constitution only that the independence of the judges may be an essential safeguard against the effects of occasional ill humors in the society. These sometimes extend no farther than to the injury of the private rights of particular classes of citizens, by unjust and partial laws. Here also the firmness of the judicial magistracy is of vast importance in mitigating the severity and confining the operation of such laws. It not only serves to moderate the immediate mischiefs of those which may have been passed, but it operates as a check upon the legislative body in passing them; who, perceiving that obstacles to the success of iniquitous intention are to be expected from the scruples of the courts, are in a manner compelled, by the very motives of the injustice they meditate, to qualify their attempts. This is a circumstance calculated to have more influence upon the character of our governments than but few may be aware of. The benefits of the integrity and moderation of the judiciary have already been felt in more states than one; and though they may have displeased those whose sinister expectations they may have disappointed, they must have commanded the esteem and applause of all the virtuous and disinterested. Considerate men, of every description, ought to prize whatever will tend to beget or fortify that temper in the courts; as no man can be sure that he may not be tomorrow the victim of a spirit of injustice by which he may be a gainer today. And every man must now feel that the inevitable tendency of such a spirit is to sap the foundations of the public and private confidence, and to introduce in its stead universal distrust and distress.

That inflexible and uniform adherence to the rights of the Constitution, and of individuals, which we perceive to be indispensable in the courts of justice, can certainly not be expected from judges who hold their offices by a temporary commission. Periodical appointments, however regulated, or by whomsoever made, would, in some way or other, be fatal to their necessary independence. If the power of making them was committed either to the executive or legislature, there would be danger of an improper complaisance to the branch which possessed it; if to both, there would be an unwillingness to hazard the displeasure of either; if to the people, or to persons chosen by them for the special purpose, there would be too great a disposition to consult popularity, to justify a reliance that nothing would be consulted but the Constitution and the laws.

There is yet a further and a weighty reason for the permanency of the judicial offices, which is deducible from the nature of the qualifications they require. It has been frequently remarked, with great propriety, that a voluminous code of laws is one of the inconveniences necessarily connected with the advantages of a free government. To avoid an arbitrary discretion in the courts, it is indispensable that they should be bound down by strict rules and precedents, which serve to define and point out their duty in every particular case that comes before them; and it will readily be conceived from the variety of controversies which grow out of the folly and wickedness of mankind that the records of those precedents must unavoidably swell to a very considerable bulk, and must demand long and laborious study to acquire a competent knowledge of them. Hence it is that there can be but few men in the society who will have sufficient skill in the laws to qualify them for the stations of judges. And making the proper deductions for the ordinary depravity of human nature, the number must be still smaller of those who unite the requisite integrity with the requisite knowledge. These considerations apprise us that the government can have no great option between fit characters; and that a temporary duration in office, which would naturally discourage such characters from quitting a lucrative line of practice to accept a seat on the bench, would have a tendency to throw the administration of justice into hands less able, and less well qualified, to conduct it with utility and dignity. In the present circumstances of this country, and in those in which it is likely to be for a long time to come, the disadvantages on this score would be greater than they may at first sight appear; but it must be confessed that they are far inferior to those which present themselves under the other aspects of the subject.

Upon the whole, there can be no room to doubt that the Convention acted wisely in copying from the models of those constitutions which have established *good behavior* as the tenure of their judicial offices, in point of duration; and that so far from being blamable on this account, their plan would have been inexcusably defective, if it had wanted this important feature of good government. The experience of Great Britain affords an illustrious comment on the excellence of the institution.

PUBLIUS

7. ON THE CONSTITUTION[1]

By THOMAS JEFFERSON

A. ON SHAYS'S REBELLION

To COLONEL EDWARD CARRINGTON[2]

PARIS, January 16, 1787

DEAR SIR,

... The tumults in America I expected would have produced in Europe an unfavorable opinion of our political state. But it has not. On the contrary, the small effect of these tumults seems to have given more confidence in the firmness of our governments. The interposition of the people themselves on the side of government has had a great effect on the opinion here. I am persuaded myself that the good sense of the people will always be found to be the best army. They may be led astray for a moment but will soon correct themselves. The people are the only censors of their governors; and even their errors will tend to keep these to the true principles of their institution. To punish these errors too severely would be to suppress the only safeguard of the public liberty. The way to prevent these irregular interpositions of the people is to give them full information of their affairs through the channel of the public papers and to contrive that those papers should penetrate the whole mass of the people. The basis of our governments being the opinion of the people, the very first object should be to keep that right; and were it left to me to decide whether we should have a government without newspapers, or newspapers without a government, I should not hesitate a moment to prefer the latter. But I should mean that every man should receive those papers and be capable of reading them. I am convinced that those societies (as the Indians) which live without government enjoy in their general mass an infinitely greater degree of happiness than those who live under the European governments. Among the former, public opinion is in

1. *The Writings of Thomas Jefferson*, ed. H. A. Washington (New York, 1861), II, 99–100, 104–5, 217–18, 260, 328–32, 404–5, 585–87.

2. Colonel Edward Carrington (1749–1810), Revolutionary soldier, member of the Congress of the Confederation, friend of Jefferson and of Washington, member of the committee that reported the Ordinance of 1787.

the place of law and restrains morals as powerfully as laws ever did anywhere. Among the latter, under pretense of governing, they have divided their nations into two classes, wolves and sheep. I do not exaggerate. This is a true picture of Europe. Cherish, therefore, the spirit of our people and keep alive their attention. Do not be too severe upon their errors but reclaim them by enlightening them. If once they become inattentive to the public affairs, you and I, and Congress and assemblies, judges and governors, shall all become wolves. . . .

To James Madison

Paris, January 30, 1787

Dear Sir,

. . . I am impatient to learn your sentiments on the late troubles in the eastern states. So far as I have yet seen, they do not appear to threaten serious consequences. Those states have suffered by the stoppage of the channels of their commerce, which have not yet found other issues. This must render money scarce and make the people uneasy. This uneasiness has produced acts absolutely unjustifiable; but I hope they will provoke no severities from their governments. A consciousness of those in power that their administration of the public affairs has been honest may, perhaps, produce too great a degree of indignation; and those characters, wherein fear predominates over hope, may apprehend too much from these instances of irregularity. They may conclude too hastily that nature has formed man insusceptible of any other government than that of force, a conclusion not founded in truth nor

experience. Societies exist under three forms, sufficiently distinguishable. 1. Without government, as among our Indians. 2. Under governments, wherein the will of everyone has a just influence, as is the case in England, in a slight degree, and in our states, in a great one. 3. Under governments of force, as is the case in all other monarchies and in most of the other republics. To have an idea of the curse of existence under these last, they must be seen. It is a government of wolves over sheep. It is a problem, not clear in my mind, that the first condition is not the best. But I believe it to be inconsistent with any great degree of population. The second state has a great deal of good in it. The mass of mankind under that enjoys a precious degree of liberty and happiness. It has its evils, too, the principal of which is the turbulence to which it is subject. But weigh this against the oppressions of monarchy, and it becomes nothing. *Malo periculosam libertatem quam quietam servitutem.*[3] Even this evil is productive of good. It prevents the degeneracy of government and nourishes a general attention to the public affairs. I hold it that a little rebellion, now and then, is a good thing and as necessary in the political world as storms in the physical. Unsuccessful rebellions, indeed, generally establish the encroachments on the rights of the people, which have produced them. An observation of this truth should render honest republican governors so mild in their punishment of rebellions as not to discourage them too much. It is a medicine necessary for the sound health of government. . . .

B. ON THE CONSTITUTION, 1787

To E. Carrington

Paris, August 4, 1787

Dear Sir,

Since mine of the 16th of January, I have been honored by your favors of

3. "I prefer perilous liberty to peaceful slavery."

April the 24th and June the 9th. I am happy to find that the states have come so generally into the schemes of the federal convention, from which, I am sure, we shall see wise propositions. I confess, I do not go as far in the reforms thought necessary, as some of my correspondents in America; but if the convention should adopt such propositions, I shall suppose them necessary. My general plan would be to make the states one as to everything connected with foreign nations, and several as to everything purely domestic. But with all the imperfections of our present government, it is without comparison the best existing, or that ever did exist. Its greatest defect is the imperfect manner in which matters of commerce have been provided for. It has been so often said, as to be generally believed, that Congress have no power by the Confederation to enforce anything; for example, contributions of money. It was not necessary to give them that power expressly; they have it by the law of nature. When two parties make a compact, there results to each a power of compelling the other to execute it. Compulsion was never so easy as in our case, where a single frigate would soon levy on the commerce of any state the deficiency of its contributions; nor more safe than in the hands of Congress, which has always shown that it would wait, as it ought to do, to the last extremities, before it would execute any of its powers which are disagreeable. I think it very material to separate, in the hands of Congress, the executive and legislative powers, as the judiciary already are, in some degree. This, I hope, will be done. The want of it has been the source of more evil than we have experienced from any other cause. Nothing is so embarrassing nor so mischievous, in a great assembly, as the details of execution. The smallest trifle of that kind occupies as long as the most important act of legislation and takes place of everything else. Let any man recollect, or look over, the files of Congress; he will observe the most important propositions hanging over, from week to week, and month to month, till the occasions have passed them, and the things never done. I have ever viewed the executive details as the greatest cause of evil to us, because they

in fact place us as if we had no federal head, by diverting the attention of that head from great to small objects; and, should this division of power not be recommended by the convention, it is my opinion Congress should make it itself, by establishing an executive committee. . . .

To John Adams[4]
PARIS, August 30, 1787

DEAR SIR,

. . . I have news from America as late as July the 19th. Nothing had transpired from the federal convention. I am sorry they began their deliberations by so abominable a precedent as that of tying up the tongues of their members. Nothing can justify this example but the innocence of their intentions and ignorance of the value of public discussions. I have no doubt that all their other measures will be good and wise. It is really an assembly of demigods. General Washington was of opinion that they should not separate till October. . . .

To James Madison
PARIS, December 20, 1787

DEAR SIR,

. . . I like much the general idea of framing a government, which should go on of itself, peaceably, without needing continual recurrence to the state legislatures. I like the organization of the government into legislative, judiciary, and executive. I like the power given the legislature to levy taxes, and for that reason solely I approve of the greater House being chosen by the people directly. For though I think a House so chosen will be very far inferior to the present Congress, will be very illy qualified to legislate for the Union, for foreign nations, etc., yet this evil does not weigh against the good of preserving inviolate the fundamental principle that the people are not to be taxed but by

4. Then United States minister to Great Britain.

representatives chosen immediately by themselves. I am captivated by the compromise of the opposite claims of the great and little states, of the latter to equal, and the former to proportional influence. I am much pleased, too, with the substitution of the method of voting by person, instead of that of voting by states; and I like the negative given to the Executive, conjointly with a third of either House; though I should have liked it better had the judiciary been associated for that purpose or invested separately with a similar power. There are other good things of less moment. I will now tell you what I do not like. First, the omission of a bill of rights, providing clearly, and without the aid of sophism, for freedom of religion, freedom of the press, protection against standing armies, restriction of monopolies, the eternal and unremitting force of the habeas corpus laws, and trials by jury in all matters of fact triable by the laws of the land, and not by the laws of nations. To say, as Mr. Wilson does, that a bill of rights was not necessary, because all is reserved in the case of the general government which is not given, while in the particular ones, all is given which is not reserved, might do for the audience to which it was addressed; but it is surely a *gratis dictum*,[5] the reverse of which might just as well be said; and it is opposed by strong inferences from the body of the instrument, as well as from the omission of the cause of our present Confederation, which had made the reservation in express terms. It was hard to conclude, because there has been a want of uniformity among the states as to the cases triable by jury, because some have been so incautious as to dispense with this mode of trial in certain cases; therefore, the more prudent states shall be reduced to the same level of calamity. It would have been much more just and wise to have concluded the other way, that as most of the states had preserved with

jealousy this sacred palladium of liberty, those who had wandered should be brought back to it; and to have established general right rather than general wrong. For I consider all the ill as established which may be established. I have a right to nothing which another has a right to take away; and Congress will have a right to take away trials by jury in all civil cases. Let me add that a bill of rights is what the people are entitled to against every government on earth, general or particular; and what no just government should refuse or rest on inference.

The second feature I dislike, and strongly dislike, is the abandonment, in every instance, of the principle of rotation in office, and most particularly in the case of the President. Reason and experience tell us that the first magistrate will always be re-elected if he may be re-elected. He is then an officer for life. This once observed, it becomes of so much consequence to certain nations, to have a friend or a foe at the head of our affairs, that they will interfere with money and with arms. A Galloman,[6] or an Angloman, will be supported by the nation he befriends. If once elected, and at a second or third election outvoted by one or two votes, he will pretend false votes, foul play, hold possession of the reins of government, be supported by the states voting for him, especially if they be the central ones lying in a compact body themselves and, separating their opponents; and they will be aided by one nation in Europe, while the majority are aided by another. The election of a President of America, some years hence, will be much more interesting to certain nations of Europe than ever the election of a king of Poland was. Reflect on all the instances in history, ancient and modern, of elective monarchies, and say if they do not give foundation for my fears; the Roman emperors, the popes while they were of

5. "Mere assertion."

6. Partisan of France.

any importance, the German emperors till they became hereditary in practice, the kings of Poland, the deys of the Ottoman dependencies. It may be said that if elections are to be attended with these disorders, the less frequently they are repeated the better. But experience says that, to free them from disorder, they must be rendered less interesting by a necessity of change. No foreign power, nor domestic party, will waste their blood and money to elect a person who must go out at the end of a short period. The power of removing every fourth year by the vote of the people is a power which they will not exercise, and if they were disposed to exercise it, they would not be permitted. The king of Poland is removable every day by the diet. But they never remove him. Nor would Russia, the emperor, etc., permit them to do it. Smaller objections are the appeals on matters of fact as well as laws; and the binding all persons, legislative, executive, and judiciary, by oath, to maintain that constitution. I do not pretend to decide what would be the best method of procuring the establishment of the manifold good things in this constitution, and of getting rid of the bad. Whether by adopting it, in hopes of future amendment; or after it shall have been duly weighed and canvassed by the people, after seeing the parts they generally dislike, and those they generally approve, to say to them, "We see now what you wish. You are willing to give to your federal government such and such powers; but you wish, at the same time, to have such and such fundamental rights secured to you, and certain sources of convulsion taken away. Be it so. Send together deputies again. Let them establish your fundamental rights by a sacrosanct declaration, and let them pass the parts of the constitution you have approved. These will give powers to your federal government sufficient for your happiness."

This is what might be said and would probably produce a speedy, more perfect, and more permanent form of government. At all events, I hope you will not be discouraged from making other trials, if the present one should fail. We are never permitted to despair of the commonwealth. I have thus told you freely what I like, and what I dislike, merely as a matter of curiosity; for I know it is not in my power to offer matter of information to your judgment, which has been formed after hearing and weighing everything which the wisdom of man could offer on these subjects. I own, I am not a friend to a very energetic government. It is always oppressive. It places the governors indeed more at their ease at the expense of the people. The late rebellion in Massachusetts has given more alarm than I think it should have done. Calculate that one rebellion in thirteen states in the course of eleven years is but one for each state in a century and a half. No country should be so long without one. Nor will any degree of power in the hands of government prevent insurrections. In England, where the hand of power is heavier than with us, there are seldom half a dozen years without an insurrection. In France, where it is still heavier, but less despotic, as Montesquieu supposes, than in some other countries, and where there are always two or three hundred thousand men ready to crush insurrections, there have been three in the course of the three years I have been here, in every one of which greater numbers were engaged than in Massachusetts, and a great deal more blood was spilt. In Turkey, where the sole nod of the despot is death, insurrections are the events of every day. Compare again the ferocious depredations of their insurgents, with the order, the moderation, and the almost self-extinguishment of ours. And say, finally, whether peace is best preserved by giving energy to the government or information to the people. This last is the most certain and the most legitimate engine of government. Educate and inform the whole mass of the people. Enable them to see that it is their interest to preserve peace and order, and they will preserve them. And it requires no very high degree of education to convince them of this. They are the only sure reliance for the preservation of our liberty. After all, it is my principle that the will of the majority should prevail. If they approve the proposed constitution in all its parts, I shall concur in it

cheerfully, in hopes they will amend it, whenever they shall find it works wrong. This reliance cannot deceive us, as long as we remain virtuous; and I think we shall be so, as long as agriculture is our principal object, which will be the case, while there remain vacant lands in any part of America. When we get piled upon one another in large cities, as in Europe, we shall become corrupt as in Europe, and go to eating one another as they do there. . . .

C. ON RATIFICATION AND NEEDED CHANGES, 1788–89

To COLONEL CARRINGTON

PARIS, May 27, 1788

DEAR SIR,

. . . I learn with great pleasure the progress of the new Constitution. Indeed I have presumed it would gain on the public mind, as I confess it has on my own. At first, though I saw that the great mass and groundwork was good, I disliked many appendages. Reflection and discussion have cleared off most of these. You have satisfied me as to the query I had put to you about the right of direct taxation. My first wish was that nine states would adopt it in order to insure what was good in it, and that the others might, by holding off, produce the necessary amendments. But the plan of Massachusetts[7] is far preferable, and will, I hope, be followed by those who are yet to decide. There are two amendments only which I am anxious for: 1. A bill of rights, which it is so much the interest of all to have that I conceive it must be yielded. The 1st amendment proposed by Massachusetts will in some degree answer this end, but not so well. It will do too much in some instances,

and too little in others.[8] It will cripple the Federal Government in some cases where it ought to be free, and not restrain in some others where restraint would be right. The 2nd amendment which appears to me essential is the restoring the principle of necessary rotation, particularly to the Senate and presidency: but most of all to the last. Re-eligibility makes him an officer for life, and the disasters inseparable from an elective monarchy render it preferable, if we cannot tread back that step, that we should go forward and take refuge in a hereditary one. Of the correction of this article, however, I entertain no present hope, because I find it has scarcely excited an objection in America. And if it does not take place ere long, it assuredly never will. The natural progress of things is for liberty to yield and government to gain ground. As yet our spirits are free. Our jealousy is only put to sleep by the unlimited confidence we all repose in the person to whom we all look as our President. After him inferior

7. The Massachusetts convention ratified the Constitution and proposed nine changes which its representatives in the new Congress were instructed to seek to have added as constitutional amendments.

8. "That it be explicitly declared, that all powers not expressly delegated by the aforesaid Constitution are reserved to the several states, to be by them exercised" (*The Debates in the Several State Conventions on the Adoption of the Federal Constitution*, ed. Jonathan Elliot [5 vols.; Washington, 1901], II, 177). Cf. the Constitution, Amendment X.

characters may perhaps succeed and awaken us to the danger which his merit has led us into. For the present, however, the general adoption is to be prayed for, and I wait with great anxiety for the news from Maryland and South Carolina, which have decided before this, and with that Virginia, now in session, may give the ninth vote of approbation. There could then be no doubt of North Carolina, New York, and New Hampshire. But what do you propose to do with Rhode Island? As long as there is hope, we should give her time. I cannot conceive but that she will come to rights in the long run. Force, in whatever form, would be a dangerous precedent. . . .

To F. Hopkinson[9]

Paris, March 13, 1789

Dear Sir,

. . . You say that I have been dished up to you as an anti-federalist, and ask me if it be just. My opinion was never worthy enough of notice to merit citing; but, since you ask it, I will tell it to you. I am not a federalist, because I never submitted the whole system of my opinions to the creed of any party of men whatever, in religion, in philosophy, in politics, or in anything else, where I was capable of thinking for myself. . . . If I could not go to heaven but with a party, I would not go there at all. Therefore, I am not of the party of federalists. But I am much farther from that of the anti-federalists. I approved, from the first moment, of the great mass of what is in the new Constitution; the consolidation of the government; the organization into executive, legislative, and judiciary; the subdivision of the legislative; the happy compromise of interest between the great and little states, by the different manner of voting in the different Houses; the

9. Francis Hopkinson (1737–91), musician, author, lawyer, statesman; signer of the Declaration of Independence.

voting by persons instead of states; the qualified negative on laws given to the executive, which, however, I should have liked better if associated with the judiciary also, as in New York; and the power of taxation. I thought at first that the latter might have been limited. A little reflection soon convinced me it ought not to be. What I disapproved from the first moment, also, was the want of a bill of rights, to guard liberty against the legislative as well as the executive branches of the government; that is to say, to secure freedom in religion, freedom of the press, freedom from monopolies, freedom from unlawful imprisonment, freedom from a permanent military, and a trial by jury, in all cases determinable by the laws of the land. I disapproved, also, the perpetual re-eligibility of the President. To these points of disapprobation I adhere. My first wish was that the nine first conventions might accept the Constitution, as the means of securing to us the great mass of good it contained, and that the four last might reject it, as the means of obtaining amendments. But I was corrected in this wish, the moment I saw the much better plan of Massachusetts, and which had never occurred to me. With the respect to the declaration of rights, I suppose the majority of the United States are of my opinion; for I apprehend, all the anti-federalists and a very respectable proportion of the federalists, think that such a declaration should now be annexed. The enlightened part of Europe have given us the greatest credit for inventing the instrument of security for the rights of the people and have been not a little surprised to see us so soon give it up. With respect to the re-eligibility of the President, I find myself differing from the majority of my countrymen; for I think there are but three states out of the eleven which have desired an alteration of this. And indeed, since the thing is established, I would wish it not to be altered during the life of our great leader, whose executive talents are superior to those, I believe, of any man in the world, and who, alone, by the authority of his name and the confidence reposed in his perfect integrity, is fully qualified to put the new government so under way, as to secure it against the efforts of opposition. But, having derived from our error all the good there was in it, I hope we shall correct it, the moment we can no longer have the same name at the helm. . . .

8. ANTI-FEDERALIST OPPOSITION TO THE CONSTITUTION[1]

By The "Federal Farmer"

EDITORS' NOTE.—These letters are ascribed by Ford and by E. C. Burnett, the historian of the Continental Congresses, to Richard Henry Lee. Burnett remarks that these letters became a sort of textbook for the opposition to the immediate ratification of the Constitution (*Dictionary of American Biography*, XI, 120).

The plan of government proposed by the convention appears to be a plan retaining some federal features; but to be the first important step, and to aim strongly at one consolidated government of the United States. It leaves the powers of government and the representation of the people so unnaturally divided between the general and state governments that the operations of our system must be very uncertain. My uniform federal attachments, and the interest I have in the protection of property, and a steady execution of the laws will convince you that, if I am under any bias at all, it is in favor of any general system which shall promise those advantages. The instability of our laws increases my wishes for firm and steady government; but, then, I can consent to no government which, in my opinion, is not calculated equally to preserve the rights of all orders of men in the community. My object has been to join with those who have endeavored to supply the defects in the forms of our governments by a

steady and proper administration of them. Though I have long apprehended that fraudulent debtors and embarrassed men, on the one hand, and men, on the other, unfriendly to republican equality, would produce an uneasiness among the people and prepare the way not for cool and deliberate reforms in the governments but for changes calculated to promote the interests of particular orders of men. Acquit me, sir, of any agency in the formation of the new system; I shall be satisfied with seeing if it shall be adopted with a prudent administration. Indeed, I am so much convinced of the truth of Pope's maxim that "that which is best administered is best" that I am much inclined to subscribe to it from experience. I am not disposed to unreasonably contend about forms. I know our situation is critical, and it behooves us to make the best of it. A federal government of some sort is necessary. We have suffered the present to languish; and whether the Confederation was capable or not originally of answering any valuable purposes, it is now but of little importance. I will pass by the men, and states, who have been particularly instrumental in preparing the way for a change and, perhaps, for governments

1. *Pamphlets on the Constitution of the United States . . . 1787–1788*, ed. P. L. Ford (Brooklyn, New York, 1888), pp. 279–81, 281–88, 288–89, 294–95, 296–97, 298–99, 300–303, 305–6, 306–7, 309, 310–13, 315–18, 319–25.

not very favorable to the people at large. A constitution is now presented which we may reject or which we may accept with or without amendments, and to which point we ought to direct our exertions is the question. To determine this question with propriety, we must attentively examine the system itself and the probable consequences of either step. This I shall endeavor to do, so far as I am able, with candor and fairness and leave you to decide upon the propriety of my opinions, the weight of my reasons, and how far my conclusions are well drawn. Whatever may be the conduct of others, on the present occasion, I do not mean hastily and positively to decide on the merits of the Constitution proposed. I shall be open to conviction and always disposed to adopt that which, all things considered, shall appear to me to be most for the happiness of the community. It must be granted that if men hastily and blindly adopt a system of government, they will as hastily and as blindly be led to alter or abolish it; and changes must ensue, one after another, till the peaceable and better part of the community will grow weary with changes, tumults, and disorders, and be disposed to accept any government, however despotic, that shall promise stability and firmness.

The first principal question that occurs is whether, considering our situation, we ought to precipitate the adoption of the proposed Constitution? If we remain cool and temperate, we are in no immediate danger of any commotions; we are in a state of perfect peace and in no danger of invasions; the state governments are in full exercise of their powers; and our governments answer all present exigencies, except the regulation of trade, securing credit, in some cases, and providing for the interest, in some instances, of the public debts; and whether we adopt a change three or nine months hence can make but little odds with the private circumstances of individuals; their happiness and prosperity, after all, depend principally upon their own exertions. We are hardly recovered from a long and distressing war. The farmers, fishermen, etc., have not fully repaired the waste made by it. Industry and frugality are again assuming their proper station. Private debts are lessened, and public debts incurred by the war have been, by various ways, diminished; and the public lands have now become a productive source for diminishing them much more. I know uneasy men who, with very much to precipitate, do not admit all these facts; but they are facts well known to all men who are thoroughly informed in the affairs of this country. . . .

Nothing but the passions of ambitious, impatient, or disorderly men, I conceive, will plunge us into commotions, if time should be taken fully to examine and consider the system proposed. Men who feel easy in their circumstances, and such as are not sanguine in their expectations relative to the consequences of the proposed change, will remain quiet under the existing governments. Many commercial and moneyed men who are uneasy, not without just cause, ought to be respected and by no means unreasonably disappointed in their expectations and hopes; but as to those who expect employments under the new Constitution; as to those weak and ardent men who always expect to be gainers by revolutions, and whose lot it generally is to get out of one difficulty into another, they are very little to be regarded; and as to those who designedly avail themselves of this weakness and ardor, they are to be despised. It is natural for men who wish to hasten the adoption of a measure to tell us, "Now is the crisis"— now is the critical moment which must be seized or all will be lost; and to shut the door against free inquiry, whenever conscious the thing presented has defects in it, which time and investigation will probably discover. This has been the custom of tyrants and their dependents in all ages. If it is true, what has been so often said, that the people of this country cannot change their condition for the worse, I presume it still behooves them to endeavor deliberately to change it for the better. The fickle and ardent in any community are the proper tools for establishing despotic government. But it is deliberate and thinking men who must establish and secure governments on free principles. Before they decide on the plan proposed, they will inquire whether it will probably be a blessing or a curse to this people.

The present moment discovers a new face in our affairs. Our object has been, all along, to reform our federal system and to strengthen our governments—to establish peace, order, and justice in the community—but a new object now presents. The plan of government now proposed is evidently calculated totally to change, in time, our condition as a people. Instead of being thirteen republics, under a federal head, it is clearly designed to make us one consolidated government. Of this, I think, I shall fully convince you in my following letters on this subject. This consolidation of the states has been the object of several men in this country for some time past. Whether such a change can ever be effected, in any manner; whether it can be effected without convulsions and civil wars; whether such a change will not totally destroy the liberties of this country—time only can determine.

To have a just idea of the government before us, and to show that a consolidated one is the object in view, it is necessary not only to examine the plan but also its history, and the politics of its particular friends.

The Confederation was formed when great confidence was placed in the voluntary exertions of individuals and of the respective states; and the framers of it, to guard against usurpation, so limited and checked the powers that, in many respects, they are inadequate to the exigencies of the Union. We find, therefore, members of Congress urging alterations in the federal system almost as soon as it was adopted. It was early proposed to vest Congress with powers to levy an impost, to regulate trade, etc., but such was known to be the caution of the states in parting with power that the vestment even of these was proposed to be under several checks and limitations. During the war the general confusion and the introduction of paper money infused in the minds of people vague ideas respecting government and credit. We expected too much from the return of peace, and, of course, we have been disappointed. Our governments have been new and unsettled; and several legislatures, by making tender, suspension, and paper-money laws, have given just cause of uneasiness to creditors. By these and other causes, several orders of men in the community have been prepared, by degrees, for a change of government; and this very abuse of power in the legislatures, which in some cases has been charged upon the democratic part of the community, has furnished aristocratical men with those very weapons, and those very means, with which, in great measure, they are rapidly effecting their favorite object. And should an oppressive government be the consequence of the proposed change, prosperity may reproach not only a few overbearing, unprincipled men but those parties in the states which have misused their powers.

The conduct of several legislatures, touching paper-money and tender laws, has prepared many honest men for changes in government which otherwise they would not have thought of—when by the evils, on the one hand, and by the secret instigations of artful men, on the other, the minds of men were become sufficiently uneasy, a bold step was taken, which is usually followed by a revolution or a civil war. A general convention for mere commercial purposes was moved for—the authors of this measure saw that the people's attention was turned solely to the amendment of the federal system; and that, had the idea of a total change been started, probably no state would have appointed members to the convention. The idea of destroying, ultimately, the state government, and forming one consolidated system, could not have been admitted—convention, therefore, merely for vesting in Congress power to regulate trade was proposed. This was pleasing to the commercial towns; and the landed people had little or no concern about it. September, 1786, a few men from the middle states met at Annapolis and hastily proposed a convention to be held in May, 1787, for the purpose, generally, of amending the Confederation—this was done before the delegates of Massachusetts and of the other states arrived—still not a word was said about destroying the old constitution, and making a new one. The states still unsuspecting, and not aware that they were passing the Rubicon, appointed members to the new convention for the sole and express purpose of revising and amending the Confederation—and, probably, not one man in ten thousand in the United States, till within these ten or twelve days, had an idea that the old ship was to be destroyed, and he put to the alternative of embarking in the new ship presented or of being left in danger of sinking. The states, I believe, universally supposed the convention would report alterations in the Confederation, which would pass an examination in Congress, and, after being agreed to there, would be confirmed by all the legislatures or be rejected. Virginia made a very respectable appointment and placed at the head of it the first man in America. In this appointment there was a mixture of political characters; but Pennsylvania appointed principally those men who are esteemed aristocratical. Here the favorite moment for changing the government was evidently discerned by a few men, who seized it with address. Ten other states appointed, and though they chose men principally connected with commerce and the judicial department, yet they appointed many good republican characters—had they all attended, we should now see, I am persuaded, a better system presented. The nonattendance of eight or nine men, who were appointed members of the convention, I shall ever consider as a very unfortunate event to the United States. Had they attended, I am pretty clear that the result of the convention would not have had that strong tendency to aristocracy now discernible in every part of the plan. There would not have been so great an accumulation of powers, especially as to the internal police of this country in a few hands as the Constitution reported proposes to vest in them —the young visionary men, and the consolidating aristocracy, would have been more restrained than they have been. Eleven states met in the convention, and after four months' close attention presented the new Constitution, to be adopted or rejected by the people. The uneasy and fickle part of the community may be prepared to receive any form of government; but I presume the enlightened and substantial part will give any constitution presented for their adoption a candid and thorough examination and silence those designing or empty men who weakly and rashly attempt to precipitate the adoption of a system of so much importance. We shall view the convention with proper respect—and, at the same time that we reflect there were men of abilities and integrity in it, we must recollect how disproportionately the democratic and aristocratic parts of the community were represented. Perhaps the judicious friends and opposers of the new Constitution will agree that it is best to let it rely solely on its own merits, or be condemned for its own defects.

In the first place, I shall premise that

the plan proposed is a plan of accommodation—and that it is in this way only, and by giving up a part of our opinions, that we can ever expect to obtain a government founded in freedom and compact. This circumstance candid men will always keep in view in the discussion of this subject.

The plan proposed appears to be partly federal, but principally, however, calculated ultimately to make the states one consolidated government.

The first interesting question therefore suggested is how far the states can be consolidated into one entire government on free principles. In considering this question, extensive objects are to be taken into view, and important changes in the forms of government to be carefully attended to in all their consequences. The happiness of the people at large must be the great object with every honest statesman, and he will direct every movement to this point. If we are so situated as a people as not to be able to enjoy equal happiness and advantages under one government, the consolidation of the states cannot be admitted.

There are three different forms of free government under which the United States may exist as one nation; and now is, perhaps, the time to determine to which we will direct our views. 1. Distinct republics connected under a federal head. In this case the respective state governments must be the principal guardians of the people's rights and exclusively regulate their internal police; in them must rest the balance of government. The Congress of the states, or federal head, must consist of delegates amenable to, and removable by, the respective states: This Congress must have general directing powers; powers to require men and moneys of the states; to make treaties, peace and war; to direct the operations of armies, etc. Under this federal modification of government, the powers of Congress would be rather advisory or recommendatory than coercive. 2. We may do away with the federal state governments and form or consolidate all the states into one entire government, with one executive, one judiciary, and one legislature, consisting of senators and representatives collected from all parts of the Union. In this case there would be a complete consolidation of the states. 3. We may consolidate the states as to certain national objects, and leave them severally distinct independent republics, as to internal police generally. Let the general government consist of an executive, a judiciary, and a balanced legislature, and its powers extend exclusively to all foreign concerns, causes arising on the seas to commerce, imports, armies, navies, Indian affairs, peace and war, and to a few internal concerns of the community; to the coin, post offices, weights and measures, a general plan for the militia, to naturalization, *and perhaps to bankruptcies*, leaving the internal police of the community, in other respects, exclusively to the state governments; as the administration of justice in all causes arising internally, the laying and collecting of internal taxes, and the forming of the militia according to a general plan prescribed. In this case there would be a complete consolidation, *quod* certain objects only.

Touching the first, or federal, plan, I do not think much can be said in its favor. The sovereignty of the nation, without coercive and efficient powers to collect the strength of it, cannot always be depended on to answer the purposes of government; and in a congress of representatives of foreign states, there must necessarily be an unreasonable mixture of powers in the same hands.

As to the second, or complete, consolidating plan, it deserves to be carefully considered at this time by every American. If it be impracticable, it is a fatal error to model our governments, directing our views ultimately to it.

The third plan, or partial consolidation, is, in my opinion, the only one that can secure the freedom and happiness of this people. I once had some general ideas that the second plan was practicable, but from long attention, and the proceedings of the convention, I am fully satisfied that this third plan is the only one we can with safety and propriety proceed upon. Making this the standard to point out, with candor and fairness, the parts of the new Constitution which appear to be improper is my object. (The convention appears to have proposed the partial consolidation evidently with a view to collect all powers ultimately in the United States into one entire government; and from its views in this respect, and from the tenacity of the small states to have an equal vote in the Senate, probably originated the greatest defects in the proposed plan. . . .

The essential parts of a free and good government are a full and equal representation of the people in the legislature, and the jury trial of the vicinage in the administration of justice—a full and equal representation is that which possesses the same interests, feelings, opinions, and views the people themselves would were they all assembled—a fair representation, therefore, should be so regulated that every order of men in the community, according to the common course of elections, can have a share in it—in order to allow professional men, merchants, traders, farmers, mechanics, etc., to bring a just proportion of their best-informed men respectively into the legislature, the representation must be considerably numerous. We have about two hundred state senators in the United States, and a less number than that of federal representatives cannot, clearly, be a full representation of this people, in the affairs of internal taxation and police, were there but one legislature for the whole Union. The representation cannot be equal, or the situation of the people proper for one government only —if the extreme parts of the society can-

not be represented as fully as the central. It is apparently impracticable that this should be the case in this extensive country—it would be impossible to collect a representation of the parts of the country five, six, and seven hundred miles from the seat of government. . . .

The great object of a free people must be so to form their government and laws, and so to administer them, as to create a confidence in, and respect for, the laws; and thereby induce the sensible and virtuous part of the community to declare in favor of the laws and to support them without an expensive military force. I wish, though I confess I have not much hope, that this may be the case with the laws of Congress under the new Constitution. . . . I wish the system adopted with a few alterations; but those, in my mind, are essential ones; if adopted without, every good citizen will acquiesce, though I shall consider the duration of our governments, and the liberties of this people, very much dependent on the administration of the general government. A wise and honest administration may make the people happy under any government; but necessity only can justify even our leaving open avenues to the abuse of power, by wicked, unthinking, or ambitious men. I will examine, first, the organization of the proposed government, in order to judge; 2d, with propriety, what powers are improperly, at least prematurely, lodged in it. I shall examine, 3d, the undefined powers; and 4th, those powers, the exercise of which is not secured on safe and proper ground.

First. As to the organization—the House of Representatives, the democratic branch, as it is called, is to consist of sixty-five members; that is, about one representative for fifty thousand inhabitants, to be chosen biennially—the federal legislature may increase this number to one for each thirty thousand inhabitants, abating fractional numbers in each state. Thirty-three representatives will make a quorum for doing business, and a majority of those present determine the sense of the House. I have no idea that the interests, feelings, and opinions of three or four millions of people, especially touching internal taxation, can be collected in such a House. In the nature of things, nine times in ten, men of the elevated classes in the community only can be chosen. Connecticut, for instance, will have five representatives—not one man in a hundred of those who form the democratic branch in the state legislature will, on a fair computation, be one of the five. The people of this country, in one sense, may all be democratic; but if we make the proper distinction between the few men of wealth and abilities, and consider them, as we ought, as the natural aristocracy of the country, and the great body of the people, the middle and lower classes, as the democracy, this federal representative branch will have but very little democracy in it, even this small representation is not secured on proper principles. . . .

In considering the practicability of having a full and equal representation of the people from all parts of the Union, not only distances and different opinions, customs and views, common in extensive tracts of country, are to be taken into view, but many differences peculiar to eastern, middle, and southern states. These differences are not so perceivable among the members of Congress, and men of general information in the states, as among the men who would properly form the democratic branch. The eastern states are very democratic and composed chiefly of moderate freeholders; they have but few rich men and no slaves. The southern states are composed chiefly of rich planters and slaves; they have but few moderate freeholders, and the prevailing influence in them is generally a dissipated aristocracy. The middle states partake partly of the eastern and partly of the southern character. . . .

The House of Representatives is on the plan of consolidation, but the Senate is entirely on the federal plan; and Delaware will have as much constitutional influence in the Senate as the largest state in the Union; and in this Senate are lodged legislative, executive, and judicial powers. Ten states in this Union urge that they are small states, nine of which were present in the convention. They were interested in collecting large powers into the hands of the Senate, in which each state still will have its equal share of power. I suppose it was impracticable for the three large states, as they were called, to get the Senate formed on any other principles. But this only proves that we cannot form one general government on equal and just principles—and proves that we ought not to lodge in it such extensive powers before we are convinced of the practicability of organizing it on just and equal principles. . . .

In the judicial department, powers ever kept distinct in well-balanced governments are no less improperly blended in the hands of the same men—in the judges of the Supreme Court is lodged the law, the equity, and the fact. It is not necessary to pursue the minute organical parts of the general government proposed. There were various interests in the convention to be reconciled, especially of large and small states; of carrying and noncarrying states; and of states more and states less democratic—vast labor and attention were by the convention bestowed on the organization of the parts of the Constitution offered; still, it is acknowledged, there are many things radically wrong in the essential parts of this Constitution—but it is said that these are the result of our situation. On a full examination of the subject, I believe it; but what do the laborious inquiries and determination of the convention prove? If they prove anything, they prove that we cannot consolidate the states on proper principles. The organization of the government presented proves that we cannot form a general government in which all power can be safely lodged; and a little attention to the parts of the one proposed will make it appear very evident that all the powers proposed to be lodged in it will not be then well deposited, either for the purposes of government or the preservation of liberty. I will suppose no abuse of power in those cases, in which the abuse of it is not well guarded against. I will suppose the words authorizing the general government to regulate the elections of its own members struck out of the plan, or free district elections, in each state, amply secured. That the small representation provided for shall be as fair and equal as it is capable of being made—I will suppose the judicial department regulated on pure principles, by future laws, as far as it can be by the Constitution and consistent with the situation of the country—still there will be an unreasonable accumulation of powers in the general government if all be granted, enumerated in the plan proposed. The plan does not present a well-balanced government. The senatorial branch of the legislative and the executive are substantially united, and the President, or the state executive magistrate, may aid the senatorial interest when weakest, but never can effectually support the democratic, however it may be opposed. The excellency, in my mind, of a well-balanced government is that it consists of distinct branches, each sufficiently strong and independent to keep its own station and to aid either of the other branches which may occasionally want aid. . . .

In the second place it is necessary, therefore, to examine the extent and the probable operations of some of those extensive powers proposed to be vested in this government. These powers, legislative, executive, and judicial, respect internal as well as external objects. Those respecting external objects, as all foreign concerns, commerce, imposts, all causes arising on the seas, peace and war, and Indian affairs, can be lodged nowhere else, with any propriety, but in this government. Many powers that respect internal objects ought clearly to be lodged in it; as those to regulate trade between the states, weights and measures, the coin or current moneys, post offices, naturalization, etc. These powers may be exercised without essentially affecting the internal police of the respective states. But powers to lay and collect internal taxes, to form the militia, to make bankruptcy laws, and to decide on appeals, questions arising on the internal laws of the respective states, are of a very serious nature and carry with them almost all other powers. These taken in connection with the others, and powers to raise armies and build navies, proposed to be lodged in this government, appear to me to comprehend all the essential powers in this community, and those which will be left to the states will be of no great importance.

A power to lay and collect taxes at discretion is, in itself, of very great importance. By means of taxes, the government may command the whole or any part of the subject's property. Taxes may be of various kinds; but there is a strong distinction between external and internal taxes. External taxes are import duties, which are laid on imported goods; they may usually be collected in a few seaport towns, and of a few individuals, though ultimately paid by the consumer; a few officers can collect them, and they can be carried no higher than trade will bear or smuggling permit—that in the very nature of commerce, bounds are set to them. But internal taxes, as poll and land taxes, excises, duties on all written instruments, etc., may fix themselves on every person and species of property in the community; they may be carried to any lengths, and, in proportion as they are extended, numerous officers must be employed to assess them and to enforce the collection of them. In the United Netherlands the general government has complete powers as to external taxation;

but as to internal taxes, it makes requisitions on the provinces. Internal taxation in this country is more important, as the country is so very extensive. As many assessors and collectors of federal taxes will be above three hundred miles from the seat of the federal government as will be less. Besides, to lay and collect taxes, in this extensive country, must require a great number of congressional ordinances, immediately operating upon the body of the people; these must continually interfere with the state laws, and thereby produce disorder and general dissatisfaction, till the one system of laws or the other, operating on the same subjects, shall be abolished. These ordinances alone, to say nothing of those respecting the militia, coin, commerce, federal judiciary, etc., will probably soon defeat the operations of the state laws and governments.

Should the general government think it politic, as some administration (if not all) probably will, to look for a support in a system of influence, the government will take every occasion to multiply laws and officers to execute them, considering these as so many necessary props for its own support. Should this system of policy be adopted, taxes more productive than the impost duties will, probably, be wanted to support the government and to discharge foreign demands, without leaving anything for the domestic creditors. The internal sources of taxation then must be called into operation, and internal tax laws and federal assessors and collectors spread over this immense country. All these circumstances considered, is it wise, prudent, or safe, to vest the powers of laying and collecting internal taxes in the general government, while imperfectly organized and inadequate; and to trust to amending it hereafter, and making it adequate to this purpose? It is not only unsafe but absurd to lodge power in a government before it is fitted to receive it. It is confessed that this power and

representation ought to go together. Why give the power first? Why give the power to the few who, when possessed of it, may have address enough to prevent the increase of representation? Why not keep the power and, when necessary, amend the Constitution and add to its other parts this power and a proper increase of representation at the same time? Then men who may want the power will be under strong inducements to let in the people, by their representatives, into the government, to hold their due proportion of this power. If a proper representation be impracticable, then we shall see this power resting in the states, where it at present ought to be, and not inconsiderately given up. . . .

. . . Powers to lay and collect taxes and to raise armies are of the greatest moment; for carrying them into effect, laws need not be frequently made, and the yeomanry, etc., of the country ought substantially to have a check upon the passing of these laws; this check ought to be placed in the legislatures or, at least, in the few men the common people of the country will, probably, have in Congress, in the true sense of the word, "from among themselves." It is true, the yeomanry of the country possess the lands, the weight of property, possess arms, and are too strong a body of men to be openly offended—and, therefore, it is urged, they will take care of themselves, that men who shall govern will not dare pay any disrespect to their opinions. It is easily perceived that if they have not their proper negative upon passing laws in Congress, or on the passage of laws relative to taxes and armies, they may in twenty or thirty years be, by means imperceptible to them, totally deprived of that boasted weight and strength. This may be done in a great measure by Congress, if disposed to do it, by modeling the militia. Should one-fifth or one-eighth part of the men capable of bearing arms be made a select militia, as has been proposed, and those the young and ardent part of the community, possessed of but little or no property, and all the others put upon a plan that will render them of no importance, the former will answer all the purposes of an army, while the latter will be defenseless. The state must train the militia in such form and according to such systems and rules as Congress shall prescribe; and the only actual influence the respective states will have respecting the militia will be in appointing the officers. I see no provision made for calling out the *posse comitatus* for executing the laws of the Union, but provision is made for Congress to call forth the militia for the execution of them—and the militia in general, or any select part of it, may be called out under military officers, instead of the sheriff to enforce an execution of federal laws, in the first instance, and thereby introduce an entire military execution of the laws. I know that powers to raise taxes, to regulate the military strength of the community on some uniform plan, to provide for its defense and internal order, and for duly executing the laws must be lodged somewhere; but still we ought not so to lodge them as evidently to give one order of men in the community undue advantages over others; or commit the many to the mercy, prudence, and moderation of the few. And so far as it may be necessary to lodge any of the peculiar powers in the general government, a more safe exercise of them ought to be secured, by requiring the consent of two-thirds or three-fourths of Congress thereto—until the federal representation can be increased, so that the democratic members in Congress may stand some tolerable chance of a reasonable negative, in behalf of the numerous, important, and democratic part of the community. . . .

There are some powers proposed to be lodged in the general government in the judicial department, I think very unnecessarily, I mean powers respecting questions arising upon the internal laws

of the respective states. It is proper the federal judiciary should have powers coextensive with the federal legislature—that is, the power of deciding finally on the laws of the Union. By Art. III, Sec. 2, the powers of the federal judiciary are extended (among other things) to all cases between a state and citizens of another state—between citizens of different states—between a state or the citizens thereof, and foreign states, citizens or subjects. Actions in all these cases, except against a state government, are now brought and finally determined in the law courts of the states respectively, and, as there are no words to exclude these courts of their jurisdiction in these cases, they will have concurrent jurisdiction with the inferior federal courts in them; and, therefore, if the new Constitution be adopted without any amendment in this respect, all those numerous actions, now brought in the state courts between our citizens and foreigners, between citizens of different states, by state governments against foreigners, and by state governments against citizens of other states, may also be brought in the federal courts; and an appeal will lay in them from the state courts or federal inferior courts to the supreme judicial court of the Union. In almost all these cases, either party may have the trial by jury in the state courts; except paper-money and tender laws, which are wisely guarded against in the proposed Constitution; justice may be obtained in these courts on reasonable terms; they must be more competent to proper decisions on the laws of their respective states than the federal states can possibly be. I do not, in any point of view, see the need of opening a new jurisdiction in these causes—of opening a new scene of expensive lawsuits, of suffering foreigners, and citizens of different states, to drag each other many hundred miles into the federal courts. . . .

I confess, in the constitution of this supreme court, as left by the Constitution, I do not see a spark of freedom or a shadow of our own or the British common law.

This court is to have appellate jurisdiction in all the other cases before mentioned. Many sensible men suppose that cases before mentioned respect as well the criminal cases as the civil ones mentioned antecedently in the Constitution; if so, an appeal is allowed in criminal cases—contrary to the usual sense of law. How far it may be proper to admit a foreigner or the citizen of another state to bring actions against state governments which have failed in performing so many promises made during the war is doubtful. How far it may be proper so to humble a state, as to oblige it to answer to an individual in a court of law, is worthy of consideration; the states are now subject to no such actions; and this new jurisdiction will subject the states, and many defendants, to actions and processes which were not in the contemplation of the parties when the contract was made; all engagements existing between citizens of different states, citizens and foreigners, states and foreigners, and states and citizens of other states were made the parties contemplating the remedies then existing on the laws of the states—and the new remedy proposed to be given in the federal courts can be founded on no principle whatever. . . .

Third, there appears to me to be not only a premature deposit of some important powers in the general government—but many of those deposited there are undefined and may be used to good or bad purposes as honest or designing men shall prevail. By Art. I, Sec. 2, representatives and direct taxes shall be apportioned among the several states, etc.—same art., Sec. 8, the Congress shall have powers to lay and collect taxes, duties, etc., for the common defense and general welfare, but all duties, imposts, and excises shall be uniform throughout the United States. By the first recited clause, direct taxes shall be apportioned on the states. This seems to favor the idea suggested by some sensible men and writers that Congress, as to direct taxes, will only have power to make requisitions; but the latter clause, power to lay and collect taxes, etc., seems clearly to favor the contrary opinion, and, in my mind, the true one, the Congress shall have power to tax immediately individuals, without the intervention of the state legislatures; in fact, the first clause appears to me only to provide that each state shall pay a certain portion of the tax, and the latter to provide that Congress shall have power to lay and collect taxes, that is, to assess upon, and to collect of, the individuals in the state, the state's quota; but these still I consider as undefined powers, because judicious men understand them differently.

It is doubtful whether the Vice-President is to have any qualifications; none are mentioned; but he may serve as President, and, it may be inferred, he ought to be qualified therefore as the President; but the qualifications of the President are required only of the person to be elected President. By Art. II, Sec. 2, "But the Congress may by law vest the appointment of such inferior officers as they think proper in the President alone, in the courts of law, or in the heads of the departments." Who are inferior officers? May not a Congress disposed to vest the appointment of all officers in the President, under this clause, vest the appointment of almost every officer in the President alone, and destroy the check mentioned in the first part of the clause and lodged in the Senate. It is true, this check is badly lodged, but then some check upon the first magistrate in appointing officers ought, it appears by the opinion of the convention, and by the general opinion, to be established in the Constitution. By Art. III, Sec. 2, the Supreme Court shall have appellate jurisdiction as to law and facts with such exceptions, etc., to what extent is it intended the exceptions shall be carried. Congress may carry them so far as to annihilate substantially the appellate jurisdiction, and the clause be rendered of very little importance.

Fourth. There are certain rights which we have always held sacred in the United States, and recognized in all our constitutions, and which, by the adoption of the new Constitution in its present form, will be left unsecured. By Article VI, the proposed Constitution, and the laws of the United States, which shall be made in pursuance thereof; and all treaties made, or which shall be made under the authority of the United States, shall be the supreme law of the land, and the judges in every state shall be bound thereby, anything in the constitution or laws of any state to the contrary notwithstanding.

It is to be observed that, when the people shall adopt the proposed Constitution, it will be their last and supreme act; it will be adopted not by the people of New Hampshire, Massachusetts, etc., but by the people of the United States; and wherever this Constitution, or any part of it, shall be incompatible with the ancient customs, rights, the laws, or the constitutions heretofore established in the United States, it will entirely abolish them and do them away. And not only this, but the laws of the United States which shall be made in pursuance of the federal Constitution will be also supreme laws, and wherever they shall be incompatible with those customs, rights, laws, or constitutions heretofore established, they will also entirely abolish them and do them away.

By the article before recited, treaties also made under the authority of the United States shall be the supreme law. It is not said that these treaties shall be made in pursuance of the Constitution—nor are there any constitutional bounds set to those who shall make them. The President and two-thirds of the Senate will be empowered to make treaties indefinitely, and when these treaties shall be made, they will also abolish all laws and state constitutions incompatible with them. This power in the President and Senate is absolute, and the judges will be bound to allow full force to whatever rule, article, or thing the President and Senate shall establish by treaty, whether it be practicable to set any bounds to those who make treaties, I am not able to say; if not, it proves that this power ought to be more safely lodged.

The federal Constitution, the laws of Congress made in pursuance of the Constitution, and all treaties must have full force and effect in all parts of the United States; and all other laws, rights, and constitutions which stand in their way must yield. It is proper the national laws should be supreme, and superior to state or district laws; but then the national laws ought to yield to unalienable or fundamental rights—and national laws, made by a few men, should extend only to a few national objects. This will not be the case with the laws of Congress. To have any proper idea of their extent, we must carefully examine the legislative, executive, and judicial powers proposed to be lodged in the general government and consider them in connection with a general clause in Art. I, Sec. 8, in these words (after enumerating a number of powers): "To make all laws which shall be necessary and proper for carrying into execution the foregoing powers, and all other powers vested by this constitution in the government of the United States, or in any department or officer thereof." The powers of this government, as has been observed, extend to internal as well as external objects, and to those objects to which all others are subordinate; it is almost impossible to have a just conception of their powers, or of the extent and number of the laws which may be deemed necessary and proper to carry them into effect, till we shall come to exercise those powers and make the laws. In making laws to carry those powers into effect, it is to be expected that a wise and prudent Congress will pay respect to the opinions of a free people and bottom their laws on those principles which have been considered as essential and fundamental in the British and in our government. But a Congress of a different character will not be bound by the Constitution to pay respect to those principles.

It is said that when people make a constitution, and delegate powers, that all powers not delegated by them to those who govern are reserved in the people; and that the people, in the present case, have reserved in themselves, and in their state governments, every right and power not expressly given by the federal Constitution to those who shall administer the national government. It is said, on the other hand, that the people, when they make a constitution, yield all power not expressly reserved to themselves. The truth is, in either case, it is mere matter of opinion, and men usually take either side of the argument as will best answer their purposes. But the general presumption being that men who govern will, in doubtful cases, construe laws and constitutions most favorably for increasing their own powers; all wise and prudent people, in forming constitutions, have drawn the line, and carefully described the powers parted with and the powers reserved. By the state constitutions, certain rights have been reserved in the people; or, rather, they have been recognized and established in such a manner that state legislatures are bound to respect them and to make no laws infringing upon them. The state legislatures are obliged to take notice of the bills of rights of their respective states. The bills of rights, and the state constitutions, are fundamental compacts only between those who govern and the people of the same state. . . .

On the whole, the position appears to me to be undeniable that this bill of rights ought to be carried farther, and

some other principles established, as a part of this fundamental compact between the people of the United States and their federal rulers.

It is true, we are not disposed to differ much, at present, about religion; but when we are making a constitution, it is to be hoped, for ages and millions yet unborn, why not establish the free exercise of religion as a part of the national compact. There are other essential rights which we have justly understood to be the rights of freemen; as freedom from hasty and unreasonable search warrants, warrants not founded on oath, and not issued with due caution, for searching and seizing men's papers, property, and persons. The trial by jury in civil causes, it is said, varies so much in the several states that no words could be found for the uniform establishment of it. If so, the federal legislation will not be able to establish it by any general laws. I confess I am of opinion it may be established, but not in that beneficial manner in which we may enjoy it, for the reasons before mentioned. When I speak of the jury trial of the vicinage, or the trial of the fact in the neighborhood, I do not lay so much stress upon the circumstance of our being tried by our neighbors; in this enlightened country men may be probably impartially tried by those who do not live very near them; but the trial of facts in the neighborhood is of great importance in other respects. Nothing can be more essential than the cross-examining witnesses, and generally before the triers of the facts in question. The common people can establish facts with much more ease with oral than written evidence; when trials of facts are removed to a distance from the homes of the parties and witnesses, oral evidence becomes intolerably expensive, and the parties must depend on written evidence, which to the common people is expensive and almost useless; it must be frequently taken *ex parte* and but very seldom leads to the proper discovery of truth.

The trial by jury is very important in another point of view. It is essential in every free country that common people should have a part and share of influence, in the judicial as well as in the legislative department. To hold open to them the offices of senators, judges, and offices to fill which an expensive education is required cannot answer any valuable purposes for them; they are not in a situation to be brought forward and to fill those offices; these, and most other offices of any considerable importance, will be occupied by the few. The few, the well-born, etc., as Mr. Adams calls them, in judicial decisions as well as in legislation, are generally disposed, and very naturally too, to favor those of their own description.

The trial by jury in the judicial department, and the collection of the people by their representatives in the legislature, are those fortunate inventions which have procured for them, in this country, their true proportion of influence and the wisest and most fit means of protecting themselves in the community. Their situation, as jurors and representatives, enables them to acquire information and knowledge in the affairs and government of the society; and to come forward, in turn, as the sentinels and guardians of each other. I am very sorry that even a few of our countrymen should consider jurors and representatives in a different point of view, as ignorant, troublesome bodies, which ought not to have any share in the concerns of government.

I confess I do not see in what cases the Congress can, with any pretense of right, make a law to suppress the freedom of the press; though I am not clear that Congress is restrained from laying any duties whatever on printing, and from laying duties particularly heavy on certain pieces printed, and perhaps Congress may require large bonds for the payment of these duties. Should the printer say the freedom of the press was secured by the Constitution of the state in which he lived, Congress might, and perhaps, with great propriety, answer, that the federal Constitution is the only compact existing between them and the people; in this compact the people have named no others, and therefore Congress, in exercising the powers assigned them, and in making laws to carry them into execution, are restrained by nothing beside the federal Constitution, any more than a state legislature is restrained by a compact between the magistrates and people of a county, city, or town of which the people, in forming the state constitution, have taken no notice.

It is not my object to enumerate rights of inconsiderable importance; but there are others, no doubt, which ought to be established as a fundamental part of the national system.

It is worthy of observation that all treaties are made by foreign nations with a confederacy of thirteen states—that the western country is attached to thirteen states—thirteen states have jointly and severally engaged to pay the public debts. Should a new government be formed of nine, ten, eleven, or twelve states, those treaties could not be considered as binding on the foreign nations who made them. However, I believe the probability to be that if nine states adopt the Constitution, the others will.

It may also be worthy of our examination how far the provision for amending this plan, when it shall be adopted, is of any importance. No measures can be taken toward amendments, unless two-thirds of the Congress, or two-thirds of the legislature of the several states shall agree. While power is in the hands of the people, or democratic part of the community, more especially as at present, it is easy, according to the general course of human affairs, for the few influential men in the community to obtain conventions, alterations in government, and to persuade the common people that they may change for the better and to get from them a part of the power. But when power is once transferred from the many to the few, all changes become extremely difficult; the government, in this case, being beneficial to the few, they will be exceedingly artful and adroit in preventing any measures which may lead to a change; and nothing will produce it but great exertions and severe struggles on the part of the common people. Every man of reflection must see that the change now proposed is a transfer of power from the many to the few, and the probability is the artful and ever active aristocracy will prevent all peaceful measures for changes, unless when they shall discover some favorable moment to increase their own influence. I am sensible thousands of men in the United States are disposed to adopt the proposed Constitution, though they perceive it to be essentially defective, under an idea that amendments of it may be obtained when necessary. This is a pernicious idea; it argues a servility of character totally unfit for the support of free government; it is very repugnant to that perpetual jealousy respecting liberty, so absolutely necessary in all free states, spoken of by Mr. Dickinson. . . .

There are, however, in my opinion, many good things in the proposed system. It is founded on elective principles, and the deposit of powers in different hands is essentially right. The guards against those evils we have experienced in some states in legislation are valuable indeed; but the value of every feature in this system is vastly lessened for the want of that one important feature in a free government, a representation of the people. Because we have sometimes abused democracy, I am not among those men who think a democratic branch a nuisance; which branch shall be sufficiently numerous to admit some of the best-informed men of each order in the community into the administration of government.

While the radical defects in the proposed system are not so soon discovered, some temptations to each state, and to many classes of men to adopt it, are very visible. It uses the democratic language of several of the state constitutions, particularly that of Massachusetts; the eastern states will receive advantages so far as the regulation of trade, by a bare majority, is committed to it. Connecticut and New Jersey will receive their share of a general impost. The middle states will receive the advantages surrounding the seat of government. The southern states will receive protection, and have their Negroes represented in the legislature, and large back countries will soon have a majority in it. This system promises a large field of employment to military gentlemen and gentlemen of the law; and in case the government shall be executed without convulsions, it will afford security to creditors, to the clergy, salary-men, and others depending on money payments. So far as the system promises justice and reasonable advantages, in these respects, it ought to be supported by all honest men; but whenever it promises unequal and improper advantages to any particular states, or orders of men, it ought to be opposed.

I have, in the course of these letters, observed that there are many good things in the proposed Constitution, and I have endeavored to point out many important defects in it. I have admitted that we want a federal system—that we have a system presented which, with several alterations, may be made a tolerably good one—I have admitted there is a well-founded uneasiness among creditors and mercantile men. In this situation of things, you ask me what I think ought to be done. My opinion in this case is only the opinion of an individual and, so far only as it corresponds with the opinions of the honest and substantial part of the community, is it entitled to consideration. Though I am fully satisfied that the state conventions ought most seriously to direct their exertions to altering and amending the system proposed before they shall adopt it—yet I have not sufficiently examined the subject, or formed an opinion, how far it will be practicable for those conventions to carry their amendments. As to the idea that it will be in vain for those conventions to attempt amendments, it cannot be admitted; it is impossible to say whether they can or not until the attempt shall be made; and when it shall be determined, by experience, that the conventions cannot agree in amendments, it will then be an important question before the people of the United States, whether they will adopt or not the system proposed in its present form. This subject of consolidating the states is new; and because forty or fifty men have agreed in a system to suppose the good sense of this country, an enlightened nation must adopt it without examination and, though in a state of profound peace, without endeavoring to amend those parts they perceive are defective, dangerous to freedom, and destructive of the valuable principles of republican government—is truly humiliating. It is true there may be danger in delay; but there is danger in adopting the system in its present form; and I see the danger in either case will arise principally from the conduct and views of two very unprincipled parties in the United States—two fires, between which the honest and substantial people have long found themselves situated. One party is composed of little insurgents, men in debt, who want no law, and who want a share of the property of others; these are called Levellers, Shaysites, etc. The other party is composed of a few, but more dangerous men, with their servile dependents; these avariciously grasp at all power and property; you may discover in all the actions of these men an evident dislike to free and equal government, and they will go systematically to work to change, essentially, the forms of government in this country; these are called aristocrats, m——ites, etc., etc. Between these two parties is the weight of the community; the men of middling property, men not in debt, on the one hand, and men, on the other, content with republican governments, and not aiming at immense fortunes, offices, and power. In 1786 the little insurgents, the Levellers, came forth, invaded the rights of others, and attempted to establish governments according to their wills. Their movements evidently gave encouragement to the other party, which, in 1787, has taken the political field, and with its fashionable dependents, and the tongue and the pen, is endeavoring to establish in a great haste a politer kind of government. These two parties, which will probably be opposed or united as it may suit their interests and views, are really insignificant compared with the solid, free, and independent part of the community. It is not my intention to suggest that either of these parties, and the real friends of the proposed Constitution, are the same men. The fact is, these aristocrats support and hasten the adoption of the proposed Constitution merely because they think it is a stepping stone to their favorite object. I think I am well founded in this idea; I think the general politics of these men support it, as well as the common observation among them that, the proffered plan [being] the best that can be got at present, it will do for a few years and lead to something better. The sensible and judicious part of the community will carefully weigh all these circumstances; they will view the late convention as a respectable body of men—America probably never will see an assembly of men, of a like number, more respectable. But the members of the convention met without knowing the sentiments of one man in ten thousand in these states respecting the new ground taken. Their doings are but the first attempts in the most important scene ever opened. Though each individual in the state conventions will not, probably, be so respectable as each individual in the federal convention, yet as the state conventions will probably consist of fifteen hundred or two thousand men of abilities, and versed in the science of government, collected from all parts of the community and from all orders of men, it must be acknowledged that the weight of respectability will be in them. In them will be collected the solid sense and the real political character of the country. Being revisers of the subject, they will possess peculiar advantages. To say that these conventions ought not to attempt, coolly and deliberately, the revision of the system, or that they cannot amend it, is very foolish or very assuming. If these conventions, after examining the system, adopt it, I shall be perfectly satisfied, and wish to see men make the administration of the government an equal blessing to all orders of men. I believe the great body of our people to be virtuous and friendly to good government, to the protection of liberty and property; and it is the duty of all good men, especially of those who are placed as sentinels to guard their rights—it is their duty to examine into the prevailing politics of parties and to disclose them—while they avoid exciting undue suspicions, to lay facts before the people which will enable them to form a proper judgment. Men who wish the people of this country to determine for themselves, and deliberately to fit the government to their situation, must feel some degree of indignation at those attempts to hurry the adoption of a system and to shut the door against examination. The very attempts create suspicions that those who make them have secret views or see some defects in the system which, in the hurry of affairs, they expect, will escape the eye of a free people.

What can be the views of those gentlemen in Pennsylvania who precipitated decisions on this subject? What can be the views of those gentlemen in Boston who countenanced the printers in shutting up the press against a fair and free investigation of this important system in the usual way? The members of the convention have done their duty—why should some of them fly to their states—almost forget a propriety of behavior, and precipitate measures for the adoption of a system of their own making? I confess candidly, when I consider these circumstances in connection with the unguarded parts of the system I have mentioned, I feel disposed to proceed with very great caution and to pay more attention than usual to the conduct of particular characters. If the Constitution presented be a good one, it will stand the test with a well-informed people: all are agreed that there shall be state conventions to examine it; and we must believe it will be adopted, unless we suppose it is a bad one, or that those conventions will make false divisions respecting it. I admit improper measures are taken against the adoption of the system as well for it—all who object to the plan proposed ought to point out the defects objected to, and to propose those amendments with which they can accept it, or to propose some other system of government, that the public mind may be known and that we may be brought to agree in some system of government to strengthen and execute the present or to provide a substitute. I consider the field of inquiry just opened and that we are to look to the state conventions for ultimate decisions on the subject before us; it is not to be presumed that they will differ about small amendments and lose a system when they shall have made it substantially good; but, touching the essential amendments, it is to be presumed the several conventions will pursue the most rational measures to agree in and obtain them; and such defects as they shall discover and not remove, they will probably notice, keep them in view as the groundwork of future amendments, and, in the firm and manly language which every free people ought to use, will suggest to those who may hereafter administer the government that it is their expectation that the system will be so organized by legislative acts, and the government so administered, as to render those defects as little injurious as possible. Our countrymen are entitled to an honest and faithful government; to a government of laws and not of men; and also to one of their choosing—as a citizen of the country, I wish to see these objects secured and licentious, assuming, and overbearing men restrained; if the Constitution or social compact be vague and unguarded, then we depend wholly upon the prudence, wisdom, and moderation of those who manage the affairs of government; or on what, probably, is equally uncertain and precarious, the success of the people oppressed by the abuse of government, in receiving it from the hands of those who abuse it, and placing it in the hands of those who will use it well.

In every point of view, therefore, in which I have been able, as yet, to contemplate this subject, I can discern but one rational mode of proceeding relative to it: and that is to examine it with freedom and candor, to have state conventions some months hence, which shall examine coolly every article, clause, and word in the system proposed, and to adopt it with such amendments as they shall think fit. How far the state conventions ought to pursue the mode prescribed by the federal convention of adopting or rejecting the plan in toto, I leave it to them to determine. Our examination of the subject hitherto has been rather of a general nature. The republican characters in the several states who wish to make this plan more adequate to security of liberty and property, and to the duration of the principles of a free government, will, no doubt, collect their opinions to certain points and accurately define those alterations and amendments they wish; if it shall be found they essentially disagree in them, the conventions will then be able to determine whether to adopt the plan as it is, or what will be proper to be done.

Under these impressions, and keeping in view the improper and unadvisable lodgment of powers in the general government, organized as it at present is, touching internal taxes, armies, and militia, the elections of its own members, causes between citizens of different states, etc., and the want of a more perfect bill of rights, etc., I drop the subject for the present, and when I shall have leisure to revise and correct my ideas respecting it, and to collect into points the opinions of those who wish to make the system more secure and safe, perhaps I may proceed to point out particularly for your consideration the amendments which ought to be ingrafted into this system, not only in conformity to my own but the deliberate opinions of others —you will with me perceive that the objections to the plan proposed may, by a more leisurely examination, be set in a stronger point of view, especially the important one, that there is no substantial representation of the people provided for in a government in which the most essential powers, even as to the internal police of the country, is proposed to be lodged.

I think the honest and substantial part of the community will wish to see this system altered, permanency and consistency given to the Constitution we shall adopt; and therefore they will be anxious to apportion the powers to the features and organizations of the government and to see abuse in the exercise of power more effectually guarded against. It is suggested that state officers, from interested motives, will oppose the Constitution presented. I see no reason for this, their places in general will not be affected, but new openings to offices and places of profit must evidently be made by the adoption of the Constitution in its present form. . . .

UNIT IV

ECONOMIC PROBLEMS OF THE NEW REPUBLIC

IN EVERY society it has to be decided what goods and services will be produced, how production will be organized, and how the total product will be distributed throughout the population. But it is obvious that these decisions may be made in many different ways and with reference to many different ends. In primitive societies they may be taken under the influence of customary habits which are so binding that we can hardly call these decisions "rational" at all; or they may be made in modern times with the self-consciousness of people who are trying to remodel the world they live in. The responsibility for shaping economic policy may be centered in a temple of priests, a royal council, a clique of ruling families, a parliament, a congress, or a dictator. Finally, it should be clear that the ends which the makers of policy have in mind are never merely economic. They may choose to sacrifice economic wealth to national defense. They may prefer guns to butter because they intend to make war. They may diversify their economy because they dislike the social effects of too much concentration. They may prevent a factory from being erected in a particular place because it spoils the view or compel all factories to abolish smoke nuisances because they pollute the air. They may decide to reduce leisure because it leads to idleness and sin or to increase it because it leads to health and happiness. Economic activity, in short, reflects the habits and values which prevail at any given time and may be influenced by any social end which seems desirable or just.

In eighteenth-century America, as in Britain, economic decisions were being taken under conditions of increasing freedom from the kind of controls which had characterized earlier centuries. The first introduction to this volume pointed the contrast between the regulated life of Jacobean England and the much more liberal tendencies of the end of the century. In political theory these impulses were generalized by Locke, and we have seen the progress of that side of the liberal tradition in later history. The same faith in freedom may be seen in various economic writings, in the decay of the old system of industrial regulation, and in the growing demands of entrepreneurs for more elbow room. It was in the midst of this experience that Adam Smith prepared and published his *Inquiry into the Nature and Causes of the Wealth of Nations*—a book which initiated the study of political economy as a formal science and which demanded the revision of traditional thinking along the lines suggested by liberal ideas. It was

Smith's achievement to divine the needs of an expanding business community, to organize the scattered tendencies of previous thought into a great synthesis of his own, and to present it as a standard of wisdom by which economic error might be judged. The doctrines of economic liberalism, like those of political liberalism, are essential to the understanding of American history.

Smith's ideas were one influence among the many which affected the economic decisions of the new American government. As a government which inherited the unfunded debts of the war, which was keenly aware of the economic disorders of the Confederation period, and which needed a revenue before it could govern at all, Washington's administration was at once faced with the problems of economic policy. But each of these questions involved more than an economic calculation, as Alexander Hamilton, the secretary of the treasury, well understood. His proposals for their solution embodied a political philosophy, a Federalist strategy, and a sectional preference, as well as an economic program. The same variety of motives may be seen among his opponents, of whom Jefferson became the chief.

Compared with either a sixteenth-century or a twentieth-century planner of economic policy, Hamilton and Jefferson were both working within the assumptions of an individualistic age. Hamilton's appreciation of Smith's writings, notwithstanding his deviation from them over tariff policy, and Jefferson's laissez faire views, may both be contrasted with the very different assumptions of earlier or later periods. But in terms of their own times they reflected radically different choices about the interests which government should serve and the manner in which it should serve them.

Hamilton had no confidence in the ability of the mass of the people to judge their own interest. He believed that the benefits of prosperity would be maximized for all by a careful attention to the interests of the creditor, commercial, and manufacturing classes. He attached the greatest importance to any arrangement which would strengthen the new government, either by wedding the interests of his favored classes to its operations or by demonstrating its authority through a tax which would fall among people who needed a reminder. He was naturally supported by all the friends of sound business and strong government and was as naturally opposed by farmers, planters, champions of democracy, and any who disliked centralized authority. Jefferson's democratic sentiments and distrust of government have already been studied. He was also, by early conviction, a philosopher whose faith in America's future was centered in her independent farmers. With these convictions he rallied around himself the various elements of opposition.

The first document in this section is an extract from Hamilton's *Report on the Public Credit*. He explains why it is so important for the government to honor its contracts, rejects the sugges-

346

tion that there should be any discrimination between the original and the final holders of the debt, and urges the national government to assume the state debts. The adoption of this program was vigorously resisted by those who resented the activities of speculators and by states with small debts. Any solution would have been open to objections. Hamilton's solution undoubtedly succeeded in restoring the public credit. The only question was whether it did so in the best manner, and that was not a subject on which agreement was possible.

This reading is followed by extracts from the remarkable *Report on Manufactures*, a document whose arguments were to be influential for more than a century. Hamilton's case for protection should be compared with the views of Adam Smith, which in other respects he follows so closely. A nation of farmers and merchants could see little defense in 1791 for a tariff which was designed in the interests of manufacturers, but Hamilton's arguments were to find strong support in the generation after 1815.

Jefferson gives his version of the issues which underlay his opponent's policies in the paper entitled "Remarks on the Hamiltonian System." Like any other piece of controversial literature, it ought to be read with caution. The "Merits of Agriculture" includes two statements by Jefferson, one in 1782, the other in 1816, after the American economy had undergone considerable changes. Those parts of Jefferson's Inaugural Address which refer to agriculture may be used to illustrate his views at a time which was roughly midway between these dates (1801).

The section ends with a selection from the arguments for and against the creation of a United States Bank. It was another of those issues which brought out all the differences in the viewpoints of Hamilton and Jefferson —Hamilton, the admirer of English institutions, the patron of a business community, the exponent of vigorous national government; Jefferson, the critic of every pennyworth of suffering in a pound sterling, the planter who saw in the bank a plot to confound the simple and enrich the shrewd, the philosopher who objected on principle to any enlargement of governmental power.

Although Jefferson's party defeated the Federalists in 1800 and remained in power for a quarter of a century, it was Hamilton's views which were more in line with future economic development. This was already apparent in Jefferson's lifetime, when the dreams of an agrarian republic had begun to fade, and the Republican party, which Jefferson had organized in the nineties, adopted both a protective tariff and a second national bank in 1816. But the Jeffersonian conception of democratic justice and government, which had become the heritage of a political party in the course of the conflict with federalism, outlived him. It was this creed—passing through numerous changes as all creeds do— which was to be repeatedly invoked by farming and laboring classes in their conflicts with business enterprise.

SECTION A. PROBLEMS OF ECONOMIC LIBERALISM

I. AN INQUIRY INTO THE NATURE AND CAUSES OF THE WEALTH OF NATIONS

By ADAM SMITH

EDITORS' NOTE.—Adam Smith (1723–90) was born at Kirkcaldy, Scotland, where his father had been comptroller of the customs. After study at the universities of Glasgow and Oxford, he served as professor of logic and of moral philosophy at the University of Glasgow from 1751 to 1763. In this period Smith wrote *The Theory of Moral Sentiments* (1759), which expressed the thesis that sympathy rather than enlighted self-interest or utility plays the primary role in human relations. From 1764 to 1766 he traveled, chiefly in France, and became acquainted with the leading physiocrats, whose beliefs included the contention that there is a natural economic order and that agriculture was the true basis of national wealth. At this time he began writing *The Wealth of Nations*, which appeared in 1776 and became the foundation of modern classical economic thought.

Franklin, Jefferson, and Hamilton were well acquainted with *The Wealth of Nations*. Indeed, Jefferson recommended it in 1790 as an excellent book in political economy. From 1789 to 1818 six editions were published in the United States, the last of which is said to have consisted of probably one thousand copies.

Materials from *The Wealth of Nations* have been selected and reorganized around the three topics, "The Wealth of a Nation Explained," "Economic Liberalism: The Ideal," and "Economic Liberalism: The Reality."

THE WEALTH OF NATIONS EXPLAINED[1]
INTRODUCTION AND PLAN OF THE WORK

The annual labor of every nation is the fund which originally supplies it with all the necessaries and conveniences of life which it annually consumes, and which consist always either in the immediate produce of that labor or in what is purchased with that produce from other nations.

According, therefore, as this produce, or what is purchased with it, bears a greater or smaller proportion to the number of those who are to consume it, the nation will be better or worse supplied with all the necessaries and conveniences for which it has occasion.

But this proportion must in every nation be regulated by two different circumstances: first, by the skill, dexterity, and judgment with which its labor is generally applied; and, secondly, by the proportion between the number of those who are employed in useful labor and that of those who are not so employed. Whatever be the soil, climate, or extent of territory of any particular nation, the

1. Adam Smith, *An Inquiry into the Nature and Causes of the Wealth of Nations* (New York, 1937), pp. (in order of their inclusion) lvii–lx, 3–9, 10–12, 734–35, 13–19, 259–60, 321–22, and 325–27. Reprinted by permission of the Modern Library, New York.

abundance or scantiness of its annual supply must, in that particular situation, depend upon those two circumstances.

The abundance or scantiness of this supply too seems to depend more upon the former of those two circumstances than upon the latter. Among the savage nations of hunters and fishers, every individual who is able to work is more or less employed in useful labor and endeavors to provide, as well as he can, the necessaries and conveniences of life for himself, or such of his family or tribe as are either too old, or too young, or too infirm to go hunting and fishing. Such nations, however, are so miserably poor that, from mere want, they are frequently reduced, or, at least, think themselves reduced, to the necessity sometimes of directly destroying, and sometimes of abandoning, their infants, their old people, and those afflicted with lingering diseases to perish with hunger or to be devoured by wild beasts. Among civilized and thriving nations, on the contrary, though a great number of people do not labor at all, many of whom consume the produce of ten times, frequently of a hundred times more labor than the greater part of those who work; yet the produce of the whole labor of the society is so great that all are often abundantly supplied, and a workman, even of the lowest and poorest order, if he is frugal and industrious, may enjoy a greater share of the necessaries and conveniences of life than it is possible for any savage to acquire.

The causes of this improvement in the productive powers of labor, and the order, according to which its produce is naturally distributed among the different ranks and conditions of men in the society, make the subject of the First Book of this Inquiry.

Whatever be the actual state of the skill, dexterity, and judgment with which labor is applied in any nation, the abundance or scantiness of its annual supply must depend, during the continuance of that state, upon the proportion between the number of those who are annually employed in useful labor and that of those who are not so employed. The number of useful and productive laborers, it will hereafter appear, is everywhere in proportion to the quantity of capital stock which is employed in setting them to work and to the particular way in which it is so employed. The Second Book, therefore, treats of the nature of capital stock, of the manner in which it is gradually accumulated, and of the different quantities of labor which it puts into motion, according to the different ways in which it is employed.

Nations tolerably well advanced as to skill, dexterity, and judgment in the application of labor have followed very different plans in the general conduct or direction of it; and those plans have not all been equally favorable to the greatness of its produce. The policy of some nations has given extraordinary encouragement to the industry of the country; that of others to the industry of towns. Scarce any nation has dealt equally and impartially with every sort of industry. Since the downfall of the Roman Empire, the policy of Europe has been more favorable to arts, manufactures, and commerce, the industry of towns, than to agriculture, the industry of the country. The circumstances which seem to have introduced and established this policy are explained in the Third Book.

Though those different plans were, perhaps, first introduced by the private interests and prejudices of particular orders of men, without any regard to, or foresight of, their consequences upon the general welfare of the society, yet they have given occasion to very different theories of political economy, of which some magnify the importance of that industry which is carried on in towns, others of that which is carried on in the country. Those theories have had a considerable influence, not only upon the opinions of men of learning, but upon the public conduct of princes and sovereign states. I have endeavored, in the Fourth Book, to explain, as fully and distinctly as I can, those different theories and the principal effects which they have produced in different ages and nations.

To explain in what has consisted the revenue of the great body of the people, or what has been the nature of those funds, which, in different ages and nations, have supplied their annual consumption, is the object of these Four first Books. The Fifth and last Book treats of the revenue of the sovereign, or commonwealth. In this book I have endeavored to show, first, what are the necessary expenses of the sovereign, or commonwealth; which of those expenses ought to be defrayed by the general contribution of the whole society; and which of them, by that of some particular part only, or of some particular members of it: secondly, what are the different methods in which the whole society may be made to contribute toward defraying the expenses incumbent on the whole society, and what are the principal advantages and inconveniences of each of those methods: and, thirdly and lastly, what are the reasons and causes which have induced almost all modern governments to mortgage some part of this revenue, or to contract debts, and what have been the effects of those debts upon the real wealth, the annual produce of the land and labor of the society.[2]

BOOK I

OF THE CAUSES OF IMPROVEMENT IN THE PRODUCTIVE POWERS OF LABOR AND OF THE ORDER ACCORDING TO WHICH ITS PRODUCE IS NATURALLY DISTRIBUTED AMONG THE DIFFERENT RANKS OF THE PEOPLE

CHAPTER I

OF THE DIVISION OF LABOR

The greatest improvement in the productive powers of labor and the greater part of the skill, dexterity, and judgment with which it is anywhere directed, or applied, seem to have been the effects of the division of labor.

The effects of the division of labor, in the general business of society, will be more easily understood by considering in what manner it operates in some particular manufactures. It is commonly supposed to be carried furthest in some very trifling ones; not perhaps that it really is carried further in them than in others of more importance: but in those

2. In defining the wealth of a nation as "the annual produce of the land and labor of the society," Smith's usage differs from common usage today. His definition really corresponds to the modern definition of a nation's annual income, whereas the term "wealth" is now used for the value of the capital resources used to produce the income (i.e., the machines, the land, the resources, the transport facilities, etc.).

trifling manufactures which are destined to supply the small wants of but a small number of people, the whole number of workmen must necessarily be small; and those employed in every different branch of the work can often be collected into the same workhouse and placed at once under the view of the spectator. In those great manufactures, on the contrary, which are destined to supply the great wants of the great body of the people, every different branch of the work employs so great a number of workmen that it is impossible to collect them all into the same workhouse. We can seldom see more, at one time, than those employed in one single branch. Though in such manufactures, therefore, the work may really be divided into a much greater number of parts than in those of a more trifling nature, the division is not near so obvious and has accordingly been much less observed.

To take an example, therefore, from a very trifling manufacture, but one in which the division of labor has been very often taken notice of, the trade of the pin-maker; a workman not educated to this business (which the division of labor has rendered a distinct trade), nor acquainted with the use of the machinery employed in it (to the invention of which the same division of labor has probably given occasion), could scarce, perhaps, with his utmost industry, make one pin in a day, and certainly could not make twenty. But in the way in which this business is now carried on, not only the whole work is a peculiar trade, but it is divided into a number of branches, of which the greater part are likewise peculiar trades. One man draws out the wire, another straightens it, a third cuts it, a fourth points it, a fifth grinds it at the top for receiving the head; to make the head requires two or three distinct operations; to put it on is a peculiar business, to whiten the pins is another; it is even a trade by itself to put them into the paper; and the important business of making a pin is, in this manner, divided into about eighteen distinct operations, which, in some manufactories, are all performed by distinct hands, though in others the same man will sometimes perform two or three of them. I have seen a small manufactory of this kind where ten men only were employed, and where some of them consequently performed two or three distinct operations. But though they were very poor, and therefore but indifferently accommodated with the necessary machinery, they could, when they exerted themselves, make among them about twelve pounds of pins in a day. There are in a pound upward of four thousand pins of a middling size. Those ten persons, therefore, could make among them upward of forty-eight thousand pins in a day. Each person, therefore, making a tenth part of forty-eight thousand pins, might be considered as making four thousand eight hundred pins in a day. But if they had all wrought separately and independently,

and without any of them having been educated to this peculiar business, they certainly could not each of them have made twenty, perhaps not one pin in a day; that is, certainly, not the two hundred and fortieth, perhaps not the four thousand eight hundredth part of what they are at present capable of performing in consequence of a proper division and combination of their different operations.

In every other art and manufacture the effects of the division of labor are similar to what they are in this very trifling one; though, in many of them, the labor can neither be so much subdivided nor reduced to so great a simplicity of operation. The division of labor, however, so far as it can be introduced, occasions, in every art, a proportionable increase of the productive powers of labor. The separation of different trades and employments from one another seems to have taken place in consequence of this advantage. This separation too is generally carried furthest in those countries which enjoy the highest degree of industry and improvement, what is the work of one man in a rude state of society being generally that of several in an improved one. In every improved society, the farmer is generally nothing but a farmer; the manufacturer, nothing but a manufacturer. The labor too which is necessary to produce any one complete manufacture is almost always divided among a great number of hands. How many different trades are employed in each branch of the linen and woolen manufactures, from the growers of the flax and the wool, to the bleachers and smoothers of the linen, or to the dyers and dressers of the cloth! The nature of agriculture, indeed, does not admit of so many subdivisions of labor, nor of so complete a separation of one business from another, as manufactures. It is impossible to separate so entirely the business of the grazier from that of the corn farmer, as the trade of the carpenter is commonly separated from that of the smith. The spinner is almost always a distinct person from the weaver; but the plowman, the harrower, the sower of the seed, and the reaper of the corn are often the same. The occasions for those different sorts of labor returning with the different seasons of the year, it is impossible that one man should be constantly employed in any one of them. This impossibility of making so complete and entire a separation of all the different branches of labor employed in agriculture is perhaps the reason why the improvement of the productive powers of labor in this art does not always keep pace with their improvement in manufactures. The most opulent nations, indeed, generally excel all their neighbors in agriculture as well as in manufactures; but they are commonly more distinguished by their superiority in the latter than in the former. Their lands are in general better cultivated and, having more labor and expense bestowed upon them, produce more in proportion to the extent and natural fertility of the ground. But this superiority of produce is seldom much more than in proportion to the superiority of labor and expense. In agriculture the labor of the rich country is not always much more productive than that of the poor; or, at least, it is never so much more productive, as it commonly is in manufactures. The corn[3] of the rich country, therefore, will not always, in the same degree of goodness, come cheaper to market than that of the poor. The corn of Poland, in the same degree of goodness, is as cheap as that of France, notwithstanding the superior opulence and improvement of the latter country. The corn of France is, in the corn provinces, fully as good and, in most years, nearly about the same price with the corn of England, though in opulence

3. The English use the word "corn" for what Americans call small grain (wheat, oats, rye, barley, etc.).

and improvement France is perhaps inferior to England. The cornlands of England, however, are better cultivated than those of France, and the cornlands of France are said to be much better cultivated than those of Poland. But though the poor country, notwithstanding the inferiority of its cultivation, can, in some measure, rival the rich in the cheapness and goodness of its corn, it can pretend to no such competition in its manufactures; at least if those manufactures suit the soil, climate, and situation of the rich country. The silks of France are better and cheaper than those of England, because the silk manufacture, at least under the present high duties upon the importation of raw silk, does not so well suit the climate of England as that of France. But the hardware and the coarse woolens of England are beyond all comparison superior to those of France, and much cheaper too in the same degree of goodness. In Poland there are said to be scarce any manufactures of any kind, a few of those coarser household manufactures excepted, without which no country can well subsist.

This great increase of the quantity of work which, in consequence of the division of labor, the same number of people are capable of performing is owing to three different circumstances; first, to the increase of dexterity in every particular workman; secondly, to the saving of the time which is commonly lost in passing from one species of work to another; and, lastly, to the invention of a great number of machines which facilitate and abridge labor and enable one man to do the work of many.

First, the improvement of the dexterity of the workman necessarily increases the quantity of the work he can perform; and the division of labor, by reducing every man's business to some one simple operation, and by making this operation the sole employment of his life, necessarily increases very much the dexterity of the workman. A common smith, who, though accustomed to handle the hammer, has never been used to make nails, if upon some particular occasion he is obliged to attempt it, will scarce, I am assured, be able to make above two or three hundred nails in a day, and those, too, very bad ones. A smith who has been accustomed to make nails, but whose sole or principal business has not been that of a nailer, can seldom with his utmost diligence make more than eight hundred or a thousand nails in a day. I have seen several boys under twenty years of age who had never exercised any other trade but that of making nails, and who, when they exerted themselves, could make, each of them, upward of two thousand three hundred nails in a day. The making of a nail, however, is by no means one of the simplest operations. The same person blows the bellows, stirs or mends the fire as there is occasion, heats the iron, and forges every part of the nail. In forging the head, too, he is obliged to change his tools. The different operations into which the making of a pin, or of a metal button, is subdivided are all of them much more simple, and the dexterity of the person, of whose life it has been the sole business to perform them, is usually much greater. The rapidity with which some of the operations of those manufactures are performed exceeds what the human hand could, by those who had never seen them, be supposed capable of acquiring.

Secondly, the advantage which is gained by saving the time commonly lost in passing from one sort of work to another is much greater than we should at first view be apt to imagine it. It is impossible to pass very quickly from one kind of work to another that is carried on in a different place and with quite different tools. A country weaver who cultivates a small farm must lose a good deal of time in passing from his loom to the field and from the field to his loom. When the two trades can be carried on in the same workhouse, the loss of time is no doubt much less. It is even in this case, however, very considerable. A man commonly saunters a little in turning his hand from one sort of employment to another. When he first begins the new work, he is seldom very keen and hearty; his mind, as they say, does not go to it, and for some time he rather trifles than applies to good purpose. The habit of sauntering and of indolent careless application, which is naturally, or rather necessarily, acquired by every country workman who is obliged to change his work and his tools every half-hour, and to apply his hand in twenty different ways almost every day of his life, renders him almost always slothful and lazy and incapable of any vigorous application even on the most pressing occasions. Independent, therefore, of his deficiency in point of dexterity, this cause alone must always reduce considerably the quantity of work which he is capable of performing.

Thirdly, and lastly, everybody must be sensible how much labor is facilitated and abridged by the application of proper machinery. It is unnecessary to give any example. I shall only observe, therefore, that the invention of all those machines by which labor is so much facilitated and abridged seems to have been originally owing to the division of labor. Men are much more likely to discover easier and readier methods of attaining any object when the whole attention of their minds is directed toward that single object than when it is dissipated among a great variety of things. But, in consequence of the division of labor, the whole of every man's attention comes naturally to be directed toward some one very simple object. It is naturally to be expected, therefore, that some one or other of those who are employed in each particular branch of labor should soon find out easier and readier methods of performing their own particular work, wherever the nature of it admits of such improvement. A great part of the machines made use of in those manufactures in which labor is most subdivided were originally the inventions of common workmen, who, being each of them employed in some very simple operation, naturally turned their thoughts toward finding out easier and readier methods of performing it. . . .

. . . All the improvements in machinery, however, have by no means been the inventions of those who had occasion to use the machines. Many improvements have been made by the ingenuity of the makers of the machines, when to make them became the business of a peculiar trade; and some by that of those who are called philosophers or men of speculation, whose trade it is not to do anything but to observe everything; and who, upon that account, are often capable of combining together the powers of the most distant and dissimilar objects. In the progress of society, philosophy or speculation becomes, like every other employment, the principal or sole trade and occupation of a particular class of citizens. Like every other employment, too, it is subdivided into a great number of different branches, each of which affords occupation to a peculiar tribe or class of philosophers; and this subdivision of employment in philosophy, as well as in every other business, improves dexterity and saves time. Each individual becomes more expert in his own peculiar branch, more work is done upon the whole, and the quantity of science is considerably increased by it.

It is the great multiplication of the productions of all the different arts, in consequence of the division of labor, which occasions, in a well-governed society, that universal opulence which extends itself to the lowest ranks of the people. Every workman has a great quantity of his own work to dispose of beyond what he himself has occasion for; and every other workman being exactly in the same situation, he is enabled to exchange a great quantity of his own goods for a great quantity or, what comes to the same thing, for the price of a great quantity of theirs. He supplies them abundantly with what they have occasion for, and they accommodate him as amply with what he has occasion for, and a general plenty diffuses itself through all the different ranks of the society.

Observe the accommodation of the most common artificer or day-laborer in a civilized and thriving country, and you will perceive that the number of people of whose industry a part, though but a small part, has been employed in procuring him this accommodation exceeds all computation. The woolen coat, for example, which covers the day-laborer, as coarse and rough as it may appear, is the produce of the joint labor of a great multitude of workmen. The shepherd, the sorter of the wool, the wool-comber or carder, the dyer, the scribbler, the spinner, the weaver, the fuller, the dresser, with many others, must all join their different arts in order to complete even this homely production. How many merchants and carriers, besides, must have been employed in transporting the materials from some of those workmen to others who often live in a very distant part of the country! How much commerce and navigation in particular, how many shipbuilders, sailors, sail-makers, rope-makers, must have been employed in order to bring together the different drugs made use of by the dyer, which often come from the remotest corners of the world! What a variety of labor too is necessary in order to produce the tools of the meanest of those workmen! To say nothing of such complicated machines as the ship of the sailor, the mill of the fuller, or even the loom of the weaver, let us consider only what a variety of labor is requisite in order to form that very simple machine, the shears with which the shepherd clips the wool. The miner, the builder of the furnace for smelting the ore, the feller of the timber, the burner of the charcoal to be made use of in the smelting-house, the brickmaker, the bricklayer, the workmen who attend the furnace, the millwright, the forger, the smith, must all of them join their different arts in order to produce them. Were we to examine, in the same manner, all the different parts of his dress and household furniture, the coarse linen shirt which he wears next his skin, the shoes which cover his feet, the bed which he lies on, and all the different parts which compose it, the kitchengrate at which he prepares his victuals, the coals which he makes use of for that purpose, dug from the bowels of the earth and brought to him perhaps by a long sea and a long land carriage, all the other utensils of his kitchen, all the furniture of his table, the knives and forks, the earthen or pewter plates upon which he serves up and divides his victuals, the different hands employed in preparing his bread and his beer, the glass window which lets in the heat and the light and keeps out the wind and the rain, with all the knowledge and art requisite for preparing that beautiful and happy invention, without which these northern parts of the world could scarce have afforded a very comfortable habitation, together with the tools of all the different workmen employed in producing those different conveniences; if we examine, I say, all these things, and consider what a variety of labor is employed about each of them, we shall be sensible that, without the assistance and co-operation of many thousands, the very meanest person in a civilized country could not be provided, even according to, what we very falsely imagine, the easy and simple manner in which he is commonly accommodated. Compared, indeed, with the more extravagant luxury of the great, his accommodation must no doubt appear extremely simple and easy; and yet it may be true, perhaps, that the accommodation of a European prince does not always so much exceed that of an industrious and frugal peasant, as the accommodation of the latter exceeds that of many an African king, the absolute master of the lives and liberties of ten thousand naked savages.

In the progress of the division of labor, the employment of the far greater part of those who live by labor, that is, of the great body of the people, comes to be confined to a few very simple operations, frequently to one or two. But the understandings of the greater part of men are necessarily formed by their ordinary employments. The man whose whole life is spent in performing a few simple operations, of which the effects too are, perhaps, always the same, or very nearly the same, has no occasion to exert his understanding or to exercise his invention in finding out expedients for removing difficulties which never occur. He naturally loses, therefore, the habit of such exertion and generally becomes as stupid and ignorant as it is possible for a human creature to become. The torpor of his mind renders him, not only incapable of relishing or bearing a part in any rational conversation, but of conceiving any generous, noble, or tender sentiment, and consequently of forming any just judgment concerning many even of the ordinary duties of private life. Of the great and extensive interests of his country he is altogether incapable of judging; and, unless very particular pains have been taken to render him otherwise, he is equally incapable of defending his country in war. The uniformity of his stationary life naturally corrupts the courage of his mind and makes him regard with abhorrence the irregular, uncertain, and adventurous life of a soldier. It corrupts even the activity of his body and renders him incapable of exerting his strength with vigor and perseverance in any other employment than that to which he has been bred. His dexterity at his own particular trade seems, in this manner, to be acquired at the expense of his intellectual, social, and martial virtues. But in every improved and civilized society this is the state into which the laboring poor, that is, the great body of the people, must necessarily fall, unless government takes some pains to prevent it.

Chapter II
OF THE PRINCIPLE WHICH GIVES OCCASION TO THE DIVISION OF LABOR

This division of labor, from which so many advantages are derived, is not originally the effect of any human wisdom which foresees and intends that general opulence to which it gives occasion. It is the necessary, though very slow and gradual, consequence of a certain propensity in human nature which has in view no such extensive utility; the propensity to truck, barter, and exchange one thing for another.

Whether this propensity be one of those original principles in human nature, of which no further account can be given, or whether, as seems more probable, it be the necessary consequence of the faculties of reason and speech, it belongs not to our present subject to inquire. It is common to all men, and to be found in no other race of animals, which seem to know neither this nor any other species of contracts. Two greyhounds, in running down the same hare, have sometimes the appearance of acting in some sort of concert. Each turns her toward his companion or endeavors to intercept her when his companion turns her toward himself. This, however, is not the effect of any contract but of the accidental concurrence of their passions in the same object at that particular time. Nobody ever saw a dog make a fair and deliberate exchange of one bone for another with another dog. Nobody ever saw one animal by its gestures and natural cries signify to another, "This is mine; that yours; I am willing to give this for that." When an animal wants to obtain something either of a man or of another animal, it has no other means of persuasion but to gain the favor of those whose service it requires. A puppy fawns upon its dam, and a spaniel endeavors by a thousand attractions to engage the attention of its master who is at dinner when it wants to be fed by him. Man sometimes uses the same arts with his brethren and, when he has no other means of engaging them to act according to his inclinations, endeavors by every servile and fawning attention to obtain their good will. He has not time, however, to do this upon every occasion. In civilized society he stands at all times in need of the co-operation and assistance of great multitudes, while his whole life is scarce sufficient to gain the friendship of a few persons. In almost every other race of animals each individual, when it is grown up to maturity, is entirely independent and in its natural state has occasion for the assistance of no other living creature. But man has almost constant occasion for the help of his brethren, and it is in vain for him to expect it from their benevolence only. He will be more likely to prevail if he can interest their self-love in his favor and show them that it is for their own advantage to do for him what he requires of them. Whoever offers to another a bargain of any kind proposes to do this. "Give me that which I want, and you shall have this which you want," is the meaning of every such offer; and it is in this manner that we obtain from one another the far greater part of those good offices which we stand in need of. It is not from the benevolence of the butcher, the brewer, or the baker that we expect our dinner but from their regard to their own interest. We address ourselves, not to their humanity, but to their self-love, and never talk to them of our own necessities but of their advantages. Nobody but a beggar chooses to depend chiefly upon the benevolence of his fellow-citizens. Even a beggar does not depend upon it entirely. The charity of well-disposed people, indeed, supplies him with the whole fund of his subsistence. But though this principle ultimately provides him with all the necessaries of life which he has occasion for, it neither does nor can provide him with them as he has occasion for them. The greater part of his occasional wants are supplied in the same manner as those of other people, by treaty, by barter, and by purchase. With the money which one man gives him he purchases food. The old clothes which another bestows upon him he exchanges for other old clothes which suit him better, or for lodging, or for food, or for money, with which he can buy either food, clothes, or lodging, as he has occasion.

As it is by treaty, by barter, and by purchase that we obtain from one another the greater part of those mutual good offices which we stand in need of, so it is this same trucking disposition which originally gives occasion to the division of labor. In a tribe of hunters or shepherds a particular person makes bows and arrows, for example, with more readiness and dexterity than any other. He frequently exchanges them for cattle or for venison with his companions; and he finds at last that he can in this manner get more cattle and venison than if he himself went to the field to catch them. From a regard to his own interest, therefore, the making of bows and arrows grows to be his chief business, and he becomes a sort of armorer. Another excels in making the frames and covers of their little huts or movable houses. He is accustomed to be of use in this way to his neighbors, who reward him in the same manner with cattle and with venison, till at last he finds it his interest to dedicate himself entirely to this employment and to become a sort of house carpenter. In the same manner a

third becomes a smith or a brazier; a fourth, a tanner or dresser of hides or skins, the principal part of the clothing of savages. And thus the certainty of being able to exchange all that surplus part of the produce of his own labor, which is over and above his own consumption, for such parts of the produce of other men's labor as he may have occasion for encourages every man to apply himself to a particular occupation and to cultivate and bring to perfection whatever talent or genius he may possess for that particular species of business.

The difference of natural talents in different men is, in reality, much less than we are aware of; and the very different genius which appears to distinguish men of different professions, when grown up to maturity, is not upon many occasions so much the cause as the effect of the division of labor. The difference between the most dissimilar characters, between a philosopher and a common street porter, for example, seems to arise not so much from nature, as from habit, custom, and education. When they came into the world, and for the first six or eight years of their existence, they were, perhaps, very much alike, and neither their parents nor playfellows could perceive any remarkable difference. About that age, or soon after, they come to be employed in very different occupations. The difference of talents comes then to be taken notice of, and widens by degrees, till at last the vanity of the philosopher is willing to acknowledge scarce any resemblance. But without the disposition to truck, barter, and exchange, every man must have procured to himself every necessary and convenience of life which he wanted. All must have had the same duties to perform, and the same work to do, and there could have been no such difference of employment as could alone give occasion to any great difference of talents.

As it is this disposition which forms that difference of talents, so remarkable among men of different professions, so it is this same disposition which renders that difference useful. Many tribes of animals acknowledged to be all of the same species derive from nature a much more remarkable distinction of genius than what, antecedent to custom and education, appears to take place among men. By nature a philosopher is not in genius and disposition half so different from a street porter as a mastiff is from a greyhound, or a greyhound from a spaniel, or this last from a shepherd's dog. Those different tribes of animals, however, though all of the same species, are of scarce any use to one another. The strength of the mastiff is not in the least supported either by the swiftness of the greyhound, or by the sagacity of the spaniel, or by the docility of the shepherd's dog. The effects of those different geniuses and talents, for want of the power or disposition to barter and exchange, cannot be brought into a common stock and do not in the least contribute to the better accommodation and convenience of the species. Each animal is still obliged to support and defend itself, separately and independently, and derives no sort of advantage from that variety of talents with which nature has distinguished its fellows. Among men, on the contrary, the most dissimilar geniuses are of use to one another; the different produces of their respective talents, by the general disposition to truck, barter, and exchange, being brought, as it were, into a common stock, where every man may purchase whatever part of the produce of other men's talents he has occasion for.

Chapter III

THAT THE DIVISION OF LABOR IS LIMITED BY THE EXTENT OF THE MARKET

As it is the power of exchanging that gives occasion to the division of labor, so the extent of this division must always be limited by the extent of that power

or, in other words, by the extent of the market. When the market is very small, no person can have any encouragement to dedicate himself entirely to one employment, for want of the power to exchange all that surplus part of the produce of his own labor, which is over and above his own consumption, for such parts of the produce of other men's labor as he has occasion for.

There are some sorts of industry, even of the lowest kind, which can be carried on nowhere but in a great town. A porter, for example, can find employment and subsistence in no other place. A village is by much too narrow a sphere for him; even an ordinary market town is scarce large enough to afford him constant occupation. In the lone houses and very small villages which are scattered about in so desert a country as the Highlands of Scotland, every farmer must be butcher, baker, and brewer for his own family. In such situations we can scarce expect to find even a smith, a carpenter, or a mason, within less than twenty miles of another of the same trade. The scattered families that live at eight or ten miles distance from the nearest of them must learn to perform themselves a great number of little pieces of work, for which, in more populous countries, they would call in the assistance of those workmen. Country workmen are almost everywhere obliged to apply themselves to all the different branches of industry that have so much affinity to one another as to be employed about the same sort of materials. A country carpenter deals in every sort of work that is made of wood; a country smith in every sort of work that is made of iron. The former is not only a carpenter but a joiner, a cabinetmaker, and even a carver in wood, as well as a wheelwright, a ploughwright, a cart- and wagon-maker. The employments of the latter are still more various. It is impossible there should be such a trade as even that of a nailer in the remote and inland parts of the Highlands of Scotland. Such a workman at the rate of a thousand nails a day, and three hundred working days in the year, will make three hundred thousand nails in the year. But in such a situation it would be impossible to dispose of one thousand, that is, of one day's work in the year.

As by means of water carriage a more extensive market is opened to every sort of industry than what land carriage alone can afford it, so it is upon the seacoast, and along the banks of navigable rivers, that industry of every kind naturally begins to subdivide and improve itself, and it is frequently not till a long time after that those improvements extend themselves to the inland parts of the country. A broad-wheeled wagon, attended by two men, and drawn by eight horses, in about six weeks' time carries and brings back between London and Edinburgh near four-ton weight of goods. On about the same time a ship navigated by six or eight men, and sailing between the ports of London and Leith, frequently carries and brings back two-hundred-ton weight of goods. Six or eight men, therefore, by the help of water carriage, can carry and bring back in the same time the same quantity of goods between London and Edinburgh, as fifty broad-wheeled wagons, attended by a hundred men, and drawn by four hundred horses. Upon two hundred tons of goods, therefore, carried by the cheapest land carriage from London to Edinburgh, there must be charged the maintenance of a hundred men for three weeks, and both the maintenance, and, what is nearly equal to the maintenance, the wear and tear of four hundred horses as well as of fifty great wagons. Whereas, upon the same quantity of goods carried by water, there is to be charged only the maintenance of six or eight men, and the wear and tear of a ship of two hundred tons burthen, together with the value of the superior risk, or the difference of the insurance between land and water carriage. Were there no other communication between those two places, therefore, but by land carriage, as no goods could be transported from the one to the other, except such whose price was very considerable in proportion to their weight, they could carry on but a small part of that commerce which at present subsists between them, and consequently could give but a small part of that encouragement which they at present mutually afford to each other's industry. There could be little or no commerce of any kind between the distant parts of the world. What goods could bear the expense of land carriage between London and Calcutta? Or if there were any so precious as to be able to support this expense, with what safety could they be transported through the territories of so many barbarous nations? Those two cities, however, at present carry on a very considerable commerce with each other, and, by mutually affording a market, give a good deal of encouragement to each other's industry.

Since such, therefore, are the advantages of water carriage, it is natural that the first improvements of art and industry should be made where this convenience opens the whole world for a market to the produce of every sort of labor and that they should always be much later in extending themselves into the inland parts of the country. The inland parts of the country can for a long time have no other market for the greater part of their goods but the country which lies round them and separates them from the seacoast and the great navigable rivers. The extent of their market, therefore, must for a long time be in proportion to the riches and populousness of that country, and consequently their improvement must always be posterior to the improvement of that country. In our North American colonies the plantations have constantly followed either the seacoast or the banks of navigable rivers and have scarce anywhere extended themselves to any considerable distance from both. . . .

In that rude state of society in which there is no division of labor, in which exchanges are seldom made, and in which every man provides everything for himself, it is not necessary that any stock should be accumulated or stored up beforehand, in order to carry on the business of the society. Every man endeavors to supply by his own industry his own occasional wants as they occur. When he is hungry, he goes to the forest to hunt; when his coat is worn out, he clothes himself with the skin of the first large animal he kills; and when his hut begins to go to ruin, he repairs it, as well as he can, with the trees and the turf that are nearest it.

But when the division of labor has once been thoroughly introduced, the produce of a man's own labor can supply but a very small part of his occasional wants. The far greater part of them are supplied by the produce of other men's labor, which he purchases with the produce, or what is the same thing, with the price of the produce of his own. But this purchase cannot be made till such time as the produce of his own labor has not only been completed but sold. A stock of goods of different kinds, therefore, must be stored up somewhere sufficient to maintain him, and to supply him with the materials and tools of his work, till such time, at least, as both these events can be brought about. A weaver cannot apply himself entirely to his peculiar business unless there is beforehand stored up somewhere, either in his own possession or in that of some other person, a stock sufficient to maintain him, and to supply him with the materials and tools of his work, till he has not only completed but sold

his web. This accumulation must, evidently, be previous to his applying his industry for so long a time to such a peculiar business.

As the accumulation of stock must, in the nature of things, be previous to the division of labor, so labor can be more and more subdivided in proportion only as stock is previously more and more accumulated. The quantity of materials which the same number of people can work up increases in a great proportion as labor comes to be more and more subdivided; and, as the operations of each workman are gradually reduced to a greater degree of simplicity, a variety of new machines come to be invented for facilitating and abridging those operations. As the division of labor advances, therefore, in order to give constant employment to an equal number of workmen, an equal stock of provisions, and a greater stock of materials and tools than what would have been necessary in a ruder state of things must be accumulated beforehand. But the number of workmen in every branch of business generally increases with the division of labor in that branch, or rather it is the increase of their number which enables them to class and subdivide themselves in this manner.

As the accumulation of stock is previously necessary for carrying on this great improvement in the productive powers of labor, so that accumulation naturally leads to this improvement. The person who employs his stock in maintaining labor necessarily wishes to employ it in such a manner as to produce as great a quantity of work as possible. He endeavors, therefore, both to make among his workmen the most proper distribution of employment and to furnish them with the best machines which he can either invent or afford to purchase. His abilities in both these respects are generally in proportion to the extent of his stock or to the number of people whom it can employ. The quantity of industry, therefore, not only increases in every country with the increase of the stock which employs it, but, in consequence of that increase, the same quantity of industry produces a much greater quantity of work. ...

Capitals[4] are increased by parsimony and diminished by prodigality and misconduct.

Whatever a person saves from his revenue he adds to his capital and either employs it himself in maintaining an additional number of productive hands or enables some other person to do so, by lending it to him for an interest, that is, for a share of the profits. As the capital of an individual can be increased only by what he saves from his annual revenue or his annual gains, so the capital of a society, which is the same with that of all the individuals who compose it, can be increased only in the same manner.

Parsimony, and not industry, is the immediate cause of the increase of capital. Industry, indeed, provides the subject which parsimony accumulates. But whatever industry might acquire, if parsimony did not save and store up, the capital would never be the greater.

Parsimony, by increasing the fund which is destined for the maintenance of productive hands, tends to increase the number of those hands whose labor adds to the value of the subject upon which it is bestowed. It tends therefore to increase the exchangeable value of the annual produce of the land and labor of the country. It puts into motion an additional quantity of industry, which gives an additional value to the annual produce.

What is annually saved is as regularly consumed as what is annually spent, and nearly in the same time too; but it is consumed by a different set of people.

4. I.e., accumulations of stock.

That portion of his revenue which a rich man annually spends is in most cases consumed by idle guests, and menial servants, who leave nothing behind them in return for their consumption. That portion which he annually saves, as for the sake of the profit it is immediately employed as a capital, is consumed in the same manner, and nearly in the same time too, but by a different set of people, by laborers, manufacturers, and artificers, who reproduce with a profit the value of their annual consumption. His revenue, we shall suppose, is paid him in money. Had he spent the whole, the food, clothing, and lodging which the whole could have purchased would have been distributed among the former set of people. By saving a part of it, as that part is for the sake of the profit immediately employed as a capital either by himself or by some other person, the food, clothing, and lodging which may be purchased with it are necessarily reserved for the latter. The consumption is the same, but the consumers are different.

By what a frugal man annually saves, he not only affords maintenance to an additional number of productive hands, for that or the ensuing year, but, like the founder of a public workhouse, he establishes, as it were, a perpetual fund for the maintenance of an equal number in all times to come. The perpetual allotment and destination of this fund, indeed, is not always guarded by any positive law, by any trust-right or deed of mortmain. It is always guarded, however, by a very powerful principle, the plain and evident interest of every individual to whom any share of it shall ever belong. No part of it can ever afterward be employed to maintain any but productive hands, without an evident loss to the person who thus perverts it from its proper destination.

The prodigal perverts it in this manner. By not confining his expense within his income, he encroaches upon his capital. Like him who perverts the revenues of some pious foundation to profane purposes, he pays the wages of idleness with those funds which the frugality of his forefathers had, as it were, consecrated to the maintenance of industry. By diminishing the funds destined for the employment of productive labor, he necessarily diminishes, so far as it depends upon him, the quantity of that labor which adds a value to the subject upon which it is bestowed, and, consequently, the value of the annual produce of the land and labor of the whole country, the real wealth and revenue of its inhabitants. If the prodigality of some was not compensated by the frugality of others, the conduct of every prodigal, by feeding the idle with the bread of the industrious, tends not only to beggar himself but to impoverish his country....

Great nations are never impoverished by private, though they sometimes are by public prodigality and misconduct. The whole, or almost the whole, public revenue is in most countries employed in maintaining unproductive hands. Such are the people who compose a numerous and splendid court, a great ecclesiastical establishment, great fleets and armies, who in time of peace produce nothing, and in time of war acquire nothing which can compensate the expense of maintaining them, even while the war lasts. Such people, as they themselves produce nothing, are all maintained by the produce of other men's labor. When multiplied, therefore, to an unnecessary number, they may in a particular year consume so great a share of this produce as not to leave a sufficiency for maintaining the productive laborers, who should reproduce it next year. The next year's produce, therefore, will be less than that of the foregoing, and if the same disorder should continue, that of the third year will be still less than that of the second. Those unproductive

hands, who should be maintained by a part only of the spare revenue of the people, may consume so great a share of their whole revenue, and therefore oblige so great a number to encroach upon their capitals, upon the funds destined for the maintenance of productive labor, that all the frugality and good conduct of individuals may not be able to compensate the waste and degradation of produce occasioned by this violent and forced encroachment.

This frugality and good conduct, however, is upon most occasions, it appears from experience, sufficient to compensate, not only the private prodigality and misconduct of individuals but the public extravagance of government. The uniform, constant, and uninterrupted effort of every man to better his condition, the principle from which public and national, as well as private opulence is originally derived, is frequently powerful enough to maintain the natural progress of things toward improvement, in spite both of the extravagance of government and of the greatest errors of administration. Like the unknown principle of animal life, it frequently restores health and vigor to the constitution, in spite, not only of the disease, but of the absurd prescriptions of the doctor.

The annual produce of the land and labor of any nation can be increased in its value by no other means but by increasing either the number of its productive laborers or the productive powers of those laborers who had before been employed. The number of its productive laborers, it is evident, can never be much increased, but in consequence of an increase of capital, or of the funds destined for maintaining them. The productive powers of the same number of laborers cannot be increased, but in consequence either of some addition and improvement to those machines and instruments which facilitate and abridge labor; or of a more proper division and distribution of employment. In either case an additional capital is almost always required. It is by means of an additional capital only that the undertaker of any work can either provide his workmen with better machinery or make a more proper distribution of employment among them. When the work to be done consists of a number of parts, to keep every man constantly employed in one way requires a much greater capital than where every man is occasionally employed in every different part of the work. When we compare, there-fore, the state of a nation at two different periods and find that the annual produce of its land and labor is evidently greater at the latter than at the former, that its lands are better cultivated, its manufactures more numerous and more flourishing, and its trade more extensive, we may be assured that its capital must have increased during the interval between those two periods and that more must have been added to it by the good conduct of some than had been taken from it either by the private misconduct of others or by the public extravagance of government. . . .

ECONOMIC LIBERALISM: THE IDEAL[5]
BOOK IV
OF SYSTEMS OF POLITICAL ECONOMY

INTRODUCTION

Political economy, considered as a branch of the science of a statesman or legislator, proposes two distinct objects: first, to provide a plentiful revenue or subsistence for the people or, more properly, to enable them to provide such a revenue or subsistence for themselves; and, secondly, to supply the state or commonwealth with a revenue sufficient for the public services. It proposes to enrich both the people and the sovereign.

The different progress of opulence in different ages and nations has given occasion to two different systems of political economy, with regard to enriching the people. The one may be called the system of commerce; the other, that of agriculture. I shall endeavor to explain both as fully and distinctly as I can and shall begin with the system of commerce. It is the modern system and is best understood in our own country and in our own times.

5. Smith, *op. cit.*, pp. (in order of their inclusion) 397–401, 415, 417–26, 650–51, 308, and 55–62.

CHAPTER I
OF THE PRINCIPLE OF THE COMMERCIAL OR MERCANTILE SYSTEM

That wealth consists in money, or in gold and silver, is a popular notion which naturally arises from the double function of money as the instrument of commerce and as the measure of value. In consequence of its being the instrument of commerce, when we have money, we can more readily obtain whatever else we have occasion for than by means of any other commodity. The great affair, we always find, is to get money. When that is obtained, there is no difficulty in making any subsequent purchase. In consequence of its being the measure of value, we estimate that of all other commodities by the quantity of money which they will exchange for. We say of a rich man that he is worth a great deal, and of a poor man that he is worth very little money. A frugal man, or a man eager to be rich, is said to love money; and a careless, a generous, or a profuse man is said to be indifferent about it. To grow rich is to get money; and wealth and money, in short, are, in common language, considered as in every respect synonymous.

A rich country, in the same manner as a rich man, is supposed to be a country abounding in money; and to heap up gold and silver in any country is supposed to be the readiest way to enrich it. For some time after the discovery of America, the first inquiry of the Spaniards, when they arrived upon any unknown coast, used to be, if there was any gold or silver to be found in the neighborhood. By the information which they received, they judged whether it was worth while to make a settlement there or if the country was worth the conquering. Plano Carpino, a monk sent as ambassador from the king of France to one of the sons of the famous Genghis Khan, says that the Tartars used frequently to ask him if there was plenty of sheep and oxen in the kingdom of France? Their inquiry had the same object with that of the Spaniards. They wanted to know if the country was rich enough to be worth the conquering. Among the Tartars, as among all other nations of shepherds, who are generally ignorant of the use of money, cattle are the instruments of commerce and the measures of value. Wealth, therefore, according to them, consisted in cattle, as according to the Spaniards it consisted in gold and silver. Of the two, the Tartar notion, perhaps, was the nearest to the truth.

Mr. Locke remarks a distinction between money and other movable goods. All other movable goods, he says, are of so consumable a nature that the wealth which consists in them cannot be much depended on, and a nation which abounds in them one year may, without any exportation, but merely by their own waste and extravagance, be in great want of them the next. Money, on the contrary, is a steady friend, which, though it may travel about from hand to hand, yet if it can be kept from going out of the country, is not very liable to be wasted and consumed. Gold and silver, therefore, are, according to him, the most solid and substantial part of the movable wealth of a nation, and to multiply those metals ought, he thinks, upon that account, to be the great object of its political economy.

Others admit that if a nation could be separated from all the world, it would be of no consequence how much or how little money circulated in it. The consumable goods which were circulated by means of this money would only be exchanged for a greater or a smaller number of pieces; but the real wealth or poverty of the country, they allow, would depend altogether upon the abundance or scarcity of those consumable goods. But it is otherwise, they think, with countries which have connections with foreign nations, and which are obliged to carry on foreign wars, and to maintain fleets and armies in distant countries. This, they say, cannot be done but by sending abroad money to pay them with; and a nation cannot send much money abroad unless it has a good deal at home. Every such nation, therefore, must endeavor in time of peace to accumulate gold and silver, that, when occasion requires, it may have wherewithal to carry on foreign wars.

In consequence of these popular notions, all the different nations of Europe have studied, though to little purpose, every possible means of accumulating gold and silver in their respective countries. Spain and Portugal, the proprietors of the principal mines which supply Europe with those metals, have either prohibited their exportation under the severest penalties or subjected it to a considerable duty. The like prohibition seems anciently to have made a part of the policy of most other European nations. It is even to be found, where we should least of all expect to find it, in some old Scotch acts of Parliament, which forbid under heavy penalties the carrying gold or silver *forth of the king-*

dom. The like policy anciently took place both in France and England.

When those countries became commercial, the merchants found this prohibition, upon many occasions, extremely inconvenient. They could frequently buy more advantageously with gold and silver than with any other commodity the foreign goods which they wanted, either to import into their own or to carry to some other foreign country. They remonstrated, therefore, against this prohibition as hurtful to trade.

They represented, first, that the exportation of gold and silver, in order to purchase foreign goods, did not always diminish the quantity of those metals in the kingdom. That, on the contrary, it might frequently increase that quantity; because, if the consumption of foreign goods was not thereby increased in the country, those goods might be re-exported to foreign countries, and, being there sold for a large profit, might bring back much more treasure than was originally sent out to purchase them. Mr. Mun compares this operation of foreign trade to the seed time and harvest of agriculture. "If we only behold," says he, "the actions of the husbandman in the seed time, when he casteth away much good corn into the ground, we shall account him rather a madman than a husbandman. But when we consider his labors in the harvest, which is the end of his endeavors, we shall find the worth and plentiful increase of his actions."

They represented, secondly, that this prohibition could not hinder the exportation of gold and silver, which, on account of the smallness of their bulk in proportion to their value, could easily be smuggled abroad. That this exportation could only be prevented by a proper attention to what they called the balance of trade. That when the country exported to a greater value than it imported, a balance became due to it from foreign nations, which was necessarily paid to it in gold and silver, and

thereby increased the quantity of those metals in the kingdom. But that when it imported to a greater value than it exported, a contrary balance became due to foreign nations, which was necessarily paid to them in the same manner, and thereby diminished that quantity. That in this case to prohibit the exportation of those metals could not prevent it, but, only by making it more dangerous, render it more expensive. That the exchange was thereby turned more against the country which owed the balance than it otherwise might have been; the merchant who purchased a bill upon the foreign country being obliged to pay the banker who sold it, not only for the natural risk, trouble, and expense of sending the money thither, but for the extraordinary risk arising from the prohibition. But that the more the exchange was against any country, the more the balance of trade became necessarily against it; the money of that country becoming necessarily of so much less value, in comparison with that of the country to which the balance was due. . . .

The importation of gold and silver is not the principal, much less the sole, benefit which a nation derives from its foreign trade. Between whatever places foreign trade is carried on, they all of them derive two distinct benefits from it. It carries out that surplus part of the produce of their land and labor for which there is no demand among them and brings back in return for it something else for which there is a demand. It gives a value to their superfluities by exchanging them for something else which may satisfy a part of their wants and increase their enjoyments. By means of it, the narrowness of the home market does not hinder the division of labor in any particular branch of art or manufacture from being carried to the highest perfection. By opening a more extensive market for whatever part of the produce of their labor may exceed the home consumption, it encourages them to improve its productive powers, and to augment its annual produce to the utmost, and thereby to increase the real revenue and wealth of the society. These great and important services foreign trade is continually occupied in performing to all the different countries between which it is carried on. They all derive great benefit from it, though that in which the merchant resides generally derives the greatest, as he is generally more employed in supplying the wants, and carrying out the superfluities of his own, than of any other particular country. To import the gold and silver which may be wanted, into the countries which have no mines, is, no doubt, a part of the business of foreign commerce. It is, however, a most insignificant part of it. A country which carried on foreign trade merely upon this account could scarce have occasion to freight a ship in a century. . . .

I thought it necessary, though at the hazard of being tedious, to examine at full length this popular notion that wealth consists in money or in gold and silver. Money in common language, as I have already observed, frequently signifies wealth; and this ambiguity of expression has rendered this popular notion so familiar to us that even they, who are convinced of its absurdity, are very apt to forget their own principles and in the course of their reasonings to take it for granted as a certain and undeniable truth. Some of the best English writers upon commerce set out with observing that the wealth of a country consists, not in its gold and silver only, but in its lands, houses, and consumable goods of all different kinds. In the course of their reasonings, however, the lands, houses, and consumable goods seem to slip out of their memory, and the strain of their argument frequently supposes that all wealth consists in gold and silver and that to multiply those metals is

the great object of national industry and commerce.

The two principles being established, however, that wealth consisted in gold and silver and that those metals could be brought into a country which had no mines only by the balance of trade or by exporting to a greater value than it imported, it necessarily became the great object of political economy to diminish as much as possible the importation of foreign goods for home consumption and to increase as much as possible the exportation of the produce of domestic industry. Its two great engines for enriching the country, therefore, were restraints upon importation and encouragements to exportation.

The restraints upon importation were of two kinds.

First, Restraints upon the importation of such foreign goods for home consumption as could be produced at home, from whatever country they were imported.

Secondly, Restraints upon the importation of goods of almost all kinds from those particular countries with which the balance of trade was supposed to be disadvantageous.

Those different restraints consisted sometimes in high duties and sometimes in absolute prohibitions.

Exportation was encouraged sometimes by drawbacks, sometimes by bounties, sometimes by advantageous treaties of commerce with foreign states, and sometimes by the establishment of colonies in distant countries.

Drawbacks were given upon two different occasions. When the home manufactures were subject to any duty or excise, either the whole or a part of it was frequently drawn back upon their exportation; and when foreign goods liable to a duty were imported in order to be exported again, either the whole or a part of this duty was sometimes given back upon such exportation.

Bounties were given for the encouragement either of some beginning manufactures, or of such sorts of industry of other kinds as were supposed to deserve particular favor.

By advantageous treaties of commerce, particular privileges were procured in some foreign state for the goods and merchants of the country beyond what were granted to those of other countries.

By the establishment of colonies in distant countries, not only particular privileges, but a monopoly was frequently procured for the goods and merchants of the country which established them.

The two sorts of restraints upon importation above-mentioned, together with these four encouragements to exportation, constitute the six principal means by which the commercial system proposes to increase the quantity of gold and silver in any country by turning the balance of trade in its favor. I shall consider each of them in a particular chapter and, without taking much further notice of their supposed tendency to bring money into the country, I shall examine chiefly what are likely to be the effects of each of them upon the annual produce of its industry. According as they tend either to increase or diminish the value of this annual produce, they must evidently tend either to increase or diminish the real wealth and revenue of the country.

Chapter II

OF RESTRAINTS UPON THE IMPORTATION FROM FOREIGN COUNTRIES OF SUCH GOODS AS CAN BE PRODUCED AT HOME

By restraining, either by high duties, or by absolute prohibitions, the importation of such goods from foreign countries as can be produced at home, the monopoly of the home market is more or less secured to the domestic industry employed in producing them. Thus the prohibition of importing either live cattle or salt provisions from foreign coun-

tries secures to the graziers of Great Britain the monopoly of the home market for butcher's meat. The high duties upon the importation of corn, which in times of moderate plenty amount to a prohibition, give a like advantage to the growers of that commodity. The prohibition of the importation of foreign woolens is equally favorable to the woolen manufacturers. The silk manufacture, though altogether employed upon foreign materials, has lately obtained the same advantage. The linen manufacture has not yet obtained it but is making great strides toward it. Many other sorts of manufacturers have, in the same manner, obtained in Great Britain either altogether or very nearly a monopoly against their countrymen. The variety of goods of which the importation into Great Britain is prohibited, either absolutely or under certain circumstances, greatly exceeds what can easily be suspected by those who are not well acquainted with the laws of the customs.

That this monopoly of the home market frequently gives great encouragement to that particular species of industry which enjoys it, and frequently turns toward that employment a greater share of both the labor and stock of the society than would otherwise have gone to it, cannot be doubted. But whether it tends either to increase the general industry of the society or to give it the most advantageous direction is not, perhaps, altogether so evident.

The general industry of the society never can exceed what the capital of the society can employ. As the number of workmen that can be kept in employment by any particular person must bear a certain proportion to his capital, so the number of those that can be continually employed by all the members of a great society must bear a certain proportion to the whole capital of that society and never can exceed that proportion. No regulation of commerce can increase the quantity of industry in any society beyond what its capital can maintain. It can only divert a part of it into a direction into which it might not otherwise have gone; and it is by no means certain that this artificial direction is likely to be more advantageous to the society than that into which it would have gone of its own accord.

Every individual is continually exerting himself to find out the most advantageous employment for whatever capital he can command. It is his own advantage, indeed, and not that of society, which he has in view. But the study of his own advantage naturally or, rather, necessarily leads him to prefer that employment which is most advantageous to the society.

First, every individual endeavors to employ his capital as near home as he can and consequently as much as he can in the support of domestic industry, provided always that he can thereby obtain the ordinary or not a great deal less than the ordinary profits of stock.

Thus, upon equal or nearly equal profits, every wholesale merchant naturally prefers the home trade to the foreign trade of consumption and the foreign trade of consumption to the carrying trade. In the home trade his capital is never so long out of his sight as it frequently is in the foreign trade of consumption. He can know better the character and situation of the persons whom he trusts, and if he should happen to be deceived, he knows better the laws of the country from which he must seek redress. In the carrying trade the capital of the merchant is, as it were, divided between two foreign countries, and no part of it is ever necessarily brought home or placed under his own immediate view and command. The capital which an Amsterdam merchant employs in carrying corn from Königsberg to Lisbon, and fruit and wine from Lisbon to Königsberg, must generally be the one-half of it at Königsberg and the other half at Lisbon. No part of it need ever come to Amsterdam. The natural residence of such a merchant should either be at Königsberg or Lisbon, and it can only be some very particular circumstances which can make him prefer the residence of Amsterdam. The uneasiness, however, which he feels at being separated so far from his capital generally determines him to bring part both of the Königsberg goods which he destines for the market of Lisbon, and of the Lisbon goods which he destines for that of Königsberg, to Amsterdam: and though this necessarily subjects him to a double charge of loading and unloading, as well as to the payment of some duties and customs, yet, for the sake of having some part of his capital always under his own view and command, he willingly submits to this extraordinary charge; and it is in this manner that every country which has any considerable share of the carrying trade becomes always the emporium, or general market, for the goods of all the different countries whose trade it carries on. The merchant, in order to save a second loading and unloading, endeavors always to sell in the home market as much of the goods of all those different countries as he can and thus, so far as he can, to convert his carrying trade into a foreign trade of consumption. A merchant, in the same manner, who is engaged in the foreign trade of consumption, when he collects goods for foreign markets, will always be glad, upon equal or nearly equal profits, to sell as great a part of them at home as he can. He saves himself the risk and trouble of exportation, when, so far as he can, he thus converts his foreign trade of consumption into a home trade. Home is in this manner the center, if I may say so, round which the capitals of the inhabitants of every country are continually circulating, and toward which they are always tending, though by particular causes they may sometimes be driven off and repelled from it toward more distant employments. But a capital employed in the home trade, it has already been shown, necessarily puts into motion a greater quantity of domestic industry and gives revenue and employment to a greater number of the inhabitants of the country than an equal capital employed in the foreign trade of consumption; and one employed in the foreign trade of consumption has the same advantage over an equal capital employed in the carrying trade. Upon equal, or only nearly equal, profits, therefore, every individual naturally inclines to employ his capital in the manner in which it is likely to afford the greatest support to domestic industry and to give revenue and employment to the greatest number of people of his own country.

Secondly, every individual who employs his capital in the support of domestic industry necessarily endeavors so to direct that industry that its produce may be of the greatest possible value.

The produce of industry is what it adds to the subject or materials upon which it is employed. In proportion as the value of this produce is great or small, so will likewise be the profits of the employer. But it is only for the sake of profit that any man employs a capital in the support of industry; and he will always, therefore, endeavor to employ it in the support of that industry of which the produce is likely to be of the greatest value, or to exchange for the greatest quantity either of money or of other goods.

But the annual revenue of every society is always precisely equal to the exchangeable value of the whole annual produce of its industry, or rather is precisely the same thing with that exchangeable value. As every individual, therefore, endeavors as much as he can both to employ his capital in the support of domestic industry, and so to direct that industry that its produce may be of the greatest value, every individual necessarily labors to render the annual revenue of the society as great as he can. He generally, indeed, neither intends to promote the public interest nor knows how much he is promoting it. By preferring the support of domestic to that of foreign industry, he intends only his own security; and by directing that industry in such a manner as its produce may be of the greatest value, he intends only his own gain, and he is in this, as in many other cases, led by an invisible hand to promote an end which was no part of his intention. Nor is it always the worse for the society that it was no part of it. By pursuing his own interest, he frequently promotes that of the society more effectually than when he really intends to promote it. I have never known much good done by those who affected to trade for the public good. It is an affectation, indeed, not very common among merchants, and very few words need be employed in dissuading them from it.

What is the species of domestic industry which his capital can employ, and of which the produce is likely to be of the greatest value, every individual, it is evident, can, in his local situation, judge much better than any statesman or lawgiver can do for him. The statesman, who should attempt to direct private people in what manner they ought to employ their capitals, would not only load himself with a most unnecessary attention but assume an authority which could safely be trusted not only to no single person but to no council or senate whatever, and which would nowhere be so dangerous as in the hands of a man who had folly and presumption enough to fancy himself fit to exercise it.

To give the monopoly of the home market to the produce of domestic industry, in any particular art of manufacture, is in some measure to direct private people in what manner they ought to employ their capitals and must, in almost all cases, be either a useless or a hurtful regulation. If the produce of domestic can be brought there as cheap as that of foreign industry, the regulation is evidently useless. If it cannot, it must generally be hurtful. It is the maxim of every prudent master of a family never to attempt to make at home what it will cost him more to make than to buy. The tailor does not attempt to make his own shoes but buys them of the shoemaker. The shoemaker does not attempt to make his own clothes but employs a tailor. The farmer attempts to make neither the one nor the other but employs those different artificers. All of them find it for their interest to employ their whole industry in a way in which they have some advantage over their neighbors and to purchase with a part of its produce, or what is the same thing, with the price of a part of it, whatever else they have occasion for.

What is prudence in the conduct of every private family can scarce be folly in that of a great kingdom. If a foreign country can supply us with a commodity cheaper than we ourselves can make it, better buy it of them with some part of the produce of our own industry, employed in a way in which we have some advantage. The general industry of the country, being always in proportion to the capital which employs it, will not thereby be diminished, no more than that of the above-mentioned artificers, but only left to find out the way in which it can be employed with the greatest advantage. It is certainly not employed to the greatest advantage when it is thus directed toward an object which it can buy cheaper than it can make. The value of its annual produce is certainly more or less diminished when it is thus turned away from producing commodities evidently of more value than the commodity which it is directed to produce. According to the supposition, that commodity could be purchased from foreign countries cheaper than it can be made at home. It could,

therefore, have been purchased with a part only of the commodities or, what is the same thing, with a part only of the price of the commodities, which the industry employed by an equal capital would have produced at home, had it been left to follow its natural course. The industry of the country, therefore, is thus turned away from a more, to a less, advantageous employment, and the exchangeable value of its annual produce, instead of being increased, according to the intention of the lawgiver, must necessarily be diminished by every such regulation.

By means of such regulations, indeed, a particular manufacture may sometimes be acquired sooner than it could have been otherwise and after a certain time may be made at home as cheap or cheaper than in the foreign country. But though the industry of the society may be thus carried with advantage into a particular channel sooner than it could have been otherwise, it will by no means follow that the sum total, either of its industry, or of its revenue, can ever be augmented by any such regulation. The industry of the society can augment only in proportion as its capital augments, and its capital can augment only in proportion to what can be gradually saved out of its revenue. But the immediate effect of every such regulation is to diminish its revenue, and what diminishes its revenue is certainly not very likely to augment its capital faster than it would have augmented of its own accord had both capital and industry been left to find out their natural employments.

Though for want of such regulations the society should never acquire the proposed manufacture, it would not, upon that account, necessarily be the poorer in any one period of its duration. In every period of its duration its whole capital and industry might still have been employed, though upon different objects, in the manner that was the most advantageous at the time. In every period its revenue might have been the greatest which its capital could afford, and both capital and revenue might have been augmented with the greatest possible rapidity.

The natural advantages which one country has over another in producing particular commodities are sometimes so great that it is acknowledged by all the world to be in vain to struggle with them. By means of glasses, hotbeds, and hotwalls, very good grapes can be raised in Scotland, and very good wine too can be made of them at about thirty times the expense for which at least equally good can be brought from foreign countries. Would it be a reasonable law to prohibit the importation of all foreign wines, merely to encourage the making of claret and burgundy in Scotland? But if there would be a manifest absurdity in turning toward any employment thirty times more of the capital and industry of the country than would be necessary to purchase from foreign countries an equal quantity of the commodities wanted, there must be an absurdity, though not altogether so glaring, yet exactly of the same kind, in turning toward any such employment a thirtieth, or even a three hundredth, part more of either. Whether the advantages which one country has over another be natural or acquired is in this respect of no consequence. As long as the one country has those advantages, and the other wants them, it will always be more advantageous for the latter rather to buy of the former than to make. It is an acquired advantage only, which one artificer has over his neighbor, who exercises another trade; and yet they both find it more advantageous to buy of one another than to make what does not belong to their particular trades.

It is thus that every system which endeavors either, by extraordinary encouragements, to draw toward a particular species of industry a greater share of the capital of the society than what would naturally go to it or, by extraordinary restraints, to force from a particular species of industry some share of the capital which would otherwise be employed in it is in reality subversive of the great purpose which it means to promote. It retards, instead of accelerating, the progress of the society toward real wealth and greatness and diminishes, instead of increasing, the real value of the annual produce of its land and labor.

All systems either of preference or of restraint, therefore, being thus completely taken away, the obvious and simple system of natural liberty establishes itself of its own accord. Every man, as long as he does not violate the laws of justice, is left perfectly free to pursue his own interest his own way and to bring both his industry and capital into competition with those of any other man or order of men. The sovereign is completely discharged from a duty, in the attempting to perform which he must always be exposed to innumerable delusions, and for the proper performance of which no human wisdom or knowledge could ever be sufficient—the duty of superintending the industry of private people and of directing it toward the employments most suitable to the interest of the society. According to the system of natural liberty, the sovereign has only three duties to attend to; three duties of great importance, indeed, but plain and intelligible to common understandings: first, the duty of protecting the society from the violence and invasion of other independent societies; secondly, the duty of protecting, as far as possible, every member of the society from the injustice or oppression of every other member of it, or the duty of establishing an exact administration of justice; and, thirdly, the duty of erecting and maintaining certain public works and certain public institutions which it can never be for the interest of any individual, or small number of individuals, to erect and maintain, because the profit could never repay the expense to any individual or small number of individuals, though it may frequently do much more than repay it to a great society. . . .

To restrain private people, it may be said, from receiving in payment the promissory notes of a banker, for any sum whether great or small, when they themselves are willing to receive them; or, to restrain a banker from issuing such notes, when all his neighbors are willing to accept of them, is a manifest violation of that natural liberty which it is the proper business of law, not to infringe, but to support. Such regulations may, no doubt, be considered as in some respect a violation of natural liberty. But those exertions of the natural liberty of a few individuals, which might endanger the security of the whole society, are, and ought to be, restrained by the laws of all governments; of the most free, as well as of the most despotical. The obligation of building party walls, in order to prevent the communication of fire, is a violation of natural liberty, exactly of the same kind with the regulations of the banking trade which are here proposed. . . .

Book I: Chapter VII
OF THE NATURAL AND MARKET PRICE OF COMMODITIES

. . . When the price of any commodity is neither more nor less than what is sufficient to pay the rent of the land, the wages of the labor, and the profits of the stock employed in raising, preparing, and bringing it to market, according to their natural rates, the commodity is then sold for what may be called its natural price.

The commodity is then sold precisely for what it is worth, or for what it really costs the person who brings it to market; for though in common language what is called the prime cost of any commodity does not comprehend the profit of the person who is to sell it again, yet if he sells it at a price which does not allow him the ordinary rate of profit in his neighborhood, he is evidently a loser by the trade, since by employing his stock in some other way he might have made that profit. His profit, besides, is his revenue, the proper fund of his subsistence. As, while he is preparing and bringing the goods to market, he advances to his workmen their wages, or their subsistence, so he advances to himself, in the same manner, his own subsistence, which is generally suitable to the profit which he may reasonably expect from the sale of his goods. Unless they yield him this profit, therefore, they do not repay him what they may very properly be said to have really cost him.

Though the price, therefore, which leaves him this profit is not always the lowest at which a dealer may sometimes sell his goods, it is the lowest at which he is likely to sell them for any considerable time; at least where there is perfect liberty, or where he may change his trade as often as he pleases.

The actual price at which any commodity is commonly sold is called its market price. It may either be above, or below, or exactly the same with its natural price.

The market price of every particular commodity is regulated by the proportion between the quantity which is actually brought to the market and the demand of those who are willing to pay the natural price of the commodity, or the whole value of the rent, labor, and profit which must be paid in order to bring it thither. Such people may be called the effectual demanders, and their demand the effectual demand, since it may be sufficient to effectuate the bringing of the commodity to market. It is different from the absolute demand. A very poor man may be said in some sense to have a demand for a coach and six; he might like to have it; but his demand is not an effectual demand, as the commodity can never be brought to market in order to satisfy it.

When the quantity of any commodity which is brought to market falls short of the effectual demand, all those who are willing to pay the whole value of the rent, wages, and profit which must be paid in order to bring it thither cannot be supplied with the quantity which they want. Rather than want it altogether, some of them will be willing to give more. A competition will immediately begin among them, and the market price will rise more or less above the natural price, according as either the greatness of the deficiency or the wealth and wanton luxury of the competitors happen to animate more or less the eagerness of the competition. Among competitors of equal wealth and luxury the same deficiency will generally occasion a more or less eager competition, according as the acquisition of the commodity happens to be of more or less importance to them. Hence the exorbitant price of the necessaries of life during the blockade of a town or in a famine.

When the quantity brought to market exceeds the effectual demand, it cannot be all sold to those who are willing to pay the whole value of the rent, wages, and profit which must be paid in order to bring it thither. Some part must be sold to those who are willing to pay less, and the low price which they give for it must reduce the price of the whole. The market price will sink more or less below the natural price, according as the greatness of the excess increases more or less the competition of the sellers, or according as it happens to be more or less important to them to get immediately rid of the commodity. The same excess in the importation of perishable will occasion a much greater competition than in that of durable commodities; in the importation of oranges, for example, than in that of old iron.

When the quantity brought to market is just sufficient to supply the effectual demand and no more, the market price naturally comes to be either exactly, or as nearly as can be judged of, the same with the natural price. The whole quantity upon hand can be disposed of for this price and cannot be disposed of for more. The competition of the different dealers obliges them all to accept of this price but does not oblige them to accept of less.

The quantity of every commodity brought to market naturally suits itself to the effectual demand. It is the interest of all those who employ their land, labor, or stock, in bringing any commodity to market, that the quantity never should exceed the effectual demand; and it is the interest of all other people that it never should fall short of that demand.

If at any time it exceeds the effectual demand, some of the component parts of its price must be paid below their natural rate. If it is rent, the interest of the landlords will immediately prompt them to withdraw a part of their land; and if it is wages or profit, the interest of the laborers in the one case, and of their employers in the other, will prompt them to withdraw a part of their labor or stock from this employment. The quantity brought to market will soon be no more than sufficient to supply the effectual demand. All the different parts of its price will rise to their natural rate, and the whole price to its natural price.

If, on the contrary, the quantity brought to market should at any time fall short of the effectual demand, some of the component parts of its price must rise above their natural rate. If it is rent, the interest of all other landlords will naturally prompt them to prepare more land for the raising of this commodity; if it is wages or profit, the interest of all other laborers and dealers will soon prompt them to employ more labor and stock in preparing and bringing it to market. The quantity brought thither will soon be sufficient to supply the effectual demand. All the different parts of its price will soon sink to their natural rate, and the whole price to its natural price.

The natural price, therefore, is, as it were, the central price, to which the prices of all commodities are continually gravitating. Different accidents may sometimes keep them suspended a good deal above it, and sometimes force them down even somewhat below it. But whatever may be the obstacles which hinder them from settling in this center of repose and continuance, they are constantly tending toward it.

The whole quantity of industry annually employed in order to bring any commodity to market naturally suits itself in this manner to the effectual demand. It naturally aims at bringing always that precise quantity thither which may be sufficient to supply, and no more than supply, that demand.

But in some employments the same quantity of industry will in different years produce very different quantities of commodities; while in others it will produce always the same, or very nearly the same. The same number of laborers in husbandry will, in different years, produce very different quantities of corn, wine, oil, hops, etc. But the same number of spinners and weavers will every year produce the same or very nearly the same quantity of linen and woolen cloth. It is only the average produce of the one species of industry which can be suited in any respect to the effectual demand; and, as its actual produce is frequently much greater and frequently much less than its average produce, the quantity of the commodities brought to market will sometimes exceed a good deal, and sometimes fall short a good deal, of the effectual demand. Even though that demand therefore should continue always the same, their market price will be liable to great fluctuations, will sometimes fall a good deal below, and sometimes rise a good deal above, their natural price. In the other species of industry, the produce of equal quantities of labor being always the same, or very nearly the same, it can be more exactly suited to the effectual demand. While that demand continues the same, therefore, the market price of the commodities is likely to do so too, and to be either altogether, or as nearly as can be judged of, the same with the natural price. That the price of linen and woolen cloth is liable neither to such frequent nor to such great variations as the price of corn, every man's experience will inform him. The price of the one species of commodities varies only with the variations in the demand: That of the other varies not only with the variations in the demand but with the much greater and more frequent variations in the quantity of what is brought to market in order to supply that demand.

The occasional and temporary fluctuations in the market price of any commodity fall chiefly upon those parts of its price which resolve themselves into wages and profit. That part which resolves itself into rent is less affected by them. A rent certain in money is not in the least affected by them either in its rate or in its value. A rent which consists either in a certain proportion or in a certain quantity of the rude produce is no doubt affected in its yearly value by all the occasional and temporary fluctuations in the market price of that rude produce; but it is seldom affected by them in its yearly rate. In settling the terms of the lease, the landlord and the farmer endeavor, according to their best judgment, to adjust that rate, not to the temporary and occasional, but to the average and ordinary price of the produce.

Such fluctuations affect both the value and the rate either of wages or of profit, according as the market happens to be either overstocked or understocked with commodities or with labor; with work done, or with work to be done. A public mourning raises the price of black cloth (with which the market is almost always understocked upon such occasions) and augments the profits of the merchants who possess any considerable quantity of it. It has no effect upon the wages of the weavers. The market is understocked with commodities, not with labor; with work done, not with work to be done. It raises the wages of journeymen tailors. The market is here understocked with labor. There is an effectual demand for more labor, for more work to be done than can be had. It sinks the price of colored silks and cloths and thereby reduces the profits of the merchants who have any considerable quantity of them upon hand. It sinks too the wages of the workmen employed in preparing such commodities, for which all demand is stopped for six months, perhaps for a twelvemonth. The market is here overstocked both with commodities and with labor.

But though the market price of every particular commodity is in this manner continually gravitating, if one may say so, toward the natural price, yet sometimes particular accidents, sometimes natural causes, and sometimes particular regulations of police, may, in many commodities, keep up the market price, for a long time together, a good deal above the natural price.

When by an increase in the effectual demand, the market price of some particular commodity happens to rise a good deal above the natural price, those who employ their stocks in supplying that market are generally careful to conceal this change. If it was commonly known, their great profit would tempt so many new rivals to employ their stocks in the same way that, the effectual demand being fully supplied, the market price would soon be reduced to the natural price and perhaps for some time even below it. If the market is at a great

distance from the residence of those who supply it, they may sometimes be able to keep the secret for several years together and may so long enjoy their extraordinary profits without any new rivals. Secrets of this kind, however, it must be acknowledged, can seldom be long kept;[6] and the extraordinary profits can last very little longer than they are kept.

Secrets in manufactures are capable of being longer kept than secrets in trade. A dyer who has found the means of producing a particular color with materials which cost only half the price of those commonly made use of, may, with good management, enjoy the advantage of his discovery as long as he lives, and even leave it as a legacy to his posterity. His extraordinary gains arise from the high price which is paid for his private labor. They properly consist in the high wages of that labor. But as they are repeated upon every part of his stock, and as their whole amount bears, upon that account, a regular proportion to it, they are commonly considered as extraordinary profits of stock.

Such enhancements of the market price are evidently the effects of particular accidents, of which, however, the operation may sometimes last for many years together.

Some natural productions require such a singularity of soil and situation that all the land in a great country which is fit for producing them may not be sufficient to supply the effectual demand. The whole quantity brought to market, therefore, may be disposed of to those who are willing to give more than what is sufficient to pay the rent of the land which produced them, together with the wages of the labor, and the profits of the stock which were em-

6. Note that the word "profit" is being used in two senses. Here *extraordinary profit* implies something beyond the *ordinary rate of profit* as discussed above. Modern economists differentiate between the two, applying the term "profit" to the first and interest to the latter.

ployed in preparing and bringing them to market, according to their natural rates. Such commodities may continue for whole centuries together to be sold at this high price; and that part of it which resolves itself into the rent of land is in this case the part which is generally paid above its natural rate. The rent of the land which affords such singular and esteemed productions, like the rent of some vineyards in France of a peculiarly happy soil and situation, bears no regular proportion to the rent of other equally fertile and equally well-cultivated land in its neighborhood. The wages of the labor and the profits of the stock employed in bringing such commodities to market, on the contrary, are seldom out of their natural proportion to those of the other employments of labor and stock in their neighborhood.

Such enhancements of the market price are evidently the effect of natural causes which may hinder the effectual demand from ever being fully supplied, and which may continue, therefore, to operate forever.

A monopoly granted either to an individual or to a trading company has the same effect as a secret in trade or manufactures. The monopolists, by keeping the market constantly understocked, by never fully supplying the effectual demand, sell their commodities much above the natural price and raise their emoluments, whether they consist in wages or profit, greatly above their natural rate.

7. In this sentence Smith succumbs to a common absurdity. The highest price a monopolist could get would be by selling *only one* item to the highest bidder. Though he might make a large profit on that unit (actually this is doubtful, owing to the great cost of producing but one unit), he will find that he will make a larger *total profit* by selling more units at a lower profit per unit. In other words, the monopolist sells not at the highest price which can be got but at whatever price will yield him the greatest total profit.

The price of monopoly is upon every occasion the highest which can be got.[7] The natural price, or the price of free competition, on the contrary, is the lowest which can be taken, not upon every occasion indeed, but for any considerable time together. The one is upon every occasion the highest which can be squeezed out of the buyers, or which, it is supposed, they will consent to give; the other is the lowest which the sellers can commonly afford to take and at the same time continue their business.

The exclusive privileges of corporations, statutes of apprenticeship, and all those laws which restrain, in particular employments, the competition to a smaller number than might otherwise go into them have the same tendency, though in a less degree. They are a sort of enlarged monopolies and may frequently, for ages together and in whole classes of employments, keep up the market price of particular commodities above the natural price and maintain both the wages of the labor and the profits of the stock employed about them somewhat above their natural rate.

Such enhancements of the market price may last as long as the regulations of police which give occasion to them.

The market price of any particular commodity, though it may continue long above, can seldom continue long below, its natural price. Whatever part of it was paid below the natural rate, the persons whose interest it affected would immediately feel the loss and would immediately withdraw either so much land, or so much labor, or so much stock, from being employed about it that the quantity brought to market would soon be no more than sufficient to supply the effectual demand. Its market price, therefore, would soon rise to the natural price. This at least would be the case where there was perfect liberty.

ECONOMIC LIBERALISM: THE REALITY[8]

The whole annual produce of the land and labor of every country, or what comes to the same thing, the whole price of that annual produce, naturally divides itself, it has already been observed, into three parts: the rent of land, the wages of labor, and the profits of stock; and constitutes a revenue to three different orders of people: to those who live by rent, to those who live by wages, and to those who live by profit. These are the three great, original, and constituent orders of every civilized society, from whose revenue that of every other order is ultimately derived.

The interest of the first of those three great orders, it appears from what has been just now said, is strictly and inseparably connected with the general interest of the society. Whatever either promotes or obstructs the one necessarily promotes or obstructs the other. When the public deliberates concerning any regulation of commerce or police, the proprietors of land never can mislead it, with a view to promote the interest of their own particular order; at least, if they have any tolerable knowledge of that interest. They are, indeed, too often defective in this tolerable knowledge. They are the only one of the three orders whose revenue costs them neither labor nor care but comes to them, as it were, of its own accord and independent of any plan or project of their own. That indolence, which is the natural effect of the ease and security of their situation, renders them too often not only ignorant but incapable of that application of mind which is necessary in order to foresee and understand the consequences of any public regulation.

The interest of the second order, that of those who live by wages, is as strictly connected with the interest of the society as that of the first. The wages of the laborer, it has already been shown, are never so high as when the demand for labor is continually rising, or when the quantity employed is every year increasing considerably. When this real wealth of the society becomes stationary, his wages are soon reduced to what is barely enough to enable him to bring up a family or to continue the race of laborers. When the society declines, they fall even below this. The order of proprietors may, perhaps, gain more by the prosperity of the society than that of laborers; but there is no order that suffers so cruelly from its decline. But though the interest of the laborer is strictly connected with that of the society, he is incapable either of comprehending that interest or of understanding its connection with his own. His condition leaves him no time to receive the necessary information, and his education and habits are commonly such as to render him unfit to judge even though he was fully informed. In the public deliberations, therefore, his voice is little heard and less regarded, except upon some particular occasions, when his clamor is animated, set on, and supported by his employers, not for his, but their own particular purposes.

His employers constitute the third order—that of those who live by profit. It is the stock that is employed for the sake of profit which puts into motion the greater part of the useful labor of every society. The plans and projects of the employers of stock regulate and direct all the most important operations of labor, and profit is the end proposed by all those plans and projects. But the rate of profit does not, like rent and wages, rise with the prosperity and fall with the declension of the society. On the contrary, it is naturally low in rich, and high in poor countries, and it is always highest in the countries which are going

8. Smith, *op. cit.*, pp. (in order of their inclusion) 248–50, 128–29, 456, 459, 460–62, 429–39, and 625–26.

fastest to ruin. The interest of this third order, therefore, has not the same connection with the general interest of the society as that of the other two. Merchants and master-manufacturers are, in this order, the two classes of people who commonly employ the largest capitals, and who by their wealth draw to themselves the greatest share of the public consideration. As during their whole lives they are engaged in plans and projects, they have frequently more acuteness of understanding than the greater part of country gentlemen. As their thoughts, however, are commonly exercised rather about the interest of their own particular branch of business than about that of the society, their judgment, even when given with the greatest candour (which it has not been upon every occasion), is much more to be depended upon with regard to the former of those two objects than with regard to the latter. Their superiority over the country gentlemen is not so much in their knowledge of the public interest as in their having a better knowledge of their own interest than he has of his. It is by this superior knowledge of their own interest that they have frequently imposed upon his generosity and persuaded him to give up both his own interest and that of the public from a very simple but honest conviction that their interest, and not his, was the interest of the public. The interest of the dealers, however, in any particular branch of trade or manufactures, is always in some respects different from, and even opposite to, that of the public. To widen the market and to narrow the competition is always the interest of the dealers. To widen the market may frequently be agreeable enough to the interest of the public; but to narrow the competition must always be against it and can serve only to enable the dealers, by raising their profits above what they naturally would be, to levy, for their own benefit, an absurd tax upon the rest of their fellow-citizens. The

proposal of any new law or regulation of commerce which comes from this order ought always to be listened to with great precaution and ought never to be adopted till after having been long and carefully examined, not only with the most scrupulous, but with the most suspicious attention. It comes from an order of men whose interest is never exactly the same with that of the public, who have generally an interest to deceive and even to oppress the public, and who accordingly have, upon many occasions, both deceived and oppressed it. . . .[9]

People of the same trade seldom meet together, even for merriment and diversion, but the conversation ends in a conspiracy against the public or in some contrivance to raise prices. It is impossible indeed to prevent such meetings, by any law which either could be executed, or would be consistent with liberty and justice. But though the law cannot hinder people of the same trade from sometimes assembling together, it ought to do nothing to facilitate such assemblies, much less to render them necessary.

A regulation which obliges all those of the same trade in a particular town to enter their names and places of abode in a public register facilitates such assemblies. It connects individuals who might never otherwise be known to one another and gives every man of the trade a direction where to find every other man of it.

A regulation which enables those of the same trade to tax themselves in order to provide for their poor, their sick, their widows and orphans, by giving them a common interest to manage, renders such assemblies necessary.

9. An early use of Smith in the United States is evidenced by the reference to *The Wealth of Nations* in an 1809 labor conspiracy trial in New York when the counsel defending the union asserted that Smith had found in Britain that "the master-tradesmen are in permanent conspiracy against the workmen" just as was true in the case before the court.

An incorporation not only renders them necessary but makes the act of the majority binding upon the whole. In a free trade an effectual combination cannot be established but by the unanimous consent of every single trader, and it cannot last longer than every single trader continues of the same mind. The majority of a corporation can enact a bylaw with proper penalties which will limit the competition more effectually and more durably than any voluntary combination whatever.

The pretense that corporations are necessary for the better government of the trade is without any foundation. The real and effectual discipline which is exercised over a workman is not that of his corporation but that of his customers. It is the fear of losing their employment which restrains his frauds and corrects his negligence. An exclusive corporation necessarily weakens the force of this discipline. A particular set of workmen must then be employed, let them behave well or ill. It is upon this account that in many large incorporated towns no tolerable workmen are to be found, even in some of the most necessary trades. If you would have your work tolerably executed, it must be done in the suburbs, where the workmen, having no exclusive privilege, have nothing but their character to depend upon, and you must then smuggle it into the town as well as you can.

It is in this manner that the policy of Europe, by restraining the competition in some employments to a smaller number than would otherwise be disposed to enter into them, occasions a very important inequality in the whole of the advantages and disadvantages of the different employments of labor and stock. . . .

Nothing, however, can be more absurd than this whole doctrine of the balance of trade, upon which not only these restraints but almost all the other regulations of commerce are founded. When two places trade with one another, this doctrine supposes that, if the balance be even, neither of them either loses or gains; but if it leans in any degree to one side, that one of them loses, and the other gains in proportion to its declension from the exact equilibrium. Both suppositions are false. A trade which is forced by means of bounties and monopolies may be, and commonly is, disadvantageous to the country in whose favor it is meant to be established, as I shall endeavor to show hereafter. But that trade which, without force or constraint, is naturally and regularly carried on between any two places is always advantageous, though not always equally so, to both.

By advantage or gain, I understand not the increase of the quantity of gold and silver but that of the exchangeable value of the annual produce of the land and labor of the country, or the increase of the annual revenue of its inhabitants. . . .

It is a losing trade, it is said, which a workman carries on with the alehouse; and the trade which a manufacturing nation would naturally carry on with a wine country may be considered as a trade of the same nature. I answer that the trade with the alehouse is not necessarily a losing trade. In its own nature it is just as advantageous as any other, though, perhaps, somewhat more liable to be abused. The employment of a brewer, and even that of a retailer of fermented liquors, are as necessary divisions of labor as any other. It will generally be more advantageous for a workman to buy of the brewer the quantity he has occasion for than to brew it himself, and, if he is a poor workman, it will generally be more advantageous for him to buy it, by little and little, of the retailer, than a large quantity of the brewer. He may no doubt buy too much of either, as he may of any other dealers in his neighborhood, of the butcher, if he is a glutton, or of the draper, if he affects to be a beau among his companions. It is advantageous to the great body of workmen, notwithstanding, that all these trades should be free, though this freedom may be abused in all of them and is more likely to be so, perhaps, in some than in others.... The restraints upon the wine trade in Great Britain, besides, do not so much seem calculated to hinder the people from going, if I may say so, to the alehouse, as from going where they can buy the best and cheapest liquor. They favor the wine trade of Portugal and discourage that of France. The Portuguese, it is said, indeed, are better customers for our manufactures than the French and should therefore be encouraged in preference to them. As they give us their custom, it is pretended, we should give them ours. The sneaking arts of underling tradesmen are thus erected into political maxims for the conduct of a great empire, for it is the most underling tradesmen only who make it a rule to employ chiefly their own customers. A great trader purchases his goods always where they are cheapest and best, without regard to any little interest of this kind.

By such maxims as these, however, nations have been taught that their interest consisted in beggaring all their neighbors. Each nation has been made to look with an invidious eye upon the prosperity of all the nations with which it trades and to consider their gain as its own loss. Commerce, which ought naturally to be among nations, as among individuals, a bond of union and friendship, has become the most fertile source of discord and animosity. The capricious ambition of kings and ministers has not, during the present and the preceding century, been more fatal to the repose of Europe than the impertinent jealousy of merchants and manufacturers. The violence and injustice of the rulers of mankind is an ancient evil, for which, I am afraid, the nature of human affairs can scarce admit of a remedy. But the mean rapacity, the monopolizing spirit of merchants and manufacturers, who neither are, nor ought to be, the rulers of mankind,

though it cannot perhaps be corrected, may very easily be prevented from disturbing the tranquillity of anybody but themselves.

That it was the spirit of monopoly which originally both invented and propagated this doctrine cannot be doubted, and they who first taught it were by no means such fools as they who believed it. In every country it always is and must be the interest of the great body of the people to buy whatever they want of those who sell it cheapest. The proposition is so very manifest that it seems ridiculous to take any pains to prove it; nor could it ever have been called in question had not the interested sophistry of merchants and manufacturers confounded the common sense of mankind. Their interest is, in this respect, directly opposite to that of the great body of the people. As it is the interest of the freemen of a corporation to hinder the rest of the inhabitants from employing any workmen but themselves, so it is the interest of the merchants and manufacturers of every country to secure to themselves the monopoly of the home market. Hence in Great Britain, and in most other European countries, the extraordinary duties upon almost all goods imported by alien merchants. Hence the high duties and prohibitions upon all those foreign manufactures which can come into competition with our own. Hence too the extraordinary restraints upon the importation of almost all sorts of goods from those countries with which the balance of trade is supposed to be disadvantageous; that is, from those against whom national animosity happens to be most violently inflamed.

The wealth of a neighboring nation, however, though dangerous in war and politics, is certainly advantageous in trade. In a state of hostility it may enable our enemies to maintain fleets and armies superior to our own; but in a state of peace and commerce it must likewise enable them to exchange with us to a greater value, and to afford a better market, either for the immediate produce of our own industry or for whatever is purchased with that produce. As a rich man is likely to be a better customer to the industrious people in his neighborhood than a poor, so is likewise a rich nation. A rich man, indeed, who is himself a manufacturer is a very dangerous neighbor to all those who deal in the same way. All the rest of the neighborhood, however, by far the greatest number, profit by the good market which his expense affords them. They even profit by his underselling the poorer workmen who deal in the same way with him. The manufacturers of a rich nation, in the same manner, may no doubt be very dangerous rivals to those of their neighbors. This very competition, however, is advantageous to the great body of the people, who profit greatly besides by the good market which the great expense of such a nation affords them in every other way. Private people who want to make a fortune never think of retiring to the remote and poor provinces of the country but resort either to the capital or to some of the great commercial towns. They know that, where little wealth circulates, there is little to be got, but that where a great deal is in motion, some share of it may fall to them. The same maxims which would in this manner direct the common sense of one, or ten, or twenty individuals should regulate the judgment of one, or ten, or twenty millions and should make a whole nation regard the riches of its neighbors as a probable cause and occasion for itself to acquire riches. A nation that would enrich itself by foreign trade is certainly most likely to do so when its neighbors are all rich, industrious, and commercial nations. A great nation surrounded on all sides by wandering savages and poor barbarians might, no doubt, acquire riches by the cultivation of its own lands, and by its own interior

commerce, but not by foreign trade. It seems to have been in this manner that the ancient Egyptians and the modern Chinese acquired their great wealth. The ancient Egyptians, it is said, neglected foreign commerce, and the modern Chinese, it is known, hold it in the utmost contempt and scarce deign to afford it the decent protection of the laws. The modern maxims of foreign commerce, by aiming at the impoverishment of all our neighbors, so far as they are capable of producing their intended effect, tend to render that very commerce insignificant and contemptible....

There seem, however, to be two cases in which it will generally be advantageous to lay some burden upon foreign, for the encouragement of domestic industry.

The first is when some particular sort of industry is necessary for the defense of the country. The defense of Great Britain, for example, depends very much upon the number of its sailors and shipping. The act of navigation, therefore, very properly endeavors to give the sailors and shipping of Great Britain the monopoly of the trade of their own country, in some cases, by absolute prohibitions, and in others by heavy burdens upon the shipping of foreign countries. The following are the principal dispositions of this act.

First, all ships of which the owners, masters, and three-fourths of the mariners are not British subjects are prohibited, upon pain of forfeiting ship and cargo, from trading to the British settlements and plantations or from being employed in the coasting trade of Great Britain.

Secondly, a great variety of the most bulky articles of importation can be brought into Great Britain only, either in such ships as are above described, or in ships of the country where those goods are produced, and of which the owners, masters, and three-fourths of the mariners are of that particular country; and when imported even in ships of this latter kind, they are subject to double aliens duty. If imported in ships of any other country, the penalty is forfeiture of ship and goods. When this act was made, the Dutch were, what they still are, the great carriers of Europe, and by this regulation they were entirely excluded from being the carriers to Great Britain or from importing to us the goods of any other European country.

Thirdly, a great variety of the most bulky articles of importation are prohibited from being imported, even in British ships, from any country but that in which they are produced, under pain of forfeiting ship and cargo. This regulation too was probably intended against the Dutch. Holland was then, as now, the great emporium for all European goods, and, by this regulation, British ships were hindered from loading in Holland the goods of any other European country.

Fourthly, salt fish of all kinds, whale fins, whalebone, oil, and blubber, not caught by and cured on board British vessels, when imported into Great Britain, are subjected to double aliens duty. The Dutch, as they are still the principal, were then the only fishers in Europe that attempted to supply foreign nations with fish. By this regulation, a very heavy burden was laid upon their supplying Great Britain.

When the act of navigation was made, though England and Holland were not actually at war, the most violent animosity subsisted between the two nations. It had begun during the government of the Long Parliament, which first framed this act, and it broke out soon after in the Dutch wars during that of the Protector and of Charles the Second. It is not impossible, therefore, that some of the regulations of this famous act may have proceeded from national animosity. They are as wise, however, as if they had all been dictated by the most deliberate wisdom. National animosity at that particular time aimed at the very same object which the most deliberate wisdom would have recommended, the diminution of the naval power of Holland, the only naval power which could endanger the security of England.

The act of navigation is not favorable to foreign commerce, or to the growth of that opulence which can arise from it. The interest of a nation in its commercial relations to foreign nations is, like that of a merchant with regard to the different people with whom he deals, to buy as cheap and to sell as dear as possible. But it will be most likely to buy cheap when, by the most perfect freedom of trade, it encourages all nations to bring to it the goods which it has occasion to purchase; and, for the same reason, it will be most likely to sell dear when its markets are thus filled with the greatest number of buyers. The act of navigation, it is true, lays no burden upon foreign ships that come to export the produce of British industry. Even the ancient aliens duty, which used to be paid upon all goods exported as well as imported, has, by several subsequent acts, been taken off from the greater part of the articles of exportation. But if foreigners, either by prohibitions or high duties, are hindered from coming to sell, they cannot always afford to come to buy; because, coming without a cargo, they must lose the freight from their own country to Great Britain. By diminishing the number of sellers, therefore, we necessarily diminish that of buyers and are thus likely not only to buy foreign goods dearer but to sell our own cheaper than if there was a more perfect freedom of trade. As defense, however, is of much more importance than opulence, the act of navigation is, perhaps, the wisest of all the commercial regulations of England.

The second case in which it will generally be advantageous to lay some burden upon foreign for the encouragement of domestic industry is when some tax is imposed at home upon the produce of the latter. In this case, it seems reasonable that an equal tax should be imposed upon the like produce of the former. This would not give the monopoly of the home market to domestic industry, nor turn toward a particular employment a greater share of the stock and labor of the country, than what would naturally go to it. It would only hinder any part of what would naturally go to it from being turned away by the tax into a less natural direction, and would leave the competition between foreign and domestic industry, after the tax, as nearly as possible upon the same footing as before it. In Great Britain, when any such tax is laid upon the produce of domestic industry, it is usual at the same time, in order to stop the clamorous complaints of our merchants and manufacturers that they will be undersold at home, to lay a much heavier duty upon the importation of all foreign goods of the same kind.

This second limitation of the freedom of trade according to some people should, upon some occasions, be extended much farther than to the precise foreign commodities which could come into competition with those which had been taxed at home. When the necessaries of life have been taxed in any country, it becomes proper, they pretend, to tax not only the like necessaries of life imported from other countries but all sorts of foreign goods which can come into competition with anything that is the produce of domestic industry. Subsistence, they say, becomes necessarily dearer in consequence of such taxes; and the price of labor must always rise with the price of the laborers' subsistence. Every commodity, therefore, which is the produce of domestic industry, though not immediately taxed itself, becomes dearer in consequence of such taxes, because the labor which produces it becomes so. Such taxes, therefore, are really equivalent, they say, to a tax upon every particular commodity produced at home. In order to put domestic upon the same footing with foreign industry, therefore, it becomes necessary, they think, to lay some duty upon every foreign commodity, equal to this enhancement of the price of the home commodities with which it can come into competition.

Whether taxes upon the necessaries of life, such as those in Great Britain upon soap, salt, leather, candles, etc., necessarily raise the price of labor, and consequently that of all other commodities, I shall consider hereafter, when I come to treat of taxes. Supposing, however, in the meantime, that they have this effect, and they have it undoubtedly, this general enhancement of the price of all commodities, in consequence of that of labor, is a case which differs in the two following respects from that of a particular commodity, of which the price was enhanced by a particular tax immediately imposed upon it.

First, it might always be known with great exactness how far the price of such a commodity could be enhanced by such a tax; but how far the general enhancement of the price of labor might affect that of every different commodity about which labor was employed could never be known with any tolerable exactness. It would be impossible, therefore, to proportion with any tolerable exactness the tax upon every foreign, to this enhancement of the price of every home commodity.

Secondly, taxes upon the necessaries of life have nearly the same effect upon the circumstances of the people as a poor soil and a bad climate. Provisions are thereby rendered dearer in the same manner as if it required extraordinary labor and expense to raise them. As in the natural scarcity arising from soil and climate, it would be absurd to direct the people in what manner they ought to employ their capitals and industry, so is it likewise in the artificial scarcity arising from such taxes. To be left to accommodate, as well as they could, their industry to their situation, and to find out those employments in which, notwithstanding their unfavorable circumstances, they might have some advantage either in the home or in the foreign market, is what in both cases would evidently be most for their advantage. To lay a new tax upon them, because they are already overburdened with taxes, and because they already pay too dear for the necessaries of life, to make them likewise pay too dear for the greater part of other commodities is certainly a most absurd way of making amends.

Such taxes, when they have grown up to a certain height, are a curse equal to the barrenness of the earth and the inclemency of the heavens; and yet it is in the richest and most industrious countries that they have been most generally imposed. No other countries could support so great a disorder. As the strongest bodies only can live and enjoy health under an unwholesome regimen, so the nations only that in every sort of industry have the greatest natural and acquired advantages can subsist and prosper under such taxes. Holland is the country in Europe in which they abound most, and which from peculiar circumstances continues to prosper, not by means of them, as has been most absurdly supposed, but in spite of them.

As there are two cases in which it will generally be advantageous to lay some burden upon foreign for the encouragement of domestic industry, so there are two others in which it may sometimes be a matter of deliberation; in the one, how far it is proper to continue the free importation of certain foreign goods; and in the other, how far, or in what manner, it may be proper to restore that free importation after it has been for some time interrupted.

The case in which it may sometimes be a matter of deliberation how far it is proper to continue the free importation of certain foreign goods is when some foreign nation restrains by high duties or prohibitions the importation of some of our manufactures into their country. Revenge in this case naturally dictates retaliation, and that we should impose the like duties and prohibitions upon the importation of some or all of their manufactures into ours. Nations accordingly seldom fail to retaliate in this manner. The French have been particularly forward to favor their own manufactures by restraining the importation of such foreign goods as could come into competition with them. In this consisted a great part of the policy of Mr. Colbert,[10] who, notwithstanding his great abilities, seems in this case to have been imposed upon by the sophistry of merchants and manufacturers, who are always demanding a monopoly against their countrymen. It is at present the opinion of the most intelligent men in France that his operations of this kind have not been beneficial to his country. That minister, by the tariff of 1667, imposed very high duties upon a great number of foreign manufactures. Upon his refusing to moderate them in favor of the Dutch, they in 1671 prohibited the importation of the wines, brandies, and manufactures of France. The war of 1672 seems to have been in part occasioned by this commercial dispute. The peace of Nimeguen put an end to it in 1678 by moderating some of those duties in favor of the Dutch, who in consequence took off their prohibition. It was about the same time that the French and English began mutually to oppress each other's industry, by the like duties and prohibitions, of which the French, however, seem to have set the first example. The

10. Jean Baptiste Colbert (1619–83) was a French statesman who thought that the national wealth might be increased by the encouragement of industry. He used the method of strongly centralized regulation. He set up model factories. He tried to standardize the production of certain staple commodities, and any infraction of these standards was to be punished. Receipts from a high protective tariff were to be used to develop roads and canals to benefit trade.

spirit of hostility which has subsisted between the two nations ever since has hitherto hindered them from being moderated on either side. In 1697 the English prohibited the importation of bonelace, the manufacture of Flanders. The government of that country, at that time under the dominion of Spain, prohibited in return the importation of English woolens. In 1700 the prohibition of importing bonelace into England was taken off upon condition that the importation of English woolens into Flanders should be put on the same footing as before.

There may be good policy in retaliations of this kind, when there is a probability that they will procure the repeal of the high duties or prohibitions complained of. The recovery of a great foreign market will generally more than compensate the transitory inconveniency of paying dearer during a short time for some sorts of goods. To judge whether such retaliations are likely to produce such an effect does not, perhaps, belong so much to the science of a legislator, whose deliberations ought to be governed by general principles which are always the same, as to the skill of that insidious and crafty animal, vulgarly called a statesman or politician, whose councils are directed by the momentary fluctuations of affairs. When there is no probability that any such repeal can be procured, it seems a bad method of compensating the injury done to certain classes of our people to do another injury ourselves, not only to those classes, but to almost all the other classes of them. When our neighbors prohibit some manufacture of ours, we generally prohibit, not only the same, for that alone would seldom affect them considerably, but some other manufacture of theirs. This may no doubt give encouragement to some particular class of workmen among ourselves and, by excluding some of their rivals, may enable them to raise their price in the home market. Those workmen, however, who

suffered by our neighbors' prohibition will not be benefited by ours. On the contrary, they and almost all the other classes of our citizens will thereby be obliged to pay dearer than before for certain goods. Every such law, therefore, imposes a real tax upon the whole country, not in favor of that particular class of workmen who were injured by our neighbors' prohibition, but of some other class.

The case in which it may sometimes be a matter of deliberation how far, or in what manner, it is proper to restore the free importation of foreign goods, after it has been for some time interrupted, is, when particular manufactures, by means of high duties or prohibitions upon all foreign goods which can come into competition with them, have been so far extended as to employ a great multitude of hands. Humanity may in this case require that the freedom of trade should be restored only by slow gradations and with a good deal of reserve and circumspection. Were those high duties and prohibitions taken away all at once, cheaper foreign goods of the same kind might be poured so fast into the home market as to deprive all at once many thousands of our people of their ordinary employment and means of subsistence. The disorder which this would occasion might no doubt be very considerable. It would in all probability, however, be much less than is commonly imagined, for the two following reasons:

First, all those manufactures of which any part is commonly exported to other European countries without a bounty could be very little affected by the freest importation of foreign goods. Such manufactures must be sold as cheap abroad as any other foreign goods of the same quality and kind, and consequently must be sold cheaper at home. They would still, therefore, keep possession of the home market, and though a capricious man of fashion might sometimes prefer foreign wares, merely because they were foreign, to cheaper and better goods of the same kind that were made at home, this folly could, from the nature of things, extend to so few that it could make no sensible impression upon the general employment of the people. But a great part of all the different branches of our woolen manufacture, of our tanned leather, and of our hardware are annually exported to other European countries without any bounty, and these are the manufactures which employ the greatest number of hands. The silk, perhaps, is the manufacture which would suffer the most by this freedom of trade, and after it the linen, though the latter much less than the former.

Secondly, though a great number of people should, by thus restoring the freedom of trade, be thrown all at once out of their ordinary employment and common method of subsistence, it would by no means follow that they would thereby be deprived either of employment or subsistence. By the reduction of the army and navy at the end of the late war, more than a hundred thousand soldiers and seamen, a number equal to what is employed in the greatest manufactures, were all at once thrown out of their ordinary employment; but, though they no doubt suffered some inconveniency, they were not thereby deprived of all employment and subsistence. The greater part of the seamen, it is probable, gradually betook themselves to the merchant service as they could find occasion, and in the meantime both they and the soldiers were absorbed in the great mass of the people and employed in a great variety of occupations. Not only no great convulsion but no sensible disorder arose from so great a change in the situation of more than a hundred thousand men, all accustomed to the use of arms, and many of them to rapine and plunder. The number of vagrants was scarce any-

where sensibly increased by it, even the wages of labor were not reduced by it in any occupation, so far as I have been able to learn, except in that of seamen in the merchant service. But if we compare together the habits of a soldier and of any sort of manufacturer, we shall find that those of the latter do not tend so much to disqualify him from being employed in a new trade as those of the former from being employed in any. The manufacturer has always been accustomed to look for his subsistence from his labor only: the soldier to expect it from his pay. Application and industry have been familiar to the one; idleness and dissipation to the other. But it is surely much easier to change the direction of industry from one sort of labor to another than to turn idleness and dissipation to any. To the greater part of manufactures besides, it has already been observed, there are other collateral manufactures of so similar a nature that a workman can easily transfer his industry from one of them to another. The greater part of such workmen too are occasionally employed in country labor. The stock which employed them in a particular manufacture before will still remain in the country to employ an equal number of people in some other way. The capital of the country remaining the same, the demand for labor will likewise be the same, or very nearly the same, though it may be exerted in different places and for different occupations. Soldiers and seamen, indeed, when discharged from the king's service, are at liberty to exercise any trade, within any town or place of Great Britain or Ireland. Let the same natural liberty of exercising what species of industry they please be restored to all His Majesty's subjects, in the same manner as to soldiers and seamen; that is, break down the exclusive privileges of corporations and repeal the statute of apprenticeship,[11] both which are real encroach-

11. The Statute of Laborers and Apprentices

ments upon natural liberty, and add to these the repeal of the law of settlements, so that a poor workman, when thrown out of employment either in one trade or in one place, may seek for it in another trade or in another place, without the fear either of a prosecution or of a removal, and neither the public nor the individuals will suffer much more from the occasional disbanding some particular classes of manufacturers than from that of soldiers. Our manufacturers have no doubt great merit with their country, but they cannot have more than those who defend it with their blood, nor deserve to be treated with more delicacy.

To expect, indeed, that the freedom of trade should ever be entirely restored in Great Britain is as absurd as to expect that an Oceana or Utopia[12] should ever be established in it. Not only the prejudices of the public but, what is much more unconquerable, the private interests of many individuals irresistibly oppose it. Were the officers of the army to oppose with the same zeal and unanimity any reduction in the number of forces, with which master-manufacturers set themselves against every law that is likely to increase the number of their rivals in the home market; were the former to animate their soldiers, in the same manner as the latter inflame their workmen, to attack with violence and outrage the proposers of any such regulation; to attempt to reduce the army

would be as dangerous as it has now become to attempt to diminish in any respect the monopoly which our manufacturers have obtained against us. This monopoly has so much increased the number of some particular tribes of them that, like an overgrown standing army, they have become formidable to the government, and upon many occasions intimidate the legislature. The member of Parliament who supports every proposal for strengthening this monopoly is sure to acquire not only the reputation of understanding trade but great popularity and influence with an order of men whose numbers and wealth render them of great importance. If he opposes them, on the contrary, and still more if he has authority enough to be able to thwart them, neither the most acknowledged probity, nor the highest rank, nor the greatest public services can protect him from the most infamous abuse and detraction, from personal insults, nor sometimes from real danger, arising from the insolent outrage of furious and disappointed monopolists.

The undertaker of a great manufacture, who, by the home markets being suddenly laid open to the competition of foreigners, should be obliged to abandon his trade, would no doubt suffer very considerably. That part of his capital which had usually been employed in purchasing materials and in paying his workmen might, without much difficulty, perhaps, find another employment. But that part of it which was fixed in workhouses, and in the instruments of trade, could scarce be disposed of without considerable loss. The equitable regard, therefore, to his interest requires that changes of this kind should never be introduced suddenly but slowly, gradually, and after a very long warning. The legislature, were it possible that its deliberations could be always directed, not by the clamorous importunity of partial interests, but by an extensive view of the general good, ought

in 1563, so far as it was concerned with apprenticeship, put legal authority behind a system of guild apprenticeship which was beginning to break up. The act regulated the employing and training of labor. For example, it was required that the period of apprenticeship must be at least seven years long, and no one might exercise a craft unless he had been apprenticed.

12. *Oceana* is the title of a work by James Harrington (1611–77) which sets forth the author's conception of the ideal government for England. *Utopia* was a book written by Sir Thomas More (1478–1535) in which he described an imaginary island on which perfection had been achieved in politics, laws, and social arrangements.

upon this very account, perhaps, to be particularly careful neither to establish any new monopolies of this kind nor to extend further those which are already established. Every such regulation introduces some degree of real disorder into the constitution of the state, which it will be difficult afterward to cure without occasioning another disorder. . . .

It is unnecessary, I imagine, to observe, how contrary such regulations are to the boasted liberty of the subject, of which we affect to be so very jealous; but which, in this case, is so plainly sacrificed to the futile interests of our merchants and manufacturers.[13]

The laudable motive of all these regulations is to extend our own manufactures, not by their own improvement, but by the depression of those of all our neighbors, and by putting an end, as much as possible, to the troublesome competition of such odious and disagreeable rivals. Our master-manufacturers think it reasonable that they themselves should have the monopoly of the ingenuity of all their countrymen. Though by restraining, in some trades, the number of apprentices which can be employed at one time, and by imposing the necessity of a long apprenticeship in all trades, they endeavor, all of them, to confine the knowledge of their respective employments to as small a number as possible; they are unwilling, however, that any part of this small number should go abroad to instruct foreigners.

Consumption is the sole end and purpose of all production, and the interest of the producer ought to be attended to only so far as it may be necessary for promoting that of the consumer. The maxim is so perfectly self-evident that it would be absurd to attempt to prove it.

13. This paragraph and all those which follow were first inserted by Smith in the third British edition of *The Wealth of Nations* (1784). Thus the remarks should be read as a reflection of his added experience as commissioner of customs and as an observation drawn after the close of the American Revolution.

But in the mercantile system, the interest of the consumer is almost constantly sacrificed to that of the producer; and it seems to consider production, and not consumption, as the ultimate end and object of all industry and commerce.

In the restraints upon the importation of all foreign commodities which can come into competition with those of our own growth, or manufacture, the interest of the home consumer is evidently sacrificed to that of the producer. It is altogether for the benefit of the latter that the former is obliged to pay that enhancement of price which this monopoly almost always occasions.

It is altogether for the benefit of the producer that bounties are granted upon the exportation of some of his productions. The home consumer is obliged to pay, first, the tax which is necessary for paying the bounty and, secondly, the still greater tax which necessarily arises from the enhancement of the price of the commodity in the home market.

By the famous treaty of commerce with Portugal, the consumer is prevented by high duties from purchasing of a neighboring country a commodity which our own climate does not produce but is obliged to purchase it of a distant country, though it is acknowledged that the commodity of the distant country is of a worse quality than that of the near one. The home consumer is obliged to submit to this inconveniency, in order that the producer may import into the distant country some of his productions upon more advantageous terms than he would otherwise have been allowed to do. The consumer, too, is obliged to pay whatever enhancement in the price of those very productions this forced exportation may occasion in the home market.

But in the system of laws which has been established for the management of our American and West Indian colonies, the interest of the home consumer has been sacrificed to that of the producer with a more extravagant profusion than in all our other commercial regulations. A great empire has been established for the sole purpose of raising up a nation of customers who should be obliged to buy from the shops of our different producers all the goods with which these could supply them. For the sake of that little enhancement of price which this monopoly might afford our producers, the home consumers have been burdened with the whole expense of maintaining and defending that empire. For this purpose, and for this purpose only, in the two last wars, more than two hundred millions have been spent, and a new debt of more than a hundred and seventy millions has been contracted over and above all that had been expended for the same purpose in former wars. The interest of this debt alone is not only greater than the whole extraor-

dinary profit, which, it ever could be pretended, was made by the monopoly of the colony trade, but than the whole value of that trade, or than the whole value of the goods, which at an average have been annually exported to the colonies.

It cannot be very difficult to determine who have been the contrivers of this whole mercantile system; not the consumers, we may believe, whose interest has been entirely neglected; but the producers, whose interest has been so carefully attended to; and among this latter class our merchants and manufacturers have been by far the principal architects. In the mercantile regulations, which have been taken notice of in this chapter, the interest of our manufacturers has been most peculiarly attended to; and the interest, not so much of the consumers, as that of some other sets of producers, has been sacrificed to it.

SECTION B. THE HAMILTONIAN AND JEFFERSONIAN SYSTEMS

1. FIRST REPORT ON THE PUBLIC CREDIT[1]

By ALEXANDER HAMILTON

EDITORS' NOTE.—Alexander Hamilton (1757–1804), first secretary of the treasury under President Washington. This *Report*, made in January, 1790, precipitated the first important political conflict after the establishment of the new government and thus contributed to the new drawing of party lines in Congress and in the country.

Hamilton begins his *Report* by quoting a congressional resolution that "an adequate provision for the support of the public credit is a matter of high importance to the honor and prosperity of the United States."

He then suggests that the United States will need to borrow in time of public danger, indicates that the success of such borrowing requires good credit, and points out the ill consequences to a country of unsound or questionable credit. The main part of the *Report*, which is given here, follows; the last sections, which are omitted from this extract, consider alternative plans for putting the total debt upon a sound financial footing and recommend means of raising the revenues necessary for annual payments of interest and principal.

... If the maintenance of public credit, then, be truly so important, the next inquiry which suggests itself is by what means it is to be effected. The ready answer to which question is, by good faith, by a punctual performance of contracts. States, like individuals, who observe their engagements are respected and trusted; while the reverse is the fate of those who pursue an opposite conduct.

Every breach of the public engagements, whether from choice or necessity, is, in different degrees, hurtful to public credit. When such a necessity does truly exist, the evils of it are only to be palliated by a scrupulous attention, on the part of the government, to carry the violation no further than the necessity absolutely requires, and to manifest, if the nature of the case admit of it, a sincere disposition to make reparation whenever circumstances shall permit. But, with every possible mitigation, credit must suffer, and numerous mischiefs ensue. It is, therefore, highly important, when an appearance of necessity seems to press upon the public councils, that they should examine well its reality, and be perfectly assured that there is no method of escaping from it, before they yield to its suggestions. For, though it cannot safely be affirmed that occasions have never existed, or may not exist, in which violations of the public faith, in this respect, are inevitable; yet there is great reason to believe that they exist far less frequently than precedents indicate; and are oftenest either pre-

1. *Reports of the Secretary of the Treasury of the United States* (Washington, 1837), I, 4-6, 7-8, 9-10, 11-12, 14, 15.

tended, through levity or want of firmness, or supposed, through want of knowledge. Expedients might often have been devised to effect, consistently with good faith, what has been done in contravention of it. Those who are most commonly creditors of a nation are, generally speaking, enlightened men; and there are signal examples to warrant a conclusion that, when a candid and fair appeal is made to them, they will understand their true interest too well to refuse their concurrence in such modifications of their claims as any real necessity may demand.

While the observance of that good faith, which is the basis of public credit, is recommended by the strongest inducements of political expediency, it is enforced by considerations of still greater authority. There are arguments for it which rest on the immutable principles of moral obligation. And in proportion as the mind is disposed to contemplate, in the order of Providence, an intimate connection between public virtue and public happiness will be its repugnancy to a violation of those principles.

This reflection derives additional strength from the nature of the debt of the United States. It was the price of liberty. The faith of America has been repeatedly pledged for it, and with solemnities that give peculiar force to the obligation. There is, indeed, reason to regret that it has not hitherto been kept; that the necessities of the war, conspiring with inexperience in the subjects of finance, produced direct infractions; and that the subsequent period has been a continued scene of negative violation, or noncompliance. But a diminution of this regret arises from the reflection that the last seven years have exhibited an earnest and uniform effort on the part of the government of the Union to retrieve the national credit, by doing justice to the creditors of the nation; and that the embarrassments of a defective constitu-

tion, which defeated this laudable effort, have ceased.

From this evidence of a favorable disposition given by the former government, the institution of a new one, clothed with powers competent to calling forth the resources of the community, has excited correspondent expectations. A general belief accordingly prevails that the credit of the United States will quickly be established on the firm foundation of an effectual provision for the existing debt. The influence which this has had at home is witnessed by the rapid increase that has taken place in the market value of the public securities. From January to November, they rose thirty-three and a third per cent; and from that period to this time, they have risen fifty per cent more; and the intelligence from abroad announces effects proportionably favorable to our national credit and consequence.

It cannot but merit particular attention that, among ourselves, the most enlightened friends of good government are those whose expectations are the highest.

To justify and preserve their confidence; to promote the increasing respectability of the American name; to answer the calls of justice; to restore landed property to its due value; to furnish new resources both to agriculture and commerce; to cement more closely the union of the states; to add to their security against foreign attack; to establish public order on the basis of an upright and liberal policy—these are the great and invaluable ends to be secured by a proper and adequate provision, at the present period, for the support of public credit.

To this provision we are invited, not only by the general considerations which have been noticed, but by others of a more particular nature. It will procure to every class of the community some important advantages, and remove some no less important disadvantages.

The advantage to the public creditors from the increased value of that part of their property which constitutes the public debt needs no explanation.

But there is a consequence of this, less obvious, though not less true, in which every other citizen is interested. It is a well-known fact that in countries in which the national debt is properly funded, and an object of established confidence, it answers most of the purposes of money. Transfers of stock or public debt are there equivalent to payments in specie; or, in other words, stock, in the principal transactions of business, passes current as specie. The same thing would, in all probability, happen here under the like circumstances.

The benefits of this are various and obvious:

First. Trade is extended by it, because there is a larger capital to carry it on, and the merchant can, at the same time, afford to trade for smaller profits; as his stock, which, when unemployed, brings him in an interest from the government, serves him also as money when he has a call for it in his commercial operations.

Secondly. Agriculture and manufactures are also promoted by it, for the like reason that more capital can be commanded to be employed in both, and because the merchant, whose enterprise in foreign trade gives to them activity and extension, has greater means for enterprise.

Thirdly. The interest of money will be lowered by it, for this is always in a ratio to the quantity of money and to the quickness of circulation. This circumstance will enable both the public and individuals to borrow on easier and cheaper terms.

And from the combination of these effects, additional aids will be furnished to labor, to industry, and to arts of every kind. But these good effects of a public debt are only to be looked for, when, by being well funded, it has acquired an adequate and stable value; till then, it has rather a contrary tendency. The fluctuation and insecurity incident to it in an unfunded state render it a mere commodity and a precarious one. As such, being only an object of occasional and particular speculation, all the money applied to it is so much diverted from the more useful channels of circulation, for which the thing itself affords no substitute, so that, in fact, one serious inconvenience of an unfunded debt is that it contributes to the scarcity of money....

Having now taken a concise view of the inducements to a proper provision for the public debt, the next inquiry which presents itself is: What ought to be the nature of such a provision? This requires some preliminary discussions.

It is agreed on all hands that that part of the debt which has been contracted abroad, and is denominated the foreign debt, ought to be provided for according to the precise terms of the contracts relating to it. The discussions which can arise, therefore, will have reference essentially to the domestic part of it, or to that which has been contracted at home. It is to be regretted that there is not the same unanimity of sentiment on this part as on the other.

The Secretary has too much deference for the opinions of every part of the community not to have observed one, which has more than once made its appearance in the public prints, and which is occasionally to be met with in conversation. It involves this question: Whether a discrimination ought not to be made between original holders of the public securities, and present possessors by purchase? Those who advocate a discrimination are for making a full provision for the securities of the former at their nominal value but contend that the latter ought to receive no more than the cost to them and the interest. And the idea is sometimes suggested of making good the difference to the primitive possessor.

In favor of this scheme, it is alleged

that it would be unreasonable to pay twenty shillings in the pound to one who had not given more for it than three or four. And it is added that it would be hard to aggravate the misfortune of the first owner, who, probably through necessity, parted with his property at so great a loss, by obliging him to contribute to the profit of the person who had speculated on his distresses.

The Secretary, after the most mature reflection on the force of this argument, is induced to reject the doctrine it contains as equally unjust and impolitic; as highly injurious, even to the original holders of public securities; as ruinous to public credit.

It is inconsistent with justice, because, in the first place, it is a breach of contract, a violation of the rights of a fair purchaser.

The nature of the contract, in its origin, is that the public will pay the sum expressed in the security to the first holder or his assignee. The intent in making the security assignable is that the proprietor may be able to make use of his property by selling it for as much as it may be worth in the market and that the buyer may be safe in the purchase.

Every buyer, therefore, stands exactly in the place of the seller, has the same right with him to the identical sum expressed in the security, and, having acquired that right by fair purchase, and in conformity to the original agreement and intention of the government, his claim cannot be disputed without manifest injustice.

That he is to be considered as a fair purchaser, results from this: whatever necessity the seller may have been under was occasioned by the government in not making a proper provision for its debts. The buyer had no agency in it and therefore ought not to suffer. He is not even chargeable with having taken an undue advantage. He paid what the commodity was worth in the market and took the risks of reimbursement upon himself. He of course gave a fair equivalent and ought to reap the benefit of his hazard; a hazard which was far from inconsiderable, and which, perhaps, turned on little less than a revolution in government.

That the case of those who parted with their securities from necessity is a hard one cannot be denied; but, whatever complaint of injury, or claim of redress, they may have, respects the government solely. They have not only nothing to object to the persons who relieved their necessities, by giving them the current price of their property, but they are even under an implied condition to contribute to the reimbursement of those persons. They knew that, by the terms of the contract with themselves, the public were bound to pay, to those to whom they should convey their title, the sums stipulated to be paid to them; and that, as citizens of the United States, they were to bear their proportion of the contribution for that purpose. This, by the act of assignment, they tacitly engage to do; and, if they had an option, they could not, with integrity or good faith, refuse to do it, without the consent of those to whom they sold.

But, though many of the original holders sold from necessity, it does not follow that this was the case with all of them. It may well be supposed that some of them did it either through want of confidence in an eventual provision or from the allurements of some profitable speculation. . . .

But there is still a point of view in which it will appear perhaps even more exceptionable than in either of the former. It would be repugnant to an express provision of the Constitution of the United States. This provision is that "all debts contracted, and engagements entered into, before the adoption of that constitution, shall be as valid against the United States under it as under the confederation"; which amounts to a constitutional ratification of the contracts respecting the debt in the state in which they existed under the confederation; and, resorting to that standard, there can be no doubt that the rights of assignees and original holders must be considered as equal. In exploding thus fully the principle of discrimination, the Secretary is happy in reflecting that he is only the advocate of what has been already sanctioned by the formal and express authority of the government of the Union in these emphatic terms: "The remaining class of creditors," say Congress, in their circular address to the states, of the 26th of April, 1783, "is composed partly of such of our fellow-citizens as originally lent to the public the use of their funds, or have since manifested most confidence in their country by receiving transfers from the lenders; and partly of those whose property has been either advanced or assumed for the public service. To discriminate the merits of these several descriptions of creditors would be a task equally unnecessary and invidious. If the voice of humanity plead more loudly in favor of some than of others, the voice of policy, no less than of justice, pleads in favor of all. A wise nation will never permit those who relieve the wants of their country, or who rely most on its faith, its firmness, and its resources, when either of them is distrusted, to suffer by the event."

The Secretary, concluding that a discrimination between the different classes of creditors of the United States cannot, with propriety, be made, proceeds to examine whether a difference ought to be permitted to remain between them and another description of public creditors—those of the states individually. The Secretary, after mature reflection on this point, entertains a full conviction that an assumption of the debts of the particular states by the Union, and a like provision for them as for those of the Union, will be a measure of sound policy and substantial justice.

It would, in the opinion of the Secretary, contribute, in an eminent degree, to an orderly, stable, and satisfactory arrangement of the national finances. Admitting, as ought to be the case, that a provision must be made, in some way or other, for the entire debt, it will follow that no greater revenues will be required, whether that provision be made wholly by the United States, or partly by them and partly by the states separately. . . .

If all the public creditors receive their dues from one source, distributed with an equal hand, their interests will be the same; and, having the same interests, they will unite in the support of the fiscal arrangements of the government; as these, too, can be made with more convenience where there is no competition. These circumstances combined will insure to the revenue laws a more ready and more satisfactory execution.

If, on the contrary, there are distinct provisions, there will be distinct interest, drawing different ways. That union and concert of views among the creditors, which in every government is of great importance to their security, and to that of public credit, will not only not exist but will be likely to give place to mutual jealousy and opposition; and from this cause, the operation of the systems which may be adopted both by the particular states and by the Union, with relation to their respective debts, will be in danger of being counteracted.

There are several reasons which render it probable that the situation of the state creditors would be worse than that of the creditors of the Union, if there be not a national assumption of the state debts. Of these it will be sufficient to mention two: One, that a principal branch of revenue is exclusively vested in the Union; the other, that a state must always be checked in the imposition of taxes on articles of consumption, from the want of power to extend the same regulation to the other states, and from the tendency of partial duties to injure its industry and commerce. Should the state creditors stand upon a less eligible footing than the others, it is unnatural to expect they would see with pleasure a provision for them. The influence which their dissatisfaction might have could not but operate injuriously, both for the creditors and the credit of the United States. Hence it is even the interest of the creditors of the Union that those of the individual states should be comprehended in a general provision. Any attempt to secure to the former either exclusive or peculiar advantages would materially hazard their interests. Neither would it be just that one class of the public creditors should be more favored than the other. The object for which both descriptions of the debt were contracted are in the main the same. Indeed, a great part of the particular debts of the states has arisen from assumptions by them on account of the Union; and it is most equitable that there should be the same measure of retribution for all....

The result of the foregoing discussions is this: That there ought to be no discrimination between the original holders of the debt and present possessors by purchase; that it is expedient there should be an assumption of the state debts by the Union and that the arrears of interest should be provided for on an equal footing with the principal.

The next inquiry in order, toward determining the nature of a proper provision, respects the quantum of the debt and the present rates of interest.

The debt of the Union is distinguishable into foreign and domestic.

The foreign debt, as stated in Schedule B, amounts to:

Principal $10,070,307.00
Bearing an interest of four, and
    partly an interest of five per cent
Arrears of interest to the last of
    December, 1789.............. 1,640,071.62
Making together $11,710,378.62

The domestic debt may be sub-
    divided into liquidated and un-
    liquidated; principal and interest
The principal of the liquidated
    part, as stated in the Schedule C,
    amounts to $27,383,917.74
Bearing an interest of six per cent
The arrears of interest, as stated in
    the Schedule D, to the end of
    1790, amount to............. 13,030,168.20
Making together $40,414,085.94

The unliquidated part of the domestic debt, which consists chiefly of the Continental bills of credit, is not ascertained but may be estimated at 2,000,000 dollars.

These several sums constitute the whole of the debt of the United States, amounting together to $54,124,464.56....

2. REMARKS ON THE HAMILTONIAN SYSTEM[1]

By Thomas Jefferson

... But a short review of facts ... will show that the contests of that day were contests of principle between the advocates of republican and those of kingly government and that, had not the former made the efforts they did, our government would have been, even at this early day, a very different thing from what the successful issue of those efforts have made it.

The alliance between the states under the old Articles of Confederation, for the purpose of joint defense against the aggression of Great Britain, was found insufficient, as treaties of alliance generally are, to enforce compliance with their mutual stipulations; and these, once fulfilled, that bond was to expire of it-

1. Thomas Jefferson, "The Anas," based upon notes kept by Jefferson when secretary of state, from *Writings* ..., ed. H. A. Washington (New York, 1861), IX, 88–97.

self, and each state to become sovereign and independent in all things. Yet it could not but occur to everyone that these separate independencies, like the petty states of Greece, would be eternally at war with each other and would become at length the mere partisans and satellites of the leading powers of Europe. All then must have looked forward to some further bond of union, which would insure eternal peace and a political system of our own, independent of that of Europe. Whether all should be consolidated into a single government, or each remain independent as to internal matters, and the whole form a single nation as to what was foreign only, and whether that national government should be a monarchy or republic, would of course divide opinions, according to the constitutions, the habits, and the circumstances of each individual. Some officers of the army, as it has always been said and believed (and Steuben and Knox have ever been named as the leading agents),[2] trained to monarchy by military habits, are understood to have proposed to General Washington to decide this great question by the army before its disbandment and to assume himself the crown on the assurance of their support. The indignation with which he is said to have scouted this parricide proposition was equally worthy of his virtue and wisdom. The next effort was (on suggestion of the same individuals, in the moment of their separation) the establishment of a hereditary order under the name of the Cincinnati,[3] ready prepared by that distinction to be ingrafted into the future frame of government, and placing General

Washington still at their head. The General ... determined to use all his endeavors for its total suppression. But he found it so firmly riveted in the affections of the members that, strengthened as they happened to be by an adventitious occurrence of the moment, he could effect no more than the abolition of its hereditary principle. ...

The want of some authority which should procure justice to the public creditors, and an observance of treaties with foreign nations, produced, some time after, the call of a convention of the states at Annapolis. Although, at this meeting, a difference of opinion was evident on the question of a republican or kingly government, yet so general through the states was the sentiment in favor of the former that the friends of the latter confined themselves to a course of obstruction only, and delay, to everything proposed; they hoped that nothing being done, and all things going from bad to worse, a kingly government might be usurped and submitted to by the people as better than anarchy and wars internal and external, the certain consequences of the present want of a general government. The effect of their maneuvers, with the defective attendance of deputies from the states, resulted in the measure of calling a more general convention, to be held at Philadelphia. At this, the same party exhibited the same practices, and with the same views of preventing a government of concord, which they foresaw would be republican, and of forcing through anarchy their way to monarchy. But the mass of that convention was too honest, too wise, and too steady to be baffled and misled by their maneuvers. One of these was a form of government proposed by Colonel Hamilton, which would have been in fact a compromise between the two parties of royalism and republicanism. According to this, the executive and one branch of the legislature were to be during good behavior, i.e., for life,

2. Baron Friedrich Wilhelm von Steuben (1730–94), Prussian officer, professional soldier, inspector general of the Continental Army, and Henry Knox (1750–1806), of Boston, major general of the Continental Army and later secretary of war under President Washington.
3. Order of officers of the Continental Army and their eldest male descendants or, if direct male heirs were lacking, collateral descendants.

and the governors of the states were to be named by these two permanent organs. This, however, was rejected; on which Hamilton left the convention, as desperate, and never returned again until near its final conclusion. These opinions and efforts, secret or avowed, of the advocates for monarchy, had begotten great jealousy through the states generally; and this jealousy it was which excited the strong opposition to the conventional constitution; a jealousy which yielded at last only to a general determination to establish certain amendments as barriers against a government either monarchical or consolidated. In what passed through the whole period of these conventions, I have gone on the information of those who were members of them, being absent myself on my mission to France.

I returned from that mission in the first year of the new government, having landed in Virginia in December, 1789, and proceeded to New York in March, 1790, to enter on the office of Secretary of State. Here, certainly, I found a state of things which, of all I had ever contemplated, I the least expected. I had left France in the first year of her revolution, in the fervor of natural rights, and zeal for reformation. My conscientious devotion to these rights could not be heightened, but it had been aroused and excited by daily exercise. The President received me cordially, and my colleagues and the circle of principal citizens apparently with welcome. The courtesies of dinner parties given me, as a stranger newly arrived among them, placed me at once in their familiar society. But I cannot describe the wonder and mortification with which the table conversations filled me. Politics was the chief topic, and a preference of kingly over republican government was evidently the favorite sentiment. An apostate I could not be, nor yet a hypocrite; and I found myself, for the most part, the only advocate on the republi-

can side of the question, unless among the guests there chanced to be some member of that party from the legislative Houses. Hamilton's financial system had then passed. It had two objects; 1st, as a puzzle, to exclude popular understanding and inquiry; 2d, as a machine for the corruption of the legislature; for he avowed the opinion that man could be governed by one of two motives only, force or interest; force, he observed, in this country was out of the question, and the interests, therefore, of the members must be laid hold of, to keep the legislative in unison with the executive. And with grief and shame it must be acknowledged that his machine was not without effect; that even in this, the birth of our government, some members were found sordid enough to bend their duty to their interest, and to look after personal rather than public good.

It is well known that during the war the greatest difficulty we encountered was the want of money or means to pay our soldiers who fought, or our farmers, manufacturers, and merchants who furnished the necessary supplies of food and clothing for them. After the expedient of paper money had exhausted itself, certificates of debt were given to the individual creditors, with assurance of payment so soon as the United States should be able. But the distresses of these people often obliged them to part with these for the half, the fifth, and even a tenth of their value; and speculators had made a trade of cozening them from the holders by the most fraudulent practices, and persuasions that they would never be paid. In the bill for funding and paying these, Hamilton made no difference between the original holders and the fraudulent purchasers of this paper. Great and just repugnance arose at putting these two classes of creditors on the same footing, and great exertions were used to pay the former the full value, and to the latter, the price only which they had paid, with interest. But this would have prevented the game which was to be played, and for which the minds of greedy members were already tutored and prepared. When the trial of strength on these several efforts had indicated the form in which the bill would finally pass, this being known within doors sooner than without, and especially than to those who were in distant parts of the Union, the base scramble began. Couriers and relay horses by land, and swift-sailing pilot boats by sea, were flying in all directions. Active partners and agents were associated and employed in every state, town, and country neighborhood, and this paper was bought up at five shillings, and even as low as two shillings in the pound, before the holder knew that Congress had already provided for its redemption at par. Immense sums were thus filched from the poor and ignorant, and fortunes accumulated by those who had themselves been poor enough before. Men thus enriched by the dexterity of a leader would follow of course the chief who was leading them to fortune and become the zealous instruments of all his enterprises.

This game was over, and another was on the carpet at the moment of my arrival; and to this I was most ignorantly and innocently made to hold the candle. This fiscal maneuver is well known by the name of the Assumption. Independently of the debts of Congress, the states had during the war contracted separate and heavy debts; and Massachusetts particularly, in an absurd attempt, absurdly conducted, on the British post of Penobscott: and the more debt Hamilton could rake up, the more plunder for his mercenaries. This money, whether wisely or foolishly spent, was pretended to have been spent for general purposes, and ought, therefore, to be paid from the general purse. But it was objected that nobody knew what these debts were, what their amount, or what their proofs. No matter; we will

guess them to be twenty millions. But of these twenty millions, we do not know how much should be reimbursed to one state, or how much to another. No matter; we will guess. And so another scramble was set on foot among the several states, and some got much, some little, some nothing. But the main object was obtained, the phalanx of the Treasury was reinforced by additional recruits. This measure produced the most bitter and angry contest ever known in Congress, before or since the Union of the states. I arrived in the midst of it. But a stranger to the ground, a stranger to the actors on it, so long absent as to have lost all familiarity with the subject, and as yet unaware of its object, I took no concern in it. The great and trying question, however, was lost in the House of Representatives. So high were the feuds excited by this subject that on its rejection business was suspended. Congress met and adjourned from day to day without doing anything, the parties being too much out of temper to do business together. The eastern members particularly, who, with Smith from South Carolina,[4] were the principal gamblers in these scenes, threatened a secession and dissolution. Hamilton was in despair. As I was going to the President's one day, I met him in the street. He walked me backward and forward before the President's door for half an hour. He painted pathetically the temper into which the legislature had been wrought; the disgust of those who were called the creditor states; the danger of the *secession* of their members, and the separation of the states. He observed that the members of the administration ought to act in concert; that though this question was not of my department, yet a common duty should make it a common concern; that the President was the

4. "Eastern members" refers to those from New England and, perhaps, New York. William Smith represented South Carolina in Congress (1789–99).

center on which all administrative questions ultimately rested, and that all of us should rally around him, and support, with joint efforts, measures approved by him; and that the question having been lost by a small majority only, it was probable that an appeal from me to the judgment and discretion of some of my friends might effect a change in the vote, and the machine of government, now suspended, might be again set into motion. I told him that I was really a stranger to the whole subject; that, not having yet informed myself of the system of finances adopted, I knew not how far this was a necessary sequence; that undoubtedly, if its rejection endangered a dissolution of our Union at this incipient stage, I should deem that the most unfortunate of all consequences, to avert which all partial and temporary evils should be yielded. I proposed to him, however, to dine with me the next day, and I would invite another friend or two, bring them into conference together, and I thought it impossible that reasonable men, consulting together coolly, could fail, by some mutual sacrifices of opinion, to form a compromise which was to save the Union. The discussion took place. I could take no part in it but an exhortatory one, because I was a stranger to the circumstances which should govern it. But it was finally agreed that, whatever importance had been attached to the rejection of this proposition, the preservation of the Union and of concord among the states was more important, and that therefore it would be better that the vote of rejection should be rescinded, to effect which, some members should change their votes. But it was observed that this pill would be peculiarly bitter to the southern states, and that some concomitant measure should be adopted, to sweeten it a little to them. There had before been propositions to fix the seat of government either at Philadelphia, or at Georgetown on the Potomac; and it was thought that by giving it to Phila-

delphia for ten years, and to Georgetown permanently afterward, this might, as an anodyne, calm in some degree the ferment which might be excited by the other measure alone. So two of the Potomac members (White and Lee, but White with a revulsion of stomach almost convulsive),[5] agreed to change their votes, and Hamilton undertook to carry the other point. In doing this, the influence he had established over the eastern members, with the agency of Robert Morris with those of the middle states,[6] effected his side of the engagement; and so the Assumption was passed, and twenty millions of stock divided among favored states, and thrown in as a pabulum to the stock jobbing herd. This added to the number of votaries to the Treasury, and made its chief the master of every vote in the legislature, which might give to the government the direction suited to his political views.

I know well, and so must be understood, that nothing like a majority in Congress had yielded to this corruption. Far from it. But a division, not very unequal, had already taken place in the honest part of that body, between the parties styled republican and federal. The latter being monarchists in principle, adhered to Hamilton of course, as their leader in that principle, and this mercenary phalanx, added to them, insured him always a majority in both Houses: so that the whole action of legislature was now under the direction of the Treasury. Still the machine was not complete. The effect of the funding system, and of the Assumption, would be temporary; it would be lost with the loss of the individual members whom it has enriched, and some engine of influence more permanent must be contrived, while these myrmidons were yet in

5. Alexander White (1738–1804), and Richard Bland Lee (1761–1827), uncle of Robert E. Lee.

6. Robert Morris (1734–1806), financier of the American Revolution, member of the Federal Convention of 1787, prominent American businessman and land speculator.

place to carry it through all opposition. This engine was the Bank of the United States. All that history is known, so I shall say nothing about it. While the government remained at Philadelphia, a selection of members of both Houses were constantly kept as directors who, on every question interesting to that institution, or to the views of the federal head, voted at the will of that head; and, together with the stockholding members, could always make the federal vote that of the majority. By this combination, legislative expositions were given to the constitution, and all the administrative laws were shaped on the model of England, and so passed. And from this influence we were not relieved, until the removal from the precincts of the bank, to Washington.[7]

Here then was the real ground of the opposition which was made to the course of administration. Its object was to preserve the legislature pure and independent of the executive, to restrain the administration to republican forms and principles, and not permit the Constitution to be construed into a monarchy, and to be warped, in practice, into all the principles and pollutions of their favorite English model. Nor was this an opposition to General Washington. He was true to the republican charge confided to him; and has solemnly and repeatedly protested to me, in our conversations, that he would lose the last drop of his blood in support of it; and he did this the oftener and with the more earnestness, because he knew my suspicions of Hamilton's designs against it, and wished to quiet them. For he was not aware of the drift or of the effect of Hamilton's schemes. Unversed in financial projects and calculations and budgets, his approbation of them was bottomed on his confidence in the man.

But Hamilton was not only a monarchist, but for a monarchy bottomed on corruption. In proof of this, I will relate an anecdote, for the truth of which

7. In 1800.

I attest the God who made me. Before the President set out on his southern tour in April, 1791, he addressed a letter of the fourth of that month, from Mount Vernon, to the Secretaries of State, Treasury, and War, desiring that if any serious and important cases should arise during his absence, they would consult and act on them. And he requested that the Vice-President should also be consulted. This was the only occasion on which that officer was ever requested to take part in a cabinet question. Some occasion for consultation arising, I invited those gentlemen (and the Attorney-General, as well as I remember) to dine with me, in order to confer on the subject. After the cloth was removed, and our question agreed and dismissed, conversation began on other matters and, by some circumstance, was led to the British constitution, on which Mr. Adams observed, "Purge that constitution of its corruption, and give to its popular branch equality of representation, and it would be the most perfect constitution ever devised by the wit of man." Hamilton paused and said, "Purge it of its corruption, and give to its popular branch equality of representation, and it would become an *impracticable* government: as it stands at present, with all its supposed defects, it is the most perfect government which ever existed." And this was assuredly the exact line which separated the political creeds of these two gentlemen. The one was for two hereditary branches and an honest elective one; the other, for a hereditary king, with a House of Lords and Commons corrupted to his will, and standing between him and the people. Hamilton was, indeed, a singular character. Of acute understanding, disinterested, honest, and honorable in all private transactions, amiable in society, and duly valuing virtue in private life, yet so bewitched and perverted by the British example as to be under thorough conviction that corruption was essential to the government of a nation....

3. REPORT ON MANUFACTURES, DECEMBER, 1791[1]

By ALEXANDER HAMILTON

The Secretary of the Treasury, in obedience to the order of the House of Representatives, of the 15th day of January, 1790, has applied his attention, at as early a period as his other duties would permit, to the subject of manufactures; and particularly to the means of promoting such as will tend to render the United States independent of foreign nations for military and other essential supplies; and he thereupon respectfully submits the following report:

The expediency of encouraging manufactures in the United States, which was not long since deemed very questionable, appears at this time to be pretty generally admitted. The embarrassments which have obstructed the progress of our external trade have led to serious reflections on the necessity of enlarging the sphere of our domestic commerce. The restrictive regulations, which, in foreign markets, abridge the vent of the increasing surplus of our agricultural produce, serve to beget an earnest desire that a more extensive demand for that surplus may be created at home; and the complete success which has rewarded manufacturing enterprise, in some valuable branches, conspiring with the promising symptoms which attend some less mature essays in others, justify a hope that the obstacles to the growth of this species of industry are less formidable than they were apprehended to be; and that it is not difficult to find, in its further extension, a full indemnification for any external disadvantages which are or may be experienced, as well as an accession of resources, favorable to national independence and safety.

There still are, nevertheless, respectable patrons of opinions unfriendly to the encouragement of manufactures. The following are, substantially, the arguments by which these opinions are defended.

"In every country (say those who entertain them), agriculture is the most beneficial and productive object of human industry. This position, generally, if not universally true, applies with peculiar emphasis to the United States, on account of their immense tracts of fertile territory uninhabited and unimproved. Nothing can afford so advantageous an employment for capital and labor as the conversion of this extensive wilderness into cultivated farms. Nothing, equally with this, can contribute to the population, strength, and real riches of the country.

"To endeavor, by the extraordinary patronage of government, to accelerate the growth of manufactures is, in fact, to endeavor by force and art to transfer the natural current of industry from a more to a less beneficial channel. Whatever has such a tendency must necessarily be unwise; indeed, it can hardly ever be wise in a government to attempt to give a direction to the industry of its citizens. This, under the quick-sighted guidance of private interest, will, if left to itself, infallibly find its own way to the most profitable employment; and it is by such employment that the public prosperity will be most effectually promoted. To leave industry to itself, therefore, is, in almost every case, the soundest as well as the simplest policy.

"This policy is not only recommended to the United States by considerations which affect all nations; it is, in a manner, dictated to them by the imperious force of a very peculiar situation. The smallness of their population, compared with their territory; the constant allurements to emigration from the settled to the unsettled parts of the country; the facility with which the less independent

1. *Reports of the Secretary of the Treasury of the United States* (Washington, 1837), I, 78–82, 83, 85, 86–92, 104, 105, 106, 107, 108, 109, 110, 113, 114, 115, 117–18, 119, 130–32.

condition of an artisan can be exchanged for the more independent condition of a farmer: these, and similar causes, conspire to produce, and for a length of time must continue to occasion, a scarcity of hands for manufacturing occupation, and dearness of labor generally. To these disadvantages for the prosecution of manufactures, a deficiency of pecuniary capital being added, the prospect of a successful competition with the manufactures of Europe must be regarded as little less than desperate. Extensive manufactures can only be the offspring of a redundant—at least of a full population. Till the latter shall characterize the situation of this country, it is vain to hope for the former.

"If, contrary to the natural course of things, an unseasonable and premature spring can be given to certain fabrics, by heavy duties, prohibitions, bounties, or by other forced expedients, this will only be to sacrifice the interests of the community to those of particular classes. Besides the misdirection of labor, a virtual monopoly will be given to the persons employed on such fabrics; and an enhancement of price, the inevitable consequence of every monopoly, must be defrayed at the expense of the other parts of the society. It is far preferable that those persons should be engaged in the cultivation of the earth; and that we should procure, in exchange for its productions, the commodities with which foreigners are able to supply us in greater perfection, and upon better terms."

This mode of reasoning is founded upon facts and principles which have certainly respectable pretensions. If it had governed the conduct of nations more generally than it has done, there is room to suppose that it might have carried them faster to prosperity and greatness than they have attained by the pursuit of maxims too widely opposite. Most general theories, however, admit of numerous exceptions; and there are few, if any, of the political kind, which

do not blend a considerable portion of error with the truths they inculcate.

I. In order to form an accurate judgment how far that which has been just stated ought to be deemed liable to a similar imputation, it is necessary to advert carefully to the considerations which plead in favor of manufactures, and which appear to recommend the special and positive encouragement of them in certain cases, and under certain reasonable limitations.

It ought readily to be conceded that the cultivation of the earth, as the primary and most certain source of national supply, as the immediate and chief source of subsistence to man, as the principal source of those materials which constitute the nutriment of other kinds of labor, as including a state most favorable to the freedom and independence of the human mind—one, perhaps, most conducive to the multiplication of the human species—has intrinsically a strong claim to pre-eminence over every other kind of industry. But that it has a title to anything like an exclusive predilection, in any country, ought to be admitted with great caution; that it is even more productive than every other branch of industry requires more evidence than has yet been given in support of the position. That its real interests, precious and important as (without the help of exaggeration) they truly are, will be advanced, rather than injured, by the due encouragement of manufactures, may, it is believed, be satisfactorily demonstrated. And it is also believed that the expediency of such encouragement, in a general view, may be shown to be recommended by the most cogent and persuasive motives of national policy.

It has been maintained that agriculture is not only the most productive but the only productive species of industry. The reality of this suggestion, in either respect, has, however, not been verified by any accurate detail of facts and calculations; and the general arguments which are adduced to prove it are rather subtle and paradoxical than solid or convincing.

Those which maintain its exclusive productiveness are to this effect:

Labor bestowed upon the cultivation of land produces enough not only to replace all the necessary expenses incurred in the business, and to maintain the persons who are employed in it, but to afford, together with the ordinary profit on the stock or capital of the farmer, a net surplus or rent for the landlord or proprietor of the soil. But the labor of artificers does nothing more than replace the stock which employs them (or which furnished materials, tools, and wages), and yield the ordinary profit upon that stock. It yields nothing equivalent to the rent of the land; neither does it add anything to the total value of the whole annual produce of the land and labor of the country. The additional value given to those parts of the produce of land which are wrought into manufactures is counterbalanced by the value of those other parts of that produce which are consumed by the manufacturers. It can, therefore, only be by saving or parsimony, not by the positive productiveness of their labor, that the classes of artificers can, in any degree, augment the revenue of the society.

To this it has been answered—

1. "That inasmuch as it is acknowledged that manufacturing labor reproduces a value equal to that which is expended or consumed in carrying it on, and continues in existence the original stock or capital employed, it ought, on that account alone, to escape being considered as wholly unproductive. That though it should be admitted, as alleged, that the consumption of the produce of the soil, by the classes of artificers or manufacturers, is exactly equal to the value added by their labor to the materials upon which it is exerted, yet it would not thence follow that it added nothing to the revenue of the society or to the aggregate value of the annual produce of its land and labor. If the consumption for any given period amounted to a given sum, and the increased value of the produce manufactured, in the same period, to a like sum, the total amount of the consumption and production, during that period, would be equal to the two sums, and consequently double the value of the agricultural produce consumed; and though the increment of value produced by the classes of artificers should, at no time, exceed the value of the produce of the land consumed by them, yet there would be, at every moment, in consequence of their labor, a greater value of goods in the market than would exist independent of it."

2. "That the position, that artificers can augment the revenue of a society only by parsimony, is true in no other sense than in one which is equally applicable to husbandmen or cultivators. It may be alike affirmed of all these classes that the fund acquired by their labor, and destined for their support, is not, in an ordinary way, more than equal to it. And hence it will follow that augmentation of the wealth or capital of the community (except in the instances of some extraordinary dexterity or skill), can only proceed, with respect to any of them, from the savings of the more thrifty and parsimonious."

3. "That the annual produce of the land and labor of a country can only be increased in two ways—by some improvement in the productive powers of the useful labor which actually exists within it, or by some increase in the quantity of such labor. That, with regard to the first, the labor of artificers being capable of greater subdivision and simplicity of operation than that of cultivators, it is susceptible, in a proportionably greater degree, of improvement in its productive powers, whether to be derived from an accession of skill or

from the application of ingenious machinery: in which particular, therefore, the labor employed in the culture of land can pretend to no advantage over that engaged in manufactures. That, with regard to an augmentation of the quantity of useful labor, this, excluding adventitious circumstances, must depend essentially upon an increase of capital, which again must depend upon the savings made out of the revenues of those who furnish or manage that which is at any time employed, whether in agriculture or in manufactures, or in any other way."

But while the exclusive productiveness of agricultural labor has been thus denied and refuted, the superiority of its productiveness has been conceded without hesitation. As this concession involves a point of considerable magnitude, in relation to maxims of public administration, the grounds on which it rests are worthy of a distinct and particular examination.

One of the arguments made use of in support of the idea may be pronounced both quaint and superficial: it amounts to this—That in the productions of the soil, nature co-operates with man; and that the effect of their joint labor must be greater than that of the labor of man alone.

This, however, is far from being a necessary inference. It is very conceivable that the labor of man alone, laid out upon a work requiring great skill and art to bring it to perfection, may be more productive, in value, than the labor of nature and man combined, when directed toward more simple operations and objects; and when it is recollected to what an extent the agency of nature, in the application of the mechanical powers, is made auxiliary to the prosecution of manufactures, the suggestion which has been noticed loses even the appearance of plausibility.

It might also be observed, with a contrary view, that the labor employed in agriculture is, in a great measure, periodical and occasional, depending on seasons, and liable to various and long intermissions; while that occupied in many manufactures is constant and regular, extending through the year, embracing, in some instances, night as well as day. It is also probable that there are among the cultivators of land more examples of remissness than among artificers. The farmer, from the peculiar fertility of his land, or some other favorable circumstance, may frequently obtain a livelihood, even with a considerable degree of carelessness in the mode of cultivation; but the artisan can with difficulty effect the same object, without exerting himself pretty equally with all those who are engaged in the same pursuit. And if it may likewise be assumed as a fact that manufactures open a wider field to exertions of ingenuity than agriculture, it would not be a strained conjecture that the labor employed in the former, being at once more constant, more uniform, and more ingenious, that that which is employed in the latter, will be found, at the same time, more productive.

But it is not meant to lay stress on observations of this nature; they ought only to serve as a counterbalance to those of a similar complexion. Circumstances so vague and general, as well as so abstract, can afford little instruction in a matter of this kind. . . .

It is extremely probable that on a full and accurate development of the matter, on the ground of fact and calculation, it would be discovered that there is no material difference between the aggregate productiveness of the one and of the other kind of industry; and that the propriety of the encouragements which may, in any case, be proposed to be given to either, ought to be determined upon considerations irrelative to any comparison of that nature.

II. But, without contending for the superior productiveness of manufacturing industry, it may conduce to a better judgment of the policy which ought to be pursued ... to evince ... that the establishment and diffusion of manufactures have the effect of rendering the total mass of useful and productive labor in a community greater than it would otherwise be....

It is now proper to proceed a step further and to enumerate the principal circumstances, from which it may be inferred that manufacturing establishments not only occasion a positive augmentation of the produce and revenue of the society but that they contribute essentially to rendering them greater than they could possibly be without such establishments. These circumstances are—

1. The division of labor.
2. An extension of the use of machinery.
3. Additional employment to classes of the community not ordinarily engaged in the business.
4. The promoting of emigration from foreign countries.
5. The furnishing greater scope for the diversity of talents and dispositions, which discriminate men from each other.
6. The affording a more ample and various field for enterprise.
7. The creating, in some instances, a new, and securing, in all, a more certain and steady demand for the surplus produce of the soil.

Each of these circumstances has a considerable influence upon the total mass of industrious effort in a community; together, they add to it a degree of energy and effect which is not easily conceived. Some comments upon each of them, in the order in which they have been stated, may serve to explain their importance.

1. AS TO THE DIVISION OF LABOR

It has justly been observed that there is scarcely anything of greater moment in the economy of a nation than the proper division of labor. The separation of occupations causes each to be carried to a much greater perfection than it could possibly acquire if they were blended. This arises principally from three circumstances.

1st. The greater skill and dexterity naturally resulting from a constant and undivided application to a single object....

2d. The economy of time, by avoiding the loss of it, incident to a frequent transition from one operation to another of a different nature....

3d. An extension of the use of machinery. A man occupied on a single object will have it more in his power, and will be more naturally led to exert his imagination in devising methods to facilitate and abridge labor, than if he were perplexed by a variety of independent and dissimilar operations. Besides this, the fabrication of machines, in numerous instances, becoming itself a distinct trade, the artist who follows it has all the advantages which have been enumerated for improvement in his particular art; and, in both ways, the invention and application of machinery are extended.

And, from these causes united, the mere separation of the occupation of the cultivator from that of the artificer, has the effect of augmenting the productive powers of labor, and, with them, the total mass of the produce or revenue of a country. In this single view of the subject, therefore, the utility of artificers or manufacturers, toward promoting an increase of productive industry, is apparent.

2. AS TO AN EXTENSION OF THE USE OF MACHINERY; A POINT WHICH, THOUGH PARTLY ANTICIPATED, REQUIRES TO BE PLACED IN ONE OR TWO ADDITIONAL LIGHTS

The employment of machinery forms an item of great importance in the general mass of national industry. It is an artificial force brought in aid of the natural force of man; and, to all the purposes of labor, is an increase of hands—an accession of strength, unencumbered, too, by the expense of maintaining the laborer. May it not, therefore, be fairly inferred that those occupations which give greatest scope to the use of this auxiliary contribute most to the general stock of industrious effort and, in consequence, to the general product of industry?

It shall be taken for granted (and the truth of the position referred to observation) that manufacturing pursuits are susceptible, in a greater degree, of the application of machinery than those of agriculture. If so, all the difference is lost to a community which, instead of manufacturing for itself, procures the fabrics requisite to its supply from other countries. The substitution of foreign for domestic manufactures is a transfer to foreign nations of the advantages accruing from the employment of machinery, in the modes in which it is capable of being employed with most utility and to the greatest extent.

The cotton mill, invented in England within the last twenty years, is a signal illustration of the general proposition which has just been advanced. In consequence of it, all the different processes for spinning cotton are performed by means of machines which are put in motion by water, and attended chiefly by women and children; and by a smaller number of persons, in the whole, than are requisite in the ordinary mode of spinning. And it is an advantage of great moment that the operations of this mill continue, with convenience, during the night as well as through the day. The prodigious effect of such a machine is easily conceived. To this invention is to be attributed, essentially, the immense progress which has been so suddenly made in Great Britain in the various fabrics of cotton.

3. AS TO THE ADDITIONAL EMPLOYMENT OF CLASSES OF THE COMMUNITY NOT ORIGINALLY ENGAGED IN THE PARTICULAR BUSINESS

This is not among the least valuable of the means by which manufacturing institutions contribute to augment the general stock of industry and production. In places where those institutions prevail, besides the persons regularly engaged in them, they afford occasional and extra employment to industrious individuals and families who are willing to devote the leisure resulting from the intermissions of their ordinary pursuits to collateral labors, as a resource for multiplying their acquisitions or their enjoyments. The husbandman himself experiences a new source of profit and support from the increased industry of his wife and daughters, invited and stimulated by the demands of the neighboring manufactories.

Besides this advantage of occasional employment to classes having different occupations, there is another, of a nature allied to it, and of a similar tendency. This is the employment of persons who would otherwise be idle and, in many cases, a burden on the community, either from the bias of temper, habit, infirmity of body, or some other cause, indisposing or disqualifying them for the toils of the country. It is worthy of particular remark that, in general, women and children are rendered more useful, and the latter more early useful, by manufacturing establishments, than they would otherwise be. Of the number of persons employed in the cotton manufactories of Great Britain, it is computed that four-sevenths, nearly, are women and children; of whom the greatest proportion are children, and many of them of a tender age.

And thus it appears to be one of the attributes of manufactures, and one of no small consequence, to give occasion to the exertion of a greater quantity of industry, even by the same number of persons, where they happen to prevail, than would exist if there were no such establishments.

4. AS TO THE PROMOTING OF EMIGRATION FROM FOREIGN COUNTRIES

Men reluctantly quit one course of occupation and livelihood for another, unless invited to it by very apparent and proximate advantages. Many who would go from one country to another, if they had a prospect of continuing with more benefit the callings to which they have been educated, will often not be tempted to change their situation by the hope of doing better in some other way. Manufacturers who, listening to the powerful invitations of a better price for their fabrics or their labor; of greater cheapness of provisions and raw materials; of an exemption from the chief part of the taxes, burdens, and restraints which they endure in the Old World; of greater personal independence and consequence, under the operation of a more equal government; and of what is far more precious than mere religious toleration— a perfect equality of religious privileges—would probably flock from Europe to the United States, to pursue their own trades or professions, if they were once made sensible of the advantages they would enjoy, and were inspired with an assurance of encouragement and employment, will with difficulty be induced to transplant themselves, with a view to becoming cultivators of land.

If it be true, then, that it is the interest of the United States to open every possible avenue to emigration from abroad, it affords a weighty argument for the encouragement of manufactures; which, for the reasons just assigned, will have the strongest tendency to multiply the inducements to it.

Here is perceived an important resource, not only for extending the population, and, with it, the useful and productive labor of the country, but likewise for the prosecution of manufactures, without deducting from the number of hands which might otherwise be drawn to tillage; and even for the indemnification of agriculture, for such as might happen to be diverted from it. Many, whom manufacturing views would induce to emigrate, would afterward yield to the temptations which the particular situation of this country holds out to agricultural pursuits; and while agriculture would, in other respects, derive many signal and unmingled advantages from the growth of manufactures, it is a problem whether it would gain or lose, as to the article of the number of persons employed in carrying it on.

5. AS TO THE FURNISHING GREATER SCOPE FOR THE DIVERSITY OF TALENTS AND DISPOSITIONS, WHICH DISCRIMINATE MEN FROM EACH OTHER

This is a much more powerful mean of augmenting the fund of national industry than may at first sight appear. It is a just observation that minds of the strongest and most active powers for their proper objects fall below mediocrity, and labor without effect, if confined to uncongenial pursuits; and it is thence to be inferred that the results of human exertion may be immensely increased by diversifying its objects. When all the different kinds of industry obtain in a community, each individual can find his proper element and can call into activity the whole vigor of his nature; and the community is benefited by the services of its respective members, in the manner in which each can serve it with most effect.

If there be anything in a remark often to be met with, namely, that there is, in the genius of the people of this country, a peculiar aptitude for mechanic improvements, it would operate as a forcible reason for giving opportunities to the exercise of that species of talent, by the propagation of manufactures.

6. AS TO THE AFFORDING A MORE AMPLE AND VARIOUS FIELD FOR ENTERPRISE

This also is of greater consequence in the general scale of national exertion than might perhaps, on a superficial view, be supposed, and has effects not altogether dissimilar from those of the circumstance last noticed. To cherish and stimulate the activity of the human mind, by multiplying the objects of enterprise, is not among the least considerable of the expedients by which the wealth of a nation may be promoted. Even things in themselves not positively advantageous sometimes become so by their tendency to provoke exertion. Every new scene which is opened to the busy nature of man to rouse and exert itself is the addition of a new energy to the general stock of effort.

The spirit of enterprise, useful and prolific as it is, must necessarily be contracted or expanded, in proportion to the simplicity or variety of the occupations and productions which are to be found in a society. It must be less in a nation of mere cultivators than in a nation of cultivators and merchants; less in a nation of cultivators and merchants than in a nation of cultivators, artificers, and merchants.

7. AS TO THE CREATING, IN SOME INSTANCES, A NEW, AND SECURING, IN ALL, A MORE CERTAIN AND STEADY DEMAND FOR THE SURPLUS PRODUCE OF THE SOIL

This is among the most important of the circumstances which have been indicated. It is a principal mean by which the establishment of manufactures contributes to an augmentation of the produce or revenue of a country and has an immediate and direct relation to the prosperity of agriculture.

It is evident that the exertions of the husbandman will be steady or fluctuating, vigorous or feeble, in proportion to the steadiness or fluctuation, adequateness or inadequateness, of the markets on which he must depend for the vent of the surplus which may be produced by his labor; and that such surplus, in the ordinary course of things, will be greater or less in the same proportion.

For the purpose of this vent, a domestic market is greatly to be preferred to a foreign one; because it is, in the nature of things, far more to be relied upon.

It is a primary object of the policy of nations to be able to supply themselves with subsistence from their own soils; and manufacturing nations, as far as circumstances permit, endeavor to procure from the same source the raw materials necessary for their own fabrics. This disposition, urged by the spirit of monopoly, is sometimes even carried to an injudicious extreme. It seems not always to be recollected that nations who have neither mines nor manufactures can only obtain the manufactured articles of which they stand in need by an exchange of the products of their soils; and that, if those who can best furnish them with such articles are unwilling to give a due course to this exchange, they must, of necessity, make every possible effort to manufacture for themselves; the effect of which is that the manufacturing nations abridge the natural advantages of their situation, through an unwillingness to permit the agricultural countries to enjoy the advantages of theirs, and sacrifice the interests of a mutually beneficial intercourse to the vain project of selling everything and buying nothing.

But it is also a consequence of the policy which has been noted that the foreign demands for the products of agricultural countries is, in a great degree, rather casual and occasional than certain or constant. To what extent injurious interruptions of the demand for some of the staple commodities of the United States may have been experienced from that cause must be referred to the judgment of those who are engaged in carrying on the commerce of the country; but it may be safely affirmed that such interruptions are, at times, very inconveniently felt, and that cases not unfrequently occur in which markets are so confined and restricted as to render the demand very unequal to the supply.

Independently, likewise, of the artificial impediments which are created by the policy in question, there are natural causes tending to render the external demand for the surplus of agricultural nations a precarious reliance. The differences of seasons in the countries which are the consumers make immense differences in the produce of their own soils in different years and, consequently, in the degrees of their necessity for foreign supply. Plentiful harvests with them, especially if similar ones occur at the same time in the countries which are the furnishers, occasion, of course, a glut in the markets of the latter.

Considering how fast and how much the progress of new settlements in the United States must increase the surplus produce of the soil, and weighing seriously the tendency of the system which prevails among most of the commercial nations of Europe; whatever dependence may be placed on the force of natural circumstances to counteract the effects of an artificial policy, there appear strong reasons to regard the foreign demand for that surplus as too uncertain a reliance and to desire a substitute for it in an extensive domestic market.

To secure such a market there is no other expedient than to promote manufacturing establishments. Manufacturers, who constitute the most numerous class, after the cultivators of land, are for that reason the principal consumers of the surplus of their labor.

This idea of an extensive domestic market for the surplus produce of the soil is of the first consequence. It is, of all things, that which most effectually conduces to a flourishing state of agriculture. If the effect of manufactories

should be to detach a portion of the hands which would otherwise be engaged in tillage, it might possibly cause a smaller quantity of lands to be under cultivation; but by their tendency to procure a more certain demand for the surplus produce of the soil, they would, at the same time, cause the lands which were in cultivation to be better improved and more productive. And while, by their influence, the condition of each individual farmer would be meliorated, the total mass of agricultural production would probably be increased; for this must evidently depend as much upon the degree of improvement, if not more, than upon the number of acres under culture.

It merits particular observation that the multiplication of manufactories not only furnishes a market for those articles which have been accustomed to be produced in abundance in a country, but it likewise creates a demand for such as were either unknown, or produced in inconsiderable quantities. The bowels, as well as the surface of the earth, are ransacked for articles which were before neglected. Animals, plants, and minerals acquire a utility and value which were before unexplored.

The foregoing considerations seem sufficient to establish, as general propositions, that it is the interest of nations to diversify the industrious pursuits of the individuals who compose them; that the establishment of manufactures is calculated not only to increase the general stock of useful and productive labor but even to improve the state of agriculture in particular; certainly to advance the interests of those who are engaged in it. There are other views that will be hereafter taken of the subject, which it is conceived will serve to confirm these inferences.

III. Previously to a further discussion of the objections to the encouragement of manufactures, which have been stated, it will be of use to see what can be said in reference to the particular situation of the United States, against the conclusions appearing to result from what has been already offered.

It may be observed (and the idea is of no inconsiderable weight) that, however true it might be, a state which, possessing large tracts of vacant and fertile territory, was, at the same time, secluded from foreign commerce would find its interest and the interest of agriculture in diverting a part of its population from tillage to manufactures; yet it will not follow that the same is true of a state which, having such vacant and fertile territory, has, at the same time, ample opportunity of procuring from abroad, on good terms, all the fabrics of which it stands in need, for the supply of its inhabitants. The power of doing this at least secures the great advantage of a division of labor, leaving the farmer free to pursue, exclusively, the culture of his land, and enabling him to procure with its products the manufactured supplies requisite either to his wants or to his enjoyments. And though it should be true that, in settled countries, the diversification of industry is conducive to an increase in the productive powers of labor, and to an augmentation of revenue and capital; yet it is scarcely conceivable that there can be anything of so solid and permanent advantage to an uncultivated and unpeopled country as to convert its wastes into cultivated and inhabited districts. If the revenue, in the meantime, should be less, the capital, in the event, must be greater.

To these observations, the following appears to be a satisfactory answer—

1st. If the system of perfect liberty to industry and commerce were the prevailing system of nations, the arguments which dissuade a country in the predicament of the United States from the zealous pursuits of manufactures would doubtless have great force. . . . If one nation were in a condition to supply manufactured articles on better terms than another, that other might find an abundant indemnification in a superior capacity to furnish the produce of the soil. . . .

But the system which has been mentioned is far from characterizing the general policy of nations. The prevalent one has been regulated by an opposite spirit. The consequence of it is that the United States are, to a certain extent, in the situation of a country precluded from foreign commerce. They can, indeed, without difficulty, obtain from abroad the manufactured supplies of which they are in want; but they experience numerous and very injurious impediments to the emission and vent of their own commodities. . . .

If Europe will not take from us the products of our soil, upon terms consistent with our interest, the natural remedy is to contract, as fast as possible, our wants of her.

2d. The conversion of their waste into cultivated lands is certainly a point of great moment in the political calculations of the United States. . . .

But it does by no means follow that the progress of new settlements would be retarded by the extension of manufactures. The desire of being an independent proprietor of land is founded on such strong principles in the human breast that, where the opportunity of becoming so is as great as it is in the United States, the proportion will be small of those whose situations would otherwise lead to it who would be diverted from it toward manufactures. And it is highly probable, as already intimated, that the accessions of foreigners, who, originally drawn over by manufacturing views, would afterward abandon them for agricultural, would be more than an equivalent for those of our own citizens who might happen to be detached from them.

The remaining objections to a particular encouragement of manufactures in the United States now require to be examined.

One of these turns on the proposition

that industry, if left to itself, will naturally find its way to the most useful and profitable employment. Whence it is inferred that manufactures, without the aid of government, will grow up as soon and as fast as the natural state of things and the interest of the community may require.

Against the solidity of this hypothesis, in the full latitude of the terms, very cogent reasons may be offered. These have relation to the strong influence of habit and the spirit of imitation; the fear of want of success in untried enterprises; the intrinsic difficulties incident to first essays toward a competition with those who have previously attained to perfection in the business to be attempted; the bounties, premiums, and other artificial encouragements, with which foreign nations second the exertions of their own citizens, in the branches in which they are to be rivaled....

The objections which are commonly made to the expediency of encouraging, and to the probability of succeeding in, manufacturing pursuits in the United States, having now been discussed, the considerations ... recommending that species of industry to the patronage of the government will be materially strengthened by a few general and some particular topics....

1. There seems to be a moral certainty that the trade of a country which is both manufacturing and agricultural will be more lucrative and prosperous than that of a country which is merely agricultural....

... Two important inferences are to be drawn: one, that there is always a higher probability of a favorable balance of trade, in regard to countries in which manufactures founded on the basis of a thriving agriculture flourish, than in regard to those which are confined wholly, or almost wholly, to agriculture; the other (which is also a consequence of the first) that countries of the former description are likely to possess more pecuniary wealth, or money, than those of the latter....

Previous to the Revolution, the quantity of coin possessed by the colonies which now compose the United States appeared to be inadequate to their circulation; and their debt to Great Britain was progressive. Since the Revolution, the states in which manufactures have most increased have recovered fastest from the injuries of the late war and abound most in pecuniary resources....

Not only the wealth, but the independence and security of a country, appear to be materially connected with the prosperity of manufactures. Every nation, with a view to those great objects, ought to endeavor to possess within itself all the essentials of national supply. These comprise the means of subsistence, habitation, clothing, and defense....

To these general considerations are added some of a more particular nature....

It is not uncommon to meet with an opinion that, though the promoting of manufactures may be the interest of a part of the Union, it is contrary to that of another part. The northern and southern regions are sometimes represented as having adverse interests in this respect. Those are called manufacturing, these agricultural states; and a species of opposition is imagined to subsist between the manufacturing and agricultural interests.

This idea of an opposition between those two interests is the common error of the early periods of every country; but experience gradually dissipates it. Indeed, they are perceived so often to succor and to befriend each other that they come at length to be considered as one, a supposition which has been frequently abused and is not universally true. Particular encouragements of particular manufactures may be of a nature to sacrifice the interests of landholders to those of manufacturers; but it is nevertheless a maxim, well established by experience, and generally acknowledged, where there has been sufficient experience, that the aggregate prosperity of manufactures and the aggregate prosperity of agriculture are intimately connected. In the course of the discussion which has had place, various weighty considerations have been adduced, operating in support of that maxim. Perhaps the superior steadiness of the demand of a domestic market, for the surplus produce of the soil, is, alone, a convincing argument of its truth....

The extensive cultivation of cotton can, perhaps, hardly be expected, but from the previous establishment of domestic manufactories of the article; and the surest encouragement and vent for the others would result from similar establishments in respect to them....

A full view having now been taken of the inducements to the promotion of manufactures in the United States, accompanied with an examination of the principal objections which are commonly urged in opposition, it is proper, in the next place, to consider the means by which it may be effected....

In order to a better judgment of the means proper to be resorted to by the United States, it will be of use to advert to those which have been employed with success in other countries. The principal of these are:

1. Protecting duties, or duties on those foreign articles which are the rivals of the domestic ones intended to be encouraged....

2. Prohibitions of rival articles, or duties equivalent to prohibitions....

3. Prohibitions of the exportation of the materials of manufacture....

4. Pecuniary bounties....

5. Premiums....

6. The exemption of the materials of manufactures from duty....

7. Drawbacks of the duties which are imposed on the materials of manufactures....

8. The encouragement of new inventions and discoveries at home, and of the introduction into the United States of such as may have been made in other countries; particularly those which relate to machinery....

9. Judicious regulations for the inspection of manufactured commodities....

10. The facilitating of pecuniary remittances from place to place....

11. The facilitating of the transportation of commodities....

The great copiousness of the subject of this report has insensibly led to a more lengthy preliminary discussion than was originally contemplated or intended. It appeared proper to investigate principles, to consider objections, and to endeavor to establish the utility of the thing proposed to be encouraged, previous to a specification of the objects which might occur, as meriting or requiring encouragement, and of the measures which might be proper in respect to each. The first purpose having been fulfilled, it remains to pursue the second.

In the selection of objects, five circumstances seem entitled to particular attention: the capacity of the country to furnish the raw material; the degree in which the nature of the manufacture admits of a substitute for manual labor in machinery; the facility of execution; the extensiveness of the uses to which the article can be applied; its subserviency to other interests, particularly the great one of national defense. There are, however, objects to which these circumstances are little applicable, which, for some special reasons, may have a claim to encouragement.

A designation of the principal raw material of which each manufacture is composed will serve to introduce the remarks upon it; as, in the first place,

IRON

... The average price, before the Revolution, was about sixty-four dollars per ton; at present, it is about eighty; a rise which is chiefly to be attributed to the increase of manufactures of the material. ...

The United States already, in a great measure, supply themselves with nails and spikes. They are able, and ought certainly to do it entirely. The first and most laborious operation, in this manufacture, is performed by water mills; and of the persons afterward employed, a great proportion are boys, whose early habits of industry are of importance to the community, to the present support of their families, and to their own future comfort. It is not less curious than true that in certain parts of the country the making of nails is an occasional family manufacture.

The expediency of an additional duty on these articles is indicated by an important fact. About 1,800,000 pounds of them were imported into the United States in the course of a year ending the 30th of September, 1790. A duty of two cents per pound would, it is presumable, speedily put an end to so considerable an importation; and it is, in every view, proper that an end should be put to it. ... [Here other commodities such as copper, lead, coal, wood, skins, grain, flax, hemp, cotton, wool, silk, glass, gunpowder, printed books, and refined sugars and chocolate are discussed.]

The foregoing heads comprise the most important of the several kinds of manufactures which have occurred as requiring, and, at the same time, as most proper for public encouragement; and such measures for affording it, as have appeared best calculated to answer the end, have been suggested.

The observations which have accompanied this delineation of objects supersede the necessity of many supplementary remarks. One or two, however, may not be altogether superfluous.

Bounties are, in various instances, proposed as one species of encouragement.[2]

It is a familiar objection to them that

they are difficult to be managed and liable to frauds; but neither that difficulty nor this danger seems sufficiently great to countervail the advantages of which they are productive, when rightly applied; and it is presumed to have been shown that they are, in some cases, particularly in the infancy of new enterprises, indispensable.

It will, however, be necessary to guard, with extraordinary circumspection, the manner of dispensing them. The requisite precautions have been thought of; but to enter into the detail would swell this report, already voluminous, to a size too inconvenient.

If the principle shall not be deemed inadmissible, the means of avoiding an abuse of it will not be likely to present insurmountable obstacles. There are useful guides from practice in other quarters.

It shall, therefore, only be remarked here, in relation to this point, that any bounty which may be applied to the manufacture of an article, cannot, with safety, extend beyond those manufactories at which the making of the article is a regular trade. It would be impossible to annex adequate precautions to a benefit of that nature, if extended to every private family in which the manufacture was incidentally carried on; and its being a merely incidental occupation which engages a portion of time that would otherwise be lost, it can be advantageously carried on without so special an aid.

The possibility of a diminution of the revenue may also present itself as an objection to the arrangements which have been submitted.

But there is no truth which may be more firmly relied upon than that the interests of the revenue are promoted by whatever promotes an increase of national industry and wealth.

In proportion to the degree of these is the capacity of every country to contribute to the public treasury; and where the capacity to pay is increased, or even

---

2. In the preceding pages he urged that protective duties be levied on specific manufactured goods.

is not decreased, the only consequence of measures which diminish any particular resource is a change of the object. If, by encouraging the manufacture of an article at home, the revenue which has been wont to accrue from its importation should be lessened, an indemnification can easily be found, either out of the manufacture itself, or from some other object which may be deemed more convenient.

The measures, however, which have been submitted, taken aggregately, will, for a long time to come, rather augment than decrease the public revenue.

There is little room to hope that the progress of manufactures will so equally keep pace with the progress of population as to prevent even a gradual augmentation of the product of the duties on imported articles.

As, nevertheless, an abolition, in some instances, and a reduction, in others, of

duties which have been pledged for the public debt, is proposed, it is essential that it should be accompanied with a competent substitute. In order to [do] this, it is requisite that all the additional duties which shall be laid be appropriated, in the first instance, to replace all defalcations which may proceed from any such abolition or diminution. It is evident, at first glance, that they will not only be adequate to this but will yield a considerable surplus. This surplus will serve—

First. To constitute a fund for paying the bounties which have been decreed.

Secondly. To constitute a fund for the operations of a board to be established for promoting arts, agriculture, manufactures, and commerce. Of this institution, different intimations have been given in the course of this report. An outline of a plan for it shall now be submitted. . . .

4. THE MERITS OF AGRICULTURE[1]

By Thomas Jefferson

PART I—1782

We never had had an interior trade of any importance. Our exterior commerce has suffered very much from the beginning of the present contest. During this time we have manufactured within our families the most necessary articles of clothing. Those of cotton will bear some comparison with the same kinds of manufacture in Europe; but those of wool, flax, and hemp are very coarse, unsightly, and unpleasant; and such is our attachment to agriculture and such our preference for foreign manufactures that, be it wise or unwise, our people will certainly return as soon as they can

1. Part I is from Jefferson's *Notes on the State of Virginia* (London, 1787), pp. 273-75; Part II is from Jefferson's letter to Benjamin Austin, January 9, 1816, in *The Writings of Thomas Jefferson*, ed. H. A. Washington (New York, 1861), VI, 521-23.

to the raising raw materials and exchanging them for finer manufactures than they are able to execute themselves.

The political economists of Europe have established it as a principle that every state should endeavor to manufacture for itself; and this principle, like many others, we transfer to America, without calculating the difference of circumstance which should often produce a difference of result. In Europe the lands are either cultivated, or locked up against the cultivator. Manufacture must therefore be resorted to of necessity, not of choice, to support the surplus of their people. But we have an immensity of land courting the industry of the husbandman. Is it best then that all our citizens should be employed in its improvement, or that one half should be called off from that to exercise manufactures and handicraft arts for the other? Those who labor in the earth are the chosen people of God, if he ever had a chosen people, whose breasts he has made his peculiar deposit for substantial and genuine virtue. It is the focus in which he keeps alive that sacred fire, which otherwise might escape from the face of the earth. Corruption of morals in the mass of cultivators is a phenomenon of which no age nor nation has furnished an example. It is the mark set on those who, not looking up to heaven, to their own soil and industry, as does the husbandman, for their subsistence, depend for it on the casualties and caprice of customers. Dependence begets subservience and venality, suffocates the germ of virtue, and prepares fit tools for the designs of ambition. This, the natural progress and consequence of the arts, has sometimes perhaps been retarded by accidental circumstances; but, generally speaking, the proportion which the aggregate of the other classes of citizens bears in any state to that of its husbandmen is the proportion of its unsound to its healthy parts, and is a good enough barometer whereby to measure its degree of corruption. While we have land to labor then, let us never wish to see our citizens occupied at a workbench, or twirling a distaff. Carpenters, masons, smiths, are wanting in husbandry; but for the general operations of manufacture, let our workshops remain in Europe. It is better to carry provisions and materials to workmen there than bring them to the provisions and materials, and with them their manners and principles. The loss by the transportation of commodities across the Atlantic will be made up in happiness and permanence of government. The mobs of great cities add just so much to the support of pure government, as sores do to the strength of the human body. It is the manners and spirit of a people which preserve a republic in vigor. A degeneracy in these is a canker which

soon eats to the heart of its laws and constitution....

PART II—1816

... You tell me I am quoted by those who wish to continue our dependence on England for manufactures. There was a time when I might have been so quoted with more candor, but within the thirty years which have since elapsed, how are circumstances changed! We were then in peace. Our independent place among nations was acknowledged. A commerce which offered the raw material in exchange for the same material after receiving the last touch of industry was worthy of welcome to all nations. It was expected that those especially to whom manufacturing industry was important would cherish the friendship of such customers by every favor, by every inducement, and particularly cultivate their peace by every act of justice and friendship. Under this prospect the question seemed legitimate, whether, with such an immensity of unimproved land, courting the hand of husbandry, the industry of agriculture, or that of manufactures, would add most to the national wealth. And the doubt was entertained on this consideration chiefly, that to the labor of the husbandman a vast addition is made by the spontaneous energies of the earth on which it is employed: for one grain of wheat committed to the earth, she renders twenty, thirty, and even fifty fold, whereas to the labor of the manufacturer nothing is added. Pounds of flax, in his hands, yield, on the contrary, but pennyweights of lace. This exchange, too, laborious as it might seem, what a field did it promise for the occupations of the ocean; what a nursery for that class of citizens who were to exercise and maintain our equal rights in that element. This was the state of things in 1785, when the *Notes on Virginia* were first printed; when, the ocean being open to all nations, and their common right in it acknowledged and exercised under regulations sanctioned by the assent and usage of all, it was thought that the doubt might claim some consideration. But who in 1785 could foresee the rapid depravity which was to render the close of that century the disgrace of the history of men? Who could have imagined that the two most distinguished in the rank of nations, for science and civilization, would have suddenly descended from that honorable eminence, and setting at defiance all those moral laws established by the Author of nature between nation and nation, as between man and man, would cover earth and sea with robberies and piracies, merely because strong enough to do it with temporal impunity; and that under this disbandment of nations from social order, we should have been despoiled of a thousand ships, and have thousands of our citizens reduced to Algerine slavery. Yet all this has taken place. One of these nations interdicted to our vessels all harbors of the globe without having first proceeded to some one of hers, there paid a tribute proportioned to the cargo, and obtained her license to proceed to the port of destination. The other declared them to be lawful prize if they had touched at the port, or been visited by a ship of the enemy nation. Thus were we completely excluded from the ocean. Compare this state of things with that of '85, and say whether an opinion founded in the circumstances of that day can be fairly applied to those of the present. We have experienced what we did not then believe, that there exists both profligacy and power enough to exclude us from the field of interchange with other nations: that to be independent for the comforts of life we must fabricate them

ourselves. We must now place the manufacturer by the side of the agriculturist. The former question is suppressed, or rather assumes a new form. Shall we make our own comforts, or go without them, at the will of a foreign nation? He, therefore, who is now against domestic manufacture must be for reducing us either to dependence on that foreign nation, or to be clothed in skins, and to live like wild beasts in dens and caverns. I am not one of these; experience has taught me that manufactures are now as necessary to our independence as to our comfort; and if those who quote me as of a different opinion will keep pace with me in purchasing nothing foreign where an equivalent of domestic fabric can be obtained, without regard to difference of price, it will not be our fault if we do not soon have a supply at home equal to our demand, and wrest that weapon of distress from the hand which has wielded it. If it shall be proposed to go beyond our own supply, the question of '85 will then recur, will our *surplus* labor be then most beneficially employed in the culture of the earth, or in the fabrications of art? We have time yet for consideration, before that question will press upon us; and the maxim to be applied will depend on the circumstances which shall then exist; for in so complicated a science as political economy, no one axiom can be laid down as wise and expedient for all times and circumstances, and for their contraries. Inattention to this is what has called for this explanation, which reflection would have rendered unnecessary with the candid, while nothing will do it with those who use the former opinion only as a stalking horse, to cover their disloyal propensities to keep us in eternal vassalage to a foreign and unfriendly people....

5. AGAINST THE CONSTITUTIONALITY OF THE BANK OF THE UNITED STATES[1]

By THOMAS JEFFERSON

EDITORS' NOTE.—On December 14, 1790, Alexander Hamilton recommended that Congress charter the first Bank of the United States. The bill was passed by early February, 1791, and Washington, before deciding to sign or veto it, requested the members of his cabinet to submit written opinions concerning it. Both Attorney-General Randolph and Jefferson urged the President to veto the bill, arguing, on slightly different grounds, that Congress lacked power to create such an institution. For Hamilton's rebuttal see pages 421–26. Eventually Washington signed the bill on the ground that he would follow the advice of the man (Hamilton) with whose department the institution would be most closely connected.

February 15, 1791

The bill for establishing a national bank undertakes among other things:

1. To form the subscribers into a corporation.

2. To enable them in their corporate capacities to receive grants of land; and so far is against the laws of *mortmain*.[2]

3. To make alien subscribers capable of holding lands; and so far is against the laws of *alienage*.

4. To transmit these lands, on the death of a proprietor, to a certain line of successors; and so far changes the course of *descents*.

5. To put the lands out of the reach of forfeiture or escheat; and so far is against the laws of *forfeiture* and *escheat*.

6. To transmit personal chattels to successors in a certain line; and so far is against the laws of *distribution*.

7. To give them the sole and exclusive right of banking under the national authority; and so far is against the laws of monopoly.

8. To communicate to them a power to make laws paramount to the laws of the states; for so they must be construed, to protect the institution from the control of the state legislatures; and so, probably, they will be construed.

I consider the foundation of the Constitution as laid on this ground: That "all powers not delegated to the United States, by the Constitution, nor prohibited by it to the states, are reserved to the states or to the people" (XIIth Amendment).[3] To take a single step beyond the boundaries thus specially drawn around the powers of Congress is to take possession of a boundless field of power, no longer susceptible of any definition.

The incorporation of a bank, and the powers assumed by this bill, have not, in my opinion, been delegated to the United States by the Constitution.

I. They are not among the powers

1. Thomas Jefferson, *Writings* ..., ed. H. A. Washington, VII, 555–61.

2. Here Jefferson stated in a footnote his opinion that, though the Constitution permitted Congress to hold land for certain purposes, it did not authorize Congress to empower corporations to do so. Mortmain (literally, "dead hand") originally referred to the condition by which, according to medieval canon law, lands once in possession of the church remained church property forever.

3. Actually Amendment X. Jefferson calls it Amendment XII because it was the last of the twelve amendments proposed by the First Congress (under the Constitution) in 1789. Ratification of ten of these proposed amendments was completed by the necessary number of states late in 1791, some months after Jefferson wrote this opinion.

specially enumerated: for these are: 1st. A power to lay taxes for the purpose of paying the debts of the United States; but no debt is paid by this bill, nor any tax laid. Were it a bill to raise money, its origination in the Senate would condemn it by the Constitution.

2d. "To borrow money." But this bill neither borrows money nor insures the borrowing it. The proprietors of the bank will be just as free as any other money-holders to lend or not to lend their money to the public. The operation proposed in the bill, first, to lend them two millions, and then to borrow them back again, cannot change the nature of the latter act, which will still be a payment, and not a loan, call it by what name you please.

3d. To "regulate commerce with foreign nations, and among the states, and with the Indian tribes." To erect a bank, and to regulate commerce, are very different acts. He who erects a bank creates a subject of commerce in its bills; so does he who makes a bushel of wheat or digs a dollar out of the mines; yet neither of these persons regulates commerce thereby. To make a thing which may be bought and sold is not to prescribe regulations for buying and selling. Besides, if this was an exercise of the power of regulating commerce, it would be void, as extending as much to the internal commerce of every state, as to its external. For the power given to Congress by the Constitution does not extend to the internal regulation of the commerce of a state (that is to say of the commerce between citizen and citizen), which remain exclusively with its own legislature; but to its external commerce only, that is to say, its commerce with another state, or with foreign nations, or with the Indian tribes. Accordingly the bill does not propose the measure as a regulation of trade, but as "productive of considerable advantages to trade." Still less are these powers covered by any other of the special enumerations.

II. Nor are they within either of the general phrases, which are the two following:

1. To lay taxes to provide for the general welfare of the United States, that is to say, "to lay taxes for *the purpose* of providing for the general welfare." For the laying of taxes is the *power,* and the general welfare the *purpose* for which the power is to be exercised. They are not to lay taxes *ad libitum*[4] *for any purpose they please* but only *to pay the debts or provide for the welfare of the Union.* In like manner, they are not *to do anything they please* to provide for the general welfare but only to *lay taxes* for that purpose. To consider the latter phrase, not as describing the purpose of the first, but as giving a distinct and independent power to do any act they please, which might be for the good of the Union, would render all the preceding and subsequent enumerations of power completely useless.

It would reduce the whole instrument to a single phrase, that of instituting a Congress with power to do whatever would be for the good of the United States; and, as they would be the sole judges of the good or evil, it would be also a power to do whatever evil they please.

It is an established rule of construction where a phrase will bear either of two meanings to give it that which will allow some meaning to the other parts of the instrument and not that which would render all the others useless. Certainly no such universal power was meant to be given them. It was intended to lace them up straitly within the enumerated powers, and those without which, as means, these powers could not be carried into effect. It is known that the very power now proposed *as a means* was rejected *as an end* by the Convention which formed the Constitution. A proposition was made to them to authorize Congress to open canals, and an

4. "At pleasure."

amendatory one to empower them to incorporate. But the whole was rejected, and one of the reasons for rejection urged in debate was that then they would have a power to erect a bank, which would render the great cities, where there were prejudices and jealousies on the subject, adverse to the reception of the Constitution.[5]

5. On the next to the last working day of the Federal Convention (September 14), while that body was making last-minute changes in the draft reported by the Committee on Style, Franklin proposed giving Congress power to cut canals. Madison suggested that the motion be enlarged into a power "to grant charters of incorporation where the interest of the United States might require and the legislative provisions of individual states may be incompetent." After some debate the motion was limited to canals and defeated, 3 ayes, 8 noes. In the debate Rufus King, answering James Wilson's argument that congressional power to incorporate was necessary to prevent a state from obstructing the general welfare, replied as follows: "The states will be prejudiced and divided into parties by it. In Philadelphia and New York it will be referred to the establishment of a bank, which has been a subject of contention in these cities. In other places it will be referred to mercantile monopolies." Wilson answered that, "as to banks, he did not think with Mr. King that the power in that point of view would excite the prejudices and parties apprehended" (Madison's "Notes," September 14, 1787, in *Documents Illustrative of the Formation of the Union,* pp. 724–25).

The "contention" over bank charters had been especially virulent in Pennsylvania between 1784 and 1787; Wilson had been in the thick of the fight in behalf of the Bank of North America. This institution, chartered originally by the Congress of the Confederation on December 31, 1781, early in 1782 had also acquired a charter from Pennsylvania. In 1785 the Pennsylvania Assembly revoked the charter; only in March, 1787, did the state see fit to grant a new and more restrictive charter. In the meantime the bank operated under the congressional act, though Delaware kindly granted the bank a charter, too. In the controversy over the proposed revocation of the charter in 1785, James Wilson developed very ably the thesis that the congressional act of incorporation was constitutional; he based his argument upon the theory that "the United States have general rights, general powers, and general obligations not derived from any par-

2. The second general phrase is "to make all laws *necessary* and proper for carrying into execution the enumerated powers." But they can all be carried into execution without a bank. A bank therefore is not *necessary* and consequently not authorized by this phrase.

It has been urged that a bank will give great facility or convenience in the collection of taxes. Suppose this were true: yet the Constitution allows only the names which are *"necessary,"* not those which are merely "convenient" for effecting the enumerated powers. If such a latitude of construction be allowed to this phrase as to give any nonenumerated power, it will go to every one, for there is not one which ingenuity may not torture into a *convenience* in some instance *or other*, to *some one* of so long a list of enumerated powers. It would swallow up all the delegated powers and reduce the whole to one power, as before observed. Therefore it was that the Constitution restrained them to the *necessary* means, that is to say, to those means without which the grant of power would be nugatory.

But let us examine this convenience and see what it is. The report on this subject, page 3, states the only *general* convenience to be the preventing the transportation and retransportation of money between the states and the treasury (for I pass over the increase of circulating medium, ascribed to it as a want, and which, according to my ideas of paper money, is clearly a demerit). Every state will have to pay a sum of tax money into the treasury; and the treasury will have to pay, in every state, a part of the interest on the public debt and salaries to the officers of government resident in that state. In most of the states there will still be a surplus of tax

ticular states, nor from all the particular states taken separately, but resulting from the union of the whole" (James Wilson, *Selected Political Essays . . . ,* ed. R. G. Adams [New York, 1930], p. 132).

money to come up to the seat of government for the officers residing there. The payments of interest and salary in each state may be made by treasury orders on the state collector. This will take up the great export of the money he has collected in his state, and consequently prevent the great mass of it from being drawn out of the state. If there be a balance of commerce in favor of that state against the one in which the government resides, the surplus of taxes will be remitted by the bills of exchange drawn for that commercial balance. And so it must be if there was a bank. But if there be no balance of commerce, either direct or circuitous, all the banks in the world could not bring up the surplus of taxes, but in the form of money. Treasury orders, then, and bills of exchange may prevent the displacement of the main mass of the money collected, without the aid of any bank; and, where these fail, it cannot be prevented even with that aid.

Perhaps, indeed, bank bills may be a more *convenient* vehicle than treasury orders. But a little *difference* in the degree of *convenience* cannot constitute the necessity which the Constitution makes the ground for assuming any non-enumerated power.

Besides, the existing banks will, without a doubt, enter into arrangements for lending their agency, and the more favorable, as there will be a competition among them for it; whereas the bill delivers us up bound to the national bank, who are free to refuse all arrangement, but on their own terms, and the public not free, on such refusal, to employ any other bank. That of Philadelphia, I believe, now does this business by their post notes, which, by an arrangement with the treasury, are paid by any state collector to whom they are presented. This expedient alone suffices to prevent the existence of that *necessity* which may justify the assumption of a nonenumerated power as a means for carrying into effect an enumerated one. The thing may be done, and has been done, and well done, without this assumption; therefore, it does not stand on that degree of *necessity* which can honestly justify it.

It may be said that a bank whose bills would have a currency all over the states would be more convenient than one whose currency is limited to a single state. So it would be still more convenient that there should be a bank whose bills should have a currency all over the world. But it does not follow from this superior conveniency that there exists anywhere a power to establish such a bank or that the world may not go on very well without it.

Can it be thought that the Constitution intended that for a shade or two of *convenience*, more or less, Congress should be authorized to break down the most ancient and fundamental laws of the several states; such as those against mortmain, the laws of alienage, the rules of descent, the acts of distribution, the laws of escheat and forfeiture, the laws of monopoly? Nothing but a necessity invincible by any other means can justify such a prostitution of laws, which constitute the pillars of our whole system of jurisprudence. Will Congress be too strait-laced to carry the Constitution into honest effect, unless they may pass over the foundation laws of the state government for the slightest convenience of theirs?

The negative of the President is the shield provided by the Constitution to protect against the invasions of the legislature: 1. The right of the executive. 2. Of the judiciary. 3. Of the states and state legislatures. The president is the case of a right remaining exclusively with the states, and consequently one of those intended by the Constitution to be placed under its protection.

It must be added, however, that unless the President's mind on a view of everything which is urged for and against this bill is tolerably clear that it is unauthorized by the Constitution; if the pro and the con hang so even as to balance his judgment, a just respect for the wisdom of the legislature would naturally decide the balance in favor of their opinion. It is chiefly for cases where they are clearly misled by error, ambition, or interest that the Constitution has placed a check in the negative of the President.

6. FOR THE CONSTITUTIONALITY OF THE BANK OF THE UNITED STATES[1]

By ALEXANDER HAMILTON

...In entering upon the argument, it ought to be premised that the objections of the Secretary of State and Attorney-General[2] are founded on a general denial of the authority of the United States to erect corporations. The latter, indeed, expressly admits, that if there be anything in the bill which is not warranted by the Constitution, it is the clause of incorporation.

Now it appears to the Secretary of the Treasury that this *general principle* is *inherent* in the very *definition* of government and *essential* to every step of the progress to be made by that of the United States, namely: That every power vested in a government is in its nature *sovereign* and includes, by *force of the term*, a right to employ all the *means* requisite and fairly applicable to the attainment of the *ends* of such power, and which are not precluded by restrictions and exceptions specified in the Constitution, or not immoral, or not contrary to the *essential ends* of political society....

...The circumstance that the powers of sovereignty are in this country divided between the national and state governments does not afford the distinction required. It does not follow from this that each of the portion of *powers* delegated to the one or to the other is not sovereign with *regard to its proper objects*. It will only *follow* from it that each has sovereign power as to *certain things* and not as to *other things*. To deny that the government of the United States has sovereign power, as to its declared purposes and trusts, because its power does not extend to all cases, would be equally to deny that the state governments have sovereign power in any case, because their power does not extend to every case. The tenth section of the first article of the Constitution exhibits a long list of very important things which they may not do. And thus the United States would furnish the singular spectacle of a *political society* without *sovereignty*, or of a *people governed* without *government*.

If it would be necessary to bring proof to a proposition so clear, as that which affirms that the powers of the federal government, as to *its objects*, were sovereign, there is a clause of its Constitution which would be decisive. It is that which declares that the Constitution, and the laws of the United States made in pursuance of it, and all treaties made, or which shall be made, under their authority, shall be the *supreme law of the land*. The power which can create the *supreme law of the land* in *any case* is doubtless *sovereign* as to such case.

This general and indisputable principle puts at once an end to the *abstract* question whether the United States have power to erect a *corporation;* that is to say, to give a *legal* or *artificial capacity* to one or more persons, distinct from the *natural*. For it is unquestionably in-

1. Alexander Hamilton, *Works ...*, ed. J. C. Hamilton (New York, 1851), IV, 105–6, 107–8, 109–11, 113, 123–24, 127–28, 129, 130–31, 132–33.
2. Edmund Randolph (cf. p. 266).

cident to *sovereign power* to erect corporations, and consequently to *that* of the United States, in *relation* to the *objects* intrusted to the management of the government. The difference is this: where the authority of the government is general, it can create corporations in *all cases;* where it is confined to certain branches of legislation, it can create corporations *only* in those cases. ...

... It is not denied that there are *implied* as well as *express powers* and that the *former* are as effectually delegated as the *latter.* And for the sake of accuracy it shall be mentioned that there is another class of powers which may be properly denominated *resulting powers.* It will not be doubted that, if the United States should make a conquest of any of the territories of its neighbors, they would possess sovereign jurisdiction over the conquered territory. This would be rather a result, from the whole mass of the powers of the government, and from the nature of political society, than a consequence of either of the powers specially enumerated. ...

... It is conceded that *implied powers* are to be considered as delegated equally with *express ones.* Then it follows that, as a power of erecting a corporation may as well be *implied* as any other thing, it may as well be employed as an *instrument* or *mean* of carrying into execution any of the specified powers, as any other *instrument* or *mean* whatever. The only question must be, in this, as in every other case, whether the mean to be employed or, in this instance, the corporation to be erected, has a natural relation to any of the acknowledged objects or lawful ends of the government. Thus a corporation may not be erected by Congress for superintending the police of the city of Philadelphia, because they are not authorized to *regulate* the *police* of that city. But one may be erected in relation to the collection of taxes, or to the trade with foreign countries, or to the trade between the states, or with the Indian tribes; because it is the province of the federal government to *regulate* those objects, and because it is incident to a general *sovereign* or *legislative* power to *regulate* a thing, to employ all the means which relate to its regulation to the best and greatest advantage. ...

Through this mode of reasoning respecting the right of employing all the means requisite to the execution of the specified powers of the government, it is objected that none but necessary and proper means are to be employed; and the Secretary of State maintains that no means are to be considered as *necessary* but those without which the grant of the power would be *nugatory.* Nay, so far does he go in his restrictive interpretation of the *word,* as even to make the case of the *necessity* which shall warrant the constitutional exercise of the power to depend on *casual* and *temporary* circumstances; an idea which alone refutes the construction. The *expediency* of exercising a particular power, at a particular time, must, indeed, depend on circumstances; but the constitutional right of exercising it must be uniform and invariable, the same today as tomorrow.

All the arguments, therefore, against the constitutionality of the bill derived from the accidental existence of certain state banks—institutions which happen to exist today and, for aught that concerns the government of the United States, may disappear tomorrow—must not only be rejected as fallacious but must be viewed as demonstrative that there is a *radical* source of error in the reasoning.

It is essential to the being of the national government that so erroneous a conception of the meaning of the word *necessary* should be exploded.

It is certain that neither the grammatical nor popular sense of the term requires that construction. According to both, *necessary* often means no more than *needful, requisite, incidental, useful,* or *conducive to.* It is a common mode of expression to say that it is *necessary* for a government or a person to do this or that thing, when nothing more is intended or understood than that the interests of the government or person require, or will be promoted by, the doing of this or that thing. The imagination can be at no loss for exemplifications of the use of the word in this sense. And it is the true one in which it is to be understood as used in the Constitution. The whole turn of the clause containing it indicates that it was the intent of the Convention, by that clause, to give a liberal latitude to the exercise of the specified powers. The expressions have peculiar comprehensiveness. They are, "to make all *laws* necessary and proper for *carrying into execution the foregoing powers*, and *all other powers* vested by the Constitution in the *government* of the United States, or in any *department* or *officer* thereof."

To understand the word as the Secretary of State does would be to depart from its obvious and popular sense and to give it a restrictive operation, an idea never before entertained. It would be to give it the same force as if the word *absolutely* or *indispensably* had been prefixed to it.

Such a construction would beget endless uncertainty and embarrassment. The cases must be palpable and extreme, in which it could be pronounced, with certainty, that a measure was absolutely necessary, or one, without which, the exercise of a given power would be nugatory. There are few measures of any government which would stand so severe a test. To insist upon it would be to make the criterion of the exercise of any implied power a *case of extreme necessity;* which is rather a rule to justify the overleaping of the bounds of constitutional authority than to govern the ordinary exercise of it. . . .

The *degree* in which a measure is necessary can never be a *test* of the legal right to adopt it; that must be a matter of opinion and can only be a *test* of expediency. The *relation* between the *measure* and the *end;* between the *nature* of the *mean* employed toward the execution of a power and the object of that power, must be the criterion of constitutionality, not the more or less of *necessity* or *utility. . . .*

This restrictive interpretation of the word *necessary* is also contrary to this sound maxim of construction; namely, that the powers contained in a constitution of government, especially those which concern the general administration of the affairs of a country, its finances, trade, defense, etc., ought to be construed liberally in advancement of the public good. This rule does not depend on the particular form of a government, or on the particular demarcation of the boundaries of its powers, but on the nature and objects of government itself. The means by which national exigencies are to be provided for, national inconveniences obviated, national prosperity promoted, are of such infinite variety, extent, and complexity, that there must of necessity be great latitude of discretion in the selection and application of those means. Hence, consequently, the necessity and propriety of exercising the authorities intrusted to a government on principles of liberal construction. . . .

But the doctrine which is contended for is not chargeable with the consequences imputed to it. It does not affirm that the national government is sovereign in all respects but that it is sovereign to a certain extent; that is, to the extent of the objects of its specified powers.

It leaves, therefore, a criterion of what is constitutional and of what is not so. This criterion is the *end*, to which the measure relates as a *mean*. If the *end* be clearly comprehended within any of the specified powers, and if the measures have an obvious relation to that *end*, and is not forbidden by a particular provision of the Constitution, it may safely be deemed to come within the compass of the national authority. There is also this further criterion, which may materially assist the decision: Does the proposed measure abridge a pre-existing right of any state or of any individual? If it does not, there is a strong presumption in favor of its constitutionality, and slighter relations to any declared object of the Constitution may be permitted to turn the scale. . . .

It is presumed to have been satisfactorily shown in the course of the preceding observations:

1. That the power of the government, *as* to the objects intrusted to its management, is, in its nature, sovereign.

2. That the right of erecting corporations is one inherent in, and inseparable from, the idea of sovereign power.

3. That the position that the government of the United States can exercise no power but such as is delegated to it by its Constitution does not militate against this principle.

4. That the word *necessary*, in the general clause, can have no *restrictive* operation derogating from the force of this principle; indeed, that the degree in which a measure is or is not *necessary* cannot be a *test* of *constitutional right* but of *expediency only*.

5. That the power to erect corporations is not to be considered as an *independent* or *substantive* power but as an *incidental* and *auxiliary* one and was therefore more properly left to implication than expressly granted.

6. That the principle in question does not extend the power of the government beyond the prescribed limits, because it only affirms a power to *incorporate* for purposes *within the sphere* of the *specified powers*.

And, lastly, that the right to exercise such a power in certain cases is unequivocally granted in the most *positive* and *comprehensive* terms. To all which it only remains to be added that such a power has actually been exercised in two very eminent instances; namely, in the erection of two governments; one northwest of the River Ohio, and the other southwest—the last independent of any antecedent compact. . . .

It shall now be endeavored to be shown that there is a power to erect one of the kind proposed by the bill. This will be done by tracing a natural and obvious relation between the institution of a bank and the objects of several of the enumerated powers of the government; and by showing that, *politically* speaking, it is necessary to the effectual execution of one or more of those powers. . . .

To establish such a right, it remains to show the relation of such an institution to one or more of the specified powers of the government. Accordingly it is affirmed that it has a relation, more or less direct. to the power of collecting taxes, to that of borrowing money, to that of regulating trade between the states, and to those of raising and maintaining fleets and armies. To the two former the relation may be said to be immediate; and in the last place it will be argued that it is clearly within the provision which authorizes the making of all *needful rules and regulations* concerning the *property* of the United States, as the same has been practiced upon by the government.

A bank relates to the collection of taxes in two ways—*indirectly*, by increasing the quantity of circulating medium and quickening circulation, which facilitates the means of paying directly, by creating a *convenient species* of medium in which they are to be paid. . . .

A bank has a direct relation to the power of borrowing money, because it is a usual, and in sudden emergencies an essential, instrument in the obtaining of loans to government.

A nation is threatened with war; large sums are wanted on a sudden to make the necessary preparation. Taxes are laid for the purpose, but it requires time to obtain the benefit of them. Anticipation is indispensable. If there be a bank, the supply can at once be had. If there be none, loans from individuals must be sought. The progress of these is often too slow for the exigency; in some situations they are not practicable at all. Frequently, when they are, it is of great consequence to be able to anticipate the product of them by advance from a bank. . . .

Let it then be supposed that the necessity existed (as but for a casualty would be the case), that proposals were made for obtaining a loan; that a number of individuals came forward and said, "We are willing to accommodate the government with the money"; with what we have in hand, and the credit we can raise upon it, we doubt not of being able to furnish the sum required, but in order to do this it is indispensable that we should be incorporated as a bank. This is essential toward putting it in our power to do what is desired, and we are obliged on that account to make it the *consideration* or *condition* of the loan.

Can it be believed that a compliance with this proposition would be unconstitutional? . . .

The institution of a bank has also a natural relation to the regulation of trade between the states, in so far as it is conducive to the creation of a convenient medium of *exchange* between them, and to the keeping up a full circulation, by preventing the frequent displacement of the metals in reciprocal remittances. Money is the very hinge on which commerce turns. And this does not merely mean gold and silver; many other things have served the purpose, with different degrees of utility. Paper has been extensively employed. . . .

The Secretary of State further argues that if this was a regulation of commerce, it would be void, as *extending as much to the internal commerce of every state as to its external*. But what regula-

tion of commerce does not extend to the internal commerce of every state? What are all the duties upon imported articles, amounting to prohibitions, but so many bounties upon domestic manufactures, affecting the interests of different classes of citizens, in different ways? What are all the provisions in the Coasting Act which relate to the trade between district and district of the same state? In short, what regulation of trade between the states but must affect the internal trade of each state? What can operate upon the whole but must extend to every part?

The relation of a bank to the execution of the powers that concern the common defense has been anticipated. It has been noted that, at this very moment, the aid of such an institution is essential to the measures to be pursued for the protection of our frontiers.

It now remains to show that the incorporation of a bank is within the operation of the provision which authorizes Congress to make all needful rules and regulations concerning the property of the United States. But it is previously necessary to advert to a distinction which has been taken by the Attorney-General.

He admits that the word *property* may signify personal property, however acquired, and yet asserts that it cannot signify money arising from the sources of revenue pointed out in the Constitution, "because," says he, "the disposal and regulation of money is the final cause for raising it by taxes."

But it would be more accurate to say that the *object* to which money is intended to be applied is the *final cause* for raising it than that the disposal and regulation of it is *such*.

The support of government—the support of troops for the common defense—the payment of the public debt, are the true *final causes* for raising money. The disposition and regulation of it, when raised, are the steps by which it is applied to the *ends* for which it was raised, not the *ends* themselves. Hence, therefore, the money to be raised by taxes, as well as any other personal property, must be supposed to come within the meaning, as they certainly do within the letter, of authority to make all needful rules and regulations concerning the property of the United States. . . .

A hope is entertained that it has, by this time, been made to appear, to the satisfaction of the President, that a bank has a natural relation to the power of collecting taxes—to that of regulating trade—to that of providing for the common defense—and that, as the bill under consideration contemplates the government in the light of a joint proprietor of the stock of the bank, it brings the case within the provision of the clause of the Constitution which immediately respects the property of the United States.

Under a conviction that such a relation subsists, the Secretary of the Treasury, with all deference, conceives, that it will result as a necessary consequence from the position, that all the specified powers of government are sovereign, as to the proper objects; that the incorporation of a bank is a constitutional measure; and that the objections taken to the bill, in this respect, are ill founded. . . .

7. FIRST INAUGURAL ADDRESS, 1801[1]

By Thomas Jefferson

Friends and Fellow-Citizens:

Called upon to undertake the duties of the first executive office of our country, I avail myself of the presence of that portion of my fellow-citizens which is here assembled to express my grateful thanks for the favor with which they have been pleased to look toward me, to declare a sincere consciousness that the task is above my talents, and that I approach it with those anxious and awful presentiments which the greatness of the charge and the weakness of my powers so justly inspire. A rising nation, spread over a wide and fruitful land, traversing all the seas with the rich productions of their industry, engaged in commerce with nations who feel power and forget right, advancing rapidly to destinies beyond the reach of mortal eye—when I contemplate these transcendent objects, and see the honor, the happiness, and the hopes of this beloved country committed to the issue and the auspices of this day, I shrink from the contemplation and humble myself before the magnitude of the undertaking. Utterly, indeed, should I despair did not the presence of many whom I here see remind me that in the other high authorities provided by our Constitution I shall find resources of wisdom, of virtue, and of zeal on which to rely under all difficulties. To you, then, gentlemen, who are charged with the sovereign functions of legislation, and to those associated with you, I look with encouragement for that guidance and support which may enable us to steer with safety the vessel in which we are all embarked amidst the conflicting elements of a troubled world.

During the contest of opinion through which we have passed, the animation of discussions and of exertions has sometimes worn an aspect which might impose on strangers unused to think freely and to speak and to write what they think; but this being now decided by the voice of the nation, announced according to the rules of the Constitution, all will, of course, arrange themselves under the will of the law, and unite in common efforts for the common good. All, too, will bear in mind this sacred principle,

1. *A Compilation of the Messages and Papers of the Presidents, 1789–1897*, ed. James D. Richardson (Washington, 1896), I, 321–24.

that though the will of the majority is in all cases to prevail, that will to be rightful must be reasonable; that the minority possess their equal rights, which equal law must protect, and to violate would be oppression. Let us, then, fellow-citizens, unite with one heart and one mind. Let us restore to social intercourse that harmony and affection without which liberty and even life itself are but dreary things. And let us reflect that, having banished from our land that religious intolerance under which mankind so long bled and suffered, we have yet gained little if we countenance a political intolerance as despotic, as wicked, and capable of as bitter and bloody persecutions. During the throes and convulsions of the ancient world, during the agonizing spasms of infuriated man, seeking through blood and slaughter his long-lost liberty, it was not wonderful that the agitation of the billows should reach even this distant and peaceful shore; that this should be more felt and feared by some and less by others and should divide opinions as to measures of safety. But every difference of opinion is not a difference of principle. We have called by different names brethren of the same principle. We are all Republicans, we are all Federalists. If there be any among us who would wish to dissolve this Union or to change its republican form, let them stand undisturbed as monuments of the safety with which error of opinion may be tolerated where reason is left free to combat it. I know, indeed, that some honest men fear that a republican government cannot be strong, that this government is not strong enough; but would the honest patriot, in the full tide of successful experiment, abandon a government which has so far kept us free and firm on the theoretic and visionary fear that this government, the world's best hope, may by possibility want energy to preserve itself? I trust not. I believe this, on the contrary, the strongest government on earth. I believe it the only one where every man, at the call of the law, would fly to the standard of the law and would meet invasions of the public order as his own personal concern. Sometimes it is said that man cannot be trusted with the government of himself. Can he, then, be trusted with the government of others? Or have we found angels in the forms of kings to govern him? Let history answer this question.

Let us, then, with courage and confidence pursue our own Federal and Republican principles, our attachment to union and representative government. Kindly separated by nature and a wide ocean from the exterminating havoc of one-quarter of the globe; too high-minded to endure the degradations of the others; possessing a chosen country, with room enough for our descendants to the thousandth and thousandth generation; entertaining a due sense of our equal right to the use of our own faculties, to the acquisitions of our own industry, to honor and confidence from our fellow-citizens, resulting not from birth but from our actions and their sense of them; enlightened by a benign religion, professed, indeed, and practiced in various forms, yet all of them inculcating honesty, truth, temperance, gratitude, and the love of man; acknowledging and adoring an overruling Providence, which by all its dispensations proves that it delights in the happiness of man here and his greater happiness hereafter—with all these blessings, what more is necessary to make us a happy and prosperous people? Still one thing more, fellow-citizens—a wise and frugal government, which shall restrain men from injuring one another, shall leave them otherwise free to regulate their own pursuits of industry and improvement, and shall not take from the mouth of labor the bread it has earned. This is the sum of good government, and this is necessary to close the circle of our felicities.

About to enter, fellow-citizens, on the exercise of duties which comprehend everything dear and valuable to you, it is proper you should understand what I deem the essential principles of our government and, consequently, those which ought to shape its administration. I will compress them within the narrowest compass they will bear, stating the general principle, but not all its limitations. Equal and exact justice to all men, of whatever state or persuasion, religious or political; peace, commerce, and honest friendship with all nations, entangling alliances with none; the support of the state governments in all their rights, as the most competent administrations for our domestic concerns and the surest bulwarks against anti-republican tendencies; the preservation of the General Government in its whole constitutional vigor, as the sheet anchor of our peace at home and safety abroad; a jealous care of the right of election by the people— a mild and safe corrective of abuses which are lopped by the sword of revolution where peaceable remedies are unprovided; absolute acquiescence in the decisions of the majority, the vital principle of republics, from which is no appeal but to force, the vital principle and immediate parent of despotism; a well-disciplined militia, our best reliance in peace and for the first moments of war, till regulars may relieve them; the supremacy of the civil over the military authority; economy in the public expense that labor may be lightly burthened; the honest payment of our debts and sacred preservation of the public faith; encouragement of agriculture and of commerce as its handmaid; the diffusion of information and arraignment of all abuses at the bar of the public reason; freedom of religion; freedom of the press, and freedom of person under the protection of the habeas corpus, and trial by juries impartially selected. These principles form the bright constellation which has gone before us and guided our steps through an age of revolution and reformation. The wisdom of our sages and blood of our heroes have been devoted to their attainment. They should be the creed of our political faith, the text of civic instruction, the touchstone by which to try the services of those we trust; and should we wander from them in moments of error or of alarm, let us hasten to retrace our steps and to regain the road which alone leads to peace, liberty, and safety.

I repair, then, fellow-citizens, to the post you have assigned me. With experience enough in subordinate offices to have seen the difficulties of this the greatest of all, I have learned to expect that it will rarely fall to the lots of imperfect man to retire from this station with the reputation and the favor which bring him into it. Without pretensions to that high confidence you reposed in our first and greatest revolutionary character, whose pre-eminent services had entitled him to the first place in his country's love and destined for him the fairest page in the volume of faithful history, I ask so much confidence only as may give firmness and effect to the legal administration of your affairs. I shall often go wrong through defect of judgment. When right, I shall often be thought wrong by those whose positions will not command a view of the whole ground. I ask your indulgence for my own errors, which will never be intentional, and your support against the errors of others, who may condemn what they would not if seen in all its parts. The approbation implied by your suffrage is a great consolation to me for the past, and my future solicitude will be to retain the good opinion of those who have bestowed it in advance, to conciliate that of others by doing them all the good in my power, and to be instrumental to the happiness and freedom of all. . . .

March 4, 1801

UNIT V

CONSTITUTIONAL PROBLEMS OF THE
NEW REPUBLIC

AS SOON as Americans began to put the Constitution into practice, problems of interpretation quickly appeared. The terms of the document had to be explored, decisions taken about their meaning, and applications made to the various circumstances of national life. Here we deal with the development of this process during the formative years—the period which extends from 1789 into the long span of years when John Marshall was chief justice of the Supreme Court.

Of the many problems which arose, three will be discussed in this introduction. The subject of the first is the scope of federal power. Was the grant of powers to be interpreted "strictly" or "loosely"? Second, who was to decide whether a particular course of action was in accordance with the Constitution or not? Was there a final arbiter of the Constitution, and, if so, where? Finally, what kind of freedom was guaranteed to individuals under the Constitution? These were issues around which a great deal of controversy centered, and the decisions which emerged were of the utmost consequence for future history.

First, how broad were the powers of the national government? The intention had been to create a federal government, and the authors of the Constitution had followed certain principles in making their distribution of power. Among other provisions, they had prohibited the national government from doing some things; they had specifically authorized it to do others; and they had given it some discretion in order to carry out its specific powers. But the wording of these prohibitions and permissions was very general. Had Congress the legal power to charter a national bank? We have seen that Hamilton said "Yes," and Jefferson, "No." Had a state the legal power to tax the operations of a national bank? We shall see that Maryland said "Yes" and Marshall, "No." What was involved in the power of Congress to regulate interstate commerce? The words of the original document gave no certain answer. These were questions which led different people to form radically different conclusions about the nature of the Constitution. We have only to recall the controversies associated with the term "consolidated government" to realize that opinion would be deeply divided. Yet it was possible, with very plausible logic, to argue that either point of view—the doctrine of strict, or the doctrine of loose, construction —was authorized by the terms of the Constitution.

A statement of the doctrine of strict construction will be found in the following papers. It is a prominent feature of the Kentucky and Virginia Resolutions of 1798, a protest made by the Republican opposition against the Federalist use of national power, which had culminated in the passage of the Alien and Sedition Acts. In this case, the view that the national government was exceeding its power was reinforced by a theory which held that the Constitution had been created by states and that the action of the national authorities amounted to a breach of this original compact between the states.

It was one of Marshall's achievements to counter these arguments with an interpretation which freed the national government from any possibility of subordination to state governments, and then proceeded to argue for a broad construction of its powers. This reasoning may be traced in the brilliant but bitterly controversial decision in the case of *McCulloch* v. *Maryland*. This case involved the constitutionality of the second Bank of the United States, which Congress had chartered in 1811, and the power of a state to tax its operations. Marshall first disposed of the argument that the Constitution owed its creation to the action of states. This is an argument which can be held in many forms, some of which, as may be seen in the case of the Kentucky and Virginia Resolves, are somewhat ambiguous in their practical consequences. But its obvious tendency, as was clearly demonstrated by the counsel for Maryland

in this case, was to enlarge the scope of state authority and to abridge the scope of federal authority. Marshall's technique was to eliminate this risk at its source by insisting that the Constitution was not the creation of states but of the whole American people. He regarded the ratifying conventions, which adopted the Constitution, not as agencies of states, but as representatives of the American nation.

Having protected himself in this way, he then insisted that the national government was fully as sovereign within its sphere as the states were within theirs; that Congress, by virtue of this sovereignty, had a wide range of choice over the means it might use to implement its specific powers; and that the states had no right to interfere with these means. The bank was such a means. The state tax on its note issue was unlawful.

This summary of the issues involved in one of Marshall's judgments may help the student to analyze others for himself. An equally famous example of the same liberal construction of federal powers will be found in *Gibbons* v. *Ogden*, a decision of 1824 which destroyed a state monopoly of steamboat navigation and cleared the way for the federal regulation of interstate commerce. At a time when the first loyalty of many citizens was still to their state, Marshall was determined to map out a broad course for the future development of national power.

The second problem developed out of the first. Given these disagreements about the interpretation of the Constitution, who was authorized to settle them? We know today that the power of deciding whether the acts of the different agencies of government are constitutional or not is exercised by the courts and that in the last resort, the Supreme Court, through the process of "judicial review," is the final judge. But there is no explicit provision for this tremendous power in the Constitution. It is the result of an interpretation which has won acceptance through the violence of civil war and the pressure of practical necessity. A radical critic of our own times would describe it as an usurpation of power. Advocates of state rights before the Civil War were equally critical. In the period which concerns us at least three answers to the question were possible. It could be said that the courts were the final judge; that the states were the final judge; or that there was no final judge.

The state-rights position was a natural deduction from the view that the Constitution was a compact between states, each of which reserved to itself the right to decide when breaches of the compact were being committed. This was the theory of the Kentucky and Virginia Resolves. The authors of these resolutions may have left some doubt in the reader's mind about what was meant by the right of the state to "interpose," but they were unambiguous in rejecting the claim of a federal court to be the final arbiter.

The view that there was no final judge may be regarded as a deduction flowing from the widely held faith in the separation of powers. It could be said that the main organs of government, both national and state, were all of equal authority, in the sense that they were equally bound by the Constitution and equally entitled to decide the limits of constitutional action within their own provinces.

Both these positions may seem unsatisfactory to the modern student; one because it creates as many judges as there are states, and the other as many judges as there are organs. He is inclined to think that in practice they would lead to chaos. But, in so thinking, he is following the logic of the interpretation which has eventually driven them out of the field. The fact is that the Constitution itself was not explicit, and a plausible case could be made for each.

Here again it was Marshall who made the most powerful contribution to the ultimate victory of judicial review. In the widest sense of the words, this term simply refers to a fundamental principle of British constitutionalism. It means the duty of an independent judiciary to test the legality of all proceedings which come before it. But in the special sense in which the term has come to be applied to the American Constitution, it means the duty to test the acts of all legislative bodies, courts, and officials, by reference to the written Constitution. The Supreme Court refuses to be bound by anything but its own interpretation of the Constitution, and it maintains it against all authorities. Marshall created the legal foundations for this position by holding invalid the highest exercise of legislative authority in the United States, an act of Congress. This was the outstanding feature of the case, *Marbury* v. *Madison* (1803). The vitality of the principle of judicial review in the period before the Civil War does not depend, however, on the annulment of acts of Congress—of which this case and the Dred Scott decision (1857) are the only examples—but on the repeated assertion of federal supervision over the acts of state legislatures, courts, and officials. In all but one of the cases from which extracts are printed in this unit, it was held that an act of a state legislature was unconstitutional. This power of judicial review has profound consequences for those who believe that democracy is a system of government in which the will of the majority, as reflected in the votes of its elected representatives, ought to prevail. It leads to the charge that the judiciary is in a position to substitute its own political opinions for those of democratic majorities.

The third problem refers to those fundamental rights of the individual which were guaranteed by the Constitution. It might be admitted that no liberties are absolute. But what limitations were intended, and by what standards were they to be justified? When, for example, does an act of Congress constitute an interference with the freedom of speech guaranteed by the First Amendment? This was one of the issues which underlay the agitation over the Alien and Sedition Acts. When does an act of a state legislature amount to an interference with freedom of contract? In *Fletcher* v. *Peck* and in *Dartmouth College* v. *Woodward*, Marshall may be studied in the role of the economic individualist. He is defending the freedom of individuals and corporations to make contracts in the faith that legislative bodies will not disturb them. This is obviously another burning issue for a people that seeks to reconcile individual freedom with the general welfare.

In studying all these constitutional questions, there are several considerations which the student should keep in mind. First, he should attempt to identify the political and economic interests which may lie behind the constitutional argument. Politicians will naturally prefer an interpretation which is appropriate to their purposes and to the situation in which they find themselves. A region which stands to benefit by an extension of federal authority will be tempted to find such an authority in the Constitution. A party in opposition may see the Constitution in quite a different light when it finds itself in office. From this point of view, what determines the adoption of a particular interpretation is not a dispassionate quest for constitutional truth but an interested desire for constitutional protection.

Second, he should acquaint himself with the species of logic employed by judicial persons. Judges are responsible not to a party but to the community. They are appointed on terms which are intended to make them immune from political pressure, and they are expected to expound the rules of law in accordance with the standards of a technical profession. It is observable, however, that the objectivity attainable by the judiciary is not absolute. For one thing, the convictions which they have acquired previous to their appointment are frequently a recommendation to the persons appointing them, and these influences may sometimes be seen in their judgments. For another, it is misleading to assume, as we frequently do, that the judicial function is merely to apply a known body of law. There is an element of lawmaking which is inseparable from the work of applying any system of law, and, the more ambiguous the law, the more conspicuous this element becomes. There are features about the American Constitution which are exceedingly ambiguous. It

would be much more accurate to say that John Marshall "created" constitutional law than to say that he "applied" it.

Lastly, the student should attempt to acquire a balanced appreciation of the implications involved in this process of interpreting the Constitution. It is notoriously easy to see one side of a question to the exclusion of others; for example, to see the advantages of Marshall's great influence for the stable and flexible development of American life, while overlooking the objections felt by either the defenders of state rights or the champions of democratic majorities. The only corrective is a willingness to examine all the consequences of the arguments employed.

1. ALIEN AND SEDITION ACTS, 1798[1]

EDITORS' NOTE.—In the spring of 1798 war with France seemed very close. The French Directory had outraged American susceptibilities by its treatment of a diplomatic mission from this country, a full account of which had been given to the American press. The popular reaction to the XYZ affair—as the incident was called—gave the Federalists a great advantage over the Republicans, who had often been apologists for the First French Republic. In this atmosphere Congress passed the four acts usually called the Alien and Sedition Acts. The Natu-

ralization Act required from prospective citizens of the United States fourteen years' residence rather than five. The Alien and Alien Enemies Acts gave the President power to deport aliens whom he considered dangerous. The Sedition Act dealt with conspiracy against the government and with the subject of seditious libel. To the Jeffersonian critics of the acts, it seemed as if the Federalists were simply arming themselves with illegal powers in the hope of smashing their domestic political opponents.

A. AN ACT CONCERNING ALIENS, JUNE 25, 1798

SECTION 1. Be it enacted by the Senate and House of Representatives of the United States of America in Congress assembled, That it shall be lawful for the President of the United States at any time during the continuance of this act to *order* all such *aliens* as he shall judge dangerous to the peace and safety of the United States, or shall have reasonable grounds to suspect are concerned in any treasonable or secret machinations against the government thereof, to depart out of the territory of the United States, within such time as shall be expressed in such order, which order shall be served on such alien by delivering him a copy thereof, or leaving the same at his usual abode, and returned to the office of the Secretary of State, by the marshal or other person to whom the same shall be directed. And in case any alien, so ordered to depart, shall be found at large within the United States after

the time limited in such order for his departure, and not having obtained a *license* from the President to reside therein, or having obtained such *license* shall not have conformed thereto, every such alien shall, on conviction thereof, be imprisoned for a term not exceeding three years, and shall never after be admitted to become a citizen of the United States. . . .

SEC. 2. And be it further enacted, That it shall be lawful for the President of the United States, whenever he may deem it necessary for the public safety, to order to be removed out of the territory thereof, any alien who may or shall be in prison in pursuance of this act; and to cause to be arrested and sent out of the United States such of those aliens as shall have been ordered to depart therefrom and shall not have obtained a license as aforesaid, in all cases where, in the opinion of the President, the public safety requires a speedy removal. And

1. *U.S. Statutes at Large*, I, 570-71, 596-97.

if any alien so removed or sent out of the United States by the President shall voluntarily return thereto, unless by permission of the President of the United States, such alien, on conviction thereof, shall be imprisoned so long as, in the opinion of the President, the public safety may require. . . .

B. SEDITION ACT, JULY 14, 1798

SECTION 1. Be it enacted by the Senate and House of Representatives of the United States of America, in Congress assembled, That if any persons shall unlawfully combine or conspire together, with intent to oppose any measure or measures of the government of the United States, which are or shall be directed by proper authority, or to impede the operation of any law of the United States, or to intimidate or prevent any person holding a place or office in or under the government of the United States, from undertaking, performing, or executing his trust or duty; and if any person or persons, with intent as aforesaid, shall counsel, advise, or attempt to procure any insurrection, riot, unlawful assembly, or combination, whether such conspiracy, threatening, counsel, advice, or attempt shall have the proposed effect or not, he or they shall be deemed guilty of a high misdemeanor, and on conviction, before any court of the United States having jurisdiction thereof, shall be punished by a fine not exceeding five thousand dollars, and by imprisonment during a term not less than six months nor exceeding five years; and further, at the discretion of the court may be holden to find sureties for his good behavior in such sum, and for such time, as the said court may direct.

SEC. 2. And be it further enacted, That if any person shall write, print, utter, or publish, or shall cause or procure to be written, printed, uttered, or published, or shall knowingly and willingly assist or aid in writing, printing, uttering, or publishing any false, scandalous, and malicious writing or writings against the government of the United States, or either house of the Congress of the United States, or the President of the United States, with intent to defame the said government, or either house of the said Congress, or the said President, or to bring them, or either of them, into contempt or disrepute; or to excite against them, or either or any of them, the hatred of the good people of the United States, or to stir up sedition within the United States, or to excite any unlawful combinations therein, for opposing or resisting any law of the United States, or any act of the President of the United States, done in pursuance of any such law, or of the powers in him vested by the Constitution of the United States, or to resist, oppose, or defeat any such law or act, or to aid, encourage or abet any hostile designs of any foreign nation against the United States, their people or government, then such person, being thereof convicted before any court of the United States having jurisdiction thereof, shall be punished by a fine not exceeding two thousand dollars, and by imprisonment not exceeding two years.

SEC. 3. And be it further enacted and declared, That if any person shall be prosecuted under this act, for the writing or publishing any libel aforesaid, it shall be lawful for the defendant, upon the trial of the cause, to give in evidence in his defense, the truth of the matter contained in the publication charged as a libel. And the jury who shall try the cause shall have a right to determine the law and the fact, under the direction of the court, as in other cases.

SEC. 4. And be it further enacted, That this act shall continue and be in force until the third day of March, one thousand eight hundred and one, and no longer: *provided,* That the expiration of the act shall not prevent or defeat a prosecution and punishment of any offense against the law during the time it shall be in force.

2. THE KENTUCKY AND VIRGINIA RESOLUTIONS[1]

EDITORS' NOTE.—In 1798 some extremists proposed to Jefferson that Virginia and North Carolina should lead a southern secession from the Union. Jefferson rejected such ideas, pointing out to John Taylor of Caroline that the supremacy of the Federalists was likely to be brief and that secession would lead to new secessions until each state stood alone. He also remarked: "Seeing that we must have somebody to quarrel with, I had rather keep our New England associates for that purpose, than to see our bickerings transferred to others. . . . A little patience and we shall see the reign of witches pass over" (*Writings,* ed. Ford, VII, 265).

The Republicans decided to protest against the acts. It was desirable that Jefferson, then Vice-President and a chief target for Federalist abuse, should not appear openly in the agitation. He was, however, the author of the resolutions which were eventually passed, with significant modifications, by the Kentucky legislature in November, 1798. While Kentucky was acting, Madison, with aid from Jefferson and W. C. Nicholas, was drafting a somewhat milder set of resolutions than Jefferson's which were subsequently adopted by the legislature of Virginia.

The reaction to the resolutions north of the Potomac was largely unfavorable. No state legislature came to the support of Virginia and Kentucky. At the next session the legislatures of these states reiterated their stand, the Kentuckians in a relatively short resolution, the Virginians in the long and able "Report" written by Madison.

The Resolutions were important primarily as a vigorous protest against legislation dangerous to liberty. They also served as a means of expression for the Republican agitation which culminated in the triumph of Jefferson's party in 1800–1801. But the stress which they laid upon the compact theory of the Union, the idea of the states as final judges of the violation of the compact, and the ideas of "interposition" and "nullification" were to be given a new significance by South Carolina in the 1830's.

A. KENTUCKY RESOLUTIONS, NOVEMBER 16, 1798

I. *Resolved,* That the several states composing the United States of America are not united on the principle of unlimited submission to their general government; but that by compact under the style and title of a Constitution for the United States and of amendments thereto, they constituted a general government for special purposes, delegated to

1. N. S. Shaler, *Kentucky: A Pioneer Commonwealth* (Boston, 1884), pp. 410, 413–16; *Debates in the Several State Conventions,* ed. J. Elliot (Washington, 1863), IV, 528–29, 533, 534, 537, 538–39, 545, 547–50, 551–52.

that government certain definite powers, reserving each state to itself, the residuary mass of right to their own self-government; and that, whensoever the general government assumes undelegated powers, its acts are unauthoritative, void, and of no force. That to this compact each state acceded as a state, and is an integral party, its co-states forming, as to itself, the other party: that the government created by this compact was not made the exclusive or final judge of the extent of the powers delegated to itself; since that would have made its discretion, and not the Constitution, the measure of its powers, but that, as in all other cases of compact among parties having no common judge, each party has an equal right to judge for itself, as well of infractions as of the mode and measure of redress. . . .[2]

VII. *Resolved*, That the construction applied by the general government (as is evinced by sundry of their proceedings) to those parts of the Constitution of the United States which delegate to Congress a power to lay and collect taxes, duties, imposts, and excises; to pay the debts, and provide for the common defense, and general welfare of the United States, and to make all laws which shall be necessary and proper for carrying into execution the powers vested by the Constitution in the government of the United States, or any department thereof, goes to the destruction of all the limits prescribed to their power by the Constitution: that words meant by that instrument to be subsidiary only to the execution of the limited powers ought not to be so construed as themselves to give unlimited powers, nor a part so to be taken as to destroy the whole residue of the instrument: that the proceedings of the general govern-

ment under color of these articles will be a fit and necessary subject for revisal and correction at a time of greater tranquillity, while those specified in the preceding resolutions call for immediate redress.

VIII. *Resolved*, That the preceding Resolutions be transmitted to the senators and representatives in Congress from this Commonwealth, who are hereby enjoined to present the same to their respective Houses, and to use their best endeavors to procure, at the next session of Congress, a repeal of the aforesaid unconstitutional and obnoxious acts.[3]

IX. *Resolved*, lastly, That the governor of this Commonwealth be, and is hereby authorized and requested to communicate the preceding Resolutions to the legislatures of the several states, to assure them that this Commonwealth considers Union for specified national purposes, and particularly for those specified in their late Federal Compact, to be friendly to the peace, happiness, and prosperity of all the states; that faithful to that compact according to the plain intent and meaning in which it was understood and acceded to by the several parties, it is sincerely anxious for its preservation; that it does also believe that, to take from the states all the powers of self-government, and transfer them to a general and consolidated gov-

3. Compare this resolution and the last part of the ninth with the analogous provisions in Jefferson's draft which follows: (8) "*Resolved*, That a committee of conference and correspondence be appointed, who shall have in charge to communicate the preceding resolutions to the legislatures of the several states . . ." and (9) "*Resolved*, That the said committee be authorized to communicate by writings or personal conferences at any times or places whatever, with any person or persons who may be appointed by any one or more co-states to correspond or confer with them; and that they lay their proceedings before the next session of Assembly." The differences in procedure indicate a considerable "toning-down" by the Kentuckians of Jefferson's propositions, and the adoption of a more practicable, if less consistent, procedure.

2. The omitted resolutions, II–VI inclusive, declared void all congressional legislation which made criminal acts other than those so enumerated in the Constitution; specifically they denounced the Sedition and Alien Acts.

ernment, without regard to the special delegations and reservations solemnly agreed to in that compact, is not for the peace, happiness, or prosperity of these states; and that, therefore, this Commonwealth is determined, as it doubts not its co-states are, tamely to submit to undelegated and consequently unlimited powers in no man or body of men on earth;[4] that if the acts before specified should stand, these conclusions would flow from them; that the general government may place any act they think proper on the list of crimes and punish it themselves, whether enumerated or not enumerated by the Constitution as cognizable by them; that they may transfer its cognizance to the President or any other person, who may himself be the accuser, counsel, judge, and jury, whose suspicions may be the evidence, his order the sentence, his officer the executioner, and his breast the sole record of the transaction; that a very numerous and valuable description of the inhabitants of these states being by this precedent reduced as outlaws to the absolute dominion of one man, and the barrier of the Constitution thus swept away from us all, no rampart now remains against

4. Here the Kentucky resolutions omit the following significant clauses in Jefferson's draft: "that in cases of an abuse of the delegated powers, the members of the general government, being chosen by the people, a change by the people would be the constitutional remedy; but, where powers are assumed which have not been delegated, a nullification of the act is the rightful remedy; that every state has a natural right in cases not within the compact (*casus non foederis*) to nullify of their own authority all assumption of power by others within their limits; that nevertheless this commonwealth from motives of regard and respect for its co-states has wished to communicate with them on the subject; that with them alone it is proper to communicate, they alone being parties to the contract, and solely authorized to judge in the last resort of the powers exercised under it, Congress being not a party, but merely the creature of the compact, and subject as to its assumption of power to the final judgment of those by whom, and for whose use itself and its powers were all created and modified. . . ."

the passions and the powers of a majority of Congress, to protect from a like exportation or other more grievous punishment the minority of the same body, the legislature, judges, governors, and counselors of the states, nor their other peaceable inhabitants who may venture to reclaim the constitutional rights and liberties of the state and people, or who for other causes, good or bad, may be obnoxious to the views or marked by the suspicions of the President, or be thought dangerous to his or their elections or other interests, public or personal; that the friendless alien has indeed been selected as the safest subject of a first experiment, but the citizen will soon follow, or rather has already followed; for, already has a sedition act marked him as its prey; that these and successive acts of the same character, unless arrested on the threshold, may tend to drive these states into revolution and blood,[5] and will furnish new calumnies against Republican governments, and new pretexts for those who wish it to be believed that man cannot be governed but by a rod of iron; that it would be a dangerous delusion were a confidence in the men of our choice to silence our fears for the safety of our rights; that confidence is everywhere the parent of despotism; free government is founded in jealousy and not in confidence; it is jealousy and not confidence which prescribes limited constitutions to bind down those whom we are obliged to trust with power; that our Constitution has accordingly fixed the limits to which and no further our confidence may go; and let the honest advocate of confidence read the Alien and Sedition Acts, and say if the Constitution has not been wise in fixing limits to the government it created, and whether we should be wise in destroying those limits; let him

5. The Jefferson draft here reads: "Unless arrested at the threshold, necessarily drive these states into revolution and blood."

say what the government is if it be not a tyranny, which the men of our choice have conferred on the President, and the President of our choice has assented to and accepted over the friendly strangers, to whom the mild spirit of our country and its laws had pledged hospitality and protection; that the men of our choice have more respected the bare suspicions of the President than the solid rights of innocence, the claims of justification, the sacred force of truth, and the forms and substance of law and justice. In questions of power then let no more be heard of confidence in man, but bind him down from mischief by the claims of the Constitution. That this Commonwealth does therefore call on its co-states for an expression of their sentiments on the acts concerning aliens, and for the punishment of certain crimes herein before specified, plainly declaring whether these acts are or are not authorized by the Federal Compact. And it doubts not that their sense will be so announced as to prove their attachment unaltered to limited government, whether general or particular, and that the rights and liberties of their co-states will

be exposed to no dangers by remaining embarked on a common bottom with their own; that they will concur with this Commonwealth in considering the said acts as so palpably against the Constitution as to amount to an undisguised declaration, that the compact is not meant to be the measure of the powers of the general government, but that it will proceed in the exercise over these states of all powers whatsoever; that they will view this as seizing the rights of the states and consolidating them in the hands of the general government with a power assumed to bind the states (not merely in cases made Federal) but in all cases whatsoever, by laws made, not with their consent, but by others against their consent; that this would be to surrender the form of government we have chosen, and to live under one deriving its powers from its own will, and not from our authority; and that the co-states, recurring to their natural right in cases not made Federal, will concur in declaring these acts void and of no force,[6] and will each unite with this Commonwealth in requesting their repeal at the next session of Congress. . . .

B. VIRGINIA RESOLUTIONS, DECEMBER 24, 1798

Resolved, That the General Assembly of Virginia doth unequivocally express a firm resolution to maintain and defend the Constitution of the United States, and the Constitution of this state, against every aggression, either foreign or domestic; and that they will support the government of the United States in all measures warranted by the former.

That this Assembly most solemnly declares a warm attachment to the union of the states, to maintain which it pledges its powers; and that, for this end, it is their duty to watch over and oppose

6. Here the Jefferson draft reads as follows: "and will each take measures of its own for providing that neither these acts, nor any other of the General Government not plainly and intentionally authorized by the Constitution, shall be exercised within their respective territories."

every infraction of those principles which constitute the only basis of that union, because a faithful observance of them can alone secure its existence and the public happiness.

That this Assembly doth explicitly and peremptorily declare that it views the powers of the federal government as resulting from the compact to which the states are parties, as limited by the plain sense and intention of the instrument constituting that compact, as no further valid than they are authorized by the grants enumerated in that compact; and that, in case of a deliberate, palpable, and dangerous exercise of other powers, not granted by the said compact, the states, who are parties thereto, have the right, and are in duty bound, to interpose, for arresting the progress of the evil, and for maintaining, within their respective limits, the authorities, rights, and liberties, appertaining to them.

That the General Assembly doth also express its deep regret that a spirit has, in sundry instances, been manifested by the federal government to enlarge its powers by forced constructions of the constitutional charter which defines them; and that indications have appeared of a design to expound certain general phrases (which, having been copied from the very limited grant of powers in the former Articles of Confederation, were the less liable to be misconstrued) so as to destroy the meaning and effect of the particular enumeration which necessarily explains and limits the general phrases, and so as to consolidate the states, by degrees, into one sovereignty, the obvious tendency and inevitable result of which would be to transform the present republican system of the United States into an absolute or, at best, a mixed monarchy.

That the General Assembly doth particularly PROTEST against the palpable and alarming infractions of the Constitution, in the two late cases of the "Alien and Sedition Acts," passed at the last session of Congress; the first of which exercises a power nowhere delegated to the federal government, and which, by uniting legislative and judicial powers to those of executive, subverts the general principles of free government, as well as the particular organization and positive provisions of the federal Constitution; and the other of which acts exercises, in like manner, a power not delegated by the Constitution, but, on the contrary, expressly and positively forbidden by one of the amendments thereto—a power which, more than any other, ought to produce universal alarm, because it is leveled against the right of freely examining public characters and measures, and of free communication among the people thereon, which has ever been justly deemed the only effectual guardian of every other right.

That this state having, by its Conven-

tion, which ratified the federal Constitution, expressly declared that, among other essential rights, "the liberty of conscience and the press cannot be canceled, abridged, restrained, or modified, by any authority of the United States," and from its extreme anxiety to guard these rights from every possible attack of sophistry and ambition, having, with other states, recommended an amendment for that purpose, which amendment was, in due time, annexed to the Constitution—it would mark a reproachful inconsistency, and criminal degeneracy, if an indifference were now shown to the most palpable violation of one of the rights thus declared and secured, and to the establishment of a precedent which may be fatal to the other.

That the good people of this commonwealth, having ever felt, and continuing to feel, the most sincere affection for their brethren of the other states; the truest anxiety for establishing and perpetuating the union of all; and the most scrupulous fidelity to that Constitution, which is the pledge of mutual friendship, and the instrument of mutual happiness—the General Assembly doth solemnly appeal to the like dispositions in the other states, in confidence that they will concur with this commonwealth in declaring, as it does hereby declare, that the acts aforesaid are unconstitutional; and that the necessary and proper measures will be taken *by each* for co-operating with this state, in maintaining unimpaired the authorities, rights, and liberties, reserved to the states respectively, or to the people.

That the governor be desired to transmit a copy of the foregoing resolutions to the executive authority of each of the other states, with a request that the same may be communicated to the legislature thereof and that a copy be furnished to each of the senators and representatives representing this state in the Congress of the United States....

C. THE MASSACHUSETTS REPLY, FEBRUARY 9, 1799

The legislature of Massachusetts, having taken into serious consideration the resolutions of the state of Virginia. . . .

. . . deem it their duty solemnly to declare that, while they hold sacred the principle, that consent of the people is the only pure source of just and legitimate power, they cannot admit the right of the state legislatures to denounce the administration of that government to which the people themselves, by a solemn compact, have exclusively committed their national concerns. That, although a liberal and enlightened vigilance among the people is always to be cherished, yet an unreasonable jealousy of the men of their choice, and a recurrence to measures of extremity upon groundless or trivial pretexts, have a strong tendency to destroy all rational liberty at home, and to deprive the United States of the most essential advantages in relations abroad. That this legislature are persuaded that the decision of all cases in law and equity arising under the Constitution of the United States, and the construction of all laws made in pursuance thereof, are exclusively vested by the people in the judicial courts of the United States.

That the people, in that solemn compact which is declared to be the supreme law of the land, have not constituted the state legislatures the judges of the acts or measures of the federal government but have confided to them the power of proposing such amendments of the Constitution as shall appear to them necessary to the interests, or conformable to the wishes, of the people whom they represent.

That, by this construction of the Constitution, an amicable and dispassionate remedy is pointed out for any evil which experience may prove to exist, and the peace and prosperity of the United States may be preserved without interruption.

But, should the respectable state of Virginia persist in the assumption of the right to declare the acts of the national government unconstitutional, and should she oppose successfully her force and will to those of the nation, the Constitution would be reduced to a mere cipher, to the form and pageantry of authority, without the energy of power; every act of the federal government which thwarted the views or checked the ambitious projects of a particular state, or of its leading and influential members, would be the object of opposition and of remonstrance; while the people, convulsed and confused by the conflict between two hostile jurisdictions, enjoying the protection of neither, would be wearied into a submission to some bold leader, who would establish himself on the ruins of both.

The legislature of Massachusetts, although they do not themselves claim the right, nor admit the authority of any of the state governments, to decide upon the constitutionality of the acts of the federal government, still, lest their silence should be construed into disapprobation, or at best into a doubt as to the constitutionality of the acts referred to by the state of Virginia; and as the General Assembly of Virginia has called for an expression of their sentiments—do explicitly declare, that they consider the acts of Congress, commonly called "The Alien and Sedition Acts," not only constitutional but expedient and necessary. . . .

This construction of the Constitution, and of the existing law of the land, as well as the act complained of, the legislature of Massachusetts most deliberately and firmly believe, results from a just and full view of the several parts of the Constitution; and they consider that act to be wise and necessary, as an audacious and unprincipled spirit of falsehood and abuse had been too long unremittingly exerted for the purpose of perverting public opinion, and threatened to undermine and destroy the whole fabric of government.

The legislature further declare that in the foregoing sentiments they have expressed the general opinion of their constituents, who have not only acquiesced without complaint in those particular measures of the federal government but have given their explicit approbation by re-electing those men who voted for the adoption of them. Nor is it apprehended that the citizens of this state will be accused of supineness, or of an indifference to their constitutional rights; for

while, on the one hand, they regard with due vigilance the conduct of the government, on the other, their freedom, safety, and happiness require that they should defend that government and its constitutional measures against the open or insidious attacks of any foe, whether foreign or domestic.

And, lastly, that the legislature of Massachusetts feel a strong conviction, that the several United States are connected by a common interest, which ought to render their union indissoluble; and that this state will always co-operate with its confederate states in rendering that union productive of mutual security, freedom, and happiness. . . .

D. THE NEW HAMPSHIRE REPLY, JUNE 14, 1799

The committee to take into consideration the resolutions of the General Assembly of Virginia, dated December 21, 1798; also certain resolutions of the legislature of Kentucky, of the 10th November, 1798, report as follows:

The legislature of New Hampshire, having taken into consideration certain resolutions of the General Assembly of Virginia, dated December 21, 1798; also certain resolutions of the legislature of Kentucky, of the 10th of November, 1798:

Resolved, That the legislature of New Hampshire unequivocally express a firm resolution to maintain and defend the Constitution of the United States, and the constitution of this state, against every aggression, either foreign or domestic, and that they will support the government of the United States in all measures warranted by the former.

That the state legislatures are not the proper tribunals to determine the constitutionality of the laws of the general government; that the duty of such decision is properly and exclusively confided

to the judicial department.

That, if the legislature of New Hampshire, for mere speculative purposes, were to express an opinion on the acts of the general government, commonly called "The Alien and Sedition Bills," that opinion would unreservedly be that those acts are constitutional, and, in the present critical situation of our country, highly expedient.

That the constitutionality and expediency of the acts aforesaid have been very ably advocated and clearly demonstrated by many citizens of the United States, more especially by the minority of the General Assembly of Virginia. The legislature of New Hampshire, therefore, deem it unnecessary, by any train of arguments, to attempt further illustration of the propositions, the truth of which, it is confidently believed, at this day, is very generally seen and acknowledged.

Which report, being read and considered, was unanimously received and accepted, one hundred and thirty-seven members being present. . . .

E. KENTUCKY RESOLUTIONS, FEBRUARY 22, 1799

Resolved, That this Commonwealth considers the federal Union, upon the

terms and for the purposes specified in the late compact, conducive to the liberty and happiness of the several states. That it does now unequivocally declare its attachment to the Union, and to that compact, agreeably to its obvious and real intention, and will be among the last to seek its dissolution. That, if those who administer the general government be permitted to transgress the limits fixed by that compact, by a total disregard to the special delegations of power therein contained, an annihilation of the state governments, and the creation, upon their ruins, of a general consolidated government, will be the inevitable consequence. That the principle and construction, contended for by sundry of the state legislatures, that the general government is the exclusive judge of the extent of the powers delegated to it, stop not short of *despotism*—since the discretion of those who administer the government, and not the *Constitution*, would be the measure of their powers. That the several states who formed that instrument, being sovereign and independent, have the unquestionable right to judge of the infraction; and, *That a nullification, by those sovereignties, of all unauthorized acts done under color of that instrument, is the rightful remedy*. That

this commonwealth does, under the most deliberate reconsideration, declare, that the said Alien and Sedition Laws are, in their opinion, palpable violations of the said Constitution; and, however cheerfully it may be disposed to surrender its opinion to a majority of its sister-states, in matters of ordinary or doubtful policy, yet, in momentous regulations like the present, which so vitally wound the best rights of the citizen, it would consider a silent acquiescence as highly criminal. That, although this Commonwealth, as a party to the federal compact, will bow to the laws of the Union, yet it does, at the same time, declare, that it will not now, or ever hereafter, cease to oppose, in a constitutional manner, every attempt, at what quarter soever offered, to violate that compact. And finally, in order that no pretext or arguments may be drawn from a supposed acquiescence, on the part of this Commonwealth, in the constitutionality of those laws, and be thereby used as precedents for similar future violations of the federal compact, this Commonwealth does now enter against them its solemn PROTEST....

F. MADISON'S REPORT ON THE VIRGINIA RESOLUTIONS

The resolution declares, *first*, That "it views the powers of the federal government as resulting from the compact to which the states are parties"; in other words, that the federal powers are derived from the Constitution; and that the Constitution is a compact to which the states are parties.

Clear as the position must seem that the federal powers are derived from the Constitution, and from that alone, the committee are not unapprized of a late doctrine which opens another source of federal powers, not less extensive and important than it is new and unexpected. The examination of this doctrine will be most conveniently connected with a review of a succeeding resolution. The

committee satisfy themselves here with briefly remarking that, in all the contemporary discussions and comments which the Constitution underwent, it was constantly justified and recommended on the ground that the powers not given to the government were withheld from it; and that, if any doubt could have existed on this subject, under the original text of the Constitution, it is removed, as far as words could remove it, by the Twelfth Amendment, now a part of the Constitution, which expressly declares, "that the powers not delegated to the United States by the Constitution, nor prohibited by it to the states, are reserved to the states respectively, or to the people."

The other position involved in this branch of the resolution, namely, "that the states are parties to the Constitution," or compact, is, in the judgment of the committee, equally free from objection. It is indeed true that the term "states" is sometimes used in a vague sense, and sometimes in different senses, according to the subject to which it is applied. Thus it sometimes means the separate sections of territory occupied by the political societies within each; sometimes the particular governments established by those societies; sometimes those societies as organized into those particular governments; and lastly, it means the people composing those political societies, in their highest sovereign capacity. Although it might be wished that the perfection of language admitted less diversity in the signification of the same words, yet little inconvenience is produced by it, where the true sense can be collected with certainty from the different applications. In the present instance, whatever different construction of the term "states," in the resolution, may have been entertained, all will at least concur in the last mentioned; because in that sense the Constitution was submitted to the "states"; in that sense the "states" ratified it; and in that sense of the term "states," they are consequently parties to the compact from which the powers of the federal government result.

The next position is that the General Assembly views the powers of the federal government "as limited by the plain sense and intention of the instrument constituting that compact," and "as no further valid than they are authorized by the grants therein enumerated." It does not seem possible that any just objection can lie against either of these clauses. The first amounts merely to a declaration that the compact ought to have the interpretation plainly intended by the parties to it; the other, to a declaration that it ought to have the execu-

tion and effect intended by them. If the powers granted be valid, it is solely because they are granted; and if the granted powers are valid because granted, all other powers not granted must not be valid.

The resolution, having taken this view of the federal compact, proceeds to infer, "That, in case of a deliberate, palpable, and dangerous exercise of other powers, not granted by the said compact, the states, who are parties thereto, have the right, and are in duty bound, to interpose for arresting the progress of the evil, and for maintaining, within their respective limits, the authorities, rights, and liberties, appertaining to them."

It appears to your committee to be a plain principle, founded in common sense, illustrated by common practice, and essential to the nature of compacts, that, where resort can be had to no tribunal superior to the authority of the parties, the parties themselves must be the rightful judges, in the last resort, whether the bargain made has been pursued or violated. The Constitution of the United States was formed by the sanction of the states, given by each in its sovereign capacity. It adds to the stability and dignity, as well as to the authority, of the Constitution, that it rests on this legitimate and solid foundation. The states, then, being the parties to the constitutional compact, and in their sovereign capacity, it follows of necessity that there can be no tribunal, above their authority, to decide, in the last resort, whether the compact made by them be violated; and consequently, that, as the parties to it, they must themselves decide, in the last resort, such questions as may be of sufficient magnitude to require their interposition.

It does not follow, however, because the states, as sovereign parties to their constitutional compact, must ultimately decide whether it has been violated, that such a decision ought to be interposed either in a hasty manner or on doubtful and inferior occasions. Even in the case of ordinary conventions between different nations, where, by the strict rule of interpretation, a breach of a part may be deemed a breach of the whole—every part being deemed a condition of every other part, and of the whole—it is always laid down that the breach must be both wilful and material, to justify an application of the rule. But in the case of an intimate and constitutional union, like that of the United States, it is evident that the interposition of the parties, in their sovereign capacity, can be called for by occasions only deeply and essentially affecting the vital principles of their political system.

The resolution has, accordingly, guarded against any misapprehension of its object, by expressly requiring, for such an interposition, "the case of a deliberate, palpable, and dangerous breach of the Constitution, by the exercise of powers not granted by it." It must be a case not of a light and transient nature but of a nature dangerous to the great purposes for which the Constitution was established. It must be a case, moreover, not obscure or doubtful in its construction but plain and palpable. Lastly, it must be a case not resulting from a partial consideration or hasty determination but a case stamped with a final consideration and deliberate adherence. It is not necessary, because the resolution does not require that the question should be discussed, how far the exercise of any particular power, ungranted by the Constitution, would justify the interposition of the parties to it. As cases might easily be stated, which none would contend ought to fall within that description—cases, on the other hand, might, with equal ease, be stated, so flagrant and so fatal as to unite every opinion in placing them within the description.

But the resolution has done more than guard against misconstruction, by expressly referring to cases of a deliberate, palpable, and dangerous nature. It specifies the object of the interposition, which it contemplates, to be solely that of arresting the progress of the evil of usurpation and of maintaining the authorities, rights, and liberties, appertaining to the states as parties to the Constitution.

From this view of the resolution, it would seem inconceivable that it can incur any just disapprobation from those who, laying aside all momentary impressions, and recollecting the genuine source and object of the Federal Constitution, shall candidly and accurately interpret the meaning of the General Assembly. If the deliberate exercise of dangerous powers, palpably withheld by the Constitution, could not justify the parties to it in interposing even so far as to arrest the progress of the evil, and thereby to preserve the Constitution itself, as well as to provide for the safety of the parties to it, there would be an end to all relief from usurped power, and a direct subversion of the rights specified or recognized under all the state constitutions, as well as a plain denial of the fundamental principle on which our independence itself was declared.

But it is objected that the judicial authority is to be regarded as the sole expositor of the Constitution in the last resort; and it may be asked for what reason the declaration by the General Assembly, supposing it to be theoretically true, could be required at the present day and in so solemn a manner.

On this objection it might be observed, first, that there may be instances of usurped power, which the forms of the Constitution would never draw within the control of the judicial department; secondly, that, if the decision of the judiciary be raised above the authority of the sovereign parties to the Constitution, the decisions of the other departments, not carried by the forms of the Constitution before the judiciary, must be equally authoritative and final with the decisions of that department. But the proper answer to the objection is that the resolution of the General Assembly relates to those great and extraordinary cases in which all the forms of the Constitution may prove ineffectual against infractions dangerous to the essential rights of the parties to it. The resolution supposes that dangerous powers, not delegated, may not only be usurped and executed by the other departments but that the judicial department, also, may exercise or sanction dangerous powers beyond the grant of the Constitution; and, consequently, that the ultimate right of the parties to the Constitution, to judge whether the compact has been dangerously violated, must extend to violations by one delegated authority as well as by another—by the judiciary as well as by the executive, or the legislature.

However true, therefore, it may be, that the judicial department is, in all questions submitted to it by the forms of the Constitution, to decide in the last resort, this resort must necessarily be deemed the last in relation to the authorities of the other departments of the government; not in relation to the rights of the parties to the constitutional compact, from which the judicial, as well as the other departments, hold their delegated trusts. On any other hypothesis, the delegation of judicial power would annul the authority delegating it; and the concurrence of this department with the others in usurped powers, might subvert forever, and beyond the possible reach of any rightful remedy, the very Constitution which all were instituted to preserve....

... In the official report on manufactures by the late secretary of the treasury, made on the fifth of December, 1791 ... it is expressly contended to belong "to the discretion of the national legislature to pronounce upon the objects which concern the general welfare, and for which, under that description, an appropriation of money is requisite and proper. And there seems to be no room for a doubt that, whatever concerns the general interests of learning, of agriculture, of manufactures, and of commerce, is within the sphere of national councils as far as regards an application of money." The latter report assumes the same latitude of power in the national councils, and applies it to the encouragement of agriculture, by means of a society to be established at the seat of government. Although neither of these reports may have received the sanction of a law carrying it into effect, yet, on the other hand, the extraordinary doctrine contained in both has passed without the slightest positive mark of disapprobation from the authority to which it was addressed.

Now, whether the phrases in question be construed to authorize every measure relating to the common defense and general welfare, as contended by some, or every measure only in which there might be an application of money, as suggested by the caution of others—the effect must substantially be the same, in destroying the import and force of the particular enumeration of powers which follows these general phrases in the Constitution; for it is evident that there is not a single power whatever which may not have some reference to the common defense or the general welfare; nor a power of any magnitude which, in its exercise, does not involve, or admit, an application of money. The government, therefore, which possesses power in either one or other of these extents is a government without the limitations formed by a particular enumeration of powers; and, consequently, the meaning and effect of this particular enumeration is destroyed by the exposition given to these general phrases.

This conclusion will not be affected by an attempt to qualify the power over the "general welfare," by referring it to cases where the general welfare is beyond the reach of the separate provisions by the individual states, and leaving to these their jurisdiction in cases to which their separate provisions may be competent; for, as the authority of the individual states must in all cases be incompetent to general regulations operating through the whole, the authority of the United States would be extended to every object relating to the general welfare, which might, by any possibility, be provided for by the general authority. This qualifying construction, therefore, would have little, if any, tendency to circumscribe the power claimed under the latitude of the term "general welfare."

The true and fair construction of this expression, both in the original and existing federal compacts, appears to the committee too obvious to be mistaken. In both, the Congress is authorized to provide money for the common defense and general welfare. In both is subjoined to this authority an enumeration of the cases to which their power shall extend. Money cannot be applied to the general welfare otherwise than by an application of it to some particular measure, conducive to the general welfare. Whenever, therefore, money has been raised by the general authority, and is to be applied to a particular measure, a question arises whether the particular measure be within the enumerated authorities vested in Congress. If it be, the money requisite for it may be applied to it. If it be not, no such application can be made. This fair and obvious interpretation coincides with, and is enforced by, the clause in the Constitution which declares that "no money shall be drawn from the treasury but in consequence of appropriations made by law." An appropriation of money to the general welfare would be deemed rather a mockery than an observance of this constitutional injunction. ...

3. *MARBURY* v. *MADISON*[1]

EDITORS' NOTE. — John Marshall (1755–1835) fought in the Revolution and then practiced law in Richmond, Virginia, before becoming, in 1801, chief justice of the United States. He served in this capacity until his death in 1835. During the period of law practice Marshall was active in public life. He was a member of the Virginia Assembly, the Virginia Executive Council, and the Virginia convention which ratified the Federal Constitution. He was one of President Adams' XYZ commissioners to France, a member of Congress, and secretary of state under Adams. He was outstanding in his loyalty to Washington and Adams during their terms as President. Marshall is best known, of course, for his creative development of our constitutional law during his years as chief justice. His influence was such that he commonly carried the Court with him; and he found it necessary to dissent in only one of the great constitutional cases decided during his term of office. *The Life of John Marshall,* ed. Albert U. Beveridge (4 vols.; Boston, 1916–19), is one of the classics of American biography and is a study

1. 1 Cranch 137 (1803). Decisions are cited by reference first to volume, then to name of reports, and then to page of reports. Reports may be named for the reporter who recorded the cases or for a jurisdiction.

of the times as well as of Marshall. It furnishes the background for the cases included in this unit.

William Marbury was one of the Federalists appointed to judicial office by the retiring President Adams. His commission embodying the appointment had been signed and sealed but had not been delivered. On Jefferson's inauguration, Madison, as secretary of state, refused to give Marbury the commission. Marbury began proceedings in the Supreme Court to secure an order, called a *mandamus*, directing Madison to give him the commission. For his right to start proceedings in the Supreme Court he relied on a section of the Judiciary Act of 1789.

It is, then, the opinion of the Court,

1st. That by signing the commission of Mr. Marbury, the President of the United States appointed him a justice of peace, for the country of Washington, in the district of Columbia; and that the seal of the United States, affixed thereto by the secretary of state, is conclusive testimony of the verity of the signature, and of the completion of the appointment; and that the appointment conferred on him a legal right to the office for the space of five years.

2dly. That, having this legal title to the office, he has a consequent right to the commission; a refusal to deliver which, is a plain violation of that right, for which the laws of his country afford him a remedy....

This, then, is a plain case for a mandamus, either to deliver the commission, or a copy of it from the record; and it only remains to be inquired whether it can issue from this court.

The act to establish the judicial courts of the United States authorizes the Supreme Court "to issue writs of mandamus, in cases warranted by the principles and usages of law, to any courts appointed, or persons holding office, under the authority of the United States."

The secretary of state, being a person holding an office under the authority of the United States, is precisely within the letter of the description; and if this court is not authorized to issue a writ of mandamus to such an officer, it must be because the law is unconstitutional and therefore absolutely incapable of conferring the authority and assigning the duties which its words purport to confer and assign.

The Constitution vests the whole judicial power of the United States in one supreme court and such inferior courts as Congress shall, from time to time, ordain and establish. This power is expressly extended to all cases arising under the laws of the United States and, consequently, in some form, may be exercised over the present case because the right claimed is given by a law of the United States.

In the distribution of this power it is declared that "the Supreme Court shall have original jurisdiction in all cases affecting ambassadors, other public ministers and consuls, and those in which a state shall be a party. In all other cases, the Supreme Court shall have appellate jurisdiction."

It has been insisted, at the bar, that as the original grant of jurisdiction, to the supreme and inferior courts, is general, and the clause, assigning original jurisdiction to the Supreme Court, contains no negative or restrictive words, the power remains to the legislature, to assign original jurisdiction to that court, in other cases than those specified in the article which has been recited, provided those cases belong to the judicial power of the United States.

If it had been intended to leave it in the discretion of the legislature to apportion the judicial power between the supreme and inferior courts according to the will of that body, it would certainly have been useless to have proceeded further than to have defined the judicial power and the tribunals in which it should be vested. The subsequent part of the section is mere surplusage—is entirely without meaning—if such is to be the construction. If Congress remains at liberty to give this court appellate jurisdiction, where the Constitution has declared their jurisdiction shall be original, and original jurisdiction where the Constitution has declared it shall be appellate, the distribution of jurisdiction, made in the Constitution, is form without substance.

Affirmative words are often, in their operation, negative of other objects than those affirmed; and in this case, a negative or exclusive sense must be given to them, or they have no operation at all.

It cannot be presumed that any clause in the Constitution is intended to be without effect; and, therefore, such a construction is inadmissible, unless the words require it.

If the solicitude of the convention, respecting our peace with foreign powers, induced a provision that the Supreme Court should take original jurisdiction in cases which might be supposed to affect them; yet the cause would have proceeded no further than to provide for such cases, if no further restriction on the powers of Congress had been intended. That they should have appellate jurisdiction in all other cases, with such exceptions as Congress might make, is no restriction, unless the words be deemed exclusive of original jurisdiction.

When an instrument organizing, fundamentally, a judicial system divides it into one supreme and so many inferior courts as the legislature may ordain and establish, then enumerates its powers, and proceeds so far to distribute them, as to define the jurisdiction of the Supreme Court by declaring the cases in which it shall take original jurisdiction, and that in others it shall take appellate jurisdiction, the plain import of the words seems to be that in one class of cases its jurisdiction is original and not appellate; in the other it is appellate and not original. If any other construction would render the clause inoperative, that is an additional reason for rejecting such other construction and for adhering to their obvious meaning. To enable this Court, then, to issue a mandamus, it must be shown to be an exercise of appellate jurisdiction or to be necessary to enable them to exercise appellate jurisdiction.

It has been stated at the bar that the appellate jurisdiction may be exercised in a variety of forms, and that, if it be the will of the legislature that a mandamus should be used for that purpose, that will must be obeyed. This is true, yet the jurisdiction must be appellate, not original. It is the essential criterion of appellate jurisdiction, that it revises and corrects the proceedings in a cause already instituted and does not create that cause. Although, therefore, a mandamus may be directed to courts, yet to issue such a writ to an officer for the delivery of a paper is, in effect, the same as to sustain an original action for that paper and, therefore, seems not to belong to appellate but to original jurisdiction. Neither is it necessary in such a case as this to enable the Court to exercise its appellate jurisdiction. The authority, therefore, given to the Supreme Court by the act establishing the judicial courts of the United States, to issue writs of mandamus to public officers, appears not to be warranted by the Constitution; and it becomes necessary to inquire whether a jurisdiction, so conferred, can be exercised.

The question whether an act, repugnant to the Constitution, can become the law of the land is a question deeply interesting to the United States but, happily, not of an intricacy proportioned to its interest. It seems only necessary to recognize certain principles, supposed to have been long and well established, to decide it.

That the people have an original right to establish, for their future government, such principles as, in their opinion, shall most conduce to their own happiness is the basis on which the whole American fabric has been erected. The exercise of this original right is a very great exertion; nor can it, nor ought it, to be frequently repeated. The principles, therefore, so established, are deemed fundamental. And as the authority, from which they proceed, is supreme, and can seldom act, they are designed to be permanent.

This original and supreme will organizes the government and assigns to different departments their respective powers. It may either stop here or establish certain limits not to be transcended by those departments.

The government of the United States is of the latter description. The powers of the legislature are defined and limited; and that those limits may not be mistaken or forgotten, the Constitution is written. To what purpose are powers limited, and to what purpose is that limitation committed to writing, if these limits may, at any time, be passed by those intended to be restrained? The distinction between a government with limited and unlimited powers is abolished if those limits do not confine the persons on whom they are imposed, and if acts prohibited and acts allowed are of equal obligation. It is a proposition too plain to be contested that the Constitution controls any legislative act repugnant to it or that the legislature may alter the Constitution by an ordinary act.

Between these alternatives there is no middle ground. The Constitution is either a superior paramount law, unchangeable by ordinary means, or it is on a level with ordinary legislative acts and, like other acts, is alterable when the legislature shall please to alter it.

If the former part of the alternative be true, then a legislative act contrary to the Constitution is not law; if the latter part be true, then written constitutions are absurd attempts, on the part of the people, to limit a power in its own nature illimitable.

Certainly, all those who have framed written constitutions contemplate them as forming the fundamental and paramount law of the nation, and, consequently, the theory of every such government must be, that an act of the legislature repugnant to the Constitution is void.

This theory is essentially attached to a written constitution and is, consequently, to be considered, by this court, as one of the fundamental principles of our society. It is not, therefore, to be lost sight of in the further consideration of this subject.

If an act of the legislature repugnant to the Constitution is void, does it, notwithstanding its invalidity, bind the courts and oblige them to give it effect? Or, in other words, though it be not law, does it constitute a rule as operative as if it was a law? This would be to overthrow, in fact, what was established in theory and would seem, at first view, an absurdity too gross to be insisted on. It shall, however, receive a more attentive consideration.

It is, emphatically, the province and duty of the judicial department to say what the law is. Those who apply the rule to particular cases must of necessity expound and interpret that rule. If two laws conflict with each other, the courts must decide on the operation of each.

So if a law be in opposition to the Constitution, if both the law and the Constitution apply to a particular case, so that the court must either decide that case conformably to the law, disregarding the Constitution, or conformably to the Constitution, disregarding the law, the court must determine which of these conflicting rules governs the case. This is of the very essence of judicial duty. If, then, the courts are to regard the Constitution, and the Constitution is superior to any ordinary act of the legislature, the Constitution, and not such ordinary act, must govern the case to which they both apply.

Those, then, who controvert the principle that the Constitution is to be considered, in court, as a paramount law are reduced to the necessity of maintaining that courts must close their eyes on the Constitution and see only the law.

This doctrine would subvert the very foundation of all written constitutions. It would declare that an act which, according to the principles and theory of our government, is entirely void, is yet, in practice, completely obligatory. It would declare that if the legislature shall do what is expressly forbidden, such act, notwithstanding the express prohibition, is in reality effectual. It would be giving to the legislature a practical and real omnipotence, with the same breath which professes to restrict their powers within narrow limits. It is prescribing limits and declaring that those limits may be passed at pleasure.

That it thus reduces to nothing what we have deemed the greatest improvement on political institutions, a written constitution would of itself be sufficient, in America, where written constitutions have been viewed with so much reverence, for rejecting the construction. But the peculiar expressions of the Constitution of the United States furnish additional arguments in favor of its rejection.

The judicial power of the United States is extended to all cases arising under the Constitution. Could it be the intention of those who gave this power to say that, in using it, the Constitution should not be looked into? That a case arising under the Constitution should be decided without examining the instrument under which it arises?

This is too extravagant to be maintained.

In some cases, then, the Constitution must be looked into by the judges. And if they can open it at all, what part of it are they forbidden to read or to obey?

There are many other parts of the Constitution which serve to illustrate this subject. It is declared that "no tax or duty shall be laid on articles exported from any state." Suppose a duty on the export of cotton, of tobacco, or of flour; and a suit instituted to recover it. Ought judgment to be rendered in such a case? Ought the judges to close their eyes on the Constitution and only see the law?

The Constitution declares that "no bill of attainder or *ex post facto* law shall be passed." If, however, such a bill should be passed and a person should be prosecuted under it, must the court condemn to death those victims whom the Constitution endeavors to preserve?

"No person," says the Constitution, "shall be convicted of treason, unless on the testimony of two witnesses to the same *overt* act, or on confession in open court." Here the language of the Constitution is addressed especially to the courts. It prescribes, directly for them, a rule of evidence not to be departed from. If the legislature should change that rule and declare one witness, or a confession out of court, sufficient for conviction, must the constitutional principle yield to the legislative act?

From these, and many other selections which might be made, it is apparent that the framers of the Constitution contemplated that instrument as a rule for the government of *courts* as well as of the legislature.

Why otherwise does it direct the judges to take an oath to support it? This oath certainly applies, in an especial manner, to their conduct in their official character. How immoral to impose it on them, if they were to be used as the instruments, and the knowing instruments, for violating what they swear to support!

The oath of office, too, imposed by the legislature is completely demonstrative of the legislative opinion on this subject. It is in these words: "I do solemnly swear that I will administer justice, without respect to persons, and do equal right to the poor and to the rich; and that I will faithfully and impartially discharge all the duties incumbent on me as, according to the best of my abilities and understanding, agreeably to the Constitution, and laws of the United States."

Why does a judge swear to discharge his duties agreeably to the Constitution of the United States if that Constitution forms no rule for his government? If it is closed upon him, and cannot be inspected by him? If such be the real state of things, this is worse than solemn mockery. To prescribe, or to take this oath, becomes equally a crime.

It is also not entirely unworthy of observation that, in declaring what shall be the supreme law of the land, the Constitution itself is first mentioned; and not the laws of the United States generally, but those only which shall be made in pursuance of the Constitution have that rank.

Thus, the particular phraseology of the Constitution of the United States confirms and strengthens the principle, supposed to be essential to all written constitutions, that a law repugnant to the Constitution is void and that courts, as well as other departments, are bound by that instrument.

The rule must be discharged.[2]

2. The motion for a writ of mandamus must be denied.

4. *FLETCHER* v. *PECK*[1]

EDITORS' NOTE.—In 1795 the Georgia legislature provided for the sale of thirty-five million acres of the state's land at a cent and a half an acre, subject to Indian claims. Bribery on behalf of the purchasing land companies secured the passage of the act. The companies promptly sold their land at an average of fourteen cents an acre to purchasers throughout the states. In 1796 a new Georgia legislature repealed the act of 1795. Because of national concern over possible Indian disorders, Congress some three years later provided for the purchase of the lands and for protection to Indians and consideration of the claims of others. After years of controversy, Congress, in 1814, appropriated five million dollars to compensate the purchasers of these Yazoo lands.

Fletcher of New Hampshire bought some of these lands from Peck of Boston in 1803. He immediately started an action against Peck in the United States Circuit Court in Boston on the ground that Peck's title was not good. Peck won a favorable decision in 1807; and Fletcher got a writ of error from the Supreme Court, directing the lower court to send a record of the case for review to the Supreme Court. Fletcher was the plaintiff in the lower court, Peck was the defendant. As the decision in the lower court was against Fletcher, he is known as the plaintiff in error, and Peck as the defendant in error, in the Supreme Court. The principal questions here were raised in the

1. 6 Cranch 87 (1810).

lower court by demurrer, a statement which admits for purposes of argument all the facts stated in a complaint or answering plea but denies that they have the legal consequences claimed for them. It is contrasted with a denial, which denies facts, and with a justification, which states new facts by way of explanation.

Mr. Justice William Johnson (1771–1834), of South Carolina, after a po-

litical and judicial career in his state, was appointed by Jefferson, in 1804, to the Supreme Court. He was a supporter of federal authority. As he intimates in his concurring opinion, the case was evidently a friendly one, to test the standing of the disputed land claims, in view of the controversy in Congress over compensation to claimants.

MARSHALL, CH. J., delivered the opinion of the Court as follows:

The pleadings being now amended, this cause comes on again to be heard on sundry demurrers and on a special verdict.

The suit was instituted on several covenants contained in a deed made by John Peck, the defendant in error, conveying to Robert Fletcher, the plaintiff in error, certain lands which were part of a large purchase made by James Gunn and others, in the year 1795, from the state of Georgia, the contract for which was made in the form of a bill passed by the legislature of that state.

The first count in the declaration[2] set forth a breach in the second covenant contained in the deed. The covenant is "that the legislature of the state of Georgia, at the time of passing the act of sale aforesaid, had good right to sell and dispose of the same, in manner pointed out by the said act." The breach assigned is that the legislature had no power to sell.

The plea in bar sets forth the constitution of the state of Georgia and avers that the lands sold by the defendant to the plaintiff were within that state. It then sets forth the granting act and avers the power of the legislature to sell and dispose of the premises as pointed out by the act.

2. Item of complaint in the statement of complaint.

To this plea the plaintiff below demurred, and the defendant joined in demurrer....

In the constitution of Georgia, adopted in the year 1789, the court can perceive no restriction on the legislative power, which inhibits the passage of the act of 1795. The court cannot say that, in passing that act, the legislature has transcended its powers and violated the Constitution. In overruling the demurrer, therefore, to the first plea, the circuit court committed no error.

The 3d covenant is that all the title which the state of Georgia ever had in the premises had been legally conveyed to John Peck, the grantor.

The 2d count assigns, in substance, as a breach of this covenant, that the original grantees from the state of Georgia promised and assured divers members of the legislature, then sitting in general assembly, that if the said members would assent to, and vote for, the passing of the act, and if the said bill should pass, such members should have a share of, and be interested in, all the lands purchased from the said state by virtue of such law. And that divers of the said members, to whom the said promises were made, were unduly influenced thereby, and, under such influence, did vote for the passing of the said bill; by reason whereof, the said law was a nullity, etc., and so the title of the state of Georgia did not pass to the said Peck, etc.

The plea to this count, after protesting that the promises it alleges were not made, avers that until after the purchase made from the original grantees by James Greenleaf, under whom the said Peck claims, neither the said James Greenleaf, nor the said Peck, nor any of the mesne vendors[3] between the said Greenleaf and Peck, had any notice or knowledge that any such promises or assurances were made by the said original grantees, or either of them, to any of the members of the legislature of the state of Georgia.

To this plea the plaintiff demurred generally, and the defendant joined in the demurrer.

That corruption should find its way into the governments of our infant republics, and contaminate the very source of legislation, or that impure motives should contribute to the passage of a law, or the formation of a legislative contract, are circumstances most deeply to be deplored. How far a court of justice would, in any case, be competent, on proceedings instituted by the state itself, to vacate a contract thus formed, and to annul rights acquired, under that contract, by third persons having no notice of the improper means by which it was obtained, is a question which the court would approach with much circumspection. It may well be doubted how far the validity of a law depends upon the motives of its framers, and how far the particular inducements, operating on members of the supreme sovereign power of a state, to the formation of a contract by that power, are examinable in a court of justice. If the principle be conceded, that an act of the supreme sovereign power might be declared null by a court, in consequence of the means which procured it, still would there be much difficulty in saying to what extent those means must be applied to produce this effect. Must it be direct corruption, or would interest or undue influence of any

kind be sufficient? Must the vitiating cause operate on a majority, or on what number of the members? Would the act be null, whatever might be the wish of the nation, or would its obligation or nullity depend upon the public sentiment?

If the majority of the legislature be corrupted, it may well be doubted whether it be within the province of the judiciary to control their conduct, and, if less than a majority act from impure motives, the principle by which judicial interference would be regulated is not clearly discerned. . . .

This solemn question cannot be brought thus collaterally and incidentally before the Court. It would be indecent, in the extreme, upon a private contract, between two individuals, to enter into an inquiry respecting the corruption of the sovereign power of a state. If the title be plainly deduced from a legislative act, which the legislature might constitutionally pass, if the act be clothed with all the requisite forms of a law, a court, sitting as a court of law, cannot sustain a suit brought by one individual against another, founded on the allegation that the act is a nullity, in consequence of the impure motives which influenced certain members of the legislature which passed the law. The circuit court, therefore, did right in overruling this demurrer.

The 4th covenant in the deed is that the title to the premises has been, in no way, constitutionally or legally impaired by virtue of any subsequent act of any subsequent legislature of the state of Georgia.

The third count recites the undue means practiced on certain members of the legislature, as stated in the second count, and then alleges that, in consequence of these practices, and of other causes, a subsequent legislature passed an act annulling and rescinding the law under which the conveyance to the original grantees was made, declaring that conveyance void, and asserting the title

3. Intermediate sellers.

454

of the state to the lands it contained. The count proceeds to recite at large this rescinding act and concludes with averring that, by reason of this act, the title of the said Peck in the premises was constitutionally and legally impaired and rendered null and void.

After protesting, as before, that no such promises were made as stated in this count, the defendant again pleads that himself and the first purchaser under the original grantees, and all intermediate holders of the property, were purchasers without notice. To this plea there is a demurrer and joinder.

The importance and the difficulty of the questions presented by these pleadings are deeply felt by the Court. The lands in controversy vested absolutely in James Gunn and others, the original grantees, by the conveyance of the governor, made in pursuance of an act of assembly, to which the legislature was fully competent. Being thus in full possession of the legal estate, they, for a valuable consideration, conveyed portions of the land to those who were willing to purchase. If the original transaction was infected with fraud, these purchasers did not participate in it, and had no notice of it. They were innocent. Yet the legislature of Georgia has involved them in the fate of the first parties to the transaction, and, if the act be valid, has annihilated their rights also.

The legislature of Georgia was a party to this transaction; and for a party to pronounce its own deed invalid, whatever cause may be assigned for its invalidity, must be considered as a mere act of power, which must find its vindication in a train of reasoning not often heard in courts of justice.

But the real party, it is said, are the people, and when their agents are unfaithful, the acts of those agents cease to be obligatory. It is, however, to be recollected that the people can act only by these agents and that, while within the powers conferred on them, their acts must be considered as the acts of the

people. If the agents be corrupt, others may be chosen, and, if their contracts be examinable, the common sentiment, as well as common usage of mankind, points out a mode by which this examination may be made and their validity determined.

If the legislature of Georgia was not bound to submit its pretensions to those tribunals which are established for the security of property, and to decide on human rights, if it might claim to itself the power of judging in its own case, yet there are certain great principles of justice, whose authority is universally acknowledged, that ought not to be entirely disregarded.

If the legislature be its own judge in its own case, it would seem equitable that its decision should be regulated by those rules which would have regulated the decision of a judicial tribunal. The question was, in its nature, a question of title, and the tribunal which decided it was either acting in the character of a court of justice, and performing a duty usually assigned to a court, or it was exerting a mere act of power in which it was controlled only by its own will.

If a suit be brought to set aside a conveyance obtained by fraud, and the fraud be clearly proved, the conveyance will be set aside, as between the parties; but the rights of third persons, who are purchasers without notice, for a valuable consideration, cannot be disregarded. Titles which, according to every legal test, are perfect are acquired with that confidence which is inspired by the opinion that the purchaser is safe. If there be any concealed defect, arising from the conduct of those who had held the property long before he acquired it, of which he had no notice, that concealed defect cannot be set up against him. He has paid his money for a title good at law; he is innocent, whatever may be the guilt of others, and equity will not subject him to the penalties attached to that guilt. All titles would be insecure, and the intercourse between man and man would be very seriously obstructed, if this principle be overturned. A court of chancery,[4] therefore, had a bill been brought to set aside the conveyance made to James Gunn and others, as being obtained by improper practices with the legislature, whatever might have been its decision as respected the original grantees, would have been bound, by its own rules, and by the clearest principles of equity, to leave unmolested those who were purchasers, without notice, for a valuable consideration.

If the legislature felt itself absolved from those rules of property which are common to all the citizens of the United States, and from those principles of equity which are acknowledged in all our courts, its act is to be supported by its power alone, and in the same power may divest any other individual of his lands, if it shall be the will of the legislature so to exert it.

It is not intended to speak with disrespect of the legislature of Georgia, or of its acts. Far from it. The question is a general question and is treated as one. For although such powerful objections to a legislative grant, as are alleged against this, may not again exist, yet the principle, on which alone this rescinding act is to be supported, may be applied to every case to which it shall be the will of any legislature to apply it. The principle is this: that a legislature may, by its own act, divest the vested estate of any man whatever, for reasons which shall, by itself, be deemed sufficient.

In this case the legislature may have had ample proof that the original grant was obtained by practices which can never be too much reprobated, and

4. A court specializing in the administration of that branch of the English law known as equity, which had been developed by English chancelors in the English court of chancery, in order to supplement the deficiencies of the older common law.

which would have justified its abrogation so far as respected those to whom crime was imputable. But the grant, when issued, conveyed an estate in fee-simple to the grantee, clothed with all the solemnities which law can bestow. This estate was transferrable; and those who purchased parts of it were not stained by that guilt which infected the original transaction. Their case is not distinguishable from the ordinary case of purchasers of a legal estate without knowledge of any secret fraud which might have led to the emanation of the original grant. According to the well-known course of equity, their rights could not be affected by such fraud. Their situation was the same, their title was the same, with that of every other member of the community who holds land by regular conveyances from the original patentee.

Is the power of the legislature competent to the annihilation of such title and to a resumption of the property thus held? The principle asserted is that one legislature is competent to repeal any act which a former legislature was competent to pass and that one legislature cannot abridge the powers of a succeeding legislature. The correctness of this principle, so far as respects general legislation, can never be controverted. But, if an act be done under a law, a succeeding legislature cannot undo it. The past cannot be recalled by the most absolute power. Conveyances have been made, those conveyances have vested legal estates, and, if those estates may be seized by the sovereign authority, still, that they originally vested is a fact and cannot cease to be a fact. When, then, a law is in its nature a contract, when absolute rights have vested under that contract, a repeal of the law cannot divest those rights; and the act of annulling them, if legitimate, is rendered so by a power applicable to the case of every individual in the community.

It may well be doubted whether the

nature of society and of government does not prescribe some limits to the legislative power; and, if any be prescribed, where are they to be found, if the property of an individual, fairly and honestly acquired, may be seized without compensation. To the legislature all legislative power is granted; but the question, whether the act of transferring the property of an individual to the public, be in the nature of the legislative power, is well worthy of serious reflection. It is the peculiar province of the legislature to prescribe general rules for the government of society; the application of those rules to individuals in society would seem to be the duty of other departments. How far the power of giving the law may involve every other power, in cases where the Constitution is silent, never has been, and perhaps never can be, definitely stated.

The validity of this rescinding act, then, might well be doubted, were Georgia a single sovereign power. But Georgia cannot be viewed as a single, unconnected, sovereign power, on whose legislature no other restrictions are imposed than may be found in its own constitution. She is a part of a large empire; she is a member of the American union; and that union has a constitution, the supremacy of which all acknowledge, and which imposes limits to the legislatures of the several states, which none claim a right to pass. The Constitution of the United States declares that no state shall pass any bill of attainder, *ex post facto* law, or law impairing the obligation of contracts.

Does the case now under consideration come within this prohibitory section of the Constitution?

In considering this very interesting question, we immediately ask ourselves, What is a contract? Is a grant a contract? A contract is a compact between two or more parties and is either executory or executed. An executory contract is one in which a party binds himself to do, or not to do, a particular thing; such was the law under which the conveyance was made by the governor. A contract executed is one in which the object of contract is performed; and this, says Blackstone, differs in nothing from a grant. The contract between Georgia and the purchasers was executed by the grant. A contract executed, as well as one which is executory, contains obligations binding on the parties. A grant, in its own nature, amounts to an extinguishment of the right of the grantor and implies a contract not to reassert that right. A party is, therefore, always estopped by his own grant.

Since, then, in fact, a grant is a contract executed, the obligation of which still continues, and since the Constitution uses the general term "contract," without distinguishing between those which are executory and those which are executed, it must be construed to comprehend the latter as well as the former. A law annulling conveyances between individuals, and declaring that the grantors should stand seized of their former estates, notwithstanding those grants, would be as repugnant to the Constitution as a law discharging the vendors of property from the obligation of executing their contracts by conveyances. It would be strange if a contract to convey was secured by the Constitution, while an absolute conveyance remained unprotected.

If, under a fair construction of the Constitution, grants are comprehended under the term "contracts," is a grant from the state excluded from the operation of the provision? Is the clause to be considered as inhibiting the state from impairing the obligation of contracts between two individuals, but as excluding from that inhibition contracts made with itself? The words themselves contain no such distinction. They are general and are applicable to contracts of every description. If contracts made with the state are to be exempted from their operation, the exception must arise from the character of the contracting party, not from the words which are employed.

Whatever respect might have been felt for the state sovereignties, it is not to be disguised that the framers of the Constitution viewed, with some apprehension, the violent acts which might grow out of the feelings of the moment; and that the people of the United States, in adopting that instrument, have manifested a determination to shield themselves and their property from the effects of those sudden and strong passions to which men are exposed. The restrictions on the legislative power of the states are obviously founded in this sentiment; and the Constitution of the United States contains what may be deemed a bill of rights for the people of each state....

It is, then, the unanimous opinion of the Court that, in this case, the estate having passed into the hands of a purchaser for a valuable consideration, without notice, the state of Georgia was restrained, either by general principles which are common to our free institutions, or by the particular provisions of the Constitution of the United States, from passing a law whereby the estate of the plaintiff in the premises so purchased would be constitutionally and legally impaired and rendered null and void. In overruling the demurrer to the 3d plea, therefore, there is no error....

JOHNSON, J. In this case I entertain, on two points, an opinion different from

that which has been delivered by the Court.

I do not hesitate to declare that a state does not possess the power of revoking its own grants. But I do it on a general principle, on the reason and nature of things: a principle which will impose laws even on the Deity....

I have thrown out these ideas that I may have it distinctly understood that my opinion on this point is not founded on the provision in the Constitution of the United States, relative to laws impairing the obligation of contracts....

There can be no solid objection to adopting the technical definition of the word "contract," given by Blackstone. The etymology, the classical signification, and the civil law idea of the word, will all support it. But the difficulty arises on the word "obligation," which certainly imports an existing moral or physical necessity. Now, a grant or conveyance by no means necessarily implies the continuance of an obligation, beyond the moment of executing it. It is most generally but the consummation of a contract....

I have been very unwilling to proceed to the decision of this cause at all. It appears to me to bear strong evidence, upon the face of it, of being a mere feigned case. It is our duty to decide on the rights, but not on the speculations of parties. My confidence, however, in the respectable gentlemen who have been engaged for the parties has induced me to abandon my scruples, in the belief that they would never consent to impose a mere feigned case upon this Court.

5. DARTMOUTH COLLEGE v. WOODWARD[1]

EDITORS' NOTE.—Dartmouth College, supported by private endowments, was incorporated by royal charter in 1769. Rights and obligations

created by the charter later passed to the state of New Hampshire. A church fight in the community, commenced in 1783, spread to the college and became more and more lively. It led to

1. 4 Wheaton 518 (February 2, 1819).

the removal of President Wheelock in 1815 by action of the trustees. The participants in the controversy had already become identified with the two political parties of the time. The Republicans replaced the Federalists in control of the state in 1816. Thereupon they modified the college charter by increasing the number of trustees, adding a board of overseers, and replacing the self-perpetuating board of trustees provided for in the charter by these new bodies, controlled by state appointment. In effect the private college was turned into a state university, as it was called. The secretary of the college sided with President Wheelock, now reinstated, and the trustees appointed under the new law. He had the records and seal of the institution in his possession. To test the rights of the parties to the dispute, the old trustees brought this action against the secretary, Woodward, on the ground that the new trustees, under whom Woodward was serving, were wrongfully retaining the records and seal. The new trustees of the university won in the state courts.

On the ground that rights protected by the federal Constitution were in question, the old trustees of the college secured a writ of error from the Supreme Court of the United States. Daniel Webster (1782–1852), a Dartmouth graduate, appeared on their behalf. He had already developed the practice which was to make him the most famous lawyer of his day. His arguments in *Dartmouth College* v. *Woodward*, in *Gibbons* v. *Ogden*, and in other cases were important contributions to the development of the federal system.

... The opinion of the Court was delivered by MARSHALL, Ch. J.

This is an action of trover,[2] brought by the Trustees of Dartmouth College against William H. Woodward, in the state court of New Hampshire, for the book of records, corporate seal, and other corporate property, to which the plaintiffs allege themselves to be entitled. A special verdict, after setting out the rights of the parties, finds for the defendant, if certain acts of the legislature of New Hampshire, passed on the 27th of June, and on the 18th of December 1816, be valid, and binding on the trustees, without their assent, and not repugnant to the Constitution of the United States; otherwise, it finds for the plaintiffs. The superior court of judicature of New Hampshire rendered a judgment upon this verdict for the defendant, which judgment has been brought before this Court by writ of error. The single question now to be considered is: Do the acts to which the verdict refers violate the Constitution of the United States?

This Court can be insensible neither to the magnitude nor delicacy of this question. The validity of a legislative act is to be examined; and the opinion of the highest law tribunal of a state is to be revised—an opinion which carries with it intrinsic evidence of the diligence, of the ability, and the integrity, with which it was formed. On more than one occasion, this Court has expressed the cautious circumspection with which it approaches the consideration of such questions; and has declared that, in no doubtful case, would it pronounce a legislative act to be contrary to the Constitution. But the American people have said, in the Constitution of the United

2. An old Anglicized French name for a legal action brought against a defendant for alleged misappropriation of property.

States, that "no state shall pass any bill of attainder, *ex post facto* law, or law impairing the obligation of contracts." In the same instrument, they have also said, "that the judicial power shall extend to all cases in law and equity arising under the Constitution." On the judges of this Court, then, is imposed the high and solemn duty of protecting, from even legislative violation, those contracts which the Constitution of our country has placed beyond legislative control; and, however irksome the task may be, this is a duty from which we dare not shrink....

It can require no argument to prove that the circumstances of this case constitute a contract. An application is made to the crown for a charter to incorporate a religious and literary institution. In the application, it is stated that large contributions have been made for the object, which will be conferred on the corporation, as soon as it shall be created. The charter is granted, and on its faith the property is conveyed. Surely, in this transaction every ingredient of a complete and legitimate contract is to be found. The points for consideration are: (1) Is this contract protected by the Constitution of the United States? (2) Is it impaired by the acts under which the defendant holds?

1. On the first point, it has been argued that the word "contract," in its broadest sense, would comprehend the political relations between the government and its citizens, would extend to offices held within a state, for state purposes, and to many of those laws concerning civil institutions, which must change with circumstances, and be modified by ordinary legislation; which deeply concern the public, and which, to preserve good government, the public judgment must control....

The general correctness of these observations cannot be controverted. That the framers of the Constitution did not intend to restrain the states in the regu-

lation of their civil institutions, adopted for internal government, and that the instrument they have given us is not to be so construed, may be admitted....

A corporation is an artificial being, invisible, intangible, and existing only in contemplation of law. Being the mere creature of law, it possesses only those properties which the charter of its creation confers upon it, either expressly, or as incidental to its very existence. These are such as are supposed best calculated to effect the object for which it was created. Among the most important are immortality, and, if the expression may be allowed, individuality; properties by which a perpetual succession of many persons are considered as the same and may act as a single individual. They enable a corporation to manage its own affairs, and to hold property, without the perplexing intricacies, the hazardous and endless necessity, of perpetual conveyances for the purpose of transmitting it from hand to hand. It is chiefly for the purpose of clothing bodies of men, in succession, with these qualities and capacities, that corporations were invented and are in use. By these means, a perpetual succession of individuals are capable of acting for the promotion of the particular object, like one immortal being. But this being does not share in the civil government of the country, unless that be the purpose for which it was created. Its immortality no more confers on it political power, or a political character, than immortality would confer such power or character on a natural person. It is no more a state instrument than a natural person exercising the same powers would be. If, then, a natural person, employed by individuals in the education of youth, or for the government of a seminary in which youth is educated, would not become a public officer, or be considered as a member of the civil government, how is it, that this artificial being, created by law, for the purpose of being employed by the same individuals, for the same purposes, should become a part of the civil government of the country? Is it because its existence, its capacities, its powers, are given by law? Because the government has given it the power to take and to hold property, in a particular form, and for particular purposes, has the government a consequent right substantially to change that form, or to vary the purposes to which the property is to be applied? This principle has never been asserted or recognized and is supported by no authority. Can it derive aid from reason?

The objects for which a corporation is created are universally such as the government wishes to promote. They are deemed beneficial to the country; and this benefit constitutes the consideration and, in most cases, the sole consideration of the grant. In most eleemosynary institutions, the object would be difficult, perhaps unattainable, without the aid of a charter of incorporation. Charitable or public-spirited individuals, desirous of making permanent appropriations for charitable or other useful purposes, find it impossible to effect their design securely and certainly, without an incorporating act. They apply to the government, state their beneficent object, and offer to advance the money necessary for its accomplishment, provided the government will confer on the instrument which is to execute their designs the capacity to execute them. The proposition is considered and approved. The benefit to the public is considered as an ample compensation for the faculty it confers, and the corporation is created. If the advantages to the public constitute a full compensation for the faculty it gives, there can be no reason for exacting a further compensation by claiming a right to exercise over this artificial being a power which changes its nature, and touches the fund, for the security and application of which it was created. There can be no reason for implying in

a charter, given for a valuable consideration, a power which is not only not expressed, but is in direct contradiction to its express stipulations. . . .

From this review of the charter, it appears that Dartmouth College is an eleemosynary institution, incorporated for the purpose of perpetuating the application of the bounty of the donors, to the specified objects of that bounty; that its trustees or governors were originally named by the founder, and invested with the power of perpetuating themselves; that they are not public officers, nor is it a civil institution, participating in the administration of government; but a charity-school, or a seminary of education, incorporated for the preservation of its property, and the perpetual application of that property to the objects of its creation.

Yet a question remains to be considered, of more real difficulty, on which more doubt has been entertained, than on all that have been discussed. The founders of the college, at least those whose contributions were in money, have parted with the property bestowed upon it, and their representatives have no interest in that property. The donors of land are equally without interest, so long as the corporation shall exist. Could they be found, they are unaffected by any alteration in its constitution, and probably regardless of its form, or even of its existence. The students are fluctuating, and no individual among our youth has a vested interest in the institution which can be asserted in a court of justice. Neither the founders of the college, nor the youth for whose benefit it was founded, complain of the alteration made in its charter or think themselves injured by it. The trustees alone complain, and the trustees have no beneficial interest to be protected. Can this be such a contract as the Constitution intended to withdraw from the power of state legislation? Contracts, the parties to which have a vested beneficial interest, and those only, it has been said, are the objects about which the Constitution is solicitous and to which its protection is extended. . . .

According to the theory of the British constitution, their Parliament is omnipotent. To annul corporate rights might give a shock to public opinion, which that government has chosen to avoid; but its power is not questioned. Had Parliament, immediately after the emanation of this charter, and the execution of those conveyances which followed it, annulled the instrument, so that the living donors would have witnessed the disappointment of their hopes, the perfidy of the transaction would have been universally acknowledged. Yet, then, as now, the donors would have no interest in the property; then, as now, those who might be students would have had no rights to be violated; then, as now, it might be said that the trustees, in whom the rights of all were combined, possessed no private, individual, beneficial interests in the property confided to their protection. Yet the contract would, at that time, have been deemed sacred by all. What has since occurred to strip it of its inviolability? Circumstances have not changed it. In reason, in justice, and in law, it is now what it was in 1769.

This is plainly a contract to which the donors, the trustees, and the crown (to whose rights and obligations New Hampshire succeeds) were the original parties. It is a contract made on a valuable consideration. It is a contract for the security and disposition of property. It is a contract, on the faith of which real and personal estate has been conveyed to the corporation. It is, then, a contract within the letter of the Constitution, and within its spirit also, unless the fact that the property is invested by the donors in trustees, for the promotion of religion and education, for the benefit of persons who are perpetually changing, though the objects remain the same, shall create a particular exception, taking this case out of the prohibition contained in the Constitution.

It is more than possible that the preservation of rights of this description was not particularly in the view of the framers of the Constitution, when the clause under consideration was introduced into that instrument. It is probable that interferences of more frequent occurrence, to which the temptation was stronger, and of which the mischief was more extensive, constituted the great motive for imposing this restriction on the state legislatures. But although a particular and a rare case may not, in itself, be of sufficient magnitude to induce a rule, yet it must be governed by the rule, when established, unless some plain and strong reason for excluding it can be given. It is not enough to say that this particular case was not in the mind of the convention, when the article was framed, nor of the American people, when it was adopted. It is necessary to go further, and to say that, had this particular case been suggested, the language would have been so varied as to exclude it, or it would have been made a special exception. The case, being within the words of the rule, must be within its operation likewise, unless there be something in the literal construction, so obviously absurd or mischievous, or repugnant to the general spirit of the instrument, as to justify those who expound the Constitution in making it an exception.

On what safe and intelligible ground can this exception stand? There is no expression in the Constitution, no sentiment delivered by its contemporaneous expounders, which would justify us in making it. In the absence of all authority of this kind, is there, in the nature and reason of the case itself, that which would sustain a construction of the Constitution not warranted by its words? Are contracts of this description of a character to excite so little interest that

462

we must exclude them from the provisions of the Constitution as being unworthy of the attention of those who framed the instrument? Or does public policy so imperiously demand their remaining exposed to legislative alteration, as to compel us, or rather permit us, to say that these words, which were introduced to give stability to contracts, and which in their plain import comprehend this contract, must yet be so construed as to exclude it?

Almost all eleemosynary corporations, those which are created for the promotion of religion, of charity, or of education, are of the same character. The law of this case is the law of all. In every literary or charitable institution, unless the objects of the bounty be themselves incorporated, the whole legal interest is in trustees and can be asserted only by them. The donors, or claimants of the bounty, if they can appear in court at all, can appear only to complain of the trustees. In all other situations, they are identified with, and personated by, the trustees; and their rights are to be defended and maintained by them. Religion, charity, and education are, in the law of England, legatees or donees, capable of receiving bequests or donations in this form. They appear in court and claim or defend by the corporation. Are they of so little estimation in the United States that contracts for their benefit must be excluded from the protection of words, which in their natural import include them? Or do such contracts so necessarily require new modeling by the authority of the legislature that the ordinary rules of construction must be disregarded in order to leave them exposed to legislative alteration?

All feel that these objects are not deemed unimportant in the United States. The interest which this case has excited proves that they are not. The framers of the Constitution did not deem them unworthy of its care and protection. They have, though in a different mode, manifested their respect for science, by reserving to the government of the Union the power "to promote the progress of science and useful arts, by securing for limited times, to authors and inventors, the exclusive right to their respective writings and discoveries." They have, so far, withdrawn science, and the useful arts, from the action of the state governments. Why then should they be supposed so regardless of contracts made for the advancement of literature as to intend to exclude them from provisions made for the security of ordinary contracts between man and man? No reason for making this supposition is perceived.

If the insignificance of the object does not require that we should exclude contracts respecting it from the protection of the Constitution; neither, as we conceive, is the policy of leaving them subject to legislative alteration so apparent as to require a forced construction of that instrument in order to effect it. These eleemosynary institutions do not fill the place, which would otherwise be occupied by government, but that which would otherwise remain vacant. They are complete acquisitions to literature. They are donations to education; donations which any government must be disposed rather to encourage than to discountenance. It requires no very critical examination of the human mind to enable us to determine that one great inducement to these gifts is the conviction felt by the giver that the disposition he makes of them is immutable. It is probable that no man ever was, and that no man ever will be, the founder of a college, believing at the time than an act of incorporation constitutes no security for the institution; believing that it is immediately to be deemed a public institution, whose funds are to be governed and applied, not by the will of the donor, but by the will of the legislature. All such gifts are made in the pleasing, perhaps delusive, hope that the charity will flow forever in the channels which the givers have marked out for it. If every man finds in his own bosom strong evidence of the universality of this sentiment, there can be but little reason to imagine that the framers of our Constitution were strangers to it and that, feeling the necessity and policy of giving permanence and security to contracts, of withdrawing them from the influence of legislative bodies, whose fluctuating policy, and repeated interferences, produced the most perplexing and injurious embarrassments, they still deemed it necesssary to leave these contracts subject to those interferences. . . .

The opinion of the Court, after mature deliberation, is that this is a contract, the obligation of which cannot be impaired without violating the Constitution of the United States. This opinion appears to us to be equally supported by reason and by the former decisions of this Court.

2. We next proceed to the inquiry, whether its obligation has been impaired by those acts of the legislature of New Hampshire, to which the special verdict refers? . . .

On the effect of this law, two opinions cannot be entertained. Between acting directly, and acting through the agency of trustees and overseers, no essential difference is perceived. The whole power of governing the college is transferred from trustees, appointed according to the will of the founder, expressed in the charter, to the executive of New Hampshire. The management and application of the funds of this eleemosynary institution, which are placed by the donors in the hands of trustees named in the charter, and empowered to perpetuate

themselves, are placed by this act under the control of the government of the state. The will of the state is substituted for the will of the donors, in very essential operation of the college. This is not an immaterial change. The founders of the college contracted, not merely for the perpetual application of the funds which they gave, to the objects for which those funds were given; they contracted also, to secure that application by the constitution of the corporation. They contracted for a system which should, so far as human foresight can provide, retain forever the government of the literary institution they had formed, in the hands of persons approved by themselves. This system is totally changed. The charter of 1769 exists no longer. It is reorganized, and reorganized in such a manner, as to convert a literary institution, molded according to the will of its founders, and placed under the control of private literary men, into a machine entirely subservient to the will of government. This may be for the advantage of this college in particular, and may be for the advantage of literature in general; but it is not according to the will of the donors, and is subversive of that contract, on the faith of which their property was given. . . .

It results from this opinion, that the acts of the legislature of New Hampshire, which are stated in the special verdict found in this cause, are repugnant to the Constitution of the United States; and that the judgment on this special verdict ought to have been for the plaintiffs. The judgment of the state court must, therefore, be reversed.

6. *McCULLOCH* v. *MARYLAND*[1]

EDITORS' NOTE.—After the War of 1812, the Republicans kept power but

1. 4 Wheaton 316 (1819).

turned to Federalist policies—internal improvements, protective tariff, national bank, a strong national government. Jefferson and Marshall had been hostile to each other. Now the prevailing ideas were congenial to Marshall. In 1816 Congress incorporated the second Bank of the United States. The bank commenced operations in 1817. In 1818 a crippling stamp tax, directed in effect only at the bank's branch in Baltimore, was imposed by the legislature of Maryland and enforced by Maryland authorities. Similar action was taken in Ohio and threatened elsewhere. Maryland brought an action at law against McCulloch, cashier of the Baltimore branch bank, to collect penalties for refusal to pay the Maryland tax. Maryland won in the state courts,

and McCulloch, for the bank, secured a writ of error from the federal Supreme Court.

Webster, again, was on the winning side. His argument followed Hamilton's opinion supporting the validity of the bill to establish the first Bank of the United States; his theory also influenced Marshall's opinion. However, William Pinkney (1764–1822), on the same side, made a more original contribution to Marshall's opinion. In vetoing a bill to recharter the second bank, in 1832, President Jackson expressed his disagreement with both Hamilton and Marshall.

March 7th, 1819. MARSHALL, Ch. J., delivered the opinion of the Court:

In the case now to be determined, the defendant, a sovereign state, denies the obligation of a law enacted by the legislature of the Union, and the plaintiff, on his part, contests the validity of an act which has been passed by the legislature of that state. The Constitution of our country, in its most interesting and vital parts, is to be considered; the conflicting powers of the government of the Union and of its members, as marked in that Constitution, are to be discussed; and an opinion given which may essentially influence the great operations of the government. No tribunal can approach such a question without a deep sense of its importance and of the awful responsibility involved in its decision. But it must be decided peacefully, or remain a source of hostile legislation, perhaps, of hostility of a still more serious nature; and if it is to be so decided, by this tribunal alone can the decision be made. On the Supreme Court of the United States has the Constitution of our country devolved this important duty.

The first question made in the cause is:

Has Congress power to incorporate a bank? It has been truly said that this can scarcely be considered as an open question, entirely unprejudiced by the former proceedings of the nation respecting it. The principle now contested was introduced at a very early period of our history, has been recognized by many successive legislatures, and has been acted upon by the judicial department, in cases of peculiar delicacy, as a law of undoubted obligation. . . .

In discussing this question, the counsel for the state of Maryland have deemed it of some importance, in the construction of the Constitution, to consider that instrument, not as emanating from the people, but as the act of sovereign and independent states. The powers of the general government, it has been said, are delegated by the states, who alone are truly sovereign; and must be exercised in subordination to the states, who alone possess supreme dominion. It would be difficult to sustain this proposition. The convention which framed the Constitution was indeed elected by the state legislatures. But the instrument, when it came from their hands, was a mere proposal, without obligation, or pretensions to it. It was reported to the then existing congress of the United States, with a request that it might "be submitted to a convention of delegates, chosen in each state by the people thereof, under the recommendation of its legislature, for their assent and ratification." This mode of proceeding was adopted: and by the convention, by congress, and by the state legislatures, the instrument was submitted to the *people*. They acted upon it in the only manner in which they can act safely, effectively, and wisely on such a subject by assembling in convention. It is true, they assembled in their several states—and where else should they have assembled? No political dreamer was ever wild enough to think of breaking down the lines which separate the states, and of compounding the American people into one common mass. Of consequence, when they act, they act in their states. But the measures they adopt do not, on that account, cease to be the measures of the people themselves, or become the measures of the state governments.

From these conventions, the Constitution derives its whole authority. The government proceeds directly from the people; is "ordained and established," in the name of the people; and is declared to be ordained, "in order to form a more perfect union, establish justice, insure domestic tranquillity, and secure the blessings of liberty to themselves and to their posterity." The assent of the states, in their sovereign capacity, is implied, in calling a convention, and thus submitting that instrument to the people. But the people were at perfect liberty to accept or reject it; and their act was final. It required not the affirmance, and could not be negatived, by the state governments. The Constitution, when thus adopted, was of complete obligation, and bound the state sovereignties.

It has been said that the people had already surrendered all their powers to the state sovereignties and had nothing more to give. But, surely, the question whether they may resume and modify the powers granted to government does not remain to be settled in this country. Much more might the legitimacy of the general government be doubted had it been created by the states. The powers delegated to the state sovereignties were to be exercised by themselves, not by a distinct and independent sovereignty, created by themselves. To the formation of a league, such as was the confederation, the state sovereignties were certainly competent. But when, "in order to form a more perfect union," it was deemed necessary to change this alliance into an effective government, possessing great and sovereign powers, and acting directly on the people, the necessity of referring it to the people, and of deriving its powers directly from them, was felt and acknowledged by all. The government of the Union, then (whatever may be the influence of this fact on the case), is, emphatically and truly, a government of the people. In form, and in substance, it emanates from them. Its powers are granted by them, and are to be exercised directly on them, and for their benefit.

This government is acknowledged by all, to be one of enumerated powers. The principle that it can exercise only the powers granted to it would seem too apparent to have required to be enforced by all those arguments, which its enlightened friends, while it was depending before the people, found it necessary to urge; that principle is now universally admitted. But the question respecting the extent of the powers actually granted is perpetually arising, and will probably continue to arise, so long as our system shall exist. In discussing these questions, the conflicting powers of the general and state governments must be brought into view, and the supremacy of their respective laws, when they are in opposition, must be settled.

If any one proposition could command the universal assent of mankind, we might expect it would be this—that the government of the Union, though limited in its powers, is supreme within its sphere of action. This would seem to result, necessarily, from its nature. It is the government of all; its powers are delegated by all; it represents all, and acts for all. Though any one state may be willing to control its operations, no state is willing to allow others to control them. The nation, on those subjects on which it can act, must necessarily bind its component parts. But this question is not left to mere reason: the people have, in express terms, decided it, by saying, "this Constitution, and the laws of the United States, which shall be made in pursuance thereof," "shall be the supreme law of the land," and by requiring that the members of the state legislatures, and the officers of the executive and judicial departments of the states, shall take the oath of fidelity to it. The government of the United States, then, though limited in its powers, is supreme; and its laws, when made in pursuance of the Constitution, form the supreme law of the land, "anything in the Constitution or laws of any state to the contrary notwithstanding."

Among the enumerated powers, we do not find that of establishing a bank or creating a corporation. But there is no phrase in the instrument which, like the Articles of Confederation, excludes incidental or implied powers; and which requires that everything granted shall be expressly and minutely described. Even the Tenth Amendment, which was framed for the purpose of quieting the excessive jealousies which had been excited, omits the word "expressly," and declares only that the powers "not delegated to the United States, nor prohibited to the states, are reserved to the states or to the people"; thus leaving the question, whether the particular power which may become the subject of contest has been delegated to the one government, or prohibited to the other, to depend on a fair construction of the whole instrument. The man who drew and adopted this amendment had experienced the embarrassments resulting from the insertion of this word in the Articles of Confederation, and probably omitted it, to avoid those embarrassments. A constitution, to contain an accurate detail of all the subdivisions of which its great powers will admit, and of all the means by which they may be carried into execution, would partake of the prolixity of a legal code, and could scarcely be embraced by the human mind. It would, probably, never be understood by the public. Its nature, therefore, requires that only its great outlines should be marked, its important objects designated, and the minor ingredients which compose those objects, be deduced from the nature of the objects themselves. That this idea was entertained by the framers of the American Constitution is not only to be inferred from the nature of the instrument but from the language. Why else were some of the limitations, found in the ninth section of the first article, introduced? It is also, in some degree, warranted, by their having omitted to use any restrictive term which might prevent its receiving a fair and just interpretation. In considering this question, then, we must never forget that it is a *constitution* we are expounding.

Although, among the enumerated powers of government, we do not find the word "bank" or "incorporation," we find the great powers, to lay and collect taxes; to borrow money; to regulate commerce; to declare and conduct a war; and to raise and support armies and navies. The sword and the purse, all the external relations, and no inconsiderable portion of the industry of the nation, are intrusted to its government. It can never be pretended that these vast powers draw after them others of inferior importance, merely because they are inferior. Such an idea can never be advanced. But it may with great reason be contended that a government, intrusted with such ample powers, on the due execution of which the happiness and prosperity of the nation so vitally depends, must also be intrusted with ample means for their execution. The power being given, it is the interest of the nation to facilitate its execution. It can never be their interest, and cannot be presumed to have been their intention, to clog and embarrass its execution by withholding the most appropriate means. Throughout this vast republic, from the St. Croix to the Gulf of Mexico, from the Atlantic to the Pacific, revenue is to be collected and expended, armies are to be marched and supported. The exigencies of the nation may require that the treasure raised in the north should be transported to the south, that raised in the east, conveyed to the west, or that this order should be reversed. Is that construction of the Constitution to be preferred which would render these operations difficult, hazardous, and expensive? Can we adopt that construction (unless the words imperiously require it) which would impute to the framers of that instrument, when granting these powers for the public good, the intention of impeding their exercise, by withholding a choice of means? If, indeed, such be the mandate of the Constitution, we have only to obey; but that instrument does not profess to enumerate the means by which the powers it confers may be executed; nor does it prohibit the creation of a corporation, if the existence of such a being be essential, to the beneficial exercise of those powers. It is, then, the subject of fair inquiry, how far such means may be employed.

It is not denied that the powers given to the government imply the ordinary means of execution. That, for example, of raising revenue, and applying it to national purposes, is admitted to imply the power of conveying money from place to place, as the exigencies of the nation may require, and of employing the usual means of conveyance. But it is denied that the government has its choice of means or that it may employ the most convenient means, if, to employ them, it be necessary to erect a corporation. On what foundation does this argument rest? On this alone: the power of creating a corporation is one appertaining to sovereignty and is not expressly conferred on Congress. This is true. But all legislative powers appertain to sovereignty. The original power of giving the law on any subject whatever is a sovereign power; and if the government of the Union is restrained from creating a corporation, as a means for performing its functions, on the single reason that the creation of a corporation is an act of sovereignty; if the sufficiency of this reason be acknowledged, there would be some difficulty in sustaining the authority of Congress to pass other laws for the accomplishment of the same objects. The government which has a right to do an act, and has imposed on it the duty of performing that act, must, according to the dictates of reason, be allowed to select the means; and those who contend that it may not select any appropriate means, that one particular mode of effecting the object is excepted, take upon themselves the burden of establishing that exception.

The creation of a corporation, it is said, appertains to sovereignty. This is admitted. But to what portion of sovereignty does it appertain? Does it belong to one more than to another? In America, the powers of sovereignty are divided between the government of the Union and those of the states. They are each sovereign, with respect to the objects committed to it, and neither sovereign, with respect to the objects committed to the other. We cannot comprehend that train of reasoning which would maintain that the extent of power granted by the people is to be ascertained, not by the nature and terms of the grant, but by its date. Some state constitutions were formed before, some since that of the United States. We cannot believe that their relation to each other is in any degree dependent upon this circumstance. Their respective powers must, we think, be precisely the same, as if they had been formed at the same time. Had they been formed at the same time, and had the people conferred on the general government the power contained in the Constitution, and on the states the whole residuum of power, would it have been asserted that the government of the Union was not sovereign, with respect to those objects which were intrusted to it, in relation to which its laws were declared to be supreme? If this could not have been asserted, we cannot well comprehend the process of reasoning which maintains that a power appertaining to sovereignty cannot be connected with that vast portion of it which is granted to the general government, so far as it is calculated to subserve the legitimate objects of that government. The power of creating a corporation, though appertaining to sovereignty, is not, like the power of making war, or levying taxes, or of regulating commerce, a great substantive and independent power, which cannot be implied as incidental to other powers, or used as a means of executing them. It is never the end for which other powers are exercised, but a means by which other objects are accomplished. No contributions are made to charity, for the sake of an incorporation, but a corporation is created to administer the charity; no seminary of learning is instituted, in order to be incorporated, but the corporate character is conferred to subserve the purposes of education. No city was ever built with the sole object of being incorporated, but is incorporated as affording the best means of being well governed. The power of creating a corporation is never used for its own sake, but for the purpose of effecting something else. No sufficient reason is, therefore, perceived, why it may not pass as incidental to those powers which are expressly given, if it be a direct mode of executing them.

But the Constitution of the United States has not left the right of Congress to employ the necessary means, for the execution of the powers conferred on the government, to general reasoning. To its enumeration of powers is added that of making "all laws which shall be necessary and proper, for carrying into execution the foregoing powers, and all other powers vested by this Constitution, in the government of the United States, or in any department thereof." The counsel for the state of Maryland have urged various arguments to prove that this clause, though, in terms, a grant of power, is not so, in effect; but is really restrictive of the general right, which might otherwise be implied, of selecting means for executing the enumerated powers. . . .

But the argument on which most reliance is placed is drawn from that peculiar language of this clause. Congress is not empowered by it to make all laws, which may have relation to the powers conferred on the government, but such only as may be "*necessary and proper*" for carrying them into execution. The word "*necessary*" is considered as controlling the whole sentence, and as limiting the right to pass laws for the execution of the granted powers, to such as are indispensable, and without which the power would be nugatory. That it excludes the choice of means, and leaves to Congress, in each case, that only which is most direct and simple.

Is it true that this is the sense in which the word "necessary" is always used? Does it always import an absolute physical necessity, so strong, that one thing to which another may be termed necessary, cannot exist without that other? We think it does not. If reference be had to its use, in the common affairs of the world, or in approved authors, we find that it frequently imports no more than that one thing is convenient, or useful, or essential to another. To employ the means necessary to an end is generally understood as employing any means calculated to produce the end and not as being confined to those single means, without which the end would be entirely unattainable. Such is the character of human language that no word conveys to the mind, in all situations, one single definite idea; and nothing is more common than to use words in a figurative sense. Almost all compositions contain words which, taken in their rigorous sense, would convey a meaning different from that which is obviously intended. It is essential to just construction that many words which import something excessive should be understood in a more mitigated sense—in that sense which common usage justifies. The word "necessary" is of this description. It has not a fixed character, peculiar to itself. It admits of all degrees of comparison and is often connected with other words, which increase or diminish the impression the mind receives of the urgency it imports. A thing may be necessary, very necessary, absolutely or indispensably necessary. To no mind would the same idea be conveyed by these several phrases. The comment on the word is well illustrated by the passage cited at the bar, from the tenth section of the first article of the Constitution. It is, we think, impossible to compare the sentence which prohibits a state from laying "imposts, or duties on imports or exports, except what may be *absolutely* necessary for executing its inspection laws," with that which authorizes Congress "to make all laws which shall be necessary and proper for carrying into execution" the powers of the general government, without feeling a conviction that the convention understood itself to change materially the meaning of the word "necessary," by prefixing the word "absolutely." This word, then, like others, is used in various senses; and, in its construction, the subject, the context, the intention of the person using them, are all to be taken into view.

Let this be done in the case under consideration. The subject is the execution of those great powers on which the welfare of a nation essentially depends. It must have been the intention of those who gave these powers to insure, so far as human prudence could insure, their beneficial execution. This could not be done by confiding the choice of means to such narrow limits as not to leave it in the power of Congress to adopt any which might be appropriate, and which were conducive to the end. This provision is made in a constitution, intended to endure for ages to come, and consequently, to be adapted to the various *crises* of human affairs. To have prescribed the means by which government should, in all future time, execute its powers, would have been to change, entirely, the character of the instrument, and give it the properties of a legal code. It would have been an unwise attempt to provide, by immutable rules, for exigencies which, if foreseen at all, must have been seen dimly, and which can be best provided for as they occur. To have declared that the best means shall not be used, but those alone, without which the power given would be nugatory, would have been to deprive the legislature of the capacity to avail itself of experience, to exercise its reason, and to accommodate its legislation to circumstances. . . .

In ascertaining the sense in which the word "necessary" is used in this clause of the Constitution, we may derive some aid from that with which it is associated. Congress shall have power "to make all laws which shall be necessary and proper to carry into execution" the powers of the government. If the word "necessary" was used in that strict and rigorous sense for which the counsel for the state of Maryland contend, it would be an extraordinary departure from the usual course of the human mind, as exhibited in composition, to add a word, the only possible effect of which is to qualify that strict and rigorous meaning; to present to the mind the idea of some choice of means of legislation not strained and compressed within the narrow limits for which gentlemen contend.

But the argument which most conclusively demonstrates the error of the construction contended for by the counsel for the state of Maryland is founded on the intention of the convention, as manifested in the whole clause. To waste time and argument in proving that, without it, Congress might carry its powers into execution would be not much less idle than to hold a lighted taper to the sun. As little can it be required to prove that, in the absence of this clause, Congress would have some choice of means. That it might employ those which, in its judgment, would most advantageously effect the object to be accomplished. That any means adapted to the end, any means which tended directly to the execution of the constitutional powers of the government, were in themselves constitutional. This clause, as construed by the state of Maryland, would abridge, and almost annihilate, this useful and necessary right of the legislature to select its means. That this could not be intended is, we should think, had it not been already controverted, too apparent for controversy.

We think so for the following reasons: 1st. The clause is placed among the powers of Congress, not among the limitations on those powers. 2d. Its terms purport to enlarge, not to diminish, the powers vested in the government. It purports to be an additional power, not a restriction on those already granted. No reason has been, or can be, assigned for thus concealing an intention to narrow the discretion of the national legislature, under words which purport to enlarge it. The framers of the Constitution wished its adoption, and well knew that it would be endangered by its strength, not by its weakness. Had they been capable of using language which would convey to the eye one idea and, after deep reflection, impress on the mind another, they would rather have disguised the grant of power than its limitation. If, then, their intention had been, by this clause, to restrain the free use of means which might otherwise have been implied, that intention would have been inserted in another place and would have been expressed in terms resembling these. "In carrying into execution the foregoing powers, and all others," etc., "no laws shall be passed but such are necessary and proper." Had the intention been to make this clause restrictive, it would unquestionably have been so in form as well as in effect.

The result of the most careful and attentive consideration bestowed upon this clause is that, if it does not enlarge, it cannot be construed to restrain the powers of Congress, or to impair the right of the legislature to exercise its best judgment in the selection of measures to carry into execution the constitutional powers of the government. If no other motive for its insertion can be suggested, a sufficient one is found in the desire to remove all doubts respecting the right to legislate on that vast mass of incidental powers which must be involved in the Constitution, if that instrument be not a splendid bauble.

We admit, as all must admit, that the powers of the government are limited and that its limits are not to be transcended. But we think the sound construction of the Constitution must allow to the national legislature that discretion with respect to the means by which the powers it confers are to be carried into execution which will enable that body to perform the high duties assigned to it in the manner most beneficial to the people. Let the end be legitimate, let it be within the scope of the Constitution, and all means which are appropriate, which are plainly adapted to that end, which are not prohibited, but consist with the letter and spirit of the Constitution, are constitutional.

That a corporation must be considered as a means not less usual, not of higher dignity, not more requiring a particular specification than other means, has been sufficiently proved. . . .

If a corporation may be employed, indiscriminately with other means, to carry into execution the powers of the government, no particular reason can be assigned for excluding the use of a bank if required for its fiscal operations. To use one must be within the discretion of Congress, if it be an appropriate mode of executing the powers of government. That it is a convenient, a useful, and essential instrument in the prosecution of its fiscal operations is not now a subject of controversy. All those who have been concerned in the administration of our finances have concurred in representing its importance and necessity; and so strongly have they been felt that statesmen of the first class, whose previous opinions against it had been confirmed by every circumstance which can fix the human judgment, have yielded those opinions to the exigencies of the nation. Under the confederation, Congress, justifying the measure by its necessity, transcended, perhaps, its powers, to obtain the advantage of a bank; and our own legislation attests the universal conviction of the utility of this measure. The time has passed away when it can be necessary to enter into any discussion in order to prove the importance of this instrument as a means to effect the legitimate objects of the government.

But were its necessity less apparent, none can deny its being an appropriate measure; and, if it is, the degree of its necessity, as has been very justly observed, is to be discussed in another place. Should Congress, in the execution of its powers, adopt measures which are prohibited by the Constitution; or should Congress, under the pretext of executing its powers, pass laws for the accomplishment of objects not intrusted to the government; it would become the painful duty of this tribunal, should a case requiring such a decision come before it, to say that such an act was not the law of the land. But where the law is not prohibited, and is really calculated to effect any of the objects intrusted to the government, to undertake here to inquire into the degree of its necessity would be to pass the line which circumscribes the judicial department and to tread on legislative ground. This Court disclaims all pretensions to such a power.

After this declaration, it can scarcely be necessary to say that the existence of state banks can have no possible influence on the question. No trace is to be found in the Constitution of an intention to create a dependence of the government of the Union on those of the states for the execution of the great powers assigned to it. Its means are adequate to its ends; and on those means alone was it expected to rely for the accomplishment of its ends. To impose on it the necessity of resorting to means which it cannot control, which another government may furnish or withhold, would render its course precarious, the result of its measures uncertain, and create a dependence on other governments which might disappoint its most important designs, and is incompatible with the language of the Constitution. But, were it otherwise, the choice of means implies a right to choose a national bank in preference to state banks, and Congress alone can make the election. . . .

It being the opinion of the court that the act incorporating the bank is constitutional and that the power of establishing a branch in the state of Maryland might be properly exercised by the bank itself, we proceed to inquire—

2. Whether the state of Maryland may, without violating the Constitution, tax that branch? That the power of taxation is one of vital importance; that it is retained by the states; that it is not abridged by the grant of a similar power to the government of the Union; that it is to be concurrently exercised by the two governments—are truths which have never been denied. But such is the paramount character of the Constitution that its capacity to withdraw any subject from the action of even this power is admitted. The states are expressly forbidden to lay any duties on imports or exports except what may be absolutely necessary for executing their inspection laws. If the obligation of this prohibition must be conceded—if it may restrain a state from the exercise of its taxing power on imports and exports—the same paramount character would seem to restrain, as it certainly may restrain, a state from such other exercise of this power, as is in its nature incompatible with, and repugnant to, the constitutional laws of the Union. A law absolutely repugnant to another as entirely repeals that other as if express terms of repeal were used.

On this ground, the counsel for the bank place its claim to be exempted from the power of a state to tax its operations. There is no express provision for the case, but the claim has been sustained on a principle which so entirely pervades the Constitution, is so intermixed with the materials which compose it, so interwoven with its web, so blended with its texture, as to be incapable of being separated from it without rending it into shreds. This great principle is that the Constitution and the laws made in pursuance thereof are supreme; that they control the Constitution and laws of the respective states and cannot be controlled by them. From this, which may be almost termed an axiom, other propositions are deduced as corollaries, on the truth or error of which, and on their application to this case, the cause has been supposed to depend. These are: 1st. That a power to create implies a power to preserve; 2d. That a power to destroy, if wielded by a different hand, is hostile to, and incompatible with, these powers to create and to preserve; 3d. That, where this repugnancy exists, that authority which is supreme must control, not yield to that over which it is supreme. . . .

The sovereignty of a state extends to everything which exists by its own authority or is introduced by its permission; but does it extend to those means which are employed by Congress to carry into execution powers conferred on that body by the people of the United States? We think it demonstrable that it does not. Those powers are not given by the people of a single state. They are given by the people of the United States, to a government whose laws, made in pursuance of the Constitution, are declared to be supreme. Consequently, the people of a single state cannot confer a sovereignty which will extend over them.

If we measure the power of taxation residing in a state by the extent of sovereignty which the people of a single state possess, and can confer on its government, we have an intelligible standard, applicable to every case to which the power may be applied. We have a principle which leaves the power of taxing the people and property of a state unimpaired, which leaves to a state the command of all its resources, and which places beyond its reach all those powers which are conferred by the people of the United States on the government of the Union, and all those means which are given for the purpose of carrying those powers into execution. We have a principle which is safe for the states and safe for the Union. We are relieved, as we ought to be, from clashing sovereignty; from interfering powers; from a repugnancy between a right in one government to pull down what there is an acknowledged right in another to build up; from the incompatibility of a right in one government to destroy what there is a right in another to preserve. We are not driven to the perplexing inquiry, so unfit for the judicial department, what degree of taxation is the legitimate use, and what degree may amount to the abuse of the power. The attempt to use it on the means employed by the government of the Union, in pursuance of the Constitution, is itself an abuse, because it is the usurpation of a power which the people of a single state cannot give. We find, then, on just theory, a total failure of this original right to tax the means employed by the government of the Union, for the execution of its powers. The right never existed, and the question whether it has been surrendered cannot arise.

But, waiving this theory for the present, let us resume the inquiry, whether this power can be exercised by the respective states consistently with a fair construction of the Constitution? That the power to tax involves the power to destroy; that the power to destroy may defeat and render useless the power to create; that there is a plain repugnance in conferring on one government a power to control the constitutional measures of another, which other, with respect to those very measures, is declared to be supreme over that which exerts the control, are propositions not to be denied. But all inconsistencies are to be reconciled by the magic of the word *confidence*. Taxation, it is said, does not necessarily and unavoidably destroy. To carry it to the excess of destruction, would be an abuse, to presume which, would banish that confidence which is essential to all government. But is this a case of confidence? Would the people of any one state trust those of another with a power to control the most insignificant operations of their state government? We know they would not. Why, then, should we suppose that the people of any one state should be willing to trust those of another with a power to control the operations of a government to which they have confided their most important and most valuable interests? In the legislature of the Union alone are all represented. The legislature of the Union alone, therefore, can be trusted by the people with the power of controlling measures which concern all, in the confidence that it will not be abused. This, then, is not a case of confidence, and we must consider it as it really is. . . .

The Court has bestowed on this subject its most deliberate consideration. The result is a conviction that the states have no power, by taxation or otherwise, to retard, impede, burden, or in any manner control, the operations of the constitutional laws enacted by Congress to carry into execution the powers vested in the general government. This is, we think, the unavoidable consequence of that supremacy which the Constitution has declared. We are unanimously of opinion that the law passed by the legislature of Maryland, imposing a tax on the Bank of the United States, is unconstitutional and void.

This opinion does not deprive the states of any resources which they originally possessed. It does not extend to a tax paid by the real property of the bank, in common with the other real property within the state, nor to a tax imposed on the interest which the citizens of Maryland may hold in this institution, in common with other property of the same description throughout the state. But this is a tax on the operations of the bank and is, consequently, a tax on the operation of an instrument employed by the government of the Union to carry its powers into execution. Such a tax must be unconstitutional. . . .

7. *GIBBONS* v. *OGDEN*[1]

EDITORS' NOTE.—Robert Fulton and his backer, Chancellor Robert R. Livingston, were in 1798 granted a twenty-year monopoly of steamboat navigation in New York if they would build a streamboat within a year that would make four miles an hour upstream on the Hudson. The monopoly was provided for by the New York legislature. It was renewed from year to year and considered a joke. After some success on the Seine in Paris in 1803, Fulton and his backer satisfied the condition of the grant in 1807. The legislature then confirmed the monopoly and increased its term to thirty years if two more boats should be put into operation in New York. Fulton and Livingston increased considerably the number of boats in New York waters and started a similar enterprise, with a similar monopoly, from the Territory of Orleans, on the Mississippi. By the time of the decision in *Gibbons* v. *Ogden*, steamboat transportation, with its advantages for upstream navigation, was helping to keep the western part of the country in the United States. Monopolies like those given Fulton were granted by a number of states, and they were frequently followed by conflicts, countermonopolies, and other retaliatory measures.

Thus, from 1811 on, the monopoly rights of Fulton and Livingston, and later of Ogden, who purchased from them a right to run ferryboats between New York and specified New Jersey points, were threatened by competitors, some of whom were encouraged by retaliatory acts passed by Connecticut and New Jersey. After preliminary skirmishing, Ogden in 1819 sued in the New York Court of Chancery to get an injunction against a competitor, a court order prohibiting Gibbons from running steamboats, without authority from the owners of the monopoly, between New Jersey and New York. Gibbons claimed that he was protected by the terms of a federal license to engage in the coasting trade. Ogden won in 1820 in the New York courts.

The case was taken to the Supreme Court, not by writ of error but by appeal. A suit for injunction is heard by a court of chancery, as a matter of equity. A jury is ordinarily not used in an equity proceeding, and the record used by the reviewing court differs from that used in reviewing an action at law. The review of an equity proceeding is called an appeal; the person seeking the review (Gibbons) is called the appellant, and the other party the appellee, or, sometimes, the respondent.

Though the appeal was taken in 1820, *Gibbons* v. *Ogden* was not argued in the Supreme Court until 1824. In the interval the importance of steamboat navigation continued to increase. Webster made perhaps his most influential argument, on behalf of Gibbons, and contributed to the opinion in which Marshall started the long and important development of interpretation of the commerce clause of the Constitution.

1. 9 Wheaton 1 (1824).

MARSHALL, Ch. J., delivered the opinion of the Court and, after stating the case, proceeded as follows:

The appellant contends that this decree is erroneous, because the laws which purport to give the exclusive privilege it sustains are repugnant to the Constitution and laws of the United States. They are said to be repugnant—1st. To that clause in the Constitution which authorizes Congress to regulate commerce. 2d. To that which authorizes Congress to promote the progress of science and useful arts.

The state of New York maintains the constitutionality of these laws; and their legislature, their council of revision, and their judges, have repeatedly concurred in this opinion. It is supported by great names—by names which have all the titles to consideration that virtue, intelligence, and office can bestow. No tribunal can approach the decision of this question without feeling a just and real respect for that opinion which is sustained by such authority; but it is the province of this Court, while it respects, not to bow to it implicitly; and the judges must exercise, in the examination of the subject, that understanding which Providence has bestowed upon them, with that independence which the people of the United States expect from this department of the government.

As preliminary to the very able discussions of the Constitution, which we have heard from the bar, and as having some influence on its construction, reference has been made to the political situation of these states, anterior to its formation. It has been said that they were sovereign, were completely independent, and were connected with each other only by a league. This is true. But when these allied sovereigns converted their league into a government, when they converted their congress of ambassadors, deputed to deliberate on their common concerns, and to recommend measures of general utility, into a legislature, empowered to enact laws on the most interesting subjects, the whole character in which the states appear underwent a change, the extent of which must be determined by a fair consideration of the instrument by which that change was effected.

This instrument contains an enumeration of powers expressly granted by the people to their government....

The words are, "Congress shall have power to regulate commerce with foreign nations, and among the several states, and with the Indian tribes." The subject to be regulated is commerce; and our Constitution being, as was aptly said at the bar, one of enumeration, and not of definition, to ascertain the extent of the power, it becomes necessary to settle the meaning of the word. The counsel for the appellee would limit it to traffic, to buying and selling, or the interchange of commodities, and do not admit that it comprehends navigation. This would restrict a general term, applicable to many objects, to one of its significations. Commerce, undoubtedly, is traffic, but it is something more—it is intercourse. It describes the commercial intercourse between nations, and parts of nations, in all its branches, and is regulated by prescribing rules for carrying on that intercourse. The mind can scarcely conceive a system for regulating commerce between nations which shall exclude all laws concerning navigation, which shall be silent on the admission of the vessels of the one nation into the ports of the other, and be confined to prescribing rules for the conduct of individuals, in the actual employment of buying and selling, or of barter. If commerce does not include navigation, the government of the Union has no direct power over that subject and can make no law prescribing what shall constitute American vessels or requiring that they shall be navigated by American seamen. Yet this power has been exercised from the commencement of the government, has been exercised with the consent of all, and has been understood by all to be a commercial regulation. All America understands, and has uniformly understood, the word "commerce" to comprehend navigation. It was so understood, and must have been so understood, when the Constitution was framed. The power over commerce, including navigation, was one of the primary objects for which the people of America adopted their government and must have been contemplated in forming it. The convention must have used the word in that sense, because all have understood it in that sense; and the attempt to restrict it comes too late. . . .

The word used in the Constitution, then, comprehends, and has been always understood to comprehend, navigation within its meaning; and a power to regulate navigation is as expressly granted as if that term had been added to the word "commerce." To what commerce does this power extend? The Constitution informs us to commerce "with foreign nations, and among the several states, and with the Indian tribes." It has, we believe, been universally admitted that these words comprehend every species of commercial intercourse between the United States and foreign nations. No sort of trade can be carried on between this country and any other to which this power does not extend. It has been truly said that commerce, as the word is used in the Constitution, is a unit, every part of which is indicated by the term.

If this be the admitted meaning of the word, in its application to foreign nations, it must carry the same meaning throughout the sentence and remain a unit, unless there be some plain intelligible cause which alters it. The subject to which the power is next applied is to commerce "among the several states." The word "among" means intermingled with. A thing which is among others is intermingled with them. Commerce among the states cannot stop at the external boundary line of each state but may be introduced into the interior. It is not intended to say that these words comprehend that commerce, which is completely internal, which is carried on between man and man in a state, or between different parts of the same state, and which does not extend to or affect other states. Such a power would be inconvenient and is certainly unnecessary. Comprehensive as the word "among" is, it may very properly be restricted to that commerce which concerns more states than one. The phrase is not one which would probably have been selected to indicate the completely interior traffic of a state, because it is not an apt phrase for that purpose; and the enumeration of the particular classes of commerce to which the power was to be extended would not have been made had the intention been to extend the power to every description. The enumeration presupposes something not enumerated; and that something, if we regard the language or the subject of the sentence, must be the exclusively internal commerce of a state. The genius and character of the whole government seem to be that its action is to be applied to all the external concerns of the nation, and to those internal concerns which affect the states generally, but not to those which are completely within a particular state, which do not affect other states, and with which it is not necessary to interfere for the purpose of executing some of the general powers of the government. The completely internal commerce of a state, then, may be considered as reserved for the state itself.

But in regulating commerce with foreign nations, the power of Congress does not stop at the jurisdictional lines of the several states. It would be a very useless power if it could not pass those lines. The commerce of the United States with foreign nations is that of the whole United States; every district has a right

477

to participate in it. The deep streams which penetrate our country in every direction pass through the interior of almost every state in the Union and furnish the means of exercising this right. If Congress has the power to regulate it, that power must be exercised whenever the subject exists. If it exists within the states, if a foreign voyage may commence or terminate at a port within a state, then the power of Congress may be exercised within a state.

This principle is, if possible, still more clear, when applied to commerce "among the several states." They either join each other, in which case they are separated by a mathematical line, or they are remote from each other, in which case other states lie between them. What is commerce "among" them; and how is it to be conducted? Can a trading expedition between two adjoining states commence and terminate outside of each? And if the trading intercourse be between two states remote from each other, must it not commence in one, terminate in the other, and probably pass through a third? . . .

We are now arrived at the inquiry—what is this power? It is the power to regulate, that is, to prescribe the rule by which commerce is to be governed. This power, like all others vested in Congress, is complete in itself, may be exercised to its utmost extent, and acknowledges no limitations other than are prescribed in the Constitution. These are expressed in plain terms and do not affect the questions which arise in this case, or which have been discussed at the bar. If, as has always been understood, the sovereignty of Congress, though limited to specified objects, is plenary as to those objects, the power over commerce with foreign nations, and among the several states, is vested in Congress as absolutely as it would be in a single government, having in its constitution the same restrictions on the exercise of the power as are found in the Constitution of the United States. . . .

But it has been urged, with great earnestness, that although the power of Congress to regulate commerce with foreign nations, and among the several states, be coextensive with the subject itself, and have no other limits than are prescribed in the Constitution, yet the states may severally exercise the same power within their respective jurisdictions. In support of this argument, it is said that they possessed it as an inseparable attribute of sovereignty, before the formation of the Constitution, and still retain it, except so far as they have surrendered it by that instrument; that this principle results from the nature of the government and is secured by the Tenth Amendment; that an affirmative grant of power is not exclusive, unless in its own nature it be such that the continued exercise of it by the former possessor is inconsistent with the grant, and that this is not of that description. The appellant, conceding these postulates, except the last, contends that full power to regulate a particular subject implies the whole power and leaves no residuum; that a grant of the whole is incompatible with the existence of a right in another to any part of it. Both parties have appealed to the Constitution, to legislative acts, and judicial decisions and have drawn arguments from all these sources to support and illustrate the propositions they respectively maintain. . . .

In our complex system, presenting the rare and difficult scheme of one general government, whose action extends over the whole, but which possesses only certain enumerated powers, and of numerous state governments, which retain and exercise all powers not delegated to the Union, contests respecting power must arise. Were it even otherwise, the measures taken by the respective governments to execute their acknowledged powers would often be of the same description and might, sometimes, interfere.

This, however, does not prove that the one is exercising, or has a right to exercise, the powers of the other. . . .

It has been contended by the counsel for the appellant that, as the word "to regulate" implies in its nature full power over the thing to be regulated, it excludes, necessarily, the action of all others that would perform the same operation on the same thing. That regulation is designed for the entire result, applying to those parts which remain as they were, as well as to those which are altered. It produces a uniform whole, which is as much disturbed and deranged by changing what the regulating power designs to leave untouched, as that on which it has operated. There is great force in this argument, and the Court is not satisfied that it has been refuted.

Since, however, in exercising the power of regulating their own internal affairs, whether of trading or police, the states may sometimes enact laws, the validity of which depends on their interfering with, and being contrary to, an act of Congress passed in pursuance of the Constitution, the Court will enter upon the inquiry whether the laws of New York, as expounded by the highest tribunal of that state, have, in their application to this case, come into collision with an act of Congress and deprived a citizen of a right to which that act entitles him. Should this collision exist, it will be immaterial whether those laws were passed in virtue of a concurrent power "to regulate commerce with foreign nations and among the several states," or in virtue of a power to regulate their domestic trade and police. In one case and the other, the acts of New York must yield to the law of Congress; and the decision sustaining the privilege they confer, against a right given by a law of the Union, must be erroneous. This opinion has been frequently expressed in this Court and is founded as well on the nature of the government as on the words of the Constitution. In

argument, however, it has been contended that, if a law passed by a state, in the exercise of its acknowledged sovereignty, comes into conflict with a law passed by Congress in pursuance of the Constitution, they affect the subject, and each other, like equal opposing powers. But the framers of our Constitution foresaw this state of things and provided for it by declaring the supremacy not only of itself but of the laws made in pursuance of it.

The nullity of any act inconsistent with the Constitution is produced by the declaration that the Constitution is the supreme law. The appropriate application of that part of the clause which confers the same supremacy on laws and treaties is to such acts of the state legislatures as do not transcend their powers, but, though enacted in the execution of acknowledged state powers, interfere with, or are contrary to, the laws of Congress, made in pursuance of the Constitution, or some treaty made under the authority of the United States. In every such case, the act of Congress, or the treaty, is supreme; and the law of the state, though enacted in the exercise of powers not controverted, must yield to it.

In pursuing this inquiry at the bar, it has been said that the Constitution does not confer the right of intercourse between state and state. That right derives its source from those laws whose authority is acknowledged by civilized man throughout the world. This is true. The Constitution found it an existing right and gave to Congress the power to regulate it. In the exercise of this power, Congress has passed "an act for enrolling or licensing ships or vessels to be employed in the coasting trade and fisheries, and for regulating the same." The counsel for the respondent contend that this act does not give the right to sail from port to port but confines itself to regulating a pre-existing right, so far only as to confer certain privileges on enrolled and licensed vessels in its exercise.

It will at once occur that, when a legislature attaches certain privileges and exemptions to the exercise of a right over which its control is absolute, the law must imply a power to exercise the right. The privileges are gone if the right itself be annihilated. It would be contrary to all reason, and to the course of human affairs, to say that a state is unable to strip a vessel of the particular privileges attendant on the exercise of a right, and yet may annul the right itself; that the state of New York cannot prevent an enrolled and licensed vessel, proceeding from Elizabethtown, in New Jersey, to New York, from enjoying, in her course, and on her entrance into port, all the privileges conferred by the act of Congress; but can shut her up in her own port and prohibit altogether her entering the waters and ports of another state. To the court it seems very clear that the whole act on the subject of the coasting trade, according to those principles which govern the construction of statutes, implies, unequivocally, an authority to license vessels to carry on the coasting trade. . . .

But all inquiry into this subject seems to the Court to be put completely at rest by the act already mentioned, entitled, "an act for the enrolling and licensing of steamboats." This act authorizes a steamboat employed, or intended to be employed, only in a river or bay of the United States, owned wholly or in part by an alien, resident within the United States, to be enrolled and licensed as if the same belonged to a citizen of the United States. This act demonstrates the opinion of Congress, that steamboats may be enrolled and licensed, in common with vessels using sails. They are, of course, entitled to the same privileges and can no more be restrained from navigating waters and entering ports which are free to such vessels than if they were wafted on their voyage by the winds instead of being propelled by the agency of fire. The one element may be as legitimately used as the other for every commercial purpose authorized by the laws of the Union; and the act of a state inhibiting the use of either, to any vessel having a license under the act of Congress, comes, we think, in direct collision with that act.

As this decides the cause, it is unnecessary to enter in an examination of that part of the Constitution which empowers Congress to promote the progress of science and the useful arts. . . .

The conclusion to which we have come depends on a chain of principles which it was necessary to preserve unbroken; and although some of them were thought nearly self-evident, the magnitude of the question, the weight of character belonging to those from whose judgment we dissent, and the argument at the bar demanded that we should assume nothing.

Powerful and ingenious minds, taking, as postulates, that the powers expressly granted to the government of the Union are to be contracted, by construction, into the narrowest possible compass, and that the original powers of the states are retained, if any possible construction will retain them, may, by a course of well-digested but refined and metaphysical reasoning, founded on these premises, explain away the Constitution of our country and leave it a magnificent structure, indeed, to look at but totally unfit for use. They may so entangle and perplex the understanding as to obscure principles which were before thought quite plain and induce doubts where, if the mind were to pursue its own course, none would be perceived. In such a case, it is peculiarly necessary to recur to safe and fundamental principles, to sustain those principles, and, when sustained, to make them the tests of the arguments to be examined.

UNIT VI

THE BEGINNINGS OF AMERICAN FOREIGN POLICY

INDEPENDENCE meant that an American foreign policy was required. What problems confronted the early administrations, and what principles governed their conduct of foreign affairs? A full study of the record between Washington's inauguration and Monroe's message to Congress would include much that is not indicated in these readings. It might begin with an analysis of the position in 1789—the year which saw a new government installed in Washington and an old government destroyed in Paris. It would examine the outstanding problems in America's relations with the three imperialist powers in this hemisphere and then turn to the impact of the French Revolution on world politics. It would trace the development of American foreign policy during the generation of European war between 1792 and 1815, dealing, in turn, with the initial declaration of neutrality; the definition of America's relations with the two European neighbors that were cramping and jostling her development; the undeclared war with France; the good fortune which cast Louisiana into Jefferson's lap; and the pressures which eventually entangled an indignant and aggressive nation in the final phase of the Napoleonic Wars. A second chapter would assess the postwar position in America and Europe, sketch the definition of the Canadian and the obliteration of the Florida boundaries, and then examine the sequence of events which culminated in Monroe's message to Congress. Taken as a whole, this would be a history of growing power and self-confidence, marked by an immense acquisition of territory, a successful pressure on the resistance of northern and southern obstacles to westward expansion, and a developing sense of America's special destiny in this hemisphere. It would also take full account of all those factors outside America's control which facilitated this development.

The papers printed here are in no sense a substitute for such an investigation. They are selections which illuminate a few of the factors which entered into the making of policy.

The decisions in the early years were taken by leaders who saw all issues within the framework of our need for independence and unity. Washington's letter to Laurens is quoted as an example of his insight into the realities which govern policy-making in a world of independent states. The same freedom from illusions about "the common maxims of national policy" is a conspicuous feature of the Farewell Address. Washington's foreign policy centered around the preservation of

481

the Union. His declaration of neutrality, his diplomacy with France, England, and Spain, and his warnings against permanent alliances were all directed to this end. In the Farewell Address, issued at a time when internal unity was being threatened by the clamor for intervention in European affairs, he stated those convictions about the special character of America's interests which were to exert such a tremendous influence in later days.

The Jefferson papers on Louisiana are a reminder, however, that some interests may be more important than freedom from entangling alliances. Jefferson's grasp of the issues created by the French acquisition of Louisiana was no less realistic than Washington's handling of the issues which had confronted him. Though Jefferson was as anxious as Washington or Adams to keep America out of war, he was quick to point out the infallible logic which converted a friend of France into an ally of Britain the moment that France took possession of New Orleans. It was Napoleon's decision to sell a territory which British sea power was bound to cut off as soon as war reopened that enabled Jefferson both to preserve his country's neutrality and to double its size.

In the nationalist aftermath of the War of 1812, many Americans were unwilling to abandon those designs on Florida which had been prominent for more than a decade. The inadequacy of Spanish rule gave some color of legality to intervention. In 1818 Andrew Jackson openly invaded Spanish territory without a declaration of war, destroyed a Negro fort, killed a band of Indians, captured a couple of Spanish forts, hanged an Indian chief who took refuge on a ship flying the British flag, and executed two British civilians. This behavior, which has been delicately described by an American historian as "not strictly in accord with international procedure," branded Jackson as an outlaw in European eyes and as a national hero in the American West. John Quincy Adams, in the face of a strong inclination on the part of the administration to disavow Jackson, succeeded in having his conduct upheld. The British government took the view that its subjects had forfeited any claim to protection; the Spanish government began to consider the prudence of selling Florida before it was stolen.

The independence which Adams showed on this occasion was reasserted in a dramatic and comprehensive form a few years later. It was in 1823 that the sense of America's special interests and responsibilities in relation to the Old World was elevated to the dignity of a doctrine.

The victors of the Napoleonic Wars conceived themselves as having saved the world for "legitimacy." In the system of congresses which followed the defeat of Napoleon, the Continental powers undertook to prevent liberal revolutions in Naples and Spain. When Europe seemed secure, the diplomats of Europe met at Verona, late in 1822, to consider restoring the authority of the Spanish monarch in his rebellious American colonies. George Canning, who had been appointed the British minister of foreign affairs when Lord Castlereagh committed suicide, was contemptuous of the system of post-Napoleonic alliances. He also saw greater commercial advantage for Britain in an independent Latin America than in a Latin America locked within the mercantile pattern of the Spanish colonial system. He therefore suggested to Richard Rush, American minister to Britain, that Great Britain and the United States co-operate to exclude any but Spanish forces from the fight to restore Latin America to Spanish allegiance. Canning's first oral suggestions to Rush set in motion a correspondence and papers out of which the Monroe Doctrine finally emerged. This "doctrine" was originally only part of three paragraphs in President Monroe's message of December 12, 1823. It remains as one of the few persistent factors in our diplomacy, though through the years it has altered materially, and we have refused to be bound by our own precedents or to apply the doctrine with consistency in all circumstances. The Monroe Doctrine has been one of the most enigmatic and explosive parts of American foreign policy.

1. ALLIANCES AND NATIONAL INTEREST[1]

By GEORGE WASHINGTON

EDITORS' NOTE.—Henry Laurens (1724–92) was a planter, merchant, and politician of South Carolina. He was president of the Second Continental Congress from November, 1777, to December, 1778. He was captured by the British, imprisoned in the Tower of London, and later exchanged for Lord Cornwallis. He was one of the commissioners for negotiating peace with Great Britain. Chosen a delegate to the Constitutional Convention of 1787, he did not serve because of failing health. This letter to Laurens accompanied Washington's official letter to Congress, which was concerned only with military affairs. For this official letter see *Washington's Writings*, ed. Fitzpatrick, XIII, 223–44; or *The Writings of George Washington*, ed. W. C. Ford (14 vols.; New York, 1889–93), VII, 239.

TO HENRY LAURENS, PRESIDENT OF CONGRESS

November 14, 1778

DEAR SIR:

This will be accompanied by an official letter on the subject of the proposed expedition against Canada. You will perceive I have only considered it in a military light; indeed, I was not authorized to consider it in any other; and I am not without apprehensions that I may be thought, in what I have done, to have exceeded the limits intended by Congress. But my solicitude for the public welfare which I think deeply interested in this affair will, I hope, justify me in the eyes of all those who view things through that just medium.

I do not know, Sir, what may be your sentiments in the present case; but, whatever they are, I am sure I can confide in your honor and friendship and shall not hesitate to unbosom myself to you on a point of the most delicate and important nature.

The question of the Canadian expedition in the form it now stands appears to me one of the most interesting that has

hitherto agitated our national deliberations. I have one objection to it, untouched in my public letter, which is, in my estimation, insurmountable and alarms all my feelings for the true and permanent interests of my country. This is the introduction of a large body of French troops into Canada, and putting them in possession of the capital of that province, attached to them by all the ties of blood, habits, manners, religion, and former connection of government. I fear this would be too great a temptation to be resisted by any power actuated by the common maxims of national policy. Let us realize for a moment the striking advantages France would derive from the possession of Canada; the acquisition of an extensive territory abounding in supplies for the use of her islands; the opening a vast source of the most beneficial commerce with the Indian nations, which she might then monopolize; the having ports of her own on this continent independent on the precarious good will of an ally; the engrossing the whole trade of Newfoundland whenever she pleased, the finest nursery of seamen in the world;

1. *Washington's Writings*, ed. Fitzpatrick, XIII, 254–57.

the security afforded to her islands; and, finally, the facility of aweing and controlling these states, the natural and most formidable rival of every maritime power in Europe. Canada would be a solid acquisition to France on all these accounts and because of the numerous inhabitants, subjects to her by inclination, who would aid in preserving it under her power against the attempt of every other.

France, acknowledged for some time past the most powerful monarchy in Europe by land, able now to dispute the empire of the sea with Great Britain, and if joined with Spain, I may say certainly superior, possessed of New Orleans on our right, Canada on our left, and seconded by the numerous tribes of Indians on our rear from one extremity to the other, a people so generally friendly to her and whom she knows so well how to conciliate, would, it is much to be apprehended, have it in her power to give law to these states.

Let us suppose that when the five thousand French troops (and under the idea of that number twice as many might be introduced) were entered the city of Quebec, they should declare an intention to hold Canada, as a pledge and surety for the debts due to France from the United States [or, under other specious pretenses hold the place till they can find a bone for contention], and [in the meanwhile] should excite the Canadians to engage in supporting [their pretenses and claims], what should we be able to say with only four or five thousand men to carry on the dispute? It may be supposed that France would not choose to renounce our friendship by a step of this kind, as the consequence would probably be a reunion with England on some terms or other; and the loss of what she had acquired, in so violent and unjustifiable a manner, with all the advantages of an alliance with us. This in my opinion is too slender a security against the measure to be relied on. The truth of the position will entirely depend on naval events.

If France and Spain should unite and obtain a decided superiority by sea, a reunion with England would avail very little and might be set at defiance. France, with a numerous army at command, might throw in what number of land forces she thought proper to support her pretensions; and England, without men, without money, and inferior on her favorite element, could give no effectual aid to oppose them. Resentment, reproaches, and submission seem to be all that would be left us. Men are very apt to run into extremes; hatred to England may carry some into an excess of confidence in France, especially when motives of gratitude are thrown into the scale. Men of this description would be unwilling to suppose France capable of acting so ungenerous a part. I am heartily disposed to entertain the most favorable sentiments of our new ally and to cherish them in others to a reasonable degree; but it is a maxim founded on the universal experience of mankind that no nation is to be trusted farther than it is bound by its interest; and no prudent statesman or politician will venture to depart from it. In our circumstances we ought to be particularly cautious, for we have not yet attained sufficient vigor and maturity to recover from the shock of any false step into which we may unwarily fall.

If France should even engage in the scheme, in the first instance with the purest intentions, there is the greatest danger that, in the progress of the business, invited to it by circumstances and, perhaps, urged on by the solicitations and wishes of the Canadians, she would alter her views.

As the Marquis clothed his proposition when he spoke of it to me, it would seem to originate wholly with himself; but it is far from impossible that it had its birth in the Cabinet of France and was put into this artful dress to give it the readier currency. I fancy that I read in the countenances of some people on this occasion more than the disinterested zeal of allies. I hope I am mistaken and that my fears of mischief make me refine too much and awaken jealousies that have no sufficient foundation.

But upon the whole, Sir, to waive every other consideration, I do not like to add to the number of our national obligations. I would wish as much as possible to avoid giving a foreign power new claims of merit for services performed to the United States and would ask no assistance that is not indispensable.

2. THE FAREWELL ADDRESS, SEPTEMBER 17, 1796[1]

By George Washington

EDITORS' NOTE.—Even during his first term as President, Washington was feeling the effect of age, and at the end of that term he had wanted to retire from public office. Although he was persuaded to accept a second term as President, Washington sent this address to the newspapers in time to forestall any demand that he serve a third term. As is indicated by the letter from Washington to Hamilton, also included here, help was enlisted in matters of both content and style. Although both Madison and Hamilton made some suggestions, the evidence indicates that Washington was the real author of this valedictory to the American people. The Farewell Address is one of the great state papers of American history.

A. TO ALEXANDER HAMILTON

September 1, 1796

My dear Sir:

About the middle of last week I wrote to you, and that it might escape the eye of the inquisitive (for some of my letters have lately been pried into) I took the liberty of putting it under a cover to Mr. Jay.

Since then, revolving on the paper that was inclosed therein, on the various matters it contained, and on the first expression of the advice or recommendation which was given in it, I have regretted that another subject (which in my estimation is of interesting concern to the well-being of this country) was not touched upon also. I mean education *generally* as one of the surest means of enlightening and giving just ways of thinking to our citizens, but particularly the establishment of a university, where the youth from *all parts* of the United States might receive the polish of erudition in the arts, sciences, and belle-lettres, and where those who were disposed to run a political course might not only be instructed in the theory and principles but (this seminary being at the seat of the general government) where the legislature would be in session half the year, and the interests and politics of the nation of course would be discussed; they would lay the surest foundation for the practical part also.

But that which would render it of the highest importance, in my opinion, is that the juvenile period of life, when friendships are formed and habits established that will stick by one, the youth, or young men, from different parts of the United States would be assembled together and would by degrees discover that there was not that cause for those jealousies and prejudices which one part of the Union had imbibed against an-

1. *Washington's Writings*, ed. Fitzpatrick, XXXV, 198–201, 214–15, 215–16, 216–17, 217–30, 231–32, 232–33, 233–36, 237–38.

other part; of course, sentiments of more liberality in the general policy of the country would result from it. What but the mixing of people from different parts of the United States during the war rubbed off these impressions? A century in the ordinary intercourse would not have accomplished what the seven years' association in arms did; but, that ceasing, prejudices are beginning to revive again and never will be eradicated so effectually by any other means as the intimate intercourse of characters in early life, who, in all probability, will be at the head of the councils of this country in a more advanced stage of it.

To show that this is no *new* idea of mine, I may appeal to my early communications to Congress; and to prove how seriously I have reflected on it since, and how well disposed I have been, and still am, to contribute my aid toward carrying the measure into effect, I inclose you the extract of a letter from me to the governor of Virginia on this subject and a copy of the resolves of the legislature of that state in consequence thereof.

I have not the smallest doubt that this donation (when the navigation is in complete operation, which it certainly will be in less than two years), will amount to twelve or £1500 sterling a year and become a rapidly increasing fund. The proprietors of the Federal City have talked of doing something handsome toward it likewise; and if Congress would appropriate some of the western lands to the same uses, funds sufficient, and of the most permanent and increasing sort, might be so established as to invite the ablest professors in Europe to conduct it.

Let me pray you, therefore, to introduce a section in the address expressive of these sentiments and recommendatory of the measure, without any mention, however, of my proposed personal contribution to the plan.

Such a section would come in very properly after the one which relates to our religious obligations, or in a preceding part, as one of the recommendatory measures to counteract the evils arising from geographical discriminations. With affectionate regard, etc.

B. THE FAREWELL ADDRESS

Friends and Fellow-Citizens:

The period for a new election of a citizen to administer the executive government of the United States being not far distant, and the time actually arrived when your thoughts must be employed in designating the person who is to be clothed with that important trust, it appears to me proper, especially as it may conduce to a more distinct expression of the public voice, that I should now apprize you of the resolution I have formed to decline being considered among the number of those out of whom a choice is to be made....

... The acceptance of, and continuance hitherto in, the office to which your suffrages have twice called me have been a uniform sacrifice of inclination to the opinion of duty and to a deference for what appeared to be your desire. I con-

stantly hoped that it would have been much earlier in my power, consistently with motives which I was not at liberty to disregard, to return to that retirement from which I had been reluctantly drawn. The strength of my inclination to do this, previous to the last election, had even led to the preparation of an address to declare it to you; but mature reflection on the then perplexed and critical posture of our affairs with foreign nations, and the unanimous advice of persons entitled to my confidence, impelled me to abandon the idea....

... The impressions with which I first undertook the arduous trust were explained on the proper occasion. In the discharge of this trust, I will only say that I have, with good intentions, contributed toward the organization and administration of the government the best exertions of which a very fallible judgment was capable. Not unconscious, in the outset, of the inferiority of my qualifications, experience in my own eyes, perhaps still more in the eyes of others, has strengthened the motives to diffidence of myself; and every day the increasing weight of years admonishes me more and more that the shade of retirement is as necessary to me as it will be welcome. Satisfied that, if any circumstances have given peculiar value to my services, they were temporary, I have the consolation to believe that, while choice and prudence invite me to quit the political scene, patriotism does not forbid it....

...If benefits have resulted to our country from these [my] services, let it always be remembered to your praise, and as an instructive example in our annals, that, under circumstances in which the passions agitated in every direction were liable to mislead, amidst appearances sometimes dubious, vicissitudes of fortune often discouraging, in situations in which not unfrequently want of success has countenanced the spirit of criticism, the constancy of your support was the essential prop of the efforts and a guaranty of the plans by which they were effected. Profoundly penetrated with this idea, I shall carry it with me to my grave as a strong incitement to unceasing vows that Heaven may continue to you the choicest tokens of its beneficence; that your Union and brotherly affection may be perpetual; that the free Constitution, which is the work of your hands, may be sacredly maintained; that its administration in every department may be stamped with wisdom and virtue; that, in fine, the happiness of the people of these states, under the auspices of liberty, may be made complete by so careful a preservation and so prudent a use of this blessing as will acquire to them the glory of recommending it to the applause, the affection,

and adoption of every nation which is yet a stranger to it.

Here, perhaps, I ought to stop. But a solicitude for your welfare, which cannot end but with my life, and the apprehension of danger, natural to that solicitude, urge me on an occasion like the present to offer to your solemn contemplation, and to recommend to your frequent review, some sentiments which are the result of much reflection of no inconsiderable observation, and which appear to me all important to the permanency of your felicity as a people. These will be offered to you with the more freedom as you can only see in them the disinterested warnings of a parting friend who can possibly have no personal motive to bias his counsel. Nor can I forget, as an encouragement to it, your indulgent reception of my sentiments on a former and not dissimilar occasion.

Interwoven as is the love of liberty with every ligament of your hearts, no recommendation of mine is necessary to fortify or confirm the attachment.

The unity of government which constitutes you one people is also now dear to you. It is justly so, for it is a main pillar in the edifice of your real independence, the support of your tranquillity at home, your peace abroad, of your safety, of your prosperity, of that very liberty which you so highly prize. But as it is easy to foresee that, from different causes and from different quarters, much pains will be taken, many artifices employed, to weaken in your minds the conviction of this truth; as this is the point in your political fortress against which the batteries of internal and external enemies will be most constantly and actively (though often covertly and insidiously) directed, it is of infinite moment that you should properly estimate the immense value of your national Union to your collective and individual happiness; that you should cherish a cordial, habitual, and immovable attachment to it, accustoming yourselves to think and speak of it as of the palladium of your political safety and prosperity, watching for its preservation with jealous anxiety, discountenancing whatever may suggest even a suspicion that it can in any event be abandoned, and indignantly frowning upon the first dawning of every attempt to alienate any portion of our country from the rest or to enfeeble the sacred ties which now link together the various parts.

For this you have every inducement of sympathy and interest. Citizens by birth or choice, of a common country, that country has a right to concentrate your affections. The name of AMERICAN, which belongs to you, in your national capacity, must always exalt the just pride of patriotism more than any appellation derived from local discriminations. With slight shades of difference, you have the same religion, manners, habits, and political principles. You have in a common cause fought and triumphed together. The independence and liberty you possess are the work of joint councils and joint efforts, of common dangers, sufferings, and successes.

But these considerations, however powerfully they address themselves to your sensibility, are greatly outweighed by those which apply more immediately to your interest. Here every portion of our country finds the most commanding motives for carefully guarding and preserving the Union of the whole.

The *North*, in an unrestrained intercourse with the *South*, protected by the equal laws of a common government, finds in the productions of the latter great additional resources of maritime and commercial enterprise and precious materials of manufacturing industry. The *South*, in the same intercourse, benefitting by the agency of the *North*, sees its agriculture grow and its commerce expand. Turning partly into its own channels the seamen of the *North*, it finds its particular navigation invigor-

ated; and while it contributes, in different ways, to nourish and increase the general mass of the national navigation, it looks forward to the protection of a maritime strength, to which itself is unequally adapted. The *East*, in a like intercourse with the *West*, already finds, and in the progressive improvement of interior communications by land and water will more and more find, a valuable vent for the commodities which it brings from abroad or manufactures at home. The *West* derives from the *East* supplies requisite to its growth and comfort, and, what is perhaps of still greater consequence, it must of necessity owe the *secure* enjoyment of indispensable *outlets* for its own productions to the weight, influence, and the future maritime strength of the Atlantic side of the Union, directed by an indissoluble community of interest as *one nation*. Any other tenure by which the *West* can hold this essential advantage, whether derived from its own separate strength or from an apostate and unnatural connection with any foreign power, must be intrinsically precarious.

While then every part of our country thus feels an immediate and particular interest in Union, all the parts combined cannot fail to find in the united mass of means and efforts greater strength, greater resource, proportionably greater security from external danger, a less frequent interruption of their peace by foreign nations; and, what is of inestimable value! they must derive from Union an exemption from those broils and wars between themselves which so frequently afflict neighboring countries not tied together by the same government, which their own rivalships alone would be sufficient to produce but which opposite foreign alliances, attachments, and intrigues would stimulate and embitter. Hence likewise they will avoid the necessity of those overgrown military establishments which under any form of government are inauspicious to liberty and which are to be regarded as particularly hostile to republican liberty. In this sense it is that your Union ought to be considered as a main prop of your liberty and that the love of the one ought to endear to you the preservation of the other.

These considerations speak a persuasive language to every reflecting and virtuous mind and exhibit the continuance of the UNION as a primary object of patriotic desire. Is there a doubt whether a common government can embrace so large a sphere? Let experience solve it. To listen to mere speculation in such a case were criminal. We are authorized to hope that a proper organization of the whole, with the auxiliary agency of governments for the respective subdivisions, will afford a happy issue to the experiment. 'Tis well worth a fair and full experiment. With such powerful and obvious motives to Union, affecting all parts of our country, while experience shall not have demonstrated its impracticability, there will always be reason to distrust the patriotism of those who in any quarter may endeavor to weaken its bands.

In contemplating the causes which may disturb our Union, it occurs as matter of serious concern that any ground should have been furnished for characterizing parties by *geographical* discriminations: *northern* and *southern;* *Atlantic* and *western;* whence designing men may endeavor to excite a belief that there is a real difference of local interests and views. One of the expedients of party to acquire influence, within particular districts, is to misrepresent the opinions and aims of other districts. You cannot shield yourselves too much against the jealousies and heart-burnings which spring from these misrepresentations. They tend to render alien to each other those who ought to be bound together by fraternal affection. The inhabitants of our western country have lately had a useful lesson on this head.

They have seen, in the negotiation by the executive, and in the unanimous ratification by the Senate of the treaty with Spain, and in the universal satisfaction at that event throughout the United States, a decisive proof how unfounded were the suspicions propagated among them of a policy in the general government and in the Atlantic states unfriendly to their interests in regard to the MISSISSIPPI. They have been witnesses to the formation of two treaties, that with Great Britain and that with Spain, which secure to them everything they could desire, in respect to our foreign relations, toward confirming their prosperity. Will it not be their wisdom to rely for the preservation of [*sic*] these advantages on the UNION by which they were procured? Will they not henceforth be deaf to those advisers, if such there are, who would sever them from their brethren and connect them with aliens?

To the efficacy and permanency of your Union, a government for the whole is indispensable. No alliances, however strict between the parts, can be an adequate substitute. They must inevitably experience the infractions and interruptions which all alliances in all times have experienced. Sensible of this momentous truth, you have improved upon your first essay by the adoption of a constitution of government better calculated than your former for an intimate Union and for the efficacious management of your common concerns. This government, the offspring of our own choice uninfluenced and unawed, adopted upon full investigation and mature deliberation, completely free in its principles, in the distribution of its powers, uniting security with energy, and containing within itself a provision for its own amendment, has a just claim to your confidence and your support. Respect for its authority, compliance with its laws, acquiescence in its measures, are duties enjoined by the fundamental maxims of true liberty. The basis of our political systems is the right of the people to make and to alter their constitutions of government. But the Constitution which at any time exists, till changed by an explicit and authentic act of the whole people, is sacredly obligatory upon all. The very idea of the power and the right of the people to establish government presupposes the duty of every individual to obey the established government.

All obstructions to the execution of the laws, all combinations and associations, under whatever plausible character, with the real design to direct, control, counteract, or awe the regular deliberation and action of the constituted authorities, are destructive of this fundamental principle and of fatal tendency. They serve to organize faction, to give it an artificial and extraordinary force, to put in the place of the delegated will of the nation the will of a party, often a small but artful and enterprising minority of the community; and, according to the alternate triumphs of different parties, to make the public administration the mirror of the ill-concerted and incongruous projects of faction rather than the organ of consistent and wholesome plans digested by common councils and modified by mutual interests. However combinations or associations of the above description may now and then answer popular ends, they are likely, in the course of time and things, to become potent engines by which cunning, ambitious, and unprincipled men will be enabled to subvert the power of the people and to usurp for themselves the reins of government, destroying afterward the very engines which have lifted them to unjust dominion.

Toward the preservation of your government and the permanency of your present happy state, it is requisite, not only that you steadily discountenance irregular oppositions to its acknowledged authority, but also that you resist with care the spirit of innovation upon its principles, however specious the pretexts. One method of assault may be to effect, in the forms of the Constitution, alterations which will impair the energy of the system and thus to undermine what cannot be directly overthrown. In all the changes to which you may be invited, remember that time and habit are at least as necessary to fix the true character of governments as of other human institutions; that experience is the surest standard by which to test the real tendency of the existing constitution of a country; that facility in changes upon the credit of mere hypotheses and opinion exposes to perpetual change, from the endless variety of hypotheses and opinion; and remember, especially, that for the efficient management of your common interests, in a country so extensive as ours, a government of as much vigor as is consistent with the perfect security of liberty is indispensable. Liberty itself will find in such a government, with powers properly distributed and adjusted, its surest guardian. It is indeed little else than a name where the government is too feeble to withstand the enterprises of faction, to confine each member of the society within the limits prescribed by the laws and to maintain all in the secure and tranquil enjoyment of the rights of person and property.

I have already intimated to you the danger of parties in the state, with particular reference to the founding of them on geographical discriminations. Let me now take a more comprehensive view and warn you in the most solemn manner against the baneful effects of the spirit of party generally.

This spirit, unfortunately, is inseparable from our nature, having its root in the strongest passions of the human mind. It exists under different shapes in all governments, more or less stifled, controlled, or repressed; but, in those of the popular form, it is seen in its greatest rankness and is truly their worst enemy.

The alternate dominion of one faction over another, sharpened by the spirit of revenge natural to party dissension, which in different ages and countries has perpetuated the most horrid enormities, is itself a frightful despotism. But this leads at length to a more formal and permanent despotism. The disorders and miseries which result gradually incline the minds of men to seek security and repose in the absolute power of an individual; and sooner or later the chief of some prevailing faction more able or more fortunate than his competitors turns this disposition to the purposes of his own elevation on the ruins of public liberty.

Without looking forward to an extremity of this kind (which nevertheless ought not to be entirely out of sight), the common and continual mischiefs of the spirit of party are sufficient to make it the interest and the duty of a wise people to discourage and restrain it.

It serves always to distract the public councils and enfeeble the public administration. It agitates the community with ill-founded jealousies and false alarms, kindles the animosity of one part against another, foments occasionally riot and insurrection. It opens the door to foreign influence and corruption, which find a facilitated access to the government itself through the channels of party passions. Thus the policy and the will of one country are subjected to the policy and will of another.

There is an opinion that parties in free countries are useful checks upon the administration of the government and serve to keep alive the spirit of liberty. This within certain limits is probably true, and in governments of a monarchical cast patriotism may look with indulgence, if not with favor, upon the spirit of party. But in those of the popular character, in governments purely elective, it is a spirit not to be encouraged.

From their natural tendency, it is certain there will always be enough of that spirit for every salutary purpose. And there being constant danger of excess, the effort ought to be, by force of public opinion, to mitigate and assuage it. A fire not to be quenched, it demands a uniform vigilance to prevent its bursting into a flame, lest instead of warming it should consume.

It is important, likewise, that the habits of thinking in a free country should inspire caution in those intrusted with its administration to continue themselves within their respective constitutional spheres, avoiding in the exercise of the powers of one department to encroach upon another. The spirit of encroachment tends to consolidate the powers of all the departments in one and thus to create, whatever the form of government, a real despotism. A just estimate of that love of power and proneness to abuse it which predominates in the human heart is sufficient to satisfy us of the truth of this position. The necessity of reciprocal checks in the exercise of political power, by dividing and distributing it into different depositories and constituting each a guardian of the public weal against invasions by the others, has been evinced by experiments ancient and modern, some of them in our country and under our own eyes. To preserve them must be as necessary as to institute them. If, in the opinion of the people, the distribution or modification of the constitutional powers be in any particular wrong, let it be corrected by an amendment in the way which the Constitution designates. But let there be no change by usurpation; for though this, in one instance, may be the instrument of good, it is the customary weapon by which free governments are destroyed. The precedent must always greatly overbalance in permanent evil any partial or transient benefit which the use can at any time yield.

Of all the dispositions and habits

which lead to political prosperity, religion and morality are indispensable supports. In vain would that man claim the tribute of patriotism who should labor to subvert these great pillars of human happiness, these firmest props of the duties of men and citizens. The mere politician, equally with the pious man, ought to respect and to cherish them. A volume could not trace all their connections with private and public felicity. Let it simply be asked where is the security for property, for reputation, for life, if the sense of religious obligation *desert* the oaths, which are the instruments of investigation in courts of justice? And let us with caution indulge the supposition that morality can be maintained without religion. Whatever may be conceded to the influence of refined education on minds of peculiar structure, reason and experience both forbid us to expect that national morality can prevail in exclusion of religious principle.

'Tis substantially true that virtue or morality is a necessary spring of popular government. The rule indeed extends with more or less force to every species of free government. Who that is a sincere friend to it can look with indifference upon attempts to shake the foundation of the fabric.

Promote then, as an object of primary importance, institutions for the general diffusion of knowledge. In proportion as the structure of a government gives force to public opinion, it is essential that public opinion should be enlightened.

As a very important source of strength and security, cherish public credit. One method of preserving it is to use it as sparingly as possible, avoiding occasions of expense by cultivating peace but remembering also that timely disbursements to prepare for danger frequently prevent much greater disbursements to repel it; avoiding likewise the accumulation of debt, not only by shunning occasions of expense, but by vigorous exertions in time of peace to discharge the debts which unavoidable wars may have occasioned, not ungenerously throwing upon posterity the burthen which we ourselves ought to bear. The execution of these maxims belongs to your representatives, but it is necessary that public opinion should cooperate....

... Observe good faith and justice toward all nations. Cultivate peace and harmony with all. Religion and morality enjoin this conduct; and can it be that good policy does not equally enjoin it? It will be worthy of a free, enlightened, and, at no distant period, a great nation to give to mankind the magnanimous and too novel example of a people always guided by an exalted justice and benevolence. Who can doubt that in the course of time and things the fruits of such a plan would richly repay any temporary advantages which might be lost by a steady adherence to it? Can it be that Providence has not connected the permanent felicity of a nation with its virtue? The experiment, at least, is recommended by every sentiment which ennobles human nature. Alas! is it rendered impossible by its vices?

In the execution of such a plan nothing is more essential than that permanent, inveterate antipathies against particular nations and passionate attachments for others should be excluded and that in place of them just and amicable feelings toward all should be cultivated. The nation, which indulges toward another a habitual hatred, or a habitual fondness, is in some degree a slave. It is a slave to its animosity or to its affection, either of which is sufficient to lead it astray from its duty and its interest. Antipathy in one nation against another disposes each more readily to offer insult and injury, to lay hold of slight causes of umbrage, and to be haughty and intractable when accidental or trifling occasions of dispute occur....

...So likewise, a passionate attach-

493

ment of one nation for another produces a variety of evils. Sympathy for the favorite nation, facilitating the illusion of an imaginary common interest, in cases where no real common interest exists, and infusing into one the enmities of the other, betrays the former into a participation in the quarrels and wars of the latter without adequate inducement or justification. It leads also to concessions to the favorite nation of privileges denied to others, which is apt doubly to injure the nation making the concessions, by unnecessarily parting with what ought to have been retained, and by exciting jealousy, ill-will, and a disposition to retaliate, in the parties from whom equal privileges are withheld. And it gives to ambitious, corrupted, or deluded citizens (who devote themselves to the favorite nation) facility to betray or sacrifice the interests of their own country, without odium, sometimes even with popularity, gilding with the appearances of a virtuous sense of obligation a commendable deference for public opinion, or a laudable zeal for public good, the base or foolish compliances of ambition, corruption, or infatuation. . . .

. . . Against the insidious wiles of foreign influence (I conjure you to believe me, fellow-citizens) the jealousy of a free people ought to be *constantly* awake, since history and experience prove that foreign influence is one of the most baneful foes of republican government. But that jealousy to be useful must be impartial, else it becomes the instrument of the very influence to be avoided instead of a defense against it. Excessive partiality for one foreign nation and excessive dislike of another cause those whom they actuate to see danger only on one side and serve to veil and even second the arts of influence on the other. Real patriots who may resist the intrigues of the favorite are liable to become suspected and odious, while its tools and dupes usurp the applause and confidence of the people to surrender their interests.

The great rule of conduct for us, in regard to foreign nations, is in extending our commercial relations to have with them as little *political* connection as possible. So far as we have already formed engagements, let them be fulfilled with perfect good faith. Here let us stop.

Europe has a set of primary interests which to us have none, or a very remote relation. Hence she must be engaged in frequent controversies, the causes of which are essentially foreign to our concerns. Hence therefore it must be unwise in us to implicate ourselves, by artificial ties, in the ordinary vicissitudes of her politics or the ordinary combinations and collisions of her friendships or enmities.

Our detached and distant situation invites and enables us to pursue a different course. If we remain one people, under an efficient government, the period is not far off when we may defy material injury from external annoyance; when we may take such an attitude as will cause the neutrality we may at any time resolve upon to be scrupulously respected; when belligerent nations, under the impossibility of making acquisitions upon us, will not lightly hazard the giving us provocation; when we may choose peace or war, as our interest guided by our justice shall counsel.

Why forgo the advantages of so peculiar a situation? Why quit our own to stand upon foreign ground? Why, by interweaving our destiny with that of any part of Europe, entangle our peace and prosperity in the toils of European ambition, rivalship, interest, humor, or caprice?

'Tis our true policy to steer clear of permanent alliances with any portion of the foreign world. So far, I mean, as we are now at liberty to do it, for let me not be understood as capable of patronizing infidelity to existing engagements (I hold the maxim no less applicable to public than to private affairs that honesty is always the best policy). I repeat it, therefore: let those engagements be observed in their genuine sense. But, in my opinion, it is unnecessary and would be unwise to extend them.

Taking care always to keep ourselves, by suitable establishments, on a respectably defensive posture, we may safely trust to temporary alliances for extraordinary emergencies.

Harmony, liberal intercourse with all nations, are recommended by policy, humanity, and interest. But even our commercial policy should hold an equal and impartial hand, neither seeking nor granting exclusive favors or preferences; consulting the natural course of things; diffusing and diversifying by gentle means the streams of commerce but forcing nothing; establishing with powers so disposed; in order to give to trade a stable course, to define the rights of our merchants, and to enable the government to support them; conventional rules of intercourse, the best that present circumstances and mutual opinion will permit, but temporary, and liable to be from time to time abandoned or varied, as experience and circumstances shall dictate; constantly keeping in view that 'tis folly in one nation to look for disinterested favors from another; that it must pay with a portion of its independence for whatever it may accept under that character; that, by such acceptance, it may place itself in the condition of having given equivalents for nominal favors and yet of being reproached with ingratitude for not giving more. There can be no greater error than to expect, or calculate, upon real favors from nation to nation. 'Tis an illusion which experience must cure, which a just pride ought to discard.

In offering to you, my countrymen, these counsels of an old and affectionate friend, I dare not hope they will make the strong and lasting impression I could wish; that they will control the usual current of the passions or prevent our nation from running the course which has hitherto marked the destiny of nations. But if I may even flatter myself that they may be productive of some partial benefit, some occasional good, that they may now and then recur to moderate the fury of party spirit, to warn against the mischiefs of foreign intrigue, to guard against the impostures of pretended patriotism, this hope will be a full recompense for the solicitude for your welfare by which they have been dictated....

... Though, in reviewing the incidents of my administration, I am unconscious of intentional error, I am nevertheless too sensible of my defects not to think it probable that I may have committed many errors. Whatever they may be, I fervently beseech the Almighty to avert or mitigate the evils to which they may tend. I shall also carry with me the hope that my country will never cease to view them with indulgence and that, after forty-five years of my life dedicated to its service, with an upright zeal, the faults of incompetent abilities will be consigned to oblivion as myself must soon be to the mansions of rest.

Relying on its kindness in this as in other things, and actuated by that fervent love toward it which is so natural to a man who views in it the native soil of himself and his progenitors for several generations, I anticipate with pleasing expectation that retreat in which I promise myself to realize, without alloy, the sweet enjoyment of partaking, in the midst of my fellow-citizens, the benign influence of good laws under a free government, the ever favorite object of my heart and the happy reward, as I trust, of our mutual cares, labors, and dangers.

3. ON THE LOUISIANA PURCHASE[1]

By THOMAS JEFFERSON

EDITORS' NOTE.—Robert R. Livingston (1746–1813), the recipient of the first of these letters from Jefferson, served on the committee to draft the Declaration of Independence, was appointed by Jefferson, United States minister to France, and with James Monroe negotiated the sale of Louisiana to the United States by France. John Breckinridge (1760–1806), the recipient of the second of these letters of Jefferson, was for a long time Jefferson's lieutenant and friend, had done much to secure passage of the Kentucky Resolutions of 1798, and served for a brief period as President Jefferson's attorney-general.

TO R. R. LIVINGSTON

April 18, 1802

... The cession of Louisiana and the Floridas by Spain to France works most sorely on the United States. On this subject the Secretary of State has written to you fully, yet I cannot forbear recurring to it personally, so deep is the impression it makes on my mind. It completely reverses all the political relations of the United States and will form a new epoch in our political course. Of all nations of any consideration, France is the one which, hitherto, has offered the fewest points on which we could have any conflict of right and the most points of a communion of interests. From these causes, we have ever looked to her as our *natural friend*, as one with which we never could have an occasion of difference. Her growth, therefore, we viewed as our own, her misfortunes ours. There is on the globe one single spot, the possessor of which is our natural and habitual enemy. It is New Orleans, through which the produce of three-eighths of our territory must pass to market, and from its fertility it will ere long yield more than half of our whole produce and contain more than half of our in-habitants. France, placing herself in that door, assumes to us the attitude of defiance. Spain might have retained it quietly for years. Her pacific dispositions, her feeble state, would induce her to increase our facilities there, so that her possession of the place would be hardly felt by us, and it would not, perhaps, be very long before some circumstance might arise which might make the cession of it to us the price of something of more worth to her. Not so can it ever be in the hands of France; the impetuosity of her temper, the energy and restlessness of her character, placed in a point of eternal friction with us, and our character, which, though quiet and loving peace and the pursuit of wealth, is high-minded, despising wealth in competition with insult or injury, enterprising and energetic as any nation on earth; these circumstances render it impossible that France and the United States can continue long friends when they meet in so irritable a position. They, as well as we, must be blind if they do not see this; and we must be very improvident if we do not begin to make arrangements on that hypothesis. The day that France takes possession of New Orleans fixes the sentence which is to restrain her forever within her low-water mark. It seals the union of two nations, who, in conjunction, can maintain exclusive posses-

1. Microfilm reproduction, Reel 42, University of Chicago Library, of the *Papers of Thomas Jefferson*, Library of Congress, Vol. 122, fols. 21077–80; and Reel 46, Vol. 134, fols. 23144–46.

sion of the ocean. From that moment, we must marry ourselves to the British fleet and nation. We must turn all our attention to a maritime force, for which our resources place us on very high ground; and, having formed and connected together a power which may render reinforcement of her settlements here impossible to France, make the first cannon which shall be fired in Europe the signal for tearing up any settlement she may have made, and for holding the two continents of America in sequestration for the common purposes of the united British and American nations. This is not a state of things we seek or desire. It is one which this measure, if adopted by France, forces on us as necessarily, as any other cause, by the laws of nature, brings on its necessary effect. It is not from a fear of France that we deprecate this measure proposed by her. For however greater her force is than ours, compared in the abstract, it is nothing in comparison of ours when to be exerted on our soil. But it is from a sincere love of peace and a firm persuasion that, bound to France by the interests and the strong sympathies still existing in the minds of our citizens, and holding relative positions which insure their continuance, we are secure of a long course of peace. Whereas the change of friends, which will be rendered necessary if France changes that position, embarks us necessarily as a belligerent power in the first war of Europe. In that case, France will have held possession of New Orleans during the interval of a peace, long or short, at the end of which it will be wrested from her. Will this short-lived possession have been an equivalent to her for the transfer of such a weight into the scale of her enemy? Will not the amalgamation of a young, thriving nation continue to that enemy the health and force which are at present so evidently on the decline? And will a few years' possession of New Orleans add

equally to the strength of France? She may say she needs Louisiana for the supply of her West Indies. She does not need it in time of peace, and in war she could not depend on them, because they would be so easily intercepted. I should suppose that all these considerations might, in some proper form, be brought into view of the government of France. Though stated by us, it ought not to give offense, because we do not bring them forward as a menace but as consequences not controllable by us but inevitable from the course of things. We mention them, not as things which we desire by any means, but as things we deprecate; and we beseech a friend to look forward and to prevent them for our common interest.

If France considers Louisiana, however, as indispensable for her views, she might perhaps be willing to look about for arrangements which might reconcile it to our interests. If anything could do this, it would be the ceding to us the island of New Orleans and the Floridas. This would certainly, in a great degree, remove the causes of jarring and irritation between us and perhaps for such a length of time as might produce other means of making the measure permanently conciliatory to our interests and friendships. It would, at any rate, relieve us from the necessity of taking immediate measures for countervailing such an operation by arrangements in another quarter. But still we should consider New Orleans and the Floridas as no equivalent for the risk of a quarrel with France, produced by her vicinage.

I have no doubt you have urged these considerations, on every proper occasion, with the government where you are. They are such as must have effect if you can find means of producing thorough reflection on them by that government. The idea here is that the troops sent to St. Domingo were to proceed to Louisiana after finishing their work in that island.[2] If this were the arrangement, it will give you time to return again and again to the charge. For the conquest of St. Domingo will not be a short work. It will take considerable time and wear down a great number of soldiers. Every eye in the United States is now fixed on this affair of Louisiana. Perhaps nothing since the Revolutionary War has produced more uneasy sensations through the body of the nation. Notwithstanding temporary bickerings which have taken place with France, she has still a strong hold on the affection of our citizens generally. I have thought it not amiss, by way of supplement to the letters of the Secretary of State, to write you this private one to impress you with the importance we affix to this transaction. . . .

TO JOHN BRECKINRIDGE

August 12, 1803

. . . Our information as to the country is very incomplete. We have taken measures to obtain it in full as to the settled part, which I hope to receive in time for Congress. The boundaries which I deem not admitting question are the high lands on the western side of the Mississippi inclosing all its waters, the Missouri, of course, and terminating in the line drawn from the northwestern point of the Lake of the Woods to the nearest source of the Mississippi, as lately settled between Great Britain and the United States. We have some claims to extend on the seacoast westwardly to the Rio Norte or Bravo,[3] and, better, to go eastwardly to the Rio Perdido, between Mobile and Pensacola, the ancient boundary of Louisiana. These claims will be a subject of negotiation with Spain, and if, as soon as she is at war, we push them strongly with one hand, holding out a price in the other, we shall certainly obtain the Floridas, and all in good time. In the meanwhile, without waiting for permission, we shall enter into the exercise of the natural right we have always insisted on with Spain, to wit, that of a nation holding the upper part of streams, having a right of innocent passage through them to the ocean. We shall prepare her to see us practice on this, and she will not oppose it by force.

Objections are raising to the eastward against this vast extent of our boundaries, and propositions are made to exchange Louisiana, or a part of it, for the Floridas. But, as I have said, we shall get the Floridas without, and I would not give one inch of the waters of the Mississippi to any nation, because I see in a light very important to our peace the exclusive right to its navigation, and the admission of no nation into it, but as into the Potomac or Delaware, with our consent and under our police. These Federalists see in this acquisition the formation of a new confederacy, embracing all the waters of the Mississippi, on both sides of it, and a separation of its eastern waters from us. These combinations depend on so many circumstances which we cannot foresee that I place little reliance on them. We have seldom seen neighborhood produce affection among nations. The reverse is almost the universal truth. Besides, if it should become the great interest of those nations to separate from this, if their happiness should depend on it so strongly as to induce them to go through that convulsion, why should the Atlantic states dread it? But especially why should we, their present inhabitants, take side in such a question? When I view the Atlantic states, procuring for those on the eastern waters of the Mississippi friendly instead of hostile neighbors on its western waters, I do not view it as an Eng-

2. Napoleon had sent French troops to subdue the revolt led by Toussaint L'Ouverture.

3. The Rio Grande del Norte (Great River of the North), now the boundary between Mexico and the United States; Rio Bravos (Ferocious River).

lishman would the procuring future blessings for the French nation, with whom he has no relations of blood or affection. The future inhabitants of the Atlantic and Mississippi states will be our sons. We leave them in distinct but bordering establishments. We think we see their happiness in their union, and we wish it. Events may prove it otherwise; and if they see their interest in separation, why should we take side with our Atlantic rather than our Mississippi descendants? It is the elder and the younger son differing. God bless them both and keep them in union if it be for their good but separate them if it be better.

The inhabited part of Louisiana, from Point Coupée to the sea, will of course be immediately a territorial government and soon a state. But, above that, the best use we can make of the country for some time will be to give establishments in it to the Indians on the east side of the Mississippi, in exchange for their present country, and open land offices in the last, and thus make this acquisition the means of filling up the eastern side instead of drawing off its population. When we shall be full on this side, we may lay off a range of states on the western bank from the head to the mouth, and so, range after range, advancing compactly as we multiply.

This treaty must, of course, be laid before both houses, because both have important functions to exercise respect-

ing it. They, I presume, will see their duty to their country in ratifying and paying for it, so as to secure a good which would otherwise probably be never again in their power. But I suppose they must then appeal to *the nation* for an additional article to the Constitution, approving and confirming an act which the nation had not previously authorized. The Constitution has made no provision for our holding foreign territory, still less for incorporating foreign nations into our Union. The Executive, in seizing the fugitive occurrence which so much advances the good of their country, have done an act beyond the Constitution. The Legislature in casting behind them metaphysical subtleties, and risking themselves like faithful servants, must ratify and pay for it, and throw themselves on their country for doing for them unauthorized what we know they would have done for themselves had they been in a situation to do it. It is the case of a guardian, investing the money of his ward in purchasing an important adjacent territory; and saying to him when of age, I did this for your good; I pretend to no right to bind you; you may disavow me, and I must get out of the scrape as I can; I thought it my duty to risk myself for you. But we shall not be disavowed by the nation, and their act of indemnity will confirm and not weaken the Constitution by more strongly marking out its lines.[4] . . .

4. THE MONROE DOCTRINE

A. THOMAS JEFFERSON TO ALEXANDER, BARON VON HUMBOLDT[1]

December 6, 1813

. . . I think it most fortunate that your travels in those countries [Mexico and

the northern coast of South America] were so timed as to make them known to the world in the moment they were

1. Microfilm reproduction, Reel 78, University of Chicago Library, of the *Papers of Thomas Jefferson,* Library of Congress, Vol. 200, fol. 35554. This letter of Jefferson to Humboldt in 1813 indicates the existence in the United States before 1823 of principles later incorporated in the Monroe Doctrine.

4. On August 18 Jefferson wrote Breckinridge that word from France made it undesirable to raise constitutional questions and suggested the desirability of having all friends of the treaty present on the first day of the session (*Papers of Thomas Jefferson,* Reel 46, Vol. 134, fol. 23172.

about to become actors on its stage. That they will throw off their European dependence I have no doubt, but in what kind of government their revolution will end is not so certain. History, I believe, furnishes no example of a priest-ridden people maintaining a free civil government. This marks the lowest grade of ignorance of which their civil as well as religious leaders will always avail themselves for their own purposes. The vicinity of New Spain to the United States and their consequent intercourse may furnish schools for the higher, and example for the lower, classes of their citizens. And Mexico, where we learn from you that men of science are not wanting, may revolutionize itself under better auspices than the southern provinces. These last, I fear, must end in military despotisms. The different casts [sic] of their inhabitants, their mutual hatreds and jealousies, their profound ignorance and bigotry, will be played off by cunning leaders, and each be made the instrument of enslaving the others. But of all this you can best judge, for in truth we have little knowledge of them to be depended on but through you.

But in whatever government they end, they will be *American* governments, no longer to be involved in the never ceasing broils of Europe. The European nations constitute a separate division of the globe; their localities make them part of a distinct system; they have a set of interests of their own in which it is our business never to engage ourselves. America has a hemisphere to itself. It must have its separate system of interests which must not be subordinated to those of Europe. The insulated state in which nature has placed the American continent should so far avail it that no spark of war kindled in the other quarters of the globe should be wafted across the wide oceans which separated us from them. And it will be so. In fifty years more the United States will contain fifty millions of inhabitants, and fifty years are soon gone over. The peace of 1763 is within that period. I was then twenty years old and of course remember well all the transactions of the war preceding it. And you will live to see the epoch now equally ahead of us, and the numbers which will then be spread over the other parts of the American hemisphere, catching long before that the principles of our portion of it and concurring with us in the maintenance of the same system. ...

B. JOHN QUINCY ADAMS, SECRETARY OF STATE, TO MR. MIDDLETON, MINISTER TO RUSSIA[2]

July 5, 1820

... The League of Peace, so far as it was a covenant of organized governments, has proved effectual to its purposes by an experience of five years. Its only interruption has been in this hemisphere, though between nations strictly European; by the invasion of the Portuguese on the territory claimed by Spain, but already lost to her, on the eastern shore of the Rio de la Plata. This aggression, too, the European alliance have undertaken to control; and in connection with it they have formed projects hitherto abortive of interposing in the revolutionary struggle between Spain and her South American colonies.

As a compact between governments it is not improbable that the European alliance will last as long as some of the states who are parties to it. The warlike passions and propensities of the present age find their principal ailment, not in the enmities between nation and nation, but in the internal dissensions between

2. John Bassett Moore, *A Digest of International Law* (Washington, 1906), VI, 377-79. Like Jefferson's letter to Humboldt, printed above, this letter reveals in American policy before 1823 ideas which were included in the Monroe Doctrine.

the component parts of all. The war is between nations and their rulers.

The Emperor Alexander may be considered as the principal patron and founder of the League of Peace. His interest is the more unequivocal in support of it. His empire is the only party to the compact free from that internal fermentation which threatens the existence of all the rest. His territories are the most extensive, his military establishment the most stupendous, his country the most improvable and thriving of them all. He is therefore naturally the most obnoxious to the jealousy and fears of his associates, and his circumstances point his policy to a faithful adhesion to the general system, with a strong reprobation of those who would resort to special and partial alliances, from which any one member of the league should be excluded. This general tendency of his policy is corroborated by the mild and religious turn of his individual character. He finds a happy coincidence between the dictates of his conscience and the interest of his empire. And as from the very circumstance of his preponderancy, partial alliances might be most easily contracted by him, from the natural resort of the weak for succor to the strong, by discountenancing all such partial combinations he has the appearance of discarding advantages entirely within his command and reaps the glory of disinterestedness while most efficaciously providing for his own security.

Such is accordingly the constant indication of the Russian policy since the peace of Paris in 1815. The neighbors of Russia which have the most to dread from her overshadowing and encroaching power are Persia, Turkey, Austria, and Prussia; the two latter of which are members of the European and even of the Holy Alliance, while the two former are not only extra-European in their general policy, but of religions which excluded them from ever becoming parties, if not from ever deriving benefit from that singular compact.

The political system of the United States is also essentially extra-European. To stand in firm and cautious independence of all entanglement in the European system has been a cardinal point of their policy under every administration of their government, from the peace of 1783 to this day. If at the original adoption of their system there could have been any doubt of its justice or its wisdom, there can be none at this time. Every year's experience rivets it more deeply in the principles and opinions of the nation. Yet in proportion as the importance of the United States as one of the members of the general society of civilized nations increases in the eyes of the others, the difficulties of maintaining this system and the temptations to depart from it increase and multiply with it. The Russian government has not only manifested an inclination that the United States should concur in the general principles of the European league, but a direct though unofficial application has been made by the present Russian minister here that the United States should become formal parties to the Holy Alliance.[3] It has been suggested, as inducement to obtain their compliance, that this compact bound the parties to no specific engagement of anything. That it was a pledge of mere principles—that its real as well as its professed purpose was merely the general preservation of peace—and it was intimated that if any question should arise between the United States and other

3. The most significant European alliance of this period was the Quadruple Alliance composed originally of the Great Powers which defeated Napoleon—Great Britain, Russia, Prussia, and Austria. Often confused with the Quadruple Alliance was the so-called "Holy Alliance," formed by the rulers of Russia, Prussia, and Austria in 1815. The popular confusion of the Holy with the Quadruple Alliance made the former seem more important than it really was; it came to symbolize a combination of absolute monarchs against popular liberties.

governments of Europe, the Emperor Alexander, desirous of using his influence in their favor, would have a substantial motive and justification for interposing if he could regard them as *his allies*, which, as parties to the Holy Alliance, he would.

It is possible that overtures of a similar character may be made to you; but, whether they should be or not, it is proper to apprize you of the light in which they have been viewed by the President. No direct refusal has been signified to Mr. Poletica. It is presumed that none will be necessary. His instructions are not to make the proposal in form unless with a prospect that it will be successful. It might, perhaps, be sufficient to answer that the organization of our government is such as not to admit of our acceding formally to that compact. But it may be added that the President, approving its general principles and thoroughly convinced of the benevolent and virtuous motives which led to the conception and presided at the formation of this system by the Emperor Alexander, believes that the United States will more effectually contribute to the great and sublime objects for which it was concluded by abstaining from a formal participation in it than they could as stipulated members of it. As a general declaration of principles, disclaiming the impulses of vulgar ambition and unprincipled aggrandizement and openly proclaiming the peculiarly Christian maxims of mutual benevolence and brotherly love to be binding upon the intercourse between nations no less than upon that of individuals, the United States not only give their hearty assent to the articles of the Holy Alliance but will be among the most earnest and conscientious in observing them. But independent of the prejudices which have been excited against this instrument in the public opinion, which time and an experience of its good effects will gradually wear away, it may be observed that, for the repose of Europe as well as of America, the European and American political system should be kept as separate and distinct from each other as possible. If the United States as members of the Holy Alliance could acquire a right to ask the influence of its most powerful member in their controversies with other states, the other members must be entitled in return to ask the influence of the United States, for themselves or against their opponents, in the deliberations of the league they would be entitled to a voice and in exercising their right must occasionally appeal to principles which might not harmonize with those of any European member of the bond. This consideration alone would be decisive for declining a participation in that league, which is the President's absolute and irrevocable determination, although he trusts that no occasion will present itself rendering it necessary to make that determination known by an explicit refusal.

C. JOHN QUINCY ADAMS, SECRETARY OF STATE, TO MR. NELSON, MINISTER TO SPAIN[4]

April 28, 1823

In the war between France and Spain, now commencing, other interests, peculiarly ours, will, in all probability, be deeply involved. Whatever may be the issue of this war as between those two European powers, it may be taken for granted that the dominion of Spain upon the American continents, north and south, is irrevocably gone. But the islands of Cuba and Puerto Rico still remain nominally, and so far really, dependent upon her, that she yet possesses the power of transferring her own dominion over them, together with the possessions of them, to others. These islands, from their local position, are

4. Moore, *op. cit.*, pp. 380–81.

natural appendages to the North American continent, and one of them (Cuba) almost in sight of our shores, from a multitude of considerations has become an object of transcendent importance to the commercial and political interests of our Union. Its commanding position, with reference to the Gulf of Mexico and the West India seas; the character of its population; its situation midway between our southern coast and the island of St. Domingo; its safe and capacious harbor of the Havana, fronting a long line of our shores destitute of the same advantage; the nature of its productions and of its wants, furnishing the supplies and needing the returns of a commerce immensely profitable and mutually beneficial, give it an importance in the sum of our national interests with which that of no other foreign territory can be compared, and little inferior to that which binds the different members of this Union together. Such, indeed, are, between the interests of that island and of this country, the geographical, commercial, moral, and political relations, formed by nature, gathering, in the process of time, and even now verging

to maturity, that, in looking forward to the probable course of events, for the short period of half a century, it is scarcely possible to resist the conviction that the annexation of Cuba to our Federal Republic will be indispensable to the continuance and integrity of the Union itself.

It is obvious, however, that for this event we are not yet prepared. Numerous and formidable objections to the extension of our territorial dominions beyond sea present themselves to the first contemplation of the subject; obstacles to the system of policy by which alone that result can be compassed and maintained are to be foreseen and surmounted, both from at home and abroad; but there are laws of political as well as of physical gravitation; and if an apple, severed by the tempest from its native tree, cannot choose but fall to the ground, Cuba, forcibly disjoined from its own unnatural connection with Spain, and incapable of self-support, can gravitate only toward the North American Union, which, by the same law of nature, cannot cast her off from its bosom. . . .

D. RICHARD RUSH, MINISTER TO ENGLAND, TO JOHN QUINCY ADAMS, SECRETARY OF STATE[5]

LONDON, August 19, 1823

(Rec'd 9th October)

No. 323

SIR,

When my interview with Mr. Canning on Saturday was about to close, I transiently asked him whether, notwithstanding the late news from Spain, we might not hope that the Spaniards would get the better of all their difficulties. I had allusion to the defection of Ballasteros,[6] in Andalusia, an event seeming to threaten with new dangers the constitutional cause. His reply was general, im-

porting nothing more than his opinion of the increased difficulties and dangers with which, undoubtedly, this event was calculated to surround the Spanish cause.

Pursuing the topic of Spanish affairs, I remarked that, should France ultimately effect her purposes in Spain, there was at least the consolation left that Great Britain would not allow her to go further and lay her hands upon the Spanish colonies, bringing them, too, under her grasp. I here had in my mind the sentiments promulgated upon this

5. Proceedings of the Massachusetts Historical Society, Second Series (Boston, 1902), XV, 412–15.

6. General Alva Ballasteros, a leader in the constitutional movement in Spain (1820–22) and chief military support of the Cádiz constitution. Andalusia is the southwest province of Spain of which Cádiz is the chief port.

subject in Mr. Canning's note to the British ambassador at Paris of the 31st of March, during the negotiations that preceded the invasion of Spain. It will be recollected that the British government say in this note that time and the course of events appeared to have substantially decided the question of the separation of these colonies from the mother-country, although their formal recognition as independent states by Great Britain might be hastened or retarded by external circumstances, as well as by the internal condition of those new states themselves; and that as His Britannic Majesty disclaimed all intention of appropriating to himself the smallest portion of the late Spanish possessions in America, he was also satisfied that no attempt would be made by France to bring any of them under *her* dominion, either by conquest or by cession from Spain.

By this we are to understand, in terms sufficiently distinct, that Great Britain would not be passive under such an attempt by France; and Mr. Canning, on my having referred to this note, asked me what I thought my government would say to going hand in hand with this, in the same sentiment; not, as he added, that any concert in action under it could become necessary between the two countries, but that the simple fact of our being known to hold the same sentiment would, he had no doubt, by its moral effect, put down the intention on the part of France, admitting that she should ever entertain it. This belief was founded, he said, upon the large share of the maritime power of the world which Great Britain and the United States shared between them, and the consequent influence which the knowledge that they held a common opinion upon a question on which such large maritime interests, present and future, hung, could not fail to produce upon the rest of the world.

I replied that in what manner my government would look upon such a suggestion I was unable to say, but that I would communicate it in the same informal manner in which he threw it out. I said, however, that I did not think I should do so with full advantage, unless he would at the same time enlighten me as to the precise situation in which His Majesty's government stood at this moment in relation to those new states, and especially on the material point of their own independence.

He replied that Great Britain certainly never again intended to lend her instrumentality or aid, whether by mediation or otherwise, toward making up the dispute between Spain and her colonies, but that, if this result could still be brought about, she would not interfere to *prevent* it. Upon my intimating that I had supposed that all idea of Spain ever recovering her authority over the colonies had long since gone by, he explained by saying that he did not mean to controvert that opinion, for he, too, believed that the day had arrived when all America might be considered as lost to Europe, so far as the tie of political dependence was concerned. All that he meant was that, if Spain and the colonies should still be able to bring the dispute, not yet totally extinct between them, to a close upon terms satisfactory to both sides, and which should at the same time secure to Spain commercial or other advantages not extended to other nations, that Great Britain would not object to a compromise in this spirit of preference to Spain. All that she would ask would be to stand upon as favored a footing as any other nation after Spain. Upon my again alluding to the improbability of the dispute ever settling down now even upon this basis, he said that it was not his intention to maintain such a position and that he had expressed himself as above rather for the purpose of indicating the feeling which this cabinet still had toward Spain in relation to the controversy than of predicting results.

Wishing, however, to be still more

specifically informed, I asked whether Great Britain was at this moment taking any step, or contemplating any, which had reference to the recognition of these states, this being the point in which we felt the chief interest.

He replied that she had taken none whatever, as yet, but was upon the eve of taking one, not final, but preparatory, and which would still leave her at large to recognize or not, according to the position of events at a future period. The measure in question was to send out one or more individuals under authority from this government to South America, not strictly diplomatic, but clothed with powers in the nature of a commission of inquiry, and which in short he described as analogous to those exercised by our own commissioners in 1817, and that upon the result of this commission much might depend as to the ulterior conduct of Great Britain. I asked whether I was to understand that it would comprehend all the new states, or which of them, to which he replied that for the present it would be limited to Mexico.

Reverting to his first idea, he again said that he hoped that France would not, should even events in the Peninsula be favorable to her, extend her views to South America for the purpose of reducing the colonies, nominally, perhaps, for Spain, but in effect to subserve ends of her own; but that, in case she should meditate such a policy, he was satisfied that the knowledge of the United States being opposed to it, as well as Great Britain, could not fail to have its influ-ence in checking her steps. In this way he thought good might be done by prevention, and peaceful prospects all round increased. As to the form in which such knowledge might be made to reach France, and even the other powers of Europe, he said, in conclusion, that that might probably be arranged in a manner that would be free from objection.

I again told him that I would convey his suggestions to you for the information of the President and impart to him whatever reply I might receive. My own inference rather is that his proposition was a fortuitous one; yet he entered into it, I thought, with some interest and appeared to receive with a corresponding satisfaction the assurance I gave him that it should be made known to the President. I did not feel myself at liberty to express any opinion unfavorable to it and was as careful to give none in its favor.

Mr. Canning mentioned to me, at this same interview, that a late confidential dispatch which he had seen from Count Nesselrode to Count Lieven, dated, I think, in June, contained declarations respecting the Russian ukase, relative to the northwest coast, that were satisfactory; that they went to show that it would probably not be executed in a manner to give cause of complaint to other nations and that, in particular, it had not yet been executed in any instance under orders issued by Russia subsequently to its first promulgation....

E. GEORGE CANNING, BRITISH FOREIGN MINISTER, TO RICHARD RUSH[7]

FOREIGN OFFICE, August 20, 1823
PRIVATE AND CONFIDENTIAL
MY DEAR SIR,

Before leaving town I am desirous of bringing before you in a more distinct,

7. *Proceedings of the Massachusetts Historical Society, Second Series*, XV, 415–16.

but still in an unofficial and confidential shape, the question which we shortly discussed the last time that I had the pleasure of seeing you.

Is not the moment come when our governments might understand each other as to the Spanish-American colonies? And if we can arrive at such an understanding, would it not be expedient for ourselves, and beneficial for all the world, that the principles of it should be clearly settled and plainly avowed?

For ourselves we have no disguise.

1. We conceive the recovery of the colonies by Spain to be hopeless.

2. We conceive the question of the recognition of them, as independent states, to be one of time and circumstances.

3. We are, however, by no means disposed to throw any impediment in the way of an arrangement between them and the mother-country by amicable negotiation.

4. We aim not at the possession of any portion of them ourselves.

5. We could not see any portion of them transferred to any other power with indifference.

If these opinions and feelings are, as I firmly believe them to be, common to your government with ours, why should we hesitate mutually to confide them to each other, and to declare them in the face of the world?

If there be any European power which cherishes other projects, which looks to a forcible enterprise for reducing the colonies to subjugation, on the behalf or in the name of Spain, or which meditates the acquisition of any part of them to itself, by cession or by conquest, such a declaration on the part of your government and ours would be at once the most effectual and the least offensive mode of intimating our joint disapprobation of such projects.

It would at the same time put an end to all the jealousies of Spain with respect to her remaining colonies and to the agitation which prevails in those colonies, an agitation which it would be but humane to allay, being determined (as we are) not to profit by encouraging it.

Do you conceive that, under the power which you have recently received, you are authorized to enter into negotiation and to sign any convention upon this subject? Do you conceive, if that be not within your competence, you could exchange with me ministerial notes upon it?

Nothing could be more gratifying to me than to join with you in such a work, and, I am persuaded, there has seldom, in the history of the world, occurred an opportunity when so small an effort of two friendly governments might produce so unequivocal a good and prevent such extensive calamities.

I shall be absent from London but three weeks at the utmost but never so far distant but that I can receive and reply to any communication within three or four days. . . .

F. RICHARD RUSH TO JOHN QUINCY ADAMS[8]

LONDON, August 23, 1823

SIR:

I yesterday received from Mr. Canning a note headed "private and confidential," setting before me in a more distinct form the proposition respecting South American affairs which he communicated to me in conversation on the sixteenth instant, as already reported in my dispatch number 323. I lose no time in transmitting a copy of his note, as

8. Richard Rush, *A Residence at the Court of London* . . . (2d ser.; London, 1845), II, 415–17.

well as a copy of my answer, written and sent today.

In framing the answer on my own judgment alone, I feel that I have had a task of some embarrassment and shall be happy if it receive the President's approbation.

I believe that this government has the subject of Mr. Canning's proposition much at heart, and certainly his note bears upon the face of it a character of earnestness as well as cordiality toward the government of the United States which cannot escape notice.

I have therefore thought it proper to meet this spirit, as far as I could, consistently with other and paramount considerations.

These I conceived to be chiefly twofold: first, the danger of pledging my government to any measure of foreign policy which might in any degree, now or hereafter, implicate it in the federative system of Europe; and, secondly, I have felt myself alike without warrant to take a step which might prove exceptionable in the eyes of France, with whom our pacific and friendly relations remain, I presume, undisturbed, whatever may be our speculative abhorrence of her attack upon the right of self-government in Spain.

In framing my answer, I had also to consider what was due to Spain herself; and I hope that I have not overlooked what was due to the colonies.

The whole subject is novel and open to views on which I have deliberated anxiously. If my answer shall be thought, on the whole, to bear properly on all the public considerations which belong most materially to the occasion, it will be a source of great satisfaction to me.

The tone of earnestness in Mr. Canning's note naturally starts the inference that the British cabinet cannot be without its serious apprehensions that ambitious enterprises are meditated against the independence of the new Spanish-American states; whether by France alone, or in conjunction with the Continental powers, I cannot now say on any authentic grounds.

I have the honor to remain

With very great respect,

Your obedient servant,

RICHARD RUSH

The Honorable
JOHN QUINCY ADAMS
Secretary of State

G. JAMES MONROE, PRESIDENT, TO THOMAS JEFFERSON, OAKHILL[9]

October 17, 1823

DEAR SIR,

I transmit to you two dispatches which were receiv'd from Mr. Rush while I was lately in Washington which involve interests of the highest importance. They contain two letters from Mr. Canning, suggesting designs of the Holy Alliance against the independence of South America and proposing a co-operation between Great Britain and the United States in support of it against the members of that alliance. The project aims in the first instance at a mere expression of opinion, somewhat in the abstract, but which, it is expected by Mr. Canning, will have a great political effect by defeating the combination. By Mr. Rush's answers, which are also inclosed, you will see the light in which he

views the subject and the extent to which he may have gone. Many important considerations are involved in this proposition. 1st. Shall we entangle ourselves, at all, in European politics and wars, on the side of any power, against others, presuming that a concert by agreement, of the kind proposed, may lead to that result? 2d. If a case can exist in which a sound maxim may and ought to be departed from, is not the present instance precisely that case? 3d. Has not the epoch arrived when Great Britain must take her stand, either on the side of the monarchs of Europe or of the United States and, in consequence, either in favor of despotism or of liberty, and may it not be presumed that, aware of that necessity, her government has seized on the present occurrence as that which it deems the most

9. *Proceedings of the Massachusetts Historical Society, Second Series,* XV, 375.

suitable to announce and mark the commencement of that career.

My own impression is that we ought to meet the proposal of the British govt. and to make it known that we would view an interference on the part of the European powers, and especially an attack on the colonies by them, as an attack on ourselves, presuming that, if they succeeded with them, they would extend it to us. I am sensible however of the extent and difficulty of the question

and shall be happy to have yours, and Mr. Madison's opinions on it. I do not wish to trouble either of you with small objects, but the present one is vital, involving the high interests for which we have so long and so faithfully and harmoniously contended together. Be so kind as to inclose to him the dispatches, with an intimation of the motive. With great respect, etc.

JAMES MONROE

Recd. Oct. 23

H. THOMAS JEFFERSON TO JAMES MONROE, PRESIDENT[10]

October 24, 1823

The question presented by the letters you have sent me is the most momentous which has ever been offered to my contemplation since that of Independence. That made us a nation; this sets our compass and points the course which we are to steer through the ocean of time opening on us. And never could we embark upon it under circumstances more auspicious. Our first and fundamental maxim should be: never to entangle ourselves in the broils of Europe; our second: never to suffer Europe to intermeddle with cis-Atlantic affairs. America, North and South, has a set of interests distinct from those of Europe and particularly her own. She should therefore have a system of her own, separate and apart from that of Europe. While the last is laboring to become the domicile of despotism, our endeavor should surely be to make our hemisphere that of freedom.

One nation, most of all, could disturb us in this pursuit; she now offers to lead, aid, and accompany us in it. By acceding to her proposition, we detach her from the bands of despots, bring her mighty weight into the scale of free government, and emancipate a continent at one stroke,

which might otherwise linger long in doubt and difficulty. Great Britain is the nation which can do us the most harm of any one, or all on earth; and with her on our side we need not fear the whole world. With her, then, we should most sedulously cherish a cordial friendship; and nothing would tend more to knit our affections than to be fighting once more, side by side, in the same cause. Not that I would purchase even her amity at the price of taking part in her wars.

But the war in which the present proposition might engage us, should that be its consequence, is not her war, but ours. Its object is to introduce and establish the American system of keeping out of our land all foreign powers—of never permitting those of Europe to intermeddle with the affairs of our nations. It is to maintain our own principle, not to depart from it. And if, to facilitate this, we can effect a division in the body of the European powers, and draw over to our side its most powerful member, surely we should do it. But I am clearly of Mr. Canning's opinion that it will prevent instead of provoking war. With Great Britain withdrawn from their scale and shifted into that of our two continents, all Europe combined would not undertake such a war, for how would they propose to get at either enemy without superior fleets? Nor is

10. Microfilm reproduction, Reel 91, University of Chicago Library, of the *Papers of Thomas Jefferson*, Library of Congress, Vol. 225, fols. 40185–86.

the occasion to be slighted which this proposition offers of declaring our protest against the atrocious violations of the rights of nations by the interference of any one in the internal affairs of another, so flagitiously begun by Bonaparte, and now continued by the equally lawless Alliance calling itself Holy.

But we have, first, to ask ourselves a question. Do we wish to acquire to our own confederacy any one or more of the Spanish provinces? I candidly confess that I have ever looked on Cuba as the most interesting addition which could ever be made to our system of states. The control which, with Florida point, this island would give us over the Gulf of Mexico, and the countries and the isthmus bordering on it, as well as all those whose waters flow into it, would fill up the measure of our political well-being. Yet, as I am sensible that this can never be obtained, even with her own consent, but by war, and its independence, which is our second interest (and especially its independence of England), can be secured without it, I have no hesitation in abandoning my first wish to future chances, and accepting its independence, with peace and the friendship of England, rather than its association, at the expense of war and her enmity.

I could honestly, therefore, join in the declaration proposed that we aim not at the acquisition of any of those possessions, that we will not stand in the way of any amicable arrangement between them and the mother-country; but that we will oppose, with all our means, the forcible interposition of any other power, as auxiliary, stipendiary, or under any other form or pretext, and most especially their transfer to any power by conquest, cession, or acquisition in any other way. I should think it, therefore, advisable that the Executive should encourage the British government to a continuance in the dispositions expressed in these letters by an assurance of his concurrence with them as far as his authority goes; and that, as it may lead to war, the declaration of which [sic] requires an act of Congress, the case shall be laid before them for consideration at their first meeting and under the reasonable aspect in which it is seen by himself.

I have been so long weaned from political subjects, and have so long ceased to take any interest in them, that I am sensible I am not qualified to offer opinions on them worthy of any attention. But the question now proposed involves consequences so lasting, and effects so decisive, of our future destinies as to rekindle all the interest I have heretofore felt on such occasions and to induce me to the hazard of opinions, which will prove only my wish to contribute still my mite toward anything which may be useful to our country. And, praying you to accept it at only what it is worth, I add the assurance of my constant and affectionate friendship and respect.

THOMAS JEFFERSON

I. CABINET DEBATE ON THE CANNING PROPOSALS[11]

WASHINGTON, November 7th.—Cabinet meeting at the President's from half-past one till four. Mr. Calhoun, Secretary of War, and Mr. Southard, Secretary of the Navy, present. The subject for consideration was the confidential proposals of the British Secretary of State, George Canning, to R. Rush, and the correspondence between them relating to the projects of the Holy Alliance upon South America. There was much conversation, without coming to any definite point. The object of Canning appears to have been to obtain some public pledge from the government of the United States, ostensibly against the

11. John Quincy Adams, *Memoirs of . . . Comprising Portions of His Diary from 1795 to 1848*, ed. Charles Francis Adams (Philadelphia, 1875), VI, 177–79.

forcible interference of the Holy Alliance between Spain and South America; but really or especially against the acquisition to the United States themselves of any part of the Spanish-American possessions.

Mr. Calhoun inclined to giving a discretionary power to Mr. Rush to join in a declaration against the interference of the Holy Allies, if necessary, even if it should pledge us not to take Cuba or the province of Texas; because the power of Great Britain being greater than ours to *seize* upon them, we should get the advantage of obtaining from her the same declaration we should make ourselves.

I thought the cases not parallel. We have no intention of seizing either Texas or Cuba. But the inhabitants of either or both may exercise their primitive rights and solicit a union with us. They will certainly do no such thing to Great Britain. By joining with her, therefore, in her proposed declaration, we give her a substantial and perhaps inconvenient pledge against ourselves and really obtain nothing in return. Without entering now into the inquiry of the expediency of our annexing Texas or Cuba to our Union, we should at least keep ourselves free to act as emergencies may arise and not tie ourselves down to any principle which might immediately afterward be brought to bear against ourselves....

I remarked that the communications recently received from the Russian minister, Baron Tuyll, afforded, as I thought, a very suitable and convenient opportunity for us to take our stand against the Holy Alliance and at the same time to decline the overture of Great Britain. It would be more candid, as well as more dignified, to avow our principles explicitly to Russia and France than to come in as a cockboat in the wake of the British man-of-war.

This idea was acquiesced in on all sides....

J. OBSERVATION ON COMMUNICATIONS RECENTLY RECEIVED FROM THE MINISTER OF RUSSIA, NOVEMBER 27, 1823[12]

The government of the United States of America is [essentially] *Republican*. By their Constitution it is provided that "The United States shall guarantee to every state in this Union, a *Republican form* of government, and shall protect each of them from invasion."

[The principles of this form of polity are: (1) that the institution of government, to be lawful, must be pacific, that is, founded upon the consent and by the agreement of those who are governed; and (2) that each nation is exclusively the judge of the government best suited to itself, and that no other nation can justly interfere by force to impose a different government upon it. The first of these principles may be designated as the principle of *liberty*—the second as the principle of national *independence*—they are both principles of *peace* and of good will to men.]

[A necessary consequence of the second of these principles is that] the United States recognize in other nations the right which they claim and exercise for themselves, of establishing and of modifying their own governments, according to their own judgments, and views of their interests, not encroaching upon the rights of others.

Aware that the monarchical principle of government is different from theirs, the United States have never sought a conflict with it, for interests not their own. Warranted by the principle of national independence, which forms one of the bases of their political institutions, they have desired peace, commerce, and

12. *Proceedings of the Massachusetts Historical Society, Second Series*, XV, 405–8. These observations were drafted by Adams on November 25 but carried the date line of November 27 in the Department of State.

honest friendship with all other nations, and entangling alliances with none.

From all the combinations of European politics relative to the distribution of power or the administration of government, the United States have studiously kept themselves aloof. They have not sought, by the propagation of their principles, to disturb the peace or to intermeddle with the policy of any part of Europe. In the independence of nations they have respected the organization of their governments, however different from their own, and, [republican to the last drop of blood in their veins,] they have thought it no sacrifice of their principles to cultivate with sincerity and assiduity peace and friendship even with the most absolute monarchies and their sovereigns.

To the revolution and war which has severed the immense territories, on the American [*territories*] continents heretofore subject to the dominion of Spain from the yoke of that power, the United States have observed an undeviating neutrality. So long as the remotest prospect existed that Spain by negotiation or by arms could recover the possession she had once held of those countries, the United States forbore to inquire by what title she had held them, and how she had fulfilled toward them the duties of all governments to the people under their charge. When the South American nations, after successfully declaring their independence, had maintained it, until no rational doubt could remain that the dominion of Spain over them was irrecoverably lost, the United States recognized them as independent nations and have entered into those relations with them, commercial and political, incident to that condition—relations the more important to the interests of the United States, as the whole of those emancipated regions are situated in their own hemisphere, and as the most extensive, populous, and powerful of the new nations are in their immediate vicinity;

and one of them bordering upon the territories of this Union.

To the contest between Spain and South America all the European powers have also remained neutral. The maritime nations have freely entered into commercial intercourse with the South Americans, which they could not have done while the colonial government of Spain existed. The neutrality of Europe was one of the foundations upon which the United States formed their judgment, in recognizing the South American independence; they considered, and still consider, that from this neutrality the European nations cannot rightfully depart.

Among the powers of Europe, Russia is one with whom the United States have entertained the most friendly and mutually beneficial intercourse. Through all the vicissitudes of war and revolution, of which the world for the last thirty years has been the theater, the good understanding between the two governments has been uninterrupted. The Emperor Alexander in particular has not ceased to manifest sentiments of friendship and good-will to the United States from the period of his accession to the throne to this moment, and the United States, on their part, have as invariably shown the interest which they take in his friendship and the solicitude with which they wish to retain it.

In the communications recently received from the Baron de Tuyll, so far as they relate to the immediate objects of intercourse between the two governments, the President sees with high satisfaction the avowal of unabated cordiality and kindness toward the United States on the part of the Emperor.

With regard to the communications which relate to the affairs of Spain and Portugal, and to those of South America, while sensible of the candor and frankness with which they are made, the President indulges the hope that they are not intended *either* to mark an era either of change, in the friendly dispositions of the Emperor toward the United States or of hostility to the principles upon which their governments are founded; or of deviation from the system of neutrality hitherto observed by him and his allies in the contest between Spain and America.

To the notification that the Emperor, in conformity with the *political principles* maintained by himself and his allies, has determined to receive no agent from any of the governments *de facto*, which have been recently formed in the New World it has been thought sufficient to answer that the United States, faithful to *their* political principles, have recognized and now consider them as the governments of independent nations.

To the signification of the Emperor's hope and desire that the United States should continue to observe the neutrality which they have proclaimed between Spain and South America, the answer has been that the neutrality of the United States will be maintained, as long as that of Europe, apart from Spain, shall continue and that they hope that of the imperial government of Russia will be continued.

[To the confidential communication from the Baron de Tuyll, of the extract, dated St. Petersburg, 30 August 1823. So far as it relates to the affairs of Spain and Portugal, the only remark which it is thought necessary to make is of the great satisfaction with which the President has noticed *that* paragraph, which contains the frank and solemn admissions that *"the undertaking of the allies yet demands a last apology to the eyes of Europe."*]

In the general declarations that the allied monarchs will never compound and never will even treat with the *revolution* and that their policy has only for its object by *forcible* interposition to guarantee the tranquillity of *all the states of which the civilized world is composed*, the President wishes to perceive sentiments, the application of which is limited, and intended in their results to be limited, to the affairs of Europe.

That the sphere of their operations was not intended to embrace the United States of America, nor any portion of the American hemisphere.

And, finally, deeply desirous as the United States are of preserving the general peace of the world, their friendly intercourse with all the European nations, and especially the most cordial harmony and good-will with the imperial government of Russia, it is due as well to their own unalterable sentiments, as to the explicit avowal of them, called for by the communications received from the Baron de Tuyll, to declare

That the United States of America, and their government, could not see with indifference the forcible interposition of any European power, other than Spain, either to restore the dominion of Spain over her emancipated colonies in America, or to establish monarchical governments in those countries, or to transfer any of the possessions heretofore or yet subject to Spain in the American hemisphere to any other European power.

DEPARTMENT OF STATE
WASHINGTON, 27 November 1823

K. THE MONROE DOCTRINE, BEING EXTRACTS FROM THE PRESIDENT'S SEVENTH ANNUAL MESSAGE[13]

WASHINGTON, December 2, 1823

Fellow-Citizens of the Senate and House of Representatives:

... At the proposal of the Russian imperial government, made through the minister of the Emperor residing here, a full power and instructions have been transmitted to the minister of the United

13. James Richardson, *Messages and Papers of the Presidents* ..., II, 209, 217-19.

States at St. Petersburg to arrange by amicable negotiation the respective rights and interests of the two nations on the northwest coast of this continent. A similar proposal had been made by His Imperial Majesty to the government of Great Britain, which has likewise been acceded to. The government of the United States has been desirous by this friendly proceeding of manifesting the great value which they have invariably attached to the friendship of the Emperor and their solicitude to cultivate the best understanding with his government. In the discussions to which this interest has given rise and in the arrangements by which they may terminate the occasion has been judged proper for asserting, as a principle in which the rights and interests of the United States are involved, that the American continents, by the free and independent condition which they have assumed and maintain, are henceforth not to be considered as subjects for future colonization by any European powers. . . .

It was stated at the commencement of the last session that great effort was then making in Spain and Portugal to improve the condition of the people of those countries and that it appeared to be conducted with extraordinary moderation. It need scarcely be remarked that the result has been so far very different from what was then anticipated. Of events in that quarter of the globe with which we have so much intercourse and from which we derive our origin, we have always been anxious and interested spectators. The citizens of the United States cherish sentiments the most friendly in favor of the liberty and happiness of their fellow-men on that side of the Atlantic. In the wars of the European powers in matters relating to themselves we have never taken any part, nor does it comport with our policy so to do. It is only when our rights are invaded or seriously menaced that we resent injuries or make preparation

for our defense. With the movements in this hemisphere we are of necessity more immediately connected, and by causes which must be obvious to all enlightened and impartial observers. The political system of the allied powers is essentially different in this respect from that of America. This difference proceeds from that which exists in their respective governments; and to the defense of our own, which has been achieved by the loss of so much blood and treasure, and matured by the wisdom of their most enlightened citizens, and under which we have enjoyed unexampled felicity, this whole nation is devoted. We owe it, therefore, to candor and to the amicable relations existing between the United States and those powers to declare that we should consider any attempt on their part to extend their system to any portion of this hemisphere as dangerous to our peace and safety. With the existing colonies or dependencies of any European power we have not interfered and shall not interfere. But with the governments who have declared their independence and maintained it, and whose independence we have, on great consideration and on just principles, acknowledged, we could not view any interposition for the purpose of oppressing them, or controlling in any other manner their destiny, by any European power in any other light than as the manifestation of an unfriendly disposition toward the United States. In the war between those new governments and Spain we declared our neutrality at the time of their recognition, and to this we have adhered, and shall continue to adhere, provided no change shall occur which, in the judgment of the competent authorities of this government, shall make a corresponding change on the part of the United States indispensable to their security.

The late events in Spain and Portugal show that Europe is still unsettled. Of this important fact no stronger proof can be adduced than that the allied powers should have thought it proper, on any principle satisfactory to themselves, to have interposed by force in the internal concerns of Spain. To what extent such interposition may be carried, on the same principle, is a question in which all independent powers whose governments differ from theirs are interested, even those most remote, and surely none more so than the United States. Our policy in regard to Europe, which was adopted at an early stage of the wars which have so long agitated that quarter of the globe, nevertheless remains the same, which is not to interfere in the internal concerns of any of its powers; to consider the government *de facto* as the legitimate government for us; to cultivate friendly relations with it, and to preserve those relations by a frank, firm, and manly policy, meeting in all instances the just claims of every power, submitting to injuries from none. But in regard to those continents circumstances are eminently and conspicuously different. It is impossible that the allied powers should extend their political system to any portion of either continent without endangering our peace and happiness; nor can anyone believe that our southern brethren, if left to themselves, would adopt it of their own accord. It is equally impossible, therefore, that we should behold such interposition in any form with indifference. If we look to the comparative strength and resources of Spain and those new governments, and their distance from each other, it must be obvious that she can never subdue them. It is still the true policy of the United States to leave the parties to themselves, in the hope that other powers will pursue the same course. . . .

L. JAMES MONROE, PRESIDENT, TO THOMAS JEFFERSON, DECEMBER, 1823[14]

Dear Sir,

Shortly after the receipt of yours of the 24th of October, and while the subject treated in it was under consideration, the Russian minister drew the attention of the govt. to the same subject, though in a very different sense from that in which it had been done by Mr. Canning. Baron Tuyll announced in an official letter, and as was understood by order of the Emperor, that having heard that the republic of Columbia had appointed a minister to Russia, he wished it to be distinctly understood that he would not receive him, nor would he receive any minister from any of the new govts. *de facto*, of which the New World had been recently the theater. On another occasion, he observed that the Emperor had seen with great satisfaction the declaration of this govt., when those new govts. were recognized, that it was the intention of the United States to remain neutral. He gave this intimation for the purpose of expressing the wish of his master that we would persevere in the same policy. He communicated soon afterward an extract of a letter from his govt., in which the conduct of the allied powers, in regard to Naples, Spain, and Portugal, was reviewed, and that policy explained, distinctly avowing their determination to crush all revolutionary movements and thereby to preserve order in the civilized world. The terms "civilized world" were probably intended to be applied to Europe only, but admitted an application to this hemisphere also. These communications were received as proofs of candor and friendly disposition to the United States, but were nevertheless answered in a manner equally explicit, frank, and direct to each point. In regard to neutrality it was observed, when that sentiment was declared, that the other powers of Europe had not taken side with Spain—that they were then neu-

14. *Proceedings of the Massachusetts Historical Society, Second Series,* XV, 411–12.

tral—if they should change their policy, the state of things, on which our neutrality was declared, being altered, we would not be bound by that declaration but might change our policy also. Informal notes, or rather a procès-verbal, of what passed in conference, to such effect, were exchanged between Mr. Adams and the Russian minister, with an understanding, however, that they should be held confidential.

When the character of these communications, of that from Mr. Canning and that from the Russian minister, is considered, and the time when made, it leaves little doubt that some project against the new govts. is contemplated. In what form is uncertain. It is hoped that the sentiments expressed in the message will give a check to it. We certainly meet, in full extent, the proposition of Mr. Canning and in the mode to give it the greatest effect. If his govt. makes a similar declaration, the project will, it may be presumed, be abandoned. By taking the step here, it is done in a manner more conciliatory with and respectful to Russia and the other powers than if taken in England, and as it is thought with more credit to our govt. Had we moved in the first instance in England, separated as she is in part, from those powers, our union with her, being marked, might have produced irritation with them. We know that Russia dreads a connection between the United States and Great Britain, or harmony in policy.

Moving on our own ground, the apprehension that, unless she retreats, that effect may be produced may be a motive with her for retreating. Had we moved in England, it is probable that it would have been inferred that we acted under her influence, and at her instigation, and thus have lost credit as well with our southern neighbors as with the allied powers.

There is some danger that the British govt., when it sees the part we have taken, may endeavor to throw the whole burden on us and profit, in case of such interposition of the allied powers, of her neutrality at our expense. But I think that this would be impossible after what has passed on the subject; besides it does not follow, from what has been said, that we should be bound to engage in the war in such event. Of this intimations may be given, should it be necessary. A messenger will depart for England with dispatches for Mr. Rush in a few days, who will go on to St. Petersburg with others to Mr. Middleton. And considering the crisis, it has occurred that a special mission, of the first consideration from the country, directed to England in the first instance, with power to attend any congress that may be convened on the affairs of South America or Mexico might have the happiest effect. You shall hear from me further on this subject.

Very sincerely your friend
[no signature]
[*Indorsed:*] "*Recd. Dec. 11.*"

UNIT VII

EQUALITY IN JACKSONIAN DEMOCRACY

IT WAS in the Age of Jackson that the equalitarian character of American democracy received its fullest expression. The doctrine that "all men are created equal" had been proclaimed in 1776; but the republic of Washington, Adams, and the Virginian dynasty was aristocratic by comparison with the impatient, full-blooded democracy of the next generation. Old hierarchies were swept away by tremendous movements of population. The expansion of farming, commerce, transportation, and manufacturing was spreading economic opportunity far and wide. Pioneer democracy, surging westward across a continent, made every eastern community feel the wash of its leveling spirit. There was probably never a time in American history when the conditions of life approximated more closely to equality or when the average American felt so confident in his capacity to deal with any problem under the sun.

In the first section of this unit we have printed several selections from the pen of one of those European observers who have brought a fresh mind and a comprehensive philosophy to the study of American institutions. Tocqueville's *Democracy in America*, like Bryce's *American Commonwealth*, is one of those works in which

Americans may see themselves as others see them. Tocqueville thought of American democracy as a portent of the fate which lay ahead of Europe. He believed that the tendency toward equality of condition would be general throughout western Europe, and he studied it here to see what could be learned from our experience. As a friendly observer, he admired much in what he saw; but he was greatly concerned about the dangers to liberty and sound morality which seemed to him to lurk behind the drift toward equality. It might be helpful to warn the general reader that Tocqueville's mind was attracted to general ideas and adroit in conjuring with them; but there were several points at which his ingenious logic parted company with reality.

From this analysis of democracy in all its aspects, we turn to some specific issues in Jacksonian America. All of them, in one form or another, reflect the influence exerted on the mind of this age by the idea of equality.

In the field of constitutional law and practice, nothing is more conspicuous than the resistance to anything which savored of "aristocracy." It took many forms: the rejection of property qualifications for office; the extension of the elective principle to offices which had been appointive; the denial that democratic administration needs the services of experts; the jealousy of legislative caucuses; the exaltation of the presidential office as the embodiment of the popular will. Of all these attempts to implement the sovereignty of the people, we have selected one example—the adoption of manhood suffrage. This is the period in which the eastern states, with their deeper class distinctions, gave the vote to propertyless laborers. In the seventeenth century a handful of Levellers in England had raised this issue and then been swept aside (see p. 40). Property qualifications of some sort had always been considered an indispensable qualification. In the western states, where manhood suffrage generally prevailed, most of the settlers did in fact own property. In the eastern states John Adams, Daniel Webster, Joseph Story, Madison, Monroe, Marshall, and Randolph had all gone on record as opponents of manhood suffrage. In the passages quoted here, which are taken from the records of a constitutional convention held in New York in 1821, Chancellor Kent extols the virtues of the freeholders as the true custodians of republican liberty and dwells at length on the folly of meddling with the best of constitutions. But he was defending a lost cause.

The potency of the same doctrine of equality is evident in the claims which labor was making for fairer treatment. This problem had not yet acquired the proportions which industrialism was to give it in later years, but the elements of unrest and organi-

zation were already present eastern cities, and the gr of the laboring classes were important factor in the cal of Democratic politicians. Running through all their protests against excessive hours and miserable wages is the conviction that a republic of "free and equal" citizens owes its workers a better lot than slavery. The Preamble of the Mechanics' Union of Trade Associations (1827) and the Resolutions of the New York Mechanics (1829) are good examples of the use of the natural rights philosophy to justify a reasonable reward for toil. We have attached to these labor documents two of the early judicial decisions about the legal rights of unions. Neither the inherited law nor the current maxims of business enterprise were at all favorable to the vigorous use of a union's bargaining power. The decision in the case of *Commonwealth* v. *Hunt* (1842) took an important step along the road toward fuller recognition by freeing the union involved from a charge of criminal conspiracy.

The grievances of the working classes also included the lack of educational opportunity. Two pleas for public education are included here; one by a committee of workingmen in Philadelphia, the other by Horace Mann, whose success in Massachusetts in developing enthusiasm for free schools provided a model for other states. Mann strikes the familiar distinction between the Europe of privileged classes and suffering masses and the America in which all have an equal chance to earn and an equal security in the fruits of their labor. But he warns his readers that, without the aid of that "great equalizer of men," universal education, new forms of privilege will soon falsify the American boast.

Mann's worries, which were connected with the rising power of capital, lead us into the politics of business enterprise. Jacksonian democracy inherited the economic individualism, and the suspicion of economic privilege, which had distinguished Jeffersonian democracy. It was dealing with an economy which had changed considerably since Jefferson's day—the growth of agriculture being counterbalanced by the rapid growth of a business community—but there is a real comparison between the conflicting policies of Jackson and Clay and those of Jefferson and Hamilton in the earlier generation. To Jackson's followers, the farmers, the poorer planters, and the laboring classes, Clay's "American system" lent itself to the creation of what Adam Smith had called a "system of preference" and what Americans usually inveighed against as "monopoly" or "special privilege." They resisted governmental bias in the name of "equal justice." This protest was most dramatically expressed in the conflict over the re-chartering of the United States Bank. The extracts which follow include samples of Clay's and Jackson's opinions about the role of government in the economic system, together with arguments for and against the services of banking corporations.

The Jacksonians did not envisage equality of opportunity as something which required the enlargement of the state's role in the life of the community, but they did place on record one important judicial decision which protected the state power from invasion by private rights. This has usually been considered the most significant feature of the Charles River Bridge case.

In the last section we turn from the world of practical politics to the moral philosophy of two men of letters. You will have read Tocqueville's opinion about the influence of equality on the moral standards of democracies. While praising some of its results, he believed that its tendency to exalt material well-being would be fatal to some kinds of excellence, and he was particularly fearful of the tyranny of mass opinion. Thoreau and Emerson should be studied here as men who were grappling with the problems of moral responsibility in a free society. Both were repelled by the materialism of American life; neither was under the least temptation to take his opinions from the mass. Thoreau is represented here by his essay *On Civil Disobedience*; Emerson, by *Man the Reformer*. Perhaps in Emerson's case a word of warning is necessary. It would be foolish to try to uncover, by logical excavation, the hidden springs which nourished his sentiments. His style has more in common with poetry, or prophecy, than with the ordinary language of reason. But his position is worth examining. If he were alive today, he would be trying to conquer communism with kindness, war with love.

p. 330 quote?

931 F. II actual
case.

Substantive
Evolution !
  states reduced in power
Contract iner

Criticism   * see 334, 336

MCL

M = 1000   C = 100
L = 50

SECTION A. THE NATURE OF EQUALITARIAN SOCIETY

1. ON DEMOCRACY IN AMERICA[1]

By ALEXIS DE TOCQUEVILLE

EDITORS' NOTE.—This work was written in the 1830's by a young French aristocrat, Alexis de Tocqueville. His major purpose was to ease the transition to the more equalitarian society which he thought inevitable and to preserve therein as much as possible of the essence of human freedom, of its habits and its institutions. The first part of *Democracy in America* (1835) ranks with the best descriptions of American democracy. The second part (1840) portrays "the general features of democratic societies." As Tocqueville put it, "America is only my setting, democracy is the subject." In his description Tocqueville made some factual errors, his speculations about the future were not all realized, and he displays some bias against the more democratic elements of Andrew Jackson's America.

Tocqueville was reared a Catholic; he studied in the *lycée* and the law school. He was a liberal, ambitious young apprentice magistrate who was also a serious student of society. Guizot's lectures on the history of civilization in France led Tocqueville to his subject; the July Revolution (1830) impelled him and his friend Beaumont to visit America, where modern democracy had had its greatest development. In nine months they visited all sections and met many of the leaders of politics and thought. Tocqueville gathered a vast amount of data from which he sought to arrive at the basic principles of modern democratic society rather than merely to describe American government. Consequently, he oversimplified and overgeneralized. Frequently he contrasts aristocratic and democratic society, setting up an idealized version of each in order to assess modern democracy as he thought it would develop in America and in Europe. While asserting that it was useless to fight against the inevitable trend toward greater equality in modern society, Tocqueville admired the "masculine virtues" of medieval feudalism and hoped that the democratic society of the future would preserve analogous values. Implicit in his work is a theory of history which finds the explanation of historical causation in a combination of "general causes" and the influence of individual choice. Tocqueville holds out the hope that man is free, within limits, to fashion society and himself in the image of his higher values.

1. With the exception of a few passages having separate citations, these extracts are taken from Alexis de Tocqueville, *Democracy in America*, ed. Francis Bowen (4th ed.; Cambridge, Mass., 1864), I, 107–8, 109–10, 111, 115–16, 118–19, 120–21, 302–7, 310, 313–14, 319–23, 330–32, 335–38, 343–44; II, 1–3, 5–6, 8–13, 37–39, 114–21, 124–27, 128–30, 132–36, 193–97, 325–29, 330, 331–34, 344–47, 356–58, 360–64, 380–81, 383–86, 391–93, 397–400, 400–401, 404–7, 410–12.

No fully satisfactory translation of *Democracy in America* exists in English. The edition from which most of these extracts were taken is the Francis Bowen "correction" of the classic English translation by Henry Reeve; the recent edition by Professor Phillips Bradley (New York, 1945) probably represents Tocqueville's meaning most accurately and has useful introductory material and notes. For those who wish to possess a less expensive, though abridged, version which gives practi-

cally all that is important in the *Democracy*, the original Reeve translation edited by Professor Henry S. Commager in the "Galaxy Edition of the World's Classics" (New York, 1947) is recommended. The scholar who wants to know just what influenced Tocqueville and his friend Beaumont while they were in the United States will read George W. Pierson's *Tocqueville and Beaumont in America* (New York, 1938).

AUTHOR'S PREFACE

THE PURPOSE OF THE "DEMOCRACY IN AMERICA"[2]

... During my stay in the United States, nothing struck me more forcibly than the general equality of condition among the people. ... The more I advanced in the study of American society, the more I perceived that this equality of condition is the fundamental fact from which all others seem to be derived and the central point at which all my observations constantly terminated.

I then turned my thoughts to our own hemisphere and thought that I discerned there something analogous to the spectacle which the New World presented to me. I observed that equality of condition, though it has not there reached the extreme limit which it seems to have attained in the United States, is constantly approaching it; and that the democracy which governs American communities seems to be rising rapidly into power in Europe.

At that moment I conceived the idea of the book which you are going to read.

That a great democratic revolution is going on among us is evident to all, but

all do not look at it in the same light. Some consider it something novel but accidental and hope that it may yet be checked; others think it irresistible because it seems to them the most continuous, the oldest, and the most permanent tendency that is to be found in history. ...

The gradual development of equality of conditions is, therefore, a Providential fact. It has the chief characteristics of such a fact; it is universal, it is lasting, it constantly eludes all human interference, and all events, as well as all men, contribute to its progress. ...

If the men of our time should be convinced, by attentive observation and sincere reflection, that the gradual and progressive development of equality is at once the past and the future of their history, this discovery alone would confer upon the change the sacred character of a divine decree. To attempt to check democracy would then seem a struggle against God himself; and the nations would be constrained to make the best of the social conditions imposed upon them by Providence. ...

To educate the democracy; to revive, if possible, its faith; to purify its morals; to direct its energies; to substitute by

2. This Preface was retranslated by Robert E. and Mary P. Keohane from Tocqueville, *De la démocratie en Amérique* (13th ed.; Paris, 1850), I, 1–2, 5–7, 15–16, 19.

degrees competence for inexperience and an understanding of its true interests for blind instincts; to adapt its government to time and place; and to modify it according to men and circumstances—such is the first duty imposed in our time upon those who direct society. A new science of politics is needed for a new world. . . .

It seems to me beyond doubt that, like the Americans, we shall arrive, sooner or later, at an almost complete equality of condition. But I do not conclude from this that we shall ever necessarily be led to draw the same political consequences which the Americans have derived from a similar social organization. I am far from supposing that they have found the only form of government which a democracy may adopt; but, as the inspiration of laws and manners in the two countries is the same, it is of tremendous interest for us to know what it has produced in each of them.

It is not, then, merely to satisfy a legitimate curiosity that I have examined America; I wished to find there instruction by which we may benefit. Anyone who thinks that I wanted to write a panegyric would be strangely mistaken; whoever reads this book will be convinced that such has not been my design. Nor has my object been to advocate this type of government in general, for I am one of those who believe that absolute excellence is almost never found in any system of laws. I have not even pretended to judge whether the social revolution, which I believe to be irresistible, is beneficial or sinister to mankind. I have acknowledged this revolution to be an accomplished fact, or on the eve of its accomplishment . . . and I have selected the nation in which its development has been the most peaceful and the most complete in order to see clearly its natural consequences and to find out, if possible, the means of rendering it profitable to mankind. I confess that, in America, I saw more than America; I sought there an image of democracy itself, with its inclinations, its character, its prejudices, and its passions in order to learn what we have to hope or to fear from its progress. . . .

I conclude by pointing out myself what many readers will consider the principal defect of the work. This book is written to favor the views of no particular party, and, in composing it, I have entertained no designs of serving or attacking any party. I have undertaken, not to see differently from others, but to look further, and, while they are busied for the next day only, I have turned my thoughts to the future.

THE POLITICAL AIM OF THE *DEMOCRACY IN AMERICA*[3]

. . . I have sought to show what a democratic people is in our time and, by this strictly accurate picture, to produce a twofold effect on my contemporaries. To those who imagine an ideal democracy a dazzling dream which they think it easy to realize, I undertake to show that they have painted their picture in false colors; that the democratic government they advocate, if it is of real advantage to those who can support it, has not the noble features they ascribe to it; and, moreover, that this government can be maintained only on certain conditions of intelligence, private morality, and faith which we do not possess and which we must work to obtain before we can secure their political results.

To those for whom the word "democracy" is synonymous with disturbance, anarchy, spoliation, and murder, I have attempted to show that democracy may be reconciled with respect for property, with deference for rights, with safety to freedom, with reverence

3. Translated from Tocqueville's letter of February 21, 1835, to his boyhood friend, Eugene Stoffels, in *Œuvres et correspondance inédites d'Alexis de Tocqueville*, ed. Gustave de Beaumont (Paris, 1861), I, 427–29.

for religion; that, if democratic government fosters less than another some of the finer possibilities of the human spirit, it has its great and noble aspects; and that perhaps, after all, it is the will of God to bestow a lesser grade of happiness upon all men than to grant a greater share of it to a smaller number and to bring a few to the verge of perfection. I have undertaken to demonstrate to them that, whatever their opinion on this point may be, it is too late to deliberate; that society is advancing and dragging them along with it toward equality of conditions; that the sole remaining alternative lies between evils henceforth irresistible; that the question is not whether aristocracy or democracy can be maintained but whether we are to live under a democratic society, devoid indeed of poetry and greatness, but at least orderly and moral, or under a democratic society, lawless and depraved, abandoned to the frenzy of revolution or subjected to a yoke heavier than any of those which have crushed mankind since the fall of the Roman Empire.

I have sought to calm the ardor of the former class of persons and, without discouraging them, to point out the only path before them. I have sought to allay the terrors of the latter and to bend their minds to the idea of an inevitable future, so that with less impetuosity, on the one hand, and less resistance, on the other, society may advance more peaceably to the necessary fulfilment of its destiny. This is the fundamental idea of the book—an idea which connects all its other ideas in a single web.... There are, however, as yet very few persons who understand it. Many people of opposite opinions are pleased with it, not because they understand me, but because they find in my book, considered on one side only, certain arguments favorable to their own passion of the moment. But I have confidence in the future, and I hope the day will come when everybody will see clearly what a few only perceive at present....

POLITICAL EFFECTS OF DECENTRALIZED ADMINISTRATION IN THE UNITED STATES[4]

Centralization is a word in general and daily use, without any precise meaning being attached to it. Nevertheless, there exist two distinct kinds of centralization which it is necessary to discriminate with accuracy.

Certain interests are common to all parts of a nation, such as the enactment of its general laws and the maintenance of its foreign relations. Other interests are peculiar to certain parts of the nation, such, for instance, as the business of the several townships. When the power which directs the former or general interests is concentrated in one place

4. The passage here quoted is a part of Tocqueville's discussion of American state government and, as such, is inserted between his treatments of American local and national government. The reader should note carefully Tocqueville's usage of "administration" and "government."

or in the same persons, it constitutes a centralized government. To concentrate in like manner into one place the direction of the latter or local interests constitutes what may be termed a centralized administration.

Upon some points these two kinds of centralization coincide; but, by classifying the objects which fall more particularly within the province of each, they may easily be distinguished.

It is evident that a centralized government acquires immense power when united to centralized administration. Thus combined, it accustoms men to set their own will habitually and completely aside; to submit, not only for once, or upon one point, but in every respect, and at all times. Not only, therefore, does this union of power subdue them compulsorily, but it affects their ordinary habits; it isolates them and then influences each separately. . . .

We have shown that, in the United States, there is no centralized administration and no hierarchy of public functionaries. Local authority has been carried farther than any European nation could endure without great inconvenience, and it has even produced some disadvantageous consequences in America. But, in the United States, the centralization of the government is perfect; and it would be easy to prove that the national power is more concentrated there than it has ever been in the old nations of Europe. Not only is there but one legislative body in each state—not only does there exist but one source of political authority—but numerous assemblies in districts or counties have not, in general, been multiplied, lest they should be tempted to leave their administrative duties and interfere with the government. In America the legislature of each state is supreme; nothing can impede its authority—neither privileges, nor local immunities, nor personal influence, nor even the empire of reason, since it represents that majority which claims to be the sole organ of reason. Its own determination is, therefore, the only limit to its action. In juxtaposition with it, and under its immediate control, is the representative of the executive power, whose duty it is to constrain the refractory to submit by superior force. The only symptom of weakness lies in certain details of the action of the government. The American republics have no standing armies to intimidate a discontented minority; but, as no minority has as yet been reduced to declare open war, the necessity of·an army has not been felt. The state usually employs the officers of the township or the county to deal with the citizens. . . .

The want of a centralized government will not, then, as has often been asserted, prove the destruction of the republics of the New World; far from the American

governments being not sufficiently centralized, I shall prove hereafter that they are too much so. The legislative bodies daily encroach upon the authority of the government, and their tendency, like that of the French Convention, is to appropriate it entirely to themselves. The social power thus centralized is constantly changing hands, because it is subordinate to the power of the people. It often forgets the maxims of wisdom and foresight in the consciousness of its strength. Hence arises its danger. Its vigor, and not its impotence, will probably be the cause of its ultimate destruction. . . . In America the power which conducts the administration is far less regular, less enlightened, and less skilful, but a hundred-fold greater, than in Europe. In no country in the world do the citizens make such exertions for the common weal. I know of no people who have established schools so numerous and efficacious, places of public worship better suited to the wants of the inhabitants, or roads kept in better repair. Uniformity or permanence of design, the minute arrangement of details, and the perfection of administrative system must not be sought for in the United States; what we find there is the presence of a power which, if it is somewhat wild, is at least robust, and an existence checkered with accidents, indeed, but full of animation and effort.

Granting, for an instant, that the villages and counties of the United States would be more usefully governed by a central authority, which they had never seen, than by functionaries taken from among them—admitting, for the sake of argument, that there would be more security in America, and the resources of society would be better employed there, if the whole administration centered in a single arm—still the *political* advantages which the Americans derive from their decentralized system would induce me to prefer it to the contrary plan. It profits me but little, after all, that a vigilant authority always protects the tranquillity of my pleasures, and constantly averts all dangers from my path, without my care or concern, if this same authority is the absolute master of my liberty and my life, and if it so monopolizes movement and life that, when it languishes, everything languishes around it; that, when it sleeps, everything must sleep; and that, when it dies, the state itself must perish. . . .

It is not the *administrative* but the *political* effects of decentralization that I most admire in America. In the United States the interests of the country are everywhere kept in view; they are an object of solicitude to the people of the whole Union, and every citizen is as warmly attached to them as if they were his own. He takes pride in the glory of his nation; he boasts of its success, to which he conceives himself to have contributed; and he rejoices in the general prosperity by which he profits. The feeling he entertains toward the state is analogous to that which unites him to his family, and it is by a kind of selfishness that he interests himself in the welfare of his country.

To the European, a public officer represents a superior force; to an American, he represents a right. In America, then, it may be said that no one renders obedience to man but to justice and to law. If the opinion which the citizen entertains of himself is exaggerated, it is at least salutary; he unhesitatingly confides in his own powers, which appear to him to be all-sufficient. When a private individual meditates an undertaking, however directly connected it may be with the welfare of society, he never thinks of soliciting the co-operation of the government; but he publishes his plan, offers to execute it, courts the assistance of other individuals, and struggles manfully against all obstacles. Undoubtedly he is often less successful than the state might have been in his position; but, in the end, the sum of these private undertakings far exceeds all that the government could have done.

As the administrative authority is within the reach of the citizens, whom in some degree it represents, it excites neither their jealousy nor hatred; as its resources are limited, everyone feels that he must not rely solely on its aid. Thus, when the administration thinks fit to act within its own limits, it is not abandoned to itself, as in Europe; the duties of private citizens are not supposed to have lapsed because the estate has come into action; but everyone is ready, on the contrary, to guide and support it. This action of individuals, joined to that of the public authorities, frequently accomplishes what the most energetic centralized administration would be unable to do. . . .

I believe that provincial institutions are useful to all nations, but nowhere do they appear to me to be more necessary than amongst a democratic people. In an aristocracy, order can always be maintained in the midst of liberty; and, as the rulers have a great deal to lose, order is to them a matter of great interest. In like manner, an aristocracy protects the people from the excesses of despotism, because it always possesses an organized power ready to resist a despot. But a democracy without provincial institutions has no security against these evils. How can a populace, unaccustomed to freedom in small concerns, learn to use it temperately in great affairs? What resistance can be offered to tyranny in a country where each individual is weak, and where the citizens are not united by any common interest? Those who dread the license of the mob, and those who fear absolute power, ought alike to desire the gradual development of provincial liberties.

I am also convinced that democratic nations are most likely to fall beneath the yoke of a centralized administration, for several reasons, amongst which is the following.

The constant tendency of these nations is to concentrate all the strength of the government in the hands of the only power which directly represents the people; because, beyond the people, nothing is to be perceived but a mass of equal individuals. But, when the same power already has all the attributes of government, it can scarcely refrain from penetrating into the details of the administration, and an opportunity of doing so is sure to present itself in the long run, as was the case in France. In the French Revolution there were two impulses in opposite directions, which must never be confounded; the one was favorable to liberty, the other to despotism. Under the ancient monarchy, the king was the sole author of the laws; and, below the power of the sovereign, certain vestiges of provincial institutions, half-destroyed, were still distinguishable. These provincial institutions were incoherent, ill arranged, and frequently absurd; in the hands of the aristocracy, they had sometimes been converted into instruments of oppression. The Revolution declared itself the enemy at once of royalty and of provincial institutions; it confounded in indiscriminate hatred all that had preceded it—despotic power and the checks to its abuses; and its tendency was at once to republicanize and to centralize. This double character of the French Revolution is a fact which has been adroitly handled by the friends of absolute power. Can they be accused of laboring in the cause of despotism when they are defending that centralized administration which was one of the great innovations of the Revolution? In this manner, popularity may be united with hostility to the rights of the people, and the secret slave of tyranny may be the professed lover of freedom. . . .

CHAPTER XIV

WHAT ARE THE REAL ADVANTAGES WHICH AMERICAN SOCIETY DERIVES FROM A DEMOCRATIC GOVERNMENT[5]

Before entering upon the present chapter, I must remind the reader of what I have more than once observed in this book. The political constitution of the United States appears to me to be one of the forms of government which a democracy may adopt; but I do not regard the American Constitution as the best, or as the only one, which a democratic people may establish. In showing the advantages which the Americans derive from the government of democracy, I am therefore very far from affirming, or believing, that similar advantages can be obtained only from the same laws.

GENERAL TENDENCY OF THE LAWS UNDER THE AMERICAN DEMOCRACY AND INSTINCTS OF THOSE WHO APPLY THEM

The defects and weaknesses of a democratic government may readily be discovered; they are demonstrated by flagrant instances, whilst its salutary influence is insensible and, so to speak, occult. A glance suffices to detect its faults, but its good qualities can be discerned only by long observation. The laws of the American democracy are frequently defective or incomplete; they sometimes attack vested rights or sanction others which are dangerous to the

5. In this, as in many other passages, Tocqueville uses in his analysis two types—one might almost use Max Weber's phrase, "ideal types"—of society whose contrasts bring out the salient characteristics of the Western society of the future. Here Tocqueville places into juxtaposition the rude but vigorous aristocratic order of the eleventh- or twelfth-century France with the equalitarian "mass state" which he thought was likely to emerge. This recurring note in the *Democracy* gave point to the remark attributed to Guizot and addressed to Tocqueville, "You judge 'democracy' like an aristocrat who has been vanquished and is convinced that his conqueror is right."

community; and, even if they were good, their frequency would still be a great evil. How comes it, then, that the American republics prosper and continue?

In the consideration of laws, a distinction must be carefully observed between the end at which they aim and the means by which they pursue that end; between their absolute and their relative excellence. If it be the intention of the legislator to favor the interests of the minority at the expense of the majority, and if the measures he takes are so combined as to accomplish the object he has in view with the least possible expense of time and exertion, the law may be well drawn up, although its purpose is bad; and, the more efficacious it is, the more dangerous it will be.

Democratic laws generally tend to promote the welfare of the greatest possible number, for they emanate from the majority of the citizens, who are subject to error, but who cannot have an interest opposed to their own advantage. The laws of an aristocracy tend, on the contrary, to concentrate wealth and power in the hands of the minority, because an aristocracy, by its very nature, constitutes a minority. It may therefore be asserted, as a general proposition, that the purpose of a democracy in its legislation is more useful to humanity than that of an aristocracy. This is, however, the sum total of its advantages.

Aristocracies are infinitely more expert in the science of legislation than democracies ever can be. They are possessed of a self-control which protects them from the errors of temporary excitement; and they form far-reaching designs, which they know how to mature till a favorable opportunity arrives. Aristocratic government proceeds with the dexterity of art; it understands how to make the collective force of all its laws converge at the same time to a given point. Such is not the case with democracies, whose laws are almost always ineffective or inopportune. The means of democracy are therefore more imperfect than those of aristocracy, and the measures which it unwittingly adopts are frequently opposed to its own cause; but the object it has in view is more useful.

Let us now imagine a community so organized by nature, or by its constitution, that it can support the transitory action of bad laws and that it can await, without destruction, the *general tendency* of its legislation; we shall then conceive how a democratic government, notwithstanding its faults, may be best fitted to produce the prosperity of this community. This is precisely what has occurred in the United States; and I repeat, what I have before remarked, that the great advantage of the Americans consists in their being able to commit faults which they may afterward repair.

An analogous observation may be made respecting public officers. It is easy to perceive that the American democracy frequently errs in the choice of the individuals to whom it intrusts the power of the administration; but it is more difficult to say why the state prospers under their rule. In the first place, it is to be remarked, that if, in a democratic state, the governors have less honesty and less capacity than elsewhere, the governed are more enlightened and more attentive to their interests. As the people in democracies are more constantly vigilant in their affairs, and more jealous of their rights, they prevent their representatives from abandoning that general line of conduct which their own interests prescribe. In the second place, it must be remembered that, if the democratic magistrate is more apt to misuse his power, he possesses it for a shorter time. But there is yet another reason which is still more general and conclusive. It is no doubt of importance to the welfare of nations that they should be governed by men of talents and virtue; but it is perhaps still more important for them that the interests of those men should not differ from the interests of the community at large; for, if such were the case, their virtues might become almost useless, and their talents might be turned to a bad account. I have said that it is important that the interests of the persons in authority should not differ from or oppose the interests of the community at large; but I do not insist upon their having the same interests as the whole population, because I am not aware that such a state of things ever existed in any country.

No political form has hitherto been discovered which is equally favorable to the prosperity and the development of all the classes into which society is divided. These classes continue to form, as it were, so many distinct communities in the same nation; and experience has shown that it is no less dangerous to place the fate of these classes exclusively in the hands of any one of them than it is to make one people the arbiter of the destiny of another. When the rich alone govern, the interest of the poor is always endangered; and, when the poor make the laws, that of the rich incurs very serious risks. The advantage of democracy does not consist, therefore, as has sometimes been asserted, in favoring the prosperity of all, but simply in contributing to the well-being of the greatest number.

The men who are intrusted with the direction of public affairs in the United States are frequently inferior, both in capacity and morality, to those whom an aristocracy would raise to power. But their interest is identified and confounded with that of the majority of their fellow-citizens. They may frequently be faithless and frequently mistaken; but they will never systematically adopt a line of conduct hostile to the majority; and they cannot give a dangerous or exclusive tendency to the government.

The maladministration of a demo-cratic magistrate, moreover, is an isolated fact, which has influence only during the short period for which he is elected. Corruption and incapacity do not act as common interests, which may connect men permanently with one another. A corrupt or incapable magistrate will not concert his measures with another magistrate, simply because the latter is as corrupt and incapable as himself; and these two men will never unite their endeavors to promote the corruption and inaptitude of their remote posterity. The ambition and the maneuvers of the one will serve, on the contrary, to unmask the other. The vices of a magistrate, in democratic states, are usually wholly personal.

But, under aristocratic governments, public men are swayed by the interest of their order, which, if it is sometimes confounded with the interests of the majority, is very frequently distinct from them. This interest is the common and lasting bond which unites them together; it induces them to coalesce and combine their efforts to attain an end which is not always the happiness of the greatest number; and it serves not only to connect the persons in authority with each other but to unite them with a considerable portion of the community, since a numerous body of citizens belong to the aristocracy, without being invested with official functions. The aristocratic magistrate is therefore constantly supported by a portion of the community as well as by the government of which he is a member.

The common purpose which, in aristocracies, connects the interest of the magistrates with that of a portion of their contemporaries identifies it also with that of future generations; they labor for the future as well as for the present. The aristocratic magistrate is urged at the same time, toward the same point, by the passions of the community, by his own, and, I may almost add, by those of his posterity. Is it, then, wonderful that he does not resist such repeated impulses? And, indeed, aristocracies are often carried away by their class spirit without being corrupted by it; and they unconsciously fashion society to their own ends, and prepare it for their own descendants.

The English aristocracy is perhaps the most liberal which has ever existed, and no body of men has ever, uninterruptedly, furnished so many honorable and enlightened individuals to the government of a country. It cannot, however, escape observation that, in the legislation of England, the interests of the poor have been often sacrificed to the advantage of the rich and the rights of the majority to the privileges of a few. The consequence is that England, at the present day, combines the extremes of good and evil fortune in the bosom of her society; and the miseries and privations of her poor almost equal her power and renown.

In the United States, where the public officers have no class interests to promote, the general and constant influence of the government is beneficial, although the individuals who conduct it are frequently unskilful and sometimes contemptible. There is, indeed, a secret tendency in democratic institutions, which makes the exertions of the citizens subservient to the prosperity of the community, in spite of their vices and mistakes; whilst in aristocratic institutions there is a secret bias which, notwithstanding the talents and virtues of those who conduct the government, leads them to contribute to the evils which oppress their fellow-creatures. In aristocratic governments public men may frequently do harm without intending it, and in democratic states they bring about good results which they never thought of.

PUBLIC SPIRIT IN THE UNITED STATES

...I am certainly far from affirming that, in order to obtain this result, the exercise of political rights should be immediately granted to all men. But I maintain that the most powerful, and perhaps the only, means which we still possess of interesting men in the welfare of their country is to make them partakers in the government. At the present time, civic zeal seems to me to be inseparable from the exercise of political rights; and I think that the number of citizens will be found to augment or decrease in Europe in proportion as those rights are extended....

NOTION OF RIGHTS IN THE UNITED STATES

... The government of the democracy brings the notion of political rights to the level of the humblest citizens, just as the dissemination of wealth brings the notion of property within the reach of all men; to my mind, this is one of its greatest advantages. I do not say it is easy to teach men how to exercise political rights; but I maintain that, when it is possible, the effects which result from it are highly important; and I add that, if there ever was a time at which such an attempt ought to be made, that time is now. Do you not see that religious belief is shaken, and the divine notion of right is declining?—that morality is debased, and the notion of moral right is therefore fading away? Argument is substituted for faith, and calculation for the impulses of sentiment. If, in the midst of this general disruption, you do not succeed in connecting the notion of right with that of private interest, which is the only immutable point in the human heart, what means will you have of governing the world except by fear? When I am told that the laws are weak and the people are turbulent, that passions are excited and the authority of virtue is paralyzed, and therefore no measures must be taken to increase the rights of the democracy, I reply, that, for these very reasons, some measures of the kind ought to be taken; and I believe that governments are still more interested in taking them than society at large, for governments may perish, but society cannot die. . . .

ACTIVITY WHICH PERVADES ALL PARTS OF THE BODY POLITIC IN THE UNITED STATES; INFLUENCE WHICH IT EXERCISES UPON SOCIETY

. . . The cares of politics engross a prominent place in the occupations of a citizen in the United States, and almost the only pleasure which an American knows is to take a part in the government and to discuss its measures. This feeling pervades the most trifling habits of life; even the women frequently attend public meetings and listen to political harangues as a recreation from their household labors. Debating clubs are, to a certain extent, a substitute for theatrical entertainments; an American cannot converse, but he can discuss; and his talk falls into a dissertation. He speaks to you as if he was addressing a meeting; and, if he should chance to become warm in the discussion, he will say "Gentlemen" to the person with whom he is conversing.

In some countries the inhabitants seem unwilling to avail themselves of the political privileges which the law gives them; it would seem that they set too high a value upon their time to spend it on the interests of the community; and they shut themselves up in a narrow selfishness, marked out by four sunk fences and a quickset hedge. But if an American were condemned to confine his activity to his own affairs, he would be robbed of one-half of his existence; he would feel an immense void in the life which he is accustomed to lead, and his wretchedness would be unbearable. I am persuaded that, if ever a despotism should be established in America, it will be more difficult to overcome the habits which freedom has formed than to conquer the love of freedom itself.

This ceaseless agitation which democratic government has introduced into the political world influences all social intercourse. I am not sure that, upon the whole, this is not the greatest advantage of democracy; and I am less inclined to applaud it for what it does than for what it causes to be done.

It is incontestable that the people frequently conduct public business very ill; but it is impossible that the lower orders should take a part in public business without extending the circle of their ideas and quitting the ordinary routine of their thoughts. The humblest individual who co-operates in the government of society acquires a certain degree of self-respect; and, as he possesses authority, he can command the services of minds more enlightened than his own. He is canvassed by a multitude of applicants, and, in seeking to deceive him in a thousand ways, they really enlighten him. He takes a part in political undertakings which he did not originate but which give him a taste for undertakings of the kind. New improvements are daily pointed out to him in the common property, and this gives him the desire of improving that property which is his own. He is perhaps neither happier nor better than those who came before him, but he is better informed and more active. I have no doubt that the democratic institutions of the United States, joined to the physical constitution of the country, are the cause (not the direct, as is so often asserted, but the indirect cause) of the prodigious commercial activity of the inhabitants. It is not created by the laws, but the people learn how to promote it by the experience derived from legislation.

When the opponents of democracy assert that a single man performs what he undertakes better than the government of all, it appears to me that they are right. The government of an individual, supposing an equality of knowledge on either side, is more consistent, more persevering, more uniform, and more accurate in details than that of a multitude, and it selects with more discrimination the men whom it employs. If any deny this, they have never seen a democratic government or have judged upon partial evidence. It is true that, even when local circumstances and the dispositions of the people allow democratic institutions to exist, they do not display a regular and methodical system of government. Democratic liberty is far from accomplishing all its projects with the skill of an adroit despotism. It frequently abandons them before they have borne their fruits, or risks them when the consequences may be dangerous; but in the end it produces more than any absolute government; if it does fewer things well, it does a greater number of things. Under its sway, the grandeur is not in what the public administration does but in what is done without it or outside of it. Democracy does not give the people the most skilful government, but it produces what the ablest governments are frequently unable to create; namely, an all-pervading and restless activity, a superabundant force, and an energy which is inseparable from it, and which may, however unfavorable circumstances may be, produce wonders. These are the true advantages of democracy.

In the present age, when the destinies of Christendom seem to be in suspense, some hasten to assail democracy as a hostile power, whilst it is yet growing; and others already adore this new deity which is springing forth from chaos. But both parties are imperfectly acquainted with the object of their hatred or their worship; they strike in the dark and distribute their blows at random.

We must first understand what is wanted of society and its government. Do you wish to give a certain elevation to the human mind and teach it to regard the things of this world with generous feelings, to inspire men with a scorn of mere temporal advantages, to form and nourish strong convictions, and keep alive the spirit of honorable devotedness? Is it your object to refine the habits, embellish the manners, and cultivate the arts, to promote the love of poetry, beauty, and glory? Would you constitute a people fitted to act powerfully upon all other nations and prepared for those high enterprises which, whatever be their results, will leave a name forever famous in history? If you believe such to be the principal object of society, avoid the government of the democracy, for it would not lead you with certainty to the goal.

But if you hold it expedient to divert the moral and intellectual activity of man to the production of comfort, and the promotion of general well-being; if a clear understanding be more profitable to man than genius; if your object be not to stimulate the virtues of heroism, but the habits of peace; if you had rather witness vices than crimes, and are content to meet with fewer noble deeds, provided offenses be diminished in the same proportion; if, instead of living in the midst of a brilliant society, you are contented to have prosperity around you; if, in short, you are of opinion that the principal object of a government is not to confer the greatest possible power and glory upon the body of the nation but to insure the greatest enjoyment, and to avoid the most misery, to each of the individuals who compose it—if such be your desire, then equalize the conditions of men and establish democratic institutions.

But if the time be past at which such a choice was possible, and if some power superior to that of man already hurries us, without consulting our wishes, toward one or the other of these two governments, let us endeavor to make the best of that which is allotted to us, and, by finding out both its good and its evil tendencies, be able to foster the former and repress the latter to the utmost.

Chapter XV

UNLIMITED POWER OF THE MAJORITY IN THE
UNITED STATES AND ITS CONSEQUENCES

... I hold it to be an impious and detestable maxim that, politically speaking, the people have a right to do anything; and yet I have asserted that all authority originates in the will of the majority. Am I, then, in contradiction with myself?

A general law, which bears the name of justice, has been made and sanctioned, not only by a majority of this or that people, but by a majority of mankind. The rights of every people are therefore confined within the limits of what is just. A nation may be considered as a jury which is empowered to represent society at large and to apply justice, which is its law. Ought such a jury, which represents society, to have more power than the society itself, whose laws it executes?

When I refuse to obey an unjust law, I do not contest the right of the majority to command, but I simply appeal from the sovereignty of the people to the sovereignty of mankind. Some have not feared to assert that a people can never outstep the boundaries of justice and reason in those affairs which are peculiarly its own and that, consequently, full power may be given to the majority by which they are represented. But this is the language of a slave.

A majority taken collectively is only an individual, whose opinions, and frequently whose interests, are opposed to those of another individual, who is styled a minority. If it be admitted that a man possessing absolute power may misuse that power by wronging his adversaries, why should not a majority be liable to the same reproach? Men do not change their characters by uniting with each other; nor does their patience in the presence of obstacles increase with their strength. For my own part, I cannot believe it; the power to do everything, which I should refuse to one of my equals, I will never grant to any number of them.

I do not think that, for the sake of preserving liberty, it is possible to combine several principles in the same government so as really to oppose them to one another. The form of government which is usually termed *mixed* has always appeared to me a mere chimera. Accurately speaking, there is no such thing as a *mixed government*, in the sense usually given to that word, because, in all communities, some one principle of action may be discovered which preponderates over the others. England, in the last century—which has been especially cited as an example of this sort of government—was essentially an aristocratic state, although it comprised some great elements of democracy; for the laws and customs of the country were such that the aristocracy could not but preponderate in the long run and direct public affairs according to its own will. The error arose from seeing the interests of the nobles perpetually contending with those of the people, without considering the issue of the contest, which was really the important point. When a community actually has a mixed government—that is to say, when it is equally divided between adverse principles—it must either experience a revolution or fall into anarchy.

I am therefore of opinion that social power superior to all others must always be placed somewhere; but I think that liberty is endangered when this power finds no obstacle which can retard its course and give it time to moderate its own vehemence.

Unlimited power is in itself a bad and dangerous thing. Human beings are not competent to exercise it with discretion. God alone can be omnipotent, because his wisdom and his justice are always equal to his power. There is no power on earth so worthy of honor in itself, or clothed with rights so sacred, that I would admit its uncontrolled and all-predominant authority. When I see that the right and the means of absolute command are conferred on any power whatever, be it called a people or a king, an aristocracy or a democracy, a monarchy or a republic, I say there is the germ of tyranny, and I seek to live elsewhere, under other laws.

In my opinion, the main evil of the present democratic institutions of the United States does not arise, as is often asserted in Europe, from their weakness but from their irresistible strength. I am not so much alarmed at the excessive liberty which reigns in that country as at the inadequate securities which one finds there against tyranny....

EFFECTS OF THE OMNIPOTENCE OF THE MAJORITY UPON THE ARBITRARY AUTHORITY OF AMERICAN PUBLIC OFFICERS

A *distinction* must be drawn between tyranny and arbitrary power. Tyranny may be exercised by means of the law itself, and in that case it is not arbitrary; arbitrary power may be exercised for the public good, in which case it is not tyrannical. Tyranny usually employs arbitrary means, but, if necessary, it can do without them.

In the United States the omnipotence of the majority, which is favorable to the legal despotism of the legislature, likewise favors the arbitrary authority of the magistrate. The majority has absolute power both to make the law and to watch over its execution; and as it has equal authority over those who are in power, and the community at large, it considers public officers as its passive agents and readily confides to them the task of carrying out its designs. The details of their office, and the privileges which they are to enjoy, are rarely defined beforehand. It treats them as a master does his servants, since they are always at work in his sight, and he can direct or reprimand them at any instant....

POWER EXERCISED BY THE MAJORITY IN AMERICA UPON OPINION

...I know of no country in which there is so little independence of mind and real freedom of discussion as in America. In any constitutional state in Europe, every sort of religious and political theory may be freely preached and disseminated; for there is no country in Europe so subdued by any single authority as not to protect the man who raises his voice in the cause of truth from the consequences of his hardihood. If he is unfortunate enough to live under an absolute government, the people are often upon his side; if he inhabits a free country, he can, if necessary, find a shelter behind the throne. The aristocratic part of society supports him in some countries, and the democracy in others. But in a nation where democratic institutions exist, organized like those of the United States, there is but one authority, one element of strength and success, with nothing beyond it.

In America the majority raises formidable barriers around the liberty of opinion; within these barriers, an author may write what he pleases, but woe to him if he goes beyond them. Not that he is in danger of an *auto da fé,* but he is exposed to continued obloquy and persecution. His political career is closed forever, since he has offended the only authority which is able to open it. Every sort of compensation, even that of celebrity, is refused to him. Before publishing his opinions, he imagined that he held them in common with others; but no sooner has he declared them than he is loudly censured by his opponents, whilst those who think like him, without having the courage to speak out, abandon him in silence. He yields at length, overcome by the daily effort which he has to make, and subsides into silence, as if he felt remorse for having spoken the truth....

THE GREATEST DANGERS OF THE AMERICAN REPUBLICS PROCEED FROM THE OMNIPOTENCE OF THE MAJORITY

Governments usually perish from impotence or from tyranny. In the former case, their power escapes from them; it is wrested from their grasp in the latter. Many observers who have witnessed the anarchy of democratic states have imagined that the government of those states was naturally weak and impotent. The truth is that, when war is once begun between parties, the government loses its control over society. But I do not think that a democratic power is naturally without force or resources; say, rather, that it is almost always by the abuse of its force, and the misemployment of its resources, that it becomes a failure. Anarchy is almost always produced by its tyranny or its mistakes but not by its want of strength.

It is important not to confound stability with force, or the greatness of a thing with its duration. In democratic republics the power which directs society is not stable, for it often changes hands and assumes a new direction. But, whichever way it turns, its force is almost irresistible. The governments of the American republics appear to me to be as much centralized as those of the absolute monarchies of Europe and more energetic than they are. I do not, therefore, imagine that they will perish from weakness.

If ever the free institutions of America are destroyed, that event may be attributed to the omnipotence of the majority, which may at some future time urge the minorities to desperation, and oblige them to have recourse to physical force. Anarchy will then be the result, but it will have been brought about by despotism.[6] ...

CONCLUSION TO VOLUME I[7]
THE UNITED STATES AND RUSSIA

... Today there are two great peoples who, starting from different points, seem to approach the same destiny; they are the Russians and the Anglo-Americans. Both of them have grown in obscurity, and, while men were looking the other way, they suddenly reach the first rank of nations. At almost the same time the world became aware of their birth and of their greatness.

All other peoples seem to have nearly reached the limits of their potentialities, and to have nothing left to do but to maintain their present status. But these two people are growing; all others have stopped or progress only with the greatest effort; these alone follow with ease and celerity a course whose limit the eye cannot yet detect.

The American battles the obstacles of nature; the Russian, those of man. The former combats the wilderness and savagery, the latter, civilization with all its weapons. American conquests are won with the laborer's plowshare; Russian triumphs, with the soldier's sword. To

6. At this point Tocqueville quoted from *The Federalist*, No. 51, the passage beginning "It is of great importance..." on p. 314. He follows this quotation with another from Jefferson on the more immediate danger of tyranny from the legislature than from the executive ("though that will come"), adding his own comment: "I am glad to cite the opinion of Jefferson upon this subject rather than that of any other, because I consider him the most powerful advocate democracy has ever had."

7. Translated from *Démocratie*, I, 504–5. Or see Bowen, *op. cit.*, I, 558–59. This amazing prophecy is the conclusion to the first part of the *Démocratie*, which was published at Paris early in 1835.

attain its ends, the American relies upon personal interest and allows free scope to the unguided energy and common sense of individuals. The Russian somehow concentrates the power of society in one man. The method of the former is freedom; of the latter, servitude.

Their starting-point is different, their ways are diverse, yet each of them seems called by the secret design of Providence to control, some day, the destinies of half the world.

SECOND PART. FIRST BOOK

INFLUENCE OF DEMOCRACY UPON THE ACTION OF INTELLECT IN THE UNITED STATES

CHAPTER I

PHILOSOPHICAL METHOD OF THE AMERICANS

I think that in no country in the civilized world is less attention paid to philosophy than in the United States. The Americans have no philosophical school of their own, and they care but little for all the schools into which Europe is divided, the very names of which are scarcely known to them.

Yet it is easy to perceive that almost all the inhabitants of the United States conduct their understanding in the same manner and govern it by the same rules; that is to say, without ever having taken the trouble to define the rules, they have a philosophical method common to the whole people.

To evade the bondage of system and habit, of family maxims, class opinions, and, in some degree, of national prejudices; to accept tradition only as a means of information, and existing facts only as a lesson to be used in doing otherwise and doing better; to seek the reason of things for one's self and in one's self alone; to tend to results without being bound to means, and to aim at the substance through the form—such are the principal characteristics of what I shall call the philosophical method of the Americans.

But if I go further and seek amongst these characteristics the principal one which includes almost all the rest, I discover that, in most of the operations of mind, each American appeals only to the individual effort of his own understanding.

America is therefore one of the countries where the precepts of Descartes are least studied and are best applied. Nor is this surprising. The Americans do not read the works of Descartes, because their social condition deters them from speculative studies; but they follow his maxims, because this same social condition naturally disposes their minds to adopt them.

In the midst of the continual movement which agitates a democratic community, the tie which unites one generation to another is relaxed or broken; every man there readily loses all trace of the ideas of his forefathers or takes no care about them.

Men living in this state of society cannot derive their belief from the opinions of the class to which they belong; for, so to speak, there are no longer any classes, or those which still exist are composed of such mobile elements that the body can never exercise any real control over its members.

As to the influence which the intellect of one man may have on that of another, it must necessarily be very limited in a country where the citizens, placed on an equal footing, are all closely seen by each other; and where, as no signs of incontestable greatness or superiority are perceived in any one of them, they are constantly brought back to their own reason as the most obvious and proximate source of truth. It is not only confidence in this or that man which is destroyed but the disposition for trusting the authority of any man whatsoever. Everyone shuts himself up in his own breast and affects from that point to judge the world.

The practice which obtains amongst the Americans, of fixing the standard of their judgment in themselves alone, leads them to other habits of mind. As they perceive that they succeed in resolving without assistance all the little difficulties which their practical life presents, they readily conclude that everything in the world may be explained and that nothing in it transcends the limits of the understanding. Thus they fall to denying what they cannot comprehend, which leaves them but little faith for whatever is extraordinary and an almost insurmountable distaste for whatever is supernatural. As it is on their own testimony that they are accustomed to rely, they like to discern the object which engages their attention with extreme clearness; they therefore strip off as much as possible all that covers it, they rid themselves of whatever separates them from it, they remove whatever conceals it from sight, in order to view it more closely and in the broad light of day. This disposition of mind soon leads them to contemn forms, which they regard as useless and inconvenient veils placed between them and the truth.

The Americans, then, have not required to extract their philosophical method from books; they have found it in themselves. The same thing may be remarked in what has taken place in Europe. This same method has only been established and made popular in Europe in proportion as the condition of society has become more equal, and men have grown more like each other. . . .

If it be asked why, at the present day, this same method is more rigorously followed and more frequently applied by the French than by the Americans, although the principle of equality is no less complete and of more ancient date amongst the latter people, the fact may be attributed to two circumstances which it is first essential to have clearly understood.

It must never be forgotten that religion gave birth to Anglo-American society. In the United States religion is therefore mingled with all the habits of the nation and all the feelings of patriotism, whence it derives a peculiar force. To this reason another of no less power may be added: in America religion has, as it were, laid down its own limits. Religious institutions have remained wholly distinct from political institutions, so that former laws have been easily changed whilst former belief has remained unshaken. Christianity has therefore retained a strong hold on the public mind in America; and I would more particularly remark that its sway is not only that of a philosophical doctrine which has been adopted upon inquiry but of a religion which is believed without discussion. In the United States, Christian sects are infinitely diversified and perpetually modified; but Christianity itself is an established and irresistible fact, which no one undertakes either to attack or to defend. The Americans, having admitted the principal doctrines of the Christian religion without inquiry, are obliged to accept in like manner a great number of moral truths originating in it and connected with it. Hence the activity of individual analysis is restrained within narrow limits, and many of the most important of human opinions are removed from its influence.

The second circumstance to which I have alluded is that the social condition and the constitution of the Americans are democratic, but they have not had a democratic revolution. They arrived upon the soil they occupy in nearly the condition in which we see them at the present day, and this is of considerable importance.

There are no revolutions which do not shake existing belief, enervate authority, and throw doubts over commonly received ideas. The effect of all revolutions is, therefore, more or less, to surrender men to their own guidance and to open to the mind of every man a void and almost unlimited range of speculation. When equality of conditions succeeds a protracted conflict between the different classes of which the elder society was composed, envy, hatred, and uncharitableness, pride and exaggerated self-confidence, seize upon the human heart and plant their sway in it for a time. This, independently of equality itself, tends powerfully to divide men—to lead them to mistrust the judgment of each other and to seek the light of truth nowhere but in themselves. Everyone then attempts to be his own sufficient guide and makes it his boast to form his own opinions on all subjects. Men are no longer bound together by ideas but by interests; and it would seem as if human opinions were reduced to a sort of intellectual dust, scattered on every side, unable to collect, unable to cohere....

Chapter II

OF THE PRINCIPAL SOURCE OF BELIEF AMONG DEMOCRATIC NATIONS

At different periods dogmatical belief is more or less common. It arises in different ways, and it may change its object and its form; but under no circumstances will dogmatical belief cease to exist, or, in other words, men will never cease to entertain some opinions on trust and without discussion. If everyone undertook to form all his own opinions, and to seek for truth by isolated paths struck out by himself alone, it would follow that no considerable number of men would ever unite in any common belief.

But obviously without such common belief no society can prosper—say, rather, no society can exist; for, without ideas held in common, there is no common action, and, without common action, there may still be men, but there is no social body. In order that society should exist and a fortiori that a society

should prosper, it is required that all the minds of the citizens should be rallied and held together by certain predominant ideas; and this cannot be the case unless each of them sometime draws his opinions from the common source and consents to accept certain matters of belief already formed.

If I now consider man in his isolated capacity, I find dogmatical belief is not less indispensable to him in order to live alone than it is to enable him to cooperate with his fellows. If man were forced to demonstrate for himself all the truths of which he makes daily use, his task would never end. He would exhaust his strength in preparatory demonstrations without ever advancing beyond them. As, from the shortness of his life, he has not the time, nor, from the limits of his intelligence, the capacity, to accomplish this, he is reduced to take upon trust a number of facts and opinions which he has not had either the time or the power to verify for himself but which men of greater ability have sought out or which the world adopts. On this groundwork he raises for himself the structure of his own thoughts; he is not led to proceed in this manner by choice but is constrained by the inflexible law of his condition. There is no philosopher of so great parts in the world but that he believes a million of things on the faith of other people and supposes a great many more truths than he demonstrates.

This is not only necessary but desirable. A man who should undertake to inquire into everything for himself could devote to each thing but little time and attention. His task would keep his mind in perpetual unrest, which would prevent him from penetrating to the depth of any truth or of grappling his mind firmly to any conviction. His intellect would be at once independent and powerless. He must therefore make his choice from amongst the various objects of human belief, and adopt many opinions without discussion, in order to search the better into that smaller number which he sets apart for investigation. It is true that whoever receives an opinion on the word of another does so far enslave his mind, but it is a salutary servitude which allows him to make a good use of freedom.

A principle of authority must then always occur, under all circumstances, in some part or other of the moral and intellectual world. Its place is variable, but a place it necessarily has. The independence of individual minds may be greater, or it may be less; unbounded it cannot be. Thus the question is, not to know whether any intellectual authority exists in the ages of democracy, but simply where it resides and by what standard it is to be measured.

I have shown in the preceding chapter how the equality of conditions leads men to entertain a sort of instinctive incredulity of the supernatural and a very lofty and often exaggerated opinion of the human understanding. The men who live at a period of social equality are not therefore easily led to place that intellectual authority to which they bow either beyond or above humanity. They commonly seek for the sources of truth in themselves or in those who are like themselves. This would be enough to prove that, at such periods, no new religion could be established and that all schemes for such a purpose would be not only impious but absurd and irrational. It may be foreseen that a democratic people will not easily give credence to divine missions; that they will laugh at modern prophets; and that they will seek to discover the chief arbiter of their belief within, and not beyond, the limits of their kind.

When the ranks of society are unequal, and men unlike each other in condition, there are some individuals wielding the power of superior intelligence, learning, and enlightenment, whilst the multitude are sunk in ignorance and prejudice. Men living at these aristocratic periods are therefore naturally induced to shape their opinions by the standard of a superior person, or superior class of persons, whilst they are averse to recognize the infallibility of the mass of the people.

The contrary takes place in ages of equality. The nearer the people are drawn to the common level of an equal and similar condition, the less prone does each man become to place implicit faith in a certain man or a certain class of men. But his readiness to believe the multitude increases, and opinion is more than ever mistress of the world. Not only is common opinion the only guide which private judgment retains amongst a democratic people, but amongst such a people it possesses a power infinitely beyond what it has elsewhere. At periods of equality, men have no faith in one another, by reason of their common resemblance; but this very resemblance gives them almost unbounded confidence in the judgment of the public; for it would not seem probable, as they are all endowed with equal means of judging, but that the greater truth should go with the greater number.

When the inhabitant of a democratic country compares himself individually with all those about him, he feels with pride that he is the equal of any one of them; but, when he comes to survey the totality of his fellows, and to place himself in contrast with so huge a body, he is instantly overwhelmed by the sense of his own insignificance and weakness. The same equality which renders him independent of each of his fellow-citizens, taken severally, exposes him alone and unprotected to the influence of the greater number. The public has therefore, among a democratic people, a singular power, which aristocratic nations cannot conceive of; for it does not persuade to certain opinions, but it enforces them and infuses them into the intellect by a sort of enormous pressure of the minds of all upon the reason of each.

In the United States the majority undertakes to supply a multitude of ready-made opinions for the use of individuals, who are thus relieved from the necessity of forming opinions of their own. Everybody there adopts great numbers of theories, on philosophy, morals, and politics, without inquiry, upon public trust; and if we look to it very narrowly, it will be perceived that religion herself holds sway there much less as a doctrine of revelation than as a commonly received opinion.

The fact that the political laws of the Americans are such that the majority rules the community with sovereign sway materially increases the power which that majority naturally exercises over the mind. For nothing is more customary in man than to recognize superior wisdom in the person of his oppressor. This political omnipotence of the majority in the United States doubtless augments the influence which public opinion would obtain without it over the minds of each member of the community; but the foundations of that influence do not rest upon it. They must be sought for in the principle of equality itself, not in the more or less popular institutions which men living under that condition may give themselves. The intellectual dominion of the greater number would probably be less absolute amongst a democratic people governed by a king than in the sphere of a pure democracy, but it will always be extremely absolute; and, by whatever political laws men are governed in the ages of equality, it may be foreseen that faith in public opinion will become a species of religion there, and the majority its ministering prophet.

Thus intellectual authority will be different, but it will not be diminished; and, far from thinking that it will disappear, I augur that it may readily acquire too much preponderance and confine the action of private judgment within narrower limits than are suited either to the greatness or the happiness of the human race. In the principle of equality I very clearly discern two tendencies; the one leading the mind of every man to untried thoughts, the other which would prohibit him from thinking at all. And I perceive how, under the dominion of certain laws, democracy would extinguish that liberty of the mind to which a democratic social condition is favorable; so that, after having broken all the bondage once imposed on it by ranks or by men, the human mind would be closely fettered to the general will of the greatest number.

If the absolute power of a majority were to be substituted, by democratic nations, for all the different powers which checked or retarded overmuch the energy of individual minds, the evil would only have changed character. Men would not have found the means of independent life; they would simply have discovered (no easy task) a new physiognomy of servitude. There is—and I cannot repeat it too often—there is here matter for profound reflection to those who look on freedom of thought as a holy thing, and who hate not only the despot but despotism. For myself, when I feel the hand of power lie heavy on my brow, I care but little to know who oppresses me; and I am not the more disposed to pass beneath the yoke because it is held out to me by the arms of a million of men. . . .

Chapter VIII

HOW EQUALITY SUGGESTS TO THE AMERICANS THE IDEA OF THE INDEFINITE PERFECTIBILITY OF MAN

Equality suggests to the human mind several ideas which would not have originated from any other source, and it modifies almost all those previously entertained. I take as an example the idea of human perfectibility, because it is one of the principal notions that the intellect can conceive, and because it constitutes of itself a great philosophical theory, which is everywhere to be traced by its consequences in the conduct of human affairs.

Although man has many points of resemblance with the brutes, one trait is peculiar to himself—he improves; they are incapable of improvement. Mankind could not fail to discover this difference from the beginning. The idea of perfectibility is therefore as old as the world; equality did not give birth to it but has imparted to it a new character.

When the citizens of a community are classed according to rank, profession, or birth, and when all men are constrained to follow the career which chance has opened before them, everyone thinks that the utmost limits of human power are to be discerned in proximity to himself, and no one seeks any longer to resist the inevitable law of his destiny. Not, indeed, that an aristocratic people absolutely deny man's faculty of self-improvement, but they do not hold it to be indefinite; they can conceive amelioration but not change. They imagine that the future condition of society may be better but not essentially different, and, whilst they admit that humanity has made progress, and may still have some to make, they assign to it beforehand certain impassable limits.

Thus, they do not presume that they have arrived at the supreme good or at absolute truth (what people or what man was ever wild enough to imagine it?), but they cherish a persuasion that they have pretty nearly reached that degree of greatness and knowledge which our imperfect nature admits of; and, as nothing moves about them, they are willing to fancy that everything is in its fit place. Then it is that the legislator affects to lay down eternal laws; that kings and nations will raise none but imperishable monuments; and that the present generation undertakes to spare generations to come the care of regulating their destinies.

In proportion as castes disappear and the classes of society approximate—as manners, customs, and laws vary, from the tumultuous intercourse of men—as new facts arise—as new truths are brought to light—as ancient opinions are dissipated, and others take their place—the image of an ideal but always fugitive perfection presents itself to the human mind. Continual changes are then every instant occurring under the observation of every man. The position of some is rendered worse, and he learns but too well that no people and no individual, how enlightened soever they may be, can lay claim to infallibility. The condition of others is improved, whence he infers that man is endowed with an indefinite faculty of improvement. His reverses teach him that none have discovered absolute good—his success stimulates him to the never ending pursuit of it. Thus, forever seeking, forever falling to rise again—often disappointed but not discouraged—he tends unceasingly toward that unmeasured greatness so indistinctly visible at the end of the long track which humanity has yet to tread.

It can hardly be believed how many facts naturally flow from the philosophical theory of the indefinite perfectibility of man, or how strong an influence it exercises even on those who, living entirely for the purposes of action and not of thought, seem to conform their actions to it without knowing anything about it.

I accost an American sailor and inquire why the ships of his country are built so as to last but for a short time; he answers without hesitation that the art of navigation is every day making such rapid progress that the finest vessel would become almost useless if it lasted beyond a few years. In these words, which fell accidentally and on a particular subject from an uninstructed man, I recognize the general and systematic idea upon which a great people direct all their concerns.

Aristocratic nations are naturally too apt to narrow the scope of human perfectibility; democratic nations, to expand it beyond reason. . . .

SECOND BOOK

INFLUENCE OF DEMOCRACY ON THE FEELINGS OF THE AMERICANS

CHAPTER I

WHY DEMOCRATIC NATIONS SHOW A MORE ARDENT AND ENDURING LOVE OF EQUALITY THAN OF LIBERTY

The first and most intense passion which is produced by equality of condition is, I need hardly say, the love of that equality. My readers will therefore not be surprised that I speak of this feeling before all others.

Everybody has remarked that, in our time, and especially in France, this passion for equality is every day gaining ground in the human heart. It has been said a hundred times that our contemporaries are far more ardently and tenaciously attached to equality than to freedom; but, as I do not find that the causes of the fact have been sufficiently analyzed, I shall endeavor to point them out.

It is possible to imagine an extreme point at which freedom and equality would meet and be confounded together. Let us suppose that all the people take a part in the government and that each one of them has an equal right to take a part in it. As no one is different from his fellows, none can exercise a tyrannical power; men will be perfectly free, because they are all entirely equal; and they will all be perfectly equal, because they are entirely free. To this ideal state democratic nations tend. This is the only complete form that equality can assume upon earth; but there are a thousand others which, without being equally perfect, are not less cherished by those nations.

The principle of equality may be established in civil society without prevailing in the political world. Equal rights may exist of indulging in the same pleasures, of entering the same professions, of frequenting the same places; in a word, of living in the same manner and seeking wealth by the same means—although all men do not take an equal share in the government. A kind of equality may even be established in the political world, though there should be no political freedom there. A man may be the equal of all his countrymen save one, who is the master of all without distinction, and who selects equally from among them all the agents of his power. Several other combinations might be easily imagined by which very great equality would be united to institutions more or less free or even to institutions wholly without freedom.

Although men cannot become absolutely equal unless they are entirely free; and consequently equality, pushed to its furthest extent, may be confounded with freedom, yet there is good reason for distinguishing the one from the other. The taste which men have for liberty and that which they feel for equality are, in fact, two different things; and I am not afraid to add that, amongst democratic nations, they are two unequal things.

Upon close inspection, it will be seen that there is in every age some peculiar and preponderating fact with which all others are connected; this fact almost always gives birth to some pregnant idea or some ruling passion which attracts to itself and bears away in its course all the feelings and opinions of the time: it is like a great stream toward which each of the neighboring rivulets seems to flow.

Freedom has appeared in the world at different times and under various forms; it has not been exclusively bound to any social condition, and it is not confined to democracies. Freedom cannot, therefore, form the distinguishing characteristic of democratic ages. The peculiar and preponderating fact which marks those ages as its own is the equality of condition; the ruling passion of men in those periods is the love of this equality. Ask not what singular charm the men of democratic ages find in being equal or what special reasons they may have for clinging so tenaciously to equality rather than to the other advantages which society holds out to them: equality is the distinguishing characteristic of the age they live in; that, of itself, is enough to explain that they prefer it to all the rest.

But, independently of this reason, there are several others which will at all times habitually lead men to prefer equality to freedom.

If a people could ever succeed in destroying, or even in diminishing, the equality which prevails in its own body, they could do so only by long and laborious efforts. Their social condition must be modified, their laws abolished, their opinions superseded, their habits changed, their manners corrupted. But political liberty is more easily lost; to neglect to hold it fast is to allow it to escape. Men therefore cling to equality not only because it is dear to them; they also adhere to it because they think it will last forever.

That political freedom may compromise in its excesses the tranquillity, the property, the lives of individuals, is obvious even to narrow and unthinking minds. On the contrary, none but attentive and clear-sighted men perceive the perils with which equality threatens us, and they commonly avoid pointing them

out. They know that the calamities they apprehend are remote, and flatter themselves that they will only fall upon future generations, for which the present generation takes but little thought. The evils which freedom sometimes brings with it are immediate; they are apparent to all, and all are more or less affected by them. The evils which extreme equality may produce are slowly disclosed; they creep gradually into the social frame; they are seen only at intervals; and at the moment at which they become most violent, habit already causes them to be no longer felt.

The advantages which freedom brings are only shown by the lapse of time, and it is always easy to mistake the cause in which they originate. The advantages of equality are immediate, and they may always be traced from their source.

Political liberty bestows exalted pleasures, from time to time, upon a certain number of citizens. Equality every day confers a number of small enjoyments on every man. The charms of equality are every instant felt and are within the reach of all; the noblest hearts are not insensible to them, and the most vulgar souls exult in them. The passion which equality creates must therefore be at once strong and general. Men cannot enjoy political liberty unpurchased by some sacrifices, and they never obtain it without great exertions. But the pleasures of equality are self-proffered: each of the petty incidents of life seems to occasion them; and, in order to taste them, nothing is required but to live.

Democratic nations are at all times fond of equality, but there are certain epochs at which the passion they entertain for it swells to the height of fury. This occurs at the moment when the old social system, long menaced, is overthrown after a severe intestine struggle, and the barriers of rank are at length thrown down. At such times, men pounce upon equality as their booty, and they cling to it as to some precious treasure which they fear to lose. The passion for equality penetrates on every side into men's hearts, expands there, and fills them entirely. Tell them not that, by this blind surrender of themselves to an exclusive passion, they risk their dearest interests; they are deaf. Show them not freedom escaping from their grasp, whilst they are looking another way; they are blind, or, rather, they can discern but one object to be desired in the universe.

What I have said is applicable to all democratic nations; what I am about to say concerns the French alone. Amongst most modern nations, and especially amongst all those of the continent of Europe, the taste and the idea of freedom only began to exist and to be developed at the time when social conditions were tending to equality and as a consequence of that very equality. Absolute kings were the most efficient levelers of ranks amongst their subjects. Amongst these nations equality preceded freedom: equality was therefore a fact of some standing when freedom was still a novelty; the one had already created customs, opinions, and laws belonging to it, when the other, alone and for the first time, came into actual existence. Thus the latter was still only an affair of opinion and of taste, whilst the former had already crept into the habits of the people, possessed itself of their manners, and given a particular turn to the smallest actions in their lives. Can it be wondered at that the men of our own time prefer the one to the other?

I think that democratic communities have a natural taste for freedom; left to themselves, they will seek it, cherish it, and view any privation of it with regret. But for equality, their passion is ardent, insatiable, incessant, invincible; they call for equality in freedom, and, if they cannot obtain that, they still call for equality in slavery. They will endure poverty, servitude, barbarism; but they will not **endure aristocracy.**

This is true at all times and especially in our own day. All men and all powers seeking to cope with this irresistible passion will be overthrown and destroyed by it. In our age, freedom cannot be established without it, and despotism itself cannot reign without its support.

CHAPTER II

OF INDIVIDUALISM[8] IN DEMOCRATIC COUNTRIES

I have shown how it is that, in ages of equality, every man seeks for his opinions within himself. I am now to show how it is that, in the same ages, all his feelings are turned toward himself alone. Individualism is a novel expression, to which a novel idea has given birth. Our fathers were only acquainted with selfishness (*égoïsme*). Selfishness is a passionate and exaggerated love of self which leads a man to connect everything with himself and to prefer himself to everything in the world. Individualism is a mature and calm feeling which disposes each member of the community to sever himself from the mass of his fellows and to draw apart with his famliy and his friends, so that, after he has thus formed a little circle of his own, he willingly leaves society at large to itself. Selfishness originates in blind instinct: individualism proceeds from erroneous judgment more than from depraved feelings; it originates as much in deficiencies of mind as in perversity of heart.

Selfishness blights the germ of all virtue: individualism, at first, only saps the virtues of public life; but, in the long run, it attacks and destroys all others and is at length absorbed in downright selfishness. Selfishness is a vice as old as the world, which does not belong to one

8. Here, in Henry Reeve's translation, is the first use of the word "individualism" in the English language. The shift in its meaning from that of this passage to that of F. J. Turner's essay on the frontier (Vol. II), and of Herbert Hoover's "Rugged Individualism" speech of 1928 (Vol. II), is a provocative and significant one.

form of society more than to another; individualism is of democratic origin, and it threatens to spread in the same ratio as the equality of condition.

Amongst aristocratic nations, as families remain for centuries in the same condition, often on the same spot, all generations become, as it were, contemporaneous. A man almost always knows his forefathers and respects them; he thinks he already sees his remote descendants, and he loves them. He willingly imposes duties on himself toward the former and the latter; and he will frequently sacrifice his personal gratifications to those who went before and to those who will come after him. Aristocratic institutions have, moreover, the effect of closely binding every man to several of his fellow-citizens. As the classes of an aristocratic people are strongly marked and permanent, each of them is regarded by its own members as a sort of lesser country, more tangible and more cherished than the country at large. As, in aristocratic communities, all the citizens occupy fixed positions, one above the other, the result is that each of them always sees a man above himself whose patronage is necessary to him and, below himself, another man whose co-operation he may claim. Men living in aristocratic ages are therefore almost always closely attached to something placed out of their own sphere, and they are often disposed to forget themselves. It is true that, in these ages, the notion of human fellowship is faint and that men seldom think of sacrificing themselves for mankind; but they often sacrifice themselves for other men. In democratic times, on the contrary, when the duties of each individual to the race are much more clear, devoted service to any one man becomes more rare; the bond of human affection is extended, but it is relaxed.

Amongst democratic nations new families are constantly springing up, others are constantly falling away, and all that remain change their condition; the woof of time is every instant broken, and the track of generations effaced. Those who went before are soon forgotten; of those who will come after, no one has any idea: the interest of man is confined to those in close propinquity to himself. As each class approximates to other classes, and intermingles with them, its members become indifferent and as strangers to one another. Aristocracy had made a chain of all the members of the community, from the peasant to the king; democracy breaks that chain and severs every link of it.

As social conditions become more equal, the number of persons increases who, although they are neither rich nor powerful enough to exercise any great influence over their fellows, have nevertheless acquired or retained sufficient education and fortune to satisfy their own wants. They owe nothing to any man, [and] they expect nothing from any man; they acquire the habit of always considering themselves as standing alone, and they are apt to imagine that their whole destiny is in their own hands.

Thus, not only does democracy make every man forget his ancestors, but it hides his descendants and separates his contemporaries from him; it throws him back forever upon himself alone and threatens in the end to confine him entirely within the solitude of his own heart. . . .

CHAPTER IV
THAT THE AMERICANS COMBAT THE EFFECTS OF INDIVIDUALISM BY FREE INSTITUTIONS

Despotism, which is of a very timorous nature, is never more secure of continuance than when it can keep men asunder; and all its influence is commonly exerted for that purpose. No vice of the human heart is so acceptable to it as selfishness; a despot easily forgives his subjects for not loving him, provided they do not love each other. He does not ask them to assist him in governing the state; it is enough that they do not aspire to govern it themselves. He stigmatizes as turbulent and unruly spirits those who would combine their exertions to promote the prosperity of the community; and, perverting the natural meaning of words, he applauds as good citizens those who have no sympathy for any but themselves.

Thus the vices which despotism produces are precisely those which equality fosters. These two things mutually and perniciously complete and assist each other. Equality places men side by side, unconnected by any common tie; despotism raises barriers to keep them asunder: the former predisposes them not to consider their fellow-creatures; the latter makes general indifference a sort of public virtue.

Despotism, then, which is at all times dangerous, is more particularly to be feared in democratic ages. It is easy to see that in those same ages men stand most in need of freedom. When the members of a community are forced to attend to public affairs, they are necessarily drawn from the circle of their own interests and snatched at times from self-observation. As soon as a man begins to treat of public affairs in public, he begins to perceive that he is not so independent of his fellow-men as he had at first imagined and that, in order to obtain their support, he must often lend them his co-operation. . . .

The Americans have combated by free institutions the tendency of equality to keep men asunder, and they have subdued it. The legislators of America did not suppose that a general representation of the whole nation would suffice to ward off a disorder at once so natural to the frame of democratic society and so fatal; they also thought that it would be well to infuse political life into each portion of the territory, in order to multiply to an infinite extent opportunities of acting in concert for all the members of the community and to make them constantly feel their mutual dependence on each other. The plan was a wise one. The general affairs of a country only engage the attention of leading politicians, who assemble from time to time in the same places; and, as they often lose sight of each other afterward, no lasting ties are established between them. But if the object be to have the local affairs of a district conducted by the men who reside there, the same persons are always in contact, and they are, in a manner, forced to be acquainted and to adapt themselves to one another.

It is difficult to draw a man out of his own circle to interest him in the destiny of the state, because he does not clearly understand what influence the destiny of the state can have upon his own lot. But if it be proposed to make a road cross the end of his estate, he will see at a glance that there is a connection between this small public affair and his greatest private affairs; and he will discover, without its being shown to him, the close tie which unites private to general interest. Thus, far more may be done by intrusting to the citizens the administration of minor affairs than by surrendering to them the control of important ones, toward interesting them in the public welfare and convincing them that they constantly stand in need one of another in order to provide for it. A brilliant achievement may win for you the favor of a people at one stroke; but to earn the love and respect of the population which surrounds you, a long succession of little services rendered and of obscure good deeds—a constant habit of kindness and an established reputation for disinterestedness—will be required. Local freedom, then, which leads a great number of citizens to value the affection of their neighbors and of their kindred, perpetually brings men together, and forces them to help one another, in spite of the propensities which sever them. . . .

It would be unjust to suppose that the patriotism and the zeal which every American displays for the welfare of his fellow-citizens are wholly insincere. Although private interest directs the greater part of human actions in the United States, as well as elsewhere, it does not regulate them all. I must say that I have often seen Americans make great and real sacrifices to the public welfare; and I have remarked a hundred instances in which they hardly ever failed to lend faithful support to each other. The free institutions which the inhabitants of the United States possess, and the political rights of which they make so much use, remind every citizen, and in a thousand ways, that he lives in society. They every instant impress upon his mind the notion that it is the duty, as well as the interest, of men to make themselves useful to their fellow-creatures; and as he sees no particular ground of animosity to them, since he is never either their master or their slave, his heart readily leans to the side of kindness. Men attend to the interests of the public, first by necessity, afterward by choice; what was intentional becomes an instinct, and, by dint of working for the good of one's fellow-citizens, the habit and the taste for serving them are at length acquired.

Many people in France consider equality of condition as one evil, and political freedom as a second. When they are obliged to yield to the former, they strive at least to escape from the latter. But I contend that, in order to combat the evils which equality may produce, there is only one effectual remedy—namely, political freedom.

CHAPTER V

OF THE USE WHICH THE AMERICANS MAKE OF PUBLIC ASSOCIATIONS IN CIVIL LIFE

I do not propose to speak of those political associations by the aid of which men endeavor to defend themselves against the despotic action of a majority, or against the aggressions of regal power. That subject I have already treated. If each citizen did not learn, in proportion as he individually becomes more feeble, and consequently more incapable of preserving his freedom single-handed, to combine with his fellow-citizens for the purpose of defending it, it is clear that tyranny would unavoidably increase together with equality.

Those associations only which are formed in civil life, without reference to political objects, are here adverted to. The political associations which exist in the United States are only a single feature in the midst of the immense assemblage of associations in that country. Americans of all ages, all conditions, and all dispositions constantly form associations. They have not only commercial and manufacturing companies, in which all take part, but associations of a thousand other kinds—religious, moral, serious, futile, general or restricted, enormous or diminutive. The Americans make associations to give entertainments, to found seminaries, to build inns, to construct churches, to diffuse books, to send missionaries to the antipodes; they found in this manner hospitals, prisons, and schools. If it be proposed to inculcate some truth, or to foster some feeling, by the encouragement of a great example, they form a society. Wherever, at the head of some new undertaking, you see the government in France, or a man of rank in England, in the United States you will be sure to find an association. . . .

A government might perform the part of some of the largest American companies; and several states, members of the Union, have already attempted it; but what political power could ever carry on the vast multitude of lesser undertakings which the American citizens perform every day with the assistance of the principle of association? It is easy to foresee that the time is drawing near when man will be less and less able to produce, of himself alone, the commonest necessaries of life. The task of the governing power will therefore perpetually increase, and its very efforts will extend it every day. The more it stands in the place of associations, the more will individuals, losing the notion of combining together, require its assistance; these are causes and effects which unceasingly create each other. Will the administration of the country ultimately assume the management of all the manufactures which no single citizen is able to carry on? And if a time at length arrives when, in consequence of the extreme subdivision of landed property, the soil is split into an infinite number of parcels, so that it can only be cultivated by companies of husbandmen, will it be necessary that the head of the government should leave the helm of state to follow the plow? The morals and the intelligence of a democratic people would be as much endangered as its business and manufactures if the government ever wholly usurped the place of private companies.

Feelings and opinions are recruited, the heart is enlarged, and the human mind is developed only by the reciprocal influence of men upon each other. I have shown that these influences are almost null in democratic countries; they must therefore be artificially created, and this can only be accomplished by associations.

When the members of an aristocratic community adopt a new opinion, or conceive a new sentiment, they give it a station, as it were, beside themselves, upon the lofty platform where they stand; and opinions or sentiments so conspicuous to the eyes of the multitude are easily introduced into the minds or hearts of all around. In democratic countries the governing power alone is naturally in a condition to act in this manner; but it is easy to see that its action is always inadequate and often dangerous. A government can no more be competent to keep alive and to renew the circulation of opinions and feelings amongst a great people than to manage all the speculations of productive industry. No sooner does a government attempt to go beyond its political sphere, and to enter upon this new track, than it exercises, even unintentionally, an insupportable tyranny; for a government can only dictate strict rules, the opinions which it favors are rigidly enforced, and it is never easy to discriminate between its advice and its commands. Worse still will be the case if the government really believes itself interested in preventing all circulation of ideas; it will then stand motionless and oppressed by the heaviness of voluntary torpor. Governments, therefore, should not be the only active powers; associations ought, in democratic nations, to stand in lieu of those powerful private individuals whom the equality of conditions has swept away.

As soon as several of the inhabitants of the United States have taken up an opinion or a feeling which they wish to promote in the world, they look out for mutual assistance and, as soon as they have found each other out, they combine. From that moment they are no longer isolated men but a power seen from afar, whose actions serve for an example and whose language is listened to. The first time I heard in the United States that a hundred thousand men had bound themselves publicly to abstain from spirituous liquors, it appeared to me more like a joke than a serious engagement; and I did not at once perceive why these temperate citizens could not content themselves with drinking water by their own firesides. I at last understood that these hundred thousand Americans, alarmed by the progress of drunkenness around them, had made up their minds to patronize temperance. They acted just in the same way as a man of high rank who should dress very plainly, in order to inspire the humbler orders with a contempt of luxury. It is probable that, if these hundred thousand men had lived in France, each of them would singly have memorialized the government to watch the public houses all over the kingdom.

Nothing, in my opinion, is more deserving of our attention than the intellectual and moral associations of America. The political and industrial associations of that country strike us forcibly; but the others elude our observation, or, if we discover them, we understand them imperfectly, because we have hardly ever seen anything of the kind. It must, however, be acknowledged that they are as necessary to the American people as the former, and perhaps more so. In democratic countries the science of association is the mother of science; the progress of all the rest depends upon the progress it has made.

Amongst the laws which rule human societies, there is one which seems to be more precise and clear than all others. If men are to remain civilized, or to become so, the art of associating together must grow and improve in the same ratio in which the equality of conditions is increased.

CHAPTER VI

OF THE RELATION BETWEEN PUBLIC ASSOCIATIONS AND THE NEWSPAPERS

When men are no longer united amongst themselves by firm and lasting ties, it is impossible to obtain the co-operation of any great number of them, unless you can persuade every man whose help you require that his private interest obliges him voluntarily to unite his exertions to the exertions of all the others. This can be habitually and conveniently effected only by means of a newspaper; nothing but a newspaper can drop the same thought into a thousand minds at the same moment. A newspaper is an adviser who does not require to be sought but who comes of his own accord and talks to you briefly every day of the common weal, without distracting you from your private affairs.

Newspapers therefore become more necessary in proportion as men become more equal and individualism more to be feared. To suppose that they only serve to protect freedom would be to diminish their importance; they maintain civilization. I shall not deny that, in democratic countries, newspapers frequently lead the citizens to launch together into very ill-digested schemes; but, if there were no newspapers, there would be no common activity. The evil which they produce is therefore much less than that which they cure.

The effect of a newspaper is not only to suggest the same purpose to a great number of persons but to furnish means for executing in common the designs which they may have singly conceived. The principal citizens who inhabit an aristocratic country discern each other from afar; and, if they wish to unite their forces, they move toward each other, drawing a multitude of men after them. It frequently happens, on the contrary, in democratic countries, that a great number of men who wish or who want to combine cannot accomplish it, because, as they are very insignificant and lost amidst the crowd, they cannot see, and know not where to find, one another. A newspaper then takes up the notion or the feeling which had occurred simultaneously, but singly, to each of them. All are then immediately guided toward this beacon; and these wandering minds, which had long sought each other in darkness, at length meet and unite. The newspaper brought them together, and the newspaper is still necessary to keep them united. . . .

CHAPTER XX

HOW AN ARISTOCRACY MAY BE CREATED BY MANUFACTURERS

I have shown how democracy favors the growth of manufactures and increases without limit the number of the manufacturing classes. We shall now see by what side road manufacturers may possibly, in their turn, bring men back to aristocracy.

It is acknowledged that, when a workman is engaged every day upon the same details, the whole commodity is produced with greater ease, promptitude, and economy. It is likewise acknowledged that the cost of production of manufactured goods is diminished by the extent of the establishment in which they are made and by the amount of capital employed or of credit. These truths had long been imperfectly discerned, but in our time they have been demonstrated. They have been already applied to many very important kinds of manufactures, and the humblest will gradually be governed by them. I know of nothing in politics which deserves to fix the attention of the legislator more closely than these two new axioms of the science of manufactures.

When a workman is unceasingly and exclusively engaged in the fabrication of one thing, he ultimately does his work with singular dexterity; but, at the same time, he loses the general faculty of applying his mind to the direction of the work. He every day becomes more adroit and less industrious; so that it may be said of him that, in proportion as the workman improves, the man is degraded. What can be expected of a man who has spent twenty years of his life in making heads for pins? and to what can that mighty human intelligence, which has so often stirred the world, be applied in him, except it be to investigate the best method of making pins' heads? When a workman has spent a considerable portion of his existence in this manner, his thoughts are forever set upon the object of his daily toil; his body has contracted certain fixed habits, which it can never shake off: in a word, he no longer belongs to himself but to the calling which he has chosen. It is in vain that laws and manners have been at pains to level all the barriers round such a man and to open to him on every side a thousand different paths to fortune; a theory of manufactures more powerful than manners and laws binds him to a craft, and frequently to a spot, which he cannot leave. It assigns to him a certain place in society, beyond which he cannot go; in the midst of universal movement, it has rendered him stationary.

In proportion as the principle of the division of labor is more extensively applied, the workman becomes more weak, more narrow-minded, and more dependent. The art advances; the artisan recedes. On the other hand, in proportion as it becomes more manifest that the productions of manufactures are by so much the cheaper and better as the manufacture is larger, and the amount of capital employed more considerable, wealthy and educated men come forward to embark in manufactures, which were heretofore abandoned to poor or ignorant handicraftsmen. The magnitude of the efforts required, and the importance of the results to be obtained, attract them. Thus, at the very time at which the science of manufactures lowers the class of workmen, it raises the class of masters.

While the workman concentrates his faculties more and more upon the study of a single detail, the master surveys an extensive whole, and the mind of the latter is enlarged in proportion as that of the former is narrowed. In a short time, the one will require nothing but physical strength without intelligence; the other stands in need of science, and almost of genius, to insure success. This man resembles more and more the administrator of a vast empire—that man, a brute.

The master and the workman have then here no similarity, and their differences increase every day. They are only connected as the two rings at the extremities of a long chain. Each of them fills the station which is made for him and which he does not leave; the one is continually, closely, and necessarily dependent upon the other and seems as much born to obey as that other is to command. What is this but aristocracy?

As the conditions of men constituting the nation become more and more equal, the demand for manufactured commodities becomes more general and extensive; and the cheapness which places these objects within the reach of slender fortunes becomes a great element of success. Hence, there are every day more men of great opulence and education who devote their wealth and knowledge to manufactures and who seek, by opening large establishments, and by a strict division of labor, to meet the fresh demands which are made on all sides. Thus, in proportion as the mass of the nation turns to democracy, that particular class which is engaged in manufactures becomes more aristocratic. Men grow more alike in the one, more different in the other; and inequality increases in the less numerous class in the same ratio in which it decreases in the community. Hence it would appear, on searching to the bottom, that aristocracy should naturally spring out of the bosom of democracy.

But this kind of aristocracy by no means resembles those kinds which preceded it. It will be observed at once that, as it applies exclusively to manufactures and to some manufacturing callings, it is a monstrous exception in the general aspect of society. The small aristocratic societies which are formed by some manufacturers in the midst of the immense democracy of our age contain, like the great aristocratic societies of former ages, some men who are very opulent and a multitude who are wretchedly poor. The poor have few means of escaping from their condition and becoming rich; but the rich are constantly becoming poor, or they give up business when they have realized a fortune. Thus the elements of which the class of the poor is composed are fixed; but the elements of which the class of the rich is composed are not so. To say the truth, though there are rich men, the class of rich men does not exist; for these rich individuals have no feelings or purposes in common, no mutual traditions or mutual hopes; there are individuals, therefore, but no definite class.

Not only are the rich not compactly united amongst themselves but there is no real bond between them and the poor. Their relative position is not a permanent one; they are constantly drawn together or separated by their interests. The workman is generally dependent on the master, but not on any particular master. These two men meet in the factory but know not each other elsewhere; and, whilst they come into contact on one point, they stand very wide apart on all others. The manufacturer asks nothing of the workman but his labor; the workman expects nothing from him but his wages.[9] The one contracts no obligation to protect, nor the other to defend; and they are not permanently connected either by habit or duty. The aristocracy created by business rarely settles in the midst of the manufacturing population which it directs; the object is not to govern that population but to use it. An aristocracy thus constituted can have no great hold upon those whom it employs; and, even if it succeed in retaining them at one moment, they escape the next. It knows not how to will, and it cannot act.

The territorial aristocracy of former ages was either bound by law or thought itself bound by usage to come to the relief of its servingmen and to succor their distresses. But the manufacturing aristocracy of our age first impoverishes and debases the men who serve it and then abandons them to be supported by the

9. Here is an interesting anticipation of the passage in the *Communist Manifesto* eight years later where the phrase, "no other nexus between man and man than naked self-interest, than callous 'cash-payment,'" expresses the same essential idea.

charity of the public. This is a natural consequence of what has been said before. Between the workman and the master there are frequent relations but no real association.

I am of opinion, upon the whole, that the manufacturing aristocracy which is growing up under our eyes is one of the harshest which ever existed in the world;

but, at the same time, it is one of the most confined and least dangerous. Nevertheless, the friends of democracy should keep their eyes anxiously fixed in this direction; for if ever a permanent inequality of conditions and aristocracy again penetrate into the world, it may be predicted that this is the gate by which they will enter. . . .

THIRD BOOK

INFLUENCE OF DEMOCRACY ON MANNERS PROPERLY SO CALLED

CHAPTER XXII

WHY DEMOCRATIC NATIONS ARE NATURALLY DESIROUS OF PEACE, AND DEMOCRATIC ARMIES OF WAR

. . . The equality of conditions and the manners as well as the institutions resulting from it do not exempt a democratic people from the necessity of standing armies, and their armies always exercise a powerful influence over their fate. It is therefore of singular importance to inquire what are the natural propensities of the men of whom these armies are composed.

Amongst aristocratic nations, especially amongst those in which birth is the only source of rank, the same inequality exists in the army as in the nation; the officer is noble, the soldier is a serf; the one is naturally called upon to command, the other to obey. In aristocratic armies the private soldier's ambition is therefore circumscribed within very narrow limits. Nor has the ambition of the officer an unlimited range. An aristocratic body not only forms a part of the scale of ranks in the nation but it contains a scale of ranks within itself; the members of whom it is composed are placed one above another, in a particular and unvarying manner. Thus, one man is born to the command of a regiment, another to that of a company; when once they have reached the utmost object of their hopes, they stop of their own accord and remain contented with their lot.

There is, besides, a strong cause which, in aristocracies, weakens the of-

ficer's desire of promotion. Amongst aristocratic nations, an officer, independently of his rank in the army, also occupies an elevated rank in society; the former is almost always, in his eyes, only an appendage to the latter. A nobleman who embraces the profession of arms follows it less from motives of ambition than from a sense of the duties imposed on him by his birth. He enters the army in order to find an honorable employment for the idle years of his youth and to be able to bring back to his home and his peers some honorable recollections of military life; but his principal object is not to obtain by that profession either property, distinction, or power, for he possesses these advantages in his own right and enjoys them without leaving his home.

In democratic armies all the soldiers may become officers, which makes the desire of promotion general and immeasurably extends the bounds of military ambition. The officer, on his part, sees nothing which naturally and necessarily stops him at one grade more than at another; and each grade has immense importance in his eyes, because his rank in society almost always depends on his rank in the army. Amongst democratic nations it often happens that an officer has no property but his pay and no distinction but that of military honors; consequently, as often as his duties change, his fortune changes, and he becomes, as it were, a new man. What was only an appendage to his position in aristocratic armies has thus become the main point, the basis of his whole condition.

Under the old French monarchy, officers were always called by their titles of nobility; they are now always called by the title of their military rank. This little change in the forms of language suffices to show that a great revolution has taken place in the constitution of society and in that of the army.

In democratic armies the desire of advancement is almost universal; it is ardent, tenacious, perpetual; it is strengthened by all other desires and only extinguished with life itself. But it is easy to see that, of all armies in the world, those in which advancement must be slowest in time of peace are the armies of democratic countries. As the number of commissions is naturally limited, whilst the number of competitors is almost unlimited, and as the strict law of equality is over all alike, none can make rapid progress—many can make no progress at all. Thus, the desire of advancement is greater, and the opportunities of advancement fewer, there than elsewhere. All the ambitious spirits of a democratic army were consequently ardently desirous of war, because war makes vacancies and warrants the violation of that law of seniority which is the sole privilege natural to democracy.

We thus arrive at this singular consequence that, of all armies, those most ardently desirous of war are democratic armies, and, of all nations, those most fond of peace are democratic nations; and what makes these facts still more extraordinary is that these contrary effects are produced at the same time by the principle of equality.

All the members of the community, being alike, constantly harbor the wish and discover the possibility of changing their condition and improving their welfare; this makes them fond of peace, which is favorable to industry, and allows every man to pursue his own little undertakings to their completion.

On the other hand, this same equality makes soldiers dream of fields of battle, by increasing the value of military honors in the eyes of those who follow the profession of arms, and by rendering those honors accessible to all. In either case, the inquietude of the heart is the same, the taste for enjoyment as insatiable, the ambition of success as great—the means of gratifying it alone are different.

These opposite tendencies of the nation and the army expose democratic communities to great dangers. When a military spirit forsakes a people, the profession of arms immediately ceases to be held in honor, and military men fall to the lowest rank of the public servants; they are little esteemed and no longer understood. The reverse of what takes place in aristocratic ages then occurs; the men who enter the army are no longer those of the highest but of the lowest rank. Military ambition is only indulged when no other is possible. Hence arises a circle of cause and consequence from which it is difficult to escape; the best part of the nation shuns the military profession because that profession is not honored, and the profession is not honored because the best part of the nation has ceased to follow it.

It is then no matter of surprise that democratic armies are often restless, ill-tempered, and dissatisfied with their lot, although their physical condition is commonly far better, and their discipline less strict, than in other countries. The soldier feels that he occupies an inferior position, and his wounded pride either stimulates his taste for hostilities which would render his services necessary or gives him a desire for revolution, during which he may hope to win by force of arms the political influence and personal importance now denied him.

The composition of democratic armies makes this last-mentioned danger much to be feared. In democratic communities almost every man has some property to preserve; but democratic armies are generally led by men without property, most of whom have little to lose in civil broils. The bulk of the nation is naturally much more afraid of revolutions than in the ages of aristocracy, but the leaders of the army much less so.

Moreover, as amongst democratic nations (to repeat what I have just remarked), the wealthiest, best educated, and ablest men seldom adopt the military profession, the army, taken collectively, eventually forms a small nation by itself, where the mind is less enlarged, and habits are more rude, than in the nation at large. Now, this small uncivilized nation has arms in its possession and alone knows how to use them; for, indeed, the pacific temper of the community increases the danger to which a democratic people is exposed from the military and turbulent spirit of the army. Nothing is so dangerous as an army amidst an unwarlike nation; the excessive love of the whole community for quiet continually puts the constitution at the mercy of the soldiery.

It may therefore be asserted, generally speaking, that, if democratic nations are naturally prone to peace from their interests and their propensities, they are constantly drawn to war and revolutions by their armies. Military revolutions, which are scarcely ever to be apprehended in aristocracies, are always to be dreaded amongst democratic nations. These perils must be reckoned amongst the most formidable which beset their future fate, and the attention of statesmen should be sedulously applied to find a remedy for the evil. . . .

No protracted war can fail to endanger the freedom of a democratic country. Not indeed that, after every victory, it is to be apprehended that the victorious generals will possess themselves by force of the supreme power after the manner of Sylla and Caesar; the danger is of another kind. War does not always give over democratic communities to military government, but it must invariably and immeasurably increase the powers of civil government; it must almost compulsorily concentrate the direction of all men and the management of all things in the hands of the administration. If it lead not to despotism by sudden violence, it prepares men for it more gently by their habits. All those who seek to destroy the liberties of a democratic nation ought to know that war is the surest and the shortest means to accomplish it. This is the first axiom of the science. . . .

I am of opinion that a restless and turbulent spirit is an evil inherent in the very constitution of democratic armies and beyond hope of cure. The legislators of democracies must not expect to devise any military organization capable by its influence of calming and restraining the military profession; their efforts would exhaust their powers before the object could be attained.

The remedy for the vices of the army is not to be found in the army itself but in the country. Democratic nations are naturally afraid of disturbance and of despotism; the object is to turn these natural instincts into intelligent, deliberate, and lasting tastes. When men have at last learned to make a peaceful and profitable use of freedom and have felt its blessings—when they have conceived a manly love of order and have freely submitted themselves to discipline—these same men, if they follow the profession of arms, bring into it, unconsciously and almost against their will, these same habits and manners. The general spirit of the nation, being infused into the spirit peculiar to the army, tempers the opinions and desires engendered by military life or represses them by the mighty force of public opinion. Teach but the citizens to be educated, orderly, firm, and free, and the soldiers will be disciplined and obedient.

Any law which, in repressing the turbulent spirit of the army, should tend to diminish the spirit of freedom in the nation, and to overshadow the notion of law and right, would defeat its object; it would do much more to favor than to defeat the establishment of military tyranny.

After all, and in spite of all precautions, a large army amidst a democratic people will always be a source of great danger; the most effectual means of diminishing that danger would be to reduce the army, but this is a remedy which all nations are not able to apply.

Chapter XXIII

WHICH IS THE MOST WARLIKE AND MOST REVOLUTIONARY CLASS IN DEMOCRATIC ARMIES

It is of the essence of a democratic army to be very numerous in proportion to the people to which it belongs, as I shall hereafter show. On the other hand, men living in democratic times seldom choose a military life. Democratic nations are therefore soon led to give up the system of voluntary recruiting for that of compulsory enlistment. The necessity of their social condition compels them to resort to the latter means, and it may easily be foreseen that they will all eventually adopt it.

When military service is compulsory, the burden is indiscriminately and equally borne by the whole community. This is another necessary consequence of the social condition of these nations and of their notions. The government may do almost whatever it pleases, provided it appeals to the whole community at once; it is the unequal distribution of the weight, not the weight itself, which commonly occasions resistance. But, as military service is common to all the citizens, the evident consequence is that each of them remains but for a few years on active duty. Thus it is in the nature of things that the soldier in democracies only passes through the army, whilst, among most aristocratic nations, the military profession is one which the soldier adopts, or which is imposed upon him, for life.

This has important consequences.

Amongst the soldiers of a democratic army, some acquire a taste for military life; but the majority, being enlisted against their will, and ever ready to go back to their homes, do not consider themselves as seriously engaged in the military profession and are always thinking of quitting it. Such men do not contract the wants, and only half partake in the passions, which that mode of life engenders. They adapt themselves to their military duties, but their minds are still attached to the interests and the duties which engaged them in civil life. They do not therefore imbibe the spirit of the army, or, rather, they infuse the spirit of the community at large into the army and retain it there. Amongst democratic nations, the private soldiers remain most like civilians; upon them the habits of the nation have the firmest hold and public opinion has most influence. It is through the private soldiers, especially, that it may be possible to infuse into a democratic army the love of freedom and the respect for rights, if these principles have once been successfully inculcated on the people at large. The reverse happens amongst aristocratic nations, where the soldiery have eventually nothing in common with their fellow-citizens, and where they live amongst them as strangers and often as enemies.

In aristocratic armies the officers are the conservative element, because the officers alone have retained a strict connection with civil society and never forgo their purpose of resuming their place in it sooner or later; in democratic armies, the private soldiers stand in this position, and from the same cause....

Chapter XXV

OF DISCIPLINE IN DEMOCRATIC ARMIES

It is a very common opinion, especially in aristocratic countries, that the great social equality which prevails in democracies ultimately renders the private soldier independent of the officer and thus destroys the bond of discipline.

This is a mistake, for there are two kinds of discipline, which it is important not to confound.

When the officer is noble and the soldier a serf—one rich, the other poor—the one educated and strong, the other ignorant and weak—the strictest bond of obedience may easily be established between the two men. The soldier is broken in to military discipline, as it were, before he enters the army; or, rather, military discipline is nothing but an enhancement of social servitude. In aristocratic armies the soldier will soon become insensible to everything but the orders of his superior officers; he acts without reflection, triumphs without enthusiasm, and dies without complaint. In this state he is no longer a man, but he is still a formidable animal trained for war.

A democratic people must despair of ever obtaining from soldiers that blind, minute, submissive, and invariable obedience which an aristocratic people may impose on them without difficulty. The state of society does not prepare them for it, and the nation might be in danger of losing its natural advantages if it sought artificially to acquire advantages of this particular kind. Amongst democratic communities military discipline ought not to attempt to annihilate the free action of the faculties; all that can be done by discipline is to direct it; the obedience thus inculcated is less exact, but it is more eager and more intelligent. It has its root in the will of him who obeys; it rests not only on his instinct but on his reason, and, consequently, it will often spontaneously become more strict as danger requires. The discipline of an aristocratic army is apt to be relaxed in war, because that discipline is founded upon habits, and war disturbs those habits. The discipline of a democratic army, on the contrary, is strengthened in sight of the enemy, because every soldier then clearly perceives that he must be silent and obedient in order to conquer.

The nations which have performed the greatest warlike achievements knew no other discipline than that which I speak of. Amongst the ancients none were admitted into the armies but freemen and citizens, who differed but little from one another, and were accustomed to treat each other as equals. In this respect, it may be said that the armies of antiquity were democratic, although they came out of the bosom of aristocracy; the consequence was that in those armies a sort of fraternal familiarity prevailed between the officers and the men. Plutarch's lives of great commanders furnish convincing instances of the fact. The soldiers were in the constant habit of freely addressing their general, and the general listened to and answered whatever the soldiers had to say; they were kept in order by language and by example far more than by constraint or punishment; the general was as much their companion as their chief. I know not whether the soldiers of Greece and Rome ever carried the minutiae of military discipline to the same degree of perfection as the Russians have done; but this did not prevent Alexander from conquering Asia—and Rome, the world.

Chapter XXVI

SOME CONSIDERATIONS ON WAR IN DEMOCRATIC COMMUNITIES

When the principle of equality is spreading, not only amongst a single nation, but amongst several neighboring nations at the same time, as is now the case in Europe, the inhabitants of these different countries, notwithstanding the dissimilarity of language, of customs, and of laws, still resemble each other in their equal dread of war and their common love of peace. It is in vain that ambition or anger puts arms in the hands of princes; they are appeased in spite of themselves by a species of general apathy and good will, which makes the sword drop from their grasp, and wars become more rare.

As the spread of equality, taking place in several countries at once, simultaneously impels their various inhabitants to follow manufactures and commerce, not only do their tastes become similar, but their interests are so mixed and entangled with one another that no nation can inflict evils on other nations without those evils falling back upon itself; and all nations ultimately regard war as a calamity almost as severe to the conqueror as to the conquered.

Thus, on the one hand, it is extremely difficult in democratic times to draw nations into hostilities; but, on the other, it is almost impossible that any two of them should go to war without embroiling the rest. The interests of all are so interlaced, their opinions and their wants so much alike, that none can remain quiet when the others stir. Wars therefore become more rare, but, when they break out, they spread over a larger field. . . .

FOURTH BOOK
INFLUENCE OF DEMOCRATIC IDEAS AND FEELINGS ON POLITICAL SOCIETY

CHAPTER II
THAT THE OPINIONS OF DEMOCRATIC NATIONS ABOUT GOVERNMENT ARE NATURALLY FAVORABLE TO THE CONCENTRATION OF POWER

The notion of secondary powers, placed between the sovereign and his subjects, occurred naturally to the imagination of aristocratic nations, because those communities contained individuals or families raised above the common level and apparently destined to command by their birth, their education, and their wealth. This same notion is naturally wanting in the minds of men in democratic ages, for converse reasons: it can only be introduced artificially, it can only be kept there with difficulty; whereas they conceive, as it were without thinking upon the subject, the notion of a single and central power, which governs the whole community by its direct influence. Moreover, in politics as well as in philosophy and in religion, the intellect of democratic nations is peculiarly open to simple and general notions. Complicated systems are repugnant to it, and its favorite conception is that of a great nation composed of citizens all formed upon one pattern and all governed by a single power.

The very next notion to that of a single and central power which presents itself to the minds of men in the ages of equality is the notion of uniformity of legislation. As every man sees that he differs but little from those about him, he cannot understand why a rule which is applicable to one man should not be equally applicable to all others. Hence the slightest privileges are repugnant to his reason; the faintest dissimilarities in the political institutions of the same people offend him, and uniformity of legislation appears to him to be the first condition of good government.

I find, on the contrary, that this notion of a uniform rule, equally binding on all the members of the community, was almost unknown to the human mind in aristocratic ages; it was either never broached, or it was rejected.

These contrary tendencies of opinion ultimately turn on both sides to such blind instincts and ungovernable habits that they still direct the actions of men, in spite of particular exceptions. Notwithstanding the immense variety of conditions in the Middle Ages, a certain number of persons existed at that period in precisely similar circumstances; but this did not prevent the laws then in force from assigning to each of them distinct duties and different rights. On the contrary, at the present time, all the powers of government are exerted to impose the same customs and the same laws on populations which have as yet but few points of resemblance.

As the conditions of men become equal amongst a people, individuals seem of less, and society of greater, importance; or, rather, every citizen, being assimilated to all the rest, is lost in the crowd, and nothing stands conspicuous but the great and imposing image of the people at large. This naturally gives the men of democratic periods a lofty opinion of the privileges of society and a very humble notion of the rights of individuals; they are ready to admit that the interests of the former are everything, and those of the latter nothing. They are willing to acknowledge that the power which represents the community has far more information and wisdom than any of the members of that community; and that it is the duty, as well as the right, of that power to guide as well as govern each private citizen.

If we closely scrutinize our contemporaries and penetrate to the root of their political opinions, we shall detect some of the notions which I have just pointed out, and we shall perhaps be surprised to find so much accordance between men who are so often at variance.

The Americans hold that, in every state, the supreme power ought to emanate from the people; but, when once that power is constituted, they can conceive, as it were, no limits to it, and they are ready to admit that it has the right to do whatever it pleases. They have not the slightest notion of peculiar privileges granted to cities, families, or persons; their minds appear never to have foreseen that it might be possible not to apply with strict uniformity the same laws to every part of the state and to all its inhabitants.

These same opinions are more and more diffused in Europe; they even insinuate themselves amongst those nations which most vehemently reject the principle of the sovereignty of the people. Such nations assign a different origin to the supreme power, but they ascribe to that power the same characteristics. Amongst them all, the idea of intermediate powers is weakened and obliterated; the idea of rights inherent in certain individuals is rapidly disappearing from the minds of men; the idea of the omnipotence and sole authority of society at large rises to fill its place. These ideas take root and spread in proportion as social conditions become more equal and men more alike; they are produced by equality, and in turn they hasten the progress of equality....

CHAPTER III

THAT THE SENTIMENTS OF DEMOCRATIC NATIONS ACCORD WITH THEIR OPINIONS IN LEADING THEM TO CONCENTRATE POLITICAL POWER

If it be true that, in ages of equality, men readily adopt the notion of a great central power, it cannot be doubted, on the other hand, that their habits and sentiments predispose them to recognize such a power and to give it their support. This may be demonstrated in a few words, as the greater part of the reasons to which the fact may be attributed have been previously stated.

As the men who inhabit democratic countries have no superiors, no inferiors, and no habitual or necessary partners in their undertakings, they readily fall back upon themselves and consider themselves as beings apart. I had occasion to point this out at considerable length in treating of individualism. Hence such men can never, without an effort, tear themselves from their private affairs to engage in public business; their natural bias leads them to abandon the latter to the sole visible and permanent representative of the interests of the community, that is to say, to the state. Not only are they naturally wanting in a taste for public business, but they have frequently no time to attend to it. Private life in democratic times is so busy, so excited, so full of wishes and of work, that hardly any energy or leisure remains to each individual for public life. I am the last man to contend that these propensities are unconquerable, since my chief object in writing this book has been to combat them. I only maintain that, at the present day, a secret power is fostering them in the human heart and that, if they are not checked, they will wholly overgrow it.

I have also had occasion to show how the increasing love of well-being and the fluctuating character of property cause democratic nations to dread all violent disturbances. The love of public tranquillity is frequently the only passion which these nations retain, and it becomes more active and powerful amongst them in proportion as all other passions droop and die. This naturally disposes the members of the community constantly to give or to surrender additional rights to the central power, which alone seems to be interested in defending them by the same means that it uses to defend itself.

As, in periods of equality, no man is compelled to lend his assistance to his fellow-men, and none has any right to expect much support from them, everyone is at once independent and powerless. These two conditions, which must never be either separately considered or confounded together, inspire the citizen of a democratic country with very contrary propensities. His independence fills him with self-reliance and pride amongst his equals; his debility makes him feel from time to time the want of some outward assistance which he cannot expect from any of them, because they are all impotent and unsympathizing. In this predicament he naturally turns his eyes to that imposing power which alone rises above the level of universal depression. Of that power his wants and especially his desires continually remind him, until he ultimately views it as the sole and necessary support of his own weakness.

This may more completely explain what frequently takes place in democratic countries, where the very men who are so impatient of superiors patiently submit to a master, exhibiting at once their pride and their servility.

The hatred which men bear to privilege increases in proportion as privileges become fewer and less considerable, so that democratic passions would seem to burn most fiercely just when they have least fuel. I have already given the reason of this phenomenon. When all conditions are unequal, no inequality is so great as to offend the eye; whereas the slightest dissimilarity is odious in the midst of general uniformity: the more complete this uniformity is, the more insupportable does the sight of such a difference become. Hence it is natural that the love of equality should constantly increase together with equality itself and that it should grow by what it feeds on.

This never dying, ever kindling hatred, which sets a democratic people against the smallest privileges, is peculiarly favorable to the gradual concentration of all political rights in the hands of the representative of the state alone. The sovereign, being necessarily and incontestably above all the citizens, excites not their envy, and each of them thinks that he strips his equals of the prerogative which he concedes to the crown. The man of a democratic age is extremely reluctant to obey his neighbor who is his equal; he refuses to acknowledge superior ability in such a person; he mistrusts his justice and is jealous of his power; he fears and he contemns him; and he loves continually to remind him of the common dependence in which both of them stand to the same master.

Every central power, which follows its natural tendencies, courts and encourages the principle of equality; for equality singularly facilitates, extends, and secures the influence of a central power.

In like manner it may be said that every central government worships uniformity. Uniformity relieves it from inquiry into an infinity of details, which must be attended to if rules have to be adapted to different men, instead of indiscriminately subjecting all men to the same rule; thus the government likes what the citizens like and naturally hates what they hate. These common sentiments, which, in democratic nations, constantly unite the sovereign and every member of the community in one and the same conviction, establish a secret and lasting sympathy between them. The faults of the government are pardoned for the sake of its tastes; public confidence is only reluctantly withdrawn in the midst even of its excesses and its errors; and it is restored at the first call. Democratic nations often hate those in whose hands the central power is vested, but they always love that power itself.

Thus, by two separate paths, I have reached the same conclusion. I have shown that the principle of equality suggests to men the notion of a sole, uniform, and strong government. I have now shown that the principle of equality imparts to them a taste for it. To governments of this kind the nations of our age are therefore tending. They are drawn thither by the natural inclination of mind and heart; and, in order to reach that result, it is enough that they do not check themselves in their course.

I am of opinion that, in the democratic ages which are opening upon us, individual independence and local liberties will ever be the products of art; that centralization will be the natural government.

Chapter V

THAT AMONGST THE EUROPEAN NATIONS OF OUR TIME THE SOVEREIGN POWER IS INCREASING, ALTHOUGH THE SOVEREIGNS ARE LESS STABLE

... There exists amongst the modern nations of Europe one great cause, independent of all those which have already been pointed out, which perpetually contributes to extend the agency or to strengthen the prerogative of the supreme power, though it has not been sufficiently attended to. I mean the growth of manufactures, which is fostered by the progress of social equality. Manufacturers generally collect a multitude of men on the same spot, amongst whom new and complex relations spring up. These men are exposed by their calling to great and sudden alternations of plenty and want, during which public tranquility is endangered. It may also happen that these employments sacrifice the health, and even the life, of those who gain by them or of those who live by them. Thus, the manufacturing classes require more regulation, superintendence, and restraint than the other classes of society, and it is natural that the powers of government should increase in the same proportion as those classes. ...

As a nation becomes more engaged in manufactures, the want of roads, canals, harbors, and other works of a semipublic nature which facilitate the acquisition of wealth is more strongly felt; and, as a nation becomes more democratic, private individuals are less able, and the state more able, to execute works of such magnitude. I do not hesitate to assert that the manifest tendency of all governments at the present time is to take upon themselves alone the execution of these undertakings, by which means they daily hold in closer dependence the population which they govern.

On the other hand, in proportion as the power of a state increases, and its necessities are augmented, the state consumption of manufactured produce is always growing larger; and these commodities are generally made in the arsenals or establishments of the government. Thus, in every kingdom, the ruler becomes the principal manufacturer; he collects and retains in his service a vast number of engineers, architects, mechanics, and handicraftsmen.

Not only is he the principal manufacturer, but he tends more and more to become the chief, or, rather, the master, of all other manufacturers. As private persons become powerless by becoming more equal, they can effect nothing in manufactures without combination; but the government naturally seeks to place these combinations under its own control.

It must be admitted that these collective beings, which are called companies, are stronger and more formidable than a private individual can ever be and that they have less of the responsibility of their own actions; whence it seems reasonable that they should not be allowed to retain so great an independence of the supreme government as might be conceded to a private individual. . . .

Amongst all European nations there are some kinds of associations or companies which cannot be formed until the state has examined their by-laws and authorized their existence. In several others, attempts are made to extend this rule to all associations; the consequences of such a policy, if it were successful, may easily be foreseen.

If once the sovereign had a general right of authorizing associations of all kinds upon certain conditions, he would not be long without claiming the right of superintending and managing them, in order to prevent them from departing from the rules laid down by himself. In this manner, the state, after having reduced all who are desirous of forming associations into dependence, would proceed to reduce into the same condition all who belong to associations already formed—that is to say, almost all the men who are now in existence.

Governments thus appropriate to themselves and convert to their own purposes the greater part of this new power which manufacturing interests have in our time brought into the world. Manufactures govern us; they govern manufactures.

I attach so much importance to all that I have just been saying that I am tormented by the fear of having impaired my meaning in seeking to render it more clear. If the reader thinks that the examples I have adduced to support my observations are insufficient or ill chosen—if he imagines that I have anywhere exaggerated the encroachments of the supreme power and, on the other hand, that I have underrated the extent of the sphere which still remains open to the exertions of individual independence—I entreat him to lay down the book for a moment and to turn his mind to reflect upon the subjects I have attempted to explain. Let him attentively examine what is taking place in France and in other countries, let him inquire of those about him, let him search himself, and I am much mistaken if he does not arrive, without my guidance, and by other paths, at the point to which I have sought to lead him.

He will perceive that, for the last half-century, centralization has everywhere been growing up in a thousand different ways. Wars, revolutions, conquests, have served to promote it; all men have labored to increase it. In the course of the same period, during which men have succeeded each other with singular rapidity at the head of affairs, their notions, interests, and passions have been infinitely diversified; but all have, by some means or other, sought to centralize. This instinctive centralization has been the only settled point amidst the extreme mutability of their lives and their thoughts.

If the reader, after having investigated

these details of human affairs, will seek to survey the wide prospect as a whole, he will be struck by the result. On the one hand, the most settled dynasties shaken or overthrown, the people everywhere escaping by violence from the sway of their laws—abolishing or limiting the authority of their rulers or their princes; the nations which are not in open revolution restless at least and excited—all of them animated by the same spirit of revolt: and, on the other hand, at this very period of anarchy, and amongst these untractable nations, the incessant increase of the prerogative of the supreme government, becoming more centralized, more adventurous, more absolute, more extensive—the people perpetually falling under the control of the public administration—led insensibly to surrender to it some further portion of their individual independence, till the very men who from time to time upset a throne and trample on a race of kings bend more and more obsequiously to the slightest dictate of a clerk. Thus, two contrary revolutions appear, in our days, to be going on; the one continually weakening the supreme power, the other as continually strengthening it. At no other period in our history has it appeared so weak or so strong. . . .

CHAPTER VI

WHAT SORT OF DESPOTISM DEMOCRATIC NATIONS HAVE TO FEAR

. . . Democratic governments may become violent, and even cruel, at certain periods of extreme effervescence or of great danger; but these crises will be rare and brief. When I consider the petty passions of our contemporaries, the mildness of their manners, the extent of their education, the purity of their religion, the gentleness of their morality, their regular and industrious habits, and the restraint which they almost all observe in their vices no less than in their virtues, I have no fear that they will meet with tyrants in their rulers but rather with guardians.

I think, then, that the species of oppression by which democratic nations are menaced is unlike anything which ever before existed in the world; our contemporaries will find no prototype of it in their memories. I seek in vain for an expression which will accurately convey the whole of the idea I have formed of it; the old words "despotism" and "tyranny" are inappropriate. The thing itself is new, and, since I cannot name, I must attempt to define it.

I seek to trace the novel features under which despotism may appear in the world. The first thing that strikes the observation is an innumerable multitude of men, all equal and alike, incessantly endeavoring to procure the petty and paltry pleasures with which they glut their lives. Each of them, living apart, is as a stranger to the fate of all the rest—his children and his private friends constitute to him the whole of mankind; as for the rest of his fellow-citizens, he is close to them, but he sees them not—he touches them, but he feels them not; he exists but in himself and for himself alone; and if his kindred still remain to him, he may be said, at any rate, to have lost his country.

Above this race of men stands an immense and tutelary power which takes upon itself alone to secure their gratifications and to watch over their fate. That power is absolute, minute, regular, provident, and mild. It would be like the authority of a parent, if, like that authority, its object was to prepare men for manhood; but it seeks, on the contrary, to keep them in perpetual childhood; it is well content that the people should rejoice, provided they think of nothing but rejoicing. For their happiness such a government willingly labors, but it chooses to be the sole agent and the only arbiter of that happiness; it provides for their security, foresees and supplies their necessities, facilitates their pleasures, manages their principal concerns, directs their industry, regulates the descent of property, and subdivides their inheritances: what remains but to spare them all the care of thinking and all the trouble of living?

Thus, it every day renders the exercise of the free agency of man less useful and less frequent; it circumscribes the will within a narrower range and gradually robs a man of all the uses of himself. The principle of equality has prepared men for these things; it has predisposed men to endure them, and oftentimes to look on them as benefits.

After having thus successively taken each member of the community in its powerful grasp, and fashioned him at will, the supreme power then extends its arm over the whole community. It covers the surface of society with a network of small complicated rules, minute and uniform, through which the most original minds and the most energetic characters cannot penetrate to rise above the crowd. The will of man is not shattered but softened, bent, and guided; men are seldom forced by it to act, but they are constantly restrained from acting. Such a power does not destroy, but it prevents existence; it does not tyrannize, but it compresses, enervates, extinguishes, and stupefies a people, till each nation is reduced to be nothing better than a flock of timid and industrious animals, of which the government is the shepherd.

I have always thought that servitude of the regular, quiet, and gentle kind which I have just described might be combined more easily than is commonly believed with some of the outward forms of freedom and that it might even establish itself under the wing of the sovereignty of the people. . . .

Chapter VII

CONTINUATION OF THE PRECEDING CHAPTERS

I believe that it is easier to establish an absolute and despotic government amongst a people in which the conditions of society are equal than amongst any other; and I think that, if such a government were once established amongst such a people, it would not only oppress men but would eventually strip each of them of several of the highest qualities of humanity. Despotism, therefore, appears to me peculiarly to be dreaded in democratic times. I should have loved freedom, I believe, at all times, but in the time in which we live I am ready to worship it.

On the other hand, I am persuaded that all who shall attempt, in the ages upon which we are entering, to base freedom upon aristocratic privilege will fail; that all who shall attempt to draw and to retain authority within a single class will fail. At the present day, no ruler is skilful or strong enough to found a despotism by re-establishing permanent distinctions of rank amongst his subjects; no legislator is wise or powerful enough to preserve free institutions if he does not take equality for his first principle and his watchword. All of our contemporaries who would establish or secure the independence and the dignity of their fellow-men must show themselves the friends of equality, and the only worthy means of showing themselves as such is to be so; upon this depends the success of their holy enterprise. Thus, the question is not how to reconstruct aristocratic society but how to make liberty proceed out of that democratic state of society in which God has placed us.

These two truths appear to me simple, clear, and fertile in consequences; and they naturally lead me to consider what kind of free government can be established amongst a people in which social conditions are equal.

It results, from the very constitution of democratic nations and from their necessities, that the power of government amongst them must be more uniform, more centralized, more extensive, more searching, and more efficient than in other countries. Society at large is naturally stronger and more active, the individual more subordinate and weak; the former does more, the latter less; and this is inevitably the case.

It is not, therefore, to be expected that the range of private independence will ever be as extensive in democratic as in aristocratic countries; nor is this to be desired; for, amongst aristocratic nations, the mass is often sacrificed to the individual and the prosperity of the greater number to the greatness of the few. It is both necessary and desirable that the government of a democratic people should be active and powerful; and our object should not be to render it weak or indolent but solely to prevent it from abusing its aptitude and its strength.

The circumstance which most contributed to secure the independence of private persons in aristocratic ages was that the supreme power did not affect to take upon itself alone the government and administration of the community; those functions were necessarily partially left to the members of the aristocracy: so that, as the supreme power was always divided, it never weighed with its whole weight and in the same manner on each individual.

Not only did the government not perform everything by its immediate agency but, as most of the agents who discharged its duties derived their power, not from the state, but from the circumstance of their birth, they were not perpetually under its control. The government could not make or unmake them in an instant, at pleasure, or bend them in strict uniformity to its slightest caprice—this was an additional guaranty of private independence.

I readily admit that recourse cannot be had to the same means at the present time; but I discover certain democratic expedients which may be substituted for them. Instead of vesting in the government alone all the administrative powers of which corporations and nobles have been deprived, a portion of them may be intrusted to secondary public bodies temporarily composed of private citizens; thus the liberty of private persons will be more secure, and their equality will not be diminished. . . .

Aristocratic countries abound in wealthy and influential persons who are competent to provide for themselves and who cannot be easily or secretly oppressed; such persons restrain a government within general habits of moderation and reserve. I am well aware that democratic countries contain no such persons naturally; but something analogous to them may be created by artificial means. I firmly believe that an aristocracy cannot again be founded in the world; but I think that private citizens, by combining together, may constitute bodies of great wealth, influence, and strength, corresponding to the persons of an aristocracy. By this means, many of the greatest political advantages of aristocracy would be obtained, without its injustice or its dangers. An association for political, commercial, or manufacturing purposes, or even for those of science and literature, is a powerful and enlightened member of the community which cannot be disposed of at pleasure or oppressed without remonstrance, and which, by defending its own rights against the encroachments of the government, saves the common liberties of the country.

In periods of aristocracy every man is always bound so closely to many of his fellow-citizens that he cannot be assailed without their coming to his assistance. In ages of equality, every man naturally stands alone; he has no hereditary friends whose co-operation he may demand; no class upon whose sympathy he may rely; he is easily got rid of, and he is trampled on with impunity. At the present time, an oppressed member of the community has therefore only one method of self-defense—he may appeal to the whole nation; and, if the whole nation is deaf to his complaint, he may appeal to mankind: the only means he has of making this appeal is by the press. Thus, the liberty of the press is infinitely more valuable amongst democratic nations than amongst all others; it is the only cure for the evils which equality may produce. Equality sets men apart and weakens them; but the press places a powerful weapon within every man's reach, which the weakest and loneliest of them all may use. Equality deprives a man of the support of his connections; but the press enables him to summon all his fellow-countrymen and all his fellow-men to his assistance. Printing has accelerated the progress of equality, and it is also one of its best correctives.

I think that men living in aristocracies may, strictly speaking, do without the liberty of the press; but such is not the case with those who live in democratic countries. To protect their personal independence I trust not to great political assemblies, to parliamentary privilege, or to the assertion of popular sovereignty. All these things may, to a certain extent, be reconciled with personal servitude. But that servitude cannot be complete if the press is free; the press is the chief democratic instrument of freedom.

Something analogous may be said of the judicial power. It is a part of the essence of judicial power to attend to private interests and to fix itself with predilection on minute objects submitted to its observation; another essential quality of judicial power is never to volunteer its assistance to the oppressed but always to be at the disposal of the humblest of those who solicit it; their complaint, however feeble they may themselves be, will force itself upon the ear of justice and claim redress, for this is inherent in the very constitution of courts of justice.

A power of this kind is therefore peculiarly adapted to the wants of freedom at a time when the eye and finger of the government are constantly intruding into the minutest details of human actions and when private persons are at once too weak to protect themselves and too much isolated for them to reckon upon the assistance of their fellows. The strength of the courts of law has ever been the greatest security which can be offered to personal independence; but this is more especially the case in democratic ages; private rights and interests are in constant danger if the judicial power does not grow more extensive and more strong to keep pace with the growing equality of conditions. . . .

I believe that there are such things as justifiable resistance and legitimate rebellion. I do not therefore assert, as an absolute proposition, that the men of democratic ages ought never to make revolutions; but I think that they have especial reason to hesitate before they embark in them and that it is far better to endure many grievances in their present condition than to have recourse to so perilous a remedy.

I shall conclude by one general idea which comprises not only all the particular ideas which have been expressed in the present chapter but also most of those which it is the object of this book to treat of. In the ages of aristocracy which preceded our own, there were private persons of great power and a social authority of extreme weakness. The outline of society itself was not easily discernible and constantly confounded with the different powers by which the community was ruled. The principal efforts of the men of those times were required to strengthen, aggrandize, and secure the supreme power and, on the other hand, to circumscribe individual independence within narrower limits and to subject private interests to the interests of the public. Other perils and other cares await the men of our age. Amongst the greater part of modern nations, the government, whatever may be its origin, its constitution, or its name, has become almost omnipotent, and private persons are falling, more and more, into the lowest stage of weakness and dependence.

In olden society everything was different; unity and uniformity were nowhere to be met with. In modern society everything threatens to become so much alike that the peculiar characteristics of each individual will soon be entirely lost in the general aspect of the world. Our forefathers were ever prone to make an improper use of the notion that private rights ought to be respected; and we are naturally prone, on the other hand, to exaggerate the idea that the interest of a private individual ought always to bend to the interest of the many.

The political world is metamorphosed; new remedies must henceforth be sought for new disorders. To lay down extensive but distinct and settled limits to the action of the government; to confer certain rights on private persons and to secure to them the undisputed enjoyment of those rights; to enable individual man to maintain whatever independence, strength, and original power he still possesses; to raise him by the side of society at large and uphold him in that position—these appear to me the main objects of legislators in the ages upon which we are now entering.

It would seem as if the rulers of our time sought only to use men in order to make things great; I wish that they would try a little more to make great men; that they would set less value on the work and more upon the workman; that they would never forget that a nation cannot long remain strong when every man belonging to it is individually weak and that no form or combination of social polity has yet been devised to make an energetic people out of a community of pusillanimous and enfeebled citizens.

I trace amongst our contemporaries two contrary notions which are equally injurious. One set of men can perceive nothing in the principle of equality but the anarchical tendencies which it engenders: they dread their own free agency; they fear themselves. Other thinkers, less numerous but more enlightened, take a different view: beside that track which starts from the principle of equality to terminate in anarchy, they have at last discovered the road which seems to lead men to inevitable servitude. They shape their souls beforehand to this necessary condition; and, despairing of remaining free, they already do obeisance in their hearts to the master who is soon to appear. The former abandon freedom because they think it dangerous; the latter, because they hold it to be impossible.

If I had entertained the latter conviction, I should not have written this book, but I should have confined myself to deploring in secret the destiny of mankind. I have sought to point out the dangers to which the principle of equality exposes the independence of man, because I firmly believe that these dangers are the most formidable, as well as the least foreseen, of all those which futurity holds in store; but I do not think that they are insurmountable.

The men who live in the democratic ages upon which we are entering have naturally a taste for independence; they are naturally impatient of regulation, and they are wearied by the permanence even of the condition they themselves prefer. They are fond of power; but they are prone to despise and hate those who wield it, and they easily elude its grasp by their own mobility and insignificance.

These propensities will always manifest themselves, because they originate in the groundwork of society, which will undergo no change; for a long time they will prevent the establishment of any despotism, and they will furnish fresh weapons to each succeeding generation which shall struggle in favor of the liberty of mankind. Let us, then, look forward to the future with that salutary fear which makes men keep watch and ward for freedom, not with that faint and idle terror which depresses and enervates the heart.

CHAPTER VIII
GENERAL SURVEY OF THE SUBJECT

... We may naturally believe that it is not the singular prosperity of the few, but the greater well-being of all, which is most pleasing in the sight of the Creator and Preserver of men. What appears to me to be man's decline is, to His eye, advancement; what afflicts me is acceptable to Him. A state of equality is perhaps less elevated, but it is more just; and its justice constitutes its greatness and its beauty. I would strive, then, to raise myself to this point of the Divine contemplation and thence to view and to judge the concerns of men.

No man, upon the earth, can as yet affirm, absolutely and generally, that the new state of the world is better than its former one; but it is already easy to perceive that this state is different. Some vices and some virtues were so inherent in the constitution of an aristocratic nation, and are so opposite to the character of a modern people, that they can never be infused into it; some good tendencies and some bad propensities which were unknown to the former are natural to the latter; some ideas suggest themselves spontaneously to the imagination of the one which are utterly repugnant to the mind of the other. They are like two distinct orders of human beings, each of which has its own merits and defects, its own advantages and its own evils. Care must therefore be taken not to judge the state of society which is now coming into existence by notions derived from a state of society which no longer exists; for, as these states of society are exceedingly different in their structure, they cannot be submitted to a just or fair comparison. It would be scarcely more reasonable to require of our contemporaries the peculiar virtues which originated in the social condition of their forefathers, since that social condition is itself fallen and has drawn into one promiscuous ruin the good and evil which belonged to it.

But as yet these things are imperfectly understood. I find that a great number of my contemporaries undertake to make a selection from amongst the institutions, the opinions, and the ideas which originated in the aristocratic constitution of society as it was; a portion of these elements they would willingly relinquish, but they would keep the remainder and transplant them into their new world. I apprehend that such men are wasting their time and their strength in virtuous but unprofitable efforts. The object is, not to retain the peculiar advantages which the inequality of conditions bestows upon mankind, but to secure the new benefits which equality may supply. We have not to seek to make ourselves like our progenitors but to strive to work out that species of greatness and happiness which is our own.

For myself, who now look back from this extreme limit of my task, and discover from afar, but at once, the various objects which have attracted my more attentive investigation upon my way, I am full of apprehensions and of hopes. I perceive mighty dangers which it is possible to ward off—mighty evils which may be avoided or alleviated; and I cling with a firmer hold to the belief, that, for democratic nations to be virtuous and prosperous, they require but to will it.

I am aware that many of my contemporaries maintain that nations are never their own masters here below and that they necessarily obey some insurmountable and unintelligent power arising from anterior events, from their race, or from the soil and climate of their country. Such principles are false and cowardly; such principles can never produce aught but feeble men and pusillanimous nations. Providence has not created mankind entirely independent or entirely free. It is true that around every man a fatal circle is traced beyond which he cannot pass, but within the wide verge of that circle he is powerful and free; as it is with man, so with communities. The nations of our time cannot prevent the conditions of men from becoming equal; but it depends upon themselves whether the principle of equality is to lead them to servitude or freedom, to knowledge or barbarism, to prosperity or wretchedness.

SECTION B. PROPERTY AND SUFFRAGE

1. DEBATE IN THE NEW YORK CONSTITUTIONAL
CONVENTION, 1821[1]

EDITORS' NOTE.—The removal of property qualifications for voting, which was substantially accomplished by this convention, was a decisive step in the movement toward a greatly expanded suffrage. After 1821 only five states retained property qualifications, and these were removed in the next three decades (Kirk Harold Porter, *A History of Suffrage in the United States* [Chicago, 1918], pp. 54, 59, 110).

CHANCELLOR KENT.[2] I am in favor of the amendment which has been submitted by my honorable colleague from Albany; and I must beg leave to trespass for a few moments upon the patience of the committee while I state the reasons which have induced me to wish that the senate should continue, as heretofore, the representative of the landed interest and exempted from the control of universal suffrage. I hope what I may have to say will be kindly received, for it will be well intended. But, if I thought otherwise, I should still prefer to hazard the loss of the little popularity which I might have in this house, or out of it, than to hazard the loss of the approbation of my own conscience.

I have reflected upon the report of the select committee with attention and with anxiety. We appear to be disregarding the principles of the constitution, under which we have so long and so happily lived, and to be changing some of its essential institutions. I cannot but think that the considerate men who have studied the history of republics, or are read in lessons of experience, must look with concern upon our apparent disposition to vibrate from a well-balanced government to the extremes of the democratic doctrines. Such a broad proposition as that contained in the report, at the distance of ten years past, would have struck the public mind with astonishment and terror. So rapid has been the career of our vibration.

Let us recall our attention, for a moment, to our past history.

This state has existed for forty-four years under our present constitution, which was formed by those illustrious sages and patriots who adorned the Revolution. It has wonderfully fulfilled all the great ends of civil government. Dur-

1. *Reports of the Proceedings and Debates of the Convention of 1821 Assembled for the Purpose of Amending the Constitution of the State of New York* ... (Albany, 1821), pp. 219-22, 178-80.

2. James Kent (1763-1847), son of a lawyer, a graduate in 1781 of Yale, began to practice law in New York in 1785. Appointed to the New York Supreme Court in 1798, Kent began the practice of publishing the decisions of the court, and these decisions are important contributions to American jurisprudence. Because of a provision of the 1821 constitution which required the retirement of judges at the age of sixty, Kent in 1823 retired from the Court. He then for the second time became a professor of law at Columbia College but soon resigned. At this time his son persuaded Kent to prepare the lectures for publication. Kent reluctantly undertook the work, greatly expanded and completely re-wrote them, and between 1826 and 1830 published the four famous volumes, *Commentaries on American Law*. During the remaining seventeen years of his life, Kent prepared five more editions of the work.

ing that long period we have enjoyed, in an eminent degree, the blessings of civil and religious liberty. We have had our lives, our privileges, and our property protected. We have had a succession of wise and temperate legislatures. The code of our statute law has been again and again revised and corrected, and it may proudly bear a comparison with that of any other people. We have had, during that period (though I am, perhaps, not the fittest person to say it), a regular, stable, honest, and enlightened administration of justice. All the peaceable pursuits of industry, and all the important interests of education and science, have been fostered and encouraged. We have trebled our numbers within the last twenty-five years, have displayed mighty resources, and have made unexampled progress in the career of prosperity and greatness.

Our financial credit stands at an enviable height; and we are now successfully engaged in connecting the great lakes with the ocean by stupendous canals, which excite the admiration of our neighbors and will make a conspicuous figure even upon the map of the United States.

These are some of the fruits of our present government; and yet we seem to be dissatisfied with our condition, and we are engaged in the bold and hazardous experiment of remodeling the constitution. Is it not fit and discreet—I speak as to wise men—is it not fit and proper that we should pause in our career and reflect well on the immensity of the innovation in contemplation? Discontent in the midst of so much prosperity, and with such abundant means of happiness, looks like ingratitude and as if we were disposed to arraign the goodness of Providence. Do we not expose ourselves to the danger of being deprived of the blessings we have enjoyed? When the husbandman has gathered in his harvest, and has filled his barns and his granaries with the fruits of

his industry, if he should then become discontented and unthankful, would he not have reason to apprehend that the Lord of the harvest might come in his wrath and with his lightning destroy them?

The senate has hitherto been elected by the farmers of the state—by the free and independent lords of the soil, worth at least $250 in freehold estate, over and above all debts charged thereon. The governor has been chosen by the same electors, and we have hitherto elected citizens of elevated rank and character. Our assembly has been chosen by freeholders, possessing a freehold of the value of $50, or by persons renting a tenement of the yearly value of $5, and who have been rated and actually paid taxes to the state. By the report before us, we propose to annihilate, at one stroke, all those property distinctions and to bow before the idol of universal suffrage. That extreme democratic principle, when applied to the legislative and executive departments of government, has been regarded with terror by the wise men of every age because in every European republic, ancient and modern, in which it has been tried, it has terminated disastrously and been productive of corruption, injustice, violence, and tyranny. And dare we flatter ourselves that we are a peculiar people who can run the career of history, exempted from the passions which have disturbed and corrupted the rest of mankind? If we are like other races of men, with similar follies and vices, then I greatly fear that our posterity will have reason to deplore, in sackcloth and ashes, the delusion of the day.

It is not my purpose at present to interfere with the report of the committee, so far as respects the qualifications of electors for governor and members of assembly. I shall feel grateful if we may be permitted to retain the stability and security of a senate, bottomed upon the freehold property of the state. Such a body, so constituted, may prove a sheet anchor amidst the future factions and storms of the republic. The great leading and governing interest of this state is, at present, the agricultural; and what madness would it be to commit that interest to the winds. The great body of the people are now the owners and actual cultivators of the soil. With that wholesome population we always expect to find moderation, frugality, order, honesty, and a due sense of independence, liberty, and justice. It is impossible that any people can lose their liberties by internal fraud or violence, so long as the country is parceled out among freeholders of moderate possessions, and those freeholders have a sure and efficient control in the affairs of the government. Their habits, sympathies, and employments necessarily inspire them with a correct spirit of freedom and justice; they are the safest guardians of property and the laws. We certainly cannot too highly appreciate the value of the agricultural interest. It is the foundation of national wealth and power. According to the opinion of her ablest political economists, it is the surplus produce of the agriculture of England that enables her to support her vast body of manufacturers, her formidable fleets and armies, and the crowds of persons engaged in the liberal professions and the cultivation of the various arts.

Now, sir, I wish to preserve our senate as the representative of the landed interest. I wish those who have an interest in the soil to retain the exclusive possession of a branch in the legislature as a stronghold in which they may find safety through all the vicissitudes which the state may be destined, in the course of Providence, to experience. I wish them to be always enabled to say that their freeholds cannot be taxed without their consent. The men of no property, together with the crowds of dependents connected with great manufacturing and commercial establishments, and the motley and undefinable population of crowded ports, may, perhaps, at some future day, under skilful management, predominate in the assembly, and yet we should be perfectly safe if no laws could pass without the free consent of the owners of the soil. That security we at present enjoy; and it is that security which I wish to retain.

The apprehended danger from the experiment of universal suffrage applied to the whole legislative department is no dream of the imagination. It is too mighty an excitement for the moral constitution of men to endure. The tendency of universal suffrage is to jeopardize the rights of property and the principles of liberty. There is a constant tendency in human society, and the history of every age proves it; there is a tendency in the poor to covet and to share the plunder of the rich; in the debtor to relax or avoid the obligation of contracts; in the majority to tyrannize over the minority and trample down their rights; in the indolent and the profligate to cast the whole burthens of society upon the industrious and the virtuous; and *there is a tendency in ambitious and wicked men to inflame these combustible materials*. It requires a vigilant government, and a firm administration of justice, to counteract that tendency. "Thou shalt not covet"; "Thou shalt not steal," are divine injunctions induced by this miserable depravity of our nature. Who can undertake to calculate with any precision how many millions of people this great state will contain in the course of this and the next century, and who can estimate the future extent and magnitude of our commercial ports? The disproportion between the men of property and the men of no property will be in every society in a ratio to its commerce, wealth, and population. We are no longer to remain plain and simple republics of farmers like the New England colonists or the Dutch settlements on the Hudson. We are fast becoming a great nation, with great commerce, manufactures, population, wealth, luxuries, and with the vices and miseries that they engender. One-seventh of the population of the city of Paris at this day subsists on charity, and one-third of the inhabitants of that city die in the hospitals; what would become of such a city with universal suffrage? France has upward of four, and England upward of five millions of manufacturing and commercial laborers without property. Could these kingdoms sustain the weight of universal suffrage? The radicals in England, with the force of that mighty engine, would at once sweep away the property, the laws, and the liberties of that island like a deluge.

The growth of the city of New York is enough to startle and awaken those who are pursuing the *ignis fatuus* of universal suffrage.

In 1773 it had 21,000 souls.
In 1801 it had 60,000 do.
In 1806 it had 76,000 do.
In 1820 it had 123,000 do.

It is rapidly swelling into the unwieldly population, and with the burdensome pauperism, of a European metropolis. New York is destined to become the future London of America; and in less than a century that city, with the operation of universal suffrage and under skilful direction, will govern this state.

The notion that every man that works a day on the road, or serves an idle hour in the militia, is entitled as of right to an equal participation in the whole power of the government is most unreasonable and has no foundation in justice. We had better at once discard from the report such a nominal test of merit. If such persons have an equal share in one branch of the legislature, it is surely as much as they can in justice or policy demand. Society is an association for the protection of property as well as of life, and the individual who contributes only one

cent to the common stock ought not to have the same power and influence in directing the property concerns of the partnership as he who contributes his thousands. He will not have the same inducements to care, and diligence, and fidelity. His inducements and his temptation would be to divide the whole capital upon the principles of an agrarian law.

Liberty, rightly understood, is an inestimable blessing, but liberty without wisdom, and without justice, is no better than wild and savage licentiousness. The danger which we have hereafter to apprehend is not the want, but the abuse, of liberty. We have to apprehend the oppression of minorities and a disposition to encroach on private right—to disturb chartered privileges—and to weaken, degrade, and overawe the administration of justice; we have to apprehend the establishment of unequal and, consequently, unjust systems of taxation and all the mischiefs of a crude and mutable legislation. A stable senate, exempted from the influence of universal suffrage, will powerfully check these dangerous propensities, and such a check becomes the more necessary, since this Convention has already determined to withdraw the watchful eye of the judicial department from the passage of laws.

We are destined to become a great manufacturing as well as commercial state. We have already numerous and prosperous factories of one kind or another, and one master-capitalist with his one hundred apprentices, and journeymen, and agents, and dependents will bear down at the polls an equal number of farmers of small estates in his vicinity who cannot safely unite for their common defense. Large manufacturing and mechanical establishments can act in an instant with the unity and efficacy of disciplined troops. It is against such combinations, among others, that I think we ought to give to the freeholders, or those who have interest in land, one branch of the legislature for their asylum and their comfort. Universal suffrage, once granted, is granted forever and never can be recalled. There is no retrograde step in the rear of democracy. However mischievous the precedent may be in its consequences, or however fatal in its effects, universal suffrage never can be recalled or checked but by the strength of the bayonet. We stand, therefore, this moment, on the brink of fate, on the very edge of the precipice. If we let go our present hold on the senate, we commit our proudest hopes and our most precious interests to the waves.

It ought further to be observed that the senate is a court of justice in the last resort. It is the last depository of public and private rights, of civil and criminal justice. This gives the subject an awful consideration and wonderfully increases the importance of securing that house from the inroads of universal suffrage. Our country freeholders are exclusively our jurors in the administration of justice, and there is equal reason that none but those who have an interest in the soil should have any concern in the composition of that court. As long as the senate is safe, justice is safe, property is safe, and our liberties are safe. But when the wisdom, the integrity, and the independence of that court is lost, we may be certain that the freedom and happiness of this state are fled forever.

I hope, sir, we shall not carry desolation through all the departments of the fabric erected by our fathers. I hope we shall not put forward to the world a new constitution as will meet with the scorn of the wise and the tears of the patriot....

The report having been read—

MR. N. SANDFORD[3] took the floor. The question before us is the right of suffrage—who shall, or who shall not, have

the right to vote. The committee have presented the scheme they thought best; to abolish all existing distinctions and make the right of voting uniform. Is this not right? Where did these distinctions arise? They arose from British precedents. In England they have their three estates, which must always have their separate interests represented. Here there is but one estate—the people. To me the only qualifications seem to be the virtue and morality of the people; and if they may be safely intrusted to vote for one class of our rulers, why not for all? In my opinion, these distinctions are fallacious. We have the experience of almost all the other states against them. The principle of the scheme now proposed is that those who bear the burthens of the state should choose those that rule it. There is no privilege given to property as such; but those who contribute to the public support we consider as entitled to a share in the election of rulers. The burthens are annual, and the elections are annual, and this appears proper. To me, and the majority of the committee, it appeared the only reasonable scheme that those who are to be affected by the acts of the government should be annually entitled to vote for those who administer it. Our taxes are of two sorts, on real and personal property. The payment of a tax on either, we thought, equally entitled a man to a vote, and thus we intended to destroy the odious distinctions of property which now exist. But we have considered personal service, in some cases, equivalent to a tax on personal property, as in work on the high roads. This is a burthen and should entitle those subject to it to equivalent privileges. The road duty is equal to a poll tax on every male citizen, of twenty-one years, of 62½ cents per annum, which is about the value of each inividual's work on the road. This work is a burden imposed by the legislature—a duty required by rulers, and which should entitle those sub-

3. Nathan Sandford, forty-two years of age when he attended this convention as a delegate, was a farmer and a native citizen of the state.

ject to it to a choice of those rulers. Then, sir, the militia next presents itself; the idea of personal service, as applicable to the road duty, is, in like manner, applicable here; and this criterion has been adopted in other states. In Mississippi mere enrolment gives a vote. In Connecticut, as is proposed here, actual service, and that without the right of commutation, is required. The duty in the militia is obligatory and onerous. The militiaman must find his arms and accouterments and lose his time. But, after admitting all these persons, what restrictions, it will be said, are left on the right of suffrage? 1st. The voter must be a citizen. 2d. The service required must be performed within the year, on the principle that taxation is annual, and election annual; so that, when the person ceases to contribute or serve, he ceases to vote.

A residence is also required. We propose the term of six months, because we find it already in the constitution; but we propose this residence in the state and not in the county or town, so that, wherever a voter may be at the time of election, he may vote there, if he has been a resident of the state for six months. The object of this was to enable those who move, as very many do, in the six months preceding an election, out of the town or ward in which they have resided, to retain the right of voting in their new habitations. The term of six months is deemed long enough to qualify those who come into our state from abroad to understand and exercise the privileges of a citizen here. Now, sir, this scheme will embrace almost the whole male population of the state. There is perhaps no subject so purely matter of opinion as the question how far the right of suffrage may be safely carried. We propose to carry it almost as far as the male population of the state. The Convention may perhaps think this too broad. On this subject we have much experience; yet there are respectable

citizens who think this extension of suffrage unfavorable to the rights of property. Certainly this would be a fatal objection, if well founded; for any government, however constituted, which does not secure property to its rightful owners is a bad government. But how is the extension of the right of suffrage unfavorable to property? Will not our laws continue the same? Will not the administration of justice continue the same? And, if so, how is private property to suffer? Unless these are changed, and upon them rest the rights and security of property, I am unable to perceive how property is to suffer by the extension of the right of suffrage. But we have abundant experience on this point in other states. Now, sir, in many of the states the right of suffrage has no restriction; every male inhabitant votes. Yet what harm has been done in those states? What evil has resulted to them from this cause? The course of things in this country is for the extension and not the restriction of popular rights. I do not know that in Ohio or Pennsylvania, where the right of suffrage is universal, there is not the same security for private rights and private happiness as elsewhere. Every gentleman is aware that the scheme now proposed is derived from the law calling this Convention, and in the constitution of this body we have the first fruits of the operation of the principle of extensive suffrage—and will anyone say that this example is not one evincing the discretion with which our people exercise this right? In our town meetings too, throughout the state, we have the same principle. In our town elections we have the highest proof of the virtue and intelligence of our people; they assemble in town meetings as a pure democracy and choose their officers and local legislatures, if I may so call them; and if there is any part of our public business well done, it is that done in town meetings. Is not this a strong practical lesson of the beneficial operation of this principle? This scheme has been proposed by a majority of the committee; they think it safe and beneficial, founded in just and rational principles, and in the experience of this and neighboring states. The committee have no attachment, however, to this particular scheme and are willing to see it amended or altered if it shall be judged for the interest of the people.

Mr. Ross.[4] Mr. Chairman. In assigning the reasons which influenced the select committee in making the report now under consideration, I shall rely much on the honorable gentlemen with whom I had the pleasure to be associated on that committee. But, sir, feeling a responsibility in common with the members of that committee, I may perhaps be permitted to state, as concisely as I can, in addition to the views just submitted by the honorable chairman of that committee (Mr. N. Sandford), some of the motives which led to the provisions contained in that report. The subject now submitted may be viewed as one of deep and interesting importance; inasmuch as it discriminates who among our fellow-citizens shall be allowed to exercise the high privilege of designating, by their votes, who shall represent them in their wants and their wishes, in the various and multiplied concerns of legislation and civil government. In every free state the electors ought to form the basis, the soil, from which everything is to spring, relating to the administration of their political concerns. Otherwise it could not be denominated a government of the people. This results from the immutable principle that civil government is instituted for the benefit of the governed. Consequently all, at least, who contribute to the support or defense of the state have a just claim to exercise the elective privi-

4. John Ross, thirty-six years of age when he attended this convention as a delegate, had been born in Connecticut and practiced medicine in New York.

lege, if consistent with the safety and welfare of the citizens. It is immaterial whether that support or defense of the state be by the payment of money or by personal service, which are precisely one and the same thing—that of taxation. Assuming this, then, as the basis, as being the least objectionable of any other, we are furnished with certain data by which the right to vote can be determined. By entering them in a register, we are able to test the qualification of electors without resorting to the multiplication of oaths, which under the present constitution had grown into a most corrupting and alarming evil. After the most full and attentive consideration of the subject, the committee were led to the conclusion that this would be the most simple and practical mode of ascertaining, with certainty, who are entitled to the privilege of electors. At the same time it gives a liberal extension to that privilege, which, unquestionably, a vast majority of our constituents will demand at our hands, and which we can have no wish to withhold, unless to perpetuate those odious distinctions which have hitherto so long and so justly been complained of. This is one of the crying evils for which we were sent here to provide a remedy. It is not to be expected, sir, that any general rules can be devised that will extend to every possible case that it would be desirable to include, nor is it possible to exclude all who might abuse the privilege. Where evils must necessarily exist, the great object of this Convention, I trust, will be to choose the least—to settle down on such general principles as will result in conferring on the people of this state the greatest possible sum of happiness and prosperity.

That all men are free and equal, according to the usual declarations, applies to them only in a state of nature and not after the institution of civil government; for them many rights, flowing from a natural equality, are necessarily abridged, with a view to produce the greatest amount of security and happiness to the whole community. On this principle the right of suffrage is extended to white men only. But why, it will probably be asked, are blacks to be excluded? I answer: because they are seldom, if ever, required to share in the common burthens or defense of the state. There are also additional reasons; they are a peculiar people, incapable, in my judgment, of exercising that privilege with any sort of discretion, prudence, or independence. They have no just conceptions of civil liberty. They know not how to appreciate it and are consequently indifferent to its preservation.

2. A PLEA FOR A WIDER SUFFRAGE[1]

EDITORS' NOTE.—Published from 1811 to 1849 at Baltimore, the *Niles Register* has no equal as a source of the daily current of events and ideas in the United States during the Jacksonian Age. Until his death, Hezekiah Niles (1777–1839) owned, edited, and wrote almost all of this famous magazine. A Pennsylvania Quaker, Niles became a printer in his youth. He began very early to write newspaper articles, and from 1805 to 1811, with a partner, he owned and edited a Baltimore daily paper, the *Evening Post*. When this paper was sold to pay the creditors, Niles founded the magazine which bears his name. His most warmly held convictions were his faith in the rule of the majority and his ardent patriotism (see Norval Neil Luxon, *Niles Weekly Register, News Magazine of the Nineteenth Century* [Baton Rouge, 1947]).

We observe that, in several of the states, discussions are going on which have for their purpose an extension of the right of suffrage—to which we wish success. In looking at some of the state constitutions, we have much cause to wonder that, in this enlightened day, so many barriers should be placed between the people at large and their local governments—as though it were necessary to have a body of patricians to stand between the plebeians and power! But, yet, the right of suffrage is so common in other states that it is not valued as it should be. Whatsoever is most estimable, whatsoever most delightful—even the enjoyment of health, the acquisition of wealth, or the society of lovely woman—loses a large part of its zest from complete possession; and hence it is that that which nations have waded through oceans of blood to obtain, that for which America contended in a seven years' cruel war with the "mother-country" to secure to herself, is, in some places, enjoyed so much as a matter of course that very little reverence or respect is paid to it. The inestimable right is exercised with indifference or from favoritism. The choice of a sheriff to execute the law produces ten times the bustle of the election of an officer who is to make the law. This should not be so. We may have our friends at elections but never ought to forget that our first duty is to serve ourselves in a serious selection of persons best qualified by their wisdom to discern the wants and wishes of the people of a state and vested with virtue sufficient to pursue its interests to their consummation in defiance of the intrigues of party or the clamors of unworthy men. When the ballot is thus

1. *Niles Register*, XIX, 115–16.

used, it brings about revolutions without confusion, which cannot be accomplished in a different state of things, except through force and arms. In the state of Massachusetts a convention is about to be chosen to change the constitution of the commonwealth; and so quietly has this great affair proceeded that nothing more than the simple fact that a convention is to be called is known out of the state. There is no anxiety about the matter—no convulsion is expected to grow out of it—for the people are acting for themselves. How different would be our feelings if such measures were in progress in a foreign country with which we had an intimate connection? We should all be gaping for news and every day expect to hear of a civil war. Paine said: "It was better to go to the place of voting than the field of battle"; and, if the right of suffrage is regarded as it ought and dispensed as it should be, it is hardly possible that any serious contention can arise among the people of a free state.

We hold it to be the natural right of every citizen, who is bound by the law to render personal services to the state or aid its revenue by money drawn from his pocket, to vote for those who may require such services or cause such exactions—and that persons so elected are responsible to such electors for their good conduct, legislative or executive. The possession of a certain quantity of property is, by no means, necessary to an acquirement of the right of suffrage. If the law for such purpose relates to things of small value, it tempts to fraud; if it respects large amounts, it forms an aristocracy. Party and partisans can make freeholders by hundreds without hazard or loss—and, when personal property is the criterion, a single watch may make fifty voters in one day. We know that such things have been done, and must believe that they will continue to be done, so long as offices are desired by men who ought not to have them. So

every man liable to fight the battles of his country, or to pay taxes to support its government, should be a qualified voter.

In Virginia (the names of states are mentioned only for examples) none but freeholders have the right of suffrage. In New York the same description of persons elect the governor and senate. In Pennsylvania all vote who pay taxes. In Maryland nothing but citizenship is required—not even a record of the voter as such. Objections may lie to either of these modes the freehold suffrage represents property, always best able to protect itself, at the cost of liberty, and even life, to be involved in its legislation; poll taxes may not be desirable, and without them many must be disfranchised; and universal suffrage, without check or control, but the opinions of the judges of election, is liable to the most disgraceful frauds—for a minority may easily rule, if resolved to appear as the majority, in populous districts where the places of polling are adjacent to one another.

In corporate cities and towns, it has been contended by many that their local government should represent property only. There is some feasibility in this proposition, but it will not bear the touchstone of truth. Property is nothing unless it is occupied and made productive; and it must be defended to render it valuable. It is the consumer that pays the tax on every article subject to taxation; thus, the tenant pays the tax of the landlord, and even the boarder the rent of the tenant. A house makes nothing—it will not, of itself, produce one cent's value in a hundred years; it is the occupant that gives value to it—the income which it brings for the accommodation afforded. No prudent man will build a house without estimating the taxes to which it is to be liable, as well as the rent which it may produce, unless he builds it for his own use; and then he estimates the taxes in its cost to him, just as if he imported a bag of coffee for his own table on which he knew he would have to pay five cents per lb. duty. And yet the right of suffrage should not be made too cheap; some act should be done by which a person may become possessed of it.

As a general principle, then, we hold it to be equitable that every citizen who may be called into the military service of a state, at the hazard of his life, by privation or exposure in battle, or who is liable to a poll or other taxes on his person or property, should have the right of voting for any office in the gift of the people; and a vote in one district should have the same weight as a vote in another district—not as it is in Maryland, etc., where one vote, in certain counties, has twenty times the influence of a like vote in other counties: but this high privilege should be carefully guarded that it may be rightfully exercised. Something should be done by which the legal voters should be recorded and known to those they elect as responsible to perform the duties of citizens. In Pennsylvania, etc., this is accomplished by a small poll tax; and no one can vote who has not paid a tax which was assessed six months previous to the election, except the sons of persons so qualified, between the ages of twenty-one and twenty-two years. If a state wants revenue, and will admit people to vote on paying their portion of it, per-

haps a poll tax, as one means of a system, is as proper a mode of raising it as any other; but, if that be thought inexpedient, the names of all the voters should at least be recorded, at their own expense or that of the state, in their respective districts, say, six months anterior to an election—which record should be handed over to the judges of their election districts, and if the name of an applicant to vote should not be found thereon (unless in special and well-defined exceptions), his vote should not be received. And every person offering his name for record should prove his citizenship and qualify that he had not had it recorded in any other district, except in the case of a removal, when he should distinctly state the same, of which a proper entry should be made.

This procedure would cause little trouble. Persons paying taxes would be electors *ipso facto*, their names being recorded; and all others would have to give in their names but once in their lifetime, but in consequence of a removal. It would affect transient persons only who have nothing at stake and prevent them and others from voting several times, at different polls, at the same election, as may easily be done in large cities or populous districts. Thus would the purity of suffrage be defended—the poor citizen be protected in his rights, and wandering persons be debarred the privilege that exclusively belongs to settled inhabitants.

SECTION C. THE BEGINNINGS OF ORGANIZED LABOR

1. THE BOSTON CARPENTERS' STRIKE, 1825[1]

EDITORS' NOTE.—The Boston house carpenters' strike of 1825, in which about six hundred journeymen participated, was the first great strike in which the ten-hour day was the principal issue. The strike failed largely because the capitalists took the position that they would not engage any master-carpenters who accepted the demands made by the striking journeymen (see John R. Commons *et al.*, *History of Labor in the United States* [New York, 1918], I, 158–62).

A. RESOLUTIONS OF JOURNEYMEN CARPENTERS

Notice to house carpenters and housewrights in the country. An advertisement having appeared in the papers of this city, giving information that there is at this time a great demand for workmen in this branch of mechanical business in this city, it is considered a duty to state for the benefit of our brethren of the trade that we are not aware of any considerable demand for labor in this business, as there is, at this time, a very considerable number of journeymen carpenters who are out of employ, and the probable inducement which led to the communication referred to arises from a disposition manifested on the part of the builders in this city to make their own terms as to the price of labor and the number of hours' labor which shall hereafter constitute a day's work. It being a well-known fact that the most unreasonable requirements have been hitherto exacted with regard to the terms of labor of journeymen mechanics in this city; and it is further well known that in the cities of New York, Philadelphia, Baltimore, and most of the other cities a much more liberal and equitable course of policy has been adopted by the master-builders, on this subject, giving to their journeymen that fair and liberal support to which they are unquestionably entitled. It is an undoubted fact that, on the present system, it is impossible for a journeyman housewright and house carpenter to maintain a family at the present time with the wages which are now usually given to the journeymen house carpenters in this city.

April 16

B. RESOLUTIONS OF MASTER-CARPENTERS

Resolved, That we learn with surprise and regret that a large number of those who are employed as journeymen in this city have entered into a combination for the purpose of altering the time of commencing and terminating their daily labor from that which has been customary from time immemorial, thereby lessening the amount of labor each day in a very considerable degree.

Resolved, That we consider such a combination as unworthy of that useful and industrious class of the community who are engaged in it; that it is fraught with numerous and pernicious evils, not

1. Reprinted by permission of the publishers, The Arthur H. Clark Company, from *A Documentary History of American Industrial Society*, ed. John R. Commons *et al* (Cleveland, 1910), VI, 78, 76–77, 79–81.

only as respects their employers, but the public at large, and especially themselves; for all journeymen of good character and of skill may expect very soon to become masters and, like us, the employers of others; and by the measure which they are now inclined to adopt they will entail upon themselves the inconvenience to which they seem desirous that we should now be exposed!

Resolved, That we consider the measure proposed, as calculated to exert a very unhappy influence on our apprentices—by seducing them from that course of industry and economy of time to which we are anxious to inure them. That it will expose the journeymen themselves to many temptations and improvident practices from which they are happily secure, while they attend to that wise and salutary maxim of mechanics, "Mind your business." That we consider idleness as the most deadly bane to usefulness and honorable living; and knowing (such is human nature that, where there is no necessity, there is no exertion, we fear and dread the consequences of such a measure upon the morals and well-being of society.

Resolved, That we cannot believe this project to have originated with any of the faithful and industrious sons of New England but are compelled to consider it an evil of foreign growth, and one which, we hope and trust, will not take root in the favored soil of Massachusetts. And especially that our city, the early rising and industry of whose inhabitants are universally proverbial, may not be infested with the unnatural production.

Resolved, That if such a measure were ever to be proper and necessary, the time has not yet arrived when it is so; if it would ever be just, it cannot be at a time like the present, when builders have generally made their engagements and contracts for the season, having predicated their estimats and prices upon the original state of things in reference to journeymen. And we appeal therefor to the good sense, the honesty, and justice of all who are engaged in this combination, and ask them to review their doings, contemplate their consequences, and then act as becomes men of sober sense and of prudence.

Resolved, finally, That we will make no alteration in the manner of employing journeymen as respects the time of commencing and leaving work and that we will employ no man who persists in adhering to the project of which we complain.

COMMITTEE

C. RESOLUTIONS OF "GENTLEMEN ENGAGED IN BUILDING"

Resolved, That we view with regret the late proceedings of a portion of the journeymen carpenters of this city terminating in a combination to curtail the usual number of working hours.

Resolved, That these proceedings are a departure from the salutary and steady usages which have prevailed in this city, and all New England, from time immemorial, by an adherence to which apprentices and journeymen, accustomed to industrious and temperate habits, have, in their turn, become thriving and respectable masters, and the great body of our mechanics have been enabled to acquire property and respectability, with a just weight and influence in society; that if this confederacy should be countenanced by the community, it must, of consequence, extend to and embrace all the working classes in every department in town and country, thereby effecting a most injurious change in all the modes of business, and in the operations of agriculture and commerce, opening a wide door for idleness and vice, and finally commuting the present condition of the mechanical classes, made happy and prosperous by frugal, orderly, temperate, and ancient habits, for that degraded state by which, in other countries, many of these classes are obliged to leave their homes, bringing with them their feelings and habits and a spirit of discontent and insubordination to which our native mechanics have hitherto been strangers.

Resolved, That, while it is admitted every man is free to make such contract in respect to time and wages as he may think for his interest, it is also considered that all combinations by any classes of citizens intended to regulate or effect the value of labor by abridging its duration are in a high degree unjust and injurious to all other classes, inasmuch as they give an artificial and unnatural turn to business and tend to convert all its branches into monopolies. If the journeymen carpenters, by an example which other trades shall follow, effect an unnatural rise in the price of labor, their employers, who vend salt, sugar, and other necessaries, must indemnify themselves by similar combinations or suspend their employment.

Resolved, That we do highly approve of the firmness, temperance, and intelligence manifested by the master-carpenters in their proceedings and indulge a strong hope that they will produce a due effect upon the well-disposed among the journeymen, and that those, upon reflection, will be satisfied that a perseverance in their present course will, in the end, produce a reaction ruinous only to themselves.

Resolved, That it is expedient for those concerned in building the present season to support the master-carpenters, on the ground by them taken, at whatever sacrifice or inconvenience, and to this end extend the time for the fulfilment of their contracts, and even to suspend, if necessary, building altogether, and that we can foresee no loss or inconvenience arising from such suspensions equal to what must result from permitting such combinations to be effectual.

Resolved, That we cordially and sincerely invite and entreat the journeymen to retrace their steps and return to their business and to realize by their industry and perseverance in the good old way the fair advantages which are now promised by full employment and good wages to all who will embrace them, and we cannot doubt that all who think themselves worthy of becoming masters will perceive their true interest in conforming to this advice. But, if contrary to expectation they should persevere in the present determination, we hereby agree and pledge ourselves to each other not to employ any such journeymen or any other master-carpenter who shall yield to their pretensions.

Voted, That the resolutions now adopted be published in the papers of this city and that Messrs. John Bellows, Josiah Marshall, John D. Williams, Samuel Perkins, and Amos Lawrence be a committee to present them to the Building Committee of Faneuil Hall Market for their concurrence and to deposit the same in convenient public places for the signatures of such citizens as may approve them and that fifty copies be printed for this purpose.

H. G. OTIS, *Chairman*
W. H. ELIOT, *Secretary*

2. PREAMBLE OF THE MECHANICS' UNION OF TRADE ASSOCIATIONS, 1827[1]

EDITORS' NOTE.—The strike of the Philadelphia journeymen carpenters, which these resolutions accompanied, failed, but it aroused a spirit of resistance which led to the federation of the city's unions into the Mechanics' Union of Trade Associations. This association, perhaps the first of its kind in the nation, sponsored a city-wide Working Men's Political party in 1828, which for about three years held the balance of power in Philadelphia politics.

When the disposition and efforts of one part of mankind to oppress another have become too manifest to be mistaken and too pernicious in their consequences to be endured, it has often been found necessary for those who feel aggrieved to associate for the purpose of affording to each other mutual protection from oppression.

We, the journeymen mechanics of the city and county of Philadelphia, conscious that our condition in society is lower than justice demands it should be, and feeling our inability, individually, to ward off from ourselves and families those numerous evils which result from an unequal and very excessive accumulation of wealth and power into the hands of a few, are desirous of forming an association which shall avert as much as possible those evils which poverty and incessant toil have already inflicted, and which threaten ultimately to overwhelm and destroy us. And, in order that our views may be properly understood, and the justness of our intention duly appreciated, we offer to the public the following summary of our reasons, principles, and objects.

If unceasing toils were actually requisite to supply us with a bare, and in many instances wretched, subsistence; if the products of our industry, or an equitable proportion of them, were appropriated to our actual wants and comfort, then would we yield without a murmur to the stern and irrevocable decree of necessity. But this is infinitely wide of the fact. We appeal to the most intelligent of every community and ask—Do not you, and all society, depend solely for subsistence on the products of human industry? Do not those who labor, while acquiring to themselves thereby only a scanty and penurious support, likewise maintain in affluence and luxury the rich who never labor?

Do not all the streams of wealth which flow in every direction and are emptied into and absorbed by the coffers of the unproductive, exclusively take their rise in the bones, marrow, and muscles of the industrious classes? In return for which, exclusive of a bare subsistence (which likewise is the product of their own industry), they receive—not anything!

Is it just? Is it equitable that we should waste the energies of our minds and bodies, and be placed in a situation of such unceasing exertion and servility as must necessarily, in time, render the benefits of our liberal institutions to us inaccessible and useless, in order that the products of our labor may be accumulated by a few into vast pernicious masses, calculated to prepare the minds of the possessors for the exercise of lawless rule and despotism, to overawe the meager multitude, and fright away that shadow of freedom which still lingers among us? Are we who confer almost every blessing on society never to be treated as freemen and equals and never

1. *Ibid.*, V, 84–90.

be accounted worthy of an equivalent, in return for the products of our industry? Has the Being who created us given us existence only with the design of making it a curse and a burthen to us, while at the same time he has conferred upon us a power with which tenfold more of blessings can be created than it is possible for society either to enjoy or consume? No! at the present period, when wealth is so easily and abundantly created that the markets of the world are overflowing with it, and when, in consequence thereof, and of the continual development and increase of scientific power, the demand for human labor is gradually and inevitably diminishing, it cannot be necessary that we, or any portion of society, should be subjected to perpetual slavery. But a ray of intelligence on this subject has gone forth through the working world, which the ignorance and injustice of oppressors, aided by the most powerful and opposing interests, cannot extinguish; and, in consequence thereof, the day of human emancipation from haggard penury and incessant toil is already dawning. The spirit of freedom is diffusing itself through a wider circle of human intellect; it is expanding in the bosoms of the mass of mankind and preparing them to cast off the yoke of oppression and servility, wherever and by whatever means it has been riveted upon them.

As freemen and republicans, we feel it a duty incumbent on us to make known our sentiments fearlessly and faithfully on any subject connected with the general welfare; and we are prepared to maintain that all who toil have a natural and unalienable right to reap the fruits of their own industry; and that they who by labor (the only source) are the authors of every comfort, convenience, and luxury are in justice entitled to an equal participation, not only in the meanest and the coarsest, but likewise the richest and the choicest of them all. The principles upon which the insti-

tution shall be founded are principles, alike, of the strictest justice and the most extended philanthropy. Believing that, whatever is conducive to the real prosperity of the greatest numbers, must in the nature of things conduce to the happiness of all, we cannot desire to injure nor take the smallest unjust advantage, either of that class of the community called employers or of any other portion. It is neither our intention nor desire to extort inequitable prices for our labor; all we may demand for this shall not exceed what can be clearly demonstrated to be a fair and full equivalent. If we demand more, we wrong the society of which we are members, and if society require us to receive less, she injures and oppresses us.

With respect to the relation existing between employers and the employed, we are prepared, we think, to demonstrate that it is only through an extremely limited view of their real interests that the former can be induced to attempt to depreciate the value of human labor. The workman is not more dependent upon his wages for the support of his family than they are upon the demand for the various articles they fabricate or vend. If the mass of the people were enabled by their labor to procure for themselves and families a full and abundant supply of the comforts and conveniences of life, the consumption of articles, particularly of dwellings, furniture, and clothing, would amount to at least twice the quantity it does at present, and of course the demand, by which alone employers are enabled either to subsist or accumulate, would likewise be increased in an equal proportion. Each would be enabled to effect twice the quantity of sales or loans which he can effect at present, and the whole industry of a people, consisting of their entire productive powers, whether manual or scientific, together with all their capital, might be put into a full, healthful, and profitable action.

The workman need not languish for want of employment, the vender for sales, nor the capitalist complain for want of profitable modes of investment. It is therefore the real interest (for instance) of the hatter that every man in the community should be enabled to clothe his own head and those of his family with an abundant supply of the best articles of that description; because the flourishing demand, thereby created, and which depends altogether on the ability of the multitude to purchase, is that which alone enables him to pay his rent and support his family in comfort.

The same may be said with respect to the tailor, the shoemaker, the carpenter, the cabinetmaker, the builder, and indeed of every other individual in society who depends for subsistence or accumulation upon the employment of his skill, his labor, or his capital. All are dependent on the demand which there is for the use of their skill, service, or capital, and the demand must ever be regulated by the ability or inability of the great mass of the people to purchase and consume. If, therefore, as members of the community, they are desirous to prosper, in vain will they expect to succeed unless the great body of the community is kept in a healthy, vigorous, and prosperous condition.

No greater error exists in the world than the notion that society will be benefited by deprecating [sic] the value of human labor. Let this principle (as at this day in England) be carried towards its full extent, and it is in vain that scientific power shall pour forth its inexhaustible treasures of wealth upon the world. Its products will all be amassed to glut the overflowing storehouses and useless hoards of its insatiable monopolizers, while the mechanic and productive classes, who constitute the great mass of the population, and who have wielded the power and labored in the production of this immense abundance, having no other resource for subsistence than what they derive from the miserable pittance, which they are compelled by competition to receive in exchange for their inestimable labor, must first begin to pine, languish, and suffer under its destructive and withering influence. But the evil stops not here. The middling classes next, venders of the products of human industry, will begin to experience its deleterious effects. The demand for their articles must necessarily cease from the forced inability of the people to consume; trade must in consequence languish, and losses and failures become the order of the day. At last the contagion will reach the capitalist, throned as he is, in the midst of his ill-gotten abundance, and his capital, from the most evident and certain causes, will become useless, unemployed, and stagnant, himself the trembling victim of continual alarms from robberies, burnings, and murder, the unhappy and perhaps ill-fated object of innumerable imprecations, insults, and implacable hatred from the wronged, impoverished, and despairing multitude. The experience of the most commercial parts of the world sufficiently demonstrates that this is the natural, inevitable, and, shall we not say, righteous consequences of a principle whose origin is injustice and an unrighteous depreciation of the value and abstraction of the products of human labor—a principle which, in its ultimate effects, must be productive of universal ruin and misery and destroy alike the happiness of every class and individual in society.

The real object, therefore, of this association is to avert, if possible, the desolating evils which must inevitably arise from a depreciation of the intrinsic value of human labor; to raise the mechanical and productive classes to that condition of true independence and inequality [sic] which their practical skill and ingenuity, their immense utility to the nation and their growing intelligence are beginning imperiously to demand: to promote, equally, the happiness, prosperity, and welfare of the whole community—to aid in conferring a due and full proportion of that invaluable promoter of happiness, leisure, upon all its useful members; and to assist, in conjunction with such other institutions of this nature as shall hereafter be formed throughout the union, in establishing a just balance of power, both mental, moral, political, and scientific, between all the various classes and individuals which constitute society at large. . . .

3. RESOLUTIONS OF THE NEW YORK MECHANICS, 1829[1]

. . . *Resolved*, That the Creator has made all equal.

Resolved, That in the first formation of government, no man gives up to others his original right of soil and becomes a smith, a weaver, a builder, or other mechanic or laborer without receiving a guaranty that reasonable toil shall enable him to live as comfortably as others.

Resolved, That the rights of the rich, or, in other words, the employer, are not greater now than they were then.

Resolved, That the rights of the poor, or the employed, are not less.

Resolved, That those who now undertake to exact an excessive number of hours of toil for a day's work are aggressors upon the rights of their fellow-citizens, invaders of their happiness, and justly obnoxious to the indignation of every honest man in the community.

Resolved, That we will not labor for any man more than the just and reasonable time of ten hours a day; and that if our employers are determined to make the experiment, which can longest be suspended, business with them, or with us, the supply of the wants of nature for ourselves and families, we will hold them responsible, as we also hold ourselves, to the good sense of our fellow-citizens, for the wrongs we may suffer at their hands.

Resolved, That a committee of fifty persons be appointed to devise the means of assisting those who may require it in consequence of fulfilling the foregoing resolutions and that they make report at a future meeting.

Resolved, That the same committee be authorized and instructed to call another meeting as soon as they shall deem it expedient.

Resolved, That the names of those who shall hereafter work more than ten hours a day, or require or receive it, shall be published in the public papers as soon as they shall be ascertained. . . .

4. *PEOPLE* v. *FISHER*[2]

The opinion of the court was rendered by SAVAGE, C. J. . . .

Whatever disputes may exist among political economists upon the point, I think there can be no doubt, in a legal sense, but what the wages of labor compose a material portion of the value of manufactured articles. The products of mechanical labor compose a large proportion of the materials with which trade is carried on. By trade, I now understand traffic or mutual dealings between members of the same community, or internal trade. Coarse boots and shoes are made in many parts of our country; not for particular persons who are to wear them, but as an article of trade and commerce. Probably such is the case in Geneva, where this offense was committed. If journeymen bootmakers, by extravagant demands for wages, so enhance the price of boots made in *Geneva*, for instance, that boots made elsewhere, in *Auburn*, for example, can be sold cheaper, is not such an

1. *Ibid.*, V, 147–48.

2. 14 Wendell 10 (Supreme Court, New York, 1835).

act injurious to trade? It is surely so to the trade of Geneva in that particular article, and that, I apprehend, is all that is necessary to bring the offense within the statute. It is important to the best interests of society that the price of labor be left to regulate itself, or rather be limited by the demand for it. Combinations and confederacies to *enhance* or *reduce* the prices of labor, or of any articles of trade or commerce, are injurious. They may be oppressive by compelling the public to give more for an article of necessity or of convenience than it is worth; or, on the other hand, of compelling the labor of the mechanic for less than its value. Without any officious and improper interference on the subject, the price of labor or the wages of mechanics will be regulated by the demand for the manufactured article and the value of that which is paid for it; but the right does not exist either to enhance the price of the article, or the wages of the mechanic, by any forced and artificial means. The man who owns an article of trade or commerce is not obliged to sell it for any particular price, nor is the mechanic obliged by law to labor for any particular price. He may say that he will not make coarse boots for less than one dollar per pair, but *he has no right to say that no other mechanic shall make them for less*. The cloth merchant may say that he will not sell his goods for less than so much per yard, but has no right to say that any other merchant shall not sell for a less price. If one individual does not possess such a right over the conduct of another, no number of individuals can possess such a right. All combinations therefore to effect such an object are injurious, not only to the individual particularly oppressed, but to the public at large. In the present case, an industrious man was driven out of employment by the unlawful measures pursued by the defendants, and an injury done to the community, by diminishing the quantity of productive labor, and of internal trade. In so far as the individual sustains an injury, the remedy by indictment is taken away by our revised statutes, and the sufferer is left to his action on the case; but in so far as the public are concerned, in the embarrassment to trade by the discouragement of industry, the defendants are liable to punishment by indictment.

If combinations of this description are lawful in *Geneva*, they are so in every other place. If the bootmakers may say that boots shall not be made for less than one dollar per pair, it is optional with them to say that ten or even fifty dollars shall be paid, and no man can wear a pair of boots without giving such price as the journeyman bootmakers may choose to require. This, I apprehend, would be a monopoly of the most odious kind. The journeymen mechanics might, by fixing their own wages, regulate the price of all manufactured articles, and the community be enormously taxed. Should the journeymen bakers refuse to work, unless for enormous wages, which the master-bakers could not afford to pay, and should they compel all the journeymen in a city to stop work, the whole population must be without bread. So of journeymen tailors, or mechanics of any description. Such combinations would be productive of derangement and confusion, which certainly must be considered "injurious to trade." Such consequences would follow were such combinations universal. It is true that no great danger is to be apprehended on account of the impracticability of such universal combinations. But if universally or even generally entered into, they would be prejudicial to trade and to the public; they are wrong in each particular case. Truth is that industry requires no such means to support it. Competition is the life of trade. If the defendants cannot make coarse boots for less than one dollar per pair, let them refuse to do so; but let them not directly or indirectly undertake to say that others shall not do the work for a less price. It may be that *Pennock*, from greater industry or greater skill, made more profit by making boots at seventy-five cents per pair than the defendants at a dollar. He had a right to work for what he pleased. His employer had a right to employ him for such price as they could agree upon. The interference of the defendants was unlawful; its tendency is not only to individual oppression, but to public inconvenience and embarrassment.

I am of opinion that the offense is indictable and that the judgment of the general sessions of Ontario County should be reversed. . . .

5. *COMMONWEALTH* v. *HUNT*[1]

SHAW, C. J. Considerable time has elapsed since the argument of this case. It has been retained long under advisement, partly because we were desirous of examining, with some attention, the great number of cases cited at the argument, and others which have presented themselves in course, and partly because we considered it a question of great importance to the Commonwealth, and one which had been much examined and considered by the learned judge of the municipal court.

We have no doubt that, by the operation of the constitution of this Commonwealth, the general rules of the common law, making conspiracy an indictable offense, are in force here and that this is included in the description of laws which had, before the adoption of the constitution, been used and approved in the Province, Colony, or State of Massachusetts Bay, and usually practiced in the courts of law. . . .

But the great difficulty is in framing any definition or description, to be drawn from the decided cases, which shall specifically identify this offense— a description broad enough to include all cases punishable under this description without including acts which are not punishable. Without attempting to review and reconcile all the cases, we are of opinion that as a general description, though perhaps not a precise and accurate definition, a conspiracy must be a combination of two or more persons, by some concerted action, to accomplish some criminal or unlawful purpose, or to accomplish some purpose, not in itself criminal or unlawful, by criminal or unlawful means. . . .

From this view of the law respecting conspiracy, we think it an offense which especially demands the application of that wise and humane rule of the common law that an indictment shall state, with as much certainty as the nature of the case will admit, the facts which constitute the crime intended to be charged. This is required to enable the defendant to meet the charge and prepare for his defense and, in case of acquittal or conviction, to show by the record the identity of the charge, so that he may not be indicted a second time for the same offense. It is also necessary, in order that a person, charged by the grand jury for one offense, may not substantially be convicted, on his trial, of another. This fundamental rule is confirmed by the Declaration of Rights, which declares that no subject shall be held to answer for any crime or offense until the same is fully and plainly, substantially and formally, described to him. . . .

We are here carefully to distinguish between the confederacy set forth in the indictment and the confederacy or association contained in the constitution of the Boston Journeymen Bootmakers' Society, as stated in the little printed book which was admitted as evidence at the trial. Because, though it was thus admitted as evidence, it would not warrant a conviction for anything not stated in the indictment. . . .

1. 4 Metcalf 111 (Massachusetts, 1842).

Stripped then of these introductory recitals and alleged injurious consequences, and of the qualifying epithets attached to the facts, the averment is this: that the defendants and others formed themselves into a society and agreed not to work for any person who should employ any journeyman or other person not a member of such society after notice given him to discharge such workman.

The manifest intent of the association is to induce all those engaged in the same occupation to become members of it. Such a purpose is not unlawful. It would give them a power which might be exerted for useful and honorable purposes or for dangerous and pernicious ones. If the latter were the real and actual object, and susceptible of proof, it should have been specially charged. Such an association might be used to afford each other assistance in times of poverty, sickness, and distress; or to raise their intellectual, moral, and social condition; or to make improvement in their art; or for other proper purposes. Or the association might be designed for purposes of oppression and injustice. But, in order to charge all those who become members of an association with the guilt of a criminal conspiracy, it must be averred and proved that the actual, if not the avowed, object of the association was criminal. An association may be formed, the declared objects of which are innocent and laudable, and yet they may have secret articles, or an agreement communicated only to the members, by which they are banded together for purposes injurious to the peace of society or the rights of its members. Such would undoubtedly be a criminal conspiracy, on proof of the fact, however meritorious and praiseworthy the declared objects might be. The law is not to be hoodwinked by colorable pretenses. It looks at truth and reality through whatever disguise it may assume. But to make such an association, ostensibly innocent, the subject of prosecution as a criminal conspiracy, the secret agreement, which makes it so, is to be averred and proved as the gist of the offense. But when an association is formed for purposes actually innocent, and afterward its powers are abused, by those who have the control and management of it, to purposes of oppression and injustice, it will be criminal in those who thus misuse it, or give consent thereto, but not in the other members of the association. In this case, no such secret agreement, varying the objects of the association from those avowed, is set forth in this count of the indictment.

Nor can we perceive that the objects of this association, whatever they may have been, were to be attained by criminal means. The means which they proposed to employ, as averred in this count, and which, as we are now to presume, were established by the proof, were that they would not work for a person who, after due notice, should employ a journeyman not a member of their society. Supposing the object of the association to be laudable and lawful, or at least not unlawful, are these means criminal? The case supposes that these persons are not bound by contract but free to work for whom they please, or not to work if they so prefer. In this state of things we cannot perceive that it is criminal for men to agree together to exercise their own acknowledged rights, in such a manner as best to subserve their own interests. One way to test this is to consider the effect of such an agreement, where the object of the association is acknowledged on all hands to be a laudable one. Suppose a class of workmen, impressed with the manifold evils of intemperance, should agree with each other not to work in a shop in which ardent spirit was furnished, or not to work in a shop with anyone who used it, or not to work for an employer who should, after notice, employ a journeyman who habitually used it. The consequences might be the same. A workman who should still persist in the use of ardent spirit would find it more difficult to get employment; a master employing such a one might, at times, experience inconvenience in his work in losing the services of a skilful but intemperate workman. Still, it seems to us that as the object would be lawful, and the means not unlawful, such an agreement could not be pronounced a criminal conspiracy. . . .

Suppose a baker in a small village had the exclusive custom of his neighborhood and was making large profits by the sale of his bread. Supposing a number of those neighbors, believing the price of his bread too high, should propose to him to reduce his prices, or, if he did not, that they would introduce another baker; and, on his refusal, such other baker should, under their encouragement, set up a rival establishment and sell his bread at lower prices; the effect would be to diminish the profit of the former baker and to the same extent to impoverish him. And it might be said and proved that the purpose of the associates was to diminish his profits, and thus impoverish him, though the ultimate and laudable object of the combination was to reduce the cost of bread to themselves and their neighbors. The same thing may be said of all competition in every branch of trade and industry; and yet it is through that competition that the best interests of trade and industry are promoted. It is scarcely necessary to allude to the familiar instances of opposition lines of conveyance, rival hotels, and the thousand other instances, where each strives to gain custom to himself, by ingenious improvements, by increased industry, and by all the means by which he may lessen the price of commodities, and thereby diminish the profits of others.

We think, therefore, that associations may be entered into, the object of which is to adopt measures that may have a tendency to impoverish another, that is, to diminish his gains and profits, and yet so far from being criminal or unlawful, the object may be highly meritorious and public-spirited. The legality of such an association will therefore depend upon the means to be used for its accomplishment. If it is to be carried into effect by fair or honorable and lawful means, it is, to say the least, innocent; if by falsehood or force, it may be stamped with the character of conspiracy. . . .

SECTION D. PUBLIC EDUCATION

1. A PLEA FOR PUBLIC EDUCATION[1]

EDITORS' NOTE.—Organized labor demanded not only better wages and hours but also better educational opportunities, and their support of the movement for an improved free public-school system was extremely influential. This plea for public education was made in 1830 by the Philadelphia Working Men's Committee.

Report of the Joint Committees of the City and County of Philadelphia, appointed September, 1829, to ascertain the state of public instruction in Pennsylvania and to digest and propose such improvements in education as may be deemed essential to the intellectual and moral prosperity of the people. . . .

After devoting all the attention to the subject, and making every inquiry which their little leisure and ability would permit, they are forced into the conviction that there is great defect in the educational system of Pennsylvania and that much remains to be accomplished before it will have reached that point of improvement which the resources of the state would justify and which the intellectual condition of the people and the preservation of our republican institutions demand.

With the exception of this city and county, the city and incorporated borough of Lancaster, and the city of Pittsburgh, erected into "school districts" since 1818, it appears that the entire state is destitute of any provisions for public instruction except those furnished by the enactment of 1809. This law requires the assessors of the several counties to ascertain and return the number of children whose parents are unable, through poverty, to educate them; and such children are permitted to be instructed at the most convenient schools at the expense of their respective counties. . . .

It is true the state is not without its colleges and universities, several of which have been fostered with liberal supplies from the public purse. Let it be observed, however, that the funds so applied have been appropriated exclusively for the benefit of the wealthy, who are thereby enabled to procure a liberal education for their children upon lower terms than it could otherwise be afforded them. Funds thus expended may serve to engender an aristocracy of talent and place knowledge, the chief element of power, in the hands of the privileged few but can never secure the common prosperity of a nation nor confer intellectual as well as political equality on a people.

The original element of despotism is a monopoly of talent, which consigns the multitude to comparative ignorance and secures the balance of knowledge on the side of the rich and the rulers. If then the healthy existence of a free government be, as the committee believe, rooted in the will of the American people, it follows as a necessary consequence, of a government based upon that will, that this monopoly should be broken up and that the means of equal

1. *A Documentary History of American Industrial Society*, ed. John R. Commons *et al.*, V, 94–101.

knowledge (the only security for equal liberty) should be rendered, by legal provision, the common property of all classes.

In a republic the people constitute the government and, by wielding its powers in accordance with the dictates, either of their intelligence or their ignorance, of their judgment or their caprices, are the makers and the rulers of their own good or evil destiny. They frame the laws and create the institutions that promote their happiness or produce their destruction. If they be wise and intelligent, no laws but what are just and equal will receive their approbation or be sustained by their suffrages. If they be ignorant and capricious, they will be deceived by mistaken or designing rulers into the support of laws that are unequal and unjust.

It appears, therefore, to the committees that there can be no real liberty without a wide diffusion of real intelligence; that the members of a republic should all be alike instructed in the nature and character of their equal rights and duties as human beings and as citizens; and that education, instead of being limited as in our public poor schools, to a simple acquaintance with words and ciphers, should tend, as far as possible, to the production of a just disposition, virtuous habits, and a rational self-governing character.

When the committees contemplate their own condition and that of the great mass of their fellow-laborers, when they look around on the glaring inequality of society, they are constrained to believe that, until the means of equal instruction shall be equally secured to all, liberty is but an unmeaning word, and equality an empty shadow, whose substance to be realized must first be planted by an equal education and proper training in the minds, in the habits, in the manners, and in the feelings of the community....

The principal points in which the bill for establishing common schools, accompanying this report, differs from the existing system of free schools are as follows:

1. Its provisions, instead of being limited to three single districts, are designed to extend throughout the Commonwealth. 2d. It places the managers of the public schools immediately under the control and suffrage of the people. 3d. Its benefits and privileges will not, as at present, be limited as an act of charity to the poor alone but will extend equally and of right to all classes and be supported at the expense of all. 4th. It lays a foundation for infantile, as well as juvenile, instruction. And, lastly, it leaves the door open to every possible improvement which human benevolence and ingenuity may be able to introduce....

2. THE IMPORTANCE OF UNIVERSAL, FREE, PUBLIC EDUCATION[1]

By HORACE MANN

EDITORS' NOTE.— Horace Mann (1796–1859) was the principal leader of the successful movement to extend

1. Horace Mann, *Lectures and Annual Reports on Education*, ed. Mrs. Mary Mann (Cambridge, 1867), III, 663, 664–66, 666–68, 668–70, 686–87, 688–89.

and strengthen free public schools. Mann's parents lived on a small Massachusetts farm, and the educational facilities available to Mann were bitterly unsatisfactory to him. After graduation in 1819 from Brown University and legal training in the famous Litchfield, Connecticut, law school, Mann was for fourteen years a successful lawyer. He served in the state legislature from 1827 to 1837. In 1837 Massachusetts established a state board of education, and Mann, giving up a profitable legal practice, became the board's first full-time secretary. His vigorous action during his twelve years in this post transformed the state's schools. The minimum school year was increased to six months, fifty new free high schools were established,

religious instruction was kept out of the public schools, and appropriations were doubled. From 25 per cent of the total expenditure on education, appropriations for public schools increased to 64 per cent. Mann was interested in other reform movements. He succeeded John Quincy Adams in the House of Representatives in 1848 as an antislavery Whig, and he was the unsuccessful Free Soil candidate for the governorship in 1852. He spent his last years as president of Antioch College in Ohio.

Another cardinal object which the government of Massachusetts, and all the influential men in the state, should propose to themselves is the physical well-being of all the people—the sufficiency, comfort, competence, of every individual in regard to food, raiment, and shelter. And these necessaries and conveniences of life should be obtained by each individual for himself, or by each family for themselves, rather than accepted from the hand of charity or extorted by poor-laws. It is not averred that this most desirable result can, in all instances, be obtained; but it is, nevertheless, the end to be aimed at. True statesmanship and true political economy, not less than true philanthropy, present this perfect theory as the goal, to be more and more closely approximated by our imperfect practice. The desire to achieve such a result cannot be regarded as an unreasonable ambition; for, though all mankind were well fed, well clothed, and well housed, they might still be but half-civilized. . . .

According to the European theory, men are divided into classes—some to toil and earn, others to seize and enjoy. According to the Massachusetts theory, all are to have an equal chance for earning and equal security in the enjoyment of what they earn. The latter tends to

equality of condition; the former, to the grossest inequalities. Tried by any Christian standard of morals, or even by any of the better sort of heathen standards, can anyone hesitate, for a moment, in declaring which of the two will produce the greater amount of human welfare, and which, therefore, is the more conformable to the divine will? The European theory is blind to what constitutes the highest glory as well as the highest duty of a state. Its advocates and admirers are forgetful of that which should be their highest ambition and proud of that which constitutes their shame. How can anyone possessed of the attributes of humanity look with satisfaction upon the splendid treasures, the golden regalia, deposited in the Tower of London or in Windsor Palace, each "an India in itself," while thousands around are dying of starvation or have been made criminals by the combined forces of temptation and neglect? The present condition of Ireland cancels all the glories of the British crown. The brilliant conception which symbolizes the nationality of Great Britain as a superb temple, whose massive and grand proportions are upheld and adorned by the four hundred and thirty Corinthian columns of the aristocracy, is turned into a loathing and a scorn when we behold the five millions of paupers that cower and shiver at its base. The galleries and fountains of Versailles, the Louvre of Paris, her Notre Dame, and her Madeleine, though multiplied by thousands in number and in brilliancy, would be no atonement for the hundred thousand Parisian *ouvriers* without bread and without work. The galleries of painting and of sculpture at Rome, at Munich, or at Dresden, which body forth the divinest ideals ever executed or ever conceived, are but an abomination in the sight of Heaven and of all good men, while actual, living beings—beings that have hearts to palpitate, and nerves to agonize, and affections to be crushed or corrupted—are experimenting all around them upon the capacities of human nature for suffering and for sin. Where standards like these exist, and are upheld by council and by court, by fashion and by law, *Christianity is yet to be discovered;* at least, it is yet to be applied in practice to the social condition of men.

Our ambition as a state should trace itself to a different origin and propose to itself a different object. Its flame should be lighted at the skies. Its radiance and its warmth should reach the darkest and the coldest abodes of men. It should seek the solution of such problems as these: To what extent can competence displace pauperism? How nearly can we free ourselves from the low-minded and the vicious, not by their expatriation, but by their elevation? To what extent can the resources and powers of Nature be converted into human welfare, the peaceful arts of life be advanced, and the vast treasures of human talent and genius be developed? How much of suffering, in all its forms, can be relieved? or, what is better than relief, how much can be prevented? Cannot the classes of crimes be lessened, and the number of criminals in each class be diminished? ...

I suppose it to be the universal sentiment of all those who mingle any ingredient of benevolence with their notions on political economy that vast and overshadowing private fortunes are among the greatest dangers to which the happiness of the people in a republic can be subjected. Such fortunes would create a feudalism of a new kind, but one more oppressive and unrelenting than that of the Middle Ages. The feudal lords in England and on the Continent never held their retainers in a more abject condition of servitude than the great majority of foreign manufacturers and capitalists hold their operatives and laborers at the present day. The means employed are different; but the similarity in results is striking. What force did then, money does now. The villein of the Middle Ages had no spot of earth on which he could live, unless one were granted to him by his lord. The operative or laborer of the present day has no employment, and therefore no bread, unless the capitalist will accept his services. The vassal had no shelter but such as his master provided for him. Not one in five thousand of English operatives or farm laborers is able to build or own even a hovel; and therefore they must accept such shelter as capital offers them. The baron prescribed his own terms to his retainers; those terms were peremptory, and the serf must submit or perish. The British manufacturer or farmer prescribes the rate of wages he will give to his work people; he reduces these wages under whatever pretext he pleases; and they, too, have no alternative but submission or starvation. In some respects, indeed, the condition of the modern dependent is more forlorn than that of the corresponding serf class in former times. Some attributes of the patriarchal relation did spring up between the lord and his lieges to soften the harsh relations subsisting between them. Hence came some oversight of the condition of children, some relief in sickness, some protection and support in the decrepitude of age. But only in instances comparatively few have kindly offices smoothed the rugged relation between British capital and British labor. The children of the work people are abandoned to their fate; and notwithstanding the privations they suffer, and the dangers they threaten, no power in the realm has yet been able to secure them an education; and when the adult laborer is prostrated by sickness, or eventually worn out by toil and age, the poorhouse, which has all along been his destination, becomes his destiny.

Now, two or three things will doubtless be admitted to be true, beyond all controversy, in regard to Massachusetts. By its industrial condition, and its business operations, it is exposed, far beyond any other state in the Union, to the fatal extremes of overgrown wealth and desperate poverty. Its population is far more dense than that of any other state. It is four or five times more dense than the average of all the other states taken together; and density of population has always been one of the proximate causes of social inequality. According to population and territorial extent, there is far more capital in Massachusetts—capital which is movable and instantaneously available—than in any other state in the Union; and probably both these qualifications respecting population and territory could be omitted without endangering the truth of the assertion. . . .

Now, surely nothing but universal education can counterwork this tendency to the domination of capital and the servility of labor. If one class possesses all the wealth and the education, while the residue of society is ignorant and poor, it matters not by what name the relation between them may be called; the latter, in fact and in truth, will be the servile dependents and subjects of the former. But, if education be equably diffused, it will draw property after it by the strongest of all attractions; for such a thing never did happen, and never can happen, as that an intelligent and practical body of men should be permanently poor. Property and labor in different classes are essentially antagonistic; but property and labor in the same class are essentially fraternal. The people of Massachusetts have, in some degree, appreciated the truth that the unexampled prosperity of the state—its comfort, its competence, its general intelligence and virtue—is attributable to the education, more or less perfect, which all its people have received. But are they sensible of a fact equally important; namely, that it is to this same education that two-thirds of the people are indebted for not being today the vassals of as severe a tyranny, in the form of capital, as the lower classes of Europe are bound to in the form of brute force?

Education, then, beyond all other devices of human origin, is the great equalizer of the conditions of men—the balance wheel of the social machinery. I do not here mean that it so elevates the moral nature as to make men disdain and abhor the oppression of their fellowmen. This idea pertains to another of its atributes. But I mean that it gives each man the independence and the means by which he can resist the selfishness of other men. It does better than to disarm the poor of their hostility toward the rich; it prevents being poor. Agrarianism is the revenge of poverty against wealth. The wanton destruction of the property of others—the burning of hayricks and cornricks, the demolition of machinery because it supersedes hand labor, the sprinkling of vitriol on rich dresses—is only agrarianism run mad. Education prevents both the revenge and the madness. On the other hand, a fellow-feeling for one's class or caste is the common instinct of hearts not wholly sunk in selfish regards for person or for family. The spread of education, by enlarging the cultivated class or caste, will open a wider area over which the social feelings will expand; and, if this education should be universal and complete, it would do more than all things else to obliterate factitious distinctions in society. . . .

The necessity of general intelligence —that is, of education (for I use the terms as substantially synonymous, because general intelligence can never exist without general education, and general education will be sure to produce general intelligence)—the necessity of general intelligence under a republican form of government, like most other very important truths, has become a very trite one. It is so trite, indeed, as to have lost much of its force by its familiarity. Almost all the champions of education seize upon this argument, first of all, because it is so simple as to be understood by the ignorant and so strong as to convince the skeptical. Nothing would be easier than to follow in the train of so many writers, and to demonstrate by logic, by history, and by the nature of the case that a republican form of government, without intelligence in the people, must be on a vast scale what a madhouse without superintendent or keepers would be on a small one—the despotism of a few succeeded by universal anarchy, and anarchy by despotism, with no change but from bad to worse. . . .

But, in the possession of this attribute of intelligence, elective legislators will never far surpass their electors. By a natural law, like that which regulates the equilibrium of fluids, elector and elected, appointer and appointee, tend to the same level. It is not more certain that a wise and enlightened constituency will refuse to invest a reckless and profligate man with office, or discard him if accidentally chosen, than it is that a foolish or immoral constituency will discard or eject a wise man. This law of assimilation between the choosers and the chosen results, not only from the fact that the voter originally selects his representative according to the affinities of good or of ill, of wisdom or of folly, which exist between them, but if the

legislator enacts or favors a law which is too wise for the constituent to understand, or too just for him to approve, the next election will set him aside as certainly as if he had made open merchandise of the dearest interests of the people by perjury and for a bribe. And if the infinitely Just and Good, in giving laws to the Jews, recognized the "hardness of their hearts," how much more will an earthly ruler recognize the baseness or wickedness of the people when his heart is as hard as theirs! In a republican government legislators are a mirror reflecting the moral countenance of their constituents. And hence it is that the establishment of a republican government, without well-appointed and efficient means for the universal education of the people, is the most rash and foolhardy experiment ever tried by man. Its fatal results may not be immediately developed, [and] they may not follow as the thunder follows the lightning, for time is an element in maturing them, and the calamity is too great to be prepared in a day; but, like the slow-accumulating avalanche, they will grow more terrific by delay and at length, though it may be at a late hour, will overwhelm with ruin whatever lies athwart their path. It may be an easy thing to make a republic, but it is a very laborious thing to make republicans; and woe to the republic that rests upon no better foundations than ignorance, selfishness, and passion! Such a republic may grow in numbers and in wealth. As an avaricious man adds acres to his lands, so its rapacious government may increase its own darkness by annexing provinces and states to its ignorant domain. Its armies may be invincible, and its fleets may strike terror into nations on the opposite sides of the globe at the same hour. Vast in its extent, and enriched with all the prodigality of Nature, it may possess every capacity and opportunity of being great and of doing good. But, if such a republic be devoid of intelligence, it will only the more closely resemble an obscene giant who has waxed strong in his youth, and grown wanton in his strength; whose brain has been developed only in the region of the appetites and passions and not in the organs of reason and conscience; and who, therefore, is boastful of his bulk alone and glories in the weight of his heel and in the destruction of his arm. Such a republic, with all its noble capacities for beneficence, will rush with the speed of a whirlwind to an ignominious end; and all good men of aftertimes would be fain to weep over its downfall did not their scorn and contempt at its folly and its wickedness repress all sorrow for its fate. . . .

1. THE AMERICAN SYSTEM[1]

By HENRY CLAY

EDITORS' NOTE.—Henry Clay (1777–1852), influential Whig political leader and opponent of Jackson, was born on the Virginia frontier but lived his mature years in Kentucky. This speech was delivered in Cincinnati, Ohio, on August 3, 1830.

...With respect to the American system, which demands your undivided approbation, and in regard to which you are pleased to estimate much too highly my service, its great object is to secure the independence of our country, to augment its wealth, and to diffuse the comforts of civilization throughout society. That object, it has been supposed, can be best accomplished by introducing, encouraging, and protecting the arts among us. It may be called a system of real reciprocity, under the operation of which one citizen or one part of the country can exchange one description of the produce of labor with another citizen or another part of the country for a different description of the produce of labor. It is a system which develops, improves, and perfects the capabilities of our common country and enables us to avail ourselves of all the resources with which Providence has blest us. To the laboring classes it is invaluable, since it increases and multiplies the demands for their industry and gives them an option of employments. It adds power and strength to our union by new ties of interest, blending and connecting together all its parts in creating an interest with each in the prosperity of the whole. It secures to our own country, whose skill and enter-prise, properly fostered and sustained, cannot be surpassed, those vast profits which are made in other countries by the operation of converting the raw material into manufactured articles. It naturalizes and creates within the bosom of our country all the arts and, mixing the farmer, manufacturer, mechanic, artist, and those engaged in other vocations together, admits of those mutual exchanges so conducive to the prosperity of all and everyone, free from the perils of sea and war—all this it effects, whilst it nourishes and leaves a fair scope to foreign trade. Suppose we were a nation that clad ourselves, and made all the implements necessary to civilization, but did not produce our own bread, which we brought from foreign countries, although our own was capable of producing it under the influence of suitable laws of protection, ought not such laws to be enacted? The case supposed is not essentially different from the real state of things which led to the adoption of the American system.

That system has had a wonderful success. It has more than realized all the hopes of its founders. It has completely falsified all the predictions of its opponents. It has increased the wealth, and power, and population of the nation. It has diminished the price of articles of consumption and has placed them within the reach of a far greater number of our people than could have found means

1. *Life and Speeches of the Hon. Henry Clay* ..., ed. Daniel Mallory (New York, 1857), I, 647–52, 659–61, 662–63, 664–67.

to command them if they had been manufactured abroad instead of at home.

But it is useless to dwell on the argument in support of this beneficent system before this audience. It will be of more consequence here to examine some of the objections which are still urged against it and the means which are proposed to subvert it. These objections are now principally confined to its operation upon the great staple of cotton wool, and they are urged with most vehemence in a particular state. If the objections are well founded, the system should be modified, as far as it can consistently with interest, in other parts of the Union. If they are not well founded, it is to be hoped they will be finally abandoned.

In approaching the subject, I have thought it of importance to inquire what was the profit made upon capital employed in the culture of cotton at its present reduced price. The result has been information that it nets from seven to eighteen per cent per annum, varying according to the advantage of situation and the degree of skill, judgment, and industry applied to the production of the article. But the lowest rate of profit, in the scale, is more than the greatest amount which is made on capital employed in the farming portions of the Union.

If the cotton planter have any just complaint against the expediency of the American system, it must be founded on the fact that he either sells *less* of his staple, or sells at *lower* prices, or purchases for consumption, articles at *dearer* rates, or of *worse* qualities, in consequence of that system, than he would do if it did not exist. If he would neither sell more of his staple, nor sell it at better prices, nor could purchase better or cheaper articles for consumption, provided the system did not exist, then he has no cause, on the score of its burdensome operation, to complain of the system but must look to other

sources for the grievances which he supposes afflict him.

As respects the sale of his staple, it would be indifferent to the planter whether one portion of it was sold in Europe and the other in America, provided the aggregate of both were equal to all that he could sell in one market, if he had but one, and provided he could command the same price in both cases. The double market would indeed be something better for him, because of its greater security in time of war as well as in peace and because it would be attended with less perils and less charges. If there be an equal amount of the raw material manufactured, it must be immaterial to the cotton planter, in the sale of the article, whether there be two theaters of the manufacture, one in Europe and the other in America, or but one in Europe; or if there be a difference, it will be in favor of the two places of manufacture, instead of one, for reasons already assigned and others that will be hereafter stated.

It could be of no advantage to the cotton planter if all the cotton now manufactured both in Europe and America was manufactured exclusively in Europe, and an amount of cotton fabrics should be brought back from Europe equal to both what is now brought from there and what is manufactured in the United States together. Whilst he would gain nothing, the United States would lose the profit and employment resulting from the manufacture of that portion which is now wrought up by the manufacturers of the United States.

Unless, therefore, it can be shown that, by the reduction of import duties and the overthrow of the American system and by limiting the manufacture of cotton to Europe, a greater amount of the raw material would be consumed than is at present, it is difficult to see what interest, so far as respects the sale of that staple, the cotton planter has in the subversion of that system. If a reduction of duties would admit of larger investments in British or European fabrics of cotton, and their subsequent importation into this country, this additional supply would take the place, if consumed, of an equal amount of American manufactures and consequently would not augment the general consumption of the raw material. Additional importation does not necessarily imply increased consumption, especially when it is effected by a policy which would impair the ability to purchase and consume.

Upon the supposition just made, of a restriction to Europe of the manufacture of cotton, would more or less of the article be consumed than now is? More could not be, unless, in consequence of such a monopoly of the manufacture, Europe could sell more than she now does. But to what countries could she sell more? She gets the raw material now unburdened by any duties except such moderate ones as her policy, not likely to be changed, imposes. She is enabled thereby to sell as much of the manufactured article as she can find markets for in the states within her own limits or in foreign countries. The destruction of the American manufacture would not induce her to sell cheaper, but might enable her to sell dearer, than she now does. The ability of those foreign countries to purchase and consume would not be increased by the annihilation of our manufactures and the monopoly of European manufacture. The probability is that those foreign countries, by the fact of that monopoly and some consequent increase of price, would be worse and dearer supplied than they now are under the operation of a competition between America and Europe in their supply.

At most, the United States, after the transfer from their territory to Europe of the entire manufacture of the article, could not consume of European fabrics from cotton a greater amount than they now derive from Europe and from manufactures within their own limits.

But it is confidently believed that the consumption of cotton fabrics, on the supposition which has been made, within the United States would be much less than it is at present. It would be less, because the American consumer would not possess the means or ability to purchase as much of the European fabric as he now does to buy the American. Europe purchases but little of the produce of the northern, middle, and western regions of the United States. The staple productions of those regions are excluded from her consumption by her policy or by her native supplies of similar productions. The effect, therefore, of obliging the inhabitants of those regions to depend upon the cotton manufactures of Europe for necessary supplies of the article would be alike injurious to them and to the cotton grower. They would suffer from their inability to supply their wants, and there would be a consequent diminution of the consumption of cotton. By the location of the manufacture in the United States, the quantity of cotton consumed is increased, and the more numerous portion of their inhabitants, who would not be otherwise sufficiently supplied, are abundantly served. That this is the true state of things I think cannot be doubted by any reflecting and unprejudiced man. The establishment of manufactures within the United States enables the manufacturer to sell to the farmer, the mechanic, the physician, the lawyer, and all who are engaged in other pursuits of life; and these, in their turns, supply the manufacturer with subsistence and whatever else his wants require. Under the influence of the protecting policy, many new towns have been built, and old ones enlarged. The population of these places draw their subsistence from the farming interests of our country, their fuel from our forests and coal mines, and the raw materials from which they fashion and fabricate from the cotton planter and the mines of our country. These mutual exchanges, so animating and invigorating to the industry of the people of the United States, could not possibly be effected between America and Europe if the latter enjoyed the monopoly of manufacturing.

It results, therefore, that, so far as the sale of the great southern staple is concerned, a greater quantity is sold and consumed, and consequently better prices are obtained, under the operation of the American system than would be without it. Does that system oblige the cotton planter to buy dearer or worse articles of consumption than he could purchase if it did not exist?

The same cause of American and European competition, which enables him to sell more of the produce of his industry and at better prices, also enables him to buy cheaper and better articles for consumption. It cannot be doubted that the tendency of the competition between the European and American manufacturer is to reduce the price and improve the quality of their respective fabrics, whenever they come into collision. This is the immutable law of all competition. If the American manufacture were discontinued, Europe would then exclusively furnish those supplies which are now derived from the establishments in both continents; and the first consequence would be an augmentation of the demand, beyond the supply, equal to what is now manufactured in the United States, but which, in the contingency supposed, would be wrought in Europe. If the destruction of the American manufactures were sudden, there would be a sudden and probably a considerable rise in the European fabrics. Although, in the end, they might be again reduced, it is not likely that the ultimate reduction of the prices would be to such rates as if both the workshops of America and Europe remained sources of supply. There would also be a sudden reduction in the price of the raw material, in consequence of the cessation of American demand. And this reduction would be permanent, if the supposition be correct that there would be a diminution in the consumption of cotton fabrics, arising out of the inability, on the part of large portions of the people of the United States, to purchase those of Europe.

That the effect of competition between the European and American manufacture has been to supply the American consumer with cheaper and better articles, since the adoption of the American system, notwithstanding the existence of causes which have obstructed its fair operation and retarded its full development, is incontestable. Both the freeman and the slave are now better and cheaper supplied than they were prior to the existence of that system. Cotton fabrics have diminished in price, and been improved in their texture, to an extent that it is difficult for the imagination to keep pace with. Those partly of cotton and partly of wool are also better and cheaper supplied. The same observation is applicable to those which are exclusively wrought of wool, iron, or glass. In short, it is believed that there is not one item of the tariff inserted for the protection of native industry which has not fallen in price. The American competition has tended to keep down the European rival fabric, and the European has tended to lower the American.

Of what then can the South Carolina planter justly complain in the operation of this system? What is there in it which justifies the harsh and strong epithets which some of her politicians have applied to it? What is there in her condition which warrants their assertion that she is oppressed by a government to which she stands in the mere relation of a colony?

She is oppressed by a great reduction in the price of manufactured articles of consumption.

She is oppressed by the advantage of two markets for the sale of her valuable staple and for the purchase of objects required by her wants.

She is oppressed by better prices for that staple than she could command if the system to which they object did not exist.

She is oppressed by the option of purchasing cheaper and better articles, the produce of the hands of American freemen, instead of dearer and worse articles, the produce of the hands of British subjects.

She is oppressed by the measures of a government in which she has had, for many years, a larger proportion of power and influence, at home and abroad, than any state in the whole Union in comparison with the population. . . .

If anything could be considered as settled, under the present constitution of our government, I had supposed that it was its authority to construct such internal improvements as may be deemed by Congress necessary and proper to carry into effect the power granted to it. For nearly twenty-five years, the power has been asserted and exercised by the government. For the last fifteen years it has been often controverted in Congress, but it has been invariably maintained, in that body, by repeated decisions, pronounced, after full and elaborate debate, and at intervals of time implying the greatest deliberation. Numerous laws attest the existence of the power; and no less than twenty-odd laws have been passed in relation to a single work. This power, necessary to all parts of the Union, is indispensable to the West. Without it, this section can never enjoy any part of the benefit of a regular disbursement of the vast revenues of the United States. . . .

Yet we are told that this power can no longer be exercised without an amendment of the Constitution! On the occasion in South Carolina, to which I have already adverted, it was said that the tariff and internal improvements are intimately connected and that the death-blow which it was hoped the one had received will finally destroy the other. I concur in the opinion that they are intimately, if not indissolubly, united. Not connected together, with the fraudulent intent which has been imputed, but by their nature, by the tendency of each to advance the objects of the other, and of both to augment the sum of national prosperity.

If I could believe that the executive message, which was communicated to Congress upon the application of the veto to the Maysville road, really expressed the opinion of the President of the United States, in consequence of the unfortunate relations which have existed between us, I would forbear to make any observation upon it. . . . It is impossible that the veto message should express the opinions of the President, and I prove it by evidence derived from himself. Not forty days before that message was sent to Congress, he approved a bill embracing appropriations to various objects of internal improvement and, among others, to improve the navigation of Conneaut Creek. Although somewhat acquainted with the geography of our country, I declare I did not know of the existence of such a stream until I read the bill. I have since made it an object of inquiry and have been told that it rises in one corner of Pennsylvania and is discharged into Lake Erie, in a corner of the state of Ohio, and that the utmost extent to which its navigation is susceptible of improvement is about seven miles. Is it possible that the President could conceive *that a national* object, and that the improvement of a great thoroughfare, on which the mail is transported for some eight or ten states and territories, is not a national consideration? The power to improve the navigation of watercourses, nowhere expressly recognized in the Constitution, is infinitely more doubtful than the establishment of mail roads, which is explicitly authorized in that instrument! Did not the President, during the canvass which preceded his election, in his answer to a letter from Governor Ray, of Indiana, written at the instance of the senate of that respectable state, expressly refer to his votes given in the Senate of the United States, for his opinion as to the power of the general government and inform him that his opinion remained unaltered? And do we not find, upon consulting the journals of the Senate, that, among other votes affirming the existence of the power, he voted for an appropriation to the Chesapeake and Delaware Canal, which is only about fourteen miles in extent? And do we not know that it was at that time, like the Maysville road now, in progress of execution under the direction of a company incorporated by a state? And that, whilst the Maysville road had a connection with roads east of Maysville and southwest of Lexington, the turnpiking of which was contemplated, that canal had no connection with any other existing canal.

The veto message is perfectly irreconcilable with the previous acts, votes, and opinions of General Jackson. It does not express *his* opinions, but those of his advisers and counselors, and especially those of his cabinet. If we look at the composition of that cabinet, we cannot doubt it. Three of the five who, I believe, compose it (whether the postmaster-general be one or not, I do not know) are known to be directly and positively opposed to the power; a fourth, to use a term descriptive of the favorite policy of one of them, is a *non-committal*, and, as to the fifth, good Lord deliver us from such friendship as *his* internal improvements. Further, I have heard it from good authority (but I will not vouch for it, although I believe it to be true) that some of the gentlemen from the South waited upon the President, whilst he held the Maysville bill under consideration, and told him if he approved of that bill, the South would no longer approve of him but oppose his administration.

I cannot, therefore, consider the message as conveying the sentiments and views of the President. It is impossible. It is the work of his cabinet; and if, unfortunately, they were not practically irresponsible to the people of the United States, they would deserve severe animadversions for having prevailed upon the President, in the precipitation of business, and perhaps without his spectacles, to put his name to *such* a paper and send it forth to Congress and to the nation. Why, I have read that paper again and again; and I never can peruse it without thinking of diplomacy, and the name of Talleyrand, Talleyrand, Talleyrand, perpetually recurring. It seems to have been written in the spirit of an accommodating soul, who, being determined to have fair weather in any contingency, was equally ready to cry out, "Good lord, good devil." Are you for internal improvements? You may extract from the message texts enough to support your opinion. Are you against them? The message supplies you with abundant authority to countenance your views. Do you think that a long and uninterrupted current of concurring decisions ought to settle the question of a controverted power? So the authors of the message affect to believe. But ought any precedents, however numerous, to be allowed to establish a doubtful power? The message agrees with him who thinks not. . . .

Let us glance at a few only of the reasons, if reasons they can be called, of this piebald message. The first is that the exercise of the power has produced discord, and, to restore harmony to the national councils, it should be abandoned, or, which is tantamount, the Constitution must be amended. The President is therefore advised to throw himself into the minority. Well—did that revive harmony? When the question was taken in the House of the people's Representatives, an obstinate majority still voted for the bill, the objections in the message notwithstanding. And in the Senate the representatives of the states, a refractory majority, stood unmoved. But does the message mean to assert that no great measure, about which public sentiment is much divided, ought to be adopted in consequence of that division? Then none can ever be adopted. Apply this new rule to the case of the American Revolution. The colonies were rent into implacable parties—the Tories everywhere abounded and in some places outnumbered the Whigs. This continued to be the state of things throughout the revolutionary contest. Suppose some timid, time-serving Whig had, during its progress, addressed the public and, adverting to the discord which prevailed and to the expediency of restoring harmony in the land, had proposed to abandon or postpone the establishment of our liberty and independence until all should agree in asserting them. The late war was opposed by a powerful and talented party; what would have been thought of President Madison if, instead of a patriotic and energetic message recommending it as the only alternative to preserve our honor and vindicate our right, he had come to Congress with a proposal that we should continue to submit to the wrongs and degradation inflicted upon our country by a foreign power because we were, unhappily, greatly divided? What would have become of the settlement of the Missouri question, the tariff, the Indian bill of the last session, if the existence of a strong and almost equal division in the public councils ought to have prevented their adoption? The principle is nothing more nor less than a declaration that the right of the majority to govern must yield to the perseverance, respectability, and numbers of the minority. It is in keeping with the nullifying doctrines of South Carolina and is such a principle as might be expected to be put forth by such a cabinet. The government of the United States, at this juncture, exhibits a most remarkable spectacle. *It is that of a majority of the nation having put the powers of government into the hands of the minority.* If anyone can doubt this, let him look back at the elements of the executive, at the presiding officers of the two houses, at the composition and the chairmen of the most important committees, who shape and direct the public business in Congress. Let him look, above all, *at measures*, the necessary consequences of such an anomalous state of things—internal improvements gone, or going; the whole American system threatened, and the triumphant shouts of anticipated victory sounding in our ears. Georgia, extorting from the fears of an affrighted majority of Congress an Indian bill, which may prostrate all the laws, treaties, and policy which have regulated our relations with the Indians from the commencement of our government; and politicians in South Carolina, at the same time, brandishing the torch of civil war and pronouncing unbounded eulogiums upon the President, for the good he has done and the still greater good which they expect at his hands, and the sacrifice of the interests of the majority.

Another reason assigned in the Maysville message is the desire of paying the national debt. By an act passed in the year 1817, an annual appropriation was made of ten millions of dollars, which were vested in the commissioners of the sinking fund, to pay the principal and interest of the public debt. . . . Under the operation of that act, nearly one hundred and fifty millions of the principal and interest of the public debt were paid, prior to the commencement of the present administration. During that of Mr. Adams, between forty and fifty were paid, whilst larger appropriations of money and land were made, to objects of internal improvements, than ever had been made by all preceding administrations together. There only remained about fifty millions to be paid when the present chief magistrate entered on the duties of that office, and a considerable portion of that cannot be discharged during the present official term.

The redemption of the debt is, therefore, the work of Congress; the President has nothing to do with it, the secretary of the treasury being directed annually to pay the ten millions to the commissioners of the sinking fund, whose duty it is to apply the amount to the extinguishment of the debt. The secretary himself has no more to do with the operation than the hydrants through which the water passes to the consumption of the population of this city. He turns the cock on the first of January, and the first of July, in each year, and the public treasure is poured out to the public creditor from the reservoir, filled by the wisdom of Congress. It is evident, from this just view of the matter, that Congress, to which belongs the care of providing the ways and means, was as competent as the President to determine what portion of their constituents' money could be applied to the improvement of their condition. As much of the public debt as can be paid will be discharged in four years by the operation of the sinking fund. I have seen, in some late paper, a calculation of the delay which would have resulted, in its payment, from the appropriation to the Maysville road, and it was less than one week! How has it happened, that, under the administration of Mr. Adams, and during every year of it, such large and liberal appropriations could be made for internal improvements without touching the fund devoted to the public debt and

that this administration should find itself balked in its first year?

The veto message proceeds to insist that the Maysville and Lexington road is not a national but a local road, of sixty miles in length, and confined within the limits of a particular state. If, as that document also asserts, the power can, in *no case*, be exercised until it shall have been explained and defined by an amendment of the Constitution, the discrimination of national and local roads would seem to be altogether unnecessary. What is or is not a national road, the message supposes, may admit of controversy and is not susceptible of precise definition. The difficulty which its authors imagine grows out of their attempt to substitute a rule founded upon the extent and locality of the road, instead of the *use* and *purposes* to which it is applicable. If the road facilitates, in a considerable degree, the transportation of the mail to a considerable portion of the Union, and at the same time promotes internal commerce among several states and may tend to accelerate the movement of armies and the distribution of the munitions of war, it is of national consideration. Tested by this, the true rule, the Maysville road was undoubtedly national. It connects the largest body, perhaps, of fertile land in the Union, with the navigation of the Ohio and Mississippi rivers and with the canals of the states of Ohio, Pennsylvania, and New York. It begins on the line which divides the state of Ohio and Kentucky, and, of course, quickens trade and intercourse between them. Tested by the character of other works, for which the President, as a senator, voted, or which were approved by him only about a month before he rejected the Maysville bill, the road was undoubtedly national.

But this view of the matter, however satisfactory it ought to be, is imperfect. It will be admitted that the Cumberland road is national. It is completed no farther than Zanesville, in the state of Ohio. On reaching that point, two routes present themselves for its further extension, both national, and both deserving of execution. One leading northwestwardly, through the states of Ohio, Indiana, and Illinois, to Missouri, and the other southwestwardly, through the states of Ohio, Kentucky, Tennessee, and Alabama, to the Gulf of Mexico. Both have been long contemplated. Of the two, the southwestern is the most wanted, in the present state of population, and will probably always be of the greatest use. But the northwestern route is in progress of execution beyond Zanesville, and appropriations toward part of it were sanctioned by the President at the last session. National highways can only be executed in sections, at different times. So the Cumberland road was and continues to be constructed. Of all the parts of the southwestern route, the road from Maysville to Lexington is most needed, whether we regard the amount of transportation and traveling upon it or the impediments which it presents in the winter and spring months. It took my family four days to reach Lexington from Maysville in April, 1829.

The same scheme which has been devised and practiced to defeat the tariff has been adopted to undermine internal improvements. They are to be attacked in detail. Hence the rejection of the Maysville road, the Fredericktown road, and the Louisville Canal. But is this fair? Ought each proposed road to be viewed separately and detached? Ought it not to be considered in connection with other great works which are in progress of execution or are projected? The policy of the foes indicates what ought to be the policy of the friends of the power.

The blow aimed at internal improvements has fallen with unmerited severity upon the state of Kentucky. No state in the union has ever shown more generous devotion to its preservation and to the support of its honor and its interest than she has. During the late war, her sons fought gallantly by the side of the President, on the glorious eighth of January, when he covered himself with unfading laurels. Wherever the war raged, they were to be found among the foremost in battle, freely bleeding in the service of their country. They have never threatened nor calculated the value of this happy union. Their representatives in Congress have constantly and almost unanimously supported the power, cheerfully voting for large appropriations to works of internal improvements in other states. Not one cent of the common treasure has been expended on any public road in that state. They contributed to the elevation of the President, under a firm conviction, produced by his deliberate acts, and his solemn assertions, that he was friendly to the power. Under such circumstances, have they not just and abundant cause of surprise, regret, and mortification at the late unexpected decision?

Another mode of destroying the system, about which I fear I have detained you too long, which its foes have adopted, is to assail the character of its friends. Can you otherwise account for the spirit of animosity with which I am pursued? A sentiment this morning caught my eye, in the shape of a Fourth of July toast, proposed at the celebration of that anniversary in South Carolina, by a gentleman whom I never saw and to whom I am a total stranger. With humanity, charity, and Christian benevolence unexampled, he wished that I might be driven so far beyond the frigid regions of the northern zone that all hell could not thaw me! Do you believe it was against *me*, this feeble and frail form, tottering with age, this lump of perishing clay, that all this kindness was directed? No, no, no. It was against the measures of policy which I have espoused, against the system which I have labored to uphold, that it was aimed. If I had been opposed to the tariff, and internal improvements, and in favor of the

South Carolina doctrine of nullification, the same worthy gentleman would have wished that I might be ever fanned by soft breezes, charged with aromatic odors—that my path might be strewed with roses, and my abode be an earthly paradise. I am now a private man, the humblest of the humble, possessed of no office, no power, no patronage, no subsidized press, no post-office department to distribute its effusions, no army, no navy, no official corps to chant my praises and to drink, in flowing bowls, my health and prosperity. I have nothing but the warm affections of a portion of the people and a fair reputation, the only inheritance derived from my father, and almost the only inheritance which I am desirous of transmitting to my children.

The present chief magistrate has done me much wrong, but I have freely forgiven him. He believed, no doubt, that I had done him previous wrong. Although I am unconscious of it, he had *that* motive for his conduct toward me. But others, who had joined in the hue and cry against me, had no such pretext. Why then am I thus pursued, my words perverted and distorted, my acts misrepresented? Why do more than a hundred presses daily point their cannon at me and thunder forth their peals of abuse and detraction? It is not against me. That is impossible. A few years more, and this body will be where all is still and silent. It is against the principles of civil liberty, against the tariff and internal improvements, to which the better part of my life has been devoted, that this implacable war is waged. My enemies flatter themselves that those systems may be overthrown by my destruction. Vain and impotent hope! My existence is not of the smallest consequence to their preservation. They will survive me. Long, long after I am gone, whilst the lofty hills encompass this fair city, the offspring of those measures shall remain; whilst the beautiful river that sweeps by its walls shall continue to bear upon its proud bosom the wonders which the immortal genius of Fulton, with the blessings of Providence, has given; whilst truth shall hold its sway among men, those systems will invigorate the industry and animate the hopes of the farmer, the mechanic, the manufacturer, and all other classes of our countrymen.

People of Ohio here assembled—mothers, daughters, sons, and sires—when reclining on the peaceful pillow of repose, and communing with your own hearts, ask yourselves if I ought to be the unremitting object of perpetual calumny? If, when the opponents of the late President gained the victory on the fourth of March, 1829, the war ought not to have ceased, quarters been granted, and prisoners released? Did not those opponents obtain all the honors, offices, and emoluments of government; the power, which they have frequently exercised, of rewarding whom they pleased and punishing whom they could? Was not all this sufficient? Does it all avail not, while Mordecai, the Jew, stands at the king's gate?

I thank you, fellow-citizens, again and again, for the numerous proofs you have given me of your attachment and confidence. And may your fine city continue to enjoy the advantages of the enterprise, industry, and public spirit of its mechanics and other inhabitants, until it rises in wealth, extent, and prosperity with the largest of our Atlantic capitals.

2. CONGRESSIONAL REPORT ON THE SECOND BANK OF THE UNITED STATES[1]

By The Ways and Means Committee, House of Representatives

EDITORS' NOTE.—There was a division of opinion among Jackson's supporters about the United States Bank and paper money. Those who supported the bank were responsible for this favorable report in 1830 by the Ways and Means Committee of the House of Representatives. George McDuffie (1790–1851), chairman at this time of the committee, was an erratic and influential politician from South Carolina. The son of poor upland farmers, McDuffie was helped by an employer to obtain an education. He began his law practice in 1814, was a member of the House of Representatives from 1821 to 1834, governor of his state in 1834, and United States senator from 1842 to 1846. McDuffie broke with Jackson on the bank and nullification, vehemently supporting both of these.

It must be assumed as the basis of all sound reasoning on this subject that the existence of a paper currency, issued by banks deriving their charters from the state governments, cannot be prohibited by Congress. Indeed, bank credit and bank paper are so extensively interwoven with the commercial operations of society that, even if Congress had the constitutional power, it would be utterly impossible to produce so entire a change in the monetary system of the country as to abolish the agency of banks of discount, without involving the community in all the distressing embarrassments usually attendant on great political revolutions, subverting the titles to private property. The sudden withdrawal of some hundred millions of bank credit would be equivalent in its effects to the arbitrary and despotic transfer of the property of one portion of the community to another, to the extent, probably, of half that amount. Whatever, therefore, may be the advantages of a purely metallic currency, and whatever the objections to a circulating medium partly composed of bank paper, the committee consider that they are precluded by the existing state of things from instituting a comparison between them, with a view to any practical result.

If they were not thus precluded, and it were submitted to them as an original question, whether the acknowledged and manifold facilities of bank credit and bank paper are not more than counterbalanced by the distressing vicissitudes in trade incident to their use, they are by no means prepared to say that they would not give a decided preference to the more costly and cumbersome medium.

But the question really presented for their determination is not between a metallic and a paper currency but between a paper currency of uniform value, and subject to the control of the only power competent to its regulation, and a paper currency of varying and

1. *Register of Debates in Congress ... of the First Session of the Twenty-second Congress Together with an Appendix Containing Important State Papers and Public Documents ...* (Washington, 1833), VIII, 132–39, 142–43.

fluctuating value, and subject to no common or adequate control whatever. On this question it would seem that there could scarcely exist a difference of opinion; and that this is substantially the question involved in considering the expediency of a national bank will satisfactorily appear by a comparison of the state of the currency previous to the establishment of the present bank and its condition for the last ten years.

Soon after the expiration of the charter of the first Bank of the United States, an immense number of local banks sprang up under the pecuniary exigencies produced by the withdrawal of so large an amount of bank credit, as necessarily resulted from the winding-up of its concerns—an amount falling very little short of fifteen millions of dollars. These banks, being entirely free from the salutary control which the Bank of the United States had recently exercised over the local institutions, commenced that system of imprudent trading and excessive issues which speedily involved the country in all the embarrassments of a disordered currency. The extraordinary stimulus of a heavy war expenditure, derived principally from loans, and a corresponding multiplication of local banks, chartered by the double score in some of the states, hastened the catastrophe which must have occurred, at no distant period, without these extraordinary causes. The last year of the war presented the singular and melancholy spectacle of a nation abounding in resources, a people abounding in self-devoting patriotism, and a government reduced to the very brink of avowed bankruptcy, solely for the want of a national institution which, at the same time that it would have facilitated the government loans and other treasury operations, would have furnished a circulating medium of general credit in every part of the Union. In this view of the subject, the committee are fully sustained by the opinion of Mr.

Dallas, then Secretary of the Treasury, and by the concurring and almost unanimous opinion of all parties in Congress; for, whatever diversity of opinion prevailed as to the proper basis and organization of a bank, almost everyone agreed that a national bank, of some sort, was indispensably necessary to rescue the country from the greatest of financial calamities.

The committee will now present a brief exposition of the state of the currency at the close of the war, of the injury which resulted from it, as well to the government as to the community, and their reasons for believing that it could not have been restored to a sound condition, and cannot now be preserved in that condition, without the agency of such an institution as the Bank of the United States.

The price current appended to this report will exhibit a scale of depreciation in the local currency, ranging through various degrees to 20, and even to 25, per cent. Among the principal eastern cities, Washington and Baltimore were the points at which the depreciation was greatest. The paper of the banks in these places was from 20 to 22 per cent below par. At Philadelphia the depreciation was considerably less, though even there it was from 17 to 18 per cent. In New York and Charleston it was from 7 to 10 per cent. But in the interior of the country, where banks were established, the depreciation was even greater than at Washington and Baltimore. In the western part of Pennsylvania, and particularly at Pittsburgh, it was 25 per cent. These statements, however, of the relative depreciation of bank paper at various places, as compared with specie, give a very inadequate idea of the enormous evils inflicted upon the community by the excessive issues of bank paper. No proposition is better established than that the value of money, whether it consists of specie or paper, is depreciated in exact proportion to the increase of its quantity, in any given state of the demand for it. If, for example, the banks, in 1816, doubled the quantity of the circulating medium by their excessive issues, they produced a general degradation of the entire mass of the currency, including gold and silver, proportioned to the redundancy of the issues, and wholly independent of the relative depreciation of bank paper at different places, as compared with specie. The nominal money price of every article was, of course, 100 per cent higher than it would have been but for the duplication of the quantity of the circulating medium. Money is nothing more nor less than the measure by which the relative value of all articles of merchandise is ascertained. If, when the circulating medium is fifty millions, an article should cost one dollar, it would certainly cost two, if, without any increase of the uses of a circulating medium, its quantity should be increased to one hundred millions. This rise in the price of commodities, or depreciation in the value of money, as compared with them, would not be owing to the want of credit in the bank bills of which the currency happened to be composed. It would exist though these bills were of undoubted credit, and convertible into specie at the pleasure of the holder, and would result simply from the redundancy of their quantity. It is important to a just understanding of the subject that the relative depreciation of bank paper at different places, as compared with specie, should not be confounded with this general depreciation of the entire mass of the circulating medium, including specie. Though closely allied, both in their causes and effects, they deserve to be separately considered.

The evils resulting from the relative depreciation of bank paper at different places are more easily traced to their causes, more palpable in their nature, and consequently more generally understood by the community. Though much less ruinous than the evils resulting from the general depreciation of the whole currency, they are yet of sufficient magnitude to demand a full exposition.

A very serious evil, already hinted at, which grew out of the relative depreciation of bank paper at the different points of importation, was its inevitable tendency to draw all the importation of foreign merchandise to the cities where the depreciation was greatest and divert them from those where the currency was comparatively sound. If the Bank of the United States had not been established, and the government had been left without any alternative but to receive the depreciated local currency, it is difficult to imagine the extent to which the evasion of the revenue laws would have been carried. Every state would have had an interest to encourage the excessive issues of its banks, and increase the degradation of its currency, with a view to attract foreign commerce. Even in the condition which the currency had reached in 1816, Boston and New York and Charleston would have found it advantageous to derive their supplies of foreign merchandise through Baltimore; and commerce would undoubtedly have taken that direction had not the currency been corrected. To avoid this injurious diversion of foreign imports, Massachusetts and New York and South Carolina would have been driven, by all the motives of self-defense and self-interest, to degrade their respective currencies at least to a par with the currency of Baltimore; and thus a rivalry in the career of depreciation would have sprung up, to which no limit can be assigned. As the tendency of this state of things would have been to cause the largest portion of the revenue to be collected at a few places, and in the most depreciated of the local currency, it would have followed that a very small part of that revenue would have been disbursed at the points where it was collected. The government would consequently have been compelled to sustain a heavy loss upon the transfer of its funds to the points of expenditure. The annual loss which would have resulted from these causes alone cannot be estimated at a less sum than two millions of dollars.

But the principal loss which resulted from the relative depreciation of bank paper at different places, and its want of general credit, was that sustained by the community in the great operations of commercial exchange. The extent of these operations annually may be safely estimated at sixty millions of dollars. Upon this sum the loss sustained by the merchants and planters and farmers and manufacturers was not probably less than an average of 10 per cent, being the excess of the rate of exchange beyond its natural rate in a sound state of the currency, and beyond the rate to which it has been actually reduced by the operations of the Bank of the United States. It will be thus perceived that an annual tax of six millions of dollars was levied from the industrious and productive classes by the large moneyed capitalists in our commercial cities who were engaged in the business of brokerage. A variously depreciated currency, and a fluctuating state of the exchanges, open a wide and abundant harvest to the money brokers; and it is not, therefore, surprising that they should be opposed to an institution which, at the same time that it has relieved the community from the enormous tax just stated, has deprived them of the enormous profits which they derived from speculating in the business of exchange. In addition to the losses sustained by the community in the great operations of exchange, extensive losses were suffered throughout the interior of the country, in all the smaller operations of trade, as well as by the failure of the numerous paper banks, puffed into a factitious credit by fraudulent artifices, and having no substantial basis of capital to insure the redemption of their bills.

But no adequate conception can be formed of the evils of a depreciated currency, without looking beyond the relative depreciation, at different places, to the general depreciation of the entire mass. It appears from the report of Mr. Crawford, the Secretary of the Treasury, in 1820, that, during the general suspension of specie payments by the local banks in the years 1815 and 1816, the circulating medium of the United States had reached the aggregate amount of one hundred and ten millions of dollars, and that in the year 1819 it had been reduced to forty-five millions of dollars, being a reduction of 59 per cent in the short period of four years. The committee are inclined to the opinion that the severe and distressing operation of restoring a vicious currency to a sound state, by the calling-in of bank paper and the curtailment of bank discounts, had carried the reduction of the currency in 1819 to a point somewhat lower than was consistent with the just requirements of the community for a circulating medium and that the bank discounts have been gradually enlarged since that time, so as to satisfy those requirements. It will be assumed, therefore, that the circulating medium of the United States has been fifty-five millions of dollars for the last ten years, taking the average.

Even upon this assumption it will follow that the national currency has been 100 per cent more valuable for the last ten years than it was in 1816. In other words, two dollars would purchase no more of any commodity in 1816 than one dollar has been capable of purchasing at any time since 1819. It is obvious, therefore, that the depreciation of the paper of particular banks, at any particular time, as compared with specie, furnishes no criterion by which to ascertain the general depreciation of the whole currency, including specie, as compared with the value of that currency at a different period. A specie dollar in 1816 would purchase no more than half as much as a paper dollar will purchase at present.

Having endeavored to explain thus briefly the general depreciation resulting from a redundant currency, the committee will now proceed to point out some of the injurious consequences which have resulted from those great changes in the standard of value which have been unavoidably produced by the correction of the redundancy.

An individual who borrowed a sum of money in 1816 and paid it in 1820 evidently returned to the lender double the value received from him; and one who paid a debt in 1820 which he had contracted in 1816, as evidently paid double the value he had stipulated to pay, though nominally the same amount in money. It is in this way that fluctuations in the quantity and value of the currency interfere, in the most unjust and injurious manner, between debtor and creditor.

And when banks have the power of suspending specie payments, and of arbitrarily contracting and expanding their issues, without any general control, they exercise a more dangerous and despotic power over the property of the community than was ever exercised by the most absolute government. In such a state of things, every man in the community holds his property at the mercy of money-making corporations, which have a decided interest to abuse their power.

By a course of liberal discounts and excessive issues for a few years, followed by a sudden calling-in of their debts and contraction of their issues, they would have the power of transferring the property of their debtors to themselves almost without limit. Debts contracted when their discounts were liberal, and the currency of course depreciated, would be collected when their discounts were almost suspended, and the cur-

rency of course unnaturally appreciated; and in this way the property of the community might pass under the hammer, from its rightful owners to the banks, for less than one-half its intrinsic value. If the committee have not greatly mistaken the matter, there is more of history than of speculation in what they have here presented to the consideration of the House.

It is impossible to form anything like an accurate estimate of the injuries and losses sustained by the community, in various ways, by the disorders and fluctuations of the currency, in the period which intervened between the expiration of the old bank charter, and the establishment of the present bank. But some tolerable notion may be formed of the losses sustained by the government in its fiscal operations during the war.

The committee have given this part of the subject an attentive and careful examination; and they cannot estimate the pecuniary losses of the government, sustained exclusively for the want of a sound currency, and an efficient system of finance, at a sum less than forty-six millions of dollars. If they shall make this apparent, the House will have something like a standard for estimating the individual losses of the community.

The government borrowed, during the short period of the war, eighty millions of dollars, at an average discount of 15 per cent, giving certificates of stock, amounting to eighty millions of dollars, in exchange for sixty-eight millions of dollars in such bank paper as could be obtained. In this statement, treasury notes are considered as stock at 20 per cent discount. Upon the very face of the transaction, therefore, there was a loss of twelve millions of dollars, which would, in all probability, have been saved, if the treasury had been aided by such an institution as the Bank of the United States. But the sum of sixty-eight millions of dollars, received by the government, was in a depreciated currency, not more than half as valuable as that in which the stock given in exchange for it has been and will be redeemed. Here, then, is another loss of thirty-four millions, resulting, incontestably and exclusively, from the depreciation of the currency, and making, with the sum lost by the discount, forty-six millions of dollars. While, then, the government sustained this great pecuniary loss in less than three years of war, amounting annually to more than the current expenses of the government in time of peace, it is worth while to inquire who are the persons who profited, to this enormous amount, by the derangement of the currency. It will be found that the whole benefit of this speculation upon the necessities of the government was realized by stockjobbers and money brokers, the very same class of persons who profited so largely by the business of commercial exchanges, in consequence of the disorders of the currency, and who have the same interest in the recurrence of those disorders as lawyers have in litigation, or physicians in the diseases of the human frame. Having presented these general views of the evils which existed previous to the establishment of the Bank of the United States, it remains for the committee to inquire how far this institution has effected a remedy of those evils. . . .

Human wisdom has never effected, in any other country, a nearer approach to uniformity in the currency than that which is made by the use of the precious metals. If, therefore, it can be shown that the bills of the United States Bank are of equal value with silver at all points of the Union, it would seem that the proposition is clearly made out that the bank has accomplished "the great end of establishing a uniform and sound currency." It is not denied that the bills of the mother-bank, and of all its branches, are invariably and promptly redeemed in specie, whenever presented at the offices by which they have been respectively issued, and at which, upon their face, they purport to be payable. Nor is it denied that the bills of the bank, and of all the branches, are equal to specie in their respective spheres of circulation. Bills, for example, issued by the mother-bank are admitted to be equal to silver in Pennsylvania, and all those parts of the adjacent states of which Philadelphia is the market. But it is contended that these bills, not being redeemable at Charleston and New Orleans, are not of equal value with silver to the merchant who wishes to purchase cotton with them in those cities. Now, if the Philadelphia merchant had silver, instead of bank bills, he certainly could not effect his purchases with it in Charleston or New Orleans, without having the silver conveyed to those places; and it is equally certain that he could not have it conveyed there without paying for its transportation and insurance. These expenses constitute the natural rate of exchange between those cities and indicate the exact sum which the merchant would give as a premium for a bill of exchange, to avoid the trouble and delay of transporting his specie. It is obvious, therefore, that, even for these distant operations of commerce, silver would be no more valuable than the bills of the bank; for these would purchase a bill of exchange on either of the cities mentioned, precisely as well as silver. If the operation should be reversed, and the planter of Louisiana or South Carolina should desire to place his funds in Philadelphia, with a view to purchase merchandise, he would find the bills of the branch bank, in either of those states, entirely equivalent to silver in effecting his object. Even, therefore, if the bank had not reduced the rate of the exchanges, it might be safely asserted that its bills would be of equal value with silver at every point in the Union, and for every purpose, whether local or general.

But it is impossible to exhibit anything

like a just view of the beneficial operations of the bank without adverting to the great reduction it has effected, and the steadiness it has superinduced, in the rate of the commercial exchanges of the country. Though this branch of the business of the bank has been the subject of more complaint, perhaps, than any other, the committee have no hesitation in saying it has been productive of the most signal benefits to the community and deserves the highest commendation. It has been already stated that it has saved the community from the immense losses resulting from a high and fluctuating state of the exchanges. It now remains to show its effect in equalizing the currency. In this respect it has been productive of results more salutary than were anticipated by the most sanguine advocates of the policy of establishing the bank. It has actually furnished a circulating medium more uniform than specie. This proposition is susceptible of the clearest demonstration. If the whole circulating medium were specie, a planter of Louisiana who should desire to purchase merchandise in Philadelphia would be obliged to pay 1 per cent, either for a bill of exchange on this latter place or for the transportation and insurance of his specie. His specie at New Orleans, where he had no present use for it, would be worth 1 per cent less to him than it would be in Philadelphia, where he had a demand for it. But, by the aid of the Bank of the United States, one-half of the expense of transporting specie is now saved to him. The bank, for one-half of 1 per cent, will give him a draught upon the mother-bank at Philadelphia, with which he can draw either the bills of that bank or specie at his pleasure. In like manner, the bank and its branches will give draughts from any point of the Union to any other where offices exist, at a percentage greatly less than it would cost to transport specie, and in many instances at par. If the merchant or planter, however, does not choose to purchase a draught from the bank, but prefers transmitting the bills of the office where he resides to any distant point, for commercial purposes, although these bills are not strictly redeemable at the point to which they are transmitted, yet, as they are receivable in payment of all dues to the government, persons will be generally found willing to take them at par; and, if they should not, the bank will receive them frequently at par, and always at a discount much less than would pay the expense of transporting specie. The fact that the bills of the bank and its branches are indiscriminately receivable at the custom-houses and land offices in payment of duties, and for the public lands, has an effect in giving uniformity to the value of these bills, which merits a more full and distinct explanation.

For all the purposes of the revenue, it gives to the national currency that perfect uniformity, that ideal perfection, to which a currency of gold and silver, in so extensive a country, could have no pretensions. A bill issued at Missouri is of equal value with specie at Boston, in payment of duties; and the same is true of all other places, however distant, where the bank issues bills, and the government collects its revenue. When it is, moreover, considered that the bank performs, with the most scrupulous punctuality, the stipulation to transfer the funds of the government to any point where they may be wanted, free of expense, it must be apparent that the committee are correct, to the very letter, in stating that the bank has furnished, both to the government and to the people, a currency of absolute uniform value in all places, for all the purposes of paying the public contributions and disbursing the public revenue. And when it is recollected that the government annually collects and disburses more than twenty-three millions of dollars, those who are at all familiar with the subject will at once perceive that bills which are of absolutely uniform value for this vast operation must be very nearly so for all the purposes of general commerce.

Upon the whole, then, it may be confidently asserted that no country in the world has a circulating medium of greater uniformity than the United States and that no country, of anything like the same geographical extent, has a currency at all comparable to that of the United States on the score of uniformity. The committee have seen the statement of an intelligent traveler who has visited almost every part of Europe, exhibiting the great variations of the currency in different parts of the same empire or kingdom. In Russia the bills of the Bank of St. Petersburg have a very limited circulation. At Riga, and throughout Courland, Livonia, and all the southern parts of the empire, the currency is exclusively of silver coins. In Denmark the notes of the Bank of Copenhagen are current only in Zealand, the other islands, and Jutland but will not pass at all in Sleswig and Holstein, which constitute the best portion of the kingdom. Since the Congress of Vienna, Germany is divided into thirty-nine separate states, each having a distinct currency, though represented in the diet at Frankfort. Out of the territory in which these several currencies are issued, they are mere articles of merchandise, which circumstance has given rise in every town to a numerous and distinct class of tradesmen called money-changers. How far these separate and unconnected currencies have a tendency to embarrass commerce may be inferred from the fact that a traveler going from St. Petersburg to Calais will lose, upon the unavoidable changes of money, an average of six per cent. In France the bills of the bank are of such large denominations as to be adapted only to the greater operations of commerce and are principally confined to the bankers and extensive traders in Paris. The general currency is silver; and, to avoid the trouble of carrying this to distant parts of the kingdom, gold pieces, or bills of exchange, which are preferable, are purchased at a premium of from $1\frac{1}{2}$ to 4 per cent. After this brief review of the currencies of Europe, the committee will barely state, as a conclusive vindication of our currency from the imputation of unsoundness, that there is no point in the Union at which a bill of the United States Bank, issued at the opposite extremity of the country, is at a discount of more than one-fourth of 1 per cent. . . .

One of the most important purposes which the bank was designed to accomplish, and which, it is confidently believed, no other human agency could have effected under our federative system of government, was the enforcement of specie payments on the part of numerous local banks deriving their charters from the several states, and whose paper, irredeemable in specie, and illimitable in its quantity, constituted the almost entire currency of the country. Amidst a combination of the greatest difficulties, the bank has almost completely succeeded in the performance of this arduous, delicate, and painful duty. With exceptions, too inconsiderable to merit notice, all the state banks in the Union have resumed specie payments. Their bills, in the respective spheres of their circulation, are of equal value with gold and silver; while, for all the operations of commerce beyond that sphere, the bills or checks of the Bank of the United States are even more valuable than specie. And even in the very few instances in which the paper of state banks is depreciated, those banks are winding up their concerns; and it may be safely said that no citizen of the Union is under the necessity of taking depreciated paper because a sound currency cannot be obtained. North Carolina is believed to be the only state where paper of the local banks is irredeemable in specie and consequently depreciated. Even there, the depreciation is only 1 or 2 per cent, and, what is more important, the paper of the Bank of the United States can be obtained by all those who desire it and have an equivalent to give for it.

The committee are aware that the opinion is entertained by some that the local banks would, at some time or other, either voluntarily or by the coercion of the state legislatures, have resumed specie payments. In the very nature of things this would seem to be an impossibility. It must be remembered that no banks ever made such large dividends as were realized by the local institutions during the suspension of specie payments. A rich and abundant harvest of profit was opened to them, which the resumption of specie payments must inevitably blast. While permitted to give their own notes, bearing no interest, and not redeemable in specie, in exchange for better notes bearing interest, it is obvious that the more paper they issued, the higher would be their profits. The most powerful motive that can operate upon moneyed corporations would have existed to prevent the state banks from putting an end to the very state of things from which their excessive profits proceeded. Their very nature must have been changed, therefore, before they could have been induced to co-operate, voluntarily, in the restoration of the currency. It is quite as improbable that the state legislatures would have compelled the banks to do their duty. It has already been stated that the tendency of a depreciated currency to attract importations to the points of greatest depreciation, and to lighten the relative burdens of federal taxation, would naturally produce among the states a rivalry in the business of excessive bank issues. But there remains to be stated a cause of more general operation, which would have prevented the inter-position of the state legislatures to correct those issues.

The banks were, directly and indirectly, the creditors of the whole community; and the resumption of specie payments necessarily involved a general curtailment of discounts, and withdrawal of credit, which would produce a general and distressing pressure upon the entire class of debtors. These constituted the largest portion of the population of all the states where specie payments were suspended and bank issues excessive. Those, therefore, who controlled public opinion in the states where the depreciation of the local paper was greatest, were interested in the perpetuation of the evil. Deep and deleterious, therefore, as the disease evidently was in many of the states, their legislatures could not have been expected to apply a remedy so painful as the compulsion of specie payments would have been, without the aid of the Bank of the United States. And here it is worthy of special remark that, while that bank has compelled the local banks to resume specie payments, it has most materially contributed, by its direct aid and liberal arrangements, to enable them to do so, and that with the least possible embarrassment to themselves and distress to the community. If the state legislatures had been ever so anxious to compel the banks to resume specie payments, and the banks ever so willing to make the effort, the committee are decidedly of the opinion that they could not have done it, unaided by the Bank of the United States, without producing a degree of distress incomparably greater than has been actually experienced. They will conclude their remarks on this branch of the subject by the obvious reflection, that if Congress, at the close of the war, had left it to the states to restore the disordered currency, his important function of sovereignty would have been left with those from whom the Constitution has expressly taken it, and by whom it could not be bene-ficially or effectually exercised. But an-other idea, of considerable plausibility, is not without its advocates. It is said that this government, by making the resump-tion and continuance of specie pay-ments the condition upon which the state banks should receive the govern-ment deposits, might have restored the currency to a state of uniformity. With-out stopping to give their reasons for believing that specie payments could not have been restored in this way and that, even if they could, a uniform currency of general credit throughout the Union would not have been provided, the com-mittee will proceed to give their reasons for thinking that such a connection be-tween the federal government and the state banks would be exceedingly dan-gerous to the purity of both. While there is a national bank, bound by its character to perform certain stipulated duties, and entitled to receive the gov-ernment deposits as a compensation, fixed by the law creating the charter, and only to be forfeited by the failure to perform those duties, there is nothing in the connection at all inconsistent with the independence of the bank and the purity of the government. The country has a deep interest that the bank should maintain specie payments, and the gov-ernment an additional interest that it should keep the public funds safely, and transfer them, free of expense, wherever they may be wanted. The government, therefore, has no power over the bank but the salutary power of enforcing a compliance with the terms of its charter. Everything is fixed by the law, and nothing left to arbitrary discretion. It is true that the Secretary of the Treasury, with the sanction of Congress, would have the power to prevent the bank from using its power unjustly and op-pressively, and to punish any attempt, on the part of the directors, to bring the pecuniary influence of the institution to bear upon the politics of the country, by

withdrawing the government deposits from the offending branches; but this power would not be lightly exercised by the treasury, as its exercise would necessarily be subject to be reviewed by Congress. It is, in its nature, a salutary corrective, creating no undue depend-ence on the part of the bank.

But the state of things would be wide-ly different if there was no national bank and it was left to the discretion of the Secretary of the Treasury to select the local banks in which the government deposits should be made. All the state banks would, in that case, be competi-tors for the favor of the treasury; and no one, who will duly consider the nature of this sort of patronage, can fail to per-ceive that, in the hands of an ambitious man, not possessed of perfect purity and unbending integrity, it would be im-minently dangerous to the public lib-erty. The state banks would enter the lists of political controversy, with a view to obtain this patronage; and very little sagacity is required to foresee that, if there should ever happen to be an ad-ministration disposed to use its patronage to perpetuate its power, the public funds would be put in jeopardy by being de-posited in banks unworthy of confi-dence, and the most extensive corrup-tion brought to bear upon the elections throughout the Union. A state of things more adverse to the purity of the gov-ernment, a power more liable to be abused, can scarcely be imagined. If five millions of dollars were annually placed in the hands of the Secretary of the Treasury, to be distributed at his discre-tion, for the purposes of internal im-provement, it would not invest him with a more dangerous and corrupting power.

In connection with this branch of the subject, the committee will briefly ex-amine the grounds of a complaint, some-times made against the Bank of the United States. It is alleged that this bank, availing itself of the government deposits, consisting in some places principally of local paper, makes heavy and oppressive draughts on the local banks for specie, and thus compels them to curtail their discounts, to the great injury of the community. In the first place, it is to be remarked that one of the highest duties of the bank—the great object for which it was established—was to prevent the excessive issues of local paper; and this duty can only be performed by enforcing upon the state banks the payment of specie for any excess in their issues. . . .

It is sometimes alleged that the present stockholders are large capitalists and, as the stock of the bank is some 20 per cent above par, that a renewal of the charter would be equivalent to a grant to them of 20 per cent upon their capital. It is true that a small proportion of the capital of the company belongs to very wealthy men. Something more than two millions of that owned in the United States belongs to persons holding upward of one hundred thousand dollars each. It is also true that foreigners own seven millions, or one-fifth of the capital. But, on the other hand, it is to be remarked that the government, in trust for the people of the United States, holds seven millions; that persons owning less than five thousand dollars each, hold four million six hundred and eighty-two thousand; and that persons owning between five and ten thousand dollars each, hold upward of three millions. It is also worthy of remark that a very considerable portion of the stock, very nearly six millions, is held by trustees and guardians, for the use of females and orphan children, and charitable and other institutions. Of the twenty-eight millions of the stock which is owned by individuals, only three million four hundred and fifty-three thousand is now held by the original subscribers. All the rest has been purchased at the market prices; a large portion of it, probably, when those prices were higher than at present. Most of the investments made by wills and deeds and decrees in equity, for the use of females and minors, are believed to have been made when the stock was greatly above par. From this brief analysis, it will appear that there is nothing in the character or situation of the stockholders which should make it desirable to deprive them of the advantages which they have fairly gained, by an application of their capital to purposes highly beneficial, as the committee have attempted to show, to the government and people of the United States. If foreigners own seven millions of the stock of the bank, our own government owns as much; if wealthy men own more than two millions, men in moderate circumstances own between seven and eight millions; and widows, orphans, and institutions devoted to charitable and other purposes own nearly six millions.

But the objection that the stock is owned by men of large capital would apply with equal if not greater force to any bank that could be organized. In the very nature of things, men who have large surplus capitals are the principal subscribers at the first organization of a bank. Farmers and planters, merchants and manufacturers, having an active employment for their capitals, do not choose to be the first adventurers in a bank project. Accordingly, when the present bank went into operation, it is believed that most of the capital was owned by large capitalists, and under a much more unequal distribution than exists at present. The large amount of stock now held in trust for females and minors has been principally, if not entirely, purchased since the bank went into operation; and the same remark is generally applicable to the stock in the hands of small holders. It is only when the character of a bank is fully established, and when its stock assumes a steady value, that these descriptions of persons make investments in it.

It is morally certain, therefore, that, if another distinct institution were created on the expiration of the present charter, there would be a much greater portion of its capital subscribed by men of large fortunes, than is now owned by persons of this description, of the stock of the United States Bank. Indeed, it might be confidently predicted that the large capitalists who now hold stock in that bank would, from their local position and other advantages, be the first to forestall the subscriptions to the new bank, while the small stockholders, scattered over the country, would be probably excluded, and the females and minors, and others interested in trust investments made by decrees in equity, would be almost necessarily excluded, as the sanction of a court could scarcely be obtained, after the passage of the new act of incorporation, in time to authorize a subscription.

To destroy the existing bank, therefore, after it has rendered such signal services to the country, merely with a view to incorporate another, would be an act rather of cruelty and caprice than of justice and wisdom, as it regards the present stockholders. It is no light matter to depreciate the property of individuals, honestly obtained, and usefully employed, to the extent of five million six hundred thousand dollars, and the property of the government, to the extent of one million four hundred thousand dollars, purely for the sake of change. It would indicate a fondness for experiment, which a wise government will not indulge upon slight considerations.

But the great injury which would result from the refusal of Congress to renew the charter of the present bank would, beyond all question, be that which would result to the community at large. It would be difficult to estimate the extent of the distress which would naturally and necessarily result from the sudden withdrawal of more than forty millions of credit, which the community now enjoys from the bank. But this would not be the full extent of the operation. The Bank of the United States, in winding up its concerns, would not only withdraw its own paper from circulation, and call in its debts, but would unavoidably make such heavy draughts on the local institutions for specie as very greatly to curtail their discounts. The pressure upon the active, industrious, and enterprising classes, who depend most on the facilities of bank credit, would be tremendous. A vast amount of property would change hands at half its value, passing under the hammer, from the merchants, manufacturers, and farmers, to the large moneyed capitalists, who always stand ready to avail themselves of the pecuniary embarrassments of the community. The large stockholders of the present bank, the very persons whose present lawful gains it would be the object of some to cut off, having a large surplus money capital thrown upon their hands, would be the very first to speculate upon the distresses of the community, and build up princely fortunes upon the ruins of the industrious and active classes. On the other hand, the females and minors, and persons in moderate circumstances, who hold stock in the institution, would sustain an injury, in no degree mitigated by the general distress of the community.

A very great and solemn question will be presented to Congress when they come to decide upon the expediency of renewing the charter of the present bank. That institution has succeeded in carrying the country through the painful process necessary to cure a deep-seated disease in the national currency. The nation, after having suffered the almost convulsive agonies of this necessary remedy, is now restored to perfect health. In this state of things it will be for Congress to decide whether it is the part of wisdom to expose the country to a degree of suffering almost equal to that which it has already suffered, for the purpose of bringing back that very derangement of the currency which has been remedied by a process as necessary as it was distressing. . . .

Extract of a letter from an intelligent merchant in Charleston, South Carolina, to the chairman of the Committee of Ways and Means, illustrating the exchange operations of the Bank of the United States.

"This effect of diminishing the vast difference of exchange between the various points of the country was evidently produced by the bank. The advantages produced by this institution in the intercourse between the western and Atlantic states can be duly appreciated only by one who sees passing before him the actual operation of the system of exchange it has created. For example, Lexington, in Kentucky, annually accumulates a large surplus of funds to her credit in Charleston, derived from the sale of horses, hogs, and other livestock, driven to that as well as to other southern markets by her citizens. Philadelphia is indebted to Charleston for exchange remitted, dividends on bank stock, etc., and Lexington is indebted to Philadelphia for merchandise. Without the transportation of a single piece of coin, Lexington draws on Charleston, and remits the check to Philadelphia in payment of her debt there, which operation adjusts the balance between the three points of the triangle almost without expense or trouble. Could such facilities be obtained from any other than an institution having branches in different parts of the Union, acting as copartners in one concern? Local banks, whatever might be their willingness, could not accommodate in the same manner and to a like extent. . . .

"The discounting of bills on the low terms established by the branch bank at this place is a great benefit to the agricultural interest, particularly in enhancing the price of cotton and rice; and, were the bank to stop its operations, there is no saying how far these staples would be depressed. The private dealers in exchange would take the place of the bank in that business, and their profits on bills would be taken out of the pockets of the planters, as the merchants would always regulate the price they would give for an agricultural production by the high or low rate at which they could negotiate their bills. On account of its connection with all parts of the Union, the bank affords this important advantage to the public: it is always a purchaser and always a seller of exchanges at fixed and low rates and thus prevents extortion by private dealers. . . .

"Before this bank went into operation, exchange was from 8 to 10 per cent either for or against Charleston, which was a loss to the planter to that amount on all the produce of Georgia and South Carolina, and, indeed you might say, all the produce of the southern and western states. . . .

"If the Bank of the United States were destroyed, the local banks would again issue their paper to an excessive amount; and, while a few adventurous speculators would be much benefited by such an issue, the honest and unsuspecting citizens of our country would, finally, be the losers. If we look back to what took place in New York, Pennsylvania, the western states, and even in our own state, we shall see the grossest impositions committed by banks, commencing with a few thousand dollars in specie, buying up newspapers to puff them as specie-paying banks, in order to delude the public, and, after getting their bills in circulation, blowing up, and leaving the unsuspecting planter and farmer victims of a fraud, by which they were deprived of the hard earnings of years of honest industry. But, sir, I believe the bank owes a great deal of the opposition which exists, and has existed, to the fact that it has put down these fraudulent institutions, got up by combinations and conspiracies of speculators, and who, after receiving large dividends, managed to destroy the credit of their own paper, and, by the agency of brokers, bought it up at half its nominal value.

"Since I last wrote you, I had a conversation with a gentleman in the confidence of some of the moneyed men of the North; and he says they are determined to break up the United States Bank, to enable them to use their money to advantage, as that institution gives so many facilities to the community as to deprive them of their former profits....

"There is another consideration: the distress would be immense which a refusal to renew the charter would produce among those who are indebted to the institution; for I find that to this branch the planters owe upward of a million dollars, and, I have no hesitation in saying, as safe a debt as is owing to any bank in the Union. But if the bank should wind up its affairs, these planters could not get credit from other institutions; and, as the bank can sue in the United States court, where judgment is obtained almost at once, property would be greatly depressed, and moneyed men would buy it up for half its value. Throughout the Union, all classes would suffer, except those who should hold up their money to go into the brokerage business, or buy property at a sacrifice. If I were sure the bank would not be rechartered, I would convert my property into money, with a view of dealing in exchange. I could make a vast fortune by it."

3. VETO OF THE BANK RENEWAL BILL[1]

By ANDREW JACKSON

WASHINGTON, July 10, 1832

To the Senate:

The bill "to modify and continue" the act entitled "An act to incorporate the subscribers to the Bank of the United States" was presented to me on the 4th July instant. Having considered it with that solemn regard to the principles of the Constitution which the day was calculated to inspire, and come to the conclusion that it ought not to become a law, I herewith return it to the Senate, in which it originated, with my objections.

A bank of the United States is in many respects convenient for the government and useful to the people. Entertaining this opinion, and deeply impressed with the belief that some of the powers and privileges possessed by the existing bank are unauthorized by the Constitution, subversive of the rights of the states, and dangerous to the liberties of the people, I felt it my duty at an early period of my Administration to call the attention of Congress to the practicability of organizing an institution combining all its advantages and obviating these objections. I sincerely regret that in the act before me I can perceive none of those modifications of the bank charter which are necessary, in my opinion, to make it compatible with justice, with sound policy, or with the Constitution of our country.

The present corporate body, denominated the president, directors, and company of the Bank of the United States, will have existed at the time this act is intended to take effect twenty years. It enjoys an exclusive privilege of banking under the authority of the general

1. *A Compilation of Messages and Papers of the Presidents, 1789–1897,* ed. James D. Richardson (Washington, 1896), II, 576–91.

government, a monopoly of its favor and support, and, as a necessary consequence, almost a monopoly of the foreign and domestic exchange. The powers, privileges, and favors bestowed upon it in the original charter, by increasing the value of the stock far above its par value, operated as a gratuity of many millions to the stockholders.

An apology may be found for the failure to guard against this result in the consideration that the effect of the original act of incorporation could not be certainly foreseen at the time of its passage. The act before me proposes another gratuity to the holders of the same stock, and in many cases to the same men, of at least seven millions more. This donation finds no apology in any uncertainty as to the effect of the act. On all hands it is conceded that its passage will increase at least 20 or 30 per cent more the market price of the stock, subject to the payment of the annuity of $200,000 per year secured by the act, thus adding in a moment one-fourth to its par value. It is not our own citizens only who are to receive the bounty of our government. More than eight millions of the stock of this bank are held by foreigners. By this act the American Republic proposes virtually to make them a present of some millions of dollars. For these gratuities to foreigners and to some of our own opulent citizens the act secures no equivalent whatever. They are the certain gains of the present stockholders under the operation of this act, after making full allowance for the payment of the bonus.

Every monopoly and all exclusive privileges are granted at the expense of the public, which ought to receive a fair equivalent. The many millions which this act proposes to bestow on the stockholders of the existing bank must come directly or indirectly out of the earnings of the American people. It is due to them, therefore, if their government sell monopolies and exclusive privileges, that they should at least exact for them as much as they are worth in open market. The value of the monopoly in this case may be correctly ascertained. The twenty-eight millions of stock would probably be at an advance of 50 per cent and command in market at least $42,000,000, subject to the payment of the present bonus. The present value of the monopoly, therefore, is $17,000,000, and this the act proposes to sell for three millions, payable in fifteen annual instalments of $200,000 each.

It is not conceivable how the present stockholders can have any claim to the special favor of the government. The present corporation has enjoyed its monopoly during the period stipulated in the original contract. If we must have such a corporation, why should not the government sell out the whole stock and thus secure to the people the full market value of the privileges granted? Why should not Congress create and sell twenty-eight millions of stock, incorporating the purchasers with all the powers and privileges secured in this act and putting the premium upon the sales into the Treasury?

But this act does not permit competition in the purchase of this monopoly. It seems to be predicated on the erroneous idea that the present stockholders have a prescriptive right not only to the favor but to the bounty of government. It appears that more than a fourth part of the stock is held by foreigners and the residue is held by a few hundred of our own citizens, chiefly of the richest class. For their benefit does this act exclude the whole American people from competition in the purchase of this monopoly and dispose of it for many millions less than it is worth. This seems the less excusable because some of our citizens not now stockholders petitioned that the door of competition might be opened and offered to take a charter on terms much more favorable to the government and country.

But this proposition, although made by men whose aggregate wealth is believed to be equal to all the private stock in the existing bank, has been set aside, and the bounty of our government is proposed to be again bestowed on the few who have been fortunate enough to secure the stock and at this moment wield the power of the existing institution. I cannot perceive the justice or policy of this course. If our government must sell monopolies, it would seem to be its duty to take nothing less than their full value, and, if gratuities must be made once in fifteen or twenty years, let them not be bestowed on the subjects of a foreign government nor upon a designated and favored class of men in our own country. It is but justice and good policy, as far as the nature of the case will admit, to confine our favors to our own fellow-citizens and let each in his turn enjoy an opportunity to profit by our bounty. In the bearings of the act before me upon these points I find ample reasons why it should not become a law.

It has been urged as an argument in favor of rechartering the present bank that the calling in its loans will produce great embarrassment and distress. The time allowed to close its concerns is ample, and, if it has been well managed, its pressure will be light, and heavy only in case its management has been bad. If, therefore, it shall produce distress, the fault will be its own, and it would furnish a reason against renewing a power which has been so obviously abused. But will there ever be a time when this reason will be less powerful? To acknowledge its force is to admit that the bank ought to be perpetual, and as a consequence the present stockholders and those inheriting their rights as successors be established a privileged order, clothed both with great political power and enjoying immense pecuniary advantages from their connection with the government.

The modifications of the existing charter proposed by this act are not such, in my view, as make it consistent with the rights of the states or the liberties of the people. The qualification of the right of the bank to hold real estate, the limitation of its power to establish branches, and the power reserved to Congress to forbid the circulation of small notes are restrictions comparatively of little value or importance. All the objectionable principles of the existing corporation, and most of its odious features, are retained without alleviation. . . .

By documents submitted to Congress at the present session it appears that on the 1st of January, 1832, of the twenty-eight millions of private stock in the corporation, $8,405,500 were held by foreigners, mostly of Great Britain. The amount of stock held in the nine western and southwestern states is $140,200, and in the four southern states is $5,623,100, and in the middle and eastern states is about $13,522,000. The profits of the bank in 1831, as shown in a statement to Congress, were about $3,455,598; of this there accrued in the nine western states about $1,640,048; in the four southern states about $352,507, and in the middle and eastern states about $1,463,041. As little stock is held in the West, it is obvious that the debt of the people in that section to the bank is principally a debt to the eastern and foreign stockholders; that the interest they pay upon it is carried into the eastern states and into Europe, and that it is a burden upon their industry and a drain of their currency, which no country can bear without inconvenience and occasional distress. To meet this burden and equalize the exchange operations of the bank, the amount of specie drawn from those states through its branches within the last two years, as shown by its official reports, was about $6,000,000. More than half a million of this amount does not stop in the eastern states but passes on to Europe to pay the dividends of the foreign stockholders. In the principle of taxation recognized by this act the western states find no adequate compensation for this perpetual burden on their industry and drain of their currency. The branch bank at Mobile made last year $95,140, yet under the provisions of this act the state of Alabama can raise no revenue from these profitable operations, because not a share of the stock is held by any of her citizens. Mississippi and Missouri are in the same condition in relation to the branches at Natchez and St. Louis, and such, in a greater or less degree, is the condition of every western state. The tendency of the plan of taxation which this act proposes will be to place the whole United States in the same relation to foreign countries which the western states now bear to the eastern. When by a tax on resident stockholders the stock of this bank is made worth 10 or 15 per cent more to foreigners than to residents, most of it will inevitably leave the country.

Thus will this provision in its practical effect deprive the eastern as well as the southern and western states of the means of raising a revenue from the extension of business and great profits of this institution. It will make the American people debtors to aliens in nearly the whole amount due to this bank, and send across the Atlantic from two to five millions of specie every year to pay the bank dividends.

In another of its bearings this provision is fraught with danger. Of the twenty-five directors of this bank, five are chosen by the government and twenty by the citizen stockholders. From all voice in these elections the foreign stockholders are excluded by the charter. In proportion, therefore, as the stock is transferred to foreign holders the extent of suffrage in the choice of directors is curtailed. Already is almost a third of the stock in foreign hands and not represented in elections. It is constantly passing out of the country, and this act will accelerate its departure. The entire control of the institution would necessarily fall into the hands of a few citizen stockholders, and the ease with which the object would be accomplished would be a temptation to designing men to secure that control in their own hands by monopolizing the remaining stock. There is danger that a president and directors would then be able to elect themselves from year to year and without responsibility or control manage the whole concerns of the bank during the existence of its charter. It is easy to conceive that great evils to our country and its institutions might flow from such a concentration of power in the hands of a few men irresponsible to the people.

Is there no danger to our liberty and independence in a bank that in its nature has so little to bind it to our country? The president of the bank has told us that most of the state banks exist by its forbearance. Should its influence become concentered, as it may under the operation of such an act as this, in the hands of a self-elected directory whose interests are identified with those of the foreign stockholders, will there not be cause to tremble for the purity of our elections in peace and for the independence of our country in war? Their power would be great whenever they might choose to exert it; but if this monopoly were regularly renewed every fifteen or twenty years on terms proposed by themselves, they might seldom in peace put forth their strength to influence elections or control the affairs of the nation. But if any private citizen or public functionary should interpose to curtail its powers or prevent a renewal of its privileges, it cannot be doubted that he would be made to feel its influence.

Should the stock of the bank principally pass into the hands of the subjects of a foreign country, and should we unfortunately become involved in a war with that country, what would be our condition? Of the course which would be pursued by a bank almost wholly owned by the subjects of a foreign power, and managed by those whose interests, if not affections, would run in the same direction, there can be no doubt. All its operations within would be in aid of the hostile fleets and armies without. Controlling our currency, receiving our public moneys, and holding thousands of our citizens in dependence, it would be more formidable and dangerous than the naval and military power of the enemy.

If we must have a bank with private stockholders, every consideration of sound policy and every impulse of American feeling admonishes that it should be *purely American*. Its stockholders should be composed exclusively of our own citizens, who at least ought to be friendly to our government and willing to support it in times of difficulty and danger. So abundant is domestic capital that competition in subscribing for the stock of local banks has recently led almost to riots. To a bank exclusively of American stockholders, possessing the powers and privileges granted by this act, subscriptions for $200,000,000 could be readily obtained. Instead of sending abroad the stock of the bank in which the government must deposit its funds and on which it must rely to sustain its credit in times of emergency, it would rather seem to be expedient to prohibit its sale to aliens under penalty of absolute forfeiture.

It is maintained by the advocates of the bank that its constitutionality in all its features ought to be considered as settled by precedent and by the decision of the Supreme Court. To this conclusion I cannot assent. Mere precedent is a dangerous source of authority and should not be regarded as deciding questions of constitutional power except where the acquiescence of the people and the states can be considered as well settled. So far from this being the case on this subject, an argument against the bank might be based on precedent. One Congress, in 1791, decided in favor of a bank; another, in 1811, decided against it. One Congress, in 1815, decided against a bank; another, in 1816, decided in its favor. Prior to the present Congress, therefore, the precedents drawn from that source were equal. If we resort to the states, the expressions of legislative, judicial, and executive opinions against the bank have been probably to those in its favor as four to one. There is nothing in precedent, therefore, which, if its authority were admitted, ought to weigh in favor of the act before me.

If the opinion of the Supreme Court covered the whole ground of this act, it ought not to control the co-ordinate authorities of this government. The Congress, the Executive, and the Court must each for itself be guided by its own opinion of the Constitution. Each public officer who takes an oath to support the Constitution swears that he will support it as he understands it and not as it is understood by others. It is as much the duty of the House of Representatives, of the Senate, and of the President to decide upon the constitutionality of any bill or resolution which may be presented to them for passage or approval as it is of the supreme judges when it may be brought before them for judicial decision. The opinion of the judges has no more authority over Congress than the opinion of Congress has over the judges, and on that point the President is independent of both. The authority of the Supreme Court must not, therefore, be permitted to control the Congress or the Executive when acting in their legislative capacities, but to have only such influence as the force of their reasoning may deserve.

But in the case relied upon, the Supreme Court have not decided that all the features of this corporation are compatible with the Constitution. It is true that the Court have said that the law incorporating the bank is a constitutional exercise of power by Congress; but, taking into view the whole opinion of the court and the reasoning by which they have come to that conclusion, I understand them to have decided that, inasmuch as a bank is an appropriate means for carrying into effect the enumerated powers of the general government, therefore the law incorporating it is in accordance with that provision of the Constitution which declares that Congress shall have power "to make all laws which shall be necessary and proper for carrying those powers into execution." Having satisfied themselves that the word *"necessary"* in the Constitution means *"needful,"* *"requisite,"* *"essential,"* *"conducive to,"* and that *"a bank"* is a convenient, a useful, and an essential instrument in the prosecution of the government's "fiscal operations," they conclude that to "use one must be within the discretion of Congress" and that "the act to incorporate the Bank of the United States is a law made in pursuance of the Constitution"; "but," say they, *"where the law is not prohibited and is really calculated to effect any of the objects intrusted to the government, to undertake here to inquire into the degree of its necessity would be to pass the line which circumscribes the judicial department and to tread on legislative ground."*

The principle here affirmed is that the "degree of its necessity," involving all the details of a banking institution, is a question exclusively for legislative consideration. A bank is constitutional, but it is the province of the Legislature to determine whether this or that particular power, privilege, or exemption is "necessary and proper" to enable the bank to discharge its duties to the government, and from their decision there is no appeal to the courts of justice. Under the decision of the Supreme Court, therefore, it is the exclusive province of Congress and the President to decide whether the particular features of this act are *necessary* and *proper* in order to enable the bank to perform conveniently and efficiently the public duties assigned to it as a fiscal agent, and therefore constitutional, or *unnecessary* and *improper*, and therefore unconstitutional.

Without commenting on the general principle affirmed by the Supreme Court, let us examine the details of this act in accordance with the rule of legislative action which they had laid down. It will be found that many of the powers and privileges conferred on it cannot be supposed necessary for the purpose for which it is proposed to be created and are not, therefore, means necessary to attain the end in view, and consequently not justified by the Constitution.

The original act of incorporation, section 21, enacts that "no other bank shall be established by any future law of the United States during the continuance of the corporation hereby created, for which the faith of the United States is hereby pledged: *Provided,* Congress may renew existing charters for banks within the District of Columbia not increasing the capital thereof, and may also establish any other bank or banks in said District with capitals not exceeding in the whole $6,000,000 if they shall deem it expedient." This provision is continued in force by the act before me fifteen years from the 3d of March, 1836.

If Congress possessed the power to establish one bank, they had power to establish more than one if in their opinion two or more banks had been "necessary" to facilitate the execution of the powers delegated to them in the Constitution. If they possessed the power to establish a second bank, it was a power derived from the Constitution to be exercised from time to time, and at any time when the interests of the country or the emergencies of the government might make it expedient. It was possessed by one Congress as well as another, and by all Congresses alike, and alike at every session. But the Congress of 1816 have taken it away from their successors for twenty years, and the Congress of 1832 proposes to abolish it for fifteen years more. It cannot be "*necessary*" or "*proper*" for Congress to barter away or divest themselves of any of the powers vested in them by the Constitution to be exercised for the public good. It is not "*necessary*" to the efficiency of the bank, nor is it "*proper*" in relation to themselves and their successors. They may *properly* use the discretion vested in them, but they may not limit the discretion of their successors. This restriction on themselves and grant of a monopoly to the bank is therefore unconstitutional. . . .

On two subjects only does the Constitution recognize in Congress the power to grant exclusive privileges or monopolies. It declares that "Congress shall have power to promote the progress of science and useful arts by securing for limited times to authors and inventors the exclusive right to their respective writings and discoveries." Out of this express delegation of power have grown our laws of patents and copyrights. As the Constitution expressly delegates to Congress the power to grant exclusive privileges in these cases as the means of executing the substantive power "to promote the progress of science and useful arts," it is consistent with the fair rules of construction to conclude that such a power was not intended to be granted as a means of accomplishing any other end. On every other subject which comes within the scope of congressional power there is

an ever living discretion in the use of proper means, which cannot be restricted or abolished without an amendment of the Constitution. Every act of Congress, therefore, which attempts by grants or monopolies or sale of exclusive privileges for a limited time, or a time without limit, to restrict or extinguish its own discretion in the choice of means to execute its delegated powers is equivalent to a legislative amendment of the Constitution and palpably unconstitutional. . . .

The government of the United States have no constitutional power to purchase lands within the states except "for the erection of forts, magazines, arsenals, dockyards, and other needful buildings," and even for these objects only "by the consent of the legislature of the state in which the same shall be." By making themselves stockholders in the bank and granting to the corporation the power to purchase lands for other purposes, they assume a power not granted in the Constitution and grant to others what they do not themselves possess. It is not *necessary* to the receiving, safekeeping, or transmission of the funds of the government that the bank should possess this power, and it is not *proper* that Congress should thus enlarge the powers delegated to them in the Constitution. . . .

The government is the only "*proper*" judge where its agents should reside and keep their offices, because it best knows where their presence will be "*necessary*." It cannot, therefore, be "*necessary*" or "*proper*" to authorize the bank to locate branches where it pleases to perform the public service, without consulting the government, and contrary to its will. The principle laid down by the Supreme Court concedes that Congress cannot establish a bank for purposes of private speculation and gain, but only as a means of executing the delegated powers of the general government. By the same principle a branch bank cannot constitutionally be established for other than public purposes. The power which this act gives to establish two branches in any state, without the injunction or request of the government and for other than public purposes, is not *"necessary"* to the due *execution* of the powers delegated to Congress.

The bonus which is exacted from the bank is a confession upon the face of the act that the powers granted by it are greater than are *"necessary"* to its character of a fiscal agent. The government does not tax its officers and agents for the privilege of serving it. The bonus of a million and a half required by the original charter and that of three millions proposed by this act are not exacted for the privilege of giving "the necessary facilities for transferring the public funds from place to place within the United States or the Territories thereof, and for distributing the same in payment of the public creditors without charging commission or claiming allowance on account of the difference of exchange," as required by the act of incorporation, but for something more beneficial to the stockholders. The original act declares that it (the bonus) is granted "in consideration of the exclusive privileges and benefits conferred by this act upon the said bank," and the act before me declares it to be "in consideration of the exclusive benefits and privileges continued by this act to the said corporation for fifteen years, as aforesaid." It is therefore for "exclusive privileges and benefits" conferred for their own use and emolument and not for the advantage of the government, that a bonus is exacted. These surplus powers for which the bank is required to pay cannot surely be *"necessary"* to make it the fiscal agent of the Treasury. If they were, the exaction of a bonus for them would not be *"proper."*

It is maintained by some that the bank is a means of executing the constitutional power "to coin money and regulate the value thereof." Congress have established a mint to coin money and passed laws to regulate the value thereof. The money so coined, with its value so regulated, and such foreign coins as Congress may adopt are the only currency known to the Constitution. But if they have other power to regulate the currency, it was conferred to be exercised by themselves and not to be transferred to a corporation. If the bank be established for that purpose, with a charter unalterable without its consent, Congress have parted with their power for a term of years, during which the Constitution is a dead letter. It is neither necessary nor proper to transfer its legislative power to such a bank, and therefore unconstitutional.

By its silence, considered in connection with the decision of the Supreme Court in the case of McCulloch against the state of Maryland, this act takes from the states the power to tax a portion of the banking business carried on within their limits, in subversion of one of the strongest barriers which secured them against federal encroachments. Banking, like farming, manufacturing, or any other occupation or profession, is *a business*, the right to follow which is not originally derived from the laws. Every citizen and every company of citizens in all of our states possessed the right until the state legislatures deemed it good policy to prohibit private banking by law. If the prohibitory state laws were now repealed, every citizen would again possess the right. The state banks are a qualified restoration of the right which has been taken away by the laws against banking, guarded by such provisions and limitations as in the opinion of the state legislatures the public interest requires. These corporations, unless there be an exemption in their charter, are, like private bankers and banking companies, subject to state taxation. The manner in which these taxes shall be laid depends wholly on legislative discretion. It may be upon the bank, upon the stock, upon the profits, or in any other mode which the sovereign power shall will.

Upon the formation of the Constitution the states guarded their taxing power with peculiar jealousy. They surrendered it only as it regards imports and exports. In relation to every other object within their jurisdiction, whether persons, property, business, or professions, it was secured in as ample a manner as it was before possessed. All persons, though United States officers, are liable to a poll tax by the states within which they reside. The lands of the United States are liable to the usual land tax, except in the new states, from whom agreements that they will not tax unsold lands are exacted when they are admitted into the Union. Horses, wagons, any beasts or vehicles, tools, or property belonging to private citizens, though employed in the service of the United States, are subject to state taxation. Every private business, whether carried on by an officer of the general government or not, whether it be mixed with public concerns or not, even if it be carried on by the government of the United States itself, separately or in partnership, falls within the scope of the taxing power of the state. Nothing comes more fully within it than banks and the business of banking, by whomsoever instituted and carried on. Over this whole subject matter it is just as absolute, unlimited, and uncontrollable as if the Constitution had never been adopted, because in the formation of that instrument it was reserved without qualification.

The principle is conceded that the states cannot rightfully tax the operations of the general government. They cannot tax the money of the government deposited in the state banks nor the agency of those banks remitting it; but will any man maintain that their mere selection to perform this public service for the general government would exempt the state banks and their ordinary business from state taxation? Had the United States, instead of establishing a bank at Philadelphia, employed a private banker to keep and transmit their funds, would it have deprived Pennsylvania of the right to tax his bank and his usual banking operations? It will not be pretended. Upon what principle, then, are the banking establishments of the Bank of the United States and their usual banking operations to be exempted from taxation? It is not their public agency or the deposits of the government which the states claim a right to tax, but their banks and their banking powers, instituted and exercised within state jurisdiction for their private emolument—those powers and privileges for which they pay a bonus, and which the states tax in their own banks. The exercise of these powers within a state, no matter by whom or under what authority, whether by private citizens in their original right, by corporate bodies created by the states, by foreigners or the agents of foreign governments located within their limits, forms a legitimate object of state taxation. From this and like sources, from the persons, property, and business that are found residing, located, or carried on under their jurisdiction, must the states, since the surrender of their right to raise a revenue from imports and exports, draw all the money necessary for the support of their governments and the maintenance of their independence. There is no more appropriate subject of taxation than banks, banking, and bank stocks, and none to which the states ought more pertinaciously to cling.

It cannot be *necessary* to the character of the bank as a fiscal agent of the government that its private business should be exempted from that taxation to which all the state banks are liable, nor can I conceive it *"proper"* that the substantive and most essential powers reserved by the states shall be thus attacked and annihilated as a means of executing the powers delegated to the general government. It may be safely assumed that none of those sages who had an agency in forming or adopting our Constitution ever imagined that any portion of the taxing power of the states not prohibited to them nor delegated to Congress was to be swept away and annihilated as a means of executing certain powers delegated to Congress.

If our power over means is so absolute that the Supreme Court will not call in question the constitutionality of an act of Congress the subject of which "it is not prohibited, and is really calculated to effect any of the objects intrusted to the government," although, as in the case before me, it takes away powers expressly granted to Congress and rights scrupulously reserved to the states, it becomes us to proceed in our legislation with the utmost caution. Though not directly, our own powers and the rights of the states may be indirectly legislated away in the use of means to execute substantive powers. We may not enact that Congress shall not have the power of exclusive legislation over the District of Columbia, but we may pledge the faith of the United States that as a means of executing other powers it shall not be exercised for twenty years or forever. We may not pass an act prohibiting the states to tax the banking business carried on within their limits, but we may, as a means of executing our powers over other objects, place that business in the hands of our agents and then declare it exempt from state taxation in their hands. Thus may our own powers and the rights of the states, which we cannot directly curtail or invade, be frittered away and extinguished in the use of means employed by us to execute other powers. That a bank of the United States, competent to all the duties which may be required by the government, might be so organized

as not to infringe on our own delegated powers or the reserved rights of the states I do not entertain a doubt. Had the Executive been called upon to furnish the project of such an institution, the duty would have been cheerfully performed. In the absence of such a call it was obviously proper that he should confine himself to pointing out those prominent features in the act presented which in his opinion make it incompatible with the Constitution and sound policy. A general discussion will now take place, eliciting new light and settling important principles; and a new Congress, elected in the midst of such discussion, and furnishing an equal representation of the people according to the last census, will bear to the Capitol the verdict of public opinion, and, I doubt not, bring this important question to a satisfactory result.

Under such circumstances the bank comes forward and asks a renewal of its charter for a term of fifteen years upon conditions which not only operate as a gratuity to the stockholders of many millions of dollars but will sanction any abuses and legalize any encroachments.

Suspicions are entertained and charges are made of gross abuse and violation of its charter. An investigation unwillingly conceded and so restricted in time as necessarily to make it incomplete and unsatisfactory discloses enough to excite suspicion and alarm. In the practices of the principal bank partially unveiled, in the absence of important witnesses, and in numerous charges confidently made and as yet wholly uninvestigated there was enough to induce a majority of the committee of investigation—a committee which was selected from the most able and honorable members of the House of Representatives—to recommend a suspension of further action upon the bill and a prosecution of the inquiry. As the charter had yet four years to run, and as a renewal now was not necessary to the successful prosecution of its business, it was to have been expected that the bank itself, conscious of its purity and proud of its character, would have withdrawn its application for the present and demanded the severest scrutiny into all its transactions. In their declining to do so there seems to be an additional reason why the functionaries of the government should proceed with less haste and more caution in the renewal of their monopoly.

The bank is professedly established as an agent of the executive branch of the government, and its constitutionality is maintained on that ground. Neither upon the propriety of present action nor upon the provisions of this act was the Executive consulted. It has had no opportunity to say that it neither needs nor wants an agent clothed with such powers and favored by such exemptions. There is nothing in its legitimate functions which makes it necessary or proper. Whatever interest or influence, whether public or private, has given birth to this act, it cannot be found either in the wishes or necessities of the executive department, by which present action is deemed premature, and the powers conferred upon its agent not only unnecessary but dangerous to the government and country.

It is to be regretted that the rich and powerful too often bend the acts of government to their selfish purposes. Distinctions in society will always exist under every just government. Equality of talents, of education, or of wealth cannot be produced by human insti-

tutions. In the full enjoyment of the gifts of Heaven and the fruits of superior industry, economy, and virtue, every man is equally entitled to protection by law; but when the laws undertake to add to these natural and just advantages artificial distinctions, to grant titles, gratuities, and exclusive privileges, to make the rich richer and the potent more powerful, the humble members of society—the farmers, mechanics, and laborers—who have neither the time nor the means of securing like favors to themselves, have a right to complain of the injustice of their government. There are no necessary evils in government. Its evils exist only in its abuses. If it would confine itself to equal protection, and, as Heaven does its rains, shower its favors alike on the high and the low, the rich and the poor, it would be an unqualified blessing. In the act before me there seems to be a wide and unnecessary departure from these just principles.

Nor is our government to be maintained or our Union preserved by invasions of the rights and powers of the several states. In thus attempting to make our general government strong, we make it weak. Its true strength consists in leaving individuals and states as much as possible to themselves—in making itself felt, not in its power, but in its beneficence; not in its control, but in its protection; not in binding the states more closely to the center, but leaving each to move unobstructed in its proper orbit....

4. HISTORY OF PAPER MONEY[1]

By WILLIAM M. GOUGE

EDITORS' NOTE.—This was probably the most thorough and systematic at-

1. William M. Gouge, *A Short History of Paper Money and Banking in the United States* ... (Philadelphia, 1833), pp. 1–7, 41–44, 84–86, 123–28.

tack on banks and paper money which was made in the Age of Jackson. The book was circulated very widely. The first edition was exhausted by 1834, a paper edition selling for twenty-five cents was published in 1835, and serialized editions appeared in many newspapers. Editions were published both in England and on the Continent. William M. Gouge (1796–1863) was an economist, journalist, and government worker. In 1823, with a partner, Gouge owned and edited the *Philadelphia Gazette* and for about a year in 1841 edited the *Journal of Banking* in Philadelphia. During part of Jackson's administration, Gouge was employed by the Treasury Department and prepared many of its important reports. He was often consulted, both by the national government and by state governments, about financial policy.

CHAPTER I

IMPORTANCE OF THE SUBJECT

In an address to the stockholders of the United States Bank, at their meeting in 1828, Mr. N. Biddle, the president of that institution, stated that, of five hundred and forty-four banks in the United States, one hundred and forty-four had been openly declared bankrupt, and about fifty more had suspended business.

Mr. Gallatin, in his "Considerations on the Currency and Banking System," published in 1831, gives a list of 329 state banks then in operation having nominal capitals of the amount of $108,301,898, which, added to the capital of the United States Bank, made the whole nominal capital of these institutions upward of one hundred and forty-three millions of dollars.

These banks issue notes which serve as substitutes for coin.

They grant credits on their books and transfer the amount of credit from one merchant to another.

They receive money on deposit.

They buy and sell bills of exchange.

They discount mercantile notes.

They buy and sell public stocks.

All these are important functions, and, if only one of them be ill performed, the community must suffer inconvenience.

The banks are scattered through nearly all the states and territories which compose our Union; but they may all be embraced in one view, inasmuch as they all substitute paper for specie, and credit for cash, and are all endowed with privileges which individuals do not possess.

By their various operations, immediate and remote, they must affect, for good or for evil, every individual in the country. Banking is not a local, temporary, or occasional cause. It is general and permanent. Like the atmosphere, it presses everywhere. Its effects are felt alike in the palace and the hovel.

To the customs of trade which banking introduces, all are obliged to conform. A man may, indeed, neither borrow money from the banks nor deposit money in their vaults; but if he buys or sells, it is with the medium which they furnish, and in all his contracts he must have reference to the standard of value which they establish. There is no legal disability to carrying on commerce in the old-fashioned safe way; but the customs of banking have introduced a practical disability. It is no longer possible for the merchant to buy and sell for ready money only, or for real money. He must give and take credit, and give and take paper money, or give up business.

Bank paper is not a legal tender in the discharge of private debts; but it has become, in point of fact, the only actual tender, and the sudden refusal of creditors to receive it would put it out of the power of debtors to comply with their engagements.

Credit, the great rival of cash, is completely controlled by the banks and distributed by them as suits their discretion.

These institutions may contribute little to the production of wealth; but they furnish the means to many for the acquisition of wealth; they appear to be the chief regulating cause of the present distribution of wealth and, as such, are entitled to particular attention.

"In copying England," says Mr. Jefferson, "we do not seem to consider that like premises induce like consequences. The *Bank mania* is one of the most threatening of these imitations; it is raising up a monied aristocracy in our country which has already set the government at defiance, and, although forced to yield a little on the first essay of their strength, their principles are unyielded and unyielding. They have taken deep root in the hearts of that class from which our legislators are drawn, and the sop to Cerberus, from fable has become history. Their principles take hold of the good, their pelf of the bad, and, thus, those whom the Constitution has placed as guards to its portals are sophisticated or suborned from their duties. That paper money has some advantages must be admitted, but its abuses are also inveterate; and that it, by breaking up the measure of value, makes a lottery of all private property cannot be denied. Shall we ever be able to put a constitutional veto upon it?"

"In most disquisitions upon the noxious tendency of banks," says another writer,[2] "much stress has been laid upon the injuries they have a power to inflict by excessive loans and consequent bankruptcy and by creating and circulating a permanent excess of currency. Could these two evils be avoided, many believe that banks would be innoxious. I regret to differ. I am not of those who imagine that banks incorporated with a liberal capital will ever endanger their solvency by extending their loans; nor of those who believe that banks controlled by specie payment can circulate a *permanent* excess of paper. And yet, I think, I can perceive a portentous power that they exercise over commercial enterprise. I am of opinion that they can circulate a *temporary* excess of paper, which, from time to time, finds a corrective in a run upon the banks for specie; that this temporary excess is succeeded by a temporary deficiency, one extreme invariably tending to another; that the consequences of this alternate excess and deficiency are, in the former case, to impart an undue excitement and, in the latter, an undue depression to commercial enterprise; that the effect of the former is to create an unnatural facility in procuring money and to enhance unnaturally the price of commodities, while that of the latter is to produce an artificial scarcity and to cheapen prices artificially; that the victims of these vibrations are the great body of merchants, whose capital and average deposits cannot always command discounts; that the gainers are a few intelligent and shrewd capitalists, the magnitude of whose deposits commands enormous discounts at all times, and who, being behind the curtain, know when to buy and when to sell. I am of opinion that these vibrations inflict evils which close not with mercantile speculation; that they tend to unhinge and disorder the regular routine of commerce and introduce at one moment a spirit of wild and daring speculation and, at another, a prostration of confidence and stagnation of business; that these feelings are transferred from the counting-house to the fireside; that the visionary profits of one day stimulate extravagance, and the positive losses of another engender spleen, irritation, restlessness, a spirit of gambling and domestic inquietude.

"I appeal to the commercial history of our country, during the last seven years,

2. Letter to Mr. Gallatin, by Publicola, New York, 1815.—AUTHOR'S NOTE.

and to the aching hearts of many of my fellow-citizens, for the truth of these reflections.

"I wish not to be misunderstood. Let no one suppose me so weak as to attribute every unfortunate speculation, and every fluctuation in prices, to an undue management or organization of our banking institutions. That would be a folly, from the imputation of which I trust the preceding remarks will rescue me. There are commercial fluctuations, and they are wholesome. They invigorate enterprise, and their benefits are directly felt by all. There are banking fluctuations, and they are highly deleterious. They intoxicate enterprise, only to enfeeble it; and the benefits are restricted to a few.

"This evil of banking fluctuation ends not with the mercantile community. It extends to everything that commercial enterprise reaches. It injures the farmer and the mechanic, in the precise ratio of the vacillations of public feeling.

"The injuries which it has inflicted have been as universal as the insinuation of bank paper; and the peculiar manner of its operation renders it doubly distressing. It does not affect the wealthy man, because he can always control discounts; but it falls with single and dreadful severity upon the industrious poor man, whose capital is not sufficient to command permanent accommodations; upon the inexperienced, who purchase knowledge by a sacrifice of property; and upon the merchant, whose skill and sagacity are superior to his wealth. . . . Against a power so tremendous, what barrier has been erected? Against a power which, at different periods, has baffled the legislative wisdom of our revolutionary sages, of the governments of Europe, and of Great Britain, what check have we imposed? THE INTEREST ACCOUNT OF EACH BANK. As well might Canute have controlled the waves of the ocean with a breath."

"Of all aristocracies," said a Committee of the New York Legislature, in 1818, "none more completely enslave a people than that of money; and in the opinion of your committee, no system was ever better devised so perfectly to enslave a community, as that of the present mode of conducting banking establishments. Like the Siren of the fable, they entice to destroy. They hold the purse strings of society; and, by monopolizing the whole of the circulating medium of the country, they form a precarious standard, by which all property in the country, houses, lands, debts and credits, personal and real estate of all descriptions, are valued; thus rendering the whole community dependent on them; proscribing every man who dares to expose their unlawful practices. If he happens to be out of their reach, so as to require no favors from them, his friends are made the victims. So no one dares complain.

"The committee, on taking a general view of our state, and comparing those parts where banks have been for some time established, with those that have had none, are astonished at the alarming disparity. They see, in the one case, the desolations they have made in societies that were before prosperous and happy; the ruin they have brought on an immense number of the most wealthy farmers, and they and their families suddenly hurled from wealth and independence into the abyss of ruin and despair.

"If the facts stated in the foregoing be true, and your committee have no doubt they are, together with others equally reprehensible and to be dreaded, such as that their influence too frequently, nay, often, already begins to assume a species of dictation altogether alarming, and unless some judicious remedy is provided by legislative wisdom, we shall soon witness attempts to control all selections to offices in our counties, nay, the elections to the very legislature. Senators and members of Assembly will be indebted to the banks for their seats in this Capitol, and thus the wise end of our civil institutions will be prostrated in the dust of corporations of their own raising."

Not a few of those who have a personal interest in the continuance of the system acknowledge and deplore the evils it produces. Indeed, we have found no men more sensible of those evils than some of the officers of banks. They retain their offices on the same principle that they would, if they lived in England, retain offices under a government they could not approve. To the established system of a country, whether political or commercial, men may deem it expedient, perhaps believe it necessary, to conform; but this need not prevent their discovering the necessity for reformation.

One of these gentlemen, Mr. John White, the cashier of the United States Branch Bank at Baltimore, makes the following candid and correct statement, in a letter to the late Secretary of the Treasury, under date of February 15th, 1830.

"Looking back to the peace, a short period, fresh in the memory of every man, the wretched state of the currency for the two succeeding years cannot be overlooked; the disasters of 1819, which seriously affected the circumstances, property, and industry of every district in the United States, will long be recollected. A sudden and pressing scarcity of money prevailed in the spring of 1822; numerous and very extensive failures took place at New York, Savannah, Charleston, and New Orleans in 1825; there was a great convulsion among banks and other monied institutions in the state of New York in 1826; the scarcity of money among traders in that state, and eastward, in the winter of 1827 and 1828, was distressing and alarming; failures of banks in Rhode Island and North Carolina, and amongst the manufactur-

ers of New England and this state, characterize the last year; and intelligence is just received of the refusal of some of the principal banks of Georgia to redeem their notes with specie—a lamentable and rapid succession of evil and untoward events, prejudicial to the progress of productive industry, and causing a baleful extension of embarrassment, insolvency, litigation, and dishonesty, alike subversive of social happiness and morals. Every intelligent mind must express regret and astonishment at the recurrence of these disasters in tranquil times, and bountiful seasons, amongst an enlightened, industrious, and enterprising people, comparatively free from taxation, unrestrained in our pursuits, possessing abundance of fertile lands and valuable minerals, with capital and capacity to improve, and an ardent disposition to avail ourselves of these great bounties.

"Calamities of an injurious and demoralizing nature, occurring with singular frequency, amidst a profusion of the elements of wealth, are well calculated to inspire and enforce the conviction that there is something radically erroneous in our monetary system, were it not that the judgment hesitates to yield assent when grave, enlightened, and patriotic senators have deliberately announced to the public, in a recent report, that our system of money is in the main excellent and that in most of its great principles no innovation can be made with advantage."

The "grave, enlightened, and patriotic senators," to whom Mr. White alludes, are those who, with Mr. Smith, of Maryland, at their head, made a report, in the year 1830, in which they represented certain kinds of bank paper as being as good as gold and even better. If their opinion is correct, it ought to be confirmed. If it is not correct, its erroneousness ought to be exposed; for error in such a subject as this may be productive of incalculable mischief. . . .

CHAPTER IX

OF BANKS AS CORPORATIONS

Against corporations of every kind, the objection may be brought that whatever power is given to them is so much taken from either the government or the people.

As the object of charters is to give to members of companies powers which they would not possess in their individual capacity, the very existence of monied corporations is incompatible with equality of rights.

Corporations are unfavorable to the progress of national wealth. As the Argus eyes of private interest do not watch over their concerns, their affairs are much more carelessly and much more expensively conducted than those of individuals. What would be the condition of the merchant who should trust everything to his clerks, or of the farmer who should trust everything to his laborers? Corporations are obliged to trust everything to stipendiaries, who are oftentimes less trustworthy than the clerks of the merchant or the laborers of the farmer.

Such are the inherent defects of corporations that they never can succeed, except when the laws or circumstances give them a monopoly or advantages partaking of the nature of a monopoly. Sometimes they are protected by direct inhibitions to individuals to engage in the same business. Sometimes they are protected by an exemption from liabilities to which individuals are subjected. Sometimes the extent of their capital or of their credit gives them control of the market. They cannot, even then, work as cheap as the individual trader, but they can afford to throw away enough money in the contest to ruin the individual trader, and then they have the market to themselves.

If a poor man suffers aggression from a rich man, the disproportion of power is such that it may be difficult for him to obtain redress; but if a man is aggrieved by a corporation, he may have all its stockholders, all its clerks, and all its protégés for parties against him. Corporations are so powerful as frequently to bid defiance to government.

If a man is unjust, or an extortioner, society is, sooner or later, relieved from the burden by his death. But corporations never die.

What is worst of all (if worse than what has already been stated be possible) is that want of moral feeling and responsibility which characterizes corporations. A celebrated English writer expressed the truth, with some roughness, but with great force, when he declared that "corporations have neither bodies to be kicked, nor souls to be damned."

All these objections apply to our American banks.

They are protected, in most of the states, by direct inhibitions on individuals engaging in the same business.

They are exempted from liabilities to which individuals are subjected. If a poor man cannot pay his debts, his bed is, in some of the states, taken from under him. If that will not satisfy his creditors, his body is imprisoned. The shareholders in a bank are entitled to all the gain they can make by banking operations; but if the undertaking chances to be unsuccessful, the loss falls on those who have trusted them. They are responsible only for the amount of stock they may have subscribed.

For the old standard of value, they substitute the new standard of bank credit. Would government be willing to trust to corporations the fixing of our standards and measures of length, weight, and capacity? Or are our standards and measures of value of less importance than our standards and measures of other things?

They coin money out of paper. What has always been considered one of the most important prerogatives of government has been surrendered to the banks.

In addition to their own funds, they have the whole of the spare cash of the community to work upon.

The credit of every businessman depends on their nod. They have it in their power to ruin any merchant to whom they may become inimical.

We have laws against usury; but if it was the intention of the legislature to encourage usurious dealings, what more efficient means could be devised than that of establishing incorporated paper-money banks?

Government extends the credit of these institutions, by receiving their paper as an equivalent for specie, and exerts its whole power to protect and cherish them. Whoever infringes any of the chartered privileges of the banks is visited with the severest penalties.

Supposing banking to be a thing good in itself, why should bankers be exempted from liabilities to which farmers, manufacturers, and merchants are subjected? It will not surely be contended that banking is more conducive than agriculture, manufactures, and commerce to the progress of national wealth.

Supposing the subscribers to banks to be substantial capitalists, why should artificial power be conferred on them by granting them a charter? Does not wealth of itself confer sufficient advantages on the rich man? Why should the competition among capitalists be diminished, by forming them into companies, and uniting their wealth in one mass.

Supposing the subscribers to banks to be speculators without capital—what is there so praiseworthy in their design of growing rich without labor that government should exert all its powers to favor the undertaking?

Why should corporations have greater privileges than simple co-partnerships?

On what principle is it that, in a professedly republican government, immunities are conferred on individuals in a collective capacity that are refused to individuals in their separate capacity?

To test this question fairly, let us suppose that a proposition were made to confer on fourteen individuals in Philadelphia, and three or four hundred individuals in other parts of the country, the exclusive privileges which three or four hundred incorporated banks now possess. How many citizens would be found who would not regard such a proposition with horror. Yet privileges conferred on corporations are more pernicious, because there is less moral feeling in the management of their concerns. As directors of a company men will sanction actions of which they would scorn to be guilty in their private capacity. A crime which would press heavily on the conscience of one man becomes quite endurable when divided among many.

We take much pride to ourselves for having abolished entails, and justly, in so far as the principle is concerned; but it seems to be lost sight of by many that entails can prove effective only when the land is of limited extent, as in Great Britain; or where the mass of the population are serfs, as in Russia. In those districts of our country where Negro slavery prevails, entails, aided by laws of primogeniture, would have kept estates in a few hands; but in the middle and northern states, a hundred ways would have been contrived for breaking the succession. If direct attempts had proved unsuccessful, the land would have been let on leases of 99 or 999 years, which would have been nearly the same in effect as disposing of them in fee simple. The abundance of land prevents its being monopolized. Supposing the whole extent of country, from the Atlantic to the Pacific, and north of the thirty-ninth degree of latitude, parceled out among a few great feudatories; those feudatories, in order to derive a revenue from their domains, would be forced to lease them in a manner which would give the tenants the whole usufruct of the terrene; for the quit rent would be only an annual payment, instead of a payment of the whole in advance.

But the floating capital of the country is limited in amount. This, from the condition of things, may be monopolized. A small portion of the community have already, through the agency of banking operations, got possession of a great part of this floating capital and are now in a fair way of getting possession of much of the remainder. Fixed and floating capital must be united to produce income, but he who has certain possession of one of these elements of revenue will not long remain without the other.

The difference between England and the United States is simply this: in the former country, exclusive privileges are conferred on individuals who are called lords; in the latter, exclusive privileges are conferred on corporations which are called banks. The effect on the people of both countries is the same. In both the many live and labor for the benefit of the few. . . .

CHAPTER XX

SUMMARY VIEW OF THE ADVANTAGES WHICH THE SYSTEM GIVES TO SOME MEN OVER OTHERS

If two individuals should trade with one another on the same principle that the banks trade with the community, it would soon be seen on which side the advantage lay. If A should pay interest on all the notes he gave, and finally pay the notes themselves with his own wealth, and if B should receive interest on all the notes he issued, and finally pay the notes themselves with A's wealth, A's loss and B's gain would be in proportion to the amount of transactions between them.

This is the exact principle of American banking operations; but, owing to the multitude of persons concerned, the nature of the transaction is not discovered by the public. Regard the whole banking interest as one body corporate, and the whole of the rest of the community as one body politic, and it will be seen that the body politic pays interest to the body corporate for the whole amount of notes received, while the body corporate finally satisfies the demands of the body politic by transferring the body politic's own property to its credit.

In private credit there is a reciproc-ity of burdens and of benefits. Substantial wealth is given when goods are sold, and substantial wealth is received when payment is made, and an equivalent is allowed for the time during which payment is deferred. If A took a note from B, indorsed by the richest man in the country, he would require interest for the time for which payment was postponed. But the banking system reverses this natural order. The interest which is due to the productive classes that receive the bank notes is paid to the banks that issue them.

If the superior credit the banks enjoy grew out of the natural order of things, it would not be a subject of complaint. But the banks owe their credit to their charters—to special acts of legislation in their favor and to their notes being made receivable in payment of dues to government. The kind of credit which is created for them by law, being equipollent with cash in the market, enables them to transfer an equal amount of substantial wealth from the productive classes to themselves, giving the productive classes only representatives of credit, or evidences of debt, in return for the substantial wealth which they part with.

To test the banking principle fairly, let us bring down our minds from a country to a county, and, to give definiteness to our ideas, let us, in all instances, make round numbers the basis of our calculation.

Suppose a county to contain a thousand families of ten persons each, and each family to be worth 5,000 dollars. The wealth of the community is, then, 5,000,000 dollars. One-tenth of this wealth, or 500 dollars for each family, we will suppose to be in silver money. The rest is in land, houses, and various commodities. The state of credit in this county is as sound as the state of the currency. The distribution of wealth is left to natural laws. The *production* and *acquisition* of riches are never separated. Every man enjoys what he produces and what he saves; and no man enjoys what is produced or what is saved by another. We will suppose the income of this community to be 1,000,000 dollars, or 1,000 dollars a year for each family, and that 700,000 dollars of this aggregate income is derived from industry, and the rest from capital, profits being at the rate of 6 per cent.

In this county are ten men of a speculative turn of mind who grow tired of working and saving and wish to grow rich in some more easy way. They apply to the legislature for a charter for a bank, with a nominal capital of 100,000 dollars, divided into a thousand shares of 100 dollars each; and their prayer is granted. It is provided in the charter that, as soon as five dollars shall be paid on each share, the bank shall commence operations. The payment of the other instalments is, according to the custom of Pennsylvania, left to the discretion of the directors.

The business of banking is new in this county, and as none clearly understand its operation but the ten speculators, they subscribe for the whole of the stock, or for one hundred shares each. Each of them pays down 500 dollars, making the whole capital paid in 5,000 dollars.

The bank then commences business and issues notes to the amount of 25,000 dollars. By the contrivance of "convertibility," and by another contrivance by which they are made receivable in payment of dues to government, the notes become current. The notes are borrowed by the speculators. Each speculator has then 2,500 dollars at command instead of 500. It is true, he pays interest to the bank as a borrower; but he receives the same interest back as a stockholder. It is evident that the equality of wealth is destroyed. The possession of a monied capital so much greater than that of his neighbors will give him advantages in trade equal to double the amount of interest. But, estimating his advantages as equal to only 6 per cent, his annual income is increased from 1,000 dollars to 1,120, his 500 dollars formerly yielding him but 30 dollars a year, and now, by their conversion into bank stock, yielding him 150 dollars; for, each metallic dollar is, by this contrivance, made to produce to him as much as five did formerly....

CHAPTER XXIX

PROBABLE CONSEQUENCES OF THE CONTINUANCE OF THE PRESENT SYSTEM

To infer that, because a system produces great evil, it must soon give way would be to argue in opposition to all experience. If mere suffering could produce reformation, there would be little misery in the world.

Too many individuals have an interest in incorporated paper-money banks to suffer the truth in relation to such institutions to have free progress. Too many prejudices remain in the minds of a multitude who have no such interest to permit the truth to have its proper effect.

It is, therefore, rational to conclude that the present system may, at least with modifications, continue to be the system of the country—not forever, as some seem to think, but for a period which cannot be definitely calculated. It is also rational to conclude that the effect it will have on society in time to come will be similar to the effect it has had in time past. We have, then, in the present state of the country the means of judging of its future condition.

No system of policy that can be devised can prevent the United States from advancing in wealth and population. Our national prosperity has its seat in natural causes which cannot be effectually counteracted by any human measures, excepting such as would convert the government into a despotism like that of Turkey, or reduce the nation to a state of anarchy resembling that of some countries of South America.

Our wealth and population will increase till they become equal for each square mile to the wealth and population of the continent of Europe.

We are now very far from this limit. Under a good system, we cannot reach it in less than one or two hundred years. Under a bad system, in not less, perhaps, than three or four hundred.

If we had a political system as bad as that of Great Britain, with its hereditary aristocracy, its laws of entail and primogeniture, its manufacturing guilds, its incorporated commercial companies, its large standing army, its expensive navy, its church establishment, its borough-mongering, its pensions and its sinecures, our advancement would be seriously retarded. But our wealth and population would, notwithstanding, continue to increase, till they should bear the same ratio to the natural resources of the country that the wealth and population of Great Britain have to the natural resources of that island.

The progress of opulence in the United States in the next forty or fifty years will probably be very great. Many of the natural sources of wealth are as yet unappropriated. In no part of the country has their productiveness been fully developed. The people have now sufficient capital to turn their land and labor to more profit than was possible in any previous period of our country's history.

The daily improvements in productive machinery, and especially in the application of steam power, the discoveries in science, the introduction of new composts and new courses of crops in agriculture, the extension of roads and canals, have all a tendency to increase the wealth of the country, till the aggregate shall be enormous.

But this increase of wealth will be principally for the benefit of those to whom an increase of riches will bring no increase of happiness, for they have already wealth enough or more than enough. Their originally small capitals have, in the course of a few years, been doubled, trebled, and, in some instances, quadrupled. They have now large capitals, which will go on increasing in nearly the same ratio.

As no kind of property is prevented from being the prize of speculation by laws of entail, it is not easy to set bounds to the riches which some of our citizens may acquire. Their incomes may be equal to those of the most wealthy of the European nobility. Think, for a moment, of the immense accession of wealth certain families in the neighborhood of large cities and other improving towns must receive, from the conversion of tracts of many acres into building lots. For ground which cost them but one hundred dollars an acre, they may get ten thousand dollars, twenty thousand dollars, or twenty-five thousand dollars. This will be without any labor or expenditure of capital on their part. The land will be increased in value, by the improvements made around it at the expense of other men.

But this is but one of the ways in which the wealth of the rich will increase. It has heretofore been found that capital invested in lots, even in the neighborhood of the most flourishing towns, doubles itself less rapidly than capital devoted to other purposes of speculation. In whatever way it may be employed, the capital of the rich will, in the aggregate, increase in nearly the ratio of compound interest.

The vicissitudes of fortune will be, as they have been in past years, many and great, but they will tend to increase the inequality of social condition by throwing the wealth of several rich men into the hands of one. It is seldom that the vicissitudes of fortune distribute the wealth of a few among the many.

An increase in the number of banks must be expected. If the system is to be *perpetual*, an increase in the number of these institutions would not, in some respects, be an evil; for seven hundred banks could circulate no more paper than three hundred and fifty. But every new bank is a new center of speculation; and one kind of stock-jobbing gives birth to another. We shall have new schemes for growing rich without labor—similar perhaps to the British bubble companies of 1825—perhaps to the former speculations in Washington City lots—perhaps to the recent speculations in Pennsylvania coal lands. The present rage for railroad stock shows that part of our population already want something to be crazy about—or rather want something by which to set their neighbors crazy. The old modes of speculation no longer afford full employment for their time and talents.

Nearly all the secondary operations of society will tend to increase the disparity between the rich and poor as different classes of the community, and not a small proportion of the rich will, in due time, become as luxurious and as corrupt, as ostentatious and as supercil-

ious, as the "first circles" in the most dissipated capitals of Europe.

Their early habits of industry and economy cleave to some of the rich men of the present day. Hence they are as useful and as modest members of society as many who are in moderate circumstances. But when their immense wealth passes, as pass it must in a few years, to their heirs, who know not the value of money, because they never knew the want of it, it will be lavished in every way which corrupt inclination can dictate.

While some will be enormously rich, there will be a considerable number in a state of comfort, as in Great Britain, and very many in a state of disconsolate poverty. Some years must, indeed, elapse, before the number of paupers and criminals, and of persons whose condition borders on pauperism, will bear the same proportion to population in Europe and America. In our immense extent of uncultivated land, the poor have a place to fly to; but the spirit of speculation will follow them there. We need not wait till the country is fully peopled to experience a measure of these evils. While some parts of the Union will have all the simplicity, the rudeness, and the poverty of new settlements; others will exhibit all the splendor and licentiousness, and misery and debasement of the most populous districts of Europe.

The beginning of this state of things is already observable. According to the estimates of Mr. Niles, the number of paupers in the maritime counties of the United States was, in 1815, in the proportion of one to every 130 inhabitants; and, in 1821, in the proportion of two to every 130.

The published accounts do not give the number of *persons* admitted into the almshouses or committed to the prisons of Philadelphia in the course of the year; but the number of commitments of criminals and vagrants amounts to three or four thousand annually, and the number of *admissions* into the almshouse is equally considerable. As the same person may be *admitted* or *committed* several times, we cannot give the exact number of either paupers or criminals. But at one time last winter, there were upward of sixteen hundred poor persons in the Spruce Street Almshouse; and many more were receiving outdoor relief.[3]

In some years the public expenditures on account of the poor in Philadelphia exceed the expenditures on the same account in Liverpool.

Some of the members of a commission appointed about twelve years ago to inquire into the causes and extent of pauperism in Philadelphia estimated the cost of relieving the poor at between four hundred and five hundred thousand dollars a year. In this estimate was included what is given in private charity, as well as what is given in public; and an allowance was made for rent of almshouses and hospitals, or for interest on the first cost of land and buildings set apart for the use of the poor. At that time the population of the city and suburbs did not much exceed one hundred and twenty thousand.

We may increase the legal provision for the relief of the indigent and multiply almshouses and hospitals. But nothing of this kind can supply the want of just laws and of equal institutions.

Efforts may be made in various ways to diffuse the blessings of education, and to promote moral and religious improvement. But these efforts will only alleviate our social evils; they cannot cure them.

In no small degree will the public distress be increased by well-meant but ill-directed attempts to give relief. There is a class of politicians (and they are unfortunately numerous and powerful) who have for each particular social evil a legal remedy. They are willing to leave nothing to nature; the law must do everything.

This is, most unfortunately, the kind of legislation which public distress is almost sure to produce. Instead of tracing its cause to some *positive* institution, the removal of which, though it might not immediately relieve distress, would prevent its recurrence, men set themselves to heaping law upon law, and institution upon institution. They in this resemble quacks who apply lotions to the skin to cure diseases of the blood, or of the digestive organs, occasioned by intemperate living.

These projects of relief and efforts at corrective legislation will be numberless in multitude and diversified in character; but, as they will not proceed on the principle of "removing the cause that the effect may cease," they will ultimately increase the evils they are intended to cure.

5. *CHARLES RIVER BRIDGE* v. *WARREN BRIDGE*[1]

EDITORS' NOTE.—The Charles River Bridge between Boston and Charlestown had been opened in 1786. It was owned by the Charles River Bridge Company under a charter which would expire in 1856. In 1828, however, Massachusetts incorporated another company to build and operate the Warren Bridge adjacent to the Charles River Bridge. The Charles River Bridge Company sought an injunction against

---

3. Part of this pauperism and criminality must be attributed to European institutions, as the character of the subjects was formed before they migrated to America. Another part is of domestic origin.—AUTHOR'S NOTE.

1. 11 Peters 420 (1837).

the building of the rival bridge and, when this was denied in the Massachusetts courts, appealed to the United States Supreme Court on writ of error. Justice Taney, who wrote the opinion of the Court, is famous for his opinion in the Dred Scott case of 1857. Justice Story, who wrote the dissent, was, next to Marshall, the most powerful conservative influence in the judiciary. He was profoundly convinced that the protection of property was the first duty of government, that a minority of able men should decide public pol-icy, and that democracy by the time of Jackson had been proved a complete failure. Daniel Webster, who represented the Charles River Bridge Company before the Supreme Court, Chancellor Kent of New York (see above, p. 567), and the conservatives, who had hoped that the Federalists and the Whigs would protect them from the Jeffersonians and Jacksonians were alarmed and unhappy about the decision of this case (see Arthur M. Schlesinger, Jr., *The Age of Jackson* [Boston, 1946], pp. 322–27).

Taney, Ch. J., delivered the opinion of the Court.

The questions involved in this case are of the gravest character, and the Court have given to them the most anxious and deliberate consideration. The value of the right claimed by the plaintiffs is large in amount; and many persons may, no doubt, be seriously affected in their pecuniary interests by any decision which the Court may pronounce; and the questions which have been raised as to the power of the several states, in relation to the corporations they have chartered, are pregnant with important consequences, not only to the individuals who are concerned in the corporate franchises, but to the communities in which they exist. The Court are fully sensible that it is their duty, in exercising the high powers conferred on them by the Constitution of the United States, to deal with these great and extensive interests with the utmost caution, guarding, so far as they have the power to do so, the rights of property and at the same time carefully abstaining from any encroachment on the rights reserved to the states. . . .

Borrowing, as we have done, our system of jurisprudence from the English law, and having adopted, in every other case, civil and criminal, its rules for the construction of statutes, is there anything in our local situation or in the nature of our political institutions which should lead us to depart from the principle where corporations are concerned? Are we to apply to acts of incorporation a rule of construction differing from that of the English law and, by implication, make the terms of a charter in one of the states more unfavorable to the public than upon an act of Parliament, framed in the same words, would be sanctioned in an English court? Can any good reason be assigned for excepting this particular class of cases from the operation of the general principle and for introducing a new and adverse rule of construction in favor of corporations, while we adopt and adhere to the rules of construction known to the English common law, in every other case, without exception? We think not; and it would present a singular spectacle if, while the courts in England are restraining, within the strictest limits, the spirit of monopoly and exclusive privileges in nature of monopolies and confining corporations to the privileges plainly given to them in their charter, the courts of this country should be found enlarging these privileges by implication and construing a statute more unfavorably to the public and to the rights of the community than would be done in a like case in an English court of justice. . . .

The object and end of all government is to promote the happiness and prosperity of the community by which it is established; and it can never be assumed that the government intended to diminish its power of accomplishing the end for which it was created. And, in a country like ours, free, active, and enterprising, continually advancing in numbers and wealth, new channels of communication are daily found necessary, both for travel and trade, and are essential to the comfort, convenience, and prosperity of the people. A state ought never to be presumed to surrender this power, because, like the taxing power, the whole community have an interest in preserving it undiminished. And when a corporation alleges that a state has surrendered, for seventy years, its power of improvement and public accommodation, in a great and important line of travel, along which a vast number of its citizens must daily pass, the community have a right to insist, in the language of this Court, above quoted, "that its abandonment ought not to be presumed, in a case, in which the deliberate purpose of the state to abandon it does not appear." The continued existence of a government would be of no great value if, by implications and presumptions, it was disarmed of the powers necessary to accomplish the ends of its creation, and the functions it was designed to perform transferred to the hands of privileged corporations. The rule of construction announced by the Court was not confined to the taxing power, nor is it so limited in the opinion delivered. On the contrary, it was distinctly placed on the ground that the interests of the community were concerned in preserving, undiminished, the power then in question; and whenever any power of the state is said to be surrendered or diminished, whether it be the taxing power, or any other affecting the public interest, the same principle applies, and the rule of construction must be the same. No one will question that the interests of the great body of the people of the state would, in this instance, be affected by the surrender of this great line of travel to a single corporation, with the right to exact toll, and exclude competition, for seventy years. While the rights of private property are sacredly guarded, we must not forget that the community also have rights and that the happiness and well-being of every citizen depends on their faithful preservation.

Adopting the rule of construction above stated as the settled one, we proceed to apply it to the charter of 1785 to the proprietors of the Charles River bridge. This act of incorporation is in the usual form, and the privileges such as are commonly given to corporations of that kind. It confers on them the ordinary faculties of a corporation, for the purpose of building the bridge; and establishes certain rates of toll, which the company are authorized to take: this is the whole grant. There is no exclusive privilege given to them over the waters of Charles River, above or below their bridge; no right to erect another bridge themselves, nor to prevent other persons from erecting one, no engagement from the state that another shall not be erected; and no undertaking not to sanction competition, nor to make improvements that may diminish the amount of its income. Upon all these subjects, the charter is silent; and nothing is said in it about a line of travel, so much insisted on in the argument, in which they are to have exclusive privileges. No words are used, from which an intention to grant any of these rights can be inferred; if the plaintiff is entitled to them, it must be implied, simply, from the nature of the grant and cannot be inferred from the words by which the grant is made.

The relative position of the Warren bridge has already been described. It does not interrupt the passage over the Charles River bridge, nor make the way to it, or from it, less convenient. None of the faculties or franchises granted to that corporation have been revoked by the legislature; and its right to take the tolls granted by the charter remains unaltered. In short, all the franchises and rights of property, enumerated in the charter, and there mentioned to have been granted to it, remain unimpaired. But its income is destroyed by the Warren bridge, which, being free, draws off the passengers and property which would have gone over it and renders their franchise of no value. This is the gist of the complaint; for it is not pretended that the erection of the Warren bridge would have done them any injury, or in any degree affected their right of property, if it had not diminished the amount of their tolls. In order, then, to entitle themselves to relief, it is necessary to show that the legislature contracted not to do the act of which they complain; and that they impaired, or, in other words, violated, that contract by the erection of the Warren bridge.

The inquiry, then, is, does the charter contain such a contract on the part of the state? Is there any such stipulation to be found in that instrument? It must be admitted on all hands that there is none; no words that even relate to another bridge, or to the diminution of their tolls, or to the line of travel. If a contract on that subject can be gathered from the charter, it must be by implication and cannot be found in the words used. Can such an agreement be implied? The rule of construction before stated is an answer to the question: in charters of this description, no rights are taken from the public, or given to the corporation, beyond those which the words of the charter, by their natural and proper construction, purport to convey. There are no words which import such a contract

as the plaintiffs in error contend for, and none can be implied. . . . The whole community are interested in this inquiry, and they have a right to require that the power of promoting their comfort and convenience and of advancing the public prosperity, by providing safe, convenient, and cheap ways for the transportation of produce, and the purposes of travel, shall not be construed to have been surrendered or diminished by the state; unless it shall appear by plain words, that it was intended to be done. . . .

Indeed, the practice and usage of almost every state in the Union, old enough to have commenced the work of internal improvement, is opposed to the doctrine contended for on the part of the plaintiffs in error. Turnpike roads have been made in succession, on the same line of travel; the later ones interfering materially with the profits of the first. These corporations have, in some instances, been utterly ruined by the introduction of newer and better modes of transportation and traveling. In some cases, railroads have rendered the turnpike roads on the same line of travel so entirely useless that the franchise of the turnpike corporation is not worth preserving. Yet in none of these cases have the corporation supposed that their privileges were invaded, or any contract violated on the part of the state. Amid the multitude of cases which have occurred, and have been daily occurring, for the last forty or fifty years, this is the first instance in which such an implied contract has been contended for, and this Court called upon to infer it from an ordinary act of incorporation containing nothing more than the usual stipulations and provisions to be found in every such law. The absence of any such controversy, when there must have been so many occasions to give rise to it, proves that neither states, nor individuals, nor corporations, ever imagined that such a contract could be implied from such charters. It shows that the men who voted for these laws never imagined that they were forming such a contract; and if we maintain that they have made it, we must create it by a legal fiction, in opposition to the truth of the fact and the obvious intention of the party. We cannot deal thus with the rights reserved to the states and, by legal intendments and mere technical reasoning, take away from them any portion of that power over their own internal police and improvement, which is so necessary to their well-being and prosperity.

And what would be the fruits of this doctrine of implied contracts, on the part of the states, and of property in a line of travel, by a corporation, if it would now be sanctioned by this court? To what results would it lead us? If it is to be found in the charter to this bridge, the same process of reasoning must discover it, in the various acts which have been passed, within the last forty years, for turnpike companies. And what is to be the extent of the privileges of exclusion on the different sides of the road? The counsel who have so ably argued this case have not attempted to define it by any certain boundaries. How far must the new improvement be distant from the old one? How near may you approach, without invading its rights in the privileged line? If this Court should establish the principles now contended for, what is to become of the numerous railroads established on the same line of travel with turnpike companies and which have rendered the franchises of the turnpike corporations of no value? Let it once be understood that such charters carry with them these implied contracts and give this unknown and undefined property in a line of traveling; and you will soon find the old turnpike corporations awakening from their sleep and calling upon this Court to put down the improvements which have taken their place. The millions of prop-

erty which have been invested in railroads and canals, upon lines of travel which had been before occupied by turnpike corporations, will be put in jeopardy. We shall be thrown back to the improvements of the last century and obliged to stand still, until the claims of the old turnpike corporations shall be satisfied; and they shall consent to permit these states to avail themselves of the lights of modern science and to partake of the benefit of those improvements which are now adding to the wealth and prosperity, and the convenience and comfort, of every other part of the civilized world. Nor is this all. This Court will find itself compelled to fix, by some arbitrary rule, the width of this new kind of property in a line of travel; for, if such a right of property exists, we have no lights to guide us in marking out its extent, unless, indeed, we resort to the old feudal grants, and to the exclusive rights of ferries, by prescription, between towns; and are prepared to decide that when a turnpike road from one town to another, had been made, no railroad or canal, between these two points, could afterward be established. This Court are not prepared to sanction principles which must lead to such results. . . .

The judgment of the supreme judicial court of the commonwealth of Massachusetts, dismissing the plaintiffs' bill, must, therefore, be affirmed, with costs.

STORY, J., dissenting. . . .

Some of the questions involved in the case are of local law. And here, according to the known principles of this court, we are bound to act upon that law, however different from, or opposite to, the jurisprudence of other states it either is, or may be, supposed to be. . . .

Is the charter to receive a strict or liberal construction? Are any implications to be made beyond the express terms? . . .

It is a well-known rule in the construction of private grants, if the meaning of the words be doubtful, to construe them most strongly against the grantor.... Why is this rule adopted? Plainly, because a grant is a contract and is to be interpreted according to its fair meaning. It would be to the dishonor of the government that it should pocket a fair consideration and then quibble as to the obscurities and implications of its own contract.... I put it to the common sense of every man whether if, at the moment of granting the charter, the legislature had said to the proprietors, "You shall build the bridge; you shall bear the burdens; you shall be bound by the charges; and your sole reimbursement shall be from the tolls of forty years; and yet we will not even guarantee you any certainty of receiving any tolls; on the contrary, we reserve to ourselves the full power and authority to erect other bridges, toll or free bridges, according to our own free will and pleasure, contiguous to yours, and having the same *termini* with yours; and if you are successful, we may thus supplant you, divide, destroy your profits, and annihilate your tolls, without annihilating your burdens." If, I say, such had been the language of the legislature, is there a man living, of ordinary discretion or prudence, who would have accepted such a charter upon such terms? I fearlessly answer, "No." There would have been such a gross inadequacy of consideration and such a total insecurity of all the rights of property, under such circumstances, that the project would have dropped stillborn. And I put the question further, whether any legislature, meaning to promote a project of permanent, public utility (such as this confessedly was), would ever have dreamed of such a qualification of its own grant, when it sought to enlist private capital and private patronage to insure the accomplishment of it.... But it is said that there is no prohibitory covenant in the charter, and no implications are to be made of any such prohi-

bition. The proprietors are to stand upon the letter of their contract, and the maxim applies, *de non apparentibus et non existentibus, eadem est lex*. And yet it is conceded that the legislature cannot revoke or resume this grant. Why not, I pray to know? There is no negative covenant in the charter; there is no express prohibition to be found there. The reason is plain. The prohibition arises by natural, if not by necessary implication. It would be against the first principles of justice to presume that the legislature reserved a right to destroy its own grant. That was the doctrine in *Fletcher* v. *Peck*, 6 Cranch 87, in this Court and in other cases turning upon the same great principle of political and constitutional duty and right. Can the legislature have power to do that indirectly which it cannot do directly? If it cannot take away, or resume, the franchise itself, can it take away its whole substance and value? ...

No principle is better established than the principle that, when a thing is given or granted, the law giveth, impliedly, whatever is necessary for the taking and enjoying the same....

What objection can there be to implications if they arise from the very nature and objects of the grant? If it be indispensable to the full enjoyment of the right to take toll that it should be exclusive within certain limits, is it not just and reasonable that it should be so construed? ...

Besides, in this very case, it is admitted on all sides that, from the defective language and wording of the charter, no power is directly given to the proprietors to erect the bridge; and yet it is agreed that the power passes by necessary implication from the grant, for otherwise it would be utterly void. The argument, therefore, surrenders the point as to the propriety of making implications and reduces the question to the mere consideration of what is a necessary implication....

Although the legislature have an unlimited power to grant franchises by the constitution of Massachusetts, they are not intrusted with any general sovereign power to recall or resume them. On the contrary, there is an express prohibition in the bill of rights in that constitution restraining the legislature from taking any private property, except on two conditions; first, that it is wanted for public use; and, secondly, that due compensation is made....

I maintain that, upon the principles of common reason and legal interpretation, the present grant carries with it a necessary implication that the legislature shall do no act to destroy or essentially to impair the franchise; that (as one of the learned judges of the state court expressed it) there is an implied agreement that the state will not grant another bridge between Boston and Charlestown, so near as to draw away the custom from the old one; and (as another learned judge expressed it) that there is an implied agreement of the state to grant the undisturbed use of the bridge and its tolls, so far as respects any acts of its own, or of any persons acting under its authority.

SECTION F. MORAL RESPONSIBILITY AND THE INDIVIDUAL

1. ON CIVIL DISOBEDIENCE[1]

By HENRY DAVID THOREAU

EDITORS' NOTE.—Henry David Thoreau (1817–62), like his friend Emerson, lived in Concord, Massachusetts. His work has made him one of the best-known American writers. His love of nature is shown in the famous *Walden* (1854), and his love of justice and individual freedom is revealed in this essay on civil disobedience. First published in 1847 under the title *Resistance to Civil Government*, it has more commonly been given the title *Essay on Civil Disobedience*.

I heartily accept the motto, "That government is best which governs least"; and I should like to see it acted up to more rapidly and systematically. Carried out, it finally amounts to this, which also I believe: "That government is best which governs not at all"; and, when men are prepared for it, that will be the kind of government which they will have. Government is at best but an expedient; but most governments are usually, and all governments are sometimes, inexpedient. The objections which have been brought against a standing army, and they are many and weighty, and deserve to prevail, may also at last be brought against a standing government. The standing army is only an arm of the standing government. The government itself, which is only the mode which the people have chosen to execute their will, is equally liable to be abused and perverted before the people can act through it. Witness the present Mexican War, the work of comparatively a few individuals using the standing government as their tool, for, in the outset, the people would not have consented to this measure.

This American government—what is

it but a tradition, though a recent one, endeavoring to transmit itself unimpaired to posterity, but each instant losing some of its integrity? It has not the vitality and force of a single living man, for a single man can bend it to his will. It is a sort of wooden gun to the people themselves; and, if ever they should use it in earnest as a real one against each other, it will surely split. But it is not the less necessary for this, for the people must have some complicated machinery or other, and hear its din, to satisfy that idea of government which they have. Governments show thus how successfully men can be imposed on, even impose on themselves, for their own advantage. It is excellent, we must all allow; yet this government never of itself furthered any enterprise but by the alacrity with which it got out of its way. *It* does not keep the country free. *It* does not settle the West. *It* does not educate. The character inherent in the American people has done all that has been accomplished, and it would have done somewhat more if the government had not sometimes got in its way. For government is an expedient by which men would fain succeed in letting one another alone; and, as has been said, when it is most expedient, the governed

1. *Aesthetic Papers*, ed. Elizabeth P. Peabody (Boston, 1849), pp. 189–211.

are most let alone by it. Trade and commerce, if they were not made of India rubber, would never manage to bounce over the obstacles which legislators are continually putting in their way; and, if one were to judge these men wholly by the effects of their actions, and not partly by their intentions, they would deserve to be classed and punished with those mischievous persons who put obstructions on the railroads.

But, to speak practically and as a citizen, unlike those who call themselves no-government men, I ask for, not at once no government, but *at once* a better government. Let every man make known what kind of government would command his respect, and that will be one step toward obtaining it.

After all, the practical reason why, when the power is once in the hands of the people, a majority are permitted, and for a long period continue, to rule, is not because they are most likely to be in the right, nor because this seems fairest to the minority, but because they are physically the strongest. But a government in which the majority rule in all cases cannot be based on justice, even as far as men understand it. Can there not be a government in which majorities do not virtually decide right and wrong, but conscience?—in which majorities decide only those questions to which the rule of expediency is applicable? Must the citizen ever for a moment, or in the least degree, resign his conscience to the legislator? Why has every man a conscience, then? I think that we should be men first and subjects afterward. It is not desirable to cultivate a respect for the law so much as for the right. The only obligation which I have a right to assume is to do at any time what I think right. It is truly enough said that a corporation has no conscience, but a corporation of conscientious men is a corporation *with* a conscience. Law never made men a whit more just; and, by means of their respect for it, even the

well-disposed are daily made the agents of injustice. A common and natural result of an undue respect for law is that you may see a file of soldiers, colonel, captain, corporal, privates, powder-monkeys and all, marching in admirable order over hill and dale to the wars, against their wills, aye, against their common sense and consciences, which makes it very steep marching indeed and produces a palpitation of the heart. They have no doubt that it is a damnable business in which they are concerned; they are all peaceably inclined. Now, what are they? Men at all? or small movable forts and magazines, at the service of some unscrupulous man in power? Visit the Navy Yard, and behold a marine, such a man as an American government can make, or such as it can make a man with its black arts, a mere shadow and reminiscence of humanity, a man laid out alive and standing, and already, as one may say, buried under arms with funeral accompaniments, though it may be

Not a drum was heard, nor a funeral note,
    As his corse to the ramparts we hurried;
Not a soldier discharged his farewell shot
    O'er the grave where our hero we buried.

The mass of men serve the state thus, not as men mainly, but as machines, with their bodies. They are the standing army, and the militia, jailers, constables, *posse comitatus*, etc. In most cases there is no free exercise whatever of the judgment or of the moral sense; but they put themselves on a level with wood and earth and stones; and wooden men can perhaps be manufactured that will serve the purpose as well. Such command no more respect than men of straw or a lump of dirt. They have the same sort of worth only as horses and dogs. Yet such as these even are commonly esteemed good citizens. Others, as most legislators, politicians, lawyers, ministers, and office-holders, serve the state chiefly with their heads; and, as they rarely make any moral distinctions, they are as likely to serve the devil, without intending it, as God. A very few, as heroes, patriots, martyrs, reformers in the great sense, and *men*, serve the state with their consciences also, and so necessarily resist it for the most part; and they are commonly treated by it as enemies. A wise man will only be useful as a man and will not submit to be "clay" and "stop a hole to keep the wind away" but leave that office to his dust at least—

I am too high-born to be propertied,
  To be a secondary at control,
Or useful serving-man and instrument
  To any sovereign state throughout the
    world.

He who gives himself entirely to his fellow-men appears to them useless and selfish; but he who gives himself partially to them is pronounced a benefactor and philanthropist.

How does it become a man to behave toward this American government today? I answer that he cannot without disgrace be associated with it. I cannot for an instant recognize that political organization as *my* government which is the *slave's* government also.

All men recognize the right of revolution, that is, the right to refuse allegiance to and to resist the government, when its tyranny or its inefficiency are great and unendurable. But almost all say that such is not the case now. But such was the case, they think, in the Revolution of '75. If one were to tell me that this was a bad government because it taxed certain foreign commodities brought to its ports, it is most probable that I should not make an ado about it, for I can do without them; all machines have their friction, and possibly this does enough good to counterbalance the evil. At any rate, it is a great evil to make a stir about it. But when the friction comes to have its machine, and oppression and robbery are organized, I say, let us not have such a machine any longer.

In other words, when a sixth of the population of a nation which has undertaken to be the refuge of liberty are slaves, and a whole country is unjustly overrun and conquered by a foreign army, and subjected to military law, I think that it is not too soon for honest men to rebel and revolutionize. What makes this duty the more urgent is the fact that the country so overrun is not our own but ours is the invading army.

Paley, a common authority with many on moral questions, in his chapter on the "Duty of Submission to Civil Government," resolves all civil obligation into expediency; and he proceeds to say that "so long as the interest of the whole society requires it, that is, so long as the established government cannot be resisted or changed without public inconveniency, it is the will of God that the established government be obeyed, and no longer. . . . This principle being admitted, the justice of every particular case of resistance is reduced to a computation of the quantity of the danger and grievance on the one side, and of the probability and expense of redressing it on the other." Of this, he says, every man shall judge for himself. But Paley appears never to have contemplated those cases to which the rule of expediency does not apply, in which a people, as well as an individual, must do justice, cost what it may. If I have unjustly wrested a plank from a drowning man, I must restore it to him though I drown myself. This, according to Paley, would be inconvenient. But he that would save his life, in such a case, shall lose it. This people must cease to hold slaves, and to make war on Mexico, though it cost them their existence as a people.

In their practice, nations agree with Paley; but does anyone think that Massachusetts does exactly what is right at the present crisis?

A drab of state, a cloth-o'-silver slut,
  To have her train borne up, and her
    soul trail in the dirt.

Practically speaking, the opponents to a reform in Massachusetts are not a hundred thousand politicians at the South, but a hundred thousand merchants and farmers here, who are more interested in commerce and agriculture than they are in humanity and are not prepared to do justice to the slave and to Mexico, *cost what it may*. I quarrel not with far-off foes but with those who, near at home, co-operate with and do the bidding of those far away, and without whom the latter would be harmless. We are accustomed to say that the mass of men are unprepared; but improvement is slow, because the few are not materially wiser or better than the many. It is not so important that many should be as good as you as that there be some absolute goodness somewhere, for that will leaven the whole lump. There are thousands who are *in opinion* opposed to slavery and to the war, who yet in effect do nothing to put an end to them; who, esteeming themselves children of Washington and Franklin, sit down with their hands in their pockets and say that they know not what to do, and do nothing; who even postpone the question of freedom to the question of free trade and quietly read the prices-current along with the latest advices from Mexico, after dinner, and, it may be, fall asleep over them both. What is the price-current of an honest man and patriot today? They hesitate, and they regret, and sometimes they petition; but they do nothing in earnest and with effect. They will wait, well disposed, for others to remedy the evil that they may no longer have it to regret. At most, they give only a cheap vote, and a feeble countenance and Godspeed, to the right, as it goes by them. There are nine hundred and ninety-nine patrons of virtue to one virtuous man; but it is easier to deal with the real possessor of a thing than with the temporary guardian of it.

All voting is a sort of gaming, like checkers or backgammon, with a slight moral tinge to it, a playing with right and wrong, with moral questions; and betting naturally accompanies it. The character of the voters is not staked. I cast my vote, perchance, as I think right; but I am not vitally concerned that that right should prevail. I am willing to leave it to the majority. Its obligation, therefore, never exceeds that of expediency. Even voting *for the right* is *doing* nothing for it. It is only expressing to men feebly your desire that it should prevail. A wise man will not leave the right to the mercy of chance nor wish it to prevail through the power of the majority. There is but little virtue in the action of masses of men. When the majority shall at length vote for the abolition of slavery, it will be because they are indifferent to slavery, or because there is but little slavery left to be abolished by their vote. *They* will then be the only slaves. Only *his* vote can hasten the abolition of slavery who asserts his own freedom by his vote.

I hear of a convention to be held at Baltimore, or elsewhere, for the selection of a candidate for the presidency, made up chiefly of editors and men who are politicians by profession; but I think, what is it to any independent, intelligent, and respectable man what decision they may come to; shall we not have the advantage of his wisdom and honesty, nevertheless? Can we not count upon some independent votes? Are there not many individuals in the country who do not attend conventions? But, no; I find that the respectable man, so called, has immediately drifted from his position, and despairs of his country, when his country has more reason to despair of him. He forthwith adopts one of the candidates thus selected as the only *available* one, thus proving that he is himself *available* for any purposes of the demagogue. His vote is of no more worth than that of any unprincipled foreigner or hireling native who may have been bought. Oh, for a man who is a *man* and, as my neighbor says, has a bone in his back which you cannot pass your hand through! Our statistics are at fault; the population has been returned too large. How many *men* are there to a square thousand miles in this country? Hardly one. Does not America offer any inducement for men to settle here? The American has dwindled into an Odd Fellow—one who may be known by the development of his organ of gregariousness, and a manifest lack of intellect and cheerful self-reliance; whose first and chief concern, on coming into the world, is to see that the almshouses are in good repair; and, before yet he has lawfully donned the virile garb, to collect a fund for the support of the widows and orphans that may be; who, in short, ventures to live only by the aid of the mutual insurance company, which has promised to bury him decently.

It is not a man's duty, as a matter of course, to devote himself to the eradication of any, even the most enormous, wrong; he may still properly have other concerns to engage him; but it is his duty, at least, to wash his hands of it and, if he gives it no thought longer, not to give it practically his support. If I devote myself to other pursuits and contemplations, I must first see, at least, that I do not pursue them sitting upon another man's shoulders. I must get off him first that he may pursue his contemplations too. See what gross inconsistency is tolerated. I have heard some of my townsmen say, "I should like to have them order me out to help put down an insurrection of the slaves, or to march to Mexico—see if I would go"; and yet these very men have each, directly by their allegiance, and so indirectly, at least, by their money, furnished a substitute. The soldier is applauded who refuses to serve in an unjust war by those who do not refuse to sustain the unjust government which makes the war; is applauded by those whose own

act and authority he disregards and sets at nought; as if the state were penitent to that degree that it hired one to scourge it while it sinned but not to that degree that it left off sinning for a moment. Thus, under the name of order and civil government, we are all made at last to pay homage to and support our own meanness. After the first blush of sin comes its indifference; and from immoral it becomes, as it were, *un*moral and not quite unnecessary to that life which we have made.

The broadest and most prevalent error requires the most disinterested virtue to sustain it. The slight reproach to which the virtue of patriotism is commonly liable, the noble are most likely to incur. Those who, while they disapprove of the character and measures of a government, yield to it their allegiance and support are undoubtedly its most conscientious supporters and so frequently the most serious obstacles to reform. Some are petitioning the state to dissolve the Union, to disregard the requisitions of the President. Why do they not dissolve it themselves—the union between themselves and the state—and refuse to pay their quota into its treasury? Do not they stand in the same relation to the state that the state does to the Union? And have not the same reasons prevented the state from resisting the Union which have prevented them from resisting the state?

How can a man be satisfied to entertain an opinion merely and enjoy *it?* Is there any enjoyment in it if his opinion is that he is aggrieved? If you are cheated out of a single dollar by your neighbor, you do not rest satisfied with knowing that you are cheated, or with saying that you are cheated, or even with petitioning him to pay you your due; but you take effectual steps at once to obtain the full amount and see that you are never cheated again. Action from principle—the perception and the performance of right—changes things and relations; it is essentially revolutionary and does not consist wholly with anything which was. It not only divides states and churches; it divides families; aye, it divides the *individual*, separating the diabolical in him from the divine.

Unjust laws exist; shall we be content to obey them, or shall we endeavor to amend them, and obey them until we have succeeded, or shall we transgress them at once? Men generally, under such a government as this, think that they ought to wait until they have persuaded the majority to alter them. They think that, if they should resist, the remedy would be worse than the evil. But it is the fault of the government itself that the remedy *is* worse than the evil. *It* makes it worse. Why is it not more apt to anticipate and provide for reform? Why does it not cherish its wise minority? Why does it cry and resist before it is hurt? Why does it not encourage its citizens to be on the alert to point out its faults and *do* better than it would have them? Why does it always crucify Christ and excommunicate Copernicus and Luther and pronounce Washington and Franklin rebels?

One would think that a deliberate and practical denial of its authority was the only offense never contemplated by government; else, why has it not assigned its definite, its suitable and proportionate penalty? If a man who has no property refuses but once to earn nine shillings for the state, he is put in prison for a period unlimited by any law that I know and determined only by the discretion of those who placed him there; but if he should steal ninety times nine shillings from the state, he is soon permitted to go at large again.

If the injustice is part of the necessary friction of the machine of government, let it go, let it go; perchance it will wear smooth—certainly the machine will wear out. If the injustice has a spring, or a pulley, or a rope, or a crank, exclusively for itself, then perhaps you may consider whether the remedy will not be worse than the evil; but if it is of such a nature that it requires you to be the agent of injustice to another, then, I say, break the law. Let your life be a counterfriction to stop the machine. What I have to do is to see, at any rate, that I do not lend myself to the wrong which I condemn.

As for adopting the ways which the state has provided for remedying the evil, I know not of such ways. They take too much time, and a man's life will be gone. I have other affairs to attend to. I came into this world, not chiefly to make this a good place to live in, but to live in it, be it good or bad. A man has not everything to do but something; and, because he cannot do *everything*, it is not necessary that he should do *something* wrong. It is not my business to be petitioning the governor or the legislature any more than it is theirs to petition me; and, if they should not hear my petition, what should I do then? But in this case the state has provided no way; its very constitution is the evil. This may seem to be harsh and stubborn and unconciliatory; but it is to treat with the utmost kindness and consideration the only spirit that can appreciate or deserve it. So is all change for the better, like birth and death which convulse the body.

I do not hesitate to say that those who call themselves abolitionists should at once effectually withdraw their support, both in person and property, from the government of Massachusetts and not wait till they constitute a majority of one before they suffer the right to prevail through them. I think that it is enough if they have God on their side, without waiting for that other one. Moreover, any man more right than his neighbors constitutes a majority of one already.

I meet this American government, or its representative the state government, directly, and face to face, once a year, no more, in the person of its tax-gatherer; this is the only mode in which a man situated as I am necessarily meets it; and it then says distinctly, "Recognize me"; and the simplest, the most effectual, and, in the present posture of affairs, the indispensablest mode of treating with it on this head, of expressing your little satisfaction with and love for it, is to deny it then. My civil neighbor, the tax-gatherer, is the very man I have to deal with—for it is, after all, with men and not with parchment that I quarrel—and he has voluntarily chosen to be an agent of the government. How shall he ever know well what he is and does as an officer of the government, or as a man, until he is obliged to consider whether he shall treat me, his neighbor, for whom he has respect, as a neighbor and well-disposed man, or as a maniac and disturber of the peace, and see if he can get over this obstruction to his neighborliness without a ruder and more impetuous thought or speech corresponding with his action? I know this well, that if one thousand, if one hundred, if ten men whom I could name—if ten *honest* men only—aye, if *one* honest man, in this state of Massachusetts, *ceasing to hold slaves*, were actually to withdraw from this co-partnership, and be locked up in the county jail therefor, it would be the abolition of slavery in America. For it matters not how small the beginning may seem to be; what is once well done is done forever. But we love better to talk about it; that, we say, is our mission. Reform keeps many scores of newspapers in its service but not one man. If my esteemed neighbor, the state's ambassador, who will devote his days to the settlement of the question of human rights in the Council Chamber, instead of being threatened with the prisons of Carolina, were to sit down the prisoner of Massachusetts, that state which is so anxious to foist the sin of slavery upon her sister—though at present she can discover only an act of inhospitality to be the ground of a quarrel with her—the legislature would not wholly waive the subject the following winter.

Under a government which imprisons any unjustly, the true place for a just man is also a prison. The proper place today, the only place which Massachusetts has provided for her freer and less desponding spirits, is in her prisons, to be put out and locked out of the state by her own act, as they have already put themselves out by their principles. It is there that the fugitive slave, and the Mexican prisoner on parole, and the Indian come to plead the wrongs of his race, should find them; on that separate, but more free and honorable ground, where the state places those who are not *with* her but *against* her—the only house in a slave state in which a free man can abide with honor. If any think that their influence would be lost there, and their voices no longer afflict the ear of the state, that they would not be as an enemy within its walls; they do not know by how much truth is stronger than error, nor how much more eloquently and effectively he can combat injustice who has experienced a little in his own person. Cast your whole vote, not a strip of paper merely, but your whole influence. A minority is powerless while it conforms to the majority; it is not even a minority then; but it is irresistible when it clogs by its whole weight. If the alternative is to keep all just men in prison, or give up war and slavery, the state will not hesitate which to choose. If a thousand men were not to pay their tax bills this year, that would not be a violent and bloody measure, as it would be to pay them, and enable the state to commit violence and shed innocent blood. This is, in fact, the definition of a peaceable revolution, if any such is possible. If the tax-gatherer, or any other public officer, asks me, as one has done, "But what shall I do?" my answer is, "If you really wish to do anything, resign your office." When the subject has refused allegiance, and the officer has resigned his office, then the revolution is accomplished. But even suppose blood should flow. Is there not a sort of blood shed when the conscience is wounded? Through this wound a man's real manhood and immortality flow out, and he bleeds to an everlasting death. I see this blood flowing now.

I have contemplated the imprisonment of the offender, rather than the seizure of his goods—though both will serve the same purpose—because they who assert the purest right, and consequently are most dangerous to a corrupt state, commonly have not spent much time in accumulating property. To such the state renders comparatively small service, and a slight tax is wont to appear exorbitant, particularly if they are obliged to earn it by special labor with their hands. If there were one who lived wholly without the use of money, the state itself would hesitate to demand it of him. But the rich man—not to make any invidious comparison—is always sold to the institution which makes him rich. Absolutely speaking, the more money, the less virtue; for money comes between a man and his objects and obtains them for him; and it was certainly no great virtue to obtain it. It puts to rest many questions which he would otherwise be taxed to answer; while the only new question which it puts is the hard but superfluous one, how to spend it. Thus his moral ground is taken from under his feet. The opportunities of living are diminished in proportion as what are called the "means" are increased. The best thing a man can do for his culture when he is rich is to endeavor to carry out those schemes which he entertained when he was poor. Christ answered the Herodians according to their condition. "Show me the tribute money," said he—and one took a penny out of his pocket. If you use money which has the image of Caesar on it, and which he has made current and valuable, that

is, *if you are men of the state*, and gladly enjoy the advantages of Caesar's government, then pay him back some of his own when he demands it; "Render therefore to Caesar that which is Caesar's, and to God those things which are God's"—leaving them no wiser than before as to which was which; for they did not wish to know.

When I converse with the freest of my neighbors, I perceive that, whatever they may say about the magnitude and seriousness of the question, and their regard for the public tranquillity, the long and the short of the matter is that they cannot spare the protection of the existing government, and they dread the consequences of disobedience to it to their property and families. For my own part, I should not like to think that I ever rely on the protection of the state. But, if I deny the authority of the state when it presents its tax bill, it will soon take and waste all my property, and so harass me and my children without end. This is hard. This makes it impossible for a man to live honestly and at the same time comfortably in outward respects. It will not be worth the while to accumulate property; that would be sure to go again. You must hire or squat somewhere, and raise but a small crop, and eat that soon. You must live within yourself and depend upon yourself, always tucked up and ready for a start, and not have many affairs. A man may grow rich in Turkey even, if he will be in all respects a good subject of the Turkish government. Confucius said: "If a state is governed by the principles of reason, poverty and misery are subjects of shame; if a state is not governed by the principles of reason, riches and honors are the subjects of shame." No; until I want the protection of Massachusetts to be extended to me in some distant southern port, where my liberty is endangered, or until I am bent solely on building up an estate at home by peaceful enterprise, I can afford to refuse allegiance to Massachusetts and her right to my property and life. It costs me less in every sense to incur the penalty of disobedience to the state than it would to obey. I should feel as if I were worth less in that case.

Some years ago the state met me in behalf of the church and commanded me to pay a certain sum toward the support of a clergyman whose preaching my father attended but never I myself. "Pay it," it said, "or be locked up in the jail." I declined to pay. But, unfortunately, another man saw fit to pay it. I did not see why the schoolmaster should be taxed to support the priest, and not the priest the schoolmaster; for I was not the state's schoolmaster, but I supported myself by voluntary subscription. I did not see why the lyceum should not present its tax bill, and have the state to back its demand, as well as the church. However, at the request of the selectmen, I condescended to make some such statement as this in writing: "Know all men by these presents, that I, Henry Thoreau, do not wish to be regarded as a member of any incorporated society which I have not joined." This I gave to the town clerk; and he has it. The state, having thus learned that I did not wish to be regarded as a member of that church, has never made a like demand on me since, though it said that it must adhere to its original presumption that time. If I had known how to name them, I should then have signed off in detail from all the societies which I never signed on to; but I did not know where to find a complete list.

I have paid no poll tax for six years. I was put into a jail once on this account, for one night; and, as I stood considering the walls of solid stone, two or three feet thick, the door of wood and iron, a foot thick, and the iron grating which strained the light, I could not help being struck with the foolishness of that institution which treated me as if I were mere flesh and blood and bones to be locked up. I wondered that it should have concluded at length that this was the best use it could put me to and had never thought to avail itself of my services in some way. I saw that, if there was a wall of stone between me and my townsmen, there was a still more difficult one to climb or break through before they could get to be as free as I was. I did not for a moment feel confined, and the walls seemed a great waste of stone and mortar. I felt as if I alone of all my townsmen had paid my tax. They plainly did not know how to treat me but behaved like persons who are underbred. In every threat and in every compliment there was a blunder, for they thought that my chief desire was to stand the other side of that stone wall. I could not but smile to see how industriously they locked the door on my meditations, which followed them out again without let or hinderance, and *they* were really all that was dangerous. As they could not reach me, they had resolved to punish my body; just as boys, if they cannot come at some person against whom they have a spite, will abuse his dog. I saw that the state was half-witted, that it was timid as a lone woman with her silver spoons, and that it did not know its friends from its foes, and I lost all my remaining respect for it and pitied it.

Thus the state never intentionally confronts a man's sense, intellectual or moral, but only his body, his senses. It is not armed with superior wit or honesty but with superior physical strength. I was not born to be forced. I will breathe after my own fashion. Let us see who is the strongest. What force has a multitude? They only can force me who obey a higher law than I. They force me to become like themselves. I do not hear of *men* being *forced* to live this way or that by masses of men. What sort of life were that to live? When I meet a government which says to me, "Your money or your life," why should I be in haste to give it my money? It may be in a great strait and not know what to do; I cannot help that. It must help itself; do as I do. It is not worth the while to snivel about it. I am not responsible for the successful working of the machinery of society. I am not the son of the engineer. I perceive that, when an acorn and a chestnut fall side by side, the one does not remain inert to make way for the other, but both obey their own laws, and spring and grow and flourish as best they can, till one, perchance, overshadows and destroys the other. If a plant cannot live according to its nature, it dies; and so a man.

The night in prison was novel and interesting enough. The prisoners in their shirt sleeves were enjoying a chat and the evening air in the doorway when I entered. But the jailer said, "Come, boys, it is time to lock up"; and so they dispersed, and I heard the sound of their steps returning into the hollow apartments. My room mate was introduced to me by the jailer as "a first-rate fellow and a clever man." When the door was locked, he showed me where to hang my hat, and how he managed matters there. The rooms were whitewashed once a month; and this one, at least, was the whitest, most simply furnished, and probably the neatest apartment in the town. He naturally wanted to know where I came from and what brought me there; and, when I had told him, I asked him in my turn how he came there, presuming him to be an honest man, of course; and, as the world goes, I believe he was. "Why," said he, "they accuse me of burning a barn; but I never did it." As near as I could discover, he had probably gone to bed in a barn when drunk, and smoked his pipe there; and so a barn was burned. He had the reputation of being a clever man, had been there some three months waiting for his trial to come on, and would have to wait as much longer; but he was quite domesticated and contented, since he got his board for nothing and thought that he was well treated.

He occupied one window, and I the other; and I saw, that, if one stayed there long, his principal business would be to look out the window. I had soon read all the tracts that were left there and examined where former prisoners had broken out, and where a grate had been sawed off, and heard the history of the various occupants of that room; for I found that even here there was a history and a gossip which never circulated beyond the walls of the jail. Probably this is the only house in the town where verses are composed, which are afterward printed in a circular form, but not published. I was shown quite a long list of verses which were composed by some young men who had been detected in an attempt to escape who avenged themselves by singing them.

I pumped my fellow-prisoner as dry as I could, for fear I should never see him again; but at length he showed me which was my bed and left me to blow out the lamp.

It was like traveling into a far country, such as I had never expected to behold, to lie there for one night. It seemed to me that I never had heard the town clock strike before, nor the evening sounds of the village; for we slept with the windows open, which were inside the grating. It was to see my native village in the light of the Middle Ages, and our Concord was turned into a Rhine stream, and visions of knights and castles passed before me. They were the voices of old burghers that I heard in the streets. I was an involuntary spectator and auditor of whatever was done and said in the kitchen of the adjacent village inn—a wholly new and rare experience to me. It was a closer view of my native town. I was fairly inside of it. I never had seen its institutions before. This is one of its peculiar institutions, for it is a shire town. I began to comprehend what its inhabitants were about.

In the morning our breakfasts were put through the hole in the door, in small oblong-square tin pans, made to fit, and holding a pint of chocolate, with brown bread, and an iron spoon. When they called for the vessels again, I was green enough to return what bread I had left; but my comrade seized it and said that I should lay that up for lunch or dinner. Soon after, he was let out to work at haying in a neighboring field, whither he went every day, and would not be back till noon; so he bade me goodday, saying that he doubted if he should see me again.

When I came out of prison—for some-one interfered and paid the tax—I did not perceive that great changes had taken place on the common, such as he observed who went in a youth and emerged a tottering and gray-headed man; and yet a change had to my eyes come over the scene—the town, and state, and country—greater than any that mere time could effect. I saw yet more distinctly the state in which I lived. I saw to what extent the people among whom I lived could be trusted as good neighbors and friends; that their friend-ship was for summer weather only; that they did not greatly purpose to do right; that they were a distinct race from me by their prejudices and superstitions, as the Chinamen and Malays are; that, in their sacrifices to humanity, they ran no risks, not even to their property; that, after all, they were not so noble but they treated the thief as he had treated them, and hoped, by a certain outward observ-ance and a few prayers, and by walking in a particular straight though useless path from time to time, to save their souls. This may be to judge my neigh-bors harshly; for I believe that most of them are not aware that they have such an institution as the jail in their village.

It was formerly the custom in our village, when a poor debtor came out of jail, for his acquaintances to salute him looking through their fingers, which were crossed to represent the grating of a jail window, "How do ye do?" My neighbors did not thus salute me but first looked at me, and then at one another, as if I had returned from a long journey. I was put into jail as I was going to the shoemaker's to get a shoe which was mended. When I was let out the next morning, I proceeded to finish my errand, and, having put on my mended shoe, joined a huckleberry party, who were impatient to put themselves under my conduct; and in half an hour—for the horse was soon tackled—was in the midst of a huckleberry field, on one of our highest hills, two miles off; and then the state was nowhere to be seen.

This is the whole history of "My Prisons."

I have never declined paying the high-way tax, because I am as desirous of being a good neighbor as I am of being a bad subject; and, as for supporting schools, I am doing my part to educate my fellow-countrymen now. It is for no particular item in the tax bill that I refuse to pay it. I simply wish to refuse allegiance to the state, to withdraw and stand aloof from it effectually. I do not care to trace the course of my dollar, if I could, till it buys a man, or a musket to shoot one with—the dollar is innocent— but I am concerned to trace the effects of my allegiance. In fact, I quietly de-clare war with the state, after my fash-ion, though I will still make what use and get what advantage of her I can, as is usual in such cases.

If others pay the tax which is de-manded of me, from a sympathy with the state, they do but what they have already done in their own case, or rather they abet injustice to a greater extent than the state requires. If they pay the tax from a mistaken interest in the indi-vidual taxed, to save his property or prevent his going to jail, it is because they have not considered wisely how far they let their private feelings interfere with the public good.

This, then, is my position at present. But one cannot be too much on his guard in such a case, lest his action be biased by obstinacy or an undue regard for the opinions of men. Let him see that he does only what belongs to himself and to the hour.

I think sometimes: Why, this people mean well; they are only ignorant; they would do better if they knew how; why give your neighbors this pain to treat you as they are not inclined to? But I think, again, this is no reason why I should do as they do or permit others to suffer much greater pain of a different kind. Again, I sometimes say to myself: When many millions of men, without heat, without ill-will, without personal feeling of any kind, demand of you a few shillings only, without the possibility, such is their constitution, of retracting or altering their present demand, and without the possibility, on your side, of appeal to any other millions, why expose yourself to this overwhelming brute force? You do not resist cold and hunger, the winds and the waves, thus obstinately; you quietly submit to a thousand similar necessities. You do not put your head into the fire. But just in proportion as I regard this as not wholly a brute force, but partly a human force, and consider that I have relations to those millions as to so many millions of men, and not of mere brute or inanimate things, I see that appeal is possible, first and instantaneously, from them to the Maker of them, and, secondly, from them to themselves. But, if I put my head deliberately into the fire, there is no appeal to fire or to the Maker of fire, and I have only myself to blame. If I could convince myself that I have any right to be satisfied with men as they are, and to treat them accordingly, and not according, in some respects, to my requisitions and expectations of what they and I ought to be, then, like a good Mussulman and fatalist, I should en-

deavor to be satisfied with things as they are, and say it is the will of God. And, above all, there is this difference between resisting this and a purely brute or natural force—that I can resist this with some effect; but I cannot expect, like Orpheus, to change the nature of the rocks and trees and beasts.

I do not wish to quarrel with any man or nation. I do not wish to split hairs, to make fine distinctions, or set myself up as better than my neighbors. I seek rather, I may say, even an excuse for conforming to the laws of the land. I am but too ready to conform to them. Indeed, I have reason to suspect myself on this head; and each year, as the tax-gatherer comes round, I find myself disposed to review the acts and position of the general and state governments, and the spirit of the people, to discover a pretext for conformity. I believe that the state will soon be able to take all my work of this sort out of my hands, and then I shall be no better a patriot than my fellow-countrymen. Seen from a lower point of view, the Constitution, with all its faults, is very good; the law and the courts are very respectable; even this state and this American government are, in many respects, very admirable and rare things, to be thankful for, such as a great many have described them; but seen from a point of view a little higher, they are what I have described them; seen from a higher still, and the highest, who shall say what they are, or that they are worth looking at or thinking of at all?

However, the government does not concern me much, and I shall bestow the fewest possible thoughts on it. It is not many moments that I live under a government, even in this world. If a man is thought-free, fancy-free, imagination-free, that which *is not* never for a long time appearing *to be* to him, unwise rulers or reformers cannot fatally interrupt him.

I know that most men think differently from myself; but those whose lives are by profession devoted to the study of these or kindred subjects content me as little as any. Statesmen and legislators, standing so completely within the institution, never distinctly and nakedly behold it. They speak of moving society but have no resting-place without it. They may be men of a certain experience and discrimination, and have no doubt invented ingenious and even useful systems, for which we sincerely thank them; but all their wit and usefulness lie within certain not very wide limits. They are wont to forget that the world is not governed by policy and expediency. Webster never goes behind government and so cannot speak with authority about it. His words are wisdom to those legislators who contemplate no essential reform in the existing government; but for thinkers, and those who legislate for all time, he never once glances at the subject. I know of those whose serene and wise speculations on this theme would soon reveal the limits of his mind's range and hospitality. Yet, compared with the cheap professions of most reformers, and the still cheaper wisdom and eloquence of politicians in general, his are almost the only sensible and valuable words, and we thank Heaven for him. Comparatively, he is always strong, original, and, above all, practical. Still his quality is not wisdom but prudence. The lawyer's truth is not Truth, but consistency, or a consistent expediency. Truth is always in harmony with herself and is not concerned chiefly to reveal the justice that may consist with wrongdoing. He well deserves to be called, as he has been called, the Defender of the Constitution. There are really no blows to be given by him but defensive ones. He is not a leader but a follower. His leaders are the men of '87. "I have never made an effort," he says, "and never propose to make an effort; I have never countenanced an effort, and never mean to countenance an effort, to

disturb the arrangement as originally made, by which the various states came into the Union." Still thinking of the sanction which the Constitution gives to slavery, he says, "Because it was a part of the original compact—let it stand." Notwithstanding his special acuteness and ability, he is unable to take a fact out of its merely political relations and behold it as it lies absolutely to be disposed of by the intellect—what, for instance, it behooves a man to do here in America today with regard to slavery, but ventures, or is driven, to make some such desperate answer as the following, while professing to speak absolutely, and as a private man—from which what new and singular code of social duties might be inferred? "The manner," says he, "in which the government of those states where slavery exists are to regulate it is for their own consideration, under their responsibility to their constituents, to the general laws of propriety, humanity, and justice, and to God. Associations formed elsewhere, springing from a feeling of humanity, or any other cause, have nothing whatever to do with it. They have never received any encouragement from me, and they never will."

They who know of no purer sources of truth, who have traced up its stream no higher, stand, and wisely stand, by the Bible and the Constitution, and drink at it there with reverence and humility; but they who behold where it comes trickling into this lake or that pool gird up their loins once more and continue their pilgrimage toward its fountainhead.

No man with a genius for legislation has appeared in America. They are rare in the history of the world. There are orators, politicians, and eloquent men by the thousand; but the speaker has not yet opened his mouth to speak who is capable of settling the much-vexed questions of the day. We love eloquence for its own sake and not for any truth which it may utter or any heroism it may inspire. Our legislators have not yet learned the comparative value of free trade and of freedom, of union, and of rectitude, to a nation. They have no genius or tlaent for comparatively humble questions of taxation and finance, commerce and manufactures and agriculture. If we were left solely to the wordy wit of legislators in Congress for our guidance, uncorrected by the seasonable experience and the effectual complaints of the people, America would not long retain her rank among the nations. For eighteen hundred years, though perchance I have no right to say it, the New Testament has been written; yet where is the legislator who has wisdom and practical talent enough to avail himself of the light which it sheds on the science of legislation?

The authority of government, even such as I am willing to submit to—for I will cheerfully obey those who know and can do better than I, and in many things even those who neither know nor can do so well—is still an impure one; to be strictly just, it must have the sanction and consent of the governed. It can have no pure right over my person and property but what I concede to it. The progress from an absolute to a limited monarchy, from a limited monarchy to a democracy, is a progress toward a true respect for the individual. Is a democracy, such as we know it, the last improvement possible in government? Is it not possible to take a step further toward recognizing and organizing the rights of man? There will never be a really free and enlightened state, until the state comes to recognize the individual as a higher and independent power, from which all its own power and authority are derived, and treats him accordingly. I please myself with imagining a state at last which can afford to be just to all men and to treat the individual with respect as a neighbor, which even would not think it inconsistent with its own repose if a few were to live aloof from it, not meddling with it, nor embraced by it, who fulfilled all the duties of neighbors and fellowmen. A state which bore this kind of fruit, and suffered it to drop off as fast as it ripened, would prepare the way for a still more perfect and glorious state, which also I have imagined, but not yet anywhere seen.

2. MAN THE REFORMER[1]

By Ralph Waldo Emerson

EDITORS' NOTE.—Ralph Waldo Emerson (1803–82) is one of the most famous of American philosophers, writers, and lecturers. After three years as a minister in Boston, Emerson spent his life as writer and lecturer in what would today be called the field of adult education. His characteristic trust in the individual and his hope that from the improvement of the individual a better society would result are evident in this essay.

Mr. President and Gentlemen:

I wish to offer to your consideration some thoughts on the particular and general relations of man as a reformer. I shall assume that the aim of each young

1. Ralph Waldo Emerson, *Nature, Addresses, and Lectures* (Boston, 1884), pp. 217–44.

man in this association is the very highest that belongs to a rational mind. Let it be granted that our life, as we lead it, is common and mean; that some of those offices and functions for which we were mainly created are grown so rare in society that the memory of them is only kept alive in old books and in dim traditions; that prophets and poets, that beautiful and perfect men, we are not now, no, nor have even seen such; that some sources of human instruction are almost unnamed and unknown among us; that the community in which we live will hardly bear to be told that every man should be open to ecstasy or a divine illumination, and his daily walk elevated by intercourse with the spiritual world. Grant all this, as we must, yet I suppose none of my auditors will deny that we ought to seek to establish ourselves in such disciplines and courses as will deserve that guidance and clearer communication with the spiritual nature. And, further, I will not dissemble my hope that each person whom I address has felt his own call to cast aside all evil customs, timidities, and limitations and to be in his place a free and helpful man, a reformer, a benefactor, not content to slip along through the world like a footman or a spy, escaping by his nimbleness and apologies as many knocks as he can, but a brave and upright man who must find or cut a straight road to everything excellent in the earth and not only go honorably himself but make it easier for all who follow him to go in honor and with benefit.

In the history of the world the doctrine of reform had never such scope as at the present hour. Lutherans, Hernhutters, Jesuits, Monks, Quakers, Knox, Wesley, Swedenborg, Bentham, in their accusations of society, all respected something—church or state, literature or history, domestic usages, the market town, the dinner table, coined money. But now all these and all things else hear the trumpet and must rush to judgment—Christianity, the laws, commerce, schools, the farm, the laboratory; and not a kingdom, town, statute, rite, calling, man, or woman but is threatened by the new spirit.

What if some of the objections whereby our institutions are assailed are ex-treme and speculative, and the reformers tend to idealism? That only shows the extravagance of the abuses which have driven the mind into the opposite extreme. It is when your facts and persons grow unreal and fantastic by too much falsehood that the scholar flies for refuge to the world of ideas and aims to recruit and replenish nature from that source. Let ideas establish their legitimate sway again in society, let life be fair and poetic, and the scholars will gladly be lovers, citizens, and philanthropists.

It will afford no security from the new ideas that the old nations, the laws of centuries, the property and institutions of a hundred cities, are built on other foundations. The demon of reform has a secret door into the heart of every lawmaker, of every inhabitant of every city. The fact that a new thought and hope have dawned in your breast should apprise you that in the same hour a new light broke in upon a thousand private hearts. That secret which you would fain keep—as soon as you go abroad, lo! there is one standing on the doorstep to tell you the same. There is not the most bronzed and sharpened money-catcher who does not, to your consternation almost, quail and shake the moment he hears a question prompted by the new ideas. We thought he had some semblance of ground to stand upon; that such as he at least would die hard; but he trembles and flees. Then the scholar says: "Cities and coaches shall never impose on me again; for, behold, every solitary dream of mine is rushing to fulfilment! That fancy I had and hesitated to utter because you would laugh—the broker, the attorney, the market-man, are saying the same thing. Had I waited a day longer to speak, I had been too late. Behold, State Street thinks, and Wall Street doubts, and begins to prophesy!"

It cannot be wondered at that this general inquest into abuses should arise in the bosom of society, when one considers the practical impediments that stand in the way of virtuous young men. The young man, on entering life, finds the way to lucrative employments blocked with abuses. The ways of trade are grown selfish to the borders of theft and supple to the borders (if not beyond the borders) of fraud. The employments of commerce are not intrinsically unfit for a man or less genial to his faculties; but these are now in their general course so vitiated by derelictions and abuses at which all connive that it requires more vigor and resources than can be expected of every young man, to right himself in them; he is lost in them; he cannot move hand or foot in them. Has he genius and virtue? the less does he find them fit for him to grow in, and, if he would thrive in them, he must sacrifice all the brilliant dreams of boyhood and youth as dreams; he must forget the prayers of his childhood and must take on him the harness of routine and obsequiousness. If not so minded, nothing is left him but to begin the world anew, as he does who puts the spade into the ground for food. We are all implicated, of course, in this charge; it is only necessary to ask a few questions as to the progress of the articles of commerce from the fields where they grew, to our houses, to become aware that we eat and drink and wear perjury and fraud in a hundred commodities. How many articles in daily consumption are furnished us from the West Indies; yet it is said that in the Spanish islands the venality of the officers of the government has passed into usage and that no article passes into our ships which has not been fraudulently cheapened. In the Spanish islands every agent or factor of the Americans, unless he be a consul, has taken oath that he is a Catholic or has caused a priest to make that declaration for him. The abolitionist has shown us our dreadful debt to the southern Negro. In the island of Cuba, in addition to the ordinary abominations of slavery, it appears only men are bought for the plantations, and one dies in ten every year, of these miserable bachelors, to yield us sugar. I leave for those who have the knowledge the part of sifting the oaths of our custom-houses; I will not inquire into the oppression of the sailors; I will not pry into the usages of our retail trade. I content myself with the fact that the general system of our trade (apart from the blacker traits, which, I hope, are exceptions denounced and unshared by all reputable men) is a system of selfishness; is not dictated by the high sentiments of human nature; is not measured by the exact law of reciprocity, much less by the sentiments of love and heroism, but is a system of distrust, of concealment, of superior keenness, not of giving but of taking advantage. It is not that which a man delights to unlock to a noble friend, which he meditates on with joy and self-approval in his hour of love and aspiration, but rather what he then puts out of sight, only showing the brilliant result, and atoning for the manner of acquiring by the manner of expending it. I do not charge the merchant or the manufacturer. The sins of our trade belong to no class, to no individual. One plucks, one distributes, one eats. Everybody partakes, everybody confesses—with cap and knee volunteers his confession, yet none feels himself accountable. He did not create the abuse; he cannot alter it. What is he? An obscure private person who must get his bread. That is the vice—that no one feels himself called to act for man but only as a fraction of man. It happens therefore that all such ingenious souls as feel within themselves the irrepressible strivings of a noble aim, who by the law of their nature must act simply, find these ways of trade unfit for them, and they come forth from it. Such cases are becoming more numerous every year.

But, by coming out of trade, you have

not cleared yourself. The trail of the serpent reaches into all the lucrative professions and practices of man. Each has its own wrongs. Each finds a tender and very intelligent conscience a disqualification for success. Each requires of the practitioner a certain shutting of the eyes, a certain dapperness and compliance, an acceptance of customs, a sequestration from the sentiments of generosity and love, a compromise of private opinion and lofty integrity. Nay, the evil custom reaches into the whole institution of property, until our laws which establish and protect it seem not to be the issue of love and reason but of selfishness. Suppose a man is so unhappy as to be born a saint, with deep perceptions but with the conscience and love of an angel, and he is to get his living in the world; he finds himself excluded from all lucrative works; he has no farm, and he cannot get one; for to earn money enough to buy one requires a sort of concentration toward money which is the selling himself for a number of years, and to him the present hour is as sacred and inviolable as any future hour. Of course, whilst another man has no land, my title to mine, your title to yours, is at once vitiated. Inextricable seem to be the twinings and tendrils of this evil, and we all involve ourselves in it the deeper by forming connections, by wives and children, by benefits and debts.

Considerations of this kind have turned the attention of many philanthropic and intelligent persons to the claims of manual labor as a part of the education of every young man. If the accumulated wealth of the past generation is thus tainted—no matter how much of it is offered to us—we must begin to consider if it were not the nobler part to renounce it and to put ourselves into primary relations with the soil and nature and, abstaining from whatever is dishonest and unclean, to take each of us bravely his part, with his own hands, in the manual labor of the world.

But it is said, "What! Will you give up the immense advantages reaped from the division of labor and set every man to make his own shoes, bureau, knife, wagon, sails, and needle? This would be to put men back into barbarism by their own act." I see no instant prospect of a virtuous revolution; yet I confess I should not be pained at a change which threatened a loss of some of the luxuries or conveniences of society, if it proceeded from a preference of the agricultural life out of the belief that our primary duties as men could be better discharged in that calling. Who could regret to see a high conscience and a purer taste exercising a sensible effect on young men in their choice of occupation and thinning the ranks of competition in the labors of commerce, of law, and of state? It is easy to see that the inconvenience would last but a short time. This would be great action, which always opens the eyes of men. When many persons shall have done this, when the majority shall admit the necessity of reform in all these institutions, their abuses will be redressed, and the way will be open again to the advantages which arise from the division of labor, and a man may select the fittest employment for his peculiar talent again without compromise.

But, quite apart from the emphasis which the times give to the doctrine that the manual labor of society ought to be shared among all the members, there are reasons proper to every individual why he should not be deprived of it. The use of manual labor is one which never grows obsolete, and which is inapplicable to no person. A man should have a farm or a mechanical craft for his culture. We must have a basis for our higher accomplishments, our delicate entertainments of poetry and philosophy, in the work of our hands. We must have an antagonism in the tough world for all the variety of our spiritual faculties, or they will not be born. Manual labor is the study of the external world. The advantage of riches remains with him who procured them, not with the heir. When I go into my garden with a spade, and dig a bed, I feel such an exhilaration and health that I discover that I have been defrauding myself all this time in letting others do for me what I should have done with my own hands. But not only health but education is in the work. Is it possible that I, who get indefinite quantities of sugar, hominy, cotton, buckets, crockery ware, and letter paper by simply signing my name once in three months to a check in favor of John Smith and Co., traders, get the fair share of exercise to my faculties by that act which nature intended for me in making all these far-fetched matters important to my comfort. It is Smith himself, and his carriers, and dealers, and manufacturers; it is the sailor, the hidedrogher, the butcher, the Negro, the hunter, and the planter who have intercepted the sugar of the sugar and the cotton of the cotton. They have got the education; I only the commodity. This were all very well if I were necessarily absent, being detained by work of my own, like theirs, work of the same faculties; then should I be sure of my hands and feet; but now I feel some shame before my wood-chopper, my plowman, and my cook, for they have some sort of self-sufficiency they can contrive without my aid to bring the day and year round, but I depend on them and have not earned by use a right to my arms and feet.

Consider further the difference between the first and second owner of property. Every species of property is preyed on by its own enemies, as iron by rust; timber by rot; cloth by moths; provisions by mold, putridity, or vermin; money by thieves; an orchard by insects; a planted field by weeds and the inroad of cattle; a stock of cattle by hunger; a road by rain and frost; a bridge by freshets. And whoever takes any of these things into his possession takes the charge of defending them from this troop of enemies or of keeping them in repair. A man who supplies his own want, who builds a raft or a boat to go a-fishing, finds it easy to calk it, or put in a tholepin, or mend the rudder. What he gets only as fast as he wants for his own ends does not embarrass him or take away his sleep with looking after. But when he comes to give all the goods he has year after year collected in one estate to his son—house, orchard, plowed land, cattle, bridges, hardware, woodenware, carpets, cloths, provisions, books, money—and cannot give him the skill and experience which made or collected these, and the method and place they have in his own life, the son finds his hands full—not to use these things but to look after them and defend them from their natural enemies. To him they are not means but masters. Their enemies will not remit; rust, mold, vermin, rain, sun, freshet, fire, all seize their own, fill him with vexation, and he is converted from the owner into a watchman or a watchdog to this magazine of old and new chattels. What a change! Instead of the masterly good humor and sense of power and fertility of resource in himself; instead of those strong and learned hands, those piercing and learned eyes, that supple body, and that mighty and prevailing heart which the father had, whom nature loved and feared, whom snow and rain, water and land, beast and fish, seemed all to know and to serve—we have now a puny, protected person, guarded by walls and curtains, stoves and down beds, coaches, and menservants and womenservants from the earth and the sky, and who, bred to depend on all these, is made anxious by all that endangers those possessions and is forced to spend so much time in guarding them that he has quite lost sight of their original use, namely, to help him to his ends—to the prosecution of his love, to the helping of his friend, to the worship of his God, to the enlargement of his knowledge, to the serving of his country, to the indulgence of his sentiment; and he is now what is called a rich man— the menial and runner of his riches.

Hence it happens that the whole interest of history lies in the fortunes of the poor. Knowledge, virtue, power, are the victories of man over his necessities, his march to the dominion of the world. Every man ought to have this opportunity to conquer the world for himself. Only such persons interest us, Spartans, Romans, Saracens, English Americans, who have stood in the jaws of need and have by their own wit and might extricated themselves and made man victorious.

I do not wish to overstate this doctrine of labor or insist that every man should be a farmer any more than that every man should be a lexicographer. In general, one may say that the husbandman's is the oldest and most universal profession and that, where a man does not yet discover in himself any fitness for one work more than another, this may be preferred. But the doctrine of the farm is merely this: that every man ought to stand in primary relations with the work of the world, ought to do it himself and not to suffer the accident of his having a purse in his pocket or his having been bred to some dishonorable and injurious craft to sever him from those duties; and for this reason, that labor is God's education; that he only is a sincere learner, he only can become a master who learns the secrets of labor and who, by real cunning, extorts from nature its scepter.

Neither would I shut my ears to the plea of the learned professions, of the poet, the priest, the lawgiver, and men of study generally; namely, that in the experience of all men of that class the amount of manual labor which is necessary to the maintenance of a family indisposes and disqualifies for intellectual exertion. I know it often, perhaps usually, happens that where there is a fine organization, apt for poetry and philosophy, that individual finds himself compelled to wait on his thoughts; to waste several days that he may enhance and glorify one; and is better taught by a moderate and dainty exercise, such as rambling in the fields, rowing, skating, hunting, than by the downright drudgery of the farmer and the smith. I would not quite forget the venerable counsel of the Egyptian mysteries, which declared that "there were two pairs of eyes in man, and it is requisite that the pair which are beneath should be closed, when the pair that are above them perceive, and that when the pair above are closed, those which are beneath should be opened." Yet I will suggest that no separation from labor can be without some loss of power and of truth to the seer himself; that, I doubt not, the faults and vices of our literature and philosophy, their too great fineness, effeminacy, and melancholy, are attributable to the enervated and sickly habits of the literary class. Better that the book should not be quite so good, and the bookmaker abler and better, and not himself often a ludicrous contrast to all that he has written.

But granting that for ends so sacred and dear some relaxation must be had, I think that if a man find in himself any strong bias to poetry, to art, to the contemplative life, drawing him to these things with a devotion incompatible with good husbandry, that man ought to reckon early with himself and, respecting the compensations of the Universe, ought to ransom himself from the duties of economy by a certain rigor and privation in his habits. For privileges so rare and grand, let him not stint to pay a great tax. Let him be a cenobite, a pauper, and, if need be, celibate also. Let him learn to eat his meals standing and to relish the taste of fair water and black bread. He may leave to others the costly conveniences of housekeeping and large hospitality and the possession of works of art. Let him feel that genius is a hospitality and that he who can create works of art needs not collect them. He must live in a chamber and postpone his self-indulgence, forewarned and forearmed against that frequent misfortune of men of genius—the taste for luxury. This is the tragedy of genius: attempting to drive along the ecliptic with one horse of the heavens and one horse of the earth, there is only discord and ruin and downfall to chariot and charioteer.

The duty that every man should assume his own vows, should call the institutions of society to account, and examine their fitness to him, gains in emphasis if we look at our modes of living. Is our housekeeping sacred and honorable? Does it raise and inspire us, or does it cripple us instead? I ought to be armed by every part and function of my household, by all my social function, by my economy, by my feasting, by my voting, by my traffic. Yet I am almost no party to any of these things. Custom does it for me, gives me no power therefrom, and runs me in debt to boot. We spend our incomes for paint and paper, for a hundred trifles, I know not what, and not for the things of a man. Our expense is almost all for conformity. It is for cake that we run in debt; it is not the intellect, not the heart, not beauty, not worship, that costs so much. Why needs any man be rich? Why must he have horses, fine garments, handsome apartments, access to public houses and places of amusement? Only for want of thought. Give his mind a new image, and he flees into a solitary garden or garret to enjoy it, and is richer with that dream than the fee of a county could make him. But we are first thoughtless and then find that we are moneyless. We are first sensual and then must be rich. We dare not trust our wit for making our house

pleasant to our friend, and so we buy ice-creams. He is accustomed to carpets, and we have not sufficient character to put floor cloths out of his mind whilst he stays in the house, and so we pile the floor with carpets. Let the house rather be a temple of the Furies of Lacedaemon, formidable and holy to all, which none but a Spartan may enter or so much as behold. As soon as there is faith, as soon as there is society, comfits and cushions will be left to slaves. Expense will be inventive and heroic. We shall eat hard and lie hard; we shall dwell like the ancient Romans in narrow tenements, whilst our public edifices, like theirs, will be worthy for their proportion of the landscape in which we set them, for conversation, for art, for music, for worship. We shall be rich to great purposes; poor only for selfish ones.

Now what help for these evils? How can the man who has learned but one art procure all the conveniences of life honestly? Shall we say all we think? Perhaps with his own hands. Suppose he collects or makes them ill—yet he has learned their lesson. If he cannot do that? Then perhaps he can go without. Immense wisdom and riches are in that. It is better to go without than to have them at too great a cost. Let us learn the meaning of economy. Economy is a high, humane office, a sacrament, when its aim is grand; when it is the prudence of simple tastes, when it is practiced for freedom, or love, or devotion. Much of the economy which we see in houses is of a base origin and is kept out of sight. Parched corn eaten today that I may have roast fowl to my dinner on Sunday is a baseness; but parched corn and a house with one apartment, that I may be free of all perturbations, that I may be serene and docile to what the mind shall speak, and girt and road-ready for the lowest mission of knowledge or good will, is frugality for gods and heroes.

Can we not learn the lesson of self-help? Society is full of infirm people who incessantly summon others to serve them. They contrive everywhere to exhaust for their single comfort the entire means and appliances of that luxury to which our invention has yet attained. Sofas, ottomans, stoves, wine, game fowl, spices, perfumes, rides, the theater, entertainments—all these they want, they need, and whatever can be suggested more than these they crave also, as if it was the bread which should keep them from starving; and, if they miss any one, they represent themselves as the most wronged and most wretched persons on earth. One must have been born and bred with them to know how to prepare a meal for their learned stomach. Meantime they never bestir themselves to serve another person; not they! They have a great deal more to do for themselves than they can possibly perform, nor do they once perceive the cruel joke of their lives, but the more odious they grow, the sharper is the tone of their complaining and craving. Can anything be so elegant as to have few wants and to serve them one's self, so as to have somewhat left to give, instead of being always prompt to grab? It is more elegant to answer one's own needs than to be richly served; inelegant perhaps it may look today, and to a few, but it is an elegance forever and to all.

I do not wish to be absurd and pedantic in reform. I do not wish to push my criticism on the state of things around me to that extravagant mark that shall compel me to suicide or to an absolute isolation from the advantages of civil society. If we suddenly plant our foot and say, "I will neither eat nor drink nor wear nor touch any food or fabric which I do not know to be innocent, or deal with any person whose whole manner of life is not clear and rational," we shall stand still. Whose is so? Not mine; not thine; not his. But I think we must clear ourselves each one by the interrogation, whether we have earned our bread today by the hearty contribution of our energies to the common benefit; and we must not cease to tend to the correction of flagrant wrongs, by laying one stone aright every day.

But the idea which now begins to agitate society has a wider scope than our daily employments, our households, and the institutions of property. We are to revise the whole of our social structure, the state, the school, religion, marriage, trade, science, and explore their foundations in our own nature; we are to see that the world not only fitted the former men but fits us, and to clear ourselves of every usage which has not its roots in our own mind. What is a man born for but to be a reformer, a remaker of what man has made; a renouncer of lies; a restorer of truth and good, imitating that great Nature which embosoms us all, and which sleeps no moment on an old past, but very hour repairs herself, yielding us every morning a new day, and with every pulsation a new life? Let him renounce everything which is not true to him, and put all his practices back on their first thoughts, and do nothing for which he has not the whole world for his reason. If there are inconveniences and what is called ruin in the way, because we have so enervated and maimed ourselves, yet it would be like dying of perfumes to sink in the effort to reattach the deeds of every day to the holy and mysterious recesses of life.

The power which is at once spring and regulator in all efforts of reform is the conviction that there is an infinite worthiness in man, which will appear at the call of worth, and that all particular reforms are the removing of some impediment. Is it not the highest duty that man should be honored in us? I ought not to allow any man, because he has broad lands, to feel that he is rich in my presence. I ought to make him feel that I can do without his riches, that I cannot be bought—neither by comfort, neither by pride—and though I be utterly penniless, and receiving bread from him, that he is the poor man beside me. And if, at the same time, a woman or a child discovers a sentiment of piety, or a juster way of thinking than mine, I ought to confess it by my respect and obedience, though it go to alter my whole way of life.

The Americans have many virtues, but they have not faith and hope. I know no two words whose meaning is more lost sight of. We use these words as if they were as obsolete as Selah and Amen. And yet they have the broadest meaning and the most cogent application to Boston in this year. The Americans have little faith. They rely on the power of a dollar; they are deaf to a sentiment. They think you may talk the north wind down as easily as raise society; and no class is more faithless than the scholars or intellectual men. Now if I talk with a sincere wise man, and my friend, with a poet, with a conscientious youth who is still under the dominion of his own wild thoughts, and not yet harnessed in the team of society to drag with us all in the ruts of custom, I see at once how paltry is all this generation of unbelievers and what a house of cards their institutions are, and I see what one brave man, what one great thought executed, might effect. I see that the reason of the distrust of the practical man in all theory is his inability to perceive the means whereby we work. Look, he says, at the tools with which this world of yours is to be built. As we cannot make a planet, with atmosphere, rivers, and forests, by means of the best carpenters' or engineers' tools, with chemist's laboratory and smith's forge to boot—so neither can we ever construct that heavenly society you prate of out of foolish, sick, selfish men and women, such as we know them to be. But the believer not only beholds his heaven to be possible but already to begin to exist—not by the men or materials the statesman uses but by men transfigured and raised above themselves by the power of principles. To principles something else is possible than transcends all the power of expedients.

Every great and commanding moment in the annals of the world is the triumph of some enthusiasm. The victories of the Arabs after Mahomet, who, in a few years, from a small and mean beginning, established a larger empire than that of Rome, is an example. They did they knew not what. The naked Derar, horsed on an idea, was found an overmatch for a troop of Roman cavalry. The women fought like men, and conquered the Roman men. They were miserably equipped, miserably fed. They were Temperance troops. There was neither brandy nor flesh needed to feed them. They conquered Asia, and Africa, and Spain, on barley. The Caliph Omar's walking-stick struck more terror into those who saw it than another man's sword. His diet was barley bread; his sauce was salt; and oftentimes by way of abstinence he ate his bread without salt. His drink was water. His palace was built of mud; and when he left Medina to go to the conquest of Jerusalem, he rode on a red camel, with a wooden platter hanging at his saddle, with a bottle of water and two sacks, one holding barley, and the other dried fruits.

But there will dawn ere long on our politics, on our modes of living, a nobler morning than that Arabian faith, in the sentiment of love. This is the one remedy for all ills, the panacea of nature. We must be lovers, and at once the impossible becomes possible. Our age and history, for these thousand years, has not been the history of kindness, but of selfishness. Our distrust is very expensive. The money we spend for courts and prison is very ill laid out. We make, by distrust, the thief, and burglar, and incendiary, and by our court and jail we keep him so. An acceptance of the sentiment of love throughout Christendom for a season would bring the felon and the outcast to our side in tears, with the devotion of his faculties to our service. See this wide society of laboring men and women. We allow ourselves to be served by them, we live apart from them, and meet them without a salute in the streets. We do not greet their talents, nor rejoice in their good fortune, nor foster their hopes, nor in the assembly of the people vote for what is dear to them. Thus we enact the part of the selfish noble and king from the foundation of the world. See, this tree always bears one fruit. In every household, the peace of a pair is poisoned by the malice, slyness, indolence, and alienation of domestics. Let any two matrons meet, and observe how soon their conversation turns on the troubles from their "help," as our phrase is. In every knot of laborers the rich man does not feel himself among his friends—and at the polls he finds them arrayed in a mass in distinct opposition to him. We complain that the politics of masses of the people are controlled by designing men, and let in opposition to manifest justice and the common weal, and to their own interest. But the people do not wish to be represented or ruled by the ignorant and base. They only vote for these, because they were asked with the voice and assemblance of kindness. They will not vote for them long. They inevitably prefer wit and probity. To use an Egyptian metaphor, it is not their will for any long time "to raise the nails of wild beasts, and to depress the heads of the sacred birds." Let our affection flow out to our fellows; it would operate in a day the greatest of all revolutions. It is better to work on institutions by the sun than by the wind. The state must consider the poor man, and all voices must speak for him. Every child that is born must have a just chance for his bread. Let the amelioration in our laws of property proceed from the conces-

sion of the rich, not from the grasping of the poor. Let us begin by habitual imparting. Let us understand that the equitable rule is that no one should take more than his share, let him be ever so rich. Let me feel that I am to be a lover. I am to see to it that the world is the better for me and to find my reward in the act. Love would put a new face on this weary old world in which we dwell as pagans and enemies too long, and it would warm the heart to see how fast the vain diplomacy of statesmen, the impotence of armies, and navies, and lines of defense, would be superseded by this unarmed child. Love will creep where it cannot go, will accomplish that by imperceptible methods—being its own lever, fulcrum, and power—which force could never achieve. Have you not seen in the woods, in a late autumn morning, a poor fungus or mushroom— a plant without any solidity, nay, that seemed nothing but a soft mush or jelly —by its constant, total, and inconceivably gentle pushing, manage to break its way up through the frosty ground, and actually to lift a hard crust on its head? It is the symbol of the power of kindness. The virtue of this principle in human society in application to great interests is obsolete and forgotten. Once or twice in history it has been tried in illustrious instances, with signal success. This great, overgrown, dead Christendom of ours still keeps alive at least the name of a lover of mankind. But one day all men will be lovers; and every calamity will be dissolved in the universal sunshine.

Will you suffer me to add one trait more to this portrait of man the reformer? The mediator between the spiritual and the actual world should have a great prospective prudence. An Arabian poet describes his hero by saying,

> Sunshine was he
> In the winter day;
> And in the midsummer
> Coolness and shade.

He who would help himself and others should not be a subject of irregular and interrupted impulses of virtue but a continent, persisting, immovable person —such as we have seen a few scattered up and down in time for the blessing of the world; men who have in the gravity of their nature a quality which answers to the flywheel in a mills, which distributes the motion equably over all the wheels and hinders it from falling unequally and suddenly in destructive shocks. It is better that joy should be spread over all the day in the form of strength than that it should be concentrated into ecstacies, full of danger and followed by reactions. There is a sublime prudence which is the very highest that we know of man, which, believing in a vast future—sure of more to come than is yet seen—postpones always the present hour to the whole life; postpones talent to genius, and special results to character. As the merchant gladly takes money from his income to add to his capital, so is the great man very willing to lose particular powers and talents, so that he gain in the elevation of his life. The opening of the spiritual senses disposes men ever to greater sacrifices, to leave their signal talents, their best means and skill of procuring a present success, their power and their fame—to cast all things behind, in the insatiable thirst for divine communications. A purer fame, a greater power, rewards the sacrifice. It is the conversion of our harvest into seed. As the farmer casts into the ground the finest ears of his grain, the time will come when we too shall hold nothing back but shall eagerly convert more than we now possess into means and powers, when we shall be willing to sow the sun and the moon for seeds.

UNIT VIII

THE CRISIS IN THE FEDERAL UNION

AT LEAST two classes of people, of all those who have interested themselves in the Civil War, have good reason to be troubled by it. For the historian who struggles to find an adequate explanation, it bristles with stubborn problems; for the democrat who holds to his faith in the possibility of government by agreement, it stands as a bleak commentary on human frailty.

The spirit of successful political compromise which had characterized the government of the United States during the first sixty years of its history was shattered during the decade preceding Lincoln's election. Many of the issues around which controversy raged had appeared before, without war resulting. Why did war finally come? Did a simple humanitarianism devour itself? Was the war made inevitable by the accumulation of rivalries in economic policy? Was it the result of violent displacements in the sectional balance of power? Of competing philosophies, which no ingenuity could bridge? Could better leadership have averted it? Why were all the aggressive impulses of the various factions eventually inflamed and all the resources of compromise exhausted? Lincoln's proposition in his Second Inaugural Address is that "both parties deprecated war, but one of them would *make* war rather than

let the nation survive, and the other would *accept* war rather than let it perish, and the war came." Lincoln said that the slavery interest was somehow the cause of the war and regarded American slavery as perhaps "one of those offenses which, in the providence of God, must needs come, but which . . . He now wills to remove and that He gives to both North and South this terrible war as the woe due to those by whom the offense came."

This tremendous national tragedy is a warning to all who seek a democratic basis for world government today. How can dissimilar interests be reconciled within a framework of union? What can be achieved by constitutional devices like the veto? What are the minimum conditions for cooperation when minorities—themselves great communities—suffer from a galling sense of insecurity?

Controversy about the nature of the union was as old as the Union itself. We have seen how Virginians and Kentuckians in 1798, and New Englanders a few years later, had developed a doctrine of state rights in opposition to the nationalist interpretation. The view that each state had the right to decide whether the terms of the Constitution were being kept could be invoked to justify a power of veto over federal action and, if need be, a right to secede. This was the position adopted by South Carolina in the Nullification Ordinance of 1832; and what one state was prepared to threaten in that year eleven states chose to execute in 1860–61.

The South Carolina doctrine was the work of John C. Calhoun, one of the greatest political figures of the Middle Period. A nationalist in his early years, he responded to the changing interests of his state by becoming in later life the leading sectionalist in southern politics. In this respect his career is an exact reversal of Daniel Webster's, who in the same period followed New England interests from sectionalism to nationalism. The point at issue between Calhoun and Webster might be stated as Calhoun asked it in 1831: Was the Constitution created by the *states*, considered as separate sovereign communities, or was it created by the *American people*, considered as one community? If the former, the sovereign powers of the states were to be invoked as a matter of last resort; if the latter, it was Calhoun's opinion that the states were left defenseless in the face of a numerical majority of the American people.

Why did Webster's sweeping attack on the state-rights doctrine seem to southerners like Calhoun to be the essence of tyranny? Many reasons are given. The southern states felt increasingly concerned about the power of the North. They were being outnumbered and outdistanced in the scramble for wealth and power. Their economic life was one-sided. Their ability to hold the Northwest within the orbit

of southern influence was dwindling. Their use of federal influence to block the economic demands of rival regions was piling up resentment. And the intellectual life of a region which had once been a center of enlightenment was now strangely cut off from the most active thought of the day. Behind the brilliant development of the Cotton Empire in the three decades before the Civil War there was a growing sense of isolation and insecurity.

One crucial factor, among all the other tendencies which were pulling North and South apart, was the slavery issue. From 1830 onward, the institution was under intense fire from the abolitionists, and many who were not abolitionists were drawn into the widening circle of critics. Some historians argue that slavery was competitively unable to keep up with free labor and that its failure to be economically profitable would eventually have forced the abolition of the system. But, if so, the political debate marched on before the economic question could resolve itself. Southerners would not accept criticism of an institution which formed the basis of their labor system and which seemed to them the only practicable solution for the racial problem. Northerners, when they were driven to think about it by the abolitionist minority, found slavery incompatible with all their cherished assumptions about democracy, progress, and industrial efficiency. Denounced and defended by its critics and supporters, slavery became an issue which wound its way into almost every crevice of national life, rousing emotions which the political process was less and less able to still. The most intolerable feature, from the southern standpoint, was the charge that slavery was sinful and that slaveholders were therefore immoral and irreligious.

In 1854 George Fitzhugh published his *Sociology for the South; or The Failure of Free Society*. This is an earnest attempt to justify the institution of slavery by exposing the cruelties and shams of free society. To study it is to measure the melancholy distance which then separated the social values of the slaveholders from those of the rest of the Union. It helps us to understand how Calhoun could pass this judgment on the deluded humanity of southerners like Jefferson: "Many in the South once believed that slavery was a moral and political evil: that folly and delusion are gone: we see it now in its true light, and regard it as the most safe and stable basis for free institutions in the world."

The slavery issue was inevitably raised by the progress of national expansion. Every westward surge of the American people upset the existing compromises and led to a new test of sectional strength. The Missouri crisis of 1819–20 was an early forecast of the trials to come. South Carolina's conduct in 1832 reflected the strains imposed by the westward development of the cotton kingdom. The expansion of the forties created a situation in which union was only just preserved by the Compromise of 1850; and within a few years of that date the problem of organizing the territories on a basis acceptable to both North and South proved fatal.

The spectacle of a great nation moving irresistibly across a continent exerted an extraordinary power over many American minds. The Jacksonian editor, John L. O'Sullivan, saw behind the advancing lines of pioneer farms, schoolhouses, courtrooms, railways, and telegraph poles the hand of a bountiful God, pouring his redeeming grace into these American vessels of mercy. But O'Sullivan could not ignore the sectional strife. After defending the annexation of Texas and looking forward to the annexation of California, he examined the charge that the drive for expansion in the Southwest was simply a southern conspiracy to extend the slave power. He rejected this explanation; but the issues involved in the great dilemma created by the aggressive survival of slavery in a free society sobered him into a mood of anxious caution. Perhaps O'Sullivan never did see that, if one is willing to be aggressive abroad, there may be little to check aggression at home.

These fears were more than justified in the aftermath of the Mexican War, when the status of slavery in the new acquisitions had to be settled. Before the forties, slavery had merely asserted its right to continue unmolested, within the limits set by Congress in the Northwest Ordinance of 1787 and the Missouri Compromise of 1820. Expansion raised the question of its extension, with southern extremists pressing for its admission everywhere in the territories and northern extremists demanding its exclusion. And where the abolitionists were concerned, the demand applied to the southern states as well as to the territories. This situation was met by the Compromise of 1850, which substituted popular sovereignty for a geographical line as the barrier between freedom and slavery in the Mexican session. California was admitted as a free state. New Mexico and Utah were empowered to decide the issue for themselves at a later date; the slave trade was abolished in the national capital; and the South won the enactment of a stricter Fugitive Slave Law.

Four years later the whole question was reopened by the Kansas-Nebraska Bill. These territories, lying in the area of the Louisiana Purchase, had been preserved from slavery by a compromise of more than thirty years' standing; but the bill through which Stephen Douglas hoped to hasten their development included a provision enabling the inhabitants to choose between freedom or slavery and thus extending to them the principle of popular sovereignty. The political reactions were immediate and immense. Attacked in the North and defended in the South, the bill precipitated a conflict marked by the appearance of a Republican party to resist the extension of slavery, severe strains within the northern and southern wings of the Democratic party, and open violence in Kansas.

Finally, after the *Dred Scott* v. *Sandford* case, when the Supreme Court decided that Congress had no authority to prohibit the institution of slavery anywhere in the territories, it seemed obvious to the Republican party—which had just seen the inauguration of a Democratic president—that all branches of the national government were now acting under the southern influence. Then the famous Lincoln-Douglas debates exposed the bankruptcy of the existing political compromise proposals.

The party platforms of 1860 reveal the Democratic party, whose national character was blasted away by sectional pressure, splintered into two factions—the one nominating Douglas, the other Breckinridge. The Republican party, sectional from its origin, nominated Lincoln. Its platform shrewdly combined those economic demands which southern influence had steadfastly resisted with a double pledge in relation to slavery: no extension in the territories; no interference with slavery in the southern states. A fourth group nominated John Bell.

The election of a "Black Republican" was the signal for the secession of seven southern states. The Mississippi Resolutions on Secession may be studied as an example of the procedure employed and of the arguments used in justification. While the issues of union and secession, peace and war, still trembled in the balance, Lincoln was inaugurated on March 4. The First Inaugural Address sought to avert the impending tragedy but effected no change. Further efforts to find a compromise made no progress, while the air grew heavy with the threat of war. It was in this atmosphere, when momentous consequences hung upon the smallest acts, that the incident occurred at Fort Sumter.

Lincoln's personal desire to see slavery ultimately abolished had been made plain enough before his election, but he and his party had assured the South that there was no intention of attacking the institution within the states. In his First Inaugural Address and in his letter to Horace Greeley, he endeavored to demonstrate that the preservation of the Union, and not the abolition of slavery, was the paramount consideration. In 1862 the pressure of the diplomatic situation, combined with the demands of the radical Republicans, led to the Emancipation Proclamation. This was an act of executive authority in time of emergency, and it applied only to some of the slaves in rebellious states. It was the passage of the Thirteenth Amendment in December, 1865, which formally abolished the institution of slavery throughout the Union.

The questions which are raised by our great national tragedy do not yield to simple answers. Here we have a war that Americans managed to create all by themselves without being dragged into it by any foreign entanglements. What responsibility must be borne by economic rivalries, by ideological differences, by political parties, by strategically placed individuals? What right had the North to prevent secession? What had the South to fear from the North by staying within the Union? What immediate losses did the South accept by leaving it? What en-

couraged them to take the risk of losing all by staking all?

The Civil War, like many another appeals to arms, raised at least one new problem for every old issue of which it disposed. Numerous questions appeared as to the extent to which belligerency increases the power of the government over the individual. In several respects it appeared that the Bill of Rights had been set aside, at least temporarily, by the executive and military power. The Milligan case brought some of these issues before the Supreme Court. Another problem, providing food for reflection for those who pin their faith on the legislative branches of the national government, was the conflict between the presidential and the congressional plans for reconstruction, which culminated in a congressional victory.

Reconstruction involved a redefinition of the Negro's legal position. The southern states, following the practice of pre-war days, enacted "Black Codes," similar to that of Mississippi. There was violent opposition in the North to this solution of the problem of four million former slaves. To those who thought that the war had been fought to free the slaves, this was less than freedom. To those who wanted to build their political fortunes out of the ruin of the South, this was an excellent pretext for ruthless action. The military occupation of the conquered South and the trial of war criminals had the usual dubious results and afford an interesting parallel to the present problems of occupation policies. Was Thaddeus Stevens right or was Lincoln right?

The victory of radical reconstruction led to the adoption of the Fourteenth and Fifteenth Amendments. The former defined citizenship and forbade the states to deprive individuals of life, liberty, or property without due process of law. Together, these two amendments, which were imposed upon the former Confederate states by force, were intended to enfranchise the Negro and to assure him civil rights equal to those of the whites; but, as soon as the South regained its freedom of action, every effort was made to re-establish white supremacy. Negroes were barred from voting by the grandfather clauses and poll taxes. They were intimidated by the Ku Klux Klan and the Knights of the White Camelia. They were denied social as well as political equality. The history of the effort to vindicate the rights of the Negro by appealing to the Fourteenth Amendment provides a somber commentary on the stubbornness of the racial problem.

Vast changes took place in the generation following the Civil War, both in the ways in which Americans earned a living and in their attitude toward government. These changes raised many problems. What happened to the theory of the division of powers between the federal and state governments? Did the Union victory, for example, result in discrediting the state-rights theory? To what degree had the Negro's economic, political, and social position improved by 1900, as compared with 1860? Was he better off as a freedman than as a slave? What happened during the Civil War and Reconstruction to the ideal of an agrarian democracy which the Jeffersonians had established and the Jacksonians reaffirmed? These are some of the questions about the place of the Civil War in the national history which should be kept in mind when the reader turns to the study of the later units.

SECTION A. CONTROVERSY OVER THE NATURE OF THE FEDERAL UNION

1. THE TRUE NATURE OF CONSTITUTIONAL GOVERNMENT[1]

By JOHN C. CALHOUN

EDITORS' NOTE.—John C. Calhoun (1782–1850), the brilliant South Carolina statesman and political theorist, entered national politics in 1810 and as an ardent nationalist vigorously supported the War of 1812. In the generation following that war, economic and population changes in North and South had become so marked that Calhoun shifted his position from the defense of nationalism to the support of state rights. South Carolina, in particular, was unhappy over the adoption of a series of protective tariffs by the federal government. It was in this connection that Calhoun drafted the report, part of which is here reproduced, for the South Carolina legislature in November, 1831.

It should not be thought that Calhoun was an enemy of the Union even in his most bitter sectional quarrels. He sought to save the Union, but he considered it worth saving only if the interests of his own section were protected. So notable were Calhoun's efforts on behalf of the slavery and the

aristocratic systems of the South that his concern for liberty is little noted. In fact, much of his effort after 1828 was directed to the defense of liberty as he understood it. He opposed the Mexican War because he feared that it would increase the power of government over individuals. He also apprehended that the belief in national destiny would endanger individual freedom. In the last years of his life he said: "It has been lately urged in a very respectable quarter that it is the mission of this country to spread civil and religious liberty all over the globe, and especially over this continent— even by force, if necessary. It is a sad delusion.... To preserve ... liberty it is indispensable to adopt a course of moderation and justice toward all nations."

It is clear that Calhoun believed that antislavery agitation was a menace to the liberty and interests of the South. In 1837 he admitted that "abolition and the Union cannot coexist." In the dramatic debate over the Compromise of 1850, Calhoun, a dying man, made a final plea for a national policy which would preserve the Union.

1. John C. Calhoun, "A Disquisition on Government," in *Works* ... (New York, 1855), I, 1–107.

In order to have a clear and just conception of the nature and object of government, it is indispensable to understand correctly what that constitution or law of our nature is in which government originates; or, to express it more fully and accurately, that law without which government would not, and with which it must necessarily, exist. Without this, it is as impossible to lay any solid foundation for the science of government as it would be to lay one for that of astronomy without a like understanding of that constitution or law of the material world, according to which the several bodies composing the solar system mutually act on each other and by which they are kept in their respective spheres. The first question, accordingly, to be considered is: What is that constitution or law of our nature without which government would not exist and with which its existence is necessary?

In considering this, I assume, as an incontestable fact, that man is so constituted as to be a social being. His inclinations and wants, physical and moral, irresistibly impel him to associate with his kind; and he has, accordingly, never been found, in any age or country, in any state other than the social. In no other, indeed, could he exist; and in no other—were it possible for him to exist—could he attain to a full development of his moral and intellectual faculties or raise himself, in the scale of being, much above the level of the brute creation.

I next assume, also, as a fact not less incontestable, that, while man is so constituted as to make the social state necessary to his existence and the full development of his faculties, this state itself cannot exist without government. The assumption rests on universal experience. In no age or country has any society or community ever been found, whether enlightened or savage, without government of some description.

Having assumed these, as unquestionable phenomena of our nature, I shall, without further remark, proceed to the investigation of the primary and important question: What is that constitution of our nature which, while it impels man to associate with his kind, renders it impossible for society to exist without government?

The answer will be found in the fact (not less incontestable than either of the others) that, while man is created for the social state, and is accordingly so formed as to feel what affects others as well as what affects himself, he is, at the same time, so constituted as to feel more intensely what affects him directly than what affects him indirectly through others; or, to express it differently, he is so constituted that his direct or individual affections are stronger than his sympathetic or social feelings. I intentionally avoid the expression "*selfish* feelings" as applicable to the former, because, as commonly used, it implies an unusual excess of the individual over the social feelings in the person to whom it is applied, and, consequently, something depraved and vicious. My object is to exclude such inference and to restrict the inquiry exclusively to facts in their bearings on the subject under consideration, viewed as mere phenomena appertaining to our nature—constituted as it is—and which are as unquestionable as is that of gravitation or any other phenomenon of the material world.

In asserting that our individual are stronger than our social feelings, it is not intended to deny that there are instances, growing out of peculiar relations—as that of a mother and her infant—or resulting from the force of education and habit over peculiar constitutions in which the latter have overpowered the former; but these instances are few and always regarded as something extraordinary. The deep impression they make, whenever they occur, is the strongest proof that they are regarded as exceptions to some general and well-understood law of our nature, just as some of the minor powers of the material world are apparently to gravitation.

I might go further and assert this to be a phenomenon, not of our nature only, but of all animated existence, throughout its entire range, so far as our knowledge extends. It would, indeed, seem to be essentially connected with the great law of self-preservation which pervades all that feels, from man down to the lowest and most insignificant reptile or insect. In none is it stronger than in man. His social feelings may, indeed, in a state of safety and abundance, combined with high intellectual and moral culture, acquire great expansion and force; but not so great as to overpower this all-pervading and essential law of animated existence.

But that constitution of our nature which makes us feel more intensely what affects us directly than what affects us indirectly through others necessarily leads to conflict between individuals. Each, in consequence, has a greater regard for his own safety or happiness than for the safety or happiness of others and, where these come in opposition, is ready to sacrifice the interests of others to his own. And, hence, the tendency to a universal state of conflict between individual and individual, accompanied by the connected passions of suspicion, jealousy, anger, and revenge—followed by insolence, fraud, and cruelty—and, if not prevented by some controlling power, ending in a state of universal discord and confusion, destructive of the social state and the ends for which it is ordained. This controlling power, wherever vested, or by whomsoever exercised, is GOVERNMENT.

It follows, then, that man is so constituted that government is necessary to the existence of society, and society to his existence and the perfection of his faculties. It follows, also, that government has its origin in this twofold constitution of his nature; the sympathetic or social feelings constituting the remote, and the individual or direct, the proximate, cause.

If man had been differently constituted in either particular—if, instead of being social in his nature, he had been created without sympathy for his kind, and independent of others for his safety and existence; or if, on the other hand, he had been so created as to feel more intensely what affected others than what affected himself (if that were possible), or, even, had this supposed interest been equal—it is manifest that, in either case, there would have been no necessity for government and that none would ever have existed. But, although society and government are thus intimately connected with and dependent on each other—of the two society is the greater. It is the first in the order of things and in the dignity of its object; that of society being primary, to preserve and perfect our race; and that of government secondary and subordinate, to preserve and perfect society. Both are, however, necessary to the existence and well-being of our race and equally of divine ordination.

I have said—if it were possible for man to be so constituted as to feel what affects others more strongly than what affects himself or even as strongly—because, it may be well doubted, whether the stronger feeling or affection of individuals for themselves, combined with a feebler and subordinate feeling or affection for others, is not, in beings of limited reason and faculties, a constitution necessary to their preservation and existence. If reversed—if their feelings and affections were stronger for others than for themselves, or even as strong—the necessary result would seem to be that all individuality would be lost, and boundless and remediless disorder and confusion would ensue. For each, at the same moment, intensely participating in

678

all the conflicting emotions of those around him, would, of course, forget himself and all that concerned him immediately, in his officious intermeddling) with the affairs of all others; which, from his limited reason and faculties, he could neither properly understand nor manage. Such a state of things would, as far as we can see, lead to endless disorder and confusion, not less destructive to our race than a state of anarchy. It would, besides, be remediless, for government would be impossible; or, if it could by possibility exist, its object would be reversed. Selfishness would have to be encouraged and benevolence discouraged. Individuals would have to be encouraged, by rewards, to become more selfish and deterred, by punishments, from being too benevolent; and this, too, by a government administered by those who, on the supposition, would have the greatest aversion for selfishness and the highest admiration for benevolence.

To the Infinite Being, the Creator of all, belongs exclusively the care and superintendence of the whole. He, in his infinite wisdom and goodness, has allotted to every class of animated beings its condition and appropriate functions and has endowed each with feelings, instincts, capacities, and faculties best adapted to its alloted condition. To man he has assigned the social and political state as best adapted to develop the great capacities and faculties, intellectual and moral, with which he has endowed him and has, accordingly, constituted him so as not only to impel him into the social state but to make government necessary for his preservation and well-being.

But government, although intended to protect and preserve society, has itself a strong tendency to disorder and abuse of its powers, as all experience and almost every page of history testify. The cause is to be found in the same constitution of our nature which makes government indispensable. The powers which it is necessary for government to possess, in order to repress violence and preserve order, cannot execute themselves. They must be administered by men in whom, like others, the individual are stronger than the social feelings. And, hence, the powers vested in them to prevent injustice and oppression on the part of others will, if left unguarded, be by them converted into instruments to oppress the rest of the community. That, by which this is prevented, by whatever name called, is what is meant by CONSTITUTION, in its most comprehensive sense, when applied to GOVERNMENT.

Having its origin in the same principle of our nature, *constitution* stands to *government* as *government* stands to *society* and, as the end for which society is ordained, would be defeated without government, so that for which government is ordained would, in a great measure, be defeated without constitution. But they differ in this striking particular. There is no difficulty in forming government. It is not even a matter of choice whether there shall be one or not. Like breathing, it is not permitted to depend on our volition. Necessity will force it on all communities in some one form or another. Very different is the case as to constitution. Instead of a matter of necessity, it is one of the most difficult tasks imposed on man to form a constitution worthy of the name; while, to form a perfect one—one that would completely counteract the tendency of government to oppression and abuse and hold it strictly to the great ends for which it is ordained—has thus far exceeded human wisdom and possibly ever will. From this another striking difference results. Constitution is the contrivance of man, while government is of divine ordination. Man is left to perfect what the wisdom of the Infinite ordained as necessary to preserve the race.

With these remarks, I proceed to the consideration of the important and difficult question: How is this tendency of government to be counteracted? Or, to express it more fully: How can those who are invested with the powers of government be prevented from employing them, as the means of aggrandizing themselves, instead of using them to protect and preserve society? It cannot be done by instituting a higher power to control the government and those who administer it. This would be but to change the seat of authority and to make this higher power, in reality, the government; with the same tendency, on the part of those who might control its powers, to pervert them into instruments of aggrandizement. Nor can it be done by limiting the powers of government, so as to make it too feeble to be made an instrument of abuse; for, passing by the difficulty of so limiting its powers, without creating a power higher than the government itself to enforce the observance of the limitations, it is a sufficient objection that it would, if practicable, defeat the end for which government is ordained, by making it too feeble to protect and preserve society. The powers necessary for this purpose will ever prove sufficient to aggrandize those who control it, at the expense of the rest of the community....

In answering the important question under consideration, it is not necessary to enter into an examination of the various contrivances adopted by these celebrated governments to counteract this tendency to disorder and abuse, nor to undertake to treat of constitution in its most comprehensive sense. What I propose is far more limited—to explain on what principles government must be formed, in order to resist, by its own interior structure—or, to use a single term, *organism*—the tendency to abuse of power. This structure, or organism, is what is meant by constitution, in its strict and more usual sense; and it is

this which distinguishes what are called constitutional governments from absolute. It is in this strict and more usual sense that I propose to use the term hereafter.

How government, then, must be constructed, in order to counteract, through its organism, this tendency on the part of those who make and execute the laws to oppress those subject to their operation is the next question which claims attention.

There is but one way in which this can possibly be done, and that is by such an organism as will furnish the ruled with the means of resisting successfully this tendency on the part of the rulers to oppression and abuse. Power can only be resisted by power—and tendency by tendency. Those who exercise power and those subject to its exercise—the rulers and the ruled—stand in antagonistic relations to each other. The same constitution of our nature which leads rulers to oppress the ruled—regardless of the object for which government is ordained—will, with equal strength, lead the ruled to resist, when possessed of the means of making peaceable and effective resistance. Such an organism, then, as will furnish the means by which resistance may be systematically and peaceably made on the part of the ruled, to oppression and abuse of power on the part of the rulers, is the first and indispensable step toward *forming* a constitutional government. And as this can only be effected by or through the right of suffrage (the right on the part of the ruled to choose their rulers at proper intervals, and to hold them thereby responsible for their conduct) the responsibility of the rulers to the ruled, through the right of suffrage, is the indispensable and primary principle in the *foundation* of a constitutional government. When this right is properly guarded, and the people sufficiently enlightened to understand their own rights and the interests of the community, and duly to appreciate the motives and conduct of those appointed to make and execute the laws, it is all-sufficient to give to those who elect effective control over those they have elected.

I call the right of suffrage the indispensable and primary principle, for it would be a great and dangerous mistake to suppose, as many do, that it is, of itself, sufficient to form constitutional governments. To this erroneous opinion may be traced one of the causes, why so few attempts to form constitutional governments have succeeded; and why, of the few which have, so small a number have had durable existence. It has led, not only to mistakes in the attempts to form such governments, but to their overthrow, when they have, by some good fortune, been correctly formed. So far from being, of itself, sufficient—however well guarded it might be, and however enlightened the people—it would, unaided by other provisions, leave the government as absolute as it would be in the hands of irresponsible rulers; and with a tendency, at least as strong, toward oppression and abuse of its powers; as I shall next proceed to explain.

The right of suffrage, of itself, can do no more than give complete control to those who elect over the conduct of those they have elected. In doing this, it accomplishes all it possibly can accomplish. This is its aim—and, when this is attained, its end is fulfilled. It can do no more, however enlightened the people, or however widely extended or well guarded the right may be. The sum total, then, of its effects, when most successful, is to make those elected the true and faithful representatives of those who elected them—instead of irresponsible rulers—as they would be without it; and thus, by converting it into an agency, and the rulers into agents, to divest government of all claims to sovereignty and to retain it unimpaired to the community. But it is manifest that the right of suffrage, in making these

changes, transfers, in reality, the actual control over the government from those who make and execute the laws to the body of the community and thereby places the powers of the government as fully in the mass of the community as they would be if they, in fact, had assembled, made, and executed the laws themselves without the intervention of representatives or agents. The more perfectly it does this, the more perfectly it accomplishes its ends; but, in doing so, it only changes the seat of authority, without counteracting, in the least, the tendency of the government to oppression and abuse of its powers.

If the whole community had the same interests, so that the interest of each and every portion would be so affected by the action of the government, that the laws which oppressed or impoverished one portion would necessarily oppress and impoverish all others—or the reverse—then the right of suffrage, of itself, would be all-sufficient to counteract the tendency of the government to oppression and abuse of its powers and, of course, would form, of itself, a perfect constitutional government. The interest of all being the same, by supposition, as far as the action of the government was concerned, all would have like interests as to what laws should be made and how they should be executed. All strife and struggle would cease as to who should be elected to make and execute them. The only question would be who was most fit; who the wisest and most capable of understanding the common interest of the whole. This decided, the election would pass off quietly and without party discord, as no one portion could advance its own peculiar interest without regard to the rest by electing a favorite candidate.

But such is not the case. On the contrary, nothing is more difficult than to equalize the action of the government in reference to the various and diversified interests of the community; and nothing more easy than to pervert its powers into instruments to aggrandize and enrich one or more interests by oppressing and impoverishing the others; and this too, under the operation of laws, couched in general terms—and which, on their face, appear fair and equal. Nor is this the case in some particular communities only. It is so in all; the small and the great, the poor and the rich, irrespective of pursuits, productions, or degrees of civilization—with, however, this difference: that the more extensive and populous the country, the more diversified the condition and pursuits of its population, and the richer, more luxurious, and dissimilar the people, the more difficult is it to equalize the action of the government and the more easy for one portion of the community to pervert its powers to oppress and plunder the other.

Such being the case, it necessarily results that the right of suffrage, by placing the control of the government in the community must, from the same constitution of our nature which makes government necessary to preserve society, lead to conflict among its different interests—each striving to obtain possession of its powers, as the means of protecting itself against the others—or of advancing its respective interests, regardless of the interests of others. For this struggle, a struggle will take place between the various interests to obtain a majority, in order to control the government. If no one interest be strong enough, of itself, to obtain it, a combination will be formed between those whose interests are most alike—each conceding something to the others, until a sufficient number is obtained to make a majority. The process may be slow, and much time may be required before a compact, organized majority can be thus formed; but formed it will be in time, even without preconcert or design, by the sure workings of that principle or constitution of our nature in which government itself originates.

When once formed, the community will be divided into two great parties—a major and minor—between which there will be incessant struggles on the one side to retain and on the other to obtain the majority—and, thereby, the control of the government and the advantages it confers....

As, then, the right of suffrage, without some other provision, cannot counteract this tendency of government, the next question for consideration is: What is that other provision? This demands the most serious consideration, for, of all the questions embraced in the science of government, it involves a principle the most important and the least understood, and, when understood, the most difficult of application in practice. It is, indeed, emphatically, that principle which *makes* the constitution, in its strict and limited sense.

From what has been said it is manifest that this provision must be of a character calculated to prevent any one interest, or combination of interests, from using the powers of government to aggrandize itself at the expense of the others. Here lies the evil; and just in proportion as it shall prevent, or fail to prevent it, in the same degree it will effect, or fail to effect, the end intended to be accomplished. There is but one certain mode in which this result can be secured, and that is by the adoption of some restriction or limitation which shall so effectually prevent any one interest, or combination of interests, from obtaining the exclusive control of the government as to render hopeless all attempts directed to that end. There is, again, but one mode in which this can be affected, and that is by taking the sense of each interest or portion of the community, which may be unequally and injuriously affected by the action of the government, separately, through its own majority, or in some other way by which its voice may be fairly expressed; and to require the consent of each interest either to put or to keep the government in action. This, too, can be accomplished only in one way—and that is by such an organism of the government—and, if necessary for the purpose, of the community also—as will, by dividing and distributing the powers of government, give to each division or interest, through its appropriate organ, either a concurrent voice in making and executing the laws or a veto on their execution. It is only by such an organism that the assent of each can be made necessary to put the government in motion; or the power made effectual to arrest its action when put in motion—and it is only by the one or the other that the different interests, orders, classes, or portions, into which the community may be divided, can be protected, and all conflict and struggle between them prevented—by rendering it impossible to put or to keep it in action, without the concurrent consent of all.

Such an organism as this, combined with the right of suffrage, constitutes, in fact, the elements of constitutional government. The one, by rendering those who make and execute the laws responsible to those on whom they operate, prevents the rulers from oppressing the ruled; and the other, by making it impossible for any one interest or combination of interests or class, or order, or portion of the community to obtain exclusive control, prevents any one of them from oppressing the other. It is clear that oppression and abuse of power must come, if at all, from the one or the other quarter. From no other can they come. It follows that the two, suffrage and proper organism combined, are sufficient to counteract the tendency of government to oppression and abuse of power and to restrict it to the fulfilment of the great ends for which it is ordained. . . .

It may be readily inferred from what has been stated that the effect of organism is neither to supersede nor diminish the importance of the right of suffrage

but to aid and perfect it. The object of the latter is to collect the sense of the community. The more fully and perfectly it accomplishes this, the more fully and perfectly it fulfils its end. But the most it can do, of itself, is to collect the sense of the greater number; that is, of the stronger interests, or combination of interests; and to assume this to be the sense of the community. It is only when aided by a proper organism that it can collect the sense of the entire community—of each and all its interests; of each, through its appropriate organ, and of the whole, through all of them united. This would truly be the sense of the entire community, for whatever diversity each interest might have within itself—as all would have the same interest in reference to the action of the government—the individuals composing each would be fully and truly represented by its own majority or appropriate organ, regarded in reference to the other interests. In brief, every individual of every interest might trust, with confidence, its majority or appropriate organ against that of every other interest.

It results, from what has been said, that there are two different modes in which the sense of the community may be taken; one, simply by the right of suffrage, unaided; the other, by the right through a proper organism. Each collects the sense of the majority. But one regards numbers only and considers the whole community as a unit, having but one common interest throughout, and collects the sense of the greater number of the whole as that of the community. The other, on the contrary, regards interests as well as numbers—considering the community as made up of different and conflicting interests, as far as the action of the government is concerned—and takes the sense of each, through its majority or appropriate organ, and the united sense of all as the sense of the entire community. The former of these I shall call the numerical, or absolute majority; and the latter, the concurrent, or constitutional majority. I call it the constitutional majority, because it is an essential element in every constitutional government—be its form what it may. So great is the difference, politically speaking, between the two majorities that they cannot be confounded without leading to great and fatal errors; and yet the distinction between them has been so entirely overlooked that, when the term *majority* is used in political discussions, it is applied exclusively to designate the numerical—as if there were no other. Until this distinction is recognized, and better understood, there will continue to be great liability to error in properly constructing constitutional governments, especially of the popular form, and of preserving them when properly constructed. Until then, the latter will have a strong tendency to slide, first, into the government of the numerical majority and, finally, into absolute government of some other form. To show that such must be the case, and at the same time to mark more strongly the difference between the two, in order to guard against the danger of overlooking it, I propose to consider the subject more at length.

The first and leading error which naturally arises from overlooking the distinction referred to is to confound the numerical majority with the people, and this so completely as to regard them as identical. This is a consequence that necessarily results from considering the numerical as the only majority. All admit that a popular government, or democracy, is the government of the people, for the terms imply this. A perfect government of the kind would be one which would embrace the consent of every citizen or member of the community; but as this is impracticable, in the opinion of those who regard the numerical as the only majority, and who can perceive no other way by which the sense of the people can be taken—they are compelled to adopt this as the only true basis of popular government, in contradistinction to governments of the aristocratical or monarchical form. Being thus constrained, they are, in the next place, forced to regard the numerical majority as, in effect, the entire people; that is, the greater part as the whole; and the government of the greater part as the government of the whole. It is thus the two come to be confounded, and a part made identical with the whole. And it is thus, also, that all the rights, powers, and immunities of the whole people come to be attributed to the numerical majority; and, among others, the supreme, sovereign authority of establishing and abolishing governments at pleasure.

This radical error, the consequence of confounding the two, and of regarding the numerical as the only majority, has contributed more than any other cause to prevent the formation of popular constitutional governments—and to destroy them even when they have been formed. It leads to the conclusion that, in their formation and establishment, nothing more is necessary than the right of suffrage—and the allotment to each division of the community a representation in the government, in proportion to numbers. If the numerical majority were really the people; and if to take its sense truly, were to take the sense of the people truly, a government so constituted would be a true and perfect model of a popular constitutional government; and every departure from it would detract from its excellence. But, as such is not the case—as the numerical majority, instead of being the people, is only a portion of them—such a government, instead of being a true and perfect model of the people's government, that is, a people self-governed, is but the government of a part over a part, the major over the minor portion. . . .

Nor would the division of government into separate and, as it regards each other, independent departments prevent this result. Such a division may do much to facilitate its operations and to secure to its administration greater caution and deliberation; but as each and all the departments—and, of course, the entire government—would be under the control of the numerical majority, it is too clear to require explanation that a mere distribution of its powers among its agents or representatives could do little or nothing to counteract its tendency to oppression and abuse of power. To effect this, it would be necessary to go one step further and make the several departments the organs of the distinct interests or portions of the community and to clothe each with a negative on the others. But the effect of this would be to change the government from the numerical into the concurrent majority.

Having now explained the reasons why it is so difficult to form and preserve popular constitutional government, so long as the distinction between the two majorities is overlooked, and the opinion prevails that a written constitution, with suitable restrictions and a proper division of its powers, is sufficient to counteract the tendency of the numerical majority to the abuse of its power—I shall next proceed to explain, more fully, why the concurrent majority is an indispensable element in forming constitutional governments and why the numerical majority, of itself, must, in all cases, make governments absolute.

The necessary consequence of taking the sense of the community by the concurrent majority is, as has been explained, to give to each interest or portion of the community a negative on the others. It is this mutual negative among its various conflicting interests which invests each with the power of protecting itself—and places the rights and safety of each, where only they can be securely placed, under its own guardianship. Without this there can be no systematic, peaceful, or effective resistance to the natural tendency of each to come into conflict with the others; and without this there can be no constitution. It is this negative power—the power of preventing or arresting the action of the government—be it called by what term it may, veto, interposition, nullification, check, or balance of power—which, in fact, forms the constitution. They are all but different names for the negative power. In all its forms, and under all its names, it results from the concurrent majority. Without this there can be no negative and, without a negative, no constitution. The assertion is true in reference to all constitutional governments, be their forms what they may. It is, indeed, the negative power which makes the constitution—and the positive which makes the government. The one is the power of acting—and the other the power of preventing or arresting action. The two, combined, make constitutional governments.

But, as there can be no constitution without the negative power, and no negative power without the concurrent majority, it follows, necessarily, that where the numerical majority has the sole control of the government, there can be no constitution; as constitution implies limitation or restriction—and, of course, is inconsistent with the idea of sole or exclusive power. And hence, the numerical, unmixed with the concurrent majority, necessarily forms, in all cases, absolute government. . . .

* * *

Liberty, indeed, though among the greatest of blessings, is not so great as that of protection; inasmuch as the end of the former is the progress and improvement of the race—while that of the latter is its preservation and perpetuation. And hence, when the two come into conflict, liberty must, and ever ought, to yield to protection, as the existence of the race is of greater moment than its improvement.

It follows, from what has been stated,

that it is a great and dangerous error to suppose that all people are equally entitled to liberty. It is a reward to be earned, not a blessing to be gratuitously lavished on all alike—a reward reserved for the intelligent, the patriotic, the virtuous and deserving—and not a boon to be bestowed on a people too ignorant, degraded, and vicious to be capable either of appreciating or of enjoying it. Nor is it any disparagement to liberty that such is and ought to be the case. On the contrary, its greatest praise, its proudest distinction, is that an all-wise Providence has reserved it as the noblest and highest reward for the development of our faculties, moral and intellectual. A reward more appropriate than liberty could not be conferred on the deserving, nor a punishment inflicted on the undeserving more just, than to be subject to lawless and despotic rule. This dispensation seems to be the result of some fixed law—and every effort to disturb or defeat it, by attempting to elevate a people in the scale of liberty, above the point to which they are entitled to rise, must ever prove abortive and end in disappointment. The progress of a people rising from a lower to a higher point in the scale of liberty is necessarily slow—and, by attempting to precipitate, we either retard, or permanently defeat it.

There is another error, not less great and dangerous, usually associated with the one which has just been considered. I refer to the opinion that liberty and equality are so intimately united that liberty cannot be perfect without perfect equality.

That they are united to a certain extent and that equality of citizens, in the eyes of the law, is essential to liberty in a popular government is conceded. But to go further and make equality of *condition* essential to liberty would be to destroy both liberty and progress. The reason is that inequality of condition, while it is a necessary consequence of liberty, is, at the same time, indispensable to progress. In order to understand why this is so, it is necessary to bear in mind that the mainspring to progress is the desire of individuals to better their condition and that the strongest impulse which can be given to it is to leave individuals free to exert themselves in the manner they may deem best for that purpose, as far at least as it can be done consistently with the ends for which government is ordained—and to secure to all the fruits of their exertions. Now, as individuals differ greatly from each other, in intelligence, sagacity, energy, perseverance, skill, habits of industry and economy, physical power, position, and opportunity, the necessary effect of leaving all free to exert themselves to better their condition must be a corresponding inequality between those who may possess these qualities and advantages in a high degree and those who may be deficient in them. The only means by which this result can be prevented are either to impose such restrictions on the exertions of those who may possess them in a high degree as will place them on a level with those who do not or to deprive them of the fruits of their exertions. But to impose such restrictions on them would be destructive of liberty, while to deprive them of the fruits of their exertions would be to destroy the desire of bettering their condition. It is, indeed, this inequality of condition between the front and rear ranks, in the march of progress, which gives so strong an impulse to the former to maintain their position and to the latter to press forward into their files. This gives to progress its greatest impulse. To force the front rank back to the rear, or attempt to push forward the rear into line with the front, by the interposition of the government, would put an end to the impulse and effectually arrest the march of progress.

These great and dangerous errors have their origin in the prevalent opinion that all men are born free and equal—than which nothing can be more unfounded and false. It rests upon the assumption of a fact which is contrary to universal observation in whatever light it may be regarded. It is, indeed, difficult to explain how an opinion so destitute of all sound reason ever could have been so extensively entertained, unless we regard it as being confounded with another, which has some semblance of truth—but which, when properly understood, is not less false and dangerous. I refer to the assertion that all men are equal in the state of nature, meaning, by a state of nature, a state of individuality, supposed to have existed prior to the social and political state and in which men lived apart and independent of each other. If such a state ever did exist, all men would have been, indeed, free and equal in it; that is, free to do as they please and exempt from the authority or control of others—as, by supposition, it existed anterior to society and govern-ment. But such a state is purely hypothetical. It never did nor can exist, as it is inconsistent with the preservation and perpetuation of the race. It is, therefore, a great misnomer to call it *the state of nature*. Instead of being the natural state of man, it is, of all conceivable states, the most opposed to his nature, most repugnant to his feelings, and most incompatible with his wants. His natural state is the social and political—the one for which his Creator made him, and the only one in which he can preserve and perfect his race. As, then, there never was such a state as the so-called state of nature, and never can be, it follows that men, instead of being born in it, are born in the social and political state and, of course, instead of being born free and equal, are born subject not only to parental authority but to the laws and institutions of the country where born and under whose protection they draw their first breath. . . .

2. EXCERPTS FROM HIS SECOND REPLY TO HAYNE, JANUARY 26, 1830[1]

By DANIEL WEBSTER

EDITORS' NOTE.—Daniel Webster (1782–1852) was born in New Hampshire and attended Dartmouth College. He practiced law and served in Congress from the state of his nativity, but removed to Massachusetts in 1816. Although Webster's career paralleled that of Calhoun's in time, in other respects their lives were in sharp contrast. Unlike Calhoun, Webster's early career was that of a sectionalist. During the War of 1812 he even toyed with theories of nullification. At about the time that the enthusiasm of Cal-houn for nationalism was on the wane, that of Webster began to ascend.

By 1830, Webster, as the voice of wealth and stability in New England, had adopted a position favorable to protective tariffs and a strong federal government. In later years Webster, like Calhoun, feared that unlimited nationalism, serving to mask sectional interests, might imperil the existence of the Union. This tempered Webster's utterances during the debates over the Compromise of 1850 and may have led him to sacrifice his chances for the presidency in the interest of the common good.

1. Daniel Webster, *Works* . . . (Boston, 1858), III, 270–342.

...I understand the honorable gentleman from South Carolina to maintain that it is a right of the state legislatures to interfere whenever, in their judgment, this government transcends its constitutional limits and to arrest the operation of its laws.

I understand him to maintain this right, as a right existing *under* the Constitution, not as a right to overthrow it on the ground of extreme necessity, such as would justify violent revolution.

I understand him to maintain an authority, on the part of the states, thus to interfere, for the purpose of correcting the exercise of power by the general government, of checking it, and of compelling it to conform to their opinion of the extent of its powers.

I understand him to maintain that the ultimate power of judging of the constitutional extent of its own authority is not lodged exclusively in the general government, or any branch of it, but that, on the contrary, the states may lawfully decide for themselves, and each state for itself, whether, in a given case, the act of the general government transcends its power.

I understand him to insist that, if the exigency of the case, in the opinion of any state government, require it, such state government may, by its own sovereign authority, annul an act of the general government which it deems plainly and palpably unconstitutional.

This is the sum of what I understand from him to be the South Carolina doctrine, and the doctrine which he maintains. I propose to consider it and compare it with the Constitution. Allow me to say, as a preliminary remark, that I call this the South Carolina doctrine only because the gentleman himself has so denominated it. I do not feel at liberty to say that South Carolina, as a state, has ever advanced these sentiments. I hope she has not and never may. That a great majority of her people are opposed to the tariff laws is doubtless true. That

a majority, somewhat less than that just mentioned, conscientiously believe these laws unconstitutional may probably also be true. But that any majority holds to the right of direct state interference at state discretion, the right of nullifying acts of Congress by acts of state legislation, is more than I know and what I shall be slow to believe.

That there are individuals besides the honorable gentleman who do maintain these opinions is quite certain. I recollect the recent expression of a sentiment which circumstances attending its utterance and publication justify us in supposing was not unpremeditated. "The sovereignty of the state—never to be controlled, construed, or decided on, but by her own feelings of honorable justice."

Mr. Hayne here rose and said that, for the purpose of being clearly understood, he would state that his proposition was, in the words of the Virginia resolution, as follows:

That this assembly doth explicitly and peremptorily declare that it views the powers of the federal government, as resulting from the compact to which the states are parties, as limited by the plain sense and intention of the instrument constituting that compact, as no farther valid than they are authorized by the grants enumerated in that compact; and that, in case of a deliberate, palpable, and dangerous exercise of other powers, not granted by the said compact, the states who are parties thereto have the right, and are in duty bound, to interpose, for arresting the progress of the evil, and for maintaining within their respective limits the authorities, rights, and liberties appertaining to them.

Mr. Webster resumed:

I am quite aware, Mr. President, of the existence of the resolution which the gentleman read, and has now repeated, and that he relies on it as his authority. I know the source, too, from which it is understood to have proceeded. I need not say that I have much respect for the constitutional opinions of Mr. Madison; they would weigh greatly with me always. But before the authority of his opinion be vouched for the gentleman's proposition, it will be proper to consider what is the fair interpretation of that resolution to which Mr. Madison is understood to have given his sanction. As the gentleman construes it, it is an authority for him. Possibly, he may not have adopted the right construction. That resolution declares that, *in the case of the dangerous exercise of powers not granted by the general government, the states may interpose to arrest the progress of the evil.* But how interpose, and what does this declaration purport? Does it mean no more than that there may be extreme cases, in which the people, in any mode of assembling, may resist usurpation and relieve themselves from a tyrannical government? No one will deny this. Such resistance is not only acknowledged to be just in America, but in England also Blackstone admits as much, in the theory and practice, too, of the English constitution. We, Sir, who oppose the Carolina doctrine, do not deny that the people may, if they choose, throw off any government when it becomes oppressive and intolerable and erect a better in its stead. We all know that civil institutions are established for the public benefit and that, when they cease to answer the ends of their existence, they may be changed. But I do not understand the doctrine now contended for to be that which, for the sake of distinction, we may call the right of revolution. I understand the gentlemen to maintain that, without revolution, without civil commotion, without rebellion, a remedy for supposed abuse and transgression of the powers of the general government lies in a direct appeal to the interference of the state governments.

Mr. Hayne here rose and said: He did not contend for the mere right of revolution but for the right of constitutional resistance. What he maintained was that in case of a plain, palpable violation of the Constitution by the general government, a state may interpose; and that this interposition is constitutional.

Mr. Webster resumed:

So, Sir, I understood the gentleman and am happy to find that I did not misunderstand him. What he contends for is that it is constitutional to interrupt the administration of the Constitution itself, in the hands of those who are chosen and sworn to administer it, by the direct interference, in form of law, of the states, in virtue of their sovereign capacity. The inherent right in the people to reform their government I do not deny; and they have another right, and that is to resist unconstitutional laws without overturning the government. It is no doctrine of mine that unconstitutional laws bind the people. The great question is: Whose prerogative is it to decide on the constitutionality or unconstitutionality of the laws? On that, the main debate hinges. The proposition that, in case of a supposed violation of the Constitution by Congress, the states have a constitutional right to interfere and annul the law of Congress is the proposition of the gentleman. I do not admit it. If the gentleman had intended no more than to assert the right of revolution for justifiable cause, he would have said only what all agree to. But I cannot conceive that there can be a middle course, between submission to the laws, when regularly pronounced constitutional, on the one hand, and open resistance, which is revolution or rebellion, on the other. I say the right of a state to annul a law of Congress cannot be maintained but on the ground of the inalienable right of man to resist oppression; that is to say, upon the ground of revolution. I admit that there is an ultimate violent remedy, above the Constitution and in defiance of the Constitution, which may be resorted to when a revolution is to be justified. But I do not admit that, under the Constitution and in conformity with it, there is any mode in which a state government, as a member of the Union, can interfere and stop the progress of the general government, by force of her own laws, under any circumstances whatever.

This leads us to inquire into the origin of this government and the source of its power. Whose agent is it? Is it the creature of the state legislatures or the creature of the people? If the government of the United States be the agent of the state governments, then they may control it, provided they can agree in the manner of controlling it; if it be the agent of the people, then the people alone can control it, restrain it, modify, or reform it. It is observable enough that the doctrine for which the honorable gentleman contends leads him to the necessity of maintaining not only that this general government is the creature of the states but that it is the creature of each of the states severally, so that each may assert the power for itself of determining whether it acts within the limits of its authority. It is the servant of four-and-twenty masters, of different wills and different purposes, and yet bound to obey all. This absurdity (for it seems no less) arises from a misconception as to the origin of this government and its true character. It is, Sir, the people's Constitution, the people's government, made for the people, made by the people, and answerable to the people. The people of the United States have declared that this Constitution shall be the supreme law. We must either admit the proposition or dispute their authority. The states are, unquestionably, sovereign so far as their sovereignty is not affected by this supreme law. But the state legislatures, as political bodies, however sovereign, are yet not sovereign over the people. So far as the people have given power to the general government, so far the grant is unquestionably good, and the government holds of the people and not of the state governments. We are all agents of the same supreme power, the people. The general government and the state governments derive their authority from the same source. Neither can, in relation to the other, be called primary, though one is definite and restricted, and the other general and residuary. The national government possesses those powers which it can be shown the people have conferred on it, and no more. All the rest belongs to the state governments or to the people themselves. So far as the people have restrained state sovereignty, by the expression of their will, in the Constitution of the United States, so far, it must be admitted, state sovereignty is effectually controlled. I do not contend that it is, or ought to be, controlled further. The sentiment to which I have referred propounds that state sovereignty is only to be controlled by its own "feeling of justice"; that is to say, it is not to be controlled at all, for one who is to follow his own feelings is under no legal control. Now, however men may think this ought to be, the fact is that the people of the United States have chosen to impose control on state sovereignties. There are those, doubtless, who wish they had been left without restraint; but the Constitution has ordered the matter differently. To make war, for instance, is an exercise of sovereignty; but the Constitution declares that no state shall make war. To coin money is another exercise of sovereign power; but no state is at liberty to coin money. Again, the Constitution says that no sovereign state shall be so sovereign as to make a treaty. These prohibitions, it must be confessed, are a control on the state sovereignty of South Carolina, as well as of the other states, which does not arise "from her own feelings of honorable justice." The opinion referred to, therefore, is in defiance of the plainest provisions of the Constitution.

There are other proceedings of public bodies which have already been alluded to, and to which I refer again, for the purpose of ascertaining more fully what is the length and breadth of that doctrine, denominated the Carolina doctrine, which the honorable member has now stood up on this floor to maintain. In one of them I find it resolved that "the tariff of 1828, and every other tariff designed to promote one branch of industry at the expense of others, is contrary to the meaning and intention of the federal compact; and such a dangerous, palpable, and deliberate usurpation of power, by a determined majority, wielding the general government beyond the limits of its delegated powers, as calls upon the states which compose the suffering minority, in their sovereign capacity, to exercise the powers which, as sovereigns, necessarily devolve upon them, when their compact is violated."

Observe, Sir, that this resolution holds the tariff of 1828, and every other tariff designed to promote one branch of industry at the expense of another, to be such a dangerous, palpable, and deliberate usurpation of power, as calls upon the states, in their sovereign capacity, to interfere by their own authority. This denunciation, Mr. President, you will please to observe, includes our old tariff of 1816, as well as all others; because that was established to promote the interest of the manufacturers of cotton to the manifest and admitted injury of the Calcutta cotton trade. Observe, again, that all the qualifications are here rehearsed and charged upon the tariff, which are necessary to bring the case within the gentleman's proposition. The tariff is a usurpation; it is a dangerous usurpation; it is a palpable usurpation; it is a deliberate usurpation. It is such a usurpation, therefore, as calls upon the states to exercise their right of interference. Here is a case, then, within the gentleman's principles and all his qualifications of his principles. It is a case for action. The Constitution is plainly, dan-

gerously, palpably, and deliberately violated; and the states must interpose their own authority to arrest the law. Let us suppose the state of South Carolina to express this same opinion by the voice of her legislature. That would be very imposing; but what then? Is the voice of one state conclusive? It so happens that, at the very moment when South Carolina resolves that the tariff laws are unconstitutional, Pennsylvania and Kentucky resolve exactly the reverse. *They* hold those laws to be both highly proper and strictly constitutional. And now, Sir, how does the honorable member propose to deal with this case? How does he relieve us from this difficulty, upon any principle of his? His construction gets us into it; how does he propose to get us out?

In Carolina the tariff is a palpable, deliberate usurpation; Carolina, therefore, may nullify it and refuse to pay the duties. In Pennsylvania it is both clearly constitutional and highly expedient; and there the duties are to be paid. And yet we live under a government of uniform laws and under a Constitution too which contains an express provision, as it happens, that all duties shall be equal in all the states. Does not this approach absurdity?

If there be no power to settle such questions, independent of either of the states, is not the whole Union a rope of sand? Are we not thrown back again, precisely, upon the old Confederation?

It is too plain to be argued. Four-and-twenty interpreters of constitutional law, each with a power to decide for itself, and none with authority to bind anybody else, and this constitutional law the only bond of their union! What is such a state of things but a mere connection during pleasure or, to use the phraseology of the times, *during feeling?* And that feeling, too, not the feeling of the people, who established the Constitution, but the feeling of the state governments.

In another of the South Carolina addresses, having premised that the crisis requires "all the concentrated energy of passion," an attitude of open resistance to the laws of the Union is advised. Open resistance to the laws, then, is the constitutional remedy, the conservative power of the state, which the South Carolina doctrines teach for the redress of political evils, real or imaginary. And its authors further say that, appealing with confidence to the Constitution itself, to justify their opinions, they cannot consent to try their accuracy by the courts of justice. In one sense, indeed, Sir, this is assuming an attitude of open resistance in favor of liberty. But what sort of liberty? The liberty of establishing their own opinions, in defiance of the opinions of all others; the liberty of judging and of deciding exclusively themselves, in a matter in which others have as much right to judge and decide as they; the liberty of placing their own opinions above the judgment of all others, above the laws, and above the Constitution. This is their liberty, and this is the fair result of the proposition contended for by the honorable gentleman. Or, it may be more properly said, it is identical with it rather than a result from it. . . .

Sir, the human mind is so constituted that the merits of both sides of a controversy appear very clear, and very palpable, to those who respectively espouse them; and both sides usually grow clearer as the controversy advances. South Carolina sees unconstitutionality in the tariff; she sees oppression there also, and she sees danger. Pennsylvania, with a vision not less sharp, looks at the same tariff and sees no such thing in it; she sees it all constitutional, all useful, all safe. The faith of South Carolina is strengthened by opposition, and she now not only sees, but resolves, that the tariff is palpably unconstitutional, oppressive, and dangerous; but Pennsylvania, not to be behind her neighbors, and equally willing to strengthen her own faith by a confident asseveration, resolves, also, and gives to every warm affirmative of South Carolina a plain, downright, Pennsylvania negative. South Carolina, to show the strength and unity of her opinion, brings her assembly to a unanimity, within seven voices; Pennsylvania, not to be outdone in this respect any more than in others, reduces her dissentient fraction to a single vote. Now, Sir, again, I ask the gentleman: What is to be done? Are these states both right? Is he bound to consider them both right? If not, which is in the wrong? or rather, which has the best right to decide? And if he, and if I, are not to know what the Constitution means, and what it is, till those two state legislatures, and the twenty-two others, shall agree in its construction, what have we sworn to when we have sworn to maintain it? I was forcibly struck, Sir, with one reflection, as the gentleman went on in his speech. He quoted Mr. Madison's resolutions, to prove that a state may interfere, in a case of deliberate, palpable, and dangerous exercise of a power not granted. The honorable member supposes the tariff law to be such an exercise of power; and that consequently a case has arisen in which the state may, if it sees fit, interfere by its own law. Now it so happens, nevertheless, that Mr. Madison deems this same tariff law quite constitutional. Instead of a clear and palpable violation, it is, in his judgment, no violation at all. So that, while they use his authority for a hypothetical case, they reject it in the very case before them. All this, Sir, shows the inherent futility—I had almost used a stronger word—of conceding this power of interference to the state, and then attempting to secure it from abuse by imposing qualifications of which the states themselves are to judge. One of the two things is true; either the laws of the Union are beyond the discretion and beyond the control of the states or else we have no constitution of general government and are thrust back again to the days of Confederation.

Let me here say, Sir, that if the gentleman's doctrine had been received and acted upon in New England, in the times of the embargo and nonintercourse, we should probably not now have been here. The government would very likely have gone to pieces and crumbled into dust. No stronger case can ever arise than existed under those laws; no states can ever entertain a clearer conviction than the New England states then entertained; and if they had been under the influence of that heresy of opinion, as I must call it, which the honorable member espouses, this Union would, in all probability, have been scattered to the four winds. I ask the gentleman, therefore, to apply his principles to that case; I ask him to come forth and declare, whether, in his opinion, the New England states would have been justified in interfering to break up the embargo system under the conscientious opinions which they held upon it? Had they a right to annul that law? Does he admit or deny? If what is thought palpably unconstitutional in South Carolina justifies that state in arresting the progress of the law, tell me whether that which was thought palpably unconstitutional also in Massachusetts would have justified her in doing the same thing. Sir, I deny the whole doctrine. It has not a foot of ground in the Constitution to stand on. No public man of reputation ever advanced it in Massachusetts in the warmest times or could maintain himself upon it there at any time.

I wish now, Sir, to make a remark upon the Virginia resolutions of 1798. I cannot undertake to say how these resolutions were understood by those who passed them. Their language is not a little indefinite. In the case of the exercise by Congress of a dangerous power not granted to them, the resolutions assert the right, on the part of the state, to interfere and arrest the progress of the evil. This is susceptible of more than one interpretation. It may mean no more than that the states may interfere by complaint and remonstrance or by proposing to the people an alteration of the federal Constitution. This would all be quite unobjectionable. Or it may be that no more is meant than to assert the general right of revolution, as against all governments, in cases of intolerable oppression. This no one doubts, and this, in my opinion, is all that he who framed the resolutions could have meant by it; for I shall not readily believe that he was ever of opinion that a state, under the Constitution and in conformity with it, could, upon the ground of her own opinion of its unconstitutionality, however clear and palpable she might think the case, annul a law of Congress, so far as it should operate on herself, by her own legislative power.

I must now beg to ask, Sir: Whence is this supposed right of the states derived? Where do they find the power to interfere with the laws of the Union? Sir, the opinion which the honorable gentleman maintains is a notion founded in a total misapprehension, in my judgment, of the origin of this government and of the foundation on which it stands. I hold it to be a popular government, erected by the people; those who administer it, responsible to the people; and itself capable of being amended and modified, just as the people may choose it should be. It is as popular, just as truly emanating from the people, as the state governments. It is created for one purpose; the state governments for another. It has its own powers; they have theirs. There is no more authority with them to arrest the operation of a law of Congress than with Congress to arrest the operation of their laws. We are here to administer a Constitution emanating immediately from the people and trusted by them to our administration. It is not the creature of the state governments. It is of no moment to the argument that certain acts of the state legislatures are necessary to fill our seats in this body. That is not one of their original state powers, a part of the sovereignty of the state. It is a duty which the people, by the Constitution itself, have imposed on the state legislatures and which they might have left to be performed elsewhere if they had seen fit. So they have left the choice of President with electors; but all this does not affect the proposition that this whole government, President, Senate, and House of Representatives, is a popular government. It leaves it still all its popular character. The governor of a state (in some of the states) is chosen, not directly by the people, but by those who are chosen by the people, for the purpose of performing, among other duties, that of electing a governor. Is the government of the state, on that account not a popular government? This government, Sir, is the independent offspring of the popular will. It is not the creature of state legislatures; nay, more, if the whole truth must be told, the people brought it into existence, established it, and have hitherto supported it, for the very purpose, amongst others, of imposing certain salutary restraints on state sovereignties. The states cannot now make war; they cannot contract alliance; they cannot make, each for itself, separate regulations of commerce; they cannot lay imposts; they cannot coin money. If this Constitution, Sir, be the creature of state legislatures, it must be admitted that it has obtained a strange control over the volitions of its creators.

The people, then, Sir, erected this government. They gave it a Constitution, and in that Constitution they have enumerated the powers which they bestow on it. They have made it a limited government. They have defined its authority. They have restrained it to the exercise of such powers as are granted; and all others, they declare, are reserved to the states or the people. But, Sir, they have not stopped here. If they had, they would have accomplished but half their work. No definition can be so clear, as to avoid possibility of doubt; no limitation so precise, as to exclude all uncertainty. Who, then, shall construe this grant of the people? Who shall interpret their will, where it may be supposed they have left it doubtful? With whom do they repose this ultimate right of deciding on the powers of the government? Sir, they have settled all this in the fullest manner. They have left it with the government itself, in its appropriate branches. Sir, the very chief end, the main design, for which the whole Constitution was framed and adopted, was to establish a government that should not be obliged to act through state agency, or depend on state opinion and state discretion. The people had had quite enough of that kind of government under the Confederation. Under that system, the legal action, the application of law to individuals, belonged exclusively to the states. Congress could only recommend; their acts were not of binding force, till the states had adopted and sanctioned them. Are we in that condition still? Are we yet at the mercy of state discretion and state construction? Sir, if we are, then vain will be our attempt to maintain the Constitution under which we sit.

But, Sir, the people have wisely provided, in the Constitution itself, a proper, suitable mode and tribunal for settling questions of constitutional law. There are in the Constitution grants of powers to Congress and restrictions on these powers. There are, also, prohibitions on the states. Some authority must, therefore, necessarily exist having the ultimate jurisdiction to fix and ascertain the interpretation of these grants, restrictions, and prohibitions. The Constitution has itself pointed out, ordained, and established that authority. How has it accomplished this great and essential end? By declaring, Sir, that *"the Constitution, and the laws of the United States made in pursuance thereof, shall be the supreme law of the land, anything in the constitution or laws of any state to the contrary notwithstanding."*

This, Sir, was the first great step. By this the supremacy of the Constitution and laws of the United States is declared. The people so will it. No state law is to be valid which comes in conflict with the Constitution, or any law of the United States passed in pursuance of it. But who shall decide this question of interference? To whom lies the last appeal? This, Sir, the Constitution itself decides also, by declaring, that *"the judicial power shall extend to all cases arising under the Constitution and laws of the United States."* These two provisions cover the whole ground. They are, in truth, the keystone of the arch! With these it is a government; without them it is a confederation. In pursuance of these clear and express provisions, Congress established, at its very first session, in the judicial act, a mode for carrying them into full effect, and for bringing all questions of constitutional power to the final decision of the Supreme Court. It then, Sir, became a government. It then had the means of self-protection; and but for this, it would, in all probability, have been now among things which are past. Having constituted the government, and declared its powers, the people have further said that, since somebody must decide on the extent of these powers, the government shall itself decide; subject, always, like other popular governments, to its responsibility to the people. And now, Sir, I repeat, how is it that a state legislature acquires any power to interfere? Who, or what, gives them the right to say to the people, "We, who are your agents and servants for one purpose, will undertake to decide, that your other agents and servants, appointed by you for another purpose, have tran-

scended the authority you gave them!" The reply would be, I think, not impertinent: "Who made you a judge over another's servants? To their own masters they stand or fall."

Sir, I deny this power of state legislatures altogether. It cannot stand the test of examination. Gentlemen may say that, in an extreme case, a state government might protect the people from intolerable oppression. Sir, in such a case, the people might protect themselves, without the aid of the state governments. Such a case warrants revolution. It must make, when it comes, a law for itself. A nullifying act of a state legislature cannot alter the case, nor make resistance any more lawful. In maintaining these sentiments, Sir, I am but asserting the rights of the people. I state what they have declared and insist on their right to declare it. They have chosen to repose this power in the general government, and I think it my duty to support it, like other constitutional powers.

For myself, Sir, I do not admit the competency of South Carolina, or any other state, to prescribe my constitutional duty; or to settle, between me and the people, the validity of laws of Congress, for which I have voted. I decline her umpirage. I have not sworn to support the Constitution according to her construction of its clauses. I have not stipulated, by my oath of office or otherwise, to come under any responsibility, except to the people, and those whom they have appointed to pass upon the question, whether laws, supported by my votes, conform to the Constitution of the country. And, Sir, if we look to the general nature of the case, could anything have been more preposterous than to make a government for the whole Union and yet leave its powers subject, not to one interpretation, but to thirteen or twenty-four interpretations? Instead of one tribunal, established by all, responsible to all, with power to decide for all, shall constitutional questions be left to four-and-twenty popular bodies, each at liberty to decide for itself, and none bound to respect the decisions of others; and each at liberty, too, to give a new construction on every new election of its own members? Would anything, with such a principle in it, or rather with such a destitution of all principle, be fit to be called a government? No, Sir. It should not be denominated a constitution. It should be called, rather, a collection of topics for everlasting controversy; heads of debate for a disputatious people. It would not be a government. It would not be adequate to any practical good or fit for any country to live under.

To avoid all possibility of being misunderstood, allow me to repeat again, in the fullest manner, that I claim no powers for the government by forced or unfair construction. I admit that it is a government of strictly limited powers; of enumerated, specified, and particularized powers; and that whatsoever is not granted is withheld. But notwithstanding all this, and however the grant of powers may be expressed, its limit and extent may yet, in some cases, admit of doubt; and the general government would be good for nothing, it would be incapable of long existing, if some mode had not been provided in which those doubts, as they should arise, might be peaceably, but authoritatively, solved.

And now, Mr. President, let me run the honorable gentleman's doctrine a little into its practical application. Let us look at his probable *modus operandi*. If a thing can be done, an ingenious man can tell *how* it is to be done, and I wish to be informed *how* this state interference is to be put in practice without violence, bloodshed, and rebellion. We will take the existing case of the tariff law. South Carolina is said to have made up her opinion upon it. If we do not repeal it (as we probably shall not), she will then apply to the case the remedy of her doctrine. She will, we must sup-pose, pass a law of her legislature, declaring the several acts of Congress, usually called the tariff laws, null and void, so far as they respect South Carolina, or the citizens thereof. So far all is a paper transaction and easy enough. But the collector at Charleston is collecting the duties imposed by these tariff laws. He, therefore, must be stopped. The collector will seize the goods if the tariff duties are not paid. The state authorities will undertake their rescue, the marshal, with his posse, will come to the collector's aid, and here the contest begins. The militia of the state will be called out to sustain the nullifying act. They will march, Sir, under a very gallant leader; for I believe the honorable member himself commands the militia of that part of the state. He will raise the NULLIFYING ACT on his standard and spread it out as his banner! It will have a preamble, setting forth that the tariff laws are palpable, deliberate, and dangerous violations of the Constitution! He will proceed, with this banner flying, to the custom-house in Charleston,

All the while,
Sonorous metal blowing martial sounds.

Arrived at the custom-house, he will tell the collector that he must collect no more duties under any of the tariff laws. This he will be somewhat puzzled to say, by the way, with a grave countenance, considering what hand South Carolina herself had in that of 1816. But, Sir, the collector would not, probably, desist, at his bidding. He would show him the law of Congress, the treasury instruction, and his own oath of office. He would say, he should perform his duty, come what might.

Here would ensue a pause, for they say that a certain stillness precedes the tempest. The trumpeter would hold his breath awhile, and before all this military array should fall on the custom-house, collector, clerks, and all, it is very probable some of those composing it would request of their gallant commander-in-chief to be informed a little upon the point of law; for they have, doubtless, a just respect for his opinions as a lawyer, as well as for his bravery as a soldier. They know he has read Blackstone and the Constitution, as well as Turenne and Vauban. They would ask him, therefore, something concerning their rights in this matter. They would inquire, whether it was not somewhat dangerous to resist a law of the United States. What would be the nature of their offense, they would wish to learn, if they, by military force and array, resisted the execution in Carolina of a law of the United States, and it should turn out, after all, that the law *was constitutional?* He would answer, of course, treason. No lawyer could give any other answer. John Fries, he would tell them, had learned that some years ago. How, then, they would ask, do you propose to defend us? We are not afraid of bullets, but treason has a way of taking people off that we do not much relish. How do you propose to defend us? "Look at my floating banner," he would reply; "see there the *nullifying law!*" Is it your opinion, gallant commander, they would then say, that, if we should be indicted for treason, that same floating banner of yours would make a good plea in bar? "South Carolina is a sovereign state," he would reply. That is true; but would the judge admit our plea? "These tariff laws," he would repeat, "are unconstitutional, palpably, deliberately, dangerously." That may all be so; but if the tribunal should not happen to be of that opinion, shall we swing for it? We are ready to die for our country, but it is rather an awkward business this dying without touching the ground! After all, that is a sort of hemp tax worse than any part of the tariff.

Mr. President, the honorable gentleman would be in a dilemma, like that of another great general. He would have a knot before him which he could not untie. He must cut it with his sword. He must say to his followers, "Defend yourselves with your bayonets"; and this is war—civil war....

SECTION B. SLAVERY AND EQUALITY

1. SOCIOLOGY FOR THE SOUTH OR THE FAILURE OF FREE SOCIETY[1]

By George Fitzhugh

EDITORS' NOTE.—George Fitzhugh (1806–81) was a Virginia lawyer who served for a time in the land-claim department of the attorney-general's office during the administration of President Buchanan. In his youth he was part of the aristocratic society of Alexandria. Later he moved to Port Royal in Caroline County. Fitzhugh contributed to the South a political and social justification of southern slavery. He proclaimed that the free society of northern industrialism was a failure. *Sociology for the South; or The Failure of Free Society* (1854) and *Cannibals All! or Slaves without Masters* (1857) are his most important writings. He wrote many articles for *De Bow's Review* and for other proslavery magazines, arguing, as Calhoun contended, that slavery was a positive good. About 1856 he went North and lectured at Harvard and Yale, met Harriet Beecher Stowe, and returned with renewed vigor to the task of defending slavery. He advocated public education for all free men and the introduction of some manufactures into the South.

To the People of the South:

We dedicate this little work to you, because it is a zealous and honest effort to promote your peculiar interests. Society has been so quiet and contented in the South—it has suffered so little from crime or extreme poverty, that its attention has not been awakened to the revolutionary tumults, uproar, mendicity, and crime of free society. Few are aware of the blessings they enjoy or of the evils from which they are exempt.

From some peculiarity of taste, we have for many years been watching closely the perturbed workings of free society. Its crimes, its revolutions, its sufferings, and its beggary have led us to investigate its past history as well as to speculate on its future destiny. This pamphlet has been hastily written but is the result of long observation, some research, and much reflection. Should it contain suggestions that will enlist abler pens to show that free society is a failure and its philosophy false, our highest ambition will be gratified. Believing our positions on these subjects to be true, we feel sanguine they are destined to final vindication and triumph. . . .

CHAPTER I

FREE TRADE

Political economy is the science of free society. Its theory and its history alike establish this position. Its fundamental maxims, laissez faire and *"pas trop gouverner,"* are at war with all kinds of slavery, for they in fact assert that individuals and peoples prosper most when governed least. It is not, therefore, wonderful that such a science

---

1. George Fitzhugh, *Sociology for the South; or The Failure of Free Society* (Richmond, Va., 1854), pp. iii, 7, 9-12, 29-40, 43-48, 82-87, 92, 94-95, 161-63, 169-71, 175-93.

should not have been believed or inculcated whilst slavery was universal. . . .

Until now, industry had been controlled and directed by a few minds. Monopoly in its every form had been rife. Men were suddenly called on to walk alone, to act and work for themselves without guide, advice, or control from superior authority. In the past, nothing like it had occurred; hence no assistance could be derived from books. The prophets themselves had overlooked or omitted to tell of the advent of this golden era and were no better guides than the historians and philosophers. A philosophy that should guide and direct industry was equally needed with a philosophy of morals. The occasion found and made the man. For writing a one-sided philosophy, no man was better fitted than Adam Smith. He possessed extraordinary powers of abstraction, analysis, and generalization. He was absent, secluded, and unobservant. He saw only that prosperous and progressive portion of society whom liberty or free competition benefited and mistook its effects on them for its effects on the world. He had probably never heard the old English adage, "Every man for himself, and Devil take the hindmost." This saying comprehends the whole philosophy, moral and economical, of the *Wealth of Nations.* But he and the political economists who have succeeded him seem never to have dreamed that there would have been any "hindmost." There can never be a wise moral philosopher, or a sound philosophy, till someone arises who sees and comprehends all the "things in heaven and earth." Philosophers are the most abstracted, secluded, and least observant of men. Their premises are always false, because they see but few facts; and hence their conclusions must also be false. Plato and Aristotle have today as many believers as Smith, Paley, or Locke, and between their times a hundred systems have arisen, flourished for a time, and been rejected. There is not a true moral philosophy, and from the nature of things there never can be. Such a philosophy has to discover first causes and ultimate effects, to grasp infinitude, to deal with eternity at both ends. Human presumption will often attempt this, but human intellect can never achieve it. *We* shall build up no system, attempt to account for nothing, but simply point out what is natural and universal and humbly try to justify the ways of God to man.

Adam Smith's philosophy is simple and comprehensive (*teres et rotundus*). Its leading and almost its only doctrine is that individual well-being and social and national wealth and prosperity will be best promoted by each man's eagerly pursuing his own selfish welfare unfettered and unrestricted by legal regulations, or governmental prohibitions, further than such regulations may be necessary to prevent positive crime. That some qualifications of this doctrine will not be found in his book we shall not deny; but this is his system. It is obvious enough that such a governmental policy as this doctrine would result in would stimulate energy, excite invention and industry, and bring into livelier action, genius, skill, and talent. It had done so before Smith wrote, and it was no doubt the observation of those effects that suggested the theory. His friends and acquaintances were of that class, who, in the war of the wits to which free competition invited, were sure to come off victors. His country, too, England and Scotland, in the arts of trade and in manufacturing skill, was an overmatch for the rest of the world. International free trade would benefit his country as much as social free trade would benefit his friends. This was his world, and had it been the only world his philosophy would have been true. . . .

A maxim well calculated not only to retard the progress of civilization but to occasion its retrogression has grown out of the science of political economy. "The world is too much governed" has become quite an axiom with many politicians. Now the need of law and government is just in proportion to man's wealth and enlightenment. Barbarians and savages need and will submit to but few and simple laws and little of government. The love of personal liberty and freedom from all restraint are distinguishing traits of wild men and wild beasts. Our Anglo-Saxon ancestors loved personal liberty because they were barbarians, but they did not love it half so much as North American Indians or Bengal tigers, because they were not half so savage. As civilization advances, liberty recedes; and it is fortunate for man that he loses his love of liberty just as fast as he becomes more moral and intellectual. The wealthy, virtuous, and religious citizens of large towns enjoy less of liberty than any other persons whatever, and yet they are the most useful and rationally happy of all mankind. The best-governed countries, and those which have prospered most, have always been distinguished for the number and stringency of their laws. Good men obey superior authority, the laws of God, of mortality, and of their country; bad men love liberty and violate them. It would be difficult very often for the most ingenious casuist to distinguish between sin and liberty, for virtue consists in the performance of duty and the obedience to that law or power that imposes duty, whilst sin is but the violation of duty and disobedience to such law and power. It is remarkable, in this connection, that sin began by the desire for liberty and the attempt to attain it in the person of Satan and his fallen angels. The world wants good government and a plenty of it—not liberty. It is deceptive in us to boast of our democracy, to assert the capacity of the people for self-government, and then refuse to them its exercise. In New England, and in all our large cities, where the people

govern most, they are governed best. If government be not too much centralized, there is little danger of too much government. The danger and evil with us is of too little. Carlyle says of our institutions that they are "anarchy plus a street constable." We ought not to be bandaged up too closely in our infancy; it might prevent growth and development; but the time is coming when we shall need more of government if we would secure the permanency of our institutions.

All men concur in the opinion that some government is necessary. Even the political economist would punish murder, theft, robbery, gross swindling, etc.; but they encourage men to compete with and slowly undermine and destroy one another by means quite as effective as those they forbid. We have heard a distinguished member of this school object to Negro slavery, because the protection it afforded to an inferior race would perpetuate that race, which, if left free to compete with the whites, must be starved out in a few generations. Members of Congress, of the Young American party, boast that the Anglo-Saxon race is manifestly destined to eat out all other races, as the wire-grass destroys and takes the place of other grasses. Nay, they allege this competitive process is going on throughout all nature; the weak are everywhere devouring the strong; the hardier plants and animals destroying the weaker, and the superior races of men exterminating the inferior. They would challenge our admiration for this war of nature, by which they say Providence is perfecting its own work—getting rid of what is weak and indifferent and preserving only what is strong and hardy. We see the war but not the improvement. This competitive, destructive system has been going on from the earliest records of history; and yet the plants, the animals, and the men of today are not superior to those of four thousand years ago. To restrict this destructive, competitive propensity, man was endowed with reason and enabled to pass laws to protect the weak against the strong. To encourage it is to encourage the strong to oppress the weak and to violate the primary object of all government. It is strange it should have entered the head of any philosopher to set the weak, who are the majority of mankind, to competing, contending, and fighting with the strong in order to improve their condition.

Hobbes maintains that "a state of nature is a state of war." This is untrue of a state of nature, because men are naturally associative; but it is true of a civilized state of universal liberty and free competition, such as Hobbes saw around him, and which no doubt suggested his theory. The wants of man and his history alike prove that slavery has always been part of his social organization. A less degree of subjection is inadequate for the government and protection of great numbers of human beings.

An intelligent English writer, describing society as he saw it, uses this language:

There is no disguising from the cool eye of philosophy, that all living creatures exist in a state of natural warfare; and that man (in hostility with all) is at enmity also with his own species; man is the natural enemy of man; and society, unable to change his nature, succeeds but in establishing a hollow truce by which fraud is substituted for violence.

Such is free society, fairly portrayed; such are the infidel doctrines of political economy when candidly avowed. Slavery and Christianity bring about a lasting peace, not "a hollow truce." But we mount a step higher. We deny that there is a society in free countries. They who act each for himself, who are hostile, antagonistic, and competitive, are not social and do not constitute a society. We use the term "free society" for want

of a better; but, like the term "free government," it is an absurdity: those who are governed are not free—those who are free are not social.

CHAPTER II

FAILURE OF FREE SOCIETY AND RISE OF SOCIALISM

The phenomena presented by the vassals and villeins of Europe after their liberation were the opposite of those exhibited by the wealthy and powerful classes. Pauperism and beggary, we are informed by English historians, were unknown till the villeins began to escape from their masters and attempted to practice a predatory and nomadic liberty. A liberty, we should infer from the descriptions we can get of it, very much like that of domestic animals that have gone wild—the difference in favor of the animals being that nature had made provision for them but had made none for the villeins. The new freemen were bands of thieves and beggars, infesting the country and disturbing its peace. Their physical condition was worse than when under the rule of the barons, their masters, and their moral condition worse also, for liberty had made them from necessity thieves and murderers. It was necessary to retain them in slavery, not only to support and sustain them and to prevent general mendicity, but equally necessary in order to govern them and prevent crime. The advocates of universal liberty concede that the laboring class enjoy more material comfort, are better fed, clothed, and housed as slaves than as freemen. The statistics of crime demonstrate that the moral superiority of the slave over the free laborer is still greater than his superiority in animal well-being. There never can be among slaves a class so degraded as is found about the wharves and suburbs of cities. The master requires and enforces ordinary morality and industry. We very much fear, if it were possible to indite a faithful comparison of the conduct and comfort of our free Negroes with that of the runaway Anglo-Saxon serfs, that it would be found that the Negroes have fared better and committed much less crime than the whites. But those days, the fourteenth and fifteenth centuries, were the halcyon days of vagabond liberty. The few that had escaped from bondage found a wide field and plenty of subjects for the practice of theft and mendicity. There was no law and no police adequate to restrain them, for until then their masters had kept them in order better than laws ever can. But those glorious old times have long since passed. A bloody code, a standing army, and efficient police keep them quiet enough now. Their numbers have multiplied a hundred fold, but their poverty has increased faster than their numbers. Instead of stealing and begging, and living idly in the open air, they work fourteen hours a day, cooped up in close rooms, with foul air, foul water, and insufficient and filthy food, and often sleep at night crowded in cellars or in garrets, without regard to sex. . . . How slavery could degrade men lower than universal liberty has done, it is hard to conceive; how it did and would again preserve them from such degradation is well explained by those who are loudest in its abuse. A consciousness of security, a full comprehension of his position, and a confidence in that position, and the absence of all corroding cares and anxieties, make the slave easy and self-assured in his address, cheerful, happy, and contented, free from jealousy, malignity, and envy, and at peace with all around him. His attachment to his master begets the sentiment of loyalty than which none more purifies and elevates human nature. . . .

The free laborer rarely has a house and home of his own; he is insecure of employment; sickness may overtake him at any time and deprive him of the means of support; old age is certain to overtake him, if he lives, and generally finds him without the means of subsistence; his family is probably increasing in numbers and is helpless and burdensome to him. In all this there is little to incite to virtue, much to tempt to crime, nothing to afford happiness, but quite enough to inflict misery. Man must be more than human to acquire a pure and a high morality under such circumstances.

In free society the sentiments, principles, feelings, and affections of high and low, rich and poor, are equally blunted and debased by the continual war of competition. It begets rivalries, jealousies, and hatred on all hands. The poor can neither love nor respect the rich, who, instead of aiding and protecting them, are endeavoring to cheapen their labor and take away their means of subsistence. The rich can hardly respect themselves, when they reflect that wealth is the result of avarice, caution, circumspection, and hard dealing. These are the virtues which free society in its regular operation brings forth. Its moral influence is therefore no better on the rich than on the poor. The number of laborers being excessive in all old countries, they are continually struggling with, scandalizing, and underbidding each other to get places and employment. Every circumstance in the poor man's situation in free society is one of harassing care, of grievous temptation, and of excitement to anger, envy, jealousy, and malignity. That so many of the poor should nevertheless be good and pure, kind, happy, and high-minded is proof enough that the poor class is not the worst class in society. But the rich have their temptations, too. Capital gives them the power to oppress; selfishness offers the inducement, and political economy, the moral guide of the day, would justify the oppression. Yet there are thousands of noble and generous and disinterested men in free society who employ their wealth to relieve and not to oppress the poor. Still, these are exceptions to the general rule. The effect of such society is to encourage the oppression of the poor.

The ink was hardly dry with which Adam Smith wrote his *Wealth of Nations*, lauding the benign influences of free society, ere the hunger and want and nakedness of that society engendered a revolutionary explosion that shook the world to its center. The starving artisans and laborers, and fishwomen and needle-women of Paris, were the authors of the first French revolution, and that revolution was everywhere welcomed and spread from nation to nation like fire in the prairies. The French armies met with but a formal opposition until they reached Russia. There, men had homes and houses and a country to fight for. The serfs of Russia, the undisciplined Cossacks, fought for lares and penates, their homes, their country, and their God, and annihilated an army more numerous than that of Xerxes and braver and better appointed than the tenth legion of Caesar. What should western European poor men fight for? All the world was the same to them. They had been set free to starve, without a place to rest their dying heads or to inter their dead bodies. Any change they thought would be for the better, and hailed Bonaparte as a deliverer. . . .

The Chartists and Radicals of England would in some way subvert and reconstruct society. They complain of free competition as a crying evil and may be classed with the Socialists. The high conservative party called Young England vainly endeavors, by preaching fine sentiments, to produce that good feeling between the rich and the poor, the weak and the powerful, which slavery alone can bring about. Liberty places those classes in positions of antagonism and war. Slavery identifies the interests of rich and poor, master and slave, and begets domestic affection on the one side, and loyalty and respect on the other. Young England sees clearly

enough the character of the disease but is not bold enough to propose an adequate remedy. The poor themselves are all practical Socialists and in some degree proslavery men. They unite in strikes and trades-unions and thus exchange a part of their liberties in order to secure high and uniform wages. The exchange is a prudent and sensible one; but they who have bartered off liberty are fast verging toward slavery. Slavery to an association is not always better than slavery to a single master. The professed object is to avoid ruinous under-bidding and competition with one another; but this competition can never cease whilst liberty lasts. Those who wish to be free must take liberty with this inseparable burden. Odd-Fellows' societies, temperance societies, and all other societies that provide for sick and unfortunate members are instances of socialism. The muse in England for many years has been busy in composing dissonant laborer songs, bewailing the hardships, penury, and sufferings of the poor, and indignantly rebuking the cruelty and injustice of their hard-hearted and close-fisted employers.

Dickens and Bulwer denounce the framework of society quite as loudly as Carlyle and Newman; the two latter of whom propose slavery as a remedy for existing evils. A large portion of the clergy are professed Socialists, and there is scarcely a literary man in England who is not ready to propose radical and organic changes in her social system. Germany is full of Communists; social discontent is universal, and her people are leaving en masse for America—hopeless of any amelioration at home for the future. Strange to tell, in the free states of America too, socialism and every other heresy that can be invoked to make war on existing institutions prevail to an alarming extent. Even according to our own theory of the necessity of slavery, we should not suppose that that necessity would be so soon felt in a new and sparsely settled country, where the supply of labor does not exceed the demand. But it is probable the constant arrival of emigrants makes the situation of the laborer at the North as precarious as in Europe and produces a desire for some change that shall secure him employment and support at all times. Slavery alone can effect that change; and toward slavery the North and all western Europe are unconsciously marching. The master-evil they all complain of is free competition—which is another name for liberty. Let them remove that evil, and they will find themselves slaves, with all the advantages and disadvantages of slavery. They will have attained association of labor, for slavery produces association of labor and is one of the ends all Communists and Socialists desire. A well-conducted farm in the South is a model of associated labor that Fourier might envy. One old woman nurses all the children whilst the mothers are at work; another waits on the sick, in a house set aside for them. Another washes and cooks, and a fourth makes and mends the clothing. It is a great economy of labor and is a good idea of the Socialists. Slavery protects the infants, the aged, and the sick; nay, takes far better care of them than of the healthy, the middle-aged, and the strong. They are part of the family, and self-interest and domestic affection combine to shelter, shield, and foster them. A man loves not only his horses and his cattle, which are useful to him, but he loves his dog, which is of no use. He loves them because they are his. What a wise and beneficent provision of Heaven that makes the selfishness of man's nature a protecting aegis to shield and defend wife and children, slaves and even dumb animals. The Socialists propose to reach this result too, but they never can if they refuse to march in the only road Providence has pointed out. Who will check, govern, and control their superintending authority? Who prevent his abuse of power? Who can make him kind, tender, and affectionate to the poor, aged, helpless, sick, and unfortunate? *Qui custodiat custodes?* Nature establishes the only safe and reliable checks and balances in government. Alton Locke describes an English farm, where the cattle, the horses, and the sheep are fat, plentifully fed, and warmly housed; the game in the preserves and the fish in the pond carefully provided for; and two freezing, shivering, starving, half-clad boys, who have to work on the Sabbath, are the slaves to these animals and are vainly endeavoring to prepare their food. Now it must have occurred to the author that if the boys had belonged to the owner of the farm, they too would have been well treated, happy, and contented. This farm is but a miniature of all England; every animal is well treated and provided for, except the laboring man. He is the slave of the brutes, the slave of society, produces everything and enjoys nothing. Make him the slave of one man instead of the slave of society, and he would be far better off. None but lawyers and historians are aware how much of truth, justice, and good sense there is in the notions of the Communists as to the community of property. Laying no stress on the too abstract proposition that Providence gave the world not to one man, or set of men, but to all mankind, it is a fact that all governments, in civilized countries, recognize the obligation to support the poor and thus, in some degree, make all property a common possession. The poor-laws and poor-houses of England are founded on communistic principles. Each parish is compelled to support its own poor. In Ireland this obligation weighs so heavily as in many instances to make farms valueless, the poor rates exceeding the rents. But it is domestic slavery alone that can establish a safe, efficient, and humane community of property. It did so in ancient times; it did so in feudal times; and does so now, in eastern Europe, Asia, and America. Slaves never die of hunger, seldom suffer want. Hence Chinese sell themselves when they can do no better. A southern farm is a sort of joint stock concern, or social phala[n]stery, in which the master furnishes the capital and skill, and the slaves the labor, and divide the profits, not according to each one's input, but according to each one's wants and necessities.

Socialism proposes to do away with free competition; to afford protection and support at all times to the laboring class; to bring about, at least, a qualified community of property and to associate labor. All these purposes slavery fully and perfectly attains. . . .

CHAPTER V

NEGRO SLAVERY

. . . Now, it is clear the Athenian democracy would not suit a Negro nation, nor will the government of mere law suffice for the individual Negro. He is but a grown-up child and must be governed as a child, not as a lunatic or criminal. The master occupies toward him the place of parent or guardian. We shall not dwell on this view, for no one will differ with us who thinks as we do of the Negro's capacity, and we might argue till doomsday, in vain, with those who have a high opinion of the Negro's moral and intellectual capacity.

Secondly, the Negro is improvident; will not lay up in summer for the wants of winter; will not accumulate in youth for the exigencies of age. He would become an insufferable burden to society. Society has the right to prevent this and can only do so by subjecting him to domestic slavery.

In the last place, the Negro race is inferior to the white race, and, living in their midst, they would be far outstripped or outwitted in the chase of free competition. Gradual but certain extermination would be their fate. We presume the maddest abolitionist does not think the Negro's providence of habits and money-making capacity at all to compare to those of the whites. This defect of character would alone justify enslaving him, if he is to remain here. In Africa or the West Indies, he would become idolatrous, savage, and cannibal, or be devoured by savages and cannibals. At the North he would freeze or starve.

We would remind those who deprecate and sympathize with Negro slavery that his slavery here relieves him from a far more cruel slavery in Africa, or from idolatry and cannibalism, and every brutal vice and crime that can disgrace humanity; and that it Christianizes, protects, supports, and civilizes him; that it governs him far better than free laborers at the North are governed. . . .

But abolish Negro slavery, and how much of slavery still remains. Soldiers and sailors in Europe enlist for life; here, for five years. Are they not slaves who have not only sold their liberties but their lives also? And they are worse treated than domestic slaves. No domestic affection and self-interest extend their aegis over them. No kind mistress, like a guardian angel, provides for them in health, tends them in sickness, and soothes their dying pillow. Wellington at Waterloo was a slave. He was bound to obey, or would, like Admiral Byng, have been shot for gross misconduct and might not, like a common laborer, quit his work at any moment. He had sold his liberty and might not resign without the consent of his master, the king. The common laborer may quit his work at any moment, whatever his contract; declare that liberty is an inalienable right and leave his employer to redress by a useless suit for damages. The highest and most honorable position on earth was that of the slave Wellington; the lowest, that of the free man who cleaned his boots and fed his hounds. The African cannibal, caught, Christianized, and enslaved, is as much elevated by slavery as was Wellington. The kind of slavery is adapted to the men enslaved. Wives and apprentices are slaves; not in theory only but often in fact. Children are slaves to their parents, guardians, and teachers. Imprisoned culprits are slaves. Lunatics and idiots are slaves also. Three-fourths of free society are slaves, no better treated, when their wants and capacities are estimated, than Negro slaves. The masters in free society, or slave society, if they perform properly their duties, have more cares and less liberty than the slaves themselves. "In the sweat of thy face shalt thou earn thy bread!" made all men slaves, and such all *good men* continue to be.

Negro slavery would be changed immediately to some form of peonage, serfdom, or villeinage if the Negroes were sufficiently intelligent and provident to manage a farm. No one would have the labor and trouble of management if his Negroes would pay in hires and rents one-half what free tenants pay in rent in Europe. Every Negro in the South would be soon liberated if he would take liberty on the terms that white tenants hold it. The fact that he cannot enjoy liberty on such terms seems conclusive that he is only fit to be a slave.

But for the assaults of the abolitionists, much would have been done ere this to regulate and improve southern slavery. Our Negro mechanics do not work so hard, have many more privileges and holidays, and are better fed and clothed than field hands and are yet more valuable to their masters. The slaves of the South are cheated of their rights by the purchase of northern manufactures which they could produce. Besides, if we would employ our slaves in the coarser processes of the mechanic arts and manufactures, such as brick-making, getting and hewing timber for ships and houses, iron-mining and smelting, coal-mining, grading railroads and plank roads, in the manufac-

ture of cotton, tobacco, etc., we would find a vent in new employments for their increase more humane and more profitable than the vent afforded by new states and territories. The nice and finishing processes of manufactures and mechanics should be reserved for the whites, who only are fitted for them, and thus, by diversifying pursuits and cutting off dependence on the North, we might benefit and advance the interests of our whole population. Exclusive agriculture has depressed and impoverished the South. We will not here dilate on this topic, because we intend to make it the subject of a separate essay. Free-trade doctrines, not slavery, have made the South agricultural and dependent, given her a sparse and ignorant population, ruined her cities, and expelled her people....

But far the worst feature of modern civilization, which is the civilization of free society, remains to be exposed. Whilst labor-saving processes have probably lessened by one-half, in the last century, the amount of work needed for comfortable support, the free laborer is compelled by capital and competition to work more than he ever did before and is less comfortable. The organization of society cheats him of his earnings, and those earnings go to swell the vulgar pomp and pageantry of the ignorant millionaires, who are the only great of the present day. These reflections might seem, at first view, to have little connection with Negro slavery; but it is well for us of the South not to be deceived by the tinsel glare and glitter of free society and to employ ourselves in doing our duty at home and studying the past rather than in insidious rivalry of the expensive pleasures and pursuits of men whose sentiments and whose aims are low, sensual, and groveling....

We deem this peculiar question of Negro slavery of very little importance. The issue is made throughout the world on the general subject of slavery in the abstract. The argument has commenced. One set of ideas will govern and control after awhile the civilized world. Slavery will everywhere be abolished or everywhere be reinstituted. We think the opponents of practical, existing slavery are estopped by their own admission; nay, that unconsciously, as Socialists, they are the defenders and propagandists of slavery and have furnished the only sound arguments on which its defense and justification can be rested. We have introduced the subject of Negro slavery to afford us a better opportunity to disclaim the purpose of reducing the white man anywhere to the condition of Negro slaves here. It would be very unwise and unscientific to govern white men as you would Negroes. Every shade and variety of slavery has existed in the world. In some cases there has been much of legal regulation, much restraint of the master's authority; in others, none at all. The character of slavery necessary to protect the whites in Europe should be much milder than Negro slavery, for slavery is only needed to protect the white man, whilst it is more necessary for the government of the Negro even than for his protection. But even Negro slavery should not be outlawed. We might and should have laws in Virginia, as in Louisiana, to make the master subject to presentment by the grand jury and to punishment for any inhuman or improper treatment or neglect of his slave.

We abhor the doctrine of the "Types of Mankind"; first, because it is at war with scripture, which teaches us that the whole human race is descended from a common parentage; and, secondly, because it encourages and incites brutal masters to treat Negroes, not as weak, ignorant, and dependent brethren, but as wicked beasts, without the pale of humanity. The southerner is the Negro's friend, his only friend. Let no intermeddling Abolitionist, no refined philosophy, dissolve this friendship....

CHAPTER XV

THE ASSOCIATION OF LABOR

If the Socialists had done no other good, they would be entitled to the gratitude of mankind for displaying in a strong light the advantages of the association of labor. Adam Smith, in his elaborate treatise on the "Division of Labor," nearly stumbled on the same truth. But the division of labor is a curse to the laborer, without the association of labor. Division makes labor ten times more efficient, but, by confining each workman to some simple, monotonous employment, it makes him a mere automaton and an easy prey to the capitalist. The association of labor, like all association, requires a head or ruler, and that head or ruler will become a cheat and a tyrant unless his interests are identified with the interests of the laborer. In a large factory, in free society, there is division of labor, and association too, but association and division for the benefit of the employer and to the detriment of the laborer. On a large farm whatever advances the health, happiness, and morals of the Negroes renders them more prolific and valuable to their master. It is his interest to pay them high wages in way of support, and he can afford to do so, because association renders the labor of each slave five times as productive and efficient as it would be were the slaves working separately. One man could not inclose an acre of land, cultivate it, send his crops to market, do his own cooking, washing, and mending. One man may live as a prowling beast of prey but not as a civilized being. One hundred human beings, men, women, and children, associated, will cultivate ten acres of land each, inclose it, and carry on every other operation of civilized life. Labor becomes at least twenty times as productive when a hundred associate as when one acts alone. The same is as true in other pursuits as in farming. But in free society the employer robs the laborer, and he is no better off than the prowling savage, although he might live in splendor if he got a fair proportion of the proceeds of his own labor.

We have endeavored to show, heretofore, that the Negro slave, considering his indolence and unskilfulness, often gets his fair share, and sometimes more than his share, of the profits of the farm and is exempted, besides, from the harassing cares and anxieties of the free laborer. Grant, however, that the Negro does not receive adequate wages from his master, yet all admit that in the aggregate the Negroes get better wages than free laborers; therefore, it follows that, with all its imperfections, slave society is the best form of society yet devised for the masses. When Socialists and Abolitionists, by full and fair experiments, exhibit a better, it will be time to agitate the subject of abolition.

The industrial products of black slave labor have been far greater and more useful to mankind than those of the same amount of any other labor. In a very short period the South and Southwest have been settled, cleared, fenced in, and put in cultivation by what were, a century ago, a handful of masters and slaves. This region now feeds and clothes a great part of mankind; but free trade cheats them of the profits of their labor. In the vast amount of our industrial products, we see the advantages of association; in our comparative poverty, the evils of free trade. . . .

CHAPTER XVII

LIBERTY AND FREE TRADE

These are convertible terms; two names for the same thing. Statesmen, orators, and philosophers, the Tories of England, and the Whigs of America, have been laboring incessantly for more than half a century to refute the doctrine of free trade. They all and each failed to produce a single plausible argument in reply. Not one of their books or

speeches survived a month. Not one ever was, or ever will be, quoted or relied on as authority to disprove the principles of political economy. The reason is obvious enough; they were all confused by words or afraid to make the proper issue. They first admitted liberty to be a good, and then attempted, but attempted in vain, to argue that free trade was an evil. The Socialists stumbled on the true issue but do not seem yet fully aware of the nature of their discovery. Liberty was the evil, liberty the disease, under which society was suffering. It must be restricted, competition be arrested, the strong be restrained from, instead of encouraged to oppress the weak—in order to restore society to a healthy state. To them we are indebted for our argument against free trade. We have extended it and explained its application. *They* demonstrated that social free trade was an evil, because it incited the rich and strong to oppress the weak, poor, and ignorant. *We* saw that the disparities of mental strength were greater between races and nations than between individuals in the same society. History spoke less equivocally as to the ruinout effects of international free trade than as to those of social free trade.

Events are occurring every day, especially at the North, that show that religious liberty must be restricted as well as other liberty.

Chinese idolaters are coming in swarms, too, to California. If they are to be permitted to practice their diabolical rights, the Negroes should be allowed to revert to the time-honored customs of their ancestors and immolate human victims to their devil deity. Mormonism is still a worse religious evil, which we have to deal with.

Liberty is an evil which government is intended to correct. This is the sole object of government. Taking these premises, it is easy enough to refute free trade. Admit liberty to be a good, and you leave no room to argue that free trade is an evil—because liberty is free trade.

With thinking men, the question can never arise: Who ought to be free? Because no one ought to be free. All government is slavery. The proper subject of investigation for philosophers and philanthropists is, "Is the existing mode of government adapted to the wants of its subjects?" No one will contend that Negroes, for instance, should roam at large in *puris naturalibus*, with the apes and tigers of Africa, and "worry and devour each other." Nor are they fitted for an Athenian democracy. What form of government short of domestic slavery will suit their wants and capacities? That is the true issue, and we direct the attention of Abolitionists to it. They are now striking wild and often hit the Bible and the marriage tie and the right of property and the duties of children to their parents and guardians harder blows than they do Negro slavery. They are mere anarchists and infidels. If they would take our advice, they would appear more respectable, do less harm, and might suggest some good. For domestic slavery, like all human institutions, has its imperfections—will always have them. Yet it is our duty to correct such as can be corrected, and we would do so, if the Abolitionists would let us alone or advise with us as friends, neighbors, and gentlemen. . . .

CHAPTER XIX
DECLARATION OF INDEPENDENCE AND VIRGINIA BILL OF RIGHTS

An essay on the subject of slavery would be very imperfect if it passed over without noticing these instruments. The abstract principles which they enunciate, we candidly admit, are wholly at war with slavery; we shall attempt to show that they are equally at war with all government, all subordination, all order. Men's minds were heated and blinded when they were written, as well by patriotic zeal, as by a false philosophy,

which, beginning with Locke, in a refined materialism, had ripened on the Continent into open infidelity. In England, the doctrine of prescriptive government, of the divine right of kings, had met with signal overthrow, and in France there was faith in nothing, speculation about everything. The human mind became extremely presumptuous and undertook to form governments on exact philosophical principles, just as men make clocks, watches, or mills. They confounded the moral with the physical world, and this was not strange, because they had begun to doubt whether there was any other than a physical world. Society seemed to them a thing whose movement and action could be controlled with as much certainty as the motion of a spinning wheel, provided it was organized on proper principles. It would have been less presumptuous in them to have attempted to have made a tree, for a tree is not half so complex as a society of human beings, each of whom is fearfully and wonderfully compounded of soul and body, and whose aggregate—society—is still more complex and difficult of comprehension than its individual members. Trees grow, and man may lop, trim, train, and cultivate them and thus hasten their growth and improve their size, beauty, and fruitfulness. Laws, institutions, societies, and governments grow, and men may aid their growth, improve their strength and beauty, and lop off their deformities and excrescences, by punishing crime and rewarding virtue. When society has worked long enough, under the hand of God and nature, man, observing its operations, may discover its laws and constitution. The common law of England and the constitution of England were discoveries of this kind. Fortunately for us, we adopted, with little change, that common law and that constitution. Our institutions and our ancestry were English. Those institutions were the growth and accretions of many ages, not the work of legislating philosophers.

The abstractions contained in the various instruments on which we professed, but professed falsely, to found our governments did no harm because, until abolition arose, they remained a dead letter. Now, and not till now, these abstractions have become matters of serious practical importance, and we propose to give some of them a candid but fearless examination. We find these words in the Preamble and Declaration of Independence:

We hold these truths to be self-evident: that all men are created equal; that they are endowed by their Creator with certain inalienable rights; that among them are life, liberty, and the pursuit of happiness; that, to secure these rights, governments are instituted among men, deriving their just powers from the consent of the governed; that, whenever any form of government becomes destructive of these ends, it is the right of the people to alter or abolish it and to institute a new government, laying its foundations on such principles and organizing its powers in such form as to them shall seem most likely to effect their safety and happiness.

It is, we believe, conceded on all hands that men are not born physically, morally, or intellectually equal—some are males, some females, some from birth, large, strong, and healthy, others weak, small, and sickly—some are naturally amiable, others prone to all kinds of wickednesses—some brave, others timid. Their natural inequalities beget inequalities of rights. The weak in mind or body require guidance, support, and protection; they must obey and work for those who protect and guide them— they have a natural right to guardians, committees, teachers, or masters. Nature has made them slaves; all that law and government can do is to regulate, modify, and mitigate their slavery. In the absence of legally instituted slavery, their condition would be worse under that natural slavery of the weak to the strong, the foolish to the wise and cunning. The wise and virtuous, the brave, the strong in mind and body, are by nature born to command and protect, and law but follows nature in making them rulers, legislators, judges, captains, husbands, guardians, committees, and masters. The naturally depraved class, those born prone to crime, are our brethren too; they are entitled to education, to religious instruction, to all the means and appliances proper to correct their evil propensities, and all their failings; they have a right to be sent to the penitentiary—for there, if they do not reform, they cannot at least disturb society. Our feelings and our consciences teach us that nothing but necessity can justify taking human life.

We are but stringing together truisms which everybody knows as well as ourselves, and yet, if men are created unequal in all these respects, what truth or what meaning is there in the passage under consideration? Men are not created or born equal, and circumstances and education and association tend to increase and aggravate inequalities among them from generation to generation. Generally, the rich associate and intermarry with each other, the poor do the same; the ignorant rarely associate with or intermarry with the learned; and all society shuns contact with the criminal, even to the third and fourth generations.

Men are not "born entitled to equal rights"! It would be far nearer the truth to say that "some were born with saddles on their backs, and others booted and spurred to ride them"—and the riding does them good. They need the reins, the bit, and the spur. No two men by nature are exactly equal or exactly alike. No institutions can prevent the few from acquiring rule and ascendancy over the many. Liberty and free competition invite and encourage the attempt of the strong to master the weak and insure their success.

Life and liberty are not "inalienable"; they have been sold in all countries, and in all ages, and must be sold so long as human nature lasts. It is an inexpedient and unwise and often unmerciful restraint on a man's liberty of action to deny him the right to sell himself when starving and again to buy himself when fortune smiles. Most countries of antiquity, and some, like China at the present day, allowed such sale and purchase. The great object of government is to restrict, control, and punish man "in the pursuit of happiness." All crimes are committed in its pursuit. Under the free or competitive system, most men's happiness consists in destroying the happiness of other people. This, then, is no inalienable right.

The author of the Declaration may have, and probably did mean, that all men were created with an equal title to property. Carry out such a doctrine, and it would subvert every government on earth.

In practice, in all ages, and in all countries, men had sold their liberty either for short periods, for life, or hereditarily; that is, both their own liberty and that of their children after them. The laws of all countries have, in various forms and degrees, in all times recognized and regulated this right to *alien* or sell liberty. The soldiers and sailors of the revolution had aliened both liberty and life; the wives in all America had aliened their liberty; so had the apprentices and wards at the very moment this verbose, newborn, false, and unmeaning Preamble was written.

Mr. Jefferson was an enthusiastic speculative philosopher; Franklin was wise, cunning, and judicious; he made no objection to the Declaration, as prepared by Mr. Jefferson, because, probably, he saw it would suit the occasion and supposed it would be harmless for the future. But even Franklin was too much of a physical philosopher, too utilitarian and material in his doctrines, to be relied on in matters of morals or government. We may fairly conclude that liberty is alienable; that there is a natural right to alien it, first, because the laws and institutions of all countries have recognized and regulated its alienation; and, secondly, because we cannot conceive of a civilized society, in which there were no wives, no wards, no apprentices, no sailors, and no soldiers; and none of these could there be in a country that practically carried out the doctrine that liberty is inalienable.

The soldier who meets death at the cannon's mouth does so because he has aliened both life and liberty. Nay, more, he has aliened the pursuit of happiness, else he might desert on the eve of battle and pursue happiness in some more promising quarter than the cannon's mouth. If the pursuit of happiness be inalienable, men should not be punished for crime, for all crimes are notoriously committed in the pursuit of happiness. If these abstractions have some hidden and cabalistic meaning, which none but the initiated can comprehend, then the Declaration should have been accompanied with a translation and a commentary to fit it for common use—as it stands, it deserves the tumid yet appropriate epithets which Major Lee somewhere applies to the writings of Mr. Jefferson it is "exuberantly false, and arborescently fallacious."

Nothing can be found in all history more unphilosophical, more presumptuous, more characteristic of the infidel philosophy of the eighteenth century than the language that follows that of which we have been treating. How any observant man, however unread, should have come to the conclusion that society and government were such plastic, man-created things that, starting on certain general principles, he might frame them successfully as he pleased, we are at a loss to conceive. But infidelity is blind and foolish, and infidelity then prevailed. Lay your foundations of government on what principles you please, organize its powers in what form you choose, and you cannot foresee the results. You can only tell what laws, institutions, and governments will effect when you apply them to the same race or nation under the same circumstances in which they have already been tried. But philosophy then was in chrysalis state. She has since deluged the world with blood, crime, and pauperism. She has had full sway and has inflicted much misery and done no good. The world is beginning to be satisfied that it is much safer and better to look to the past, to trust to experience, to follow nature, than to be guided by the *ignis fatuus* of a priori speculations of closet philosophers. If all men had been created equal, all would have been competitors, rivals, and enemies. Subordination, difference of caste and classes, difference of sex, age, and slavery beget peace and good will.

We were only justified in declaring our independence, because we were sufficiently wise, numerous, and strong to govern ourselves, and too distant and distinct from England to be well governed by her. . . .

The first clause of the Bill of Rights of Virginia contains language of like import with that which we have been criticizing. The fourth clause is in the following words: "That no man or set of men are entitled to exclusive or separate privileges from the rest of the community, but in consideration of public services; which, not being descendible, neither ought the offices of magistrate, legislator, or judge to be hereditary." This is very bad English and is so obscurely expressed that we can only guess at the meaning intended to be conveyed. We suppose that "exclusive or separate emoluments and privileges" was intended to apply to such harmless baubles as titles of nobility and coats-of-arms, and to petty ill-paid officers, and that the author never dreamed that hereditary property, however large, was a "separate emolument or privilege."

The author saw no objection to the right secured by law to hold five hundred subjects or Negro slaves, and ten thousand acres of land, to the exclusion of everybody else and to transmit them to one's children and grandchildren, although an exclusive hereditary privilege far transcending any held by the nobility of Europe—for the nobility of Russia do not hold such despotic sway over their serfs as we do over our Negroes and are themselves mere slaves to the emperor, whilst our slaveholders have scarcely any authority above them. We have no doubt the author, like our modern farmers, considered this "a mere circumstance" and would have told you that a man has a *natural right* to his lands and Negroes, a natural right to what belonged to his father.

Property is not a natural and divine but conventional right; it is the mere creature of society and law. In this all lawyers and publicists agree. In this country the history of property is of such recent date that the simplest and most ignorant man must know that it commenced in wrong, injustice, and violence a few generations ago and derives its only title now from the will of society through the sanction of law. Society has no right, because it is not expedient, to resume any one man's property because he abuses its possession and does not so employ it as to redound to public advantage—but if all private property, or if private property generally were so used as to injure, instead of promote public good, then society might and ought to destroy the whole institution.

From these premises it follows that government, in taxing private property, should only be limited by the public good. If the tax be so heavy as to deter the owner from improving the property, then, in general, will the whole public be injured.

False notions of the right of property, and of the duties and liabilities of property-holders, destroy all public spirit and patriotism, cripple and injure, and prevent the growth and development of the South. We feel it our duty to deflect a little from our subject to expose these errors.

Now, a natural right is a "divine right," and if we southern farmers have a divine right to our little realms and subjects, is it not hard to dispute the like right in sovereigns on a larger scale? The world discovered that the power of kings was a trust power conferred on them for the good of the people and to be exercised solely for that purpose—or else forfeited. Are we guilty of treason in suggesting that farmers have no better titles than kings and that the *law* vests them with separate property in lands and Negroes, under the belief and expectation that such separate property will redound more to public advantage than if all property were in common? We have an aristocracy with more of privilege and less of public spirit than any that we meet with in history. Less of public spirit, because they cherish that free-trade philosophy which inculcates selfishness as a moral and political duty, which teaches that the public good is best promoted when nobody attends to public affairs, but each one is intent on his own private ends. Naturally, southerners, like all slaveholders, are liberal and public-spirited. It is their philosophy that has taken away their patriotism. According to the sense in which the term "public services" is used, meaning, no doubt, official services, in the Bill of Rights, no farmer could hold his lands and Negroes a day, for they have not rendered public services as a consideration for their great, "exclusive and separate emolument and privilege." ...Constitutions should never be written till several centuries after governments have been instituted, for it requires that length of time to ascertain how institutions will operate. No matter how you define and limit, in words, the powers and duties of each department of government, they will each be sure to exercise as much power as possible and to encroach to the utmost of their ability on the powers of other departments. When the Commons were invoked to Parliament, the king had no idea they would usurp the taxing powers; but, having successfully done so, it became part of the English constitution that the people alone could tax themselves. ... In this country we shall soon have two constitutions, that a priori thing which nobody regards, and that practical constitution deduced from observation of the workings of our institutions. Whigs disregard our written Constitution when banks, tariffs, or internal improvements are in question; Democrats respect it not when there is a chance to get more territory; and Young America, the dominant party of the day, will jump through its paper obstructions with as much dexterity as harlequin does through the hoop. State governments, and senators, and representatives, and militia, and cities, and churches, and colleges, and universities, and landed property are institutions. Things of flesh and blood that know their rights "and knowing dare maintain them." We should cherish them. They will give permanence to government and security to state rights. But the abstract doctrines of nullification and secession, the general principles laid down in the Declaration of Independence, the Bill of Rights, and Constitution of the United States, afford no protection of rights, no valid limitations of power, no security to state rights. The power to construe them is the power to nullify them. Mere paper guaranties, like the constitutions of Abbé Sieyès, are as worthless as the paper on which they are written.

Our institutions, founded on such generalities and abstractions as those of which we are treating, are like a splendid edifice built upon kegs of gunpowder. The Abolitionists are trying to apply the match to the explosive materials under our parliament house; we are endeavoring to anticipate them by drenching those materials with ridicule. Nobody deems them worth the trouble of argument or the labor of removal. They will soon become incombustible and innocuous.

Property is too old and well tried an institution, too much interwoven with the feelings, interests, prejudices, and affections of man, to be shaken by the speculations of philosophers. It is only its maladministration that can endanger it. So far from wishing to shake or undermine property, we would, for the public good, give it more permanence. We do not like the Western Homestead provision of forty acres, because that entails on families poverty and ignorance and tends to depress civilization. We do not like the large entails of England, because they beget an idle, useless, and vicious aristocracy. . . . A law entailing farms of such amount as would educate families well, without putting them above the necessity of industry and ex-

ertion, would add much to national wealth, in encouraging good and permanent improvements, and would improve national character and intelligence, by securing a class of well-educated men, attached to the soil and the country. We need not fear the mad-dog cry of aristocracy; a man with an entailed estate of five hundred acres, and a coat-of-arms to boot, would not be a very dangerous character. . . . Five hundred acres of land and thirty Negroes would suffice to educate all the younger members of the family and make useful citizens of them. Primogeniture and entails have had this good effect in England. The younger sons have filled the professions, the church, the army, and the navy with able, ambitious men. It has furnished London and Liverpool with the best merchants in the world and made trade one of the most honorable professions.

It is pleasing to see the poor acquiring lands, but the pleasure is more than balanced, with all save the malicious, by seeing the rich stripped of them. Those accustomed to poverty suffer little from it. Those who have been rich are miserable when they become poor. . . .

SECTION C. WESTWARD EXPANSION AND SECTIONAL CONFLICT

1. THE GREAT NATION OF FUTURITY[1]

By JOHN L. O'SULLIVAN

EDITORS' NOTE.—This article and the next selection, entitled "Annexation," are attributed to John Louis O'Sullivan (1813–95), a Jacksonian Democrat, who achieved some prominence in American letters before the Civil War. Through the medium of the *United States Magazine and Democratic Review*, which he established in 1837, to "strike the hitherto silent strings of the democratic genius of the country," O'Sullivan presented to his readers the works of the greatest literary men of the day. In addition, he glorified all things American and was one of the first to employ the phrase "manifest destiny" in print. As chargé d'affaires to Lisbon and then as resident minister to Portugal under President Pierce, he championed manifest destiny as a foreign policy. Later in the decade he sponsored a filibustering expedition to Cuba and was twice indicted for violation of the neutrality laws.

The American people having derived their origin from many other nations, and the Declaration of National Independence being entirely based on the great principle of human equality, these facts demonstrate at once our disconnected position as regards any other nation; that we have, in reality, but little connection with the past history of any of them and still less with all antiquity, its glories, or its crimes. On the contrary, our national birth was the beginning of a new history, the formation and progress of an untried political system, which separates us from the past and connects us with the future only; and so far as regards the entire development of the natural rights of man, in moral, political, and national life, we may confidently assume that our country is destined to be *the great nation* of futurity.

It is so destined, because the principle upon which a nation is organized fixes its destiny, and that of equality is perfect, is universal. It presides in all the operations of the physical world, and it is also the conscious law of the soul—the self-evident dictate of morality, which accurately defines the duty of man to man, and consequently man's rights as man. Besides, the truthful annals of any nation furnish abundant evidence that its happiness, its greatness, its duration, were always proportionate to the democratic equality in its system of government.

How many nations have had their decline and fall because the equal rights of the minority were trampled on by the despotism of the majority; or the interests of the many sacrificed to the aristocracy of the few; or the rights and interests of all given up to the monarchy of one? These three kinds of government have figured so frequently and so

1. *The United States Magazine and Democratic Review*, VI (November, 1839), 2–3, 6.

largely in the ages that have passed away that their history, through all time to come, can only furnish a resemblance. Like causes produce like effects, and the true philosopher of history will easily discern the principle of equality, or of privilege, working out its inevitable result. The first is regenerative, because it is natural and right; the latter is destructive to society, because it is unnatural and wrong.

What friend of human liberty, civilization, and refinement can cast his view over the past history of the monarchies and aristocracies of antiquity, and not deplore that they ever existed? What philanthropist can contemplate the oppressions, the cruelties, and injustice inflicted by them on the masses of mankind and not turn with moral horror from the retrospect?

America is destined for better deeds. It is our unparalleled glory that we have no reminiscences of battlefields, but in defense of humanity, of the oppressed of all nations, of the rights of conscience, the rights of personal enfranchisement. Our annals describe no scenes of horrid carnage, where men were led on by hundreds of thousands to slay one another, dupes and victims to emperors, kings, nobles, demons in the human form called heroes. We have had patriots to defend our homes, our liberties, but no aspirants to crowns or thrones; nor have the American people ever suffered themselves to be led on by wicked ambition to depopulate the land, to spread desolation far and wide, that a human being might be placed on a seat of supremacy.

We have no interest in the scenes of antiquity, only as lessons of avoidance of nearly all their examples. The expansive future is our arena and for our history. We are entering on its untrodden space with the truths of God in our minds, beneficent objects in our hearts, and with a clear conscience unsullied by the past. We are the nation of human

progress, and who will, what can, set limits to our onward march? Providence is with us, and no earthly power can. We point to the everlasting truth on the first page of our national declaration, and we proclaim to the millions of other lands that "the gates of hell"—the powers of aristocracy and monarchy—"shall not prevail against it."

The far-reaching, the boundless future, will be the era of American greatness. In its magnificent domain of space and time, the nation of many nations is destined to manifest to mankind the excellence of divine principles; to establish on earth the noblest temple ever dedicated to the worship of the Most High—the Sacred and the True. Its floor shall be a hemisphere—its roof the firmament of the star-studded heavens, and its congregation a Union of many Republics, comprising hundreds of happy millions, calling, owning no man master, but governed by God's natural and moral law of equality, the law of brotherhood—of "peace and good will amongst men. . . ."

Yes, we are the nation of progress, of individual freedom, of universal enfranchisement. Equality of rights is the cynosure of our union of states, the grand exemplar of the correlative equality of individuals; and, while truth sheds its effulgence, we cannot retrograde without dissolving the one and subverting the other. We must onward to the fulfilment of our mission—to the entire development of the principle of our organization—freedom of conscience, freedom of person, freedom of trade and business pursuits, universality of freedom and equality. This is our high destiny, and in nature's eternal, inevitable decree of cause and effect we must accomplish it. All this will be our future history, to establish on earth the moral dignity and salvation of man—the immutable truth and beneficence of God. For this blessed mission to the nations of the world, which are shut out from the lifegiving light of truth, has America been chosen; and her high example shall smite unto death the tyranny of kings, hierarchs, and oligarchs and carry the glad tidings of peace and good will where myriads now endure an existence scarcely more enviable than that of beasts of the field. Who, then, can doubt that our country is destined to be *the great nation* of futurity?

2. ANNEXATION[1]

By John L. O'Sullivan

It is time now for opposition to the annexation of Texas to cease, all further agitation of the waters of bitterness and strife, at least in connection with this question—even though it may perhaps be required of us as a necessary condition of the freedom of our institutions that we must live on forever in a state of unpausing struggle and excitement upon some subject of party division or other. But, in regard to Texas, enough has now been given to party. It is time for the common duty of patriotism to the country to succeed—or, if this claim will not be recognized, it is at least time for common sense to acquiesce with decent grace in the inevitable and the irrevocable.

Texas is now ours. Already, before these words are written, her convention has undoubtedly ratified the acceptance, by her congress, of our proffered invitation into the Union and made the requisite changes in her already republican form of constitution to adapt it to its future federal relations. Her star and her stripe may already be said to have taken their place in the glorious blazon of our common nationality; and the sweep of our eagle's wing already includes within its circuit the wide extent of her fair and fertile land. She is no longer to us a mere geographical space—a certain combination of coast, plain, mountain, valley, forest, and stream. She is no longer to us a mere country on the map. She comes within the dear and sacred designation of our country; no longer a "*pays*," she is a part of "*la patrie*"; and that which is at once a sentiment and a virtue, patriotism, already begins to thrill for her too within the national heart. It is time then that all should cease to treat her as alien and even adverse—cease to denounce and vilify all and everything connected with her accession—cease to thwart and oppose the remaining steps for its consummation; or, where such efforts are felt to be unavailing, at least to embitter the hour of reception by all the most ungracious frowns of aversion and words of unwelcome. There has been enough of all this. It has had its fitting day during the period when, in common with every other possible question of practical policy that can arise, it unfortunately became one of the leading topics of party division, of presidential electioneering. But that period has passed, and with it let its prejudices and its passions, its discords and its denunciations, pass away too. The next session of Congress will see the representatives of the new young state in their places in both our halls of national legislation, side by side with those of the old thirteen. Let their reception into "the family" be frank, kindly, and cheerful, as befits such an occasion, as comports not less with our own self-respect than patriotic duty toward them. Ill betide those foul birds that delight to 'file their own nest, and disgust the ear with perpetual discord of ill-omened croak.

Why, were other reasoning wanting, in favor of now elevating this question of the reception of Texas into the Union, out of the lower region of our past party

1. *Ibid.*, XVII (July, 1845), 6–8, 12–14.

dissensions, up to its proper level of a high and broad nationality, it surely is to be found, found abundantly, in the manner in which other nations have undertaken to intrude themselves into it, between us and the proper parties to the case, in a spirit of hostile interference against us, for the avowed object of thwarting our policy and hampering our power, limiting our greatness and checking the fulfilment of our manifest destiny to overspread the continent allotted by Providence for the free development of our yearly multiplying millions. This we have seen done by England, our old rival and enemy; and by France, strangely coupled with her against us, under the influence of the Anglicism strongly tinging the policy of her present prime minister, Guizot. The zealous activity with which this effort to defeat us was pushed by the representatives of those governments, together with the character of intrigue accompanying it, fully constituted that case of foreign interference which Mr. Clay himself declared should and would unite us all in maintaining the common cause of our country against the foreigner and the foe. We are only astonished that this effect has not been more fully and strongly produced and that the burst of indignation against this unauthorized, insolent, and hostile interference against us has not been more general even among the party before opposed to annexation and has not rallied the national spirit and national pride unanimously upon that policy. We are very sure that if Mr. Clay himself were now to add another letter to his former Texas correspondence, he would express this sentiment and carry out the idea already strongly stated in one of them in a manner which would tax all the powers of blushing belonging to some of his party adherents. . . .

California will, probably, next fall away from the loose adhesion which, in such a country as Mexico, holds a remote province in a slight equivocal kind of dependence on the metropolis. Imbecile and distracted, Mexico never can exert any real governmental authority over such a country. The impotence of the one and the distance of the other must make the relation one of virtual independence; unless, by stunting the province of all natural growth, and forbidding that immigration which can alone develop its capabilities and fulfil the purposes of its creation, tyranny may retain a military dominion which is no government in the legitimate sense of the term. In the case of California this is now impossible. The Anglo-Saxon foot is already on its borders. Already the advance guard of the irresistible army of Anglo-Saxon emigration has begun to pour down upon it, armed with the plow and the rifle, and marking its trail with schools and colleges, courts and representative halls, mills and meeting-houses. A population will soon be in actual occupation of California, over which it will be idle for Mexico to dream of dominion. They will necessarily become independent. All this without agency of our government, without responsibility of our people—in the natural flow of events, the spontaneous working of principles, and the adaptation of the tendencies and wants of the human race to the elemental circumstances in the midst of which they find themselves placed. And they will have a right to independence—to self-government—to the possession of the homes conquered from the wilderness by their own labors and dangers, sufferings and sacrifices—a better and a truer right than the artificial title of sovereignty in Mexico a thousand miles distant, inheriting from Spain a title good only against those who have none better. Their right to independence will be the natural right of self-government belonging to any community strong enough to maintain it—distinct in position, origin, and character, and free from any mutual obligations of membership of a common political body, binding it to others by the duty of loyalty and compact of public faith. This will be their title to independence; and by this title, there can be no doubt that the population now fast streaming down upon California will both assert and maintain that independence. Whether they will then attach themselves to our Union or not is not to be predicted with any certainty. Unless the projected railroad across the continent to the Pacific be carried into effect, perhaps they may not; though, even in that case, the day is not distant when the empires of the Atlantic and Pacific would again flow together into one, as soon as their inland borders should approach each other. But that great work, colossal as appears the plan on its first suggestion, cannot remain long upbuilt. Its necessity for this very purpose of binding and holding together in its iron clasp our fast settling Pacific region with that of the Mississippi Valley—the natural facility of the route—the ease with which any amount of labor for the construction can be drawn in from the overcrowded populations of Europe, to be paid in the lands made valuable by the progress of the work itself—and its immense utility to the commerce of the world with the whole eastern coast of Asia, alone almost sufficient for the support of such a road—these considerations give assurance that the day cannot be distant which shall witness the conveyance of the representatives from Oregon and California to Washington within less time than a few years ago was devoted to a similar journey by those from Ohio; while the magnetic telegraph will enable the editors of the *San Francisco Union,* the *Astoria Evening Post,* or the *Nootka Morning News* to set up in type the first half of the President's Inaugural before the echoes of the latter half shall have died away beneath the lofty porch of the Capitol as spoken from his lips.

Away, then, with all idle French talk of *balances of power* on the American continent. There is no growth in Spanish America! Whatever progress of population there may be in the British Canadas, is only for their own early severance of their present colonial relation to the little island three thousand miles across the Atlantic; soon to be followed by annexation and destined to swell the still accumulating momentum of our progress. And whosoever may hold the balance, though they should cast into the opposite scale all the bayonets and cannon, not only of France and England, but of Europe entire, how would it kick the beam against the simple solid weight of the two hundred and fifty, or three hundred millions—and American millions—destined to gather beneath the flutter of the Stripes and Stars, in the fast-hastening year of the Lord 1945!

3. *DRED SCOTT* v. *SANDFORD*[1]

EDITORS' NOTE.—In the case of *Dred Scott* v. *Sandford*, Chief Justice Taney attempted to resolve the conflict over slavery in the territories by a sweeping affirmation of a man's right to take his property where he wills within the Union. From the beginning the case was a test of slave power, not of Dred Scott's right to freedom. The trials were sponsored by sons of Scott's earlier owner. The plaintiff, originally a slave, brought this action against the defendant, originally his master, for a trespass consisting of "gently" laying his hands upon him to restrain him. In 1834 the plaintiff was taken by the

1. 19 Howard 393 (1857), 399, 406–12, 426–27, 430, 432, 447–52.

defendant from the slave state of Missouri to the free state of Illinois; and in 1836 from Illinois to Fort Snelling, then part of the Territory of Wisconsin, now in Minnesota. In 1838 the plaintiff was taken by the defendant back to Missouri. The plaintiff brought his action in the state courts of Missouri in 1846 (*Dred Scott, a Man of Color* v. *Emerson*), and a judgment favorable to the defendant was rendered there in 1852.

Change of jurisdiction was arranged by a fictitious sale of Scott to Sandford of New York, his owner's brother, and the case was taken into the federal courts of the United States in 1854. The plaintiff claimed, first, that he had

Mr. Chief Justice TANEY delivered the opinion of the Court. . . .

It is true, every person, and every class and description of persons, who were at the time of the adoption of the Constitution recognized as citizens in the several states, became also citizens of this new political body; but none other; it was formed by them, and for them and their posterity, but for no one else. And the personal rights and privileges guaranteed to citizens of this new sovereignty were intended to embrace those only who were then members of the several state communities or who should afterward by birthright or otherwise become members, according to the provisions of the Constitution and the principles on which it was founded. It was the union of those who were at that time members of distinct and separate political communities into one political family, whose power, for certain specified purposes, was to extend over the whole territory of the United States. And it gave to each citizen rights and privileges outside of his state which he did not before posesss and placed him

become free by his residence in Illinois or in the Territory of Wisconsin or both; and, second, that, being free and having been born in the United States, he was a citizen.

A majority of the Supreme Court decided against him on both points and in doing so found it proper to hold the Missouri Compromise of 1820 unconstitutional. It is upon this point that much of the philosophical and historical interest of the case depends. It is important to note that, in finding the compromise unconstitutional, the United States Supreme Court for the first time invalidated an enactment because of its inconsistency with a due-process clause.

in every other state upon a perfect equality with its own citizens as to rights of person and rights of property; it made him a citizen of the United States.

It becomes necessary, therefore, to determine who were citizens of the several states when the Constitution was adopted. And, in order to do this, we must recur to the governments and institutions of the thirteen colonies when they separated from Great Britain and formed new sovereignties and took their places in the family of independent nations. We must inquire who, at that time, were recognized as the people or citizens of a state, whose rights and liberties had been outraged by the English government; and who declared their independence and assumed the powers of government to defend their rights by force of arms.

In the opinion of the Court the legislation and histories of the times, and the language used in the Declaration of Independence, show that neither the class of persons who had been imported as slaves nor their descendants, whether they had become free or not, were then acknowledged as a part of the people nor intended to be included in the general words used in that memorable instrument.

It is difficult at this day to realize the state of public opinion in relation to that unfortunate race which prevailed in the civilized and enlightened portions of the world at the time of the Declaration of Independence and when the Constitution of the United States was framed and adopted. But the public history of every European nation displays it in a manner too plain to be mistaken.

They had for more than a century before been regarded as beings of an inferior order and altogether unfit to associate with the white race, either in social or political relations; and so far inferior that they had no rights which the white man was bound to respect; and that the Negro might justly and lawfully be reduced to slavery for his benefit. He was bought and sold and treated as an ordinary article of merchandise and traffic whenever a profit could be made by it. This opinion was at that time fixed and universal in the civilized portion of the white race. It was regarded as an axiom in morals as well as in politics, which no one thought of disputing, or supposed to be open to dispute; and men in every grade and position in society daily and habitually acted upon it in their private pursuits, as well as in matters of public concern, without doubting for a moment the correctness of this opinion.

And in no nation was this opinion more firmly fixed or more uniformly acted upon than by the English government and English people. They not only seized them on the coast of Africa and sold them or held them in slavery for their own use but they took them as ordinary articles of merchandise to every country where they could make a profit on them and were far more extensively engaged in this commerce than any other nation in the world.

The opinion thus entertained and acted upon in England was naturally impressed upon the colonies they founded on this side of the Atlantic. And, accordingly, a Negro of the African race was regarded by them as an article of property and held and bought and sold as such in every one of the thirteen colonies which united in the Declaration of Independence and afterward formed the Constitution of the United States. The slaves were more or less numerous in the different colonies, as slave labor was found more or less profitable. But no one seems to have doubted the correctness of the prevailing opinion of the time.

The legislation of the different colonies furnishes positive and indisputable proof of this fact....

The language of the Declaration of Independence is equally conclusive:

It begins by declaring that "when, in the course of human events, it becomes necessary for one people to dissolve the political bands which have connected them with another, and to assume, among the powers of the earth the separate and equal station to which the laws of nature and nature's God entitle them, a decent respect for the opinions of mankind requires that they should declare the causes which impel them to the separation."

It then proceeds to say: "We hold these truths to be self-evident: that all men are created equal; that they are endowed by their Creator with certain inalienable rights; that among these are life, liberty, and the pursuit of happiness; that to secure these rights, governments are instituted, deriving their just powers from the consent of the governed."

The general words above quoted would seem to embrace the whole human family, and if they were used in a similar instrument at this day would be so understood. But it is too clear for dispute that the enslaved African race were not intended to be included and formed no part of the people who framed and adopted this declaration; for if the language, as understood in that day, would embrace them, the conduct of the distinguished men who framed the Declaration of Independence would have been utterly and flagrantly inconsistent with the principles they asserted; and instead of the sympathy of mankind, to which they so confidently appealed, they would have deserved and received universal rebuke and reprobation.

Yet the men who framed this declaration were great men—high in literary acquirements—high in their sense of honor, and incapable of asserting principles inconsistent with those on which they were acting. They perfectly understood the meaning of the language they used and how it would be understood by others; and they knew that it would not in any part of the civilized world be supposed to embrace the Negro race, which, by common consent, had been excluded from civilized governments and the family of nations and doomed to slavery. They spoke and acted according to the then established doctrines and principles and in the ordinary language of the day, and no one misunderstood them. The unhappy black race were separated from the white by indelible marks, and laws long before established, and were never thought of or spoken of except as property and when the claims of the owner or the profit of the trader were supposed to need protection.

This state of public opinion had undergone no change when the Constitution was adopted, as is equally evident from its provisions and language.

The brief preamble sets forth by whom it was formed, for what purposes, and for whose benefit and protection. It declares that it is formed by the *people* of the United States; that is to say, by those who were members of the different political communities in the several states; and its great object is declared to be to secure the blessings of liberty to themselves and their posterity. It speaks in general terms of the *people* of the United States, and of *citizens* of the several states, when it is providing for the exercise of the powers granted or the privileges secured to the citizen. It does not define what description of persons are intended to be included under these terms, or who shall be regarded as a citizen and one of the people. It uses them as terms so well understood that no further description or definition was necessary.

But there are two clauses in the Constitution which point directly and specifically to the Negro race as a separate class of persons and show clearly that they were not regarded as a portion of the people or citizens of the government then formed.

One of these clauses reserves to each of the thirteen states the right to import slaves until the year 1808, if it thinks proper. And the importation which it thus sanctions was unquestionably of persons of the race of which we are speaking, as the traffic in slaves in the United States had always been confined to them. And by the other provision the states pledge themselves to each other to maintain the right of property of the master by delivering up to him any slave who may have escaped from his service and be found within their respective territories. . . .

And we may here again refer, in support of this proposition, to the plain and unequivocal language of the laws of the several states, some passed after the Declaration of Independence and before the Constitution was adopted, and some since the government went into operation.

We need not refer, on this point, particularly to the laws of the present slaveholding states. . . .

No one, we presume, supposes that any change in public opinion or feeling, in relation to this unfortunate race, in the civilized nations of Europe or in this country should induce the Court to give to the words of the Constitution a more liberal construction in their favor than they were intended to bear when the instrument was framed and adopted. Such an argument would be altogether inadmissible in any tribunal called on to interpret it. If any of its provisions are deemed unjust, there is a mode prescribed in the instrument itself by which it may be amended; but, while it remains unaltered, it must be construed now as it was understood at the time of its adoption. It is not only the same in words but the same in meaning and delegates the same powers to the government and reserves and secures the same rights and privileges to the citizen; and, as long as it continues to exist in its present form, it speaks not only in the same words but with the same meaning and intent with which it spoke when it came from the hands of its framers and was voted on and adopted by the people of the United States. Any other rule of construction would abrogate the judicial character of this Court and make it the mere reflex of the popular opinion or passion of the day. This Court was not created by the Constitution for such purposes. Higher and graver trusts have been confided to it, and it must not falter in the path of duty.

What the construction was at that time, we think, can hardly admit of doubt. We have the language of the Declaration of Independence and of the Articles of Confederation, in addition to the plain words of the Constitution itself; we have the legislation of the different states before, about the time, and since the Constitution was adopted; we have the legislation of Congress, from the time of its adoption to a recent period; and we have the constant and uniform action of the Executive department, all concurring together and leading to the same result. And, if anything in rela-

tion to the construction of the Constitution can be regarded as settled, it is that which we now give to the word "citizen" and the word "people."

And upon a full and careful consideration of the subject, the Court is of opinion that, upon the facts stated in the plea in abatement, Dred Scott was not a citizen of Missouri within the meaning of the Constitution of the United States and not entitled as such to sue in its courts; and, consequently, that the circuit court had no jurisdiction of the case and that the judgment on the plea in abatement is erroneous. . . .

We proceed . . . to inquire whether the facts relied on by the plaintiff entitled him to his freedom. . . .

The act of Congress, upon which the plaintiff relies, declares that slavery and involuntary servitude, except as a punishment for crime, shall be forever prohibited in all that part of the territory ceded by France, under the name of Louisiana, which lies north of thirty-six degrees thirty minutes north latitude and not included within the limits of Missouri. And the difficulty which meets us at the threshold of this part of the inquiry is whether Congress was authorized to pass this law under any of the powers granted to it by the Constitution; for, if the authority is not given by that instrument, it is the duty of this Court to declare it void and inoperative and incapable of conferring freedom upon anyone who is held as a slave under the laws of any one of the states.

The counsel for the plaintiff has laid much stress upon that article in the Constitution which confers on Congress the power "to dispose of and make all needful rules and regulations respecting the territory or other property belonging to the United States"; but, in the judgment of the Court, that provision has no bearing on the present controversy, and the power there given, whatever it may be, is confined, and was intended to be confined, to the territory which at that time belonged to, or was claimed by, the United States and was within their boundaries as settled by the treaty with Great Britain and can have no influence upon a territory afterward acquired from a foreign government. It was a special provision for a known and particular territory, and to meet a present emergency, and nothing more.

A brief summary of the history of the times, as well as the careful and measured terms in which the article is framed, will show the correctness of this proposition. . . .

We do not mean, however, to question the power of Congress in this respect. The power to expand the territory of the United States by the admission of new states is plainly given; and in the construction of this power by all the departments of the government, it has been held to authorize the acquisition of territory, not fit for admission at the time, but to be admitted as soon as its population and situation would entitle it to admission. It is acquired to become a state and not to be held as a colony and governed by Congress with absolute authority; and, as the propriety of admitting a new state is committed to the sound discretion of Congress, the power to acquire territory for that purpose, to be held by the United States until it is in a suitable condition to become a state upon an equal footing with the other states, must rest upon the same discretion. It is a question for the political department of the government, and not the judicial; and whatever the political department of the government shall recognize as within the limits of the United States, the judicial department is also bound to recognize, and to administer in it the laws of the United States, so far as they apply, and to maintain in the territory the authority and rights of the government, and also the personal rights and rights of property of individual citizens, as secured by the Constitution. All we mean to say on this point is

that, as there is no express regulation in the Constitution defining the power which the general government may exercise over the person or property of a citizen in a territory thus acquired, the Court must necessarily look to the provisions and principles of the Constitution, and its distribution of powers, for the rules and principles by which its decision must be governed.

Taking this rule to guide us, it may be safely assumed that citizens of the United States who migrate to a territory belonging to the people of the United States cannot be ruled as mere colonists, dependent upon the will of the general government, and to be governed by any laws it may think proper to impose. The principle upon which our governments rest, and upon which alone they continue to exist, is the union of states, sovereign and independent within their own limits in their internal and domestic concerns, and bound together as one people by a general government, possessing certain enumerated and restricted powers, delegated to it by the people of the several states, and exercising supreme authority within the scope of the powers granted to it, throughout the dominion of the United States. A power, therefore, in the general government to obtain and hold colonies and dependent territories, over which they might legislate without restriction, would be inconsistent with its own existence in its present form. Whatever it acquires, it acquires for the benefit of the people of the several states who created it. It is their trustee acting for them and charged with the duty of promoting the interests of the whole people of the Union in the exercise of the powers specifically granted. . . .

But the power of Congress over the person or property of a citizen can never be a mere discretionary power under our Constitution and form of government. The powers of the government and the rights and privileges of the citizen are regulated and plainly defined by the Constitution itself. And, when the territory becomes a part of the United States, the federal government enters into possession in the character impressed upon it by those who created it. It enters upon it with its powers over the citizen strictly defined and limited by the Constitution, from which it derives its own existence, and by virtue of which alone it continues to exist and act as a government and sovereignty. It has no power of any kind beyond it; and it cannot, when it enters a territory of the United States, put off its character and assume discretionary or despotic powers which the Constitution has denied to it. It cannot create for itself a new character separated from the citizens of the United States and the duties it owes them under the provisions of the Constitution. The territory, being a part of the United States, the government and the citizen both enter it under the authority of the Constitution, with their respective rights defined and marked out; and the federal government can exercise no power over his person or property, beyond what that instrument confers, nor lawfully deny any right which it has reserved.

A reference to a few of the provisions of the Constitution will illustrate this proposition.

For example, no one, we presume, will contend that Congress can make any law in a territory respecting the establishment of religion, or the free exercise thereof, or abridging the freedom of speech or of the press, or the right of the people of the territory peaceably to assemble, and to petition the government for the redress of grievances.

Nor can Congress deny to the people the right to keep and bear arms, nor the right to trial by jury, nor compel anyone to be a witness against himself in a criminal proceeding.

These powers, and others, in relation to rights of person, which it is not nec-essary here to enumerate, are, in express and positive terms, denied to the general government; and the rights of private property have been guarded with equal care. Thus the rights of property are united with the rights of person and placed on the same ground by the Fifth Amendment to the Constitution, which provides that no person shall be deprived of life, liberty, and property without due process of law. And an act of Congress which deprives a citizen of the United States of his liberty or property, without due process of law, merely because he came himself or brought his property into a particular territory of the United States, and who had committed no offense against the laws, could hardly be dignified with the name of due process of law.

So, too, it will hardly be contended that Congress could by law quarter a soldier in a house in a territory without the consent of the owner, in time of peace; nor in time of war, but in a manner prescribed by law. Nor could they by law forfeit the property of a citizen in a territory who was convicted of treason, for a longer period than the life of the person convicted; nor take private property for public use without just compensation.

The powers over person and property of which we speak are not only not granted to Congress but are in express terms denied, and they are forbidden to exercise them. And this prohibition is not confined to the states, but the words are general and extend to the whole territory over which the Constitution gives it power to legislate, including those portions of it remaining under territorial government as well as that covered by states. It is a total absence of power everywhere within the dominion of the United States and places the citizens of a territory, so far as these rights are concerned, on the same footing with citizens of the states and guards them as firmly and plainly against any inroads which the general government might attempt under the plea of implied or incidental powers. And if Congress itself cannot do this—if it is beyond the powers conferred on the federal government—it will be admitted, we presume, that it could not authorize a territorial government to exercise them. It could confer no power on any local government, established by its authority, to violate the provisions of the Constitution.

It seems, however, to be supposed that there is a difference between property in a slave and other property and that different rules may be applied to it in expounding the Constitution of the United States. And the laws and usages of nations, and the writings of eminent jurists upon the relation of master and slave and their mutual rights and duties, and the powers which governments may exercise over it, have been dwelt upon in the argument.

But, in considering the question before us, it must be borne in mind that there is no law of nations standing between the people of the United States and their government and interfering with their relation to each other. The powers of the government and the rights of the citizen under it are positive and practical regulations plainly written down. The people of the United States have delegated to it certain enumerated powers and forbidden it to exercise others. It has no power over the person or property of a citizen but what the citizens of the United States have granted. And no laws or usages of other nations, or reasoning of statesmen or jurists upon the relations of master and slave, can enlarge the powers of the government or take from the citizens the rights they have reserved. And if the Constitution recognizes the right of property of the master in a slave, and makes no distinction between that description of property and other property owned by a citizen, no tribunal, acting under the authority of the United States, whether it be legislative, executive, or judicial, has a right to draw such a distinction or deny to it the benefit of the provisions and guaranties which have been provided for the protection of private property against the encroachments of the government.

Now, as we have already said in an earlier part of this opinion, upon a different point, the right of property in a slave is distinctly and expressly affirmed in the Constitution. The right to traffic in it, like an ordinary article of merchandise and property, was guaranteed to the citizens of the United States, in every state that might desire it, for twenty years. And the government in express terms is pledged to protect it in all future time if the slave escapes from his owner. This is done in plain words—too plain to be misunderstood. And no word can be found in the Constitution which gives Congress a greater power over slave property or which entitles property of that kind to less protection than property of any other description. The only power conferred is the power coupled with the duty of guarding and protecting the owner in his rights.

Upon these considerations it is the opinion of the Court that the act of Congress which prohibited a citizen from holding and owning property of this kind in the territory of the United States north of the line therein mentioned is not warranted by the Constitution and is therefore void; and that neither Dred Scott himself, nor any of his family, were made free by being carried into this territory; even if they had been carried there by the owner with the intention of becoming a permanent resident.

We have so far examined the case as it stands under the Constitution of the United States and the powers thereby delegated to the federal government.

But there is another point in the case which depends on state power and state law. And it is contended, on the part of the plaintiff, that he is made free by being taken to Rock Island, in the state of Illinois, independently of his residence in the territory of the United States; and, being so made free, he was not again reduced to a state of slavery by being brought back to Missouri.

Our notice of this part of the case will be very brief, for the principle on which it depends was decided in this court, upon much consideration, in the case of *Strader et al.* v. *Graham*, reported in 10th Howard, 82. In that case the slaves had been taken from Kentucky to Ohio, with the consent of the owner, and afterward brought back to Kentucky.

And this Court held that their *status* or condition, as free or slave, depended upon the laws of Kentucky, when they were brought back into that state, and not of Ohio; and that this Court had no jurisdiction to revise the judgment of a state court upon its own laws. This was the point directly before the Court, and the decision that this Court had not jurisdiction turned upon it, as will be seen by the report of the case.

So in this case. As Scott was a slave when taken into the state of Illinois by his owner, and was there held as such, and brought back in that character, his *status*, as free or slave, depended on the laws of Missouri and not of Illinois. . . .

4. SPRINGFIELD SPEECH, JUNE 26, 1857[1]

By ABRAHAM LINCOLN

EDITORS' NOTE.—The Dred Scott decision, handed down on March 6, 1857, aimed a hard blow at the efforts of Lincoln and the new Republican party to contain slavery within its existing limits. Three months later Lincoln and his fellow-Republicans of Springfield made an opportunity to answer the court and Stephen A. Douglas, whose position seemed enhanced by the Taney decision. In this speech Lincoln's logic is as important for the statements he makes on the sanctity of judicial decisions as it is upon the issues of slavery expansion. However, in the famous Lincoln-Douglas debates the slavery question received full and almost undivided attention.

. . . And now as to the Dred Scott decision. That decision declares two propositions—first, that a Negro cannot sue in the United States courts and, secondly, that Congress cannot prohibit slavery in the territories. It was made by a divided court—dividing differently on the different points. Judge Douglas does not discuss the merits of the decision, and in that respect I shall follow his example, believing I could no more improve on McLean and Curtis than he could on Taney.

He denounces all who question the correctness of that decision as offering violent resistance to it. But who resists it? Who has, in spite of the decision, declared Dred Scott free and resisted the authority of his master over him?

Judicial decisions have two uses—first, to absolutely determine the case decided; and, secondly, to indicate to the public how other similar cases will be decided when they arise. For the latter use, they are called "precedents" and "authorities."

1. Abraham Lincoln, *Complete Works* . . . , ed. John J. Nicolay and John Hay (New York, 1905), II, 319-39.

727

We believe as much as Judge Douglas (perhaps more) in obedience to, and respect for, the judicial department of government. We think its decisions on constitutional questions, when fully settled, should control not only the particular cases decided but the general policy of the country, subject to be disturbed only by amendments of the Constitution as provided in that instrument itself. More than this would be revolution. But we think the Dred Scott decision is erroneous. We know the court that made it has often overruled its own decisions, and we shall do what we can to have it to overrule this. We offer no resistance to it.

Judicial decisions are of greater or less authority as precedents according to circumstances. That this should be so accords both with common sense and the customary understanding of the legal profession.

If this important decision had been made by the unanimous concurrence of the judges, and without any apparent partisan bias, and in accordance with legal public expectation and with the steady practice of the departments throughout our history, and had been in no part based on assumed historical facts which are not really true; or, if wanting in some of these, it had been before the court more than once, and had there been affirmed and reaffirmed through a course of years, it then might be, perhaps would be, factious, nay, even revolutionary, not to acquiesce in it as a precedent.

But when, as is true, we find it wanting in all these claims to the public confidence, it is not resistance, it is not factious, it is not even disrespectful, to treat it as not having yet quite established a settled doctrine for the country. But Judge Douglas considers this view awful. Hear him:

The courts are the tribunals prescribed by the Constitution and created by the authority of the people to determine, expound, and enforce the law. Hence, whoever resists the final decision of the highest judicial tribunal aims a deadly blow at our whole republican system of government—a blow which, if successful, would place all our rights and liberties at the mercy of passion, anarchy, and violence. I repeat, therefore, that if resistance to the decisions of the Supreme Court of the United States, in a matter like the points decided in the Dred Scott case, clearly within their jurisdiction as defined by the Constitution, shall be forced upon the country as a political issue, it will become a distinct and naked issue between the friends and enemies of the Constitution—the friends and the enemies of the supremacy of the laws.

Why, this same Supreme Court once decided a national bank to be constitutional; but General Jackson, as President of the United States, disregarded the decision and vetoed a bill for a recharter, partly on constitutional ground, declaring that each public functionary must support the Constitution "as he understands it." But hear the general's own words. Here they are, taken from his veto message:

It is maintained by the advocates of the bank that its constitutionality, in all its features, ought to be considered as settled by precedent and by the decision of the Supreme Court. To this conclusion I cannot assent. Mere precedent is a dangerous source of authority and should not be regarded as deciding questions of constitutional power, except where the acquiescence of the people and the states can be considered as well settled. So far from this being the case on this subject, an argument against the bank might be based on precedent. One Congress, in 1791, decided in favor of a bank; another, in 1811, decided against it. One Congress, in 1815, decided against a bank; another, in 1816, decided in its favor. Prior to the present Congress, therefore, the precedents drawn from that source were equal. If we resort to the states, the expressions of legislative, judicial, and executive opinions against the bank have been probably to those in its favor as four to one. There is nothing in precedent, therefore, which, if its authority were admitted, ought to weigh in favor of the act before me.

I drop the quotations merely to remark that all there ever was in the way of precedent up to the Dred Scott decision, on the points therein decided, had been against that decision. But hear General Jackson further:

If the opinion of the Supreme Court covered the whole ground of this act, it ought not to control the co-ordinate aurhorities of this government. The Congress, the executive, and the court must, each for itself, be guided by its own opinion of the Constitution. Each public officer who takes an oath to support the Constitution swears that he will support it as he understands it and not as it is understood by others.

Again and again have I heard Judge Douglas denounce that bank decision and applaud General Jackson for disregarding it. It would be interesting for him to look over his recent speech and see how exactly his fierce philippics against us for resisting Supreme Court decisions fall upon his own head. It will call to mind a long and fierce political war in this country, upon an issue which, in his own language, and, of course, in his own changeless estimation, was "a distinct issue between the friends and the enemies of the Constitution," and in which war he fought in the ranks of the enemies of the Constitution.

I have said, in substance, that the Dred Scott decision was in part based on assumed historical facts which were not really true, and I ought not to leave the subject without giving some reasons for saying this; I therefore give an instance or two which I think fully sustain me. Chief Justice Taney, in delivering the opinion of the majority of the court, insists at great length that Negroes were no part of the people who made, or for whom was made, the Declaration of Independence or the Constitution of the United States.

On the contrary, Judge Curtis, in his dissenting opinion, shows that in five of the then thirteen states—to wit, New Hampshire, Massachusetts, New York, New Jersey, and North Carolina—free Negroes were voters and in proportion to their numbers had the same part in making the Constitution that the white people had. He shows this with so much particularity as to leave no doubt of its truth; and as a sort of conclusion on that point holds the following language:

The Constitution was ordained and established by the people of the United States, through the action, in each state, of those persons who were qualified by its laws to act thereon in behalf of themselves and all other citizens of the state. In some of the states, as we have seen, colored persons were among those qualified by law to act on the subject. These colored persons were not only included in the body of "the people of the United States" by whom the Constitution was ordained and established; but in at least five of the states they had the power to act, and doubtless did act, by their suffrages, upon the question of its adoption.

Again, Chief Justice Taney says:

It is difficult at this day to realize the state of public opinion in relation to that unfortunate race which prevailed in the civilized and enlightened portions of the world at the time of the Declaration of Independence and when the Constitution of the United States was framed and adopted.

And again, after quoting from the Declaration, he says:

The general words above quoted would seem to embrace the whole human family, and if they were used in a similar instrument at this day would be so understood.

In these the Chief Justice does not directly assert but plainly assumes as a fact that the public estimate of the black man is more favorable now than it was in the days of the Revolution. This assumption is a mistake. In some trifling particulars the condition of that race has been ameliorated; but as a whole, in this country, the change between then and now is decidedly the other way; and their ultimate destiny has never appeared so hopeless as in the last three or four years. In two of the five states—New Jersey and North Carolina—that then gave the free Negro the right of voting, the right has since been taken away, and in a third—New York—it has been greatly abridged; while it has not been extended, so far as I know, to a single additional state, though the number of the states has more than doubled. In those days, as I understand, masters could, at their own pleasure, emancipate their slaves; but since then such legal restraints have been made upon emancipation as to amount almost to prohibition. In those days legislatures held the unquestioned power to abolish slavery in their respective states, but now it is becoming quite fashionable for state constitutions to withhold that power from the legislatures. In those days, by common consent, the spread of the black man's bondage to the new countries was prohibited, but now Congress decides that it will not continue the prohibition, and the Supreme Court decides that it could not if it would. In those days our Declaration of Independence was held sacred by all and thought to include all; but now, to aid in making the bondage of the Negro universal and eternal, it is assailed and sneered at and construed, and hawked at and torn, till, if its framers could rise from their graves, they could not at all recognize it. All the powers of earth seem rapidly combining against him. Mammon is after him, ambition follows, philosophy follows, and the theology of the day is fast joining the cry. They have him in his prison-house; they have searched his person and left no prying instrument with him. One after another they have closed the heavy iron doors upon him; and now they have him, as it were, bolted in with a lock of a hundred keys, which can never be unlocked without the concurrence of every key—the keys in the hands of a hundred different men, and they scattered to a hundred different and distant places; and they stand musing as to what invention, in all the dominions of mind and matter, can be produced to make the impossibility of his escape more complete than it is.

It is grossly incorrect to say or assume that the public estimate of the Negro is more favorable now than it was at the origin of the government.

Three years and a half ago Judge Douglas brought forward his famous Nebraska bill. The country was at once in a blaze. He scorned all opposition and carried it through Congress. Since then he has seen himself superseded in a presidential nomination by one indorsing the general doctrine of his measure but at the same time standing clear of the odium of its untimely agitation and its gross breach of national faith; and he has seen that successful rival constitutionally elected, not by the strength of friends, but by the division of adversaries, being in a popular minority of nearly four hundred thousand votes. He has seen his chief aids in his own state, Shields and Richardson, politically speaking, successively tried, convicted, and executed for an offense not their own, but his. And now he sees his own case standing next on the docket for trial.

There is a natural disgust in the minds of nearly all white people at the idea of an indiscriminate amalgamation of the white and black races; and Judge Douglas evidently is basing his chief hope upon the chances of his being able to appropriate the benefit of this disgust to himself. If he can, by much drumming and repeating, fasten the odium of that idea upon his adversaries, he thinks he can struggle through the storm. He therefore clings to this hope, as a drowning man to the last plank. He makes an occasion for lugging it in from the opposition of the Dred Scott decision. He finds the Republicans insisting that the Declaration of Independence includes *all* men, black as well as white, and forthwith he boldly denies that it includes Negroes at all, and proceeds to argue gravely that all who contend it does do so only because they want to vote, and eat, and sleep, and marry with Negroes! He will have it that they cannot be consistent else. Now I protest against the counterfeit logic which concludes that, because I do not want a black woman for a slave, I must necessarily want her for a wife. I need not have her for either. I can just leave her alone. In some respects she certainly is not my equal; but in her natural right to eat the bread she earns with her own hands without asking leave of anyone else, she is my equal and the equal of all others.

Chief Justice Taney, in his opinion in the Dred Scott case, admits that the language of the Declaration is broad enough to include the whole human family, but he and Judge Douglas argue that the authors of that instrument did not intend to include Negroes by the fact that they did not at once actually place them on an equality with the whites. Now this grave argument comes to just nothing at all, by the other fact that they did not at once, or ever afterward, actually place all white people on an equality with one another. And this is the staple argument of both the chief justice and the senator for doing this obvious violence to the plain, unmistakable language of the Declaration.

I think the authors of that notable instrument intended to include *all* men, but they did not intend to declare all men equal *in all respects*. They did not mean to say all were equal in color, size, intellect, moral developments, or social capacity. They defined with tolerable distinctness in what respects they did consider all men created equal—equal with "certain inalienable rights, among which are life, liberty, and the pursuit of happiness." This they said, and this they meant. They did not mean to assert the obvious untruth that all were then actually enjoying that equality, nor yet that they were about to confer it immediately upon them. In fact, they had no power to confer such a boon. They meant simply to declare the right, so that enforcement of it might follow as fast as circumstances should permit.

They meant to set up a standard maxim for free society which should be familiar to all and revered by all; constantly looked to, constantly labored for, and even though never perfectly attained, constantly approximated, and thereby constantly spreading and deepening its influence and augmenting the happiness and value of life to all people of all colors everywhere. The assertion that "all men are created equal" was of no practical use in effecting our separation from Great Britain; and it was placed in the Declaration not for that but for future use. Its authors meant it to be—as, thank God, it is now proving itself—a stumbling block to all those who in after times might seek to turn a free people back into the hateful paths of despotism. They knew the proneness of prosperity to breed tyrants, and they meant, when such should reappear in this fair land and commence their vocation, they should find left for them at least one hard nut to crack.

I have now briefly expressed my view of the meaning and object of that part of the Declaration of Independence which declares that "all men are created equal."

Now let us hear Judge Douglas' view of the same subject, as I find it in the printed report of his late speech. Here it is:

No man can vindicate the character, motives, and conduct of the signers of the Declaration of Independence except upon the hypothesis that they referred to the white race alone, and not to the African, when they declared all men to have been created equal; that they were speaking of British subjects on this continent being equal to British subjects born and residing in Great

Britain; that they were entitled to the same inalienable rights, and among them were enumerated life, liberty, and the pursuit of happiness. The Declaration was adopted for the purpose of justifying the colonists in the eyes of the civilized world in withdrawing their allegiance from the British crown and dissolving their connection with the mother-country.

My good friends, read that carefully over some leisure hour and ponder well upon it; see what a mere wreck—mangled ruin—it makes of our once glorious Declaration.

"They were speaking of British subjects on this continent being equal to British subjects born and residing in Great Britain"! Why, according to this, not only Negroes but white people outside of Great Britain and America were not spoken of in that instrument. The English, Irish, and Scotch, along with white Americans, were included, to be sure, but the French, Germans, and other white people of the world are all gone to pot along with the judge's inferior races!

I had thought the Declaration promised something better than the condition of British subjects; but no, it only meant that we should be equal to them in their own oppressed and unequal condition. According to that, it gave no promise that, having kicked off the king and lords of Great Britain, we should not at once be saddled with a king and lords of our own.

I had thought the Declaration contemplated the progressive improvement in the condition of all men everywhere; but no, it merely "was adopted for the purpose of justifying the colonists in the eyes of the civilized world in withdrawing their allegiance from the British crown and dissolving their connection with the mother-country." Why, that object having been effected some eighty years ago, the Declaration is of no practical use now—mere rubbish—old wadding left to rot on the battlefield after the victory is won.

I understand you are preparing to celebrate the "Fourth," tomorrow week. What for? The doings of that day had no reference to the present; and quite half of you are not even descendants of those who were referred to at that day. But I suppose you will celebrate and will even go as far as to read the Declaration. Suppose, after you read it once in the old-fashioned way, you read it once more with Judge Douglas' version. It will then run thus: "We hold these truths to be self-evident: that all British subjects who were on this continent eighty-one years ago were created equal to all British subjects born and then residing in Great Britain."

And now I appeal to all—to Democrats as well as others—are you really willing that the Declaration shall thus be frittered away?—thus left no more, at most, than an interesting memorial of the dead past?—thus shorn of its vitality and practical value and left without the germ or even the suggestion of the individual rights of man in it?

But Judge Douglas is especially horrified at the thought of the mixing of blood by the white and black races. Agreed for once—a thousand times agreed. There are white men enough to marry all the white women, and black men enough to marry all the black women; and so let them be married. On this point we fully agree with the judge, and when he shall show that his policy is better adapted to prevent amalgamation than ours, we shall drop ours and adopt his. Let us see. In 1850 there were in the United States 405,751 mulattoes. Very few of these are the offspring of whites and free blacks; nearly all have sprung from black slaves and white masters. A separation of the races is the only perfect preventive of amalgamation; but, as an immediate separation is impossible, the next best thing is to keep them apart where they are not already together. If white and black people never get together in Kansas, they will never mix blood in Kansas. That is at least one self-evident truth. A few free colored persons may get into the free states, in any event; but their number is too insignificant to amount to much in the way of mixing blood. In 1850 there were in the free states 56,649 mulattoes; but for the most part they were not born there—they came from the slave states, ready made up. In the same year the slave states had 348,874 mulattoes, all of home production. The proportion of free mulattoes to free blacks—the only colored classes in the free states—is much greater in the slave than in the free states. It is worthy of note, too, that among the free states those which make the colored man the nearest equal to the white have proportionably the fewest mulattoes, the least of amalgamation. In New Hampshire, the state which goes farthest toward equality between the races, there are just 184 mulattoes, while there are in Virginia—how many do you think?—79,775, being 23,126 more than in all the free states together.

These statistics show that slavery is the greatest source of amalgamation, and next to it, not the elevation, but the degradation of the free blacks. Yet Judge Douglas dreads the slightest restraints on the spread of slavery, and the slightest human recognition of the Negro, as tending horribly to amalgamation.

The very Dred Scott case affords a strong test as to which party most favors amalgamation, the Republicans or the dear Union-saving Democracy. Dred Scott, his wife, and two daughters were all involved in the suit. We desired the court to have held that they were citizens so far at least as to entitle them to a hearing as to whether they were free or not; and then, also, that they were in fact and in law really free. Could we have had our way, the chances of these black girls ever mixing their blood with that of white people would have been diminished at least to the extent that it could not have been without their consent. But Judge Douglas is delighted to have them decided to be slaves and not human enough to have a hearing, even if they were free, and thus left subject to the forced concubinage of their masters and liable to become the mothers of mulattoes in spite of themselves: the very state of case that produces nine-tenths of all the mulattoes—all the mixing of blood in the nation.

Of course, I state this case as an illustration only, not meaning to say or intimate that the master of Dred Scott and his family, or any more than a percentage of masters generally, are inclined to exercise this particular power which they hold over their female slaves.

I have said that the separation of the races is the only perfect preventive of amalgamation. I have no right to say all the members of the Republican party are in favor of this, nor to say that as a party they are in favor of it. There is nothing in their platform directly on the subject. But I can say a very large proportion of its members are for it and that the chief plank in their platform—opposition to the spread of slavery—is most favorable to that separation.

Such separation, if ever effected at all, must be effected by colonization; and no political party, as such, is now doing anything directly for colonization. Party operations at present only favor or retard colonization incidentally. The enterprise is a difficult one; but "where there is a will there is a way," and what colonization needs most is a hearty will. Will springs from the two elements of moral sense and self-interest. Let us be brought to believe it is morally right, and at the same time favorable to, or at least not against, our interest to transfer the African to his native clime, and we shall find a way to do it, however great the task may be. The children of Israel, to such numbers as to include four hundred thousand fighting men, went out of Egyptian bondage in a body.

How differently the respective courses of the Democratic and Republican parties incidentally bear on the question of forming a will—a public sentiment—for colonization, is easy to see. The Republicans inculcate, with whatever of ability they can, that the Negro is a man, that his bondage is cruelly wrong, and that the field of his oppression ought not to be enlarged. The Democrats deny his manhood; deny, or dwarf to insignificance, the wrong of his bondage; so far as possible, crush all sympathy for him, and cultivate and excite hatred and disgust against him; compliment themselves as Union-savers for doing so; and call the indefinite outspreading of his bondage "a sacred right of self-government."

The plainest print cannot be read through a gold eagle; and it will be ever hard to find many men who will send a slave to Liberia, and pay his passage, while they can send him to a new country—Kansas, for instance—and sell him for fifteen hundred dollars, and the rise.

5. THE LINCOLN-DOUGLAS DEBATES, 1858[1]

EDITORS' NOTE.—For most of the decade preceding these famous debates the outstanding political figure of Illinois was Stephen Arnold Douglas (1813–61). Born in Vermont and reared there and in western New York State, Douglas went West to seek his fortune. Working with the "organization," he rose rapidly in the Democratic party. After three consecutive terms in Congress, he was in 1847 elected to the United States Senate, where he was immediately made chairman of the Committee on Territories. His marriage to a North Carolina heiress strengthened his party ties with the South. He had a very important part in making the Compromise of 1850, and he played a leading role in the passage of the Kansas-Nebraska Act of 1854. His interest in the latter act may have been influenced by his residence in Chicago and his connections with proposed western railroads. From that time Douglas was publicly and irrevocably committed to the principle of "popular sovereignty" in opposition to more extreme positions on the question of the extension of slavery into the territories. After having loyally supported Buchanan's election, Douglas broke with the new President over the attempt of the administration in 1857–58 to bring Kansas into the Union as a slave state. The Illinois members of the Republican party, which had been founded in 1854, nominated Lincoln for the Senate in 1858 as the successor to Douglas.

The campaign opened with Lincoln's acceptance of his nomination in the famous "house divided" speech at Springfield. Douglas began his campaign at Chicago and started on a tour of the state; Lincoln "trailed" him, usually speaking in each town on the same day or on the day following Douglas' appearance. A joint debate

1. *Political Debates between Hon. Abraham Lincoln and Hon. Stephen A. Douglas . . .* (Columbus, Ohio, 1860), pp. 1, 10–12, 89–90, 95–97, 215–17, 220–23, 229–30, 232–35, 238–39. Published as a campaign document by the Ohio Republican State Central Committee, the text is considered reasonably authentic, although Douglas complained that Lincoln had had an opportunity to revise his remarks while he (Douglas) had not. Actually the few changes are of a minor character.

seemed logical; it was requested by Lincoln and accepted by Douglas. Under the terms set by the latter the two contestants were to debate in one town in each of the seven congressional districts in which they had not yet spoken (thus omitting Chicago and Springfield). Except for Freeport in the north and Jonesboro in "Egypt" (the extreme southern part of Illinois), the debates were in the middle section of the state where party strength was most evenly divided and in which the victory would most likely be decided.

The election resulted in the narrow victory of the Republican state ticket, but a majority of the legislators elected were pledged to Douglas, who was duly re-elected on January 6, 1859, by a vote of 54 to 46. Although Lincoln lost the senatorship, he had become a figure of national importance. On the other hand, Douglas, by his enunciation of the "Freeport doctrine," had taken a position which, combined with southern intransigence, resulted in the split of the Democratic party in the campaign of 1860—and so probably contributed to Lincoln's election to the presidency in that year.

A. THE "HOUSE DIVIDED" SPEECH, SPRINGFIELD, JUNE 17, 1858

Mr. President and Gentlemen of the Convention:

If we could first know where we are, and whither we are tending, we could better judge what to do and how to do it. We are now far into the fifth year since a policy was initiated with the avowed object, and confident promise, of putting an end to slavery agitation. Under the operation of that policy, that agitation has not only not ceased but has constantly augmented. In my opinion, it will not cease until a crisis shall have been reached and passed. "A house divided against itself cannot stand." I believe this government cannot endure permanently half-slave and half-free. I do not expect the Union to be dissolved—I do not expect the house to fall—but I do expect it will cease to be divided. It will become all one thing or all the other. Either the opponents of slavery will arrest the further spread of it and place it where the public mind shall rest in the belief that it is in the course of ultimate extinction or its advocates will push it forward, till it shall become alike lawful in all the states, old as well as new—North as well as South.

B. DOUGLAS' ANSWER, CHICAGO, JULY 9, 1858

The framers of the Constitution well understood that each locality, having separate and distinct interests, required separate and distinct laws, domestic institutions, and police regulations adapted to its own wants and its own condition; and they acted on the presumption, also, that these laws and institutions would be as diversified and as dissimilar as the states would be numerous and that no two would be precisely alike, because the interests of no two would be precisely the same. Hence, I assert, that the great fundamental principle which underlies our complex system of state and federal governments, contemplated diversity and dissimilarity in the local institutions and domestic affairs of each and every state then in the Union or thereafter to be admitted into the Confederacy. I therefore conceive that my friend, Mr. Lincoln, has totally misapprehended the great principles upon which our government rests. Uniformity in local and domestic affairs would be destructive of state rights, of state sovereignty, of personal liberty and personal freedom. Uniformity is the parent of despotism the world over, not only in politics, but in religion. Wherever the doctrine of uniformity is proclaimed that all the states must be free or all slave, that all labor must be white or all black, that all the citizens of the different states must have the same privileges or be governed by the same regulations, you have destroyed the greatest safeguard which our institutions have thrown around the rights of the citizen.

How could this uniformity be accomplished, if it was desirable and possible? There is but one mode in which it could be obtained, and that must be by abolishing the state legislatures, blotting out state sovereignty, merging the rights and sovereignty of the states in one consolidated empire, and vesting Congress with the plenary power to make all the police regulations, domestic and local laws, uniform throughout the limits of the Republic. When you shall have done this, you will have uniformity. Then the states will all be slave or all be free; then Negroes will vote everywhere or nowhere; then you will have a Maine liquor law in every state or none; then you will have uniformity in all things, local and domestic, by the authority of the federal government. But, when you attain that uniformity, you will have converted these thirty-two sovereign, independent states into one consolidated empire, with the uniformity of disposition reigning triumphant throughout the length and breadth of the land.

From this view of the case, my friends, I am driven irresistibly to the conclusion that diversity, dissimilarity, variety in all our local and domestic institutions, is the great safeguard of our liberties and that the framers of our institutions were wise, sagacious, and pa-

triotic, when they made this government a confederation of sovereign states, with a legislature for each, and conferred upon each legislature the power to make all local and domestic institutions to suit the people it represented, without interference from any other state or from the general Congress of the Union. If we expect to maintain our liberties, we must preserve the rights and sovereignty of the states; we must maintain and carry out that great principle of self-government incorporated in the compromise measures of 1850; indorsed by the Illinois legislature in 1851; emphatically embodied and carried out in the Kansas-Nebraska Bill, and vindicated this year by the refusal to bring Kansas into the Union with a constitution distasteful to her people.

The other proposition discussed by Mr. Lincoln in his speech consists in a crusade against the Supreme Court of the United States on account of the Dred Scott decision. On this question, also, I desire to say to you unequivocally that I take direct and distinct issue with him. I have no warfare to make on the Supreme Court of the United States, either on account of that or any other decision which they have pronounced from that bench. The Constitution of the United States has provided that the powers of government (and the constitution of each state has the same provision) shall be divided into three departments—executive, legislative, and judicial. The right and the province of expounding the Constitution and constructing the law is vested in the judiciary established by the Constitution. As a lawyer, I feel at liberty to appear before the Court and controvert any principle of law while the question is pending before the tribunal; but, when the decision is made, my private opinion, your opinion, all other opinions must yield to the majesty of that authoritative adjudication. . . .

But I am equally free to say that the

reason assigned by Mr. Lincoln for resisting the decision of the Supreme Court in the Dred Scott case does not in itself meet any approbation. He objects to it because that decision declared that a Negro descended from African parents, who were brought here and sold as slaves, is not, and cannot be, a citizen of the United States. He says it is wrong, because it deprives the Negro of the benefits of that clause of the Constitution which says that citizens of one state shall enjoy all the privileges and immunities of citizens of the several states; in other words, he thinks it wrong because it deprives the Negro of the privileges, immunities, and rights of citizenship, which pertain, according to that decision, only to the white man. I am free to say to you that in my opinion this government of ours is founded on the white basis. It was made by the white man, for the benefit of the white man, to be administered by white men, in such manner as they should determine. It is also true that a Negro, an Indian, or any other man of inferior race to a white man, should be permitted to enjoy, and humanity requires that he should have the rights, privileges, and immunities which he is capable of exercising consistent with the safety of society. I would give him every right and every privilege which his capacity would enable him to enjoy, consistent with the good of the society in which he lived. But you may ask me: What are these rights and these privileges? My answer is that each state must decide for itself the nature and extent of these rights....

C. LINCOLN'S QUESTION AT THE SECOND DEBATE
FREEPORT, AUGUST 27, 1858

I now proceed to propound to the Judge the interrogatories, so far as I have framed them. I will bring forward a new instalment when I get them ready. I will bring them forward now, only reaching to number four.

The first one is:

Question 1. If the people of Kansas shall, by means entirely unobjectionable in all other respects, adopt a state constitution, and ask admission into the Union under it, *before* they have the requisite number of inhabitants according to the English Bill—some ninety-three thousand—will you vote to admit them?

Q. 2. Can the people of a United States territory, in any lawful way, against the wish of any citizen of the United States, exclude slavery from its limits prior to the formation of a state constitution?

Q. 3. If the Supreme Court of the United States shall decide that states cannot exclude slavery from their limits, are you in favor of acquiescing in, adopting, and following such decision as a rule of political action?

Q. 4. Are you in favor of acquiring additional territory, in disregard of how such acquisition may affect the nation on the slavery question? ...

D. DOUGLAS' REPLY, FREEPORT, AUGUST 27, 1858

... The next question propounded to me by Mr. Lincoln is: Can the people of a territory in any lawful way, against the wishes of any citizen of the United States, exclude slavery from their limits prior to the formation of a state constitution? I answer emphatically, as Mr. Lincoln has heard me answer a hundred times from every stump in Illinois, that in my opinion the people of a territory can, by lawful means, exclude slavery from their limits prior to the formation of a state constitution. Mr. Lincoln knew that I had answered that question over and over again. He heard me argue the Nebraska Bill on that principle all over the state in 1854, in 1855, and in 1856, and he has no excuse for pretending to be in doubt as to my position on that question. It matters not what way the Supreme Court may hereafter decide as to the abstract question whether slavery may or may not go into a territory under the Constitution, the people have the lawful means to introduce it or exclude it as they please, for the reason that slavery cannot exist a day or an hour anywhere unless it is supported by local police regulations. Those police regulations can only be established by the local legislature, and, if the people are opposed to slavery, they will elect representatives to that body who will by unfriendly legislation effectually prevent the introduction of it into their midst. If, on the contrary, they are for it, their legislation will favor its extension. Hence, no matter what the decision of the Supreme Court may be on that abstract question, still the right of the people to make a slave territory or a free territory is perfect and complete under the Nebraska Bill. I hope Mr. Lincoln deems my answer satisfactory on that point. . . .

The third question which Mr. Lincoln presented is, if the Supreme Court of the United States shall decide that a state of this Union cannot exclude slavery from its own limits, will I submit to it? I am amazed that Lincoln should ask such a question. ["A schoolboy knows better."] Yes, a schoolboy does know better. Mr. Lincoln's object is to cast an imputation upon the Supreme Court. He knows that there never was but one man in America, claiming any degree of intelligence or decency, who ever for a moment pretended such a thing. . . . He casts an imputation upon the Supreme Court of the United States, by supposing that they would violate the Constitution of the United States. I tell him that such a thing is not possible. It would be an act of moral treason that no man on the bench could ever descend to. Mr. Lincoln himself would never in his partisan feelings so far forget what was right as to be guilty of such an act.

The fourth question of Mr. Lincoln is: Are you in favor of acquiring additional territory, in disregard as to how such acquisition may affect the Union on the slavery questions? This question is very ingeniously and cunningly put.

The Black Republican creed lays it down expressly, that under no circumstances shall we acquire any more territory unless slavery is first prohibited in the country. I ask Mr. Lincoln whether he is in favor of that proposition. Are you [addressing Mr. Lincoln] opposed to the acquisition of any more territory, under any circumstances, unless slavery is prohibited in it? That he does not like to answer. When I ask him whether he stands up to that article in the platform of his party, he turns, Yankee-fashion, and without answering it, asks me whether I am in favor of acquiring territory without regard to how it may affect the Union on the slavery question. I answer that whenever it becomes necessary, in our growth and progress, to acquire more territory, that I am in favor of it, without reference to the question of slavery, and, when we have acquired it, I will leave the people free to do as they please, either to make it slave or free territory, as they prefer. It is idle to tell me or you that we have territory enough. Our fathers supposed that we had enough when our territory extended to the Mississippi River, but a few years' growth and expansion satisfied them that we needed more, and the Louisiana territory, from the west branch of the Mississippi to the British possessions, was acquired. Then we acquired Oregon, then California and New Mexico. We have enough now for the present, but this is a young and a growing nation. It swarms as often as a hive of bees, and, as new swarms are turned out each year, there must be hives in which they can gather and make their honey. In less than fifteen years, if the same progress that has distinguished this country for the last fifteen years continues, every foot of vacant land between this and the Pacific ocean, owned by the United States, will be occupied. Will you not continue to increase at the end of fifteen years as well as now? I tell you, increase and multiply and expand is the law of this nation's existence. You cannot limit this great Republic by mere boundary lines, saying, "Thus far shalt thou go, and no further." Any one of you gentlemen might as well say to a son twelve years old that he is big enough and must not grow any larger and, in order to prevent his growth, put a hoop around him to keep him to his present size. What would be the result?

Either the hoop must burst and be rent asunder or the child must die. So it would be with this great nation. With our natural increase, growing with a rapidity unknown in any other part of the globe, with the tide of emigration that is fleeing from despotism in the Old World to seek refuge in our own, there is a constant torrent pouring into this country that requires more land, more territory upon which to settle; and, just as fast as our interests and our destiny require additional territory in the North, in the South, or on the islands of the ocean, I am for it, and, when we acquire it, will leave the people, according to the Nebraska Bill, free to do as they please on the subject of slavery and every other question.

E. LINCOLN'S SPEECH, JONESBORO, SEPTEMBER 15, 1858

... The second interrogatory that I propounded to him, was this:

"Question 2. Can the people of a United States territory, in any lawful way, against the wish of any citizen of the United States, exclude slavery from its limits prior to the formation of a state constitution?"

To this Judge Douglas answered that they can lawfully exclude slavery from the territory prior to the formation of a constitution. He goes on to tell us how it can be done. As I understand him, he holds that it can be done by the territorial legislature refusing to make any enactments for the protection of slavery in the territory, and especially by adopting unfriendly legislation to it. For the sake of clearness I state it again: that they can exclude slavery from the territory, first, by withholding what he assumes to be an indispensable assistance to it in the way of legislation and, second, by unfriendly legislation. If I rightly understand him, I wish to ask your attention for a while to his position.

In the first place, the Supreme Court of the United States has decided that any congressional prohibition of slavery

in the territories is unconstitutional—that they have reached this proposition as a conclusion from their former proposition, that the Constitution of the United States expressly recognizes property in slaves, and from that other constitutional provision that no person shall be deprived of property without due process of law. Hence they reach the conclusion that as the Constitution of the United States expressly recognizes property in slaves, and prohibits any person from being deprived of property without due process of law, to pass an act of Congress by which a man who owned a slave on one side of a line would be deprived of him if he took him on the other side, is depriving him of that property without due process of law. That I understand to be the decision of the Supreme Court. I understand also that Judge Douglas adheres most firmly to that decision; and the difficulty is: How is it possible for any power to exclude slavery from the territory unless in violation of that decision? That is the difficulty....

I hold that the proposition that slavery cannot enter a new country without police regulations is historically false. It is not true at all. I hold that the history of this country shows that the institution of slavery was originally planted upon this continent *without* these "police regulations" which the Judge now thinks necessary for the actual establishment of it. Not only so, but is there not another fact—how came this Dred Scott decision to be made? It was made upon the case of a Negro being taken and actually held in slavery in Minnesota Territory, claiming his freedom because the act of Congress prohibited his being so held there. *Will the Judge pretend that Dred Scott was not held there without police regulations?* There is at least one matter of record as to his having been held in slavery in the territory, not only without police regulations, but in the teeth of congressional legislation supposed to be valid at the time. This shows that there is vigor enough in slavery to plant itself in a new country even against unfriendly legislation. It takes not only law but the *enforcement* of law to keep it out. That is the history of this country upon the subject.

I wish to ask one other question. It being understood that the Constitution of the United States guarantees property in slaves in the territories, if there is any infringement of the right of that property, would not the United States courts, organized for the government of the territory, apply such remedy as might be necessary in that case? It is a maxim held by the courts that there is no wrong without its remedy; and the courts have a remedy for whatever is acknowledged and treated as a wrong.

Again: I will ask you, my friends, if you were elected members of the legislature, what would be the first thing you would have to do before entering upon your duties? *Swear to support the Constitution of the United States.* Suppose you believe, as Judge Douglas does, that the Constitution of the United States guarantees to your neighbor the right to hold slaves in that territory—that they are his property—how can you clear your oaths unless you give him such legislation as is necessary to enable him to enjoy that property? What do you understand by supporting the constitution of a state or of the United States? Is it not to give such constitutional helps to the rights established by that Constitution as may be practically needed? Can you, if you swear to support the Constitution, and believe that the Constitution establishes a right, clear your oath without giving it support? Do you support the Constitution if, knowing or believing there is a right established under it which needs specific legislation, you withhold that legislation? Do you not violate and disregard your oath? I can conceive of nothing plainer in the world. There can be nothing in the words "support the Constitution," if you may run counter to it by refusing support to any right established under the Constitution. And what I say here will hold with still more force against the Judge's doctrine of "unfriendly legislation." How could you, having sworn to support the Constitution, and believing it guaranteed the right to hold slaves in the territories, assist in legislation *intended to defeat that right?* That would be violating your own view of the Constitution. Not only so, but, if you were to do so, how long would it take the courts to hold your votes unconstitutional and void? Not a moment.

Lastly I would ask: Is not Congress, itself, under obligation to give legislative support to any right that is established under the United States Constitution? I repeat the question: Is not Congress, itself, bound to give legislative support to any right that is established in the United States Constitution? A member of Congress swears to support the Constitution of the United States, and if he sees a right established by that Constitution which needs specific legislative protection, can he clear his oath without giving that protection? Let me ask you why many of us who are opposed to slavery upon principle give our acquiescence to a Fugitive Slave law? Why do we hold ourselves under obligations to pass such a law and abide by it when it is passed? Because the Constitution makes provision that the owners of slaves shall have the right to reclaim them. It gives the right to reclaim slaves and that right is, as Judge Douglas says, a barren right, unless there is legislation that will enforce it.

The mere declaration, "No person held to service or labor in one State under the laws thereof, escaping into another, shall in consequence of any law or regulation therein be discharged from such service or labor, but shall be delivered up on claim of the party to whom such service or labor may be due," is powerless without specific legislation to enforce it. Now, on what ground would a member of Congress who is opposed to slavery in the abstract, vote for a Fugitive law, as I would deem it my duty to do? Because there is a constitutional right which needs legislation to enforce it. And al-

though it is distasteful to me, I have sworn to support the Constitution, and having so sworn, I cannot conceive that I do support it if I withhold from that right any necessary legislation to make it practical. And if that is true in regard to a Fugitive Slave law, is the right to have fugitive slaves reclaimed any better fixed in the Constitution than the right to hold slaves in the territories? For this decision is a just exposition of the Constitution, as Judge Douglas thinks. Is the one right any better than the other? Is there any man who, while a member of Congress, would give support to the one any more than the other? If I wished to refuse to give legislative support to slave property in the territories, if a member of Congress, I could not do it, holding the view that the Constitution establishes that right. If I did it at all, it would be because I deny that this decision properly construes the Constitution. But if I acknowledge, with Judge Douglas, that this decision properly construes the Constitution, I cannot conceive that I would be less than a perjured man if I should refuse in Congress to give such protection to that property as in its nature it needed. . . .

F. DOUGLAS' SPEECH AT THE FIFTH DEBATE
GALESBURG, OCTOBER 7, 1858

. . . Now, let me ask you whether the country has any interest in sustaining this organization known as the Republican party. That party is unlike all other political organizations in this country. All other parties have been national in their character—have avowed their principles alike in the slave and free states, in Kentucky as well as Illinois, in Louisiana as well as in Massachusetts. Such was the case with the old Whig party, and such was and is the case with the Democratic party. Whigs and Democrats could proclaim their principles boldly and fearlessly in the North and in the South, in the East and in the West, wherever the Constitution ruled

and the American flag waved over American soil.

But now you have a sectional organization, a party which appeals to the northern section of the Union against the southern, a party which appeals to northern passion, northern pride, northern ambition, and northern prejudices, against southern people, the southern states, and southern institutions. The leaders of that party hope that they will be able to unite the northern states in one great sectional party and, inasmuch as the North is the strongest section, that they will thus be enabled to outvote, conquer, govern, and control the South. Hence you find that they now make speeches advocating principles and measures which cannot be defended in any slaveholding state of this Union. Is there a Republican residing in Galesburg who can travel into Kentucky and carry his principles with him across the Ohio? What Republican from Massachusetts can visit the Old Dominion without leaving his principles behind him when he crosses Mason and Dixon's line? Permit me to say to you in perfect good humor, but in all sincerity, that no political creed is sound which cannot be proclaimed fearlessly in every state of this Union where the federal Constitution is not the supreme law of the land....

I ask you, my friends, why cannot Republicans avow their principles alike everywhere? I would despise myself if I thought that I was procuring your votes by concealing my opinions and by avowing one set of principles in one part of the state and a different set in another part. If I do not truly and honorably represent your feelings and principles, then I ought not to be your senator; and I will never conceal my opinions, or modify or change them a hair's breadth, in order to get votes. I tell you that this Chicago doctrine of Lincoln's—declaring that the Negro and the white man are made equal by the Declaration of Independence and by Divine Providence—is a monstrous heresy. The signers of the Declaration of Independence never dreamed of the Negro when they were writing that document. They referred to white men, to men of European birth and European descent, when they declared the equality of all men. I see a gentleman there in the crowd shaking his head. Let me remind him that, when Thomas Jefferson wrote that document, he was the owner, and so continued until his death, of a large number of slaves. Did he intend to say in that Declaration that his Negro slaves, which he held and treated as property, were created his equals by di-

vine law and that he was violating the law of God every day of his life by holding them as slaves? It must be borne in mind that, when that Declaration was put forth, every one of the thirteen colonies were slave-holding Colonies, and every man who signed that instrument represented a slave-holding constituency. Recollect, also, that no one of them emancipated his slaves, much less put them on an equality with himself, after he signed the Declaration. On the contrary, they all continued to hold their Negroes as slaves during the Revolutionary War. Now, do you believe—are you willing to have it said—that every man who signed the Declaration of Independence declared the Negro his equal and then was hypocrite enough to continue to hold him as a slave in violation of what he believed to be the divine law? And yet, when you say that the Declaration of Independence includes the Negro, you charge the signers of it with hypocrisy.

I say to you, frankly, that in my opinion this government was made by our fathers on the white basis. It was made by white men for the benefit of white men and their posterity forever and was intended to be administered by white men in all time to come. But while I hold that under our Constitution and political system the Negro is not a citizen, cannot be a citizen, and ought not to be a citizen, it does not follow by any means that he should be a slave. On the contrary, it does follow that the Negro, as an inferior race, ought to possess every right, every privilege, every immunity which he can safely exercise consistent with the safety of the society in which he lives. Humanity requires, and Christianity commands, that you shall extend to every inferior being, and every dependent being, all the privileges, immunities, and advantages which can be granted to them consistent with the safety of society. If you ask me the nature and extent of these privileges, I answer that that is a question which the people of each state must decide for themselves. Illinois has decided that question for herself. We have said that in this state the Negro shall not be a slave nor shall he be a citizen. Kentucky holds a different doctrine. New York holds one different from either, and Maine one different from all. Virginia, in her policy on this question, differs in many respects from the others, and so on, until there are hardly two states whose policy is exactly alike in regard to the relation of the white man and the Negro. Nor can you reconcile them and make them alike. Each state must do as it pleases. Illinois had as much right to adopt the policy which we have on that subject as Kentucky had to adopt a different policy. The great principle of this government is that each state has the right to do as it pleases on all these questions, and no other state, or power on earth, has the right to interfere with us or complain of us merely because our system differs from theirs. In the Compromise Measures of 1850, Mr. Clay declared that this great principle ought to exist in the territories as well as in the states, and I reasserted his doctrine in the Kansas and Nebraska Bill in 1854.

But Mr. Lincoln cannot be made to understand, and those who are determined to vote for him, no matter whether he is a proslavery man in the South and a Negro-equality advocate in the North, cannot be made to understand how it is that in a territory the people can do as they please on the slavery question under the Dred Scott decision. Let us see whether I cannot explain it to the satisfaction of all impartial men. Chief Justice Taney has said in his opinion in the Dred Scott case that a Negro slave, being property, stands on an equal footing with other property and that the owner may carry them into United States territory the same as he does other property. Suppose any two of you, neighbors, should conclude to go to Kansas, one carrying $100,000 worth of Negro slaves and the other $100,000 worth of mixed merchandise, including quantities of liquors. You both agree that under that decision you may carry your property to Kansas, but, when you get it there, the merchant who is possessed of the liquors is met by the Maine liquor law, which prohibits the sale or use of his property, and the owner of the slaves is met by equally unfriendly legislation, which makes his property worthless after he gets it there. What is the right to carry your property into the territory worth to either when unfriendly legislation in the territory renders it worthless after you get it there? The slaveholder when he gets his slaves there finds that there is no local law to protect him in holding them, no slave code, no police regulation maintaining and supporting him in his right, and he discovers at once that the absence of such friendly legislation excludes his property from the territory, just as irresistibly as if there was a positive constitutional prohibition excluding it. . . .

G. LINCOLN'S REPLY, GALESBURG, OCTOBER 7, 1858

. . . The Judge has also detained us awhile in regard to the distinction between his party and our party. His he assumes to be a national party—ours a sectional one. He does this in asking the question whether this country has any interest in the maintenance of the Republican party? He assumes that our party is altogether sectional—that the party to which he adheres is national; and the argument is that no party can be a rightful party—can be based upon rightful principles—unless it can announce its principles everywhere. I presume that Judge Douglas could not go into Russia and announce the doctrine of our national democracy; he could not denounce the doctrine of kings and em-

743

perors and monarchies in Russia; and it may be true of this country that in some places we may not be able to proclaim a doctrine as clearly true as the truth of democracy, because there is a section so directly opposed to it that they will not tolerate us in doing so. Is it the true test of the soundness of a doctrine that in some places people won't let you proclaim it? Is that the way to test the truth of any doctrine? Why, I understood that at one time the people of Chicago would not let Judge Douglas preach a certain favorite doctrine of his. I commend to his consideration the question whether he takes that as a test of the unsoundness of what he wanted to preach.

There is another thing to which I wish to ask attention for a little while on this occasion. What has always been the evidence brought forward to prove that the Republican party is a sectional party? The main one was that in the southern portion of the Union the people did not let the Republicans proclaim their doctrines amongst them. That has been the main evidence brought forward—that they had no supporters, or substantially

none, in the slave states. The South have not taken hold of our principles as we announce them; nor does Judge Douglas now grapple with those principles. . . .

I ask his attention also to the fact that by the rule of nationality he is himself fast becoming sectional. I ask his attention to the fact that his speeches would not go as current now south of the Ohio River as they have formerly gone there. I ask his attention to the fact that he felicitates himself today that all the Democrats of the free states are agreeing with him, while he omits to tell us that the Democrats of any slave state agree with him. If he has not thought of this, I commend to his consideration the evidence in his own declaration, on this day, of his becoming sectional too. I see it rapidly approaching. Whatever may be the result of this ephemeral contest between Judge Douglas and myself, I see the day rapidly approaching when his pill of sectionalism, which he has been thrusting down the throats of Republicans for years past, will be crowded down his own throat. . . .

H. DOUGLAS' OPENING SPEECH, ALTON, OCTOBER 15, 1858

Ladies and Gentlemen:

It is now nearly four months since the canvass between Mr. Lincoln and myself commenced. On the sixteenth of June the Republican Convention assembled at Springfield and nominated Mr. Lincoln as their candidate for the United States Senate, and he, on that occasion, delivered a speech in which he laid down what he understood to be the Republican creed and the platform on which he proposed to stand during the contest.

The principal points in that speech of Mr. Lincoln's were: First, that this government could not endure permanently divided into free and slave states, as our fathers made it; that they must all become free or all become slave; all become one thing or all become the other,

otherwise this Union could not continue to exist. I give you his opinions almost in the identical language he used. His second proposition was a crusade against the Supreme Court of the United States because of the Dred Scott decision; urging as an especial reason for his opposition to that decision that it deprived the Negroes of the rights and benefits of that clause in the Constitution of the United States which guarantees to the citizens of each state all the rights, privileges, and immunities of the citizens of the several states.

On the tenth of July I returned home and delivered a speech to the people of Chicago in which I announced it to be my purpose to appeal to the people of Illinois to sustain the course I had pursued in Congress. In that speech I joined issue with Mr. Lincoln on the points which he had presented. Thus there was an issue clear and distinct made up between us on these two propositions laid down in the speech of Mr. Lincoln at Springfield and controverted by me in my reply to him at Chicago.

On the next day, the eleventh of July, Mr. Lincoln replied to me at Chicago, explaining at some length, and reaffirming the positions which he had taken in his Springfield speech. In that Chicago speech he even went further than he had before and uttered sentiments in regard to the Negro being on an equality with the white man. He adopted in support of this position the argument which Lovejoy and Codding, and other abolition lecturers had made familiar in the northern and central portions of the state, to wit: that the Declaration of Independence having declared all men free and equal, by divine law, also that Negro equality was an inalienable right, of which they could not be deprived. He insisted, in that speech, that the Declaration of Independence included the Negro in the clause, asserting that all men were created equal, and went so far as to say that if one man was allowed to take the position that it did not include the Negro, others might take the position that it did not include other men. He said that all these distinctions between this man and that man, this race and the other race, must be discarded, and we must all stand by the Declaration of Independence, declaring that all men were created equal.

The issue thus being made up between Mr. Lincoln and myself on three points, we went before the people of the state. During the following seven weeks, between the Chicago speeches and our first meeting at Ottawa, he and I addressed large assemblages of the people in many of the central counties. In my speeches I confined myself closely to those three positions which he had taken, controverting his proposition that this Union could not exist as our fathers made it, divided into free and slave states, controverting his proposition of a crusade against the Supreme Court because of the Dred Scott decision, and controverting his proposition that the Declaration of Independence included and meant the Negroes as well as the white men when it declared all men to be created equal. . . . I took up Mr. Lincoln's three propositions in my several speeches, analyzed them, and pointed out what I believed to be the radical errors contained in them. First, in regard to his doctrine that this government was in violation of the law of God, which says that a house divided against itself cannot stand, I repudiated it as a slander upon the immortal framers of our Constitution. I then said, I have often repeated, and now again assert, that in my opinion our government can endure forever, divided into free and slave states as our fathers made it—each state having the right to prohibit, abolish, or sustain slavery, just as it pleases. This government was made upon the great basis of the sovereignty of the states, the right of each state to regulate its own domestic institutions to suit itself, and that right was conferred with the understanding and expectation that, inasmuch as each locality had separate interests, each locality must have different and distinct local and domestic institutions, corresponding to its wants and interests. Our fathers knew when they made the government that the laws and institutions which were well adapted to the Green Mountains of Vermont were unsuited to the rice plantations of South Carolina. They knew then, as well as we know now, that the laws and institutions which would be well adapted to the beautiful prairies of Illinois would not be suited to the mining regions of California. They knew that in a republic as broad as this, having such a variety of soil, climate, and interest, there must necessarily be a corresponding variety of lo-

WESTWARD EXPANSION AND SECTIONAL CONFLICT

cal laws—the policy and institutions of each state adapted to its condition and wants. For this reason this Union was established on the right of each state to do as it pleased on the question of slavery and every other question; and the various states were not allowed to complain of, much less interfere with, the policy of their neighbors. . . .

You see that if this abolition doctrine of Mr. Lincoln had prevailed when the government was made, it would have established slavery as a permanent institution, in all the states, whether they wanted it or not, and the question for us to determine in Illinois now as one of the free states is whether or not we are willing, having become the majority section, to enforce a doctrine on the minority which we would have resisted with our heart's blood had it been attempted on us when we were in a minority. How has the South lost her power as the majority section in this Union, and how have the free states gained it, except under the operation of that principle which declares the right of the people of each state and each territory to form and regulate their domestic institutions in their own way. It was under that principle that slavery was abolished in New Hampshire, Rhode Island, Connecticut, New York, New Jersey, and Pennsylvania; it was under that principle that one-half of the slaveholding states became free; it was under that principle that the number of free states increased until, from being one out of twelve states, we have grown to be the majority of states of the whole Union, with the power to control the House of Representatives and Senate, and the the power, consequently, to elect a President by northern votes without the aid of a southern state. Having obtained this power under the operation of that great principle, are you now prepared to abandon the principle and declare that merely because we have the power you will wage a war against the south-

ern states and their institutions until you force them to abolish slavery everywhere. . . ?

My friends, there never was a time when it was as important for the Democratic party, for all national men, to rally and stand together as it is today. We find all sectional men giving up past differences and continuing the one question of slavery, and, when we find sectional men thus uniting, we should unite to resist them and their treasonable designs. Such was the case in 1850, when Clay left the quiet and peace of his home and again entered upon public life to quell agitation and restore peace to a distracted Union. Then we Democrats, with Cass at our head, welcomed Henry Clay, whom the whole nation regarded as having been preserved by God for the times. He became our leader in that great fight, and we rallied around him the same as the Whigs rallied around "Old Hickory" in 1832 to put down nullification. Thus you see that whilst Whigs and Democrats fought fearlessly in old times about banks, the tariff, distribution, the specie circular, and the subtreasury, all united as a band of brothers when the peace, harmony, or integrity of the Union was imperiled. It was so in 1850, when abolitionism had even so far divided this country, North and South, as to endanger the peace of the Union; Whigs and Democrats united in establishing the compromise measures of that year and restoring tranquillity and good feeling. These measures passed on the joint action of the two parties. They rested on the great principle that the people of each state and each territory should be left perfectly free to form and regulate their domestic institutions to suit themselves. You Whigs and we Democrats justified them in that principle. In 1854, when it became necessary to organize the territories of Kansas and Nebraska, I brought forward the bill on the same principle. In the Kansas-Nebraska Bill you find it declared to be the

746

true intent and meaning of the act not to legislate slavery into any state or territory, nor to exclude it therefrom, but to leave the people thereof perfectly free to form and regulate their domestic institutions in their own way. I stand on that same platform in 1858 that I did in 1850, 1854, and 1856. . . .

I answer specifically if you want a further answer and say that, while under the decision of the Supreme Court, as recorded in the opinion of Chief Justice Taney, slaves are property like all other property, and can be carried into any territory of the United States the same as any other description of property, yet when you get them there they are subject to the local law of the territory just like all other property. You will find in a recent speech delivered by that able and eloquent statesman, Hon. Jefferson Davis, at Bangor, Maine, that he took the same view of this subject that I did in my Freeport speech. He there said:

If the inhabitants of any territory should refuse to enact such laws and police regulations as would give security to their property or to his, it would be rendered more or less valueless in proportion to the difficulties of holding it without such protection. In the case of property in the labor of man, or what is usually called slave property, the insecurity would be so great that the owner could not ordinarily retain it. Therefore, though the right would remain, the remedy being withheld, it would follow that the owner would be practically debarred, by the circumstances of the case, from taking slave property into a territory where the sense of the inhabitants was opposed to its introduction. So much for the oft-repeated fallacy of forcing slavery upon any community.

You will also find that the distinguished speaker of the present House of Representatives, Hon. Jas. L. Orr, construed the Kansas and Nebraska Bill in this same way in 1856, and also that great intellect of the South, Alex. H. Stephens, put the same construction upon it in Congress that I did in my Freeport speech. The whole South are rallying to the support of the doctrine that, if the people of a territory want slavery, they have a right to have it, and, if they do not want it, that no power on earth can force it upon them. I hold that there is no principle on earth more sacred to all the friends of freedom than that which says that no institution, no law, no constitution, should be forced on an unwilling people contrary to their wishes; and I assert that the Kansas and Nebraska Bill contains that principle. It is the great principle contained in that bill. It is the principle on which James Buchanan was made President. Without that principle he never would have been made President of the United States. I will never violate or abandon that doctrine if I have to stand alone. I have resisted the blandishments and threats of power on the one side, and seduction on the other, and have stood immovably for that principle, fighting for it when assailed by northern mobs or threatened by southern hostility. I have defended it against the North and the South, and I will defend it against whoever assails it, and I will follow it wherever its logical conclusions lead me. I say to you that there is but one hope, one safety, for this country, and that is to stand immovably by that principle which declares the right of each state and each territory to decide these questions for themselves. This government was founded on that principle and must be administered in the same sense in which it was founded.

But the Abolition party really think that under the Declaration of Independence the Negro is equal to the white man and that Negro equality is an inalienable right conferred by the Almighty, and hence that all human laws in violation of it are null and void. With such men it is no use for me to argue. I hold that the signers of the Declaration of Independence had no reference to Negroes at all when they declared all men to be created equal. They did not mean Negro, nor the savage Indians, nor the Fiji Islanders, nor any other barbarous race. They were speaking of white men. They alluded to men of European birth and European descent—to white men and to none others—when they declared that doctrine. I hold that this government was established on the white basis. It was established by white men for the benefit of white men and their posterity forever and should be administered by white men and none others. But it does not follow, by any means, that merely because the Negro is not a citizen, and merely because he is not our equal, that, therefore, he should be a slave. On the contrary, it does follow that we ought to extend to the Negro race, and to all other dependent races all the rights, all the privileges, and all the immunities which they can exercise consistently with the safety of society. Humanity requires that we should give them all these privileges; Christianity commands that we should extend those privileges to them. The question then arises: What are those privileges and what is the nature and extent of them. My answer is that that is a question which each state must answer for itself. We in Illinois have decided it for ourselves. We tried slavery, kept it up for twelve years, and, finding that it was not profitable, we abolished it for that reason, and became a free state. We adopted in its stead the policy that a Negro in this state shall not be a slave and shall not be a citizen. We have a right to adopt that policy. For my part I think it is a wise and sound policy for us. You in Missouri must judge for yourselves whether it is a wise policy for you. If

you choose to follow our example, very good; if you reject it, still well, it is your business, not ours. So with Kentucky. Let Kentucky adopt a policy to suit herself. If we do not like it, we will keep away from it, and if she does not like ours let her stay at home, mind her own business and let us alone. If the people of all the states will act on that great principle, and each state mind its own business, attend to its own affairs, take care of its own Negroes, and not meddle with its neighbors, then there will be peace between the North and the South, the East and the West, throughout the whole Union. Why can we not thus have peace? Why should we thus allow a sectional party to agitate this country, to array the North against the South, and convert us into enemies instead of friends, merely that a few ambitious men may ride into power on a sectional hobby? How long is it since these ambitious northern men wished for a sectional organization? Did any one of them dream of a sectional party as long as the North was the weaker section and the South the stronger? Then all were opposed to sectional parties; but the moment the North obtained the majority in the House and Senate by the admission of California, and could elect a President without the aid of southern votes, that moment ambitious northern men formed a scheme to excite the North against the South, and make the people be governed in their votes by geographical lines, thinking that the North, being the stronger section, would outvote the South, and consequently they, the leaders, would ride into office on a sectional hobby. I am told that my hour is out. It was very short.

I. LINCOLN'S REPLY, ALTON, OCTOBER 15, 1858

...It is not true that our fathers, as Judge Douglas assumes, made this government part slave and part free. Understand the sense in which he puts it. He assumes that slavery is a rightful thing

within itself—was introduced by the framers of the Constitution. The exact truth is that they found the institution existing among us, and they left it as they found it. But, in making the government, they left this institution with many clear marks of disapprobation upon it. They found slavery among them, and they left it among them because of the difficulty— the absolute impossibility—of its immediate removal. And when Judge Douglas asks me why we cannot let it remain part slave and part free, as the fathers of the government made it, he asks a question based upon an assumption which is itself a falsehood; and I turn upon him and ask him the question, when the policy that the fathers of the government had adopted in relation to this element among us was the best policy in the world—the only wise policy—the only policy that we can ever safely continue upon—that will ever give us peace, unless this dangerous element masters us all and becomes a national institution— *I turn upon him and ask him why he could not leave it alone*. I turn and ask him why he was driven to the necessity of introducing a *new policy* in regard to it. He has himself said he introduced a new policy. He said so in his speech on the twenty-second of March of the present year, 1858. I ask him why he could not let it remain where our fathers placed it. I ask, too, of Judge Douglas and his friends why we shall not again place this institution upon the basis on which the fathers left it. I ask you, when he infers that I am in favor of setting the free and slave states at war, when the institution was placed in that attitude by those who made the Constitution, *did they make any war?* If we had no war out of it, when thus placed, wherein is the ground of belief that we shall have war out of it if we return to that policy? Have we had any peace upon this matter springing from any other basis? I maintain that we have not. I have proposed nothing more than a return to the policy of the fathers.

I confess, when I propose a certain measure of policy, it is not enough for me that I do not intend anything evil in the result, but it is incumbent on me to show that it has not a *tendency* to that result. I have met Judge Douglas in that point of view. I have not only made the declaration that I do not *mean* to produce a conflict between the states, but I have tried to show by fair reasoning, and I think I have shown to the minds of fair men, that I propose nothing but what has a most peaceful tendency. The quotation that I happened to make in that Springfield speech, that "a house divided against itself cannot stand," and which has proved so offensive to the Judge, was part and parcel of the same thing. He tries to show that variety in the domestic institutions of the different states is necessary and indispensable. I do not dispute it. I have no controversy with Judge Douglas about that. . . .

Now irrespective of the moral aspect of this question as to whether there is a right or wrong in enslaving a Negro, I am still in favor of our new territories being in such a condition that white men may find a home—may find some spot where they can better their condition— where they can settle upon new soil and better their condition in life. I am in favor of this not merely (I must say it here as I have elsewhere) for our own people who are born amongst us, but as an outlet for *free white people everywhere*, the world over—in which Hans and Baptiste and Patrick, and all other men from all the world, may find new homes and better their conditions in life.

I have stated upon former occasions, and I may as well state again, what I understand to be the real issue in this controversy between Judge Douglas and myself. On the point of my wanting to make war between the free and the slave states, there has been no issue between us. So, too, when he assumes that I am in favor of introducing a perfect social and political equality between the white and black races. These are false issues, upon which Judge Douglas has tried to force the controversy. There is no foundation in truth for the charge that I maintain either of these propositions. The real issue in this controversy—the one pressing upon every mind—is the sentiment on the part of one class that looks upon the institution of slavery *as a wrong* and of another class that *does not* look upon it as a wrong. The sentiment that contemplates the institution of slavery in this country as a wrong is the sentiment of the Republican party. It is the sentiment around which all their actions—all their arguments circle—from which all their propositions radiate. They look upon it as being a moral, social, and political wrong; and, while they contemplate it as such, they nevertheless have due regard for its actual existence among us, and the difficulties of getting rid of it in any satisfactory way and to all the constitutional obligations thrown about it. Yet having a due regard for these, they desire a policy in regard to it that looks to its not creating any more danger. They insist that it should, as far as may be, *be treated* as a wrong, and one of the methods of treating it as a wrong is to *make provision that it shall grow no larger*. They also desire a policy that looks to a peaceful end of slavery at sometime as being wrong. These are the views they entertain in regard to it as I understand them; and all their sentiments—all their arguments and propositions—are brought within this range. I have said, and I repeat it here, that if there be a man amongst us who does not think that the institution of slavery is wrong in any one of the aspects of which I have spoken, he is misplaced and ought not to be with us. And if there be a man amongst us who is so impatient of it as a wrong as to disregard its actual presence among us and the difficulty of getting rid of it suddenly in a satisfactory way, and to disregard the constitutional obligations thrown about it, that man is misplaced if he is on our platform. We disclaim sympathy with him in practical action. He is not placed properly with us.

On this subject of treating it as a wrong, and limiting its spread, let me say a word. Has anything ever threatened the existence of this Union save and except this very institution of slavery? What is it that we hold most dear amongst us? Our own liberty and prosperity. What has ever threatened our liberty and prosperity save and except this institution of slavery? If this is true, how do you propose to improve the condition of things by enlarging slavery—by spreading it out and making it bigger? You may have a wen or cancer upon your person and not be able to cut it out lest you bleed to death; but surely it is no way to cure it, to engraft it and spread it over your whole body. That is no proper way of treating what you regard a wrong. You see this peaceful way of dealing with it as a wrong—restricting the spread of it, and not allowing it to go into new countries where it has not already existed. That is the peaceful way, the old-fashioned way, the way in which the fathers themselves set us the example.

On the other hand, I have said there is a sentiment which treats it as *not* being wrong. That is the Democratic sentiment of this day. I do not mean to say that every man who stands within that range positively asserts that it is right. That class will include all who positively assert that it is right, and all who like Judge Douglas treat it as indifferent and do not say it is either right or wrong. These two classes of men fall within the general class of those who do not look upon it as a wrong. . . .

The Democratic policy in regard to that institution will not tolerate the merest breath, the slightest hint, of the least degree of wrong about it. Try it by some of Judge Douglas' arguments. He says he "don't care whether it is voted up or voted down" in the territories. I do not care myself in dealing with that expression, whether it is intended to be expressive of his individual sentiments on the subject or only of the national policy he desires to have established. It is alike valuable for my purpose. Any man can say that who does not see anything wrong in slavery, but no man can logically say it who does see a wrong in it; because no man can logically say he does not care whether a wrong is voted up or voted down. He may say he does not care whether an indifferent thing is voted up or down, but he must logically have a choice between a right thing and a wrong thing. He contends that whatever community wants slaves has a right to have them. So they have if it is not a wrong. But if it is a wrong, he cannot say people have a right to do wrong. He says that, upon the score of equality, slaves should be allowed to go in a new territory, like other property. This is strictly logical if there is no difference between it and other property. If it and other property are equal, his argument is entirely logical. But if you insist that one is wrong and the other right, there is no use to institute a comparison between right and wrong. You may turn over everything in the Democratic policy from beginning to end, whether in the shape it takes on the statute book, in the shape it takes in the Dred Scott decision, in the shape it takes in conversation, or the shape it takes in short maxim-like arguments—it everywhere carefully excludes the idea that there is anything wrong in it.

That is the real issue. That is the issue that will continue in this country when these poor tongues of Judge Douglas and myself shall be silent. It is the eternal struggle between these two principles—right and wrong—throughout the world. They are the two principles that have stood face to face from the beginning of time and will ever continue to struggle. The one is the common right of humanity and the other the divine right of kings. It is the same principle in whatever shape it develops itself. It is the same spirit that says, "You work and toil and earn bread, and I'll eat it." No matter in what shape it comes, whether from the mouth of a king who seeks to bestride the people of his own nation and live by the fruit of their labor, or from one race of men as an apology for enslaving another race, it is the same tyrannical principle. . . .

I understood I have ten minutes yet. I will employ it in saying something about this argument Judge Douglas uses, while he sustains the Dred Scott decision, that the people of the territories can still somehow exclude slavery. The first thing I ask attention to is the fact that Judge Douglas constantly said, before the decision, that whether they could or not, *was a question for the Supreme Court.* But after the Court has made the decision, he virtually says it is *not* a question for the Supreme Court but for the people. And how is it he tells us they can exclude it? He says it needs "police regulations," and that admits of "unfriendly legislation." Although it is a right established by the Constitution of the United States to take a slave into a territory of the United States and hold him as property, yet unless the territorial legislature will give friendly legislation, and, more especially, if they adopt unfriendly legislation, they can practically exclude him. Now, without meeting this proposition as a matter of fact, I pass to consider the real constitutional obligation. Let me take the gentleman who looks me in the face before me, and let us suppose that he is a member of the territorial legislature. The first thing he will do will be to swear that he will support the Constitution of the United States. His neighbor by his side in the territory has slaves and needs territorial legislation to enable him to enjoy that constitutional right. Can he withhold the legislation which his neighbor needs for the enjoyment of a right which is fixed in his favor in the Constitution of the United States which he has sworn to support? Can he withhold it without violating his oath? And, more especially, can he pass unfriendly legislation to violate his oath? Why, this is a *monstrous* sort of talk about the Constitution of the United States! *There has never been as outlandish or lawless a doctrine from the mouth of any respectable man on earth.* I do not believe it is a constitutional right to hold slaves in a territory of the United States. I believe the decision was improperly made, and I go for reversing it. Judge Douglas is furious against those who go for reversing a decision. But he is for legislating it out of all force while the law itself stands. I repeat that there has never been so monstrous a doctrine uttered from the mouth of a respectable man.

I suppose most of us (I know it of myself) believe that the people of the southern states are entitled to a congressional Fugitive Slave law—that is a right fixed in the Constitution. But it cannot be made available to them without congressional legislation. In the Judge's language, it is a "barren right" which needs legislation before it can become efficient and valuable to the persons to whom it is guaranteed. And as the right is constitutional I agree that the legislation shall be granted to it—and that not that we like the institution of slavery. We profess to have no taste for running and catching niggers—at least I profess no taste for that job at all. Why then do I yield support to a Fugitive Slave law? Because I do not understand that the Constitution, which guarantees that right, can be supported without it. And if I believed that the right to hold a slave in a territory was equally fixed in the Constitution with the right to reclaim fugitives, I should be bound to give it the legislation necessary to support it. I say that no man can deny his

obligation to give the necessary legislation to support slavery in a territory who believes it is a constitutional right to have it there. No man can who does not give the abolitionists an argument to deny the obligation enjoined by the Constitution to enact a Fugitive Slave law. Try it now. It is the strongest abolition argument ever made. I say if that Dred Scott decision is correct, then the right to hold slaves in a territory is equally a constitutional right with the right of a slaveholder to have his runaway returned. No one can show the distinction between them. The one is express, so that we cannot deny it. The other is construed to be in the Constitution, so that he who believes the decision to be correct believes in the right. And the man who argues that by unfriendly legislation, in spite of that Constitutional right, slavery may be driven from the territories cannot avoid furnishing an argument by which abolitionists may deny the obligation to return fugitives and claim the power to pass laws unfriendly to the right of the slaveholder to reclaim his fugitive. I do not know how such an argument may strike a popular assembly like this, but I defy anybody to go before a body of men whose minds are educated to estimating evidence and reasoning and show that there is an iota of difference between the constitutional right to reclaim a fugitive and the constitutional right to hold a slave in a territory, provided this Dred Scott decision is correct. I defy any man to make an argument that will justify unfriendly legislation to deprive a slaveholder of his right to hold his slave in a territory that will not equally, in all its length, breadth, and thickness, furnish an argument for nullifying the Fugitive Slave law. Why, there is not such an abolitionist in the nation as Douglas, after all.

J. DOUGLAS' SECOND SPEECH, ALTON, OCTOBER 15, 1858

... Mr. Lincoln tries to avoid the main issue by attacking the truth of my proposition, that our fathers made this government divided into free and slave states, recognizing the right of each to decide all its local questions for itself. Did they not thus make it? It is true that they did not establish slavery in any of the states or abolish it in any of them; but, finding thirteen states, twelve of which were slave and one free, they agreed to form a government uniting them together, as they stood divided into free and slave states, and to guarantee forever to each state the right to do as it pleased on the slavery question. Having thus made the government, and conferred this right upon each state forever, I assert that this government can exist as they made it, divided into free and slave states, if any one state chooses to retain slavery. He says that he looks forward to a time when slavery shall be abolished everywhere. I look forward to a time when each state shall be allowed to do as it pleases. If it chooses to keep slavery forever, it is not my business, but its own; if it chooses to abolish slavery, it is its own business—not mine. I care more for the great principle of self-government, the right of the people to rule, than I do for all the Negroes in Christendom. I would not endanger the perpetuity of this Union, I would not blot out the great inalienable rights of the white men, for all the Negroes that ever existed. Hence, I say, let us maintain this government on the principles that our fathers made it, recognizing the right of each state to keep slavery as long as its people determine, or to abolish it when they please. But Mr. Lincoln says that, when our fathers made this government, they did not look forward to the state of things now existing, and therefore he thinks the doctrine was wrong; and he quotes Brooks, of South Carolina, to prove that our fathers then thought that probably slavery would be abolished by each state acting for itself before this time. Suppose they did; suppose they did not foresee what has occurred—does that change the principles of our government? They did not probably foresee the telegraph that transmits intelligence by lightning, nor did they foresee the railroads that now form the bonds of union between the different states, or the thousand mechanical inventions that have elevated mankind. But do these things change the principles of the government? Our fathers, I say, made this government on the principle of the right of each state to do as it pleases in its own domestic affairs, subject to the Constitution, and allowed the people of each to apply to every new change of circumstances such remedy as they may see fit to improve their condition. This right they have for all time to come....

I ask you to look into these things and then tell me whether the democracy or the abolitionists are right. I hold that the people of a territory, like those of a state (I use the language of Mr. Buchanan in his letter of acceptance), have the right to decide for themselves whether slavery shall or shall not exist within their limits. The point upon which Chief Justice Taney expresses his opinion is simply this: that slaves, being property, stand on an equal footing with other property, and consequently that the owner has the same right to carry that property into a territory that he has any other, subject to the same conditions. Suppose that one of your merchants was to take fifty or one hundred thousand dollars' worth of liquors to Kansas. He has a right to go there under that decision, but when he gets there he finds the Maine liquor law in force, and what can he do with his property after he gets it there? He cannot sell it, he cannot use it, it is subject to the local law, and that law is against him, and the best thing he can do with it is to bring it back into Missouri or Illinois and sell it. If you take Negroes to Kansas, as Col. Jeff. Davis said in his Bangor speech, from which I have quoted today, you must take them there subject to the local law. If the people want the institution of slavery, they will protect and encourage it; but if they do not want it, they will withhold that protection, and the absence of local legislation protecting slavery excludes it as completely as a positive prohibition. You slaveholders of Missouri might as well understand what you know practically, that you cannot carry slavery where the people do not want it. All you have a right to ask is that the people shall do as they please; if they want slavery, let them have it; if they do not want it, allow them to refuse to encourage it.

My friends, if, as I have said before, we will only live up to this great fundamental principle, there will be peace between the North and the South. Mr.

Lincoln admits that under the Constitution on all domestic questions, except slavery, we ought not to interfere with the people of each state. What right have we to interfere with slavery any more than we have to interfere with any other question? He says that this slavery question is now the bone of contention. Why? Simply because agitators have combined in all the free states to make war upon it. Suppose the agitators in the states should combine in one-half of the Union to make war upon the railroad system of the other half? They would thus be driven to the same sectional strife. Suppose one section makes war upon any other peculiar institution of the opposite section, and the same strife is produced. The only remedy and safety is that we shall stand by the Constitution as our fathers made it, obey the laws as they are passed, while they stand the proper test and sustain the decisions of the Supreme Court and the constituted authorities.

6. PARTY PLATFORMS OF 1860

EDITORS' NOTE.—The Democratic party, holding its 1860 national convention at Charleston, South Carolina, had difficulty in organizing because the delegates from the Lower South insisted that the party as a whole must accept the principle that "slavery was right." This led to an open split in the Democratic ranks, for Stephen A. Douglas, its logical candidate, had compromised on the slavery issue in sponsoring the Kansas-Nebraska Bill.

The first round in the struggle between the Democratic factions took place in the committee on resolutions, where the vote was by states, and the

southern factions forced their opinion on slavery into the majority report. The fight was carried onto the floor of the convention, where the majority report was replaced by the minority resolutions. By the narrow vote of 165 to 138 the Douglas forces won on the floor what they had failed to carry in committee. Before the amended resolutions could be finally accepted by the convention, however, a motion was heard to divide the resolutions and vote on the first resolution, omitting from it the phrase "and we recommend, etc." Upon passage of the first resolution, a separate vote was taken on each of the following. The second resolution was defeated by a vote of 21 to 238. The remainder were passed by substantial majorities, there being expressed opposition to only one, though several of the southern delegations refused to vote on any of them.

Before these resolutions could be made the will of the convention, Mississippi, Louisiana, South Carolina, Florida, Texas, Arkansas, and Georgia withdrew wholly or in part. An effort was then made to nominate presidential and vice-presidential candidates, but it was impossible to achieve an adequate vote in the rump convention; and, finally, on the tenth day, May 3, 1860, the convention adjourned, to reconvene June 18, 1860, in Baltimore.

In Mr. Cushing's remarks reopening the convention at Baltimore he erroneously referred to the minority report as containing five instead of six resolutions. However, he accurately omitted No. 2 as having been defeated at Charleston. Against each of the other resolutions stood a motion to reconsider and table. The matter was dropped until after candidates for the presidency and vice-presidency were nominated. On June 23, the last day of the convention, the seventh of the above resolutions was introduced and adopted. Items 1, 3, 4, and 5 of the minority report were specifically approved. By implication, No. 6 was also adopted. Thus, finally, the Douglas Democratic platform was constructed. Item 2, usually printed as part of the platform, does not belong but rather

was replaced in meaning and intent by item 7.

The same afternoon the Douglas Democratic platform was adopted, but in another Baltimore hall, one body of seceding Democrats, now including the Massachusetts delegation, and with Mr. Cushing presiding, met and adopted the second majority report of the Charleston Committee on Resolutions as their platform and nominated John C. Breckinridge of Kentucky for President. Meanwhile an earlier secessionist meeting which had met in St. Andrew's Hall, Charleston, adjourned to Richmond, where they awaited the results at Baltimore. When the second Baltimore convention had finished its work, the Richmond group met and ratified the Breckinridge nomination and platform, thus bringing unity to the radical slavery Democrats.

The Republican party, which met in Chicago in 1860, adopted the platform given below (pp. 757–59) and, on the third ballot, nominated Lincoln for the presidency.

The Constitutional Union party, made up of what Lincoln called the "nice exclusive sort" of Whigs and elements of the former American or "Know-Nothing" party, met in convention at Baltimore and nominated John Bell, senator from Tennessee.

The student who desires a full account of the conventions and campaign should consult E. D. Fite, *The Presidential Campaign of 1860* (New York, 1911), or appropriate chapters in James G. Randall, *Civil War and Reconstruction* (Boston, 1937).

A. THE ORIGINS OF THE DEMOCRATIC (DOUGLAS) PLATFORM[1]

1. *Resolved*, That we, the Democracy of the Union in convention assembled, hereby declare our affirmance of the resolutions unanimously adopted and declared as a platform of principles by the Democratic Convention at Cincinnati, in the year 1856, believing that Democratic principles are unchangeable in their nature when applied to the same subject matters; and we recommend as the only further resolutions the following:

2. Inasmuch as difference of opinion exists in the Democratic party as to the nature and extent of the powers of a territorial legislature, and as to the powers and duties of Congress, under the Constitution of the United States, over the institution of slavery within the territories,

Resolved, That the Democratic party will abide by the decision of the Supreme Court of the United States upon these questions of constitutional law.

3. *Resolved*, That it is the duty of the United States to afford ample and complete protection to all its citizens, whether at home or abroad, and whether native or foreign-born.

4. *Resolved*, That one of the necessities of the age, in a military, commercial, and postal point of view, is speedy communication between the Atlantic and Pacific states; and the Democratic party pledge such constitutional government aid as will insure the construction of a railroad to the Pacific Coast at the earliest practicable period.

5. *Resolved*, That the Democratic party are in favor of the acquisition of the island of Cuba on such terms as shall be honorable to ourselves and just to Spain.

6. *Resolved*, That the enactments of state legislatures to defeat the faithful execution of the Fugitive Slave Law are hostile in character, subversive of the Constitution, and revolutionary in their effect.

* * *

7. *Resolved*, That it is in accordance with the interpretation of the Cincinnati platform, that during the existence of the territorial governments the measure of restriction, whatever it may be, imposed by the federal Constitution on the power of the territorial legislature over the subject of the domestic relations, as the same has been or shall hereafter be finally determined by the Supreme Court of the United States, should be respected by all good citizens, and enforced with promptness and fidelity by every branch of the general government.

B. DEMOCRATIC (BRECKINRIDGE) PLATFORM[2]
ADOPTED JUNE 23, 1860

Resolved, That the platform adopted by the Democratic party at Cincinnati be affirmed, with the following explanatory resolutions:

1. *Resolved*, That the government of a territory organized by an act of Congress is provisional and temporary, and during its existence all citizens of the United States have an equal right to settle with their property in a territory, without their rights either of person or property being destroyed or impaired by congressional or territorial legislation.

2. *Resolved*, That it is the duty of the federal government in all its departments to protect, when necessary, the rights of persons and property in the territories, and wherever else its constitutional authority extends.

3. *Resolved*, That when settlers in a

1. Democratic National Convention, *Official Proceedings . . . 1860 . . .* (Cleveland, 1869), pp. 47–48, 177. Resolutions 1–6 constitute the minority report, introduced April 28, 1860. Number 7 was adopted on June 23.

2. National Democratic Convention, *Proceedings of the Convention at Charleston and Baltimore . . . 1860* (Washington, 1860), p. 246.

territory having an adequate population form a state constitution, the rights of sovereignty commence, and being consummated by an admission into the Union, they stand on an equal footing with the people of other states; and that a state thus organized ought to be admitted into the federal Union, whether its constitution prohibits or recognizes the institution of slavery.

4. *Resolved*, That the Democratic party are in favor of the acquisition of the island of Cuba on such terms as shall be honorable to ourselves and just to Spain, at the earliest practicable moment.

5. *Resolved*, That the enactments of state legislatures to defeat the faithful execution of the Fugitive Slave law are hostile in character, subversive of the Constitution, and revolutionary in their effect.

6. *Resolved*, That the democracy of the United States recognize it as an imperative duty of this government to protect naturalized citizens in all their rights, whether at home or in foreign lands, to the same extent as its native-born citizens.

Whereas one of the greatest necessities of the age, in a political, commercial, postal, and military point of view, is a speedy communication between the Pacific and Atlantic Coasts: Therefore,

7. *Be it resolved*, That the Democratic party do hereby pledge themselves to use every means in their power to secure the passage of some bill, to the extent of the constitutional authority of Congress, for the construction of a Pacific railroad, from the Mississippi River to the Pacific Ocean, at the earliest practicable moment....

C. REPUBLICAN PLATFORM[3]
ADOPTED MAY 17, 1860

Resolved, That we, the delegated representatives of the Republican electors of the United States, in convention assembled, in discharge of the duty we owe to our constituents and our country, unite in the following declarations:

1. That the history of the nation, during the last four years, has fully established the propriety and necessity of the organization and perpetuation of the Republican party, and that the causes which called it into existence are permanent in their nature, and now, more than ever before, demand its peaceful and constitutional triumph.

2. That the maintenance of the principles promulgated in the Declaration of Independence and embodied in the Federal constitution, "That all men are created equal; that they are endowed by their Creator with certain inalienable rights; that among these are life, liberty, and the pursuit of happiness; that, to

secure these rights, governments are instituted among men, deriving their just powers from the consent of the governed," is essential to the preservation of our Republican institutions; and that the federal Constitution, the rights of the states, and the Union of the states, must and shall be preserved.

3. That to the Union of the states this nation owes its unprecedented increase in population, its surprising development of material resources, its rapid augmentation of wealth, its happiness at home and its honor abroad; and we hold in abhorrence all schemes for disunion, come from whatever source they may: and we congratulate the country that no Republican member of Congress has uttered or countenances the threats of disunion so often made by Democratic members, without rebuke and with applause from their political associates; and we denounce those threats of disunion, in case of a popular overthrow of their ascendancy, as denying the vital principles of a free government, and as

3. *A Political Textbook for 1860* . . . , ed. Horace Greeley and John F. Cleveland (New York, 1860), pp. 26–27.

an avowal of contemplated treason, which it is the imperative duty of an indignant people sternly to rebuke and forever silence.

4. That the maintenance inviolate of the rights of the states, and especially the right of each state to order and control its own domestic institutions according to its own judgment exclusively, is essential to that balance of powers on which the perfection and endurance of our political fabric depend; and we denounce the lawless invasion by armed force of the soil of any state or territory, no matter under what pretext, as among the gravest of crimes.

5. That the present Democratic Administration has far exceeded our worst apprehensions, in its measureless subserviency to the exactions of a sectional interest, as especially evinced in its desperate exertions to force the infamous Lecompton Constitution upon the protesting people of Kansas; in construing the personal relation between master and servant to involve an unqualified property in persons; in its attempted enforcement, everywhere, on land and sea, through the intervention of Congress and of the federal courts of the extreme pretensions of a purely local interest; and in its general and unvarying abuse of the power intrusted to it by a confiding people.

6. That the people justly view with alarm the reckless extravagance which pervades every department of the federal government; that a return to rigid economy and accountability is indispensable to arrest the systematic plunder of the public treasury by favored partisans; while the recent startling developments of frauds and corruptions at the federal metropolis show that an entire change of administration is imperatively demanded.

7. That the new dogma that the Constitution, of its own force, carries slavery into any or all of the territories of the United States, is a dangerous political heresy, at variance with the explicit provisions of that instrument itself, with contemporaneous [sic] exposition, and with legislative and judicial precedent; is revolutionary in its tendency, and subversive of the peace and harmony of the country.

8. That the normal condition of all the territory of the United States is that of freedom: that as our Republican fathers, when they had abolished slavery in all our national territory, ordained that "no person should be deprived of life, liberty, or property, without due process of law," it becomes our duty, by legislation, whenever such legislation is necessary, to maintain this provision of the Constitution against all attempts to violate it; and we deny the authority of Congress, of a territorial legislature, or of any individuals, to give legal existence to slavery in any territory of the United States.

9. That we brand the recent reopening of the African slave trade, under the cover of our national flag, aided by perversions of judicial power, as a crime against humanity and a burning shame to our country and age; and we call upon Congress to take prompt and efficient measures for the total and final suppression of that execrable traffic.

10. That in the recent vetoes, by their federal governors, of the acts of the legislatures of Kansas and Nebraska, prohibiting slavery in those territories, we find a practical illustration of the boasted Democratic principles of non-intervention and popular sovereignty embodied in the Kansas-Nebraska Bill, and a demonstration of the deception and fraud involved therein.

11. That Kansas should, of right, be immediately admitted as a state under the Constitution recently formed and adopted by her people, and accepted by the House of Representatives.

12. That, while providing revenue for the support of the general govern-

ment by duties upon imports, sound policy requires such an adjustment of these imposts as to encourage the development of the industrial interests of the whole country: and we commend that policy of national exchanges which secures to the working men liberal wages, to agriculture remunerating prices, to mechanics and manufacturers an adequate reward for their skill, labor, and enterprise, and to the nation commercial prosperity and independence.

13. That we protest against any sale or alienation to others of the public lands held by actual settlers, and against any view of the homestead policy which regards the settlers as paupers or suppliants for public bounty; and we demand the passage by Congress of the complete and satisfactory homestead measure which has already passed the House.

14. That the Republican party is opposed to any change in our naturalization laws or any state legislation by which the rights of citizenship hitherto accorded to immigrants from foreign lands shall be abridged or impaired; and in favor of giving a full and efficient protection to the rights of all classes of citizens, whether native or naturalized, both at home and abroad.

15. That appropriations by Congress for river and harbor improvements of a national character, required for the accommodation and security of an existing commerce, are authorized by the Constitution, and justified by the obligations of government to protect the lives and property of its citizens.

16. That a railroad to the Pacific Ocean is imperatively demanded by the interests of the whole country; that the federal government ought to render immediate and efficient aid in its construction; and that, as preliminary thereto, a daily overland mail should be promptly established.

17. Finally, having thus set forth our distinctive principles and views, we invite the co-operation of all citizens, however differing on other questions, who substantially agree with us in their affirmance and support.

D. CONSTITUTIONAL UNION PLATFORM[4]
ADOPTED MAY 9, 1860

WHEREAS, Experience has demonstrated that platforms adopted by the partisan conventions of the country have had the effect to mislead and deceive the people, and at the same time to widen the political divisions of the country, by the creation and encouragement of geographical and sectional parties; therefore,

Resolved, That it is both the part of patriotism and of duty *to recognize* no political principle other than THE CONSTITUTION OF THE COUNTRY, THE UNION OF THE STATES, AND THE ENFORCEMENT OF THE LAWS, and that, as representatives of the Constitutional Union men of the country in national convention assembled, we hereby pledge ourselves to maintain, protect, and defend, separately and unitedly, these great principles of public liberty and national safety, against all enemies at home and abroad, believing that thereby peace may once more be restored to the country, the rights of the people and of the states reestablished, and the government again placed in that condition, of justice, fraternity, and equality, which, under the example and Constitution of our fathers, has solemnly bound every citizen of the United States to maintain a more perfect union, establish justice, insure domestic tranquillity, provide for the common defense, promote the general welfare, and secure the blessings of liberty to ourselves and our posterity.

4. *Ibid.*, p. 29.

SECTION D. THE CIVIL WAR AND RECONSTRUCTION

1. MISSISSIPPI RESOLUTIONS ON SECESSION
NOVEMBER 30, 1860[1]

EDITOR'S NOTE.—Historically the doctrine of constitutional secession, as distinct from the Lockean right of rebellion, frequently was advanced by discontented sections. Before 1850 there was little difference between the regions of the country in this respect. Each denounced as contrary to state sovereignty any national measures against its sectional interest.

The resolutions of the Mississippi legislature of November 30, 1860, are among the most succinct statements of the causes of secession. The adoption of the resolutions preceded the adoption of the ordinance of secession which was drawn up by a convention selected to take action after the secession of South Carolina in December. That ordinance, adopted after considerable debate and in the face of determined opposition, was the formal instrument dissolving the compact between the state of Mississippi and the United States. Thus Mississippi was the first to follow South Carolina in the effort to dissolve the Union.

WHEREAS, The Constitutional Union was formed by the several states in their separate sovereign capacity for the purpose of mutual advantage and protection;

That the several states are distinct sovereignties, whose supremacy is limited so far only as the same has been delegated by voluntary compact to a federal government, and, when it fails to accomplish the ends for which it was established, the parties to the compact have the right to resume, each state for itself, such delegated powers;

That the institution of slavery existed prior to the formation of the federal Constitution, and is recognized by its letter, and all efforts to impair its value or lessen its duration by Congress, or any of the free states, is a violation of the compact of Union and is destructive of the ends for which it was ordained, but in defiance of the principles of the Union thus established, the people of the northern states have assumed a revolutionary position toward the southern states;

That they have set at defiance that provision of the Constitution which was intended to secure domestic tranquillity among the states and promote their general welfare, namely: "No person held to service or labor in one state, under the laws thereof, escaping into another, shall in consequence of any law or regulation therein, be discharged from such service or labor, but shall be delivered up on claim of the party to whom such service or labor may be due";

That they have by voluntary associations, individual agencies, and state legislation interfered with slavery as it prevails in the slave-holding states;

That they have enticed our slaves from us and, by state intervention, ob-

1. Mississippi, *Laws of the State* . . . , 1860 (Jackson, Miss., 1860), pp. 43–45.

structed and prevented their rendition under the Fugitive Slave Law;

That they continue their system of agitation obviously for the purpose of encouraging other slaves to escape from service, to weaken the institution in the slave-holding states, by rendering the holding of such property insecure, and as a consequence its ultimate abolition certain;

That they claim the right and demand its execution by Congress, to exclude slavery from the territories, but claim the right of protection for every species of property owned by themselves;

That they declare in every manner in which public opinion is expressed their unalterable determination to exclude from admittance into the Union any new state that tolerates slavery in its constitution and thereby force Congress to a condemnation of that species of property;

That they thus seek by an increase of abolition states "to acquire two-thirds of both houses," for the purpose of preparing an amendment to the Constitution of the United States, abolishing slavery in the states, and so continue the agitation that the proposed amendment shall be ratified by the legislatures of three-fourths of the states;

That they have in violation of the comity of all civilized nations, and in violation of the comity established by the Constitution of the United States, insulted and outraged our citizens when traveling among them for pleasure, health, or business, by taking their servants and liberating the same, under the forms of state laws, and subjecting their owners to degrading and ignominious punishment;

That to encourage the stealing of our property they have put at defiance that provision of the Constitution which declares that fugitives from justice into another state, on demand of the executive authority of that state from which he fled, shall be delivered up;

That they have sought to create domestic discord in the southern states by incendiary publications;

That they encouraged a hostile invasion of a southern state to excite insurrection, murder, and rapine;

That they have deprived southern citizens of their property and continue an unfriendly agitation of their domestic institutions, claiming for themselves perfect immunity from external interference with their domestic policy;

We of the southern states alone made an exception to that universal quiet;

That they have elected a majority of electors for President and Vice-President on the ground that there exists an irreconcilable conflict between the two sections of the Confederacy in reference to their respective systems of labor and in pursuance of their hostility to us and our institutions, thus declaring to the civilized world that the powers of this government are to be used for the dishonor and overthrow of the southern section of this great Confederacy. Therefore;

Be it resolved by the legislature of the state of Mississippi, That in the opinion of those who now constitute the said legislature, the secession of each aggrieved state is the proper remedy for these injuries.

J. A. P. CAMPBELL
*Speaker of the House
of Representatives*

JAMES DRANE
President of the Senate
Approved
November 30, 1860

MISSISSIPPI SECESSION ORDINANCE[2]

AN ORDINANCE to dissolve the union between the state of Mississippi and other states united with her under the compact entitled "the Constitution of the United States of America."

The people of the state of Mississippi, in convention assembled, do ordain and declare, and it is hereby ordained and declared as follows, to wit:

SECTION 1st. That all the laws and ordinances by which the said state of Mississippi became a member of the federal Union of the United States of America be, and the same are hereby, repealed, and that all obligations on the part of the said state or the people thereof to observe the same, be withdrawn, and that the said state doth hereby resume all the rights, functions, and powers which, by any of said laws or ordinances, were conveyed to the government of the said United States, and is absolved from all the obligations, restraints, and duties incurred to the said federal Union, and shall from henceforth be a free, sovereign, and independent state.

SEC. 2nd. That so much of the first section of the seventh article of the constitution of this state as requires members of the legislature, and all officers, executive and judicial, to take an oath or affirmation to support the Constitution of the United States, be, and the same is hereby, abrogated and annulled.

SEC. 3rd. That all rights acquired and vested under the Constitution of the United States, or under any act of Congress passed, or treaty made, in pursuance thereof, or under any law of this state, and not incompatible with this Ordinance, shall remain in force and have the same effect as if this Ordinance had not been passed.

SEC. 4th. That the people of the state of Mississippi hereby consent to form a federal Union with such of the states as may have seceded or may secede from the Union of the United States of America, upon the basis of the present Constitution of the said United States, except such parts thereof as embrace other portions than such seceding states.

Thus ordained and declared in convention the ninth day of January in the year of our Lord one thousand eight hundred and sixty-one.

IN TESTIMONY *of the passage of which, and the determination of the members of this Convention to uphold and maintain the state in the position she has assumed by said Ordinance, it is signed by the president and members of this convention this the fifteenth day of January, A.D., 1861.—W. S. BARRY, President.*

2. FIRST INAUGURAL ADDRESS, MARCH 4, 1861[1]

By ABRAHAM LINCOLN

Fellow-Citizens of the United States:

In compliance with a custom as old as the government itself, I appear before you to address you briefly and to take in your presence the oath prescribed by the Constitution of the United States to be taken by the President "before he enters on the execution of his office."

I do not consider it necessary at present for me to discuss those matters of administration about which there is no special anxiety or excitement.

Apprehension seems to exist among the people of the southern states that by the accession of a Republican Administration their property and their peace

2. Mississippi, *Journal of the State Convention . . . January, 1861 . . .* (Jackson, Miss., 1861), pp. 119-20.

1. *Messages and Papers of the Presidents*, ed. James D. Richardson (Washington, 1896), VI, 5-12.

and personal security are to be endangered. There has never been any reasonable cause for such apprehension. Indeed, the most ample evidence to the contrary has all the while existed and been open to their inspection. It is found in nearly all the published speeches of him who now addresses you. I do but quote from one of those speeches when I declare that—

I have no purpose, directly or indirectly, to interfere with the institution of slavery in the states where it exists. I believe I have no lawful right to do so, and I have no inclination to do so.

Those who nominated and elected me did so with full knowledge that I had made this and many similar declarations and had never recanted them; and more than this, they placed in the platform for my acceptance, and as a law to themselves and to me, the clear and emphatic resolution which I now read:

Resolved, That the maintenance inviolate of the rights of the states, and especially the right of each state to order and control its own domestic institutions according to its own judgment exclusively, is essential to that balance of power on which the perfection and endurance of our political fabric depend; and we denounce the lawless invasion by armed force of the soil of any state or territory, no matter under what pretext, as among the gravest of crimes.

I now reiterate these sentiments, and in doing so I only press upon the public attention the most conclusive evidence of which the case is susceptible that the property, peace, and security of no section are to be in any wise endangered by the now incoming Administration. I add, too, that all the protection which, consistently with the Constitution and the laws, can be given will be cheerfully given to all the states when lawfuly demanded, for whatever cause—as cheerfully to one section as to another.

There is much controversy about the delivering-up of fugitives from service or labor. The clause I now read is as plainly written in the Constitution as any other of its provisions:

No person held to service or labor in one state, under the laws thereof, escaping into another, shall in consequence of any law or regulation therein be discharged from such service or labor, but shall be delivered up on claim of the party to whom such service or labor may be due.

It is scarcely questioned that this provision was intended by those who made it for the reclaiming of what we call fugitive slaves; and the intention of the lawgiver is the law. All members of Congress swear their support to the whole Constitution—to this provision as much as to any other. To the proposition, then, that slaves whose cases come within the terms of this clause "shall be delivered up" their oaths are unanimous. Now, if they would make the effort in good temper, could they not with nearly equal unanimity frame and pass a law by means of which to keep good that unanimous oath?

There is some difference of opinion whether this clause should be enforced by national or by state authority, but surely that difference is not a very material one. If the slave is to be surrendered, it can be of but little consequence to him or to others by which authority it is done. And should anyone in any case be content that his oath shall go unkept on a merely unsubstantial controversy as to *how* it shall be kept?

Again: In any law upon this subject ought not all the safeguards of liberty known in civilized and humane jurisprudence to be introduced, so that a free man be not in any case surrendered as a slave? And might it not be well at the same time to provide by law for the enforcement of that clause in the Constitution which guarantees that "the citizens of each state shall be entitled to all privileges and immunities of citizens in the several states"?

I take the official oath today with no mental reservations and with no purpose to construe the Constitution or laws by any hypercritical rules; and while I do not choose now to specify particular acts of Congress as proper to be enforced, I do suggest that it will be much safer for all, both in official and private stations, to conform to and abide by all those acts which stand unrepealed than to violate any of them, trusting to find impunity in having them held to be unconstitutional.

It is seventy-two years since the first inauguration of a President under our national Constitution. During that period fifteen different and greatly distinguished citizens have in succession administered the executive branch of the government. They have conducted it through many perils, and generally with great success. Yet, with all this scope of precedent, I now enter upon the same task for the brief constitutional term of four years under great and peculiar difficulty. A disruption of the federal Union, heretofore only menaced, is now formidably attempted.

I hold that in contemplation of universal law and of the Constitution the union of these states is perpetual. Perpetuity is implied, if not expressed, in the fundamental law of all national governments. It is safe to assert that no government proper ever had a provision in its organic law for its own termination. Continue to execute all the express provisions of our national Constitution, and the Union will endure forever, it being impossible to destroy it except by some action not provided for in the instrument itself.

Again: If the United States be not a government proper, but an association of states in the nature of contract merely, can it, as a contract, be peaceably unmade by less than all the parties who made it? One party to a contract may violate it—break it, so to speak—but does it not require all to lawfully rescind it?

Descending from these general principles, we find the proposition that in legal contemplation the Union is perpetual confirmed by the history of the Union itself. The Union is much older than the Constitution. It was formed, in fact, by the Articles of Association in 1774. It was matured and continued by the Declaration of Independence in 1776. It was further matured, and the faith of all the then thirteen states expressly plighted and engaged that it should be perpetual, by the Articles of Confederation in 1778. And finally, in 1787, one of the declared objects for ordaining and establishing the Constitution was *"to form a more perfect Union."*

But if destruction of the Union by one or by a part only of the states be lawfully possible, the Union is *less* perfect than before the Constitution, having lost the vital element of perpetuity.

It follows from these views that no state upon its own mere motion can lawfully get out of the Union; that *resolves* and *ordinances* to that effect are legally void, and that acts of violence within any state or states against the authority of the United States are insurrectionary or revolutionary, according to circumstances.

I therefore consider that in view of the Constitution and the laws the Union is unbroken, and to the extent of my ability I shall take care, as the Constitution itself expressly enjoins upon me, that the laws of the Union be faithfully executed in all the states. Doing this I deem to be only a simple duty on my part, and I shall perform it so far as practicable unless my rightful masters, the American people, shall withhold the requisite means or in some authoritative manner direct the contrary. I trust this will not be regarded as a menace, but only as the declared purpose of the Union that it *will* constitutionally defend and maintain itself.

In doing this, there needs to be no bloodshed or violence, and there shall be none unless it be forced upon the national authority. The power confided to me will be used to hold, occupy, and possess the property and places belonging to the government and to collect the duties and imposts; but, beyond what may be necessary for these objects, there will be no invasion, no using of force against or among the people anywhere. Where hostility to the United States in any interior locality shall be so great and universal as to prevent competent resident citizens from holding the federal offices, there will be no attempt to force obnoxious strangers among the people for that object. While the strict legal right may exist in the government to enforce the exercise of these offices, the attempt to do so would be so irritating and so nearly impracticable withal that I deem it better to forego for the time the uses of such offices.

The mails, unless repelled, will continue to be furnished in all parts of the Union. So far as possible the people everywhere shall have that sense of perfect security which is most favorable to calm thought and reflection. The course here indicated will be followed unless current events and experience shall show a modification or change to be proper, and in every case and exigency my best discretion will be exercised, according to circumstances actually existing and with a view and a hope of a peaceful solution of the national troubles and the restoration of fraternal sympathies and affections.

That there are persons in one section or another who seek to destroy the Union at all events and are glad of any pretext to do it I will neither affirm nor deny; but if there be such, I need address no word to them. To those, however, who really love the Union may I not speak?

Before entering upon so grave a matter as the destruction of our national fabric, with all its benefits, its memories, and its hopes, would it not be wise to ascertain precisely why we do it? Will you hazard so desperate a step while

there is any possibility that any portion of the ills you fly from have no real existence? Will you, while the certain ills you fly to are greater than all the real ones you fly from, will you risk the commission of so fearful a mistake?

All profess to be content in the Union if all constitutional rights can be maintained. Is it true, then, that any right plainly written in the Constitution has been denied? I think not. Happily, the human mind is so constituted that no party can reach to the audacity of doing this. Think, if you can, of a single instance in which a plainly written provision of the Constitution has ever been denied. If by the mere force of numbers a majority should deprive a minority of any clearly written constitutional right, it might in a moral point of view justify revolution; certainly would if such right were a vital one. But such is not our case. All the vital rights of minorities and of individuals are so plainly assured to them by affirmations and negations, guaranties and prohibitions, in the Constitution that controversies never arise concerning them. But no organic law can ever be framed with a provision specifically applicable to every question which may occur in practical administration. No foresight can anticipate nor any document of reasonable length contain express provisions for all possible questions. Shall fugitives from labor be surrendered by national or by state authority? The Constitution does not expressly say. *May* Congress prohibit slavery in the territories? The Constitution does not expressly say. *Must* Congress protect slavery in the territories? The Constitution does not expressly say.

From questions of this class spring all our constitutional controversies, and we divide upon them into majorities and minorities. If the minority will not acquiesce, the majority must, or the government must cease. There is no other alternative, for continuing the government is acquiescence on one side or the other. If a minority in such case will secede rather than acquiesce, they make a precedent which in turn will divide and ruin them, for a minority of their own will secede from them whenever a majority refuses to be controlled by such minority. For instance, why may not any portion of a new confederacy a year or two hence arbitrarily secede again, precisely as portions of the present Union now claim to secede from it? All who cherish disunion sentiments are now being educated to the exact temper of doing this.

Is there such perfect identity of interests among the states to compose a new union as to produce harmony only and prevent renewed secession?

Plainly the central idea of secession is the essence of anarchy. A majority held in restraint by constitutional checks and limitations, and always changing easily with deliberate changes of popular opinions and sentiments, is the only true sovereign of a free people. Whoever rejects it does of necessity fly to anarchy or to despotism. Unanimity is impossible. The rule of a minority, as a permanent arrangement, is wholly inadmissible; so that, rejecting the majority principle, anarchy or despotism in some form is all that is left.

I do not forget the position assumed by some that constitutional questions are to be decided by the Supreme Court, nor do I deny that such decisions must be binding in any case upon the parties to a suit as to the object of that suit, while they are also entitled to very high respect and consideration in all parallel cases by all other departments of the government. And while it is obviously possible that such decision may be erroneous in any given case, still the evil effect following it, being limited to that particular case, with the chance that it may be overruled and never become a precedent for other cases, can better be borne than could the evils of a different practice. At the same time, the candid citizen must confess that if the policy of the government upon vital questions affecting the whole people is to be irrevocably fixed by decisions of the Supreme Court, the instant they are made in ordinary litigation between parties in personal actions the people will have ceased to be their own rulers, having to that extent practically resigned their government into the hands of that eminent tribunal. Nor is there in this view any assault upon the Court or the judges. It is a duty from which they may not shrink to decide cases properly brought before them, and it is no fault of theirs if others seek to turn their decisions to political purposes.

One section of our country believes slavery is *right* and ought to be extended, while the other believes it is *wrong* and ought not to be extended. This is the only substantial dispute. The fugitive-slave clause of the Constitution and the law for the suppression of the foreign slave trade are each as well enforced, perhaps, as any law can ever be in a community where the moral sense of the people imperfectly supports the law itself. The great body of the people abide by the dry legal obligation in both cases, and a few break over in each. This, I think, cannot be perfectly cured, and it would be worse in both cases *after* the separation of the sections than before. The foreign slave trade, now imperfectly suppressed, would be ultimately revived without restriction in one section, while fugitive slaves, now only partially surrendered, would not be surrendered at all by the other.

Physically speaking, we cannot separate. We cannot remove our respective sections from each other nor build an impassable wall between them. A husband and wife may be divorced and go out of the presence and beyond the reach of each other, but the different parts of our country cannot do this. They cannot but remain face to face, and intercourse, either amicable or hostile, must continue between them. Is it possible, then, to make that intercourse more advantageous or more satisfactory *after* separation than *before?* Can aliens make treaties easier than friends can make laws? Can treaties be more faithfully enforced between aliens than laws can among friends? Suppose you go to war, you cannot fight always; and when, after much loss on both sides and no gain on either, you cease fighting, the identical old questions, as to terms of intercourse, are again upon you.

This country, with its institutions, belongs to the people who inhabit it. Whenever they shall grow weary of the existing government, they can exercise their *constitutional* right of amending it or their *revolutionary* right to dismember or overthrow it. I cannot be ignorant of the fact that many worthy and patriotic citizens are desirous of having the national Constitution amended. While I make no recommendation of amendments, I fully recognize the rightful authority of the people over the whole subject, to be exercised in either of the modes prescribed in the instrument itself; and I should, under existing circumstances, favor rather than oppose a fair opportunity being afforded the people to act upon it. I will venture to add that to me the convention mode seems preferable, in that it allows amendments to originate with the people themselves, instead of only permitting them to take or reject propositions originated by others, not especially chosen for the purpose, and which might not be precisely such as they would wish to either accept or refuse. I understand a proposed amendment to the Constitution—which amendment, however, I have not seen—has passed Congress, to the effect that the federal government shall never interfere with the domestic institutions of the states, including that of persons held to service. To avoid misconstruction of what I have said, I depart from my purpose not to speak of particular amendments so far as to say that, holding such a provision to now be implied constitutional law, I have no objection to its being made express and irrevocable.

The Chief Magistrate derives all his authority from the people, and they have conferred none upon him to fix terms for the separation of the states. The people themselves can do this also if they choose, but the Executive as such has nothing to do with it. His duty is to administer the present government as it came to his hands and to transmit it unimpaired by him to his successor.

Why should there not be a patient confidence in the ultimate justice of the people? Is there any better or equal hope in the world? In our present differences, is either party without faith of being in the right? If the Almighty Ruler of Nations, with His eternal truth and justice, be on your side of the North, or on yours of the South, that truth and that justice will surely prevail by the judgment of this great tribunal of the American people.

By the frame of the government under which we live this same people have wisely given their public servants but little power for mischief and have with equal wisdom provided for the return of that little to their own hands at very short intervals. While the people retain their virtue and vigilance no administration by any extreme of wickedness or folly can very seriously injure the government in the short space of four years.

My countrymen, one and all, think calmly and *well* upon this whole subject. Nothing valuable can be lost by taking time. If there be an object to *hurry* any of you in hot haste to a step which you would never take *deliberately*, that object will be frustrated by taking time; but no good object can be frustrated by it. Such of you as are now dissatisfied still have the old Constitution unimpaired, and, on the sensitive point, the laws of your own framing under it; while the new administration will have no immediate power, if it would, to change either. If it were admitted that you who are dissatisfied hold the right side in the dispute, there still is no single good reason for precipitate action. Intelligence, patriotism, Christianity, and a firm reliance on Him who has never yet forsaken this favored land are still competent to adjust in the best way all our present difficulty.

In *your* hands, my dissatisfied fellow-countrymen, and not in *mine*, is the momentous issue of civil war. The government will not assail *you*. You can have no conflict without being yourselves the aggressors. *You* have no oath registered in heaven to destroy the government, while *I* shall have the most solemn one to "preserve, protect, and defend it."

I am loath to close. We are not enemies, but friends. We must not be enemies. Though passion may have strained, it must not break our bonds of affection. The mystic chords of memory, stretching from every battlefield and patriot grave to every living heart and hearthstone all over this broad land, will yet swell the chorus of the Union, when again touched, as surely they will be, by the better angels of our nature.

3. LETTER TO HORACE GREELEY[1]

By ABRAHAM LINCOLN

EDITORS' NOTE.—This letter was written in answer to "The Prayer of Twenty Millions," an open letter by Horace Greeley to Lincoln, dated August 19, 1862, complaining against Lincoln's policy of prosecuting the war merely to save the Union and demanding immediate emancipation of the slaves.

Horace Greeley (1811–72) was publisher and editor of the *New York Tribune*, which during the 1850's became the political bible for great areas of the North. He was one of the first publishers to abandon Whiggery for the Republican party. In spite of his eccentricities, Greeley and his *Tribune* were great forces in the Republican party, and his "Prayer of Twenty Millions" needed an answer.

WASHINGTON, August 22, 1862

Hon. Horace Greeley:

DEAR SIR:

I have just read yours of the nineteenth, addressed to myself through the *New York Tribune*. If there be in it any statements or assumptions of fact which I may know to be erroneous, I do not now and here controvert them. If there be in it any inferences which I may believe to be falsely drawn, I do not now and here argue against them. If there be perceptible in it an impatient and dictatorial tone, I waive it in deference to an old friend, whose heart I have always supposed to be right.

As to the policy I "seem to be pursuing," as you say, I have not meant to leave anyone in doubt.

I would save the Union. I would save it the shortest way under the Constitution. The sooner the national authority can be restored, the nearer the Union will be "the Union as it was." If there be those who would not save the Union unless they could at the same time *save* slavery, I do not agree with them. If there be those who would not save the Union unless they could at the same time *destroy* slavery, I do not agree with them. My paramount object in this

1. *The Rebellion Record*, ed. Frank Moore (New York, 1866–73), XII, 483.

struggle *is* to save the Union and is *not* either to save or destroy slavery. If I could save the Union without freeing *any* slave, I would do it; and if I could save it by freeing *all* the slaves, I would do it; and if I could do it by freeing some and leaving others alone, I would also do that. What I do about slavery and the colored race, I do because I believe it helps to save this Union; and what I forbear, I forbear because I do *not* believe it would help to save the Union. I shall do *less* whenever I shall believe what I am doing hurts the cause, and I shall do *more* whenever I shall believe doing more will help the cause. I shall try to correct errors when shown to be errors; and I shall adopt new views so fast as they shall appear to be true views. I have here stated my purpose according to my view of *official* duty, and I intend no modification of my oft-expressed *personal* wish that all men, everywhere, could be free.

Yours,

A. LINCOLN

4. THE EMANCIPATION PROCLAMATION[1]

By ABRAHAM LINCOLN

WHEREAS, on the twenty-second day of September, in the year of our Lord one thousand eight hundred and sixty-two, a proclamation was issued by the President of the United States, containing, among other things, the following, to wit:

"That on the first day of January, in the year of our Lord one thousand eight hundred and sixty-three, all persons held as slaves within any state or designated part of a state, the people whereof shall then be in rebellion against the United States, shall be then, thenceforward, and forever, free; and the Executive Government of the United States, including the military and naval authority thereof, will recognize and maintain the freedom of such persons, and will do no act or acts to repress such persons, or any of them, in any efforts they may make for their actual freedom.

"That the Executive will, on the first day of January aforesaid, by proclamation, designate the states and parts of states, if any, in which the people thereof, respectively, shall then be in rebellion against the United States; and the fact that any state, or the people thereof, shall on that day be in good faith represented in the Congress of the United States, by members chosen thereto at elections, wherein a majority of the qualified voters of such states shall have participated, shall, in the absence of strong countervailing testimony, be deemed conclusive evidence that such state, and the people thereof, are not then in rebellion against the United States."

Now, therefore, I, Abraham Lincoln, President of the United States, by virtue of the power in me vested as commander-in-chief of the army and navy of the United States, in time of actual armed rebellion against the authority and government of the United States, and as a fit and necessary war measure for suppressing said rebellion, do, on this first day of January, in the year of our Lord one thousand eight hundred and sixty-three, and in accordance with my purpose so to do, publicly proclaimed for the full period of one hundred days from the day first above mentioned, order and designate as the states and parts of states wherein the people thereof, respectively, are this day in rebellion against the United States, the following, to wit:

Arkansas, Texas, Louisiana (except the parishes of St. Bernard, Plaquemines, Jefferson, St. John, St. Charles, St. James, Ascension, Assumption, Terre Bonne, Lafourche, St. Mary, St. Martin,

1. *United States Statutes at Large*, XII, 1268.

and Orleans, including the city of New Orleans), Mississippi, Alabama, Florida, Georgia, South Carolina, North Carolina, and Virginia (except the forty-eight counties designated as West Virginia, and also the counties of Berkeley, Accomac, Northampton, Elizabeth City, York, Princess Ann, and Norfolk, including the cities of Norfolk and Portsmouth), and which excepted parts are for the present left precisely as if this proclamation were not issued.

And by virtue of the power and for the purpose aforesaid, I do order and declare that all persons held as slaves within said designated states and parts of states are, and henceforward shall be, free; and that the Executive Government of the United States, including the military and naval authorities thereof, will recognize and maintain the freedom of said persons.

And I hereby enjoin upon the people so declared to be free to abstain from all violence, unless in necessary self-defense; and I recommend to them that, all cases when allowed, they labor faithfully for reasonable wages.

And I further declare and make known that such persons, of suitable condition, will be received into the armed service of the United States to garrison forts, positions, stations, and other places, and to man vessels of all sorts in said service.

And upon this act, sincerely believed to be an act of justice, warranted by the Constitution upon military necessity, I invoke the considerate judgment of mankind and the gracious favor of Almighty God.

In witness whereof, I have hereunto set my hand and caused the seal of the United States to be affixed.

Done at the city of Washington this first day of January, in the year of our Lord one thousand eight hundred and sixty-three, and of the Independence of the United States of America the eighty-seventh.

5. GETTYSBURG ADDRESS, NOVEMBER 19, 1863[1]

By ABRAHAM LINCOLN

Fourscore and seven years ago our fathers brought forth on this continent a new nation, conceived in liberty, and dedicated to the proposition that all men are created equal.

Now we are engaged in a great civil war, testing whether that nation, or any nation so conceived and so dedicated, can long endure. We are met on a great battlefield of that war. We have come to dedicate a portion of that field as a final resting-place for those who here gave their lives that that nation might live. It is altogether fitting and proper that we should do this.

But, in a larger sense, we cannot dedicate—we cannot consecrate—we cannot hallow—this ground. The brave men, living and dead, who struggled here, have consecrated it far above our poor power to add or detract. The world will little note nor long remember what we say here, but it can never forget what they did here. It is for us, the living, rather, to be dedicated here to the unfinished work which they who fought here have thus far so nobly advanced. It is rather for us to be here dedicated to the great task remaining before us—that from these honored dead we take increased devotion to that cause for which they gave the last full measure of devotion; that we here highly resolve that these dead shall not have died in vain; that this nation, under God, shall have a new birth of freedom; and that government of the people, by the people, for the people, shall not perish from the earth.

1. Abraham Lincoln, *Complete Works . . .*, ed. John G. Nicolay and John Hay (New York, 1905), IX, 209-10.

6. SECOND INAUGURAL ADDRESS, MARCH 4, 1865[1]

By ABRAHAM LINCOLN

Fellow-Countrymen:

At this second appearing to take the oath of the presidential office there is less occasion for an extended address than there was at the first. Then a statement somewhat in detail of a course to be pursued seemed fitting and proper. Now, at the expiration of four years, during which public declarations have been constantly called forth on every point and phase of the great contest which still absorbs the attention and engrosses the energies of the nation, little that is new could be presented. The progress of our arms, upon which all else chiefly depends, is as well known to the public as to myself, and it is, I trust, reasonably satisfactory and encouraging to all. With high hope for the future, no prediction in regard to it is ventured.

On the occasion corresponding to this four years ago all thoughts were anxiously directed to an impending civil war. All dreaded it, all sought to avert it. While the inaugural address was being delivered from this place, devoted altogether to *saving* the Union without war, insurgent agents were in the city seeking to *destroy* it without war—seeking to dissolve the Union and divide effects by negotiation. Both parties deprecated war, but one of them would *make* war rather than let the nation survive, and the other would *accept* war rather than let it perish, and the war came.

One-eighth of the whole population were colored slaves, not distributed generally over the Union, but localized in the southern part of it. These slaves constituted a peculiar and powerful interest. All knew that this interest was somehow the cause of the war. To strengthen, perpetuate, and extend this interest was the object for which the insurgents would rend the Union even by war, while the government claimed no right to do more than to restrict the territorial enlargement of it. Neither party expected for the war the magnitude or the duration which it has already attained. Neither anticipated that the *cause* of the conflict might cease with or even before the conflict itself should cease. Each looked for an easier triumph and a result less fundamental and astounding. Both read the same Bible and pray to the same God, and each invokes His aid against the other. It may seem strange that any men should dare to ask a just God's assistance in wringing their bread from the sweat of other men's faces, but let us judge not that we be not judged. The prayers of both could not be answered. That of neither has been answered fully. The Almighty has His own purposes. "Woe unto the world because of offenses; for it must needs be that offenses come, but woe to that man by whom the offense cometh." If we shall suppose that American slavery is one of those offenses which, in the providence of God, must needs come, but which, having continued through His appointed time, He now wills to remove, and that He gives to both North and South this terrible war as the woe due to those by whom the offense came, shall we discern therein any departure from those divine attributes which the believers in a living God always ascribe to Him? Fondly do we hope, fervently do we pray, that this mighty scourge of war may speedily pass away. Yet, if God wills that it continue until all the wealth piled by the bondsman's two hundred and fifty years of unrequited toil shall be sunk, and until every drop of blood drawn with the lash shall be paid by another drawn with the sword,

1. *Messages and Papers of the Presidents*, ed. Richardson, VI, 276–77.

as was said three thousand years ago, so still it must be said "the judgments of the Lord are true and righteous altogether."

With malice toward none, with charity for all, with firmness in the right as God gives us to see the right, let us strive on to finish the work we are in, to bind up the nation's wounds, to care for him who shall have borne the battle and for his widow and his orphan, to do all which may achieve and cherish a just and lasting peace among ourselves and with all nations.

7. *EX PARTE* MILLIGAN[1]

EDITORS' NOTE.—On October 5, 1864, Milligan, a civilian, was arrested in Indiana by order of the military commandant of the district of Indiana. He was tried by a military court, established by authority of the President, for inciting insurrection, found guilty, and sentenced to death. His sentence was approved by the President, and the execution was set for May 19, 1865. In January, 1865, after the military trial, a grand jury impaneled by an Indiana court met but found no indictment against Milligan. On May 10, 1865, Milligan filed a petition for a writ of habeas corpus, in effect asking that the validity of his imprisonment be considered in the federal circuit court in Indiana. Under an act of Congress of March 3, 1863, President Lincoln by a proclamation of September 15, 1863, had suspended the privilege of the writ of habeas corpus where persons were held as prisoners for violations of laws punishing interference with military operations, including the kind of interference for which Milligan had been convicted by the military court. The judges of the circuit court were divided in their opinion on the legal questions presented and certified questions to the Supreme Court. The act of Congress was held by its terms to authorize a writ of habeas corpus under the circumstances, and the validity of Milligan's confinement was denied by the Supreme Court.

Mr. Justice DAVIS delivered the opinion of the Court. . . .

During the late wicked Rebellion, the temper of the times did not allow that calmness in deliberation and discussion so necessary to a correct conclusion of a purely judicial question. *Then*, considerations of safety were mingled with the exercise of power; and feelings and interests prevailed which are happily terminated. *Now* that the public safety is assured, this question, as well as all others, can be discussed and decided without passion or the admixture of any element not required to form a legal judgment. We approach the investigation of this case fully sensible of the magnitude of the inquiry and the necessity of full and cautious deliberation. . . .

The controlling question in the case is this: Upon the *facts* stated in Milligan's petition, and the exhibits filed, had the military commission mentioned in it *jurisdiction*, legally, to try and sentence him? Milligan, not a resident of one of the rebellious states, or a prisoner of war, but a citizen of Indiana for twenty years past, and never in the military or naval service, is, while at his home, arrested by the military power of the

1. 71 U.S. 2 (1866), 107, 109, 118–22, 124–27, 132–33, 135–37, 139–41.

United States, imprisoned, and, on certain criminal charges preferred against him, tried, convicted, and sentenced to be hanged by a military commission, organized under the direction of the military commander of the military district of Indiana. Had this tribunal the *legal* power and authority to try and punish this man?

No graver question was ever considered by this Court, nor one which more nearly concerns the rights of the whole people; for it is the birthright of every American citizen, when charged with crime, to be tried and punished according to law. The power of punishment is alone through the means which the laws have provided for that purpose, and, if they are ineffectual, there is an immunity from punishment, no matter how great an offender the individual may be, or how much his crimes may have shocked the sense of justice of the country or endangered its safety. By the protection of the law human rights are secured; withdraw that protection, and they are at the mercy of wicked rulers or the clamor of an excited people. If there was law to justify this military trial, it is not our province to interfere; if there was not, it is our duty to declare the nullity of the whole proceedings. The decision of this question does not depend on argument or judicial precedents, numerous and highly illustrative as they are. These precedents inform us of the extent of the struggle to preserve liberty and to relieve those in civil life from military trials. The founders of our government were familiar with the history of that struggle and secured in a written constitution every right which the people had wrested from power during a contest of ages. By that Constitution and the laws authorized by it this question must be determined. The provisions of that instrument on the administration of criminal justice are too plain and direct to leave room for misconstruction or doubt of their true meaning. Those applicable to this case are found in that clause of the original Constitution which says, "That the trial of all crimes, except in case of impeachment, shall be by jury"; and in the fourth, fifth, and sixth articles of the amendments. The fourth proclaims the right to be secure in person and effects against unreasonable search and seizure and directs that a judicial warrant shall not issue "without proof of probable cause supported by oath or affirmation." The fifth declares that "no person shall be held to answer for a capital or otherwise infamous crime unless on presentment by a grand jury, except in cases arising in the land or naval forces, or in the militia, when in actual service in time of war or public danger, nor be deprived of life, liberty, or property, without due process of law." And the sixth guarantees the right of trial by jury, in such manner and with such regulations that, with upright judges, impartial juries, and an able bar, the innocent will be saved and the guilty punished. It is in these words: "In all criminal prosecutions the accused shall enjoy the right to a speedy and public trial by an impartial jury of the state and district wherein the crime shall have been committed, which district shall have been previously ascertained by law, and to be informed of the nature and cause of the accusation, to be confronted with the witnesses against him, to have compulsory process for obtaining witnesses in his favor, and to have the assistance of counsel for his defense." These securities for personal liberty thus embodied were such as wisdom and experience had demonstrated to be necessary for the protection of those accused of crime. And so strong was the sense of the country of their importance, and so jealous were the people that these rights, highly prized, might be denied them by implication, that, when the original Constitution was proposed for adoption, it encountered severe opposition; and, but for the belief that it would be so amended as to embrace them, it would never have been ratified.

Time has proved the discernment of our ancestors; for even these provisions, expressed in such plain English words that it would seem the ingenuity of man could not evade them, are *now*, after the lapse of more than seventy years, sought to be avoided. Those great and good men foresaw that troublous times would arise, when rulers and people would become restive under restraint, and seek by sharp and decisive measures to accomplish ends deemed just and proper; and that the principles of constitutional liberty would be in peril, unless established by irrepealable law. The history of the world had taught them that what was done in the past might be attempted in the future. The Constitution of the United States is a law for rulers and people, equally in war and in peace, and covers with the shield of its protection all classes of men, at all times, and under all circumstances. No doctrine, involving more pernicious consequences, was ever invented by the wit of man than that any of its provisions can be suspended during any of the great exigencies of government. Such a doctrine leads directly to anarchy or despotism, but the theory of necessity on which it is based is false; for the government, within the Constitution, has all the powers granted to it which are necessary to preserve its existence; as has been happily proved by the result of the great effort to throw off its just authority.

Have any of the rights guaranteed by the Constitution been violated in the case of Milligan? And, if so, what are they?

Every trial involves the exercise of judicial power; and from what source did the military commission that tried him derive their authority? Certainly no part of the judicial power of the coun-try was conferred on them, because the Constitution expressly vests it "in one supreme court and such inferior courts as the Congress may from time to time ordain and establish," and it is not pretended that the commission was a court ordained and established by Congress. They cannot justify on the mandate of the President; because he is controlled by law and has his appropriate sphere of duty, which is to execute, not to make, the laws; and there is "no unwritten criminal code to which resort can be had as a source of jurisdiction."

But it is said that the jurisdiction is complete under the "laws and usages of war."

It can serve no useful purpose to inquire what those laws and usages are, whence they originated, where found, and on whom they operate; they can never be applied to citizens in states which have upheld the authority of the government, and where the courts are open and their process unobstructed. This Court has judicial knowledge that in Indiana the federal authority was always unopposed, and its courts always open to hear criminal accusations and redress grievances; and no usage of war could sanction a military trial there for any offense whatever of a citizen in civil life, in nowise connected with the military service. Congress could grant no such power; and to the honor of our national legislature be it said, it has never been provoked by the state of the country even to attempt its exercise. One of the plainest constitutional provisions was, therefore, infringed when Milligan was tried by a court not ordained and established by Congress and not composed of judges appointed during good behavior....

Another guarantee of freedom was broken when Milligan was denied a trial by jury....

It is claimed that martial law covers with its broad mantle the proceedings of this military commission. The proposition is this: that in a time of war the commander of an armed force (if in his opinion the exigencies of the country demand it, and of which he is to judge) has the power, within the lines of his military district, to suspend all civil rights and their remedies and subject citizens as well as soldiers to the rule of *his will;* and in the exercise of his lawful authority cannot be restrained, except by his superior officer or the President of the United States.

If this position is sound to the extent claimed, then when war exists, foreign or domestic, and the country is subdivided into military departments for mere convenience, the commander of one of them can, if he chooses, within his limits, on the plea of necessity, with the approval of the Executive, substitute military force for and to the exclusion of the laws and punish all persons, as he thinks right and proper, without fixed or certain rules.

The statement of this proposition shows its importance; for, if true, republican government is a failure, and there is an end of liberty regulated by law. Martial law, established on such a basis, destroys every guarantee of the Constitution and effectually renders the "military independent of and superior to the civil power"—the attempt to do which by the king of Great Britain was deemed by our fathers such an offense that they assigned it to the world as one of the causes which impelled them to declare their independence. Civil liberty and this kind of martial law cannot endure together; the antagonism is irreconcilable; and, in the conflict, one or the other must perish.

This nation, as experience has proved, cannot always remain at peace and has no right to expect that it will always have wise and humane rulers, sincerely attached to the principles of the Constitution. Wicked men, ambitious of power, with hatred of liberty and contempt of law, may fill the place once occupied by Washington and Lincoln; and if this right is conceded, and the calamities of war again befall us, the dangers to human liberty are frightful to contemplate. If our fathers had failed to provide for just such a contingency, they would have been false to the trust reposed in them. They knew—the history of the world told them—the nation they were founding, be its existence short or long, would be involved in war; how often or how long continued, human foresight could not tell; and that unlimited power, wherever lodged at such a time, was especially hazardous to freemen. For this, and other equally weighty reasons, they secured the inheritance they had fought to maintain, by incorporating in a written constitution the safeguards which *time* had proved were essential to its preservation. Not one of these safeguards can the President, or Congress, or the Judiciary disturb, except the one concerning the writ of habeas corpus.

It is essential to the safety of every government that, in a great crisis, like the one we have just passed through, there should be a power somewhere of suspending the writ of habeas corpus. In every war there are men of previously good character wicked enough to counsel their fellow-citizens to resist the measures deemed necessary by a good government to sustain its just authority and overthrow its enemies; and their influence may lead to dangerous combinations. In the emergency of the times, an immediate public investigation according to law may not be possible; and yet the peril to the country may be too imminent to suffer such persons to go at large. Unquestionably, there is then an exigency which demands that the government, if it should see fit in the exercise of a proper discretion to make arrests, should not be required to produce the persons arrested in answer to a writ of habeas corpus. The Constitution goes no further. It does not say after a writ of habeas corpus is denied a citizen that he shall be tried otherwise than by the course of the common law; if it had intended this result, it was easy by the use of direct words to have accomplished it. The illustrious men who framed that instrument were guarding the foundations of civil liberty against the abuses of unlimited power; they were full of wisdom, and the lessons of history informed them that a trial by an established court, assisted by an impartial jury, was the only sure way of protecting the citizen against oppression and wrong. Knowing this, they limited the suspension to one great right and left the rest to remain forever inviolable. But it is insisted that the safety of the country in time of war demands that this broad claim for martial law shall be sustained. If this were true, it could be well said that a country, preserved at the sacrifice of all the cardinal principles of liberty, is not worth the cost of preservation. Happily, it is not so.

It will be borne in mind that this is not a question of the power to proclaim martial law, when war exists in a community and the courts and civil authorities are overthrown. Nor is it a question what rule a military commander, at the head of his army, can impose on states in rebellion to cripple their resources and quell the insurrection. The jurisdiction claimed is much more extensive. The necessities of the service, during the late Rebellion, required that the loyal states should be placed within the limits of certain military districts and commanders appointed in them; and, it is urged, that this, in a military sense, constituted them the theater of military operations; and, as in this case, Indiana had been and was again threatened with invasion by the enemy, the occasion was furnished to establish martial law. The conclusion does not follow from the premises. If armies were collected in Indiana, they were to be employed in another locality, where the laws were obstructed and the national authority disputed. On *her* soil there was no hostile foot; if once invaded, that invasion was at an end, and with it all pretext for martial law. Martial law cannot arise from a *threatened* invasion. The necessity must be actual and present; the invasion real, such as effectually closes the courts and deposes the civil administration.

It is difficult to see how the *safety* of the country required martial law in Indiana. If any of her citizens were plotting treason, the power of arrest could secure them, until the government was prepared for their trial, when the courts were open and ready to try them. It was as easy to protect witnesses before a civil as a military tribunal; and as there could be no wish to convict, except on sufficient legal evidence, surely an ordained and established court was better able to judge of this than a military tribunal composed of gentlemen not trained to the profession of the law....

The CHIEF JUSTICE delivered the following opinion.

Four members of the Court, concurring with their brethren in the order heretofore made in this cause, but unable to concur in some important particulars with the opinion which has just been read, think it their duty to make a separate statement of their views of the whole case.

We do not doubt that the Circuit Court for the District of Indiana had jurisdiction of the petition of Milligan for the writ of habeas corpus....

The act of Congress of March 3d, 1863, comprises all the legislation which seems to require consideration in this connection. The constitutionality of this act has not been questioned and is not doubted....

It must be borne in mind that the prayer of the petition was not for an absolute discharge but to be delivered from military custody and imprisonment, and, if found probably guilty of any offense, to be turned over to the proper tribunal for inquiry and punishment; or, if not found thus probably guilty, to be discharged altogether.

And the express terms of the act of Congress required this action of the court. The prisoner must be discharged on giving such recognizance as the court should require, not only for good behavior, but for appearance, as directed by the court, to answer and be further dealt with according to law....

But the opinion which has just been read goes further and, as we understand it, asserts not only that the military commission held in Indiana was not authorized by Congress but that it was not in the power of Congress to authorize it; from which it may be thought to follow that Congress has no power to indemnify the officers who composed the commission against liability in civil courts for acting as members of it.

We cannot agree to this....

Congress has the power not only to raise and support and govern armies but to declare war. It has, therefore, the power to provide by law for carrying on war. This power necessarily extends to all legislation essential to the prosecution of war with vigor and success, except such as interferes with the command of the forces and the conduct of campaigns. That power and duty belong to the President as commander-in-chief. Both these powers are derived from the Constitution, but neither is defined by that instrument. Their extent must be determined by their nature and by the principles of our institutions....

In Indiana, for example, at the time of the arrest of Milligan and his co-conspirators, it is established by the papers in the record that the state was a military district, was the theater of military operations, had been actually invaded, and was constantly threatened with invasion. It appears, also, that a powerful secret association, composed of citizens and others, existed within the state, under military organization, conspiring against the draft, and plotting insurrection, the liberation of the prisoners of war at various depots, the seizure of the state and national arsenals, armed co-operation with the enemy, and war against the national government.

We cannot doubt that, in such a time of public danger, Congress had power, under the Constitution, to provide for the organization of a military commission and for trial by that commission of persons engaged in this conspiracy. The fact that the federal courts were open was regarded by Congress as a sufficient reason for not exercising the power; but that fact could not deprive Congress of the right to exercise it. Those courts might be open and undisturbed in the execution of their functions, and yet wholly incompetent to avert threatened danger, or to punish, with adequate promptitude and certainty, the guilty conspirators.

In Indiana the judges and officers of the courts were loyal to the government. But it might have been otherwise. In times of rebellion and civil war it may often happen, indeed, that judges and marshals will be in active sympathy with the rebels, and courts their most efficient allies.

We have confined ourselves to the question of power. It was for Congress to determine the question of expediency. And Congress did determine it. That body did not see fit to authorize trials by military commission in Indiana, but by the strongest implication prohibited them. With that prohibition we are satisfied, and should have remained silent if the answers to the questions certified had been put on that ground, without denial of the existence of a power which we believe to be constitutional and important to the public safety—a denial which, as we have already suggested, seems to draw in question the power of Congress to protect from prosecution the members of military commissions who acted in obedience to their superior officers, and whose action, whether warranted by law or not, was approved by that upright and patriotic President under whose administration the Republic was rescued from threatened destruction. . . .

8. MISSISSIPPI BLACK CODE, 1865

A. THE CIVIL RIGHTS OF FREEDMEN IN MISSISSIPPI[1]

SECTION 1. *Be it enacted by the Legislature of the State of Mississippi,* That all freedmen, free Negroes, and mulattoes may sue and be sued, implead and be impleaded in all the courts of law and equity of this state, and may acquire personal property and choses in action, by descent or purchase, and may dispose of the same, in the same manner, and to the same extent that white persons may: Provided that the provisions of this section shall not be so construed as to allow any freedman, free Negro, or mulatto to rent or lease any lands or tenements, except in incorporated towns or cities in which places the corporate authorities shall control the same.

SEC. 2. Be it further enacted, That all freedmen, free Negroes, and mulattoes may intermarry with each other, in the same manner and under the same regulations that are provided by law for white persons: Provided, that the clerk of probate shall keep separate records of the same.

SEC. 3. Be it further enacted, That all freedmen, free Negroes, and mulattoes, who do now and have heretofore lived and cohabited together as husband and wife shall be taken and held in law as legally married, and the issue shall be taken and held as legitimate for all purposes. That it shall not be lawful for any freedman, free Negro, or mulatto to intermarry with any white person; nor for any white person to intermarry with any freedman, free Negro, or mulatto; and any person who shall so intermarry shall be deemed guilty of felony and, on

1. Mississippi, *Laws of the State . . . , 1865* (Jackson, Miss., 1866), pp. 82–86.

conviction thereof, shall be confined in the state penitentiary for life; and those shall be deemed freedmen, free Negroes, and mulattoes who are of pure Negro blood, and those descended from a Negro to the third generation inclusive, though one ancestor of each generation may have been a white person.

SEC. 4. Be it further enacted, That in addition to cases in which freedmen, free Negroes, and mulattoes are now by law competent witnesses, freedmen, free Negroes, or mulattoes shall be competent in civil cases when a party or parties to the suit, either plaintiff or plaintiffs, defendant or defendants, also in cases where freedmen, free Negroes, and mulattoes is or are either plaintiff or plaintiffs, defendant or defendants, and a white person or white persons is or are the opposing party or parties, plaintiff or plaintiffs, defendant or defendants. They shall also be competent witnesses in all criminal prosecutions where the crime charged is alleged to have been committed by a white person upon or against the person or property of a freedman, free Negro, or mulatto: Provided that in all cases said witnesses shall be examined in open court on the stand, except, however, they may be examined before the grand jury, and shall in all cases be subject to the rules and tests of the common law as to competency and credibility.

SEC. 5. Be it further enacted, That every freedman, free Negro, and mulatto shall, on the second Monday of January, one thousand eight hundred and sixty-six, and annually thereafter, have a lawful home or employment, and shall have written evidence thereof, as follows, to wit: if living in any incorporated city, town, or village, a license from the mayor thereof; and if living outside of any incorporated city, town, or village, from the member of the board of police of his beat, authorizing him or her to do irregular and job work, or a written contract, as provided in section sixth of this act, which licenses may be revoked for cause, at any time, by the authority granting the same.

SEC. 6. Be it further enacted, That all contracts for labor made with freedmen, free Negroes, and mulattoes for a longer period than one month shall be in writing and in duplicate, attested and read to said freedman, free Negro, or mulatto, by a beat, city or county officers, or two disinterested white persons of the county in which the labor is to be performed, of which each party shall have one; and said contracts shall be taken and held as entire contracts, and if the laborer shall quit the service of the employer, before expiration of his term of service, without good cause, he shall forfeit his wages for that year, up to the time of quitting.

SEC. 7. Be it further enacted, That every civil officer shall, and every person may, arrest and carry back to his or her legal employer any freedman, free Negro, or mulatto who shall have quit the service of his or her employer before the expiration of his or her term of service without good cause, and said officer and person shall be entitled to receive for arresting and carrying back every deserting employee aforesaid, the sum of five dollars, and ten cents per mile from the place of arrest to the place of delivery, and the same shall be paid by the employer, and held as a set-off for so much against the wages of said deserting employee: Provided that said arrested party after being so returned may appeal to a justice of the peace or member of the board of police of the county, who on notice to the alleged employer, shall try summarily whether said appellant is legally employed by the alleged employer and has good cause to quit said employer; either party shall have the right of appeal to the county court, pending which the alleged deserted shall be remanded to the alleged employer, or otherwise disposed of as shall be right and just, and the decision of the county court shall be final.

SEC. 8. Be it further enacted, That upon affidavit made by the employer of any freedman, free Negro, or mulatto, or other credible person, before any justice of the peace or member of the board of police, that any freedman, free Negro, or mulatto, legally employed by said employer, has illegally deserted said employment, such justice of the peace or member of the board of police shall issue his warrant or warrants, returnable before himself, or other such officer, directed to any sheriff, constable, or special deputy, commanding him to arrest said deserter and return him or her to said employer, and the like proceeedings shall be had as provided in the preceding section; and it shall be lawful for any officer to whom such warrant shall be directed, to execute said warrant in any county of this state, and that said warrant may be transmitted without indorsement to any like officer of another county, to be executed and returned as aforesaid, and the said employer shall pay the cost of said warrants and arrest and return, which shall be set off for so much against the wages of said deserter.

SEC. 9. Be it further enacted, That if any person shall persuade or attempt to persuade, entice, or cause any freedman, free Negro, or mulatto to desert from the legal employment of any person, before the expiration of his or her term of service, or shall knowingly employ any such deserting freedman, free Negro, or mulatto, or shall knowingly give or sell to any such deserting freedman, free Negro, or mulatto, any food, raiment, or other thing, he or she shall be guilty of a misdemeanor and, upon conviction, shall be fined not less than twenty-five dollars and not more than two hundred dollars and the costs, and, if said fine and costs shall not be immediately paid, the court shall sentence said convict to not exceeding two months' imprisonment in the county jail, and he or she shall moreover be liable to the party injured in damages: Provided, if any person shall, or shall attempt to persuade, entice, or cause any freedman, free Negro, or mulatto to desert from any legal employment of any person, with the view to employ said freedman, free Negro, or mulatto, without the limits of this state, such person, on conviction, shall be fined not less than fifty dollars and not more than five hundred dollars and costs, and, if said fine and costs shall not be immediately paid, the court shall sentence said convict to not exceeding six months' imprisonment in the county jail.

SEC. 10. Be it further enacted, That it shall be lawful for any freedman, free Negro, or mulatto to charge any white person, freedman, free Negro, or mulatto, by affidavit, with any criminal offense against his or her person or property and upon such affidavit the proper process shall be issued and executed as if said affidavit was made by a white person, and it shall be lawful for any freedman, free Negro, or mulatto, in any action, suit, or controversy pending, or about to be instituted, in any court of law or equity of this state, to make all needful and lawful affidavits, as shall be necessary for the institution, prosecution, or defense of such suit or controversy.

SEC. 11. Be it further enacted, That the penal laws of this state, in all cases not otherwise specially provided for, shall apply and extend to all freedmen, free Negroes, and mulattoes. . . .

Approved November 25, 1865.

B. THE MISSISSIPPI APPRENTICE LAW[2]

SECTION 1. *Be it enacted by the legislature of the state of Mississippi,* That it shall be the duty of all sheriffs, justices of the peace, and other civil officers of the several counties in this state to report to the probate courts of their respective counties semiannually, at the January and July terms of said courts, all freedmen, free Negroes, and mulattoes, under the age of eighteen, within their respective counties, beats, or districts, who are orphans, or whose parent or parents have not the means, or who refuse to provide for and support said minors, and thereupon it shall be the duty of said probate court to order the clerk of said court to apprentice said minors to some competent and suitable person, on such terms as the court may direct, having a particular care to the interest of said minors: Provided, that the former owner of said minors shall have the preference when, in the opinion of the court, he or she shall be a suitable person for that purpose.

SEC. 2. Be it further enacted, That the said court shall be fully satisfied that the person or persons to whom said minor shall be apprenticed shall be a suitable person to have the charge and care of said minor and fully to protect the interest of said minor. The said court shall require the said master or mistress to execute bond and security, payable to the state of Mississippi, conditioned that he or she shall furnish said minor with sufficient food and clothing, to treat said minor humanely, furnish medical attention in case of sickness; teach or cause to be taught him or her to read and write, if under fifteen years old, and will conform to any law that may be hereafter passed for the regulation of the duties and relation of master and apprentice: Provided that said apprentice shall be bound by indenture, in case of males until they are twenty-one years old, and in case of females until they are eighteen years old.

2. *Ibid.,* pp. 86–90.

SEC. 3. Be it further enacted, That in the management and control of said apprentices, said master or mistress shall have power to inflict such moderate corporeal chastisement as a father or guardian is allowed to inflict on his or her child or ward at common law: Provided that in no case shall cruel or inhuman punishment be inflicted.

SEC. 4. Be it further enacted, That if any apprentice shall leave the employment of his or her master or mistress, without his or her consent, said master or mistress may pursue and recapture said apprentice and bring him or her before any justice of the peace of the county whose duty it shall be to remand said apprentice to the service of his or her master or mistress; and in the event of a refusal on the part of said apprentice so to return, then said justice shall commit said apprentice to the jail of said county, on failure to give bond, until the next term of the county court; and it shall be the duty of said court, at the first term thereafter, to investigate said case, and if the court shall be of opinion that said apprentice left the employment of his or her master or mistress without good cause, to order him or her to be punished, as provided for the punishment of hired freedmen, as may be from time to time provided for by law, for desertion, until he or she shall agree to return to his or her master or mistress: Provided that the court may grant continuances, as in other cases; and provided, further, that if the court shall believe that said apprentice had good cause to quit his said master or mistress, the court shall discharge said apprentice from said indenture and also enter a judgment against the master or mistress for not more than one hundred dollars, for the use and benefit of said apprentice, to be collected on execution, as in other cases.

SEC. 5. Be it further enacted, That if any person entice away any apprentice from his or her master or mistress, or shall knowingly employ an apprentice, or furnish him or her food or clothing, without the written consent of his or her master or mistress, or shall sell or give said apprentice ardent spirits, without such consent, said person so offending shall be deemed guilty of a high misdemeanor, and shall, on conviction thereof before the county court, be punished as provided for the punishment of persons enticing from their employer hired freedmen, free Negroes, or mulattoes.

SEC. 6. Be it further enacted, That it shall be the duty of all civil officers of their respective counties to report any minors within their respective counties to said probate court who are subject to be apprenticed under the provisions of this act, from time to time, as the facts may come to their knowledge, and it shall be the duty of said court, from time to time, as said minors shall be reported to them or otherwise come to their knowledge, to apprentice said minors as hereinbefore provided.

SEC. 7. Be it further enacted, That in case the master or mistress of any apprentice shall desire, he or she shall have the privilege to summon his or her said apprentice to the probate court, and thereupon, with the approval of the court, he or she shall be released from all liability as master of said apprentice, and his said bond shall be canceled, and it shall be the duty of the court forthwith to reapprentice said minor; and in the event any master of an apprentice shall die before the close of the term of service of said apprentice, it shall be the duty of the court to give the preference in reapprenticing said minor to the widow, or other member of said master's family: Provided that said widow or other member of said family shall be a suitable person for that purpose....

SEC. 10. Be it further enacted, That in all cases where the age of the freedman, free Negro or mulatto, cannot be ascertained by record testimony, the judge of the county court shall fix the age....

Approved November 22, 1865.

C. THE MISSISSIPPI VAGRANCY LAW[3]

SECTION 1. *Be it enacted by the legislature of the state of Mississippi,* That all rogues and vagabonds, idle and dissipated persons, beggars, jugglers, or persons practicing unlawful games or plays, runaways, common drunkards, common night-walkers, pilferers, lewd, wanton, or lascivious persons, in speech or behavior, common railers and brawlers, persons who neglect their calling or employment, misspend what they earn, or do not provide for the support of themselves or their families, or dependents, and all other idle and disorderly persons, including all who neglect all lawful business, or habitually misspend their time by frequenting houses of ill-fame, gaming-houses, or tippling shops, shall be deemed and considered vagrants under the provisions of this act and, on conviction thereof, shall be fined not exceeding one hundred dollars, with all accruing costs, and be imprisoned at the discretion of the court not exceeding ten days.

SEC. 2. Be it further enacted, That all freedmen, free Negroes, and mulattoes in this state, over the age of eighteen years, found on the second Monday in January, 1866, or thereafter, with no lawful employment or business, or found unlawfully assembling themselves together either in the day or night time, and all white persons so assembling with freedmen, free Negroes, or mulattoes, or usually associating with freedmen, free Negroes, or mulattoes on terms of equality, or living in adultery or fornication with a freedwoman, free Negro, or mulatto, shall be deemed vagrants and, on conviction thereof, shall be fined in the sum of not exceeding, in the case of a freedman, free Negro or mulatto, fifty dollars, and a white man two hundred dollars, and imprisoned at the discretion of the court, the free Negro not exceeding ten days, and the white man not exceeding six months. . . .

SEC. 4. Be it further enacted, That keepers of gaming-houses, houses of prostitution, all prostitutes, public or private, and all persons who derive their chief support in employments that militate against good morals or against laws shall be deemed and held to be vagrants.

SEC. 5. Be it further enacted, That all fines and forfeitures collected under the provisions of this act shall be paid into the county treasury for general county purposes, and in case any freedman, free Negro, or mulatto shall fail for five days after the imposition of any fine or forfeiture upon him or her for violation of any of the provisions of this act, to pay the same, that it shall be, and is hereby made, the duty of the sheriff of the proper county to hire out said freedman, free Negro, or mulatto to any person who will, for the shortest period of service, pay said fine or forfeiture and all costs: Provided, a preference shall be given to the employer, if there be one, in which case the employer shall be entitled to deduct and retain the amount so paid from the wages of such freedman, free Negro, or mulatto, then due or to become due; and in case such freedman, free Negro, or mulatto cannot be hired out he or she may be dealt with as a pauper.

SEC. 6. Be it further enacted, That the same duties and liabilities existing among white persons of this state shall attach to freedmen, free Negroes, and mulattoes to support their indigent families, and all colored paupers; and that, in order to secure a support for such indigent freedmen, free Negroes, and mulattoes, it shall be lawful, and it is hereby made the duty of the boards of county police of each county in this state, to levy a poll or capitation tax on each and every freedman, free Negro, or mulatto, between the ages of eighteen and sixty years, not to exceed the sum of one dol-

3. *Ibid.,* pp. 90–93.

lar annually, to each person so taxed, which tax when collected, shall be paid into the county treasurer's hands, and constitute a fund to be called the Freedman's Pauper Fund, which shall be applied by the commissioners of the poor for the maintenance of the poor of the freedman, free Negroes, and mulattoes of this state, under such regulations as may be established by the boards of county police, in the respective counties of this state.

SEC. 7. Be it further enacted, That if any freedman, free Negro, or mulatto shall fail or refuse to pay any tax levied according to the provisions of the sixth section of this act, it shall be prima facie evidence of vagrancy, and it shall be the duty of the sheriff to arrest such freedman, free Negro, or mulatto, or such person refusing or neglecting to pay such tax, and proceed at once to hire, for the shortest time, such delinquent taxpayer to anyone who will pay the said tax, with accruing costs, giving preference to the employer, if there be one.

SEC. 8. Be it further enacted, That any person feeling himself or herself aggrieved by the judgment of any justice of the peace, mayor, or alderman, in cases arising under this act, may, within five days, appeal to the next term of the county court of the proper county, upon giving bond and security in a sum not less than twenty-five nor more than one hundred and fifty dollars, conditioned to appear and prosecute said appeal, and abide by the judgment of the county court, and said appeal shall be tried *de novo* in the county court, and the decision of said court shall be final. . . .

Approved November 24, 1865.

D. THE PENAL CODE OF MISSISSIPPI[4]

SECTION 1. *Be it enacted by the legislature of the state of Mississippi,* That no freedman, free Negro, or mulatto, not in the military service of the United States government, and not licensed so to do by the board of police of his or her county, shall keep or carry firearms of any kind, or any ammunition, dirk, or bowie knife, and on conviction thereof, in the county court, shall be punished by fine, not exceeding ten dollars, and pay the costs of such proceedings, and all such arms or ammunition shall be forfeited to the informer, and it shall be the duty of every civil and military officer to arrest any freedman, free Negro, or mulatto found with any such arms or ammunition, and cause him or her to be committed for trial in default of bail.

SEC. 2. Be it further enacted, That any freedman, free Negro, or mulatto committing riots, routes, affrays, trespasses, malicious mischief, cruel treatment to animals, seditious speeches, insulting gestures, language, or acts, or assaults on

4. *Ibid.*, pp. 165–67.

any person, disturbance of the peace, exercising the function of a minister of the Gospel without a license from some regularly organized church, vending spirituous or intoxicating liquors, or committing any other misdemeanor, the punishment of which is not specifically provided for by law, shall, upon conviction thereof, in the county court, be fined, not less than ten dollars, and not more than one hundred dollars, and may be imprisoned, at the discretion of the court, not exceeding thirty days.

SEC. 3. Be it further enacted, That if any white person shall sell, lend, or give to any freedman, free Negro, or mulatto, any firearms, dirk, or bowie knife, or ammunition, or any spirituous or intoxicating liquors, such person or persons so offending, upon conviction thereof, in the county court of his or her county, shall be fined, not exceeding fifty dollars, and may be imprisoned, at the discretion of the court, not exceeding thirty days: Provided, that any master, mistress, or employe[r] of any freedman, free Negro, or mulatto may give to any freedman, free Negro, or mulatto, apprenticed to or employed by such master, mistress, or employer, spirituous or intoxicating liquors, but not in sufficient quantities to produce intoxication.

SEC. 4. Be it further enacted, That all the penal and criminal laws now in force in this state, defining offenses and prescribing the mode of punishment for crimes and misdemeanors committed by slaves, free Negroes, or mulattoes, be and the same are hereby re-enacted, and declared to be in full force and effect,

against freedmen, free Negroes, and mulattoes, except so far as the mode and manner of trial and punishment have been changed or altered by law.

SEC. 5. Be it further enacted, That if any freedman, free Negro, or mulatto, convicted of any of the misdemeanors provided against in this act, shall fail or refuse, for the space of five days after conviction, to pay the fine and costs imposed, such persons shall be hired out by the sheriff or other officer, at public outcry, to any white person who will pay said fine and all costs and take such convict for the shortest time....

Approved November 29, 1865.

9. CONSTITUTION AND RITUAL OF THE KNIGHTS OF THE WHITE CAMELIA[1]

PREAMBLE

WHEREAS, Radical legislation is subversive of the principles of the government of the United States, as originally adopted by our fathers:

And WHEREAS, Our safety and our prosperity depend on the preservation of those grand principles and believing that they can be peacefully maintained: Therefore, we adopt the following [constitution somewhat similar to that of the Klan].

[QUESTIONS ASKED THE CANDIDATE]

1. Do you belong to the white race? *Ans.*—I do.

2. Did you every marry any woman who did not, or does not, belong to the white race? *Ans.*—No.

3. Do you promise never to marry any woman but one who belongs to the white race? *Ans.*—I do.

4. Do you believe in the superiority of your race? *Ans.*—I do.

5. Will you promise never to vote for

anyone for any office of honor, profit, or trust who does not belong to your race? *Ans.*—I do.

6. Will you take a solemn oath never to abstain from casting your vote at any election in which a candidate of the Negro race shall be opposed to a white man attached to your principles, unless prevented by severe illness or any other physical disability? *Ans.*—I will.

7. Are you opposed to allowing the control of the political affairs of this country to go, in whole or in part, into the hands of the African race, and will you do everything in your power to prevent it? *Ans.*—Yes.

8. Will you devote your intelligence, energy, and influence to the furtherance and propagation of the principles of our Order? *Ans.*—I will.

9. Will you, under all circumstances, defend and protect persons of the white race in their lives, rights, and property, against all encroachments or invasions from any inferior race, and especially the African? *Ans.*—Yes.

10. Are you willing to take an oath forever to cherish these grand principles, and to unite yourself with others who,

1. *Documentary History of Reconstruction,* ed. Walter L. Fleming (Cleveland, Ohio: Arthur H. Clark Co., 1907), II, 349–54. Adopted in 1869.

like you, believing in their truth, have firmly bound themselves to stand by and defend them against all? *Ans.*—I am.

The C[ommander] shall then say: If you consent to join our Association, raise your right hand, and I will administer to you the oath which we have all taken: ....

[CHARGE TO INITIATES]

Brothers: You have been initiated into one of the most important Orders which have ever been established on this continent: an Order which, if its principles are faithfully observed and its objects diligently carried out, is destined to regenerate our unfortunate country and to relieve the white race from the humiliating condition to which it has lately been reduced in this Republic. It is necessary, therefore, that, before taking part in the labors of this Association, you should understand fully its principles and objects and the duties which devolve upon you as one of its members.

As you may have already gathered from the questions which were propounded to you, and which you have answered so satisfactorily, and from the clauses of the Oath which you have taken, our main and fundamental object is the MAINTENANCE OF THE SUPREMACY OF THE WHITE RACE in this Republic. History and physiology teach us that we belong to a race which nature has endowed with an evident superiority over all other races, and that the Maker, in thus elevating us above the common standard of human creation, has intended to give us over inferior races a dominion from which no human laws can permanently derogate. The experience of ages demonstrates that, from the origin of the world, this dominion has always remained in the hands of the Caucasian race; whilst all the other races have constantly occupied a subordinate and secondary position; a fact which triumphantly confirms this great law of nature. Powerful nations have succeed-

ed each other on the face of the world, and have marked their passage by glorious and memorable deeds; and among those who have thus left on this globe indelible traces of their splendor and greatness, we find none but descended from the Caucasian stock. We see, on the contrary, that most of the countries inhabited by the other races have remained in a state of complete barbarity; whilst the small number of those who have advanced beyond this savage existence, have, for centuries, stagnated in a semibarbarous condition of which there can be no progress or improvement. And it is a remarkable fact that, as a race of men is more remote from the Caucasian and approaches nearer to the black African, the more fatally that stamp of inferiority is affixed to its sons and irrevocably dooms them to eternal imperfectibility and degradation.

Convinced that we are of these elements of natural ethics, we know, besides, that the government of our Republic was established by white men, for white men alone, and that it never was in the contemplation of its founders that it should fall into the hands of an inferior and degraded race. We hold, therefore, that any attempt to wrest from the white race the management of its affairs in order to transfer it to control of the black population is an invasion of the sacred prerogatives vouchsafed to us by the Constitution, and a violation of the laws established by God himself; that such encroachments are subversive of the established institutions of our Republic, and that no individual of the white race can submit to them without humiliation and shame.

It, then, becomes our solemn duty, as white men, to resist strenuously and persistently those attempts against our natural and constitutional rights, and to do everything in our power in order to maintain, in this Republic, the supremacy of the Caucasian race, and restrain the black or African race to that condition of social and political inferiority for which God has destined it. This is the object for which our Order was instituted; and, in carrying it out, we intend to infringe no laws, to violate no rights, and to resort to no forcible means, except for purposes of legitimate and necessary defense.

As an essential condition of success, this Order proscribes absolutely all social equality between the races. If we were to admit persons of African race on the same level with ourselves, a state of personal relations would follow which would unavoidably lead to political equality; for it would be a virtual recognition of *status*, after which we could not consistently deny them an equal share in the administration of our public affairs. The man who is good enough to be our familiar companion is good enough also to participate in our political government; and if we were to grant the one, there could be no good reason for us not to concede the other of these two privileges.

There is another reason, Brothers, for which we condemn this social equality. Its toleration would soon be a fruitful source of intermarriage between individuals of the two races; and the result of this *miscegenation* would be gradual amalgamation and the production of a degenerate and bastard offspring, which would soon populate these states with a degraded and ignoble population, incapable of moral and intellectual development and unfitted to support a great and powerful country. We must maintain the purity of the white blood, if we would preserve for it that natural superiority with which God had ennobled it.

To avoid these evils, therefore, we take the obligation TO OBSERVE A MARKED DISTINCTION BETWEEN THE TWO RACES, not only in the relations of public affairs, but also in the more intimate dealings and intercourse of private life which, by the frequency of their occurrence, are more apt to have an influence on the attainment of the purposes of the Order.

Now that I have laid before you the objects of this Association, let me charge you specially in relation to one of your most important duties as one of its members. Our statutes make us bound to respect sedulously the rights of the colored inhabitants of this Republic, and, in every instance, to give to them whatever lawfully belongs to them. It is an act of simple justice not to deny them any of the privileges to which they are legitimately entitled; and we cannot better show the inherent superiority of our race than by dealing with them in that spirit of firmness, liberality, and impartiality which characterizes all superior organizations. Besides, it would be ungenerous for us to undertake to restrict them to the narrowest limits as to the exercise of certain rights, without conceding to them, at the same time, the fullest measure of those which we recognize as theirs; and a fair construction of a white man's duty toward them would be, not only to respect and observe their knowledged rights, but also to see that these are respected and observed by others.

From the brief explanation which I have just given you, you must have satisfied yourselves that our Association is not a political party and has no connection with any of the organized parties of the day. Nor will it lend itself to the personal advancement of individuals or listen to the cravings of any partisan spirit. It was organized in order to carry out certain great principles, from which it must never swerve by favoring private ambitions and political aspirations. These, as well as all sentiments of private enmity, animosity, and other personal feelings, we must leave at the door before we enter this council. You may meet here, congregated together, men who belong to all the political organizations which now divide, or may divide, this country; you see some whom embittered feuds and irreconcilable hatred have long and widely separated; they have all cast away these rankling feelings to unite cordially and zealously in the labors of our great undertaking. Let their example be to you a useful lesson of the disinterestedness and devotedness which should characterize our efforts for the success of our cause!

10. CIVIL RIGHTS CASES[1]

EDITORS' NOTE.—Negroes were denied admission to or accommodation in theaters, hotels, and railway cars in southern states after the Civil War. Those responsible for this discrimination were indicted or sued for penalties under a federal statute which made it a crime to deny any person within the United States "the full and equal enjoyment of the accommodations, advantages, facilities, and privileges of inns, public conveyances on land and water, theaters, and other places of public amusement; subject only to the conditions and limitations established by law, and applicable alike to citizens of every race and color, regardless of any previous condition of servitude." The act was passed on March 1, 1875. In a number of cases the question of the validity of this act was presented, by the certification of questions or by writs of error, to the Supreme Court. The act was held unconstitutional.

Mr. Justice BRADLEY delivered the opinion of the Court. . . .

The first section of the Fourteenth Amendment (which is the one relied on), after declaring who shall be citizens of the United States, and of the several states, is prohibitory in its character, and prohibitory upon the states. It declares that: "No state shall make or enforce any law which shall abridge the privileges or immunities of citizens of the United States; nor shall any state deprive any person of life, liberty, or property without due process of law; nor deny to any person within its jurisdiction the equal protection of the laws."

It is state action of a particular character that is prohibited. Individual invasion of individual rights is not the subject matter of the amendment. It has a deeper and broader scope. It nullifies and makes void all state legislation, and state action of every kind, which impairs the privileges and immunities of citizens of the United States, or which injures them in life, liberty, or property without due process of law, or which denies to any of them the equal protection of the laws. It not only does this, but, in order that the national will, thus declared, may not be a mere *brutum fulmen*, the last section of the amendment invests Congress with power to enforce it by appropriate legislation. To enforce what? To enforce the prohibition. To adopt appropriate legislation for correcting the effects of such prohibited state laws and state acts, and thus to render them effectually null, void, and innocuous. This is the legislative power conferred upon Congress, and this is the whole of it. It does not invest Congress with power to legislate upon subjects which are within the domain of state legislation; but to provide modes of relief against state legislation, or state action, of the kind referred to. It does not authorize Congress to create a code of municipal law for the regulation of private rights; but to provide modes of

1. 109 U.S. 3 (1883), 8, 10–12, 14–15, 17–18, 20–22, 25–26, 35, 42–44, 48, 57–59, 61–62.

redress against the operation of state laws, and the action of state officers, executive or judicial, when these are subversive of the fundamental rights specified in the amendment. Positive rights and privileges are undoubtedly secured by the Fourteenth Amendment; but they are secured by way of prohibition against state laws and state proceedings affecting those rights and privileges, and by power given to Congress to legislate for the purpose of carrying such prohibition into effect; and such legislation must necessarily be predicated upon such supposed state laws or state proceedings and be directed to the correction of their operation and effect. . . .

If this legislation is appropriate for enforcing the prohibitions of the amendment, it is difficult to see where it is to stop. Why may not Congress with equal show of authority enact a code of laws for the enforcement and vindication of all rights of life, liberty, and property? If it is supposable that the states may deprive persons of life, liberty, and property without due process of law (and the amendment itself does suppose this), why should not Congress proceed at once to prescribe due process of law for the protection of every one of these fundamental rights, in every possible case, as well as to prescribe equal privileges in inns, public conveyances, and theaters? The truth is that the implication of a power to legislate in this manner is based upon the assumption that if the states are forbidden to legislate or act in a particular way on a particular subject, and power is conferred upon Congress to enforce the prohibition, this gives Congress power to legislate generally upon that subject and not merely power to provide modes of redress against such state legislation or action. The assumption is certainly unsound. It is repugnant to the Tenth Amendment of the Constitution, which declares that powers not delegated to the United

States by the Constitution, nor prohibited by it to the states, are reserved to the states respectively or to the people. . . .

In this connection it is proper to state that civil rights, such as are guaranteed by the Constitution against state aggression, cannot be impaired by the wrongful acts of individuals, unsupported by state authority in the shape of laws, customs, or judicial or executive proceedings. The wrongful act of an individual, unsupported by any such authority, is simply a private wrong, or a crime of that individual; an invasion of the rights of the injured party, it is true, whether they affect his person, his property, or his reputation; but if not sanctioned in some way by the state, or not done under state authority, his rights remain in full force and may presumably be vindicated by resort to the laws of the state for redress. An individual cannot deprive a man of his right to vote, to hold property, to buy and sell, to sue in the courts, or to be a witness or a juror; he may, by force or fraud, interfere with the enjoyment of the right in a particular case; he may commit an assault against the person, or commit murder, or use ruffian violence at the polls, or slander the good name of a fellow-citizen; but, unless protected in these wrongful acts by some shield of state law or state authority, he cannot destroy or injure the right; he will only render himself amenable to satisfaction or punishment; and amenable therefore to the laws of the state where the wrongful acts are committed. Hence, in all those cases where the Constitution seeks to protect the rights of the citizen against discriminative and unjust laws of the state by prohibiting such laws, it is not individual offenses, but abrogation and denial of rights, which it denounces, and for which it clothes the Congress with power to provide a remedy. This abrogation and denial of rights, for which the states alone were or could be responsible, was the great seminal and fundamental wrong which was intended to be remedied. And the remedy to be provided must necessarily be predicated upon that wrong. It must assume that in the cases provided for, the evil or wrong actually committed rests upon some state law or state authority for its excuse and perpetration. . . .

But the power of Congress to adopt direct and primary, as distinguished from corrective, legislation, on the subject in hand, is sought, in the second place, from the Thirteenth Amendment, which abolishes slavery. This amendment declares that "neither slavery, nor involuntary servitude, except as a punishment for crime, whereof the party shall have been duly convicted, shall exist within the United States, or any place subject to their jurisdiction"; and it gives Congress power to enforce the amendment by appropriate legislation. . . .

It may be that by the Black Code (as it was called), in the times when slavery prevailed, the proprietors of inns and public conveyances were forbidden to receive persons of the African race, because it might assist slaves to escape from the control of their masters. This was merely a means of preventing such escapes and was no part of the servitude itself. A law of that kind could not have any such object now, however justly it might be deemed an invasion of the party's legal right as a citizen, and amenable to the prohibitions of the Fourteenth Amendment.

The long existence of African slavery in this country gave us very distinct notions of what it was, and what were its necessary incidents. Compulsory service of the slave for the benefit of the master, restraint of his movements except by the master's will, disability to hold property, to make contracts, to have a standing in court, to be a witness against a white person, and such like burdens and incapacities were the inseparable incidents of the institution. Severer punishments for crimes were imposed on the slave than on free persons guilty of the same offenses. Congress, as we have seen, by the Civil Rights Bill of 1866, passed in view of the Thirteenth Amendment, before the Fourteenth was adopted, undertook to wipe out these burdens and disabilities, the necessary incidents of slavery, constituting its substance and visible form; and to secure to all citizens of every race and color, and without regard to previous servitude, those fundamental rights which are the essence of civil freedom, namely, the same right to make and enforce contracts, to sue, be parties, give evidence, and to inherit, purchase, lease, sell, and convey property, as is enjoyed by white citizens. Whether this legislation was fully authorized by the Thirteenth Amendment alone, without the support which it afterward received from the Fourteenth Amendment, after the adoption of which it was re-enacted with some additions, it is not necessary to inquire. It is referred to for the purpose of showing that at that time (in 1866) Congress did not assume, under the authority given by the Thirteenth Amendment, to adjust what may be called the social rights of men and races in the community; but only to declare and vindicate those fundamental rights which appertain to the essence of citizenship, and the enjoyment or deprivation of which constitutes the essential distinction between freedom and slavery. . . .

When a man has emerged from slavery, and by the aid of beneficent legislation has shaken off the inseparable concomitants of that state, there must be some stage in the progress of his elevation when he takes the rank of a mere citizen and ceases to be the special favorite of the laws, and when his rights as a citizen, or a man, are to be protected in the ordinary modes by which other men's rights are protected. There were thousands of free colored people in this country before the abolition of slavery, enjoying all the essential rights of life, liberty, and property the same as white citizens; yet no one, at that time, thought that it was any invasion of his personal status as a freeman because he was not admitted to all the privileges enjoyed by white citizens, or because he was subjected to discriminations in the enjoyment of accommodations in inns, public conveyances, and places of amusement. Mere discriminations on account of race or color were not regarded as badges of slavery. If, since that time, the enjoyment of equal rights in all these respects has become established by constitutional enactment, it is not by force of the Thirteenth Amendment (which merely abolishes slavery), but by force of the Fourteenth and Fifteenth amendments.

On the whole we are of opinion that no countenance of authority for the passage of the law in question can be found in either the Thirteenth or Fourteenth Amendment of the Constitution; and, no other ground of authority for its passage being suggested, it must necessarily be declared void, at least so far as its operation in the several states is concerned. . . .

Mr. Justice HARLAN dissenting.

The opinion in these cases proceeds, it seems to me, upon grounds entirely too narrow and artificial. I cannot resist the conclusion that the substance and spirit of the recent amendments of the Constitution have been sacrificed by a subtle and ingenious verbal criticism. "It is not the words of the law but the internal sense of it makes the law: the letter of the law is the body; the sense and reason of the law is the soul." Constitutional provisions, adopted in the interest of liberty, and for the purpose of securing, through national legislation, if need be, rights inhering in a state of freedom, and belonging to American citizenship, have been so construed as to defeat the ends the people desired to accomplish, which

they attempted to accomplish, and which they supposed they had accomplished by changes in their fundamental law. By this I do not mean that the determination of these cases should have been materially controlled by considerations of mere expediency or policy. I mean only, in this form, to express an earnest conviction that the Court has departed from the familiar rule requiring, in the interpretation of constitutional provisions, that full effect be given to the intent with which they were adopted.

The purpose of the first section of the act of Congress of March 1, 1875, was to prevent *race* discrimination in respect of the accommodations and facilities of inns, public conveyances, and places of public amusement. . . .

That there are burdens and disabilities which constitute badges of slavery and servitude, and that the power to enforce by appropriate legislation the Thirteenth Amendment may be exerted by legislation of a direct and primary character, for the eradication, not simply of the institution, but of its badges and incidents, are propositions which ought to be deemed indisputable. . . .

Congress has not, in these matters, entered the domain of state control and supervision. It does not, as I have said, assume to prescribe the general conditions and limitations under which inns, public conveyances, and places of public amusement shall be conducted or managed. It simply declares, in effect, that since the nation has established universal freedom in this country, for all time, there shall be no discrimination, based merely upon race or color, in respect of the accommodations and advantages of public conveyances, inns, and places of public amusement.

I am of the opinion that such discrimination practiced by corporations and individuals in the exercise of their public or quasi-public functions is a badge of servitude the imposition of which

Congress may prevent under its power, by appropriate legislation, to enforce the Thirteenth Amendment; and, consequently, without reference to its enlarged power under the Fourteenth Amendment, the act of March 1, 1875, is not, in my judgment, repugnant to the Constitution.

It remains now to consider these cases with reference to the power Congress has possessed since the adoption of the Fourteenth Amendment. Much that has been said as to the power of Congress under the Thirteenth Amendment is applicable to this branch of the discussion and will not be repeated.

Before the adoption of the recent amendments, it had become, as we have seen, the established doctrine of this Court that Negroes, whose ancestors had been imported and sold as slaves, could not become citizens of a state, or even of the United States, with the rights and privileges guaranteed to citizens by the national Constitution; further, that one might have all the rights and privileges of a citizen of a state without being a citizen in the sense in which that word was used in the national Constitution, and without being entitled to the privileges and immunities of citizens of the several states. Still, further, between the adoption of the Thirteenth Amendment and the proposal by Congress of the Fourteenth Amendment, on June 16, 1866, the statute books of several of the states, as we have seen, had become loaded down with enactments which, under the guise of apprentice, vagrant, and contract regulations, sought to keep the colored race in a condition, practically, of servitude. It was openly announced that whatever might be the rights which persons of that race had, as freemen, under the guarantees of the national Constitution, they could not become citizens of a state, with the privileges belonging to citizens, except by the consent of such state; consequently, that their civil rights, as citizens of the state, depended entirely upon state legislation. To meet this new peril to the black race, that the purposes of the nation might not be doubted or defeated, and by way of further enlargement of the power of Congress, the Fourteenth Amendment was proposed for adoption. . . .

But what was secured to colored citizens of the United States—as between them and their respective states—by the national grant to them of state citizenship? With what rights, privileges, or immunities did this grant invest them? There is one, if there be no other—exemption from race discrimination in respect of any civil right belonging to citizens of the white race in the same state. That, surely, is their constitutional privilege when within the jurisdiction of other states. And such must be their constitutional right, in their own state, unless the recent amendments be splendid baubles, thrown out to delude those who deserved fair and generous treatment at the hands of the nation. Citizenship in this country necessarily imports at least equality of civil rights among citizens of every race in the same state. It is fundamental in American citizenship that, in respect of such rights, there shall be no discrimination by the state, or its officers, or by individuals or corporations exercising public functions or authority, against any citizen because of his race or previous condition of servitude. . . .

But if it were conceded that the power of Congress could not be brought into activity until the rights specified in the act of 1875 had been abridged or denied by some state law or state action, I maintain that the decision of the Court is erroneous. . . .

In every material sense applicable to the practical enforcement of the Fourteenth Amendment, railroad corporations, keepers of inns, and managers of places of public amusement are agents or instrumentalities of the state, because they are charged with duties to the public, and are amenable, in respect of their duties and functions, to governmental regulation. . . .

My brethren say that when a man has emerged from slavery, and by the aid of beneficent legislation has shaken off the inseparable concomitants of that state, there must be some stage in the progress of his elevation when he takes the rank of a mere citizen and ceases to be the special favorite of the laws, and when his rights as a citizen, or a man, are to be protected in the ordinary modes by which other men's rights are protected. It is, I submit, scarcely just to say that the colored race has been the special favorite of the laws. The statute of 1875, now adjudged to be unconstitutional, is for the benefit of citizens of every race and color. What the nation, through Congress, has sought to accomplish in reference to that race is—what had already been done in every state of the Union for the white race—to secure and protect rights belonging to them as freemen and citizens; nothing more. It was not deemed enough "to help the feeble up, but to support him after." The one underlying purpose of congressional legislation has been to enable the black race to take the rank of mere citizens. The difficulty has been to compel a recognition of the legal right of the black race to take the rank of citizens, and to secure the enjoyment of privileges belonging, under the law, to them as a component part of the people for whose welfare and happiness government is ordained. At every step, in this direction, the nation has been con-

fronted with class tyranny, which a contemporary English historian says is, of all tyrannies, the most intolerable, "for it is ubiquitous in its operation, and weighs, perhaps, most heavily on those whose obscurity or distance would withdraw them from the notice of a single despot." Today, it is the colored race which is denied, by corporations and individuals wielding public authority, rights fundamental in their freedom and citizenship. At some future time, it may be that some other race will fall under the ban of race discrimination. If the constitutional amendments be enforced, according to the intent with which, as I conceive, they were adopted, there cannot be, in this republic, any class of human beings in practical subjection to another class, with power in the latter to dole out to the former just such privileges as they may choose to grant. The supreme law of the land has decreed that no authority shall be exercised in this country upon the basis of discrimination, in respect of civil rights, against freemen and citizens because of their race, color, or previous condition of servitude. To that decree—for the due enforcement of which, by appropriate legislation, Congress has been invested with express power—everyone must bow, whatever may have been, or whatever now are, his individual views as to the wisdom or policy, either of the recent changes in the fundamental law, or of the legislation which has been enacted to give them effect.

For the reasons stated I feel constrained to withhold my assent to the opinion of the Court.

11. *PLESSY* v. *FERGUSON*[1]

EDITORS' NOTE.—Plessy was one-eighth Negro but appeared white. He occupied a vacant seat in a railway coach for white passengers, to which

1. 163 U.S. 537 (1896), 540, 542-44, 550-52, 554-64.

his ticket otherwise entitled him, on a trip in Louisiana. Refusing to move to a coach for Negro passengers at the direction of a conductor, he was ejected from the coach. Plessy was committed for trial under a Louisiana statute requiring "equal but separate" railway accommodations for white and colored people and imposing penalties on anyone for "insisting" on going into the wrong coach or compartment. On the ground that there was no appeal from a conviction, he sought to test his rights by a petition for a writ to prohibit action by the trial court, addressed to the supreme court of Louisiana. That court denied the petition on the ground that the statute was constitutional. On a writ of error, the Supreme Court of the United States affirmed the judgment.

Mr. Justice Brown, after stating the case, delivered the opinion of the Court.

This case turns upon the constitutionality of an act of the General Assembly of the state of Louisiana, passed in 1890, providing for separate railway carriages for the white and colored races. . . .

The constitutionality of this act is attacked upon the ground that it conflicts both with the Thirteenth Amendment of the Constitution, abolishing slavery, and the Fourteenth Amendment, which prohibits certain restrictive legislation on the part of the states.

1. That it does not conflict with the Thirteenth Amendment, which abolished slavery and involuntary servitude, except as a punishment for crime, is too clear for argument. Slavery implies involuntary servitude—a state of bondage; the ownership of mankind as a chattel, or at least the control of the labor and services of one man for the benefit of another, and the absence of a legal right to the disposal of his own person, property, and services. . . .

A statute which implies merely a legal distinction between the white and colored races—a distinction which is founded in the color of the two races, and which must always exist so long as white men are distinguished from the other race by color—has no tendency to destroy the legal equality of the two races, or re-establish a state of involuntary servitude. Indeed, we do not understand that the Thirteenth Amendment is strenuously relied upon by the plaintiff in error in this connection.

2. By the Fourteenth Amendment, all persons born or naturalized in the United States, and subject to the jurisdiction thereof, are made citizens of the United States and of the state wherein they reside; and the states are forbidden from making or enforcing any law which shall abridge the privileges or immunities of citizens of the United States, or shall deprive any person of life, liberty, or property without due process of law, or deny to any person within their jurisdiction the equal protection of the laws. . . .

The object of the amendment was undoubtedly to enforce the absolute equality of the two races before the law, but in the nature of things it could not have been intended to abolish distinctions based upon color, or to enforce social, as distinguished from political, equality, or a commingling of the two races upon terms unsatisfactory to either. Laws permitting, and even requiring, their separation in places where they are liable to be brought into contact do not necessarily imply the inferiority of either race to the other, and have been generally, if not universally, recognized as within the competency of the state legislatures in the exercise of their police power. The most common instance of this is connected with the establishment of separate schools for white and colored children, which has been held to be a valid exercise of the legislative power even by courts of states where the political rights of the colored race have been longest and most earnestly enforced. . . .

So far, then, as a conflict with the Fourteenth Amendment is concerned, the case reduces itself to the question whether the statute of Louisiana is a reasonable regulation, and with respect to this there must necessarily be a large discretion on the part of the legislature. In determining the question of reasonableness it is at liberty to act with reference to the established usages, customs, and traditions of the people, and with a view to the promotion of their comfort, and the preservation of the public peace and good order. Gauged by this standard, we cannot say that a law which authorizes or even requires the separation of the two races in public conveyances is unreasonable or more obnoxious to the Fourteenth Amendment than the acts of Congress requiring separate schools for colored children in the District of Columbia, the constitutionality of which does not seem to have been questioned, or the corresponding acts of state legislatures.

We consider the underlying fallacy of the plaintiff's argument to consist in the assumption that the enforced separation of the two races stamps the colored race with a badge of inferiority. If this be so, it is not by reason of anything found in the act, but solely because the colored race chooses to put that construction upon it. The argument necessarily assumes that if, as has been more than once the case, and is not unlikely to be so again, the colored race should become the dominant power in the state legislature, and should enact a law in precisely similar terms, it would thereby relegate the white race to an inferior position. We imagine that the white race, at least, would not acquiesce in this assumption. The argument also assumes that social prejudices may be overcome by legislation and that equal rights cannot be secured to the Negro except by an enforced commingling of the two races. We cannot accept this proposition. If the two races are to meet upon terms of social equality, it must be the result of natural affinities, a mutual appreciation of each other's merits, and a voluntary consent of individuals. . . . Legislation is powerless to eradicate racial instincts or to abolish distinctions based upon physical differences, and the attempt to do so can only result in accentuating the difficulties of the present situation. If the civil and political rights of both races be equal, one cannot be inferior to the other civilly or politically. If one race be inferior to the other socially, the Constitution of the United States cannot put them upon the same plane.

It is true that the question of the proportion of colored blood necessary to constitute a colored person, as distinguished from a white person, is one upon which there is a difference of opinion in the different states, some holding that any visible admixture of black blood stamps the person as belonging to the colored race (*State* v. *Chavers*, 5 Jones [N.C.]1, p. 11); others that it depends upon the preponderance of blood (*Gray* v. *State*, 4 Ohio 354; *Monroe* v. *Collins*, 17 Ohio St. 665); and still others that the predominance of white blood must only be in the proportion of three-fourths (*People* v. *Dean*, 14 Michigan 406; *Jones* v. *Commonwealth*, 80 Virginia 538). But these are questions to be determined under the laws of each state and are not properly put in issue in this case. Under the allegations of his petition it may undoubtedly become a question of importance whether, under the laws of Louisiana, the petitioner belongs to the white or colored race.

The judgment of the court below is, therefore, *Affirmed*.

Mr. Justice HARLAN dissenting. . . .

In respect of civil rights, common to all citizens, the Constitution of the United States does not, I think, permit any public authority to know the race of those entitled to be protected in the enjoyment of such rights. Every true man has pride of race, and under appropriate circumstances when the rights of others, his equals before the law, are not to be affected, it is his privilege to express such pride and to take such action based upon it as to him seems proper. But I deny that any legislative body or judicial tribunal may have regard to the race of citizens when the civil rights of those citizens are involved. Indeed, such legislation, as that here in question, is inconsistent not only with that equality of rights which pertains to citizenship, national and state, but with the personal liberty enjoyed by everyone within the United States.

The Thirteenth Amendment does not permit the withholding or the deprivation of any right necessarily inhering in freedom. It not only struck down the institution of slavery as previously existing in the United States, but it prevents the imposition of any burdens or disabilities that constitute badges of slavery or servitude. It decreed universal civil freedom in this country. This Court has so adjudged. But that amendment having been found inadequate to the protection of the rights of those who had been in slavery, it was followed by the Fourteenth Amendment, which added greatly to the dignity and glory of the American citizenship, and to the security of personal liberty, by declaring that "all persons born or naturalized in the United States, and subject to the jurisdiction thereof, are citizens of the United States and of the state wherein they reside," and that "no state shall make or enforce any law which shall abridge the privileges or immunities of citizens of the United States; nor shall any state deprive any person of life, liberty, or property without due process of law, nor deny to any person within its jurisdiction the equal protection of the laws." These two amendments, if enforced according to their true intent and meaning, will protect all the civil rights that pertain to freedom and citizenship. Finally, and to the end that no citizen should be denied, on account of

his race, the privilege of participating in the political control of his country, it was declared by the Fifteenth Amendment that "the right of citizens of the United States to vote shall not be denied or abridged by the United States or by any state on account of race, color, or previous condition of servitude."

These notable additions to the fundamental law were welcomed by the friends of liberty throughout the world. They removed the race line from our governmental systems. . . .

It was said in argument that the statute of Louisiana does not discriminate against either race but prescribes a rule applicable alike to white and colored citizens. But this argument does not meet the difficulty. Everyone knows that the statute in question had its origin in the purpose, not so much to exclude white persons from railroad cars occupied by blacks, as to exclude colored people from coaches occupied by or assigned to white persons. Railroad corporations of Louisiana did not make discrimination among whites in the matter of accommodation for travelers. The thing to accomplish was, under the guise of giving equal accommodation for whites and blacks, to compel the latter to keep to themselves while traveling in railroad passenger coaches. No one would be so wanting in candor as to assert the contrary. The fundamental objection, therefore, to the statute is that it interferes with the personal freedom of citizens. . . . If a white man and a black man choose to occupy the same public conveyance on a public highway, it is their right to do so, and no government, proceeding alone on grounds of race, can prevent it without infringing the personal liberty of each.

It is one thing for railroad carriers to furnish, or to be required by law to furnish, equal accommodations for all whom they are under a legal duty to carry. It is quite another thing for government to forbid citizens of the white and black races from traveling in the same public conveyance, and to punish officers of railroad companies for permitting persons of the two races to occupy the same passenger coach. If a state can prescribe, as a rule of civil conduct, that whites and blacks shall not travel as passengers in the same railroad coach, why may it not so regulate the use of the streets of its cities and towns as to compel white citizens to keep on one side of a street and black citizens to keep on the other? Why may it not, upon like grounds, punish whites and blacks who ride together in streetcars or in open vehicles on a public road or street? Why may it not require sheriffs to assign whites to one side of a courtroom and blacks to the other? And why may it not also prohibit the commingling of the two races in the galleries of legislative halls or in public assemblages convened for the consideration of the political questions of the day? Further, if this statute of Louisiana is consistent with the personal liberty of citizens, why may not the state require the separation in railroad coaches of native and naturalized citizens of the United States, or of Protestants and Roman Catholics?

The answer given at the argument to these questions was that regulations of the kind they suggest would be unreasonable and could not, therefore, stand before the law. Is it meant that the determination of questions of legislative power depends upon the inquiry whether the statute whose validity is questioned is, in the judgment of the courts, a reasonable one, taking all the circumstances into consideration? A statute may be unreasonable merely because a sound public policy forbade its enactment. But I do not understand that the courts have anything to do with the policy or expediency of legislation. . . .

The white race deems itself to be the dominant race in this country. And so it is, in prestige, in achievements, in education, in wealth, and in power. So, I doubt not, it will continue to be for all time, if it remains true to its great heritage and holds fast to the principles of constitutional liberty. But in view of the Constitution, in the eye of the law, there is in this country no superior, dominant, ruling class of citizens. There is no caste here. Our Constitution is color-blind and neither knows nor tolerates classes among citizens. In respect of civil rights, all citizens are equal before the law. The humblest is the peer of the most powerful. The law regards man as man and takes no account of his surroundings or of his color when his civil rights as guaranteed by the supreme law of the land are involved. It is, therefore, to be regretted that this high tribunal, the final expositor of the fundamental law of the land, has reached the conclusion that it is competent for a state to regulate the enjoyment by citizens of their civil rights solely upon the basis of race. . . .

The sure guarantee of the peace and security of each race is the clear, distinct, unconditional recognition by our governments, national and state, of every right that inheres in civil freedom, and of the equality before the law of all citizens of the United States without regard to race. State enactments, regulating the enjoyment of civil rights, upon the basis of race, and cunningly devised to defeat legitimate results of the war, under the pretense of recognizing equality of rights, can have no other result than to render permanent peace impossible, and to keep alive a conflict of races, the continuance of which must do harm to all concerned. . . .

The arbitrary separation of citizens, on the basis of race, while they are on a public highway, is a badge of servitude wholly inconsistent with the civil freedom and the equality before the law established by the Constitution. It cannot be justified upon any legal grounds.

If evils will result from the commingling of the two races upon public highways established for the benefit of all, they will be infinitely less than those that will surely come from state legislation regulating the enjoyment of civil rights upon the basis of race. We boast of the freedom enjoyed by our people above all other peoples. But it is difficult to reconcile that boast with a state of the law which, practically, puts the brand of servitude and degradation upon a large class of our fellow-citizens, our equals before the law. The thin disguise of "equal" accommodations for passengers in railroad coaches will not mislead anyone, nor atone for the wrong this day done....

I am of opinion that the statute of Louisiana is inconsistent with the personal liberty of citizens, white and black, in that state, and hostile to both the spirit and letter of the Constitution of the United States. If laws of like character should be enacted in the several states of the Union, the effect would be in the highest degree mischievous. Slavery, as an institution tolerated by law, would, it is true, have disappeared from our country, but there would remain a power in the states, by sinister legislation, to interfere with the full enjoyment of the blessings of freedom; to regulate civil rights, common to all citizens, upon the basis of race; and to place in a condition of legal inferiority a large body of American citizens, now constituting a part of the political community called the People of the United States, for whom, and by whom through representatives, our government is administered. Such a system is inconsistent with the guarantee given by the Constitution to each state of a republican form of government, and may be stricken down by congressional action, or by the courts in the discharge of their solemn duty to maintain the supreme law of the land, anything in the constitution or laws of any state to the contrary notwithstanding.

For the reasons stated, I am constrained to withhold my assent from the opinion and judgment of the majority....

578

322

682F.